FIELDING'S
CARIBBEAN
1992

Current Fielding Titles

FIELDING'S ALPINE EUROPE 1992
FIELDING'S AUSTRALIA 1992
FIELDING'S BENELUX 1992
FIELDING'S BERMUDA AND THE BAHAMAS 1992
FIELDING'S BRITAIN 1992
FIELDING'S BUDGET EUROPE 1992
FIELDING'S CARIBBEAN 1992
FIELDING'S EUROPE 1992
FIELDING'S HAWAII 1992
FIELDING'S ITALY 1992
FIELDING'S MEXICO 1992
FIELDING'S PEOPLE'S REPUBLIC OF CHINA 1992
FIELDING'S SCANDINAVIA 1992
FIELDING'S SELECTIVE SHOPPING GUIDE TO EUROPE 1992
FIELDING'S SPAIN AND PORTUGAL 1992

FIELDING'S ALASKA AND THE YUKON
FIELDING'S BUDGET ASIA Southeast Asia and the Far East
FIELDING'S CALIFORNIA
FIELDING'S FAMILY VACATIONS USA
FIELDING'S FAR EAST 2nd revised edition
FIELDING'S HAVENS AND HIDEAWAYS USA
FIELDING'S LEWIS AND CLARK TRAIL
FIELDING'S LITERARY AFRICA
FIELDING'S TRAVELER'S MEDICAL COMPANION
FIELDING'S WORLDWIDE CRUISES 5th revised edition

FIELDING'S CARIBBEAN 1992

BY **MARGARET ZELLERS**

FIELDING TRAVEL BOOKS
c/o **WILLIAM MORROW & COMPANY, INC.**
1350 Avenue of the Americas, New York, N.Y. 10019

Copyright © 1978, 1980, 1981, 1982, 1983, 1984, 1985, 1986, 1987, 1988, 1989, 1990, 1991, 1992 by Margaret Zellers

All rights reserved. No part of this book may be reproduced or utilized in any form or by any means, electronic or mechanical, including photocopying, recording or by any information storage and retrieval system, without permission in writing from the Publisher. Inquiries should be addressed to Permissions Department, William Morrow and Company, Inc., 1350 Avenue of the Americas, New York, N.Y. 10019.

Recognizing the importance of what has been written, it is the policy of William Morrow and Company, Inc., and its imprints and affiliates, to have the books we publish printed on acid-free paper, and we exert our best efforts to that end.

Library of Congress Catalog Card Number: 79-6410015
ISBN: 0-688-09320-5

Printed in the United States of America

Fourteenth Edition

1 2 3 4 5 6 7 8 9 10

Text design by Marsha Cohen/Parallelogram

Author's Note of Thanks

The Caribbean is *not* "just like home," but I feel at home in the region. Although a veneer of tourism masks some of my once-favorite places, I still have a sense of discovery as I wander around the islands. For that I give sincere thanks to the many friends and colleagues who have shared their islands and traditions, and have helped me to know the real Caribbean. When the places and its people are true to themselves, they are at their best. And it's that Caribbean—the natural one—that makes me enthusiastic about my frequent travels to and through the islands.

You'll do yourself a favor if you stray from the well-trodden tourist paths into the countryside, to local events such as flower shows, polo matches, church services, chamber of commerce meetings, and school classes to spend time with island residents not involved with tourism. Although their lives are affected by tourism, their daily focus is probably closer to some of your own interests, as is the case for me.

I've learned from many people on each island. I am grateful to them, and to government officials and businessmen—hoteliers and others—who give me the pulse of an island's economy, as well as to those who have led me on new adventures. I have also learned from my own special family—three generations who have shared Caribbean and other travels, sometimes in fact but always in conversations. My parents, my sister and brother-in-law, and my nephews John and Geoffrey have helped stretch my horizons, to see the islands through their eyes without the blinders sometimes created by my previous travels.

Although I am the only author of this book, it could not reach your hands without the help of hundreds of others. To all, I say "thank you." I hope that my words can help with your travels—and understanding.

Margaret Zellers

About the Author

Margaret Zellers is a travel journalist whose "beat" is the world. She is a respected authority on the Caribbean, an area she has known since the mid-1950s. On behalf of the government of the United States Virgin Islands, Ms. Zellers served in New York as director of their first off-island tourism office. She has also been involved with development programs for other Caribbean islands, independently and as a member of the Caribbean Tourism Organization and the Caribbean Hotel Association. She has received awards from the Caribbean Tourism Organization for "her many years of support through positive and constructive journalism," from the Caribbean Hotel Training Institute for her assistance with setting up initial contact between Switzerland's Ecole Hoteliere in Lausanne and Caribbean interests, from the Jamaica Tourist Board for distinguished reporting on the Caribbean region, and as "Travel Writer of the Year" from the Bahamas Hotel Association. She has strongly supported the U.S. government's Caribbean Basin Initiative, and participated with the White House Press Corps in President Reagan's April 1982 visit to Jamaica and Barbados on behalf of the CBI and better Caribbean-United States communication, and was in Grenada for President Reagan's visit in February 1986. Ms. Zellers frequently visits Caribbean communities to speak with schoolchildren and the general public, sharing ideas for an integrated visitor-resident experience. She serves on the Board of Directors of RARE Center, a not-for-profit organization involved with conservation education in the Caribbean and Latin America.

Margaret Zellers was one of the first five journalists to return to Cuba for reports on tourism in August 1976 and the first travel book author to include reportage on the islands' "Political Picture" and "Lifestyle" along with the expected facts on hotels, restaurants, and activities. Her coverage of Grenada documented political events in that country beginning in 1979, long before the facts gained world attention in October 1983. Her books have been the first to include detailed reporting on many of the lesser-known islands, including Anguilla, Vieques, Barbuda, and Terre de Haut, as well as offering the most comprehensive coverage of the bigger island countries.

In her profession as a travel journalist, Margaret Zellers apprenticed with the late Sydney Clark, named Dean of American Travel Writers by his colleagues and author of *All The Best in* . . . countries all over the world. In 1973, she became author, researcher, and area editor of *Fodor's Guide to the Caribbean, Bahamas and Bermuda,* a position she relinquished with the 1978 edition when she signed with William Morrow and Company to write *Fielding's Caribbean,* which she has researched and written each year since that time. She is also author of *Fielding's Alpine Europe* and writes frequent features for national magazines and major metropolitan newspapers.

Other books by the author include a series of GeoMedia Pocketguides on countries in Europe and the Caribbean, the text for Graphic Arts' photographic book on the Caribbean, and guides to small inns *(Austria—The Inn Way, Caribbean—The Inn Way,* and *Switzerland—The Inn Way)* published by GeoMedia, Westport, CT.

"The Commerce of the West India Islands is part of the American System Commerce. They can neither do without us nor we without them. The creator has placed us upon the Globe in such a situation that we have occasion for each other. We have the means of assisting each other, and politicians and artful contrivances cannot separate us."
—JOHN ADAMS
President of the United States 1797–1801

The quotation above was presented, on a plaque, by Jamaica's Prime Minister Edward Seaga to President Reagan, on the occasion of the President's visit to Jamaica and Barbados, April 7–11, 1982.

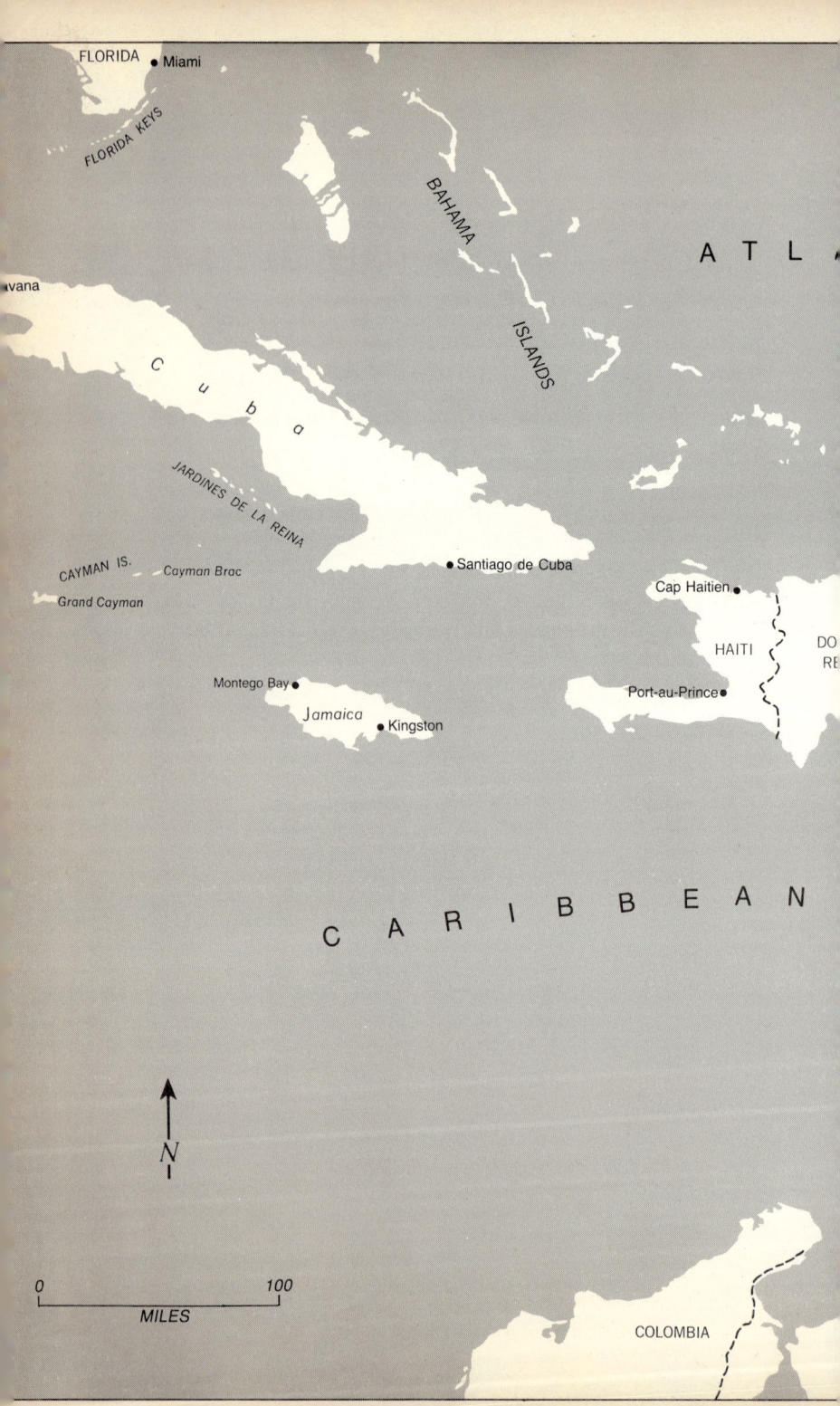

CARIBBEAN NEWSLETTER

Even before *Fielding's 1992 Caribbean* is in the bookstores in fall 1991, there have been changes on the islands. Since tourism is the major employer and an important source for hard currency, Caribbean governments and private sector entrepreneurs adjust their tourism product to meet market demands.

To keep up-to-date on news and current observations, a quarterly *Caribbean Newsletter* is available to readers who send this page together with a check for $25 to cover postage and handling for the four (4) 1992 issues to:

> Caribbean Newsletter
> c/o GeoMedia, #316
> 1771 Post Road East
> Westport, CT 06880

The *Caribbean Newsletter* is issued in November 1991, and in February, May, and August of 1992. A subscription includes all four issues.

Name: _____

Street: _____

City, State and Zip Code: _____

Free Bulletin: Owners of *Fielding's Caribbean 1992* are invited to send a self-addressed, stamped envelope to GeoMedia to receive a *one time only* special bulletin with observations effecting Caribbean travel *after* this book goes to press.

Suggestions and Comments

We're interested in making this book as useful as possible for your travels and, for that reason, we'd appreciate having some information about you—as well as your suggestions.

Islands of special interest:

Type of Accommodation:

      Hotel_____; Housekeeping_____; Low-Cost_____.

Month of intended Caribbean visit:

Intended length of stay:

Anticipated budget for the vacation:

Number of people in your party (including yourself):

Approximate ages of travelers:

under 25____; from 26–39____; from 40–50____; over 60____.

Suggestions/Comments:

WHAT'S IN THE STARS?

Stars are awarded to properties that are exceptional. The absence of stars is not necessarily a negative notice; the text usually explains details.

Although several opinions and factors have been considered when stars were awarded for this edition, the final decision in all cases is that of the author. **Author's Awards** are given for hotels and restaurants that are exceptional, even when they may not warrant five stars.

Stars are awarded only to places where staff and management attitude is positive, welcoming, and honest. Although there are very few "five star" properties in the Caribbean, if criteria used for the best European hotels are applied, there are some properties that are the best the Caribbean has to offer. In this edition, they are rewarded with five stars.

As long as Caribbean people continue to confuse good service with servility, which some resent as a remnant of slavery, gracious hospitality as it is pridefully known elsewhere will not be possible in the Caribbean.

The criteria for stars are as follows:

★★★★★ an elegant Caribbean resort with gracious service.

★★★★ exceptionally comfortable, with all holiday facilities. These properties are often large, and part of an international chain.

★★★ excellent; often a small property that is special for a specified reason.

★★ very good; often a small property with ownership involvement.

★ above average; noteworthy for a particular reason.

THE CARIBBEAN ON A CHART*
©by Margaret Zellers

	Good beaches	Tennis	Golf	Sailing charters	Scuba snorkeling	Good shopping	Local handicrafts	Nighttime action	Gambling	Big hotels	Charming inns	Good restaurants	Summer packages	Cosmopolitan	Quiet, away from all	Good medical facilities	Local currency	Information address
Anguilla, W.I.	★	★									★				★		US $1 = EC $2.65	271 Main St. Northport, NY 11768 T 516+261-1234
Antigua and Barbuda, W.I.	★	★	★	★	★	★	★	★	★	★	★	★	★	★			US $1 = EC $2.65	610 Fifth Ave. New York, NY 10020 T 212+541-4117
Aruba, N.A.	★	★		★	★	★		★	★	★		★	★				US $1 = Af 1.77	521 Fifth Ave. New York, NY 10175 T 212+426-3030
Barbados, W.I.	★	★	★	★	★	★	★	★		★	★	★	★	★			US $1 = Bds $1.98	800 Second Ave. New York, NY 10017 T 212+986-6516
Bonaire, N.A.		★		★	★			★			★	★			★		US $1 = NAf $1.77	201½ E 29th St. New York, NY 10016 T 212+799-0242
British Virgin Islands	★	★		★	★	★					★	★	★		★		US $	370 Lexington Ave. New York, NY 10017 T 212+696-0400
Cayman Islands, B.W.I.	★	★	★	★	★	★				★	★	★	★	★			US $1 = CI $.80	420 Lexington Ave. New York, NY 10017 T 212+682-5582
Cuba	★	★		★		★		★				★			★		Cuban peso	55 Queen St. E Toronto, Ont. Canada M5H 1R5 T 416+362-0700
Curaçao, N.A.		★	★		★	★		★	★	★		★	★	★			US 1$ = Naf 1.77	400 Madison Ave. New York, NY 10017 T 212+751-8266
Dominica, W.I.					★		★				★				★		US $1 = EC $2.65	℅ CTO 20 E 46th St. New York, NY 10017 T 212+682-0435
Dominican Republic	★	★	★	★	★	★		★	★	★	★	★	★	★			US $1 = 10.50 peso	℅ Consulate 1 Times Sq. Plaza New York, NY 10036 T 212+867-0833
Grenada, W.I.	★	★	★	★	★	★	★	★		★	★	★	★				US $1 = EC $2.65	820 Second Ave. New York, NY 10017 T 212+687-9554
Guadeloupe, F.W.I.	★	★	★	★	★	★	★	★	★	★	★	★	★	★			US $1 = 5.5 Fr. francs	610 Fifth Ave. New York, NY 10020 T 212+757-1125
Haiti	★	★		★	★	★	★	★	★	★	★	★	★	★			US $1 = 5 gourdes	405 Lexington Ave. New York, NY 10017 T 212+697-9767

Location													Currency	Address
Jamaica, W.I.	★	★	★	★	★	★	★	★	★	★		★	US $1 = J $12	866 Second Ave. New York, NY 10017 T 212+ 688–7650
Martinique, F.W.I.	★	★	★	★	★	★	★	★	★	★	★	★	US $1 = 5.5 Fr. francs	610 Fifth Ave. New York, NY 10020 T 212+ 757–1125
Montserrat, W.I.			★	★		★		★	★		★	★	US $1 = EC $2.65	℅ Pace, 485 Fifth Ave. New York, NY 10017 T 212+ 818–0100
Nevis, W.I.	★	★		★	★			★		★		★	US $1 = EC $2.65	414 E. 75th St New York, NY 10021 T 212+ 535–1234
Puerto Rico	★	★	★	★	★	★	★	★	★	★	★	★	US $	1290 Ave. of the Americas New York, NY 10019 T 212+ 541–6630
Saba, N.A.			★				★	★				★	US $1 = NAf 1.77	271 Main St Northport, NY 11768 T 516+ 261–7474
St. Barthélemy, F.W.I.	★	★	★	★	★	★	★	★	★	★	★	★	US $1 = 5.5 Fr. Francs	610 Fifth Ave. New York, NY 10020 T 212+ 757–1125
St. Croix, U.S.V.I.	★	★	★	★	★	★	★	★	★	★	★	★	US $	1270 Ave. of the Americas New York, NY 10020 T 212+ 582–4520
St. Eustatius, N.A.		★		★				★	★			★	US $1 = NAf 1.77	271 Main St. Northport, NY 11768 T 516+ 261–7474
St. John, U.S.V.I.	★	★	★	★		★	★		★	★	★	★	US $	1270 Ave. of the Americas New York, NY 10020 T 212+ 582–4520
St. Kitts, W.I.	★	★	★	★	★		★	★	★	★	★	★	US $1 = EC $2.65	414 E. 75th St New York, NY 10021 T 212+ 535–1234
St. Lucia, W.I.	★	★	★	★	★	★	★	★	★		★	★	US $1 = EC $2.65	820 Second Ave. New York, NY 10017 T 212+ 867–2950
St. Maarten, N.A. St. Martin, F.W.I.	★	★	★	★	★	★	★	★	★	★	★	★	NAf 1.77 or 5.5 Fr. francs	275 Seventh Ave. New York, NY 10001 T 212+ 986–0000
St. Thomas, U.S.V.I.	★	★	★	★	★	★	★	★	★	★	★	★	US $	1270 Ave. of the Americas New York, NY 10020 T 212+ 582–4520
St. Vincent, W.I.	★	★	★	★	★		★	★		★		★	US $1 = EC $2.65	801 Second Ave. New York, NY 10017 T 212+ 687–4490
Trinidad, W.I.	★	★	★	★	★	★	★	★	★	★	★	★	US $1 = TT $4.25	#1508, 25 W 43rd St. New York, NY 10036 T 212+ 719–0540
Tobago, W.I.	★	★	★	★		★	★	★	★	★	★	★	US $1 = TT $4.25	#1508, 25 W 43rd St. New York, NY 10036 T 212+ 719–0540
Turks & Caicos, B.W.I.	★		★				★					★	US $	425 Madison Ave. New York, NY 10017 T 212+ 888–4110

*Stars are given only when item noted is exceptional. Average to mediocre facilities may exist for categories where no star appears.

CONTENTS

AUTHOR'S NOTE 3

ABOUT THE AUTHOR 4

MAP 6

CARIBBEAN NEWSLETTER 9

WHAT'S IN THE STARS? 11

CARIBBEAN ON A CHART 12

THE CARIBBEAN MYSTIQUE 21

COLUMBUS AND THE CARIBBEAN 27

THIS YEAR'S BEST 30
Beaches / **30;** Budget Travel / **30;** Discoveries / **31;** Families / **31;** Food / **31;** Foreign Flavor / **31;** Gambling / **32;** Golf / **32;** Honeymoons / **32;** Luxury / **32;** Natural Surroundings / **33;** Nightlife / **33;** Sailing / **33;** Scuba Diving / **33;** Singles / **34;** Shopping / **33;** Tennis / **34;** Windsurfing / **34**

TIPS AND TOPICS FOR CARIBBEAN TRAVELING 35
Airlines / **35;** Boats and Ships / **37;** Bugs, Beetles, and Other Bothersome Things / **39;** Clothing / **39;** Cruise Ship Ports / **41;** Documents / **41;** Drinking Water / **42;** Drugs / **42;** Electric Current / **43;** Island Choices / **43;** Language / **44;** Lodging / **45;** Mail / **46;** Medical / **46;** Money Matters / **47;** Nature / **47;** Package Tours / **48;** Rack Rate / **49;** Safety / **49;** Shopping / **50;** Terms / **53;** Travel Agents / **53;** Tips for Last Minute Travel / **54;** Weather / **56**

ANEGADA (See British Virgin Islands)

ANGUILLA 59
Political Picture / **60;** Island Appearance / **60;** Lifestyle / **60;** Medical Facilities / **61;** Money Matters / **61;** Communications / **61;** Arrival / **61;** Departure / **62;** Touring Tips / **62;** Lodging / **62;** Restaurants / **68;** Natural Surroundings / **71;** Places Worth Finding / **71;** Sports / **71;** Treasures and Trifles / **72**

ANTIGUA 73
Political Picture / **75;** Island Appearance / **76;** Lifestyle / **76;** Medical Facilities / **77;** Money Matters / **77;** Communications / **77;** Arrival / **77;** Cruises / **77;** Departure / **78;** Touring Tips / **78;** Lodging / **79;** Restaurants / **90;** Natural Surroundings / **92;** Places Worth Finding / **92;** Sports / **94;** Treasures and Trifles / **96**

ARUBA 99
Political Picture / **100;** Island Appearance / **100;** Lifestyle /

101; Medical Facilities / 102; Money Matters / 102; Communications / 102; Arrival / 102; Cruises / 103; Departure / 103; Touring Tips / 103; Lodging / 103; Restaurants / 111; Natural Surroundings / 115; Places Worth Finding / 116; Sports / 117; Treasures and Trifles / 118

BARBADOS 121

Political Picture / 122; Island Appearance / 123; Lifestyle / 124; Medical Facilities / 125; Money Matters / 125; Communications / 125; Arrival / 125; Cruises / 126; Departure / 126; Touring Tips / 127; Lodging / 127; Restaurants / 142; Natural Surroundings / 145; Places Worth Finding / 147; Sports and Activities / 150; Treasures and Trifles / 151

BARBUDA 155

Political Picture / 156; Island Appearance / 156; Lifestyle /156; Medical Facilities / 156; Money Matters / 157; Communications / 157; Arrival / 157; Departure / 157; Touring Tips /157; Lodging / 157; Restaurants / 159; Natural Surroundings / 159; Places Worth Finding / 159; Sports / 160; Treasures and Trifles / 160

BEQUIA (See St. Vincent)

BONAIRE 161

Political Picture / 163; Island Appearance / 163; Lifestyle /163; Medical Facilities / 164; Money Matters / 164; Communications / 164; Arrival / 164; Cruises / 164; Departure / 164; Touring Tips / 165; Lodging / 165; Restaurants / 168; Natural Surroundings / 169; Places Worth Finding / 170; Sports / 171; Treasures and Trifles / 172

BRITISH VIRGIN ISLANDS 175

Political Picture / 176; Island Appearance / 176; Lifestyle /177; Medical Facilities / 177; Money Matters / 177; Communications / 177; Arrival / 178; Cruises / 179; Departure / 179; Touring Tips / 179; Lodging /180
Tortola / 181
Lodging / 181; Resort Islands near Tortola / 186; Restaurants on or near Tortola / 187; Natural Surroundings / 189; Places Worth Finding / 189; Sports / 190; Treasures and Trifles / 192
Anegada / 193
Jost Van Dyke / 194
Mosquito Island / 195
Necker Island / 196
Virgin Gorda / 196
Arrival / 197; Lodging / 197; Restaurants / 201; Places Worth Finding / 201; Sports / 202; Treasures / 202

CANOUAN (See St. Vincent)

CARRIACOU (See Grenada)

CAYMAN ISLANDS 203

Political Picture / 205; Island Appearance / 206; Lifestyle / 207; Medical Facilities / 207; Money Matters / 208; Communications / 208; Arrival / 209; Cruises / 209; Departure / 209; Touring Tips / 209; Lodging / 210; Restaurants / 219; Natural Surroundings / 221; Places Worth Finding / 222; Sports / 223; Treasures and Trifles / 225
The Other Caymans
Cayman Brac / 226; Little Cayman / 228

CUBA 231
Political Picture / **233**; Island Appearance / **234**; Lifestyle / **234**; Medical Facilities / **235**; Money Matters / **235**; Communications / **235**; Arrival / **235**; Departure / **236**; Touring Tips / **236**; Habana Lodging / **236**; Restaurants / **241**; Places Worth Finding / **243**
Cienfuegos / **247**;
Holguin / **248**;
Santiago de Cuba / **252**;
Trinidad / **250**;
Varadero / **260**

CURACAO 267
Political Picture / **268**; Island Appearance / **268**; Lifestyle / **268**; Medical Facilities / **269**; Money Matters / **269**; Communications / **269**; Arrival / **269**; Cruises / **270**; Departure / **270**; Touring Tips / **270**; Lodging / **271**; Restaurants / **274**; Natural Surroundings / **277**; Places Worth Finding / **277**; Sports / **279**; Treasures and Trifles / **280**

DOMINICA 283
Political Picture / **284**; Island Appearance / **284**; Lifestyle / **285**; Medical Facilities / **285**; Money Matters / **285**; Communications / **286**; Arrival / **286**; Cruises / **286**; Departure / **286**; Touring Tips / **287**; Lodging / **287**; Restaurants / **292**; Natural Surroundings / **293**; Places Worth Finding / **294**; Sports / **294**; Treasures and Trifles / **295**

DOMINICAN REPUBLIC 297
Political Picture / **299**; Island Appearance / **301**; Lifestyle / **301**; Medical Facilities / **302**; Money Matters / **302**; Communications / **303**
Santo Domingo / **304**
Cruises / **305**; Departure / **305**; Touring Tips / **306**; Lodging / **307**; Restaurants / **313**; Natural Surroundings / **316**; Places Worth Finding / **317**; Sports / **322**; Treasures and Trifles / **323**
La Romana / **325**
Puerto Plata / **329**
Sosua / **339**
Punta Cana (East End) / **343**

GRENADA 345
Political Picture / **347**; Island Appearance / **348**; Lifestyle / **349**; Medical Facilities / **349**; Money Matters / **349**; Communications / **349**; Arrival / **350**; Cruises / **350**; Departure / **351**; Touring Tips / **351**; Lodging / **352**; Restaurants / **357**; Natural Surroundings / **358**; Places Worth Finding / **359**; Sports / **361**; Treasures and Trifles / **362**
Carriacou / **363**

GUADELOUPE 367
Political Picture / **368**; Island Appearance / **369**; Lifestyle / **369**; Medical Facilities / **370**; Money Matters / **370**; Communications / **371**; Arrival / **371**; Cruises / **371**; Departure / **372**; Touring Tips / **372**; Lodging / **373**; Restaurants / **381**; Natural Surroundings / **383**; Places Worth Finding / **384**; Sports / **385**; Treasures and Trifles / **386**
Les Saintes / **387**

HAITI 391
Political Picture / **393**; Island Appearance / **394**; Lifestyle / **395**; Medical Facilities / **395**;

Money Matters / **395**; Communications / **395**; Arrival / **396**; Cruises / **396**; Departure / **396**; Touring Tips / **397**
Port-au-Prince and Petionville / **398**
  Lodging / **398**; Restaurants / **403**; Natural Surroundings / **404**; Places Worth Finding / **404**; Sports / **408**; Treasures and Trifles / **409**
Cap Haitien / **411**
Jacmel / **415**

JAMAICA **419**
Political Picture / **420**; Island Appearance / **420**; Lifestyle / **422**; Medical Facilities / **423**; Money Matters / **423**; Communications / **423**
Kingston / **426**
  Arrival / **426**; Departure / **426**; Touring Tips / **427**; Lodging / **427**; Restaurants in Kingston / **430**; Natural Surroundings / **432**; Places Worth Finding in Kingston / **433**; Sports / **435**; Treasures and Trifles / **435**
Lucea / **436**
Mandeville / **437**
Montego Bay / **439**
  Arrival / **440**; Departure / **440**; Touring Tips / **440**; Lodging / **441**; Restaurants in Montego Bay / **449**; Natural Surroundings / **451**; Places Worth Finding Around Montego Bay / **452**; Sports / **453**; Treasures and Trifles / **454**;
Negril / **455**
Ocho Rios / **463**
Runaway Bay / **475**
Port Antonio / **477**

JOST VAN DYKE (See British Virgin Islands)

MARTINIQUE **481**
Political Picture / **483**; Island Appearance / **483**; Lifestyle / **484**; Medical Facilities / **484**; Money Matters / **484**; Communications / **485**; Arrival / **485**; Cruises / **485**; Departure / **485**; Touring Tips / **486**; Lodging / **487**; Restaurants / **495**; Natural Surroundings / **499**; Places Worth Finding / **500**; Sports / **502**; Treasures and Trifles / **504**

MONTSERRAT **507**
Political Picture / **508**; Island Appearance / **508**; Lifestyle / **509**; Medical Facilities / **509**; Money Matters / **509**; Communications / **509**; Arrival / **510**; Cruises / **510**; Departure / **510**; Touring Tips / **510**; Lodging / **511**; Restaurants / **514**; Natural Surroundings / **514**; Places Worth Finding / **515**; Sports / **516**; Treasures and Trifles / **516**

MUSTIQUE (See St. Vincent)

NEVIS **519**
Political Picture / **520**; Island Appearance / **520**; Lifestyle / **520**; Medical Facilities / **521**; Money Matters / **521**; Communications / **521**; Arrival / **521**; Cruises / **522**; Departure / **522**; Touring Tips / **522**; Lodging / **522**; Restaurants / **526**; Natural Surroundings / **527**; Places Worth Finding / **527**; Sports / **528**; Treasures and Trifles / **528**

PALM ISLAND (See St. Vincent)

PETER ISLAND (See British Virgin Islands)

PETIT ST. VINCENT (See St. Vincent)

PUERTO RICO 531
Political Picture / **532;** Island Appearance / **532;** Lifestyle / **533;** Medical Facilities / **534;** Money Matters / **534;** Communications / **534;** Arrival / **534;** Cruises / **535;** Departure / **536;** Touring Tips / **536;** Lodging / **538;** Restaurants / **545;** Natural Surroundings / **549;** Places Worth Finding / **549;** Sports / **552;** Treasures and Trifles / **544**
Dorado / **556**
Southeast Coast / **559**
Ponce / **562**
Mayaguez / **564**
Culebra / **568**
Vieques / **569**

SABA 573
Political Picture / **573;** Island Appearance / **573;** Lifestyle / **575;** Medical Facilities / **575;** Money Matters / **575;** Communications / **575;** Arrival / **575;** Departure / **576;** Touring Tips / **576;** Lodging / **576;** Natural Surroundings / **578;** Places Worth Finding / **578;** Sports / **579;** Treasures and Trifles / **579**

ST. BARTHELEMY 581
Political Picture / **582;** Island Appearance / **582;** Lifestyle / **583;** Medical Facilities / **583;** Money Matters / **583;** Communications / **584;** Arrival / **584;** Cruises / **584;** Departure / **584;** Touring Tips / **584;** Lodging / **585;** Restaurants / **593;** Natural Surroundings / **596;** Places Worth Finding / **596;** Sports / **596;** Treasures and Trifles / **597**

ST. CROIX 599
Political Picture / **601;** Island Appearance / **601;** Lifestyle / **601;** Medical Facilities / **602;** Money Matters / **602;** Communications / **602;** Arrival / **602;** Cruises / **603;** Departure / **603;** Touring Tips / **604;** Lodging / **604;** Restaurants / **611;** Natural Surroundings / **612;** Places Worth Finding / **613;** Sports / **619;** Treasures and Trifles / **621**

SINT EUSTATIUS 623
Political Picture / **624;** Island Appearance / **624;** Lifestyle / **624;** Medical Facilities / **624;** Money Matters / **624;** Communications / **624;** Arrival / **625;** Cruises / **625;** Departure / **625;** Touring Tips / **625;** Lodging / **625;** Natural Surroundings / **628;** Places Worth Finding / **628;** Sports / **629;** Treasures and Trifles / **629**

ST. JOHN 631
Political Picture / **633;** Island Appearance / **633;** Lifestyle / **633;** Medical Facilities / **633;** Money Matters / **634;** Communications / **634;** Arrival and Departure / **634;** Cruises / **634;** Touring Tips / **634;** Lodging /**635;** Restaurants / **640;** Natural Surroundings / **641;** Places Worth Finding / **641;** Sports / **642;** Treasures and Trifles / **643**

ST. KITTS 645
Political Picture / **647;** Island Appearance / **647;** Lifestyle / **648;** Medical Facilities / **648;** Money Matters / **648;** Communications / **648;** Arrival / **649;** Cruises / **649;** Departure / **649;**

Touring Tips / **650**; Lodging / **650**; Restaurants / **656**; Natural Surroundings / **657**; Places Worth Finding / **658**; Sports / **660**; Treasures and Trifles / **660**

ST. LUCIA   663

Political Picture / **665**; Island Appearance / **666**; Lifestyle / **666**; Medical Facilities / **667**; Money Matters / **667**; Communications / **667**; Arrival / **668**; Cruises / **668**; Departure / **668**; Touring Tips / **668**; Lodging / **669**; Restaurants / **676**; Natural Surroundings / **679**; Places Worth Finding / **680**; Sports / **682**; Treasures and Trifles / **683**

ST. MARTIN/SINT MAARTEN   685

Political Picture / **688**; Island Appearance / **688**; Lifestyle / **689**; Medical Facilities / **689**; Money Matters / **690**; Communications / **690**; Arrival / **690**; Cruises / **691**; Departure / **691**; Touring Tips / **691**; Lodging / **692**; Restaurants / **705**; Natural Surroundings / **709**; Places Worth Finding / **709**; Sports / **711**; Treasures and Trifles / **712**

ST. THOMAS   715

Political Picture / **717**; Island Appearance / **717**; Lifestyle / **718**; Medical Facilities / **718**; Money Matters / **718**; Communications / **719**; Arrival / **719**; Cruises / **719**; Departure / **719**; Touring Tips / **720**; Lodging / **720**; Restaurants / **730**; Natural Surroundings / **732**; Places Worth Finding / **732**; Sports / **734**; Treasures and Trifles / **736**

ST. VINCENT AND ITS GRENADINES   739

Political Picture / **741**; Island Appearance / **741**; Lifestyle / **742**; Medical Facilities / **742**; Money Matters / **743**; Communications / **743**; Arrival / **743**; Cruises / **744**; Departure / **744**; Touring Tips / **744**; Lodging / **745**; Restaurants / **750**; Natural Surroundings / **750**; Places Worth Finding / **751**; Sports / **753**; Treasures and Trifles / **754**
The Grenadines / **755**
  Bequia / **756**
  Canouan / **758**
  Mayreau / **759**
  Mustique / **759**
  Palm Island / **760**
  Petit St. Vincent / **761**
  Union Island / **762**

TORTOLA (See British Virgin Islands)

TRINIDAD   765

Political Picture / **766**; Island Appearance / **766**; Lifestyle / **767**; Medical Facilities / **768**; Money Matters / **768**; Communications / **768**; Arrival / **768**; Cruises / **769**; Departure / **769**; Touring Tips / **769**; Lodging / **770**; Restaurants / **774**; Natural Surroundings / **776**; Places Worth Finding / **779**; Sports / **780**; Treasures and Trifles / **781**

TOBAGO   783

Political Picture / **784**; Island Appearance / **784**; Lifestyle / **784**; Medical Facilities / **785**; Money Matters / **785**; Communications / **785**; Arrival / **785**; Departure / **786**; Touring Tips / **786**; Lodging / **786**; Restaurants / **791**; Natural Surroundings / **791**; Places Worth Finding / **792**; Sports / **793**; Treasures and Trifles / **794**

TURKS AND CAICOS 795

Political Picture / **795**; Island Appearance / **797**; Lifestyle / **797**; Medical Facilities / **797**; Money Matters / **797**; Communications / **797**; Arrival / **797**; Cruises / **798**; Departure / **798**; Touring Tips / **798**; Lodging /**798**; Natural Surroundings / **803**; Places Worth Finding / **803**; Sports / **803**; Treasures and Trifles / **803**

UNION ISLAND (See St. Vincent)

VIRGIN GORDA (See British Virgin Islands)

U.S. REPRESENTATIVES 805

HOTEL QUICK-REFERENCE CHARTS 809

THE CARIBBEAN MYSTIQUE

Paradise. Robinson Crusoe. Romance. Escape. Caribbean islands inspire dreams. They are fantasy islands that hint at a simpler, more honest life for those who live in a fast-paced, complicated world. They are beach-fringed, sea-surrounded specks known for sensuous music, exotic lifestyle, and hedonistic pleasures.

And they are home, for a multi-hued population that watches—and sometimes participates in—rapid changes, from an agrarian economy that had fallen on hard times to a complicated lifestyle increasingly affected by (and dependent upon) "tourism." These are places that have been yanked into the 1990s, with satellite television, airplane links, and fax machines.

You've been lured by the mystique, but can you capture it? What are your chances of realizing your dreams? Many of us have—but it's not always easy. There's a very strong possibility that, if you haven't yet traveled into the area, you're imagining a place that doesn't exist. What *is* the real Caribbean?

Modern tourism got its kick-start from World War II personnel stationed in the area in the 1940s. They returned home with tales of an idyllic place where costs were low, temperatures soothing, beaches beautiful, rum good, and people were eager to please. But just as the world has changed, so dramatic changes have taken place in the islands, especially since the mid–1970s.

The 32 island communities included in this book can count, all together, less than 90,000 square miles of land and approximately 28,400,000 nationals. Cuba is the largest country, with 44,200 square miles and 9,865,000 people; some of the other islands claim less than five square miles, with populations of less than 1000.

Although the numbers are small when compared with other regions of the world, these island countries (including the Bahamas and Bermuda, which are in the Atlantic Ocean, north of the Caribbean Sea) combine—but do not always completely integrate—the major European cultures and strident African heritage. The islands were brought into the modern world by the English and Irish, French, Spanish, Dutch, Danish, Swedish, and Americans, working with Indonesians, Chinese, East and West Indians, and Africans.

The region speaks in several languages, including French, Spanish, Dutch, English-with-regional-dialects, American, domestic patois, and the Netherlands Antilles' Papiamentu, a verbal stew of Dutch, Spanish, English and words from other languages. Lifestyles vary, sometimes in relationship to languages, from island to island.

Tourism is now the most significant employer on most islands, directly and indirectly contributing almost $6 billion to island countries' coffers. Almost 10 million visitors arrived in the islands during 1991. And an increasing fleet of cruise ships brings an estimated 6.5 million people into the region.

Although always suspect (as a polluter of local mores and morals), tourism has finally earned the attention of government at the highest levels, with ministerial status in many islands and quasi-government, politically independent status on others. As islands strive to offer modern, American-style conveniences, however, many have sacrificed their natural attributes—and their environment.

These islands that appear to be stepping stones between the southern tip of Florida and the north coast of South America have a fascinating history that dates from years before the time of Christ, when the Arawak indians first paddled their canoes out of Venezuela's Orinoco River.

Island images benefit (or perhaps suffer) from million-dollar budgets allocated to advertising and publicity that have not always served their best interests. Although the pictures are spectacular, and the purchased adjectives are positive and complimentary, the impressions are flawless. The projected image makes no allowance for reality; the suggestion is that "everything's perfect in paradise." And therein lies the problem.

The islands are third world countries that have only recently emerged from abject poverty; most have more than 90% black population. The road toward independence has had its potholes and washouts. Since the late 1960s, the region has been a subject for fickle reporting as it has undergone significant changes. There has been friction while island communities were grappling with an identity crisis created, in part, by severe economic problems and by racial tensions in areas where the economic power had been held by a white minority. During these years, visitors were being invited "into the house" to pay for a "carefree" holiday on terms that were not clearly defined. There were misunderstandings—on both sides. While crises are a source for headlines, many positive improvements have not been.

In the mid-1950s, most Caribbean islands had colonial governments. The three independent countries—Haiti (1804), the Dominican Republic (1844), and Cuba (1902)—were (and are) linked by inter-migrations. And each country has its traumatic history and often tumultuous present.

Haiti's destitute economy had suffered through the controversial dictatorship of François "Papa Doc" Duvalier, who made himself President-for-life in 1964 and set up systems for his son to become President-for-life on his death in 1971, when Jean-Claude was only 19 years old. "Baby Doc" fled from his country in early 1986, leaving a legacy of turmoil from which Haiti is only just recovering.

The Dominican Republic, meanwhile, was disciplined under the 30-year rule of dictator Generalissimo Rafael Leonidas Trujillo Molino, who was murdered in 1961. Elections in spring 1990 returned the incumbent octogenarian President Joaquin Balaguer to office by a narrow margin over his octogenarian rival, self-proclaimed Marxist, Juan Bosch, but the country has severe economic and other problems.

Cuba became a Communist country soon after a January 1959 revolution put Fidel Castro in power, with strong support from the Soviets. Although the amazing changes in the Communist world may result in improved U.S.-Cuban relations (when the government for the former Soviet Union pulls back on financial support, and turns its full attention to its own troubled economy), the doors for travel are closed for most U.S. citizens as this edition goes to press.

In the 1960s, financially troubled Britain's decision to shed its colonies was more for economic reasons than for humanitarian ones. And the plan played into the hands of island politicians who felt the tug of nationhood and the appeal of independence. The West Indies Federation, conceived to build a measure of stability by uniting the former British Caribbean colonies, was staffed by West Indian-born nationals, many of whom had been educated at the liberal, often Marxist, London School of Economics.

By 1962, strong leaders in Jamaica and Trinidad & Tobago gained independence for their countries, weakening the fledgling Federation by their departure. It was dissolved soon after Barbados' independence in 1966. (It's worth noting that, after 20 years of trying to go it alone, many of the smaller once-British countries are now part of an Organization of Eastern Caribbean States, known as OECS. In May 1987, they met to work toward creating a single state. The members are Antigua–Barbuda, Dominica, St. Lucia, St. Kitts and Nevis, St. Vincent and the Grenadines, Grenada, and Montserrat; other British-linked islands are observers.)

Except for vacationers who enjoyed Robinson-Crusoe-style holidays, few people noticed these islands in the 1960s. Tourism was an infant industry. Less than a dozen intrepid dreamers had the stamina (and funds) to create a vacationers' "paradise"—on islands such as Barbuda, St. John, Young Island, Petit St. Vincent, and Palm Island. The aid packages that were occasionally dropped on islands had strings attached to the donors, and few individuals and/or corporations invested in the region.

By 1966, the remaining, economically fragile British colonies, were granted Associated Statehood as individual islands or in groups, as a step toward eventual independence. During these years, local politicians tried their wings in world political circles and many found a comfortable climate in the Marxist ideology. Support from communist Cuba was strong and strategically placed.

Grenada became independent in 1974, to be followed by Dominica (1978), St. Vincent (1979), and St. Lucia (1979). The two-island nation of Antigua-Barbuda gained independence from Britain in 1981, and St. Kitts and Nevis became one two-island country in 1983.

The former Dutch and French colonies grew in other ways. On January 1, 1986, Aruba stepped away from its Netherlands Antilles' siblings to become one element of the three-pronged Kingdom of the Netherlands. The five other Netherlands Antilles' islands (Bonaire, Curaçao, Sint Maarten, Saba, and Sint Eustatius) are a second element of the Kingdom; the Netherlands is the third. There are talks of total independence for each of the Dutch Caribbean elements by 1996, but for now, all look to tourism to drive their economies.

The French islands—Martinique and Guadeloupe, with satellites of St. Martin, Desirade, Marie-Galante, Les Saintes, and St. Barthelemy—have become full-fledged *regions* and *departements* of France, with all the attendant benefits, plus the political persuasion reaching the islands from mainland France and, to those islands's strong communist parties, from Cuba. Pro-independence elements on both Guadeloupe and Martinique continue to push for nationhood, sometimes in sympathy with each other and always with support from Cuba. For the forseeable future, these islands will remain part of France.

Following the Spanish-American war, the United States claimed Puerto Rico and, in 1917, the U.S. government purchased the formerly Danish Virgin Islands (St. Croix, St. John, and St. Thomas) for $25 million, to safeguard the Panama Canal in an increasingly complex world order. These days, the U.S. Virgin Islands make up one self-governing territory, with consulting links through the U.S. Department of Interior. Puerto Rico has unique status as a U.S. Commonwealth, with self-government and an impending prebescite for statehood, independence, or continued Commonwealth status. Both the U.S. Virgin Islands and Puerto Rico elect their own governments, and both receive preferential tax and other financial benefits with their territorial and Commonwealth status.

Of the islands covered in this book, only Anguilla, the British Virgin Islands (Virgin Gorda, Tortola, and several small islands), Montserrat, the Cayman Islands, and the Turks & Caicos islands are British colonies (now called territories), a status each has freely chosen in preference to independence.

Always given worth when wars demanded loyalties, the one-time European colonies played a crucial role at the time of U.S. independence. Their location (and their loyalties) made them useful conduits for arms and funds that flowed from Europe to the east coast of young America. These islands were to replay their role as an arena for European power plays during the first half of the 20th century, during the world wars, at a time when their economies had fallen on hard times, following the abolition of slavery and the resulting failure of the sugar crops.

Acknowledged as strategic bases for the allies, the Caribbean islands had an international value. Many island airstrips were built during those years, for the U.S. Navy airplanes. German submarines patrolled these waters, as did those of the United States and allied nations and wartime activity then, as in the 17th and 18th centuries, created some of the shipwrecks that are scuba sites today.

In the 1990s, all of the region's English-speaking islands have democratically elected governments who support a free market economy. On each of the formerly-British islands, the public (government) and private sectors are working together to build a strong country. The decisive action in Grenada in October 1983, when the U.S. rescue mission routed the Marxism that had been nurtured by Cuba and the Soviet Union with its satellites, proved to be a catharsis for the region.

Although still a goal for the few islands that have yet to achieve it, independence is now taken in stride, but free-market western-oriented economic practices are still not fully understood. Caribbean people see the advantages—and the disadvantages—of the system. Opposition parties have an appealing message when the economy falters and, while the Caribbean people are aware of the benefits of tourism, they also live with its liabilities—increasing crime, erosion of natural resources, and a beach-centered social and economic life that is not natural to their traditions. All these are factors that have an impact on the Caribbean mystique.

Caribbean islands have been pirate strongholds since the 17th century. They have long histories of smuggling. And they were nefarious ports during U.S. prohibition, when they were used for contraband liquor. Although marijuana, known as *ganja* in Jamaica and by that, or another, name on other islands, has been part of the Caribbean culture since Amerindians smoked "the weed" centuries ago, hard drugs are a modern scourge, brought to and through the islands from Columbia and other source countries. The jagged shorelines on many islands are being used today for drug drops. As anti-drug laws are enforced on the U.S. mainland, the supplies back up into the Caribbean. And the affluence resulting from drug-dealing is overwhelming for some Caribbean nationals. Drugs are as much a fact of life on idyllic Caribbean islands as they are in U.S. communities. Although the situation does not threaten most people, wise travelers should be aware of its existence. And island governments must address the problem.

Pundits no longer refer to tourism as a "non-polluting industry." On many islands, the environment is threatened by over-development. On some islands, beachside hotels dump sewage into the once-pristine sea. Plastic litter coats the roadsides; hillsides are scraped clean for developments, or leveled for airports. Until recently, little thought was given to the fragile island environment. But it is not too late for some places. The Barbados-based Caribbean Conservation Committee has spearheaded several programs for preservation and protection of both natural growth and historic buildings. Most islands have conservation groups; many have National Trust organizations. And the Philadelphia-based RARE Center for Tropical Bird Conservation, has sparked community environmental education programs on several islands.

On an economic level, Britain, Canada, and the United States have redesigned aid programs, directing them to small industries, tourism-related as well as in other areas in hopes of broadening the economic base. The United States Department of State has signed Tax Information Exchange Agreements with Barbados, Dominica, the Dominican Republic, Grenada, Jamaica, and Trinidad & Tobago, and will do so with other countries. One result is that U.S. businesspeople may deduct expenses incurred while attending seminars, meetings, and conventions in signed countries. Another is that TIEA countries are eligible to tap funds available through Puerto Rico's "section 936" for low-cost investment financing. And the Caribbean Basin Initiative, launched by President Reagan in 1982, is being revised to allow more practical support to island economies, for tourism-related projects as well as for other industry.

We who visit Caribbean countries these days benefit by learning about the host country and, perhaps, by sharing expertise on a personal basis. Many island governments make it easy, as well as pleasant, to meet island residents. The local tourist boards and many hotels can make arrangements. The owners of several of the island's inns are enthusiastic about sharing their knowledge of their homeland. If you are a member of Rotary Club, a church group, a garden club, or are a volunteer at your local library or hospital, you can find a common bond with at least one island resident. If you like to play bridge or enjoy some other hobby, meeting an island resident who shares the interest can add immeasurably to your holiday. Here are some sources for facts about the Caribbean region:

Caribbean Tourism Organization, 20 East 46th Street, New York, NY 10017, T 212+ 682–0435; and Mer Vue, Marine Gardens, Hastings, Barbados, West Indies, T 809+ 427–5242.

Caribbean Hotel Association, 18 Marseilles Street, Santurce, Puerto Rico 00907; T 809+ 725–9139.

Caribbean Central America Action, #510, 1211 Connecticut Avenue, NW, Washington, DC 20036; T 202+ 466–7464.

Caribbean Association of Industry and Commerce, Box 259, 2nd Floor, Musson Bldg., Lower Hincks St., Bridgetown, Barbados, West Indies; T 809+ 436–6385.

COLUMBUS AND THE CARIBBEAN

[The *Caribbean Newsletter,* mentioned on page 9, will have current facts about celebrations planned for the Columbus years. This is the status at press time.]

Christopher Columbus started it all—the modern development of the Caribbean region, at least. Whether or not his arrival was a blessing for the region has been hotly debated. As is too often the case in Caribbean circles, an exceptional opportunity to promote a widely-recognized event is being hog-tied in emotional trauma.

Because the intrepid explorer opened the floodgate for slavery, and documents indicate that some of his crew probably mistreated the Arawaks, Caribs, Tainos, and others they found when they arrived, many of today's Caribbean folks are curbing their enthusiasm for his arrival.

The facts remain. Christopher Columbus was the first European tourist, when he arrived in what's now called the Caribbean, in fall of 1492. He returned three times, and was followed by other Europeans, who set up plantations, imported African slaves, and carried out their wars in the seas that surrounded their Caribbean colonies and on the shores of the colonies themselves. The Europeans were the first settlers to follow the Arawak indians.

Christopher Columbus, or Cristobal Colon as he was known at home (and still is known in Spanish-speaking islands), touched land somewhere in the Bahamas (or Turks & Caicos islands) on October 12, 1492. He had left home on August 3, with 88 men, to sail west to reach—as every school child knows—the *East* Indies. Instead, he found—and named—the *West* Indies.

On that journey, he continued on to Cuba and La Espanola, now known as Hispaniola, the island occupied by Haiti and the Dominican Republic. His men's settlement, at a place they called La Navidad, is thought to be near the north coast border between the two countries.

On September 25, 1493, Columbus set out again from Spain, with 17 ships and 1500 men, returning to Spain in 1496. On this journey, he sighted and named Dominica, on Sunday, November 3, and also passed by Guadeloupe, Montserrat, Antigua, St. Martin, Santa Cruz (which became St. Croix), and San Juan Bautista, which is now known by the name given to its rich port, Puerto Rico. Some of the crew stayed on Hispaniola, establishing a second settlement, since no one survived from the first, at Isabela, also on the north coast of the Dominican Republic.

Eventually some members of that settlement went south, to flee persecution and to search for gold. A settlement was established at the mouth of the Ozama River, eventually moving across the river to the present capital of Santo Domingo, where a city was built to serve as transit port for passage to and from Central America.

On May 30, 1498, the third expedition left Spain, with six ships, sailing south, in the vicinity of Trinidad and the coast of South America. He was brought back from this journey in chains to answer charges by his enemies. Records document the Isla Santa, and remark on what would be the Gulf of Paria at the mouth of the Orinoco river, where the expedition paused on August 14.

After answering the charges and gaining his freedom, Columbus set out—dispirited and in bad health—on a fourth voyage, in 1502, with four caravelles. On this journey, he passed St. Lucia, the coast of Honduras, and then went into San Juan, before returning to Spain, where he arrived on November 7, 1504. At a point on this journey, Columbus paused at Salt River on Santa Cruz, now known as St. Croix.

His legacy in the region is far greater than the documentation of his voyages, however. Most islands claim his influence in their names, for saints, familiar sights, and relatives, as is the case with San Juan, Dominica, Grenada (for Spain's Grenada), Montserrat (for the monastery in Spain), St. Barthelemy (for his brother, Bartolome), and others.

There are few touchstones from his time, however. Not only does the tempo of these times set a pace for tearing down legends but also, scholarship about Columbus's voyages in island archives, where they exist, is limited. Libraries in Spain (with documents in Spanish) and in London, England (at the British museum) have specific records, but few have perused them with a detailed knowledge of Caribbean islands.

Among the best books about the Columbus voyages are those by Samuel Elliot Morrison, most especially *Admiral of the Ocean Seas*. For other information, look for comprehensive articles in forthcoming issues of the *National Geographic* and *Smithsonian magazines*.

Since most Caribbean islands do not have funds, or in some cases the enthusiasm, for promotion of their Columbus links, you'll be pretty much on your own to tailor your own travels. Look carefully at promotions planned for the Columbus year. Many may be excellent; some will undoubtedly be aimed at profits for the promoters.

Among the Caribbean communities with specific plans that seem well organized at press time, consider:

Bahamas: Celebrations are planned, focusing on the island of San Salvador, where Club Med expects to open a new property and on the other islands where festivals and events will be held. Although a flurry of interest greeted a new claim for landfall at Samana in the Bahamas, the Bahamian government seems ready to devote their energies and promotional funds to San Salvador, and the Bahamas in general, as the first landfall.

Dominican Republic: With a well-established claim to being a thriving community in the early 1500s, and with financial and technical support from

Spain, the country has many authentic Columbian touchstones. Bartolome Colon, Cristobal's brother, celebrated the first mass in the new world, on the banks of the Ozama River that splits the capital of Santo Domingo. He established the settlement, which was further developed by Nicholas de Ovando, appointed governor after Cristobal was taken from the settlement in chains at the end of his third voyage. And Diego Colon, a son of Cristobal, was viceroy of the Indies; he administered his holdings from Santo Domingo, where he was briefly held prisoner by Sir Francis Drake, in 1585, during one of several altercations between the Spanish and the English in those early days.

Historically, the north coast settlements are well documented, although little or nothing remains in those areas today. The south coast settlement, at the capital of Santo Domingo, is alive and well, having been rebuilt with limestone blocks from a quarry used by the original builders. Although most of the buildings have been reconstructed, they are done in authentic style. There are several exceptional museums, and a new multimillion dollar monument with museums. There will be special events, although nothing has been announced at press time.

Jamaica: The Jamaican government hopes to tie in with Columbus celebrations through the fact that his ships wrecked off the north coast. In May of 1494, at the end of the second journey, two caravelles were beached in 10 feet of water, not far from St. Ann's Bay, where they may still lie, covered in silt. Although the caravelles have not been found at press time, a group from the Institute of Nautical Archeology, affiliated with Texas A & M University, is conducting an underwater dig in hopes of finding the ships.

Puerto Rico: The historic restorations at Old San Juan benefit from Columbus celebrations, although the "admiral of the ocean seas" never settled here. Ponce de Leon was the island's first governor, although he went on (in search of the fountain of youth) to Florida. In fact, many of the 16th- and 17th-century buildings in Old San Juan are in better condition than those in Santo Domingo, capital of the Dominican Republic. Because the city was built at the tip of a peninsula, and protected by a sturdy fort, modern building could grow only on the neck of land that links the bulge to the island. There will be festivals and other celebrations throughout the year in Puerto Rico.

St. Croix: On November 14, 1493, amid the third voyage, some of the crew went ashore at Salt River, on the north coast of St. Croix, in hopes of finding fresh water. They were beaten back by hostile Indians, some of whom they captured; Columbus named the area Cabo de Flechas (cape of the arrows). The group of the Islas de Virgines (Virgin Islands) was named by Columbus. The legend claims they take their name from St. Ursula and her 11,000 virgins, who were set upon by savages on their pilgrimage to a holy site in the 11th century.

Turks & Caicos: Seminars have been held in these islands, as they work toward establishing their claim for having been the first landfall. The Caicos Passage, a 22-mile-wide channel that separates the group, has been renamed Columbus Passage. Budgetary constraints will hamper the government's ability to make a big splash.

THIS YEAR'S BEST

Each island has its own personality. Although specific traits are explained in the chapters that follow, here's a short list of my choices for:

BEACHES: My top dozen choices for wide, soft-sand, white-to-butterscotch-colored beaches would be North Shoal Bay on Anguilla, Palm to Manchebo Beach in Aruba, Cocoa Point on Barbuda, Veradero on Cuba, West Bay on Grand Cayman, Negril on Jamaica, Playa Flamenco on Culebra, Grand Anse in Grenada, Baie Longue on St. Martin, Magens Bay on St. Thomas, Great Courland Bay, known as Turtle Beach, on Tobago, and Grace Bay on Providenciales, one of the Turks and Caicos islands. Others worth noting are Half Moon Bay on Antigua, tiny Owen Island off Little Cayman, Crane Beach on Barbados, Plage Crawan on Terre-de-Haut, the Tobago Cays and Salt Whistle Bay in the Grenadine Islands, Chouchou Bay on Haiti, Playa Luquillo on Puerto Rico, Sandy Cay in the British Virgin Islands, Les Salines on Martinique, Baie de St. Jean and Gouverneur on St. Barths, Buck Island off St. Croix, Trunk Bay and Cinnamon Bay on St. John, Cockleshell/Banana Bay on St. Kitts, Ilet Pinel off St. Martin, and Sapphire Bay on St. Thomas.

BUDGET TRAVEL: Each chapter has a section called "Low-Cost Lodging," and some of the apartments and cottages mentioned under "Housekeeping Holidays" can be very inexpensive when the place is filled and the cost is split. All-inclusive resorts *can* be reasonably priced, but read the small print to be sure exactly what is covered in the cost. The best value comes when room, meals, drinks, watersports and other activities, tips, and taxes are included in the one quoted sum, and the items included are those you want. Insofar as moderately priced islands are concerned, there are only a few, namely the island of Dominica and some places in the Dominican Republic. Haiti is also reasonably priced, due to its political and other problems, but it's not suggested for timid travelers, and Trinidad and Tobago have reasonable rates at many hotels. Puerto Rico has many pleasant small places where rates are reasonable.

CAMPING: The United States Virgin Islands set the pace in 1956, when most of the island of St. John was dedicated as the 29th U.S. National Park. In addition to the Cinnamon Bay campgrounds, the island has privately-owned Maho Bay Camps. Other places with camplike facilities include Tortola, in the British Virgin Islands, where the Brewers Bay campsite patterned itself (loosely) after the St. John venture, and the island of Carriacou, part of (and north of)

Grenada, where Casada Bay has camplike facilities that are ideal for back-to-nature holidays. Both Martinique and Guadeloupe have camping vehicles for rent and designated areas where they may be parked. Individual chapters note camplike accommodations; the island government tourist offices can help with specific details.

DISCOVERIES: If you want a Robinson Crusoe experience away from the shadow of modern tourism, look into the lesser-known islands such as Dominica, Montserrat, St. Vincent, and Tobago, as well as Terre-de-Haut and Marie-Galante (off Guadeloupe), Barbuda, and several of the Grenadines islands, namely Bequia, Canouan, Union Island, and Grenada's Carriacou. Even big and cosmopolitan Trinidad is little known to most American tourists and the Turks & Caicos are almost deserted.

FAMILIES: Renting an apartment or cottage near an active resort gives flexibility, with the opportunity to cook at home to cater to family appetites. For specific places, refer to "Housekeeping Holidays" in each chapter. For teenage children, consider a Club Med or one of the family-oriented, all-inclusive resorts on Jamaica (*Boscobel*, *Jamaica-Jamaica*, or *Trelawny*, for example), or a lively area such as the north coast of the Dominican Republic, especially the Puerto Plata-Sosua-Cabarete area. In Puerto Rico, the resorts such as Hyatt's *Dorado* and *Cerromar*, or the southeast coast's *Palmas del Mar* have golf, tennis, and other activities including camps for children, as does the *Caribe Hilton*. The island of St. John or Tortola and Virgin Gorda, in the British Virgin Islands, are good for sea-oriented families where young people can sail, scuba, dive, and snorkel. With babies, consider islands that are easy to reach with one non-stop flight and where experienced nannies are available. Three worth investigating are Jamaica, Grand Cayman, and Puerto Rico. Barbados is also a good place for families, with direct (but not always non-stop) flights.

FOOD: Most islands have at least a few places that serve exceptional food. Islands with dozens of choices include Sint Maarten/St. Martin (where prices can be budget-breaking), Guadeloupe and Martinique (where spicy creole cooking coexists with classical French cuisine), Barbados, St. Lucia, and Jamaica (where plentiful local produce is nicely served in Caribbean-style restaurants), and Puerto Rico, especially the San Juan area, where the range of restaurants reflects that known in most U.S. cities. Santo Domingo, capital of the Dominican Republic, has many excellent restaurants (and most have reasonable prices); there are now a few good places, also, on the north coast, but they are geared for tourists. There are a few atmospheric and good restaurants on Aruba and Curacao, where Dutch-style often means an Indonesian *rijsttafel* (the multi-dish meal served with rice). Otherwise, count on Caribbean cuisine, which is now being presented with the appeal warranted by the fresh and colorful island-grown ingredients.

FOREIGN FLAVOR: For Spain (and speaking Spanish), try the Dominican Republic and, to a lesser degree, Puerto Rico. Although the southern group of Dutch-affiliated islands—Aruba, Bonaire, and Curacao—have the language and other reflections of the mother country, the many words—and local folk—suggest the island's proximity to South America. For French language, customs, and currency, head for Martinique, Guadeloupe, and St. Barthelemy. Most other Caribbean islands are, or have been, British-affiliated, with customs and language familiar to North American travelers.

GAMBLING: Puerto Rico and the Dominican Republic have full-fledged casinos with floor shows in many big hotels. Sint Maarten has casinos on the Dutch side only. Many of Aruba's biggest hotels have their own casinos; others are convenient to the Alhambra casino complex. Curacao also has casinos in its biggest hotels; Bonaire has one casino. Antigua's casinos are in the *St. James's Club* (European style), in the *Flamingo Hotel,* and at the government's *Halcyon Cove Hotel* (U.S.-style). On Martinique and Guadeloupe, there are French-style casinos at or near the *Meridien* hotels and, on Martinique, also at *La Batelier Hotel.* Some Barbados properties have slot machines, as do a few in Jamaica, and there's a casino in the *Jack Tar* hotel on St. Kitts and a few slot machines elsewhere. Haiti has casinos, but status is uncertain at press time. The *Caribbean Newsletter* (page 9) will update this list when warranted.

GOLF: The best courses, according to those in the know, are at *Casa de Campo* in the Dominican Republic, *Hyatt's Dorado* and *Cerromar* on the north coast of Puerto Rico, and *Palmas del Mar* on the southeast coast of Puerto Rico. There are also several good courses in Jamaica, with those at *Tryall, Half Moon,* and *Rose Hall* the most popular. There's a course near Port of Spain in Trinidad and at *Mt. Irvine* on Tobago, as well as at St. Francois on Guadeloupe and Trois Ilets on Martinique and a new 18-hole course on Nevis at the *Four Seasons* resort. The Robert Trent Jones course on the north coast of the Dominican Republic, at *Playa Dorada,* suffers from drainage problems after heavy rains, and courses on Antigua are more fun than professional as is the case, also, on Grand Cayman and Montserrat. The best course on Barbados is at *Sandy Lane.*

HONEYMOONS: Look at any issue of *Bride's* or *Modern Bride* magazines for Caribbean suggestions. Ask the government tourist offices, whose addresses are at the start of each chapter, about hotels offering honeymoon packages and check with the island hotel associations. Consider places such as *Couples* or the *Sandals* resorts on Jamaica, or *Couples* on St. Lucia. All are inclusive, with plenty of activities for couples. St. Thomas is also a popular honeymoon island. Many islands offer complete wedding arrangements, with license, preacher, flowers, and reception all part of a package. Anguilla has such a program, as do Jamaica and the United States Virgin Islands of St. Croix, St. Thomas, and St. John.

LUXURY: If you want the very best, consider *Curtain Bluff* or *Jumby Bay* on Antigua; *Malliouhana* or *Cap Juluca* on Anguilla; *Tryall* or *Round Hill* on Jamaica; the *K Club* on Barbuda (if it's open); *Sandy Lane* on Barbados; or renting a private and elegant villa on Jamaica, Barbados, or St. Barthelemy; or renting a private island such as Necker Island or Drake's Anchorage, in the British Virgin Islands, or in the Grenadines.

NATURAL SURROUNDINGS: The best islands for walks and hikes in the wilderness for birding and botanical pursuits are Dominica, Jamaica, Trinidad, Tobago, portions of Grenada, St. Lucia, and St. Vincent, and the National Parks on Guadeloupe and Martinique, as well as the National Park near El Yunque and El Foropark on Puerto Rico. See the section called "Natural Surroundings" in each chapter for specific suggestions on each island.

NIGHTLIFE: Where there are big hotels and/or casinos, there's usually some action. The best places for nightclubing are the San Juan area of Puerto Rico, plus Santo Domingo and Puerto Plata in the Dominican Republic, Martinique, Guadeloupe, and the south-coast resort area of Barbados. The price-inclusive hotels and most resort hotels (in winter season) have local evening entertainment, which is usually domestic bands or floor shows.

SAILING: The best cruising areas, because there are lots of islands within a reasonably confined area, are the British Virgin Islands, the St. Thomas-St. John area of the U.S. Virgin Islands, and the Grenadines, from St. Vincent south to Grenada. There are also well-established marinas, with bareboat and crewed yacht charters, on Martinique, Guadeloupe, and Philipsburg, Marigot and Oyster Pond on Sint Maarten/St. Martin. Antigua's English Harbour and Falmouth Harbour are also home ports for many yachts, as are Marigot Bay, Rodney Bay, and Castries on St. Lucia and marinas on the south coast of Grenada.

SCUBA DIVING: Scuba diving got its Caribbean start in St. Thomas, where the Navy's Underwater Demolition Teams trained during World War II. St. Thomas is still one of the established diving triumvirate, with Grand Cayman and Bonaire, but there are scuba divemasters available on most islands—even on tiny Saba, Sint Eustatius, and St. Kitts. See "Sports" in the chapters and refer to *Skin Diver* and other dive-focused magazines.

SHOPPING: Haitians set the pace, with their signature *naif* art, which includes colorful paintings as well as many fanciful decorative items, but colorful crafts of good quality can also be found in Guadeloupe and Martinique, where Madras fabric in the faded bronze tones is used for clothes, place mats, and other items. The U.S. Peace Corp reestablished a craft center on the southwest coast of St. Lucia, where Chinese teachers are helping with items made from woven reeds and other grasses, and other craftspeople are helping youngsters to develop skills. On Barbados and on Trinidad, artists have adapted their talent for wall hangings, as well as note cards, place mats and coasters. Dominica and Montserrat have well-made mats and baskets. There are workshops for reproductions of Jamaican Georgian-style furniture in Jamaica; the Dominican Republic also has talented artisans who make furniture of wood as well as wicker. For noteworthy resort fashions, Carole Cadogan in Barbados sets very high standards; there are also talented designers in Jamaica and Trinidad.

As for "duty-free" shopping, it's worth researching the fine points of "duty-free," if you care about finding a real bargain. Shopkeepers on some islands have boosted prices for one-time bargains so that, even though no or low duty is paid at port of entry, the cost in the shop is more than you'd pay at your hometown discount store. Among the islands with extensive selections of imports culled from world markets, investigate the U.S. Virgin Islands (especially St. Croix and St. Thomas), as well as the Dutch and French sides of Sint Maarten/St. Martin and the Dutch-affiliated islands of Aruba and Curacao. St. Lucia's Pointe Seraphine and Antigua's Heritage Quay have been created for cruise ship passengers and other tourists. Refer to the "Treasures and Trifles" sections of each chapter and to the "Shopping" comment in the next chapter (page 50).

SINGLES: Decide whether you want constant action or a few congenial people, perhaps even happy couples. Many single travelers enjoy the *Club Mediterranee* resorts and/or the other price-inclusive places (on Jamaica, Barbados, Antigua, and other islands), where meeting other guests is made easier by organized activities. If you prefer, as I do, a small hotel with a compatible group, many places included in my *GeoMedia Pocketguide to Caribbean Small Hotels* can be good. Many singles find companionship, and fun, through sports—perhaps learning a new one. Several resorts offer sports-focused weeks with tennis, golf, scuba diving, and/or sailing.

TENNIS: Most of the larger hotels have tennis courts and a few have special tennis weeks with pro-Am tournaments. Inquire about the dates for the tournaments at Antigua's *Curtain Bluff* and *Half Moon* and at Jamaica's *Tryall Hotel & Club*. Ask for details about tennis weeks at the *Hyatt's Dorado Beach* and *Cerromar* on the north coast of Puerto Rico, and at *Palmas del Mar*, also on that island. The *Coccoloba Plantation* on Anguilla has a Peter Burwash Tennis program and All American Sports manages the program for the *St. James's Club* on Antigua and Jamaica's *Half Moon Club*.

WINDSURFING: Boardsailing is big business in the islands! Investigate the "Sailboard Vacations" facilities on Aruba, the Barbados Windsurfing Resort, the several places at Cabarete on the north coast of the Dominican Republic, Rincon and other places on the west coast in Puerto Rico, and off beaches in the U. S. Virgin Islands. Sint Maarten/St. Martin has several areas for boardsailing; St. Barths has boards for rent at Baie de St. Jean; Martinique's Anse Mitan has plenty of boards and on Guadeloupe, hotels near Gosier and at St. Francois have boards for rent—as do many beachfront hotels on all islands. Ask in advance if you're passionate about the sport.

TIPS AND TOPICS FOR CARIBBEAN TRAVELING

Options for Caribbean travel are endless. The "one brand" days are over. Although travel once followed a system, as did other elements of life such as job, school, and hometown choice, these are the days of "supermarket" travel. There are as many choices as there are people choosing. How you put the elements together and budget the cost for your vacation are personal decisions.

It's possible to buy travel in as many categories as you buy your clothes or food: you can go to the fashionable boutique or quality supermarket, where you'll probably pay a premium for pre-selected merchandise, or you can go to the lowest cost factory pipe-racks or discount stores. In travel terms, you can travel deluxe—at one of the few five-star hotels in the Caribbean—or low-cost, at campsites or guest houses. You can choose a small island with a few special places or a big island with the full array. Finding the place to fit your dreams is the challenge! What follows is a list of some options.

Airlines

Puerto Rico is the Caribbean's hub, with hundreds of flights funneling through its Munoz Marin International Airport each day. *American Airlines* leads the pack, in frequency of flights to and through the Caribbean. When it won the race (with Eastern) to build Puerto Rico into a full-fledged hub, the airline conscientiously expanded its services through San Juan, using both the small-plane *American Eagle* flights and big-plane *American Airlines* flights, for the nearby islands of Anguilla, St. Thomas, St. Croix, and Sint Maarten, as well as for islands in the southern sector, such as Aruba, Curaçao, Barbados, Grenada, and Trinidad, and almost all islands between north and south.

But it was *Pan American* that first flew into the Caribbean—in the late 1920s, with flights to Cuba—and opened up the region in the 1950s. Once again, a pared-down *Pan American* is rebuilding its schedule into the Caribbean, through Puerto Rico and to other islands.

Continental Airlines is increasing its services out of U.S. cities, with frequent flights from the New York area out of Newark, New Jersey, and connections through that airport with its other U.S. flights. *Midway* flies out of Chicago and other mid-west cities; *Delta* flies through Atlanta to the islands, and there are good connections, also, from the west coast and the southwest, through Dallas, Miami, Atlanta and other cities. *Air Canada* has scheduled services from Toronto and Montreal, in addition to the several charter services from Canadian cities.

There are, in fact, thousands of flights year-around on the U.S. and Canadian carriers, on European carriers, and on the national carriers of islands such as the Caymans *(Cayman Airlines)*, Jamaica *(Air Jamaica)*, the Dutch Caribbean *(ALM,* the Dutch Antilles airline), Aruba *(Air Aruba),* and to many of the formerly British islands on Trinidad & Tobago's airline *(BWIA,* which stood for British West Indies Airways).

AUTHOR'S OBSERVATION

"Full" flights are the bane of the travelers' plans. In fact, very few flights are full when they take off. At peak travel times, nationals and others often book several flights to give themselves choices. But they only occupy one of those seats. If you can be flexible, and are traveling with carry-on baggage, *always* be willing to "stand-by" for the flight of your choice. Often you will be aboard when the plane takes off.

In addition to Puerto Rico, and those islands reached through Puerto Rico, other Caribbean islands with frequent daily non-stop flights from U. S. cities are the Dominican Republic, the Cayman Islands, and Jamaica. Each of the other islands is easily reached, in a hen-and-chickens fashion, from one or more of the major islands in its orbit. Thus Anguilla, in addition to being linked to Puerto Rico, is also linked to St. Thomas, Sint Maarten, and St. Kitts. Tiny Saba is linked to Sint Maarten and Sint Eustatius (Statia) by *Winair* (Windward Islands Air Service). St. Barthélémy (St. Barths) is linked to Sint Maarten, via *Winair* and *Air St. Barthélémy,* and to Guadeloupe via *Air Guadeloupe.* There are also flights out of St. Croix. Nevis is easily reached out of its sister island, St. Kitts (by both plane and boat), and out of Antigua, on *LIAT* (Leeward Island Air Transport) flights, as well as through St. Croix.

Culebra and Vieques are reached aboard small planes from San Juan, Puerto Rico, and from St. Croix and St. Thomas. The British Virgin Islands (Virgin Gorda and Tortola) are also reached from Puerto Rico, as well as from St. Thomas and other neighboring islands. And St. Vincent and its Grenadines as well as Grenada are easily reached through Barbados.

Deregulation of the airline industry has opened island areas (and the rest of the world) to "everyone." While the well-known U.S. and island-national airline services remain consistent, other carriers fly into the region when charter or other business makes service viable. Although "unknown" names may have suggested questionable safety and service in earlier times, these days they imply entrepreneurship; most are staffed and headed by experienced airline people who once worked for the well-known airlines.

Insofar as regional airlines are concerned, they proliferate almost as fast as the gnats known at some beaches after the twilight rains! Some of the island-based regional airlines have only a few small planes. The longtime leader for inter-island service is LIAT, formally Leeward Islands Air Transport, started over 30 years ago and still offering the best inter-island service from its base at Antigua.

> **AUTHOR'S OBSERVATION**
>
> If you are interested in visiting several islands, ask your travel agent to get details on LIAT's "Explorer" fares. There are two versions and they must be purchased outside the region. Your travel agent can issue what is known as an "MCO" for the 21-day fare that allows for visits to three islands or the one month fare that allows for visits to all islands on LIAT's system.

Yes! Island-based airline "services" can be infuriating to travelers used to the once-comfortable U.S. and European flights. However, now that deregulation has wreaked havoc with U.S. continental air service, it's safe to say that the island services are no worse than you'll find at home. The planes are small, and the people move slowly, but these airlines provide the best (and, in some cases, only) links with many of the outer islands.

When negotiating with local airline services, allow plenty of time. Be patient, but be firm. Keep your cool, no matter how infuriating the system may seem. The best results come when you reassure the people you are dealing with that they are as important as they think they are.

Boats and Ships

See "Cruise Ship Ports" below for further thoughts.
Amerindians paddled their own canoes out of the Orinoco and north through the Caribbean island chain about the time of Christ, and perhaps before. In the 15th century, Columbus sailed west to arrive at the "West" Indies, to be followed by assorted pirates, privateers, and plantation owners and workers. Boats and ships have linked these islands since the earliest years and, although the airplane now allows for thousands of travelers to touch Caribbean shores, there are some islands that are still linked to neighbors only by boat, as was the case for all, if they had any link, until the 1950s.

Today, although freighter traffic still exists, by far the greatest volume of sea traffic is on yachts, boats, and cruise ships.

> **AUTHOR'S OBSERVATION**
>
> Cruises to Caribbean islands offer the ultimate package tour! From the time you board the ship until you return to homeport, you are carried along to fascinating islands, which you can tour around or look at from afar. Food, room, entertainment, and medical care (should you want it) are all within easy reach, and someone is ever-ready to solve the few problems that may occur.

There's no doubt but that the convenience of unpacking, stowing your luggage, and letting the captain and his crew guide you from one island to the next, is the most carefree way to see these islands. Relaxing aboard the cruise that's right for you, however, requires research, unless you're flexible enough to take your chances. Some cruises are best for singles; others appeal to independent travelers who aren't searching for non-stop social life. Some cruises focus on educational seminars; others have elaborate sports programs. Some are best for couples, others are good for families, and still others are ideal for senior citizens. There are small ships that can glide into little-known islands as well as huge ships that become an island unto themselves (and mask any natural island's own personality when all the ship's passengers come ashore).

Selecting is a science. A trusted travel agent can be a one-stop source for folders, facts, and information. And the Cruise Lines International Association (#1407, 500 Fifth Ave., New York, NY 10110, T 212+ 921-0066), which represents most of the leading cruise lines and has complete information about the ships, also has good background information about the concept of cruising.

Whatever your source, these are the questions to ask:

• What are the ports? Are they the places you really want to visit or are you planning to stay aboard anyway?

• What's the homeport? Although most big ships have moved to southern U.S. ports in recent seasons and many ships base their weekly cruises in San Juan, Puerto Rico, a number of the smaller, more exclusive ships use other islands as homeport. There are ships that base in Jamaica, Martinique, Barbados, Curacao, St. Croix, and other islands.

• Is airfare from the nearest major city included in the price? Some cruise lines include airfare in the price, but how much and from where varies.

• What's the plan for shipboard entertainment? Some lines offer investment courses, cooking lessons, computer courses, instruction in golf, scuba, languages, fitness/spa regimens, and even talks by renowned authorities.

• What size is the ship? Small ships usually appeal to independent travelers; big ships have entertainment and restaurant choices akin to those at major landbased resorts.

• What size are the cabins, and what's included? Is there television? Do you care? Ask for a deck plan and check it carefully.

• How much time is allowed in ports? Unless your ship docks at a shoreside pier, be sure to subtract the time it takes to get off the ship, into town, and back aboard again.

Cruise ships seldom leave you in port long enough to get a real feel for the island. You may see a lot, but it's impossible to know much more than what the place looks like in the short time allowed. On the other hand, a cruise is an ideal way to visit several islands with a minimum of inconvenience, and no airport lines or lost luggage, so that you can select the one you like for a longer visit in the future.

[*Facts about yacht chartering are included in individual island chapters. The busiest and most complete marinas are in Antigua, the British Virgin Islands, Grenada, Guadeloupe, Martinique, St. Croix, St. Lucia, Sint Maarten, St. Thomas, and St. Vincent, but there are also good marinas on some of the other islands.*]

Bugs, Beetles, and Other Bothersome Things

"No see 'ums" are just that: they're annoying gnats whose presence can turn an idyllic spot into a torture chamber. Although they thrive at many beaches and in swampy areas, they seem to hold their conventions on beautiful coves at sunset and beaches after a heavy rain. Their favorite meal seems to be human ankles, which they enjoy at the best alfresco restaurants, especially those that are surrounded by moisture-catching grasses.

Predicting where you'll meet "no see'ums" is difficult, but it's safe to assume that they will thrive with humid weather and will flee (or die from) beach "fogging" or other manmade elimination techniques. The most effective deterrent I've found is a compact (and convenient to carry) tube of *Cutters,* sold at fishing or other outdoor stores, but any bug repellent should do.

Cockroaches, sometimes called "mahogany bugs," have become the pivot-point for many island tales, including the fact that boys on St. Thomas used to sell them, packaged as a rare find in matchboxes, to unsuspecting tourists. Times may have changed, but the cockroaches have not. They are on all islands and may be staying in your room. Although most hotels respect their clients' horror of the ugly bug, and advise maids to spray and otherwise keep them away, travelers who plan to rent a cottage, villa, or apartment might want to visit the local hardware store to pack some prevention along with other provisions.

Mosquitoes, in the same category insofar as nuisance is concerned, are easier to swat, spray or otherwise annihilate. Islands that have had serious mosquito problems in the past—Grand Cayman and St. Lucia, for example—have waged war against the annoying visitor, but mosquitoes are a scourge of tropical life. Although they've been brought under control at most places with constant spraying and other action, the best offense is a good defense. If you're usually bothered by mosquitoes, come to the islands prepared with a favorite (and effective) bug spray. On islands where there is some problem, local shops will sell the product(s) that islanders have found to be effective.

Lizards are a fact of Caribbean life. The omnipresent gecko is known throughout the islands and the larger iguana, protected for its prehistoric appearance on some islands, ends up in stew and soup in many local kitchens. Frankly, I find both animals intriguing to watch—although first-timers may be horrified. That so many people return again and again to enjoy the Caribbean is testimony to the fact that most people find the lizards to be more entertainment than nuisance.

Although the mongoose, brought into the islands by plantation owners to control the snakes, is a popular rodent found on most islands, few bigger animals were ever brought to these islands. Goats and cattle are raised for food. Wild boar can be found in the forests of the Dominican Republic, where hunting is popular sport at specified seasons, but most other islands have only birds and small rodents. For listings of specific animals, contact the local tourist offices.

Clothing

Special considerations for clothes have been discussed, when necessary, within each chapter. Check the "Lifestyle" section.

Travel light with all baggage—mental as well as physical—when you head for the Caribbean. Clothes no longer make the man—or woman. In many places, except for the expensive and chic resorts mentioned throughout the book, fancy togs are taken more as a statement of the wearer's insecurities than as a fashion parade, and their obvious mark of affluence makes the wearer fair game for high charges. After all, if you can spend that much on clothes, surely you can give a little more for tips.

Summer is the season—all year around. Lightweight cotton is best (nylon and synthetics are hot), and some summer-weight jacket or sweater will be comfortable for evenings, mountain resorts, or restaurants with Caribbean-style air-conditioning (which, from my experience, is icebox-cold). While I don't recommend a daily uniform of cut-off blue jeans for everyone, they and the denim skirt are acceptable outfits, even in the French islands, where you will find that French resort fashions are de rigueur for the French folk who live and visit here. Swinging skirts, tight shirts open at the neck, and tight pants—if you can wear them well—are the fashion. On French beaches, nothing goes. Topless bathing is acceptable at hotels in the French West Indies and nudist beaches are proliferating, but if you are of the snicker-and-giggle school, forget about it. Those who choose to go where nothing goes usually do so with elan, and those who can't handle it look sophomoric.

When a resort perpetuates the dress-for-dinner ritual, it is noted when singled out for discussion in the individual chapters, but there is no island (although there *are* a few places on some islands) where you *must* wear jacket-and-tie or gala long skirt. April through December travel gear is usually even more casual than winter wear, partly because that is the low-cost time to head south, although it is also the season when the flowers-in-bloom are spectacular.

The wardrobe difference between beaches (and bathing suits) and cities (with coverup) is magnified in the Caribbean countries with a Latin tradition. In downtown San Juan, Puerto Rico, for example, short shorts and bare-back dresses have been seen only in the past few decades—and are usually on tourists. This island, with its Spanish heritage still firmly intact in many of the villages, has the old-time European respect for public places, and certainly for churches. The same is true in the Dominican Republic, in the old part of the city of Santo Domingo. Businessmen in both these areas and in many other places throughout the Caribbean have doffed their jacket and tie (the mark of a respectable businessman) only in the past few years, and some are donning them again. Even without jacket and tie island citizens dress with dignity when they go to their cities and with appropriate pomp when they are meeting with politicians.

I've often headed into the Caribbean for a week or more with one small suitcase (carry-on size), filled with one cotton skirt (in addition to the one I wear on the plane), 2 short-sleeved shirts, 1 long-sleeved shirt (plus the one I wear), one or two cotton dresses suitable for evening, plus tennis clothes, bathing suits, beach cover-up, underwear, and sleepwear. Add to that something for sailing (long pants to ward off too much sun), plus sunglasses, suntan lotion, and personal cosmetics, and you're all set. For men, 2 pairs of trousers (khaki pants can double for evening), 2 shirts for daytime plus 2 (wear one on the plane) for evening, with bathing suits, underwear, etc., and a jacket you might wear on the plane will suffice.

Special social occasions may require something spectacular and convention cavorting has some clothing requirements that won't be on the vacation-visitor list. Coping with those situations is a matter of personal style.

AUTHOR'S OBSERVATION

Take only "easy-care" clothes—things that don't require ironing, dry-cleaning, etc. And pack a bathing suit with your carry on luggage. If your suitcase is "lost," at least you can sit on the beach while you wait for it to show up.

Cruise Ship Ports

Get as much information as you can about each island's shops, sites, and other points of interest, prior to setting off on your cruise. All the island tourist offices have quantities of information.

If you want an action-packed, lively cruise, choose one that visits the bigger, brassier islands, even though the port may seem junky, with all its tourist clutter. If you're more interested in nature and Robinson Crusoe experiences, select a smaller ship that stops at very quiet, less well-known islands. Although port facilities may be minimal on the smaller islands, they allow for a more natural island experience.

Many intineraries allow golfers, tennis players, and other sports enthusiasts enough time in port to play. If you're interested in Caribbean history, the most accessible sites are in Puerto Rico (San Juan), the Dominican Republic (Santo Domingo), Antigua (English Harbour and Shirley Heights), Dominica (Fort Shirley, near Portsmouth), Barbados (the Garrison and several sites around the island), St. Thomas (Charlotte Amalie), St. Croix (Christiansted), St. Kitts (Brimstone Hill), and Haiti (especially Cap Haitien).

Some ports have extensive, modern facilities with many shops; others are some distance from the shops and most interesting sights. Port facilities that have been improved or created since 1987 usually have efficient modern facilities with telephones, restrooms, shops, and fleets of taxis, but be sure to ask whether or not the projected facilities are all operating. Ports often receive ships before all their facilities are ready.

Most ships stop in St. Thomas and/or St. Croix, to allow shoppers who are U.S. citizens to take advantage of the extra customs allotment from those United States' islands (see the specific island chapters for shopping facts). Be aware that cruise lines sometimes have "deals" with certain shops, which may be the only ones that the cruise directors recommend. Such recommendations often mean that you'll see many of your fellow passengers in those shops, but not that those are the only good shops.

For details about specific islands, read the "Cruise" comment in each chapter.

Documents

Documents for traveling in the Caribbean are minimal. Except for Cuba, you need no visa. Haiti and the Dominican Republic require Tourist Cards, which can be purchased at the airline counter when you check in, or at the appropriate desk when you arrive in the country. For proof of citizenship, which you *will* be required to show, there's nothing to compare with your passport. Passports are not required by all Caribbean countries/islands, but they are, without doubt, the easiest means of clearing immigration without difficulties and, even more important (sometimes) than your arrival in the Caribbean, your return home to U.S. cities is often expedited *if* you have a valid U.S. passport in hand. Your passport, your immigration card (which will be provided on the plane if you have not been given one when you check in at the airport), and a return or ongoing ticket are the only documents needed for most of your Caribbean travels. A U.S. passport costs $35 and is valid for 10 years. You will need a 2¼" × 2¼" full-face photograph and a copy of your birth certificate to purchase a passport from the U.S. State Department. Your post office can assist.

A word to the wise: Formalities for leaving any Caribbean country involve paying a departure tax of varying amounts, depending on the country/island, and return of the carbon copy of the immigration form which you presented (in duplicate) on arrival.

Drinking Water

Drinking water is not the problem it once was in the countries of the Caribbean, but is a scarce commodity everywhere since sunshine is far more dependable than rain. Even the most modern places have water problems sometimes, not with purity, just with quantity. Saltwater conversion plants are obsolete as soon as they are completed; wells are exhausted in many instances, and even where the freshwater table is high, the pipes and pumps to get the water to where it is needed for consumption are often not up to the task. You will never perish from thirst (and there's always local beer and rum to drink), but you may turn on the faucet to have a trickle or nothing come out—even at luxury resorts. Most grocery stores sell bottled water, if it is not available through your hotel's bar or sundry shop.

Drugs

Selling drugs is illegal in Caribbean islands, as it is in the United States. However, the days of Prohibition—when rumrunning was a lucrative business in Bahamian and Caribbean islands—have returned to many Caribbean communities. Drugs of all sorts are readily available. Since islanders have been smoking "weed" since the Arawak and Carib Indians used to inhale smoke from leaves burned in fires, the habit is one of long standing. Marijuana is easily grown and is available "everywhere," usually by its local name, which in the case of Jamaica is "ganja." In recent years, crack, cocaine, and other drugs have also come into most Caribbean islands, in transit from Colombia and other South American sources.

In spite of the fact that it is illegal, beach vendors and others sometimes sell drugs—if buyers express an interest. Beware—and be wary. On some islands, drugs are freely offered—along with sun smocks, carved wooden items, coral jewelry, and straw baskets. I have found that a polite-but-firm "No, thank you" usually sends the salesmen elsewhere, but anyone strolling a beach or a vendors' market should be prepared for (not surprised by) the offer.

Electric Current

Electric current on almost all of the islands is sometimes on—and sometimes off. Do not head south armed with your electric razor, hair dryer, heat curlers, facial steamer, electric toothbrush, etc. and expect them to work on all islands. In some cases, the current is not the same as in the U.S.; in others, it's uneven. My advice is to return to the simple life—even to letting your wet hair dry in warm sun and tradewinds. If you *must* take your electric appliances with you, check on the need for a converter. Although you will find standard U.S. current in most hotels in the U.S. Virgins and in Puerto Rico and in a handful of other places, even on those islands, when you are at a simpler spot, the electricity may run on another current—and it may (probably will) fail completely on occasion. Always inquire at the front desk before you plug in—and risk blowing out the hotel's electric system. Overloaded electrical conduits are as much a fact of island life as saltwater conversion plants that are too small for the burgeoning demands. Instead of taking all your modern American appliances, pack a flashlight, several books of matches, and some candles, along with your toothbrush and manual razor. They'll be far more useful (and lighter to carry). Most places where you are paying a premium are places where you can expect to find a hair salon, if not on premises then at least nearby. There are also places where you can expect your appliances to work, but check with management.

Island Choices

In some ways, islands are like small towns; in other ways, they're like cosmopolitan cities. In all ways, they are different from what you know at home. Each island has its own personality and, in the bigger islands, the personality changes from shore to mountainside. Areas where tourism has developed are quite different from places untouched by the travelers' sometimes heavy foot. Places with highrise hotels and casinos are quite different from the low-lying, understated luxury that exists on other islands.

How much "foreign" flavor do you want—and enjoy? The French islands (Martinique, Guadeloupe, St. Barthelemy, the French side of the Dutch-shared island of St. Martin/Sint Maarten) have French customs. That includes dining habits and preparation of food, as well as language and currency. The Dutch-affiliated islands of Aruba, Bonaire, Curacao, Saba, Sint Eustatius, and the Dutch side of French-shared St. Martin/Sint Maarten have a few Dutch customs, notable in some of the food which takes its cue from the formerly Dutch region of Indonesia. Otherwise, the Dutch islands are 20th century modern, which seems almost "American."

The U.S. islands, with the U.S. postal and phone systems, in addition to Kentucky Fried Chicken, McDonalds, and Woolworths, are the U.S. Virgins of St. Croix, St. John, and St. Thomas, and the U.S. Commonwealth of Puerto Rico, which shares the American accoutrements, but not the language and customs (which have developed along Spanish lines). And for truly Spanish ambiance, most places in the Dominican Republic have retained the flavor, and the Spanish language.

Most of the other countries in the Caribbean have a British heritage, but each of the newly independent islands has worked its traditions into its own personality. British customs appear with the pageantry of military bands, the pomp of public appearances by government functionaries, an addiction to cricket, and a preference for afternoon teatime and polo. Barbados and Jamaica are each multi-faceted nations, with vacation villas and apartments, as well as luxury resorts, all-inclusive, action-packed places, and inns and small hotels. The two-island nations of Antigua-Barbuda, St. Kitts-Nevis, and Trinidad & Tobago have different personalities on each of their islands. The first pair is two beach-fringed islands; the second recalls the plantation days with estates that are now charming hotels; the third combines a cosmopolitan island with a beach-and-sea escape. St. Lucia and Dominica mingle styles and language from French neighbors with their British West Indian atmosphere, while the personality of St. Vincent, the face of a kite whose tail is its sand-fringed Grenadine islands, is affected by the sea. Grenada is the ninth once-British, now independent island, and the entire group is closely allied with the still British colonies of the Caymans, Anguilla, and Montserrat.

Finding the place for your perfect vacation can be a little like searching for hidden treasure. Rest assured that all the elements you're looking for exist *somewhere* in the Caribbean. I hope the information in the pages that follow will help you find out where.

Language

Do not assume that when English is spoken, it is *your* English. Every English-speaking island has its own dialect, each distinct from the other, although outsiders cannot usually distinguish one from the other. The people you meet on the streets and working in and around the hotels will be far more familiar with their own colloquial sayings and speech short cuts than they will be with yours. Funny jokes with double meaning or quick quips over the breakfast table usually leave a young waitress or waiter completely befuddled. While you are slapping your thighs with glee, they will probably be talking in muffled tones with their fellow staff members about how crazy you are.

When you are asking for something special and your waiter or waitress smiles and says "yes," don't assume that means you will get what you think you have asked for. "Yes" in reply to "Do you have scrambled eggs?" means, simply, that they do have them—there's nothing in what you have asked to suggest that you want some. The same can be true with telephone calls: "Yes" in reply to "Is Ebenezer there?" means, simply, that he is at home—but the person who answered may not know that you would like to speak to him. So it goes in the Caribbean, where local customs are different from those in your hometown.

There are a lot of words in common parlance throughout the Caribbean—and Caribbean is one of them—that have a special ring to the ear. Your pronunciation marks you immediately as "friend or foe," if not literally then certainly as one who has (or has not) taken the time to find out how things are called in the Caribbean. No one expects outsiders to be fluent in the local language, and by mimicking the intonation—and inserting an occasional "mon," we only sound like the complete outsiders we are. Of course, English is *not* the local language in the French-speaking islands (Martinique, St. Martin, Guadeloupe and her dependencies, plus Haiti), where speaking French is essential if you want to wander out of tourist troughs; or in Cuba, Puerto Rico, or the Dominican Republic, where Spanish is spoken. Speaking "pure" French or Spanish will be sufficient to be understood in the areas just mentioned, even if the local dialect is not "pure."

For words to watch, let's start with Caribbean—which is CaRIB-be-an or Ca-rib-BE-an, no one knows (or cares) for sure. Anyone who corrects you is being presumptuous since the proper pronunciation is "according to whom." I know of no move to standardize the pronunciation, but there is some feeling among the new movers of the Caribbean that the area *is* the Caribbean, not the West Indies, because factors from all the countries that fringe the Caribbean sea are coming into play in the development of this region. South America (Venezuela especially), Mexico, and certainly Cuba have their effect on the emerging nations of the Caribbean. Cuba considers itself a Latin American country, not a West Indian island—although the country *is* part of the West Indies.

Pronunciation of island names seems to confuse many travelers, so here's the list of the unusual pronunciation of some of the islands covered in this book:

Antigua: An-TEA-ga
Barbuda: Bar-BIEW-da
Barbados: Bar-BA-dos—not "the Barbados" (it's only one island)
Bequia: BECK-way
Canouan: CAN-oo-wan
Carriacou: Carry-A-coo
Grenada: Gre-NAY-da (the other pronunciation is a city in Spain; and the country's best known beach L'Anse aux Epines is pronounced vaguely Lanse-eh-pan)
Guadeloupe: GUA-dah-loop, and the dependencies are known as Les Saintes, pronounced Lay-San, with the island of Terre de Haut pronounced Tair-de-oh, all slurred together.
Jost Van Dyke: Yost Van Dyke
Nevis: NEE-vis (People who live here are Nevisians.)
Petit Saint Vincent: Petty Saint Vincent
St. Barthelemy: Best known as Saint Barths, so spelled with the French abbreviation, but pronounced San Barts
St. Croix: Saint Croy

Lodging

The more homework you do, the happier you will be with your island "home." Everything is available, from elegant villas with full staff to luxury hotels to small and special inns, and inexpensive, simply furnished guest houses. All are discussed, in detail, in the individual island chapters, with multi-room properties covered under "Hotels/Resorts." The villas and apartments are discussed under "Housekeeping Holidays," places with less than 50 rooms and unique personality under "The Inn Way," and the very inexpensive places under "Low-Cost Lodging."

> **AUTHOR'S OBSERVATION**
>
> If an inclusive price resort appeals, be sure to read the small print carefully. Although "inclusive" should mean that *everything* is included—and you will have no additional expenses, some places use the word but do not include tours, drinks, and transfers between airport and hotel. Always ask.

If you decide to rent a villa, be sure to inquire in advance about the tipping procedures and the availability of food supplies. There are variations in facilities offered. In some of the simpler places, you may want to bring a few of your favorite cooking utensils with you. At others, especially those that supply help in the form of a cook experienced with the local foods (and ways to obtain them), you can relax and enjoy being pampered.

Mail

The addresses for all hotels are included at the back of the book. Mail to the properties should always include the name of the island, and the area—either W.I. (West Indies), or N.A. (Netherlands Antilles), or F.W.I. (French West Indies), or B.V.I. (British Virgin Islands), and in the case of the Caymans, Anguilla, the British Virgins, and Montserrat, B.W.I. (British West Indies). Only Puerto Rico and the United States Virgin Islands are covered under U.S. domestic postage rates, where a regular letter at press time costs 29¢; airmail postage is not necessary since mail in the U.S. goes by air anyway. *For all other countries/islands in the Caribbean*, postage is 50¢ per half ounce up to two ounces. Reconfirm rates with your local post office. For all but the U.S. Virgin Islands and Puerto Rico, expect mail—even by air—to take at least two weeks, and sometimes as long as a month! If it takes less, consider yourself lucky. Fax machines and telex facilities are used by most hotels, especially those doing volume business in North America and Europe.

Medical Facilities

The major cruise ships offer one of the best ways for vacationers with medical problems to visit the Caribbean. Many ships have fully equipped hospitals, and there's always a doctor on board. Insofar as islands are concerned, U.S. citizens with health problems can feel comfortable on any island with direct flights to Miami—such as Grand Cayman, Montego Bay or Kingston in Jamaica, Sint Maarten/St. Martin, and the U.S. Virgin Islands. Puerto Rico has several excellent hospitals in the San Juan area. Barbados has developed a link with Healthcare International. Ask the tourist office for details. When healthcare is a major consideration, your doctor should be part of your first discussions about an island vacation. He/she can also give you the names of professional contacts. For further facts, read the "Medical Facilities" section in the individual island chapters.

Money Matters

Money matters are covered specifically within each chapter, as the facts pertain to the destination. In addition, throughout the discussions about restaurants and facilities, bouquets and brickbats have been thrown when value is good or not so good, respectively.

AUTHOR'S OBSERVATION

Keep in mind one obvious fact: the places of and in the Caribbean are in the tourism business because they want to make money—and how much value you get for the money you spend depends on you and the amount of research/homework you are willing to do.

Start with the premise that there is profit in any business that survives in the Caribbean—and that profit is being made on you, the tourist. In some countries you will have to spend U.S. dollars in special stores and for your hotel bills. In all countries, you will get the official exchange rate for your money at the banks; many stores and hotels charge a premium for their cash changing services, as is the practice all over the world. You will usually get a better exchange rate with traveler's checks than you will with U.S. dollars when you change money from U.S. currency to local. For those who intend to get off the beaten paths of tourism, having sufficient cash in the currency of the country is a courtesy to your hosts. People with "Mom and Pop" operations in small villages in the French West Indies, the hills of Dominica, or the back roads on Jamaica, Trinidad, Tobago, and elsewhere cannot and should not be expected to know the present exchange rate—and how to handle US$20 or more. You are welcome to come into the local rum shop or small store, but you will be obvious enough as an outsider; splashing down a pile of U.S. dollar bills, or even worse, a pile of local currency you haven't taken the time to figure out, is at best an inconvenience and at worst an affront.

Nature

Insofar as domestic birds and beasts are concerned, each island has its own crop. While Bonaire is respected among ornithologists for its salt ponds, which are the nesting grounds for hundreds of flamingoes, other islands such as Dominica, St. Vincent, and St. Lucia have rare and colorful endemic parrots. Bananaquits dip into the sugar bowls on terrace dining tables on many islands, and other birds can be found in rain forests and on walking tours. Hummingbirds are common on many islands, darting from flower to flower within easy glimpse from your patio, and the menacing blackbirds, known as "Cling-Cling" and by other names, are a distant relative to New England's crow. Birders should check with the government tourist offices, whose addresses are listed at the start of each chapter, for information about local bird-watching clubs and walking tours.

Package Tours

There was a time when "package tour" meant being coddled and cared for on a prescribed itinerary with someone else in charge. All you had to do was wake up in the morning and wait to be told what to do. Not so now!

These days a "package tour" can mean almost anything. It can be a special interest tour, with an experienced guide to lecture on a specific subject. It can also be several days at a Club Mediterranee, or one of Jamaica's all-inclusive hotels, and or an all-inclusive hotel on a few of the other islands, where you will be with like-minded souls on the plane and at the resort. But there are other package plans where you may never know the others who have bought your "package." You don't have to be joined at the spine with a bunch of strangers when you buy a "package."

The term refers to a multi-day vacation with at least two elements—usually air and hotel—included in one price. Although the original idea gave good value to the traveler who knew what the holiday would cost before starting the journey, and the hosts (who knew that someone was going to fill the airplane seat and hotel room), the fact is that there are many scams in the marketplace.

You'll have to read carefully and ask many questions to be sure that the package offers what you think you're buying. Remember that people who write tour promotion brochures and advertising copy are well schooled in making the "product" sound as enticing (and inexpensive) as possible. You'll have to translate their words to tell whether the bargain is as it seems—and judge whether or not the deal is ideal for you.

The original concept was implemented by what is known in the travel industry as a "wholesaler" or "tour operator," who acted as middleman to bargain with a hotel (usually one that was having trouble selling all its rooms) to buy many rooms at a bulk price and then put them together with seats on an airline by using the same technique. For that reason, most of the package holidays are offered to the bigger islands and to places that have a lot of hotel rooms. The tour operator or wholesaler would offer the package for sale through travel agents, who would earn their usual commission.

When the procedure was first enacted, some of the price saving (but by no means all of it) was passed on to you, in the form of a multi-day vacation at good value. These days, however, some hotels have put together their own all-inclusive plans, with a "middleman" who is part of their payroll, and airlines have linked their computers with one or a few companies to package the bulk of their multi-day offerings. The power-broker's role is often (but not always) played by the hosts (airline and/or hotel) who certainly have their own profit more clearly in focus than your budget, although in good situations, both are considered.

The responsibility, therefore, is on *you* to purchase what will prove to be the best package *for you*. Perhaps that means dealing directly with the hotel of your choice, and hundreds of hotels are described in the pages that follow. Always ask if the hotel has an all-inclusive plan; if you're flexible with your travel times and concerned about costs, it may pay to fit into one of them. Additional information sources are the travel section of your nearest big city newspaper and other travel-focused media. In all cases, your decision can be helped by working with the free printed material from the government tourist offices and an experienced travel agent. (See "Travel Agent" below.)

For this winter, expect to find good value package plans offered for Aruba, the Dominican Republic north coast, many hotels in Jamaica, some of the bigger hotels in Puerto Rico, and in Curacao, as well as competitive pricing on packages offered through American Airlines, Delta, and other major carriers into the region. The *Caribbean Newsletter* (see page 9) will have information about special packages when they are especially noteworthy.

Rate for Lodging

In the old days, hotels listed (and charged) one rate—or a reasonable variety of rates. Today, pricing follows market forces—supply, demand, and deal-makers. The term "rack rate" emerged as a term for the printed rate that appears on the hotel brochures put into the travel agents' and other racks for display. It is the rate that is shown on the government tourist office listing and listed at the back of this book in the charts. It is a guideline; other rates usually also apply.

Just as business travelers have traditionally paid the regular airfares, because their travel often cannot be planned far enough in advance to take advantage of promotional fares, so the "rack rate" is often paid by individual travelers who want to stay at a specific hotel at a specified time.

In many cases, it is possible to negotiate from the daily rack rate for long stays and, although the better hotels still respect the time-honored systems (and provide service that warrants the charges), many hotels will offer better daily rates on package plans and at times other than their peak season.

Safety

AUTHOR'S NOTE

Throughout the island-by-island reporting that follows, I have included comments about the "Political Picture" that should prepare you for headlines in the local newspapers and any rhetoric you may hear while visiting the islands. I have also noted, with "Author's Observations" and comments throughout the text, the few places where I feel adventuresome travelers would be happier than timid tourists.

These islands *do* look like your dream island, be it Robinson Crusoe's retreat, or "Fantasy Island," or those glorious promotion pictures you see. And the Caribbean countries *can* be like that, and usually are. But they are also developing nations, and the interweaving of "haves" and "have-nots" is difficult at best, volatile at worst. Tourists are definitely "haves," whether you think of yourselves in that category or not. The fact is, anyone basking in the sun on a Caribbean beach has paid a substantial sum to be there and, with hotel rates, to stay there. The value of the clothes in one suitcase equals far more than a month's wages for a lot of people of the Caribbean, and in fact, is closer to the equivalent of the income for a year in some places. Add to that the cameras, sports equipment, and extra trappings—and you certainly see a "have."

All island governments are conscious of the need to protect not only you, but also their own people. Yes. You will be safe in the usual vacation hotels, and probably anywhere else you choose to go. However, I believe that anyone traveling anywhere in the world these days should do so conscientiously. I would advise leaving your expensive jewelry at home, keeping rental cars locked when you park them, avoiding dark and desolate back streets, keeping card-deck-sized folds of bills out of sight, using safe deposit boxes for extra cash and valuables, keeping million dollar camera equipment out of sight when not in use (and carry it with you on the airplane, don't check it with your baggage), generally avoiding "rich" behavior unless it is so much a part of you that to do so will change your personality (and in that case, stay at one of the special enclaves for the rich that can be found on many islands).

Timid travelers will probably be happiest at the resorts with all the facilities within reach. You can take guided tours where you will have the security of the group. The rest of us will continue to live as we do at home, driving around in cars to sample restaurants, shop, and see the sights that sound interesting.

Shopping

Purchases made in the Caribbean islands are, with the exception of Puerto Rico, subject to U.S. customs' duties. Even purchases made in the U.S. Virgin Islands (St. Croix, St. John, and St. Thomas) are subject to customs duties, as a holdover from policies in place at the time the islands were purchased from Denmark (in 1917). As a result of effective lobbying, the customs allotments were changed in September 1990, and some portions of the customs regulations are under on-going review.

At press time, the per person duty-free allotment (which means the retail value amount of goods each person can bring into the United States without paying additional duties) is $1200 per person from the U.S. Virgin Islands and $600 from countries made eligible by the Caribbean Basin Initiative, namely, insofar as those covered in this book are concerned, Antigua-Barbuda, Barbados, the British Virgin Islands, Dominica, the Dominican Republic, Grenada, Haiti, Jamaica, Montserrat, the Netherlands Antilles (Aruba, Bonaire, Curacao, Sint Maarten, Saba, and Sint Eustius, also known as Statia), St. Kitts-Nevis, St. Lucia, St. Vincent and the Grenadines, and Trinidad & Tobago.

The duty-free allotment for the French West Indies (Martinique, Guadeloupe and its satellites, St. Barthelemy, and St. Martin) remains at $400. However, I suspect customs inspectors will have a hard time separating purchases you make in St. Martin from those you've made in Sint Maarten, which is just one of the convolutions of the U.S. government's customs department changes.

In addition to the bonus allotment on dutiable goods, the U.S. Virgin Islands also have a larger liquor quota. You are permitted to bring back up to five liters of liquor, plus one additional liter of spirits made in the U.S. Virgin Islands. The allotment from other Caribbean islands is one liter duty free, with duty assessed on alcohol content so that wines, for example, have lower duty than cognac.

> **AUTHOR'S OBSERVATION**
>
> In the interests of "helping U.S. friends" and catering to special factions, the new customs regulations have many confusing elements. For example, gifts mailed to others come under the postal service regulations, not the customs department regulations, according to one of my sources. If you are planning major purchases, I'd suggest getting a written statement from your nearest customs official—at least until the September 1990 changes are further clarified.

There's a 10% duty on the first $1000 over your duty-free allotment; that amount is 5% from the U.S. Virgin Islands. Items made in the U.S. Virgins may be brought to the U.S. outside of duty allotments.

Gifts valued up to $50 may be mailed every day to any recipient, but no more than one duty-free gift may be received per individual per day. From the U.S. Virgin Islands, the value for mailed gifts is $100. *Know Before You Go,* the Customs department's pamphlet about their procedures, gives details and explains the procedures. (U.S. Customs is listed in the phone book for all cities and many towns.)

"Generalized System of Preferences" (GSP) regulations apply for most of the Caribbean islands. What this weighty name implies is that many handmade items from the less-developed countries are allowed into the United States duty free. The list is specific, but among the items included are straw and handcrafted items, some leather goods, wood carvings, and paintings by island artists. If you're thinking about major purchases of island-made items, visit your nearest Customs office to look through the GSP listing in the book.

For insurance against "shoppers' bulge," pack a fold-up canvas bag, some heavy twine, and one of those small handles that clips onto the string. Even if you are not expecting to buy, you'll probably be tempted by something, and there's never enough space to hold whatever it may be.

Caribbean stores and markets can be divided into two categories: places selling luxury imports from the world's sources and places selling simple handicrafts, some of which are of very high caliber and all of which can be fun.

Most resort hotels have boutiques, but a lot of the merchandise is imported from the U.S.—and expensive. Be sure to bring enough suntan lotion; it sells at a premium to a captive audience in island shops.

Islands with the best prices and selection of luxury imports are Sint Maarten/St. Martin, St. Thomas and St. Croix (with their bonus of being U.S.), Curacao and Aruba, and perhaps the tax-free areas in the Dominican Republic.

There are also some stores with luxury imports on Antigua, Barbados, the British Virgin Islands of Tortola and Virgin Gorda, Grand Cayman, Guadeloupe and Martinique, Jamaica, St. Lucia, St. Vincent, and Trinidad.

Most of the other islands have at least one place that sells crystal, fine china and figurines, cameras and clocks, but the selection isn't extensive enough to warrant singling them out.

Insofar as the luxury imports are concerned, don't expect to find all patterns and companies represented in every island store. Although the selection of, for example, crystal or china will be representative, a favorite pattern may not be in stock. In some cases it can be ordered—but it's wiser to buy what you can see.

The Dutch islands (Aruba, Bonaire, Curacao, and Sint Maarten) are great places to buy Dutch cheeses, chocolates, tinned hams, and other products; the French islands of Martinique, Guadeloupe, St. Barthelemy, and St. Martin excel in French fashions, gourmet foods, and perfumes.

Perfumes and cosmetics can be good buys in the Caribbean. The debate about which island has the best prices continues. The solution depends, I believe, on how sharp the store owner is at merchandising. Prices rise and fall with the tradewinds, and "specials" are a response to the "better price" at some other island (or store). If you're addicted to a special scent, be sure to (1) know the hometown price and (2) buy if the island store's price is lower. I suspect that few travelers plan an itinerary on perfume prices and only cruise-ship passengers will have the opportunity for multi-port comparisons (and, if you're on a cruise, you can often do best at the special sales offered by the ship's boutique).

The best islands for quantities of quality handicrafts are Haiti, the Dominican Republic, Grenada, Jamaica, Puerto Rico, and St. John in the U.S. Virgin Islands. It's possible to find at least a few talented craftsmen on most islands, but many do not mass-produce items. Work is often "one of a kind" and best found by making inquiries after your island arrival.

Checklist for shoppers
- Have a plan for purchase, even if it's a vague one. If china is a possible purchase, have some idea of makers, styles, and hometown prices; do the same for cameras, with specific models and makes in mind.
- Know the hometown discount store's best price—before you buy an island "bargain" that isn't one.
- Contact the tourist office before you leave home for the name and address of the contact for the island's gift shop association, to write for folders and facts. If there is no association, ask the tourist office for any information about things to buy.
- If you're making a big purchase, be prepared to discuss price, even in the classiest shops. Many stores have "variable" pricing, and will give a price break depending on the merchandise, personal interrelationship, season, competition, and how sales have been going.
- Take the merchandise with you, if possible, to avoid problems with shipping, return of merchandise, and other difficulties that come with many long-distance business dealings.
- Don't be pressured into a quick sale unless you like to gamble. Beach vendors and market folk are wily (and can be entertaining) purchase partners. They know the game well—and you should too.
- Know your dollars, especially in the "dollar" countries of Jamaica, Barbados, Trinidad & Tobago, and the Eastern Caribbean group of Antigua, Grenada, Dominica, Montserrat, St. Lucia, St. Vincent where their dollars are not equal to the U.S. dollar. When you're bargaining with street vendors, it's very important to know whose dollars are being negotiated—and it's often easy to get a *very* good price if you pay in U.S. dollars (properly equated to local currency, of course).

- Be wary. Be wise. Have fun. Most island purchases are as valuable for the memories as for the merchandise.

Terms

There are some words that are commonly used throughout the Caribbean, and have been used—with no further explanation—throughout the text. At the risk of repeating the obvious for the experienced Caribbean travelers, here's what I mean when I use the word:

bohio: actually the thatched "hut" that the first settlers lived in, but used now to refer to the manmade old-style small country homes in Cuba and other countries, as well as for the thatched shade "trees" on Caribbean beaches.

guayabera: the loose, straight, long-sleeved shirt that has been a "uniform" at the best occasions at Mexico's Acapulco for decades, as well as in Cuba. The shirt has now become the fashion for men, and on most Caribbean islands/countries, can go to most evening events.

MAP: Modified American Plan, which means breakfasts and dinners included in your hotel rate.

EP: European Plan, no meals.

package tour: a tour of several days sold at an all-inclusive price, sometimes (but not always) including air fare. Be sure to read the small print carefully to be sure just what the one price *does* include.

wholesaler and/or tour operator: the person/firm that negotiates special prices with hotels for blocks of rooms, and special rates with airlines for blocks of seats, or with cruise lines for blocks of cabins, to put together the package tour. The wholesaler usually receives 20% or more from the hotel (and sometimes other concessions); your hometown travel agent will get a 10% to 15% commission on your room/tour *from the hotel or wholesaler*.

peak season: from December 16 through April 15 or thereabouts for most Caribbean hotels. That is the time of top rates.

shoulder season: In the Caribbean, the term refers to April–May and to September–October and sometimes November, and usually means good-value vacations.

off-season: the summer months. The term came into usage when Caribbean travelers were those who fled the cold winter climate. These days the "off-season," euphemistically called "the season of sweet savings" by the Caribbean Tourism Association, can be the busiest season for some areas, but the rates are lower than in winter months, sometimes as much as 40% less. Dates are usually April 16 through December 15.

Travel Agents

Although it's possible to make all your reservations yourself, directly with the airline or cruise line you choose, there's nothing to compare with the information available through a good travel agent. Time spent researching—reading books, looking at folders (which you can pick up free at any travel agency and get through the government tourist offices), talking to friends, looking at major metropolitan newspapers with good travel sections—before you go into your travel agent's office is a good investment. You then know what questions to ask, and your travel agent can be specific with answers. ASTA, the American Society of Travel Agents, is a nationwide association of individuals and firms involved with the travel industry. ASTA travel agents are professionals; your travel plans are their business. The head office for ASTA is 1101 King St., Alexandria, VA 22314, T 703+739-2782.

Deregulation of the travel industry (which means that any airline, hotel, or other purveyor is able to offer anything he chooses; there are no federal restrictions) has resulted in an avalanche of offers, with prices ranging from joke-low to alpine peaks. Sifting through everything is not easy, and your travel agent can save hours by sharing his/her expertise.

How to choose an agent? Treat a travel agent as your stock broker. Travel agents generally earn their living by commissions paid by hotels, airlines, cruise lines, and other products. Obviously, the more costly the travel, the more the agent gets paid. However, good travel agents are interested in more than just the money. They are interested in building a reliable clientele, and they do that by sharing some good tips—even when they may not put money in their pockets. I have found ASTA agents with CTC after their names to be well-informed and concerned about their clients. What does CTC mean? Certified Travel Counselor, and an agent who carries the initials after his/her name has taken courses through an umbrella organization based in the Boston area. If you want to know the CTC's in your area, write to the Institute of Certified Travel Agents, 148 Linden St., Box 56, Wellesley, MA 02181, T 617+237-0280.

Tips for Last-Minute Travel

There's always room for one more. If visions of stretching out on a sea-swept beach are all that keep you going, hang onto your dream—even when headlines holler that hotels and airplanes are full. There are ways to find your place in the sun, even at height of season, if you're willing to be flexible. You may head for some island or hotel you've never heard about, on an airline whose name hasn't become a household word, but the spirit of the Caribbean has always been one of spontaniety, and the sunshine is assured. Past seasons have seen unprecedented numbers of people heading to the Cayman Islands, Barbados, Sint Maarten, and, more recently, St. Barths, but there's still space somewhere for you.

Here are some tried and true ways to find both a room at the last minute on some sunny island and a route for getting there:

1. Secure space on the plane. Flexibility is the key. If you live near a major-city airport, going out to "stand-by" for a plane the computer says is "full" often yields a seat south. Most flights have at least a couple of "no-shows" and, if you're ready to go, you can sit in one of those seats. On the other hand, there are ways to be sure you have a reservation—even when everyone says "impossible." Flying at off-peak travel times often yields a better rate, as well as a chance for space. Even when your travel agent says "no space," you may find seats—if you're willing to invest some time in telephone calls. Most airlines serving Caribbean countries have toll-free numbers for reservations. Dial (800) 555-1212 to ask for the toll-free number from your area for *any* airline heading to a Caribbean destination. If you're reasonably flexible on where and when you go, chances are you will get seats, and it's important to secure your space on flights down to the islands and back *before* you start on your hotel space.

2. Find a hotel. It is not as awesome as it may seem. There are several non-traditional routes for finding a bed near a beach, even at height of season. Most Caribbean hotels have reservations representatives in U.S. cities. Call the government tourist office (see individual chapters) for your first choice island (the one you've been able to "reach" by plane) and ask for a list of hotel representatives with U.S. telephone numbers or consult the information at the back of this book. Many of the reps also have 800 numbers; the same system used for finding an 800 number for airlines works for the hotel representatives.

Chances are that you'll secure a room through the rep, but—if that fails— here's another route: telephone the hotel association on the island in question. Most Caribbean countries have active and effective hotel associations. A telephone call or cable to the island may seem expensive, but if you can find a room for your vacation, the investment is worth the effort. Ask for a room, specify dates, and ask for a fax reply for confirmation. If you have your heart set on a special hotel, often a direct call to that hotel can yield a room. You may catch the front desk just when they have received a cancellation. Otherwise, take your chances on the hotel, with the knowledge that you are heading south for sunshine—and that can be found on any number of beaches.

The following list includes telephone and fax numbers for members of the Caribbean Hotel Association.

Anguilla: T 809+ 497–2944, fax 809+ 497–3091
Antigua: T 809+ 462–0374, fax 809+ 462–3702
Aruba: T 011+ 297–82–2607, fax 011+ 297–82–4202
Barbados: T 809+ 426–5041, fax 809+ 429–2845
Bonaire: T 011+ 599–8593
British Virgin Islands: T 809+ 494–3514, fax 809+ 494–2226
Cayman Islands: T 809+ 949–8111, fax 809+ 949–7054
Curacao: T 011+ 599–63–6260, fax 011+ 599–63–6445
Dominica: T 809+ 498–3288
Dominican Republic: T 809+ 532–2907, fax 809+ 535–4256
Grenada: T 809+ 440–1590, fax 809+ 440–4124
Guadeloupe: T 011+ 590 88.59.99
Haiti: T 011+ 509–6–0967
Jamaica: T 809+ 926–3635, fax 809+ 926–2090
Martinique: T 011+ 596–75.09.21, fax 011+ 596+ 75.01.54
Puerto Rico: T 809+ 725–2901, fax 809+ 725–2913
St. Barthelemy: T 011+ 590 27.64.80, fax 011+ 590 27.75.47
St. Croix: T 809+ 733–7117, fax 809+ 773–5883
St. Kitts–Nevis: T 809+ 465–5304, fax 809+ 465–1106
St. Lucia: T 809+ 452–5978, fax 809+ 453–1121
St. Maarten: T 011+ 599–52–2333, fax 011+ 599–52–3915
St. Martin: T 011+ 590–87.83.88
St. Thomas/St. John: T 809+ 774–6835, fax 809+ 774–4993
St. Vincent: T 809+ 457–1072, fax 809+ 457–4567
Trinidad & Tobago: T 809+ 624–3065
Turks & Caicos: T 809+ 946–2232

3. Contact your travel agent, with the request that you be booked on one of the tours heading south. A quick flick through the Sunday travel section of your nearest metropolitan newspaper can yield the current listing of some of what's available. Vacationing this way is a little like taking a prize from the grab bag; you won't know what you've paid for until you "open the package," but at least you can go somewhere warm and sunny.

Weather

"When Lady Nugent arrived in Jamaica in 1800, she remarked to Lord Balcarres that it was a very fine day. 'I assure you that you will be tired of saying this before many days are over,' replied His Lordship," according to commentary in Basil Cracknell's *The West Indians*. Jamaican legends refer to the southeast breeze as "the doctor," and the cool winds off the land as "the undertaker," but in Papiamento, the language of the southern Netherlands Antilles, there is no word for weather. It's always perfect, and not worth talking about.

As recently as a few years ago, people "only" went south in winter months, usually to escape from snow and ice, or at least bone-chilling cold. Since affluence has traditionally been the measure of one's ability to take "time off" in winter, the rates are highest at all hotels and villas from mid-December until mid-April, with premium rates charged at some places over the Christmas holidays, and during February and March.

Wise travelers now realized, however, that weather doesn't change much year 'round in the countries bordering the Caribbean sea, a claim that cannot be made by Bermuda or even The Bahamas, since both groups of islands lie north of the Caribbean with The Bahamas southeast of the tip of Florida, sharing weather well known to Florida folks.

Summer versus winter: Although logic suggests that if Florida and Texas are hot in summer, the Caribbean islands (which lie farther south) must be hotter, that's not a fact. The Caribbean islands do lie closer to the equator, but they also lie in the path of the steady tradewinds that sent Columbus and his followers to these shores. Since they are small land masses, most islands are constantly cooled by the breeze. Average daily temperatures seldom vary as much as 10 degrees above wintertime highs. Although downtown pockets may seem steamy, the sea's nearby for cooling swims. If you're heading south primarily for sea—to be on it, in it, or under it, it doesn't matter when you go to the islands insofar as the weather is concerned. And, since most people seem willing to pay a premium for winter travel, an added bonus for summer travelers is the fact that hotel rates can be as much as 40% lower at many of the most expensive properties and at their lowest everywhere. In addition, flowering trees and local events are at their most colorful. The trees come into full bloom in summer and a full calendar of sport and festive events can be found on most islands from April through the fall.

Rainy season is a myth. Traditionally used by island folk to refer to their fall season, when the average daily rainfall tallies to the highest numbers, the "rainy season" is often one of the pleasant times to visit. The rains are usually quick and heavy showers that may douse the area late at night or early in the morning, lured to the island by its warmer temperature when the absence of

TIPS AND TOPICS FOR CARIBBEAN TRAVELING · · · 57

sunshine makes the dark sky cooler. The rains seldom effect vacationers' plans (and a daily hour of sunshine is more than enough to yield a noteworthy tan).

Tropical rain storms are a fact of island life at all times of the year; records of recent years note heavy rains in January and at other "unusual" times. While some of the drier islands—Aruba, Bonaire, and Curaçao, for example—are desertlike from lack of rain, verdant dress of Dominica's lush mountain peaks follows almost-daily showers. Just as is true in any country, the bigger islands have a varied (although always comfortably warm) climate. On Jamaica, for example, the lush foliage of Ocho Rios is testimony to that area's greater rainfall; on St. Croix, the east end is almost desertlike while the northwest area has a rain forest; and on the Dominican Republic, the increased rainfall of recent years around Puerto Plata on the north coast may be partially caused by the increase in the land temperature due to rapid building.

Hurricanes? No one can tell you they don't happen. They do—and have recently with Gilbert in September '88 and Hugo in '89. But they usually gather in the Caribbean region and pack their wallop farther north—on the shores of Florida or the Gulf of Mexico. They usually "assemble" in the late summer and early fall, but all islands benefit from tracking facilities that make it easy to know when heavy storms are predicted. You have your choice of moving to high land or leaving the island on the next flight. There's plenty of time for either action.

The answer, then, as to "When to go?" is whenever you can get packed and get away. If rates matter, plan to travel between mid-April and mid-December, when rates have dropped from winter highs.

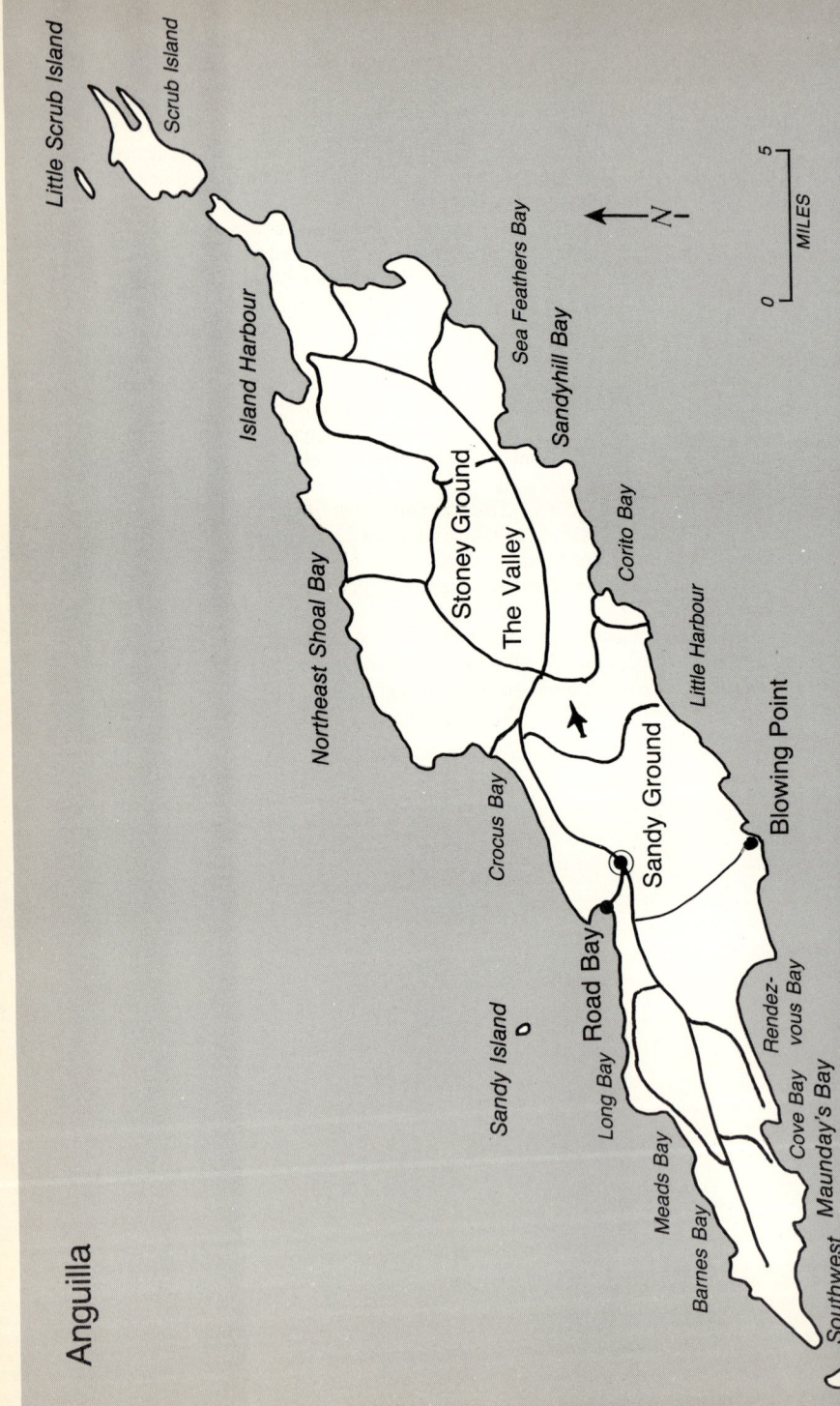

ANGUILLA

> Anguilla Department of Tourism, The Secretariat, The Valley, Anguilla, W.I., T 809+ 497–2451; Anguilla Tourist Information, 271 Main St., Northport, NY 11768, T 516+ 261–1234 or 800+ 553–4939, fax 516+ 261–9606.

$ · · · US $1 = EC $2.65
Unless otherwise noted, $ refers to U.S. currency.

There were mountains of conch shells on the beach, where the fishermen had wrenched the meat from the shell before it could be pounded tender, seasoned, and stewed to become the main feast on the dinner table. The polished pink tones of the piles of shells made a design on the cornstarch sand that separated sea from scrub growth along the shore. There were no footprints on this beach, until we swam ashore and made our own.

We had sailed to Anguilla from Sint Maarten, when a boat was the only way to reach this island—in the early 1960s. The few intrepid airplane pilots who chose to land here did so on a flat patch covered with stubble; they brought few tourists.

Not so now! Anguilla has come of age in tourism. Some of us miss the laid-back lifestyle that was the island's pace even a few years ago. Others, arriving now for the first time, still see Anguilla as "undiscovered."

It's true that, although the main road is good, the side roads are mostly packed sand carved into ruts by the trucks needed for the inevitable construction. It's also true that the finger-snapping service expected by some international travelers is hard to find on this island (or anywhere in the Caribbean, for that matter).

But the island is "with it" in the world, linked by telephone and fax machines, by several airlines (thankfully using small planes), and by shuttle boat service. The bustle and clutter of St. Martin/Sint Maarten is only a few minutes away. The sea still provides a buffer, but for how long? The modern world—and its pricing strategies—have made a mark on this small island. But for this season, at least, there are few scars.

AUTHOR'S OBSERVATION

In West Indian terms, Anguilla is a prosperous island. Anguillians care more about an outdoor life than they do about big, luxurious houses. The half-built stucco dwellings that you'll notice around the island are being constructed as spare funds and time allow. In spite of their derelict appearance, they are one sign of the island's prosperity; the many new and often luxurious hotels and rental cottages are another.

POLITICAL PICTURE: Elections held on February 28, 1989, supported the policies of the incumbent party, the Anguilla National Alliance. By the votes of his elected colleagues, Chief Minister Emile Gumbs was returned to the office he has held since March 1984. The island's other major party is the Anguilla United Party, led by a former chief minister, Ronald Webster, who was active in Anguilla's independence movement in the 1960s. Two other parties—the Anguilla Development Party and PACE—played minor roles in the peaceful election. The ANA encourages controlled tourism growth, and has shown little interest in sharing the casinos and construction mess of neighboring St. Martin.

The 35 square miles of Anguilla became a British Dependent Territory on December 20, 1980. In 1967, Anguilla was grouped with St. Kitts and Nevis as one Associated State of Britain, destined to become one independent Caribbean country. For almost 10 years, the 3-island status was a point of relative turmoil for Anguillians. The confrontation was between Anguillians and Kittitians, or more especially due to the government policies of the late premier of St. Kitts-Nevis and at that time also of Anguilla, Robert Bradshaw. For a number of reasons, one of them being that Anguillians believed that they were not getting their fair share of British government appropriations or a fair shake with government policies, Anguillians, then led by Ronald Webster, petitioned the British government to split from St. Kitts-Nevis and go it alone. Anyone who remembers the press coverage in 1969 may recall the interest shown when British paratroopers landed on the beaches of Anguilla to keep the peace. The uncomfortable alliance ended when Anguilla was granted special status on February 10, 1976, in response to petitions from its 6000 nationals.

ISLAND APPEARANCE: Most of this splinter of land is flat; the mid-section is covered with low-lying shrubs that are often parched by constant daily sunshine. The communities are loosely gathered, simple stucco houses and landholdings; there is no town of substance. Villages are often a couple of shops, an eating place, school, or church marking a crossroad. Road Bay is the exception, with its cement pier sometimes busy with ships bringing supplies for the increasing tourism facilities. The beach that lines Road Bay sees most of the island's "action," at its several small eating places, its one hotel, and the few shops and other places that cater to island residents. Most Anguillians are black.

LIFESTYLE: For most of their history, Anguillians have tilled their own plots of land, harvested their food, and earned their livelihood from the sea. A home of one's own has priority, and many partially finished buildings speckle the 16-by-4-mile island, awaiting money for eventual completion. Many Anguillians work in the States, sending (and bringing) funds home from labors abroad. Those who have remained at home are making a good living with tourism and construction as well as the time-honored business in lobsters and fish.

> **AUTHOR'S OBSERVATION**
>
> Although Anguilla has a long way to go before it challenges the commercial clutter of neighboring St. Martin/Sint Maarten, the island's once-pristine shores are breaking out in a rash of hotels, cottages, and other tourist facilities. People who visited this island even two years ago will be astounded by the changes.

MEDICAL FACILITIES: The small hospital at Crocus Bay is used to capacity by Anguillians. Airlift to Puerto Rico is recommended for emergencies.

MONEY MATTERS: U.S. currency is happily accepted, although the local currency is Eastern Caribbean dollars and cents. Be sure, when you transact business in local stores and restaurants, where the $ sign usually refers to Eastern Caribbean currency, that you know whose dollars are quoted. Always ask. One U.S. dollar equals EC$2.65.

COMMUNICATIONS are easy, by direct-dial telephone from North America. The code is 809+ 497+ 4-digit local number. Airmail (50 cents for the first ½ ounce from U.S.) can take two weeks or more. Facsimile machines are used by many hotels and businesses. From Anguilla, phone calls can be made at the Cable & Wireless office or, at a premium charge, from your hotel. Cable & Wireless sells phone cards, the size of a credit card, for use (instead of coins) with designated telephones. AT&T's USADirect dial is 1–800+ 872–2881 from Anguillian phones.

ARRIVAL can be by air or boat. *American Eagle*'s small planes make frequent flights between San Juan, Puerto Rico, and Anguilla's airport. There is also small-plane service, aboard *Winair* flights, out of Dutch Sint Maarten's international airport, and small plane flights from the French side's Grand Case airstrip. The flight between St. Martin/Sint Maarten and Anguilla takes about 7 minutes. Some Anguillian hotels arrange charters for guests arriving in Sint Maarten on international flights.

> **AUTHOR'S OBSERVATION**
>
> If you want your baggage to arrive when you do, do not check it through to Anguilla. In spite of inconvenience, the only reliable way to be sure you'll have clothes when you arrive is to carry them through any connecting airports yourself.

Shuttle boats operate, several times daily, between Marigot (the main town of French St. Martin) and Anguilla's Blowing Point dock. The fare for the 20-minute motorboat ride is $10; the taxi fare to the Marigot dock from the airport on Dutch Sint Maarten is also about $10. It is possible (and fun) to sail to Anguilla on charter boats from Sint Maarten/St. Martin, but that experience is usually a day trip out of the Dutch/French island.

AUTHOR'S OBSERVATION

A departure tax is levied, even for day trips, from both Anguilla and Sint Maarten/St. Martin. Even when you are in transit to arrive on Anguilla, you will have to pay from Sint Maarten/St. Martin. Officials are persistent about collecting the tax, which is $5 (from the Dutch side) or 10 French francs (from the French side).

DEPARTURE is either by boat from Blowing Point dock, or by air from the tidy terminal at Anguilla's Wallblake Airport. *Air BVI, LIAT, Winair, Air Anguilla, Tyden Air,* and *American Eagle* have desks at Wallblake Airport. Don't count on the few airport shops being open if you are leaving very early or late. If you have rented a car, you can avoid standing in line for check-in if you pass by the airport well in advance of your departure, to check in and get your seat assignment. The departure tax is $5.

TOURING TIPS: For **car rental,** *Connor's* is my top recommendation, not only because Maurice Connor is a trusted colleague, but because his fleet, which started with one Volkswagen in '71, now numbers over 50, with a range of styles. He gives good service, and has new, well-maintained cars. Maurice Connor can be reached from overseas by phone at 809+497–2433. There are several other car rental firms, including *Bennie's Travel and Tours,* not far from Blowing Point dock (T 809+ 497–2221); *Tripple K,* near the airport (T 809+ 497–2934); and *Roy Rogers Car Rental,* with offices also on Sint Maarten (T 809+ 497–6290). Most hotels can assist with arranging rental cars. Rental firms can write out your Anguillian driver's license, for which you pay US$6. The island bus service starts from a roadside stop a short walk up the road from the boat pier at Blowing Point. **Taxi** drivers hover around the entrance of pier and airport when arrivals are expected. Rates start high for short rides. Lore from some drivers may be worth the investment; otherwise, plan to drive yourself.

There are **boating** excursions to nearby Sandy Island and other spots. Your hotel will have details. *Boo's Cycle Rental* is one source for **motorcycles.**

AUTHOR'S OBSERVATION

Bring your favorite mosquito/sand fly repellent. The "no-see-'um" problem is not unique to Anguilla, but a place near the beach can lose a lot of romance if you have to slap and scratch.

LODGING: Anguilla offers both absolute luxury at top dollar and basic small spots, but there's not much in the middle range for prices or facilities. Entrepreneurs have consciously set out to appeal to the top of the market—and now can claim to have several of the Caribbean's most elegant new properties. Four hotels have rates that stretch well over $600 per day for two in winter season—only for room and breakfast. The best places are on soft, powdery sand beaches; most of the simpler lodgings are on or near the main road that stretches the length of the island.

It's worth noting that most seaside lodgings—even those that aspire to elegance—are at the end of dirt-and-sand rutted roads.

An 8% government tax and 10% service are added to hotel bills.

AUTHOR'S AWARDS

Spectacular *Malliouhana* reigns supreme for ultimate luxury (and pretense); *Carimar Beach Club* provides comfortable seaview apartments clustered at a nearby point on the same beach; *Easy Corner Villas* allow for easy housekeeping and offer Anguilla's best value.

Information about places-to-stay is included under Hotels/Resorts; Housekeeping Holidays, The Inn Way, and Low Cost Lodging. Stars apply to position within category. (See page 11.)

HOTELS/RESORTS range from the ultra-luxurious to simpler places. Services also stretch to extremes—from unctious to careless.

Anguilla Great House • *on Rendezvous Bay* • is reached by a dirt/sand road, passing an unsightly (and sometimes fragrant) swamp. The bedrooms stretch from the reception area (in a box-like building) in two single-story wings, arranged as a half-moon cupping the pool, beach, and bar-dining pavilion. The name-giving Great House has yet to be built. Furnishings are mock-Georgian style. A seaviewing veranda lines the five rooms in each block. The two end rooms have king-sized beds, the next two have kitchenettes, the middle room has twin beds—and all have connecting doors that allow for pairing or separate status, depending on guest wishes. Although the setting is pleasant, the patio dining area has mediocre food; the place needs trained management to reach its potential. Rendezvous Bay beach is long and beautiful, with a view toward Marigot, St. Martin. *Hotel.*

★★★★ **Cap Juluca** • *on Maunday's Bay* • claims a superb location—on a beautiful talcum-powder beach. Although the resort has been a construction site since it opened, life seems to have settled down to an upscale style with 74 luxurious rooms and 14 suites; most of the staff are skilled at pampering. Sensational Moorish-style suites are in several 2-story clusters, some with six suites and others with less. All are opulently furnished, with seaview patio or balcony, depending on level (beach or upstairs). Top rooms give the most privacy. Bathrooms are huge—and hedonistic—with two-person tubs and private adjoining solarium. Tower rooms, in middle of upper level of some units, have a spiral staircase to a totally private upper sundeck. Insofar as public space is concerned, there's an attractive shop (classy clothes and trinkets) near *Pimm's* restaurant, which is within sound of the sea, and the option for more casual dining at Chaterton's. Food at Pimm's is pretentiously elegant, in European style. Count on stratospheric cost. Tennis courts are near the suites; golf privileges have been arranged on specific days at Mullet Bay on Sint Maarten ($65 green's fee includes cart; boat transport is $35 each way); Cap Juluca's beach is gorgeous! *Resort.*

★★★★ **Cinnamon Reef** • *at Little Harbour, about midpoint on the south coast* • is a seaside enclave with good tennis courts, a small beach, some watersports, and rooms nicely furnished in Caribbean colors. Reached by a 5-minute drive on a spur road off the main route, the place is self-centered. A huge fresh water pool supplements the owner-encouraged beach bordering the lagoon. Most villas have a sea view from the living area, with the bedroom at the back, up (or down) a few steps. (You can see the sea over your toes from some of the beds.) Rooms have a telephone jack for those who want to claim a phone from the front desk. Some villas have refrigerators; all rooms have icemakers. Tea is served on the reception building's patio at 4 p.m.; dinners are served nearby, in the plant-punctuated sea-view dining terrace. *Resort.*

★★★★ **Coccoloba** • *at Barnes Bay, on the northwest coast* • gives its guests attractive lodgings overlooking a beautiful beach, with nearby pool, tennis, elegant restaurant, and a boutique. Perched on a bluff, sharing Mead's Bay beach with Malliouhana and enjoying another stretch of sand along Barnes Bay, Coccoloba puts its guests in one of several single-story buildings along the ridge that eventually slopes to the sea. Most rooms are split-level suites; the bedroom is up a few steps from living area and bathroom. Minimum-rate rooms are in the newest building, farthest from the main building, but with a small pool for renters of the deluxe suites and the few single rooms. This "Great House" is also closest to the beach and sea; other rooms require climbing steep steps down (and back up). Restaurant tables in the poolside dining area in the main building are placed so that conversation with fellow guests is easy. Menu offerings and presentation of food are exceptional (and expensive). People who like (and can afford) "the good life" will like it here. *Resort.*

★★★★★ **Malliouhana Beach Hotel** • *on Mead's Bay, on the northwest coast* • continues to warrant high praise for architecture and outlook, although I have often found some staff to seem diffident. The main buildings cap the hilltop with what some may know as "Mediterranean elegance": white stucco buildings, red tile roofs, and plenty of arches, arcades, and terraced areas. The sea-rimming blanket of white, powdery sand, and the diamond-clear sea, deserve "the best" and this place can offer it—when the human element operates at peak performance. The first-built beachside buildings are draped with multi-colored bougainvillea and other plants, as are the hillside headquarters. Patios and personal touches are perfect. The hillside mansion includes the multipooled main building and most of the balconied rooms. Tennis courts are near the beach, where watersports are offered. Guests are paying top dollar to be pampered in spectacular surroundings. Staff seems to respond to the call for perfection, but guests should be prepared to respond to service blips when they occur and to encounter sometimes haughty "service." *Resort.*

★★★ **The Mariners'** • *on Road Bay Beach* • has grown from the original attractive buildings that made it Anguilla's first new hotel (in 1983) to become a complete resort with tennis courts and pool, now operating with all-inclusive rates. The restaurant, with its beachside veranda, is a short walk toward the shore. Most of the rooms are in single-story bands, built in West Indian wood fretwork style. Connecting doors can lock or not, as guests' desire. Although some of the comfortably furnished units have kitchenettes, guests are encouraged to use the restaurant. The newer two-story blocks of rooms are slightly inland. Since the port at Road Bay, where construction materials and supplies are off-loaded, has gotten busier, the hotel is at the heart of the island's action. Several basic beachside bistros line the shore. Inquire about possible exchange dining options, under the "all-inclusive" plan. If you enjoy West Indian life, with modern comforts and Anguillian hospitality, this place can seem wonderful. Anguillian Clive Carty is in charge of on-the-spot management. *Small resort.*

★★★ **Rendezvous Bay Hotel** • *at the eastern end of Rendezvous Bay, on the south coast* • has grown from modest size, as Anguilla's first beachfront hotel, to become a multi-faceted resort, with new beachfront villas to the west, and sea-front apartments to the east of the original home, with its band of basic motel-like rooms. Very much a Gumbs family enterprise, this place has a devoted following among those who know and love a West Indian lifestyle. Now with 1990's flourishes, in the decor and fittings in the newest units, the long stretch of Rendezvous Bay's soft white sand beach and a low-key, no-pressure atmosphere remain the appeal of this place. Don't count on gourmet food in the restaurant—yet, but a rental car can take you to some of Anguilla's better mealtime goals. This place allows for beachside lodging at a more reasonable price than that charged by the ritzy pace-setters. *Hotel.*

HOUSEKEEPING HOLIDAYS can be pleasant on Anguilla, if you're self-sufficient and like plenty of quiet time. Each season sees new villas and apartments for rent, with only a few in the luxury category. Count on being able to buy fresh fish, if you're willing to follow the fishermen, and on making forays to neighboring St. Martin/Sint Maarten for staples you might choose not to bring from home. Anguillian shops are reasonably well stocked, but the selection is not extensive and prices are high.

Many of the rental facilities have more than one agent, but some of the best contacts for good listings are **Prems Real Estate,** Morgan Hill, Anguilla, British West Indies, T 809+ 497–2456; **Villa Vacations,** c/o Travel Professionals, 444 East 52nd St., New York, NY 10022, T 212+ 753–1133; and **Sunshine Villas,** Box 142, Blowing Point, Anguilla, British West Indies, T 809+ 497-6149.

★★★ **Carimar Beach Club** • *on Mead's Bay* • is a cluster of Mediterranean-style buildings, with comfortably furnished apartments on the beach next to Malliouhana. Rates put this place into luxury orbit in winter season, although you're on your own for apartment-style living. The beach is a long stretch of soft, white sand with portions sometimes carved by waves responding to a northeast wind. Operated on a condominium pattern, units are for rent in owner's absence. Two tennis courts are part of the complex. This place can be perfect, if you seek a leisurely life on Anguilla's "gold coast." *Apts.*

★★★★ **Cove Castles** • *on southwest Shoal Bay* • have distinctive (and noteworthy) architecture. Units are private condominiums—both villas and beach houses—for rent in owner's absence, with ultimate privacy. Although each beach-bordering unit is self-contained, with an upstairs bedroom that has a sensational sea view toward St. Martin, all stand like sentinels along the shore. The restaurant tucked amid the buildings at beach level serves guests' favorites in an atmosphere that hints of an exclusive private party. All units also have complete kitchen for home-cooking, when preferred. Policy has been to close for summer months. *Villas.*

★★ **Cul de Sac** • *at Blowing Point, not far from the boat dock* • claims a perch near the shore's edge, although flourishing bushes may block the view from some of the homey cottages. The dirt road leading to the lodgings snakes through scrub-growth. A small pool is the sunning spot; there's not a beach at this shore. Count on being about 15 minutes' drive from the best beaches. You'll want a car for mobility—and for sampling some of the island's restaurants. There's a cozy, low-key, relaxed atmosphere here. *Cottages.*

Dolphins • *at Sandy Hill Bay, on the southeast coast* • is a pleasantly furnished 2-bedroom home with sea view and beach below. It's in the neighborhood of *Loblolly* (see below). *Apt.*

★★ **Easy Corner Villas** • *on the hillside overlooking Road Bay* • are modern, attractive, and built for homelike vacation living. Furnishings are comfortable with modern appliances for carefree living. Often rented for a month or more, the 1- and 2-bedroom units are 2 per white stucco building. Maurice Connor (of car-rental fame) is the owner. You'll need a car for mobility and will feel as though you are in a residential area. *Apts.*

Ferry Boat Inn and Apartments • *near the Blowing Point boat dock, on the south coast* • are on the shore (no beach), with an open-to-breezes bar and restaurant that serves as social center for those renters who want one. One-bedroom apartments are furnished with basics; the 2-bedroom house can be good for families. You'll want a car for mobility. *Apts.*

★★ **Fountain Beach** • *on the north shore at Shoal Bay* • offers apartments with ceiling fans and sea view, slightly removed from the other lodgings and beachside bars at this gorgeous beach. You'll need a car to go anywhere else, but you're on one of the island's longest powdery white sand beaches, which becomes slightly more active on weekends. *Apts.*

Harbor Lights • *on the north coast, at Island Harbour* • has a few apartments, furnished with basics and within walking distance of the beach and a few restaurants. Don't count on a lot of nighttime action in this area, for this season at least. Beachside casual *Smitty's* is a gathering hub some days; *Hibernia* is the best nearby restaurant. *Apts.*

Loblolly • *overlooking Sandy Hill Bay, on the southeast coast* • is 2 apartments, upstairs and downstairs, perched on a bluff that plunges to the sea. Furnishings seem more like someone's home than a rental place. A car's essential. *Apts.*

Masara Resort • *overlooking Kartouche Bay, near the airport* • is several 1- and 2-bedroom apartments, for independent housekeeping. It's a short walk to the shore for swimming. *Apts.*

Palm Grove Apartments • *near the shore at Sea Feathers Bay* • are owned by former Chief Minister Ronald Webster and provide basic housing at what is becoming a residential area with visitor rental in mind. The independent buildings have basics and, as at other places, renting a car is a good idea.

Rainbow Reef Villas • *at the south coast, with a view toward St. Martin* • are several basic-block homes, some of them for rent in owner's absence. The shore is rocky at this point; better beaches and all restaurants require a car. *Sea Feathers* (see below) is in the same area. *Houses.*

Rose's Place • *on the north coast, east of Island Harbour* • has duplex apartments with 2 bedrooms and 2 baths at the shore. Recently built, apartments have sea view and quiet surroundings. You can walk to *Hibernia* restaurant, or down the road to the beach (*Smitty's Beach Bar* and other spots), but you'll want a car for any island touring. *Apts.*

Sea Feathers • *at the southeast coast, on Sea Feather Bay* • is an ambitious apartment and villa development that is underway. The sizable villas, the first of 25 that are planned, are often in private hands, but the 6 boxcar-style buildings near the road, a walk from the shore, hold several studio and bigger apartments that are available for rent, sale, and timeshare. Count on modern plumbing and new construction. Car required for mobility. *Apts., Villas.*

★★ **Sea Grape Villas** • *on Mead's Bay* • are large multi-level apartments amid seagrape trees at the shore, midway between Malliouhana on the eastern bluff, and Coccoloba on the western hill. Planned as a beach club with several privately owned units, the first three buildings opened in the late spring '89. Beach-level bedrooms are viewless; the best view is from the kitchen and nearby patio and living-room area. The beach is spectacular and, although not open at presstime, an alfresco restaurant is planned. This is another venture for Maurice Connor (who owns *Easy Corner Villas* and *Connor's Car Rental*), in association with Robert Carroll of Edgartown, MA. *Apts.*

Shoal Bay Resort • *on northwest Shoal Bay* • is a conglomeration of big block buildings with apartments. In an architectural "style" that's not to my taste, this place has become a blight on the landscape. Too many apartments have been wedged into a small space. The beach is still lovely, and rates here have been reasonable in recent seasons. SBV (below) is next door. *Apts.*

Shoal Bay Villas • *on the north coast, west of Island Harbour* • were planned and built by Jack Wigley, who sold to Anguillians a few years ago. With the beachside restaurant and bar as a gathering spot, guests have choice of the long lovely beach or a small pool for swimming. Apartments are in 2-story buildings on a beautiful beach, or around the pool, on the inland side of the beachfront units. Poolside units share the noise of any boisterous guests. *Apts.*

★★★ **La Sirena** • *overlooking Mead's Bay, near Sea Grape Villas* • is Mediterranean style, with 2- and 3-bedroom apartments in a cluster of white stucco buildings. The reception building holds bar and social areas, with a top level sea view dining room, reached by a spiral staircase. Pleasant fabrics and comfortable furniture complement the views from most rooms. The pool is on-premises; it's a short walk to the beach. *Apts.*

Skiffles • *on the southeast shore, not far from Road Bay* • caps a hill. Guests can walk through the brush down to the water, but there's no beach for swimming and the walk is reasonably rugged. The pool provides a cooling-off place for renters of the 5 units, 2 of which are in 2-story pink-painted buildings and one stands alone. You'll need a car; the caretaker can offer suggestions about places to see and dine. *Apts.*

THE INN WAY: Anguilla has no inns in the traditional warmly hospitable Caribbean style. The Mariners once had that feeling, but it has grown too big and lacks the management-guest concern that makes Caribbean inns special. Management at some of the apartments and villas—notably Easy Corner and Fountain Beach—share the concern often associated with good inn management. Some places mentioned under ''Low-Cost Lodging'' may seem inn-like to young travelers—or those young in spirit who want to get back to basics.

LOW-COST LODGINGS: From mid-April to mid-December, rates are lower at all places, but the costs at a few of the housekeeping places can seem reasonable even in peak winter months when divided by the maximum occupancy. Insofar as small hotels are concerned, it's possible to find a room in winter for less than $50 for two, meals extra, but the place will be basic, bordering on seedy. There are few real bargains. Some of the guest-house hotel rooms are very simple, with cotlike beds and shared bathroom. Others are in modern, boxy buildings that are not much on atmosphere but are reasonably clean, with basic furnishings. None are on beaches, although **Lloyd's** (T 497–2351), on the hillside at The Valley, is an easy stroll down the hill to the sea. Its 14 simply furnished rooms near the hospital were some of the island's first lodgings, when Anguilla welcomed visitors before tourism warranted luxury hotels. **Inter-Island Hotel** (T 497–6259) and nearby **Maybern** (T 497–6350) are reasonably modern, boxy buildings with basic rooms. Both are on the main road at South Hill, not far from Sandy Ground. **Casa Nadine** (T 497–2358), near the bakery at The Valley, and **Yellow Banana** (T 497–2626) at Stoney Ground are two others to consider. None of these places has more than 20 rooms; most have only a few; all will seem like roadside hovels to travelers used to U.S. luxury.

RESTAURANTS range from very casual places popular with local folk to extravagant luxury that can be measured by top international standards (with prices to match). All of the most elegant (and expensive) restaurants are affiliated with resorts, and accept outside guests only when the resort's guests have been accommodated. Among those places are *Pimm's* at Cap Juluca and the restaurants at *Malliouhana* and *Coccoloba*.

Count on at least $50 per person for dining at the toniest places. A complete dinner at the more casual places will range from $20 to $30, depending on your choices.

AUTHOR'S AWARDS

Hibernia, just beyond Island Harbour, is my first choice for independent dining; *Lucy's Harbour View* still claims my time for its Road Bay view and respectably good food at reasonable (for Anguilla) prices; and *Riviera,* within sound of the sea at Road Bay, is romantic and relaxing. Tops for hotel dining are *Pimm's* at Cap Juluca, plus the restaurants at Malliouhana and Coccoloba, all with very high prices.

Arlo's Place • *near Skiffles apartments* • had an iffy start, but now offers pasta, pizza, and other Italian specialties plus fish in a building reached by a dirt road off the main island road.

Aquarium • *near Easy Corner's entrance above Road Bay* • is Diedrick and Elaine Brooks's place. It's popular with residents, but lacks the beachside atmosphere that is popular with vacationers.

Barrell Stay • *on the beach at Road Bay* • is actually made of barrel "stays," or staves as many know them. Its Robinson Crusoe atmosphere makes a swim between courses seem possible, and fish, chicken, and veal bathed in special sauces are highlights.

Fish Trap • *at Island Harbour* • had lost its panache, when I checked for this edition. I'll try it again, before making any recommendations. Less than a dozen small tables freckle the porch-like terrace, where dogs and cats curl to sleep in spare space. The sea-and-fishing-boat view is best by daylight; the place is about half-an-hour's drive west from the Road Bay area, which makes a long dark drive for nighttime.

★★★★ **Hibernia** • *just east of Island Harbour* • offered *tarte de poisson, terrine de merou* (grouper), and other tasty items when I visited. Main courses include duckling, fish, and other staples, attractively served and, in my case, delicious. Classical music played softly in the background. The open-to-breezes porch and the inside room have sea view during daytime; the restaurant becomes cozy and homelike after dark. This place is worth the drive.

Johnno's • *on the beach at Road Bay* • is better for its steel band and fun than for food, although fish fries, chicken, and other filling offerings are served along with drinks.

★★ **Lucy's Harbour View** • *at the road's turning to head down from The Valley area to Road Bay* • continues to feature lobster and fish, with soups and special entrees sometimes claiming first place. Ask for a table at the edge for the best view.

Old House • *near The Valley* • makes the most of surroundings in an attractive former home to offer acceptable seafood specialties as well as other American-style fare. Open for breakfast, lunch, and dinner, the place is sometimes a gathering spot.

Oriental Restaurant • *at The Valley* • serves Chinese food with seafood emphasis in *very* simple surroundings at a crossroads.

Palm Palm • *shoreside, at Road Bay* • has been one of the group of beach shacks serving lunch and dinner in a casually Caribbean atmosphere. The fact that Lucy (of Harbour View) has taken over this spot should bode well for offerings, but my meal just after the takeover was mediocre at best. Read the menu carefully before settling in—and glance at meals that other diners have chosen before making your selection. Could be a fun experience; mine wasn't.

Pimm's • *beachside, at Cap Juluca* • is as good for atmosphere as for food. Although it's casual during daylight hours, this is no wet-bathing-suit kind of place; it's sunstruck-chic. Put a dazzling cover-up over your swim suit, if you choose not to put on designer resort clothes. Evening is elegant, with the nearby buildings floodlit and sea sounds to complement the occasional local band. Mealtime offerings are as pleasing to the eye as to the palate. Prices are high, but who cares? This place is made for memories.

Reefside • *on the beach at Shoal Bay Villas* • serves hearty food (burgers, fish, steaks, etc.) in a casual, beach-oriented setting. This place used to be called "Happy Jacks."

Ripples • *in a boxy building at Road Bay* • claims the space formerly called Dockside. Not much to look at from the outside, the place has a pub style, with a menu that features shrimp, steak, and other imports.

Riviera Restaurant • *at Road Bay* • is another of the trio of good seaside bistro-style places (along with *Palm Palm* and *Barrell Stay*). It follows the lead of the others insofar as food style is concerned, and sometimes peps up for evening entertainment.

Roy's • *at Crocus Bay* • specializes in fish as well as bar drinks. Best when some celebration is under way, this place has its followers.

Smitty's Seaside Saloon • *at Island Harbour* • comes alive on weekends and some evenings. Check on the spot if you're in the area.

The Warden's House • *near The Valley crossroads* • serves steak, afternoon tea, and snacks in a patio next to the house that gives it its name. Better for atmosphere than for food, it's a convenient touring stop.

NATURAL SURROUNDINGS: Long stretches of the coastline are rimmed with soft white sand. Since the shore slopes into the sea from most beaches, snorkeling is good. Offshore reefs keep surging seas at bay; many can be reached by an easy swim. Some of the offshore islands are good places for birding. (Chief Minister Gumbs is an avid birder and one source for tips about the best sites.) Although some dive sites are popular with entrepreneurs from busy Sint Maarten, many are still in pristine condition.

Insofar as the island's parched landscape is concerned, The Fountain, a series of caves near the northeast coast's Shoal Bay, has been designated a National Park by the Anguillian government. Archaeologists have found early Amerindian inscriptions that lead some to believe that the caves were a prized religious site for the Arawaks and other early tribes. Check with the tourist office about The Fountain's status. When its prominence was suspected, it was closed to the public until its value could be assessed by scholars—and its riches protected from invasion by tourists and residents.

PLACES WORTH FINDING are limited, and if you don't bother to get to any of them, your holiday can still be "perfect." This is a "no pressure" place. All the sights are natural, except for **Wall Blake House,** the plantation house that was restored a few years ago and has been purchased by private owners. From a paper that David Carty, Anguillian-born history buff, assembled about Wall Blake House, I learned that although the house you look at may not be the one that stood here in the 18th century, there are some foundation stones that date to 1787, and that's its claim to fame. The legends that languish around the house are almost as interesting as the architecture and the impressive restoration. There are tales of murder in the cellar, of destruction during the French invasion in 1796, of lavish living in the sugar heyday of Anguilla, and family intrigue, with bachelor brothers and unknown wives of other brothers, and, most recently, the lonely years of Miss Mary Blake, who lived here until 1976, when she died, willing the property to St. Gerard's Catholic Church. (Be sure to note the elaborate decor of the new church—you can't miss it—next door.)

SPORTS center on the sea.

Tamariain Watersports (T 497–2020) offers certification and resort **diving** courses, as well as facilities for waterskiing and sunfish for rent from their headquarters near the beach at Malliouhana and at the Mariners. *Island Watersports* has a shop at Sandy Ground/Road Bay for windsurfers, scuba, and snorkel equipment. *Ramblin' Rose,* a 44-foot yacht, sets sail daily at 10 a.m. from Road Bay. Cost for a day's sailing is $70.

Suntastic Cruises Ltd. (T 497–3400) arranges **cruises** along the coast and to neighboring islets and cays. Sport fishing can also be arranged, but don't count on top-notch fishing gear.

Neville Connor and Erviŋ Romney (T 497–2433, 497–2845, or 497–2395) can arrange for you to spend the day at Sandy Island. They operate a **boat service,** at $5 each way, plus the food and a barbecue ($7 for basics, and $13 if you want lobster). They have been charging $1.50 for drinks.

Anguillians are known for their prowess at sea. You can chat with the fishermen, when you see them at Island Harbour or other coves, and can sometimes make arrangements to go out scuba diving or snorkeling when they go.

To witness one of the special August Monday races at Mead's Bay is a special treat. Be sure to ask about any event for the deep-hulled, hand-built racing craft, with their triangular handsewn sails.

Tennis can be played on courts at Coccoloba, Malliouhana, Cap Juluca, Cinnamon Reef, and The Mariners if you are a guest at the hotel. Bring your own tennis balls and racquet unless you enjoy paying premium prices.

TREASURES AND TRIFLES are best found in the boutiques at the most luxurious hotels (Coccoloba, Cap Juluca, Malliouhana, and sometimes also at Cinnamon Reef). Insofar as locally made items are concerned, find Courtney Devonish, an accomplished artisan from Barbados who moved to Anguilla in early 1989. Some of his exceptional carvings are sold at his airport shop (which sells mostly liquor).

The **Anguilla Craft Shop** at Stoney Ground has some interesting craftwork, as well as jams, jellies, shellwork, straw work and other locally made items. Embroidery and crochet work are good quality at Elsie's, in Stoney Ground.

Remember that prices in local shops are quoted in local currency, which is Eastern Caribbean dollars, value EC$2.65 to US$1.

ANTIGUA

> Antigua and Barbuda Tourist Office, Box 363, Long and Thames sts., St. John's, Antigua, W.I., T 809+ 462–0480 or 809+ 462–2105, fax 809+ 462–2483; #311, 610 Fifth Ave., New York, NY 10020, T 212+ 541–4117, fax 212+ 757–1607; #601 2000 "N" St. N.W., Washington, DC, 20036, T 202+ 296–6310; 60 St. Clair Ave. E., Toronto, Ontario, Canada M4T 1N5, T 416+ 961–3083; 15 Thayer St., London SW1 W9TJ, England, T 01+ 486–7073.

$ · · · US $1 = EC $2.65
Unless otherwise noted, $ refers to U.S. currency.

It took only a few minutes to toss my suitcase into the back of the car, and less than that to get underway. In peak winter season, it might seem risky to arrive with no reservations—but it wasn't. For several days, I roamed around Antigua, traveling with my belongings in the back of the car, finding a room when (and where) I felt like stopping.

My first pause was at the gas station, where my comments about the loud and lively music prompted an invitation from the pump attendant to meet him later that evening. I pleaded plans, and drove away.

The second was to pick up two ladies, Flora and her daughter Rosie. They had finished their beach parade for the day. Their work is making (or buying) and selling smocks and T-shirts to sun-washed visitors who hover near the beaches.

"Business is bad," I learned before I contributed the fact that maybe people have had enough of T-shirts. It might be time to find a new product. The ubiquitous T-shirt has been the big item for the past several years, providing a sporadic living for Antiguan beach vendors—and the folks on mainland China who make the shirts.

Flora seemed confident that the cotton for the fabric comes from Antigua, but I have my doubts. The fields of Antigua don't produce enough cotton to make all the T-shirts I suspect are proferred. They're everywhere!

So are children, the hope of the future. Neatly uniformed young folks dance beside the streets early in the morning and again at midday, on their transit to the schoolhouse. On weekday midmornings, you can hear their recitations from the breeze-swept schoolrooms.

As I drove away from the tourist-focused north coast, the countryside opened up ahead of me and the landscape, in areas not yet marked for development,

looked much as it must have to Antigua's first British settlers: rolling hills blanketed in shades of green and occasional sights of the sea beyond.

Antigua is beautiful in the morning hours. Sun gilds the countryside, turning palm fronds and other growth to silver when the dawn rain reflects its beams. I followed a rainbow to St. John's, reaching the capital before cars and commerce had clogged the streets.

Breakfast was my goal; I had chosen to flee from the certain eggs-and-bacon at the hotels. In town, shutters were opening, doors were unlocked, as I stepped from street over open gutter to sidewalk in a hopping two-step that is the requisite "dance" in cluttered St. John's.

With some relief, I stepped into the enclave of Redcliffe Quay, following a smell of coffee. Since power had just failed, as happens in these islands when commerce outpaces infrastructure, I settled for iced coffee. Although breakfast was not usually offered, imaginative Bernadette suggested a bacon, lettuce, and tomato sandwich, which eventually arrived, artfully arranged by item on my plate. Another Antiguan day had officially begun.

POLITICAL PICTURE: Elections held on March 9, 1989, gave the Bird family another term in office. Although some seats were contested, 15 of the 16 seats were eventually decided for Prime Minister Vere Bird's Antigua Labour Party. The prime minister has had his hand at the helm of his own island's future for most of the past 50 years. He is the last of the Caribbean's old-time politicians, practicing a brand of politics (with favors and fund manipulation) not held in high esteem by those who operate by more conventional ethics. One of his sons, Lester Bird, serves as deputy prime minister; he is expected to assume the top office when his father is no longer able to serve. Another son, V. C. Bird Junior, is an island legend in his own time for alleged manipulation of funds and gun shipments to Colombia. Since his role as a labor leader of the 1940s, Vere Bird has been well connected to dominate his country's destiny. When Antigua became an Associated State of Britain's Caribbean community in 1967, he was the chief minister. When the island became independent, on November 1, 1981, he became the country's first prime minister. Only for one term, from 1971 (when the Progressive Labour Party won the elections and George Walter served as chief minister), has Vere Bird been "out of office."

Antigua's government spending has reached awesome levels, and the government seems to expect tourism to solve all the problems. Although the island has very little unemployment, and imports workers for its burgeoning tourism, the Bird government continues to encourage hotel and condominium projects, with a contract to an Italian firm for Heritage Quay in downtown St. John's, and rampant rumors about the intended sale of approximately 26 acres at Fort James, near the capital, to the mafia-linked Gambino family, among the more noteworthy recent ventures. The country's Marxist movement has its champion in Tim Hector, an eloquent Antiguan who has been critical of some of the Labour Party's practices. He publishes the local *Outlet* newspaper.

The United States has long had links with Antigua, most recently from World War II when the U.S. military built the landing strip still in use as the island's major airport facility. Prior to (and following) Grenada's problems in fall of '83, U.S. aid programs have given money to Antiguan projects, through the Agency for International Development and other sources.

ISLAND APPEARANCE: Although once robed in sugar cane, the hillsides are now decked out with other crops—or left in a natural state, perhaps to yield eventually to yet another tourism or development scheme. The island is not studded with tall palm trees, as some visitors expect; it has rolling hills, areas of lush tropical growth (especially in the south), and hundreds of coves where the clear sea washes soft, sandy shores. Areas around St. John's—both south around Deep Bay and north, almost from town past Dickenson Bay and around the north coast—have become building sites, with little apparent attention to zoning, ecology, or the natural attributes that have been a strong attraction for visitors to this island in recent years. Some once-remote beaches are now linked to the mainstream by roads and marred by random hotel and resort building. Although there are some high-density resort developments on coves in the south and east, these areas seem attractively out of the mainstream of the most frenetic development.

The island's strategic location amid the Caribbean chain gave it an 18th and 19th century importance for shipping. There are several sites that remain from the British colony's historic role. Included are 18th-century forts, Shirley Heights, and the restoration at English Harbor.

St. John's, the capital, may seem cluttered and confusing for the first-time visitor (as it does, also, to some of us who have been coming to this island for decades!). Most Antiguans are of African descent.

LIFESTYLE is Caribbean casual, with a veneer for tourism at resort and hotel areas as well as in St. John's when cruise ships are in port. St. John's Cathedral, at a high point of the capital, is testimony to the conservative (and religious) nature of most Antiguans, and tidy churches, often built of stone, punctuate villages in each of the country's parishes.

AUTHOR'S OBSERVATION

Although people in the countryside, away from the capital and areas devoted to tourism, are friendly and pleasant when visitors stop to talk, there's an attitude in St. John's and at the tourist areas that I find unpleasant. In town, people would just as soon walk into you as around you and a friendly "Good Morning" or another greeting is often met with silence or a puzzled look. If you drive, don't expect normal courtesies of the road. Drive defensively.

St. John's, Antigua's capital, was yanked into the 1980s in only one year, with the creation of cruise ship facilities (including a casino) at the town's waterfront, in 1988. The once sleepy town was shorn of most tradition, with Heritage Quay created in its place. The narrow streets of the 18th-century town plan are clogged and, due to construction and weekday business traffic, almost impassable.

Although the government's capitulation to tourism may make it seem unnecessary, sensitive travelers will still want to cover up the beach attire for forays into town and for island touring. When you venture away from the areas devoted to "mass tourism," you can glimpse the friendly and special qualities that have made Antigua a popular vacation place for those wise enough to have discovered it years ago.

MEDICAL FACILITIES: Holberton Hospital, on a hillside at the outskirts of the capital of St. John's, is a 220-bed hospital. Most of the larger hotels have a doctor on call, but the most serious medical problems are flown off the island—sometimes to Miami hospitals.

MONEY MATTERS: The national currency is Eastern Caribbean dollars and cents. Restaurant menus are usually listed in EC dollars, although U.S. equivalents are sometimes shown as well. Most hotel prices are in U.S. dollars. Be prepared to pay top dollar, even for mediocre meals and certainly for car rentals, watersports, and other vacationers' pursuits. Not all places accept credit cards. If using one is important for your travel budget, inquire when you make your mealtime reservation. *Always* ask whose dollars are being quoted; prices at tourist places are high enough without being bamboozled into paying in the wrong currency! (It's worth wondering why St. John's is home for so many private banks, but know that you will probably encounter long lines when you go to any one of them to cash travelers' checks.)

COMMUNICATIONS are easy by telephone from North America, with the 809 area code followed by Antigua's 46 and 5 digits. Facsimile machines are used by most hotels. There's no quality newspaper on the island, although the *Outlet* makes spicy reading about local matters. Portable radios are the best source for international news, via VOA (Voice of America), BBC (British Broadcasting Corporation) and, as a novelty, Radio Moscow via Cuba. The Cable & Wireless office on St. Mary's Street in St. John's is the place to make international calls, if you want to avoid most hotels' steep surcharges. Cable & Wireless sells phone-cards in various denominations, for use in telephones that will not accept coins. For details on AT&T's USADirect system, phone 1–800+ 874–4000 or, from Antigua, 1–412+ 553–7458 collect.

ARRIVAL at V. C. Bird International Airport is usually Caribbean style—with immigration lines seeming tedious while you wait. Immigration officials greet you with little expression and a "welcome" that borders on surly; don't count on any friendly exuberance. You'll need proof of citizenship (passport is best), plus onward ticket, and the completed immigration card which you should receive on your arrival plane.

Baggage is "dumped" in an area that is too small for the volume that passes through here especially when several planes arrive near the same time, but brace yourself, tug yours free, and take it through the customs line, where I have found officials to be efficient and pleasant.

The Tourist Office desk, near the baggage claim area, has leaflets. Staff during my recent visits were helpful, and reasonably pleasant. When they are there, they can call to find out about rooms, if you arrive without reservations.

CRUISE ships tie up at the pier on the left-hand side as they enter St. John's harbor. That pier is a short drive (or a long hot walk) from St. John's. Ships should be able to dock right in town at Heritage Quay, but harbor dredging and other problems affect that pier's use. The casino and the shops filled with luxury imports make Heritage Quay one source of amusement. History buffs will want to visit the Historical Museum in the Old Court House, in St. John's, before driving to the other side of the country to visit the restoration (to the 18th century) at English Harbour, also known as Nelson's Dockyard, and the restored buildings and fort ruins at Shirley Heights, which overlook English Harbour. Dickenson Bay beach has most of the watersports activity, as well as another casino (at Halcyon Cove hotel).

DEPARTURE: The modern airport's open-and-airy departure lounge (plus bar and a couple of shops) makes waiting for your plane reasonably comfortable, but the area can be noisy if big planes are active nearby. Count on finding crowds at the airport counters for departure check-in, and allow enough time—which usually means an hour or more—for slow processing. Be persistent with your place in line, and your questions. Local folk know the ropes and sometimes wedge the less forceful out of the way. Have US$8 ready for the departure tax, which you can pay in US$ or the equivalent in EC$.

AUTHOR'S OBSERVATION

Although there is an upstairs restaurant (before you go through airport security) and a snack-and-bar facility in the open-to-breezes waiting area, don't count on any gourmet cooking in this spot. Be prepared, also, for only tourist-type items for sale at the few shops, and don't expect much in the way of "service." You buy at your own initiative—and risk!

TOURING TIPS: Many years ago, when Antigua offered only taxis for tourists, I negotiated a **car rental** with a taxi driver named Matthew. We walked away from the taxi area, to a tree then standing near the airport parking lot, where we transacted our business—for what I have always suspected was Matthew's own car. Since that time, I have rented from *Matthew's Car Rental* (T 461–1776) many times. The firm now has several cars, most in excellent condition. Either Mr. Matthew or his representative is at the car rental desk just outside the customs area at the airport. Among the other car rental firms represented at the airport are *Jonas Rent-A-Car* (T 463–3760), *St. John's Car Rental* (T 462–4600), *Jacob's Rent-A-Car* (T 461–0399), and *Gage's Car Rental* (T 461–1071). Some are affiliated with national companies, although they seem to prefer to hide that affiliation, perhaps making direct deals to their own advantage. *Titi Rent-A-Car* (T 463–1452), at Galleon Beach Club, arranges for rental of both cars and boats. A few other hotels also have cars for rent. Inquire when you make your reservation.

Your car rental firm sells an Antiguan driver's license for $12, or EC$30.

AUTHOR'S OBSERVATION

Be prepared to negotiate, by a few minutes of casual chatter, when you rent a car. Although the line of Antiguan entrepreneurs behind the car-rental desk may seem intimidating, they're pleasant people who enjoy some idle banter. Your result may be a better rental rate, but should be an honest transaction. Protest if the first-quoted price seems high!

Roads are a national embarrassment. Most are pot-holed, with curbs crumbling. You can be assured of good roads to properties owned or of interest to the prime minister, his family, and his friends. Antiguan roads are not well posted and, although there are a few more signs than in past years, you'll have to count on a good sense of direction—or enjoy losing your way. Even when a road seems well paved, brace yourself for inevitable potholes and *do not expect Antiguan drivers to pause or turn out of your way*. Drive defensively.

Although there are several honest **taxi** drivers, tourism has created some scoundrels. Be sure to ask the tourist board people what the rate should be for your ride and then reconfirm the amount with the taxi driver *before you get into the car*. When you negotiate for a day tour always clarify whose dollars are being quoted (EC$ or US$) and don't be shy about bargaining for a better rate.

Some of the best "touring" is offshore, by **boat**. Most hotels can help arrange a day sail. Jumby Bay, on Long Island, *may* be an option for an elegant (expensive) lunch, but reservations are required—and not accepted when the hotel is fully booked.

LODGING: Recent construction has caused some shores and hillsides to break out in a rash of new hotels and housekeeping units. There seems to be little thought given to protection of the environment. Most places to stay are clustered around Dickenson Bay and the north coast, with the newest festering along Runaway Bay. In spite of the rush to build, Antigua has a visible shortage of trained staff. A domestic hospitality training program is desperately needed!

Count on having a 10% to 15% service charge and a 7% government tax added to your bill, and be sure to inquire in advance about other extra charges to avoid a shock when you check out.

AUTHOR'S AWARDS

Jumby Bay offers Antigua's ultimate luxury, with pampering on its exclusive island; *Curtain Bluff* continues to be a favorite, for its club-like atmosphere and loyal staff. *Long Bay* is a friendly, low-key, family-run place; and *Trade Winds* has proved to be a convenient and comfortable "home" for a housekeeping holiday.

Information about places to stay is included under Hotels/Resorts, Housekeeping Holidays, The Inn Way, and Low-Cost Lodging. Stars are awarded within each category. (See page 11.)

HOTELS/RESORTS: The rapid increase in hotel rooms creates a confusing range of options. When you've narrowed your choice, ask specific questions of hotel management, to be sure that the property offers those things most important for your vacation happiness.

★ **Blue Heron Beach Hotel** • *on the southwest coast, at Johnson's Point Beach* • is a few 2-story buildings with several rooms in each, next to some unsightly (and unrelated) buildings that have stood unfinished for a couple of years. Popular for price and seaside location, the Blue Heron has an on-premise restaurant and some beach equipment for rent, but check on other activities prior to your visit. This place is being managed through a British-Arab group and is used by British, European, and other guests for whom price is more important than action. The *Caribbean Newsletter* (page 9) will have an update when warranted. *Hotel.*

★★★★ **Blue Waters Beach** • *on Soldier Bay* • nestles in a cove amid one of Antigua's prized residential areas. This classic Antiguan hotel is about 15 minutes' drive from downtown St. John's and, in another direction, from the airport. The entrance road curves past the tennis courts and a spate of recently built apartments/villas that are part of the complex. The beach is pleasant, but small (and supported by a cement bulkhead); many guests stay near the pool, enjoying the grounds from lounge chairs on the lawn. Most bedrooms are in 2-story arms that reach from the main reception and restaurant area to embrace the pool, lawn, and beach. Blue Waters thrives on repeat visitors, many of them British, European, and Canadian, as well as American. Mealtimes are festive events, with occasional buffets, and a la carte offerings from the terrace as well as the newer, more formal dining room. Tea is an afternoon ritual for many guests. Brace yourself for the swarms of birds that share your breakfast and lunchtime tables. They are harmless, but can be pesky. For atmosphere and Antiguan tradition, this place gets high marks. *Resort.*

★★★★★ **Curtain Bluff** • *on the south coast, at Morris Bay near the village of Old Road* • is one of my favorite Caribbean hotels. It's definitely not glitzy, and it does aspire to keep pace with the nouveau action-plan with a new beachside cafe and fitness center. CB offers country club elegance with "old money" style, as it has done successfully for 30 years. Owners Chelle and Howard Hulford, General Manager Rob Sherman and his wife, Bernadette, and Antiguan Manager Cal Roberts lead a team of loyal employees who give this place its soul. Like the vintage wines that Howard Hulford stocks in his impressive wine cellar, CB improves with time. The luxurious blufftop suites, and completely refurbished beachfront rooms are classically comfortable. The main house, with the tone of an elegant island home, has the patio restaurant, lounge areas, and the terrace used for dancing to local bands many evenings. Bedrooms are breeze swept, with overhead fans for additional cooling. The main building and two beaches are the social centers, but there's plenty of space for privacy. The beach nearest the tennis courts has a watersports center. Operating on an all-inclusive plan, guests pay once—for everything except shop purchases and fancy wines. Following a long tradition, CB is not open as a hotel in mid-summer. *Classic resort.*

★★ **Galley Bay** • *on a half-mile of white sand beach, about 10 minutes' drive south of St. John's* • has a Robinson Crusoe feeling, helped along by its Tahitian-style "huts" and a seaside atmosphere that has always been its tradition. In addition to the thatch-roofed units, there are more traditional beachfront bedrooms. Popular with Europeans who enjoy the casual lifestyle, GB is a pleasant place for North Americans who enjoy international surroundings. There's music some evenings, and the moon and the stars most nights. This place maintains the inn-like feeling that has made it a favorite since its '50s opening. *Small resort.*

★★ **Halcyon Cove Beach Resort & Casino** • *on Dickenson Bay* • is one of the island's liveliest hotels, within a 10-minute ride from town (the trip from the airport is about 20). Tour groups—European, Canadian, and American—keep this place bouncing, and watersports, tennis, motorbikes, volleyball, horseback riding, jogging, gambling, and more give the action-oriented plenty to keep them occupied. The government owns the hotel; a Britain-based firm manages it. The casino (opened in '82) is usually the country's most active. The several 2-story blocks of rooms are near the beach, with some of them fringing the large (and some-times busy) pool. The *Warri Bar* perches on stilts in the sea, and is reached by a boardwalk: the watersports concession is at the beach, as is the beach bar, a popular meeting-and-greeting spot, especially around noontime and when the sun sets. Shops provide surcease from the sun. Halcyon Cove is good for casual, congenial types who won't mind cluttered premises. Beach vendors can be pesky. *Hotel.*

★ **Half Moon Bay** • *not far from the elegant Mill Reef complex* • claims a prized beach-bordered location—with tennis, golf (for relaxation, but not necessarily for pros), restaurants, shops, and an assortment of 100 rooms, most of which have a lovely view of the beach. Separated into north wing, middle wing, south wing, and new wing, the resort offers the most spacious accommodations (and endroom suites) in the new wing and smaller nooks in the older, least expensive rooms. Oceanfront suites are the top-rate rooms. All rooms have sunning terrace; all guests, many of whom represent middle America, have access to all facilities, which spread over several acres. Tennis enthusiasts can participate in several special tournaments. Traditionally, tournaments have been held in early January, early April, and early November, but check with the hotel for exact dates. Salt air takes its toll on some of the fittings in bathrooms and on the fabric in some of the rooms, but owners seem willing to invest in new trappings when needed. Staff seemed to need better direction when I visited; a management takeover is rumored at presstime. *Resort.*

★★ **Hawksbill Beach Hotel** • *down a sea-ended road that curves west and south from St. John's* • sits at the edge of a white sandy strand, on a 37-acre plot that is convenient to St. John's although miles away in atmosphere. The main blufftop building has the reception area, restaurant, and some rooms. The beach is a short walk down the hill. There are beach cottages and an assortment of 2-story buildings filled with rooms; "standard" rooms face the "garden" and are the backside of the superior sea view rooms. Tennis courts and watersports are daytime diversions; there's usually musical entertainment on winter season evenings. European guests like the casual atmosphere. *Hotel.*

★★★ **Jolly Beach Carib Village** • *near Valley Church Bay* • is self-contained and action-packed, with plenty of watersports offered at the beach and a swarm of beach vendors selling "everything" (which has been known to include marijuana). Lodgings can be in any of 21 buildings, each with a Caribbean island name. Top-rated rooms are usually in a building that opened, a few years ago, as a Holiday Inn. Most bedrooms are *very* small. Action focus is near the restaurants, in areas that are comfortable for lounging and at the Rendez-vous Court area. Operated on an inclusive plan, windsurfing and other watersports are a specialty. Carib Village seems to be a happy home for charter groups from Europe, North America, and elsewhere. Avoid the temptation to remain on premises *all* the time; rent a car for at least a day to see the "real" Antigua. Food is mass produced, but OK. Swiss entrepreneur Alfred Erhart's place seems to have found its niche. *Resort.*

★★★★★ **Jumby Bay** • *on its own Long Island* • provides ultimate luxury for those who put high value on exclusive, private island settings. Reached by boat from a dock near the *Beachcomber,* a few minutes' ride from the airport (and "under" the take-off path), the 300-acre island is flecked with discreetly placed buildings that include the original former home, now serving as the main Great House building, several luxuriously appointed rooms, two to a unit, and others—equally lavish—nearer the center built for small executive seminars and meetings. Opened originally by Homer Williams from Portland, OR, majority owners are now John and Harry Mariani, whose Italian vineyards provide Villa Banfi wines. The island is threaded with bicycle and walking paths, has sand-lined coves, and provides luxury with privacy. The beach is powdery white sand, and the beachside restaurant has good offerings (which include elaborate drinks) at very high prices. Walks can be enjoyed by bird-spotters; fishing *looks* good (but isn't, from shore, a fisherman friend advises); tennis courts are in good shape. Although plans to sell some units for private use might suggest a change in atmosphere, chances are the arrangement will continue the established classy quality. Count on quiet surroundings with luxurious touches, comfortable rooms, and elegant dining, especially for main house dinners. The hotel's boat makes regular crossings to the main island dock where taxis can meet you if you haven't arranged for a rental car. *Classic resort.*

★★★ **Long Bay** • *on the east coast, beyond Willikies Village* • maintains a true Antiguan spirit, which is a miracle in these days of rampant building. The hotel is naturally casual, comfortable, pleasant, and unpretentious—and I like it. Jacques and Jackie Lafaurie continue to be involved in daily management, supported by a loyal staff that includes Juliette, Sam and several others. Peak winter season finds repeaters occupying most of the 20 rooms in the main 2-story, waterfront building as well as the cottages. It's an easy stroll to the beach for pre-breakfast swims; beachside barbecues are one of the evening activities. The tennis court is in good shape; sailing and fishing are popular, with departures from the hotel pier. Food is home-style; don't expect gourmet cooking or an extensive wine selection. This is a place for those in search of an easy lifestyle beloved by those of us who knew the Caribbean before tourism shifted into high gear. *Inn-like hotel.*

★★★★★ **Mill Reef** • *at a southern bulge on the east coast* • is elegance as old money knows it. It's also a private club, at which only invited guests may lodge. Rooms in the main building have sea view, traditional "summer house" comforts, with white-painted wood walls accented with pleasant floral fabrics. This is an enclave resort, in the Newport RI, Jupiter FL, traditional Palm Beach style. Tennis, golf, fishing and boating are pastimes, as is afternoon tea. Dinner is a social occasion, alfresco at the main house. Not for everyone (because "everyone" can't get in), Mill Reef is a lifestyle. *Private resort.*

★★ **Pineapple Beach Club** • *on the east coast shore, near Willikie's Village* • is a lively inclusive resort that has flourished in the shell of property originally built in the 1960s. Yellow accents pep up the white-painted buildings and the atmosphere is "fun." The pool is near the beach and the main building, which holds the restaurant. Bedrooms are in a 2-story block of rooms to the left (when you face the sea), at the rocky end of the bay, and in newer buildings to the right, or in several single-story, sun-baked rooms near the tennis court, a few steps from the hub. The public area is open-to-breezes, and geared for sociable casually comfortable living. Be sure to ask *exactly* what's included in the one-price plan. (Long Bay hotel is at the far end of the same beach.) *Resort.*

★★ **Ramada Royal Antiguan** • *at Deep Bay, about 5 miles southwest of St. John's* • is Antigua's only highrise hotel. Italian built, the hotel was given Ramada management in mid-90. Although Ramada's policies indicate staff training, count on slow service here. The Italian-style doorknobs and other bedroom appointments are a challenge to manipulate; the view from many rooms is a scruffy hillside. Restaurants at the beach are attractive, but food hints at American fast-food style. Planned by the government to be a total resort, with hotel facilities as well as villas (for sale), this property got off to a slow start—with its casino a major drawing card. Located inland, a few minutes' walk to the Deep Bay beach, the physical plant aspires to a status not yet achieved. The lagoon in front of the hotel is a long way from becoming the intended marina. *Hotel.*

Runaway Beach • *on Runaway Bay, just north of St. John's* • offers casual beachside living. Rooms are beachfront-hotel style close to the sea and in some of the many small buildings that are part of a condo-timeshare plan. The on-premise restaurant is a separate concession, and can be quite good. The status of the beach depends on the sea swells just prior to (or during) your visit and on the number of cruise ships in port, since many passengers flock to this beach. The hub for socializing is the bar near the restaurant at the beach. The shore-rimming road curves seaside between Barrymore's Hotel and the main road near the southwest end of Dickenson Bay, past many new properties. You'll need a car, or taxi, for mobility. *Hotel.*

★★★★ **Sandals Antigua Resort** • *on Dickenson Bay, about 10 minutes' drive from St. John's* • is a newcomer for this season and bodes well for Antigua. Jamaica's indefatigable resort-builder, Gordon "Butch" Stewart, plants his well-trained Sandals team and pace-setting all-inclusive expertise on one of this country's best beaches. Totally rebuilt and refurbished, the former Anchorage and Divi resort has a couple of pleasant restaurants, an assortment of bedroom styles, and an upbeat fun-filled feeling that's helped along by the constant daytime activities and a full range of evening entertainment (with Halcyon's casino next door). Some of the bedrooms are updates of those long-known to

Anchorage visitors when they enjoyed the place as a toney upscale haven in the '50s and '60s; others are newly built. Tennis courts and watersports are on premises; boat trips and horseback riding are easily arranged. The sea view dining room is great for watching the beach parade. Count on this place to bring new (and welcomed) high standards for action-packed fun in the sun. *All-inclusive resort.*

    Sandpiper Reef Resort • *on a north-coast cove at Crosbies Estate* • has yet to reach its full potential. The property is attractive and comfortable, near Dickenson Bay and St. John's, but not in the fray. The poolside dining room has a serenely tropical atmosphere, helped along by entertainment some evenings. Menu offerings are imaginative and tasty. The total revamp of an older hotel leaves little of the past, except for terraced and balconied rooms within earshot of your neighbors. The beach is fine for sunning and sea-wallowing, but there are better strands for miles of soft sand. The Caribbean Newsletter (page 9) will have an update of status when warranted. *Hotel.*

    ★★ **St. James's Club** • *on Marmora Bay, in the southeast* • never reached its goal as a jet-set resort, in spite of a gala opening (under previous management) that saw the likes of Liza Minnelli, Joan Collins and Peter Holm (prior to their marriage and subsequent split), and other luminaries cavorting at the beach, pool, and elsewhere. Owned by Arab interests who have poured millions into this one-time Holiday Inn, the property has two beaches (one wind-swept and one manmade), plant-filled public areas, chic boutiques, music poolside (where a wind-baffle protects sunbathers from the often powerful prevailing winds), candlelit evening dining, and a disco that's lively when the house count is. Villas that offer view-full cluster living have grown like barnacles on a hillside rising from the manmade beach. There are tennis courts, horses to ride, watersports, and a yachting center that has claimed status as an international port. This place is remote from most of the Antigua action. Inquisitive guests will need a car for mobility. The *Caribbean Newsletter* (page 9) will have comments about any improvements, when warranted. *Resort.*

HOUSEKEEPING HOLIDAYS range from simple studio apartments furnished only with the basics to a few luxury homes that are available for rent in owner's absence, and include a rapidly growing number of apartments and villas that are part of condominium clusters. Several of the apartment clusters are linked with existing hotels (such as those at St. James's) and have been mentioned above. Although **La Cure Villas** (11661 San Vincente Blvd., Los Angeles, CA 90049; T 800+ 387–2726) is one source for rentals around the island, many of the places do their own booking. **Serendipity Villas** (Box 244, St. John's, Antigua, W.I., T 809+ 462–4101) has two units for rent. Be prepared for the fact that many of the new places have very thin walls, small rooms, and are built to make maximum use of land (and profitability). Privacy is sometimes sacrificed as units angle to give you a view of your neighbor's patio instead of beautiful natural scenery. If you anticipate staying on Antigua for a while, it makes sense to rent a hotel room for a few days while you wander around to see for yourself.

    Provisioning can be accomplished at Antigua's markets, although prices will be high for staples as well as imports. If you want to tackle the local market in St. John's, you can find fresh fish, fruits, and vegetables, with the black Antiguan pineapple (with smaller diamonds and a skinnier shape than the fat Hawaiian version) a succulent local product. Spices can be bought fresh, in their natural state, so bring some plastic bags to carry the goods. The good restaurants around the island are usually expensive.

★★ **Antigua Village** • *on Dickenson Bay* • is a community of many apartments. Built in late '79, the units are in 2-story clusters, nesting on the sand at what can be a narrow part of the beach that stretches along to Halcyon Cove in one direction and beyond Buccaneer Cove to Runaway Bay hotel in the other. Construction seems flimsy to me, with cracks and breakage both occupational hazards that don't really matter unless you own the place. A pool marks the center of the complex. Count on adequate but not lavish furnishings and a link on a timesharing leasing plan. The open-to-breezes on-premise cafe/restaurant and its neighboring bar are gathering spots for nautical and beach-loving types, as are other places along the busy beach. *Apts.*

★★ **Barrymore Beach Apartments** • *on Runaway Beach* • opened in the '84–'85 season, with 2-bedroom apartments in 2- and 3-story buildings. Nicely furnished, and sold as condominiums or time-share units, the apartments offer beachside living with independence. The name link is the result of the La Barrie family connection: Manager Brian Gordon and his wife, Linda, the youngest daughter of the La Barrie family. The *Satay* hut is pleasant for casual, beachside dining and staff rotates with the *DuBarry* restaurant at Barrymore. Diversions can include a stroll down the beach to Runaway Bay. *Apts.*

Blue Acres • *on a point of land along Hodges Bay Road* • is another Italian-financed apartment/villa/condo project that puts high-density "luxury" in an already crowded residential area. *Apts.*

Boon's Point • *overlooking Soldier's Bay* • uses a sugar mill cone as the focal point for a group of bluff-top villas. Units are for sale, but can be rented in owner's absence. The *Caribbean Newsletter* (page 9) will have news.

Carlisle Bay Villas • *on the south coast at Carlisle Bay* • hopes to focus on the top-flight tennis courts, which have a professional look. Intended for private ownership, the 2-story units allow for beachside living at a bay always known by locals to have cloudy, silt-filled seas. Although construction has seriously affected a lagoon area that marked the fresh well-water for the Old Road community, hopefully some ecological balance can be restored by the time this place gets in full operation. Underway since 1990, Carlisle hopes to open for this season. The *Caribbean Newsletter* (page 9) will have further news when warranted. *Apts.*

★★★ **Copper & Lumber Store** • *in English Harbour's restored area* • has 12 beautiful apartments. Originally opened on December 1, 1977, but totally refurbished in '84. The apartments have an 18th-century feeling but all modern comforts. Decor combines wood, brick walls, and patterned fabrics.

Whether you settle into *Dread Thought, Boreas, Collingwood, Agamemnon,* or any of the 5 apartments that face the harbor, or *Britannia,* with its view over the harbor and yachts bobbing at anchor, you'll need boat or car to reach a beach. Choice of rooms includes the twin-bedded units, with kitchen and living room (*Britannia* has a balcony); and the duplex units, comfortable for 4, with one bedroom upstairs with sink, and the main living area easily set up as the second bedroom. Two restaurants (one of which is a casual pub) are on the entry level. *Inn-like apts.*

★★ **Dian Bay Resort** • *on the east coast, overlooking Long Bay area* • is a cluster of free-standing 2-story buildings, each with a couple of 1- and 2-bedroom apartments, which can be sold (or rented) together or as two units. It's a hot walk down the hill to the beach (shared by Long Bay and Pineapple hotels), but there's a small pool at the hilltop. The *Crocodile* restaurant, in a villa with island-and-sea view, has made quite a name for its excellent offerings. Reservations are recommended. This is a good bet for independent folk. *Apts.*

Emerald Cove • *at Nonsuch Bay on the east coast* • is a gigantic Italian-sponsored development, which reflects a style better known at Mediterranean resorts such as those on the Italian island of Sardinia. Although plans include a tourist center, with hotel rooms and a marina, don't count on much for this season. A couple of palatial villas mark the landscape, where new roads slice hillsides and valleys. The *Caribbean Newsletter* (page 9) will have further comment, when warranted.

★★ **Falmouth Harbour Beach Apartments** • *on Falmouth Bay* • sit seaside on the protected cove and on its hillside, within a stroll from English Harbour. Most units have wood-slat terrace or porch (depending on first or second floor), with adequate modern appurtenances, including spatulas, whisks, egg beaters, and the like. Emphasis here is on do-it-yourself, with casual atmosphere that can keep you in your bathing suit or less for 24 hours a day. You can walk to the *Yacht Club,* or to the *Admiral's Inn* for dinner, or cook at home. Sailboats moor offshore (or pull up on the beach when size allows), so if the sea is your interest, you can settle in here. *Cozy apts.*

★★ **Galleon Beach** • *at Freeman's Bay* • offers a bit of everything—a beach, a haven for good food and camaraderie, and the option to do what you want to—using your own cottage as your base. The units along the beach are my favorites even though they are showing signs of wear. Each has a bedroom, a living room with sofas that can make into 2 more beds, and a connecting kitchen—all spread along the beach with a sea view (and screens over louvers). The hillside units are set up for 4, with 2 bedrooms, hillside view and breeze (an easy walk to the beach), and enough space around to merit privacy. Rental cars are a good idea if you want mobility. Yachts bob at anchor offshore; English Harbour is the next cove west; and *The Inn,* with its beachside bar/restaurant and the more elegant hilltop perch, is next door, a short drive or easy walk. Dinner served at *Colombo's* Italian restaurant, in the shoreside gathering area, runs $25 or more depending on your choices. There's island entertainment some nights and conversation with other guests the rest of the time. *Villas.*

Halcyon Heights Apartments • *on the hillside, above the Halcyon Cove hotel and Dickenson Bay* • have been sold as condominiums but are often available for rent in owner's absence. Furnished to the taste of the owner (and therefore varying from unit to unit), all apartments have balconies with sea view and modern kitchen equipment. You'll want a car for mobility; the place seems good for independent, value-conscious vacationers. *Apts.*

Heritage Hotel • *at Heritage Quay, in St. John's* • is an Italian-built cluster of 22 apartments, intended for private ownership for a market that never materialized. Opened in 1989, the 1-bedroom suites have two double beds, a bathroom with decorative Italian fixtures (that can prove infuriating for those more familiar with American standard), and color television. Studios are sitting rooms, with a pull-down bed. Although operated as a hotel, all rooms have a complete kitchen. *Apts.*

★★★ **Hodges Bay Club** • *on the north coast* • offers spacious and comfortable apartments. Some units are wedged between sea and road, on a sliver of land that gives dwellers a lovely sea view. Others are on the inland side of the road. The on-premise restaurant is one of Antigua's better dining depots. Guests can boat to nearby Prickly Pear Cay for picnics, with the help of managers Charles and Wendy Smith, who have landed here after time running Necker Island in the British Virgins. This can be an elegant island home. *Apts.*

★★ **Marina Bay Condominiums** • *on Runaway Bay, next to Dickenson Bay* • sprouted from the beach in mid-'90. With dozens of units clustered in one area, and dredged lagoons making home-side docking possible, this place appeals to boating folk. You're within walking distance of all the action at Dickenson Bay—and good beaches for swimming and other watersports. *Apts.*

★ **Pillar Rock Pavilions** • *sharing Deep Bay with Ramada Royal Antiguan* • offer 2-bedroom apartments and studios, with modern furnishings, complete kitchen facilities, and reasonably private patio. The pool is the social hub; a rental car allows for easy beach and shopping access. Barbecue nights are a weekly activity; otherwise meals are available at the *Sandcastle* restaurant near the pool. *Apts.*

Sand Haven • *on Runaway Bay beach* • is a 2-story block of apartments, with a restaurant right on the beach. Good for informal, cost-conscious travelers, this place is near plenty of resort action—but slightly removed (for peace and quiet). Popular with Canadians, and others who know good value. *Apts.*

★★★ **Siboney Beach Club** • *at Dickenson's Bay beach* • nestles amid shrubbery, aloof from the beach-busy life that surrounds it. The apartments are comfortably furnished; the choicest, in my opinion, are the top floor units closest to the sea. A small-and-pleasant pool hides in the foliage, for those who want a quiet place to read or reflect while sunning. This can be a special hideaway. *Apts.*

Time Away Beach Apartments • *on Runaway Bay* • are part of the fleet of newcomers that has moored on this sandy shore in the past couple of years. Good for independent folk who don't need showy surroundings. *Apts.*

★★ **Trade Winds Hotel & Apartments** • *the hillside, overlooking Halcyon Cove* • proved ideal on a recent visit, although management seemed in disarray. Conveniently located above Dickenson Bay, the apartment styles allow for closing off one room to make studio units, 1- and 2-bedroom units, or bedrooms only. "C" units, with kitchenette on your patio, are the least expensive. Popular with Europeans who know good value, the guests at the bar and poolside are an international mix. The French restaurant near the pool is attractive, but pricey and disorganized on the night I dined. *Pari's Pizza* is not far down the road and Dickenson Bay is within daytime walking distance, if you don't mind a hot walk down (and back up) the asphalt road. Management will drive you down, if you haven't rented a car. *Apts.*

★ **Yepton Beach Resort** • *at the shore, next to Pillar Rock* • was new for the season of '87–'88. The modern, comfortable units are part of a condominium development, where apartments are for rent in owner's absence. A car will help with mobility, but a few facilities are on the premises. There's a pool as well as the beach, but prepare for sandflies. *Apts.*

THE INN WAY: Antigua has several attractive small properties that thrive on unpretentious hospitality. In addition to the inns mentioned below, look into *Curtain Bluff, Jumby Bay, Long Bay,* and *Galleon Beach,* mentioned elsewhere in this "Lodgings" section. All have exceptional island ambience.

★★★ **Admiral's Inn** • *in the heart of English Harbour* • has been unique, since it opened as an inn in 1961. Making the most of its 18th century history, and the harbor where Admiral Nelson wandered when his H.M.S. *Boreas* was in port, the building is well maintained. The patio is popular for leisurely lunches and for sipping potions within sight and sound of yachts at anchor; the neighboring dining room shares that view (and breezes) when the heavy wood doors are latched open. Mealtime offerings are American-style; the nautical surroundings are best enjoyed by daylight, although dinners (with music) are romantic. Bedrooms vary in shape and size, responding to the 18th-century building. The best are upstairs, in the inn, with windows that open out to a view of bobbing yachts. Overhead fans swirl sea-breezes. Rooms in the annex that dates from 1775 are more modern, with air-conditioning and no sea view. This casually comfortable place is an inn worth the name. Don't count on a lot of attention from the staff, but they are there if you need them. (See "Places Worth Finding" for harbor facts.) *Inn.*

Antigua Mill Inn • *on the hillside near the airport* • refers to itself as a businessman's hotel. I have stayed here many times, and welcome some improvements in decorating and atmosphere. The better rooms are behind the pool.

Within minutes of the airport, the place is convenient for overnighting when you have an early plane to some nearby island. Rates are higher than warranted by surroundings. The *Caribbean Newsletter* (page 9) will comment on improvements, when noticeable. *Small hotel.*

Barrymore • *on Old Fort Road, not far from St. John's Center* • has expanded, to fill almost every square inch of its property with buildings, pool, and restaurant. Well known to West Indian and other businessfolk who travel these islands, the rooms are furnished with basics. Most bedrooms have air conditioners, which are essential since many overlook patio or parking lot, making everything public when doors and windows are open. *Small hotel.*

The Beachcomber • *at the northeast shore, near the airport and U.S. base* • has rooms in a 2-story building. Television is an attraction for local folk at the bar; the dining room is nearby. Located near the dock where the boat departs for ritzy *Jumby Bay,* this place is definitely non-chic—with a small beach and pool. *Small hotel.*

Catamaran • *on the shore at Falmouth Harbour* • has about a dozen rooms in various shapes and sizes, facing a busy marina with many lovely yachts anchored offshore. All bedrooms have overhead fans in this nautical setting. Most bedrooms are in several stucco buildings that ribbon the shore. Numbers 3, 4, 5, and 6 share a cement slab terrace area. Deep-sea fishing, sailing, and other water-focused events are arranged at the front desk. The restaurant features Antiguan and West Indian specialties. *Small hotel.*

★★★ **The Inn at English Harbour** • *overlooking English Harbour* • ranges from the hilltop main house and a few cottages, to the 2-story buildings of beachside apartments down the hill. There's a homelike atmosphere in the hilltop public rooms and restaurant; most daytime activity is at the beach, where the seaside bar is popular for lunch and lingering, with a view of yachts bobbing at anchor. *Galleon Beach* (see "Housekeeping Holidays") is a stroll down the beach. The airport is half-an-hour's drive; St. John's is west of the airport, across the island. *Inn, Apts.*

Lord Nelson Club • *on a beach-lined cove not far from the airport* • has a windsurfing focus. Still surviving in the old style, some of the bedrooms border on tacky. Seabreezes sweep the rooms, which are in a 2-story block next to the restaurant and bar building. If you're looking for a laid-back, casual place, and are young in fact or at heart, consider this. *Small hotel.*

LOW-COST LODGING: Although some vacationers will find that a family can vacation for reasonable cost by renting one of the apartments or villas mentioned in the "Housekeeping Holiday" section, Antigua has many small hotels and guest houses with a few rooms for rent at very reasonable rates. Ask the Tourist Board office for a copy of their booklet called *A Guide to Small Hotels and Guest Homes*. Most small spots are boxy, modern stucco buildings without much (or any) West Indian tradition, except that imparted by the owner/manager, usually an Antiguan. Most have the basics, however, and the cost is low.

Few places are on the beach, and many will require a rental car for those who aren't interested in hitchhiking or waiting in the hot sun for the occasional public bus.

Here's my selection from the many small spots with reasonable rates: **St. Mary's Court,** in a traditional West Indies house on St. Mary's Street in St. John's, might be worth thinking about for students and other budget-conscious travelers; **St. John's Court,** on the outskirts of town across the road from the *Barrymore Hotel,* has very basic accommodations at a reasonable (for high-priced Antigua) cost; **Spanish Main,** on Independence Avenue in St. John's, has a few very basic rooms—and a popular pub-like restaurant.

Insofar as other inexpensive places are concerned, I'd suggest looking before booking. Some are more like roadside stands than vacation hotels. In St. John's, check out **Bougainvillea Hotel** on All Saint's Road, **Joe Mike's Hotel,** on the second floor of a boxy building whose first floor is a store and bar/restaurant, and **Piggotsville** in the Clare Hall area.

RESTAURANTS appear each season with the growing tourism "plans." A full dinner at the best will set you back $40 or more per person. Most places close one day a week, so be sure to check the schedules; they may vary. Also inquire about luncheon service; the beachside places are almost always open, but some of the inland spots limit dining hours to evening only. One word to the wise: if you have not rented a car and are dependent on taxis, be sure to make arrangements for pick up after your mealtime is over. Some restaurants will help you find a car, but you'll be far more comfortable if you have the name and phone number of a reliable driver and have made your own arrangements for transportation.

Among the special meals worth noting at hotels are dinner at *Curtain Bluff* or the Sunday brunch at *Blue Waters. Colombo's Italian Restaurant* at Galleon Beach can be fun and *Long Bay's* beach buffets are worth the drive. Call ahead to make reservations at all the above. *Admiral's Inn* at English Harbour is acceptable for hamburgers and other offerings (including seafood salad) at lunchtime, but don't expect much in the way of gourmet cooking.

AUTHOR'S AWARDS

Casaurina gets top honors for a pleasant atmosphere, interesting menu, and good service; and *18 Carrot* has been my choice for a good in-town lunch, but check on its status.

DuBarry's • *at the Barrymore Hotel, on the outskirts of the capital* • is near the pool of the family-owned hotel. Popular with Antiguan businessfolk at noontime, the restaurant has a following for dinner, but didn't live up to my hopes on a recent visit.

★★★ **Le Bistro** • *on the north coast* • is an elegant dining option, with space at one of the 14-plus tables at a premium during the height of winter season. The langouste (local lobster) comes at top tally, and crepes suzette end the meal with a flaming flourish. Beef, duckling, and the other European-style offerings are regular fare. With cuisine that takes its tone from France (but does its cooking Antiguan style), the restaurant is pleasant—and expensive. Plan to make reservations on winter evenings when the place is popular. Monday has been traditional closing day, but check for changes.

★★★ **Casaurina** • *on the main road between St. John's and Dickenson Bay* • is a relative newcomer, where delicious meals are served in attractive surroundings—on the veranda and small inner rooms of a traditional cozy Antiguan home. White walls with green trim and accents give a feeling of space; overhead fans provide the breezes. Seafood, chicken and steak are sliced and sauced in delicate manner. Staff seemed pleasantly professional. For a special evening meal, try this.

★★ **Crocodile** • *at Dian Bay, on the east coast* • has an elaborate menu that rose to expectations when I tried it. If you go for dinner, arrive before sunset to enjoy the view.

★★ **18 Carrot** • *on Church Street in St. John's* • makes the most of a narrow street-level building with ferns, Victorian wooden latticework, and other decorator touches. Overhead fans swirl the air for cooling. Local produce has been adapted to tasty recipes (fishballs are one recommendable offering). Popular with local folk for noonday meals, the eatery is at the "back" of the Old Court House that now holds the Antigua National Museum.

Pari's Pizza • *across from Trade Winds, up the hill above Dickenson Bay* • is a bowered trattoria that appears more Italian than Caribbean. Open from mid-morning until mid-night, this place serves pizzas, pasta, and other Italian specialties. Brace yourself for the prices (like $6 for a 9″ pizza), but count on a comfortably casual atmosphere in the three-tiered shrub-surrounded hideaway.

Pizzas on the Quay • *at Redcliffe Quay in St. John's* • is a gathering spot, both for local folk and visitors, especially for families. The relaxing atmosphere benefits from pub stools at the bar plus wooden tables and chairs, both inside and on the patio. The menu includes a lot more than pizza. (Antiguan-owner, Bernadette, is the wife of Curtain Bluff's Rob Sherman.)

Brother B's • *also in the city/capital* • has made a name for itself for *very* informal island surroundings with hearty West Indian food. (This is no place for a dress-up evening.) Other casual spots to consider, for typical West Indian surroundings, are the **Oasis** and **China Garden,** both in simple West Indian houses (China Garden is on the second floor), and loved by locals.

The Victory • *at 3 Redcliffe Quay* • has pub food, seafood, and evening action, often with music. The publike atmosphere draws island regulars.

The Yard • *on a side street in downtown St. John's* • is a popular gathering spot for residents who happen to be in the capital at noontime and for vacationers who want to drop by at noon—or afternoon.

NATURAL SURROUNDINGS include several splinter islands that have broken off from the main island, especially on the eastern and southeastern shores, as well as sister-island, Barbuda, covered in its own chapter. Insofar as the landscape is concerned, the area north of St. John's has been pretty well scarred by tourism. That's where most of the development has been.

As you drive south along the west coast, however, there are some beautiful beaches. Darkwood Beach is one of the most accessible; it has a seaside restaurant. Fig Tree Drive has long been a sight touted by taxi drivers. It is, in fact, a winding road that leads through the hilliest and lushest part of the island, referred to by some as a "Rain Forest," which it is not, in fact. These "figs," incidentally, are local bananas.

Indian Town Point, on the east coast not far from Long Bay, is one of many sites where Amerindian artifacts are still being found. The rugged growth that covers portions of Boggy Peak, the island's highpoint (in the southwest), leads, I've been told, to an area with huge monoliths, which some 19th-century British thought marked an Amerindian religious site. (If you hope to visit this site, allow plenty of time to check with the tourist office and other sources to find yourself a good guide. Do not wander up this peak alone!)

For those with an interest in island formations, *Antigua Reefs, Rocks & Highroads of History*, a paperback book by H. G. Multer, M. P. Weiss, and Desmond Nicholson, is a good source for facts. Available in some local bookstores, it describes the geology and reefs, explaining the formation of the Barbuda Bank, which rises from sea level as Antigua and Barbuda islands.

Although there are a few scuba diving operators, many of the surrounding reefs are virtually virgin territory for divers. Surging seas keep visitors away from the southeastern islands when tradewinds whip across their shores, but reefs around Green Island and Bird Island are favorites for colorful fish. Lack of strong (and enforced) conservation efforts have meant that many areas are being damaged by fishermen, pollution, and plucking of reef life.

PLACES WORTH FINDING are related to the island's history as the major port for British naval activity in the 19th-century Caribbean. The restoration at English Harbour is worth the better part of a day, with time for a prowl around the hilltop ruins at Shirley Heights, overlooking the harbor, and a visit to Fort Berkeley and to Clarence House.

Antour, a tour company founded by some of the country's most knowledgeable hosts (hoteliers, personnel from another tour company, and others), can be counted on to offer professional and interesting tour services. If you'll feel more comfortable with a guide, contact them at their offices in St. John's.

A person worth finding is Desmond Nicholson, who's often at the **Antigua Historical Museum** in the Old Court House in St. John's. Desmond leads Thursday afternoon archaeology walks around some of the former Arawak sites and responds to enthusiasm from visitors interested in Antiguan lore. If you have a particular interest in the island's history, he's your best source for information. The museum holds Amerindian artifacts found around the island. Although displays may seem pretty basic for those who know something about West Indian history, they are enjoyed by Antiguans, especially schoolchildren.

This is the country's first real museum. The building is a good example of West Indian Georgian style.

English Harbour was used by Admiral Horatio Nelson as the main base for the British fleet in the 18th and early 19th centuries. English Harbour, also called **Nelson's Dockyard,** still has many of the original buildings intact. Some, such as the Admiral's Inn and the Copper & Lumber Store, have been restored and rebuilt to accommodate overnight guests. Others are marked for ambitious rebuilding. Admiral's Inn was the "Lead Cellar," where pitch was stored in barrels, with the Engineer's Office on the upper floors (where the guest rooms are now located). The Copper & Lumber Store (now apartments) was completely gutted, to be rebuilt in tasteful old style over its cisterns, which were used to hold 50 tons of fresh water in Nelson's day.

The **Guard House,** at the right of the entrance to the Dockyard, is where you will be encouraged to pay your $1 entrance fee (and where you can mail postcards in the small post office). Farther along on your right is the **Admiral's House,** now a museum on its main floor and, in fact, never the admiral's house in spite of its name. (The admiral is supposed to have quartered in a house, now gone, on the site of the present Naval Officers' Quarters.) Inside the museum, the collection ranges from amusing to interesting, with a half dozen rooms open to the sea breeze and lined with pictures, early charts, and some cabinets with Arawak Indian relics found on Antigua. There's a model of *Arabella,* a schooner built in the 1840s, and another big model in the back room, plus a 4-poster canopy bed in the other back room that looks comfortable enough to climb into. Clay pipes found at Shirley Heights are in a cabinet, and I found the photographs of the Dockyard at a 1952 party fascinating. (A sweep through the museum can take as little as 15 minutes, but is worth more time.)

AUTHOR'S OBSERVATION

If you're on a cruise ship, either ask your driver to speed here first, and get in and get out before the crowd, or make this your last stop before racing back to the ship. With a lot of tourists wandering around, it's difficult to capture the 18th and 19th centuries.

The **Galley,** in which the shop is located, was the cookhouse used by the 19th-century crew from ships being worked on at the dockyard; the **Naval Officers' Quarters,** constructed in 1815, has a cafeteria and artisan studios. The stone ground floor is part of a 600-ton cistern.

According to the small booklet, *The Romance of English Harbour,* the first reference to English Harbour was in a letter of December 9, 1671, when Sir Charles Wheler, Governor of the Leeward Islands, urged the Crown to consider English Harbour as a place for the British fleet because of its deep and huge pocket. By 1704, the Harbour was the home for the fleet, which set out from here on raids and forays over the next 100 years, the years of constant seesawing of power between British, Spanish, French, and Netherlands explorers, settlers, and pirates. By 1725 the dockyard was fitted out as a place for repairs, with the first dockyard across the harbor from the present site, at St. Helena, the shoreside spot now occupied by the Antigua Slipway, Ltd. (who incorporated some of the original slipway equipment into their modern lifts).

In the 1780s, when Admirals Rodney and Hood were battling for supremacy of the Caribbean seas, English Harbour was "filled" with the big ships that came in for work following battles. Rodney set out from here for the Battle of the Saints, fought off Dominica (when he captured the French Admiral Comte de Grasse); and Admiral Nelson set off from here, in more leisurely times, to court (and marry) Fanny Nisbet, who lived on nearby Nevis.

Clarence House, on the opposite hill, overlooking the harbour, was built in 1787, to be occupied by H.R.H. Prince William Henry, then Duke of Clarence, later King William IV. (The Duke of Clarence was commander of HMS *Pegasus*, at the time when Captain Nelson was stationed here in command of HMS *Boreas*.) Clarence House, used by the present governor of Antigua as his weekend home, is open to the public on other occasions. If the narrow gate is open, drive through and give the caretaker a small stipend for the talk he offers about the furnishings (some supplied by the National Trust) as he takes you around. Clarence House was used by Princess Margaret during her honeymoon with Antony Armstrong-Jones, and more recently was the site for a luncheon for Queen Elizabeth and Prince Philip when they visited Antigua on October 28, 1977. The building got a new roof after the hurricane of 1950 blew the older one off, but otherwise the structure is much the same as when it was built in the late 1780s.

Shirley Heights, up and out an arm of land across the bay from English Harbour, offers a spectacular view of the harbor area. It's an ideal place to walk through 18th- and 19th-century Antiguan colonial history. There's a parking area at the top, where one of the buildings has been turned into a restaurant and sipping spot (noted more for its presence than for any culinary successes). Around the Heights, there are several 18th-century ruins. For history buffs, this place warrants a few hours—but arrive either early or late in the day to avoid the strongest sun. (Some folks enjoy the hike up to the heights, but too much of the route is along the edge of the asphalt road for my time.)

Antigua provides a perfect hub for visiting **neighboring islands** on day trips or longer. Spend some time at LIAT (Leeward Islands Air Transport) offices, either at the airport or in town, to find out which flights go where. There's commuter service to Montserrat and there are frequent flights to Barbuda, although it's often difficult to confirm your return flight in Antigua (because it's controlled in Barbuda). Other nearby islands are St. Kitts, Nevis, and Dominica.

SPORTS are sea-oriented, with Antigua Sailing Week the traditional focus for yachts that converge from U.S. ports and around the Caribbean. Held at the end of April–early May, depending on Easter, the events spoke out from English Harbour, a source for **yacht charter** at all times of the year.

Nicholson Yachts has operated from English Harbour since Commander V.E.B. Nicholson sailed his family into a nearby cove on New Year's Eve, 1949, after crossing the Atlantic. He stayed, first taking day charters from Mill Reef on the family yacht and gradually acting as "captain" of a fleet of yachts for charter. These days son Rodney operates the firm that acts as land touchstone for a fleet of some 80 yachts. The U.S. office is at 432 Colombia St., Cambridge, MA 02141, T 800+ 662–6066.

For chartering your own yacht, check with yachts that tie up at English

Harbour (you can drive out to the dockyard and ask people you see there), or use the same procedure for the yachts at anchor at Falmouth Harbour. Many hotels have yachts for day charters, usually a couple anchored at Dickenson Bay. The usual cost for a day sail is about $50 per person, lunch and drinks included. Small groups may be able to negotiate a more favorable rate.

Most hotels also acknowledge the lure of the sea, even for nonsailors. A **day-sail** has become part of the hotel activities, even when the yacht is not anchored offshore. One character craft is the 63-ton *Servabo,* a Brixham trawler that made its way across the Atlantic a few years ago and bases itself (scenically) off the shores of Dickenson Bay. The Barbecue Cruise (daily except Sun. and Wed.), heads out from Buccaneer Cove at 9:30 and fills your day with snorkeling, shelling, rope swinging, calypso, dancing, rum punches, a feast of a barbecue, and plenty of sunshine (take a long-sleeved shirt and some sun screen). The ship's 1000 square feet of deck can hold a crowd, which she usually takes in season. You'll have more space and just as much fun at the shoulder season when the ship may not go out daily, but will go out a couple of times per week.

The *Jolly Roger,* relative of the successful rum-punch-party-boats that operate in Barbados, put down anchor at Dickenson Bay in late '81 and quickly picked up a following that included many of the island's expatriates who put together their own parties on board. The day or cocktail cruises are casual fun (with plenty of food and drink as well as music), and can be easily arranged from Halcyon Cove or any hotel.

Deep-sea fishing is available through several of the hotels where, if there's not a motorboat that links itself to the property, there's usually someone "on call." The watersports concession on the beach at Dickenson Bay, near the Halcyon Cove Hotel, can arrange deep-sea fishing, as can Curtain Bluff (with its own yacht), Long Bay, and people at English Harbour.

Scuba is offered by *Dive Runaway* (Box 1370, St. John's, Antigua, 809+ 462–2626) and on Dickenson Bay, as well as through many hotels' activities' desks. A 1-tank dive costs about $40; plus $15 for equipment. Introductory dive, with equipment, is $65. Trips are scheduled, but the schedule tends to be flexible when the winter rush is past. Check late in the day before you want to head out and check in well before departure time to be fitted for your equipment, if you're experienced. Novices will have pool time for instruction before they go out to dive. Introductory courses are given. Night dives with the pros can be arranged. There's a scuba contact at Blue Waters, Jolly Beach and most other hotels. Long Bay excels with it, and Curtain Bluff offers snorkeling and scuba from its beachshop.

Boardsailing, the generic name for the sport that is often called by the name of the originator (Windsurfer), is popular on most beaches. You can count on finding equipment at Dickenson Bay, Lord Nelson Inn, St. James's Club, Pineapple, Blue Waters, Jolly Beach, and Curtain Bluff. Anyone who is proficient at the sport should check with the nautical types at English Harbour to see if there are any special boardsailing regattas. (There is usually one or more planned as part of the festivities of Antigua Sailing Week, but there are events planned at other times as well.) Pros respect the on-shore winds that usually push the seas at Half Moon.

Tennis is popular at many hotels. In all cases, bring your own tennis balls—

unless you don't care how much you spend. Prices in Antigua are "astronomical," due to import costs and a captive audience. At many places, racquets can be rented and, while they may not be top quality, they make it possible to play if the mood strikes you. Curtain Bluff has a special tennis tournament in April. It has become a popular tradition, and many guests repeat the experience year after year. Half Moon has special tournaments in early January, early April, early May, and early November. Contact the hotel for details. Other places with courts in addition to Half Moon (5) and Curtain Bluff (3) are Blue Waters (1), Halcyon Beach (2), Anchorage (2), Jolly Beach (2), Jumby Bay (1), Long Bay (1), and St. James Club (5).

Golfers head to Cedar Valley Course, where the full 18 offer "an interesting game." Some hotels assist with transportation to the course, which is near St. John's, at the northern nub of the island. Antigua Beach uses the few holes of Gambles course, with the entrance just outside the hotel's driveway. The course is acceptable for exercise, but not as well maintained as the Cedar Valley 18. Half Moon has a few holes.

Horseback riding is arranged through Halcyon Cove and other Dickenson Bay hotels' activities desks. The horses lost their grazing ground when Halcyon added its new rooms. If you're at a hotel on another cove you will have to add the cost of a taxi to the cost of the ride. Figure about $50 per person for a couple of hours.

TREASURES AND TRIFLES: With the opening of the tourist enclave at Heritage Quay in St. John's in early 1989, that area and neighboring Redcliffe Quay became the shopping center for "duty free" goods. Store windows are filled with crystal, china, cameras, and other imports from world markets, but shoppers should do hometown research to be sure that the prices are, in fact, "bargains."

St. Mary's Street, which stretches from the gates of Heritage Quay, has been the main drag for shoppers, but many of the most successful shops—the few that carried island fashions and crafts of high quality—also have outlets in Heritage Quay, which seems to suggest that they may close their other places. High-quality interesting items can also be found at some hotel boutiques (Curtain Bluff, Half Moon, and Jumby Bay, for example) and at the stores and museum in English Harbour.

The ubiquitous T-shirts, straw items, and wood carvings are sold along the beaches and in most shops. They are *everywhere,* especially at English Harbour, where local hucksters make the entryway seem like running the gauntlet, especially on days when cruise ships are in St. John's.

Harmony Hall at Brown's Bay Mill, out near the entrance to Mill Reef and Half Moon Bay, set high standards for island art when it opened in late 1987. In and near a sugar mill tower that dates from 1843, items for sale include carefully selected handcrafts and paintings. Meeting standards set at their Jamaican Harmony Hall, on the north coast east of Ocho Rios, Annabella and Peter Proudlock and partners collected paintings by Caribbean artists, which are offered for sale with "Annabella boxes" (small wood boxes with island scenes on the cover), small ceramic cottages in West Indian styles, and much more. Prices range from modest (for small trinkets and notecards) to paintings and other artwork in the hundreds of dollars U.S.

Island Arts, with several outlets, is another top-quality source for Caribbean paintings and art. Nick and Gloria Waley operate the biggest and best-quality gallery from Aiton Place, in the Hodges Bay area (on the north coast), but they also have galleries at Heritage Quay (with the kind of items that appeal to cruise ship passengers), and a couple of hotels (Ramada Royal Antiguan and the St. James's Club, at press time). In addition to having special shows of Antiguan artists, the Waleys collect (and display) representative work by talented folk from other islands as well as Central and South American countries.

In the Falmouth and English Harbour area, **Seahorse Studios** and **Falmouth Harbour Studios** are two other places to visit for art and crafts.

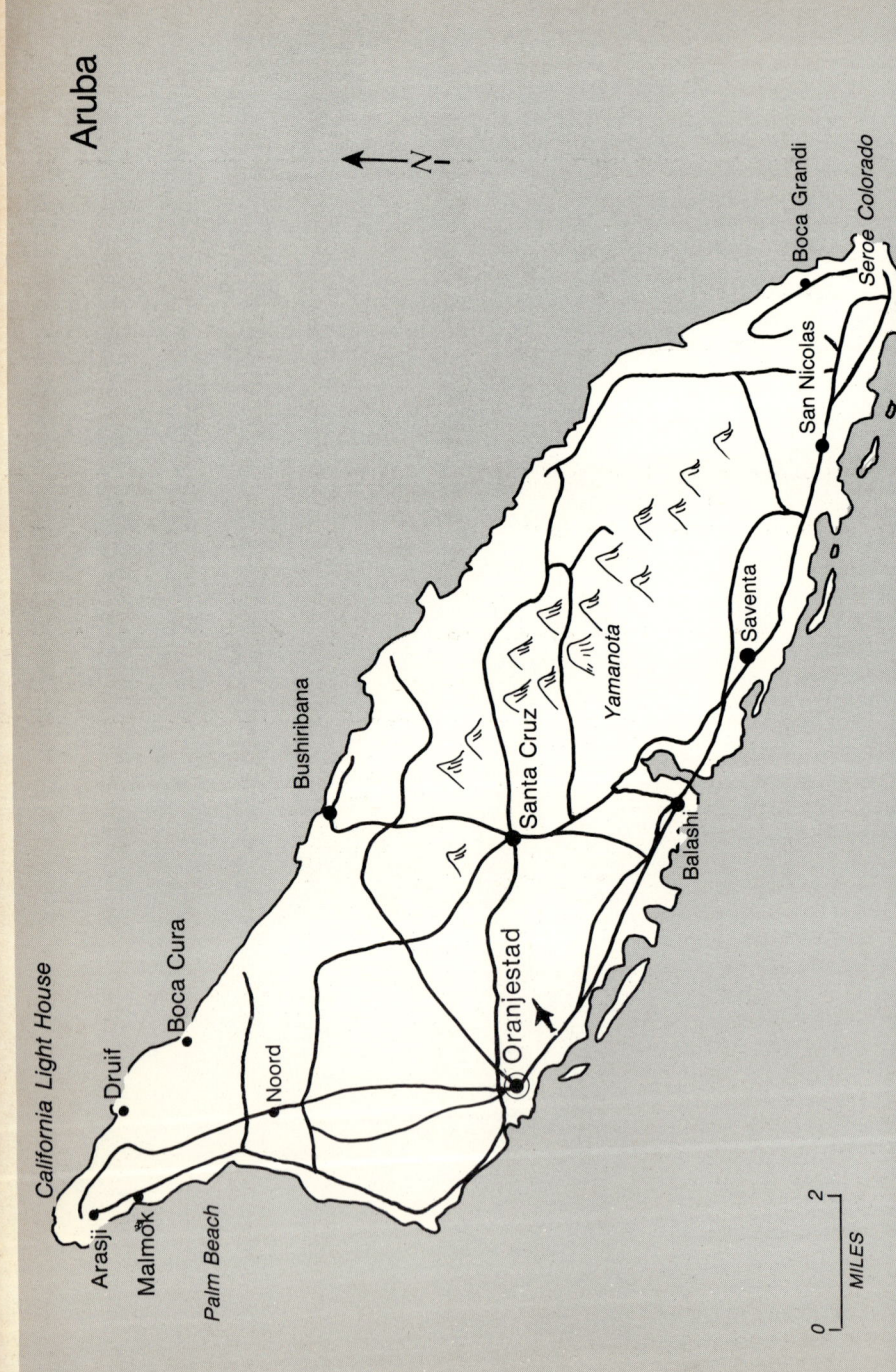

ARUBA

> Aruba Tourist Bureau, A. Shuttestraat 2, Oranjestad, Aruba, N.A., T 011+ 297–82–3777, fax; Aruba Tourist Bureau, 12th floor, 521 Fifth Ave., New York, NY 10175, T 212+ 246–3030 or 800+ 862–7822, fax 212+ 557–1614; and Oficina de Turismo de Aruba, Edificio Centro Capriles (Local C-29), Plaza Venezuela, Caracas, Venezuela.

$ · · · US $1 = Af 1.77
    Unless otherwise noted, $ refers to U.S. currency.

The warm breeze was invited through the louvers by curtains that were wrapped around a pole across the lintel. Jacobo Kock had just brought two ice cold Heineken beers from his kitchen and we sat in his neatly appointed living room to talk.

I had found Jacobo Kock—again—by reminiscing with someone at a restaurant in Oranjestad. Jacobo Kock was a night watchman at the Aruba Caribbean Hotel when I first met him, many years ago. He had taken a job as a night guard at the hotel after he was pensioned from the Lago-Exxon oil refinery. For me, Jacobo Kock doubled as "goodwill ambassador" and teacher.

We talked for almost an hour one night and, when I passed again the next night, he gave me a gift—a book about the Netherlands Antilles with an inscription that I treasure. I never took him up on his offer to meet some of his friends in his town of San Nicolas, out of the mainstream that finds tourist hotels and shops on beaches around the main town of Oranjestad, but I had driven in search of him this day—in hopes of finding him home.

His welcome was a warm one—and I learned from him again. He had retired, now, from both jobs. He was 13 when he started to work for Lago-Exxon, the refinery that opened in 1929 on the southeast shore of Dutch Aruba; he retired in the late '70s, after 36 years, with a treasured ring with two diamonds. His bright eyes were covered by thick glasses and his sight was weakening, but his love for Aruba and his natural warmth were stronger than Aruba's steady tradewinds.

When Cobo Kock was a boy, he fished. There was more rain on Aruba in those days and there were cows on the island—for milk and meat. Now most of the meat comes from South America; the produce comes from Venezuela; and the tourists—the new oil—come from North America.

San Nicolas, the southeast shore city where Jacobo Kock still lives, was for many years the prized residential area of Aruba. Although the city prospered during Aruba's successful years as an oil refining depot, it slumbers now—waiting for an infusion of funds—and perhaps of tourists—to bring it to life. A few years ago, this was where the money was, although the stores and town streets hardly hint of that today. In a style known to those who have visited the Netherlands (the mother country), bland facades greet the visitor's glance; the warmth of the home is secure within.

Since the closing of the Lago-Exxon complex outside San Nicolas, tourism has come into clear focus as a source of employment income. Today Aruba has made a commitment to tourism that includes high-rise hotels, lively gambling casinos, extensive shopping facilities with luxury items imported from all over the world, and training for Arubans in the skills for a profitable hospitality industry.

POLITICAL PICTURE: Reasonable cooperation between the public sector (government) and the private sector (hotels and other tourism interests) has apparently brought a potentially disastrous building spree under control. Although Aruba has an astounding number of new rooms, plus more projects in the works, the government seems willing to join the private sector with promotion. The MEP (Movimento Electorial de Pueblo) has mostly itself to thank for the overbuilding, since it processed most of the building permits without any apparent plan beyond the political expediency of giving jobs for construction. The AVP (Aruba Volks Party) was only in power for an interim two years, until December 1988, when the coalition government that was formed following elections returned the key positions to the MEP. Elections must be called (by the party in power) sometime before the end of 1992. The *Caribbean Newsletter* (page 9) will have an update.

The island was granted independence, and separate status within the three-part Kingdom of the Netherlands, at its own insistence, on January 1, 1986. (The kingdom includes the Netherlands, colloquially called Holland; Aruba; and the five islands of the Netherlands Antilles, namely Bonaire, Curaçao, Sint Maarten, Sint Eustatius, and Saba.) About the same time, the person who was catalyst for the independence sentiments, Betico Croes, died, Exxon's Lago oil refinery closed, leaving skilled workers without jobs, and tourism seemed at a standstill. Hundreds of nationals left Aruba for work elsewhere. Others retrained for the tourism industry, and permits were lavishly issued for new hotels. In spite of its experience with the oil refinery, Aruba has again become a single-source economy but the cooperation between the private and public (government) sectors bodes well for a cohesive tourism development plan.

ISLAND APPEARANCE: Aruba is shaped like an arrowhead, jettisoned from the tip of Colombia's Peninsula de la Guajira directly toward the coast of Venezuela. It lies a few miles north of the shore of Venezuela's Peninsula de Paraguana. Given its location, it should come as no surprise that South American influences have an impact on the Aruban culture. Unlike most other Caribbean islands, the people of Aruba retain features from a long Dutch, Spanish, and Taino culture.

There's an eerie other-worldness about the jagged and parched, cactus-studded terrain of this 72-square-mile island, and an unsettling serenity in the deep Caribbean blue that makes the horizon line far offshore. Soft, white-sand beaches stretch along portions of the leeward (southwestern) shore. Although its terrain is fascinating in an awesome way, Aruba is not a pretty island in a traditional "lush tropics" sense. The bony landscape looks more like pictures of the surface of the moon than like anything you'll see on other Caribbean islands. Mangrove trees are lush and green around some of the small islands that fleck the Barcadera Industrial Harbor and the airport area, where the Bucuti Yacht Club is located. A few of those isles are being developed for tourism. Elsewhere the indigenous Watapana trees, colloquially known as the divi-divi trees, bend at a broken-arm angle, forced there by the prevailing (and strong) tradewinds. The highest peak is the 617-foot Yamanota hill, which rises in a pyramid shape.

LIFESTYLE in Aruba is one of contrasts, depending on whether you choose to focus on the residents (who seldom wear suits to work and who enjoy the resort life on special occasions) or on the vacationers who loll on the beaches and poolside in various stages of undress (but who usually dress-up, if not in jacket or dressy dress then at least in something other than daytime clothes, for dinner at the better restaurants).

AUTHOR'S OBSERVATION

Although many Arubans speak fluent English, their national language is Papiamentu, a difficult tongue for outsiders, with words from Spanish, Portuguese, Dutch, English, French, and African dialects, with a strong overlay of Aruban independence. Dutch is Aruba's formal language, and fast-talking Americans may have to speak English slowly to be understood. People in local shops and villages often do not speak English. The humor of American jokes sometimes gets lost in the trade winds.

Be sure to inquire about special holidays and festivals while you are on the island; participation in these will be a unique experience. An event worth noting is the Bon Bini Festival held on Tuesday evenings at Fort Zoutman, on the patio, at the entrance to the Historical Museum. Food, crafts, dances, and special drinks are part of the "welcome" celebration. Some hotels (notably the Holiday Inn, Golden Tulip Aruba Caribbean, and the Talk of the Town Hotel) have special Aruban-style events. The end of February/early March carnival, held the weekend before the start of Lent, is a popular and colorful event with elaborate costumes and street parades. A pulsating Jazz Festival is held in June.

Aruba's prized asset is its people. In spite of the fact that the country looks at tourism as its financial "savior" and the source of employment, Arubans work with pride and ability. Although the money from tourism is obviously important to the economy (and the well-being of Aruba's citizens), I have the feeling that Arubans *really* enjoy the people-to-people contacts that tourism allows—as well as the cash that it puts in their pockets.

Expect to find some Dutch customs, especially those that have been translated to other Dutch-affiliated, warm-weather countries such as Indonesia, which gives Aruba rijsttafel, a multi-dish rice table that is an eating ceremony. Many holidays coincide with those celebrated in the Netherlands (Queen's birthday, etc.), and Dutch cheeses, Bols gin, Heineken and Amstel beer, and other Dutch products fill stores—and will fill you if you choose.

> **AUTHOR'S OBSERVATION**
>
> Aruba has wind, not breeze. Hair swirls constantly when you are outside, and the lovely fine sand that is wonderful underfoot becomes tiny flying pellets when stirred by the wind. Search for a sheltered spot on the beach.

MEDICAL FACILITIES: The Horatio Oduber Hospital is near most of the hotels, slightly inland on the southwest coast. It is multi-story, and looks more like one of the country's modern hotels than a hospital. Many of the doctors have trained in the Netherlands.

MONEY MATTERS: The official currency is the Aruban florin or guilder (the words are interchangeable), noted as Af or Afl and pegged to the U.S. dollar, not the Netherlands' guilder. U.S. currency is used in most tourist spots, but you may get a slightly better rate if you use the local currency.

> **AUTHOR'S OBSERVATION**
>
> Be sure to read your credit card slips carefully, especially in restaurants where the space marked "tip" is left conspicuously empty, and the Aruban custom of 5% government tax and 10% service charge is totaled for 15%, which is entered in the "taxes" space. You should know that the "service" 10% is supposed to be divided among all the staff of the place you are dining. If you want to give extra for special attention, do so, but you are not obligated to give anything more than the amount already added. Inquire if in doubt.

COMMUNICATIONS are easy by telephone with Aruba, following the normal routes for overseas calls, which, from North America, is to dial 011 + 297 + 8 and a 5-digit number. Within Aruba, hotels add a hefty premium on telephone calls from your room. To reach AT&T's USADirect operator, dial 800–1011 as a local call. For mail service, use airmail at 50 cents for the first half ounce, and consider yourself lucky if mail takes under 2 weeks. Facsimile machines are fastest and can be found at most hotels.

ARRIVAL at Aruba's Aeropuerto Internationale Reina Beatrix, named for the Queen of the Netherlands, is efficient and easy. Immigration procedures are reasonably fast if you have filled out the form usually given to you on the plane, and have it in hand with your passport (the best identification, although anything that proves place of birth will do), and return or onward air ticket.

After you have cleared Customs (usually perfunctory, for vacationers), you can negotiate for a rental car or take a taxi directly to your hotel. There are several car rental booths outside the terminal.

CRUISE ship arrivals are deposited right at the waterfront in the town of Oranjestad, the island's capital. You can easily walk to the shops, if you don't mind walking in the blazing sun. Taxis are waiting near the end of the gangplank to take you touring. Among the most popular sights, in addition to the occasional gabled architecture and Fort Zoutman in Oranjestad, are the surf-pounded rocks of the east and north coasts—and the casinos in the high-rise hotels and near Manchebo Beach.

DEPARTURE is from the left-hand side of the airport terminal, as you face it from the road. Check-in lines can be long, so allow almost 2 hours if you want some time to shop after you have passed immigration. You'll need your airline ticket, a copy of your immigration form (the original of which you surrendered on arrival), and Af17.70 or US$10. Be sure to reconfirm your flight a day before departure if you are flying at peak season. The shops in the waiting area sell Dutch cheeses and a few other imported food items, but bigger purchases must be made elsewhere.

TOURING TIPS: **Car rental** is carefree on Aruba's good roads. Even when you get lost, and find yourself on some of the dirt roads on the "back" side of the island, exploring can be fun. You can visit anything worth seeing in one day, and from that point on you will need a car only for dinners out (when you can take taxis, if you'd rather). I've had very good luck with the minimum rate from *Marco's Car Rental,* one of several firms with a booth at the airport. Other car rental firms with airport pick-up include *Budget, National, Avis,* and *Hertz.* Firms seem to present a solid front on pricing, although there's variety in style of cars and maintenance. Try shopping for good rates.

Organized **tours,** and day trips to other islands are arranged through *De Palm Tours N.V.* (142 L. G. Smith Blvd., Box 656, Aruba, N.A.; T 800+ 533–7256 or 011+ 297+ 92–4400, fax 914+ 276–3946) and/or *Pelican Tours* (Rockefellerstraat 1, Oranjestad, Aruba, N.A.; T 011+297+82–3888, fax 011+ 297+ 83–2655). DePalm's newest venture is the company's "own" island, where facilities have been built for beach parties and daytime scuba, snorkeling, windsurfing and other water-focused activities. The day on the island is available through the activities' desks at all hotels. DePalm picks you up, takes you to the ferry for the island trip, and meets you at the dock to return you to your hotel when the day is done.

If you want to enjoy the island as residents know it, board one of the yellow **buses** that stretch to San Nicolas and other areas. The buses stand at the parking area not far from the tourist office and the waterfront in Oranjestad. Bus service is good, with regular routes running along the beach-and-hotel-rimmed coast, so that you need only wait in front of your hotel for a ride into town, or in town for the ride back. The cost is about 75¢.

Taxis are plentiful, but expensive. If you are traveling with a group of several people, the cost is amortized, but if you are traveling alone or with one other person you might as well rent a car.

LODGING choices range from the ever-increasing army of high-rise, casino-punctuated big properties on Palm Beach through the low-rise, clustered resorts that flourish on Manchebo and Druif beaches, where the Alhambra Casino and shopping center provide added diversion. Included in the mix is a hotel school that operates as a full-fledged inclusive hotel (named *Bushiri*), on the outskirts of Oranjestad, and a fleet of condominiums, many of which are in basic boxy buildings, with modern kitchen equipment and plumbing, thin walls, standard bedrooms, and either balcony or porch, depending on where the unit is located. And then there is a family of small spots, once private homes in the residential Malmok area, where guests focus on sensational windsurfing, possible at the northwest coast, north of the highrise hotels.

From a total of 2318 rooms in 1985, Aruba's hospitality industry expanded to 3628 rooms for 1989—and almost doubled, to 6585 by the end of 1990. By 1992 the tally is expected to be 6833, to reach a total of 7100 by 1993! The options may seem confusing, but it pays to research—and to read the fine print. After all, it's *your* vacation!

AUTHOR'S OBSERVATION

In some cases, taxes and tips plus the cost of the meals can double the cost of what appears to be a "bargain" rate. And a few of the big hotels continue a long outdated practice of adding an "energy surcharge." Voice your protest about this sneaky method of increasing your bill! Responsible hotel management should long since have figured "energy" into room cost. I think this "energy surcharge" is a scam!

Aruba has developed into a "package plan" resort, with some very reasonable multinight holidays that include the basics of room and air fare with whatever add-ons have been negotiated between the tour operator and the hotel. Very few wise travelers pay the "rack rate" (the rate as it is given on the semi-annual rate sheet published by the tourist department and on the hotel's own rate list). Those rates continue to be high—and often not worth the $, in my opinion, for room-only, no matter how great the view. Shop carefully, to find the best value.

In addition to your room rate, all hotels add the 5% government tax and most also add 10% or 15% for service. It is not necessary to leave added tips, unless you have asked for—and received—special service.

AUTHOR'S AWARDS

Manchebo Beach and its sister-property *Bucuti* deserve special mention for the loyal, enthusiastic management and staff, and for clinging to Aruban-style hospitality in the face of all the new buildings; Hyatt's *Aruba Resort* is sensational and well-run; *Golden Tulip Aruba Caribbean* continues to be one of my favorite highrise hotels. For small spots with special hospitality, the Yarzagarays lead the group with their *Vistalmar*.

Information about places to stay is included under Hotels/Resorts, Housekeeping Holidays, The Inn Way, and Low-Cost Lodging. Stars are awarded within each category. (See page 11.)

HOTELS/RESORTS A few years ago, when the *Golden Tulip Aruba Caribbean* was totally refurbished, it marked the beginning of a new burst of hotel building. Now that project is dwarfed by the siege of new high-rise hotels, with expected U.S. style and systems. Both Hyatt and Sonesta have brought innovative tropical architecture to Aruba, and they, plus other new properties, make it worthwhile to search for good values this winter.

★★★ **Americana Aruba Hotel & Casino** • *on Palm Beach* • is a two-tower high-rise hotel, with a full range of activities and a choice of restaurants, shops, and rooms. The *Golden Tulip* and the expanding *Playa Linda* are the near neighbors, both a stroll away along the beach. The first 9-story tower of the hotel was built in '75, the second was added in early 1990. Both wedge inland from the powdery beach activity (lounges, snack bars, sports concession) to the road that stretches from town to the Malmok residential area and beyond. The huge, fantasy pool has waterfalls and other features. The lobby is attractive, with the addition of *Le Cafe,* a casual, comfortable sipping and snacking area with European overtones. There are nightclub shows and other activities, including poolside functions and entertainment at the neighboring hotels and, of course, the casino. *Stellaris* is the disco/nightclub. Insofar as rooms, most are in pretty good shape. The newest tower has all modern amenities. Expect to find the usual big hotel: modern, air-conditioned boxes, and a hotel that is often full of convention and other group business. Best value comes with package tours; check with your travel agent for the season's "deals." *Resort hotel.*

Amsterdam Manor Beach • *on the inland side of the road, northwest of the Concorde* • is starting as a small spot, with less than 50 rooms. Next door to *La Quinta,* and convenient to restaurants and the casino at the *Concorde,* the place offers standard hotel-style rooms slightly removed from the bustle of the biggies. *Hotel.*

Aruba Beach Club • *on Druif Beach between Manchebo Beach and the Divi Divi Hotel* • is primarily a time-share resort. The 133 rooms (called suites) have efficiency kitchens, although the property operates on a hotel plan, offering meals from its restaurants (and along the beach at the other hotels). Lively banter is part of the pool party when the action-oriented settle here. Interior halls are gloomy, but outdoor activity can seem fun—if you like casual surroundings. The U-shaped building cups sand and shore, and has an assortment of shops around the main floor's check-in area. *Hotel.*

★★★ **Aruba Concorde Hotel & Casino** • *on Palm Beach* • with its 500 rooms in a tower is at the Oranjestad end of the beach, about a 15-minute drive from town. The hotel operates independently from other Concorde properties. Brace yourself for the wind tunnel at the entrance. Structural problems result in a gale wind blowing through the porte cochere, so when your taxi pulls up for your grand entrance, hold your head. Dependent on convention or special group business, the hotel is often lively with visiting South American guests. The pool area is pleasant, there's plenty of action, and downstairs (below the main lobby, but on pool level), you'll find an attractive coffee shop as well as the *Adriana*

Italian restaurant that serves special dinners (at high prices) and several shops. Be sure to ask about package holidays. *Big hotel.*

★★ **Aruba Holiday Inn and Casino** • *on Palm Beach* • is huge, with a new group of Holiday Inn-style bedrooms in high-rise and low-rise buildings, and an assortment of dining rooms (*Empress of China,* with its "Chinese Rice Table" is one); *King Neptune's,* poolside, with "cookout seafood" and a water ballet is one of the special evening offerings. The *Supper Club* offers an Antillean floorshow Sun. at 8 p.m. *L'Esprit* is the disco, which can be lively when the houseguests are; the casino is nearby, and the arcade between the main lobby and the casino and restaurant area is lined with shops. Count on action, and look for package tours for best value. *Big hotel.*

★★ **Aruba Palm Beach** • *on Palm Beach, next to the Aruba Caribbean* • with its 202 rooms in a beachside tower, started life as a Sheraton. The big-name chain pulled out in August '82, and the Aruban government and the hotel's casino operator took over its operation. The downstairs coffee shop, with its Dutch decor (Delft blue-and-white plus wood) has a relatively interesting menu. On the other side of the windows that keep the coffee shop air-conditioned, the *Steak Pub* serves barbecue choices for alfresco dinners near the pool. This place seems to have a pleasant atmosphere that makes it possible to overlook the relatively casual service. There are shops, tennis courts, and the casino on the premises; a full roster of beachfront and other outdoor activities are available on the shore. Rooms are standard U.S. hotel-style and needed attention when I looked. *Big hotel.*

★★★ **Bucuti** • *beachfront neighbor, and sister Best Western–linked property, to Manchebo Beach* • was new for the season of '87–'88. Viewful rooms are comfortably appointed; each has a sea-sight from the patio or terrace and tropical tones in fabric and furniture. Most have kitchenettes. With access to all the watersports and restaurant facilities at Manchebo Beach, and a unique pool and shipwreck restaurant on the beach in front of Bucuti, guests are comfortably situated. The friendly staff makes this place special. (The Alhambra casino complex is a walk down the road—or beach—toward town.) *Hotel.*

★★ **Bushiri Bounty Hotel** • *at the edge of Oranjestad* • on a piece of shore that is shared with the island's new container port, opened for the season of '82–'83 and has built additional rooms for a total of 154. The buildings are attractive, with most rooms having harbor view. All-inclusive "Bounty" rates now make this a good value. The rooms and other facilities are modern, comfortable, and well maintained. The *Aruba Hospitality and Trades Training Center* is on the site, and some of the graduates are hired by the hotel. If you're interested in the hotel training program, it is sometimes possible to tour the facilities. Ask the manager. The pool is pleasant; you can walk into town for shopping, restaurants, etc. *Hotel.*

La Cabaña Beach and Racquet Club • *north of the Concorde, on the inland side of the shore-rimming road* • grew from its small-and-solid start to become a big-and-beautiful community, with a focus on tennis, fitness, and watersports. Planned for 500-plus studio, 1- and 2-bedroom units, the complex has choices for restaurants and other entertainment as well as Jacuzzis and a huge pool. All units are comfortably appointed, with modern equipment; the best rooms have a sea view, although the club is across the road from the beach. The *Caribbean Newsletter* (page 9) will comment about the planned casino, after it opens. All that kind of action is at nearby casinos. *Resort.*

Carnicom Hotel • *north of the Holiday Inn, at Palm Beach* • is Carnival Cruise Line's "parent" who claimed a structure that had been announced as part of another big chain's overseas endeavors and will add some of the glitz-and-glitter style that it plastered on the Cable Beach area near Nassau in the Bahamas. The 460-room property hoped to open in mid-'91, but was nowhere close when I checked at press time. The Caribbean Newsletter (page 9) will have facts when warranted.

Casa del Mar Beach Resort • *on Druif Beach* • is neighbor and time-share sister to the *Aruba Beach Club*. Tennis courts, pool, and beach activities are part of the formula that puts blocks of 32 units up at a rate that took building into '88 with a total of 107 2-bedroom, 2-bath units, each comfortable for up to four people. *Manchebo Beach* is a neighbor.

★★★ **Divi Divi Beach Hotel** • *on the beach* • is within a stroll of its sister resorts: *Tamarijn* and *Dutch Village,* and of *Aruba Beach Club, Casa del Mar, Manchebo,* and *Bucuti,* along the beach. The action center is the Alhambra casino and entertainment hub across the road. Most guests in the 204 rooms find the place comfortable, but I've noticed some slip in once-high standards. The open-to-breezes cafe-style breakfast and snacking area is operated on cafeteria style, which I find unsettling for starting your day. The only asset, in my opinion, is the beach and sea view. The hotel's policy of having a coffee cart wheeled near the rooms at some set time every morning means that you can easily get coffee or tea when you want it. Entertainment at the hotel is often Aruban-style; food service, alfresco or in the more formal dining room, is uneven, but settings are attractive. There's a pool at the beach, and all activities can be arranged through the hotel's concessionaire, who operates from an office to the right of the lobby, as you enter. Rooms stretch out to the left in a series of low-rise buildings, with the *Sandpiper Beach Bar* the hub for folks who occupy the rooms farthest from the main building. The hotel has some evening activities, but the casino is the "big time." *Resort-style hotel.*

★★ **Divi Tamarijn Beach Hotel** • *at Druif Beach* • is a grove of a dozen or so white stucco two-story buildings, with attractive brick-colored roofs, scattered along the shore. Most of the 204 rooms are comfortable; many have sea view. The first-floor rooms offer the convenience of walking right onto the beach, but they also are open for view by anyone who strolls along the shore. As you walk into the lobby, the check-in area is to your right, with the lounge area punctuated by a model and sales desk for the Dutch Village, on the inland side of the road and a time-share/condominium project that is part of the Divi Divi and Tamarijn family. Tamarijn offers good value in surroundings that are convenient to other Druif Beach hotels and a short ride from those at Palm

Beach or from the town of Oranjestad. (The name is the Dutch spelling of the fruit tree known in English as Tamarind.) *Hotel.*

★★★★ **Golden Tulip Aruba Caribbean Hotel & Casino** • *on Palm Beach* • between the Americana Aruba and the Aruba Palm Beach, was for many years the best hotel in Aruba. An early favorite, when it first opened several years ago, the hotel reclaimed luxury status as part of its adoption by Holland's Golden Tulip group. The heart of the hotel is the 120-room Barbizon wing; the Garden wing stretches toward the beach; the all-new Caribbean wing added 176 rooms. The 30 Lanai rooms that are near the tennis court sell at lowest rate. Shops, saunas, fitness equipment and 4 tennis courts offer daytime diversions; the casino, nightclub and 4 restaurants take care of evening hours. There are 39 luxury suites in addition to the hundreds of regular rooms, most with sea view, and an assortment of restaurants that range from the elegant (expensive) *French Room* to the beach- and poolside *Gazebo. The Rib Room* features beef. *Big hotel.*

★★★★ **Hyatt Regency Aruba Resort & Casino** • *on the wide beach shared by other highrises* • is a lovely property on 12 acres of land that includes a span on spectacular Palm Beach. A huge lagoon-style pool is on three levels, with waterfalls, gardens, and a spiral water slide that makes the place a welcome oasis—and no mean feat—on desertlike Aruba. Regency Club rooms are the hotel's best, with club-floor services that include continental breakfast and cocktail nibbles in the rate. Other rooms are also state-of-the-art, with the highly respected Hyatt services. Young vacationers can participate in the Camp Hyatt program, while older folks spend time shopping or in the casino. A huge and glittering casino is also an integral part of Hyatt's $52 million investment, as are three restaurants. In addition to the coffee shop equivalent, there's a seafood restaurant, and another that features South American specialties. The health club is fully equipped, with sauna, exercise machines, and other facilities. Check with Hyatt for special family and other vacation plans. *Resort hotel.*

★★★ **Manchebo Beach Resort Hotel** • *on Manchebo and Druif beaches* • is unique for Aruba. As the only totally Aruban hotel, the property has a very friendly personality, helped along by General Manager Ewald Biemans's thoughtful management and a devoted staff. Built in 1967 in the motel style that was popular at that time, the several 2-story buildings are dressed with tropical foliage. Best rooms are those with sea view; all are scheduled for new decor for this season. There are good on-site restaurants, an active windsurfing center, a pool whose borders can seem people-lined, an entertainment and dining link with *Talk of the Town Hotel,* and the most spectacular wide, white-sand beach in Aruba. Favored by Europeans, especially Dutch who have become repeat visitors, Manchebo has a personality that can appeal to Americans who like continental flavor with Caribbean sunshine. It shares a Best Western reservations affiliation with its sister properties, *Bucuti,* a few steps away, and *Talk of the Town. Resort hotel.*

Paradise Beach Village • *on the inland side of the road, north of the Concorde* • with La Quinta and Amsterdam Manor as neighbors, PBV is a reasonably small spot, with luxury suites and a pleasant restaurant, La Vie en Rose. *Hotel.*

Plantation Bay Beach Resort & Casino • *on the northwestern end of Palm Beach* • plans to open for winter '91–'92, with a multi-story U-shaped building spilling its guests into the center pool-studded area that opens out to eye-blinding white sand of Palm Beach. Although the 420-room property is not open at press time, it's expected to be in full swing by fall. The *Caribbean Newsletter* (page 9) will have after-opening comments and star rating. Plans include six restaurants, a health club, and a huge-and-glittering casino. Be sure to check on status before counting on all facilities; inquire about the special-rate packages that may announce the opening season. *Resort hotel.*

★★★ **Ramada Renaissance Hotel & Casino** • *near the other hotels on the southwest coast* • expects to accept its first guests this season, although the hotel's not open at press time. The 210-room property is a $50-million venture owned by an Aruban company, Eagle Beach Hotel N.V. Elaborate plans include an action-packed resort in the Las Vegas style, with 24-hour coffee shop, casino, dinner theater, rooftop restaurant, and convention meeting rooms. This is a bigtime project! The *Caribbean Newsletter* (page 9) will have star rating and observations when the property is open. *Resort hotel.*

★★★ **Sonesta Hotel, Beach Club & Casino** • *in Oranjestad, amid shops and restaurants* • has a Disney-World quality, with its water-filled lobby that allows for shuttle boat pick-up for transport to the resort's private island beaches. Owned by an Aruban company and managed by Sonesta, the 301-room property opened in early '91. The innovative design set a new pace for Aruban hotels, especially for in-town properties. If you tire of the two on-premise restaurants, there are several nearby dining depots that offer signing privileges for Sonesta guests. The shopping arcade claims "over 80 shops," with a range from elegant imports to tourist clutter. Watersports are available on the private island; the casino is lively when the hotel has groups/conventions and/or when a cruise ship is in port. *Resort hotel.*

★ **Talk of the Town** • *in Oranjestad* • is a motel-style place popular with business travelers (who like the convenience of those 62 rooms that have a kitchen unit). It's a member of the U.S. Best Western chain. Rooms are around the swimming pool (favored by businessmen's families whose children cavort during daytime hours), and seemed dark, partially because the overhanging roof obscures some sunshine—and shelter. Air conditioning is essential; and the hum drowns out the sound of folks socializing at the poolside bar while you're trying to sleep. The disco is called *Contempo.* Transportation is provided to Manchebo Beach for shoreside swimming; *Surfside* (with *Temptations* restaurant) is across the road. This hotel was the flagship for Ike and Grete Cohen's Aruba operations, and it is still where they maintain one of the island's venerable restaurants, also called *Talk of the Town. Hotel.*

HOUSEKEEPING HOLIDAYS offer the island's best values, and a good way for a couple or families to have a vacation. There are many inexpensive studios and apartments, most clustered in the Malmok residential area. Luxury-style villa living as it is known on some other islands is not a feature of vacation life in Aruba, except perhaps at the *Dutch Village.* When (or if) the once private homes at the Lago-Exxon executive complex, near Rogers Bay, are available for rent, they could be very comfortable lodgings for vacationers with cars. Time-share units grow like weeds. There are many clusters. Most accommodations are basic, modern apartments such as you could find in many areas in the U.S.

Caribbean Palm Village • *inland, near the church at Noord* • is a cluster of apartments in several 2-story buildings. "Free" rental cars (which you'll need to get to the beach and restaurants) are part of your room rate; you pay only the $8 daily charge for insurance. Count on basic housekeeping facilities in a sunny-suburb style. *Valentino's,* the on-premise restaurant, has good Italian-style food. *Apts.*

★★ **Dutch Village** • *near the beach, mingling with Divi's Tamarijn* • is a group of apartments built on a boomerang-shaped piece of land that shares owners with the Divi and Tamarijn. The first of the studios and 1- and 2-bedroom apartments opened in July '83, to be followed by additional units. The town house style appeals to owners who rent their units when they are elsewhere. All units are complete with modern kitchen. *Apts.*

Harbour Town • *on the waterfront in Oranjestad* • is one of the many new time-share apartment clusters. Plans include a marina and a casino, to be completed by late 1990 or early 1991, but they are not open at presstime. The first of the eventual 240 units are open. *Apts.*

Mill Resort • *a short distance inland from the beach, with a landmark Dutch (imported) mill as its namesake* • is a cluster of almost 100 apartments, intended to be sold for time-share and rented in owners' absence. Since the place is being built, its rooms and appointments are modern. The beach is a hot walk from here; a rental car makes spontaneous travel easier. *Apts.*

★★★ **Playa Linda** • *on Palm Beach, between the Americana Caribbean and the Holiday Inn* • commands a prize section of the gorgeous beach. The 1- and 2-bedroom apartments and suites are attractively furnished, and owned (or offered for sale) on time-share programs. Kitchen facilities are ultramodern, but guests with big budgets often take advantage of the many good restaurants. There's an attractive on-premises restaurant with reasonably good food, and all the beach action—and nearby hotels' casinos—are within a short walk from your room. The first 60 units were open in July '83; phase two's suites followed. *Apt. hotel.*

La Quinta • *inland, not far from Palm Beach* • is about two dozen time-share apartments that can provide a comfortable, simple home at reasonable cost. You'll want a car for touring, but you can walk across the road to the beach. *Apts.*

Sunset Village • *near Eagle Beach* • is on the inland side of the shore-rimming road, not far from Manchebo Beach. The time-share units are tidy apartments, for rent on a regular basis when the owners are not in residence. The public bus passes nearby. *Apts.*

THE INN WAY: Although Aruba doesn't have a long tradition of innkeeping, where the owner makes the time—and devotes the energy—to give personalized treatment, there are a couple of places where hospitality is exceptional.

   Sailboard Vacations • *in the Malmok residential area, at the north end of Palm Beach* • is the cover-all name for several places that used to be bed-and-breakfast inns. Among the group are *The Edge's,* with air-conditioned efficiency units gathered around a courtyard near the Jacuzzi-pool that serves as a cool-off dunking area; *Boulevard Apartments,* a few doors away from the Edge's, but with a similar set-up; *TeSoro Apartments,* with a 1-bedroom house as well as other rooms; and a few other houses. Obviously the hospitality comes with the spontaneous windsurfing interest. *Casual inns.*

   ★ **Vistalmar** • *on Bucutiweg near the airport and across the road from the small private Yacht Club* • is a long-time favorite for dependable Aruban hospitality. Alby and Katy Yarzagaray have used a formula that works for their home to help create one for you. Their two 2-story units, each with 4 apartments, are near the sea (but not a beach). Bicycles can be a means of transportation; the public bus runs nearby; rental car will give maximum freedom to roam. The kitchen facilities are modern and complete; bedrooms and bath are comfortable. Living area is on the front of your unit, facing the sea. Hedges give maximum privacy for the ground-floor level, but 2nd floor balconies overlook mangrove trees and sea. Ideal for self-sufficient folk seeking homelike surroundings in the sun. *Apts.*

LOW-COST LODGINGS: In recent years a spate of small spots have opened up, many of them clustering at the northwestern end of Palm Beach, in Malmok area. Among the best bets, in my opinion, are **Edward's Seaview Apartments** (82–6551), not far from the beach, with air-conditioned efficiency apartments, private entrances, and simple surroundings. None of the small spots is a decorator's dream, but all have the basics—at a cost that hovers around $50 for two, meals extra. Be sure to inquire about special windsurfing package plans.

RESTAURANTS on Aruba have varied personalities. There's a lot more than hotel dining to entertain you here. Those who like Oriental food will find plenty of places, and most restaurants will have good food for good value. The new Harbor Town area has several restaurants. Sophisticated, European-style dining is an "iffy" proposition here. In most cases, the atmosphere usually exceeds the culinary expertise, in my opinion. Count on finding plenty of American-style food (hamburgers, hotdogs, club sandwiches) and expect to pay high tabs in the restaurants that consider themselves gourmet.

---- AUTHOR'S AWARDS ----
Chez Mathilde, in a once-private home in Oranjestad, is the island's most elegant restaurant; *Brisas del Mar* is a humble place along the coast almost at San Nicolas, where the fresh seafood is worth the drive, and *Papiamento,* upstairs in attractive, in-town surroundings, serves "clay pot" specialties and other attractively presented entrees.

Before itemizing offerings by particular restaurants, here's a tip for self-sufficient vacationers: Plan at least one picnic, to take advantage of all the marvelous choices at the delicatessens in Oranjestad.

---- AUTHOR'S OBSERVATION ----
Be aware that credit card slips will be presented with the "service/tips" section left blank even though that fee has been included in your bill. Draw an X through those spaces unless you want to tip twice!

Adriana • *the Italian restaurant on the lower level of the Aruba Concorde Hotel* • features mostly northern Italian (lighter) cuisine, and my samplings were good. Pasta was leaden, but the veal was excellent. Wines here, as everywhere, are expensive for the European imported names, but the selection is above average. Dinner with everything can run $40 per person, but you can have a pasta plate and a glass of wine for about $20.

Bali • *at the Oranjestad waterfront, by Arnold Schuttestratt* • is an Aruban tradition that benefits from the talents of Eduardo Ellis, who has taken over this place. The floating, Indonesian-style restaurant has been a part of Aruba's dining roster for more than two decades, expanding to include a part of the pier and a flat-bottomed barge permanently moored to the waterfront. The item to order, preferably with a group of friends, is the multi-course (20 for the full "show") rice table called *rijsttafel,* with several small portions of unusual items, and one or more ice-cold Heineken beers. If you dine at midday, you'll be able to see the waterfront activity through the windows, and you'll also sense the gentle motion of the boat. Skip this place on steamy days when harbor smells settle. The interior is dark; evening atmosphere is best. Count on spending $25 per person, at least, unless you snack on appetizers.

★★ **Boonoonoos** • *in Oranjestad, not far from Papiamento restaurant* • takes its name from a celebration in the Bahamas—but its kitchen is strictly local. A fun place for an evening with friends, this air-conditioned place seemed popular with Arubans when I tried it.

★★ **Brisas del Mar** • *about half-an-hour's drive east along the south coast (on good roads) at Savaneta, near San Nicolas* • is a special, nautical spot that is a gathering place for the nearby fishermen and for Aruban families for special occasions. It's not a dress-up spot. Joe Rasmijn gives most of the credit for the success of the restaurant to his wife, Lucia, but both work hard to keep things in good shape, and there is no plan to let success go to their heads and build big. Ask for recommendations about the fresh fish if you're unsure about what to order. Everything is good.

Buccaneer • *not far from the big Palm Beach hotels* • but not as near to the shore as its name (and seafood menu) might suggest, has a devoted local following. I like the fish-tank, nautical atmosphere, even when the food is only average—and expensive. There are many who feel that this is *the* place to go if you are planning only one night away from your hotel.

Captain's Table • *on Wilhelminastraat in Oranjestad* • is a favorite for familiar fare: steak, fish, veal, and salads.

Charlie's Bar • *in San Nicolas, at Zeppenfeldstraat 56* • is a "quick-and-dirty" local bar that's popular for its juke box, snack foods, drinks, and good conversation with local folk and others who find their way here. With its down-and-out, Hemingway-style atmosphere, this is an island legend where hamburgers and lobster are only part of its claim to fame.

★★★ **Chez Mathilde** • *near the Police Station at Herrenstraat in Oranjestad* • offers one of the best dining experiences in Aruba. The core of the restaurant is the family home, refurbished (and rebuilt) to accommodate mealtime guests. Be sure to look around the walls, at pictures that show the original home. The international menu aspires to French flair, and often achieves it. The varied wine list has some excellent choices. More formal than many Aruban restaurants, this place should be first on your list, as it usually is on mine. Reservations are needed, especially at the height of the season.

★ **De Dijssel** • *on Hospitalstraat off Nassaustraat in Oranjestad* • is a Dutch-style coffee house that will make you believe you are in the Netherlands. With traditional pea soup, bitterballen, and other Dutch specialties served in cozy, air-conditioned surroundings, this pleasant place is ideal for light meals at modest cost. Pastries and breads are baked on the premises—and sold from the bakery next door. The Harsvelds, owners, maintain Dutch-strict hours: luncheon is from 12 till 2, not later.

De Olde Mill • *on the inland side of the Palm Beach road* • is a real 1804 mill from Friesland, northern Netherlands. Check its status when you arrive on the island; it changes, and on my recent visits the food has not been noteworthy. The mill stands out and it was a good place for early evening cocktails. Food bears further research.

La Dolce Vita • *on Nassaustraat at the far end from the major shopping area* • is one of a cluster of good restaurants that have opened up in former houses or small buildings. Prices are high, and food did not live up to my expectations, but the pastas are good and some of the other offerings (veal, for example) can be tasty if not too elaborately prepared.

Driftwood • *on Klipstraat, which runs parallel to Nassaustraat, in Oranjestad* • warrants mention for seafood in small, casually comfortable surroundings.

Dynasty • *in the Harbour Town area, on Oranjestad's waterfront* • is Aruba's first Japanese-Thai restaurant. Locals love it.

Gianni's Garden • *on Havenstraat in downtown Oranjestad* • is yet another Italian eatery, featuring pastas, garlic sauces, and pleasant surroundings.

★ **Mamas and Papas** • *near the stadium in Oranjestad* • is a favorite for true Aruban aficionados who know and enjoy simple surroundings and good local food. Keshiyana with a salad can be a memorable meal at this small spot, operated by the owners of Taurina.

Oriental • *at Zoutmanstraat 5* • has an extensive menu of Chinese offerings, with fried rice, wonton soup, and several Indonesian dishes as some of the standards. "Oriental Specials" combine several good offerings, as do the multi-selection "Oriental Chinese Dishes." A bonus feature here is the "Kuminda pa Hiba," which means "Take-out service," available from 10:30 a.m.–10:30 p.m. Prices for many of the full meals are under $10.

La Paloma • *near Buccaneer* • has its following for informal fare. Aruban-style seafood (spicy and sauced), special stews and flaked fish with fried plantain and spices are favorite fare.

★★★ **Papiamento** • *near the museum, in Oranjestad* • is the place Eduardo Ellis made famous, with pleasant atmosphere and good food. The stairs that lead up to the second floor deposit you in an atmospheric, multi-chambered restaurant. There's a sophisticated bar area where you can wait, if your table's not ready, and an interesting menu that includes fish and meat grilled on a blisteringly hot slab that is brought to your table for service. A costumed dance troupe performs some evenings for an Aruban folklore and fun evening. Check when you arrive to be sure to make a reservation on the right night, although food's good—and service willing—most of the time.

Le Petit Cafe • *on Schlepstraat, which is the western end of Nassaustraat* • is a popular owner-managed small spot with good food at reasonable prices. Aruban specialties are featured.

Talk of the Town • *at the western fringe of Oranjestad* • is an Aruban classic that has its devoted following. Steak and salad are favorites, although other entrees also parade on the impressive menu. Count on dark, air-conditioned surroundings with napery and U.S. style.

★★ **La Taurina** • *at Nassaustraat 149* • is one of the cluster of interesting restaurants. It opened in early '83, and now has a devoted following. The decor is Spanish, complete to the style of the chairs and certainly to the bullfight and other pictures on the wall. Paella was one of the offerings—and it was excellent. Open 6 p.m. to midnight, you can count on a bit of Spain when the doors are open.

Temptations • *at Surfside across from Talk of the Town in Oranjestad* • is part disco and part dining room. As homebase for a weekly beach party, this place *can* be fun, when the guests are. An Aruban-style menu with soup and salad as specialties. Drinks are included for the price of the evening's event. This place deserves further on-the-spot research before you book for dinner.

Warung Djawa • *on Boerhavestraat 4 in Oranjestad* • serves spicy and savory Indonesian food, as its name suggests. Although the rijsttafel is a personal favorite (with small portions of varying tastes and textures), there are many interesting offerings.

Among the many Chinese restaurants, some to try are the **Dragon Phoenix**, at Havenstraat 31; the **Mido** on Dwarsstraat; and **Kowloon**, at the corner of Emmastraat. All are an easy walk from the Nassaustraat shopping area in Oranjestad.

NATURAL SURROUNDINGS: Aruba's beauty is not that of a lush tropical island. The flat cover of sand that humps to an occasional conelike hill is baked by relentless sun. Desertlike and windswept, the countryside takes on moonscape overtones. Patches and dots of dusty green plants, including several kinds of cactus, break the beige landscape, but it's the surrounding transparent sea that appeals to most visitors. Spiky and strange looking Watapana trees, better known as divi-divi, bend to the southwest, forced there by the constant tradewinds. They can be your compass if you lose sight of the island's highest point, Yamanota (617 ft.). The two other high points, northeast of Oranjestad, are Hooiberg, at 541 feet, and the hump known as Seroe Plat, at 308 feet. It's also called Kristal Berg for the quartz that can be collected on the site.

AUTHOR'S OBSERVATION

An island tour, by *DePalm* or *Pelican Tours,* is one way to see the natural surroundings and to be sure you get some historical facts, but you can also learn plenty by reading the very helpful green sheet called "Aruba Holiday," available through your hotel and the tourist office.

Exploring by rental car is best when you get "lost" on some of the packed-sand roads along the wind-ravaged northeast coast. The caves (Fontein noted for early Amerindian drawings, Guadirikiri whose claim to fame is bats, and Huliba) are northwest of San Nicolas. And the Tunnel of Love, talked about as an underground passage (but never seen by me) is here also.

The well-paved road that passes the community of Paradera, on the route to Seroe Plat, leads also to the oft-mentioned abandoned gold mines. Since there is little left of the alluvial gold, and since the panning was done on the surface, the site isn't much to look at these days.

At Casibari, a few miles west of midisland, huge boulders perch on the sun-dried landscape. A few provide pockets for a rock garden; the area is one of the favorite picture places for scenes of the *cunucu,* as the countryside is called in Papiamentu.

Due to the constant wind, dry weather, and an unforgiving growing climate, there are few insects or birds that are indigenous to Aruba. An oval area across the road from the hotel strip has been set aside as a bird sanctuary. Aruba's tiny, brilliant green and yellow parakeets can be seen here.

Insofar as beaches are concerned, in addition to Palm Beach and Druif Beach, where most of the hotels are located, Rogers Beach and Baby Beach, both near San Nicolas, are popular with residents. (Baby Beach is especially good for snorkeling.) Privately owned Adacuri Beach, on the northeast coast, is known for its lively surf. Surfing is also popular north of Palm Beach, where the wind whips around Kudarebe, the northwestern point that is marked by the California dunes and lighthouse.

About midway on the north coast, there's a much photographed area where the rocks have been chiseled by wind, sea, and sand into "The Natural Bridge."

PLACES WORTH FINDING are mostly in Oranjestad; sights around the island are the natural ones, mentioned above. ***ORANJESTAD,*** the capital, takes its name from the Netherlands' House of Orange, and took its first importance from the fact that the wily Dutch knew the value of a fort for protection from invasions. They built **Fort Zoutman,** named after a famous Dutch rear admiral who made a name for himself in the many English-Dutch 18th-century forays. The site at Paardenbaai was a new location, far west on the south coast from where the previous commander had lived (near San Nicolas at the Commandeursbaai). Most activity took place around the fort, and as houses grew near the walls, the town expanded—just in time to be named for the House of Orange in the early 1800s. The fort's William III Tower takes its name from the regent, since the lamp that made it a lighthouse was first lit on the King's birthday. The **Aruba Historical Museum,** located in one big room of the fort, deserves at least an hour, for touchstones of this unusual island's history. It holds an interesting collection from Indian to more recent times.

One esoteric museum choice for those with special interests includes the **shell collection** of Mr. and Mrs. DeMan. They will sometimes open their home to visitors who make an appointment T 011+ 2–4246. **The Museo Numismatico** (T 297+ 82–8831) at the Instituto di Cultura on J. E. Yrausquin square holds the money and coin collection of Mario Odor. Telephone to find out when the place is open.

Head for the waterfront for wandering. The sloops and ships that tie up along the cement strip sell from their decks and charters for fishing can be arranged from the dock next to the Bali restaurant. Although you may not be in the market for vegetables from Venezuela, it is interesting to see what is sold from the boat decks.

Mar-Lab is one of the more interesting tours to come onto the Aruban activities roster. With your sneakers and bathing suit (plus cover up), you can sign on for a few hours of climbing over the rocks and snorkeling plus a visit to the "Aruba Sea-Life Park." Organized tours, with a biologist to discuss the flora and fauna, can be arranged through your hotel's activities desk.

Lago Oil & Transport Company, Ltd., a wholly owned subsidiary of Exxon, was largely responsible for the expansion of San Nicolas (the cutback in employees due to automation and the official closing of the refinery in early '85, is largely responsible for the fact that a lot of San Nicolas residents now drive taxis, or travel a long way to work at the Palm Beach and Druif Beach hotels, if they're lucky enough to get a job). The refinery opened on August 12, 1924, and used to be a transshipment port for VLCCs (Very Large Crude Carriers).

SPORTS are mostly sea-centered, with action along the shore of Palm Beach, where *De Palm Watersports* and *Pelican Tours* maintain desks at most of the big hotels. (See "Touring" for Aruban addresses of each firm's head office.)

Deep-sea fishing can be arranged from most hotels, and costs about $150 for a half day and $300 for a full day, for 4 people, with a charge of $20 per person for any extras up to 6. Captain Ricardo takes his *Gena* out in search of sailfish, blue marlin, amberjack, and other fish, and you're expected to give him any catch in lieu of a tip, as is the practice with many deep-sea fishermen.

Snorkeling can be enjoyed off shores near the hotels, but the watersports' desks provide special excursions. Beachside firms also have equipment to rent, but my suggestion is to bring your own mask and flippers if you enjoy snorkeling. The chance of your getting rental equipment that fits as well as your own is slim except, perhaps, at *Peter Hughes Dive Shop* at the Divi hotels.

Scuba instruction starts in your hotel pool, with other novices who signed up when you did. Cost for in-pool instruction and one dive is about $40 per person, but the trips to the reefs for experienced divers are $45 per person, minimum of 2, or—if there are several of you—the boat will go when you want to, at a fee you negotiate. Usual departures are at 11 and 2. If the trip is not leaving from your hotel (due to a light house count) you can stroll down the beach to one of the other bastions to sign on with their group. No matter where you start, go to the reefs or wrecks, and there are two main features with the latter. The *Antilia*, a German freighter whose captain bailed out as soon as World War II was declared, is one. The captain crept ashore on the Dutch island to surrender after he submerged his ship in about 66 feet of sand off the shore. (According to one oft-told tale, the crew then went over to Bonaire for the duration of the war.) The other wreck is the *Pedernales*, an oil tanker that happened to be trafficking between Venezuela and Aruba in May 1941. She was split at the seams by a German sub, and when her sinking site put her in a major shipping lane, her bottom was dragged to a shallow spot where she was used for target practice by U.S. marines. Now the coral that grows on her sides and the fish that hover around make the wreck fascinating for underwater viewing. The Divi hotels' focus on scuba, with *Peter Hughes Dive Shop,* was the start of the recent enthusiasm. *Scuba Aruba* (T 297+ 83–4142) also has a full range of facilities.

Sailing is aboard whatever boats are moored offshore. Recent possibilities have included *Tranquillo* and *Seaventure,* trimarans, for cruises along the west coast. *Tranquillo* takes from 8 to 25 people on an all-day cruise with a two-hour interlude to enjoy a picnic lunch, snorkeling, and swimming. *Seaventure* divides its day into segments, with two-hour morning, early-afternoon, and cocktail cruises along the west coast. De Palm and Pelican are the operators; check with them about any other boats available.

Boardsailing is possible at the Palm Beach hotels, as well as out of Divi Divi, Tamarijn, Manchebo Beach, and Aruba Beach Club, but the prized area is north of Malmok to Arasji and California Dunes. Small hotels and boarding houses in this area are hubs for surfers, as is the shore. *Sailboard Vacations* (T 297+ 82–1072), *Divi Winds* (T 297+ 83–5000), and *Rogers Windsurf* (T 297+ 82–1918) are the leaders with equipment, lessons, and events.

Golf is limited to the dry and dusty Aruba Golf Course, formerly the exclusive domain of the Lago-Exxon top staff, where "greens fees" for sand "greens," are about $10 for 18-holes, caddies are $10, and clubs rent for $6. There's a mini-golf course at the Holiday Inn.

Tennis courts speckle most of the resort hotels. Prepare yourself for windy play, even when the courts have baffles. Early morning, late in the day, or at night on those courts with lights, are the *only* times sane folk play. (The sun is too strong at other times.)

TREASURES AND TRIFLES range from the world's luxuries (carried in some of the stores in Oranjestad and in boutiques in the luxury hotels) to the ubiquitous T-shirts, books about Aruba, and some crafts. Cosmetics and lotions made from the locally grown aloe cactus are a good buy.

Attractive, interesting shopping malls have been built in recent seasons, supplementing the always popular boutique-filled area near the Alhambra casino, in the vicinity of the *Divi* hotels and Manchebo Beach. The **Seaport Village Mall,** near the *Sonesta* hotel, has almost 80 shops, including places that carry well-known clothing and accessory names such as Gucci, Givenchy, and Ralph Lauren, plus perfumes, crystal, and other luxury items.

The **Swain Wharf** area at Harbourtown Village, in Oranjestad, has several small shops that carry island-made items, such as batik clothing and wall hangings and pottery.

AUTHOR'S OBSERVATION

South American gems are imported and sold in Aruba, but do some research about quality of stones before you make your purchase. Expensive and dramatic jewelry is sold in many high-quality shops in Oranjestad and in the best hotels.

In addition to European (and American) sunglasses, binoculars, cameras, and other precision equipment, Aruban supermarkets and airport shops carry Dutch cheese, chocolate, and tinned items, as well as food imports from many of the members of the European Economic Community.

It's sometimes possible to find dramatic and colorful resort clothes, many of them European imports, but you'll have to cull through a lot of mediocre merchandise to find the best buys.

AUTHOR'S OBSERVATION

Although shops are officially open 8–12 and 2–6, Monday through Saturday, be sure to check on the afternoon hours. Some shops close Tuesday afternoons, a few on Saturday, and some small places button up completely if business is light (sometimes in spring or fall) and the staff needs a holiday. Check also on Aruban holidays.

BARBADOS

Barbados Board of Tourism, Box 242, Prescod Blvd. & Harbour Rd., Bridgetown, Barbados, W.I., T 809+427–2623, fax 809+ 426–4080; #1215, 3440 Wilshire Blvd., Los Angeles, CA 90010, T 213+380–2198; 800 Second Ave., New York, NY 10017, T 212+986–6516 or 800+ 221–9831, fax 212–573–9850; #1508, 20 Queen St. West, Toronto, Ontario, Canada M5H 3R3, T 416+979–2472, fax 416+ 979–8726; #960, 615 Dorchester West Blvd., Montreal, Quebec, Canada H3B 1P5, T 514+861–0085, fax 514+ 861–7917; 263 Tottenham Court Rd., London, England W1P 9AA, T 01+636–9448.

$ · · · US$1 = Bds$1.98
Unless otherwise noted, $ refers to U.S. currency.

When Mr. Lowe at Payne's Bay looked up from his other customers, he was surprised to see me—an obvious visitor—in his small shop. But Donald, a Barbadian I'd talked with a few minutes before, had told me that Mr. Lowe would have the candle for the special wax I needed to go with lime for medication to minister to my friend's foot full of sea urchin spines. Mr. Lowe not only had the homemade candle, he also took the time to tell me the proper sequence: lime juice first, then wax, then ignore—until the wax peels off by itself. The heat of the wax draws the spine, he said, or causes it to die through "lack of oxygen"—he wasn't sure which. But the result was no pain, no infection, and by the next day, no evidence of the encounter with the urchin.

Life in Barbados these days is a wonderful intertwining of time-honored traditions and the comforts of the 20th century. Wise visitors make time, away from the overbuilding and saturation of tourist services that plague some areas, to look around and find the essence that makes life in Barbados unique.

There's the rugged and often windy east coast shore, for example, where a spontaneous picnic—cheese, fruit, cold chicken, warm bread, and wine—can provide a memory to pull off the "experience" shelf for many years.

And there are the horse races, on weekends in winter, when most of Barbados turns out, to drape themselves over the railings that surround the track if they haven't bought admission for the bleachers (boxes are reserved for dignitaries). My best tip came from an elbow-high, wide-eyed boy who lingered at my side long enough to answer my question with a whispered reply that required a bow to hear, before I could stroll to the window to place my bet. He's also the one who tipped me off to drinking sorrel, a West Indian soft drink. He said it was better than Banks' beer, brewed in Barbados and a good post-tennis refresher.

But it was Barbara who introduced me to her friend Marva at the produce stalls, where the local fruits and vegetables were piled high, waiting for purchase. And between the two of them, I learned the many uses for Christophene, a squashlike West Indian vegetable that is marvelously mellow when boiled with butter and milk, but cucumber-crunchy when cut in slices and served as a cocktail snack. (Barbara alone shared her knowledge of how to tell when a breadfruit is ripe, and at least five recipes for fixing it.)

Many years ago, before the crop of vendors began to grow on the beaches, there was a lady who used to come along the south shore road early in the morning, singing "Fly-eeng Feesh" to the accompaniment of the wooden-wheeled cart that carried the flying fish. And hand-hewn boats made up the fleet that was pushed through the rough seas until fishermen could set sail before the first light of dawn to catch them. In the center of Bridgetown, there was a much-photographed Barbadian face, topped with a towering cauldron of boiled bark juice known as mauby, the Coca Cola of Barbados. Today the mauby is often in bottles, the fishing fleet is motorized, and the flying fish is bought from baskets at the shore, wherever the fleet comes in.

Although the island is only 21 miles long by 14 miles wide at its broadest part, people who lived in a west shore village years ago seldom got to the east. If you were born around Holetown, you stayed there. Someone in your family went out to fish for food, and perhaps someone knew that the town was named Jamestown when a landing party from the *Olive Blossom* stepped ashore long enough to pound a cross into the ground, and to carve "James, King of England and this island" on a tree. That was 1605, and it was 20 years later, after the king had granted the island to the Earl of Marlborough, that a settling party established a community. (And it was two years after that that Marlborough lost his colony to the Earl of Carlisle, and a settlement started at Carlisle Bay, where they built a bridge—at Bridgetown.) This island had always been British—until 1966 when it became independent.

AUTHOR'S OBSERVATION

Beach vendors flourish on Barbadian shores. Beware and be firm. Although local officials are striving to control the proliferation, the beach vendors are well-organized about voicing their right to make a living. The fact is no matter what they're selling (and it ranges from clothes to artwork to shell and coral jewelry to marijuana and heavier drugs), they are peskier than the sand flies that sometimes settle on the beaches at sunset. I have found that a polite-but-firm "No, thank you" even before they start their sales pitch keeps the bother to a minimum, but if you take time to look at the merchandise, you are fair game for a long "conversation," and often an overpriced purchase.

POLITICAL PICTURE: The government is based on the British system, with elections called every five years. Prime Minister Erskine Sandiford succeeded to his office following the death of Prime Minister Errol Barrow, who was elected Prime Minister in May 1986. Sandiford's party won elections held in spring of '91 and he continues as Prime Minister.

With a strong two-party system since independence from Britain in November 1966, the country now has three significant political parties. The Prime Minister's Democratic Labour Party and the Barbados Labour Party (founded by Sir Grantley Adams more than 35 years ago) were joined, in March '89, by the National Democratic Party, formed by a splinter group from the ruling Democratic Labour Party, with Dr. Richard Haynes as leader.

All three parties support free-enterprise, have strong social conscience and viable domestic programs, and acknowledge the need for labor-intensive industries. They differ in methods to achieve full employment and an improved standard of living. In spite of the differences, Barbados continues to be one of the Caribbean's most stable countries.

The country has one of the Caribbean's highest standards of living, in spite of the fact that the island does not have much in the way of natural resources.

Although the sugar industry is still an important factor in the economy, tourism and light manufacturing are the main sources for employment and hard currency. An active Industrial Development Corporation encourages joint ventures with U.S., Canadian, and other foreign companies.

Because of its location, quality communications, and worker skills, Barbados has become an administrative center for the Eastern Caribbean area. The United States Embassy in Barbados is responsible for the Eastern Caribbean countries, including Dominica, St. Lucia, St. Vincent and its Grenadines, Montserrat and Antigua. In addition, Barbados is the home for the Caribbean Development Bank, the Caribbean Association of Industry and Commerce, the the Caribbean Tourism and Research Centre, and the administrative office for Peace Corps in the Eastern Caribbean, as well as the regional office for the United States Agency for International Development (U.S. AID).

Tourism is acknowledged as the major wage earner and source for employment, whether the jobs come with construction of new hotels or with staff positions once the hotels are open. Always a popular destination for Europeans, Barbados has been a vacation center for British visitors as well as North and South Americans.

ISLAND APPEARANCE: Barbados is entirely surrounded by the Atlantic Ocean; it lies east of the Caribbean Sea, although it has many characteristics of the other islands. The usual approach by plane sweeps in toward the southwest coast and crosses the southern sector from Needham's Point (where Fort Charles has been incorporated into the grounds of the Barbados Hilton Hotel) along the coast. Those who sit on the lefthand side of the airplane have a spectacular view of Bridgetown and the coast.

Commonly referred to as "pear-shaped," the country claims about 166 square miles of limestone outcropping, rising out of the sea far east of the rest of the Caribbean chain. Laced with caves, a midsection has recently been commercialized as Harrison Caves and other portions have been set aside as nature preserves. The south coast is cluttered with tourism trappings from Oistins to Bridgetown; the west coast also has a thick border of hotels, villas, apartments, restaurants, and shops. The island rises to a bluff on the east coast, before dropping sharply to plains that stretch to the sea. Once covered with sugar cane, many acres are still devoted to the crop, which borders the country roads until it is harvested.

AUTHOR'S OBSERVATION

Barbados urgently needs an environmental plan that will be enforced, with strict zoning laws and building codes. Already, the west coast beaches are seriously eroded at some times of the year; they are slivers at others. The random building along the southwest coastal road is not only unattractive, but dangerous for both walking and driving.

Most Barbadians (98%) are of African descent; a small percentage claim early British and Scottish settlers as ancestors.

LIFESTYLE is distinctly Barbadian, with some once British traditions now firmly integrated into Barbadian patterns. Many of the hotels offer afternoon tea, a preference of British visitors as well as Barbadians, and the Police Band and mounted horse guard perform with a precision recognized as being part of a British heritage.

Cricket is a national passion, especially since Barbados has birthed several of the top cricket players—Sir Garfield Sobers, Sir Frank Worrell, John Goddard, and Everton Weeks among them. From June through January, a crop of small transistors grow from Barbadian ears, and conversation can only take place when a cricket score does not. Matches can be witnessed at Garrison Savannah and at almost any patch of sand, or island field, when enough kids can be gathered together to field a team.

The horse races, at the Barbados Turf Club on the Savannah, draw crowds of Barbadians and visitors who enjoy doing what the residents do, and the polo matches at the west coast field (near Sandy Lane) are socially acceptable events for winter high-season.

Barbadian traditions have been assembled for an entertaining evening of song, dance, and legends. "1627 and All That Sort of Thing" is a dinner-and-show event at the Barbados Museum, at the Garrison Savannah near Bridgetown, and the same producers have staged a second event called "Barbados, Barbados," based on legends about former island resident Rachel Pringle. That show takes place at Balls Plantation, in the countryside. Transportation from your hotel is included (as are dinner and drinks) in the ticket price for each of the evenings.

AUTHOR'S OBSERVATION

Some Barbadians in the "front line" of tourism seem to have succumbed to the lure of cash; sacrificing common courtesies in the process. In recent travels, I have frequently been overcharged and overhassled. Don't be surprised if you're treated rudely, especially by the airport's taxi crowd. If you feel "pushed around," voice your written complaint to the Tourist Board.

The people of the country are called Barbadians. The term "Bajan," although also used by some, seems to me to be less common these days, perhaps because it was used constantly by the British in the old days. It's a contraction of "Barbadian." "Bim" is the affectionate name for the country.

Clothes are conservative, not only on residents who will dress up to go into Bridgetown, and to church, but also on most visitors. Splashy resort wear is OK for the luxury hotels, and for special social fetes around the island, but for most roaming around, conservative, neat, and comfortable warm weather dress is appreciated by the residents who take pride in calling this place home.

MEDICAL FACILITIES: The 600-bed, multi-story Queen Elizabeth Hospital near downtown Bridgetown is overcrowded, and reportedly understaffed, although facilities are reasonably good, with private rooms as well as wards. There is ambulance service. Many doctors practicing in Barbados have received their training in England, Canada, the U.S., and European countries. Most of the hotels have at least one nearby doctor on call. Services at health clinics around the country are available free for Barbadians. Air ambulance operates from Barbados, but it's a long flight to Miami.

MONEY MATTERS: When in doubt, ask whether the price you are being quoted is in U.S. or Barbadian dollars; US$1 equals about Bds$2. Banks usually take a few cents on the dollar for their changing service, so the rate you receive is closer to Bds$1.94 for each US$1. There is a branch bank at the airport before you go through Immigration. The taxi fare you pay from the airport (or pier) to your hotel will be in Barbados dollars. Hotels here, as everywhere else in the tourist-oriented world, charge a premium for their exchange services. Most bills will be presented in Barbadian currency unless you've paid your travel agent in U.S. dollars in advance. Credit cards are accepted at many hotels, restaurants, and stores.

COMMUNICATIONS include direct dial telephone and facsimile machines, with communications from North America and elsewhere accomplished by dialing 809 area code + 42 or 43 Barbados code + 5-digit number. There is no charge for local telephone calls. Barbados External Telecommunications Ltd. (T 809+427–5200) offers worldwide communications. Local telephone service is handled through Barbados Telecommunications (Bartel.) For AT&T's USA-Direct service while in Barbados, find one of the designated telephones (there are some at the cruise ship pier) or dial 1+ 412+ 555-7458 collect to reach an AT&T operator who can assist. Airmail postage to Barbados is 50 cents for the first ½ ounce; count on mail taking two weeks at least. Facsimile machines are used by most businesses, including hotels. Television and newspapers are good quality. Both the *Barbados Advocate* and *The Nation* carry local and international news.

ARRIVAL in Barbados is businesslike and usually orderly. Grantley Adams International Airport, opened in '79, is a full-service facility with spokes to Britain and Europe as well as to the U.S., Canada, South America, and the rest of the Caribbean. When the big planes arrive, lines for immigration procedures can be long and *slow*. The Barbados Tourism and Hotel Association booth (where you can make hotel reservations if you arrive without any) is a valuable travelers' aid. I have used the on-the-spot reservation service countless times, and have found the staff efficient, helpful, and welcoming. The booth is a few steps from the airport branch of the Barbados National Bank, one place where you can change your money to local currency.

When you pass through customs (perfunctory if you seem to have only tourist trappings), you are "out the door" and at the taxi stand.

AUTHOR'S OBSERVATION

The taxi "dispatching" has been chaotic on some of my recent arrivals. Drivers seem more interested in their deals with groups (and, I suspect, the hope for bigger tips) than in taking the next in line. Dispatchers appear to give better care to their driver-friends than to those of us waiting for a single taxi.

CRUISE ship arrivals are usually at the Deep Water Harbour's pier, where taxis are waiting if you choose not to make the long (and hot) walk to the nearby shops at Pelican Village or the even longer walk into Bridgetown. If you happen to be on a ship that anchors out, the passengers are sent into shore by small boats; avoid the first-off-the-ship crush, and enjoy the view from shipside. There will be taxis around at all times. In addition to being a port of call for many cruises, Barbados is homeport for several small-ship cruises, some of which go to Palm Island in the Grenadines, Grenada, Guyana, Tobago, St. Lucia, and Martinique. The weekly departures operate fall through spring. Some of the other ships that stop here are willing to drop off (or pick up) passengers also.

Plantation houses such as Drax Hall, Villa Nova, and Sunbury House, plus botanic gardens, a wildlife park, and Harrison Caves are among the sights to see. The capital of Bridgetown can be overwhelming for first-time visitors but the shops yield treasures and the careenage and harbor area have cafes and plenty of nautical interest. Adventuresome travelers should consider making advance arrangements for renting a car, to drive around and explore.

DEPARTURE is relatively pleasant, but be prepared for l-o-n-g and slow check-in lines if you are heading out on a big plane flight. Even though your island traveling may tempt you to ignore the warning to check in more than one hour before flight time, do what you are told! If you don't appear in plenty of time, your seat may be given to a stand-by passenger, especially if you are flying one of the commuter airlines, the small plane services to neighboring islands, where seats are at a premium and wise island travelers know they can "always" get a last-minute seat. There's a departure tax of Bds$20 or US$10.

There are shops, with interesting merchandise (including Barbados Mount Gay rum and other liquor), at the airport. But know in advance that the walk from the terminal to the plane on the tarmac can seem interminable if you are laden with packages. The "in-bond" shopping pick-up desk is convenient (near the exit doors for flight departure), and the system works in Barbados. (See "Treasures and Trifles" comment.)

TOURING TIPS: Taxis are ready and willing to take you where you want to go and to pick you up after you dine, swim, tour, or whatever. Be sure to ask the going rate (and whose dollars) for the kind of tour or other journey you want *before* you get into a cab. Your hotel will be able to suggest reliable drivers. Mr. Simpson (T 809+435–6727 or 435–6303) has been my "pilot" on a couple of occasions. From his south-coast base, he has willingly (and dependably) picked me up for 6 a.m. flight departures and other assorted tasks.

AUTHOR'S OBSERVATION

Barbados offers well-organized information for visitors. The country's two newspapers—the *Advocate* and the *Nation*—are good sources for what's happening at the minute. *The Visitor* is a newssheet full of facts about restaurants and activities, and the *Barbados Tourist News* is also fact-filled. (Both are available free from hotels and at other visitor depots.)

Rental cars are the easiest way to get around if you enjoy spontaneous roaming. Rental choices range from open-to-breezes, Australian-hardy, mini-Mokes (a back-cracking small car that can seem more like a cart on wheels) to Subarus, Datsuns, Suzukis, and other more substantial cars. On several occasions I have rented from *Sunny Isle Motors* (T 809+428–8009), located in Worthing, on the island side of the road that borders the busy southwest coast. *Avis* and the other brand names make the most of their famous name by charging the highest rates in Barbados. *Dear's Garage* (T 809+429–9277 and 809+427–7853) has taxis, chauffeur-driven cars, *and* rental cars. *Sun Crest Rent-a-Car* (T 809+432–1482) has mini-Mokes, the larger sun-Moke, and enclosed cars, and *Direct Rentals* (T 809+426–3221) has Suzuki vans and cars. There are several other rental firms around the island. Each hotel has its link, and some have their own rental cars.

If you want a car during the winter peak season, it's wise to reserve when you make your hotel reservation. Driving is on the left, British-style, and a Barbadian driver's license can be purchased when you rent your car, for Bds$30 for one year. Barbadian roads are good, but often traffic-clogged, especially at business commuting hours in and around Bridgetown. The new ABC (Adams-Barrow-Cummins) highway cuts from the airport to the west coast just north of Bridgetown, avoiding most of the capital clog.

The **public bus** system is good. One route passes the airport, between Bridgetown and the east coast. Visitors should avoid public buses at commuter's hours (from 8–9:30 in the morning, around lunchtime, and from 3:30–6 p.m.), when they are needed by Barbadians to get to work or school. At other times, the service that runs along the south and west coasts can be an excursion, and an inexpensive way to get to Bridgetown or to other hotels for lunch or a day at the beach if you are not staying near one. Most buses are relatively modern; all are labeled with their destination, and bus drivers are helpful with directions if you can't figure out the place names.

LODGING: There are literally hundreds of rooms, in all shapes and sizes, and in all degrees of comfort. Always known to wise British and Europeans—

both those who seek the luxury of a private pool-studded villa and those who want a simple housekeeping room-or-two, the facilities are now very popular also with Canadians who come by packaged planeloads.

> **AUTHOR'S OBSERVATION**
>
> In a trend-setting move, the Barbados Hotel Association, in cooperation with the Barbados Tourist Board, operates a central lodging reservations service through a toll-free 800 number—800+ 462–2526 or 800+ GO–BAJAN. You and/or your travel agent can make reservations instantly by dialing that number in the U.S. and Canada. From other countries, the offices of Utell International can make reservations. Funds for the system were supplied by the Barbados Tourism Development Corporation, a group of private companies who contribute a percentage of their profits for promotion of the country's tourism. The project is to be applauded, not only for the obvious cooperation offered by the private sector, but for the service to travelers.

It's important to research carefully, not only for the facilities on the property, but with questions about the surroundings. A few properties that could be luxurious are set amid unattractive developments. Long known for low-rise luxury, the St. James (west) coast is now on the verge of overbuilding. The southwest coast is already overbuilt; it is a warren of places to stay. The general trend is for the monied visitors to head for the west coast; all others fold themselves into the less-expensive lodgings on the southwest and south coasts, where it's usually easy to walk to beach, restaurants, and other activities.

International corporations—Hilton, Marriott, Cunard-Trafalgar, Trust House Forte, and others—include local style in their Barbadian properties. In addition to the places that offer expected hotel facilities, there's a long list of apartment and villa accommodations, some of which also have a restaurant and bar area, plus entertainment and watersports. Many small and inexpensive places are also very basic; the chic small spots charge accordingly.

Be sure to ask, in advance, about additional charges to the quoted room rate. There is a 5% government tax, and most places add at least 10% as a service charge, but there may be other "extras."

> **AUTHOR'S AWARDS**
>
> *Sandy Lane*'s total overhaul makes it the country's most luxurious property, not only because its "private estate" ambience is sensational, but because European and other guests help set the tone; *Coral Reef* continues to be a personal favorite, for its traditional lifestyle; my favorite small hotel is *Ocean View,* because it's bold enough to hold on to its Barbadian heritage. A special nod goes to *Kingsley Club,* because it offers an ideal hideaway in simplest, hospitable style.

Information about places-to-stay is included under Hotels/Resorts, Housekeeping Holidays, The Inn Way, and Low-Cost Lodging. Stars are awarded within each category. (See page 11.)

HOTELS/RESORTS range from attractive small hotels nestled at secluded niches on long beaches to huge, sprawling resorts, some of which seem to have expanded solely on the whim of the current moneyman. Careful research pays off when making your travel plans. Ask a lot of questions—of your travel agent, the Barbados Tourist Board, and your friends—before booking.

Barbados Beach Village • *at Fitts Village on the west coast about 15 minutes' drive north of Bridgetown* • focuses on action, with the pool and its pavilion plus the small and busy beach offering a place for sailing and other watersports. Tennis courts are across the road, but you'll have to drive (or take the west coast bus) to Sandy Lane for golf. Count on groups; investigate special weeklong holiday plans. Don't expect the last word in housekeeping or staff attention. *Hotel.*

★★★ **Buccaneer Bay** • *at Paynes Bay, not far from Bridgetown* • is an attractive beach-and-pool-focused place, with airy central patio and pleasant social bar. Most of the air-conditioned rooms in the 2-story buildings give you a sea view; all have a small refrigerator, plus toaster and teakettle. The terrace is pleasant for sitting and sunning. The bus runs along the main shore road outside, connecting you to the string of hotels to the north and to Bridgetown, 6 miles south, if you choose not to rent a car. Entertainment is planned some evenings; ask about special package plans. *Small hotel.*

★★★★ **Cobblers Cove** • *on the west shore, in northern St. Peter's Parish* • gets high marks for congenial, comfortable surroundings. Rooms, which are suites, are gathered around the pool and main house, with the feeling of an estate. The 2-story units have bedroom, living area that opens for view, and patio or terrace depending on whether your suite is ground level or upstairs, plus all comforts. The Camelot Suite is the most luxurious, in the main house. Ably managed by Hamisch Watson, who headed southeast from Antigua's Blue Waters in '88, this enclave has been one of my long-time favorites. Among its few drawbacks is traffic along the main west coast road and limited acreage that makes finding a place to park your car (and sometimes yourself) a challenge. Although the edge of the pool may seem crowded when the hotel is full, there's a strand of sand (shared with Claudette Colbert and other noteworthy neighbors) that proves perfect for early-morning walks or twilight wandering. Music, some evenings and at the Sunday midday buffet, supplements conversations with fellow guests (usually British, with a few Americans and Canadians) for entertainment. Meals on the seaside terrace are typically tropical, with sea breezes complementing the sea sounds. Watersports are offered at the beach and touring tips are freely given by the front desk staff. *Small hotel.*

★★ **Coconut Creek Hotel** • *on the west coast, south of Holetown* • joined the Colony Club and Tamarind Cove family in early '85, in an ownership triumvirate that bespeaks quality, comforts, and Caribbean personality. A pub atmosphere in the common rooms has been this hotel's trademark since its opening several years ago with another owner's hand at the helm. The original cluster of several small cottages is saved from seeming cluttered by the fact that the units are on several levels from roadside to sea. The pool is a few steps down from the reception, dining, and drinking area, and the beach is down from that. Newer rooms, to the left of the original group as you face the sea, follow the usual 2-story plan, with sea view a prime part of each unit's decor. Evening entertainment is limited to music a few nights each week and there's the option to exchange mealtimes with the related hotels; daytimes include the opportunity to enjoy their beaches and watersports. *Small hotel.*

★★★★ **Colony Club** • *near Holetown on the west coast* • and next door to Coral Reef, settles its guests into a few 3-story banks of rooms, a few steps from the beach shared with the other west coast hotels in this area. Traditionally catering to a British clientele, Colony serves afternoon tea and takes care of its guests with time-honored traditions. Antiques and flower arrangements punctuate the public rooms and patio, and there's a pool for guests who prefer not to have sand on their toes. Evening entertainment is limited to music a few nights a week; most guests turn in early. This place would appeal to vacationers who want quality and quiet surroundings. *Hotel.*

★★★★ **Coral Reef** • *on the west coast, near Holetown* • is one of my longtime favorites. I like the fact that cottage rooms are scattered around the grounds, that flower arrangements are a feature of the public areas, that many of the staff have been here "forever," and that the property is still a family-run place—with Cynthia and Budge O'Hara now yielding most of the helmsmanship to their daughter, Karon, and sons, Mark and Patrick. The property has had an extensive refurbishing for this season, with new paint and fabrics where needed. Some bedrooms seem small; many bathrooms are distinctly '50s; and the traffic along the beach—a scourge for all the luxury hotels—is a nuisance when you're snoozing in the sun. However, the pool is very private and flourishing tropical foliage borders the beach, lending privacy to most bedrooms. The single story main house has welcoming arms of rooms; other rooms are around the grounds, in an assortment of buildings. Opened some 30-plus years ago, the hotel has Colony Club as a nextdoor neighbor, and other hotels just a stroll along the beach. All watersports are nearby, as is tennis. *Classic hotel.*

★★ **Cunard's Paradise Beach Hotel** • *on the northwest coast, about 10 minutes from downtown Bridgetown* • is a sprawling resort with a link to Cunard's cruises that can give you combination sea-and-shore holidays. Extensive renovations (and building) are constant, in a race to keep this place up to snuff. One recent modification is the inclusive plan called "Club Paradise." *The Carvery,* in the hotel's Batavia wing (one of the older buildings along the beach) has a Sunday Bajan buffet for Bds$45. The entertainment program is geared to offering you a fun-filled holiday. Watersports are available at the beach area, and buffets, music, and other special events keep the weekly calendar interesting. There's a battery of shops near the hotel's entrance, and good restaurants off the premises, but not too far away by taxi or rental car. Inquire about special plans. Some rooms offer sea view, but if it's important to you, be sure to request one; others may be hillside or back of buildings. *Resort.*

★★★ **Discovery Bay** • *on the St. James coast at Holetown* • is popular with well-heeled European guests as well as wise North Americans. Nestled at the small bridge that marks Holetown, the hotel's imposing entrance leads to a courtyard that is pool-punctuated, with two arms of rooms that stretch toward the beach and sea. A refurbishing program in late '85 added welcome improvements as well as new furniture to many rooms. Convenience to Holetown makes a car necessary only for exploring. You can walk to shops, and have a few right at the parking area for the hotel. Guests in the 84 rooms are often repeaters who call this place their winter home. The tennis court is floodlit for night play and watersports are available. *Classic hotel.*

★★★ **Divi South Winds Resort** • *on the south coast in the hotel-flecked St. Lawrence area* • a member of the Ithaca-New York-based Divi family, claims 20 acres on both sides of the coast-rimming road, with multilevel rooms, suites, and apartments clustering around the central pool. Beachside dining is Italian-style; one new restaurant features salads in a wicker, plant-filled decor; other mealtimes are complemented by a pianist, fashion shows, cabaret, or other events. There are 3 pools, 2 tennis courts, and weekly parties and other events. You're within walking distance of some of the country's best restaurants and a couple of popular nightspots, as well as shops and car rentals or bus services. *Resort.*

Eastry House Hotel and Apartments • *on a hillside, in St. Peter Parish* • is an estate, owned by Gordon and Pat Carlstrom. The once private Eastry House was first opened in the late 1950s as an elegant restaurant, with a few personalized bedrooms. In recent years, more bedrooms have been added, as have modern apartments in a separate building, and the property has a Barbadian-European atmosphere. Several rooms have a lovely sea view; all are comfortably furnished. Dinners are served in elegant style in the original main house; high tea and other beverages are served on the terrace, with a view of the sea. There's a pool near the main house, with tennis court nearby. It's a long (hot) walk along the road, down the hill, to the shore; a car makes that jaunt easier. *Small hotel & Apts.*

★★★ **Grand Barbados Beach Hotel** • *on the beach at Carlisle Bay* • is a full-service, modern, vacation and business hotel within a few minutes' drive (one mile) of the capital's core. Not only does the one-time Holiday Inn have a Barbadian personality, but it also makes the most of a wedge of beachfront, with air-conditioned and alfresco dining areas, and 29 rooms on two executive floors (6 and 7) where special staff are helpful and room amenities include color TV, minibar, hairdryers, and cosmetics. Ask for an end room for the best view, or a room in the Aquatic Club wing for the most privacy. It's over the sea at the end of the sunning pier that also holds the *Boardwalk Cafe* in midsection and *The Schooner* seafood restaurant. The *Golden Shell* dining room serves entrees with style and flair. Next door to the *Barbados Yacht Club,* across the road from the *Island Inn,* and within easy walk of the *Hilton,* Grand Barbados is a convenient base. Watersports include windsurfing and scuba instruction. Tennis is nearby. The activities desk arranges for tours, rental cars, and evening activities at the on-premises *Coral Garden* or elsewhere on the island. Sundries and reading material are available from Ross's *Holiday Shop* near the entrance; shops are also nearby. *Hotel.*

★★ **Ginger Bay Beach Club** • *on the southeast coast not far from Marriott's Sam Lord's Castle* • is lonesome on the windswept southeast coast, where management focuses on Barbadian hospitality. The white powdery beach is one of the island's best, and the attractive living units give a homey feeling to the place. Although the hotel seems remote, Bridgetown is only 25 minutes' drive along the coast road. *Small hotel.*

Half Moon • *on the busy south coast* • claims a prominent place on the sand-trimmed shoreline, and plants its guests in 1- and 2-bedroom apartments, with a garden and pool view. The 3-story building gives everyone a balcony, and the location (15 minutes from Bridgetown in one direction and 15 minutes from the airport, in the other) can be convenient if you have a car. This place has become a popular base for reasonable-to-low-cost package plans. (Buses run along the main road, but it's a few minutes' walk to the bus stop.) *Hotel.*

★★ **Heywoods Resort** • *north on the west coast* • was adopted into the Wyndham family in early 1989, but staff attitude is still a problem. (Many seemed diffident and careless.) The multi-building complex offers "everything," with 2 pools, tennis, pitch-and-putt golf, watersports facilities, a long beach (which sometimes suffers from ground swells and feet-hurting coral), tennis courts, several restaurants, shops, and activities. The 2- and 3-story plantation-style buildings are parallel to the shore, with the feeling of a town. Sugar Mill House is at the northern end of the complex, close to the Captain's Quarters and its *Captain's Table* restaurant. Other buildings—The Antillean, Little Bristol, and Calabali—have apartments, studios, and standard hotel rooms. Other restaurants include *Caroline's,* at the shore; *El Comedor,* with a Spanish tone; and *Trawlers,* for seafood. Menus (and cooking styles) seemed to cater to basic American tastes, but some improvements may have been made by the time you visit. *Club Miliki,* the disco, is lively when there's an active group in the hotel. Although the west coast public bus reaches here from the capital and the hotel operates a daily shuttle bus for shopping, a rental car gives complete freedom. The resort's a long way out; it needs package tours from Europe, Britain, Canada, and the U.S. to seem lively. *Resort.*

★★★★ **Hilton International Barbados** • *on the beach at Needham's Point* • is a 5-story, coral-stone hotel with foliage-filled inner courtyard perched on a historic site that incorporates an 18th-century fort. It has also been the social center for government and other Barbadian activities and, therefore, was *the* place for business travelers to stay. Bridgetown is 5 minutes from the hotel's door and all the facilities of a resort (beaches, tennis, pool, shops, beachside bar, entertainment, elegant dining room, and comfortable rooms—with reliable telephone links) are here. My preference for alfresco dining leads me to the Terrace for lunchtime; the enclosed *Fort Charles* room (named for the 18th-century fort that is sometimes used for parties) seems like any big city dining room, with the elaborate menu sometimes rising to expectations. Refurbishing has turned the first floor "halls" into several cozy conversation centers, with comfortable chairs and cocktail tables. Rooms in the main building have either sea or bay view. The best view is from the higher floors (where you may have to endure the vagaries of the temperamental elevators unless you want to climb the stairs). Minimum rate rooms in the "garden wing" are comfortable, and the 2-story building puts its guests closest to the beach (if you like an early morning swim) and nearest to the tennis courts. Good summer-season package plans make the hotel reasonable for well-heeled families and others; activities make this Hilton good for all ages. The nearby Mobil oil storage tanks make breezes "fragrant" when wind direction warrants, but that's no problem most of the time. *Resort hotel.*

★★ **King's Beach Hotel** • *at Mullins Bay, north on the west coast* • opened for 1989, with most rooms in a 2-story building with outstretched arms. All have beach-and-sea view and minibar; many are comfortable suites. Management encourages families, and plans some activities for young ones during school vacation times. The poolside *Calypso Court* restaurant encourages outside reservations for its informal, sometimes Bajan fare. Sports are complimentary. Many European and Canadian groups settle here. *Hotel.*

★★★ **Marriott's Sam Lord's Castle** • *at St. Philip on the east coast* • is a resort community unto itself, with 259 rooms in several buildings, plus 3 pools, tennis courts, a long beach (that is usually windy, with surf and undertow), shops, entertainment, choices for dining, and an historic main house that is the reception area (and namesake). When Marriott arrived in Barbados in '72, the expansion at this southeast spot started, from the original cottage rooms (some privately owned, rented in owner's absence, and still some of the most interesting rooms) to several wings of new rooms, furnished and appointed to expected stateside standards. This place needs groups to keep it alive (and lively), and they're often here. Castle dinners, arranged by special reservation in the elegantly furnished 19th-century mansion that was built by the legendary Sam Lord, can be an unforgettable island experience, and other meals (especially buffets) offer well-heaped, American-style service, even when the food is the hotel's version of Bajan-style. The historic original building has 10 period-appointed bedrooms. Be prepared for the hotel to be a tourist attraction for cruise passengers and others on an island tour, and know that you must have a car (or enough money to support a taxi driver) if you want mobility. You can stay here and not even know you're on Barbados. *Resort.*

Pineapple St. James Beach Club • *seaside, on the west coast* • has 100-plus rooms, in 3- and 4-story buildings, gathered around a lovely pool in an area that opens toward the seafront restaurant. The property has had several masters in its lifetime; the Ithaca-New York-based Divi group sold the property in mid-'91 to Barbadian interests. The beach is narrow and slopes gradually into the sea; the pool is pleasant for swimming. Most of the bedrooms have a sea view; the ones on the upper floors and nearest the sea are my favorites. Located midway along the west coast, the hotel is on the public bus route between Bridgetown and the north, if you choose not to rent a car or take taxis. Proposed ownership changes make it impossible to evaluate service at press time. The *Caribbean Newsletter* (page 9) will share any news. *Hotel.*

★★★★ **Royal Pavilion** • *on the west coast, north of Holetown* • occupies the site of one of the island's popular 1950s resorts. This property, sister to its southern neighbor, Glitter Bay, and also owned by British Michael Pemberton, opened for winter of '88. It's built in grand colonial style with an imposing courtyard in the main entrance building and wings of tastefully furnished rooms. The nicest, in my opinion, have sea view and are near the pool and beachside *Tabora's Cafe,* where the Moonglows play for Sunday luncheon and at other times. Pastas, pizzas, salads, and snacks are served, but I hope that netting or some other bird deterrent has been installed by the time you visit. Blackbirds came brazenly to my table. The *Palm Terrace* serves more elegant fare in its classy surroundings. This place aspires to be top quality for Barbados; it charges top prices as well. *Hotel.*

★★★ **Sandpiper Inn** • *on the west coast near Speightstown* • is a lovely west coast nest that shares a "family relationship" with the Coral Reef. This is a West Indian–style hotel, with stucco walls, and shake-shingle roofs and wood-beamed balconies stretching along the second story, with patios perfect for the garden-level rooms. All rooms cluster around the free-form pool and garden area. There's a lovely beach, plus nearby shops, and the comfort of knowing that you're at the "blue blood" section of Barbados's "gold coast." The pleasant seaside restaurant offers imaginative fare, attractively served, with sea sounds and soft breezes. *Hotel.*

Sandy Lane Resort • *on the beach of the west coast* • has been a Barbadian pace-setter since it opened in 1961. Planned and developed by Sir Ronald Tree, and his wife, Marietta, the hotel was built in the style of an elegant private estate, with an impressive porte-cochere at the entrance and the traditional "welcoming arms" staircase leading to the beachfront terrace. Built of coral limestone, the hotel has weathered nicely. After several months of being closed and totally refurbished, Sandy Lane should, once again, set high standards, under London-based Forte hotels. Bedrooms are in two wings off the main building; meals are served on the sea view terrace and the beachfront patio. Grounds are spacious, usually well-maintained, and punctuated at appropriate places with fountains, gardens, and pools. The tennis courts are near the main house; the golf course claims several acres on the inland side of the road. A soft-sand beach is the apron for the terrace, which is the stage for the steel band that plays for the Sunday buffet and on other occasions. Watersports are offered at the beach, which is public (as are all Barbados' beaches) and subject to a rash of beach vendors who can be pesky. Staff training was a big part of the plan for the re-opening, which had not taken place at press time. The hotel should warrant ★★★★★ when it reopens; the *Caribbean Newsletter* (page 9) will have my post-opening comments. *Resort.*

★★ **Southern Palms** • *on the curve of shore-road that leads through the St. Lawrence area on the busy southeast coast* • is a rambling resort that tries to offer something for everyone. The core of the resort is the *Khus Khus* bar, with its pyramid-shaped roof (it's near the pool, bordering the sandy shore). The 111 rooms are arranged in wings on both sides, with those on the first floor providing easy access to the beach and other activities (but little privacy, if you're in one of the rooms that has steady "walk-by" traffic). My preference continues to be for the rooms in the 1 to 91 block, with 2 units along the beach. Count on groups, and plenty of action that appeals to lively couples and/or those with children (especially during vacation time). There's an assortment of shops and dining depots within a few steps of your room. *Resort.*

★★ **Tamarind Cove** • *at Paynes Bay on the west coast shore* • opened in March 1970, sharing the long white sand west coast beach with neighbor Buccaneer Bay. Spacious doubles and an assortment of 1- or 2-bedroom suites cup the pool and palm-punctuated garden areas. Room service is available "24 hours a day." Thursday night is known for the barbecue and Barbadian floor show. Free service is provided for the 7-mile jaunt down the coast to Bridgetown (Mon.–Sat., in at 9:30 a.m., out at 12:30 p.m.). Watersports can be arranged at the beach. There's a tennis pro, and polo and the riding stables, plus Sandy Lane's golf, are not far along the coast. *Hotel.*

★★★★ **Treasure Beach** • *at the beach on the west coast road* • thrives under new ownership as an oasis on the busy west coast road. Lodging units are attractive studios/suites, planned in horseshoe-shape, with the pool at the center of the U that opens to the beach. Most units have a living area that opens to a patio or porch, depending on your level; all are angled to give maximum privacy, although some porches and patios are more "public" than others. The property has a loyal list of repeat visitors who think of the place as their Barbadian home, especially for winter weeks. A talented chef should bring new glory to the restaurant, which is nestled under the rooftop but open to the breezes. Inquire about the schedule for special evenings, with buffets and entertainment. I like this place, for its location, atmosphere, and hospitality. *Small hotel.*

HOUSEKEEPING HOLIDAYS range from some of the region's most luxurious homes and villas to small apartments for cost-conscious travelers. Responding to the need for apartments (and the cost and problems with staff), many island entrepreneurs have built accommodations, some of which have now turned to time-sharing and/or condominium arrangements.

Alleyne, Aguillar and Altman, a firm with offices at Derricks, on the St. James coast (T 809+432–0840, fax 809+ 432–2147), has an impressive list of villas for rent in owners' absence. There are multi-room homes with pool-punctuated lawns and several in staff as well as small and nicely furnished places that are ideal for a couple. Other sources are **Villas and Apartments Abroad** (420 Madison Ave., New York, NY 10017, T 212+759–1025, 800+ 433–3020, fax 212+ 755–8316); **La Cure Villas** (11661 San Vicente Blvd., Los Angeles, CA 90049, T 800+387–2726) **West Indies Management Company** (Box 1461, Newport, R.I. 02840, T 401+849–8012 or T 800+932–3222, fax 401+847–6290).

There are excellent supermarkets on Barbados, in addition to good places to buy fresh local vegetables. One worth driving to find is *JB's*, out on Rendezvous Hill, inland from the southwest coast hotels. In addition to being a vast emporium, the supermarket has homebaked breads, Barbados seasoning, and other "finds."

Adventuresome visitors can buy fresh fish when the catch is brought in at

Oistins on the southwest coast, or from places your maid or cook can tell you about near the home you rent. Count on finding some interesting pates, condiments, desserts, and locally baked breads at the small specialty shops that have sprung up along the west and south coasts. There's no need to bring foods from home, unless you have a craving for something special. (Be sure to add Barbadian pepper sauce as an island condiment. *Windmill* brand can be found in most markets.)

AUTHOR'S OBSERVATION

If you're not familiar with island house-renting procedures, be prepared for "your" maid or housekeeper to take charge. Some staff can give the feeling that they own the house, and you are *their* tenant, since they are there year-round (and you, presumably, are "borrowing").

Angler Apartments • *at Derrick's, near the beach on the west coast* • are for cost-conscious travelers who enjoy simple surroundings. Chandra and Roger Gosdain have furnished their units neatly, with basics. The two-bedroom apartment is comfortable for as many as 6; a one-bedroom apartment for 4; and five more modest one-bedroom units that can seem comfortable for up to 3. Convenient to nearby hotels, and on the west coast–Bridgetown bus route, these units are a place in the sun at reasonable cost. *Apts.*

★ **Asta Apartments** • *on the shore near Needham's Point* • has 60 units in a 3-story building. It shares the beach that stretches to the Hilton. Self-sufficient types can enjoy the modern but basic surroundings, a pool-punctuated courtyard that opens onto the beach, and the independence of being able to cook "at home." A restaurant featuring Barbadian-style food offers relief from household chores, and several good restaurants (*Flamboyant, Brown Sugar,* and others) are within walking distance. The road that spurs to Asta is off the main southwest coast drive; within less than 10 minutes you can be in downtown Bridgetown by public bus. Inquire about the bigger apartments if you want more space than a pleasant studio allows. All rooms have terrace or balcony, depending on which of the 3 levels you are on. *Apts.*

★ **Beachcomber Apartments** • *near Holetown, on the west coast beach* • are nine nests in a modern, boxy building that counts on the spectacular sea view and sandy setting for atmosphere. All modern equipment in the 3 on 3 apartments makes the studios and the 2-bedroom units ideal homes for extended stays. Sea and sand are the focal points; top-floor units have an unparalleled (and unobstructed) ocean view. Nestled amid west-coast luxury, this place offers the comforts of home within a short walk (or ride) of all conveniences. *Apts.*

★★ **Best Western Sandy Beach** • *wedged onto a patch of shore in the busy Worthing area* • has 50 2-bedroom and 39 1-bedroom units (many of which are privately owned, and rented in owners' absence), all attractively furnished. Those with a sea view (as opposed to a view of one of the other buildings) are my favorites. Meals are served in the beach and poolside rondavel that is the *Greenhouse*. Activities include those offered at a nearby health club, plus watersports, and a boat trip to the west coast. This place is good for families with teenage children (who can walk to most of the interesting activity). The beach is small, but the sand is soft. *Apts.*

★★★ **Casuarina Beach Hotel** • *St. Lawrence Gap* • captures a prize (but often windy) piece of shoreline, slightly removed from the building boom that has cluttered some parts of the bulge known as St. Lawrence Gap. New with the season of '81, the property occupies 7½ acres and freckles it with 3- to 4-story buildings with apartments that have balconies facing the sea or pool area. Tennis is popular; squash courts are near the entrance; watersports are offered through the on-premises contact. This place will appeal to well-heeled families who want an apartment by the sea. Although many good restaurants and some boutiques are within walking distance, the walk on the dark roadside is not recommended at night. A rental car is advisable for easy mobility; taxis are available for occasional jaunts. *Apts.*

★★★★ **Glitter Bay** • *on the beach-lined west coast* • flourishes amid tropical planting, with several elegantly furnished apartments, many of which have an unobstructed sea view. The first 21 apartments opened just before January 1, 1982, to be joined by a community of others that are angled on the grounds to give maximum privacy, in spite of being close to neighbors. The public areas—pool, dining, bar, and beach—are well-maintained, and the alfresco terrace near pool and beach is one of my favorite places to pause amid west-coast researching. A shop in the main house, part of the original Cunard estate, offers staples and some fashions, but you'll have to go outside the complex for extensive shopping and sports. Special evenings add action, especially during the season. Every effort is made to maintain the luxury ambience that the place suggests, following the tone set by the fact that the grounds were the private property of Sir Edward Cunard, who built his winter retreat here. *Apts.*

★ **Rockley Resort & Beach Club** • *along the southwest coast* • rose from the shores in December 1977 with the first of what is almost 300 apartments with full residential facilities. The apartments give renters a pool (there are several around the grounds), plus the option for the beach linked to the inland locale by free shuttle bus, and several casual eating spots. There are night-lighted tennis courts and a golf course for sports enthusiasts. *Apts.*

Sand Acres Beach Club • *on the south shore in the Maxwell area* • is a wedge of beachside apartments with a pool and easy access to a tennis court. Popular with wise British and Canadian travelers, the units have been completely refurbished to offer comfortable housekeeping, but they are far from lavish. *Apts.*

Sandhurst Apartment Hotel • *at St. Lawrence Gap* • settles into the side-by-side settlement at a bulge on the shore. If you claim one of these 21 air-conditioned units, you'll be sharing space at the sandy strand with other apartment renters about 15 minutes' drive west of Bridgetown. Hotel services are offered (housekeeping, sheets changed, etc.), and there are gardens on "your" side of the road. Some of the rooms have beach view, but the setting for all is simple. *Apts.*

★ **Sandridge** • *north, at the west coach beach* • offers comfortable apartments that can be ideal for families. Located next door to Cobblers Cove, at the northern end of the west coast, the units appeal to wise travelers who appreciate good value. Apartments at the sea-end of the building have a nice view; others are angled so they look seaward also. There's a pool near the beach, plus a bar, terrace restaurant, and minimart for food and drink. Bernie Weatherhead is your host. *Apts.*

★★★ **Sea Foam Haciendas** • *securely notched to the south coast road* • are modern apartments at the edge of the sea. When you settle on your balcony, the sea and sand are your view. Modern kitchenettes, with stools-at-counter for snacking and a table in the living/dining area for more elaborate meals, make casual shoreside living easy. Units have 2 bedrooms, are air-conditioned, and are convenient to an assortment of restaurants and other hotels, plus shops, the laundromat, and everything you need. Full maid service is included. Public bus service passes nearby. These units are very comfortable nests. *Apts.*

★★★ **Settlers Beach Hotel** • *on the west coast* • part of the trio that includes Coral Reef and Sandpiper (see comment in "Hotels" section), offers comfortable apartments with hotel services. The 22 units are in 2-story buildings at the shore, with a pool as the social center. Emphasis is on independent, relaxed living. Exchange privileges are arranged with the sister properties. Ideal for well-heeled couples or families with grown children. *Apts.*

Yellow Bird Hotel • *at St. Lawrence Gap* • is a block of apartments near many restaurants and other lodgings, and across the road from a small beach. Good value for basic housekeeping. *Apts.*

THE INN WAY: Barbados has always had attractive small inns. The recent spate of decorating and refurbishing has resulted in rebuilding some properties. The best, in my opinion, are the original Barbadian buildings, with their many layers of paint, pleasant fabrics in Caribbean colors, and homelike style. Here are some worth noting:

Atlantis • *on the wind-swept east coast* • provides a rare opportunity to see life as the upper-crust Barbadians have traditionally known it. Located on the dramatic Bathsheba coast, a favorite place for the island's "old families" to spend their holidays, Atlantis is true to its own legend. Although modernized and spruced up from its 1880's family guest house origins, a reservedly-friendly, sea-oriented atmosphere prevails. Most rooms have simple, but comfortable, furnishings and balconies that face the sea; the **Fleet View Apartments,** sharing ownership, overlook the fishing fleet that sets out in early hours from Tent Bay. This is a good spot for Barbadian food, whether it be flying fish, kingfish in special sauce, or the vegetables plucked from island farms to be sauced and served at the tables here. *Small hotel & apts.*

Bagshot House • *on the south coast road, in the St. Lawrence area* • clings to a sliver of beachfront, wedged between road and sea, amid the hubbub of a touristy coast. In business since 1946, when Eileen Robinson began opening her home for friends and kindred souls, this place is comfortable casual. Shoreside meals are served alfresco; entertainment is limited to congenial guests and special dinners some nights. Rooms vary in size and shape, with the ones that have sea view preferred. (Rooms on the road side are blasted by traffic.)

★★ **Crane Beach Hotel** • *on the southeast coast, about 30 minutes drive from Bridgetown and 15 from the airport* • is a quiet hideaway, with an oft-photographed view from the bluff-top pool and 19th-century style furnishings in bedrooms. For generations, Crane has been a favorite holiday area for Barbadians who have their main house (and business) in Bridgetown. Noteworthy for its cliffside location that sheers to a lovely wide band of white-pink sand with a band of foaming surf, the hotel is popular for Sunday brunches and midday meals when the scenery can be enjoyed, and meals can be followed (or preceeded) by a swim in sea below. At other times, this place is quiet. *Inn.*

★★★ **Island Inn** • *in Aquatic Gap, across the road from Grand Barbados Beach Hotel* • is a gem. Preserving the traditional shell of a longtime Barbadian inn, the Odles have created a special spot. Bedrooms are around the center courtyard and the small pool at the back of the property, as well as along the left side (where you look into a parking lot as you leave your room). Meals are served on the patio (and were mediocre, with snail-slow service when I sampled). Although many rooms are viewless, they are attractively furnished and decorated, with mirrors on the limestone walls. All have modern bathrooms; furnishings take their cue from Georgian antiques. Beaches are a short walk from the inn, near either Grand Barbados or the Hilton. *Inn.*

★ **Kingsley Club** • *at Cattlewash, on the windswept east coast* • is an island legend, long favored by Barbadians and others who adapt to traditional places. With a spectacular view of the wind-swept sea, and a short walk (across the road) to the long beach, Kingsley thrives on an atmosphere akin to fishing clubs in the U.S. northeast or England's Channel shore. Pretense is not part of its appeal. Sea breezes and simple living are. Guests in the 7 rooms know and enjoy a back-to-basics lifestyle, with plenty of time for reading and resting. Featuring fish and other domestic produce, mealtimes are special occasions. This place is remote and relaxing for those who enjoy reverse chic. *Inn.*

★★★ **Ocean View Hotel** • *on the busy southwest coast road, at the edge of the sea* • is stately, with a faded elegance that is part of the appeal. Sea sounds are "music" for the dining room; coffee and/or tea can be taken on the porch, where louvered shutters are raised to welcome sea breezes. Bedrooms vary in size and shape, on both sides of a narrow hallway. Although there are traffic noises for the lowest-rate rooms facing the road, furnishings are attractive and housekeeping is attentive in all rooms. The dinner theater, held at sea-level, downstairs from the entry salon and dining area, is a special feature—and fun. Flower arrangements are lovely. Swims are easy from the sliver of beach. I've stayed here happily, and intend to again. *Classic hotel.*

140 · · BARBADOS

★ **Seaview** • *on the busy southwest coast road, near Garrison Savannah* • has had a total overhaul of the historic inn's interior. Rooms are decorated in faux-Georgian style, taking advantage of the high ceilings and windows with shutters. One of the oldest hotels in Barbados, the building has wrought-iron balconies around its second floor, breeze-swept rooms, and a tradition of a thermos of ice water regularly replenished and put in your room. Better known by some for the *Tamarind Tree* and *Virginian* restaurants, on and next to these grounds, the inn expects to have a squash court and tennis court ready for this season. There's a small pool; the beach is a short walk over what used to be a natural lawn (and now seems to be a potential building site). Although room rates were breathtaking when I checked, ask about packages or other plans that may yield a more palatable price. *Small hotel.*

LOW-COST LODGING is better and more varied in Barbados than on most other islands, but some inexpensive spots border on being (or are) seedy. Check carefully. Not only are there hundreds of rooms in the clusters of simple apartments that have always been very popular with cost-conscious Canadians and British, but also there are several small hotels and guest houses with reasonable rates. Housekeeping standards vary. Some places charge more than their accommodations warrant because of location and demand; others sacrifice standards for profit, making them difficult to recommend.

For the best apartments, which can figure to reasonable rates when cost is divided among a few people, see "Housekeeping Holidays" above. What follows are a few of the most worthy guest houses and small hotels:

Abbeville Hotel • *on the inland side of the shore-rimming southwest coast road* • provides inexpensive rooms in clean, if spartan, surroundings. As one of the older hotels, the bedrooms vary in size and shape; furnishings are attic originals. Rooms in the main house have more style (and no air-conditioning); newer rooms have in-wall air conditioners. A good value for those who are satisfied with basics. The restaurant is popular for Barbadian food—with pepper sauce. The beach is across the road.

Berwyn • *in the Rockley area of the southwest coast* • has 4 rooms, 3 of them with private bathroom. The place is small, very simple, and very inexpensive. Only recommended when costs are crucial.

Caribbee Beach Hotel • *in Hastings, near Bridgetown, on the southwest coast* • sits on a narrow strip of land between the main south coast road and the sea. One of the older Barbadian hotels, Caribbee refurbishes regularly and is a good value. Inquire about special packages, and know that rates may be higher than they deserve to be.

Fairholme • *at Maxwell on the southwest coast* • is a 2-story, modestly furnished, cluster of rooms centered by gardens and a pool. You're within walking distance of the beach. Well-known to wise British and Canadian visitors, the 31-room hotel has some apartments as well as standard hotel-style rooms.

Flamboyant • *on the inland side of the south coast road, not far from Garrison Savannah* • is a personal favorite for very simple accommodations. Behind the main house that holds a well-known restaurant and in a neighboring building, the rooms are basic and sometimes rented on long-term basis. Some are apartments.

Mackston Apartments • *on the island side of the shore-rimming road, near Bridgetown* • are some of my favorite apartments, although most are rented for longer term. The 6 units are comfortably furnished, with a garden area and the convenience of the Hastings hotel/restaurant area.

Maresol Beach Apartments • *at St. Lawrence Gap* • include the original beachside 2-storied buildings, each with an apartment up and an apartment down and additional apartments across the road on the inland side. The small minimarket next to the check-in desk gives you staples and liquor at supermarket prices; the rest of your goods you can get in town—or from the fish market. Maid service is included in your rate; compassionate nannies are available for the children or grandchildren (who are encouraged at other than peak Feb. and March), and you'll find the front office staff a helpful and willing source of information. A car will help for island touring, but you can walk to plenty of dining depots, and can take the bus into Bridgetown; the beach that stretches out before you offers some action options.

Margate Gardens • *in the Hastings area of the southwest coast* • is a pleasant family-style place, punctuated with a pool for those who'd rather linger on the lawn than walk across the road to the beach. Baby-sitters and maid service are provided for guests in the self-catering units in 3-story, white-painted blocks amid the tropical gardens. Markets are nearby; atmosphere is friendly, with Jan Brown in charge.

Nautilus Beach • *on the beach near Bridgetown* • has little in the way of vacation atmosphere, but the apartments may prove suitable for anyone who wants to be near town and not far from the Hilton and Grand Barbados Beach hotels. All rooms are simply furnished; sea viewing rooms are best. Worth considering for cost and convenience.

Sea Breeze Beach Hotel • *on the Maxwell coast road, a seaside curve off the main airport-to-town route* • is a friendly, small hotel where guests have choice of pool or a span of talcum-soft sand for swimming, and home-cooked food in the dining room. The nicest rooms have sea view; all have the personality of an established property whose guests return year after year. Owned by Hazel Ann and Trevor Kent, who had shared in management of the legendary Mermaid Inn on Carriacou, this place is carefully tended. *Inn.*

Sunset Crest Resort • *on the inland side of the west coast road* • is mentioned only because the sprawling complex is so big that you can't miss it as you drive up the coast. A gathering of several boxy houses and a few 2-story "hotel" blocks, Sunset Crest is worth looking into if price is paramount. Surroundings have the look of a suburban development.

Windsurfing Resort • *on the south coast, near the town of Oistins* • adopted the former Beneston Beach Hotel and turned it into a casual, lively, windsurfers' hub to take advantage of the tradewinds that brush this coast. The shoreside bar is a popular place for surfers who also lounge on the lawn and shore when not at sea. The activity draws day enthusiasts who came for board rental as well as for camaraderie. Primarily for the young in sport and spirit, the rooms are simple; the place is sports-oriented.

RESTAURANTS around Barbados range from those in old homes with a lot of atmosphere to beachside places with little or none, with the whole roster of hotels—some of them with excellent restaurants—in the middle. Prices will be high (about $40 per person for a full meal with wine and flourishes) at the top spots, higher than they should be at some of the middle-range places, and reasonable if you are lured by local West Indian food and lucky enough to find a place that serves some. Surroundings at the best spots are eminently civilized, a hangover from the days of British rule that has become so much a fact of Barbadian life that everyone enjoys what used to be the exclusive province of the country club set.

Although Barbados has a sheaf of helpful tourist information sheets (including the weekly *Tourist News*), by far the best and most comprehensive is the annual *Ins and Outs of Barbados,* carefully researched by Sally and Keith Miller. Be sure to ask around when you arrive to track down a copy.

AUTHOR'S AWARD

Josef's continues to be my favorite, for its imaginative and tasty offerings served at a lovely shoreside setting in the St. Lawrence area; *Brown Sugar,* in the Garrison area south of Bridgetown, is another atmospheric spot, well worth an evening's outing; *Sunbury House* is the ultimate, for elegant service in a private home (by reservation, only); and the *Café Musée,* in the patio at the Barbados Museum, is a lovely place for light meals and/or tea.

Ascanio's • *on the south coast's Rockley Road* • is one place to go when you want Italian food. A menu that starts with mussels marinara, misto mare, and antipasto leads into saltimbocca romana, fettuccine Alfredo and assorted pastas, fish, and veal main courses, to finish with zabaglione and other Italian vintage desserts. The place opened by the Marconi family provides transportation if you call in advance for a reservation.

★★★ **Brown Sugar** • *next to the Island Inn, just south of Bridgetown not far from Hilton and Carlisle Bay* • is a very good bet for delicious food in lovely surroundings, amid hanging plant-filled baskets, in a restored West Indian wooden house. Lunchtime buffets draw local businessmen (who pay Bds$26.55 for the fixed-price meal); evening hours are more romantic (and a la carte). A prize place to sample substantial Barbadian food. High marks for good value, and an excellent meal with West Indian specialties.

Café Musée • *in the patio at the Barbados Museum, in the Garrison area of Bridgetown* • is a special experience, especially after a tour through the museum. Susan Wolcott opened this place about the time her *Waterfront Café* burned a few years ago and brought some good "home-cooking" with her. Expect to find delicious pastries and breads, as well as an imaginative selection of heartier fare. Best from mid-day to twilight, the restaurant closes when the museum does.

★★★ **Bagatelle** • *out Highway 2A, which runs north from Bridgetown, not along the coast, but the next main road inland, taking the left fork as you head north* • bets its atmosphere on the Great House it inhabits, which owners claim dates from 1665. The atmosphere is terrific; prices are high, but somehow I don't mind because the surroundings are special. Located in the countryside, Bagatelle is a good place for a gala (and expensive) evening out. The 5-course dinner costs Bds$60.

★★★ **Carambola** • *perched at the west coast seaside* • set its pace with original owners who then sold to Barbadian Michael Ward. Although service (up and down a hillside) has to be a nightmare for staff, the surroundings are lovely. If the quality of food holds, expect to make your essential reservations days in advance for a winter dinner. Arrive before sunset, for a beautiful view; the romantic mood arrives with candlelight. Pricey and sometimes pretentious, this place is well worth a visit for west coast residents.

★★ **Chateau Creole** • *on a spur off the main west coast road, not far from most of the west coast properties* • is a hideaway where you can settle into another world for the evening. Staff dressed in Creole costumes help the atmosphere, and dining on the terrace by candlelight can lend a romantic note. Service can be s-l-o-w; reservations are recommended (as is some gnat repellent for ankles and other areas that might be nibbled while you are dining). Specialties are stuffed whitefish (which can suffer from over cooking), and lobster Cantonese, which I enjoy. Atmosphere is tops; cooking isn't always.

David's • *on the south coast road amid the lodging cluster* • is in one of the small chattel houses resting right on the roadside, but its back area hangs over the sea. The menu is extensive, with the basics (fish chicken, beef) prepared in imaginative ways. Staff attitude is not always welcoming, but the location is convenient and pretty.

da Luciano's • *in the hotel-filled Hastings area* • has a lovely setting, with house and gardens. Garden area tables are the nicest, for my dining dollar, and the food focus is on Italian flavors for veal, chicken, fish, and beef. The dining area seems pretentious, with mirrors, dark red fabrics, and a Victorian drawing room feeling.

Flamboyant • *in the Hastings area* • is a West Indian house on the inland side of the main southwest coast road. The porch tables continue to be my favorite places. Local lobster, when you get it, is best when grilled, but fish and other specialties can also be good.

★★★★★ **Josef's** • *on the seaside in the south-coast St. Lawrence area* • commands all superlatives, whether you settle at a porch table for a leisurely midday meal or a lingering, late-night dinner. The setting, in Waverly House, a former private home, is luxurious, with overhead fans to keep you cool if the breeze lets up. Crepes fruits de mer were excellent on one try, but so were other offerings. Entrees range from barracuda with hollandaise at Bds$23 to about Bds$35 for a filet. Grilled shrimp tallied to Bds$25, and the Grand Marnier mousse was priceless (and only cost Bds$4 at lunch or Bds$5 for dinner). If you have but one meal out, try for a reservation here.

Kokos • *overlooking the sea on the shore road up the west coast, in St. James parish* • is a pleasant place that features the Barbadian version of "nouvelle cuisine." Recommended for special evening out, Kokos follows the domestic pattern of high prices and slow service, but it seems worth it. Its location amid the west coast hotels makes it popular, especially at height of season.

★★ **Luigi's** • *in Dover at one "end" of the shoreline road (not far from Casuarina Hotel)* • is fun, and the food is good. The atmosphere is attractively Italian, and the menu is filled with mouth-watering pasta, as well as some northern Italian (veal and less heavy) specialties. Wine list is interesting. A fun place to go with friends, Luigi's is worth the investment of the $25 or so a good meal will cost.

Pisces • *in the St. Lawrence area* • is one of a trio of tourist-laden recommendables. It has a seaside atmosphere that rates higher than the food, in my opinion. The fish from which it takes its name are served as specialties, all kinds, most of them fresh from the Barbados sea (and some of them "frozen fresh," I fear). Caribbean lobster is progged (and propelled by charter planc) from nearby seas. Atmosphere is pleasant; prices are the usual high.

Plantation Restaurant • *just in from the main shore-rimming road on the grounds of Caribbean Pepperpot* • follows the tradition of turning former homes into dining nooks. A social section known as *Stables* is a pub/disco popular with young (teenage) folk. Plantation's tables can be on the porch or in the house, and food is Barbadian French-style.

Raffles • *on the west coast road, near Discovery Bay Hotel at Holetown* • is a scenic spot where the elaborate menu and usually good service make the high prices seem almost worth it. Reservations are recommended at height of winter season, and it's worth stopping by to check the menu—and opening hours—at other times.

Reid's • *at the southern section of the west coast shore road* • occupies the street level of an old Barbadian house that has been spruced up for the restaurant. Pub fare and Barbadian food (flying fish, etc.) are featured in reasonably simple surroundings. Best when you dine as part of a group, the place can seem quiet when you're one of two.

The Steak House • *in a Barbadian house in the St. Lawrence area* • was the country's first steak house. It's still one of the best, with U.S. prime beef, salads, and other staples. A favorite of residents and knowing visitors, this part of the trio that includes Tamarind Tree and the Virginian is another of the Weatherhead ventures.

St. James' Steak House • *north on the west coast* • is a favorite for winter west coast visitors who crave good beef. Nestled in a small spot near the sea, the restaurant also offers fish, prepared in interesting ways.

★★★ **Sunbury** • *in the countryside, about 20 minutes' drive from most hotels* • is the private home of the Thomas's, available for lunch or dinner guests by prior reservations. Expect to find service as you would at a private party, with surroundings elegant—and guests expected to be, also. Sunbury is also open many days for tours and afternoon tea. Telephone ahead to be sure of times.

Tamarind Tree • *at the back patio of Seaview Hotel, near Bridgetown* • has a devoted Barbadian following, especially at lunchtime and for family evenings. The squash courts below the restaurant are still "in the works."

The Virginian • *in a restored house neighbor, and related to the Tamarind Tree at the Seaview Hotel* • offers its special shrimp veja and other seafood specialties, in addition to steaks, salad, and garlic bread. Its reputation as a place for good food at reasonable cost continues and the new surroundings, with high ceilings and several small rooms, are elegantly homelike.

Witch Doctor • *on the inland side, across from Pisces* • continues to be popular with local folk as well as tourists, which makes reservations advisable at peak holiday and February seasons. Island foods are sometimes offered, but informal American-style food is now featured.

NATURAL SURROUNDINGS: There's no sense of "discovery" with the natural surroundings on Barbados. Everything worth noting has been defined and signposted so that it is easily accessible for moderately adventuresome travelers. Roads are being repaved, and newly carved, on this 21- by 14-mile island, making most places easy to find. There are caves, tropical gardens, interesting rock formations, and acres of sugar cane fields.

Early morning hikes are sponsored by the Barbados National Trust and the Duke of Edinburgh's Award Scheme, on Sunday mornings from January through May and by the Outdoors Club. Further facts can usually be found in *The Visitor,* a tourist newssheet available through your hotel.

Harrison Caves can be fascinating, if you happen to arrive at other than cruise passenger time. Located near Welchman Hall Gully, the Caves officially opened with independence celebrations in November 1981. Electric carts travel along cement roadways for the tour. Lights have been discreetly hidden, but are pointed toward the most intriguing stalagmites and stalactites. Fascinating—if you like that kind of thing.

Flower Forest, at Richmond Plantation, in the Scotland area, is about an hour's drive through the countryside from Bridgetown and west coast resorts. Opened in December '83, the area is 50 acres of peace and quiet, with paths that lead past flower beds and banana groves as well as through areas planted with palms, breadfruit trees, avocadoes, mangoes, and all manner of tropical flora. The park is open from 9:30 a.m. until 5 p.m., with the early and late hours the best for visits if you hope to see any wild monkeys. There's an admission charge of Bds$6.

Welchman Hall Gully, almost in the middle of the island, east of Holetown (open daily; check at the south entrance; small fee; buy pamphlet), is a worthy goal if you are interested in tropical flora and in walking along wooded paths to find representative samples. The Barbados National Trust took over maintenance (and promotion) of this plot in 1960, and they do their utmost (often with volunteer workers) to make the grounds as interesting as possible. The original concept of the owner of this plantation was to plant as many indigenous shrubs and trees as could be found on Barbados and neighboring islands, concentrating on spice and fruit trees at the start. That was in the last half of the 1800s, when J. W. Carrington owned the plot. The work of the National Trust has concentrated on refurbishing the existing plants and adding representative worthy types. The entire excursion can take anyone with an interest at least half a day; you can wander along paths past carefully marked (and tended) flora. In sharp contrast to the usual day at the beach, this is a place for an afternoon walk on the day when you rent a car to explore the island.

Barbados Wildlife Reserve, in the northern quarter of the island, in St. Peter's Parish, is a verdant area where the local "green" monkey and other Barbadian animals flourish. Open from 10 a.m. to 5 p.m. daily, the sanctuary is a place to spot birds and wander through the mahogany forest as well as to watch the monkeys.

AUTHOR'S OBSERVATION

Novice travelers to the West Indies should be forewarned that Barbadian taxi drivers, as a group, are a very savvy lot. They know how to "work" tourists; it behooves you to know how to "handle" taxi drivers. If you don't do your homework (know approximate fares and routes *before* you get in the cab), they might do it for you—at your expense.

Bathsheba Coast is for nature lovers, and those who like salt spray as they saunter along a surf-pounded beach. This rugged northeast coast is spectacular, in my opinion, and far more worth a lingering wander than a lot of the 36 sights printed on the back of the Barbados Board of Tourism map (or the list of 50 Edward Stone assembled). What you find here is up to you, but the coast is a far cry from any of the calculated conventional nesting areas that cover most of the west coast. (It is an area favored by the old-time Barbadian families for *their* holiday weekends and weeks when they take leave from the busy life of Bridgetown.)

Andromeda Gardens, not far from Tent Bay on the Bathsheba coast (take Highway 3 from Bridgetown) should be seen at the start of your time in Barbados if you have any interest in the plants that surround you. The Bannochies (original owners of the property) have done a spectacular job of planting and pruning, so that orchids, oleanders, and varieties of hibiscus mix and mingle with the omnipresent bougainvillea, heliconia, and a host of other brilliant blooms. All set off by ferns and other greenery as well as waterfalls and guide commentary, if you ask for it.

Insofar as offshore sights are concerned, a ship was sunk a few years ago to become a fish condominium in seas off the **Barbados Marine Reserve and Museum** at Folkstone, in Holetown on the west coast. Recognized dive sites are at Dotting's Reef, a 7-mile stretch about a quarter mile this shore. There is firm legislation in place to protect all marine life and, although the seas off the east coast are strong, there are some sites off the south coast that can be visited when the winds do not make them treacherous.

PLACES WORTH FINDING include sights near the capital as well as Great Houses, as the main house of a plantation is called, if you have a special interest in early West Indian/Barbadian history (in which case, note the museums, etc., below). A rental car for a day can cover most of the island's scenic highlights. Shaped like an avocado, Barbados wears a blanket of sugarcane from December until cane cutting season in late May or June. When the cane is tall, you can drive across the midsection of the island without being able to see anything but a wall of green fronds, reminiscent—for those who have driven in England—of the narrow hedgerow-lined roads in the southwest.

AUTHOR'S OBSERVATION

Driving (on the left) around Barbados is easy, if terrifying. In spite of the people, cars, buses, donkey carts, goats, etc., that share your road, driving yourself is the best way to travel if you don't mind getting lost. Places have names, but many of them are noted only in the hearts of the Barbadians. Signs, when they appear at all, will carry village names that you may not be able to find on your map.

The main "highways" spoke out from Bridgetown, with Highway 1 running along the west coast. Highway 7 curves south to run east along the coast, and 2 through 6, some of them with A branches, stretch out through the countryside like the fingers on your hand. Some fingers are webbed, but don't count on it. You may have to backtrack to get where you want to go, if you care, and be prepared to come across new well-paved roads that are not shown on any maps. Gas is expensive, but most cars get good mileage and have fixed daily rental charges that put the total at well below what you would pay for a take-and-wait taxi.

BRIDGETOWN is bustling and more geared to shopping than to sightseeing. There was a time, not too long ago, when you could share space on the town streets with the 2-wheeled jaunty carts drawn by donkeys. They were the main means of transportation, and many of the country people came to town that way. **The Careenage** was also intriguing in those days, when the island-built sloops and schooners were hauled for repairs, to be tipped on their sides with ballast and pulleys. Modern commerce has changed some of the traditions, and where it has not, the cars block the view and the heat that rises from paved-and-clogged streets takes most of the fun out of the escapade. Exception: If there is a parade or festival that follows the marching route from Garrison Savannah to Trafalgar Square, stand along the route. The mixture of pageantry and people is not to be missed.

Trafalgar Square is worth a glimpse, which is all you'll have time to give it as you whisk by in a car. If you stand nearby to look longer, be sure to keep looking left and right so you don't get run over. Nelson cruised around this area, from his base at Antigua's English Harbour, and was well known to Barbadians, who erected the monument to him in 1813. He had visited in port, aboard his *Victory,* not long before his death, notice of which reached Barbados on December 13, 1805. Old-time Barbadians used to make a big thing about the fact that this Trafalgar Square was dedicated before the one in London, but today ties to England—and to Nelson—are not on the top of most people's minds. The square and its importance to the island's early history are relics of another era.

George Washington's brother's house is talked about, as is the former President's smallpox attack endured while here, but that's about all there is to either event. (Washington visited Barbados at age 19, before he became president. It was in the fall of 1751, and he stayed for 49 days. According to the Barbados Hilton, he was entertained at Fort Charles on November 3.) The actual house of Lawrence Washington is a matter of speculation.

Garrison Savannah, off the main road, just south of Bridgetown, is the weekend race track and site for any other big sports or ceremonial event in Barbados. If you want to witness the country at its most enthusiastic, go to the horse races or to a cricket match at Kensington Oval, being played between Barbados and any visiting country. The 50-acre Garrison parade ground has been used for training and marches since the first British soldiers were stationed in Barbados in the late 1600s. When British troops officially withdrew in 1906, the fields continued to be used for some ceremonial events and that's still the case (any taxi driver can tell you what's going on if your hotel desk doesn't seem too sure).

AUTHOR'S OBSERVATION

Make the two Barbados newspapers, the *Nation* and the *Advocate,* part of your daily diet. The news coverage can be enlightening and the *Advocate* carries current activities information. You are welcome to attend anything listed—from band concert at Hastings to flower show, tea, or open-house tour. Buying *The Bajan,* a magazine printed in Barbados, can also shed light on island activities, not only in Barbados but also on some of the neighboring specks.

Barbados Museum, at the Garrison bordering the Savannah is the locale for the lively evening dinner and show known as "1627 and All That Sort of Thing." It's well worth a visit for its historic buildings as well as for the collection of Barbadian furniture, artifacts, and paintings of the country in its early days. There is a slight entrance fee and a stroll around the grounds can be accomplished in an hour or so.

St. Ann's Fort, the rust-red building at the fringe of the Savannah, was completed in 1703. The clock tower, completed almost 100 years later, survived the 1831 hurricane that wiped out most of the underpinnings and the buildings around it and still is the point to find if you're having trouble locating the Savannah.

House Tours are an annual event, sponsored by the Barbados National Trust. They are held in the height of season during late February and early March. Check for details prior to arrival if you are interested in peeking at private life in Barbados. If there is no planned tour, you can still go to restored homes that have been opened as small museums.

Drax Hall is "the oldest plantation house in Bardados." Records show it was started by James Drax in 1650, and it has remained in the family since that time. There are antiques from Europe, as well as some interesting Barbadian furniture and appointments, typical of what was used in the elegant homes of plantation owners.

Sunbury Plantation House (daily, 10 a.m.–4:30 p.m.; Bds$8) is a 300-year-old estate house furnished with lovely antiques, some of which were made in Barbados. Privately owned, the house has a courtyard where lunch, coffee, and tea are served.

Villa Nova (Mon.–Fri., 10 a.m.–4 p.m. small fee) opened to the public in 1976, after the present owners had purchased it from the late Lord Avon, better known as Sir Anthony Eden. The plantation house was built in 1834, and Queen Elizabeth stayed here during a visit when Eden was owner. The furnishings are a varied lot, many of them interesting antiques showing Barbadian adaptations of styles popular in Europe in the early 1800s.

St. Nicholas Abbey (Mon.–Fri., 10 a.m.–3 p.m.; Bds$5) is "one of the oldest plantation mansions in Barbados," having been built between 1650 and 1660. The Jacobean Plantation house is a treasure, even without a glimpse at the antique-filled interior. But if Lt. Col. Stephen Cave (owner) is around when you visit, you are in for an afternoon you won't soon forget. Plan some time to walk around the grounds.

(Fees charged for entrance to each of the above house-museums go toward the projects of the **Barbados National Trust,** a prime mover for restoration of Barbadian treasures just before many homes and areas were about to be taken over or torn down to make way for '70s commerce.)

SPORTS AND ACTIVITIES range from hiking and horseback riding, tennis and golf, to parasailing (which is swinging from a parachute while being towed through the air by a sea-skimming boat), scuba diving, board sailing, regular sailing, and all manner of other watersports.

For guidelines, you'll find most of the activity at or near the resort hotels (for the obvious reason that visitors congregate there) and you can partake, even if you are staying at another place. All beaches in Barbados are public, and open to everyone. Roads reach most beaches—the powdery, sandy ones on the calm west coast and the beaches pounded by rugged Atlantic surf that rolls in from Africa to the east coast. The southwest coast beaches are the most crowded, due to the concentration of places to stay (and proximity to the city). Only

North Point is beachless and desolate. (Its rugged terrain looks like a moonscape.)

Scuba is offered through many west coast resorts, with concessions available at Cunard's Paradise Beach, Coral Reef, Sandy Lane, and other hotels. There is a watersports center at the Hilton Hotel, where divers usually set out from the beach shared with the Grand Barbados Beach Hotel after the in-pool lesson or check out. Sandy Beach offers a resort certification course through *Sandy Beach Watersports,* and has had some scuba package-holidays in recent seasons. As a general practice, reef dives take place off the southwest and west coasts, with two prime underwater sights being the *Berwyn* tug, wrecked at Carlisle Bay, and the Greek freighter, S.S. *Stavronikita,* blown up almost according to plan at the west coast Folkstone Underwater Park.

The *Atlantis* submarine makes it possible for non-swimmers to see the underwater sights. The 50-foot submersible, with its crew of 2, sinks into the sea, allowing passengers to look out one of the 16 "viewports," airplane fashion, to see the underwater world. The Canadian-Barbadian venture is based at Bridgetown's Careenage.

Snorkeling is usually good in Folkstone Park and some of the other west-coast areas, and often also off the southwest shore, but winds can make quite a difference in the wave action and churning seas cloud up the area, as all snorkelers know. There is equipment available for rent, but chances are your own fits better (and will cost less).

Boardsailing, also known as windsurfing, is very popular, especially off the south coast shores. The Barbados Windsurfing Club in Maxwell, and Silver Sands Hotel, near the airport and Long Bay, are two hubs, but Grand Bay and other hotels in the resort areas also have boards.

Golfers head for Sandy Lane, or perhaps the course at Rockley. The Sandy Lane course is the "top of the line" for golfers in Barbados, with 18 holes ranging over 6986 yards and maintenance usually good. You'll find plenty of Barbadians willing to go a round, so check with the golf pro if you want partners. There are golf carts, as well as class A and class B caddies. If you're here for the winter, look into the monthly (or longer) memberships. Sign-up times are required at height of season, and it's a good idea to check in at all times of the year.

Tennis is popular, with the courts at the Hilton, at Marriott's Sam Lord's Castle, Sandy Lane, Sunset Crest, Paradise Beach, and other hotels sometimes available for outside guests. Be sure to check in advance, and set a time with the pro. The situation with ball boys is not as efficient as I have seen it on some other island courts, but if you have the services of a ball boy, he should be tipped from 50¢ to US$1, depending on how much you've made him run around. By all means, bring your own tennis balls. If they are available at all for local purchase, they are very expensive. (A can of tennis balls is a good gift for island tennis enthusiasts.)

Horseback riding can be arranged through the activities desk at any hotel. There are stables in the Bridgetown area, as well as out in mid-island. The horse races (for viewers) are held at the Garrison Savannah near Bridgetown and the polo matches are held at the fields not far from Sandy Lane, on the west coast.

Sailing on bigger boats can be arranged through some of the west coast hotels. The Barbados Yacht Club might be of interest to yachtsmen who have a link with a hometown club, but races that are held on many weekends are often only for members and guests (but anyone can enjoy the sight of the yachts sailing along the west coast on their regular races). Day-long and cocktail cruises can be arranged through some of the resort hotels on the west coast.

Vanessa Ann, a tall ship based in Bridgetown harbor, takes passengers to sea for morning, dinner, and evening cruises. Hotels have details.

The *Jolly Roger,* Barbadian lawyer Clyde Turney's venture, offers a fun-filled, lively few hours on a pirate ship. The character yacht has sister ships (one on Antigua with plans for other islands), but this is where the idea got its start. Full complements of lively guests sign on for a 4-hour cruise along the shore (about $25 for steak barbecue lunch plus rum punch, and pick up and delivery to your hotel). One of the boats is a 106-foot cargo ship that became a pirate craft after a metamorphosis in late 1977, to break into the season in early '78. Included in the summer "Best of Barbados" package tour, the trip should be part of your own plans even if you haven't bought that summer bargain week. It's fun, focused on savoring sun and sea (and plenty of punch). (In case you think the name comes from pirate fame, the folks who own her claim that it is adapted from French—"la jolie rougere," translated as the pretty red one, referring to the character craft's trademark red sails.) Special arrangements can be made for sunset cruising, which may be on a regular schedule if you're here at height of season.

Deep-sea fishing is possible, with some boats available for half-day or full-day outings. Your hotel can put you in touch with people they know to be reliable, and you should expect to pay about $150 for 4 to 6 people for a half day, and $300 or so for a full day. The sport is not a major one in seas off Barbados, but you might enjoy a day at sea.

TREASURES AND TRIFLES   are scattered all over the island. All the resort hotels have at least a few shops. There are several quality shops in a cluster at the entrance to Marriott's Sam Lord's Castle Resort (which is a good idea, because you're pretty far away from everything when you stay here); the Hilton offers a curve of boutiques with interesting items; Sandy Lane's boutique also has top-line fashions (usually, also, high-priced); and the shops at the entrance to Sandpiper and Tamarind Cove are attractive (with decorator items as well as some clothes and high-quality Barbadian-made items).

Although the biggest shops are in downtown Bridgetown, many of them have branches that join specialty boutiques at the resort communities along the southwest coast as well as at Holetown and Speightstown and the Sunset Crest shopping malls on the west coast and at shopping centers on the southwest coast. Items for sale include things for visitors and items needed and purchased by people who live here. The two are not, as is the case in some islands, mutually exclusive. Top department stores compare with the best of their kind in many mainland cities, with imports from England and other places sharing shelf space with more and more things made locally, or in other Caribbean countries.

BARBADOS

> **AUTHOR'S OBSERVATION**
> One purchase that is useful, attractive, and helpful to a local cause is the illustrated map with commentary printed through the Barbados National Trust and available at Cloister Bookshop on Hincks Street in Bridgetown, and at other outlets.

In general, the boutiques and resortwear shops are at hubs at Holetown and Speightstown on the west coast, where branches of some of the big shops are supplemented (even surpassed) by boutiques with colorful fashions. Prices are high, but happily, so is quality. Even at Pelican Village (see below) and the few random shops around Bridgetown and along the beaches, I find quality has standardized and is better than it had been. A branch of the **Barbados Handicraft Shop** is prominent at Dover (selling mats, hats, baskets, T-shirts, and other locally made items).

Dorly's rum packages its product in a special bottle shaped like a Barbados Harbour policeman. For about Bds$10, the rum makes a nice memento (which won't look nearly as hokey when you get it home). The rum is available in supermarkets and, at about the same price, in the duty-free liquor purchase places after you pass through immigration and security at the airport.

> **AUTHOR'S OBSERVATION**
> The "in-bond" shopping system works well in Barbados. You can buy (in the better stores) in-bond for delivery to plane or ship, at a tax-free purchase price. If you buy far enough in advance of your departure (2 days, at least), airport delivery *should* be problem-free. The pick-up point for in-bond purchases is just inside the departure terminal, after you have passed security and immigration.

Pelican Village offers an assortment of merchandise focused for the tourist. When the first crop of shops assembled under the peak roofs near the end of the Deep Water Pier (so that tourists could fall off the ship and into the shelves of the shops), merchandise was mostly handmade, lovingly if not professionally inspired. There's a high degree of professionalism in some of the work, especially that of Courtney Devonish, who has expanded his metier from the clay that he learned to mold as a boy to include fascinating wood sculpture. His shop, **C.O.D. Pottery,** is not far from the Government Handicraft Center, just outside the Pelican Village complex. **ArmBer Shop** (#24) is a good place for ready-made sundresses. Armin and Beryl (husband and wife) can make clothes to order, given a few days. Interesting shells are for sale at the **Marine Shop** (#25), and at **Sunny Isle** (#27) investigate the current crop of colorful string dolls, doorstops, mobiles, and handmade puppets with cork legs and winning personalities (for Bds$16). Some real treasures from the Pelican Village shops are the handmade clay figures of Barbados Harbour police and the regular police that are made by **Campbell Skeete.** Look for his small shop (#10) to the right as you face the restaurant with the street at your back.

Best of Barbados is a family enterprise run by Jimmy and Jill Walker and daughter Charlotte Hingston. Jill's Barbadian designs and drawings are featured. They'll greet you from all sides, in several shops around the island. After you've seen something of this country, you will realize that she has captured a lot of the local color. Quality of the prints for framing, her screen prints on children's clothes, and whatever craftwork she offers will be above the local average. A set of 4 coasters of Jill Walker prints makes a good gift as do the tableware, clothes, and accessories. This is a quality source for one-stop gift shopping.

Batik Caribe, with studios at St. Vincent, has outlets around the country, most of them at tourist hubs. Look for Batik at Sam Lord's, the Hilton, Gulf House on Broad Street in Bridgetown, and at Na Desie Apartment Hotel, across from Sunset Crest #1 on the west coast. The colorful fabrics are stitched into resortwear or sold by the yard for wraps and/or stitching yourself.

Barbadian supermarkets offer one of the best sources for good (and local) gifts for homefolks. Although Goddard's and Simpsons and some of the smaller markets have some stocks, the one-stop source if you have a car is **JB's MasterMart** at Sargent Village, not far inland from the south coast road. Specialties to search for include the pepper sauce (which is mouth-burning hot), stocked near the catsup and other condiments, and sherry-pepper sauce, better known in Bermuda but now made in Barbados also. (*Windmill* is one reliable brand for pepper sauce.)

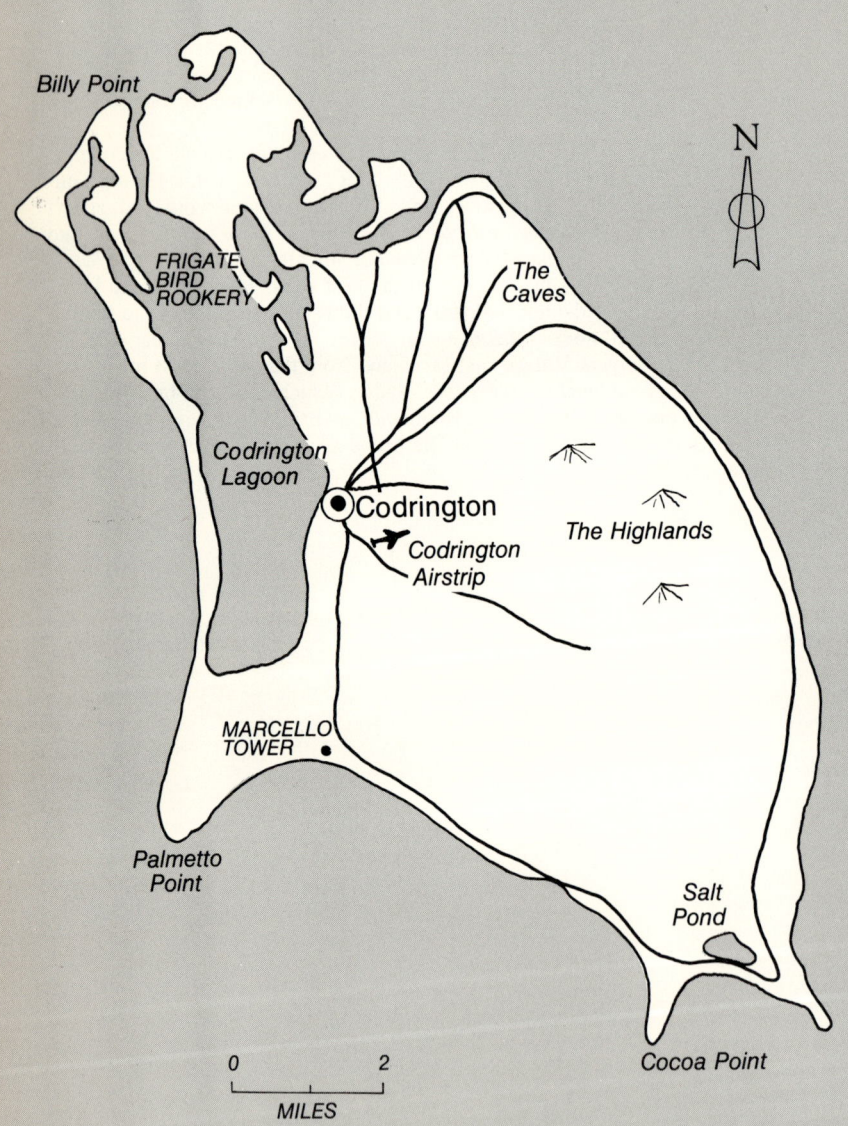

BARBUDA

> Antigua and Barbuda Tourist Office, Box 363, Long St., Antigua, W.I., T 809+462–0480 or 462–2105, fax 809+462–2483; Suite 311, 610 Fifth Ave., New York, NY 10020, T 212+541–4117, fax 212+757–1607; Suite 601, 2000 N St., N.W., Washington, DC 20036, T 202+296–6310; 60 St. Clair Ave. E., Toronto, Ontario, Canada M4T 1N5, T 416+961–3083; 15 Thayer St., London SW1 W9TJ, England, T 01+486–7073.

$ · · · US$1 = EC$2.65
Unless otherwise noted, $ refers to U.S. currency.

Soft sand makes a slalom course out of the "road," and a rim between my route and the limpid sea. "My" sturdy Hustler, borrowed a few minutes earlier from a bemused Barbudan, is a suitable companion for exploring. I have total confidence in the car, and the beauty of the surroundings sets my mind at ease. It doesn't matter that the "road" is a sand track and that I'm not sure where I'm going.

"All the roads lead back to here," I was told earlier, as I leveraged into the driver's seat to bounce away in my borrowed chariot. Profit Burton, who had helped arrange the rental of the jeep, promised I'd find "some of the most gorgeous beach you ever see." He's right!

This is an unusual island. The 62 square miles are a coral pancake, cooking on the Caribbean sea. The commerce and tourism of Antigua are a respectable 25 miles away, too far to see clearly and much too different to feel.

Barbuda is the kind of island that helps to manufacture dreams. Almost 30 years ago William Cody Kelly pictured his remote resort on the south coast beach, and more recently, others have spotted this spectacular spot—and set some plans in motion. Fortunately, rumors move faster than reality.

The island came into focus for those who watched a CBS "60 Minutes" television show in early '83, when Morley Safer reported on the "Sovereign Order of New Aragon." Taking its cue—and its name—from a group formed in 718 in Spain, the new "Sovereign Order" proved to be a "Sicilian doctor and part-time Prince" who tried to buy some Barbudan land as a retreat for a small and elite group of the world's wealthy.

Their plan never materialized—although the gossip certainly did—only to receive a challenge in mid-1987 from treasure hunter Mel Fisher's mind-boggling scheme for a dive-in, action-packed resort. Barbuda is that kind of place. Marked, inevitably, for future development, the island stands serene, slightly seedy, and silent—in seas that separate it from the commercial developments of other less idyllic spots and with long and beautiful beaches that are, in a word, spectacular.

AUTHOR'S OBSERVATION

Not to be confused with Barbados or Bermuda, the island's name is pronounced Bar-*biew*-da.

POLITICAL PICTURE: Barbuda is part of the two-island country of Antigua-Barbuda, which became independent from Britain on November 1, 1983. The 1500 Barbudians take their independence seriously, although their style of politics is difficult for most outsiders to understand. For many years, Burton was the name to know, since Burtons run most of the businesses on this quiet island. Barbuda's causes are now championed at government meetings in Antigua's capital, St. John's, by a delegate who supports the exploitive policies approved by Antigua-Barbuda's Prime Minister, Vere C. Bird. (See "Political Picture" for Antigua.) Barbudians have been vocal in their requests for attention from the country's government, for funds for road building and other services. A few Barbudians have also been very active in potential money-making schemes of their own—from fish processing to selling of sand to other ventures popular on isolated islands. From time to time, there is talk of independence, but those plans are dormant at present. So is most of the activity on the island.

ISLAND APPEARANCE Barbuda seems to lie flat on the sea, with scrub growth prickling from its surface in some sectors. Don't expect areas of palm trees; few trees grow that high. Only naturalists and the most avid island aficionados will be intrigued by Barbuda, since there's little or no development except for the hullabaloo along Coco Beach, where a legendary resort carves its place. The main town of Codrington is a collection of modest, sun-baked buildings, a few of which are local bars favored by fishermen when seas are too rough for their work. The few roads are mile after mile of packed sand occasionally with an asphalt layer; most of the shoreline is rimmed with wide, white-to-pink soft-sand beaches. This is definitely an outpost island! Most Barbudians claim African ancestors.

LIFESTYLE is very relaxed, with the quiet village of Codrington the one community. There are only two resorts where visitors stay pretty much to themselves, sinking into the sea or hiking through the flatlands in search of birds to spot and game to shoot.

MEDICAL FACILITIES Although there's no big hospital, and serious medical problems warrant chartering a plane to fly to Puerto Rico or Miami, the small Springview Hospital benefits from the Coco Point Fund, incorported in New York as a not-for-profit chartered organization, and thoughtful attention from guests and friends of Coco Point, who have arranged for donations of hospital supplies and grants for purchase of needed supplies and equipment.

MONEY MATTERS are handled in Eastern Caribbean currency, with U.S. dollars happily accepted (and sometimes required) at hotels. If you think you want EC currency, change money at banks on Antigua; it's difficult to find a place to change money on Barbuda.

COMMUNICATIONS are best by arriving in person. There's no phone service. Radio calls are possible from Antigua. Coco Point resort has communications links through its New York office (see listing at back of book).

ARRIVAL is via small plane from Antigua, usually on LIAT, as Antigua-based Leeward Islands Air Transport is known. The flight takes about 20 minutes. Be sure to reconfirm your departing LIAT flight when you arrive; it may be difficult to find anyone who can help with reconfirmation at other times. Coco Point has its own well-equipped, comfortable small jet to meet its guests. The K-Club does also, when it is open. You'll be met on arrival in Antigua.

DEPARTURE from Codrington's airport is casual. It's a good idea to arrive early, even if the tiny air "terminal" is not open, because many folks arrive without reservations and are sometimes served on a "first come, first served" basis. If you are connecting to an away-from-Antigua flight, be sure LIAT knows that you have connections to make.

TOURING TIPS: Waddalli Marke (462–2227) takes day trips from Antigua, offering a tour, picnic lunch, and flights. Profit Burton is one of the enterprising "tour operators" on Barbuda. He's often at the airport to meet the planes. His small van loads with visitors and the tour depends on the wishes of the group insofar as how much beach time, picnic time, and driving/sightseeing is involved. Rental cars are not easy to find. I latched onto a privately-owned Hustler jeep for my touring, and found it reminiscent of driving in deserts in other countries. Cost depends on your bargaining abilities.

LODGING is either pricey luxury or humble places that charge more than they're worth, in my opinion.

HOTELS/RESORTS are limited to two as this edition goes to press, but there are rumors of other big developments to come. It will take time for plans to materialize, but the *Caribbean Newsletter* (page 9) will give facts for the most realistic rumors when warranted.

★★★★★ **Coco Point Lodge** • *at Coco Point, on the south shore* • is one of the Caribbean's special spots, with a mystique that belies its appearance. Old money and the inwardly secure love it; nouveau riche are sometimes put off by the basic "architecture" and laid-back atmosphere. To some, it seems to be a put-on for the life of luxury; to others it is a dream come true. The spectacular beach cannot be questioned; it is one of the Caribbean's best, longest, and whitest—and is what drew Cincinnati's William Cody Kelly and a college friend here, when they were flying around the Caribbean to find "the perfect" island. In the early 1960s friends at Antigua's exclusive Mill Reef Club suggested that Kelly investigate this island; the first buildings at Coco Point began to grow soon thereafter. A couple of hurricanes washed away the earliest efforts, but the Kellys and friends persevered. What stands now is a remote enclave of unpretentious lodgings where an inclusive price (over $1000 per day for two, with taxes and tips included) gives you food, drink, tennis courts, boats for fishing and sailing, snorkel equipment, hunting hints, and assorted other diversions. (Bring your own scuba gear.) Bedrooms are in one of several ranch-style houses, most draped in shrubs, flowers, and other tropical growth that thrive when there's rain (which isn't often). The villas are comfortably furnished for beach-side living, all units offer a beach and seaview from patio and living area, and most have enviable privacy. Some sleeping areas share a common living room, an acceptable arrangement for families and/or close friends. The resort is self-contained, with emphasis on the good life as the key to comfort. No phones. No cars. No gala nightlife, but "yes" to pleasant surroundings in which to relax—and revive. The only planned activity is a weekly Sunfish Sailboat race; its purpose is as a casual meet-and-greet opportunity. Meals are served in the main house, where the bar and terrace become the social hub from late afternoon onward. A private house party atmosphere makes this place appealing for those comfortable in a WASP country club setting. *Clublike resort.*

The K Club • *on the long beach shared with Coco Point* • is a sensation—which has had hiccups since it "opened" as the 1980s became the '90s. The premature opening was, I suspect, because the contractors were liable for substantial penalties if they didn't have units ready by December 1989. Reportedly built out of pique at his reception (and treatment) at Coco Point, Italian Aldo Pinto and Mariuccia Mandelli, best known for her Krizia haute couture, have poured millions into this planned pace-setter. The spacious villas have the elegance of luxurious island homes, with fluffy towels, expensive sheets, and other accoutrements, and an upscale atmosphere that is difficult (impossible?) for the Barbudian staff to understand. Bathrooms are lavish; living areas viewful and relaxing. The beach is, quite simply, spectacular! And the intended sybaritic lifestyle could be enjoyed by those willing to pay the astounding price tag, if they're also willing to overlook the obvious gaffes in service and hospitality. The route to reach this place has been a rutted and often-dusty packed-sand road—for a bumpy 20-minute drive from Codrington's airport—but there's talk of a private plane from Antigua to a private airstrip (as is the case for Coco Point). The golf course might be ready for this season; the *Caribbean Newsletter* will have a status report on this place, which aspires to be ★★★★★-plus when it hits its stride. *Exclusive resort.*

HOUSEKEEPING HOLIDAYS are back to basics on Barbuda. Bring staples with you or plan to buy them (at high prices) in Antigua. There's little in the markets of Codrington. Fresh fish and lobster are available, depending on your bargaining ability. The few places are best appreciated by those who *want* out-of-the-way lodgings in camplike style.

The Earls • *near Codrington* • includes one 4-bedroom villa and two 1-bedroom studio apartments that can be linked through connecting doors if a family wants the whole unit. There's also a "cottage" in Codrington. The villa and studio apartments are about a mile from town; all are a few minutes' drive from the airport. Don't expect to find lavish furnishings. The emphasis is on very informal living with sun, sand, sea, and nature as prime attractions. Your cook will come to the beach with you to cook out, if you wish. These lodgings are only worth pursuing if you are Robinson Crusoe or similarly self-sufficient.

THE INN WAY: There's only one place even close to claiming inn-like status, and it falls short of the mark (for hospitality).

Sunset View Resort • *near Codrington and the shore* • is a small and very modest hotel. Although the physical plan is pleasant, with 2-story buildings angled around a small pool, the buildings were set so that essential breezes are cut off by construction. They stand on parched land, a long hot walk from town or from the shore, which makes a taxi or some vehicle essential. Rooms have modern conveniences, which may or may not be in good condition. The patio is open to breezes and pleasant for meals and socializing.

LOW-COST LODGING: It's sometimes possible to find a room in a local home at very modest cost. The only reliable way to arrange these accommodations, however, is to fly here to see for yourself. Some homes do not have hot water; most will not offer private bathrooms. The very simple facilities seem best for back-packing types.

RESTAURANTS are limited to the hotels, at this point, but the best bet is a lobster grilled on the beach.

NATURAL SURROUNDINGS: Although it's one of two islands (Antigua is the other) that rise from the now submerged Barbuda Bank, this low-lying "platter" is only limestone rock. Its high point reaches 147 feet, in an area known as The Highlands. Caves north of that area, near the northeastern shore, have not been thoroughly explored by scholars who might recognize markings and other findings. Similar underground caves on Anguilla, however, are thought to be one of the region's earliest and most important Amerindian religious sites. Birders focus on the Frigate Bird Rookery, in the northwestern area on Codrington Lagoon, but there are an estimated 150 species of birds spotted elsewhere around the island—until development sends them elsewhere.

Fishermen have long respected and made a good living from the sea. Caribbean lobsters are a crop of value, and reefs are now coming into focus for scuba divers since almost 100 shipwrecks lie in surrounding seas.

At this writing there are no professionally organized diving facilities, although adventuresome (and experienced) divers are among the island's few visitors.

PLACES WORTH FINDING are those offered by nature. The village of Codrington is a cluster of homes with a few shops for goods for local consumption. By all means go to the pink beach, where tiny shells pave the shoreline.

SPORTS are available for Coco Point's guests, through the facilities at the hotel. Other visitors should be content with swimming and snorkeling, unless you are a scuba enthusiast and want to bring your own equipment. There are a couple of scuba pros on Barbuda. The best source is the Catamaran, a shoreside inn opened by some American scuba enthusiasts. When boats anchor off Le Village Soleil, it's sometimes possible to go for a day's sail.

TREASURES AND TRIFLES are best found on Antigua. There are a few shops at Antigua's airport, if you don't have time to go into St. John's.

BONAIRE

> Bonaire Tourist Bureau, Kaya Simon Bolivar 12, Kralendijk, Bonaire, N.A., T 011+599+7−8322, fax 011+5997−8408; Bonaire Government Tourist Information Office, c/o Resorts Management, 201½ E. 29th St., New York, NY 10016, T 212+799−0242 or 800+826−6247, fax 212+689−1598; 815A Queen St. E., Toronto, Ont., Canada M4M 1H8, T 416+465−2958.

$ · · · US$1 = NAf 1.77
Unless otherwise noted, U.S. equivalents are figured at this rate.

The room was dark when Dee Scarr's commentary put animation into the colorful slides that paraded across the screen. There were pictures of fish eagerly feeding on clouds of "breadcrumbs," nibbling hot dogs or pieces of cheese, being stroked, and becoming friends with divers whom they return to "visit" when the boat appears. "People are in the sea because of technology," she explains, "and not because we are natural friends or natural enemies of any of the sea creatures. Therefore, they do not fear us naturally."

It was about 9 p.m., and those who shared the small, shoreside room with me were heading out early in the morning for an eagerly anticipated scuba diving experience. Dee has been sharing her "Touch of the Sea" technique with divers from Florida to Caymans and on to Bonaire. Her ecologically oriented talk tells divers how friendly the fish are, how fragile their lifestyle (especially when we intrude), how one recognizable fish turned up at a dive site some distance from his first "home," and of how she and others had tracked the travels of their underwater friends from one area off Bonaire's coral hump to another.

The staghorn coral and parade of fish that help light up the liquid atmosphere around Bonaire are a fact of life. They've been swirling for centuries around this coral reef that rises high enough—and stretches long enough—to hold houses, road, an airport, and a couple of small hotels. But you are still living on a reef . . . and you're the most recent intruder.

The underwater landscape has been growing forever, and the flamingos that fly here every day from an unknown nightly nesting spot have a longer tenancy than we do. They have a say over what changes are made and there are others who speak for the sea fans, the elkhorn coral, and the strands of growth in the majestic underwater arboretum.

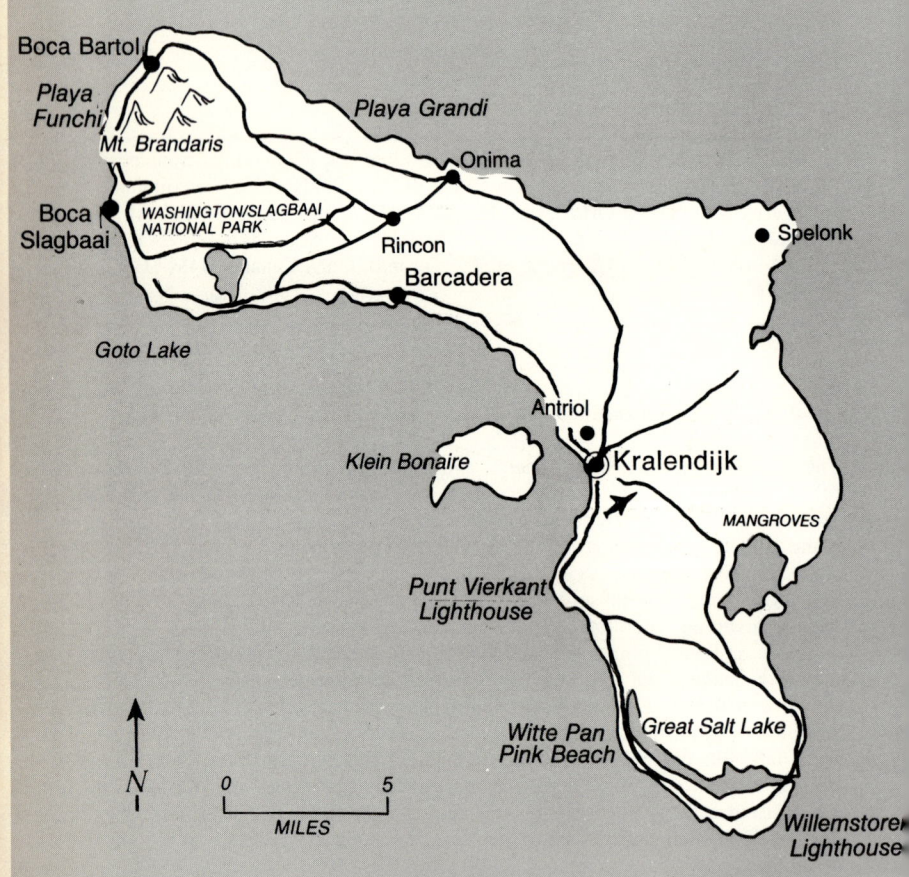

Father Candidas, or Vater Candidas as he is known on Bonaire, seems to be the resident expert on the birds. He has tracked an awesome number, and sometimes shares his knowledge with visitors who make an appointment to learn from him. His best source, he says, is a bird book in Dutch that is now being translated into English, but there's no substitute for spending hours roaming the bony landscape of this island, pith helmet on head, binoculars at the ready, flask of water in a pocket, and conversation at a standstill. The birds are here; usually people are not.

The natural Bonaire is a special island whose true value is often overlooked. It could be the Caribbean's Galapagos.

POLITICAL PICTURE: As one of the Netherlands Antilles (with Curacao and the three S-islands, Saba, Statia, and Sint Maarten, to the north), Bonaire shares guidance and aid from the mother country (Holland). Bonaire also shares in the plans, agreed to at meetings held in the Netherlands in spring of '83, for Aruba's split from its sister islands on January 1, 1986, and the independence of the rest of the group and Aruba in 1996. The 10,022 people that live on this 112-square-mile, boomerang-shaped, coral outcropping elect one representative to the Staten that meets in Curaçao to discuss policies and regulations for the five islands. The local government, however, is strictly a Bonairean affair, with elections held every four years. The most recent elections, in April 1991, supported plans for development, and those plans are moving along at a good pace.

Tourism is the main hard-currency source for the island, with Venezuelans and other South American visitors making an impact on an island that is being "discovered" by increasing numbers of North Americans. As is the case with neighbor islands Aruba and Curaçao, South America's effect on this island is immediately obvious, not only with language (Spanish is spoken by many), but also with business.

ISLAND APPEARANCE: "Parched" and "dry" are the two words that come to mind. Although fascinating from the air, because the surrounding reefs turn the seas several shades of blue and the shoreline is etched white in some areas, the island seems desertlike; it is not lush or palm studded. Your airport exit puts you within a few minutes' drive of the half dozen streets of town, all fringed with reasonably standard stucco block buildings in a style popular for island commerce in the '50s and '60s. There are only a few buildings in town with the interesting architecture of Dutch colonial days, although some of the newest resorts are setting an interesting pace for modern style. Washington-Slagbaai National Park is a protected area of corrugated terrain, with trees, scrub-brush, and cactus that thrive in the dry climate, as well as salt ponds and waterholes that are favorite nesting areas for birds. There are also salt ponds in the southern sector of this boomerang-shaped island. Although there are several sandy coves, they do not have the long, wide, white-sand borders found on some other islands.

LIFESTYLE is Caribbean in a Dutch framework. Because the island (in size and population) is not large, local customs are akin to those in many small rural towns. Life for Bonaireans is conservative, and—although casual dress is common for everyone—visitors should cover up their beach attire when going into the small town of Kralendijk. At official government functions, guests will dress up, but that is about the only time you will see male residents in coat and tie, or women in long dresses (and even that does not always happen these days). Since this is a warm and sunny, beach-oriented outdoor place, casual clothes can go almost everywhere.

MEDICAL FACILITIES: Although the island is small, the hospital in Kralendijk has a decompression chamber in recognition of its scuba appeal. Doctors have trained in the Netherlands and the facilities are well maintained.

MONEY MATTERS involve the Netherlands Antilles florin or guilder, noted as NAf or Afl (for Antilles' florin). Most restaurants, shops, and hotels quote prices in the local currency but will take U.S. currency (and give change in guilders). Hotels will expect you to pay in dollars if you are from the United States. Change currency at the bank for the best rate; hotels usually charge a few points.

COMMUNICATIONS are reasonably easy by overseas telephone service, but not all lodgings have phones, and room phones are rare. Direct dial to Bonaire is 011+ 599+ 7+ 4-digit Bonaire number. From Bonaire, calls can be made by credit card from the Landsradio office in Kralendijk and from the airport. AT&T's USADirect service is reached by dialing 001+800+872–2881 from telephones in Bonaire. There are excellent radio services, but one result of the nearness to the South American coast is that most of the stations are in Spanish.

ARRIVAL by air often follows a 25-minute flight (at about 3000 feet) from Curaçao, unless you fly in from Miami on one of ALM Antillean Airline's 2½ hour flights, or come by cruise ship (see below). American Airlines has a link through its San Juan, Puerto Rico, hub. Smaller planes continue to provide the regular service, with frequent flights from Aruba and Curaçao as well as from South American cities. The boxy, modern airport terminal was opened in '79, having been financed with European Common Market funds. Arrival formalities are perfunctory if you have flown in from one of the other Dutch islands; if you are arriving from outside the region, you need to show your proof of citizenship (passport is best), plus return or onward tickets. There are car rental services as well as taxis at the airport.

CRUISE ships dock at the main town of Kralendijk, within easy walking distance of the few shops, the several restaurants, and the Divi Flamingo Beach Resort. Scuba diving, birding, and hiking in the National Park are the main attractions.

DEPARTURE is reasonably easy at the small, neat terminal, especially when you make your official Netherlands Antilles exit from a connecting flight in Curacao. There's a pleasant bar area with tables and chairs for relaxing during the inevitable delay with planes. The departure tax is NAf17.70 or US$10. The inter-island tax for sister Dutch-affiliated islands is US$5.65.

TOURING TIPS **Car rental** makes sense on Bonaire. If you're planning to tour Washington Park, be sure to ask for a rugged, jeep-style vehicle since there are 20-plus miles of unpaved roads. On a few recent visits, I rented from *Bonaire Car Rental* at the airport, but other firms also have airport desks, and rates are pretty much the same with all. *Dollar Rent-a-car* (T 599+7-8888, fax 599+7-8877) is another to try. Main roads are good and driving is easy—with plenty of pausing places if you want to take pictures or go for a picnic. Unless you're staying at Divi Flamingo Beach or like being locked into where you *are* staying (except for scuba experiences), you'll need a car for getting around. **Taxis** are available, but not always where and when you want one. Honda **scooters** can be rented through most *Budget Car Rental* offices and Yamahas can be rented at *Happy Chappy Rentals* (Kaya Hellmund 27), which is also a dive shop. If you want an organized **tour,** *Bonaire Sightseeing* (T 599+7-8300, fax 599+7-8118) offers them, with a half-day each for the northern or the southern part of the island, at about $12 for each half.

LODGING is limited to a few hotels and a couple of dozen informal guest houses where scuba diving is the main topic of conversation. With the opening of *The Point* and *Harbour Village,* Bonaire has its first new-and-big resorts.

Most lodgings add the 8% government tax and a 10% service charge to your bill, but always ask about other possible charges to avoid last minute surprises.

AUTHOR'S AWARDS

Captain Don's Habitat is a longtime favorite, for its truly Bonairean personality and the new and comfortable villa suites; *Divi Flamingo* continues to be one of the Divi group's best hotels; and I give a pre-opening award to *The Point* for the glitzy pace it will set for Bonaire, with its lagoons, casino, and other trappings.

Information about places-to-stay is included under Hotels/Resorts, Housekeeping Holidays, The Inn Way, and Low-Cost Lodging. Stars are awarded within each category. (See page 11.)

HOTELS/RESORTS have leapt into a new league this season, with the Harbour Village and plans for The Point. Expect a few start-up problems for the new places this season.

★★★ **Captain Don's Habitat** • *at the shore, near Bonaire Beach Hotel* • has attractive villas along the rocky shore and rooms with modern comforts (and more space than the original cluster), plus restaurants and the always active scuba program. This place has a long and legendary history, having been opened by Don Stewart, who was the first to focus on diving off Bonaire more than 20 years ago. His original hotel, with its "Monks' Cell" dormitory-style dwellings, was a very casual place where many folks had happy vacations before the Caribbean became so homogenized. To keep up with the times, Habitat has cleaned up its act, but all the "personality" has not yet been swept away.

Comfortably casual sea-and-scuba-oriented folk could enjoy this place. The new villas have all comforts. *Inn & Apts.*

★★★ **Divi Flamingo Beach Resort & Casino** • *on the shore on the fringe of Kralendijk* • has grown from a modest start more than 20 years ago, with buildings that had been a prisoner-of-war detention camp, to become a complete and comfortable resort. Some rooms (101–115 and 116–124) perch at the shore, suspended over the splashing waves. Others, the newest of the lot, are fully air-conditioned studios with private sunning area. Standard rooms (4–9 and 22–26), part of the original core, are simply furnished (and dark), but all guests have easy access to the sea-based *Chibi Chibi* restaurant or the *Calabas Terrace* for meals, the *Flamingo Nest* deck bar for lingering, and two pools and the sea (but not much of a beach) for lolling. One pool, at the town edge of the resort, is centered by the casino and what's known as *Club Flamingo*. Lounge chairs fleck pool sides and the cement piers that stretch, fingerlike, into the sea. Two dive piers, brackets on the property, are touchstones for the dive boats (and enthusiasts) who make the most of the extensive *Peter Hughes Dive Bonaire* on-premises facilities. (This is an ideal scuba diving place for experts or beginners.) For night action, there's the *Flamingo Casino and Players Lounge*. You can walk to town in about 10 minutes, and there are a couple of on-premises shops for essentials. This property offers warm hospitality to those who like seaside action (or want to be with others who do). *Resort.*

★★★ **Harbour Village Beach Resort** • *at the marina, northwest of town* • has aspirations to be a total resort, although some of its planned facilities are not yet in full swing. "Sonesta" was the management name tagged to the hotel before it opened, but by early 1991, local owners had taken over management—as well as sales of the units, which can be rented in owners' absence. The resort includes 63 guest rooms and suites, plus 44 villas, in 1- and 2-story buildings clustered at or near the shoreline. Watersports include scuba and windsurfing, as well as boating options. A pleasant freshwater pool supplements the beach-and-sea for swimmers. Check on the status of the fitness center and the casino/nightclub, if they're important for your holiday happiness. Neither are open at presstime. The *Caribbean Newsletter* (page 9) will have comments as plans progress. *Resort.*

The Point • *near the airport, Kralendijk, and the shore* • is an elaborate creation that includes lagoons lacing the property, swinging foot bridges (that can move to let yachts pass), and a casino on its own tiny island. The Concorde's Robert Parker picked up this site when a Venezuelan effort ran out of cash; but progress has been slow since the fanfare that greeted his purchase. Almost 200 rooms and suites are in the plans for houseguests who can play at the casino or along the white sand-bordered shore. Shops, restaurants, and a full range of activities are part of the plan when this place is in full swing. The *Caribbean Newsletter* (page 9) will have an update, after the official opening. Ask specific questions about status of facilities before making your deposit.

Sorobon Beach Resort • *remote, on a southeast shore* • is a naturalist resort, started by owners who moved south from their resort with a similar theme on Sint Maarten. Several chalets provide housing for a carefree group of guests whose holiday has an unfettered focus. The place has been successful enough to warrant added facilities in recent years. For those who choose to "vacation in the buff," this may be a place to find. *Resort.*

★ **Sunset Beach Hotel and Casino** • *on the shore, about 5 minutes' drive from town* • knew a previous "life" as the Bonaire Beach Hotel. Extensive (and much-needed) refurbishing of the motel-style rooms gives the place a lift. The main building holds a small casino, as well as a few shops and the dining room. Bedrooms range in blocks to the left of the building as you face the sea (from the parking area). The tennis courts are farther to the left; beach activities include rental sailboats, scuba diving (including lessons), windsurfing, and snorkeling. A shoreside dining terrace has been used for breakfasts, informal lunches and barbecue evenings. Expect to find British and European guests, as well as Canadians and people from the U.S. lured here by value-full package plans. *Hotel.*

HOUSEKEEPING HOLIDAYS on Bonaire give you independence, but you'll want to bring some of the basics from home (or load up when you pass through Curacao or Aruba). You *can* buy staples in Bonaire, but selection depends on recent shipments since there's not a big local populace to assure well-stocked shelves and prices are high. One U.S.-based source for housekeeping units is **Carib Vacations** (9181 Heathridge Dr., West Palm Beach, FL 33411, T 407+793–8016 or 800+666–8016); an island-based source is **Hugo Gerharts** (Kralendijk, Bonaire, N.A.; T 011+599+7-8300).

Bachelor's Beach Apartments • *not far from the airport, on the road that leads away from Kralendijk* • are attractive, with 1- and 2-bedroom units furnished with wicker. The tiny "lawn" that stretches to the sea is coral shale, and you're on the rocks (no beach), as is the case with most places along Bonaire's shoreline. Clean, neat, and well kept when I looked in. *Apts.*

Bonaire Beach Bungalows • *just down the road from Bachelor's* • has 1- and 2-bedroom apartments in free-standing buildings, with 4 units in 2-story buildings. The clear water that is at the shore is ideal for scuba diving, as reported by the guests I talked with when I visited. Be prepared to at least nod "hello" to your neighbors; you'll hear them anyway. *Apts.*

Sand Dollar Condotel and Beach Club • *next to Bonaire Beach Hotel* • is over 200 ondominiums and town houses, with a couple of entrances from the parking area. Intended for private ownership, many units are available for rent in owners' absence. In addition to the pool and tennis courts, ownership plans a more extensive shopping complex (some stores are already in place) and a casino, which is not open at press time. For details on exactly what's on-premises when you plan to visit, ask management. The *Caribbean Newsletter* (page 9) will have further facts when warranted. *Apts.*

Sunset Oceanfront Apartments • *on the harbor, north of town* • is a building of a dozen 1- and 2-bedroom apartments, with a "neighborhood" feeling. *Apts.*

THE INN WAY usually means back-to-nature for Bonaire. The overwhelming ambience is scuba-focused, especially at the small spots that usually carry the imprint of the owner-diver. Until it added the new villa suites, *Captain Don's* met my criteria for an inn, insofar as hospitality is concerned. Although the place is too big to be a cozy inn, it still maintains the friendly atmosphere that gave it its early fame.

Here are several to try, for a scuba-inn:

Black Durgeon Inn • *on the shore, not far from Kralendijk* • is another small spot devoted to divers. With less than a dozen rooms, each with a kitchenette of sorts and basic furnishings that include a purring air-conditioning unit, this place is popular with folks who prefer informal housekeeping to flashy resorts. Don't bring much luggage; most rooms are small.

Buddy's Dive Resort • *near Habitat and Sand Dollar, on the Leeward Coast* • is a group of modern seafront apartments, both 1- and 2-bedroom units in a low, white stucco building. The units have all modern conveniences, including air-conditioning, and are some of what's planned to be a 72-unit community. *Apts.*

Carib Inn • *at the shore* • has 10 rooms in its building, with small pool and pleasant patio where diving enthusiasts congregate. This is another of Bonaire's small dive-oriented lodgings. Meals are not offered at the premises (which means that folks without one of the cooking units will have to find a friend who cooks or sample the local restaurants).

Sunset Inn • *on the beach* • has kitchenettes in 2 of its half-dozen rooms and cable television in all rooms. Casual and dive-oriented (as are most small spots on this island), this place can be ideal for self-sufficient scuba enthusiasts who can stroll to a couple of nearby dive operations. Kralendijk is a short walk away.

LOW-COST LODGINGS: The least expensive places are private rooms for rent and the tourist office is the best source for what's available. Inquire, also, about the older rooms at Habitat and Buddy's Dive Resort (see above). They rent at low cost. Some of the cottages and apartments come to very reasonable cost when shared by several people, and rates—as on all the islands—are much lower from mid-April through mid-December than the winter time, peak-season top rates. **Hotel Rochaline,** in Kralendijk, has, I hope, had a desperately needed overhaul by the time you visit. Be sure to ask; the *Caribbean Newsletter* (page 9) will have news when warranted, but when I checked for this edition, the place looked like a welfare hotel. The rooms were dirty and small. Take a look at the kitchen before eating in the once pleasant *Lisboa* restaurant.

RESTAURANTS on Bonaire can be comfortably entertaining, but expensive for a captive audience of tourists. Most of the dining depots are in the town of Kralendijk, with a few places at hotels or other spots nearby. When *Sonesta* and *The Point* are in full swing, their restaurants may be noteworthy. Seafood is usually fresh from surrounding seas; steaks are flown in (and have been frozen); and you can expect to find Dutch/Indonesian offerings on some menus. The listing is often in Dutch; prices will be in local currency (and someone will need a converter or a quick mind to tabulate if you want to pay in U.S. dollars).

★★★ **Beefeater** • *in a small Bonairean house on Kaya Grandi, across from the Tourist Office* • has a devoted following. The place is known for its steaks. Atmosphere is friendly, and reservations are recommended if you want to dine at locally fashionable 8 p.m. or later. The place is closed on Tuesdays.

★★★★ **Bistro des Amis** • *on Kaya L. D. Gerharts, off Kaya Grandi in Kralendijk* • where I enjoyed an exceptionally good poisson du jour (fish of the day) is my "best bet" for Bonaire. Its escargot are pungently seasoned, and the aroma of garlic lends a true bistro note. Reservations are recommended. Lucielle, the owner, is Bonairean, but the atmosphere is definitely French, from the wine to the decor and the leisurely dining. Don't plan on Sun. when the place is closed; otherwise stop by anytime after 6:30 p.m. or so. After 11 p.m. there's dancing, but dining is limited to snacks.

★★★ **Zeezicht** • *Seaview, on the shore* • is a convenient rendezvous if you're in town with friends. Its location gives lingerers plenty to watch, especially if you have a table on the building's front porch. The second floor becomes a disco most evenings. Specialties include the full fish menu, Chinese favorites, some Indonesian items and other interesting offerings leading up to the local lobster (served at 11 to 35 NAf, depending on style and size). Worth a visit if you're not discouraged by flies around your food.

Among the eating possibilities at hotels, the **Chibi-Chibi** and the **Calabas Terrace** at Divi Flamingo Beach have food and service that will be familiar for American tastes. All the expecteds parade on the menu (steak, chicken, fish), and usually appear dressed in recognizable fashions. The setting (at the sea, within sound of wave splash if conversations permit hearing) is pleasant; prices are high; and food is acceptable. The dining terrace at Sand Dollar is called the Green Parrot; its menu is hamburgers, etc.

Residents seem to enjoy **China Garden,** in a former home on Breedestraat, and Kaya Grandi, but I don't head to small Caribbean islands for Chinese food and haven't tried it. Ask at the Tourist Board about any newcomers.

NATURAL SURROUNDINGS The reference to the "Caribbean's Galapagos" in the introduction to this chapter is not an idle comment. Significant portions of Bonaire's 112 square miles, measuring 3 to 7 miles at the widest expanse and about 24 miles long, and all of the 1500 acres of Klein Bonaire, the rocky, beach-rimmed speck just out of the harbor at Kralendijk, are set aside as nature preserves where unusual birds and lizards thrive. As many as 135 bird species have been counted, with the flocks of elegant flamingos nesting in the salinas (salt ponds) of the Washington-Slagbaai National Park, at Goto Meer, and near Pekel Meer in the south, and the indigenous Lora parrot, now endangered although once considered a pest, finding protection in the park. Insofar as lizards are concerned, the ubiquitous geckos are "everywhere," but the Anolis, with a yellow dewlap, and the large blue lizard are unique to Bonaire.

> **AUTHOR'S OBSERVATION**
> The concise and fact-filled articles in the pink *Bonaire Holiday* tourist newspaper, available through the tourist office and most hotels, are good sources for background about Bonaire's natural assets. Contact the tourist office for a copy prior to your arrival on the island.

Washington/Slagbaai National Park, at the northwestern nub of the island, started with about 5000 acres of rugged, arid land that was dotted with scrub, cactus, and divi-divi trees. In the original acreage, once a private estate, there is a waterhole that draws interesting birds. The preserve now includes an additional tract, bringing its total size to about 13,500 acres. In addition to being laced with rutted roads, in those places where there are any roads at all, hiking and walking paths lead to remote areas.

> **AUTHOR'S OBSERVATION**
> A broad-brimmed hat, plenty of effective sunblock, comfortable (preferbly lightweight) walking shoes, and a water flask are as essential as your binoculars if you're hiking in this hot and arid terrain.

Tickets are sold (about $2 for adults; less for children) at the gate house, which also holds a small museum, where the main road enters the park area. Conservationists should try to track down a copy of the *Field Guide of the Washington National Park,* published by the Netherlands Antilles Park Foundation.

The Bonaire Marine Park surrounds the island, from the shore to a depth of about 200 feet. The protected area received its impetus from the World Wildlife Fund, which expressed interest (and provided seed money) for the Bonaire project, now managed by the Netherlands Antilles National Foundation, locally known as STINAPA, an acronyn for its tongue-twisting Dutch name. Reef management has become the study for biologists, including those from the Caribbean Marine Biological Institute in Curacao, and study projects are widely acknowledged for their importance to preservation of Bonaire's natural surroundings in light of a developing tourism. Divers and snorkelers are (and will be) enchanted by the complex life under the sea in this area that has been touted as "one of the three best scuba areas in the world."

PLACES WORTH FINDING are few, and not nearly as interesting in my opinion as what nature has given to this special spot.

KRALENDIJK, the small capital, is two streets wide, with a few arms reaching inland; it is the hub of the island's "developed" area, which is the west coast. Except for the shops, there's not much of visitor interest in town. Even the boxy stucco buildings, most of them air-conditioned for staff survival, are not much to look at; there's a small selection of the Dutch architecture adapted to the Caribbean climate that you see in Willemstad, Curacao, or even

Aruba's Oranjestad. **Instituto Folklore Bonaire** on Helmundweg, in the fort (Mon., Wed., Fri. 8 a.m.–12 p.m., Sat. 9 a.m.–1 p.m.) is worth some time, when you are in town, to look at the artifacts collected from Bonaire homes and grounds. In addition to a few utensils and some diagrams and comments about the earliest Indian settlers, there are some interesting musical instruments and a few costumes. (This isn't worth a special trip, but can occupy a half hour between shops.) The **Fish Market,** in the "Greek Temple" at the waterfront near Hotel Rochaline, should be visited in the morning for the best look at the catch.

Slave huts, on the southwest coast, are small and, although it may be interesting to see where the workers rested (2 per hut) while they worked on the salt flats, the area is hot and stark—with acres of shallow ponds of the Antilles International Salt Company stretching out to evaporate in the sun. The Willemstoren Lighthouse marks the island's southernmost tip. If you miss seeing it, don't consider your vacation ruined, but do try to catch the flamingos.

BOPEC is the Bonaire Petroleum Corporation, a joint operation of Long Island, N.Y.'s Northville Industries and Paktank of Rotterdam. Its continuing status is in question at presstime. The firm created a furor among caring conservationists when it was proposed for Bonairean shores, but local politicians assuaged the protestors with promises that all precautions would be taken to keep the transfer of European, Mideast, and African oil to U.S. tankers a purely pipe-processed operation. No sea dumping or pipe splitting, they claim.

SPORTS on Bonaire are sea-centered. Sealife is protected and conservation is a serious concern. The water gives you a dependable visibility of 150 to 200 feet; you can get to a lot of interesting places without a boat; the water's warm enough to **scuba** without a wet suit, and there's very little current and no shark scares in the hotel or dive site areas. Add to that the fact that pros have put all their expertise into teaching you how to scuba, and you have ideal surroundings to learn—practically by osmosis.

Bonaire Scuba Center started operations in February 1981 from bases at the Bonaire Beach Hotel and an apartment. The Center has full facilities and enough equipment for up to 80 divers plus all the equipment for board sailing, glass-bottom boat trips and other watersports. Stateside contact is through Bonaire Scuba Center, Box 775, Morgan, NJ 08879; 201 + 566–8866 or 800 + 526–2370.

Habitat Dive Center and Captain Don are known to anyone who is anyone in the underwater world. (Anyone who hasn't heard the name will know it after about 5 minutes on this island.) Don Stewart is king of Bonaire's underwater caverns, but many may not know that when Captain Don came ashore on Bonaire on May 21, 1962, he intended to continue to Antigua, and more verdant island dreams. The life he found underwater here far exceeded anything he hoped to find above the ground on other islands, so he stayed. At that point, the "invaders" who had landed on Bonaire were few, and the patch of land he clung to after nine years at sea became his leap-off ledge for underwater explorations that have helped the Bonaireans realize the riches of the reefs that surround them. It is thanks largely to the pioneering (and perseverance) of Don Stewart that the scuba clan have recognized Bonaire as one of the world's top three diving resorts. His informal *Habitat,* a "total resort" for divers where even table talk is dive-centered, is a short walk from the Bonaire Beach Hotel. A team takes beginners as well as experienced divers to the sites that rim Bonaire. Divemasters change, but the program remains fascinating. Details are available through *Habitat* (1080 Port Boulevard, Miami, FL 33123, 800+327-6709).

Peter Hughes Dive Bonaire has been in operation for several years. Peter Hughes started diving and teaching in Trinidad, Roatan (Honduras), and Tobago before coming to Bonaire, where his scuba expertise led him to the Cayman Islands and now to the U.S., where he is vice-president of marine operations for the Divi Hotel group (which includes Flamingo Beach). There are few (if any) Caribbean-based scuba programs of the scope and expertise of this one, where facilities include the necessary tanks, regulators, fins, snorkels, etc., plus flattop boats, a 31-foot cruiser for longer hauls, and a 60-foot sailboat for picnics and cruising as well as diving. The U.S. contact is Divi Hotels (800+367-3484 or 607+277-3484).

Bonaire's diving opportunities are endless, and can be as easy as surveying the growth and life around the piers at the harbor of Kralendijk to heading out to Klein Bonaire, the small island that sits in the harbor, or making unscheduled dives at whim right from your hotel. Since the island *is* a coral reef, surrounded by more reefs, you can see plenty by walking in from shore.

Deep-sea fishing can be arranged out of the hotels. All equipment is available with the charter, and what you may lack in the last word in rods and reels you more than make up for with the convenience of having something with the boat.

Waterskiing is possible, through your hotel's activities' desk. Check when you get to Bonaire.

Horseback riding is offered at *Rini's Stables* (check with Cap'n Don at *Habitat*).

Boardsailing is popular with many scuba folk, and boards are appearing at Bonaire Beach and other spots. Check with the Tourist Board if the sport is important for you.

Sailing regattas have been held for the past 15-plus years in October. Started as a race for traditional island sloops, the event has become annual. Check with the tourist office if you're interested. For day and longer yacht charters, ask at the marina when you get to Bonaire.

Other sports on Bonaire are limited to **tennis** at Sunset Beach Hotel, Sand Dollar, Divi Flamingo Beach, or on the two town courts.

The sea is all—unless you include **birding** as a sport, in which case there are about 130 species to track, and the spectacular flock of flamingos, bright pink from the special algae they feed on in the salt flats. The flamingos are in residence year-round. Fall, winter, and spring are the best time for other birds.

TREASURES AND TRIFLES on Bonaire are sea-centered, and most of them are untouchable. The sights you capture with your (or a rented) underwater camera will be the best tokens of your trip to Bonaire, but if you want the more commercial items usually found in tourist resorts, you'll have to meander around Karlendijk or make a quick sweep through the selection at your hotel's boutique.

Spritzer & Fuhrmann on Kaya Grandi (the continuation of J. A. Abraham Boulevard) stocks watches, jewelry, and other luxury items at prices similar to those in Curacao and Aruba. **Littman Jewelers,** also on Kaya Grandi, also has quality merchandise. Do not expect the same extensive selection you might have seen in Aruba or Curacao (or could see on a day's flight and shopping excursion to either island), but there will be something to spend your money on. If you have your heart set on a special item, start your shopping early enough so that the store staff have time to have a selection flown over from one of the other shops.

Things Bonaire, on Kaya Grandi, has piles of T-shirts and a few locally made items, but **Aries Boutique,** at the Bonaire Shopping Gallery, has some resort clothes and coral jewelry as well as the ubiquitous T-shirt.

Fundashon Arte Industria Bonairiano, on J. A. Abraham Boulevard in town, is the local source for arts and crafts. While the assortment includes childlike shellwork, there are also a few locally made caftans, some black coral jewelry, and wraparound skirts made from fabric with island designs. The project was helped by a U.N. group devoted to encouraging, and training in, handicrafts, but my most recent look at the merchandise didn't fill me with inspiration (or desire to buy).

Cambes, one of the few local industries, makes shirts and uniforms. Although you probably won't be in the market for one of the uniforms, some of the sport shirts and leisure clothes are worth a look. Ask about the "factory outlet" shop.

Stop at the **Kralendijk Supermarket** or **Lidia's** if you're interested in local and Indonesian spices, which can be bought off the shelf along with other European Common Market (and of course Netherlands) imports.

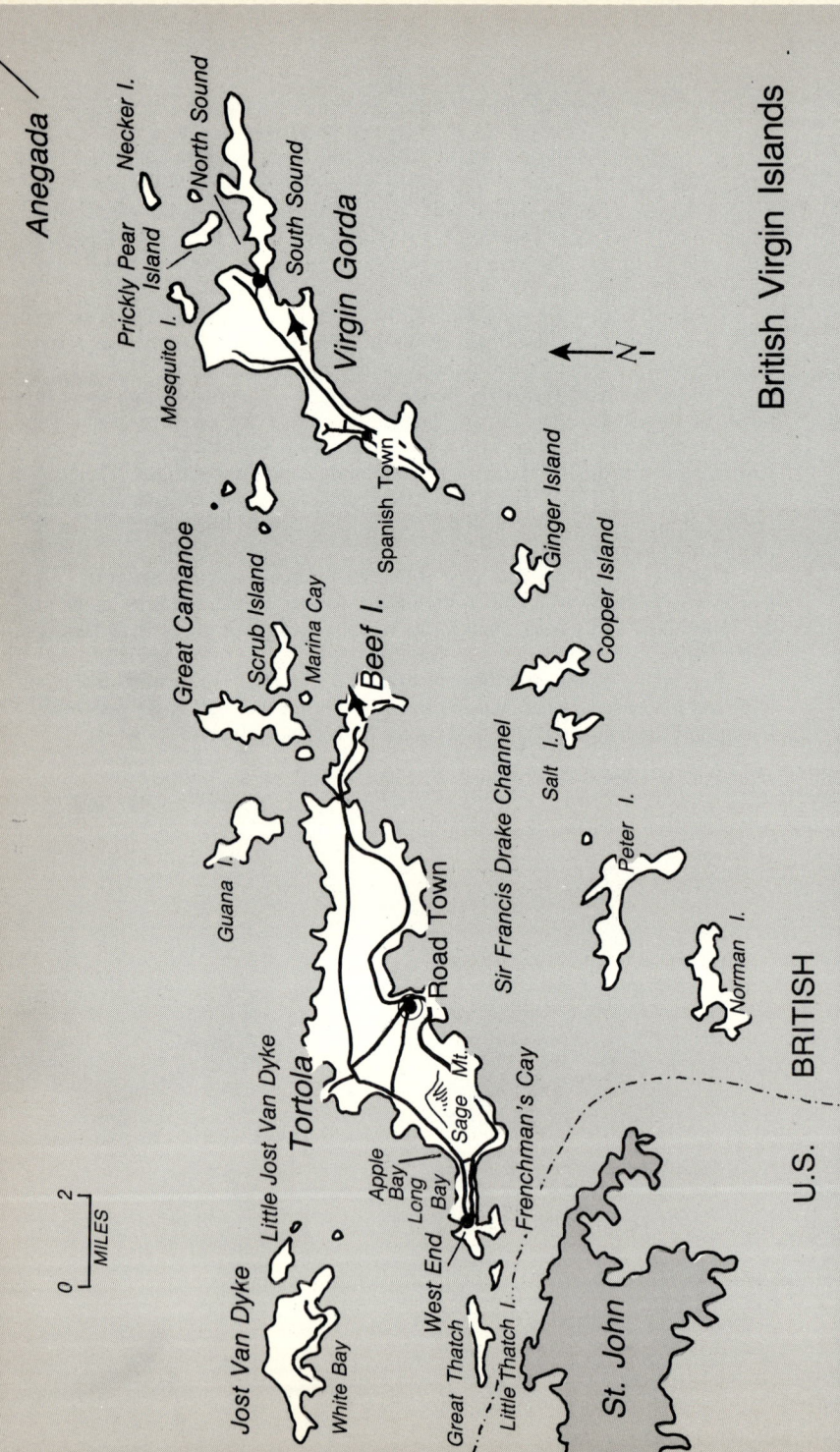

BRITISH VIRGIN ISLANDS

British Virgin Islands Tourist Board, Box 134, Road Town, Tortola, British Virgin Islands, T 809+494–3134; #511, 370 Lexington Ave., New York, NY 10017, T 212+696–0400, or 800+835–8530, fax 212+949–8250; 1686 Union St., San Francisco, CA 94132, T 415+775–0344; 801 York Mills Rd., Suite 201, Don Mills, Ont., M3B 1X7, T 416+283–2235; 26 Hockerill St., Bishops Stortford, Herts, CM23 2DW England, T 01+44 279 54969, fax 44–279–506616.

$ · · · *U.S. currency is legal tender in the British Virgins.*

See pages noted for information on: Anegada, p. 193; Beef Island, p. 178; Guana Island, p. 186; Jost Van Dyke, p. 194; Marina Cay, p. 186; Mosquito Island (Drake's Passage), p. 195; Necker Island, p. 196; Peter Island, p. 186–87; Tortola, p. 181; Virgin Gorda, p. 196.

When I hoisted myself into the passenger seat in the cabin of Keith's van, I was unsure about the cost of my ride. I didn't want to be in the van at all. I wanted a rental car, and the dudes that lounged on the counter near the "car rental" sign had pointed me toward a desk at the other end of the airport for information. The young lady behind the desk leafed through pages of firms and prices, and then linked me up with one. "Where's the car?" I asked. "In town," she answered. "Can you take me there?" I asked. "No," she said, "you'll have to take a taxi." How much? She said between $10 and $12. That's when Keith appeared.

Conversation had been easy on the roller coaster ride—up, down, and around—from the airport, over the one-car-wide, four-cars-long bridge linking Beef Island's airport and the island of Tortola, to town. The pauses, to pick up Keith's pals when they hailed our van, provided relief from the wobbling route, and an opportunity to look around at the land—and the surrounding sea.

When I handed Keith $10 at the end of my ride, he gave me back $4 without comment. I guess the fare is $6 when you rent a car, but my ride back to the airport with Benjamin-from-Budget was free; he lives out at East End. "Life's better out here," he told me. "It's quieter. Things is more spread out." And he told me about his house by the sea, with a red roof and a porch where he sits to fish.

Life is sea-centered in the British Virgins. The 60-plus sand-fringed humps that are these islands take on the personality of ships at sea, even though they do not bob at anchor. Small inns have special personalities; the managers are usually the owners, and each is always "captain" of his "ship."

It's easy, when you look out to sails on the sea, to ponder about the days of the 17th and 18th centuries, when Spanish, Dutch, French, and English ships sailed through the Anegada Passage to what we know as Sir Francis Drake Channel. The Spanish paused on Virgin Gorda to work the copper mines until they ran out; the English claimed Tortola, early enough for the Earl of Cumberland to use it as his starting point for an assault on Puerto Rico in 1596. And the English held these islands long enough to be hassled by the Dutch who swept northwest from Sint Maarten to claim the area for a while. The English stepped in again, and eventually permanently, to pepper the Danes who had taken, and were tilling, neighboring St. John, now one of the U.S. Virgin Islands.

AUTHOR'S OBSERVATION

The British Virgins continue to offer low-key holidays that focus on beach-and-sea pleasures. The style is that of an Americanized "Bermuda," without the perfect packaging and with higher costs.

POLITICAL PICTURE is a stable one in the British Virgins, with both the United Party and the Virgin Islands Party dedicated to democratic government. Chief Minister H. Lavitty Stout was elected to office following the September 30, 1986, elections, when his VIP won the majority of seats. Elections are expected soon after this edition goes to press. The British Virgins are a Dependent Territory (formerly referred to as a colony) of Britain, with self-governing status. Although both parties' policies seem similar to the outsider, there are subtle differences in the attitudes toward tourism. Both parties run tourism as a business, acknowledging that the territory has only beaches and islands as natural resources and that protection of the environment is essential.

ISLANDS' APPEARANCE: If you have a dream of what tropical islands should look like, this group will probably fit it: several small green islands rise like humps from the sea sparkling in the sun. Upon closer inspection, most of the "humps" have irregular waterlines where soft, white sand borders protected coves. It's no fluke that the British Virgins claim the best cruising grounds within the Caribbean islands! Tradewinds assure brisk breezes and island locations guarantee easy landfall. Although none of the British Virgins have a lush, tropical rain forest to compare with those found on a few of the other islands, most are covered with a respectable amount of trees, shrubs, and grasses that become green within hours of the fast and heavy rain showers that douse these islands throughout the year (usually at pre-dawn or evening hours).

The only town of note is Road Town, which has grown along its waterfront in recent years. The town is still small, with most shops and offices along two parallel roads that follow the shoreline. The fringe of yachts that gather at Road Town's marinas give the town its flavor. West End, also on Tortola, is smaller than Road Town but has grown with a new commercial (for visitors) center on the far side of the harbor from the ferry boat docks. Virgin Gorda's commercial "hub" is its marina area, on the southwest coast, near Spanish Town, a group of buildings that is the town.

LIFESTYLE is blissfully casual and uncomplicated. Since many British Virgin Islanders had experience working on other islands before their own islands turned to the hospitality industry as a business, they saw what over-development and greed can do. Most are united in the strong feeling that controlled and slow growth is the best path for the British Virgin Islands, where the population numbers about 12,500 for all the islands. Most of the resorts and hotels are on Tortola and Virgin Gorda; even the most luxurious are low-profile places.

Some U.S. methods are incorporated into the B.V.I. lifestyle, but there's a distinct sea-and-beach focus that makes things operate at their own pace—especially when "efficiency" and government offices are involved.

AUTHOR'S OBSERVATION

Virgin Gorda is one of the Caribbean's few places where cars and homes are left unlocked, with no concern for break-ins or vandalism. Life here is based on mutual respect.

Clothes are casual. Guests at Little Dix, the region's pace-setting resort, and also at Peter Island, may dress up for dinner some nights, but outfits at most other places are comfortably casual. A change of boat clothes is about as fancy as some spots get.

MEDICAL FACILITIES: Peebles Hospital, in Road Town, Tortola, is the main hospital for all the British Virgins. It has about 50 beds, and offers basic nursing care. There are small clinics, with a doctor or nurse in charge, on some of the other islands, but many of the small spots rely on boat service to Road Town for serious medical care. Medical emergencies can be flown to Puerto Rico on charter planes, from Road Town's Beef Island airport or from the airstrip on Virgin Gorda. There's no decompression chamber for scuba divers.

MONEY MATTERS focus on how fast it goes. Food and lodging cost more than their equivalents on the U.S. mainland. Credit cards are accepted at some tourist-focused places, but always ask, if paying with plastic is important. Not all places accept them. Bring traveler's checks, or cash (and be cautious with flaunting your cash as you should be wherever you travel).

COMMUNICATIONS: Direct dialing from the U.S. and elsewhere overseas is easy with the 809 area code + 49 for B.V.I. + 5-digit local phone. Cable

& Wireless sells phonecards in various denominations for use in designated public telephones that do not accept coins. For AT&T's USADirect service from the British Virgins, use any telephone to dial 1–800+872–2881 to talk with an AT&T operator. There's a dedicated USADirect telephone at the Virgin Gorda marina and others at specific places in Tortola. Facsimile machines are often used. Don't count on phones in your room. U.S.V.I. and Puerto Rico radio stations are received clearly, but bring a small radio if you want to listen to them. Some places have television, but most have other more natural priorities.

ARRIVAL techniques depend on the island you choose. You'll have at least a couple of airports (and airlines) to deal with to get to any of the islands, unless you arrive by boat/ship. San Juan, Puerto Rico, is the most important jump-off point, with easy links on *American Eagle* and *Sunaire, Air BVI, LIAT,* and other small airlines to Beef Island for Tortola and nearby islands and to Virgin Gorda for places on that island and its satellites. St. Thomas, in the U.S. Virgin Islands, is another connecting point, with dozens of flights on small planes as well as links by boat out of Charlotte Amalie, the U.S.V.I. capital, to Road Town or West End on Tortola or to Virgin Gorda. You can also get to the British Virgins relatively easily by air from Sint Maarten and from St. Croix.

AUTHOR'S OBSERVATION

If the air and boat links sound confusing, my advice is twofold: get a good map of the islands so you know where your holiday haven is located, and—when you make your reservation—ask *them* for the best route to reach the place.

If you prefer to arrive by boat, there's regular ferry service from St. Thomas, in the U.S. Virgins, from the waterfront at Charlotte Amalie, that island's capital, and from Red Hook, at the east end. Since service operates to both Road Town and West End on Tortola, it's important to read the schedule carefully so that you know your B.V.I. arrival or departure port; the two towns are about 20 minutes' drive from each other. (There are seat-in-car minivan taxis that make the land link easy.) The crossing between St. Thomas and the British Virgins takes about an hour.

Smiths Ferry Service operates several boats between Road Town and West End (both on Tortola) and Charlotte Amalie, St. Thomas, daily except Wednesday; on Wednesdays the ferry runs between Virgin Gorda and St. Thomas. *Speedy's Delight* and *Speedy's Fantasy* operate almost shuttle service between Road Town and Virgin Gorda, Road Town and St. Thomas, Road Town and St. John (U.S.V.I.), and Road Town and Virgin Gorda to Anegada.

Charter-boat folk who have picked up a yacht in the U.S. islands can get entry details from the home port operator.

Having said all that, arrivals are casual affairs—with your most formal entry at the Beef Island airport, the official B.V.I. entry point. There will be customs officials also at the ramp at West End (Tortola) for the ferries and charter yachts, at Soper's Hole (Tortola) for charter boats, and at Virgin Gorda's strip. You will be expected to have citizenship identification (passport is requested for Canadian and American visitors) and return ticket; ritual will be perfunctory, but official, and it can seem to take forever at island pace.

CRUISE LINES have "discovered" some of the British Virgins and, although none of the islands have docking facilities to accommodate the biggest ships, some cruise itineraries include Tortola and other islands, bringing passengers ashore in small boats. Your travel agent can track down cruises that include the British Virgins; they will usually be aboard ships that start cruising from San Juan, Puerto Rico. *Clipper Cruise Line*'s (T 800+325–0010) small ships cruise the U.S. and British Virgins, including Tortola, Norman Island, Virgin Gorda, and Jost Van Dyke. The *Sir Francis Drake,* (T 800+662–0090) a 3-masted schooner, makes weekly journeys through the U.S. and British Virgins, departing from St. Thomas. Beaches are the main attraction, although the water pods formed amid the huge boulders at the Baths on Virgin Gorda are also interesting.

AUTHOR'S OBSERVATION

If enjoying the Baths at their natural best is part of their fascination (as it is for me), avoid visiting when cruise ships are in the area. People roam the small area in a style reminiscent of ants at a picnic.

DEPARTURE by air, from airports on Virgin Gorda or Beef Island/Tortola, is informal and casual, since planes are often delayed. You'll be required to pay a $5 departure tax by air, even for a day trip. The departure tax for sea passengers is $4.

TOURING TIPS: The **car rental** game varies, according to your contact. Best bet is probably through your hotel, if they will handle it. I've gotten quite a runaround when trying to rent on the spot; availability of cars and the prices can vary according to the firm and the time of year. Peak-season winter prices can be high to the point of absurdity, but at slower times there's some point in leisurely conversation if you have the time. Gurghels and jeeps, both hardy cars, cope with some of the spine-cracking dirt roads that lead to some of the best beaches.

I found Ethelyn Burke at *Budget Car Rentals* (T 809+494–2639), near Village Cay marina very courteous and helpful. Her firm has normal and four-wheel drive, jeep-type cars. *Avis, Hertz,* and *National* also have local representatives. Other firms with cars to rent include *Old Salt,* (T 809+494–2352) for Gurghels; and Dennis *Alphonso Rent-A-Car* (T 809+494–3137) for jeeps, Gurghels, and Suzukis. Obtaining your driver's license is as easy as forking out $10.

Harrigan Rent-A-Cycle (T 809+495–5542) and *Hero's Bicycle Rental* (T 809+494–3536) have **mopeds** and other cycles for rent. There are no car rental desks at the Beef Island airport. Taxi drivers have that business locked up, and charge the usual fee (from $8 to $10) to drive you into town, where most firms are located. (If you make reservations in advance, some firms will arrange to meet you on arrival.) On Tortola, there are plenty of taxis for land touring. I've used Antwin George, who has a thriving business with multi-passenger small buses plus cars, but there are many other taxi drivers. Winston Smith, known to all as "Billy," uses a beautifully maintained air-conditioned car as his taxi.

In Road Town, Tortola, *Travel Plan Tours* is a full-fledged travel agent, competent at handling local and long-distance reservations, and also offering island tours. On Virgin Gorda, contact *Virgin Gorda Tours*.

Speedy's *Fantasy*, an 84-passenger **ferry**, connects Tortola and Virgin Gorda by boat and Speedy's *Delight* links Anegada. Speedy also has a road link on Virgin Gorda, with taxis and small boxy buses for bouncing around these roads.

The Peter Island ferry operates several times daily for the half hour crossing from the CSY dock to the island resort. Water taxis can be hired for personalized links to sister B.V.I.s.

There are more sailing **yachts** for charter in this area than anywhere else in the Caribbean. (Some say the world.) Check the "Sports" section for details on charter companies I have known to be reliable experts.

Most of your touring on these islands is going to be to find a beach or get to another island; there's not a lot in the way of sights to see—except for nature's best.

AUTHOR'S OBSERVATION

Be sure to contact the Tourist Board, when you're making your plans, to ask for a copy of the *British Virgin Islands Welcome Tourism Guide*, a fact-filled free pamphlet. *The Welcome*, published in Tortola, can be obtained by mail in the U.S. for $5. Write to Box 133, Road Town, Tortola. (A subscription of 6 issues is $20.)

LODGING in the British Virgins is always in a place with its own personality; there are no high-rise hotels or splashy resorts. Only a few properties have more than 50 rooms. One *(Little Dix)* is on Virgin Gorda; the others are on or near Tortola (*Prospect Reef* and *Peter Island*). All the rest are small and special places stamped with the personality of the owner/manager. Husband-and-wife teams own and/or manage most of these islands' 30-plus properties. Gala nightlife can't be found, but there's plenty of daytime sea action. Several inns nest on each of a half dozen tiny isles, which are linked by boat to their nearest bigger island. Although accommodations at some spots are surprisingly grand (air-conditioned in some cases; private bathroom in all), the lights can go out during a power failure, the supply of fresh water (which comes from rain caught in cisterns, built for that purpose) may be limited, and if you're doing the cooking, the best sources are the local fishermen and supermarkets in Tortola or St. Thomas (neighboring U.S.V.I.), where selection is varied and prices are high.

AUTHOR'S AWARDS

Little Dix Bay provides both lovely surroundings and good management in luxurious style; *Sugar Mill* is a personal favorite, among the small spots for the warm hospitality (and good food) offered by its owners and staff, and *Long Bay*'s beach and gradual improvements make it worth considering for quiet comforts.

Room rates reflect a wish for exclusivity more than the degree of elaborate facilities; they're sometimes higher than surroundings may warrant. In addition to the printed rate, most bills carry the 5% government hotel tax and a 10% or 15% service charge. Be sure to ask if that covers all "service"; at some places, staff is especially attentive and may warrant additional "appreciation."

Information about places-to-stay is included below, or following either "Tortola" or "Virgin Gorda" headings, under Hotels/Resorts, Housekeeping Holidays, The Inn Way, or Low Cost Lodging. Stars are awarded within each category. (See page 11.)

TORTOLA

This island, linked to its airport on Beef Island with a narrow bridge, is the seat of the government. It's also the island where most of the hotels are located, with about a dozen around Road Town. There are also a few at beaches on the northwest coast, a couple at West End, and some alone on tiny islands off the east end and the south coast.

HOTELS/RESORTS: Count on comfortable informality at most places, and an outdoor focus at all.

★★★ **Long Bay** • *rising from shore to hillside on the northwest coast* • claims a beautiful white-powder beach, which you'll note from the hilltop just prior to arrival. The beach "club" is the social center, with pool, plus bar and cafe-style restaurant. A second restaurant is on the hillside. Lodgings are in hillside rooms or along the beach, where the newest rooms have full comforts and easy beach-and-sea access. The entrance area seemed tacky when I checked for this edition, with a jury-rigged "arch" and seedy looking buildings. Hopefully that will have changed by the time you visit; the prices and proposed atmosphere warrant a classier look. Count on being on one of Tortola's best beaches, but expect the sand to slope gently into the sea, sometimes over solid coral rock. The *Caribbean Newsletter* (page 9) will have an update when warranted. For this season, expect soft sand, comfortable lodgings, and a few "rough" edges that keep this place from being as classy as it could be. (Bring your favorite bug repellent for the pesky "no-see-'ums" that can swarm at twilight and/or when the ground is damp.) You're about 30 minutes' drive from Road Town and almost an hour from the airport. *Small Resort.*

★★★ **Mariner Inn** • *on the fringe of Road Town* • is a yacht-oriented hotel. Although it has no beach, it does have warm hospitality (emanating from a style set by Ginny and Charlie Cary, and maintained by their well-trained staff), comfortable rooms (a total of 39, plus 2 suites, in 2 blocks of 2-story buildings), convenient location, and plenty going on. This is home port for *The Moorings* charter boat operation that now stretches to include *Treasure Isle* hotel and marinas on other Caribbean islands. Yachts are at the piers when they're not at sea. The pool is lovely, and the deck that rims it is flecked with tables where you can dine on American-style island food. The apartments can be ideal for families with grown children and for anyone who enjoys the seafaring life. Ask about the diving and sailing package holidays. *Hotel.*

Prospect Reef • *on the western border of Road Town* • opened as Tortola's biggest hotel and first resort in the late '70s with a community of 2-story buildings with several lodging units in each. Built by British-born Humphrey Kripps, the hotel was planned to house guests in an assortment of 100-plus rooms. Units include full apartments (some with 2 bedrooms), studios, and standard rooms that can be mixed and matched by locking doors. Although they were built to be sold as privately owned apartments, that plan never went smoothly. The close proximity of rooms is not always ideal for strangers. There's no beach at the hotel, but there are pools, tennis courts, shops, boats for charter at the aquatic center, and scuba and snorkel links. On-premises restaurants include a very casual harbor-level place and a seafront upstairs restaurant for more elaborate meals. Make further inquiries before booking for this season. *Hotel.*

★★ **Treasure Isle Hotel** • *tucked into the foliage on a hillside overlooking the harbor at Road Town* • gives its guests a pool (for play and scuba lessons), a choice of sun-splashed or covered terrace for lingering (and dining), pleasant public areas, and an assortment of rooms that range from the 25 motel-style (most with sea view) to something a little grander (in the 15 suites). Although now owned by *The Mariner*'s parent company, Steve Colgate's *Offshore Sailing School* has used this hotel for land base. See "Sports" for details. Guests can walk down the hill and across the road to yachting activity, or toward Road Town to sample a few of the dining and drinking depots. *Small hotel.*

Village Cay Resort • *with the marina, on the east side of Road Town* • makes the most of the marina location, with seafront elegant suites the most viewful. Other rooms have been refurbished, to make the most of whatever view is available and to provide modern (and expected) comforts. Although once a simple place for yachtsmen ashore, this place has been upgraded to offer a lot more than boat-ashore life. You're right in the middle of a lot of nautical (and shopping) activity at a place with a couple of restaurants, and within a short stroll of Road Town's center and ferry boat dock. *Small hotel.*

HOUSEKEEPING HOLIDAYS: There are literally dozens of apartments and cottages that offer kitchen facilities for those who want the independence of do-it-yourself living. In addition to the places mentioned below, check with the hotels (above) and the small places mentioned under "Low-Cost Lodging" since many of those places also have one or two apartments for rent, in addition to hotel rooms.

Because yachting has long been a fact of life for these islands, you'll find good supermarkets and other sources for stocking up on food on both Tortola and on Virgin Gorda, but don't count on a lot of markets on the other islands. Items, when you do find them, will be more expensive than your hometown supermarket. If you have some special favorites, bring them with you.

Admiralty Estate Resort • *on the hillside above Road Town* • gathers attractive units with all modern comforts around a nice pool. The road to reach George's Hollow, where the place is located, is wiggly and steep. Ask to be taken up Joe's Hill to the parking lot, where you can call for a jitney. The *Caribbean Newsletter* (page 9) will have more facts as plans continue. *Villas.*

Brandywine • *on the southeast shore* • is several homelike apartments along the shore, with a few on hillsides and elsewhere. All are privately owned, but sometimes for rent. The entrance road runs next to the shoreline buildings, with the car parking area putting you at the main door that leads to the bedroom level (2 lovely rooms). You have to go downstairs to the living room, with sunset-viewing porch over the sea. *Homelike apts.*

Fort Recovery Estates • *mid island, near the north shore* • are several fully equipped villas. Most have one bedroom, a few have two; there is one villa with several bedrooms. Maid service is included. The on-premise commissary has convenience-high prices. Although pleasant for "at home" vacations, you'll want a car for touring. *Villas.*

Frenchman's Cay Resort • *across the harbor from West End* • plants its attractive buildings up the hillside from the shoreline dock. All units have beautiful sea-and-island views. The property gathers its condominium units in a semi-circle around a small beach to offer pool-punctuated lodgings. The restaurant in the midst of the property can supplement the cooking you do at home in your choice of 1- or 2-bedroom units. The units offer a comfortable home, with tennis courts. You'll need a car. *Villas.*

Maya Cove Apartments • *at the end of a spur off the dip-and-weave route from Beef Island airport to downtown Road Town* • are good for those who like informality and share a love of the sea. Neighbors will be nautical types. The simply furnished 1-bedroom apartments have kitchenettes; the 2-bedroom unit seems more homelike. You'll need a car for land; setting out to sea is simple. *Apts.*

Nanny Cay Apartments • *at a marina, west of Road Town on the south coast* • is yacht-oriented. A rental car permits mobility; otherwise you'll need taxis. Most of the units are rented long-term, but some open up for week-long or longer rentals. Under the "Ramada" banner for a couple of years, the proposed resort never materialized. This place lapses back to its laid-back, residential style for this season. The *Caribbean Newsletter* (page 9) will have news when warranted. *Apts.*

Rockview Holiday Homes • *near West End* • accommodate from 2 to 8 people in private, viewful villas with all the comforts of home, including maid service, help with car rentals, baby-sitters, and watersports. *Houses.*

Sunset House • *on a hilltop overlooking Long Bay* • is a beautiful 10-room villa, built in Spanish-Mediterranean style. It is owned by the chief minister, is lavishly furnished, and, although clinging to a small plot, aspires to a feeling of luxury. *House.*

THE INN WAY: Even the big hotels in the British Virgins have an inn-like style, with friendly staff and management often involved with ownership. However, there are several small spots that do qualify, in my opinion, as inns, with the best traditions of inn-keeping. Standards and style vary, but all are small, personality places where the stamp of the owner(s) is immediately evident.

Cane Garden Beach Hotel • *on the northwest coast at Cane Garden Bay* • is a small spot that offers reasonable rooms (with air-conditioners and telephones) at a cluster focused on the beach and sea. The beach bar lures sailors from yachts that anchor offshore as well as day visitors from elsewhere on the island. It's an "over the mountain" ride to Road Town shops and town life. This is a laid-back, relaxing place without much pretense. *Small hotel.*

CSY Yacht Club • *near Road Town, but not within easy walking distance* • offers 8 comfortable rooms at the marina. They're usually booked by charterers either before or after cruising. The second-story open-air dining area, with the *Bilge Bar* serves casual fare while you wait for your boat to come in. OK as home port if you like the sea. (The ferry for Peter Island docks nearby.) *Guest House.*

★★ **Fort Burt** • *on a hillock on the southwestern fringe of Road Town* • commands a beautiful harbor view and has a personality all its own. The main room is balcony fringed, with bedrooms up a few steps and behind the dining area. Richard Hodgkins, formerly at Treasure Isle, manages with a friendly style that independent travelers find comfortable. This place is legend-filled, with tales told in previous editions of interest to folks who like to hear about the past. Efforts to restore the small inn's charming ambience are paying off. You'll have to hike up and down a short but steep hill to get anywhere from here, and even the pool at the hilltop is a few steps from the main area. This place is fun when other guests are. *Inn.*

Sebastians on the Beach • *on the northwest coast at Apple Bay* • claims a patch of beach as its daytime focus, for guests who stay in the newer block of beachfront rooms or the simpler, older rooms on the inland side of the seaside road. Some are on the second floor of the original (old) building; others are at the back. This place has always appealed to Robinson Crusoe types who enjoy a beachcomber-casual atmosphere. Although there are good dive shops, bring most of your own equipment if you're an avid snorkeler or scuba diver. Set at the place where the up-and-over-the-hill road meets the north coast, Sebastians is about 15 minutes' drive from Road Town. *Inn.*

★★★ **Sugar Mill Estate** • *on the northwest shore, east of Sebastians and Long Bay* • is cozy and comfortable, made so by the owners, Jinx and Jeff Morgan, and their staff. The Morgans left California in late '82 to try their hand at inn-keeping, and officially took over this place in early '83. *Islands* alfresco restaurant and a sandy sunning area with easy sea access make the shore the focus for daytime hours. The hillside restaurant is where the owners excel in the evening, with specialties for which they are famous. Count on exceptional mealtimes and warm hospitality in pleasant surroundings. Bedrooms are in several cottages (some with nice sea views) up the hillside, near a small pool on the inland side of the shore-rimming road. Sugar Mill is an island inn, in the best sense of the word. *Inn.*

LOW-COST LODGINGS: In recent seasons, several small spots have opened up. Most are operated by British Virgin Islanders who have added rooms to a local restaurant or guest house. Although rooms may be small, and furnishings simple, most of the places in Road Town are within walking distance of activities and other restaurants. The *Caribbean Newsletter* (page 9) will have additional listings when places seem worthwhile. For now, look into:

B.V.I. Aquatic Hotel • *a few minutes' walk from the West End pier* • is a 2-story block of simply furnished rooms-with-kitchenettes for basic housekeeping in an area known for its nautical working-port atmosphere. You'll need transportation to get to beaches, but you're near the ferry dock for water-linked excursions.

Castle Maria • *in Road Town* • has studios and rooms for a total of 30 units, all with private bathroom (with hot water), some with kitchenette. The 2-story building clings to a hillside, which allows for sea views from all rooms. You'll want a rental car for easy access to all beaches, and management rents them. Neighbors are the chief minister and the governor, whose homes are nearby.

Harbour View Guest House • *at remote Cane Garden Bay on the northwest coast* • offers kitchenettes in simple rooms, but don't count on every cooking convenience. Best if you are comfortable camping.

Jolly Roger Inn • *at West End* • offers a few rooms at the dock. The casual atmosphere and basic rooms appeal to campers and informal boat folk.

Maria's by the Sea • *in Road Town, on Wickham's Cay, not far from the marina* • Motel-style rooms, with reasonable comforts. Some units have kitchenette. The bar/restaurant is one source for meals. This place has a pool.

Sea View • *in Road Town, near the Fort Burt Hotel* • gives you a room with a view at modest cost. This place has grown from the popular local restaurant to include studios and rooms, as well as a small pool. Count on town noises in the evening, but know that you can walk to the center of town in minutes.

Way Side Guest House • *in Road Town* • has 20 rooms, a locally popular restaurant, and very low rates. This place has a local following.

RESORT ISLANDS NEAR TORTOLA: A map is essential to understand the lay of the land, or islands, in this case. The places that follow are best reached from Tortola's Beef Island airport, for those who are flying in to link up with the boat connection. Boat arrivals may find some places easy to reach directly from St. Thomas, in the U.S. Virgin Islands. Be sure to ask your island host when you make your reservation.

★★★ **Guana Island Club** • *on its own island that has a rock "iguana head" formation on a cliff off its western side* • has an enthusiastic following of vacationers who have found—and love—this place. Lodgings cap a hilltop, with the main house the gathering, dining, and information hub and most rooms in viewful cottages with comfortably casual appointments. Operated as a club for many years, the place now welcomes compatible outsiders who want an outpost island with a focus on nature, spectacular views, and restful surroundings. Evening action evolves from guest interests, with mellow music (from tapes) in the background. Day trippers from other BVIs are not encouraged, so the cluster community is preserved. This sixth largest of the British Virgins has been designated a nature sanctuary, north of the east end of Tortola. July is the month when a team led by Harvard University's Dr. James Lazell researches island growth and wildlife, but interested lodgers will find management friendly, and willing to give suggestions for nature walks and other pursuits throughout the year. Count on steep climbs, by foot or the Nissan Patrol car (with a surrey top), from the dock to the top-of-hill main building.

★★ **Marina Cay** • *on its own 6-acre dot off Beef Island* • is reached by Boston Whaler or its equivalent if the hotel knows you're coming. (If you're not expected, you may find yourself standing on the Beef Island pier frantically waving your arms; phoning is easier.) The place provided the anecdotes and setting for *Our Virgin Island,* a book sometimes found in paperback, written more than 30 years ago by Robb White, and a 1958 movie of the same name. Rooms are in separate villa-style buildings near the crown of the tiny island. Dining is alfresco, at the main house or at the shoreside area favored by seafaring folk who anchor offshore and row in for dinner. The focus is watersports, with a completely equipped scuba shop. Bring books and let the cares seep out; this is a good place to revive sagging spirits.

★★★★ **Peter Island Resort and Yacht Harbour** • *about 25 minutes away, aboard a deluxe ferry that strings between the island and a dock next door to the CSY marina, near Road Town* • is an 800-acre outpost that aspires to luxury, making the most of the God-given virtues of beautiful beaches and interesting island terrain. The original Scandinavian-built A-frame lodgings have been joined by beachfront rooms. The A-frame Harbour Houses hold 4 suites, each with its own sunning area; the Beach Houses have direct access to the sand and sea. Reopened, following extensive rebuilding after Hugo's visit (Sept '89), the island resort offers tennis courts, a lovely pool, beaches where you can find boardsailing and places for scuba and/or snorkeling, or bicycles for riding over the island's several trails, plus darts, billiards, Ping-Pong, and other games.

The marina welcomes classy yachts from the high seas (but reportedly discourages casual sailors with intimidating curtness). An *Ashore/Afloat* plan provides for overnights at sea. The rooms have telephone and television, plus all the modern conveniences. The 3-bedrooms, 2-bath consummate luxury of a once private villa can be yours, with 2 maids, a gardener, a minimoke (car), and use of a 46-foot Bertram sportfishing boat for about $10,000 for 6 nights for 8 people. Smaller "Sprat Bay," with room for 6, is also available as a private cottage. *Resort.*

RESTAURANTS ON OR NEAR TORTOLA: So-called international dining in the British Virgins is expensive, partly because almost everything is imported and partly because, I suspect, that's what owners/managers think the traffic will bear. The food served at some of the island inns is excellent, attractively served in tantalizing tropical settings, *but* the logistics of getting from one place to another make sampling all the best places impossible. It's highly unlikely, unless you've booked for an overnight or more, that you'll be at Virgin Gorda's Biras Creek, for example, if you're staying on Tortola. It's a long poke from anywhere except Bitter End Yacht Club, which shares its bay. Always make reservations; since most restaurants are small, head count is crucial. Dress is informal at most B.V.I. spots, but all places encourage neat but not formal attire.

The Road Town area is the action hub, for restaurants as well as for everything else. There are, however, places on the northwest coast—*Sugar Mill,* for example—that are worth making an effort to find. Eating spots range from snack places to recently-built air-conditioned pubs to take-out spots. Among the first group, check out *Cell 5,* wedged into an open space on the main road; *Pusser's* (see below) is the modern pub; and both Village Cay and The Moorings have take-out places where yachting folks can get good food to eat on board.

AUTHOR'S OBSERVATION

Expect to pay New York city prices (or higher) for food that ranges from excellent to interesting to mediocre, with quality depending on the chef—and who works on his/her day off. Don't be shy about asking to see the menu before you settle at a table.

Bing's Drop Inn Bar • *at Fat Hog's Bay, near the east end* • made its name as a late-night dancing and chatting spot for local folks and people interested in a casual evening with some action. The restaurant takes its cue from those days, with homecooked food such as conch fritters and fish stew as well as more ambitious offerings where lobster, chicken, veal, and beef are sauced and herbed. The place usually closes on Mondays; reservations are advisable.

★★★ **Brandywine Bay** • *east of Road Town* • is in a once-private home on the top of the hill (with a great view). Menu follows Italian style, taking its tone from the talented chef-host. Be sure to notice the fine art and old photos on the walls. Worth the drive a few miles out of town, even if you're not staying on the premises. Count on $40 per person at least, and more if you want good wine and flourishes.

★★ **Carib Garden** • *in Road Town* • serves meals in its tiny patio and small upstairs rooms. Mon. through Sat., Sun. for dinner only. Food is West Indian, with U.S. overtones.

Chopsticks • *on the inland side of the shore road, at Wickhams Cay* • adds Chinese techniques to island fish and conch for some tasty results. Can be fun and friendly. Szechuan style takes on added power with West Indian flair.

The Cloud Room • *perched high, with a view over Road Town and the sea* • picks you up in town and brings you home after your meal, which will be a special experience available only by reservation. Not only is the food reasonably good, with the familiar chicken, fish, and beef, presented with some flair, but a moveable roof slides back to reveal the stars and moon on the otherwise protected dining terrace. Guests from other parts of the island can rendezvous at the Stone Haves restaurant for the ride up the mountain.

Dinghy's/Santa Maria • *in view of the Village Cay marina* • has a great location, overlooking the yachts. Food is American-style, with blackened fish, steaks, chicken, and salads. Better for atmosphere than for food, this place is worth a try.

Mariner Inn • *next to The Moorings marina and around the hotel pool* • is included for those who want good, solid American fare in nice surroundings. Music most evenings makes this place fun, and the "Yachtsman's Special," often chicken or fish, is kept at reasonable cost (about $10).

Mrs. Scatliffe's • *east of Sugar Mill, at Carrot Bay* • is a typically Tortolan experience. The restaurant is in the home of the former cook at Sugar Mill, under previous owners. Drive by to see what (and if) Mrs. Scatliffe is serving, to make your reservations for the evening meal. Her choices are traditional West Indian, with home-grown vegetables and fish served in homemade sauces.

★★ **Peter Island** • *on its own island* • is nice for an excursion, since the boat ride will be parentheses around your mealtime (unless you're a houseguest). Check for the weekly program; events are planned for residents and outsiders can often be included after making advance reservations. Count on meals to be elaborate (and expensive), in keeping with the setting.

Pusser's Country Store & Pub • *in Road Town, with harbor view* • opened in its old-style surroundings in December 1986, and has become a tourist haven for shopping and "a cool one." Popular for lingering, this place takes its name (and funding) from the island's Pusser's (for the ship's purser) rum. Its waterfront location is a gathering place when cruise ships are in port.

Pusser's Landing • *near Soper's Hole Wharf at West End* • is a congenial coveside spot where dining is alfresco, at tables on the wood deck, punctuated with yellow canvas-backed chairs and umbrellas. This place is fun when the nautical types are around and pleasant at the shore at any time. Lobster and fish can be counted upon, as can cold beer and wine. A favorite for nautical types whose boats are moored nearby. (The recent rash of shops is an added diversion.)

★★★ **Skyworld** • *at the "top," on the Ridge Road* • is like dining on top of the world, with town lights way below and stars overhead for evening decor and spectacular daytime views over islands. Conch fritters and pasta join more elaborate fare for dining treats. Onion rings were praised by one loyal reader.

★★★ **Sugar Mill** • *on the northwest side of the island* • warrants a visit. What may be lacking in speedy service is more than made up for in interesting offerings on the menu. Both hosts (Jeff and Jinx Morgan) are "food-smiths" who gave up California living for island inn-keeping. This place is attractive, atmospheric—and good!

Other on-their-own-island places that welcome outsiders with advance reservations are **Marina Cay,** where you dine on the patio at the main house on the hilltop, and on Bellamy Cay the legendary **Last Resort,** a long-time favorite with yachtsmen who enjoy Tony and Jackie Snell's nautical decor, lively entertainment, and awesomely extensive buffets, complete with chafing dishes full of interesting offerings, plus roast beef and other hearty food.

NATURAL SURROUNDINGS are, in a word, spectacular! Although the tree, shrub, and plant life of these islands may seem "routine" among the Caribbean islands, the oft-touted **Baths** on Virgin Gorda—where gigantic boulders appear to have been thrown in random arrangement, cupping waterpools and carpeting them with the softest, whitest sand—are definitely worth seeing. Snorkeling is sensational in this area; the setting is unique. In fact, it's the islands themselves, their proximity to each other, and the diamond-clear seas that surround them that are most breathtaking.

The recent establishment of **National Park areas,** where sea life and ground covers are protected, bodes well for the continuing preservation. Although few of the several migrating and resident birds are dramatically colorful, there are many species that lure birders to these shores.

It is, however, the **offshore wrecks** serving as fish condominiums that are among the region's most valuable assets. Some of the most enchanting scuba diving areas at and around Tortola are on the north shore and off Guana Island, the northern part of Great Camanoe, and at Dog Island, and Scrub Island, as well as around most of the islands on the southern flank of Sir Francis Drake Channel. The *Wreck of the Rhone,* a Royal Mail packet steamer, lies off Great Harbour, Peter Island. It is a highlight!

PLACES WORTH FINDING on Tortola and the other British Virgins usually involve beaches, sea, and natural surroundings. There's not much in the way of historic buildings, at least nothing that is interesting enough to take time away from sea pursuits, unless it's a visit to Road Town's Folk Museum or a tour of the rum factory (which can be arranged through the tourist office and/or your hotel.) Because boat and plane excursions can easily get you to another island and back in a day, all the area's "places worth finding" are noted here.

Cooper Island, easy to reach by sailing or on a day trip arranged through Treasure Isle Hotel, has a gorgeous beach, some interesting trails to follow (bring sturdy shoes) for flora and fauna watching, and an attractive restaurant that offers standard fare (with seafood salad a favorite) at the beach. The grilled fish is worth ordering, and less pricey than the local lobster. Cooper Island has the capacity to create the perfect memory.

Bitter End (see "Hotel" coverage for Virgin Gorda) offers a day excursion that includes pick-up at the Virgin Gorda "mainland" dock, the use of watersports equipment, plus lunch for under $50. Although the resort has added shops, restaurants, and sports concessions that make it a hodge-podge, a visit may be worth the effort. A long day from Tortola could start with an early-morning boat ride to **Virgin Gorda.**

Anegada, an unusual island far north of Virgin Gorda, is easily reached by small plane from Beef Island airport or aboard *Speedy's Delight,* if you prefer to arrive by sea. A day here can be quite an excursion, with a lobster lunch at *The Reefs* an integral part of the plan.

As is obvious, my idea of a place worth finding in this unique cast of islands is whatever I can reach from my starting point, and that can be a cozy cove for a picnic lunch, another small inn on another small island, or the lively marinas around Road Town, Nanny Cay, or Maya Cove on Tortola or at the Yacht Harbour on Virgin Gorda.

SPORTS for the British Virgins are all wet—either on, in, or under the sea. Tortola has no golf course (nor does any other B.V.I.), and there are only a few places with decent tennis courts on Tortola. Any list of yachts-for-charter numbers well over 300, with newcomers for each season. Here's a look at sports highlights for Tortola.

Sailing on your own boat, either bare-boat (where you and your pals serve as skipper and crew) or with paid crew, is superb in this area, as any reader of *Sail, Yachting,* or any of the other boating magazines already knows. Winds are steady, islands are convenient for easy landfall, and there are exceptional coves providing safe anchorage (and often, also, special dining experiences). The entire spectrum of the British Virgins stretches over sparkling seas, with St. Thomas and St. John (two of the U.S. Virgin Islands) nearby. There are additional sources for yacht charter on Virgin Gorda; charter boat firms of note on Tortola include the following.

Caribbean Sailing Yachts, familiarly known as CSY, is reached through Box 157, Road Town, Tortola, B.V.I., phone T 809+494-2741, or its U.S. base at #106, 5402 Beaumont Center Blvd., Tampa, FL 33634, T 800+237-1137 or 813+886-6783. The boating complex at Baughers Bay gives you a couple of rooms for overnighting before and after cruising, plus a boat in the slip off the deck at your feet when you're ready to take to the high seas. Cutters, sloops, and ketches are listed as the fleet for this season. Started by a Tenafly, New Jersey, sailor/dentist, John van Ost, and now captained by son Bob, the fleet is part of a triple-based operation that finds CSY Yachts cruising from ports in the Bay Islands off Honduras as well as into the Grenadines, usually on skippered charters from CSY port at St. Vincent.

Go Vacations (T 809+495-2379) operating from their marina at Fat Hog's Bay on the east end, is a Canadian firm with both sail and motor boats for charter. Sizes for most of the yachts range from 30 feet, with 5 berths in 2 cabins, to 54 feet with 10 berths in 6 cabins. The motor boats are 35 to 42 feet long, with 3 to 5 cabins. For details contact the firm at 129 Carlingview Dr., Rexdale, Ontario, Canada M9W 5E7, T 416+674-1880.

The Moorings, Ginny and Charles Cary's venture operating out of their Mariner Inn at Wickham Cay II on the east shore of Road Harbour, is the best charter operation in the entire Caribbean, in my opinion. Charterers' briefings are professional, no-nonsense sessions, and boats are in top condition. The Carys' operation specializes in comfortable 39-51-foot sloops as part of a fleet of about 90 yachts including sloops and ketches, all fiberglass, all in top condition. All boats go in for checkup at the end of every cruise. If you have a problem on the high seas, you have the route to call—and have been advised of the spots where you're out of radio range. The Carys sailed to this spot several years ago and continue to supervise their own operation here and in Grenada and St. Lucia with conscientious daily attention. The Tortola address is Box 139, T 809+494-2331 and the U.S. contact for The Moorings, Ltd., is 1305 U.S. 19 South #402, Clearwater, FL 33546, T 813+530-5651.

Offshore Sailing School, with U.S. offices at 16731-110 McGregor, Ft. Myers, FL 33908; T 813+454-1700 or 800+221-4326, operates "learn to sail" courses and other programs from Treasure Isle on Tortola.

Nanny Cay Marina, down a dirt road near the village of West End, *Village Cay Marina* at Prospect Reef, and the *Fort Burt Marina* in Road Town provide finger piers for visiting yachts (or those that call these ports home for at least part of the year). Many of the yachts are available for individual charters, which can be arranged through the office at each place or by walking along the pier and talking to some of the boat people.

Among the regulars are *White Squall II,* (T 809+494-2564) an 80-foot schooner that was chartering for $70 per day; *Shadowfax,* a 60-foot catamaran that charters out of Treasure Isle Hotel, also for $65 per day per person; and *Foxy Lady* (T 809+494-3540) a 24-foot Seabird, and *Patsy Lady,* a 43-foot motorcruiser for fishing, both out of Nanny Cay.

Your land base will have details on all the daily charters, good for picnic and snorkel cruising, even for nonsailors.

Scuba divers have plenty of sources for diving assistance, lessons, and equipment. Allan Baskin moved his base from Haiti, to *Baskin in the Sun* (Box 108, Road Town, Tortola, B.V.I., T 809+494-2858), with its branches at Long Bay, Sugar Mill, and Prospect Reef. *Underwater Safaris* (Box 139, Road Town, Tortola, B.V.I., T 809+494-3235) operate from The Moorings docks, and *Island Diver* (T 809+494-3878) has a shop at Village Cay marina. There are many other firms, including Virgin Gorda's pace-setter Kilbride's *Underwater Tours* (see "Sports" for Virgin Gorda), but on Tortola, these are ones I can vouch for—all professionals, all ethical, and all well equipped. (Rates will be standardized, restraint of trade or not.)

Boardsailing (otherwise known as "windsurfing") is very popular in the

British Virgins. Many hotels have at least a couple of boards for guests' use. Prospect Reef takes guests to Trellis Bay for boardsailing. *Boardsailing B.V.I.* has an office there. Board rentals have been about $150 per week. If you want to be sure to have one, contact the school at Box 537, Long Look, Tortola, B.V.I., T 809+495-2447, well in advance of your arrival on the island.

Tennis is popular at the *Tennis Centre* at Prospect Reef resort, where there are several courts with good surfaces. There are also 3 courts on Peter Island and one at Long Bay. The court on Guana Island seemed OK for fun, but not for hard play.

Horseback riding can be arranged through your hotel on Tortola and on Virgin Gorda. Don't count on the best training and equipment.

Birdwatchers will be interested in spending time at the nature area at Biras Creek on Virgin Gorda, or at Guana Island, off Tortola, or wandering around Peter Island. There are also places for wandering on Tortola and elsewhere on Virgin Gorda, but you'll want a 4-wheel-drive car to get to the more remote spots since many roads are dirt, rutted and rock-pocked.

TREASURES AND TRIFLES on Tortola are easily found at shops in the Village Cay marina area and in town. On the streets of Road Town, the few small shops with anything of interest for visitors center on Main Street, one road in from the newer Wickham's Cay Road, which lines the shore (on reclaimed land).

Gourmet Galley, at Village Cay Marina, has a selection of prepared foods (at $3 to $5.25 per portion) include boeuf bourguignon, enchiladas, stuffed zucchini, chicken vindaloo (with green bananas), as well as pizza and quiche. All are sold frozen, for you to heat at home, wherever that may be. In addition to the usual stock of vegetables, casseroles and other items, you can find seasoned sea salt and Mrs. Thomas's guava jelly and other preserves.

Pusser's Company Store, in Road Town, has a "Ralph Lauren"-"Banana Republic" look about it, with few bargains in the sport-conscious clothing and other merchandise. **Sunny Caribbee,** on Main Street, is the perfect place for one-stop shopping in Tortola. You'll find a colorful selection of island produce, crafts, and paintings. The attractively packaged spices, herbs, sauces, soaps, herbal teas, well-chosen handicrafts, (many from Haiti), and other items make great gifts—and the food products can prove addictive, once tried. From its B.V.I. home, the company exports to several other islands—but this shop has the most complete selection. Sunny Caribbee's owners had a great idea and haven't lagged with attention to detail. They continue to offer quality with imagination.

Several boutiques yield something worth wearing, if you're in the market for casual resort clothes. Selections are not large, but given a little time you can probably find some treasures among bathing suits, T-shirts, sun-smocks, and other frothy items.

Delightfully Yours, on Main Street near the Post Office, has some interesting handmade items, and across the road, find **Caribbean Handprints** and **Past and Presents.** The first has screened fabrics, in bright island colors and designs, in shirts, skirts, small-fry togs, hats, handbags, and an assortment of other items. All styles and clothes are Lilly-look-alikes, if you are in the market for that traditional Florida-country club class. P & P has an eclectic collection of old items, some antiques and some that are treasures for other reasons. The selection of books—Penguin trademark, West Indian subjects, and general—is exceptional.

Little Denmark, at the Wickhams Cay end of Main Street, has a little bit of everything, from batteries and T-shirts to European imports plus straw and wicker.

The Gallerie, next door, features local artwork, with special displays given to the crushed-coral scultpure of Mel Bellamy (beautiful treasures for "at home" memories).

Inquire about two locally made products: "British Virgin Islands Caribbean Seasoning" with West Indian spices and salt from sun-dried flats harvested at Salt Island ($1.50 for a 4-oz. shakerful), and Pusser's Rum (from British pronunciation of "purser's") which reportedly sells in the U.S. for $14.95 a fifth.

At the West End, **Sopers Hole Marina** boats a multi-building shopping center, painted in several hues of sun-faded pastels. Within the complex, there's an art gallery, some places selling island crafts, and a **Pusser's Company Store,** with a slightly smaller selection of clothes and other items than you'll find in the Road Town store, but the same style.

ANEGADA

North of Virgin Gorda, Anegada is a flat slab of land that is best reached for most folks by small plane from Tortola's Beef Island Airport, about 20 miles away. Check for the schedule (which changes frequently) when you arrive at the airport, if this sounds like your kind of place. Why go? Because the white powdery-sand beaches are lovely to scuff along, and the island wears a bracelet of rugged reefs that have caught enough ships through the centuries to have some of the most exciting scuba diving areas in the British Virgins. There are about 170 residents, and not much in the way of tourist attractions. The entire island—ponds and all—covers an area about 11 miles by 3.

The first great dream for Anegada was in the late 1960s, when Englishman Kenneth Bates offered the British Virgin Islands government great schemes for development. Roads were started to lead to the hotels, elegant resorts, and second homes that would be built on land bought inexpensively from Anegadians or negotiated with the government. The plan dissolved in 1968, leaving plenty of Anegadians bitter and suspicious. When another developer appeared in the 1970s, promising "tourist and residential buildings, community facilities and the basic concepts for the use and development of part of the island that would offer every opportunity for local participation" plus "recommendations on the protection of the environment including flora and fauna, birds and fish, and on the introduction of various small, specialized industries such as a turtle breeding unit," Anegadians were ready to take another chance. Conservation and interests of the residents (both fashionable ideas of the times) had been included in the programs, and the president of the company made a good-faith donation of $10,000 toward local causes (while someone else went around collecting $500 per house to be connected to the island's power system, which had been installed by the benevolent company). The only problem with this plan was that the perpetrator was Jean Doucet, president of Sterling Bank and Trust, a conglomerate with interests also in the Bahamas, which established in Grand Cayman under that colony's 1966 tax haven laws—and went broke in the mid-1970s, leaving Anegada (and all Sterling's other projects) deprived and once more destitute. For this season, Anegada continues to offer what it always has had: a sunny flat island with a small community, the Settlement.

The Reefs • *at the shore* • is a 12-room inn that has become a beacon of sorts. It is operated by Lowell Wheatley, not far from the air strip, and you can cover the distance in a car when you arrive. Fishing folk and those who know and love the sea, and quiet shoreside surroundings, can settle in here happily—especially if Lowell speeds you out for a sportfishing day. This is a fascinating quiet spot for a getaway vacation. Motel-style units offer basic comforts and the Wheatleys offer genuine hospitality. Divers will find lots of interest. Sailors who are not experts in these seas should stay away; the reefs make the approach very tricky, as the shipwrecks testify.

JOST VAN DYKE

West of Tortola, and north of St. John, this quiet four-and-one-half-square-mile island, whose "first name" is pronounced Yost, is almost easier to reach from St. Thomas than it is from Tortola's West End or Road Town. Boats make the link; if you're booking one of the two places to stay, the management there can advise the best routing. And if you're planning on housekeeping, bring favorites from home and stock up at a supermarket in St. Thomas, or in Road Town on Tortola. There's no source for food on this small island, which is perfect for people who want to be removed from commercial threats (including any provided by electricity, which isn't available). The coves are favored anchorages for yachting types who sometimes saunter up to one of the name places to dine. (Advance reservations are necessary; ship-to-shore calls suffice for last-minute plans.)

Rudy's Mariner Inn • *on the beach at Great Harbour* • is a simple spot, with basic housekeeping facilities and a beachcomber atmosphere. The cove is a popular anchorage for cruising yachts, and the beach bar and restaurant have a steady clientele when the yachting season is in full swing. Otherwise, you'll have one of the three rooms pretty much to yourself. Robinson Crusoe would feel at home here.

Sandcastle • *on the hillside above White Bay* • has been a popular island outpost since Daphne Henderson ran the place as her home-for-guests, with her special recipes a highlight of the evening. New owners from Clearwater, Florida, continue the style; candlelit dinners draw yachting folk smart enough to call ahead for a reservation. Rooms are in four tradewind-cooled cottages, with natural surroundings made spectacular by God-given powdery sand and seas in every shade of blue. Snorkeling is good from the beach and neighboring coves; boardsailing and a day sailer are other action options.

Sandy Ground • *on the east end of the island* • is several villas on a hillside with sea view; the beautiful beach is below. Your home will have full kitchen (which you tend and take care of yourself), terra-cotta floors, a private terrace that's ideal for sunning and star-gazing, and peaceful, quiet surroundings shared only with the other guests. Reports of a clublike atmosphere among repeaters who head here as a group suggest that you'll have a better time if you fit in, or are with a clutch of your own pals.

Restaurants on Jost Van Dyke are led by **Sandcastle,** known for its good food (reservations are a *must*). For casual seaside dining, at places you'll reach by boat, the longtime leader, now with T-shirts and other items for sale, is **Foxy's Tamarind,** at Great Harbour; a relative (also popular) newcomer is **Harry's Place,** at Little Harbour. Both are casual beachside places with devoted patrons who buy T-shirts, drinks, and meals. Also look for **Abe's,** a fish place, at Little Harbour and **Ali Baba's,** at the customs house at Great Harbour. My sailing sleuth said that the pig roast at **Rudy's** (at Great Harbour) was fun; it's planned for groups by advance reservation, but sometimes others can be included. Yachtsmen should get in touch in advance to see what's planned.

MOSQUITO ISLAND

This unfortunate name is what this speck off the north coast of Virgin Gorda is called on charts, so we'll identify it that way too, but its claim to fame, both for yachtsmen and for other visitors, is Drake's Anchorage. Unless you sail in on a yacht, or make your own direct motorboat arrangements, the way to reach this speck is by motorboat from Gun Creek, a northeast cove that Virgin Gorda taxis can find.

Drake's Anchorage • *on Mosquito Island* • offers an elegantly exclusive atmosphere for folks who can enjoy a hideaway without phones, TV, or other modern-day intrusions, and don't mind undertaking the sometimes tedious journey by plane, car, and boat to get here. Although only 5 minutes by boat from Virgin Gorda, this place seems far removed from everything except naturally comfortable, pampered living. The ultimate luxury is to rent the entire 125-acre island, an idea that might appeal to executives who need a place to hold seminars, or think-tank types. (A Cousteau group is one that does.) Ten seaview, comfortable rooms are on Lime Tree Beach; two native-stone villas are pleasantly furnished and private. They are away from the main building. A windmill helped provide the island's electricity and solar panels were put in place for heating water. Vegetables and fruits for the daily meals have always been grown on the island, but the emphasis has been renewed (and the former units refurbished). Watersports are a highlight of daytime activities. Boardsailing, bonefishing, scuba diving, and snorkeling are popular. Yachting folks anchor offshore, lending their tales to evening entertainment. Remote and special, Drake's Anchorage can provide an ideal getaway island for island-seeking folks who enjoy comforts amid beautiful surroundings. The place is officially closed from mid-August to mid-November.

NECKER ISLAND

This privately owned 74-acre paradise can be yours—for a mere $5500 per day. (It was home for Princess Diana, her children, her mother, and assorted aides in April '90.) Although it's possible to share the space with as many as 20, there's agreement among those who pay the tally that the island is more comfortable with no more than 8 couples since more people means that you'll have to turn over the living room part of your suite to another twosome. Owned by British magnate Richard Branson, initiator of Virgin Atlantic Airline and owner of Virgin Atlantic *Challenger II* (a 72-foot, $2.3 million yacht that broke the transatlantic ocean speed record in July 1986), the island offers ultimate luxury. The hilltop villa has a master bedroom, 2 bedroom suites (that can be 4 bedrooms), and 5 bedrooms—plus a managing couple who are gourmet cooks, 3 maids, 2 gardeners, and an essential boatman to help you make the link to other more populous islands. Several boats and windsurfers rent with the house and 2 Jacuzzis supplement the swimming pool. (This place also has some audio-visual equipment, useful for corporate meetings if not for leisure hours.) If you love (and can afford) luxury, consider this.

VIRGIN GORDA

Simply sensational—and sensationally simple! That's what this island is. From the air, the clutter of huge boulders that fleck the southwest end look as though they had been thrown there by some giant in a fit of pique, but the northeastern stretch of the island is hilly, reasonably lush, and multi-coved. The island was mined for gold in the 17th century, but from the time the gold ran out (or the Spaniards ran away) until recent years, nothing much had happened here. Yachtsmen long have known the beaches, as soft and white as talcum powder, and The Baths, with clear pools created and sheltered by huge boulders at the shore, but it took the vision (and money and taste) of Laurance Rockefeller and his team to breathe new life into the fat Virgin, as Virgin Gorda's name translates.

Rockefeller's affection for cruising these waters, and his previous experience with the pace-setting Caneel Bay on nearby St. John, led to Little Dix Bay resort, a project that was nicknamed the "British Virgin Islands' Red Cross" for the many services Rockefeller interests' provided. In the early '50s, before the start of the Rockefeller investment, the island had no telephones, no power supply, no doctor, no paved roads, and no adequate schooling or jobs for the couple of hundred people who lived here. When the first boards and building blocks appeared on the beach at Little Dix Bay in 1961, Virgin Gorda—and, in fact, the British Virgin Islands—took the first step into the burgeoning tourism business. Although a few of its shores have been discretely trimmed with small resorts, the original natural appeal of Virgin Gorda remains. Little Dix has few peers in the Caribbean, but there are several personality places in the British Virgin Islands and elsewhere that got their start—either with staff or encouragement—from this one. Little Dix opened in 1964, built mostly by British Virgin Islanders who learned their skills on the job, from foremen and others stationed here to build the resort. The staff, many of whom had their first jobs at St. John's sister resort, Caneel Bay, returned to the British Virgins for a job in their own country. Access roads have been built, generators have been installed, the airport on Virgin Gorda was built originally for Little Dix Bay guests, a shopping center was created a few years after the hotel was opened, and the Virgin Gorda Yacht Harbour was started as an accommodation for Little Dix guests, sparked and sponsored by the Rockresort group. Visitors arriving here today, with time to complain about slow service, flickering lights or power outages, and the inevitable water shortage (the result of extended periods of sunny weather, with no rain), should pause to reflect on the miracle that there are hotels with modern comforts on this island at all. It wasn't easy—and it wasn't that long ago that things were very different here.

AUTHOR'S OBSERVATION

Be sure to bring your favorite bug spray or other nipper repellent. Sand flies and mosquitos can be pesky.

ARRIVAL on Virgin Gorda is easiest and fastest by the small planes of *Air BVI, American Eagle, Sunaire,* and others to the Virgin Gorda airstrip from Puerto Rico, St. Thomas, or St. Maarten, but some of us prefer the slower arrival by boat—to the Yacht Harbour from Road Town, Tortola, or from St. Thomas, in the U.S.V.I. No matter how you plan to arrive, count on an air/taxi/boat/taxi combination that is best handled with little or no luggage (don't bring much), and use that time to slow down and start your vacation. About the only thing you can count on is that there will be delays.

Lodgings for Virgin Gorda are grouped according to Hotel/Resorts, Housekeeping Holidays, The Inn Way, or Low-Cost Lodging. Stars are awarded within each category. (Refer to page 11 for details.)

HOTELS/RESORTS range from real luxury at Little Dix to remote resorts and simple spots, each with its own personality.

★★★ **Biras Creek** • *at North Sound* • caps a small hill, and slides down its sides to the sound. The 150-acre estate was built by a Norwegian shipping magnate who followed the lead of compatriot Torloff Smedvig, who built the original Peter Island. The main building (dining rooms; small shop with suntan lotions, etc.; bar and spectacular views) caps the hilltop, with rooms in cottages at the shore. There's a swimming pool for cottage users who don't want to do more than step off their terrace, but the real beach is reached after a short and tropical garden walk to Deep Bay. Tennis courts and the bird sanctuary supplement the snorkeling, scuba, and sailing activities. Your home, once you've completed the expedition to reach this spot, will be one of the 15 two-suite units that curve along the shore. *Small resort.*

★★ **Bitter End Yacht Club** • *reached by boat from Gun Point dock on North South* • has grown like the proverbial Topsy, with buildings added to the original off-beat, casual yacht-oriented inn to create a "something for everybody" place that seems in danger of losing its soul. The once-lovely seafront is a string of buildings and docks, for arrival and departure of day visitors and long-stay folks, and for watersports concessionaires and other purveyors. The waterfront restaurant could be in Florida or some other warm-and-sunny U.S. seaside place, both for its prices and its gimmicky food offerings, which you sample from an overkill buffet by putting your choices on a tray as you carry it along the line. Bedrooms nest in dozens of buildings blanketing the hillside. The best, for my time, are those farthest away from the waterfront clutter, to the path heading north. Although they require a longish walk, and a climb upstairs for some, they are away from any nighttime music and other noise and look out on the natural scenery of island-and-sea. Top-rate rooms are the cottages built as the former Tradewinds resort to the south (near Biras Creek). In an attempt to appeal to all travelers, this place has driven away some of its longtime nautical friends. Most true sailors opt for quieter coves. *Resort.*

Fischer's Cove Beach • *at The Valley within walking distance of the marina* • is famous for its island food, especially the lobster dinners. Native son Anderson Flax returned home to Virgin Gorda in the early '60s, after a stint as a mechanic on neighboring St. Thomas. Recognizing the budding tourism complex that had been planted by Rockresorts, Andy Flax opened his Andy's by the Sea, a small bar popular with the workers and with the few tourists who reached Virgin Gorda in those days. The place grew on the choice sand-rimmed cove that had been given to him by his grandfather and began to serve local food in simple surroundings, eventually to add 8 cottages for guests who knew and wanted good value. Now the place is a full-fledged small resort, with a seaside patio that is a restaurant (and a perfect place to catch the sunset view). Rooms are in several buildings around the grounds. (In the meantime, Andy stocked and started Virgin Gorda Tours Association, the island's first organized taxi business, and met and married his Antiguan-born wife, Norma.) *Hotel.*

★★★★★ **Little Dix Bay** • *on the shore* • continues to be a luxury retreat. Rooms are in viewful units tucked in clusters along flower-trimmed paths that meander along the beach with some units down by the tennis courts. The main gathering spot (restaurant, bar, near the beach) is open to sea breezes, with a loose-fitting thatch cap to keep the sun off. Your room will be made of purpleheart wood, colorful fabrics, and all modern comforts, including air conditioning in some units. (I have always found the overhead fan more than enough motivation for stirring the soft breezes.) There is a complete tennis complex (5 courts), with pro around in peak season months, plus watersports easily arranged here and at the Yacht Harbour, a reasonable (but hot) walk or short ride from the resort. Day boating excursions are offered through the activities desk; small shops are on premises for immediate purchases, and you have about 500 acres to meander around, book or binoculars in hand. The pace by day is leisurely, quiet, sun-and-sea-filled; entertainment some evenings is as rambunctious as a barbecue and steel band, but count on turning in early unless you bring a lively group from home, or happen to find one here. The Little Dix development pumped a reported $2.5 million into the B.V.I. economy, and the resort recognizes its responsibility to its guests—and to the people of the island—to provide what is expected (which means having its own desalinization plant, building roads, giving good wages, etc.). If you vacation at other than peak season (winter), check for the special spring, summer, and fall package holidays that link Little Dix with Caneel and sometimes with time on a yacht, for a split week or two. *Classic Resort.*

Pussers at Leverick Bay • *on a north coast cove, with a view toward Mosquito Island* • may have another name for this season, but its rapid completion in mid-'91 assures that it will exist and it was built by the Pusser clan, who have ventures on Tortola. The first glimpse, as you arrive on the winding, climbing road, is a nest of red-roofed buildings that seem to fill the hill-banked cove that had been quiet Leverick Bay. The bedrooms step up the hillside, a steep climb to and from the shore. The shore area is dedicated to buildings that hold the restaurant, shops, and other services, as well as a pool. I suspect this place might lure cruise ship visitors when they are in port. The *Caribbean Newsletter* (page 9) will have further comment, when the resort is in full swing. This place has overtones of a strictly commercial venture, but may offer valuefull package plans that would be worth investigating. View from the rooms is lovely, but I suspect that evening music and other noises will drift through your windows later than some may wish. You'll want a car or taxi for mobility. *Resort.*

HOUSEKEEPING HOLIDAYS: There are many cottages and small villas for rent around Virgin Gorda. Among those that operate with central management, and usually a restaurant, are:

Diamond Beach Club • *on the north shore* • has several villas and a small house for folks who want a housekeeping hideaway. This remote grouping is only about 15 minutes from the Yacht Harbour, but inquire about the last part of the road, which was rutted and rock-pocked dirt when I drove it. The *Caribbean Newsletter* (page 9) will have an update. *Villas.*

★ **Guavaberry-Spring Bay Vacation Homes** • *at the boulder-strewn, south part of the island* • has the look and the feel of a woodsy camp, except that your home will be well furnished, and the weather and welcome will be warm.

The beach is down the walk, the tumble of gigantic rocks known locally as "The Baths" is not far away, and there are gigantic boulders next to the main house. Highly recommended for independent housekeeping types who can stock up happily at the Virgin Gorda marina supermarket (or can bring canned goods and meat in a box from home). The small commissary on the premises copes with emergency rations. *Cottages.*

Mango Bay Resort and Paradise Villas • *on the beach on a quiet cove* • has the potential to be an elegant retreat but it will grow in slow stages. Management/ownership squabbles result in the two names for what is, in fact, one villa community. The first of the villas appeared in the late 1980s, with comfortable patios for sunning and pleasant, airy rooms in the well-equipped villas. These units can be ideal homes for vacationers in search of a sunstruck place for total relaxation. Units range from studios to 3-bedroom villas; all are served by capable maids. The beach is gorgeous; the style quiet. *Villas.*

THE INN WAY: Some of the housekeeping places have the warmth and hospitality usually associated with the best inns. However, on Virgin Gorda, there's one inn that warrants special note.

★ **Olde Yard Inn** • *inland on the island* • has offered home-grown hospitality for a couple of decades and Carol Kaufman and her team continue to do so. The octagonal room that is "the library" had been the trademark of the originators is now also a T.V. room used often, I observed, by staff. The atmosphere is casual, with the pub-like bar a popular gathering area, and the food featuring island-style cooking and fresh fish. There's nothing elaborate about the rooms or dress requirements, and your happiness here will depend on your compatibility with the owners and the mix of other guests. *Inn.*

Ocean View • *at the Virgin Gorda Marina* • has the setting and potential to be a pleasant inn, but it was short on hospitality when I visited. Bedrooms are upstairs, over the dining area and the porch/patio that seems to appeal to local folks when they take time out. Furnishings are basic, bordering on rundown. The location is wonderful—very convenient for the marina; prices are higher than services and surroundings warranted, when I checked for this edition. *Small hotel.*

LOW-COST LODGING: Places on Virgin Gorda are priced for the incomes of those who have been persevering to reach this place—and that's high. There's not much in the way of *very* low-cost lodgings, unless you shop around for a room somewhere when you arrive on the island. The best bet is to wait until the rates drop (on or about April 15) and vacation before they rise again preceding Christmas. Insofar as reasonable-for-the-BVI is concerned, the best bet is to fill every bed of a cottage rental (at which time the rate is divided by enough people to make the per person cost low). Places to consider include two 2-bedroom houses called **Rockmere** and **Vistas** • *at Little Trunk Bay* • that rent for about $1200 per week for 4 in winter and less in summer season or **Windfall Villa** • *at The Valley* • with 3 bedrooms and basic surroundings.

RESTAURANTS on Virgin Gorda range from very casual fish and lobster spots, and publike places at the marina, to hotel dining facilities that often incorporate noteworthy cuisine and interesting decor. Some of the hotels are noteworthy for meals. **Little Dix** is best for gala meals (especially dinners by candlelight) on their sea-view terraces; **Olde Yard Inn** serves imaginative entrees in pleasant surroundings; and for sheer quantity of food in American theme-restaurant style, **Bitter End** wins—with its overwhelming buffet.

Andy's Chateau de Pirate • *on the sea, near the Post Office* • serves meals for special occasions. Check to see if you can join a barbecue or another fete. This place is not always open, but when it is, it can be fun.

Bath & Turtle • *a publike place in the shopping center at the Yacht Harbour* • draws some of the boat folk who are moored at the marina, and others from elsewhere. The island regulars meet for coffee, sundowners, and casual meals. The atmosphere is informal, boaty, and friendly. It's a good place to meet with others.

Biras Creek • *on a hilltop, reached by boat and foot* • has been the traditional leader for the island, and a place popular with visiting yachtsmen who call ahead for reservations: count on gourmet cuisine.

Chez Michelle, • *in The Valley, near the Virgin Gorda Yacht Harbour* • has island-elegant surroundings in a typical West Indian small building. French-style food is served and with flair. A welcome addition to the dine-around roster, this place is one to try. I like the continental atmosphere.

Fischer's Cove • *on the beach near the harbor* • has been the island's premier seafood place since Andy Flax first started cooking the lobsters. It's still good and, informal although pricier than the place may warrant. There's a steel band some nights in winter season.

Pusser's Pub • *at Leverick Bay, on North Sound* • has traditional food such as hamburgers (which they serve in a basket—sometimes) and an impressive Sun. brunch from 12 p.m. to 2 p.m., with hot banana bread a highlight. On Sat. there's a beach barbecue. Acknowledging that many visitors don't have cars, the management arranges pick up from the Yacht Harbour and a couple of other places at about 6:30 p.m. with return at 9:30 p.m. or so.

PLACES WORTH FINDING are wonderfully natural on Virgin Gorda. There are several pristine beaches, where soft white powder sand blankets long spans. Since most of the island's landscape is still in its natural state, there's not much to distinguish the Gorda Peak Park, except that it is the highest point on the island (1370 feet), or Devil's Bay National Park, which is at the southernmost portion of the island. On the southwest shore, The Baths, so-named for the pools of clear water that collect amid mammoth boulders, are a favorite attraction, not only for long-stay visitors but for yachtsmen and, more recently, for cruise ship visitors who are brought here by jitney-bus or motor launch. (To enjoy The Baths at their best, plan to visit when the cruise passengers are elsewhere. Natural, quiet beauty is what makes this place unique.)

If you're interested in flora, climb up Gorda Peak to look for wild orchids and other island plants as well as birds. The nature walk on the grounds of Biras Creek can be pleasant relief from the more commercial parts of that complex.

There are dozens of offshore islands and islets, some of which have small resorts but most of which are virtually untrammeled. Motorboats can be arranged when you're on the spot. There are many local entrepreneurs eager to take you around the area.

SPORTS are centered on the sea, sailing and scuba, with facilities available at the Yacht Harbour as well as through people at the various hotels. **Scuba** is firmly and ably in the hands of *Kilbrides Underwater Tours,* whose acknowledged master, Bert Kilbride, lives on Saba Rock at North Sound. Two 42-foot dive boats take divers to underwater wrecks, caves, and coral forests. Resort and full certification courses are offered. A 1-tank dive is $50; the resort course $75. Little Dix is the source for **tennis,** but you should stop by to check with the pro to be sure you can get court time. That resort also has special **yacht charter** arrangements for its guests. *Misty Isle Yacht Charters* operates day sails to nearby islands and offers longer charters as well. **Fishing trips** are sometimes arranged through Little Dix in coordination with Caneel Bay resort on St. John. Check at the *Yacht Harbour* for **deep-sea fishing** arrangements; there are usually several boats available for charter. Biras Creek and Bitter End also have the full range of watersports, with sailing a prime focus at Bitter End.

TREASURES AND TRIFLES: On Virgin Gorda, the Yacht Harbour is the hub for most of the shops. Some shops started with Little Dix sponsorship, in the early days when it was all there was. In recent seasons, a separate clutch of bookstores, handicraft places, and clothes shops opened. Some of the merchandise is above average (and so is price), depending on what your shopping situation is at home. (If you are near a commercial city, you'll find the offerings paltry here.) Some of the best offerings are the spices, soaps, jams, and other **Sunny Caribbee** items. The **Commissary & Ships Store** is a supermarket-style place that also has merchandise, such as the popular fish bags and other canvas carry-alls made by Zoro of St. Thomas. Bitter End also has an assortment of gift and clothing shops.

Liquor and perfumes are good, but not usually exceptional buys. The British Virgins do not claim "freeport" or duty-free shopping, although liquor prices are better bargains than you'll find at home (and at a few of the puffed-up priced Thomas shops). You'll do even better if you pass through the neighboring American Virgins so that you can take advantage of the special one-gallon allotment and the supermarket prices, in that place that made its name (and a fortune) on duty-free liquor, etc.

CAYMAN ISLANDS

Cayman Islands Department of Tourism, P.O. Box 67, George Town, Grand Cayman, B.W.I., T 809+949–7999, fax 809+949–0623; 3440 Wilshire Blvd., #1202, Los Angeles, CA 90010, T 213+738–1968; 250 Catalonia Ave., #401, Coral Gables, FL 33134, T 305+444–6551; Box 824, Tarpon Springs, FL 34386, T 813+934–9078; Box 900024, Atlanta, GA 30329, T 404+934–3959; 980 N. Michigan Ave., #1206, Chicago, IL 60611, T 312+944–5602; Box 2602, Baltimore, MD 21215, T 301+644–0855; Box 114, Boston, MA 02117, T 617+431–7771; 420 Lexington Ave., #2733, New York, NY 10170, T 212+682–5582; 9794 Forest Lane, #569, Dallas, TX 75243, T 214+823–3838; Two Memorial City Plaza, 820 Gessner, #170, Houston, TX 77024, T 713+461–1317; E. B. Smith Travel Marketing; 234 Eglinton Ave. E., #306; Toronto, Ont., Canada M4P 1K5, T 416+485–1550; 100 Brompton Rd., London SW3 1EX, England, 071+581–9960.

$ · · · US$1 = CI$.80
Unless otherwise noted, $ refers to U.S. currency.

See pages noted for information on: Cayman Brac, p. 226; Grand Cayman, p. 208; Little Cayman, p. 228.

When he was less than five years old, Will Jackson learned to make rope, as did most people who "went to business" at the East End of Grand Cayman. Made from the unopened leaf of the thatch palm tree, rope was bartered, in 50 fathom lengths, for food and goods when they were available.

Ropemaking was an important industry on Grand Cayman as recently as the 1950s. Men, women, and children would walk long distances in the wilderness to find thatch tops that were suitable. With a smoke pan to ward off mosquitoes and a machete to hack a way through the gnarled underbrush, industrious Caymanians would walk four or five miles through swamp and over rock, returning over a similar route with the 200 or more tops they had found.

That was only the beginning. Tied in bundles of two, the tops were set in the sun to be dried before they could be stripped into strings. The true test of

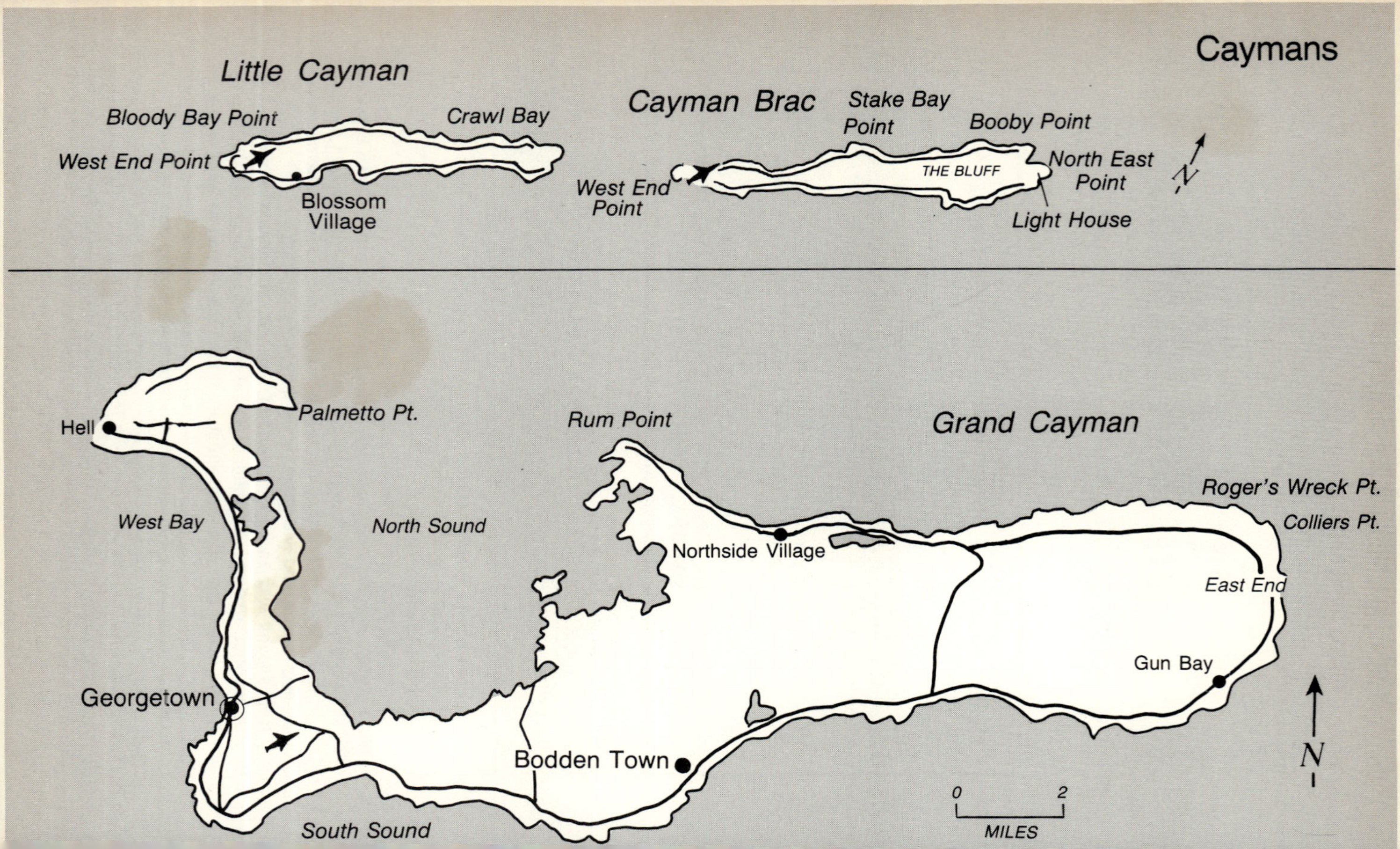

Caymans

Little Cayman

- Bloody Bay Point
- West End Point
- Crawl Bay
- Blossom Village

Cayman Brac

- West End Point
- Stake Bay Point
- Booby Point
- THE BLUFF
- North East Point
- Light House

Grand Cayman

- Hell
- West Bay
- Palmetto Pt.
- North Sound
- Rum Point
- Northside Village
- Roger's Wreck Pt.
- Colliers Pt.
- East End
- Gun Bay
- Bodden Town
- Georgetown
- South Sound

N→

0 2
MILES

ropemaking was the skill of winding the strings into strands, an art that, when practiced correctly, would keep the rope from falling apart while being wound into fathoms.

In the 1920s, according to Will Jackson, 50 fathoms of rope, known as a coil, would sell for nine English pennies. He remembers fondly his first real pair of shoes. He earned them by making rope.

Although the earliest settlements were tied to the sea, with boat building and ropemaking, it is only since the 1970s that the sea is once again the major source for Caymanians' livelihood. It is the attraction for thousands of visitors who come here each year, lured by the promise of being able to see unimagined wonders of the underwater world from the land base that seems safe and secure.

In the years of European discovery, it was the turtles that lured voyagers to these islands. So many of them used to wallow in the seas around the Caymans that ships heading back to Europe from settlements in Jamaica used to stop on the shores of Cayman Brac to pick up a supply for the crossing. This was in the earliest years; a record on June 26, 1655, notes that a ship headed to "the Kie of Manus to get some turtle for our sick people."

The name later became Kiemanus, and sometimes Caimanos, and by 1622, Caiman Isles—and still people came for the turtles. Today turtles take second place. They're being cultivated at the several-times refinanced West Bay venture called the Cayman Turtle Farm. Fishermen through the centuries captured the entire Cayman crop, and went farther afield, throughout the Caribbean and near the shores of Cuba, to return with turtles—and some say the mosquitoes that can be the scourge of Cayman life.

Cayman Brac and Little Cayman, each covered at the end of this chapter, were the first islands in this group to be sighted and settled, according to the commentary by George S. S. Hirst in his *Notes on the History of the Cayman Islands,* written in 1898 when he was commissioner. "On the tenth day of May, 1503, Christopher Columbus returning from his fourth and last voyage from the Central America Coast discovered the Lesser Cayman Islands, which on account of the prodigious number of turtles seen both in the sea and on the shores, he called Las Tortugas." Hirst adds that "very shortly after their discovery he drove his weather-beaten and sinking caravels into the harbour at St. Ann's Bay Jamaica," but not without noting in his log that his ships had passed between what could only be the Lesser Caymans. He could see two islands—and these are only 7 miles apart; Grand Cayman is about 80 miles southwest.

It's the beaches that bring people here today, and the tax haven status that makes offshore banking attractive. Both lures are the foundations on which the flourishing local economy has been built.

AUTHOR'S OBSERVATION

Don't make a move without getting your copy of the *Tourist Weekly,* published by the Cayman Free Press, a fact-filled newssheet that will tell you the latest places to eat, shop, scuba dive, dance, etc.

POLITICAL PICTURE: The elections held in November 1988 resulted in few changes: The Executive Council's Member for Tourism, Aviation, and Trade is widely respected and a strong policy leader. As a British colony, the Caymans have one of the most stable governments in the Caribbean, with 12 elected seats in their 15-member Legislative Assembly. The governor is appointed by Queen Elizabeth II and is the key member of the Assembly. The Executive Council, roughly equivalent to the United States' Presidential Cabinet, includes 4 elected officials and 4 appointed officials (the governor, chief secretary, attorney general, and financial secretary).

This three-island colony has total control over its daily affairs and quietly goes about its business, putting money from tourism and its considerable offshore banking facilities into the area's coffers to run the government and to keep the colony's infrastructure in good condition.

ISLAND APPEARANCE: The overwhelming impact is made by the long white ribbon of sand that fringes West Bay. Although the coral ridges that stretch for miles under the sea are a world of mystery, the plateaus that rise out of the sea to be the three Cayman Islands are dry, rocky, and sun baked with patches of knotted underbrush and acres of swamp where mosquito colonies have only recently been subdued. If you flex your arm, with the elbow about shoulder height, and chop it off at the shoulder, you have the shape of Grand Cayman. The eastern district is at the shoulder. West Bay Beach, also known as Seven Mile Beach, is along the outer side of the upraised arm and the clenched fist is the area shared by the communities of West Bay and Barkers, an area better known for the settlement at Hell and the Turtle Farm.

North Sound claims most of the space between fist and shoulder, while the space below the raised biceps is South Sound and Bodden Bay. The landscape of Grand Cayman is about as interesting as the skin on an average arm. There are no mountains, and hardly a hill. The island's high point, locally called The Mountain, rises only 50 feet above sea level.

In an effort to encourage domestic concern about the environment, the Cayman Islands National Trust implemented the innovative education program offered through Philadelphia-based RARE Center. The campaign focuses on protecting the Cayman Islands parrot, a Cuban parrot subspecies that has specific markings unique to the Cayman Islands. Helping Caymanians to recognize the need to protect the parrots' habitat (and thereby the natural environment) is the program's purpose. Parrots have been spotted in northeastern Grand Cayman and on Cayman Brac.

The northeastern bulge of Grand Cayman is laced with trails, most of which are in poor condition, but birders can be rewarded by walking inland from the Queen's Highway.

Marine Parks are part of a plan to preserve the fragile underwater community. Conservation legislation designated three sea categories, which are environmental regions, replenishing areas, and the recreational Marine Parks. The western shore, up to and around Villas Papagallo, and the northeast, off Rum Point, are two of the Marine Parks. Little Sound, an area in the north, is an environmental zone; Meagre Bay Pond, with a road running along its southern shore and mangroves fringing its northern limits, is a good area for birding. (For details on Little Cayman and Cayman Brac, refer to the commentary at the end of this chapter.)

LIFESTYLE in the Caymans is conservatively casual in an Americanized s easily recognized in trend-following suburbs in the U.S. midwest and south. Although British links are firmly forged, the Caymanian personality these days is so overwhelmed with the effects of the neighboring United States that many traces of a uniquely Caymanian lifestyle that were visible even a few years ago have now disappeared. While daytime activities revolve around beach and sea, the nighttime is devoted to dining out and to entertainment offered at a few of the bigger hotels. This is a low-key place that has become a haven for many who flee from northern cold and snows in search of warm weather and the sun.

AUTHOR'S OBSERVATION

A week of revelry worth noting if you like to join in local fun-and-frolic is the annual Pirate's Week, held during the last week in October. Parades, picnics, and pranks are all part of the fun, with costume parties featuring pirate traditions. Check with the Department of Tourism, and make reservations as far ahead as possible (for airline and hotel space) at what has become a popular island event.

Until 1972, the only people with Caymanian status were those with a Caymanian parent. Just being born here didn't count; your family had to have been here practically since Bodden or Ebanks, both of whom have been here "forever." (The Caymans' telephone book shows hundreds of listings of Ebankses and Boddens, and towns and shops also carry those names.) Laws were modified in 1972 and again in the early '80s, to allow foreigners to become Caymanian "by grant," if approved by the Caymanian Protection Board.

Clothes are calculatedly casual. Attire for fishing and watersports is de rigueur during the days; neatly casual resort wear is the pattern in the evenings. The most casual spots are those south of George Town and away from the Seven Mile Beach. Along the beach, guests at the high-priced hotels dress up in the traditional Caribbean visitor style, occasionally with long skirts on ladies and even a few madras jackets on men. Neat, straight shirts with no tie are acceptable in many restaurants, but there are a couple of places that aspire to the quality image, so don your best.

AUTHOR'S OBSERVATION

Although the mosquitoes and other small nibblers known as "no-see-'ums" have been brought under control, wise Caymanian travelers have some bug repellent at hand. After late-day rains or at other humid times, the pesky pinchers can ruin your plans to sit on your patio or by the pool. Be prepared.

MEDICAL FACILITIES: The government hospital, on the airport side of downtown George Town, is modern, air-conditioned, and as good as many hospitals in medium-sized towns in the U.S. or Britain (and better than some). Many of the doctors have trained in the U.S., Canada, Britain, or another country where medical schools are top-notch. There's a decompression chamber on the island, a fact of interest for scuba divers; air ambulance service reaches Miami in little more than an hour.

MONEY MATTERS: The local currency is Caymanian dollars, and most signs are posted in that currency. Before you are fooled into thinking that food and other prices are low, remember that CI$1 equals US$1.25; the "lower" prices are not lower for U.S. dollar-spenders. U.S. dollars are accepted, but some hotels encourage changing into Caymanian dollars (so they can get hard currency).

AUTHOR'S OBSERVATION

The Cayman Islands economy is based on the banking business and on tourism, and tourism brings the bodies that put life and action into the community. Although the island facilities are in good shape, be prepared for the fact that everything is geared to prying as many of your dollars from you as possible.

COMMUNICATIONS are easy between Grand Cayman and overseas, with direct-dial from North America, using 809 area code + 94 + 5-digit Caymanian number. The Cable & Wireless office in George Town is one place to make overseas phone calls without paying the hefty surcharge usually levied at hotels. Cable & Wireless sells a phonecard, about the size of a credit card, for use in public telephones that will not accept coins. The card comes in several amounts, and can be used until that amount is spent. AT&T's USADirect service is available from the Cayman Islands, by dialing 1872 to reach the AT&T operator through whom you place your call, either collect or charged to your AT&T number. Facsimile machines are used by most hotels and many other businesses. Do not count on having a phone (or radio) in your hotel room and know that phone links to Little Cayman and Cayman Brac are a challenge.

AUTHOR'S OBSERVATION

The Cayman Islands Department of Tourism produces the Caribbean's most compact, concise, and helpful printed information. The fact-packed *Cayman Islands Rates & Facts* booklet, printed annually and available free through the tourist offices, gives accurate information in a no-nonsense formula.

ARRIVAL ON GRAND CAYMAN is efficient and pleasant, to a breeze-swept and attractive airline terminal. The airport has all modern conveniences arranged in a comfortably Caribbean style. For Immigration, you must have a return or continuing ticket, so the officials know you are not planning to be a drag on the community. When you have shown identification (passport is best), and been granted entry, walk on and wait for your luggage. The taxi drivers that stand outside the airport entrance are a cut above those that hover around most Caribbean airport entrances. I've found reception warm, service pleasant, conversation enlightening—and the fee high—but somehow that seems acceptable when the service is willing.

Cayman Airways, the national link to Miami, Houston, Atlanta, Tampa, New York, and other cities, provides easy and comfortable links to Grand Cayman, and within the trio, between the big island and its sister islands of Cayman Brac and Little Cayman. *American* also has daily service linking cities to Grand Cayman through Miami. If you plan to visit all three islands, research schedules. All flights do not operate daily; advance planning will avoid disappointment. Cayman Brac's Gerald Smith Airport was lengthened in the late '70s to accommodate bigger planes, and there are sometimes direct flights from Tampa and Miami and other southern cities. *Air Jamaica* joins Cayman Airways in flights between Kingston, Jamaica, and Grand Cayman. Inquire about the "Cayman Caper," a special fare with hotels that gives a couple of days in the islands at very low fares from Miami. Your travel agent has details.

CRUISES come into the Caymans in ever increasing numbers, with passengers stepping off the ship and into George Town in some cases, and being ferried in by small boats in others. Beach and sea activities occupy most onshore time, with a barbecue beach party at the Grand Caymanian Holiday Inn a regularly scheduled event. One of the many snorkeling and scuba sites is within a short walk from the dock.

DEPARTURE by air is easy and pleasant. The airport has plenty of shops, but if you're planning on last-minute shopping, be sure to find out whether or not they'll be open when your plane departs. Security systems prevail here. It's a good idea to leave at least an hour for check-in procedures. You'll need to turn in the copy of your immigration card when you pass through the immigration area. There's a departure tax of CI$6 or US$7.50.

TOURING TIPS: Since you can walk the entire length of West Bay, otherwise known as Seven Mile Beach (although it's not 7 miles long), either in the sand or along the road, there's no pressure to rent a car unless you "must" drive around the island. The local bus makes the run along the beach-paralleling road, if your feet get tired. A Caymanian driver's permit is available through all car rental firms. It costs US$3.

Car rental firms are easy to find. *Cico/Avis Car Rentals* (T 800+331-1212 or 809+949-2468) has offices just outside the Grand Caymanian Holiday Inn and at other convenient locations. They will make arrangements for a rental car at rates that hover above CI$30 per day, including mileage. *Budget Rent-A-Car* (T 809+949-5605) has offices at Ramada Treasure Island Resort and other hotels, but my best rate for some recent travels came from picking up the car at their offices on the fringe of George Town. *Holiday Payless Rent-A-Car* (T 809+949-7074) has an office a short walk from the airport exit (turn left). There are several other firms (*Ace/Hertz* T 800+654-3131 or 809+949-2280),

Coconut Car Rental (T 800+262-6687 or 809+949-4037), and *National* (T 800+ CAR RENT or 809+949-4790, among them), and most have offices near (but not at) the airport; many have courtesy phones at the airport. You can take a **taxi** to the office (it's too far to walk with luggage), if you know in advance, and you can leave your car at the airport with ease. You simply stop at the firm's office to pay up and then drive your car to the airport, park it, and drop the keys in a box near the flight check-in area. Rates are comparable to stateside rates (without the bargains). Some firms have special rates for summer, and except at peak season, in winter, shopping around for rates may pay off. Don't count on much of a break at height of winter (certainly Christmas) when cars go at a premium. Driving is on the left.

Honda **motor scooters** can be rented from *Caribbean Motors Ltd.* (T 809+949-8878); Yamahas and mopeds are available through *Cayman Cycle Rentals* (T 809+947- 4021), through several offices along the West Coast road. Daily rates for mopeds are about $25; weekly rates figure to less per day. Since the island is flat, mopeds and other cycles (even bicycles) are easy to maneuver even when distances are long.

LODGING on Grand Cayman can be in an assortment of condominiums (many for rental in owners' absence) and other apartments as well as in several big and small hotels. Apartments range from compact studios to small houses. The islands 3000-plus rooms are almost equally divided between hotel rooms and those in housekeeping units. All buildings have a low profile; none can be "higher than a palm tree," although that restriction seems to have been exceeded in a couple of cases. A construction boom in the past 12 years has created some room-saturated clusters along West Bay beach, notably a huge Japanese project at the north end. The government wisely declared a three-year moratorium on new hotel construction along most of the west coast, effective June 1990. Most buildings have been set back from the beach and seem small in atmosphere if not in room count. Life here is geared to independent travelers who want a Bermuda-style feeling.

AUTHOR'S OBSERVATION

The beach shown in 99% of the hotel and other brochures for Grand Cayman is the l-o-n-g powdery ribbon that stretches along West Bay. It's known locally as "Seven Mile Beach," although it's not quite seven miles long. Ask whether or not your chosen spot is actually on that beach.

Of the more than 30 properties that string along Seven Mile Beach, more than half of them give you the option to cook (or be cooked for) at home. In the past couple of years, some vacation facilities have appeared at the east end, and even at the north, across North Sound, but the biggest concentration is still along West Bay. It's possible to walk all "seven" miles of West Bay Beach, so getting from one spot to another can be your day's activity. At nighttime, walking between hotels is also possible, but it's best to walk along the well-lit road, even with the steady stream of traffic that often roars along this stretch. Taxis and the public bus are available, if you don't have a car.

CAYMAN ISLANDS · · · 211

AUTHOR'S AWARDS
The *Hyatt Regency* is the Caymans' best full-fledged resort hotel; *Caribbean Club* is a long-time favorite for its traditional Caymanian style as well as its location on Seven Mile Beach; and small *Sunset House* continues to warrant special mention for low-key comfort with a scuba-focused Caribbean style.

Information about places-to-stay is included under Hotels/Resorts, Housekeeping Holidays, the Inn Way, and Low-Cost Lodging. Stars are awarded within each category. (See page 11.)

HOTELS/RESORTS include some of the international chains, namely Holiday Inn, Hyatt, Ramada, and Radisson. Traditional Caymanian style is best enjoyed, however, at several of the smaller beachside properties. A shortage of Caymanian workers has led to importation of flocks of young people from Ireland for the winter season; most of them return to work in their own country's tourism plant in summer.

Beach Club Colony • *in the midst of West Bay Beach, near the Holiday Inn* • offers old-style Caribbean atmosphere but service and maintenance seem only average. The sun-washed porch/patio has been pleasant for leisurely mealtimes, but look things over carefully before settling in. Sea view rooms, in 2-story buildings at both sides of the restaurant, are the nicest nests, in my opinion. The beachside location is ideal; and this place has potential.

★★★★ **Grand Pavilion** • *on the inland side of West Bay road* • aspires to elegance, with its grand entrance on the West Bay side of the building. The building, where Queen Elizabeth lodged during one of her visits, is a tasteful, potentially deluxe hotel, with a center courtyard and rooms furnished with copies of Georgian antiques. Well-chosen fabrics add accents to pastel-painted walls. Several rooms overlook the center courtyard where there's a pool; West Bay beach is across the road. *Le Diplomat* restaurant flirts with being the Caymans' most elegant, but both the *Terrace* and *Garden* restaurants are more Caribbean style. The property has a conference center and other amenities for small groups. *Hotel.*

★ **Holiday Inn Grand Cayman** • *at the midpoint of West Bay Beach* • was the first, and for many years the only, large hotel on the island. It is also the hub for cruise ship passengers who want beach facilities while they're in port. The cluster of snack spots, shops, and sports concessions makes this place a jumble, in my opinion, and on recent visits facilities seemed overused and were showing signs of wear. Staff has taken on a cavalier attitude that sometimes results from years of tourism and the Holiday Inn formula rooms needed attention when I checked. Used for package tours and other groups, this hotel seems to me to be a tourism "factory." *Hotel.*

★★★★ **Hyatt Regency Grand Cayman** • *on the inland side of the West Bay road* • is an "island" on an island. Almost totally self-contained, the resort provides several dining areas, shops, entertainment facilities, a courtyard pool, and the island's only golf facility (which requires a special Caymanian golf ball for short-course play). Its elevator tower is the highest building on Grand Cayman; stairways allow easy access to the several floors of rooms, all furnished in typical hotel style—with Hyatt's inimitable flourishes. The beach complex, a few minutes' walk from the main hotel, holds *Hemingway's* restaurant and is one source for daytime activities and beach-oriented evening parties. Expect to find a sunstruck chain reaction, but brace yourself for slow but willing service; this hotel—more than any other—was responsible for the Caymanian government's decision to import workers from Ireland for the winter tourist season. *Resort hotel.*

★★ **Radisson Grand Cayman** • *on West Bay beach, between the Hyatt's beach area and George Town* • is a 5-story resort complex that includes balconied oceanfront and ocean view rooms as well as less-expensive rooms with courtyard view. Since you're on Seven Mile Beach, the pool may seem superfluous, but it is an active hub. Restaurants include the Brighton Beach coffee shop equivalent, the *Regency Grill* for more expensive fare, and the *Quayside Lounge* for evening action. Hertz operates the auto rental; Don Foster has the watersports concession. Opened in 1990, the place is popular with groups and Radisson aficionados. *Resort hotel.*

★ **Ramada Treasure Island Resort** • *near George Town, at the shore* • is a multifloor, multiroom complex used for package-tour travelers and other price-conscious guests. (When its rooms are paired with airfare, you'll get the best rates.) A close owner link with the music industry has brought country music entertainers to the property. The 290 rooms are standard formula: some upper-floor rooms have a view over nearby buildings to the sea; the lower-floor rooms are dark when they're shrouded in planting. Air conditioning is essential and small balconies often give the view only toward your neighbors. Neighboring properties include Grapetree/Cocoplum and George Town Villas, whose apartment renters have access to this hotel's facilities. The on-premises *Escargot* restaurant was disappointing when I tried it. If you get a good rate, this place can be a convenient nest. The poolside bar is popular at twilight, and all rooms are equipped with minibar refrigerators. Used items are added to your bill and restocked daily. *Hotel.*

★★ **Spanish Cove** • *on the rocky shore at the northern fist of the western arm* • is "undergoing renovation" at press time. Long noted as a scuba resort, the small inn had been a meeting and gathering place for divers who wanted a no-nonsense underwater program and were content with basic rooms, a pool, and the dining area. The *Caribbean Newsletter* (page 9) will have details on a possible name-change and new facilities. Spanish Bay Villas are contiguous, but have been separately managed.

HOUSEKEEPING HOLIDAYS have been in fashion for those-in-the-know for a couple of decades or so with the only changes being the addition of more self-catering accommodations and better supplies in the local markets. When you've decided whether you want beachfront or inland location, you're only halfway there. There are countless options and only on-the-spot research during one vacation can help you be sure of the best for you for "next year." Although most of the apartments are along West Bay, there are interesting places scattered along other shores, as well as on Little Cayman and Cayman Brac.

Food costs at local markets (and restaurants) are high, but there are good stock-up stores, including complete supermarkets, near the West Bay lodgings, and some places maintain commissaries for the convenience of guests.

Among the firms specializing in apartment rentals, **Cayman Rent-A-Villa** (Box 681, Grand Cayman, B.W.I., T 809+947–4144, fax 809+949–7471) handles listings for many properties including private homes for rent in owners' absence. Some may overlap with places mentioned below. **Hospitality World,** 250 Catalonia Ave., #501, Coral Gables, FL 33134, T 800+232–1034 or 809+949–8098, also lists condominium and other rentals. Taking a room for a couple of days to look around on your own can unearth some good deals.

★ **Beachcomber** • *on the Holiday Inn side of Pan Caymanian* • has 23 nicely furnished 2- and 3-story units on West Bay Beach. All are apartments with patio or balcony and a sea view. There's a pool near the tennis courts. *Apts.*

Britannia Villas • *at the Hyatt Complex* • is a section of the vast Hyatt resort area on the inland side of West Bay Road, at the golf course. Guests in the 25 apartments are united by a golfing focus. Since the building is reasonably new so are its facilities, with hints of tony U.S. golf resorts. (The course is better known for novelty than for professional standing.) *Apts.*

★★★ **Caribbean Club** • *on West Bay Bech* • appeals to those who prefer a well-cared-for "antique" to a modern copy. The color scheme, with the pink stucco walls of the 18 cottages and the yellow beach umbrellas, seems a bit abrupt, but there's no question about the low-key high quality of this place. Maids are pleasant, surroundings are comfortable, and the food and wine served in the Caribbean Club's refurbished European-style dining room is some of the island's best. *Cottages.*

★★ **Cayman Kai** • *on the north coast* • offers several types of accommodations scattered around a peninsula. Inquire about the status of the ferry boat that sometimes links the resort with the outskirts of George Town across North Sound. The drive from town takes about 45 minutes. Incorporating the beach made famous for some of us with the legendary Rum Point inn, Cayman Kai offers self-atering accommodations in the cluster of units that are near the registration desk plus dining area, small boutique, and scuba center, in addition to interesting wood-frame buildings known as *Sea Lodges* and other units in another cluster known as the *Island Houses.* The original core has the dining room and upstairs bar area, near the pool, and is conducive to casual conversations and conviviality, with entertainment some evenings. Scuba diving is featured and, although the place took a pounding from Hurricane Gilbert's seas (in September '88), things are now in good shape. *Cottages & apts.*

★ **Christopher Columbus Apartments** • *on West Bay Beach* • are in single, 2- and 3-story buildings with a beachside pool that is popular with guests staying in the beige-and-brown buildings. The units were built as condominiums, for rent in owners' absence. The penthouse is the prize. The tennis court is across the road. *Apts.*

★★ **Colonial Club** • *on West Bay Beach* • is a half-dozen 3-story buildings with 2- and 3-bedroom apartments furnished for sunstruck living. There's a heated pool at this Brian Butler project. *Apts.*

Coral Caymanian • *on West Bay Beach* • has a few beach-oriented apartments and a couple of hotel rooms. On land owned by the Kickconnell family (and waiting, I suspect, for a buyer who'll pay the price), the single-story buildings date from the Cayman's earliest interest in tourism. Units have few modern flourishes. With booking best negotiated on the spot, or during one visit for your next, the rooms have easy access to the beach. *Apts.*

★★ **Discovery Point Club** • *at the north end of West Bay* • is a comfortable complex of condominium units, some for rent in owners' absence. A good bet, slightly removed from the busiest hubs. *Apts.*

George Town Villas • *on the West Bay side of George Town* • successfully wall out the neighboring villa clusters that join them on the northern fringe of town. Cupped in the rim of 3-story, balconied buildings are lawn, pool, and beach—the social and sunning spots for lodgers. Near neighbors are *Poinsetta*, *Grapetree/Cocoplum*, and the *Ramada*. Each villa has 2 bedrooms, bath, and full kitchen; rooms on the second floor have a better view. Once you're inside the cluster, it's possible to overlook the clutter of building on the outside. *Apts.*

Grapetree/Cocoplum • *at the fringe of George Town* • is a 3-story condominium family, with 1- and 2-bedroom units, plus some 2-bedroom penthouses. Many of the units are full-time residences. There's a tennis court, but the beach is nothing spectacular at this end of West Bay. You're at the action hub that is *Ramada Treasure Island,* with its resort facilities. *Apts.*

★★★ **The Great House** • *on West Bay Beach* • is a 1988 addition to the parade of properties that borders the beach. Built for an "upscale market," the 26 suites are on a 3½ acre piece of land next to Plantana, walled off from the traffic of West Bay Road by planting and a courtyard. This place aspires to elegance, taking its cues from the traditional West Indian Great House style. Planned for private ownership, the units are rented in owners' absence. Developer Martyn Bould was also involved with *Plantana,* mentioned below.

★ **Harbour Heights** • *north of midway on powdery West Bay Beach* • has settled into its piece of coastline, giving guests in the 45 units a sense of home. Apartments are in 3 sections, linked to L-shape, offering 2-bedroom, 2-bath lodgings with maid service. Some units are on long-term lease. Nice location; good deal.

Heritage Club • *at the northern part of Seven Mile Beach* • is one of several recently built apartment clusters, with a central pool as well as the beach for swimming and tennis courts on the premises. Comfortably furnished, the place is small enough to have a neighborhood atmosphere. *Apts.*

Indies Suites • *across the road from the beach* • offer reasonably priced 1- and 2-bedroom suites in a pool-punctuated setting, inland from the shore. The motel-style rooms have T.V., telephone, and kitchenettes, although management provides complimentary continental breakfast for guests. Popular with cost-conscious self-sufficient travelers who care more about being in the Caymans than having a classy address. *Hotel.*

★★ **Islands Club** • *on Seven Mile Beach* • is a classy collection of 2-bedroom townhouses, most of which are used by the owners or on long-term rental. Full kitchens can take care of mealtimes, but *Le Diplomat* at Grand Pavilion is just across the road inland and other restaurants are nearby. Tennis courts are on premise; the beach is the front lawn. *Apts.*

Island Pine Villas • *on the beach* • are attractive 1- and 2-bedroom units, at the town end of the famed strand. Overhead fans are often enough for air-cooling, but units also have air conditioners. More reasonable than many spots, the units are comfortable—not lavish. *Apts.*

★★★ **Lacovia** • *at West Bay Beach* • is a 5-story building filled with apartments that give residents a sea view and easy access to the beach. A red-tile roof marks this place. You're in the mainstream, but within an enclave that seems removed from it. *Apts.*

★ **Limetree Bay** • *on the inland side of the West Bay Road* • is across the road from the Governor's beachside house. The hub is the pool and a central clubhouse with sauna, card room, laundry room, and a proclivity to be booked for private parties by members when they have more friends than they can fit into their studio, 1-bedroom, 2-bedroom, or townhouse apartments. All 72 apartments are fully furnished, usually by the owners. Other accouterments include 2 night-lighted tennis courts, putting green, shuffleboard, and boat dock for entrance into the lagoon and eventual settings out to sea. *Apts.*

★ **London House** • *Box 1356, West Bay Beach, Grand Cayman* • opened in '79 on the long and lovely band of sand that stretches all the way down to the outskirts of George Town, a good span for joggers. The sea view apartments are efficiently equipped with full kitchen facilities, plus living room with dining area and comfortable bedrooms. Balconies and patios (depending on whether you're on the first or second floor) have a view over the freshwater pool and sea. Ask for a room away from the pool if you're bothered by other people's exuberance. The 2-bedroom apartments (16 of them) can easily handle a family, but reserve early for the 1-bedroom units. There are only 3, and they go fast in season. *Apts.*

Morritt's Tortuga Club • *at the east end, half-an-hour's drive from George Town* • has a legendary history that's hard to feel these days. (Tortuga Club was one of the island's best inns in its "first life," in the early 1960s, when it was created and operated by a couple from the U.S.) Several owners later, the place has become a condominium complex, with some units for rent in owners' absence. There are tennis courts, in addition to pool and the beach. Although you're a long way from town, you're near some of the best dive sites. The *Caribbean Newsletter* (page 9) will have an update when warranted, but inquire about status of construction before booking here.

★★★ **Pan-Cayman House** • *on West Bay Beach* • has 10 apartments offering solid comforts. One of the early settlers on this shore, this place puts a high priority on giving people peace and quiet, with action options only a few feet away along the length of Seven Mile Beach. Separated from the Caribbean Club by Turtle Run, a palatial private home discreetly camouflaged by branches from beachside trees that bend to the white sand, Pan-Cayman House has its own homey atmosphere. All rooms, upstairs or sand level, have a sea view—and if you want to be able to walk from your living room out to the sea with no steps up or down, request the ground level, and brace yourself for footfall overhead. *Apts.*

★★ **Plantana** • *on the West Bay coast* • puts its guests into apartments in a 3-story beige-and-brown building with screened porches, and a pool. Just south of Harbour Heights, the location puts you within a convenient beach stroll to other West Bay lodgings, activities, and restaurants. *Apts.*

The Retreat at Rum Point • *on a north coast beach* • has recovered (and rebuilt) after Hurricane Gilbert's September '88 visit, and is open this season. The Retreat and its neighbor, Cayman Kai, are a self-contained community across North Sound from West Bay and most other lodgings. Watersports (including scuba) are prime pursuits for the action oriented. *Villas & Apts.*

★ **Seascape** • *next to Lacovia* • is small, nice, and older than most of the West Bay newcomers. There's a market not too far away. Not for fussy folk, this spot can be great for those who like an "old shoe" comfort. *Apts.*

★ **Silver Sands** • *on West Bay Beach* • sprawls at the sandy shore beyond Victoria House on the north end of the beach and just before the sign announcing small West Bay Village and the town cemetery. There's a freshwater pool, a nice lawn, a few tennis courts, and a "total resort" feeling tucked onto this piece of shoreline. *Apts.*

★ **Spanish Bay Villas** • *at the northern tip of the west coast* • stand next to Spanish Cove diving resort and offer self-catering accommodations with easy access to the dive boats and other watersports activities. The single-story units stretch back from the shore, providing a measure of privacy according to the angle with the neighboring unit. Utilities are modern; a car is advisable for mobility. Villas Pappagallo and its restaurant are reasonably near neighbors. *Apts.*

★ **Tarquynn Manor** • *on West Bay Beach* • has 20 2-bedroom condominiums for rent in owners' absence. The location is a drawing card, as is the fact that one bedroom in each unit faces the sea (the other is on the inland side), and that charges are more reasonable than many places on Seven Mile Beach. Opened in '77, this place has settled well. *Apts.*

★ **Victoria House** • *at the north end of Seven Mile Beach* • has 25 air-conditioned apartments and lures some folks south with good-value long-term rentals during summer months. Furnishings are modern, nothing spectacular but certainly more than adequate. Your fully electric kitchen has refrigerator and freezer. Studios and 1-bedroom units are perfect for 2, and perhaps for 3; but if you're 4 or more, search out a 2-bedroom unit or the penthouse rooms, in spite of the climb. The front office (which is on the left side as you face the property) is a fountain of information, with a bulletin board that posts the best and newest eating places with their menus and often a guest comment or two. Tennis courts are on the roadside. When you're here, you're within bicycling distance of the village of West Bay and a long sandy stroll of 4 miles or more to the hotels near George Town. *Apts.*

★★ **Villas of Galleon** • *at West Bay Beach* • have grown at the beach north of the Holiday Inn. The 1-, 2-, and 3-bedroom units are angled to give most lodgers a sea view from the balcony or patio. The upper rooms are preferred because the view is unobstructed and you're unaffected by the beach traffic. Dining depots are an easy sand-scuffing stroll from "home." *Apts.*

Villas Pappagallo • *at the north end of the western peninsula* • offers 45 units in 3 banks of buildings at the shore. They're available for sale, but you can rent them for your vacation home. You're about 10 miles from George Town, a fact that makes car rental essential for mobility. The restaurant (see below) on the inland side of the road is attractive, a popular in-season gathering spot. Spanish Cove is nearby; and plans for this place include tennis courts, and more units. The pool's in place; there's no beach. *Apts.*

★★★ **West Indian Club** • *on West Bay, near Royal Palms* • can seem comfortable, if you want homelike surroundings with the convenience of your own maid and apartment. Royal palms line the drive to the entrance of the pseudo-plantation-style pink building. The atmosphere of the 9 apartments is traditional Caribbean style. Little has been forgotten by the owners, whose apartment you will use (at a fee) in their absence. There's a thatched bohio on the beach for sun shelter, with wood and plank seats for guest-gathering and one hammock in the middle. Seven Mile Beach awaits. *Apts.*

THE INN WAY: The few traditional inns that offer personal Caymanian hospitality have a scuba-diving focus. Although a few of the housekeeping units do have management that seems willing to make the extra effort to be hospitable, most people seem to treat their property as a money machine and their work as a "job." The places that are exceptionally friendly are usually owner managed. For vacationers who enjoy a measure of independence, and are comfortable taking the initiative with questions about island activities, some of the small spots mentioned under "Low-Cost Lodgings" offer good values, but there are no inns in the accepted European or British style.

★★ **Sunset House** • *on the shore, south of George Town* • is a cozy, comfortable place where "luxury" means having a telephone in your room. A few of the rooms are upstairs, over the main reception area; others (#401–403 on the ground level and #404–406 upstairs) are in a separate block with a nice sea view. Although the old West Indian house that used to mark this property has disappeared in favor of the newer buildings, there's still a pleasant Caymanian, scuba-and-sea-oriented atmosphere here. *Inn.*

LOW-COST LODGING: Although some of the best values come with multi-person rentals of apartments, there are also several small spots that have reasonable rates and some rooms-for-rent that are listed with the Cayman Tourist Office in George Town. Most of the less expensive places are not on beaches, and many offer very casual lodgings for people who are primarily interested in diving. Here are a few places to consider:

Ambassadors Inn • *south of George Town* • is a divers' resort that offers 15 basic rooms and plenty of diving conversation. The 2-story building is across the road from the Grand Old House, one of Cayman's best known (and most expensive) restaurants. On the inland side of the road, a short walk to a bit of sand, you'll have to drive to departure points for the best dive sites. *Inn.*

Eldemire's Guest House • *south of George Town, on the inland side of the road* • has only 4 rooms and an apartment. One of the favorite small spots through the years, the place is "in demand" so book well in advance. *Guesthouses.*

Grama's Bed & Breakfast • *not on the beach, but pool-punctuated* • offers home-like surroundings and doesn't take credit cards. Rooms are basic, in various shapes and sizes. Rooms with ceiling fans are less expensive than those with air-conditioning units, but all are inexpensive and informal. *Guesthouse.*

Island House Resort • *on West Bay* • is a small spot with about a dozen rooms and a small restaurant and bar for socializing. Most rooms have air conditioners; all have ceiling fans. The beach is outside the door—and snorkeling is good nearby. *Inn.*

Seaview Hotel • *within walking distance of downtown* • has a saltwater pool for swimming and overhead fans to work with air conditioners for air cooling. Rooms are basic, but the price is right for many. The piano bar is active some evenings; otherwise guests group to go elsewhere. *Small hotel.*

Windsor House Apartment • *near George Town* • is part of the private home of Mr. and Mrs. Bernard St. Aubyn and has been popular for those in search of an independent "home." You can walk into George Town to pick up the bus for West Bay beach, or walk to one of the dive resorts etched on the coast south of the capital.

Windjammer Hotel • *on the inland side of the road that rims Seven Mile Beach, not far from town* • is a small spot with an often-active nightclub and small dining depot. Rooms have kitchenettes, T.V., and air conditioners, although the ceiling fans often provide enough air swirl. *Small hotel.*

RESTAURANTS on Grand Cayman are increasing with each season, but more is not necessarily better. Folks who know (and crave) the top-rated cuisine of Europe, or even major cities in the U.S., may be disappointed by the quality here, and appalled by the prices.

Most of the restaurants follow the U.S. tradition, with steaks, chicken, and other staples surrounded by iceberg lettuce salads, rolls and butter, and the usual, or pizza parlors and spaghetti houses with the expected Italian pastas. **Tony Romas** is here (for ribs and chicken). There are a couple of restaurants that aspire to haute cuisine and several small spots that serve West Indian/Caymanian-style food. Among the latter, look for **Sheila's** on Goring Avenue in George Town, as well as **Welly's Cool Spot, Island House, Lillian's Snacks,** the **Blue Marlin,** and the **Turning Point.** Most of the new shopping centers that are flecking the inland side of West Bay Road (to accommodate the condominium- and villa-renters) have some variety of restaurant, and you'll see **Burger King, Kentucky Fried Chicken, Wendys, Pizza Hut,** and other U.S. fast-food chains. Most snack spots feature hamburgers, pizza, grilled cheese, and the like. There are several good ice-cream places, both in town at **Triffles Ice Cream Emporium** at the Elizabethan Centre, not far from the post office, and along West Bay Road at Venezia, **Coconut Place, Cones,** and other spots.

Most restaurants add a 15% gratuity (and present your bill in Caymanian currency, which makes the total seem like less than its U.S. equivalent).

AUTHOR'S AWARDS

Le Diplomat provides world-class good offerings in elegant surroundings; the *Cracked Conch* is the best place to try the island staple of conch in congenial, casual comfort.

★ **Almond Tree** • *near George Town, at the south end of West Bay* • has a casual, Caribbean atmosphere that makes for pleasant dining (on once-frozen seafood and U.S.-style offerings). The tropical drinks, turtle, conch, and fish dishes are worth sampling. Entertainment on some evenings focuses on West Indian tunes by a local musician.

★★★ **Caribbean Club** can be nice for the gala evening, although my meal on a recent evening was not the greatest. Book ahead to be sure of a reservation, and come with plenty of cash. It's easy to spend over $50 per person, if you have wine and all the trimmings. Escargot are pungent; stuffed crab Maryland is well worth trying; and the scampi are my favorite. Conch fritters, a local specialty, seems a curious twist for a classy restaurant, but they're good. Wine list is extensive (and expensive). Candlelight at dinner lends a nice note.

★★ **Cracked Conch** • *at Selkirk Plaza across from Lacovia Apartments on West Bay Road* • is a casual, friendly local spot created for visitors, as well as a way of cooking conch. The light batter-fried "cracked" conch is a *must* and, if your stomach can take it, join it with conch fritters for an appetizer. The popular fisherman's platter is a plateful! I recommend a cold beer with this food.

Grand Old House • *south of George Town* • is owned by Chef Tell from Philadelphia, whose tv promotion and recipes make this one of the islands most popular (and expensive) restaurants. The original building was known as the Petra Plantation Great House. Now its porches are speckled with tables for those who want to dine with the sea breezes (inside rooms are also set up). The surroundings are attractive and if your on-the-spot questions yield positive replies, it's worth making a reservation.

L'Escargot • *at Ramada Treasure Island Hotel* • was a disappointment, with presumptuous surroundings, high prices, and mediocre menu offerings.

Lighthouse • *past Bodden Town in Breakers* • is a place for a day you've rented a car; it serves interesting seafood specialties in way-out seaside surroundings. Call Peggy Burgos (originally from Canada) if you want to find out what's special—and that can include special dinners on holidays. Reservations are essential for dinnertime; you can take a chance for lunch.

Lobster Pot • *upstairs and seaside near Bob Soto's scuba center* • is popular with residents and regular visitors. The location sets the tone—which is not fancy, but is pricey for the seafood meals, simply served. The food *is* good, if you like local fish and lobster. Mervin Cumber and Clemens Guetler oversee this operation as well as the Periwinkle (see below). For casual surroundings seaside, try it.

Ristorante Pappagalo • *at the northern end of the west coast* • seemed overpriced, with a menu that read better than the chef's abilities warranted on my visit. Although a Mexican architect used Jamaican bamboo for the building, I felt a Polynesian atmosphere was created by the thatched roof over the bar area. The menu features northern Italian recipes, with veal, seafood, and sauces as well as the familiar pastas. German beer is served in the *Flamingo Lounge*. Waiters were dressed in tuxedos for the opening salvo, but that costume may defer to the warm climate as the restaurant mellows.

The Wharf • *seaside, at the fringe of George Town* • puts its reputation on the lobster (good and expensive) and imaginative offerings by creative chef Wolfgang Kluth. The stuffed turtle steak rouladen and the Cayman conch chowder were prize winners at the Caymanian Pirates Week Culinary Competition years ago. Purchase of this place, in early '81, by a group of long-time (and enthusiastic) Caymanian residents with other involvements in the islands' tourism plan, assures a fun-filled place. Count on some entertainment—and at least a $40 tab.

Grand Cayman is flecked with snacking places, not only in George Town, but also along the road out to West End. One local spot is **Morgan's Harbour.** This is not a place for fancy clothes and pretentions, but it is a place to get good seafood in very casual surroundings. This place, and a couple of other eateries, are popular with fishermen and others who like the sea. **Borden's Pizza Hut,** in George Town, is good—if you like pizzas. It's a popular local spot.

NATURAL SURROUNDINGS are mostly water soaked. The landscape of Grand Cayman is of limited interest—except for two areas set aside as bird sanctuaries. Colliers Bay Pond, between Gun Bay and the Tortuga Club, facing the East End Channel, is one area; the other is centered on Meagre Bay Pond, near the south coast, east of Bodden Town. The island's official bird list includes 53 species, with the yellow-faced grassquit among the favorites. (Many of the most colorful birds are shown on postage stamps and most have been documented in *Birds of the Cayman Islands,* a book by Particia Bradley and Yves-Jacques Rey-Millet.)

Ironshore, the name for the spiky dark rocks, that are the natural cementing of clifflike limestone with the remains of shells and coral, makes up portions of the land. Elsewhere, the landscape is studded with cactus, dry brush, and sandy expanses. The few palms near the beaches have been planted for effect, while others that grow in the wild have given Caymanians the source for rope in times past. Planted more recently, Australian pines add a soft green fringe to the inland side of the sands along West Bay.

The Pirate Caves, near Bodden Town, midway on the south coast, are commercial and not of much interest. The Bay Caves at Spott's Bay have been closed to the public.

The Cayman Islands have never had a botanic garden, as was the case on most other islands where the English settled, but they are surrounded by one of the Caribbean's most exciting underwater gardens—flourishing in a natural state amid the reefs and walls that ring these islands.

The turtles found in large quantities in the 16th century, and coveted by sailors for their ability to survive at sea long enough to be cooked for meals, were almost eradicated by the 1950s. Indiscriminate harvesting of both turtles and eggs depleted the crop, and natural predators, such as the birds who pluck the eggs for their nests on the beach, played their role. In 1973, the Green Turtles, Loggerheads, Hawksbills and others were listed as endangered species, meaning that no turtle products may be brought into the United States.

Coral pulverized by wind and sea becomes the soft sand beaches, with the most impressive one along West Bay. There are small beaches at Smith's Cove, on the south coast, east of George Town, and at many areas around the island, but West Bay's Seven Mile Beach is the most popular strand.

The offshore reefs have always commanded respect, whether fared or fawned over. Acknowledged as a valuable natural resource for today's scuba divers, they brought terror to the hearts of 17th-century sailors whose ships were spiked—and often split—upon them.

From the West Bay anchorages to the East End Channel and from North Sound to South Sound and Bodden Bay, the seas off the coral blanket that is

Grand Cayman are spectacular. Being able to see for 200 feet underwater is nothing special in Caymanian waters and, while at least 22 dive sites are noted in the official literature from the Cayman Islands Department of Tourism, the seas surrounding Cayman Brac and Little Cayman offer many unusual sights in areas best known to only a few divers.

Popular diving sites include the 325 wrecks that are submerged in the seas, festering with coral and embellished with colorful fish. One of the favorite "sights" for 1984 was Paquet Cruises' *Rhapsody,* a 24,000-ton ship that ran aground on a Caymanian sandbar during a March 28 storm and sat there for a few months! The underwater sights off the North Wall, which is the result of a ridge of Cuba's Sierra Maestra some 200 miles away, make the seas off the northwestern shore fascinating when they're calm enough for scuba. Sting Ray City, at the mouth of North Sound, is another source of underwater magic. The reefs at West Bay are almost always ideal (although not as exciting, according to some experts). Little Drop-Off, a relatively easy swim about 100 yards from shore, hides a submerged schooner, and trims its gnarled stern with purple sea fans, tube sponges, coral, and fish. Off George Town, the wreck of the 375-foot *Balboa* is "buried" in about 35 feet of water and the *Oro Verde,* sunk with ceremony in spring '80, has its collection of special fish.

AUTHOR'S OBSERVATION

Caymanian authorities have legislated strict diving regulations—and controls on the motorboats and big ships that anchor around here. Rules are enforced, but a lot of damage by anchors and coral pluckers had already disadvantaged some reefs.

PLACES WORTH FINDING are limited, if you're expecting historic forts and buildings. Since these islands were out of the mainstream of 17th- and 18th-century development, and their landscape was too harsh to warrant much attention for plantations, no impressive forts were built. The **Cayman Turtle Farm,** once known as Mariculture, might be of interest for the life history of the Green Turtle and a look at the growing pens. The entrance to the "farm" is through a small shop, which sets the project's commercial tone.

AUTHOR'S OBSERVATION

Because turtles are an endangered species according to U.S. conservation laws, U.S. customs will confiscate turtle purchases. CTF officials are trying to work out a special dispensation since these turtles are harvested from a farm where they are cultivated, but nothing's happened yet.

Although there are experienced professionals to take you on a tour and provide background information, they are not always available. If you crave more than cursory facts, inquire about special tours. Otherwise, you can wander around the breeding and growing areas on your own, with the booklet sold in the shop as your guide.

The first of the female turtles raised in the compound crawled up onto the fabricated beach in mid-1975 to lay her first batch of eggs. The following year, 29 turtles laid 15,186 eggs, and the hatch rate was recorded at over 88%, and now the Turtle Farm seems to be firmly established. The booklet explains that there are almost 60,000 turtles, most of whom live in 40 tanks ranging from 30 to 70 feet in diameter, and that the water changes in the large tanks every hour and in the small tanks every 5 minutes. The place is fascinating if you are interested in the life cycle of the turtle and in the process that has evolved here for its cultivation and harvesting for the world market. (The turtle steaks you can eat in restaurants around town probably come from here.)

Underwater sights can be enjoyed by all. The 28-passenger *Atlantis*, a submarine that takes participants down to about 50 feet below sea level, operates on a regular basis. The cost has been about $50. Deeper dives on the submarine operated by *Research Submersible Ltd.* down to 800 feet below, can be arranged for about $250 per person. That special experience takes about 2 hours from boat-boarding to return-to-shore.

The Cayman Maritime Museum and Shop, announced with some fanfare in mid-'87, is a commercial venture of Herbert Humphreys Jr. (owner of the Holiday Inn) and partners. Located on the waterfront in George Town, convenient to cruise passengers and other tourists, the "museum" is built with elements reminiscent of West Indian forts. Among the displays that focus on the islands' swashbuckling past are a pirate robot who talks of his escapades, a display about Caymanian turtles, a gold bar to lift, and Amerindian artifacts.

SPORTS: Scuba, snorkeling, and watersports are the main reason for coming to the Caymans, and *Ocean Realm, Undercurrent,* and *Skin Diver* magazines and *Underwater USA* in a newspaper format, regularly extoll the virtues.

―――――――――― **AUTHOR'S OBSERVATION** ――――――――――
Dive Cayman, a book by island diver and photographer Nancy Sefton, is well worth purchasing prior to your arrival here for diving. Cost is $10, and orders can be placed with Undersea Photo Supply of Cayman, Ltd., Box 1151, Grand Cayman, B.W.I.

Only Bonaire rivals this island for top-notch facilities and a single focus, but the options for entertainment for hours *above* water are much greater here. (St. Thomas has top-notch facilities and a lot of other things on its mind.)

Bob Soto (T 800+262–7686, fax 809+947–4631) is a time-honored Cayman name for **scuba diving.** His name is on the Caymans' largest firm, which he sold a few years ago to Ron Kipp and others. There are several shops, including ones at the Holiday Inn Grand Cayman on West Bay and at North Church Street at the Lobster Pot restaurant and branches at Cayman Islander, Grand Pavilion, and the Scuba Centre. Rates for a morning 2-tank dive are about $50 with tanks, belt, and other equipment; a 1-tank dive in the afternoon is about $40; night dive is $40 for 2 hours; 3 hours in the pool for beginners is the starting session, and only 6 novices go out at a time, with 2 instructors. A "resort course," to allow you to go from beginner to diver-with-supervision, costs about $85. In addition to arranging for the lessons (contracted for, and paid for, in U.S.$), the shop at the Grand Caymanian has a selection of T-shirts, fins, masks, fish cards to wear around your neck so you can recognize what you're seeing, and the interesting *Guide to Corals & Fishes* by Idaz and Gerry Greenberg (published by Seahawk Press and sold for $8). It's plastic, and perfect for underwater reading.

> **AUTHOR'S OBSERVATION**
> Underwater photographers should check on dates for the Nikonos Shoot Out, a fun-filled spring contest for underwater shots, with grand prizes.

Surfside Water Sports (T 800+543–6828, fax 809+949–8639) offers the full roster, with a scuba resort course at $80, the 6-day full scuba certification course with boat trips and equipment included at $350. You can learn to sail, and then rent a boat with a pal at set fees on record in the surfside office. This is also the source for **parasailing** (where you swing from a parachute high in the sky while being towed by a speedboat skimming the sea below). Among other Grand Cayman firms that specialize in scuba diving, Dan Foster's *Dive Grand Cayman Ltd.* (T 809+949–5679, fax 809+947–5133), *Parrots Landing* (T 800+448–0428, fax 809+949–0294), and *Red Sail Sports* (T 800+255–6425, fax 809+949–8808) are names to know. Stan Waterman, award-winning underwater cinematographer (*Jaws, The Deep,* and others) produced a 30-minute film while staying in the Caymans.

In addition to the places already mentioned, it's safe to say that *every* Cayman hotel, apartment, or inn has some link with the sea and local dive operators. Each season finds new enthusiasts entering the business, either after working a while with one of the long-established firms, or starting on their own from a former base in the U.S. or on some other Caribbean island.

Cayman Kai has its own scuba operator. The resort also sets up sunset cruises and picnic trips with a lobster lunch. Clint Ebanks' *Scuba Cayman Ltd.* has a 46-foot dive boat called *Queen Angel* and *Eden Diving Center,* the island's most accessible dive area just off the waterfront of George Town, is a favorite for cruise ship passengers who can walk from the pier into the water to dive.

The *Cayman Aggressor* and *Cayman Aggressor II* (Aggressor Fleet Ltd., P.O. Drawer K, Morgan City, LA 70381, T 800+348–2628) are two fully equipped dive boats with live-aboard facilities. The 1-week dive vacations go for about $1295pp, including diving opportunities limited only by the boats' itinerary, with new sites each day. Groups can charter, with Captain Wayne Hanson and crew.

Captain Marvin's Water Adventure sets out for a day from Morgan's Harbour, for picnic and snorkeling; other day trips are also offered. Your hotel's activities desk is one source for information; the tourist board office in George Town is another.

Aqua Delights at the Holiday Inn has jet skis as well as water skiing, parasailing, and all the water-amusement vehicles, including those for boardsailors.

Other dive opportunities await on Little Cayman and Cayman Brac.

Deep-sea fishing has become a drawing card for sportsmen that is almost equal to the island's lure as a scuba resort. An International Fishing Tournament, held in June, is labeled "Million Dollar Month" with cash and other prizes for winners. Contact the tournament committee (Box 878, West Wind Bldg., Grand Cayman, B.W.I.) for details. Local guides claim that marlin migrate through these waters all year, and they've been good at luring some from the seas at The Banks, about 10 miles west of Grand Cayman. About a dozen fishing boats call the Caymans home port (and stay around all year to prove it). Kent Eldemire, original owner of Casa Bertmar, is one of the most knowledgeable fishermen around, and Captain Bryan Ebanks has had good luck with his *Tashara I* and *Tashara II*. Others to look for are the *Theresia D*, *Seafaire*, and boats out at Morgan's Harbour. Most hotels can put you in touch with top fishing boat charterers, as can the watersports concessions and shops.

It seems fair to say that in the Caymans, at least, you can do anything you want to with sea and sand, at a price.

Tennis is popular with the land-based folk. There are many asphalt-type courts and some lay-cold on Grand Cayman, with most of the best courts along West Bay Beach. All of them can be played, some at a price. Check with the Grand Caymanian Holiday Inn for the biggest clump of courts; others can be found at Victoria House, Silver Sands, Cayman Kai, Beach Club Colony, Hyatt, Ramada Treasure Island, Radisson, and most of the condo clusters.

Golf arrived on Grand Cayman in a distinctly Caymanian fashion. Because the island is so flat, land sells at a premium, and water is a problem for irrigation, an unusual course was designed. Said to be "typical of those found in Scotland" in a public relations puff piece, the Britannia Golf course is 9 holes but it contains an 18-hole "Cayman Course" that requires play with a short-distance ball designed for this course by Jack Nicklaus. Although only 40 acres were available to play with (and on), designers tried to pack in the challenges of the normal 18-hole course (which requires at least 100 acres). The results can give golfers an entertaining few hours, but they won't compare with regulation championship courses elsewhere. For the opening season, those who wanted to play 18 holes were required to play from 8 to 11 a.m. (Those rules may still be in effect.) Reservations are essential. Greens fees are $25 for the Cayman course; $18.75 for the regulation 9-hole course. Check on rental clubs; it may not be worth the effort to bring your own. Telephone (809 + 949–8020) to set up starting times.

TREASURES AND TRIFLES include Cayman honey from Savannah; a few books, namely *Our Island Treasures*, *Stories Our Grandparents Told*, and *Recipes from the Cayman Islands*, which are sold in some of the gift shops; and plenty of T-shirts and "tacky tourist stuff." George Town is bubbling with boxy banks, all gleaming new and most of them the result of a change in laws in 1966 that gave the Cayman Islands tax haven status. The capital is not a quaint West Indian town in any sense of the word; it is bustling (by comparison to what it was before the 1966 legislation), new, and built for commerce. There are few bargains for shoppers, but there are shelves loaded with the usual imported china and crystal. Shops to find are **Caymania II** with "duty-free" bargains that aren't really, **Mica Boutique** for clothes, across from **Black Coral** (jewelry) and **Arabus** (men's and women's clothes). Up the road a few paces are **Topaz Jewelers** (some interesting expensive black coral and tortoiseshell work), **The Jewelry Factory** (specialists in working local stones, shells, and coral), and the **Smiths** (interesting quality jewelry and jewels). Turn right, with your back to the sea, and you will find a lot more banks. Around the corner, heading back toward the sea, you'll find **Treasure Cove** (with a branch in the Grand Caymanian, and a larger selection of Wedgwood and other imported china and crystal here), plus the **Grand Cayman Craft Market** (which isn't much, from my observation) and **English Shoppe, Ltd.** (with the imports you'd expect to find). The English Shoppe is next to Cayman Arms, at the shore, with **Brenda's** (bathing suits, summer clothes, some from U.S.) across the way.

Best bet for local art (some good, some average, some terrible—in my opinion) and Haitian imports is **Hole-in-the-Wall.**

One unique spot to shop is at the **Cayman Turtle Farm's Shop,** but know that, as of this writing, purchases may be confiscated by U.S. customs. Since most turtles are listed on U.S. customs sheets as "endangered species," customs inspectors have been instructed to confiscate items made from turtle shell. It will be hard/impossible to convince them that your purchase is made from cultivated (and therefore *not* endangered) turtles. The shop also carries T-shirts, books, postcards, and other Caymaniana.

CAYMAN BRAC

"As a boy, I used to climb up the cliff near the lighthouse to climb down the rock-face to steal eggs. I couldn't bring them home—I'd be punished if I did—so we boys used to whip them up with sugar and water, to eat them from a bowl under the trees over there." Thus I learned about one Bracker's childhood, as we talked in front of his small, neat home.

A short while earlier I had driven to that cliff face, along a dirt and rutted road that is certainly now paved. On my solitary journey toward the lighthouse, I'd met up with a Caterpiller bulldozer and a brace of workmen raking its plunder. I could not pass, so asked how long it would take for me to park, walk around them, and continue to the lighthouse, my goal for that morning. "Oh!" said one man. "That's going to take a long time."

I was disappointed. "That's okay," my new friend said. "This man will clear the road so you can drive on." He motioned to the man in the bulldozer with wheels bigger than my whole Daihatsu Charade. With a roar made less awesome by the workmen's smiles and nods, my route was cleared—in less than three minutes.

Such is the speed of progress on Cayman Brac, where man ravages in minutes an area best known, until this year, to birds and wildlife. The Brac is changing, perhaps too fast.

ISLAND APPEARANCE is dry and dusty, with some scrub growth and salt ponds where herons and egrets are among the many birds. The most interesting area for naturalists is the bluff that rises from sea level in the west to widen as it runs the length of the island, sheering as cliffs to the sea on the northeastern shore. The Caymanian parrot can sometimes be spotted here.

OTHER MATTERS: **Political picture** hangs on Grand Cayman, although a few politicians seek more tourism and development for this island. **Lifestyle** is outdoor casual, with emphasis on scuba diving for daytime activity and hotels' entertainment for evening hours. **Money matters** are conducted in Caymanian currency, with US$1 valued at CI$.80. **Communication** with the outside world is limited since there are few telephones, although all hotels have links with the U.S. and elsewhere. Forget about newspapers and instant contact with other places.

ARRIVAL on Cayman Brac is usually aboard the small plane flights of *Cayman Airways,* although there are services from southern cities on occasional jet flights for scuba diving groups. Private planes also use the airport.

TOURING TIPS include **renting a car** and driving around the island on your own. I've had very satisfactory rentals through Mrs. Scott at *S & H Car Rentals* (T 809+948-7347), who can be reached by phone from the airport. Her office is at her home at Stake Bay.

LODGING on Cayman Brac is usually in one of three hotels. A few people offer rooms in private homes or even homes for rent in owners' absence, but those are best found on the spot—perhaps this year for next, if you like what you see.

Brac Reef Beach Resort • *on the shore not far from the airstrip* • was a newcomer in '84, after its owners had sold the original Brac Reef to the Divi hotel group. The modern hotel appearance suggests services and style that are not readily available, although the diving program is in full swing with package plans the best deals as far as room rates are concerned. Don't count on much from the dining room, where evening specials are fairly basic. The bar near the pool is a popular gathering spot. If you're not a scuba diver, or hoping to become one, bring books and inner contentment to this quiet spot. *Hotel.*

Buccaneer's Inn • *on the airport road, mid-island* • is on the shore, with diving places nearby. Rooms are in a cluster of buildings, with a pool and patio bar as social centers. Air conditioning and color TV are bonuses, as are tennis facilities. *Hotel.*

Divi Tiara Beach Hotel • *on the southwest coast, near the airstrip* • follows the scuba focus for Divi hotels in Aruba, Bonaire, Barbados, New Providence in the Bahamas, and elsewhere. Most meals are served buffet style with lining up essential at prime times. Rooms are hotel style, with reasonable comforts and air conditioning. Ask for a room as far as possible from the generator to avoid the constant rumble. Most guests depart on the morning scuba expeditions, returning midafternoon. A portion of the shoreline tries to be a beach where dunking is possible in spite of the fact that coral is rough underfoot.

There are tennis facilities and bicycles for rent. A small shop is near the dining terrace and check-in area. *Hotel.*

RESTAURANTS are limited to the hotel dining rooms and a few places around the island that are better for drinks than for dinner from my experience. **Edd's Place** and a couple of other gathering spots serve local food; the **Lagoon Bar** is best for drinking. Gourmet cooking has not yet reached Cayman Brac.

NATURAL SURROUNDINGS can be fascinating for those who like their islands untrammeled. Roads run the length of the island along the north and the south coasts and branch off from the cross-island road like the tines of a fork on the heights of the Bluff. I hope the Bluff area will be declared a national park before the inevitable building for home sites swings into high gear. As of this edition, a lot of the parched dry land is best known to birds, lizards, and the island's indigenous parrot. The Western Ponds have some water birds, about 2.7 miles due east of Tiara Beach on the south coast. Land birds, including the Cayman Brac parrot and the Red-leggged Thrush, can be seen on the walking paths across the Bluff and along Major Donald Drive. There are walking paths in the area on the Bluff, near the lighthouse. One of the most interesting paths leads up the face of the cliffs from seaside Spot Bay, walking on level ground at the eastern end of the Bluff. From January through August, White-tailed Tropicbirds nest on the face of the Bluff; Brown Boobies can be seen there throughout the year.

Scuba diving is reportedly superb, with challenging and exciting sites not far from the northwestern shore.

PLACES WORTH FINDING will be the result of prowling around the island for caves or birdwatching or heading out to sea for fishing. You can stand in the shallow flats for bone fishing, taking your cue from your guide, who will probably use minnows for bait (and will toss the fish back in after the day's sport is over). Most planned entertainment focuses on beach barbecues, picnics, boat trips to Little Cayman, an occasional dance, and a swim in the saltwater pool.

LITTLE CAYMAN

A few minutes' after Cayman Airways' Short 330 landed on the grass strip on Little Cayman after the 10-minute flight from Cayman Brac I stood before Miss Nayda at the small window of the only shed in sight. It was the post office, the source for stamps for the postcards I hoped I would send. Only when I had lunged into the cab of a pick-up truck, owned by one of the half-dozen people standing around when my plane landed, did I realize that I had disrupted the morning ritual. People were waiting—not for me, but for the news, mail, and packages that had arrived when I did.

CAYMAN ISLANDS · · · 229

Although historians claim that the Lesser Caymans were first settled in the 1600s, Little Cayman, a 10-mile-by-2-mile island with a permanent population of 20, is really an outpost. Reached by boat or small planes from Cayman Brac or by Cayman Airways plane service, the island has "big time" potential for those who enjoy outpost islands.

A Caymanian aficionado advised a few years ago that the best route for on-the-spot facts for Little Cayman is to call the public telephone and ask your question of anyone who answers!

ISLAND APPEARANCE: Little Cayman is fringed by sand in some areas, especially at Point of Sand, a remarkable long stretch of beach wrapping around the eastern point to include portions of the south coast. Tarpon Lake dots the south coast, not far from tiny Owen Island, a beach-bordered speck off the southwest coast.

OTHER MATTERS: **Lifestyle** is independently back to basics. The main focus for guests is the sea—for scuba, swimming and sport fishing—although a few are lured by birds and flora. **Money matters** are conducted in Caymanian currency, as elsewhere in this British territory, with US$1 valued at CI $.80. **Communication** with the outside world focuses on the small post office at the grass airstrip, where a handful of folks congregate when planes land—for mail and news. Hotels have links with the U.S. and elsewhere, but don't count on easy access to dial telephones.

TOURING TIPS come from the residents with cars and/or pick-up trucks. They'll give you a ride to places you might want to visit—and hotels arrange pick-ups at the airport.

LODGINGS on Little Cayman are an unusual lot, each taking its cue from an independent owner/manager with a trademark personality. There are also some rooms for rent, but surveying for them is best done on-the-spot. Here are four of the established places:

Dillon's Cottages • *on the southern shore, near the west end* • are simple dwellings for independent housekeeping. Favored by divers and/or nature-lovers who have been this way before, the couple of cottages are often rented for long term. It's worth checking, if you want to set up housekeeping. *Cottages.*

Pirates Point • *on the beach, near the airstrip* • serves fare never known to pirates! Gourmet cook and owner, Gladys Howard applies tips and training from London's Cordon Bleu to locally grown produce and fresh fish, for memorable meals. Guests in the dozen rooms spend days exploring the island—birding and tracking the local lizards—or wallowing in diamond-clear seas, or diving along or snorkeling over the wall at Bloody Bay. Some guests simply enjoy this quiet, remote, and very special place. *Inn.*

Sam McCoy's Diving and Fishing Lodge • *near Spot Bay and Bloody Bay Point* • is casual and sea focused, with some rooms (but not all) having private bathroom and others sharing facilities. Informality is the keynote, with the diving—and transportation to some exceptional dive sites—included in the overnight cost, along with all meals. *Guesthouse.*

Southern Cross Club • *on the south coast, overlooking tiny Owen Island* • was established in the 1950s as a getaway hideout for sportsmen who thrived on leaving social and business pressures at home. The atmosphere still prevails, for guests who settle into one of the dozen cottages on the beach. In addition to fishing and/or scuba excursions, guests head for offshore Owen Island or a wander along the long, sandy shore. The main building is the social hub with its friendly fishermen's bar and the camplike dining area. My meal was almost inedible, but most guests come here for the outdoor offerings. This is a special spot that appeals to fisherfolk and those with outdoor interests. *Small hotel.*

NATURAL SURROUNDINGS: With only a few of its 20 miles of roads paved, the island offers much for those who prefer nature without most modern "enhancements." Unlike its soil-starved sister, Little Cayman's landscape has shades of green. The shallow lagoons that make lace out of the south side of the island are filled with bonefish. Pygmy tarpon thrive in the landlocked mangrove lagoon known as Tarpon Lake, about midway on the south coast. Seas are mined with reefs that are the pride of scuba divers and the peril of inexperienced boatmen. Bloody Bay, off the north coast, was noted as one of the world's top dive sites by Jacques Cousteau in the 1970s. Its Three Fathom Wall crests less than 20 feet below the surface about 150 yards offshore. Cumber's Caves and the caverns at Preston Bay, at the southwest tip of the island, are other diving favorites.

SPORTS on Little Cayman are sensational, if it's scuba you seek. Pros will want to bring their own regulators, gauges, and light-weight wet suits for deep dives. A light for night dives is also recommended. Diving sites include the wall at Bloody Bay, which drops from less than 20 feet to about 6000 or so, making it one of the few walls where snorkelers can enjoy a glimpse from the top. Check with resorts for diving specifics—and facts on birding, tarpon fishing and bone fishing on the flats.

CUBA

Instituto de Turismo Nacional e Internacional, Cubatur, Calle 23, #156, Vedado, Habana, Cuba. Corporación de Turismo y Comercio, Cubanacan S.A., Calle 146 entre 11 y 13, Municipio Playa, Reparto Siboney, Spartado 16046, La Habana, Cuba. In the U.S., tours are arranged through Marazul, #1311, 250 W. 57th St., New York, NY 10107, T 212+582-9570 or 800+223-5334. In Canada, Cuba Tourist Board, #705, 55 Queen St. East, Toronto, Ontario M5H 1R5, 416+362-0700; Bureau de Tourisme de Cuba, #1402, 440 Dorchester Ouest Blvd., Montreal, Quebec H2Z 1V1, T 514+875-8004.

$ · · · US$1.25 = 1 Cuban peso at the official rate
Unless otherwise noted, $ refers to U.S. currency.

AUTHOR'S OBSERVATION
At press time, there are restrictions on travel in Cuba for U.S. citizens. In general, only government officials, news-gatherers, researchers, people with close relatives in Cuba, and specific others are permitted to travel with U.S. passport. Although other U.S. citizens *can* visit the country, they are not permitted to travel under the protection offered by a U.S. passport and are liable for prosecution under the "trading with the enemy" act. For details, contact the U.S. Department of State. The *Caribbean Newsletter* (page 9) will have news when things change.

The dimly lit back room of the Bodeguita del Medio has not changed in almost 30 years. Its walls are covered with graffiti where the photographs, letters, and other memorabilia allow enough space. The boxy wood chairs still creak when you push them back on two legs; conversations are still eclectic; and the hot sauce, with its gnat-sized power-bombs of hot peppers, is still presented in an overgrown jelly jar.

On a visit in 1976, Martinez, with a cloud of white hair, was still there—and eager to reminisce about Ernest Hemingway. "We consider him a Cuban," he said with fireworks in his eyes. Hemingway is one of the few U.S. legends from the past that inspires reverence in Cubans—young and old. They love his *machismo*. It's akin to theirs—even in a socialist system that stresses equality, especially between the sexes, and spells out divisions of responsibilities in the Family Code of 1975 (Law 1289).

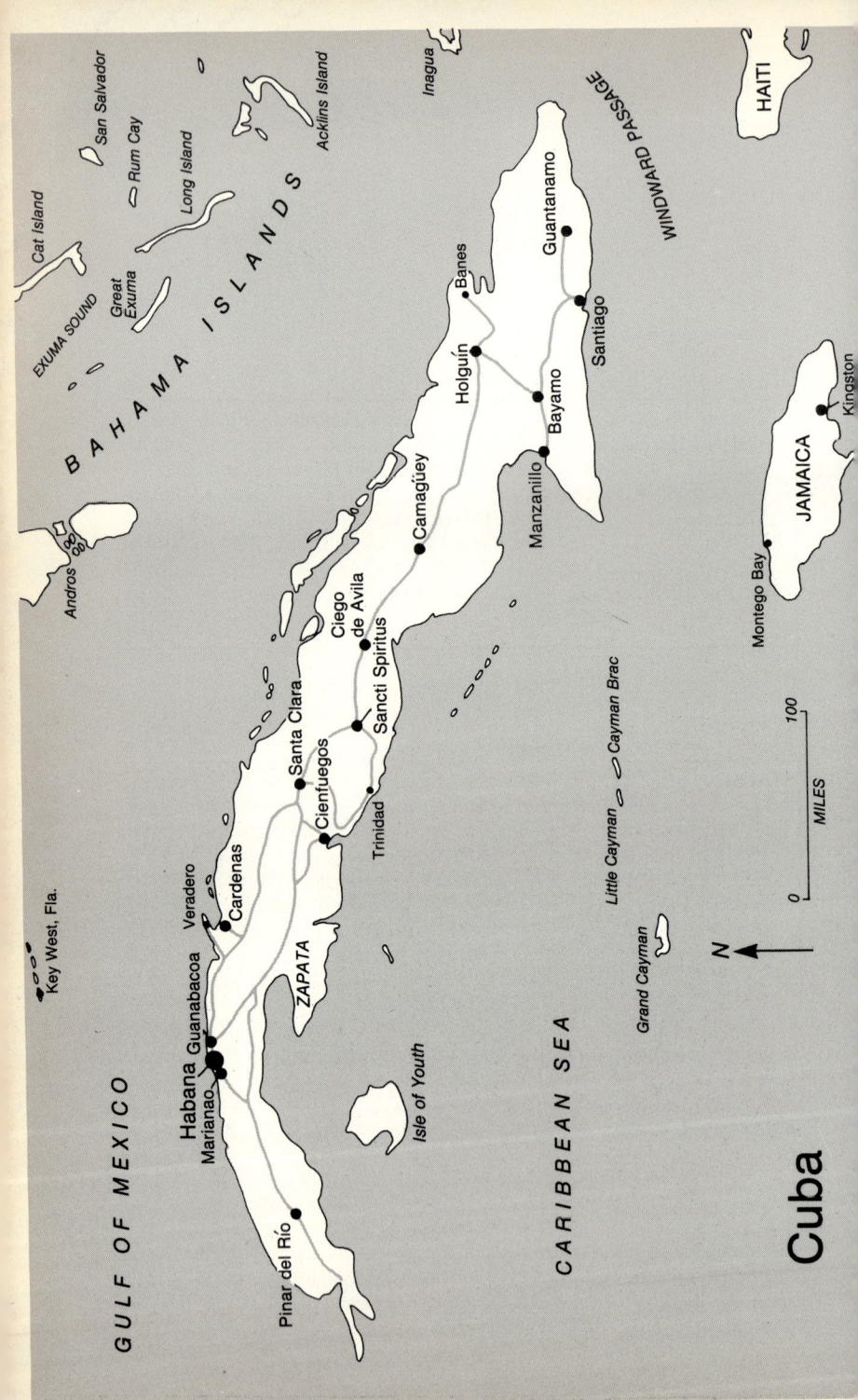

Bodeguita is a bar-restaurant, a series of closets linked by doorways with no doors in the 17th-century heart of old Habana, along a cobbled street off the Cathedral Plaza. Behind its swinging shutter-doors, the bar stretches into series of small rooms, cocoons for writers, artists, and intellectuals—aspiring and achieving.

A chair hung upside down from the ceiling in one corner. Leandro Garcia, the writer who first put Bodeguita into print, sat on it about 1924. Now no one does—obviously. And no one dresses the way *Harper's Bazaar* photographed their "Flying Down to Cuba" story—in the diaphanous "moth dress," or even as *Life* magazine pictured "A Cuban Way With Styles" in their May 5, 1968, issue. In August 1976, when I made the first of several visits to Castro's Cuba, both relics hung on the wall, surrounded by revolutionary slogans.

"That was a time of romance. You'll see a change, be we are more relaxed now," I was told soon after we'd passed a *Welcome* sign—in Spanish, Russian, English, and French.

AUTHOR'S OBSERVATION

Throughout this chapter, the name of the capital is spelled as it is in Cuba, namely Habana—and not Havana as it sounds when spoken.

POLITICAL PICTURE: Cubans refer to their government as socialist, which is explained as a step toward eventual Communism. The country built the first Marxist government in the Western Hemisphere. Well over half the population of 10 million have been born since Fidel's Revolution in 1959, and have been brought up in the socialist (communist) system with once-strong links to the Soviet Union and countries of eastern Europe. The rapid changes in the eastern European countries in the first half of 1990 seem only to have made Castro more determined to set his country on a unique course. Return of Cuban soldiers, who were sent to Angola and other countries as mercenaries, however, is certain to destabilize a country already in economic doldrums and speculation is rampant about how long Fidel's experiment can last.

Resentment against the United States, as "Yankee Imperialists" has been cultivated in the years since the Revolution. The blockade instituted by the U.S. government in 1961 served only to consolidate Cuban resentment—making resident Cubans even more determined to prove they could "go it alone." The debacle of the Playa Giron—which we refer to as the Bay of Pigs—is regarded as the "primera derrota del Imperialismo en America" (the first defeat of American Imperialism). Help offered by the Soviet Union at that time, and the financing that authoritative reports list at astounding figures, was gratefully received by Cubans, who acknowledge that their country would not have survived without that aid—and the back-breaking work, and sacrifices, of the Cuban people. Soviet technicians and professionals stepped in to fill the vacuum left by North Americans and the many educated Cubans who left Cuba in the years after the Revolution. The effect of perestroika on the Cuban economy has been significant; Soviet aid has been dramatically cut from previous levels in light of the problems faced in their own part of the world.

The Revolutionary government ruled Cuba with a Council of Ministers until a new constitution on December 2, 1976, the 20th anniversary of Fidel's arrival aboard *Granma* to start the Revolution in the Sierra Maestra mountains. At that time, constitutional government—with Poder Popular ("People Power"), which had been tried in Matanzas Province and proved workable—was implemented. The former six provinces became fourteen; Poder Popular implements policies made by the National Assembly, with Fidel as Maximum Leader, Commander in Chief, and President of both the Council of Ministers and the Council of State. The Central Committee of the Communist Party is recognized in the Cuban Constitution of 1976 (and the preamble includes a denunciation of Yankee imperialism).

AUTHOR'S OBSERVATION

By June 1991, Cuban workers were spending long hours in an attempt to complete almost 30 stadiums, apartment buildings, and other facilities for the prestigious Pan American games, held in August. The task was made all the more arduous by the fact that the Cuban economy is in disarray. Bicycles are the mode of transportation; there is not enough fuel for the public transportation system. Other shortages plague the population. The *Caribbean Newsletter* (page 9) will have information about the political picture as it changes.

ISLAND APPEARANCE: With 42,627 square miles, Cuba is the largest Caribbean island. It is also one of the most beautiful countries, with "more than 200 bays and 289 beaches." Mountain ranges add drama, with the Sierra de los Organos in the west, the Escambray mountains in the central portion, and the Sierra Maestra mountains (which were the "home" of Castro's revolution) in the east. On the north coast, Veradero Beach, which stretches east of Habana (the capital), has mystique for some Americans as a pre-Castro playground for well-heeled travelers. But it's only one of many gorgeous soft-sand beaches; the beach at Horguin is also beautiful, and there are good beaches along areas on the south coast. The Isle of Youth, formerly known as the Isle of Pines, is noteworthy for its beaches, for offshore scuba diving, and for its sometimes sensational history. The 16th-century Spanish buildings in Habana, Santiago, and Trinidad are among the most noteworthy; most are in reasonably good repair—at least from the outside. Official literature mentions "8000 species of flora, 900 kinds of fish, 300 species of birds, 4000 kinds of mollusks and 2000 kinds of insects, none of which are poisonous."

LIFESTYLE: *Senor* and *Senora* went with the revolution. Everyone now is a *companero* or *companera*. The terms are heard frequently over loudspeakers and in conversation, when you travel around the country. The appellation is roughly equivalent to "comrade," and connotes complete equality. *Adios*, with its inherent reference to God ("go with God") has given way to *hasta la vista*.

There's no class system based on wealth; power has been substituted instead. Private initiative is not an asset in the socialist system. The apparent respect (or calculated homage) for people working a level above and camaraderie with colleagues appeared to me to be more official than spontaneous.

Since the system requires regular assessment of a person's work by his or her colleagues and advancement in a profession depends on good recommendations, there is little allowance for personal "fits of pique." (This extends to visiting journalists. I have found my Cuban colleagues baffled, but always courteous, with some of my more troublesome requests.)

Clothes do not make the person in Cuba; one's loyalty and contribution to "the system" do. Soviets and other Eastern Europeans, who have been Cuba's main tourists for the past several years (on barter programs arranged by their governments), have not set much of a pace for fashion; the world-class dress of jeans and T-shirts is the style here as well. Displays of wealth or high fashion are distinctly out of place in today's Cuba; jewelry is not worn. For a week of travel, women will be comfortable with slacks, shorts, and a skirt with shirts; men should bring plain-colored trousers, short-sleeved shirts, and a guayabera or other lightweight long-sleeved shirt for dressier evenings; plus bathing suits for pool and beach, and sandals or walking shoes, of course.

MEDICAL FACILITIES: Since improved medicine was one of the priorities of the Revolution, medical standards are high. For North American visitors, charges are minimal, but must be paid in U.S. dollars or another hard currency. In the 1960s and '70s, many doctors were trained in the Soviet Union, and former Eastern bloc countries. These days, there are highly regarded medical schools in Cuba with students from many other countries. (Spain, for example, has exchange programs with Cuban-operated clinics, which are now being set up in Spain for special care for some diseases.)

MONEY MATTERS: The Cuban peso is also marked with the $-sign, and outweighs the dollar when exchanged in Cuba (where you'll invest US$1.25 for one peso). The exchange given at the hotels and banks involves a hefty chunk for the service. Officially there's no tipping in this socialist/communist country, but tips are welcome from tourists, and Cubans find they, too, must tip to get any kind of service. Keep track of your exchange slips if you expect to be transferring pesos back to dollars when you leave the country. Even with the slips, the process is tedious. At tourist shops in hotels, only U.S. dollars or other hard currency is accepted. Although some credit cards are accepted, namely Eurocard, Diners Club International, the international versions of MasterCard and Visa, no credit cards using U.S. banks are accepted. Checks drawn on U.S. banks are not accepted.

COMMUNICATIONS: It is possible to telephone Cuba from the U.S. (and more easily from Canada and other countries with normal relations with the country) through the international telephone operator. Facsimile machines are also used by some offices. But allow plenty of time for any telephone transactions. Procedures can be slow; the transmission lines are limited.

ARRIVAL: At press time, one service out of the U.S. operates from Miami, through Marazul Tours. Charter flights are arranged on *American Airlines* and *Trans Haiti*. Flights also operate with Nassau in the Bahamas, Kingston in Jamaica, and other Caribbean islands. There are several vacation flights out of

Canadian cities, especially Toronto and Montreal. There are also flights from Mexico. Habana's Jose Marti airport is about 25 minutes' drive from town. Both Cubatur and Cubanacan (see "Touring Tips" below) have representatives at the airport for plane arrivals.

Cuban visas and tourist cards are required, and are usually supplied by the firm arranging transportation into the country. Cuban-born visitors must also obtain visas, available through the nearest Cuban consulate.

DEPARTURE: Procedures are relatively easy. There's an air-conditioned bar *before* you go through immigration. Once you're processed through the exit formalities (show your passport or other identification; forfeit your immigration card), you will wait in an area that has a couple of government Tourist Shops where you can buy T-shirts, cigars, and a few other items.

TOURING TIPS: There are several options for touring. The government's *Cubatur* and the government-and-overseas-private-sector *Cubanacan* are the domestic tour operators. When you're part of an organized tour, you will probably travel in **buses.** Around the city, you can take the public buses that travel the most popular areas. Visitors can also take longer bus trips to nearby towns and other provinces. **Taxis** are available, and can be arranged through the hotels. They are carefully regulated, and reasonably inexpensive. **Rental cars** are available through Cubanacan and Cubatur. Your hotel can assist with information. Most cars are Soviet-made Ladas. (The few other cars on the road are vintage U.S. models.) **Airplane** service links many areas of the country through the network of modern, strategically placed airports. Although flights are frequent between places such as Horguin, Santiago, and the Isle of Youth, it's difficult to learn the "schedule," and delays and cancellations are frequent. Flights are primarily for the use of government officials and guests. Most Cubans cannot travel.

LODGING: In Habana, most of the hotels are former 1950s "pleasure palaces," dating from the years when Cuba was a gambling paradise easily enjoyed on a short hop from Florida, but many hotels in the resort areas are modern and often built by foreign companies to international first-class standards. In Habana, the former Hilton is the *Habana Libre* and the legendary *Nacional,* although a tired grande dame, is still welcoming guests. In beach-lined Veradero, many of the hotels are clusters of former private homes, used by those affluent enough, pre-Castro, to have a vacation beach villa. Since Veradero is the prized sun-sand-and-sea resort area, there are also newer multi-story hotels, as there are at other places designated by the government for tourist development. Many are built in the style that was popular on many Caribbean islands in the early 1970s; some now being built are typical of modern resorts in Europe. There are a few rustic resorts, used by Cuban nationals for their family vacations, that have a camplike outdoor quality. The most popular resort areas are Veradero, Horguin, and, for divers, the Isle of Youth (better known to some as the Isle of Pines), which can be reached by plane from Habana or Varadero, or by ferry from Batabano.

CUBA · · · 237

AUTHOR'S OBSERVATION
If you must have special soap, a fluffy bath towel, a face cloth, and other such tokens from the capitalistic world, bring them with you—and plan to leave them with your Cuban friends.

At press time, your room rate will have been negotiated by the tour operator who arranged your entry into the country. Most visits are multi-night vacations, where room rate and air fare are packaged as one. In this economy, where hard currency is desperately needed and Americans are thought to be rich (and profligate), rates are what the traffic will bear, but they are still far below those on other Caribbean islands.

Information about places-to-stay is included under Hotels, Housekeeping Holidays, The Inn Way, and Low-Cost Lodging. Cuban hotels have not been star-graded in this edition.

HABANA AND ENVIRONS

Most of the traditional activity centers on the capital, which is a hub for business folks, politicians, and visitors interested in Spanish and modern Cuban history. Today's Habana is a curious mixture of the place Columbus might have known and the home for Castro's brand of communism. Facilities mix buildings from the 17th century with a group of buildings from the 1950s, and several built in recent years. Refer to p. 240 for Santa Maria, p. 247 for Cienfuegos, p. 248 for Holguin, p. 252 for Santiago, p. 260 for Varadero.

HOTELS: There are many hotels in the Habana area. Several have been built in recent years, in the multi-story style, with standardized rooms and facilities.

Biocaribe • *10 minutes from downtown* • is a Cubanacan project that had not opened at press time. Planned for 120 rooms, the modern hotel will be used by European visitors and others. Air-conditioned rooms have minibar and telephone. *Hotel.*

Capri • *21 and N sts., Vedado area* • is one of the city's top hotels, used by the government to house visiting guests and by those who want to stay in one of Habana's best. Most head straight for the top—to the 17th floor, where you weave your way through an unmarked door to a small air-conditioned bar with "windows" that look out on flipping feet and diving bodies as they wallow in the water of the pool you can reach on the 18th floor. The main restaurant for hotel guests is on the 4th floor. The hotel has a cabaret nightclub show, held in what was a lively casino controlled by George Raft pre-Castro. *Hotel.*

Chateau Miramar • *in the Miramar area* • is a new, 59-room hotel planned to open in '91, but not opened at the time of my visit for this edition. The *Caribbean Newsletter* (page 9) will have further comment.

Comodoro • *near the Aquarium, in the Miramar area, at 84th St.* • is one of the newer hotels, built in Spanish-Mediterranean style, graded 4-star by the government. The upper-floor rooms that face the sea have a nice view. Count on the usual amenities (Tourist Shop, pleasant pool, and restaurants)—and tour groups. *Hotel, villas.*

Habana Libre • *23rd and L sts., Vedado area* • held the title of the top convention hotel in the Caribbean when it was managed by Hilton in the 1950s. The basic structure is still impressive, although carpet and air conditioners show signs of wear. Head up the winding staircase for the pool-level bar, where canned music peps things up while you sip your *mojito* or Cuban beer along with Cubans and other folks who gather here. The 25th floor *Sierra Maestra Restaurant* offers the ubiquitous Cuban buffet, including a huge selection of sweet desserts. Count on your room to be a '50s version of what you know as Hilton style, but be prepared for a new look for furnishings that replace those that haven't survived the 40 years (there are some that have). *Hotel.*

Inglaterra • *at the corner of San Rafael and Paseo de Marti* • provides standard services on the fringe of the old city of Habana. This is Habana's oldest hotel, having been built in the 1880s. The location is not as pleasant as some of the traditional tourism hotels, but you'll be only a short walk from the Garcia Lorca Theater and not far from the Plaza de la Catedral and the Museum of the Revolution. *Hotel.*

Nacional • *21st St. and O, in the Vedado area* • has recently been refurbished. The structure has weathered all storms since its opening in 1929–30. The pink palace still has its name etched on its "forehead," and stands, impressive, on a viewful bluff overlooking the Malecon and the sea. Used by Eastern European, Mexican, and other groups, the hotel is a city landmark with a palatial aura. Note the tiles that border the main lobby, and the Moorish-Spanish-style ceilings overhead, both of which—along with other classical attributes—I hope will survive the refurbishing. Around the fringe of the lobby, you'll find a money-changing booth, small shops for Cubans and tourists, and other activities. *Hotel.*

Riviera • *Malecon and Paseo sts., in the Vedado area* • was Miami rackets' boss Meyer Lansky's ill-timed plunge into the money market of Habana. The fountain in front of the property was added in 1978, for the 11th World Youth Festival. The high-rise hotel, about 5 minutes' taxi ride from the downtown area, opened with fanfare in 1959, at the time of the Revolution. One of the first to be refurbished, the 16-story hotel offers reasonably comfortable rooms. Air conditioners and carpets show signs of wear, but the overall impression is o.k. *Hotel.*

Victoria • *near the Rampa* • is one of the smaller hotels, with air-conditioned rooms and private bath. On the premises, there's a restaurant as well as some shops. *Hotel.*

HOUSEKEEPING HOLIDAYS: Although many of the properties in the beach-fringed Varadero area, about half an hour's drive from Habana, are former private homes confiscated by the government and now used for visitor lodgings, the kitchen facilities are often quite basic. Vacationers are encouraged to join others in the central dining rooms.

Within 20 minutes' of downtown Habana, the Marina Hemingway has become a tourist center, with the addition of several self-catering apartments and some villas that are popular with Germans and other European visitors.

Hotel El Viejo Y El Mar • *overlooking the marina* • is a 6-story block of reasonably comfortable small apartments, built to European taste. Rooms are air conditioned; balconies overlook the marina. All apartments have T.V., telephone, and kitchen, plus modern bathroom. There's a nice-sized pool, with a bar and cafe, plus a cafeteria and another restaurant off the lobby. A Tourist Shop offers trinkets and other items; there's a shopping area nearby for food, but don't count on much selection. *Hotel.*

Villa Paraiso • *at the marina* • is a collection of small air-conditioned houses, with 1, 2, or 3 bedrooms, plus kitchen, bathroom, and tv. There's 24-hour room service, plus attendants to take care of children. Guests at the villas share the facilities at El Viejo, where rental cars and watersports are available. *Villas.*

THE INN WAY: You won't find many family-owned inns in today's Cuba. Perhaps that will come, when the lifestyle changes.

LOW-COST LODGING: Since Cuba is eager to display its system for students, and since sports tourism is a primary focus, there are many ways for young people and sportspeople to vacation inexpensively. Being part of a people-to-people group is one way that is open for students, teachers, and other professional groups. Marazul Tours has details.

Colina • *near the Rampa, the hub for airline offices, banks, restaurants, and other activities* • is noted as a 3-star hotel by some. Its convenient location and standard services are its greatest assets.

Deauville • *Galiano Ave. and Malecon* • is downtown, about 5 blocks from the Prado. The 15-story traditional hotel, opened in the late 50s, was granted a casino license just before they became obsolete. Favored by Soviets and other Eastern Europeans, the hotel seems to me to be dark and dingy. The Tourist Shop on the second level is a cut below the Tourist Shops in the other hotels mentioned.

St. John's • *not far from the Colina, near the Rampa* • has air-conditioned rooms and a convenient location.

Triton • *west of the center, at 70th St., facing the water, in the Mirimar area, not far from the Hemingway Marina* • is popular with attendees at the International Conference Center, which is nearby. Bedrooms have air conditioners and private bath.

Vedado • *near the Rampa* • is another one of the smaller hotels, with air-conditioned rooms and private bath. The lobby has a Tourist Shop and restaurant.

Also used by Marazul Tours and other firms are the **Lincoln** (some air-conditioned rooms), the **Bruzon** (no air conditioning), and the **Caribbean** (no air conditioning).

HOTELS AROUND HABANA: (For Santiago de Cuba and Varadero, see pages 252 and 260 respectively). *SANTA MARIA,* a resort area built since the Revolution at a beach on the north shore, east of Habana, has several hotels.

Bacuranao • *on the north shore just before you reach Santa Maria* • is a sprawl of single-story, small and simple units. During my first visit, the property was being used for Russian and other Eastern European vacationers; signs were in Russian as well as Spanish and French, the last a hangover from a one-season use of the property by Club Mediterrannee (which had a brief hedonistic fling before folks realized the ideology conflicts with the austerity of Communism). The property hugs a small bay on which some people row boats or rubber rafts. There's a pavilion at one edge of the bay for drinks and dining. A store offers the usual Tourist Shop items. *Resort.*

Marazul • *at Santa Maria* • was one of the first in the government's plan announced in the mid-1970s to build 59 new hotels. This one opened, on a long stretch of white powder sand, in mid-1976, with an ultramodern look, helped along with white plaster walls, colorful accents, and several levels with plenty of open space to take advantage of the breezes that blow through the main areas. The lobby has plants for accents; the big dining room (where the long tables are filled with a complete buffet at mealtime) is air-conditioned. There is a big swimming pool (not as big as the "mirror" resort, *Pasacaballo,* at the south coast's Cienfuegos, but the southern resort does not have the white sand beach you find here). There are the usual public rooms, Tourist Shop (with T-shirts, rum, cigars, dolls, records, and an inventory that increases as time and talent allow), snack bar, bar, and activities desk. Rooms are clean, neat, twin-bedded, with private bath and modern plumbing, as you'd expect in any modern first-class hotel. A taxi into downtown Habana takes about 30 minutes. *Hotel.*

Villa Megano • *at Santa Maria* • shares the beach of Marazul and is a cottage-type resort built on a hillside, with some of the feeling, a colleague commented, of Las Brisas in Mexico's Acapulco. *Villas.*

Playa Hermosa • *on the north coast* • is a complex of villas available for international visitors, if some tour operator sets it up. You can walk to the beach from your 1-, 2-, or 3-bedroom house. *Villas.*

Tropico • *the easternmost resort on the north coast beaches in Habana Province* • has several villas. When I first saw the property in August 1976, Juan Manuel Martinez Tinguano was in charge, in thanks for help he gave to Fidel during the Revolution. "Built for the people" in 1959, the complex was used by Canadian groups. A notice posted on a board near the bar/dining room area urged visitors not to wear shorts in museums, and advised that bikes rent for 50 centavos per hour, tennis rackets rented for one peso per hour, and archery, basketball, badminton, and billiards were available as entertainment, in addition to rental of rowboats, sailboats, and fishing equipment, and scuba lessons. Plans for groups include a rum-tasting party at the beach and a Cuba night, as with all the resort area hotels where visitors stay for a couple of nights or longer. Rooms at Tropico are simple but adequate, with emphasis on the beach, pool, and outdoor informal life. *Resort.*

SAN ANTONIO DE LOS BANOS, about 25 minutes from the downtown area, is marked for development as a resort area.

Hotel Las Yagrumas • *near the Ariguanabo River* • is a 2-story resort, centered around its large pool. The air-conditioned rooms have T.V. and telephone, as well as reasonable modern comforts. Built with a conference room, the resort hopes to host small meetings. There are tennis and squash courts on the premises; horseback riding is offered, and bicycles and mopeds can be arranged, as can river excursions. Restaurants are o.k. *Small resort.*

RESTAURANTS IN HABANA: There have been rapid changes since my first visit to communist Cuba in August 1976. Things move fast in this country, when the project concerns tourist facilities, acknowledged as a source for hard currency. A few of the menus reflect the flair and flourishes expected with international cuisine but most food was strangely tasteless when I tried it. Offerings include fish, and pork, often stewed, as are other types of meat. Eggs are available in tourist places, as is rice. Although 7 ounces of chicken or pork every 10 days has been the allotment for Cubans, buffet tables at tourist hotels (*Libre, Riviera, Capri, Nacional,* etc.) are heaped with an assortment of cold and hot dishes, plus fresh fruit and Cuban-sweet desserts and cheese. Although visitors may tire of continuous buffets, the procedure is as much for the Cubans who splurge on a meal out as it is for the visitors—as you will note by the mealtime enthusiasm of your guides.

When you present your white currency paper with payment of bills in many bars and restaurants, you will receive a tourist discount. The procedure applies also for the costs above the basic charge at cabarets and floor shows.

Cuban beer is the common mealtime beverage (note the care with which it's poured); wine is often available by the glass, but don't expect it to be French import, unless you're prepared to pay plenty. It's more likely to be Portuguese or from communist countries.

The Cuban art of restaurant service is reappearing. In the top restaurants, the service will be as close to the "white glove" treatment of yesteryear as this socialist country can get.

Bodeguita del Medio • *on Emperado, off Cathedral Plaza* • is a classic—and another Hemingway favorite. According to the legend as told to me, the chair that hangs upside down in the back room corner is the one that Leandro Garcia, the first writer to mention Bodeguita, used to sit on, but another story claims that a peasant who used to come into the place asked that his chair be reserved when he went to heaven. The saloon doors that open onto the street swing into the bar that backs up to the cluttered kitchen where country food is prepared. Several small and crowded rooms are like closets without doors, and the atmosphere is like no place else I know. Although some of the clippings of yesteryear have been replaced by political slogans about Panama, Nicaragua, Angola, Ethiopia, and the current Cuban communist causes, the place still stands as a statement of the time. (This is one lingering place you can count on to be packed with people.)

La Cecelia • *on Fifth Ave., near 110th St. in the Miramar area* • is a former home turned restaurant. Cuban-style home cooking is the specialty; the setting is a pleasant one.

Coppelia Ice Cream Parlor • *not far from the Habana Libre and Hotel Capri* • is the place to find for Cuban-watching and for delicious ice cream. The series of Coppelia shops took its cue from the exclusive ice cream places enjoyed by the wealthy before the revolution. Coppelias are people places; this is the pace-setter.

La Floridita • *on Calle Obispo at Monserrate* • is heartily touted as a Hemingway haven. This is the place where he is supposed to have lingered with the bartenders to help perfect the daiquiri, served everywhere in modern Cuba in foamy frozen splendor. Before the Revolution, Floridita was one of two grand restaurants (*Zaragozana*, whose original owners moved to Old San Juan, Puerto Rico, was the other). Some of the bartenders who worked here in the Hemingway era are still around, but the current Cuban claims that the Floridita is "at the level of the American Bar of Paris, the Savoy of London or El Plaza of Buenos Aires" seem a bit ambitious to me, and hark back to the earlier era when an old issue of *Esquire* (with the clipping framed on the wall) called the place one of the 7 great bars. At present, the white plastic covers on the bar stools look a little too new, the tables set like animals on a merry-go-round around the pillar in the back room are not always full, and there's a lack of joy that was never a part of this place before. In the hedonistic pre-Castro days, a writer could call this "an institution of unique integrity in a city where catering to tourists has corrupted the spirit and meaning of a truly honest bar," and note that "at the Floridita, man's spirit may be elevated by conversation and companionship not entered into betrayal by his baser instincts." The potential for a "truly great bar" is here, but at the moment you'll have to content yourself with recollections of Hemingway, helped along by a lingering look at his bust in a corner. The service at Floridita is some of Cuba's best; you can count on spending the equivalent of $20 per person for a full meal.

El Emperador • *at Calle 17 between M and N, next door to the entrance for La Torre* • is smaller than famous Floridita, more intimate, with an atmosphere that is helped along by wandering guitar players (when they're performing). Prices are not quite as high as the top-floor La Torre.

El Patio • *at the Cathedral Plaza on the corner near San Ignacio and Empedrado* • was the former home of Marques Aguas Claras (as you can note on the shield at the left of the entrance). Choices for lingering include the front terrace, on the historic Plaza, and the tables around the fountain in the center courtyard. There are small, private air-conditioned dining rooms for special dinners. (Reserve by calling ahead.) Dinners will run about 8 pesos for fish (pescado), but spaghetti costs a modest 5 to 7 pesos depending on the sauce. Chicken (pollo) runs about 7, and your juice will be a couple of pesos.

La Torre • *at Calle 17 between M and N sts., on the top of the apartment building that blocks the sunset view for guests at the Hotel Capri* • is one of Cuba's top spots, complete with view over the night lights of the city and service that's up to the best. The street-level entrance is somber and the elevator ride reminiscent of that in an office building, but the sparkling lights of Habana lend a festive evening aura once you've reached the top.

Las Ruinas • *in Lenin Park, 15 miles south of the city* • is a restaurant where Fidel often entertains visiting dignitaries. Surroundings are elegant, ultramodern, and built to incorporate the ruins of walls of an old sugar mill. There's a piano, on which '40s tunes are played during dining hours, and Tiffany lamps hang at appropriate places. Note especially the 5 stained-glass panels, done by Rene Puertocarrero. Furniture harks to the 19th century, with ferns softening the austerity of a very modern new building. There is no reason to expect less than the best Cuban service and food here; you are paying for it. Dinner for 2 can cost the equivalent of $100, with wine and all flourishes, including cigars.

Sloppy Joe's • *on a side street in the old city* • is a shadow of its former self. When American visitors return in bulk to Cuba, the place may come to life again as we flock to see the '40s photos of Rudy Vallee, Alice Faye, Ray Milland, Sophie Tucker, Rosalind Russell, Cesar Romero, and Tyrone Power, among others. All were habitues of Sloppy Joe's during their visits to pre-Revolution Habana, and their photos and comments are plastered all over pillars and walls. The bar, when I visited, was empty—with a few bottles of Cuban rum in liquor cabinets once bursting with the best of the imported brands. This is a stand-up, informal place that thrives on crowds of people, but seems pitiful in their absence.

Zaragozana • *on Monserrate, not far from Floridita* • has lost most of the sparkle from its pre-Castro hedonistic days, but it is, once again, one of socialist Habana's best (and most expensive—at $20 pp) restaurants.

PLACES WORTH FINDING in Habana are touchstones for almost five centuries. The tour you take to reach Cuba will undoubtedly have sightseeing in Habana as part of its program, but during free time, you can walk, bus, or take a taxi (they wait outside the hotels) to the Cathedral Plaza, to Plaza de Armas, or to the Prado, the mall that stretches from what had been the Capitol to the Malecon. These are the three main hubs for touring in old Habana.

> **AUTHOR'S OBSERVATION**
>
> Fuel shortages have interrupted public bus services and car use, but your hotel can assist with transportation available for hard-currency-spending tourists.

La Habana's full name is San Cristobal de la Habana. After two attempts to found a city to the west, the present site became the start of the city in 1519. Llave del Nuevo Mundo (the key of the New World) was the nickname given to the early city, because of its prize location for control of the Florida and Yucatan peninsulas. The key on the seal of Habana symbolizes this fact.

All museums are closed on Mondays. Be sure to check for specific opening hours. Times change, and although most places are open sometime on Sunday, some museums open only in the morning, others only in the afternoon.

Castillo del Morro (Morro Castle), on the eastern point of the harbor entrance, is one of the city's most photographed sights. The restaurant, museum, and tourist facilities opened July 26, 1978. On my first visit to this former prison (used for Castro's political prisoners), just after it became a restaurant, I stepped over the scaffolding, walked through the potential shops and restaurants, and photographed the spectacular view across the mouth of the harbor to the city of Habana, as the first foreign journalist to visit the fort just prior to the time it was to be open for visitors. Morro Castle was built in 1589, as one of the two terminals from which the heavy chain was hung across the harbor each evening (Castillo de la Punta was the other.)

Castillo de la Punta (Castle of the Point) houses exhibitions of arms from early times, in addition to having a restaurant and other tourist facilities.

> **AUTHOR'S OBSERVATION**
>
> Check at your hotels' tour desk to see about a boat ride past La Fuerza, El Morro, La Punta, La Cabana, and La Chorrera. The excursion departs from Base Nautica near the 1830 Restaurant at Desembocadura del rio Almendares, west of the downtown area. A motorboat similar to Hemingway's *Pilar* takes a minimum of 8 people for a tour. You may have to assemble your group, but the excursion will be well worth the investment. La Habana presents a very different picture from the sea.

Museo de la Ciudad de la Habana, in the former palace of the Captains-General, on Plaza de Armas, is an opportunity to step back into another era. The minute you pass the entrance and look at the courtyard with its statue of Columbus, you are removed from Habana of the 1990s. I was told that the palace was built in 1557, was a convent, and was rebuilt as a palace in the 18th century. The huge rooms, the balconied center courtyard, and the wide staircase (with a piano on one level) attest to an earlier elegant era. Note especially the paintings of the 1800s (portraits of prominent Spaniards, and one William O'Ryan). When I wandered through on one visit, a woman guard in one of the rooms asked me if I was French. No, I replied, "United States." Her face breaking into a smile, she quietly clapped her hands. "Oh," she said, "that is so good." The exhibits paled by comparison to the welcome, but on subsequent visits I have appreciated the visual background in Cuban history.

The city of Habana was established in 1519 at the small church across from Museo de la Ciudad, on the site of what is now El Templeto. A statue of Diego Columbus, son of Christopher, stands in the front of the building; the pineapples on the pillars are the symbol of hospitality, and the Greek temple known as El Templeto was completed in 1828. Inside is a famous painting showing the first mass held in the New World, but getting to see the painting is difficult. The building is usually closed.

At the park between the Museo and El Templeto, there is a statue of Don Carlos Manuel de Cespedes, the "father of Cuba" as president of the new Cuba in 1868.

Museo de Arte Colonial de la Habana, the Museum of Colonial Art of Habana, was reopened on the Plaza de la Catedral in 1969. If only to get inside one of the oldest buildings around the 16th-century plaza you should find an hour or two to wander through the colonial rooms, to look at the silver water pitchers, with bowls, that served as elegant sinks for early settlers, the parasols and mantillas, the urns and vases of earlier times.

AUTHOR'S OBSERVATION

This area around the Cathedral Plaza is one of the most picturesque in old Habana. A cafe table at El Patio restaurant provides a perfect place for a lingering look. (The famed Bodequita del Medio, a Hemingway favorite, is around the corner along San Ignacio.)

Fraternity Park, the Latin American park, where 21 countries planted mahogany trees in soil brought from their homelands, is at one side of the big capitol building, which you will recognize because it looks like the Capitol in Washington, DC. The former seat of the government is now the Academy of Sciences. In the capitol building is **Museo Felipe Poey,** with special sections devoted to minerals, natural science, a planetarium, and archaeological finds in Cuba, in addition to areas used for special exhibitions. (During one of my recent visits, the building's interior and the lawns outside were filled with Russian heavy machinery and weapons for war.) The name "Capitolio" is still etched on the imposing building's "forehead." To the right of the former capitol, the Habana Theater performs downstairs in what had been a private club for wealthy Spaniards in the 19th century. (The *Plaza Hotel* and the *Inglaterra,* now remodeled for today's travelers, are in this area.)

Along the Prado, leading to the Malecon and the site of one of Habana's liveliest carnivals, there are lampposts and urns that "were made from the remains of Spanish ships."

As you stand at the Malecon, looking up the Prado, the **Museum of the Revolution** is on your left, in Batista's former palace. It is testimony to the feats of the revolutionaries. Exhibits fill the several stories of the building, and tanks and other war vehicles are on the lawns outside. During one visit, I noted Fidel's comments that the "Yankees took our economy, they took our best lands, our minds . . . they exploited our public services, they took the biggest part of our lands . . ." It was explained to me that "Fidel has to be hard on the United States and imperialism to break the dependence, to make the people work to accomplish the impossible." From the soldiers and tanks at the front gates to and through the exhibits of the Bay of Pigs, past Fidel's comments against Yankee imperialism, the museum stands as a school about the Revolution for young Cubans, and a reminder for the rest of us.

On the inland side of the Museum of the Revolution, there is an exhibition area showing the *Granma*, the humble ship in which Fidel made his landing on the south coast of Cuba, when he headed into the Sierra Maestra with the guerrillas.

Museo Nacional, in the Palacio de Bellas Artes, is worth as much time as you can give it. The ramps that lead to the various levels make it easy (if long) to walk to the top for the most current Cuban art, all of it representing Revolutionary themes that are popular in Cuba today. Ancient Greek, Roman, and European art is at other levels, with some interesting examples of early Cuban art and the portraits and scenes that were poular in the 18th and 19th centuries.

Not far from the railroad station, you can see one of the few remaining bits of the old city walls, most of which were destroyed in August 1863. The wall around the old city was started on February 6, 1674, and completed by the 1790s.

Casa Natal de Jose Marti, across from the central railroad station, has several small rooms lined with photographs and documents from the life of the man regarded as the "Apostle" of Cuban freedom. Marti, always regarded highly by the Cuban people, has now been adopted by the Revolution as one of its heroes. Marti traveled to Key West and Tampa, Florida, to raise money for his revolution against the Spaniards; Fidel followed his route when he traveled to Cuban communities in the United States to raise money for his Revolution in the late 1950s.

Museo de Artes Decorativas (decorative arts; Calle 17 e/e y D, Vedado) should not be missed by anyone with an interest in colonial Cuban history. The former home in which the collections of china and furniture are displayed is worth a visit for itself. Be sure to take time to look at the ceilings, walls, decoration around the windows and doors, and the elegant touches that have been refurbished before the museum was reopened after the Revolution.

Museo Historico de Guanabacoa, about 30 minutes' drive outside Habana in the suburban hills at Guanabacoa, is a folk museum, with exhibits (photographs and documents) about the early weed women and rituals of the Indians.

Parque Lenin, a favorite recreation area for Cubans, is about 15 miles south of Habana. In addition to an amphitheater for 2400 people, opportunities for horseback riding, and sports areas, there is a tourist train that runs all around the park, to the delight of Cuban children and parents. (Las Ruinas, the elegant restaurant that has been a favorite of Fidel's, is here.)

Finca Vigia, Hemingway's home at San Francisco de Paula, 30 minutes' drive out of Habana, is a musem. You can peer through the windows, but may not enter or photograph the interior. The Cubans say that Mary Hemingway donated the home; Mary Hemingway has been quoted as saying she did not.

However, it's still here—and Hemingway's beloved fishing boat, *Pilar,* is sitting on struts in the "front yard."

Ernest Hemingway bought his house in 1936, and lined the drive with palms. As you look through the windows, you can see homey chintz-covered couches and chairs, half-finished bottles of liquor, and one place where Hemingway used to write—atop his bookcase, with a view through the window. His favorite records, scattered around, seemed to include Russian folk songs, Cole Porter, Artie Shaw, and the *William Tell Overture.* In the bedroom, there's another typewriter, propped up on a fat *Who's Who in America.* His study has tiled floors, and a camel saddle, plus driftwood and other personal treasures, and in the dining room, the mahogany trestle table is surrounded by Spanish-style chunky chairs. Etched hurricane globes were on the table when I looked in. After peeking at Hemingway relics, wind around to the lookout area, atop one of the outbuildings. The view over the plains between the village and Habana is awe-inspiring.

The house, and other Hemingway spots, including Cojimar, the fishing village where he kept his boat, and which he used as the setting for *The Old Man and the Sea,* are part of a Hemingway Tour, set up and promoted by Cubatur.

The Hemingway myth is alive and well in Habana and its surroundings, not only in the Floridita and the Bodequita del Medio Cafe, but also in the annual Fishing Tournament.

MID-COUNTRY

CIENFUEGOS, in one of Cuba's pouch harbors on the south coast, is a major port, with emphasis on industry. It has also been home port for Cuba's Russian submarines and other military equipment. It was the site of the country's first fertilizer plant, built after the Revolution, and has an oil refinery in addition to being "home" for 12 sugar mills, a 600-bed hospital, a 30,000-person regional sports stadium (with complete housing for the teams), and an open classroom experimental school (no walls). The bay of this city, known as the Pearl of Cuba by those who live here, is 10 miles long. The town is named for Don Jose Cienfuegos, one of the captains-general during the 18th century, when the Spanish built a fort here to defend the area from the British. Although the harbor is one of the south coast's largest, poking deep into the land, the town was not settled until 1819 when Frenchman Louis de Clouet led a small group from New Orleans, which had recently been purchased by the United States. "The rich families used to live" on a tongue of land known as Punta Gorda before the Revolution. When I first saw this city in August 1976, there were hundreds of red and blue Fords at one of the port depots, newly arrived from Argentina to be used as taxis and government cars. Many of those cars are still in use, although fuel is hard to come by. **Palacio Valle,** and some of the other former homes along the seaside boulevard near the Hotel Jagua, are now museums, full of "chandeliers and furniture for the people."

HOTELS IN AND NEAR CIENFUEGOS are mostly modern, and resort style, enjoyed by Canadian and European groups.

Hotel Jagua • *on the shoreside where boats depart for excursions around the harbor and by water to Hotel Pasacaballo* • was finished in 1959 and "opened by the Revolution in 1960." The palatial building was started by Batista's brothers, to be a private home. Its vast halls and elegant main-floor rooms are now used as the lobby for the hotel, with an air-conditioned (cold) dining room at the back on the right, and a pool in the patio. The lunch I had here on one visit, served in the best Cuban tradition by a man who had been an expert in his profession before the Revolution and now teaches young people aspiring to be good waiters and maitres, was a fresh fruit plate (with watermelon, papaya, pineapple) followed by fresh red snapper, fried bananas, rice, and an avocado and cucumber salad, with the usual sweet dessert and thick coffee. *Resort.*

Hotel Pasacaballo • *across the harbor entrance from Castillo de Jagua* • is a mirror image of the Marazul at Santa Maria, on the north coast just outside Habana. Completed in August 1976, the hotel is reasonably modern, typical of the properties around Cuba that have an almost Scandinavian feeling, which is helped along by white walls, several open and airy plant-trimmed patios, and colorful accents. The swimming pool is *huge,* Olympic size or more, stretching out at the "back" of the hotel, with a poolside bar and lounge chairs. There are bicycles for rent, a Tourist Shop, 3 bars, beauty parlor, "nautical activities" arranged, and a magnificent view framed in the windows of the freezing cold air-conditioned dining room serving the usual Cuban fare, often accompanied by elegantly poured beer. There's a coffee shop on the lower level for snacks. Room 517, my home on one visit, is reached from lobby level by a Hitachi (Japanese) elevator, and has a pool view, plus comfortable (narrow) bed, private modern bath. *Resort.*

Rancho Luna • *near Cienfuegos, about 5 minutes' drive from Pasacaballo* • has the Escambray mountains in the background. Its location on the beach makes it a favorite with Cuban and Eastern European visitors. The one-story units stetch out along the south shore. *Hotel.*

• • •

HOLGUIN, about 2 hours' drive from Santiago, is not much of a sight-seeing goal, but it is an entirely new city, planned by the Revolution to replace the existing old city. Lenin Hospital in Holguin is one of the biggest in the country, and the town is an industrial hub (cane-cutting and lifting machinery is made here). The modern airport is the funnel for vacationers to reach Guardalavaca, a 10-year-old resort on one of the country's several powdery beaches.

HOTELS NEAR HOLGUIN include both modern, beachside resorts and an unusual mountain retreat that appeals to bird-watchers and others who like verdant surroundings.

Mayabe Hotel • *20 minutes outside Holguin* • nests on the top of a wooded hill, overlooking the plains and lake. Opened in 1972, the mountain resort lures guests who enjoy wooded walks, riding horseback, dancing to the band that plays at the alfresco music area on evenings when the house count warrants a band, and spending leisure hours in the wood-beam restaurant where beer is served in handmade pottery mugs. The bamboo and wood construction of the main building (and the check-in area where there is a television set surrounded by chairs) supports the country atmosphere. There's another bar beyond the pool, with a penned donkey that is a favorite for guests. (The donkey drinks beer.) Americans will see some similarity to small inns in U.S. mountain resorts. There are "old" rooms, with private bath and tepid water, and "new" rooms built in the same style in 1978. *Hotel.*

Hotel Guardalavaca • *35 miles north of Holguin* • is one of the modern hotels, built for resort life for groups of Eastern European or North American visitors in winter as well as for Cubans during the summer months. A completely planned resort, the hotel houses guests in three 2-story white stucco buildings with air-conditioned rooms, some with balconies and refrigerator unit, all with private bath. Wood chairs are painted white, with bright-colored cushions, and the Canadian-made hand dryer in the ladies' room almost blew me out the door. The big dining room has tables for 4 or more, air-conditioned (to freezing cold, as is the case in many Cuban dining rooms). The bar (for rum and beer) serves inside and poolside, with stools on the pool side, and chairs in the room with a red and blue colorful plexiglass wall. *Hotel.*

The beach is spectacular—a long strand of white powder gradually sloping to the sea, with rental boats (pedal, sail, row) at one end of the beach and a concession for food and rental of the separate bungalows in a nearby area that Cubans may use for their vacations at the other end of the beach. Bohios along the sand protect from the sun, if you can't find one of the several sea grape trees to call home for a day. The beach is a short stroll from the hotel.

Other hotels in and around Holguin include the **Atlantico, Villa Don Lino, Villa El Cocal,** and **Villa El Quinque,** all used for Cubanacan tourist groups from Europe and elsewhere.

• • •

EL COBRE, a village about 30 minutes out of Santiago, on the road to Holguin, is where the church of La Virgin de la Carridad (Our Lady of Charity) is located. It holds the statute of the patron Saint of Cuba that washed up out of the sea. The Revolution has allowed the church to stand, and the village to thrive on it, out of respect for the legend.

• • •

BANES, about 45 minutes' drive from Guardalavaca, is Batista's hometown, the "birthplace of the tyrant," I was told. The **Museo Regional de Arquelogia Indocubana** (Indo-Cuban museum), in an air-conditioned building that was constructed by the Banco Continental (which I was told was an American bank), holds a modest but meaningful collection of relics from the Indo-Cuban cultures. Opened in 1965, the museum shows the migration of the Arawaks, and mortars and pestles as well as other implements believed to have belonged to the Ciboney tribe (spelled Siboney elsewhere). Daggers found near tombs and maps showing where the earliest Indians lived in Cuba are also exhibits, but it was the drawings of Taino Indian life by J. Martinez, done in '73, that made the daily habits clear (with artist's license, but I suppose his imagination is as good as anyone's). Note the facial expressions on the handles broken from early Indian vessels, and the other cases that hold ceremonial cups. There are 2 canoe paddles in a case by the stairway: One is a copy of a Maisi paddle from Baracoa (the original is in a museum in the U.S.); the other is from the Bahamas and here for an unexplained reason. Photos of burial sites at Yaguajay are displayed, and necklaces—old and modern, all restrung—are hung from pins in a cabinet on the wall.

• • •

TRINIDAD, almost in the middle of Cuba's south coast, is a national monument. It was also the scene of fierce fighting during the Revolution, when guerrillas swept into town on raids from the surrounding Escambray mountains. Today, Villa de la Santisima Trinidad (Town of the Most Holy Trinity) is a tourist attraction as a city-museum that is one of the best preserved examples of 17th- and 18th-century stone houses with the familiar Spanish-style iron grates. On separate occasions, I was told that some of the stone (I suspect ballast bricks) came from Philadelphia, or from Boston, on trading ships in the early centuries of the rum triangle. Regardless of the U.S. connection, the city is the third oldest in the country, after Baracoa (1511) and Bayamo (1513). It was a thriving city in 1585, when Diego Velazquez was governor. (He established the city in 1514, about the same time as Santiago de Cuba.) At one time in recent history 37,000 people lived in this city that is about 400 kms from Habana, but during my first visit in August '76, the only visible residents were a few old people who peeked from their doorways to look at an obvious outsider, and some children, hands full of what I know elsewhere in the Caribbean as "gnips," but which are called *mamacillo* here, a fleshy grapelike fruit the size of a golf ball and a favorite of young and old.

As I munched on gnips, bought from a teenager on horseback, I wandered the cobbled streets, lined with beige-to-pink stone buildings in almost perfect examples of 17th-century building: tiled roofs, iron grills caging the windows, intricate lintels over the doors. The entire city is a museum worth seeing (in spite of the heat of the town).

Most tours will plan a visit to the **Brunet Palace,** at the "top" of town, near **La Iglesia de la Candelaria de la Popa,** which was started in 1726. Inside the palace, the riches of colonial Cuba have been preserved. You can wander past elegant furniture, religious paintings, jewelry and jewel cases, and elegant chandeliers. Note the peaked wood ceilings (built so the heat would rise) and the arched doorways to allow for the breeze. Some of the typical Cuban adaptations of European styles are obvious in the furniture, with wood frames filled with woven reed backs and seats so that breezes could circulate. Tiled floors are also impressive. The home was built in the 1750s, in the Spanish style adapted for West Indian living, with open patios. As you walk around town, ask your guide to point out the houses of the Malibran Segartes and Ortiz families, also good examples of colonial homes of wealthy settlers. The former Convent of Santa Ana has become a school of the Revolution.

• • •

PLAYA ANCON, about 15 km (20 minutes' drive) from Trinidad, on the south coast, has a few beach hotels. One, with no pool, is the same style as

Pasacaballo; another, **Costasur** has pool, beachside location, and some tourist amenities.

• • •

THE ZAPATA PENINSULA, about 100 miles south of Habana and only 25 miles west of Cienfuegos, is an intriguing and dramatic area of swamp land that has been set aside as a nature preserve. Noted since Taino Indian days for its crocodiles, the swamps are still home for an impressive collection. Now the area is developed, with attention to ecology, as a resort, with several cabins, a few restaurants (*Boca de la Laguna* and *Pio Cua* are two), and an unusual hotel. To the east of the Zapata Peninsula is Playa Giron, known to Cubans as the "primera derrota del imperialismo en America," and to Americans as the Bay of Pigs.

Guama Tourist Village, the hotel, takes its name from an Indian hero who fought the Spaniards. Reached by a 45-minute boat trip through La Laguna del Tesoro (Treasure Lake), the resort was started in 1960, opened in 1961, and is the result of Cuban ingenuity in dredging islands out of a crocodile-infested lagoon. (The crocodiles are now caged and cultivated at what you will be shown as a tourist site, where you take the boat for Guama). Your thatched hut, built in Taino Indian style, will be on one of 7 small islands. Before you picture a primitive spot, know that every unit has modern plumbing, air-cooling, comfortable beds, and the option to row your bungalow's rowboat to the main dining and dancing area or to walk along the boardwalks that weave around, linking the islands in the lagoon. Gaining a reputation for excellent fishing, Guama is a unique resort—the only one of its kind in the Caribbean. There's an Indian Museum, with life-sized bronze-colored Taino Indians in frozen action poses, on one of the islands. (The Indians are the work of Rita Longa.) You can row to the museum or go on the motor launch that brings you to the village. (The name of "my" boat on my first trip was *Alcatraz*.)

• • •

THE ISLE OF YOUTH was known as the Isle of Pines when Amos Kidder Fiske wrote in *The West Indies* (1899), that the Isle "remained uninhabited until 1828, when a military section was established there. In recent years, it has become a health resort for consumptives." Sydney Clark noted, in his *All The Best in the Caribbean 1959,* that "at the conclusion of the Spanish-American War the U.S. acquired the island, or so it was thought, from Spain. More than 10,000 Americans settled there, foreseeing a rosy future for this American island, and many of them invested heavily in real estate and in building developments. But in 1926, the United States Congress, guided and goaded by the enlightened legal mind of Elihu Root, decided that the island was and is an obvious satellite of Cuba and not, like Puerto Rico, an annexable tidbit of territory. The ambitious plan of American settlers and promoters collapsed and this lovely isle of pines and grapefruit and cool trade winds and buried pirate treasure fell into a prolonged sleep. Finally Cuba realized that she had an uncorked gold mine of holiday treasure and began to bestir herself to develop it. This trend has reached its spectacular climax, so far, in the new hotel. The Cuban government built and owns this superlative resort and it would be hard to exaggerate its beauty or its luxurious refinements." Clark's text was written at the time of the Revolution, when the Isle of Pines gained local notoriety as the place where Fidel served the 20 months before his release from his 15-year sentence, imposed at the hospital-turned-court in Santiago, in 1953.

Today the Isle of Pines is called the Isle of Youth, in recognition of the 11,000 students who work and are schooled there.

El Colony has been a hotel since the 1950s, but in those days it didn't look like this one does. Completely modernized (by workmen who I suspected were political prisoners, when I visited the Isle of Pines in '78 to see the "new" hotel in progress), the Colony has been used as a base for *Scuba Cuba* holidays. With all the modern touches—rooms with view, pool, mealtime buffets, and beach-oriented holidays—watersports enthusiasts have the opportunity to enjoy some exciting underwater sights.

SANTIAGO DE CUBA

Santiago de Cuba is known as the "hot spot" of the country—partly because of the weather in this east end valley bowl, partly because of the sentiments of the *mambises,* the field workers whose uprisings against the Spanish provided the strength for the eventual overthrow of the colonial power, and partly because this is where the Revolution got its start.

Erna Fergusson, in her *Cuba,* published in 1946, points out that the city was popular with North Americans, who used to enjoy riding "out to San Juan Hill, where Teddy Roosevelt charged; El Caney, where the Rough Riders landed; Daiquiri, of mixed memories [the beach that gave rise to the famous Barcardi rum drink which the U.S. Navy claims to have named], and Santiago itself, where our General William Shafter accepted the surrender of Spain's General Toral." Fergusson notes that "Santigueros will never forgive or forget that the United States and not Cuban troops marched in to conquer the city, and it was a Yank and not a Cuban who took the Spaniard's sword. Indeed the whole episode of surrender and occupation [in the Spanish-American War] was marked by our national genius for doing things wrong. Our officers even neglected to invite Cuban generals to participate in the surrender ceremonies." I heard some of the same comments from my Cubatur guides during my visit.

Santiago de Cuba is at the southeast end of the country, almost 2 hours' Cubana flight from Habana and about 13 hours' drive on the 8-lane highway that will eventually stretch from one end of the country to the other and already goes most of the way between the capital and the country's third oldest city.

HOTELS IN SANTIAGO have their own personalities. Where you stay will depend on where your tour operator puts you.

Casa Grande • *Plaza de la Catedral* • sits on the corner of the Plaza, diagonally across from the cathedral and is quite seedy, but very prominent. The 5th-floor open-air cabaret has music most evenings; the hotel has the aura of ages past. Historic but lacking all the modern conveniences, Casa Granda (sic) was described by Erna Fergusson, in her book *Cuba* (1946), as "Santiago's great tourist hotel, the Casa Granda, and that is not a misspelling of Grande, but the name of a family. Casa Granda's big time was when Grace Line Steamers put in regularly, bringing North Americans."

Balcon del Caribe • *near El Morro Fort* • sits atop a cliff at the shore. The 2-story blocks of rooms opened in May 1978. There's a pool for entertainment as well as an active fishing pier and nightclub. San Pedro del Mar, which opened in the '40s and is a popular open-air nightclub for music with beer or rum, is a short walk from the hotel.

La Gran Piedra • *about an hour's ride in special mountain bus* • is said to have a spectacular view. Some tours include a visit to this outpost.

Las Americas • *Santiago* • was one of the first new hotels, built in the early '70s. It is home for many groups who pass through town, but the lack of pool or any cooling-off place other than the dining rooms makes it a step below the *Hotel Versalles*. Rooms are simply but adequately furnished; they stretch out in a 2-story box just off the main road.

Hotel Santiago de Cuba • *mid-city* • is a 15-story high-rise, with facilities built under a Cubanacan partnership that creates an international-style hotel. Bedrooms are modern, comfortable, and viewful, especially if you have a suite with a balcony. Restaurants serve what you will quickly recognize is Cuban standard tourist fare. The pool is the social center; there are two tennis courts. For evening, there's a disco and piano bar. *Hotel.*

Hotel Versalles • *on a hillside, off the main road between the airport and the center of the city* • has an African atmosphere created with dark wood and raffia Cuban country-style furniture and an open, airy feeling. Newest rooms are in 2-story units near the older cabana rooms that stretch off from the center lobby building. The air-conditioned rooms have T.V. and refrigerators. In the lobby, there's a Tourist Shop. There's a good-sized pool, with poolside bar down a few steps at the other end where you can get a good view overlooking Santiago. The air-conditioned dining room under some of the living units was super-cooled during my visit (you almost need a sweater); the food was typical of the Santiago area and European tourist-oriented. Cubanacan uses this property for their tours. *Hotel.*

PLACES WORTH FINDING IN SANTIAGO DE CUBA are legion. Not only does the city's role in the Revolution yield at least a half dozen important places, but there are museums for colonial furniture plus parks and cemeteries that shed light on the Cuban revolutionary spirit.

Bosca de los Heroes, not far from Las Americas hotel, is a monument to Che Guevara. It's on the spot where Che spoke to the Santiago people for the last time. The pebbled path that you meander up to reach the angular monument on the small rise represents the rivers in the mountains of Bolivia. The trees that have been planted on the site symbolize the woods in which he was lost, and the marble slabs that make up the monument are from Bayamon. Images and names of people important to the Revolution are etched into the planes and panels, but you have to get close to the blocks to read the inscriptions. The names are of those who went with Che to Bolivia.

Fort Yarayo, built in 1868 for defense from the pirates, seems small and misplaced at its location in the outskirts of old Santiago. At that time, however, the sea filled this area.

Santa Ifigenia Cemetery stretches for miles. A hot spot in a hot city, the cemetery's main appeal is to those on a Revolution pilgrimage. The Jose Marti tomb, to the left as you face the main entrance, is lined with stones onto which some of his sayings are etched. There are 28 stones: 14 leading to the tomb and 14 behind it. Among the thoughts are those he voiced at Cajobayo when he said, "He who thinks of himself does not love his country." At Playitas, "The people are mixed with the blood of the men." At Mijial, "There is no sermon like life itself." At Rio Guayabo, "The government should be born out of the people." At Palenque, "When a people divide, they kill themselves." And at Cabezedas de Ciguatos, "Liberty is the definitive religion." Marti, considered a fighter for all Latin America, died on April 11, 1895. His tomb was started in 1949 but not dedicated until 1951. The 6 women standing around the outside of the dome represent the 6 provinces of his time, and are marked on the inside by the 6 shields of those provinces, which were Camaguey (with cattle raising), Oriente (with fruit), Pinar del Rio, Habana (bee and key), Matanzas, and Las Villas. As you look through to the flag-covered box below, note that the sun always hits the tomb because, as was explained to me, "he did not want to be in the dark." I was also told that he wanted fresh flowers and a flag on his tomb (the flowers were missing when I visited).

If you enter through the main gate at the cemetery, you will find the tomb of Carlos Manuel de Cespedes, the father of the country, straight ahead on the left. (Between the Jose Marti Monument and the de Cespedes tomb, there's a monument for Thomas Estrada Palma whom, I was told, "sold Cuba out" to the Americans. He lived 1835–1908.)

The Bacardis you pass as you wander around are of the rum family. Emilio Bacardi, who was mayor of Santiago in the early 1900s, was a fighter for independence and is acclaimed in today's Cuba for the museum in his name in downtown Santiago.

Jose Marti district, a community of prefab cement buildings on the outskirts of town, was the Soviet Union's response to the damage of Hurricane Flora, which swept through this area in 1968. The Soviets dedicated the factory in which all the cement slabs were made; 45,000 people live in the community, which has 3 primary schools, 2 secondary schools, 6 day-care centers, and a "Friendship School," where each classroom bears a country's name.

Santiago University, a modern complex of buildings between the Jose Marti district and the center of Santiago, was opened on October 10, 1947. At the time it "was built by a private society," to open with 5 areas of study available to those who paid to attend. The university was recognized by the government in 1951, offers 26 courses of study, and is crowned with a sign that says "Viva el Internacionalismo Proletario."

Ateneo Armondo Maestre, perched on a hill not far from Hotel Versalles, on the outskirts of the city, is the modern sports center. If there's anything going on, see if you can attend. Sports events will be entertaining, but the place was at its best during one of my visits when the *Sierra Maestra* (local newspaper) was having its special cultural festival.

Granjita Siboney, about 20 minutes' drive from downtown Santiago, along a route that is marked with monuments to revolutionary heroes, is a farmhouse museum. There are 6 monuments on the left and 20 on the right as you drive out to the farm; each monument has its own personality and purpose. A couple of them are shelters for the bus stop. The route was dedicated in 1973, on the 20th anniversary of the assault on the Moncada barracks. Abel Santamaria rented the property as a chicken farm, building the coops along the street to cover the cars and weapons that the Revolutionaries were assembling on the site. Your guide will point out the well in which the guns were hidden. It was at this spot that the plans were laid for the assault on the Moncada barracks (July 26, 1953). The place has been a museum since 1964 and in the several small rooms, you can see pictures of Cuba at the time of the Moncada, including a picture of a U.S. Marine urinating on the statue of Jose Marti, Fidel arguing in front of the U.S. Embassy, and a young Raul leading a strike at the university. There are issues of *El Acusador* of July 1952, the underground newspaper, with articles about the times.

Moncada Garrison has become a symbol of the Revolution, as the place Fidel, Abel Santamaria, and Raul planned to attack when they were captured in 1953. Fidel and Raul were tried, found guilty, and sent to prison on the Isle of Pines. The attack on the arsenal of the barracks was planned to gather arms for the Revolution, but Fidel was apprehended as he approached the barracks in his car. It was carnival week, and the arms they had sought to capture had been moved to make sleeping quarters for additional troops, brought into Santiago de Cuba to keep the merrymaking residents under control. After two hours of fighting, Fidel ordered withdrawal; Raul also withdrew from his base at the Palace of Justice. The Garrison is now a school, with the wing to the left as you face the vast sun-bleached yellow fort housing a museum over the former arsenal (which is now an infirmary for the schoolchildren). There's a model of the barracks and the nearby buildings showing the Batista officers' club (now the office of the Department of Education), Colonel Chaviano's house (now the offices for the TV station), and officers' and soldiers' houses, now used by families. The Military Hospital has become the School of Dentistry. In the first room to the right homage is paid to the Heroes of Independence: Carlos Manuel Cespedes, Ignacio Agramonte, Antonio Maceo, Maximo Gomez, and Jose Marti, all of whom waged their wars against the Spaniards. The explosion of the *Maine* in Habana's harbor, during the turn-of-the-century war of independence from Spain "was the excuse of the United States to enter the war," I was told. "They made intervention in Cuba for three years." The life and activities of Julio Antonio Mella, founder of the Communist Party in Cuba in 1925, are presented in another room, where I also noted that 1940 to 1950 was a "time of prostitution, gambling, assassination of leaders, and longshoremen leaders in Cuba," and "the corruption in Cuba was very great." At this time, Fidel represented workers as well as students. My guide explained that "Moncada was the only way to solve the problems of the country; Fidel showed us how bad things really were," and as you walk through the exhibits, you can note the points he made. There are photographs of revolutionaries, captured and dead. My guide noted that there were no bullet holes or blood on the uniforms although the soldiers were found dead—in the Moncada courtyard. The truck in which Fidel was brought to the provisional prison, in what is now the memorial to Abel Santamaria, is in another courtyard. As you look closely at the display cabinets, you can note the "ammunition," *cocteles molotov* made from Pepsi and olive oil bottles. Around the walls are pictures of Fidel and other revolutionaries. There is a picture of Fidel, after 22 months on the Isle of Pines (now a popular scuba resort); pictures of meetings with Melba Hernandez and Haydee Santamaria (Abel's sister), the two women who were in the mountains with Fidel (Melba was, for a while, Cuban ambassador to Vietnam and Haydee also has a high government position). There are pictures of training in Mexico, and "gathering funds for the new struggle," as well as some *Granma* landing uniforms, those worn when, on December 2, 1956, troops landed at the Golfo de Guacanayabo to head into the Sierra Maestra. A map in one room shows the routes of troops from the *Granma* landing, and copies of the underground newspapers, plus the routes of Che Guevara and Camilo Cienfuegos, who were charged with "giving the war from the east to the west" of Cuba, i.e., bringing the war to Habana and beyond. That project took about two months, from August 21, 1958, to October 7, 1958, and culminates in pictures of Fidel in Habana, talking to the people in the square around the statue of Maximo Gomez, a Dominican who fought for Cuban independence (the square is where Batista's former palace has become the Museum of the Revolution).

Museo Abel Santamaria, behind the Moncada Garrison, is a memorial museum, opened in 1975, at the former Saturnino Lora Hospital. During the attack on the Moncada Garrison, this is where Abel Santamaria, the man who bought and stocked the "chicken farm" at Siboney, waited with his men to play their part in the three-pronged attack. The messenger sent to tell them that Fidel had surrendered never reached them, and the group was captured in the hospital rooms used "to hospitalize paying patients." They are pointed out by the guide. "As was typical in those days, these patients were better cared for," I was told. The walls that separated private patients rooms have been knocked out. As you wander from one to the next you are bombarded with photos supporting Fidel's progress with his 5 projects: Tierra, Vivienda, Desempleo, Industria, and Salud (land, housing, unemployment, industry, health). Photos showing neon lights of the Savoy Bar Club, Johnny's Bar Club, and all the evils of old Habana share space with photos of old and young in abject poverty. Photos of Esso and Texaco gas pumps are prominent on one wall, along with a "Land of Sugar" ad by U.S. Rainbow candy wafers seem hopelessly out of place in a room that shows children sitting on the floors in schoolrooms, old people in decaying buildings, and all the evils the Revolution lists from 1929 to 1958. Juxtaposed with coming-out pictures of Cuban debutantes are the wide eyes of starving children, bellies distended, plight obvious.

The focal point of the museum is the room where Fidel was tried, a room that had been the teaching room "for 20 or so nurses" in 1953. On October 16, 1953, the teaching room was used to "carry out the trial of Fidel who had already confessed to being involved in the Moncada Garrison attack." The trial began in the Palace of Justice (now the offices of the *Tribuno Provincial Popular*), "but in the third session Fidel was taken out and prevented from trial." From here Fidel was sentenced to 15 years, and taken to the Isle of Youth/

Pines. My guide explained that Santiago justice used a trick (saying that Abelardo Crespo Arias, an important witness, was too ill to be moved from the hopsital) to turn the trial of Fidel into a private one. Fidel was his own defense—and his chair and the chair of the unused defense provided by the Batista state are pointed out. Comment was made about the grandeur of the furniture—"typical of that used by the bourgeoisie." This is the room where Fidel gave the famous speech that included the much quoted phrase, "Condenadme no importa, La Historia me absolverá" (Condemning me is not important, history will absolve me). The memorial garden and monument to Abel Santamaria was established in late 1978.

Casa de Frank y Joseu Pais, on a side street in the old part of Santiago, is a small museum within four humble rooms. This was the home of Frank Pais Garcia, a revolutionary who organized the underground in Santiago to meet Fidel in the Sierra Maestra mountains after his *Granma* boat landing at the shores of the Golfo de Guacanayabo. The name and face of Frank Pais are prominent in Santiago and throughout the country. His death at 22, and his contribution to the Revolution, make him a hero, praised by Fidel and revered by the Santiagueros. Frank Pais died in 1957, captured and killed on the street as he left an underground meeting at a colleague's house. "Typical of his personality, he sent the others out before him; he alone was captured and killed," I was told. Each year, on the anniversary of his death, hundreds follow the path of his coffin. On the day of his burial, his casket was covered with the Cuban flag and the 26 July flag; the 26 July song and the national anthem are sung during the march, as they were sung at his funeral.

Frank Pais Garcia was born on December 7, 1935; he lived in the house with his two brothers (Joseu was also a revolutionary; the third brother, still living, was not mentioned much). His father was a Baptist preacher; his mother died in 1977. The exhibits throughout the small house hold his school records (he was a brilliant student who went on to become a teacher, a profession he left when underground activities took too much of his time); he was beloved by his friends (and by fellow Cubans). Frank Pais met with Fidel twice—once in Mexico after Fidel left the Isle of Pines/Youth, and the second time in the Sierra Maestra, when his well-trained revolutionary forces joined those of Fidel.

Knowing Spanish is essential for full understanding of the young man who was arrested for protesting policies of the government; he attacked hunters' clubs for the arms to train the guerrilla forces that were to wage the Revolution. In the courtyard of the humble home, a garden has been planted with flowers and trees that have significance for the Revolution.

Casa Antonio Maceo, a small house on another side street not far from the main plaza, holds pictures and charts significant to Spanish Revolutionary Cuba. Maceo was a revolutionary who took part in 800 battles in the Ten Years' War (1868–1878) and 119 in the 1885 War, and was wounded 29 times. His accomplishments in leading troops over 1900 kms from Santiago to Habana, from October 22, 1895, to January 22, 1896, are noted and documented on a map to the right as you enter the house. Maceo was killed in 1896. He was a mulatto, "conscious of the racism of his time." Look around at the 19th-century house in which he was born. It has the original ceiling, and the original bricks are on the floor of the small room to the left of the entrance. In the small garden in the back you can note the U.S. printing machine, Washington Press, R. Hoe & Co., New York 1864 #2556, on which the revolutionary *El Cubano Libre* was printed.

Museo de Clandestinidad, in the former police station that was captured by Frank Pais on November 30, 1956, faces a plaza that is the site of one of Santiago's most traditional festivals, the Fiesta del Tivoli, a May festival with costumes and customs of earlier days. Dances and food are part of the festivities, but the exhibits in the museum project a serious time in Cuban history. (The 2nd-floor breeze-swept balconies provide one of the best views of old and new Santiago.) Among the exhibits that focus on Frank Pais and his underground activities are photographs of the meeting of Frank and Fidel in the Sierra Maestra. *New York Times* reporter Ted Matthews's account (Sunday, February 27, 1957) of the meeting in the Sierra Maestra—the first word the people had that Fidel was still alive—is displayed, as well as the report by UPI reporter Francis MacCarthy headlined "Muerto Fidel Castro afirma la United Press," which I was advised by my guide—the sister of one of the martyrs—was done to mislead the Cuban people. There are photographs of *Granma*, the boat used for the landing, and a display of the instructions by Fidel to the Santiagueros about how to proceed after he and his men had taken the city in the name of the Revolution. In one of the display cases are the Cuban flag, *cocteles molotov* made with Hatuey beer bottles, the green uniform that was worn for the first time with the 26 de Julio red armband in the uprising of November 30, an assortment of medicines, pipe bombs, Esso can bombs, and other items used in the 25 months of struggle that resulted in Fidel Castro's leadership of Cuba.

Museo Emilio Barcardi, in downtown Santiago, "was founded by Emilio Bacardi Moreau in 1899, opened in this location in October 1927, reestablished in 1964 under the National Council of Culture of the Revolution, and reopened for the people in 1968." Bacardi, a member of the rum family, was mayor of Santiago around 1900 and a supporter of independence. (His tomb is pointed out in Santa Ifigenia Cemetery.) The main exhibits on the street level are about the Indian heritage, showing the early settlements of the Tainos and the Siboneys (sometimes spelled Ciboney). The maces and capes of conquistadors are displayed, as well as 16th-century banners—and a wooden Santiago (St. James) on his white horse, prancing in the middle of the revolutionary exhibits. The 1810–1898 years of *autonomismo* are shown in dark halls "because there was no light on life" in those years, I was told. In the room covering 1868 to 1878, the Ten Years' War, it was pointed out to me that "Fidel says he fought the same revolution—that the revolution never stopped from that time." Personal effects of leaders are displayed—their plates, tiles, any small thing pertaining to the lives of any of the leaders, including Cespedes. There is also another printing press used for the revolutionary paper *El Cubano Libre*. Mambises (field worker) goods, their shoes made from palm fronds, hide bags, etc., are displayed in recognition of the contribution of the field workers to the Revolution. A display of two colonial cannons and countless machetes, hung at impressive intervals—fencelike around the cannons—makes its own statement. Other rooms show comments about Cuba by American officials—Breckenridge, the Platt Amendment, etc.

Upstairs is a change from the revolutionary lessons, with displays of modern Cuban art as well as some of the original items in the Bacardi collection.

Look for some of the Cuban artists: Baldomera Fuentes (1809–1877), Joaquin Cuadras (1843–1875), Manuel Vincens; and portraits by Frederico Martinez (1828–1920). Jose Joaquin Tejada (1867–1943) was a Santiago painter. It's also worth inquiring about the huge painting showing Cortez in armor on landing in Cuba, painted by Juan Emilio Hernandez Giro (1882–1953).

Mueble Colonial, the home of Diego Velazquez, on the main plaza diagonally across from the Cathedral, is the oldest house in Cuba, and one of the oldest in Latin America. It was built for Velazquez, the Spanish explorer who settled Santiago, in the early 1500s. Intricate wood-beam-and-paint ceilings, wood-screened windows with window seats where the dwellers could watch the world outside without being seen, and impressive sconces (with Russian lightbulbs) set the tone. The house was opened as a museum in 1971 to show furniture and architecture, room by room, from the 16th century through the early 20th century. In the earliest rooms there are trunks, heavy Spanish furniture, and a painting of Diego Velazquez. Note the heavy wood wardrobe that served as a closet, and the table set with ceramic plates, assembled from pieces found near this site. The Cuban bedstead and chairs in the 17th-century room show the influence of Spain; the rest of the furniture in this room is genuinely Spanish. The tapestry representing the end of the 17th century may have been made in Cuba but is certainly woven with gold thread. (The room dividers are for the museum use; at the time of Velazquez, all the living was in one big, long room.) In the 19th-century room, all the furniture was made in Cuba, with the exception of a marble-top table. Spanish, French, and English influences are obvious, and Cuban silver is used in the plates and urns in the cabinet, although some of the pieces were worked in Germany. The gold storage area, uncovered during recent excavations and remodeling, will be pointed out. It is on the far side of the courtyard, straight ahead from the entrance.

A second home has been acquired as part of the museum. It is entered from the Diego Velazquez home by walking through the carriage courtyard (look right, to the carriage doors that open out to the side street). There is Cuban furniture in most of the rooms, with styles similar to those known in Europe, except for the cane backs in chairs and settees for air circulation. In the Victorian room, the heavy sleigh bed was made in Santiago. "The father of the country slept in this bed"—that is, Manuel de Cespedes. I learned in the 20th-century room that the "bourgeoisie imported furniture from all over the world because they wanted to be in fashion" and "then is broken the development of Cuban furniture," which had filled the rooms from the earlier centuries. "The bourgeoisie show in this way how strong they are," I heard as I looked around the room filled with incredibly ornate Victoriana that looks absurd in this socialist society. (The piece de resistance was a pair of urns, with figures of Uncle Tom characters.)

Castillo del Morro, the fort at one side of the entrance to the harbor at Santiago de Cuba, is a 20-minute drive from the downtown area, past the new hotel (*Balcon del Caribe*) and the '40s-built *San Pedro del Mar,* a nightclub/dance place by the sea. The fort was built by the Spanish from 1630 to 1642. When Santiago was the capital of Cuba, this was the hub of activity, the fortress from which the pirates and others were bombarded, and the repository for arms and goods. It was past this fort that Cortez sailed on his way to Mexico, that Francisco Pizarro headed to conquer Peru, that Gonzalo Jimenez went to found

Colombia, and that Juan Ponce de Leon headed to Puerto Rico before he went on to Florida; and it was inside these walls, according to one of the pamphlets printed and distributed by Cubatur, that "many of the patriots of our war for independence were imprisoned and executed. . . ."

The fort is now a museum, restaurant, and recreation area, well worth the drive out to see the view along the way as well as the pink cast to the stones, the massive walls, the drawbridge over which you enter, and the museum. (The original town was east of El Morro. The mosquitoes drove them to the present location.)

VARADERO

This resort area is mostly a 45-km-long peninsula, "discovered in 1920 by French millionaire Irenee Dupont [sic]," who was, in fact, an American millionaire. The peninsula, with its powdery sand beach that runs almost 12 miles, was the playground of the very rich. In its pre-Revolution heyday, the villas that prickled the shore were second (or third) homes for wealthy Cubans and Americans. After the Revolution, when the government was spreading the wealth, the homeowners were given their choice of residence. Some Cubans chose to live in their Varadero homes and "give the other property to the government." Americans left. Today, the former private homes of Varadero have been grouped as hotels, with a new central building, usually at the beach, for restaurant, bar, and recreation area. The government plan for Varadero was to move the residents to the new city of Santa Marta, built on the cell system inland from the beach, and to turn all of Varadero into a tourist complex. Since the Revolution, cluster living is the communist/socialist goal.

LODGINGS at Varadero are growing faster than sugarcane in the fields, mostly as cooperative ventures arranged through Cubanacan and foreign investors, but also planned by the government. Built as hotels before the Revolution, the Internacional, the Oasis, and Kawama have been spruced up to meet modern demands, as have many villa resorts assembled from former private homes. In addition, more than 2000 new rooms in international-style hotels have been opened, or under construction, since 1990. Among the newcomers are **Hotel Paradiso** (210 rooms), **Hotel Palmeras** (501 rooms), **Hotel Tuxpan** (235 rooms), **Modulo Las Perles** (80 rooms), **Modulo Los Caneles** (60 rooms), and **Gaviota II** (105 rooms). Big news is made by Spain's **Melia Varadero,** to open this winter, and **Club Varadero,** operated by the successful Jamaica-based *SuperClubs,* on the all-inclusive formula inaugurated by John Issa. This is its first season.

Lodgings embroider the inland side of a spectacular long strand of white sand as soft as talcum powder, making it easy for visitors to stroll from one to another. In addition to the multi-story hotels, there are dozens of villa properties for self-catering, which is a vacation style that Europeans know and enjoy.

Since most Americans will be visiting Varadero as part of a group tour, the hotel base will depend on the tour operators' negotiations. You can roam from hotel to hotel, however, either by walking along the beach, taking the bus, or hiring a taxi—if you can find one. A bus runs the gamut of hotels, and a tourist "train" wiggles along the route at the height of the winter season (and perhaps at other times).

HOTELS IN VARADERO: Many of the newest hotels are comparable to deluxe and first-class hotels throughout the world. All hotels stretch along the beach, or just inland from the shore, so no further address is given in the comment below.

Arenas Blancas • *near the beach west of the Internacional* • a resort of formerly private houses, is one of the better hotels because the homes were elegant. "These people really knew how to live," a Cuban commented as we walked through one of the units. Arenas has its restaurant and entertainment area in a large former home, built in Spanish colonial style, with tile and flourishes, with a huge clay water urn, called a *tinajon*, in the gardened courtyard. The houses scattered around the linking lawns hold most of the 150 bedrooms; the main house has the Ping-Pong table, Tourist Shop, and a place to play chess, dominoes, or whatever. *Villas.*

Cabanas del Sol • *near the beach in the eastern area* • is villas with 2 or 3 bedrooms, with the option for bicycling, "nautical activities," and other resort activities arranged through the Cubatur representative. (The property abuts the houses grouped as Villa Cuba, at the east end of the strip.) *Villas.*

Caribe • *on the beach* • is a recently built 3-story hotel, which has been used mostly by Eastern European and Russian groups. Its public areas are around the central pool, which fits into the pocket of the U-shape. The beach runs along the "top" of the U. When I looked at the property, the game room was the scene of a boisterous game of pool, and there were pinball machines waiting for play. *Hotel.*

Club Varadero • *on the beach* • is Cuba's first western-style all-inclusive property, following the pattern well known in Jamaica and other Caribbean islands. In early 1991, Jamaican John Issa announced his plans to take over the property, rebuilt it to SuperClub's style, and open for winter '91–'92. Intended for the Canadian and European markets, the hotel will be ready for Americans as soon as the gates are opened. For details on this property, contact SuperClubs office in the U.S., Canada, and Jamaica. The *Caribbean Newsletter* (page 9) will have facts when the property opens. *Resort.*

Internacional • *at the middle of the stretch of accommodations* • was a popular modern hotel when it was built in the years before the Revolution. Some of the bedrooms are big, with marble baths; most are comfortable, not lavish, and some have sea view. Used primarily by groups from Canada in winter, the public facilities at the hotel include the pool (site for beginners' scuba lessons), the restaurants, with an inside air-conditioned room and a terrace in the sun used in the winter months when the international toursist season is underway, a Tourist Shop, a game room with children's activities, Cubatur activities desk (where you can sign up for tours), and that great expanse of beach just off the terrace. (The small statues of Columbus on one side and Queen Isabella wishing him farewell on the other seemed out of place to me, in today's Cuba.) The nightclub has the area's top show. *Hotel.*

Kawama • *between the western part of the beach and Laguna de Paso Malo* • is a pre-Revolution hotel, adapted to the modern concept and several small cabanas. The stone building with brick-colored tile roof is the original hotel. There's a lot of variety in architecture, but there's a congenial Caribbean hotel feeling at the thatched-roofed shelter that serves as a beachside bar. If you are not staying here, drop by for a Cuban beer mid-afternoon. *Hotel.*

Oasis • *on the far western end of the string* • is one of the pre-Revolution hotels, on a beach that will not seem like much after you've scuffed through the powder of the main strand. This end of the beach has some seaweed and rocks underfoot off-shore, and seems to be subject to the vagaries of wind and surf. Rooms are adequate, and the patio that is sometimes the dance floor on starry evenings has a small bohio for serving beer and rum drinks by the beach. There's the usual restaurant, Tourist Shop, and game room for guests who base here. *Hotel.*

Hotel Paradiso • *on the beach* • is a multi-story complex built for European visitors, adhering to the style popular on the Spanish coast. With a pool for the on-premise focus, and sea view rooms preferred, the hotel offers many resort facilities and plenty of activity. *Hotel.*

Hotel Sol Palmeras • *at the beach* • is a huge new complex with air-conditioned modern rooms in multi-story buildings, as well as very comfortable suites, gathered around a pool-patio. The restaurants offer variety in decor (but much of the same tedious Cuban-style food); watersports, tours, and other activities are easily arranged through the tour guides that accommodate groups from Europe and elsewhere. *Resort.*

Villa Cuba • *near the beach at the eastern sector.* • is several former homes on the short streets that stretch straight back from the beach, at the eastern end of the peninsula, not too far from Las Americas, the former du Pont mansion. Most of the privately owned furniture has been removed, either by the former owners or by the government, to be replaced with functional tables, chairs, beds, and bureaus. Although each house has its own kitchen, meals are rarely served "at home" unless a Cuban family or group of friends has rented the entire villa (one reason may be that food rationing makes meals difficult). There is a central area at the beach for meals and entertainment. *Villas.*

Villa Tortuga • *near the beach at the east end of the lagoon* • is former homes and small villas that in their pre-Revolution life might have been middle-class vacation homes. By comparison to the villas used as part of Villa Cuba, these places are small and boxy. *Cottages.*

RESTAURANTS IN VARADERO are developing as the tourist business warrants.

Albacora • *Calle 59 at Ave. 1 May* • is a good choice for seafood. Not only are the surroundings atmospherically simple, with fishnets, shells made into lampshades, and blue and white decor, but there's the opportunity to dine on the seaside deck, in the sunshine that is one reason I like Varadero. Try to get a table near the huge sea grape tree that shades the deck.

Castel Nuovo • *in a former home on the inland side of the road that runs along the shore* • just after you cross the bridge to the resort area, was recommended for excellent food in air-conditioned surroundings. I have not eaten here, but was told that cuisine is similar to that offered at Las Americas, at prices to match.

Las Americas is touted (not advertised, in this Communist country) with the comment "The du Pont family used to spend their winters here in unbelievable luxury. Why don't you come for lunch?" And you should. The service aspires to rival Cuba's best, even when you fill the only table in one of the several small dining rooms that now occupy the library and parlors on the main floor. The menu lists a complete range of fish, pork, eggs, and seafood—and my sampling was excellent, when I dined in the former library (amid shelves of English books that included Rose Macaulay's *Staying with Friends,* and *America Conquers Britain* by Ludwell Denney. *Let Them Live* and *Smile Please* stood next to *Sugar Facts & Figures 1952* and *Webster's Collegiate Dictionary*). The view out the window of the spectacular sea glimmering under warm sun was sharp contrast to the elegance of my surroundings. A full-course lunch or dinner can run about 20 pesos per person, with the entrees hovering around 8 pesos. Before or after your meal, weave your way down the stairs to the right as you enter to the downstairs bar that now occupies the former du Pont wine cellar. Your Cuban beer or rum will be quaffed in surroundings that have known the world's best wines.

Kastellito • *a small house on the beach near the center of the town of Varadero* • serves drinks and snacks on its porches. Because the house had character, this small spot has more atmosphere than most. It's a good place for late afternoon sipping while the sun goes down.

Coppelia ice cream is available at the center of town, near Ocho Mil Baquillas (8000 lockers), which is the government-built underground parking area with—you guessed it—8000 lockers where Cubans who come out for a swim can park their belongings. (Note the small turn-of-the-century hotel near the park on the inland side of the road. This and some of the other old Varadero buildings have been refurbished as restaurants or small hotels.)

Cueva del Pirata • *east of Las Americas* • is the area's most interesting nightspot, in my opinion. Definitely for tourists, the Pirate's Cave has real atmosphere. It is *inside* a cave, complete with nooks for sitting and sipping in niches in the rocks; waiters dress like pirates. (I could do without the huge phony spiders and trunks of gold that are tucked into other spots.) There's a floor show, and a deafening din when the music plays (rock surroundings don't offer ideal acoustics). Your tour may include a night here, but if not, take a cab to see what the place is all about.

PLACES WORTH FINDING IN VARADERO are linked with the sea or nature (as with the **Bellamar caves** near Matanzas). Most of the hotels have a tour desk, where a Cubatur representative will make arrangements for you to go scuba diving, on a glass-bottom boat ride, on an all-day boat safari with picnic lunch, to Guama on the south coast by bus, to Habana, including lunch and tours, or on an overnight excursion to Habana, including the show at Tropicana.

A tour of **Las Americas,** the home and grounds of the former estate of Irenee du Pont is the top attraction in the Varadero area when you want to get off the beach. The private lake that was the du Pont "swimming pool" has been outfitted with a bar on stilts in the center, and pedal boats and rowboats you can hire to reach it. The golf course that ranges around the grounds needs a lot of work, which it may get when the people of the Revolution find they have enough leisure time to play golf. The mansion, with its red plush, heavy wood pieces in the rooms on the main floor, still has some of the du Pont furniture, "which the du Ponts chose to leave here." Note the heavy wood ceilings, the marble floors, the huge open doorways—and the rings and rods from which heavy pull drapes used to hang. On the second floor you will see the bedrooms of the family; notice a glass-topped table with 1928 photographs of life as the du Ponts knew it—when they were building their mansion, and when they entertained the first guests. Much is made of Mr. du Pont's hobby of raising iguanas and using them for "iguana fights." There are a dozen or more photographs of the wealthy wandering around in their tropical white suits, and sometimes in more casual (always proper) attire. The only caption left intact on one of the iguana pictures reads "The competitor [no name] crouching to receive the attack." The house was built at a reported cost of 600,000 pesos; Mr. du Pont acquired the property "on the pretense of starting a hemp plantation"; he used it to entertain his friends and as a vacation home for his family. (Paint is peeling in a daughter's room and I noticed that Mr. du Pont's bedroom has the best view and breeze.) Be sure to go up to the top floor "cocktail terrace," which offers a breathtaking view in surroundings that seem Moorish.

SPORTS: Fishing has always been a Cuban favorite. During my first visit after the Revolution, in August 1976, I went to sea on the prototype of what has become a Cuban fishing boat, used for the Hemingway International Tournament, which was reinstituted for the first time after the Revolution. The *Pirana,* as the fishing boat is called, has fighting chairs and a flying bridge in a style reminiscent of Hemingway's fishing boat, the 38-foot *Pilar.* U.S., Venezuelan, Soviet, and Cuban teams participated in the Hemingway Tournament, which took place in about 20 miles of sea off Habana. The 60 boats ranged in size from 31 to 65 feet.

Scuba has developed in Cuba following professional standards. Some of the areas have been explored by American divers. Facilities are excellent on the Isle of Youth, off Trinidad, where the drop-off is not too far from the coast, and at some areas near Varadero where arrangements are made through your hotel to depart from the Base Nautica, the Yacht Club. There is a tourism official in charge of the "activity of scuba diving at a national level," and you can be sure—as with other projects that are official policies of Cuba's Communist government—the development will be orderly and for group tours.

Spear fishing is restricted in most areas, according to the government's conservation plans. At some areas, such as Cayo Lago off the Isle of Youth, where there is plenty of fish and lobster, spear fishing is permitted. There are strictly imposed seasons for lobster progging, so that the supply has time to regenerate, thus avoiding the depletion of stock that has pushed prices sky-high and made local langouste scarce in many places elsewhere in the Caribbean.

Birdwatching follows suggestions made by American birder George Harrison, who spotted 95 species in the Zapata Swamp and noted 25 endemic birds. Tours will house participants at the Zapata area as well as in the mountains.

Physical fitness programs are part of the regimentation and training for youths in the Revolution. Special sports complexes have been built in many cities around the country and the sports facilities and the housing are used to accommodate visiting teams for sports holidays. Eastern European groups and other countries sympathetic to Cuba's Communism are already using these facilities.

TREASURES AND TRIFLES are not an integral part of the Cuban economy these days. Stores for Cubans have very little merchandise and what is there is rationed. There are special stores for tourists in all the tourist hotels. In May 1978 the first "freeport" bazaar opened at the Habana Libre, to be followed by similar shops in other hotels housing international visitors. The average Cuban cannot buy in the Tourist Shops. You will find Eastern European crystal, Russian and Eastern European radios and other electronic equipment, Cuban rum and cigars, as well as some simple handicrafts, and a few other imports when shipments can be arranged. If Cubatur's plans continue, you can expect to find more in the Tourist Shops than I saw when I visited. You will find Cuban T-shirts, labeled "Tea-shirt" in one case I noticed where the shirts were made in China. Inquire especially about modern Cuban artwork, both ceramics and paintings.

Cuba 64, in old Habana, not far from the Cathedral Plaza, is a shop with a collection of handicrafts, some good, some novice quality. Plans are to upgrade the quality of the crafts, but no matter what is on display, the surroundings—an old colonial house—are attractive and worth the visit.

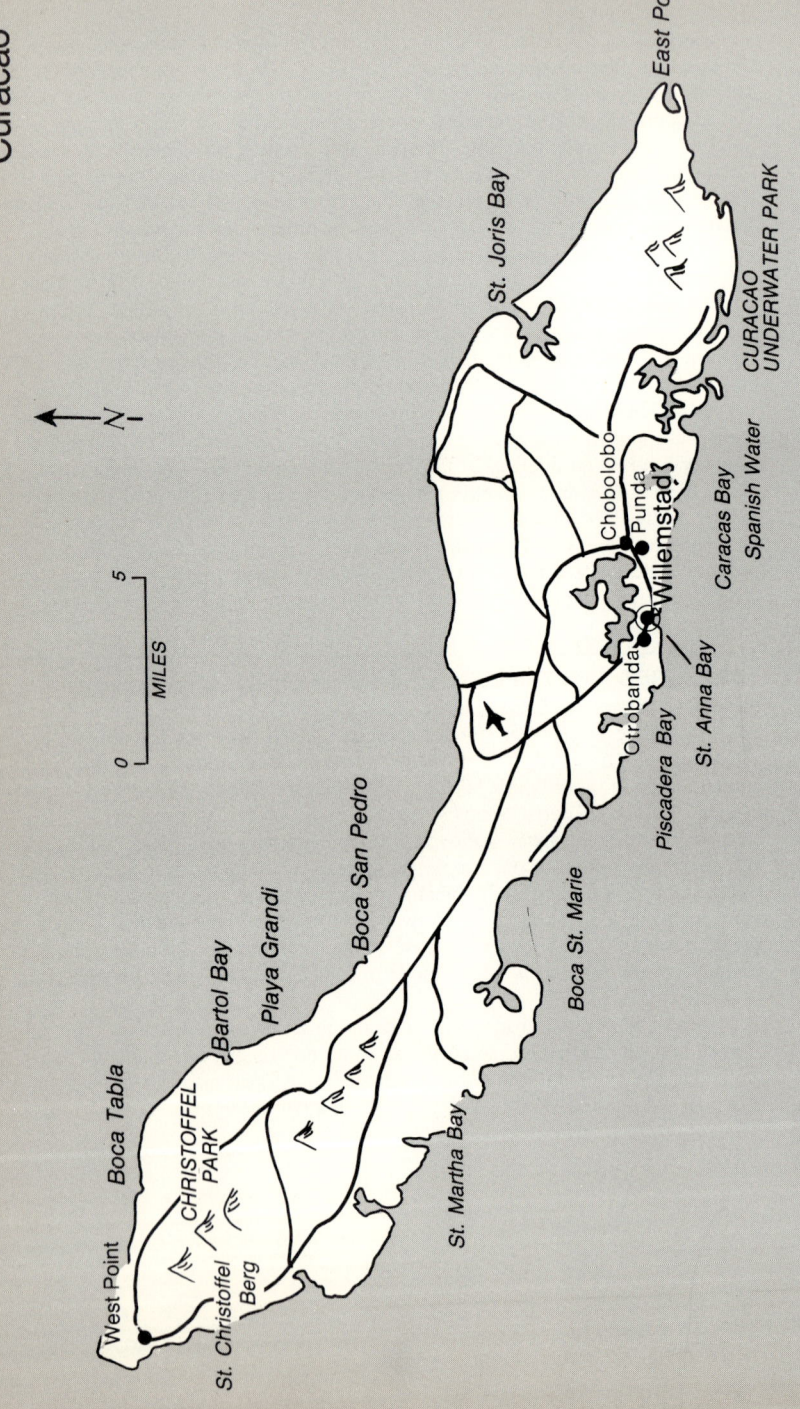

CURAÇAO

> Curaçao Tourist Board, Pietermaai, Willemstad, Curaçao, N.A., 011+599+961–6000, fax 599+961–2305; 330 Biscayne Blvd., Miami, FL 33132, T 305+374–5811; 400 Madison Ave., New York, NY 10022, T 212+751–8266 or 800+332–8266, fax 212+486–3024.

$ · · · US$1 = 1.77NAf
Unless otherwise noted, all references are to U.S. dollars.

Meridita's smile was nicer than the shrimp she brought me and the view from my perch at Westpunt made the dowdy surroundings at Playa Forti seem perfect. They didn't distract in any way from my eagerness to watch the sea below, and the children playing on the curve of sand that marks the boundary of Westpunt Baie. There's a church that punctuates the inland side of the road, and two visitors were waiting there for the bus as I curved into Playa Forti's parking area. Their scuba gear was propped against a nearby tree. We waved—and I picked them up for the ride back to Willemstad, after I had had my shrimp and a cool Heineken beer. Their bus had not yet arrived.

Meridita and I had a brief conversation when I asked her about life in the small village of Westpunt, far removed from the cosmopolitan life around the capital of Willemstad. "It's quiet," she offered, shrugging her shoulders. "I go down to town—every day, every night." It takes 25 minutes in her car, and helps explain why the traditional lifestyle once known in Curaçao is changing.

The landhuizen of Curaçao's *kunuku* (as the countryside is called) are gradually being restored, and some are open as museums or restaurants. There are almost 100 houses around the island. They have been built in the open style known in the Netherlands—where people show their best facade to those who may pass by. It was a sign of status in the mother country to have your city building standing tall since the street frontage, highly taxed, was regulated. That may apply in downtown Willemstad, but in the kunuku, the Netherlands custom of keeping the parlor curtains parted so that the outside world can see that you have a nice home, is more the way of life.

Curaçao of the kunuku, also spelled cunucu (a Papiamento word for country), is another world, far removed from the Curaçao of commerce that most see in and around Willemstad. The customs are consistently Dutch, adapted to the Caribbean. When the Spaniards settled here in the 1500s, following the island's discovery by Alonso de Ojeda, a Spanish navigator, it was gold people were looking for—and freedom from harassment. Curaçao's comfort for the world's weary is nothing new; the island has welcomed Catholics, Jews, Protestants, Moslems, famous people such as Simon Bolivar, who hid out here twice during his wars for the liberation of South America, infamous people who have changed with their professions, plus many—like us—who come to rest for a while and revive.

POLITICAL PICTURE: Curaçao is the seat of government for the 5-island Netherlands Antilles, one of the trio that makes up the Kingdom of the Netherlands. As of January 1, 1986, the three-pronged kingdom consists of the Netherlands, Aruba, and the Netherlands Antilles, a group that includes Curaçao, Bonaire, Sint Maarten, Saba, and Sint Eustatius (better known as Statia). The five-island Staten meets in Curaçao. It is made up of elected representatives from the islands. In addition, there is an Executive Council of the Netherlands Antilles. Each island has its own legislative and executive hierarchy, known as its Island Council. Elections for Island Council members are held every 4 years, most recently in April 1991. At meetings held in the Netherlands in early '83, it was agreed that Aruba would pursue its plan for compatible independence from the other five islands by 1986, and each would become "totally" independent by 1996. Although Curaçao has been the financial and commercial leader of the Netherlands Antilles, the island government grapples with severe economic problems. The Curaçao Shell refinery was adopted by Petroleos de Venezuela S.A. in October 1985, when Shell pulled out. Now called Refineria Isla (Curaçao) S.A., the operation is an important employer. A once-flourishing drydock operation is again gaining in importance, and Curaçao's government acknowledges the value of tourism and there are comprehensive plans for expansion of that industry as well as an enthusiastic plan for conservation.

ISLAND APPEARANCE: The capital, Willemstad, is picturesque, with gabled buildings that recall the architecture of Amsterdam and other Dutch cities, in spite of their pastel-colored paint. Curaçao's countryside is hauntingly beautiful. On the outskirts of the city windmills fleck the flat, parched terrain. They are not as traditional as those in the mother country, but are certainly reminiscent of Holland's expertise with wind and water—even here, where there is plenty of wind, but not much fresh water. Heading west along the good highways, the land begins to undulate into hills covered with pine trees; angular arms of huge cactus spike from the slopes. A relatively flat area—I call it "the plains"—breaks at the seashore where a rocky bay is harbor for a few island-built fishing boats. There are some beach-fringed coves, heading northwest into the countryside of this 40-mile-long sliver that sits some 40 miles off the coast of Venezuela, but the island does not have the long, soft-sand shoreline of its neighbor Aruba. Most beaches are hardpacked sand brought from the sea floor as man-made beaches. The best beach is at the Seaquarium area and there are patches of sand at most hotels, where pool-swimming is popular.

LIFESTYLE: Many traditional Dutch value systems and disciplines are still obvious in schools, in the form of government and in traditional Curaçaoan families. Influences from North and South America have been woven into this island's lifestyle in an interesting pattern. Look for the few vestiges of Netherlands' traditions in the countryside, at festivals and dance performances sponsored by community groups, and when you have the opportunity to visit with any Curaçaoan families. Dutch is the official mother tongue, but Papiamento, that verbal stew that is spoken in Aruba, Bonaire, and Curaçao (and spread to the northern Dutch triumvirate when workers who had come south to work in the oil refineries headed back north to their home islands) is taught in schools as well as spoken by the old-timers.

In spite of this island's obvious involvement with tourism, visitors are advised to consider local sensibilities and cover up beach attire for forays into town and sightseeing around the island. Basic Dutch conservatism is still a fact of many Netherlands Antilles' personalities.

AUTHOR'S OBSERVATION

Curaçao has made good use of an infusion of Netherlands'-granted funds to refurbish, repaint, and rebuild many of its historic downtown buildings. Even the once seedy shopping area looks better.

MEDICAL FACILITIES: St. Elisabeth Hospital is completely modern, with up-to-date facilities. Many of the doctors have been trained in the Netherlands. In addition to an intensive care unit and coronary care facilities, the hospital has radiology equipment and decompression chambers. It has 750 beds, in both shared and private rooms.

MONEY MATTERS involve the Netherlands Antilles florin or guilder (the words are used interchangeably), written as NAf or Afl, but U.S. dollars are accepted everywhere. Prices will be stated in local currency and sometimes, also, in U.S. dollars. A service charge of 10% or 15% is added on all bills, even when no service is involved. There's no need to leave more, unless you've asked for (and gotten) special treatment.

AUTHOR'S OBSERVATION

Look carefully at credit card slips to be sure you are not being double-billed for service (tip) and taxes.

COMMUNICATIONS are easy, via direct-dial telephone, using the 011 overseas code, plus 599 and the Curaçao phone number starting with 9. From Curaçao, AT&T's USADirect service can be used by dialing 1+800+872-2881 for AT&T operator assistsance. Other telecommunications links are also reasonably efficient, but count on mail delays. Facsimile machines are used by most hotels and many other businesses.

ARRIVAL at Curaçao International Airport is easy and efficient. *ALM, American,* and other airlines wing in here regularly from the U.S., as do flights from South America, the Netherlands, and elsewhere in Europe. There are also flights linking Sint Maarten and Aruba. You'll need proof of citizenship (passport is best), plus return or onward ticket and a filled-in Immigration card, which you will probably be given on the plane. Baggage claim is an open-to-breezes area not far from the immigration desks. Taxis gathered at the door can take you and luggage to your hotel or you can rent a car to drive the well-paved roads. The airport is about 25 minutes from Willemstad and most of the hotels.

CRUISE ships are big business for Curaçao. Passengers will probably arrive at pier facilities opened in early '83. Taxis are available for touring, but most passengers seem to flock to the shops in town even with the "Bon Bini" marketplace in Punda.

DEPARTURE by plane is relatively organized, with a vast array of shops (a Caribbean version of Holland's Schipol Airport), with top quality merchandise, at reasonably good prices. Count on finding Dutch cheese, chocolates, and Delft pottery. There's a departure tax of NAf17.50 or US$10.

TOURING TIPS: Willemstad can be toured easily on foot. The traditional walk across the Queen Emma bridge, which links Punta and Otrabanda, the two sides of the capital, means that visitors staying at the Curaçao Caribbean, Las Palmas, and Holiday Beach hotels can walk to most of the shops from the in-town stop for their shuttle-bus service. (Most hotels offer complimentary transportation into Willemstad so, if you can adjust your plans to the schedule, there's no need for the expense of taxis.)

AUTHOR'S OBSERVATION

A visit to the tourist office at Waterfort Plaza, near the walls of the Fort, should be the first stop in town. Depending on who's on duty, the staff may (or may not) offer a lot of information but they *have* the facts even when you may have to take the initiative. There's also literature to read.

Rental car firms (*Budget, National,* and others) have cars available through their desks at the airport as well as through most hotels. *Caribe Rentals* (T 61-3089) has jeeps and cars at reasonable rates, and *CAM Tropical Rentals* has mopeds. I've found Budget very helpful.

Main roads are excellent and well posted. By all means, drive out to Westpunt, making the loop using the northeast road for one swing and the west side road for another; the scenery is a fascinating combination of cactus and pines, with rolling hills, and a few sandy coves. A few historic houses have been restored in the country, and your camera can capture them.

Island **tours** are offered by *Casper Tours, Taber Tours, Daltino Tours, A.B.C. Tours,* and perhaps others by the time you arrive, but they all offer pretty much the same: a city tour, a 5½-hour island tour, a 5½-hour East Point tour (both for $20), and a night tour (for $40). Private tours cost about $20 per hour. If you are alone, a tour is a good way to meet others. However, exploring in a rental car can be easy and fun. Armed with the fact-packed yellow sheet called *Curaçao Holiday,* things are easy to find at your own pace.

Some of the nicest tours are the walking tours around the old city. Check with the tourist office.

Jeep Safari Curaçao (Box 716, Curaçao, N.A.; T 61–73829) arranges unusual tours into the kunuku, with guide if you want one and there are boat trips to Klein Curaçao, a small offshore isle.

All-day tours, including flight, to Aruba and Bonaire are well worth the investment and the challenge of adapting to flight schedules, if you want to visit all the ABCs and if the tours are still being offered while you are visiting. Boat service also links the islands for those who enjoy adventures. However, you can visit the other islands on your own at less cost if you've included the plans in your ticket from your starting point.

LODGING is mostly in hotels. Curaçao does not yet have a crop of condominiums and apartments such as has grown elsewhere, but some are being built, notably **Kadushi Cliffs,** which hopes to open this year. Casinos are a focus for a few of the hotels, with groups booking gambling vacations. Although there are small sandy coves out on the island, none of the lodgings has a very good soft-sand beach.

Expect to have a 5% government tax and at least 10% service charge added to your bill.

AUTHOR'S AWARDS

Avila has been my long-time choice for this island, because it continues to have a uniquely Curaçaoan style.

Information about places-to-stay is included under Hotels/Resorts and Low-Cost Lodging. This island has few Housekeeping Holidays and only one in the traditional sense. Stars are awarded within categories, when warranted. (See page 11.)

HOTELS/RESORTS are clustered near Willemstad, with only one out on the island.

★★★ **Avila Beach Hotel** • *at the shore on the outskirts of Willemstad* • knew a former life as the Governor's mansion. Its location, amid a number of interesting old houses that are being restored, repaired, or removed, makes it convenient to town and restaurants (although you'll need taxi, car, or bus to get to the popular shopping area). New rooms are the result of owner Nic Moller's belief that his guests want more comforts than some of the older rooms could provide. The back terrace overlooks the small beach; there's a congenial beach bar and an old world warmth about this place that I like. The staff is friendly and helpful. Newer rooms are in the 3-story addition, with those with a sea view preferred, and newest rooms will be in the new building next door, when it is finished. This place is favored by wise and worldly Europeans and other travelers. Watersports can be arranged at the beach. *Hotel.*

Coral Cliff • *about a 25-minute drive from town (and action)* • began with 35 rooms in motel-style arms but is slated for expansion and a casino. The

Caribbean Newsletter (page 9) will have details. It can be a retreat for the world-weary, and for those who want to enjoy peace and quiet at the shore. The beach is packed sand-and-shell, but pleasant for sunning and OK for swimming. The restaurant, in its own building, has a bar that offers a wonderful sunset view. Specialties included fresh seafood when I visited, and the food was excellent. (Reservations are required, to be sure they have food for you if you're driving out from town.)

★★★ **Curaçao Caribbean Hotel Casino** • *about 10 minutes' drive from downtown (shuttle-bus supplements taxis)* • had been part of the Hilton International family until late '83 acquisition by the Venezuela-based Concorde group. In early '86 Concorde pulled out, leaving management to the owner—the Curaçao government. The property has had infusions of refurbishing funds with each management team and looks pretty good. Rooms 501–3 combine as the Princess suite; if your budget can afford it, get it. It's lovely and views are great from this level. Public areas are attractive, but the "beach" area is small. The sea/swimming area is cupped in rock breakwaters; the pool is pleasant, but know that this place is popular with residents, especially on weekends when they flock here. The watersports concession is active; there is a casino to supplement the hotel's action plan; and a battery of shops line an arcade near the lobby. Inquire about packages. *Hotel.*

Holiday Beach • *on the shore* • is less than 10 minutes from town and about 5 minutes, in the other direction, from the Curaçao Caribbean and Las Palmas. The property was born as a Holiday Inn but is now government-run. Gaming package holidays are the hotel's steady business. The casino can be active when there are groups in the house, but the atmosphere without them may seem dreary. The staff seemed diffident and answers to questions were basic at best on my most recent visit. There are a couple of shops in the lobby area and a pool out by the shoreline where you can dunk in the sea (it's too shallow to really swim). The rooms with sea view are preferred. *Hotel.*

Hotel Holland • *near the airport and about 20 minutes' drive from Willemstad* • is a comfortable small hotel, but its airport location puts it away from the usual seafront action. Rooms are motel style. The place is popular for business folk. *Hotel.*

★★★ **Las Palmas** • *across the road from beach and Curaçao Caribbean Hotel Casino* • has been operating as an inclusive-price resort with several villas scattered around a hillside, and a public center that also has regular hotel rooms. Ask about plans for this season. The villas have complete kitchen, attractive living area, and a couple of bedrooms, ideal for a few friends or a family. You'll need a car for mobility, but can walk all around the premises (or take the hotel's shuttle-bus if you're willing to wait for it). There's a pool area, with a small commissary (stocking up in town is advisable) and a gameroom with video games that beep and tweet when prodded. Watersports are offered from the beach, which is a stroll down the hill, across the road, next to the *Curaçao Caribbean*. *Villas, hotel.*

Lions Dive Hotel • *near the Seaquarium, east of Willemstad* • opened in May '89. Planned for divers, and built with funding through the Lions' Club of Curaçao, this hotel features a complete divers' program, with the expected lobby shops and a small beach, plus the Seaquarium for other diversions. Rooms are reasonable size, with motel style. Diving is the main focus. *Hotel.*

Princess Beach Resort • *on Martin Luther King Blvd., southeast of town, next to the Seaquarium* • is a full-fledged resort hotel with a casino focus. A man-made beach layered along the shore and the opening of the Seaquarium has turned this coast into an active resort area. The property is appealing for divers as well as for gamblers; the restaurants and the pool area are gathering spots. General Manager Frank Maynard brings many years of hotel experience to the Princess, where rooms are modern, comfortable, and air-conditioned. *Hotel.*

Sonesta Beach Resort Curaçao • *at the shore, 15 minutes' drive from Willemstad* • intends to open by April '92, with 232 rooms. The *Caribbean Newsletter* (page 9) will have details.

Trupial Inn • *on Groot Davelaarweg, in Willemstad* • offers typically Curaçaoan hospitality in neat, clean, hotel-style surroundings. Rooms are in a standard band of stucco-walled units, and the pool, sauna, and tennis court help to compensate for the lack of beach. This can be a good base for businessmen and others who come to Curaçao for something other than sea sports. *Hotel.*

Van der Valk Plaza Hotel & Casino • *at the harbor entrance in Willemstad's Punda area* • is a highrise hotel with pool, restaurants, shops, and an eye-level view of ships entering the harbor from the fort walls that are incorporated into the building. Opened in 1957, and part of the Inter Continental group for part of its life, the hotel is now under the watchful eye of the Van der Valk family from the Netherlands. The 254-room hotel looks better than it has in several years; the view from its top-of-the-tower dining room is unusual, with the refinery's fires in full bloom. Very convenient for shops and downtown restaurants, the hotel's pool is the only swimming spot. You'll need a car, or a bus or taxi ride, to reach a beach. *Hotel.*

THE INN WAY: is best sampled in the countryside, where one of the island's historic homes has been turned into a restaurant and inn.

Landhuis Daniel • *in the center of the island, northwest of Willemstad* • is best known for its restaurant, which is popular for lunch amid a day's touring. The few guest bedrooms allow for an unmatched opportunity to enjoy life in surroundings familiar to 19th-century settlers. Bedrooms have personality; the Landhuis atmosphere is informal and pleasant. *Inn.*

LOW-COST LODGINGS are in small hotels, built in motel style, or in private homes where owners sometimes rent rooms to guests. The tourist office in

Willemstad is the best source for rooms for rent. **Bahia Inn** and **Sun Reef Village** are two places with apartments. Among the families with either an apartment with modest kitchen or rooms with kitchen privileges are the rooms at **Sink Jago**, at Panoramaweg 6, or **I Koeiman**, on Burabaweg 18, or the **De Windts**, at Parallelweg 7, all in residential areas of the capital. Check with the tourist office for other private-home suggestions.

El Conde • *Roodeweg 74, in Otrabanda* • has a few rooms with air conditioners in the heart of town. Don't count on Caribbean atmosphere. *Pension.*

Park Hotel • *on Frederikstraat in Willemstad* • offers basic hotel rooms for people who put cost above Caribbean atmosphere. Businessfolk like being in-town although life slows to "stop" when the shops close. *Hotel.*

RESTAURANTS in Curaçao are interesting and fun, although often expensive. In addition to *rijsttafel,* an Indonesian-style multi-course rice table with several tasty (often spicy) dishes, there are attractive restaurants that present European-style cuisine accompanied by good wines. Insofar as local cooking is concerned, Curaçaoans have a Dutch tradition in their kitchens, especially in the Kunuku (pronounced coo-NOO-coo), and some restaurants now offer that tradition to you. Among foods you're apt to find these days are *sopito* (a fish and coconut soup), *funchi* (cornmeal with flavorings), *zult* (pickled pigs ears), *keshi yena* (a shell of Edam cheese stuffed with Caribbean shrimp, beef, or chicken and sundry spices), and *sancocho di gallinja* (a chicken stew, country style). On tables in the authentic spots, the hot pepper sauce has the power to lift the lid from the jar, and your larynx from your throat. It may hide in an innocuous little bottle or it may be found in the familiar Indonesian spice wrapper that hints of what's inside.

For the less adventuresome, **Pizza Hut, Kentucky Fried Chicken,** and **McDonald's** have homes here, although both are in residential areas away from the usual tourist troughs.

★★★★ **Bistro Le Clochard** • *in the walls of Rif Fort on the Otrabanda side of Willemstad* • is tops, with good food attractively served in candlelit surroundings. Langouste (the local lobster), at 45NAf., and cheese fondues at 43NAf. for 2 are both recommended. The "cuisine Suisse and Française" takes its cue from the training (in Switzerland) of the Curaçaoan-born owner/chef, Freddy Berends. (His wife, Iris, is Swiss.) Lunch hours, in spite of the continental cuisine, are Dutch-rigid (from 12 p.m.–2 p.m.), with dinner service starting at 6:30 p.m. and carrying on until midnight. Comfort is the key word for clothes and cosmopolitan the word for cuisine. Count on a steep tally at dinner hours, especially if you care about wine. (The bistro is a short walk from the depot where guests are deposited by hotel-provided transportation.)

La Bistroelle • *at Zeelandia and Schottegatweg Oost* • is behind a shopping center in the residential area east of the harbor well outside downtown Willemstad. Recent visits have provided memorable food and surroundings. (Look at the photos of old Curaçao on the walls.) The location is anything but festive, and if you come here by cab, be sure to make arrangements for a pickup time.

De Taveerne • *inland on the east side of Santa Anna Bay, in a residential part of Willemstad* • would be worth visiting as a museum of sorts, even if Jerry and Christine Wielinga, and chef Kolenbracher (from the mother country), didn't serve such good food. The care that has been lavished on the decor of Landhuis Groot Davelaar is obvious to anyone intrigued by Curaçao's traditions. Reservations are advised for the 52-seat cellar restaurant in the octagonal house; there's only one seating per evening.

Fort Nassau • *overlooking Santa Anna Bay to the north and the harbor to the south* • was Fort Republic when it was completed by the Dutch in 1797. The problems with keeping things running in recent times are nothing compared to the rotating claims for ownership of this fort in the early days. The British claimed the fort in 1807, and named it Fort George, but when treaties in 1816 turned the island back to the Dutch the name became Fort Orange Nassau. Used by American antiaircraft crews in World War II, the fort opened as a restaurant in the 1950s. It still provides a viewful dining spot. It is a traditional cruise passenger goal, so it's to be avoided on cruise ship days, unless you like crowds. The *Infinity* wine "cellar" can be fun if your group is, and mealtime choices range from fish and lobster to beef. If you're driving yourself, weave through Punda and De Ruyterkade, past the new market, turning left at the stoplight but *not* at the road to go up to go over the Queen Juliana Bridge. A second left on Pareraweg to turn left on Versaillesweg will thread you up the hill (a taxi is a lot easier than driving yourself if you're poor on directions).

Fort Waakzaamheid Tavern • *across the bay from Fort Amsterdam, not far off the Otrabanda ramp from the Queen Juliana Bridge* • fits itself out in historic fashion and gives a fascinating view of Willemstad with its meals. In a country tavern atmosphere, you can dine on steaks, fish served local style, and sandwiches (lunchtime), quaffing a locally brewed Amstel beer with it all. Open lunch and dinner (daily except Tues.), the tavern does its best to recreate some of the features of its past, preserving the aura of tavern life, but adapted for modern times. Lunch runs at least $10; figure $20 and up for dinner.

Golden Star • *at Socratesstraat 2, on the corner of Dr. Maalweg and Dr. Hugenhottaweg* • has good local food, including fish and funchi (a cornmeal mush), as well as steaks, chops, and sandwiches.

★★★ **Indonesia** • *in an attractive building in a residential area on Mercuriusstraat, which is a side street in the Salina area* • is a "must." The multicourse rijsttafel, or rice table, is the specialty of the house, and one for 4 people is about 78NAf. There's a 10-course meal or 16- to 24-course fete, with each course a taste or two of meat, chicken, fish, vegetable, or some other edible, many of them spicy. For those that are not pungent themselves, there's fire-hot sauce to dab on each forkful. A memorable experience, not to be missed. (If you are one or two, there are plates that have selections of several tastes.) Open lunch and dinner. Reservations recommended. If you drive yourself, come in daylight to find the place.

★★ **Larousse** • *in a historic building on Penstraat, not far from the Avila Hotel* • makes the most of an 18th-century building and the Chaine des Rotisseurs affiliation by offering well-prepared fish and other fresh-from-Holland produce and presenting the food attractively. A tiny balcony/attic area is used for small (and private) gatherings. It's a good idea to phone ahead to ask about the evening specials and reserve a table. Count on a pricey evening.

★★★ **Le Recif** • *wedged into the walls of Rif Fort on Otrobanda* • is a few arches from Bistro Le Clochard. The small restaurant serves seafood from 12 to 2 p.m. and also at evening hours. Don't expect only fresh-caught fish. The single-subject menu here includes herring in sour cream and smoked salmon, neither of them available offshore. The snapper fillet and stewed conch are relatively local, although consigned to a freezer due to the exigencies of sporadic guest count. Even if you visit here only for the *soppitoe* (the special Curaçao fish chowder), this nook is well worth the visit (and money spent) if you are a fish eater.

The Wine Cellar • *in a portion of a historic house in Willemstad* • makes a name for itself mostly for its wine list, which carries on for pages with offerings from Germany, Italy, and the French Alsace area. Your meals are mostly steak and beef. An entrecote (steak) runs about $15, with a filet for close to $20, but count on this for a leisurely evening, and come casual. Dutchman Nico Cornelisse is your host and his haven holds about 40 people maximum. The place opens about 6 p.m., and is closed Sunday.

Landhuis Zeelandia • *about 10 minutes from the center of town, in the direction of the Princess Hotel* • offers exceptional food, for lunch and dinner. Count on spending close to NAf70 for a memorable meal, in a nicely restored historic house, built in the 1840s. Offerings have a European flair, even when they are Curaçaon specialties. The wine list had some good offerings when I checked for this edition. Call ahead for reservations at peak season (winter).

Playa Forti • *out near Westpunt* • is a halting place for many folks who drive out this way (and, also, for some of the tours that come through here) and is overrated insofar as food is concerned, if my sampling is typical. Three shrimp pierced into tacky lettuce, and one chilled (and delicious) beer, cost $6.75. *Dradu* and *mula* (local fish fried Curaçao-style with rice) was 17 NAf., or about $9.75. *Enchilada de camarones* (shrimp in a kind of pancake), and *carco stoba* (stewed conch, the "meat" that lives in that beautiful shell people like to bring home as a souvenir) are also on the menu, as are hamburgers and fried chicken. Drinks? There's *kibra hacha*, which I learned was rum, gin, and the domestic orange liqueur called "Curaçao"—and Hacha is a local hardwood tree—as well as other lethal specialties.

There are a few other spots along the west coast road, but Playa Forti is the one that seems to get all the recognition.

Chungking, Wilhelminaplein 1, is very convenient. The **Great Wall**, at the Centro Commercial Antilia, is also good.

NATURAL SURROUNDINGS: The corrugated terrain of the northwestern portion of this island prickles with an unusual combination of scrub growth, feathery pines, and cactus rising from the parched landscape like the tines of forks. As you drive west, there are some beaches along the south coast, especially at Playa Kalki where the snorkeling is good offshore. At Boca Tabla, pounding surf has carved caves into the shoreline. In addition to the flora (including orchids), which can be seen at eye level when you walk around Christoffel Park, there are Amerindian paintings on rocks at Boca Grandi. The park, which covers some 4500 acres, is also home for iguanas and birds. One trail leads to the top of Christoffel (at 1239 feet) and others thread through the grounds.

The Underwater Park is one of the prized diving areas; the small islet known as Klein Curaçao is another. Resident divemasters can also arrange for trips along the south coast, from west to east, at many sites.

PLACES WORTH FINDING are concentrated in Willemstad and its immediate environs.

Willemstad is enchanting, even though its sun-bleached pastel facades and Amsterdam-style stepped roofs cup crass commercialism. The town is photogenic, historic, and well maintained, partly because of a strong historical group, and partly because everyone here is well aware that the town of Willemstad is about all Curaçao has going for it at this point as far as something of tourist interest is concerned. It was named for King Willem II in 1647, during the early years of Dutch settlement, and its port claims to be the fifth busiest in the world! Whether the oft-told legend about the faded pastel of the buildings is true or not, the soft colors help the aura that makes this town worth looking at today. (The story is that an early governor ordered the blinding white buildings painted pastel because the white hurt his eyes!)

The **Curaçao Museum,** near the Holiday Beach on van Leeuwenhoekstraat in Otrabanda, occupies a building dating from 1853. The museum has been in operation since 1946, but its Shon Janchi Boskaljon Bandstand was reopened May 18, 1986, to be used for special island events held on the first Sunday of each month at 7:30 p.m. Named for a Curaçaoan soldier who was also a composer and bandmaster, the bandstand had been a tradition since the 1890s when it was the hub for soirees with music and socializing among the island's residents. It's hoped that the custom will be revived on the monthly Sunday evenings in which visitors are encouraged to participate.

Mikve Israel-Emanuel Synagogue, on Columbusstraat at Kerkstraat, celebrated its 250th anniversary in March 1982. It occupies most of the block and has many noteworthy items inside. With its Beth Haim Cemetery, the museum, and the baths that were uncovered in the courtyard during excavations in 1976, it is the prize touring attraction for many visitors to Curaçao. The building at #26 Kuiperstraat was the rabbi's residence, but it has been incorporated into the museum (open 9 a.m.–11:45 a.m.; 2:30 p.m.–4:45 p.m. Mon.–Fri., closed Sat. and Sun. If a cruise ship is in port on Sundays, the museum opens.)

Bolivar House, opened a couple of years ago as a museum, holds an interesting collection of the South American liberator's memorabilia.

Queen Emma Pontoon Bridge started as a toll bridge when it spanned the river in 1888. It's free today, and still in use as a footbridge, because it provides the fastest link between Otrobanda and Punda, the two halves of the city. Vehicles have to head out, up, and over the blatant 193-foot Queen Juliana Bridge (see below). The pontoon bridge and the floating schooner market that survives at harborside in spite of the new, huge, modern market that was built to improve local shopping conditions, are places worth finding in town. (The new market, where housewives shop, is air-conditioned under the vast cement cap that curves into the harbor off De Ruyterkade near the Post Office.)

Queen Juliana Bridge can't be missed—even if you want to miss it. The $30-million fixed span that sits over Curaçao like some outsized buckle was finally dedicated on April 30, 1974—after a few false starts that had the two sides stretching toward the center (red parentheses in the sky as you looked up from downtown) missing their center segment. Long after the bridge was completed, traffic had to wait for the access roads that would make it possible to head up and over this four-lane highway to cross the 270-foot wide channel between Punda and Otrobanda. The goal was to undo the hair-pulling, horn-honking traffic snarl that Queen Emma caused. The rainbow-shaped bridge took 13 years to build and was talked about for more than 45. First discussions about the need for a new route started in 1929; the bridge was finally in use in mid-1974. The approach on the Punda side leads past the American Consulate, housed in a building that was given by the Dutch in thanks for assistance and protection offered to this island during the World Wars.

The spoon shape of **Curaçao's harbor** is the center of sightseeing. In the bowl, there can be as many as 14 oil tankers, plus countless other ships for repair, and around the edges you can see the spurts of fire from the refinery. (Note this view at night from the top of the Vander Valk Plaza Hotel or the Fort Nassau restaurant for the most awesome effect.) The port of Willemstad has been called the western hemisphere's largest dry-docking facilities, and although few people are positive about the present and growing status of Cuba's south-coast Cienfuegos, this port is certainly plenty big. More than a dozen ships can be docked and serviced at one time, and you can see several tied up at the harbor docks at almost any season.

Seaquarium, on the southeast coast, just off Martin Luther King Blvd., has an amazing collection of fish and invertebrates in its multichambered complex. Restaurants, water flume rides, and shops add to the entertainment value, but the sea and sealife are the focus.

The **Curaçao National Underwater Park,** east of Caracas Bay on the southeast shore, has been open since December 14, 1983, and now includes almost 3000 acres off the south coast. Dozens of mooring buoys keep scuba and other boats from digging their anchors into the now protected black coral. The small tugboat wreck offshore has provided a popular home for colorful fish, making the scuba diving and snorkeling worthwhile. Both the Caribbean Marine Biological Institute (CARMABI) and the Netherlands Antilles National Park Foundation (STINAPA) have their headquarters not far from Las Palmas and the Curaçao Caribbean hotels.

On the day you rent a car, head for Westpunt to find any of the Curaçao beaches and ask at the tourist office, or phone ahead, before you set out to find if any of the Landhuis are open. **Landhuis Jan Kok** is a delightful country goal, for a Bols gin or an Amstel locally brewed beer or on Sundays for its island-famous Dutch pancakes; it's an old house furnished with country antiques. **Landhuis Ascension** on the northwest side of Curaçao, in Banda Bou, is a social center for the Royal (Dutch) Navy. It's open on the first Sunday of the month (for services and sightseeing), but may be visited with special permission at other times. **Landhuis Santa Maria** is well worth visiting for handicrafts made by the handicapped, as well as for a look at the landhuis and its gardens. (In Willemstad, the Curaçao Museum is in a historic house as are De Taveerne restaurant and the retreat for the Sisters of Charity, Landhuis Habaai.) There are at least 15 of the old houses, Bottelier, Klein, Sint Joris, and Santa Kruz among them, that are interesting enough to slow down to look at from the outside, and to photograph, even if you aren't encouraged to wander around.

SPORTS on Curaçao center on the sea for most visitors because of the sun, but residents are interested in the local baseball teams and soccer/football matches as well as tennis (which can be played at most hotels). **Scuba** is spectacular, they say, though the constant shipping activity has clouded some of the areas that used to be prime spots. Dr. Hans Haas made the first sports dive off Curaçao in 1939, where the Curaçao Caribbean hotel now stands. The classic wreck for this area is the Dutch ship *Orange Nassau*, easily reached with guide and group. With the opening of the dive venture at the Seaquarium complex, Curaçao joined Bonaire and other places as a fully equipped dive destination. The operation includes dive boats, the best equipment, expert instruction, and full underwater photography facilities. Be sure to inquire about special good values during summer (up to mid-December), when beginner and advanced instruction is provided in one all-inclusive fee. *Dive Curaçao* operates out of Princess Beach. *Piscadera Watersports* also arranges diving. **Deep-sea fishing** trips can be arranged, and there are some small boats for rent by the half-day or day for a **cruise** around St. Michels Bay.

Boardsailing is big business in seas around Curaçao. Check with the High Wind Center (T 61–4944) or Top Watersports (T 61–7343) for facts about board rental and upcoming events.

Golfers have little choice: The *Curaçao Golf and Squash Club,* with a 3400-yard par 36 course at Emmastad is it, and the greens are sand, but the fairways are grass. It's not worth lugging your clubs this far; rental will be about $6, with caddy at $2 for 9 holes. Open for visitors Tues.–Fri., 8 a.m.–4 p.m.

Tennis courts are available at the Curaçao Caribbean, Holiday Beach, Princess Beach, Las Palmas, and the Coral Cliff hotels. The *Curaçao Sport Club*'s 4 courts are the most interesting if you want to play with some residents. There's a charge for all night-lighted courts over and above the daytime charge levied on nonhotel guests and some hotels have tennis package holidays. Squash is possible on the 2 courts at the *Curaçao Golf and Squash Club* at the refinery.

Horseback riding is a marvelous way to get a new look at Curaçao. J. M. Pinedoe rents horses at his *Rancho Allegre* at Gr. Michiel. Both English and Western saddles are offered, as well as guides to lead you on lopes around the plantations of sandy Curaçao. (This will be a hot but fascinating couple of hours. By all means, come prepared with jeans, a long-sleeved shirt, hat, and plenty of sun screen.) Plan for an early morning sunup ride or a ride late afternoon (4–6 p.m.) to get the full flavor of desert, Caribbean-style. Make arrangements a day in advance, and be sure to settle the matter of a cab if you do not have a car to drive yourself.

TREASURES AND TRIFLES are tucked into all the nooks of the streets and plazas of a five-block area in downtown Willemstad and the shopping arcade of the Curaçao Caribbean hotel. Under the eaves of the 17th-century Dutch houses are some excellent buys—and some bargains that are not. The warning repeated throughout this book, when discussions center around "duty-free" and "free-port" shopping, applies here also. As far as cameras, binoculars, radios, tape decks, stereo equipment, etc. are concerned, be sure you know your hometown price. You may find that there's very little difference in the price you pay in Curaçao and what your local discount store can give because it buys in bulk. Camera lenses have proved to be very good buys in past seasons, but know exactly what you want and be sure that what you are looking at is the item you need—and not just a lookalike.

Recent sprucing up of Willemstad's shopping area has led to plazas, welcome resting places where you can sit at an umbrellaed cafe table while you tally your purchases and plan what to buy next. Gomezplein is one such spot.

Shops in Willemstad are open 8 a.m.–12 p.m., 2–6 p.m., Mon.–Sat., and some stay open even during the lunchtime. US$ are welcomed everywhere, and you can get your change in U.S. currency also. Credit cards are accepted in most stores.

AUTHOR'S OBSERVATION

Shops and merchandise vary. For on-the-spot information, before you set out in the bazaar-filled town, ask for (and read carefully) the yellow *Curaçao Holiday*. It's fact-filled, and issued regularly so its information is "current."

Boolchands Kohinoor, at Heerenstraat 4 B has binoculars, cameras, and other precision instruments.

As far as clothes are concerned, I do not see much in the way of bargains these days, but there are a lot of trendy fashions, some of them reasonably priced. **Aquarius,** at Breedestraat 11, is one place with top quality (and prices) for European and U.S. designer clothes. If you are in the market for snug-fitting pants and Italian, French, or English clothes, look around here to find Cardin, Courreges, Ted Lapidus, and others. Accessories are especially interesting—belts, scarves, jewelry, etc. Another store for Dior, Cardin, Oleg Cassini, and their ilk is **Jet Set** on Kerkstraat. (It does not close at lunchtime.) London's Marks & Spencer line is carried at **La Fortuna** on Heerenstraat, and you can buy Burbury and Aquascutum at **Cosmopolitan** next door on Heerenstraat.

Two stores to try for one-stop shopping are the **Yellow House** for perfumes and **New Amsterdam,** a typical department store that is stuffed with imports from everywhere and will be glad to charge any of them on whatever credit card you carry. Both stores are on Breedestraat. (The street-level shopping window of Yellow House is "standard," but look up at the 2nd floor for a glimpse at the past, with arched windows and interesting roofline trim.)

Spritzer & Fuhrmann's legend began in Willemstad, when Austrian watchmaker Charles Fuhrmann left the ship he had intended to take to South America and stayed in Curaçao in 1927. Not long after, a fellow watchmaking Austrian, Wolf Spritzer, also arrived in Curaçao, and the 2 opened a small watch repair shop in Willemstad. The natural interest in jewels and gold led to expansion into jewelry, and the jewelry caught the eye (and wallets) of servicemen stationed in Curaçao in the '40s. Business began and thrived when the postwar cruises sent people south in search of treasures and tans. In the 1980s, the stores fell on hard times; some closed. But the famous-name venture now has a new owner, and revitalized outlook. The stores are open and worth visiting again. The S & F specialties are watches and clocks, jewelry, crystal, bone china, many imported luxury items, and spectacular and very special jewelry that commands—and gets—top price.

Salas, at Salina, on the outskirts of town, is the place to head for if you are interested in books, newspapers (*The New York Times*), and magazines, in addition to a nice print of Curaçao's *Handelskade* (the waterfront) and the cookbook *This Is the Way We Cook*.

Van Dorp, with four shops on the island, also handles the daily news from its store on Breedestraat. Located near the waterfront end of the street, Van Dorp's selection of paperbacks includes the Penguin books, and the miscellany available can take care of most of the trinket needs for the remembrances for the folks back home.

Landhuis Santa Marta, on Piscaderabaai, is the craft workshop for the handicapped. When you buy here, you can find one-of-a-kind items—and help a local industry.

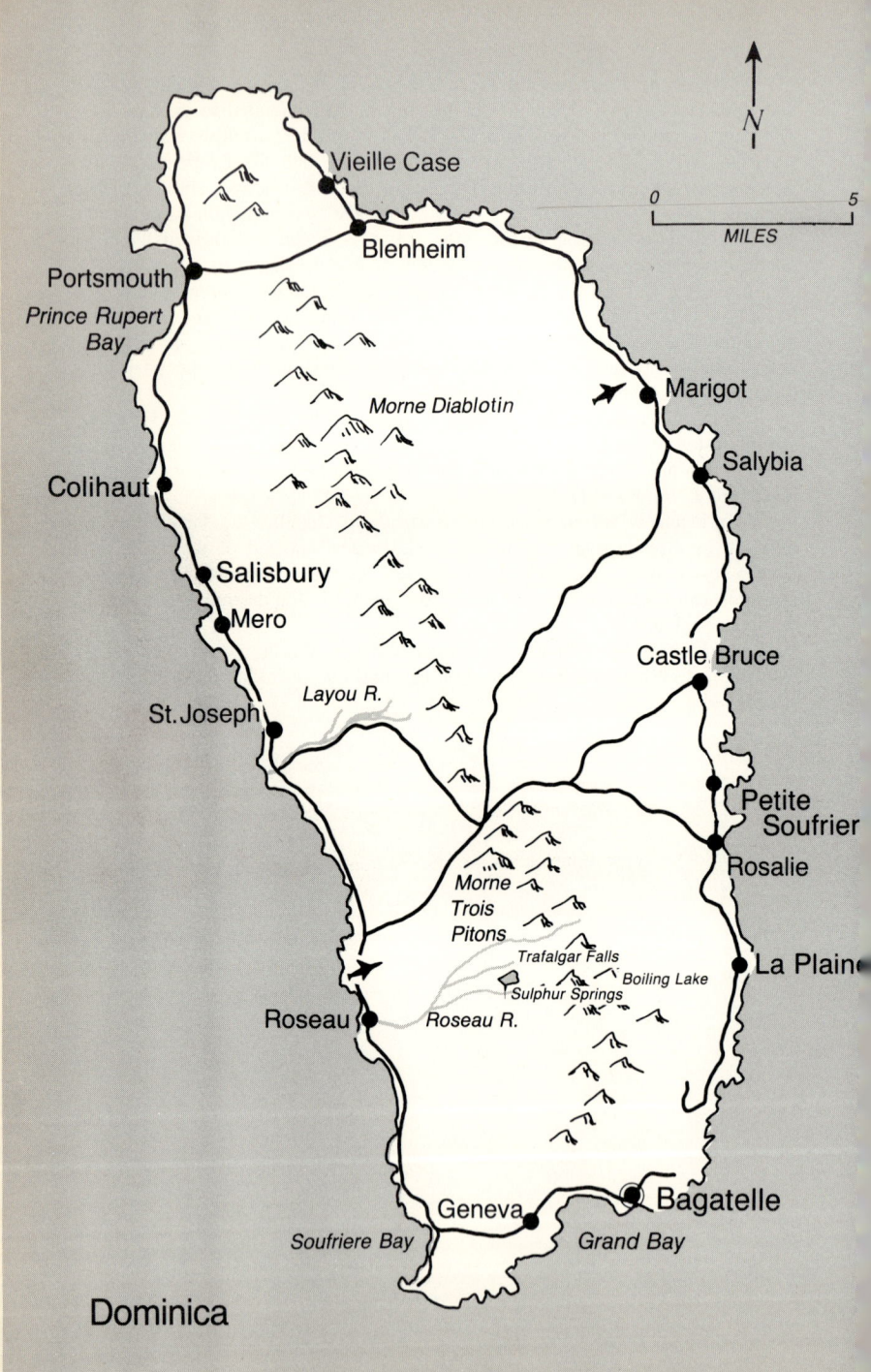

DOMINICA

Dominica Tourist Board, Box 73, Roseau, Dominica, W.I., T 809+449–2351, fax 809+448–6563; Caribbean Tourist Organization, 20 East 46th St., New York, NY 10017, T 212+682–0435, fax 212+697–4258.

$ · · · US $1 = EC $2.65
Unless otherwise noted, $ refers to U.S. currency.

With one sweep of his arm, Lennox Honychurch gathered centuries of history. His feet were firmly planted in the gray-gold sands of Douglas Bay, but his mind was in the lively Battle of Les Saintes that took place in 1782.

Lennox is Dominican. His ancestors came to this rugged but lush island decades ago, to settle as 18th-century planters, joining others who came to the New World. He is animated when he talks about the twin peaks of the Cabrits, or the ruins of the 18th-century Fort Shirley, blanketed with overgrowth between them, and of the role of Dominica in the sea battles between French and English. He is proud of his country, and he knows almost everything about its fascinating history.

The island was "given" to the Caribs by the French and the English in the treaty of Aix-la-Chapelle in 1748, when both countries were so busy battling over all the neighboring islands that they didn't have time for this one. It was the French who started nibbling first, however, after they had secured Guadeloupe about 25 miles off the north point of Dominica, and Martinique, almost the same distance off the southern shores. The British then moved in full force to claim the island as English, early in Europe's Seven Years War (1756–1763). The band of French settlers permitted to remain were instrumental in giving Dominica a brief period under the French flag in 1778, but England soon claimed Dominica again and that claim was secured by the Treaty of Versailles in 1783, when the nationality of most of the islands of the Caribbean would be decided at the tables in Europe.

When you hike to the Freshwater Lake, about two miles northeast of a small community called Laudat, and you are at the Montane Forest or the Elfin Woodland, it is difficult to imagine the turbulent history of this awesomely individualistic country. Follow the Middleham trails, from Sylvania or from Cochrane or from Providence, and you can imagine a forest primeval. Go on the river ride, perhaps in a gommier canoe, carved and cajoled—as in the days of old—from a single tree trunk. Boats gather at Portsmouth and are paddled along the river past villages and natural forest. Or take a boat from Roseau, south past Pointe Michel and Soufriere Bay, to Scotts Head, where you can dive off and swim to a white sand beach—or stand tall and look over the peninsula to see the seas of the Martinique Channel.

Dominica is many things, none of them like any other Caribbean island. This is a fiercely individualistic country, with a personality and a creativity that are more complex and capable than its small size suggests.

POLITICAL PICTURE: Elections held in mid-1990, following the British system within every five-year term, continued to support Dominica's indefatigable Prime Minister, Mary Eugenia Charles, but by a very narrow margin that astonished many Caribbean pundits. Long before the prime minister was "introduced" to the American public through television coverage at the time of the Grenada activity in October '83, she was widely respected as an eminently capable spokesperson for the needs of the underdeveloped countries of the region. Her support for the U.S. Caribbean Basin Initiative has gone far beyond campaigning for Dominica, and has included explaining the complicated plan to her Caribbean colleagues as well as meeting with key people in Washington to focus on the needs of the region.

When her Freedom Party won the hotly contested elections of June 1980, Prime Minister Charles was faced with an almost bankrupt 300-square mile nation of 80,000 people who had been courted by Cuba—and virtually ignored by the United States. Severe hurricanes in the fall of 1979 had done extensive damage, destroying countless homes, washing out roads, and ruining the agricultural industry, primarily export of coconut products, bananas, and limes, which are Dominica's main source for hard currency.

Under the Charles administration the economy has improved, but an active opposition wants faster results. U.S. and other countries' assistance with road building has helped to weave a network of paved roads throughout the country. The U.S. Agency for International Development and other aid organizations offer assistance programs for Dominica. Partnership for Productivity International has been active, as have other independent programs. Inflation has been reduced, jobs have been created, and the trade deficit that had tallied to well over $80 million in 1981 has been dramatically lowered. Efforts to encourage small, labor-intensive industries are beginning to bear fruit. Tourism efforts are focused on "the nature island of the Caribbean," conservation of natural resources is a primary concern, and the country offers much to vacationers seeking off-the-beaten-path pleasures.

ISLAND APPEARANCE: Unique among Caribbean islands, Dominica is almost entirely tropical forest. Almond-shaped, in the sea just south of French Guadeloupe's Iles des Saintes and north of French Martinique, the island's small capital of Roseau nests at the sea's edge in the southwestern sector. Portsmouth, the next largest town, on the northwest coast, has a more protected harbor and is favored by yachts and other boats. This dramatically mountainous island has few beaches. The best are along the west coast south of Portsmouth and at coves on the north coast. The beach near Scott's Head at the island's southern tip is one of the country's best. This island has been spared the glut of tourist hotels found on some of its neighbors.

> ### AUTHOR'S OBSERVATION
> *RARE Center for Tropical Bird Conservation* (1529 Walnut St., Philadelphia, PA 19102, T 215+568-0420), a not-for-profit organization affiliated with Philadelphia's Academy of Natural Sciences, has assisted with a conservation/education program to save the endangered Imperial and Red-necked parrots. A poster showing the rare Imperial Parrot, locally known as the Sisserou, is available through RARE for a contribution of $30 or more.

LIFESTYLE is individualistically Dominican, with vestiges of British traditions and French influences apparent in a population that is about 98% black. The country has a traditional agricultural society, where most of the people work the land, as has been the case through history, on plantations of bananas, limes, other citrus fruits, spices, and almost everything except sugar, which has never been a big crop on this mountainous island. A community of Carib Indian descendants lives in the northeastern area, not too far from Melville Hall airport. The Caribs have their own customs, but many have now mixed with the African population so few pure-bred Caribs remain. Chances are that you will have little to do with the true (and complex) Carib community. Dominica is more pioneer country than Caribbean resort. The customs are those of a newly emerging nation: changing. The majority of Dominica's 80,000 population have an average annual income of less than $100 per year.

Clothes for visiting Dominica should include hiking shoes, jeans, and sweaters for the mountains, where it can be cool, and a waterproof, light-weight poncho for rain. You'll want a bathing suit, and something for informal evening wear, but this is not a "lot of luggage" place. This is a West Indian island where you are encouraged to fit in, not parade like a peacock.

MEDICAL FACILITIES: Princess Margaret Hospital, located at Good Will near Roseau, was almost doubled in size with an addition completed in early 1989. Many of the doctors received their training in Britain, Canada, and the U.S., and links with medical schools in those countries allow the hospital to have access to modern equipment and techniques. Every district has its clinic, in the British tradition. Since all hotels are small and operated by Dominicans, owners have local connections with doctors.

MONEY MATTERS revolve around the Eastern Caribbean currency at a fixed value of EC$2.65 to US$1. U.S. dollars are welcomed; U.S. small change has no value. Converting some money to EC$ at your hotel or the bank will ease transactions and tips. If you choose to change money at one of the Roseau banks, allow plenty of time. Lines for service are often long and slow moving.

COMMUNICATION is reasonably easy via telephone, with direct-dial 809 area code + 44 (for Dominica) + a 5-digit number. Phone calls from Dominica can be made from your hotel or from the Cable & Wireless office in Roseau. Cable & Wireless sells phonecards in various denominations for use in designated public telephones that do not accept coins. For service with AT&T's USADirect system, dial 001 + 800 + 872-2881 to reach an AT&T operator who can place your U.S. call to your AT&T number or collect. Facsimile machines are used by some hotels, the Tourist Office, and many other businesses. Telex and radio are also available. Airmail from the U.S. takes 10 days or more and costs 50¢ for the first half-ounce.

ARRIVAL on Dominica was simplified when small Canefield Airport opened near Roseau in early '82. Built with British government assistance, until French-assisted paving came along faster, the air strip accommodates small planes. LIAT and other lines come in from Antigua, Barbados, Guadeloupe, Martinique, St. Lucia, and other nearby islands. There is also island-hopping service from St. Croix. The Canefield airport is about five minutes from Roseau's center.

Melville Hall airport, in the northeastern sector of the country, is the only airport for bigger but still small planes of LIAT and others. Although the almost two-hour ride to Roseau has been made somewhat easier by recent road improvements, it's still a long ride.

AUTHOR'S OBSERVATION

Be alert to the dollar–for–dollar exchange rate. Although most taxi drivers are scrupulously honest, I've encountered at least two who would happily have accepted U.S. dollars for a price quoted in EC currency, thereby increasing their profit by 2.65%! Always ask, before setting out on your journey, whose dollars are being quoted.

The taxi fare from Canefield to Roseau's hotels is about US$8 and the fare from Melville Hall airport to Roseau can be as little as US$13, if you arrange for a seat in a car heading to the capital. Your return trip, if you hire a taxi on your own, can cost as much as US$80! If you're staying in Roseau, consider making a day's excursion out of your trip to Melville Hall, heading up to Portsmouth in the morning to have lunch at the beach (perhaps at Coconut Beach), and then drive on to the airport, about an hour across the northern tip of the island. Be sure to negotiate the charge for the day *before* you start the journey. (See "Touring Tips" below.)

CRUISE stops are limited to small ships since port facilities are minimal, but some lines do include Roseau and Portsmouth on their itineraries. Yachtsmen favor the protected harbor of Portsmouth, on the northwest coast; Roseau is open-water. Check with the Dominica Tourist Board about cruise lines.

DEPARTURE is very easy from Canefield airport and also, after the ride, from Melville Hall. You'll be required to return a copy of the immigration form you received on arrival. Don't count on shops at the airports. There is a departure tax of EC$15.

TOURING TIPS: This island offers some of the Caribbean's most interesting opportunities for adventuresome travel. For first-timers, an experienced **taxi** driver/guide can be very helpful, not only for negotiating the roads but also for the information he should be able to give to you. Check through your hotel and/or the Tourist Office in Roseau for names of reliable guides.

Roads have been vastly improved in recent years. The road that borders the west coast, between Roseau and Portsmouth to the east coast and back to Roseau are also reasonably good, even when they climb and plummet, following the mountainous terrain.

Dominica Tours (℅ Anchorage Hotel; T 809+448–2638, fax 809+448–5680) has several special-interest options, including hikes for flora and fauna as well as mountain hikes to places such as Trois Pitons, where vegetation has flourished again, following the devastation of the hurricanes in 1979. The Armours' Dominica Tours also arrange river journeys into the back country.

Whitchurch Travel Agency (Box 71, Old St., Roseau, Dominica, West Indies, T 809+445–2181) is reliable, Dominican-style efficient, and ready to help with all your touring plans. Opportunities for touring include the rugged jungle area, with waterfalls and hiking in the National Park.

There are a few **car rental** companies, but don't expect to find the latest model autos. For Dominica driving, a sturdy jeep can be a good idea and a compact and reliable shift car has definite advantages with the steep grades in the mountains. *Shillingford Car Rental* (10 Winston Lane, Goodwill; T 809+448–3151) and *Valley Car Rental* (Box 3, Roseau; T 809+448–2279) are two of the firms that rent daily for about US$30 and weekly for around US$220. A driver's license can be obtained for US$8 and presentation of your passport and a valid hometown license.

LODGING: The capital of Roseau had all the hotels, until a few years ago. Now there are a few beachside places in Portsmouth, as well as a couple of unusual places to stay in the hillsides and wilderness of this wonderfully verdant island. Insofar as style is concerned, most of Dominica's hotels are closer to being inns than to U.S.-style hotels; there are no big hotels on Dominica. *Fort Young* and *Castaways* come closest to offering accepted hotel amenities; *Anchorage* bridges the line between hotel and inn, since it is a family-operated small hotel; and *Castaways* has some of the beach-and-watersports offerings expected at Caribbean hotels. When you plan a holiday here, consider combining a few days at one of the hotels in the capital and a few days at one of the mountain resorts. Both *Whitchurch* and *Dominica Tours* (see "Touring Tips," above) can help with plans when you arrive on Dominica if you want to look around before you make reservations.

There's a 10% government tax, and often a 10% to 15% service charge added to the room rate.

DOMINICA

AUTHOR'S AWARDS

Reigate Hall provides comfortable, viewful surroundings overlooking seaside Roseau; *Anchorage* continues to be true to itself and its Dominican heritage. *Fort Young Hotel* deserves special mention as it aspires to be the country's leader.

Information about places-to-stay is included under Hotels/Resorts, Housekeeping Holidays, The Inn Way, and Low-Cost Lodging. Stars are awarded within each category. (See page 11.)

HOTELS/RESORTS in Dominica are small, personality places, preferred by adventuresome travelers and those who enjoy natural surroundings.

★★ **Anchorage Hotel** • *a mile or so from downtown Roseau* • has been my Dominican home for several visits over many years. The site has been the Armours' family home long before they added their first rooms for guests, in the 3-story building on the south side of the pool. Both Carl and Janice created the hotel, now operated by their children who manage reservations (Yvonne), restaurant (Carla), and watersports (Fitzroy). The newer rooms are in a block along the shore, north of the pool and central building, with a squash court between rooms and road. The location makes the hotel convenient for folks who want to be in the capital; son-in-law Henry Shillingford's able guidance for tours and Fitzroy's expertise for diving make the place self-sufficient. There's entertainment some evenings, but a relaxed atmosphere encourages guests to feel "at home." *Small hotel.*

★★ **Castaways** • *at Mero, on the west coast about 30 minutes from Roseau* • has a long tradition of inn-keeping, with time out for a few years as the home for medical students. The 28 rooms with balconies are motel style, on the hillside, offering dramatic views of the countryside and sea (when pruning permits), plus expected (but not lavish) hotel comforts. The hotel needed a lot of work when I checked for this edition. The *Caribbean Newsletter* (page 9) will have further comment. Castaways gives its guests watersports at the beach, in addition to access to the hiking and other activities of the hinterlands. Management and staff do all possible to assist with vacation plans, and island produce is presented in interesting style at mealtimes. *Hotel.*

★★ **Fort Young Hotel** • *on the southern fringe of Roseau* • stands on the site of the former fort, which it absorbs. Officially opened in April 1988, the hotel punctuates its core with a pleasant pool, with the open-air dining area bordering one side of the patio (with overhead fans to swirl breezes). Bedrooms are on the outer edge, which gives most a lovely sea view from the bluff-top perch. Most of the furnishings have been made in Dominica, with local wood and straw work lending a nice touch. Bathrooms are tiny, but modern. The hotel has a loyal following of businessfolk; the Prime Minister is one of the property's owners. *Hotel.*

★ **Portsmouth Beach Hotel** • *at the west coast, just south of Portsmouth* • is a sister-property to the Armour family's Anchorage, with all the activities links. With several buildings used by American students attending the Ross Medical School, there's usually some activity in the beachfront dining area. Rooms are motel style, with overhead fans for cooling, and can seem cozy for folks who want a seaside, quiet place. There's a small pool set inland from the shore, which is bordered by a butterscotch sand beach shared with Coconut Beach Hotel. Picard's cottages are neighbors. *Hotel.*

★★ **Reigate Hall** • *in the mountains, about 10 minutes' drive above Roseau* • has a Swiss-mountain feeling. High enough above the bustle of the West Indian capital, guests can hear the birds and enjoy the mountain air. This is a home turned inn, with a well-maintained tennis court and attractively furnished rooms. (Rooms 5, 6, and 7 are among those with the best view.) Tables and chairs set amid trees offer peaceful oases. Don't expect a lot of action, except on the occasional evening when there's a bridge tournament or some other planned event. Food served in the dining room is Dominican style, with fresh-grown produce. *Hotel.*

Sisserou • *in Castle Comfort, about a mile south of Roseau* • offers basic comforts on the shore. Used by businessfolks who have appointments in the capital, the hotel's rooms seem to me to be like those of a run-down Holiday Inn. There's a pool, and all amenities are here. What this place needs is maintenance and an improvement in staff attitude. It could be a comfortable small hotel; it wasn't when I visited. (It takes its name from one of Dominica's endangered parrots.) *Hotel.*

HOUSEKEEPING HOLIDAYS: There are a few places for rent, but none is in the resort style that you may know from other islands. The best way to find a rental is to stay a few days at a hotel and ask to see what's available around the country. There are a few cottages up in the mountains at Springfield Plantation (see "The Inn Way" below), but only a few places have been built in recent years for vacationers' housekeeping.

Coconut Beach • *on the shore, south of Portsmouth* • provides some simple, single story, housekeeping apartments built near the beachside restaurant and newer back-to-basics apartments. Don't expect anything grand. This place is geared to informal living, in a style favored by Germans and other European travelers who head for the sun with a vengeance. The open air restaurant is better known for its hospitality than for its food offerings, although reasonable fare is offered. You can walk along the gray-sand beach to the Portsmouth Hotel, where the medical school students (mostly Americans) live. *Cottages.*

Picard Beach Resort • *at the shore, south of Portsmouth* • is another of the Armour family's projects, along with neighbor Portsmouth Beach and Roseau's Anchorage. The attractive natural wood cottages have louvered windows and doors, for air cooling. Kitchenettes have the basics, but few flourishes; bathrooms have modern equipment, including bidets. Popular with Europeans and wise Americans, these places are ideal for a back-to-nature holiday with some comforts. The beachside restaurant serves all meals, when you tire of cooking. Tours can be arranged through the Armour family enterprises. *Cottages.*

Sans Souci Manor • *in the mountains overlooking Roseau* • is a gathering of attractively furnished apartments adjacent to the home of John Keller, an expatriate from New York who left his now defunct Caribbean tour company. Comfortable for self-sufficient folk who love mountain scenery, sea views, and peace and quiet (as the owner does), the apartments are occasionally available for week-long rental, although they are often committed on long-term arrangements. It's worth inquiring, if you're looking for a Dominican "home." *Apts.*

Sunshine Village • *on the shore, north of Portsmouth* • is a collection of bungalows that are popular with German and other European tourists. Life here is *very* informal; watersports are offered. Expect camplike surroundings with a sea and bathing suit atmosphere. *Bungalows.*

THE INN WAY: Even Dominica's hotels have innlike qualities, but the following places have strong personalities, usually taking cues from the owner.

Emerald Pool Hotel • *in the mountains, near the Emerald Pool* • has always been a rough-cut jewel, but its status is uncertain at press time. When you're in the country, inquire—if you want a combination town and mountain vacation. The *Caribbean Newsletter* (page 9) will carry further information when warranted.

EverGreen Hotel • *in the Castle Comfort area, just south of Roseau* • has the comforts of a home turned inn. The dining area and balcony-with-chairs are pleasant public rooms. Some of the bedrooms are small and dark, requiring air conditioners for cooling. The rooms on the front of the house suffer from the noises of traffic that runs along the main coastal road. Two rooms are "under" the dining room and balcony, on the sea side but set back from the shoreline so there's not much view. Best for those already familiar with Dominica and its hospitality, this place has a following among Canadians, British, and wise Americans. *Inn.*

Layou River Hotel • *about half an hour from Roseau, and an hour or so from the airport* • is comprised of cement and stucco buildings with angular roofs that nestle into lush foliage, wrapping guests (when there are any) in air-conditioned comfort (and constant hum). Although this place might be popular with folks who enjoy tramping through the Dominican wilderness and adventuring around the Layou River, the hotel has yet to operate at full tilt. When there's worthy news about this place, the *Caribbean Newsletter* (page 9) will note it. There's a pool on the premises, and the natural pool formed by the river near the shoreline. Ideal for nature lovers, this is no place for lone travelers—unless you *really* want to be alone. *Small hotel.*

Layou Valley Inn • *in the mountains, 15 miles north of Roseau* • is a wonderfully cozy small spot favored by those who enjoy natural surroundings.

Ideally situated for hikes and known for innovative use of the plentiful island produce, Layou Valley Inn guarantees a memorable vacation for nature lovers. Tamara and Louis Holmes are your guides, advisers, and hosts. Their use of island stone, wood, and natural attributes gives a special quality. Waterfalls are your "swimming pools"; dramatic nature your "television." *Inn.*

Papillotte • *a 20-minute, 4-mile, pot-holed drive from Roseau* • offers another world, a retreat from commercial realities and a haven for those who seek comfort in surroundings that include majestic waterfalls, lush tropical growth, and warm hospitality. The place that Cuthbert and Anne Grey Bapsiste have put together gives you rustic rooms, with basic, island-made furniture, and awesome views of verdant, jungle-like nature. With mineral baths, a craft center (with some reasonable work, using local vines and grasses, as well as some wood carvings) and places for river dips and sunbathing all nearby, the drive doesn't make any difference. Food is Dominican style and the surroundings will spellbind nature lovers. *Bungalow.*

Riviere La Croix Estate Hotel • *about 15 minutes off the main mountain road and almost an hour from either Roseau or the Melville Hall Airport* • is in a state of flux. The *Caribbean Newsletter* (page 9) will have details when warranted. It's mentioned only because it was a Robinson Crusoe legend when it was operating a few years ago and, as tourism improves, someone may recreate a similar outpost retreat. *Inn.*

Springfield Plantation • *about 20 minutes' drive from Roseau, up Imperial Road* • is a special place favored by nature-lovers and used as an environment and conservation study and research center. Mr. John Archbold, long-time owner of the plantation, who gave the property to Clemson University, has a legendary history with Dominica. After 9 years in England, his mother, Ann Archbold Saunderson (who had spent her honeymoon on safari in Africa in 1902) packed up the 4 children, and left her husband and the Saunderson name to move to Bar Harbor, Maine. When John Archbold graduated from Princeton in 1934, he boarded a schooner and headed south, to land at and fall in love with Dominica. Several plantation acquisitions later, Archbold found himself in the inn-keeping business, with the 4-bedroom Victorian plantation house at Springfield Estate. In 1972, just before the bottom fell out of the banana and citrus market, and waves of independence hit Dominican shores, Springfield Plantation had expanded to 15 rooms in the original and other buildings. And about that time, taking the cue from Laurance Rockefeller's National Park grant of land on St. John in the U.S. Virgins, Archbold deeded 1200 acres of his Middleham Estate to the Dominican government through the island's Nature Conservancy. The property is part of the Dominica National Park, whose entrance is 2 miles from Springfield Plantation. Botanists, scholars, and those on independent nature studies who stay here can know that they will be well fed on island specialties. Novice travelers may be intimidated by the verdant surroundings, but adventuresome visitors will be enchanted.

Springfield Guest House, the original plantation house, perches on a bend of the old Imperial Road, at about 1163 feet, with a view of the sea and a steep slope at each "ear." Guests in the main house bedrooms (private bath with each) and the apartments use the sitting room with fireplace, and can rock on the veranda. There's a protected river pool near the house, and a small pool at Samaan (separate house with 2 double bedrooms and bath, plus living room and bedroom on the first floor). Bee House, a bamboo cottage, has two double bedrooms, plus kitchen, dining room, terrace with sea view (maid service provided), and Mount Joy is a full house, with pool in its garden, above Springfield House along the Imperial Road. Guests here have 4 bedrooms, with living room, kitchen, and veranda. *Inn, cottages.*

LOW-COST LODGING is not difficult to find on Dominica, but some accommodations are very simple/rustic, in a traditional West Indian style known throughout the Caribbean prior to the 1950s. In Roseau, both the **Continental Inn** (32 Queen Mary St.) and **Vena's** (Cork St.) rent rooms and are popular with some West Indian businessmen and others who know the area. Continental is a 2-story building with a few air-conditioned rooms, 5 of which have private bathroom. Vena's, across the road from the Tourist Office, has 3 rooms with private bathroom and others without, in what might have been a private home in earlier times.

Castle Comfort Guest House • *on the shore near Anchorage Hotel, at Roseau* • has a half-dozen small rooms, with bath. Expanded from Dorothy Perryman's shoreside home, the guest house has been enjoyed by wise British and Canadian travelers, as well as a few price-conscious Americans. The homelike atmosphere makes it easy to get help with scuba and touring arrangements, especially since Derek Perryman, the owner's son, is a skilled scuba diver. Good value and good local food are among the assets. *Guesthouse.*

Hamstead Country House • *at the north coast* • is a 2-story cement-block building with comfortable rooms and small balconies. The 6-bedroom house is near the Hampstead River, within walking distance of Batibou Beach, and about 20 minutes' drive to Portsmouth, on the west coast. *Guesthouse.*

RESTAURANTS are usually the province of the hotels, with each having its own special way of cooking the local foods. (Taxes and shipping problems make importing difficult, so don't count on steak and french fries here.) You will be offered crapaud, otherwise known as "mountain chicken," and actually the huge frogs that live in the woods of Dominica. They are delicious, almost any way they are prepared, so order them if you see them on the menu. Sweetwater crayfish, land crab, fresh fish including tritri, fried plantain (a variety of banana), pawpaw (otherwise known as papaya), mangoes, squashlike christophine, and breadfruit (a potatolike vegetable) are all offered in season. Pumpkin and callaloo are two favorite soups. (The latter is like spinach.)

Chances are you will dine where you overnight, unless you lunch at one of the other hotels when you're touring around. If you are in Roseau for lunch or dinner, check **La Robe Creole**, at the corner of Castle Street and Turkey Lane, for excellent fish and other local food, often highly spiced. When I dined there Tony and Erica Burnett-Biscombe ran the place, and the food was excellent. It's one of the top spots, for conversation as well as for good food. Others to try in Roseau are **Ti Kai,** opposite the Convent High School on the outskirts of Roseau, and **Guiyave,** on Cork Street not far from the tourist office. Both serve good local/Dominican food and are informally comfortable. **Papillote** should not be missed, if you have a car (or have made arrangements with a patient taxi driver who will wait while you dine), and reservations at **Springfield Plantation,** if you haven't chosen to stay here, will yield a memorable time. Plan for Springfield at mid-day to get full advantage of the surroundings or go up mid-afternoon for a swim (ask ahead for permission) and stay for dinner. (Same should be said for Papillote, since the falls are best, obviously, when you can see them!)

NATURAL SURROUNDINGS: Dominica's mountains are blanketed with verdant growth. Although some of the landscape is cultivated—for banana, coconut, lime and other crops—there are vast areas of virtually virgin rain forest, and hundreds of rivers and streams that occasionally drop in dramatic waterfalls.

AUTHOR'S OBSERVATION

Dominica has two endangered species of parrot that are included in a national protection plan. The Imperial Parrot, or Sisserou, is the national bird, shown on the flag of the country. Recent counts have found only 50 Sisserous. The Jacot, or Red-necked Parrot, is the second species that can be seen in the wilderness; only about 300 of them remain.

Dominica's sights are natural ones, and are ideal for birdwatchers, hikers, and botanists. Some of the jungle areas are so thick that Eric Lamb, the man who first established jeep safari jaunts in the early 1960s said "it would take a man a lifetime to clear a path through the wilderness. Some 300 rivers crisscross the steep terrain and no one knows how many waterfalls may exist in the seldom-visited interior. The interior of Dominica has as many as 60 different tree species within a 10-acre plot and is the only place where either the Sisserou (Imperial Parrot; *Amazona imperialis*) or the Red-necked parrot *(Amazona arausica),* both endangered species, can be found. Birdwatchers may also be interested in some of the other 135 species including the pigeons, doves, hummingbirds, swifts, fly-catchers, chicken-hawks, and bananaquits.

Morne Trois Pitons National Park, with the office headquarters at Victoria Street (Dominica National Park Office, Box 148, Roseau, Dominica) is a chunk of 16,000 acres (25 square miles) in the south-central part of Dominica that was established in July 1975 by an Act of the Legislature as the first part of what is intended to be an expanding National Park network. Rangers work at clearing paths, and have made great progress on the **Emerald Pool Nature Trail** (which is almost *too* developed, especially if you come in as part of a big group). The Canadian Nature Federation assisted with the project, which involved funding through several international agencies including the Canadian International Development Agency (CIDA).

Other places in the park area are the **Freshwater Lake,** in the crater of an extinct volcano, and the **Valley of Desolation,** an "other world" area where most of the vegetation has succumbed to the sulfur fumes and bubbling mud creating what is known as the **Boiling Lake,** which was discovered in 1922. It's a 4-hour hike to the Valley of Desolation. Guides for this expedition and others can be arranged through the Forestry Department. (Call the office of Felix Gregoire at 809+448–2733 to make arrangements.)

Insofar as the waters surrounding Dominica are concerned, the sights are best known to the few Dominicans who have taken up scuba diving. The areas around Portsmouth would undoubtedly yield some underwater treasures, since they were the location for sea battles, and some shipwrecks have also been noted in the southern seas, around Roseau and south to Scott's Head. One area of special interest is called the **Hot Springs,** where volcanic pressure is released through vents and the hot air/water has inhibited the sealife found in other areas.

PLACES WORTH FINDING are mostly the natural ones mentioned above, but there is an impressive restoration underway at the Cabrits, mountain peaks just north of Portsmouth where the ruins of **Fort Shirley** are being excavated. The work is intended to recall the vibrant 17th- and 18th-century history and the British/French battle of Les Saintes. At this point, the ruins are a good hiking goal for those who enjoy reflecting on the island's history. There is a small museum showing the importance of Fort Shirley in the battles between the European powers for prominence of these seas, the colonies, and therefore Europe, as well as the Arawak and Carib early history of the island.

Roseau is still truly a West Indian town. It has not capitulated to tourism. Many of its original wood and stucco buildings still stand, now in use as shops, offices, and an occasional restaurant. **The Dawbiney Market Plaza,** officially opened on February 10, 1988, has been restored to look much as it might have when it was the town's central marketplace. These days it is home for art exhibits, local produce, and tourism information. Plans are to have resident artisans ply traditional Dominican crafts of basket weaving, woodworking, pottery, and so forth.

Of particular interest for those who love the real West Indies will be the many small villages around the country where life is lived as it has been for past decades, with few flourishes. Although the Carib community in the northeast has now integrated with Dominicans and others, and it not as pure Carib as it was even a few years ago, the site may be worth visiting if you have an interest in the region's earliest Amerindians.

The road south of Roseau, on the west coast, reaches Pointe Michel, where visitors can sense the French influence that is so prevalent on this island. There are some beaches along this shore, reaching as far as Scott's Head. Grand Bay claims one of the best.

SPORTS are for the rugged individualist on this island, despite the fact that there are boat tours, fishing programs, hiking forays, and other adventures planned and provided with guide by *Whitchurch Travel Agency* or *Dominica Tours* (see "Touring Tips" above.)

Sailing is usually on a charter yacht, coming here from someplace else. If you're the captain, you can check with customs and the Roseau jetty. A rash of drug smuggling and other nefarious schemes has caused Roseau's customs' agents to be very thorough in yacht checks, but if you're not smuggling there's no problem.

Scuba diving has gained encomiums from the pros who know these Caribbean waters well. Neglected in favor of some of the better-known spots (Bonaire and the Caymans, for example), Dominica came to the attention of those who like to pioneer areas just after hurricanes, which often shift the bottom sands and uncover formerly hidden wrecks. An astounding collection of 17th- and 18th-century ships reportedly lie off Dominican shores, and many of them are yet to be discovered. Check with Fitzroy Armour at *Waitikubuli Dive Centres* (T 809+448-2638) about scuba sights and package vacations, using Anchorage, Picard cottages, or Portsmouth Beach as "home." Derek Perryman's *Dive Dominica* (T 809+448-2188), at Castle Comfort Guest House, is a prized source for local scuba lore. Divers speed from shore in a twin-engine fiberglass boat, which puts most dive sites within 20 minutes of land. The firm offers night dives and dive packages as well as resort and certification courses. Call ahead to be sure about the availability of rental equipment (which may be in short supply if you vacation at a time popular with several other divers). The Underwater Park near Portsmouth, on the northwest coast, is one dive site that is rich with offerings, but many of the most interesting locations (and those nearest Dive Dominica's head office) are off the southwest coast, near Scott's Head.

Boating trips up the coast from Roseau to Portsmouth are another option, with a canoe or flat-bottom boat trip up Indian River. The charge for a minimum of 4 is $80 ($20 per person).

Fishing, waterskiing, and zipping offshore in a **motorboat** can be arranged for $20 per hour, but don't count on all the flourishes for deep-sea fishing vessels here. Life is marvelously simple, remember?

Hiking is best with a guide, either through the National Park (check with the Roseau office for guides) or through the Tourist Office.

Safari Tours, in Land Rovers, can be called sport by some. Certainly the excursion is not for the carsick crowd, unless well laced with your most effective Dramamine equivalent.

TREASURES AND TRIFLES are limited. This is not a typical tourist island with freeport shops and the like. What has been made for tourists is priced for tourists, and because there are not too many of us in Dominica, the price is sometimes high on the old "bird in the hand" theory. The basket and handicraft shops sprinkled along the road through the Carib Reservation on the east coast do have some interesting intricately woven work, but when you ask the price (which is seldom marked) it will be priced for you—and you are a lot richer (or so the owner thinks) than he is. (There's no doubt about your income versus that of the basket weavers, but as for the entrepreneurs who are setting up the shops? In relative terms, I'm not so sure.)

In Roseau, the best woven grass rugs—and they are interesting and a long-time favorite purchase—are at **Tropicrafts,** started almost 50 years ago by Sister Berine at the Convent Industrial School. The sisters are still active in overseeing the work of those who weave the rosettes and other sections at home, as well as those who stitch the final rug together on the floor of the vast hall that is home for Tropicrafts. (Rugs can sometimes be made to order, but you will do better if you can find something in stock that is close to what you want. Be sure to measure your porch or room before you leave for Dominica.)

Caribana Handcrafts at 31 Cork Street in Roseau "offers you the best of everything'' according to its small folder, but what it stocks its shelves and rooms with are hats, mats, and woven items similar to those found at Tropicrafts.

Check the **Workshop for the Blind,** at the north edge of Roseau, for other handmade items. Prices here are worth every penny. If you buy some of the local coconut oil for sunning, *beware*. It's only for already tanned skin; novices will burn!

The *Dominica Story* by Lennox Honychurch will prove to be a valuable purchase for anyone interested in this fascinating country's history and legends. If you have difficulty finding a copy of the book in one of the stores in town, ask at the Tourist Office for assistance with tracking down a copy. You'll find it to be a true treasure.

DOMINICAN REPUBLIC

Secretaria de Estado de Turismo, Avenida George Washington, Santo Domingo, Republica Dominicana, T 809+682-8181. **Author's Note:** At presstime, the Dominican Republic's Ministry of Tourism seems in disarray. Offices in the United States have been forced to close for financial reasons. One source for further information is the Dominican Republic Mission to the United Nations, 144 East 44th St., New York, NY 10017, T 212+867-0833. The *Caribbean Newsletter* (page 9) will have further information when the problem is resolved.

$ · · · US$1 = about RD$7.50 (Dominican peso); rate fluctuates. *Unless otherwise noted, $ refers to U.S. currency.*

See pages noted for information on: Barahona, p. 305; Boca Chica, p. 311; Cabarete, p. 331; Playa Juan Dolio, p. 312; Puerto Plata, p. 331; Punta Cana, 344; La Romana (Casa de Campo), p. 326; Samana, p. 331; Santo Domingo area, p. 305; Sosua, p. 330; Housekeeping Holidays, p. 309, 327, 335.

Maria made her grand entrance, gliding across the tiled patio, her terry-cloth "train" sweeping the edge of the pool. It didn't seem to matter that her bathing suit was wet. Her arena was the courtyard of what had been the home of prominent 16th-century residents and now a 20th-century hotel in the colonial restoration area of Santo Domingo. Maria is eight years old, but her bearing was reminiscent of another Maria—Dona Maria de Toledo y Rojas, a niece of Spain's King Ferdinand and the wife of Diego Colon, son of Cristobal Colon, whom most English-speaking people know better as Christopher Columbus.

Santo Domingo makes the past come alive; not only through the performances of its children, but most vividly in the restoration of its 16th-century buildings that stand in a convenient cluster on the banks of the Ozama River in the center of the city. Columbus stands, as he has since the French cast him in bronze in 1837, on the biggest square, Plaza Colon, outside the Cathedral of Santa Maria la Menor. This is the cathedral that claims to have held the bones of Columbus until they were moved to Columbus Lighthouse in 1990. The Cathedral is still used for services for Dominican Catholics on Sundays and at

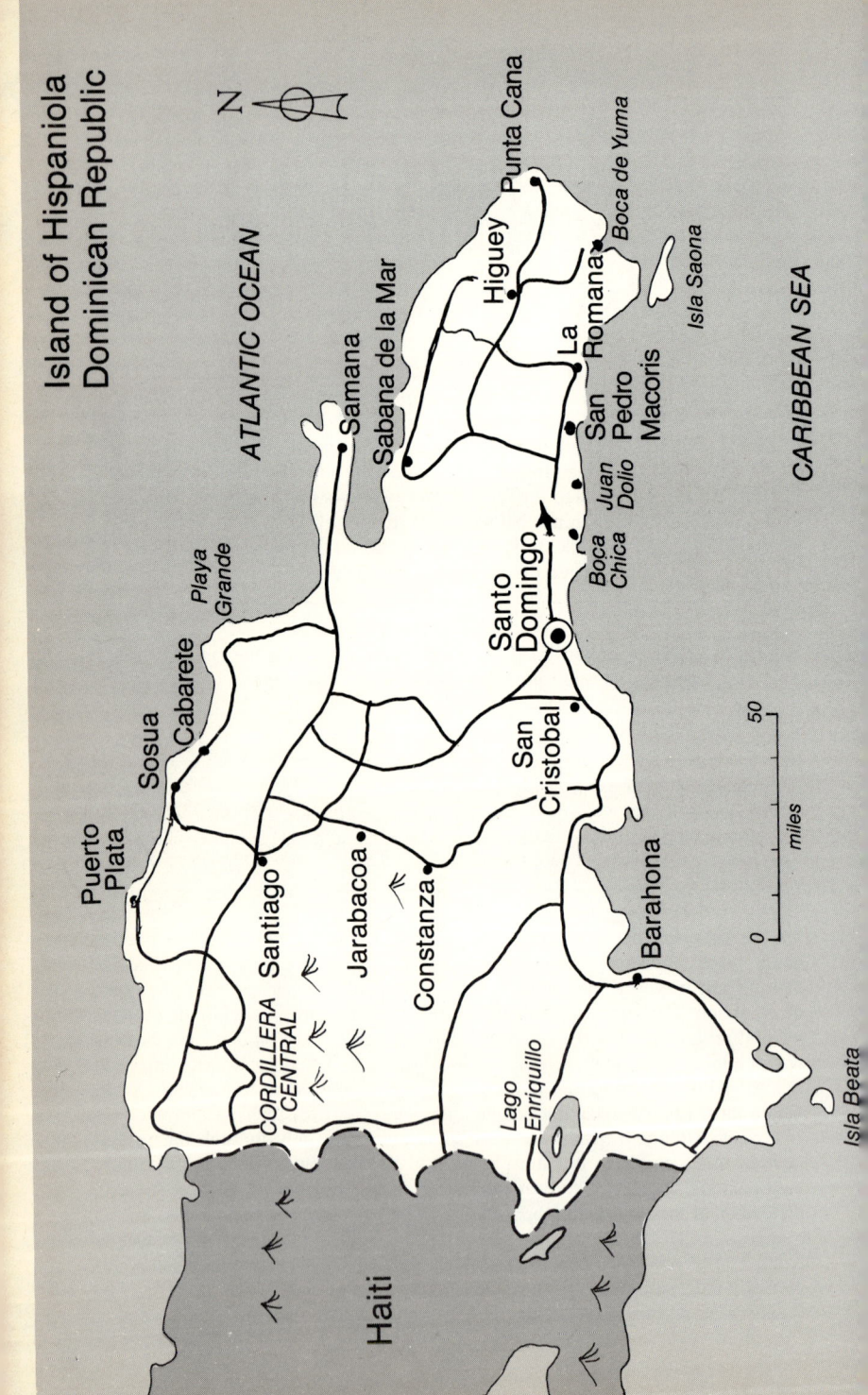

other special times. (At least four other places also claim to hold the Columbus remains—the result of a nameplate switch intended to foil the rampaging Sir Francis Drake. This has puzzled historians for centuries.)

Don Francisco Billini, who as archbishop of the cathedral in 1877 discovered the bones of Columbus (who had discovered what is now the Dominican Republic on December 5, 1492) stands on marble in another of Santo Domingo's refurbished squares. Juan Pablo Duarte, considered by Dominicans to be the father of the country, stands in a third. (Duarte met with a group of patriots and started a movement for independence from Haiti, successful in 1844.)

Today's Juans, Franciscos, Diegos, and Marias face a life quite different from that of their ancestors. About five million Dominicans share the island of Hispaniola with the country of Haiti, on a two-thirds/one-third split that gives the Dominican Republic not only the larger but also the richer portion of land. Everything grows here, including tourism—and children.

This sunny island is about 150 miles southeast of Cuba and 54 miles from the western end of Puerto Rico. It has links with both, and a multifaceted lifestyle that includes not only the city-of-salesmen and special sights but also some of the Caribbean's most complete resort communities—at La Romana, Puerto Plata, and Punta Cana—and acres of fascinating countryside, some of it with miles of soft sand beaches.

AUTHOR'S OBSERVATION

Columbus has been an important person in Dominican history, not only because he landed on the north coast, but also because his son was viceroy of Santo Domingo, soon after the city was established on the south coast. Spain continues to give financial, historical, and emotional support for extensive restoration of ancient buildings and sites and for a countrywide celebration of Columbus's voyages in 1992.

POLITICAL PICTURE: Elections held on May 16, 1990, found the incumbent president, Partido Reformista candidate Joaquin Balaguer, and Partido Liberation Dominicana candidate Juan Bosch so closely matched that a recount was required. Both men have played pivotal roles in the country's politics: Juan Bosch, who served briefly as president in 1966, is an active Marxist; Balaguer, who has served six 4-year terms as president, is a capitalist. Both men are in their 80s and have capable younger men in their parties. President Balaguer, who is 83 and blind, was declared president by a margin of less than 1% of the vote, and his administration's efforts for tourism continue.

When the 30-year reign of dictator Generalissimo Rafael Leonidas Trujillo Molina ended (with his murder in 1961), the country endured four years of tumultuous politics. This period included the brief but controversial presence, in April 1965, of U.S. troops, dispatched to help secure a peaceful democratic government. In 1966, President Joaquin Balaguer became the government's leader, with the support of the United States and a paternal presence that made it possible for him to serve three consecutive 4-year terms.

He lost the election of 1978 to Antonio Guzman, a 67-year-old cattle rancher, who was named head of the Partido Revolucionario Dominicano, with the strong support of a popular Dominican national, Jose Francisco Pena Gomez, known for his strong leftist doctrine.

In close elections of May 1982, Balaguer's Partido Reformista was again defeated by the Partido Revolucionario Dominicano, even after a controversial halt in the balloting. Following the death of Guzman, Salvador Jorge Blanco became president.

But Balaguer returned, victorious, in the May 1986 elections, when he was 78 and almost totally blind. He had defeated the incumbent PRD, whose candidate was the 51-year-old former president of the Senate, Jacobo Majluta Azar, by an estimated 43,000 votes. Balaguer assumed office in August 1986, from PRD President Salvador Jorge Blanco, who was later tried and convicted for manipulation of funds.

Since 1966, when President Balaguer became the country's leader for the first time, a middle class has been created and the standard of living has improved for many. Tourism has become the number-one employer and the major source for hard currency.

During his earlier terms, President Balaguer supported tourism development at La Romana and in Santo Domingo on the south coast and along the north coast, around Puerto Plata, where projects were initiated with loans from the World Bank, the Inter-American Development Bank, and other international lending sources. That seed money has spurred amazing private investment. Now the beach-bordered east coast is a top priority, as is a mountains-to-beach area on the southwest coast, around Barahona.

By mid-1990, the country's hotel room count had grown to 18,000—from less than 4,000 in 1981. More than 25,000 rooms will be available by 1992, for the country's gala celebration of the 500th anniversary of the Discovery of America—and Columbus's voyages to Dominican shores.

In the past year, tourism contributed about 12% of the gross domestic budget, or between $750 million and $800 million, an increase over the $675 million of the previous year. The industry employs an estimated 50,000 workers, in construction and hospitality industry services, and caters to an increasing European market, especially from Germany, Italy, and Spain.

With its acres of fertile land, and natural resources that include nickel, gold, and its people, the Dominican Republic has the potential to become self-sufficient insofar as food is concerned. It lacks distribution and marketing skills, however, and the glamour of imports from the U.S. is a key factor in the trauma facing the Dominican economy. Many Dominicans take their dollars out of their own country, and emigrate to the U.S. when they have the chance. Hurricanes and manmade problems have tested the will of the Dominicans, but the country has awesome potential and offers the Caribbean's most extensive collection of vacation facilities.

AUTHOR'S OBSERVATION

The people of the country are referred to as Dominicans, pronounced Do-MIN-i-cans; the people of the once British island of Dominica are also known as Dominicans, but the word is pronounced Do-mi-NEE-cans.

ISLAND APPEARANCE This country, which occupies the eastern two-thirds of the island of Hispaniola, is far bigger than most people realize. At 18,700 square miles, it is slightly larger than the combined states of Connecticut, Massachusetts, and Rhode Island. Since the south coast capital of Santo Domingo was settled not long after Columbus landed on the north coast, it has several of the Caribbean's most impressive 15th- and 16th-century buildings and historic sites. But there are no beaches; the capital is on a rocky coast. The best south coast beaches are east and west of the capital, near Barahona and at coves such as Boca Chica, Juan Dolio, and Bayahibe; along the east coast from Punta Cana to Macao; and along the north coast, where there are long golden-sand beaches at Playa Dorada (east of Puerto Plata) and at Playa Grande (planned for development in the years ahead) as well as on the north coast of the Samana peninsula. The central portion of the country is mountainous and, although little known to visitors, laced with hiking paths that lead through almost virgin tropical forests and areas known best to the birds and other wildlife.

AUTHOR'S OBSERVATION

Although the country is big enough to absorb many tourism enclaves without destroying its national personality, some places have been dramatically affected by uncontrolled development. The north coast, east of Puerto Plata, has areas that are cluttered with trappings for tourism; Playa Juan Dolio seems headed in that direction also. East end tourism pockets, with huge resorts surrounded by gates with guards, also tend toward enclave tourism. As development continues, the traditional Dominican way of life seems threatened—at least in tourism areas.

LIFESTYLE is that of a Latin country, in every way. Dominicans enjoy living well, and do so at every opportunity. Although there are many citizens who live on very little, there are many Dominicans who enjoy the restaurants, public beaches, and the tourist facilities, and many who have invested in the burgeoning tourism and vacation home industries. As with most places, it is easier to observe, and share, the Dominican way of life when you speak Spanish and make time to travel into the country, to places such as Santiago, Higuey, and other non-touristed places. Traditional Dominican families still treat daughters with the strict discipline of old Spain.

Dinner hour is late—9 p.m. or later—and places will be open for full meal service well after midnight. Siesta is still observed, if not for the nap time, then certainly for the closing of shops, museums, and offices, especially in and around the capital. Many reopen about 5 p.m., staying open until 9 p.m. Traffic into and out of the city will be one clue to the importance of the long and lingering lunch hour.

> **AUTHOR'S OBSERVATION**
>
> Speaking some Spanish will make a big difference in your conversational comfort. Although some people involved with tourism do speak English, the majority working in the hotels are not fluent. "No problem," which you will hear often, usually means "no action," or no problem for *me* (the speaker) because I'm not going to do anything—but plenty of problems for *you* (the listener) because nothing will be done. Travel with a sense of humor—and do what you want done yourself whenever possible.

Dominican coffee is a treat for those of us who like strong black coffee. I deplore the fact that many new hotels serve a watered-down version, calculated to please American palates. *If* you want the real thing, you will have to ask for Dominican coffee in places like the Sheraton coffee shop and some other places that try to accommodate the U.S. preference. If you want American coffee, you'll have to ask for *it* in the Dominican restaurants, or bring your own small jar of instant coffee and ask for hot water.

Clothes in the city are conservative. Business suits are proper for business calls; dark dresses—with sleeves and backs if you are going into the cathedral—are suitable for women. Resort clothes are limited to the resort areas where casual summer-fun clothes are the accepted "uniform."

MEDICAL FACILITIES: The Dominican Republic has several hospitals and dozens of clinics at population centers around the country. The biggest and most modern hospital is Jose Maria Cabral y Baez (T 809 + 583–4311), on Central, not far from the church in the mid-country town of Santiago. The Universidad Catolica Madre e Maestra Medical School (T 809 + 583–0441) uses Santiago's facility; many students from the U.S. and other countries are enrolled in their program. In addition to the hospital in Santiago, there are modern (and often overcrowded) hospitals in Santo Domingo (Hospital Marion), where there is also a Cardiovascular center (T 809 + 682–6071), and in Puerto Plata (Hospital Ricardo Limardo, T 809 + 586–2210, on avenida Juan Enrique Kunhardt), and at La Romana (Hospital Central Romana, T 809 + 687–7787). For Punta Cana, the nearest hospital is in Higuey (Hospital Nuestra Srz. de la Altagracia, T 809 + 554–2386). Although a few staff members speak English, it's worth remembering that Spanish is the language of the country.

MONEY MATTERS: The Dominican peso floats against the dollar. Denoted as RD, but appearing with the $ sign, the peso is sometimes misread as U.S. currency by U.S. visitors. *Always* ask, if you're unsure about what the $ sign means—or assume it is pesos unless you're told otherwise. Although the equivalent has been about RD$7.5 to US$1 in recent times, the rate fluctuates. Ask at the Dominican Tourist Office as well as your local bank—for the equivalent at the time you plan to travel. Even when the exchange is reasonably stable, U.S. dollars are in demand. People are eager to buy dollars, and will often give more than the official rate. Although such transactions are illegal, they are widely practiced. If you *do* buy on the street, you risk being gyped by the pros. When the currency is moving against the U.S. dollar, "What's the exchange today?"

is the first question you should ask when you arrive, and it's wise to ask it more than once—from your hotel reception (who will give you the tourism talk) to your taxi drivers to people you talk with at the markets and in the shops. Chances are you'll hear several different answers. In the casinos, if you play in dollars, they pay in dollars; if you play in pesos, they pay in pesos! Credit card purchases are converted at the official rate. Only U.S. dollars are accepted at the duty-free shops at the airport after you pass through immigration; other duty-free shops accept pesos.

AUTHOR'S OBSERVATION

It is difficult to change pesos back into dollars, so change only what you expect to spend, unless you want a lot of pesos as souvenirs. The paper money is old and falling apart; coins have little value and are seldom used.

COMMUNICATIONS: Telephone service from the U.S. to the Dominican Republic is as easy as dialing 809 and the number, but within the country you may have more difficulty. Some of the more secluded and remote places do not have phones, and at those that do, the phones don't always work. To use AT&T's USADirect service, dial 001+800+872-2881 to reach the AT&T operator who will place your call, either collect or charged to your AT&T number. Facsimile machines are used by many hotels and businesses. There is good local television (in Spanish, of course), and many Santo Domingo hotels have cable programs in English. Telex and other telecommunications facilities are available. Once again, it's important to note that Spanish is the language of the country. Non-linguists will find a phrase book a valuable companion.

LODGING: The centers for resort activities (watersports, tennis, golf, and evening action) are on the north coast around Puerto Plata, through Playa Dorada to Sosua and Cabarete; on the south coast at Boca Chica, Playa Juan Dolio, and La Romana; and on the east coast around Punta Cana. The capital, Santo Domingo, has several first-class hotels, with swimming pools, tennis, casinos, and—in one case—a European-style spa. Most hotels are modern and multistory, with the comforts expected in U.S. city hotels, but there are also smaller spots where the surroundings are basic. All lodgings have a Dominican-Spanish style, not only because the personnel speak Spanish, but also because the pace of life—with the lobby being a social center and mealtimes being late—is distinctly Dominican. Most city hotels, which are used by businesspeople and by vacationers interested in Santo Domingo's history and many restaurants, have been built since 1976, when the *Hotel Santo Domingo* was opened by Gulf+Western as the pace-setter for the new tourism thrust. (The former Gulf+Western hotels—*Hotel Santo Domingo, Hotel Hispaniola,* and *Casa de Campo* at La Romana—are now owned by the Florida-based Fajul family.)

To enjoy the best of the Dominican Republic, consider linking a few days in a beachfront hotel with a few days in Santo Domingo, for a sand-and-city combination.

Hotel bills carry a 5% government tax, 6% food and beverage tax, and 10% service charge, for a total 21% tax on your room and meal charges.

---– AUTHOR'S AWARDS ––---
In the Santo Domingo area, *Ramada Jaragua* leads with glitz and glitter, in its lobby, casino, spa, and the newest (top-rate) rooms; *Hotel Santo Domingo* maintains its traditional Dominican style. *Casa de Campo* is in a class by itself as an expansive country club with inimitable Dominican style. At Sosua, I've enjoyed *Villas Los Coralillos*.

Information about places-to-stay is included under Hotels/Resorts, Housekeeping Holidays, the Inn Way, and Low-Cost Lodging for each of the major tourism regions. Refer to the start of this chapter for page references for the regions. Stars are awarded within each category. (See page 11.)

THE SOUTH COAST

SANTO DOMINGO, the country's capital, is the pivot point for the south coast. Not only is the country's major airport a few miles east of the capital, but also the port is serve by ships from around the world as well as by an increasing number of cruise ships. In the pages that follow, we travel east along the south coast to Boca Chica, Playa Juan Dolio, and La Romana, with a tip of the hat to Barahona, west of the capital and an area marked for tourism development.

BOCA CHICA is a *very* casual beachside community, with cafes nesting amid places with rooms and beaches cluttered with chairs, watersports equipment, and other activities. Seafood dining in your bathing suit is a popular pastime. Everything in the area has grown, barnacle-style, as the popularity for watersports increases. Although the place can seem like a hornet's nest on weekends, when it seethes with sunning, swimming, disco-loving Dominicans, visitors may find the laidback lifestyle pleasant during the week.

PLAYA JUAN DOLIO, almost 90 minutes' drive from Santo Domingo, has been a favorite seaside haven for wealthy residents of Santo Domingo for more than a decade. Some have moved here full time to escape the rigors of city life; others maintain a beach home for weekend and vacation use. Although the original places were small and very basic, geared to the outdoor life, more sophisticated apartments and hotels are now being built in this area.

LA ROMANA, about two hour's drive east of the capital, has a past that gives it more prominence (and prosperity) than the capital, in the late 18th and early 19th centuries. Established by sugar barons who shipped their crop from the Dominican Republic to Puerto Rico, the town takes its name from *la romana,* the sugar scales on which the crop was weighed before shipping. Today the town's gridlike streets are usually quiet, lined with a few shops that are of more interest to residents than to visitors. If there is any activity, it is usually around the market square. The biggest attraction for visitors is at the Casa de Campo resort, and Altos de Chavon, the newly built, 16th-century village on the heights overlooking the Chavon River (see "Places Worth Finding").

BARAHONA, southwest of the capital and the hometown of a previous minister of tourism, is marked for tourism development, but nothing substantial is open at presstime.

ARRIVAL IN SANTO DOMINGO, at Aeropuerto Internacional de Las Americas, is much improved, with the opening of vast new terminal space. However, Spanish-speaking travelers familiar with South American airports will feel most at home here. In addition to proof of citizenship (passport is best) and return or onward ticket, you will need a tourist card, issued either by the carrier or at a desk when you arrive in the Dominican Republic. The charge is $10. (See page 331 on arrival at the north coast.)

The customs ritual is thorough, silent, and simple if you are not bringing anything but your own tourist trappings with you. This is one of the few places where porters are present, and pleasant (when you speak Spanish).

Brace yourself for the surge of people—taxi drivers as well as Dominicans waiting for friends and relatives—just outside the terminal doors. Plow through, hire a taxi, if you are not being met and/or haven't rented a car, and head for the shore-rimming highway west into Santo Domingo or east toward Romana and Punta Cana for the south and east coast resorts.

If you are going to La Romana (Casa de Campo resort, Altos de Chavon, and other beach areas), check as you arrive (before immigration) for the transportation. It is possible to fly out to the landing strip at Casa de Campo, but the journey takes almost as long as the hour-plus to drive by the time you connect with the pilot, claim your luggage, recheck it, and take off. *American Airlines' American Eagle* links San Juan, Puerto Rico, to Santo Domingo, as well as La Romana and Punta Cana.

Herrera is a small domestic airport, used mostly for private and charter flights, on the western side of the city of Santo Domingo. It's a ten-minute taxi ride from most Santo Domingo hotels, and is a good jump-off point for quick trips around this big country. Inquire when you arrive in Santo Domingo about flights and possible schedules.

CRUISE passengers landing on the south coast, at Santo Domingo, will be arriving at recently expanded port facilities not far from the restored area of the Old City. Taxis are available to take you where you want to go, and the omnipresent moneychangers will swarm like flies (along with trinket salespeople). For cruise facts for the north coast, turn to page 332.

DEPARTURE FROM SANTO DOMINGO Since the airport is modern, procedures are fairly routine—as long as you remember that Spanish is the language and that it's difficult (perhaps impossible) to change your unspent pesos back to dollars, even if you've held onto the currency slips, which you sometimes get. Count on a lot of bustle and long check-in lines prior to flight time. Dominicans love to come to the airport, even when they have no plans to fly.

The departure tax is US$10 or RD$15 for Dominicans.

Consolidate your carry-on. The major airlines are strict about what you can carry and about the fact that it must be in palatable portions. The duty-free shopping area, once you have passed through immigration, specializes in liquor, perfumes, Spain's Lladro figurines, leathergoods, and other imports, with a sparse collection of domestic crafts. Purchases must be made in U.S. dollars, but it's worthwhile trying to bargain about price; sometimes you'll have good results.

TOURING TIPS: Getting around the city of Santo Domingo area is easy and can be very inexpensive if you're adventuresome and/or speak Spanish. **Buses** travel the routes from the Old City to the outskirts, bordering the hotels where you're apt to be staying. The bus ride costs a modest amount. **Taxi** rates are rising but they are very reasonable dollar equivalents when paid in pesos. In addition, you can hail one of the cars that run **jitney** service along regular routes. They are called *publicos* and are very reasonable. Ask your hotel about the routes, to be sure you're standing at the right spot.

Count on spending about RD$60–70 for your taxi ride from the airport into the city, unless you've made some other arrangement. The ride takes about 40 minutes and goes along a seaside highway built in Trujillo's era, with planting restored after being battered by severe storms.

Rental cars are available, and rates vary according to the company and the kind of car. At the airport, you'll find booths for *Avis, National, Hertz, Thrifty* and *Nelly Rent-a-Car, City, Budget, Pueblo, Honda Rent-a-car,* and *Rentauto.* Most take MasterCard, Diner's Club, American Express, and BankAmericard. It will take a while for you to clear the papers for your car, and speaking Spanish will prove invaluable, not only for a rate, but also for standard negotiations—and for carefree travel around the countryside (where Spanish is the only language).

One of the best bets, and a plan that has proved popular, according to tour operators and Dominican tourism officials, is a fly/drive holiday with a car rental included with your hotel room rate and airfare. (Your travel agent or the Dominican Tourist Information Center can give you details.)

Roads are poorly marked if they are marked at all, and the official-looking maps lack many minor and new roads. Getting from Santo Domingo southeast to La Romana won't be much of a problem, once you get yourself out of the city traffic. The route is almost straight, along good roads following or just inland from the south shore. From there to Punta Cana is also a well-paved road. From Santo Domingo to Puerto Plata is a straight north-south route, but allow some time for a stop in Santiago, at least to look around, and be prepared for traffic (and cars that stop with no warning) as you approach Santo Domingo on the return run. The market stands that set up along the roadside (and serve good, strong Dominican coffee) are favorite halting spots for Dominicans, who buy fresh produce there.

There is excellent air-conditioned **coach-bus** service operated by private companies between Santo Domingo and Puerto Plata. *Metro Tours, Terra Bus,* and *Caribe Tours* have several-times-daily buses between Santo Domingo and Puerto Plata for RD$30, plus other services to Santiago and other cities. The terminal is not far from the Embajador Hotel. The air-conditioned bus ride between Santo Domingo and Puerto Plata takes about three hours fifteen minutes. If you've never been here before, this is one of the few places in the Caribbean where I think a bus tour is helpful, not only to help you get your bearings, but also to get some of the background on this historic and fascinating country. If your package holiday doesn't include a tour, and your travel agent hasn't sold you one, check with the hotel activities desk. They can certainly set you up. Small **planes** fly between Santo Domingo and Puerto Plata, La Romana, Samana, Punta Cana, and other Dominican airstrips on regular service and on charter usually from Herrara airport on the outskirts of the city.

HOTELS/RESORTS IN SANTO DOMINGO are usually modern, U.S.-city style, with several mass-produced rooms in a multi-story, boxy building. The one exception is *Hotel de Ovando,* which has colonial atmosphere in the heart of the old city. The nearest beaches are about 25 minutes' drive from the city, but most hotels have pools. Some of Santo Domingo's hotels link with air fares for good-value multi-night vacations.

AUTHOR'S OBSERVATION

Many of the big hotels have a busy and social cocktail hour, with complimentary *tapas* served in or near the lobby.

Dominican Concorde Hotel & Casino • *on Avenida Anacaona in the suburb of Mirador del Sur* • is an imposing property with a fragile personality and a sometimes bewildered staff. Built in 1977 as a Loews high-rise, the property claims a fleet of tennis courts, plus a huge pool, plenty of room for a health club, and all of nearby Paseo de los Indios, 5 miles of seaside park, to jog around. The hotel has a casino, convention hall, a tower of 316 rooms, plus shops, restaurants, and an occasionally lively nightspot. The location, about 30 minutes' drive from downtown, might be OK for convention folk who want a single hub; otherwise, it's a long way to anywhere, including most other restaurants. *Hotel.*

★★★ **El Embajador Hotel & Casino** • *on Avenida Sarasota, on the outskirts of the capital* • is popular for some U.S. visitors and gamblers as well as for South Americans and Europeans. The high-rise hotel was the country's first luxury property, when Pan Am's affiliate, Inter-Continental, opened it in the early 1950s. The property is still a good one, with infusions of funds from the present owners and the opening of an executive floor (the 5th) with concierge services. The big pool and its patio are popular with Dominicans, who enjoy spending weekends here and who use the facilities as a club, as well as with visitors. The lobby is open and active, with the reception area to the left as you enter and the casino entrance nearby. The *Jardin de Jade,* to the right off the lobby, is a popular Chinese restaurant where luncheons and dinners are served, with full ceremony if you want it. Rooms overlooking the pool also overlook a mildewed and unsightly roof (over the patio and cafe dining area), but the view in the distance is of the sea. The alfresco cafe near the pool is pleasant for breakfast as well as for lunch and early dinners; taxis can take you to other dining places. (The minimum fare is RD$20.) Tennis courts and lobby shops are here; it's a 10-plus-minute ride downtown to historic Old Santo Domingo. The hotel is now in a residential area. *Resort hotel.*

★★★ **Gran Hotel Lina** • *on Maximo Gomez at 27 Febrero* • is modern, comfortable hotel, with what has traditionally been one of the city's best restaurants and a large, and sometimes lively, casino in a neighboring room. The rooms built in 1986 in the high-rise tower include all the expected hotel comforts plus color TV and a minibar; suites are attractive, and the presidential suite is elegantly Dominican. There's a small and pleasant casino on the ground floor, not far from the refurbished, expanded, considerably improved decor of Lina's restaurant (see "Restaurants"). There are lobby shops, as well as a sauna, 2 swimming pools, Jacuzzi, and gym plus tennis court. This hotel is popular with Dominicans for their events, so there's often action around the lobby. You're within walking distance of the Museum of Dominican Man and the cultural center, as well as Plaza Criollo shops, and not far from downtown. *Hotel.*

★ **Hotel Hispaniola** • *on Avenida Independencia, across from Hotel Santo Domingo* • has been spruced up, with improvements at the casino, but is still not as "classy," in my opinion, as its more elegant sister-hotel (Santo Domingo) across the road. The hotel has a history that goes back to the days of *Paz* (peace), which is what this place was called when Argentine Dictator Juan Peron lived here in temporary exile. Favorite rooms for those who want to be near the pool are the garden suites, some of which are used on long-term lease by Dominicans. *Hotel.*

Hotel Naco and Casino • *on Av. Tiradentes, near a shopping center in the city* • offers comfortable lodgings and one of the city's casinos. Although favored by regulars and residents (rather than the usual American tourist), the hotel is well-known to business folk who appreciate the facilities. Fairly standard insofar as appearance is concerned, Naco can be convenient and comfortable. There's a pool and restaurant, with other dining choices nearby. *Hotel.*

Hostal Nicolas de Ovando • *on Calle las Damas in the Colonial City* • stands on a historic site on the east bank of the Ozama River, within easy walking distance of the Old City's many worthy sights. A casino has recently been added. The property occupies a site chosen by Nicolas de Ovando in the 16th century as the locale for the first European-style city in the New World. From 1502 to 1509, he lived in one of the houses that now make up the hotel. The Office of Cultural Patrimony took over the property and the neighboring historic house of Francisco Davila (built in the first years of the 16th century) to scrape off the abuses of ages, gut the interior, and restore what had become 3 houses (numbers 9, 11 and 13). At the present time, the bedrooms are furnished in ersatz medieval style. Although they have been plagued by a musty smell, the entire property has recently had a much needed refurbishing. There's a small pool in one of the river-rimming courtyards; the restaurant could be one of the city's best, but it continues to be "in a state of flux." *Hotel.*

★★★★ **Ramada Jaragua Resort, Casino, and European Spa** • *on the Malecon, next to the Sheraton* • is action-oriented, with beautifully furnished rooms with T.V., telephone, radio, and luxurious bathrooms. The lobby is spacious and elegant, with the casino to the left of the entrance and check-in to the right. Although there is a bar and snacking place at the casino, most of the restaurants are to your right, nearer the pool. Twilight *tapas,* the customary Spanish cocktail snacks, are offered gratis, along with entertainment most evenings. Bedrooms in the multi-story tower are best; rooms in the 2-story annex that is part of the old Jaragua hotel seem dark. The elaborate spa facilities include exercise rooms, sauna, and Jacuzzis, plus aerobics and exercise classes. Inquire about the spa package vacations. *Resort hotel.*

★★ **Hotel Santo Domingo** • *on Avenida Independencia, within sight of the sea* • was created with the elegance of a palatial Dominican home. Dominican marble floors, hand-fired tiles, and the lattice screens help establish the atmosphere created through the color and design sense of Dominican-born Oscar de la Renta and designer William Cox. Lofty air-filled courtyards have awnings at the edges and tropical plants throughout. Rooms are in two 5-story buildings, joined at one "corner," and framing courtyards. Many have sea view; others have garden view. All have modern, comfortable furnishings that are showing signs of wear and 45 of the total house count are balconied minisuites. The presidential suite occupies a top-floor corner with pool-and-sea view. As the first resort hotel in Santo Domingo, when it was built under Gulf + Western aegis in 1976, the hotel set the pace for Dominican tourism. It is now owned by the Florida-based Fajul family that also owns Hispaniola and the Casa de Campo resort. (The Dominican-American Chamber of Commerce maintains its offices here, and the place has been a favorite for businessmen who enjoy classy surroundings.) *Hotel.*

★★★ **Sheraton Santo Domingo Hotel & Casino** • *on the Avenida George Washington, the seaside boulevard popularly called the Malecon* • opened in the late 1970s. Rising 11 stories within an easy 15-minute walk from the colonial center, the Lama brothers' Sheraton has a Dominican personality, while offering the expected chain conveniences. The 361 rooms include 7 junior suites, 14 one-bedroom suites, a presidential suite, 11 rooms with sofa beds and a link to the standard rooms or suites, 5 rooms with Murphy beds for salesmen or others who want a living room look by day, and 4 rooms fitted for handicapped guests. The terrace around the pool, on the first floor (up one from the street level), is popular for business lunches, as well as daytime daliance, and *Antoine's* is one of the city's fashionable dining spots. (It can seem formidably quiet when you're one of a few dining here, however.) The shops at the entrance have good quality items, especially those in *Jaez,* where style is the keynote. The casino is to the left of the entrance. *Hotel.*

HOUSEKEEPING HOLIDAYS IN THE SANTO DOMINGO AREA are best at the beaches of Boca Chica, Juan Dolio, and elsewhere on the south coast. Most are Spanish-Dominican–style, and speaking Spanish certainly helps with the day-to-day necessities. Many of the lodgings are new, modern, fully furnished apartments and villas, part of condominium development schemes where units are available for rent in owners' absence. Other places are small, simple, and geared to an outdoor life that stands on no ceremony and isn't affected if the stove does not work (presumably because you can eat out or cook on a grill). There's not much in the city, but most of what's available will be listed through *ARAH,* a Dominican rental service with offices at 194 Avenida 27 de Febrero, Santo Domingo, D.R. It's also a good idea to check with the *American Chamber of Commerce* offices at the Hotel Santo Domingo. They will be able to give you names of realtors used to working with Americans and may know of some homes or apartments for rent. The U.S. Embassy is on Avenida Cesar Nicolas Penson, not far from the Plaza de la Cultura.

In the past couple of years, several "apart-hotels" have been built, to accommodate the increasing number of businesspeople and others who want the independence that a small kitchenette offers.

Plaza Naco • *on Av. Tiradentes, a few blocks from the Naco hotel* • was a newcomer for the '89 season. The 12-story building is filled with superior, deluxe, royale, and plaza suites, all with kitchen facilities. The plaza suites are the biggest and best, with a balcony, living area, and kitchen in addition to the bedroom. Conveniently located to shopping centers and many restaurants, this is a comfortable place for folks spending concentrated time in the capital.

Among the other apartment facilities are **Arah Apart-Hotel** (33 units; T 809+567-4267), **Delta Apart-Hotel** (69 units; T 809+535-7471), **Plaza Colonial** (108 units; T 809+687-9111); **Plaza Florida** (33 units; T 809+689-0151), **Plaza del Sol** (23 units; T 809+687-1317), and **Turey** (12 units; T 809+562-5271).

THE INN WAY is not a style popular in the Santo Domingo area. There are no "inns," in the traditional sense of small, owner-operated places with cozy, homelike atmosphere.

LOW-COST LODGING: Because of the U.S. dollar to Dominican peso ratio, hotels that are primarily for Dominicans are very inexpensive by U.S. standards. Because most hotels on the north coast have been built with North American and European tourists in mind, they are usually more expensive than the hotels in the capital. Be aware, however, that some of the hotels in the capital are geared to business traffic. They will not have the usual tourist amenities, although several do have swimming pools, and speaking Spanish is essential. Timid tourists should check carefully before booking a very inexpensive hotel; some hotels—and some of the motels on the road from the airport to town—have daytime traffic and rent rooms for the day (or by the hour). Among the small hotels used by businessmen and some tourists are:

Bolivar • *on Avenida Bolivar 62* • is not far from the Cervantes Hotel, but without a swimming pool (and, therefore, even less expensive). Further inquiries are recommended before booking one of the 16 rooms. *Hotel.*

Hotel Cervantes • *on Calle Cervantes, a side street within walking distance of the Sheraton and the Malecon* • is an inexpensive hotel with a good restaurant, pleasant pool, and easy access to major sights and shops in the city. Although rooms border on being spartan, and views *may* be over the small pool but will more likely be into neighbors' houses, the basics are here. If price is a consideration, one of the 140 rooms could be acceptable. *Hotel.*

★ **Continental** • *on Avenida Maximo Gomez* • has a small pool and *Le Jardin* restaurant. It's popular with knowledgeable businessmen who speak Spanish. Within easy walking distance to several good restaurants along the

Malecon (the seaside boulevard), the hotel is not too far from the Sheraton and the Jaragua. The best of the 100 modern hotel-style rooms have a sea view. *Hotel.*

Napolitano • *on George Washington, as the Malecon is formally called* • has one of the city's best located dining terraces, if you like cafe-style places with a good view of the Malecon pedestrian (and other) traffic. Rooms rise in a tower, with those that have a view of the sea the best bet (although they do absorb the street noises). Pizza on the hotel's terrace can be a pleasant pastime; the pool is the cooling off place after a stroll to and around the Old City. *Hotel.*

★ **San Geronimo Hotel & Casino** • *on Ave. Independencia* • is one street inland from the Malecon (near the Sheraton and others). The 72-room, multi-story hotel is modern, with comfortable, sometimes small, air-conditioned rooms, plus suites with kitchenettes. The public bus passes along for easy (and inexpensive) access to the Old City and elsewhere. *Hotel.*

SHORESIDE LODGINGS ON THE SOUTH COAST center at three main locales: Boca Chica, about a 30-minute drive along the shore, southeast of the capital and a long-time favorite for Santo Domingo residents; Playa Juan Dolio, farther east on the south coast, about an hour's drive from Santo Domingo; and the beaches near the town of La Romana, where Casa de Campo resort is joined by a couple of other places. (For hotels and facilities near La Romana, see pages 326–329; included in the coverage below is *Hotel Playa Real,* on its own beach near Juan Dolio.)

BOCA CHICA is the best beach near the capital. About 10 miles east of the airport, the area has burgeoned in recent years, in response to the new affluence of some Dominicans and their interest in investing in tourism. A series of shore-side cafes and informal lodgings line the road that runs along the beach. Among the most entertaining are *Lindomar, Picolo Italiana* (with guest-house rooms for rent), *Golden Beach* (also with rooms), *Restaurant Aircoris,* and *Guamira* (with a few simple rooms).

Boca Chica Beach Resort • *near, but not on, the beach* • is a multi-room hotel where the best rooms have seaview balconies; all the U.S.-style rooms are air-conditioned. "Superior" rooms have refrigerators; 2-room suites have 2 bathrooms and a kitchen. Operated on an "all-inclusive" plan (which means room and taxes, meals, liquor, sports equipment, and activities), the hotel is within easy strolling distance of all the cafes and activities. There's a pool in front, where the scuba clinic is given. Windsurfing is popular. Taxi fare from the airport is about $10. *Hotel.*

AUTHOR'S OBSERVATION
If you think Boca Chica sounds like your kind of place, make a visit to look things over before you book a room. This place is for the young in spirit or in fact.

PLAYA JUAN DOLIO has a beachside fun-in-the-sun focus that takes its cue from Canadian and European package-tour vacationers who have joined wealthy Dominicans on the once quiet beaches. There are hundreds of bedrooms in dozens of places to stay, with many more being built. Among the best of the lot are:

Costa Linda • *on the shore* • is in the first phase of a condominium plan, with several units open for this season. Although rooms are compact, there's everything here for light housekeeping. *Apts.*

Decameron • *at the shore* • is a big hotel with several restaurants, a casino, a disco, and plenty of action in a multi-story hotel atmosphere. Built for groups and often full of them, this place aspires to be a first-class hotel. *Hotel.*

Don Juan Beach Resort • *at the palm-studded beach* • is a 4-story, multi-room hotel where the best rooms have sea-view balconies. All are modern, in U.S. style. The activities desk can arrange for watersports and tours. There's a pool in front, near the white-sand beach. *Hotel.*

Metro Hotel and Marina • *on the beach* • has tennis courts, swimming pool, Jacuzzi, and a range of watersports from waterskiing, boardsailing, and sailing to scuba diving. The air-conditioned, modern rooms have view of either sea or pool. All have a telephone and color TV. *El Puerto* is the air-conditioned restaurant; *El Velero* is the seaside dining terrace. *Hotel.*

Palmas del Mar • *at the beach* • is a good place for a self-sufficient holiday in Spanish surroundings. Gathered around the tennis courts, with a pavilion for dancing (on the nights there is music), the apartments were designed by Manuel Del Monte, best-known to some for his tireless work on the restored area of the Old City of Santo Domingo. *Apts.*

Playa Canes • *amid the cluster of lodgings* • near the beach, has several apartments with a hotel-services feeling. There's a casual restaurant for times when guests prefer not to use the kitchenette facilities. All activities nearby. *Apts.*

Hotel Playa Real • *on the beach about a 20-minute drive east of Juan Dolio amid a flourishing palm grove* • can be a special spot for those who are seeking sea, sun, and solitude. Although the hotel is sometimes used as the luncheon stop for day tours between Santo Domingo and Altos de Chavon, most of the time things are pretty quiet. Ideal for small groups of congenial people, the hotel offers modern rooms in several buildings, a pool, pleasant alfresco dining facilities (where food was mediocre when I tried it), and unhurried atmosphere. *Hotel.*

Punta Garza Beach Club • *at the beach* • is a cluster of 2-story white stucco buildings, capped with terra cotta roofs in a style that bears a Dominican imprint. This place is popular with folks who enjoy housekeeping at the beach. *Apts.*

Sea Shells • *a short walk from the beach* • is one of this season's new spots. The modern hotel rooms are small but comfortable. There's an on-premise restaurant. *Hotel.*

Talanquera • *near the beach* • has a pool, tennis courts, and plans for a casino. The 224 modern, comfortable rooms are often booked by Canadians who found the Playa Juan Dolio area on low-cost package plans. *Hotel.*

Villas del Mar • *near the beach* • are sprinkled along the shore, down a dirt road off the main coastal road, which weaves a bit inland at this section. For a beach-focused holiday amid Spanish-speaking Dominican families who come out from Santo Domingo on weekends, this place offers comfortable surroundings. Don't count on a lot of on-premise entertainment, but there's plenty nearby. *Apts.*

RESTAURANTS IN SANTO DOMINGO are some of the Caribbean's best, and prices, compared to what people are paying elsewhere, are very reasonable when converted into pesos. Because the Dominican Republic is one of the few Caribbean countries where almost everything can be grown, raised, or caught locally (good vegetables, rice, coffee, beef, and, of course, chickens and fish), most of the meals use fresh produce and will be excellent—with specialties prepared according to tried-and-true recipes of qualified chefs. Dominicans love good food and quality surroundings and expect to pay for them.

You can still find very inexpensive, excellent food in small places in the countryside where the Dominican country people eat, and prices in Santo Domingo's well-known restaurants and at the tourist-and-otherwise popular places around the country will figure to about $20 per person for a full meal.

In sharp contrast to the situation on many Caribbean islands, the luxury restaurants in the hotels are usually dependable. Hotel Santo Domingo's *Alcazar,* Sheraton *Antoine's,* Embajador's *Le Diplomat,* and the Dominican Concorde's *La Casa* are attractive.

★ **La Bahia** • *on the Malecon near the Old City* • is the best bet for a casual place with top-notch seafood. This inauspicious-looking spot, on a corner near the port in Santo Domingo is a Dominican (and my) favorite restaurant. Tourist-type Americans are a rare commodity, but Dominican couples and families fill this place almost every evening (but not until 9 p.m. or later). Wood chairs with rush seats are pulled up to simple tables, and discreet people-watching is a pastime, if you're not lucky enough to have your own group of lively conversationalists. Camarones (shrimp) are superb; lambi (conch) is good, and the price is right—at about RD$15 per entree. This is a place to settle in for seafood Dominican style.

★★ **El Bodegon** • *at Arzobispo Merino 152, in the Old City at the corner of the Plaza, not far from the cathedral* • is an air-conditioned pocket of dining pleasure, with tile floors, dark-wood accents, and a comfortable atmosphere for enjoying award-winning meals. Try the cassoulet a la Gascona (lamb and pork stew with sausage) at RD$20, zarzuela de mariscos at RD$25 or, if you're budget-watching, spaghetti at about RD$10. Pato al higo (duck) and mero a la vasca (bass with garlic sauce) are specialties.

★★★ **Il Buco** • *next door to El Bodegon on Arzobispo Merino and not far from the Centro Dominicano de Informacion Touristica* • is well worth an evening reservation. The owner came back to the city after a few years at the Gulf + Western Casa de Campo complex and opened his special restaurant on the site of what had been La Casa Verde. Specialties include the homemade pasta, well-cooked fish, and delicious desserts displayed on a trolley that is wheeled to your table. Be sure to attempt the antipasto assortment. The place is open for lunch and very popular in the evening with Dominicans (who like to dine late). Decor, with brick walls and stucco arches, gives an Old World feeling, very fitting for a place that is a short walk from the city's historic cathedral and other buildings. Plan for a leisurely Dominican-style meal here, and know that you will part with $20 per person for a meal with full flourishes, accompanied by wine.

Cafe St. Michel • *on Lope de Vega 24* • specializes in fresh fish, cooked and served with French-style sauces. The attractive surroundings add a lot to the experience and offerings I've sampled warrant repeat visits.

★★ **Chez Francois** • *near the Cathedral in the restored Old City* • is top of my list for French cuisine, if you want to sample that in a Spanish-heritage country. Surroundings are spectacular, with antiques and other decorator touches, and the place is perfect for a late-and-elegant evening. Count on your meal costing RD$25 or so, with wine and flourishes.

Fonda de la Atarazana • *across the road from the Alcazar in downtown Santo Domingo* • is worth a stop for a cool beverage off the courtyard and a look out the window of the second-floor restaurant. If you get the right table, you'll be at eye level with Diego Columbus's home, a spectacular sight when it's night-lighted, but a good view anytime. Portions and food were heavy (country Dominican) when I tried this spot, but it's worth a visit for ambience, and for convenience when you're touring the Old City.

La Fromagerie • *at Plaza Criolla* • serves special cheese dishes, as its name suggests, but other entrees follow French style. Cozy and pleasant, this place is worth a visit.

Jai Lai • *on Avenida Independencia, inland from the Sheraton* • serves seafood and Peruvian specialties (beef) in a former home. The service has been exceptional on recent visits, and the surroundings are pleasant. The location is convenient to reach by foot before or after a stroll along the seaside Malecon (as is the Dominican custom).

★★★ **Jardin de Jade** • *at the Embajador Hotel* • is a favorite for good Chinese food in a reasonably formal setting. A daily special lunch is offered for business people and others. The smaller round tables, with the revolving circular tray in the middle, make for easy enjoyment, and the Peking duck, complete with crepes, sprouts, and sauces, is wonderful. This place is worth trying, when you want a break from more elaborate international fare.

★★★ **Lina's** • *at Gran Hotel Lina on Avenida Maximo Gomez* • is the nickname of Marcelina Aguado, the renowned creator of the restaurant. When she came from Spain, at the behest of Trujillo to be his special cook, it seemed highly unlikely that her name would denote one of the country's best hotels. From modest beginnings, selling her best-known products from a street stall, Lina's restaurant now thrives in expanded and refurbished surroundings. Zarzuela, which is seafood, including shrimp, lobster, bits of clams, with Pernod in the sauce, is worth ordering; I prefer to stick with the seafood offerings. The lunchtime fixed-price special is a true bargain. Desserts are delicious, if you like *very* sweet custards and the like.

★ **La Meson de la Cava** • *on Avenida Mirador del Sur* • better known as a nightclub near the Embajador Hotel, is also worth a dinner. Ottico Ricart, owner and chef overseer does some of the cooking himself, but your primary reason for coming here will not be only food (although the filet mignon can be superb). The place is 50 feet below the road; you pirouette down a perilous staircase that looks like it leads from a manhole cover. You can cuddle in a corner of the caves, or settle for a traditional table for two or more. Touristy? Yes, but well done and worth the investment in time and money. The nightly live music starts at 9 p.m.

Piccolo Gourmet • *on Avenida Lincoln* • is regarded by some as the finest restaurant, not only for food but also for atmosphere. Italian sauces and spices with seafood, veal, chicken, and beef cover the range of offerings. Desserts can be special and strong Dominican coffee punctuates the finale.

★ **Vesuvio** • *on the Malecon* • has been popular since its opening in 1953. Dominicans enjoying a casual night out settle into the alfresco tables near the entrance to the air-conditioned (and cold) inner sanctum, which is a favorite for family celebrations. If you plan ahead, you can have a feast of suckling pig, but otherwise settle for one of the Italian specialties (fettucine at about $4, antipasto priced by the item, and homemade manicotti) or the steaks and seafood that are still the most popular items on the menu. The appetizer cart can provide a meal in itself, but ask Enzo Bonarelli, your host, for his suggestion for the evening special. Obviously the Italian fare is dependable. With the a la carte menu, you can find an entree and skip out leaving less than $10. (Closed Wed.)

The terrace of **Napolitano Hotel,** where you can get small pizzas as well as other snacks, is one of several places along Malecon where you can join Dominicans for the late-evening hours. **El Castillo,** on the sea-side of Malecon, is another (be sure to sit outside). Horse-drawn carriages are part of the parade that passes along the shore-rimming road, and you'll find the open-to-breezes places busy until the early hours of dawn. Sample the platos tipicos which include modongo (tripe—which appears on the menu as "beef stripe") or the bollito de yucca, a cheese and ground yucca root finger-sized nibble that is deep fried and delicious—if you like that kind of thing. Strictly casual, cafe style is the atmosphere.

For easy and relatively inexpensive city dining, there are always the hotel coffee shops, but don't count on the best Dominican food there. The few offerings on the menu are Americanized beyond recognition, and you'll do better with something you know is American—a club sandwich, or fruit or avocado salad, for example. If your stomach can stand it (and mine has often) buy chicharones, pastelitos, or empanadas from the street vendors or the cafes along the Malecon. The first is fried and crispy pork rind; the second and third are little and big pastries made from yucca flour and filled with spicy ground meat. The oranges and pineapples you'll see for sale from carts, especially in the country, are always juicy and delicious.

Good local rums are *Bermudez, Sibonney,* and *Brugal,* all readily available and a lot less expensive than scotch or other imported alcohol, which carries high duty. *Presidente* and *Carona* are two of the DR's good beers.

NATURAL SURROUNDINGS: Among the islands that form the eastern rim of the Caribbean sea, only Jamaica, Puerto Rico, Martinique, Guadeloupe, and Cuba have a range of natural attributes comparable to those that can be enjoyed in the Dominican Republic. The difference between the five other places and the Dominican Republic is that this country has no organized system of national parks or trails for its mountainous midlands, making it difficult for the average visitor to find (or gather information about) the areas that might be of most interest. Spanish-speaking visitors have an advantage; many of the Dominicans who know and love their countryside are not fluent in English.

The central Cordillera mountain range offers astounding flora and fauna, cascading rivers, and forest preserves, as well as remarkable views in the areas where the verdant foliage permits a vista. The highest mountain, Pico Duarte, is almost 10,000 feet. Among the many flowers around the countryside, there are more than 300 varieties of orchids, many of them available for export through the Orchid Garden (Arroyo Hondo) at the Botanical Garden in Santo Domingo.

Those who make the 4-hour drive, between Puerto Plata and Santo Domingo (north-south), will enjoy lovely views of the country's highest mountain ranges, after passing acres of sugar cane, tobacco and other crops. Pine trees and colorful gardens are part of the scenery in the mountain valleys. Santiago, the country's second city, is surrounded by the Yaque del Norte river, in a region known as El Cibao, which is protected by mountain ranges.

In the western sector of the country, near the Haitian border, Enriquillo Lake is below sea level. The salt mines near the lake lend their salinity to the water, which is home for alligators. Iguanas and other fauna thrive in the surrounding area, which is visited only by adventuresome travelers. Also in this area, Los Patos springs join to form a river that runs parallel to the coastline.

Little is known about most of the reefs and terrain in surrounding seas. The best-known area is La Caleta, with two reefs and surroundings, which has been designated as an underwater park. Favorite sights are Los Bajos coral hills and the fish that have glommed around the *Hickory,* a ship sunk a few years ago to create a potential dive site. From La Romana, Catalina Island is surrounded by good dive sites, especially off its north coast. (The island is a Dominican Navy station.) The coral reef that runs from La Romana east to the offshore Isla Saona is a popular diving area. There are also documented sites off the east end and off the north coast, near Sosua and east of the Playa Dorada resorts.

PLACES WORTH FINDING ON THE SOUTH COAST: The 16th-century restored area of **Colonial Santo Domingo** leads the list, with the Cathedral, Casas Reales, and Casa de Colon three "requirements." Ambitious restoration projects are already underway, to put this area in prime condition for the 500th anniversary of the discovery of America, in 1992. When Miguel Diaz thought he had killed the servant of Don Bartolome Colon (Columbus), Christopher's brother, he fled from the settlement in the north, and made his way to the south coast, where he met and fell in love with an Indian princess who lived with her tribe on the banks of the Ozama. When he became despondent with longing for his friends, she urged him to go north and bring some of them back. He did, only to find that he had not, in fact, killed the servant and was not a criminal. He then waxed enthusiastic about his home in the south, and the gold mines at Jaina nearby. According to Samuel Hazard's report in his writings in 1873, Don Bartolome confirmed the fact of the mines, checked with his brother for approval, and moved the whole north coast town of Isabela south to settle New Isabela on the banks of the Ozama. Columbus is thought to have visited when he returned from Spain in August 1498; the name change came either in honor of the day (Sunday) when the town was founded or of the father of Columbus, whose name was Domingo.

Soon after Nicolas de Ovando succeeded as governor in 1502, a hurricane wiped out the town, which he ordered rebuilt on the other side of the river, where it now stands. Hazard quotes Ovideo, a 16th-century historian, as saying that "as touching the buildings, there is no city in Spain, not even Barcelona, so much to be preferred as San Domingo. The houses for the most part are stone—the situation is much better than Barcelona, by reason that the streets are much larger and wider, and without comparison straighter and more direct, being laid out with cord, compass and measure. In the midst of the city is the fortress and castle, and such houses so fair and large that they may well receive any lord or noble of Spain with his train and family, and especially is this true of that of Don Diego Columbus."

Santo Domingo's Colonial City represents a multi-million dollar investment on the part of the Dominican government, with the help of Spain and other donors, but its value is far greater to anyone interested in history. Not as authentic as Old San Juan, Puerto Rico (where the 16th- and 17th-century buildings remained to be restored), the rebuilding of the Old City of Santo Domingo has been modern, based on the old design.

Casa de Colon, also known as the **Alcazar,** is the house where Diego Colon (Columbus) lived with his bride (Dona Maria de Toledo y Rojas, a niece of King Ferdinand). The house is furnished as it might have been when they lived there in the 1500s. Most of the antiques have been donated by Spanish interests, and the handiwork (note the ceilings and tiled floors) was under the tutelage of Juan Guzman who worked with Manuel Del Monte Urraca. The tiles amid the terra cotta on the floors show a lion (Ferdinand) and a castle (Isabella).

The 3 tapestries are especially valuable. Although they are 17th-century, they depict the Columbus story. Note especially the 16th-century kitchen with tiles, and two wood benches by the fireplace. Food was carried up the narrow spiral stairs which you can climb to reach the second floor dining rooms. One room is for the children, the other more formal for adults. There are ivory-encrusted desks and other furniture in the main hall, which was used for receptions; and the view from the balconies over the Ozama can be impressive. (Squint to overlook the modern boxcars, etc.) Despite what you may be told, the Alcazar is newly built, with stones mined from an area similar to that which was used for the original building. The government invested more than $1 million in the palace they first reopened, with fanfare, on Columbus Day 1957. (Several million more has been invested recently in paving and reconstructing the Colonial City.) King Juan Carlos and his Queen Sofia were feted here first at an elegant reception during their visit in 1975, following placement of additional gifts from Spain and completion of some of the work on the nearby areas—notably La Atarazana, Calle Las Damas, and the cathedral—and several times on their visits since then.

La Atarazana is where the conquistadors and others used to bring their ships for supplies and repair. It is the first arsenal in the New World, where arms and military equipment were stored and troops were trained. Today, after tireless work by the Oficina de Patrimonio Cultural, and its former director Manuel Del Monte Urraca, who trained with others in Spain, Atarazana is catacombed with shops and small restaurants, and may eventually have some small hotels, although none have been forthcoming in recent years. Although the appearance of the area is true to the 16th century all the construction is new, using old walls and arches when they were worthy and solid, with electric wires underground and brick walks unknown to the early settlers.

Samuel Hazard comments that "the walls of the older houses are very solidly constructed either of stone or . . . mamposteria . . . glutinous earth . . . mixed with lime, and sometimes . . . with powdered stone; frames of plans are then made . . . and filled with layers of this composition, sand and lime being added. The whole is then moistened with water, well pounded and kneaded, and allowed to dry, the mould being withdrawn, leaves a firm solid wall, which, on exposure to the air, becomes hard as stone. Even the walls of the city are built in this way." And then he adds that "with the exception of the old churches, there are few really imposing buildings in the city."

As you walk from the Alcazar, along Calle Las Damas past Hostal Nicolas de Ovando, think what this street must have been like in the 16th century, when it was the area popular for the official twilight promenade for the ladies of the court. If you plan your stroll for late afternoon, notice the pink cast to the walls as the sun goes down.

Casas Reales (Tues.–Fri., 9 a.m.–12 p.m., 3–6 p.m.; Sat. 10 a.m.–6 p.m.; RD$1 adults, RD$.50 children; English-speaking guides available, booklet in English for RD$7.50), on the west side of the street (the right, as you walk south with the Alcazar at your back), is a restoration in the 16th-century style of what was the Palacio de la Real Audiencia y Chancilleria de Indias y el Palacio de los Governadores y Capitanes Generales de la Isla Espanola (Palace of the Royal Audience of the Indies and the Palace of the Governors and Captains-General of Santo Domingo). The name of Casas Reales has been noted in the earliest documents of the city, when it was mentioned that the governor and the captains-general lived on the upper floor of the northwestern part of the building; the rest of the upper floor was occupied by the room for the royal audience, while the treasury and the counting house were on street level. If you don't do more than look at the large map of the world Columbus knew, showing his voyages in colored lights (in room 1), the visit is worth it, but the furniture is impressive and the entire restoration and museum give an excellent picture of the trappings and interests of life in the 16th and 17th centuries. In room #3 are exhibits of mining, agriculture, livestock, and the uses of tobacco in the Dominican economy; then you walk through what were the stables and the powder magazine to the carriage houses, past statues of A. de Suazo and Nicolas de Ovando to reach the coin room. Created as a landmark on October 18, 1973, the museum was opened May 31, 1976, when King Juan Carlos of Spain visited the country.

Casa de Bastidas (Tues.–Sun. 9 a.m.–12 p.m., 3–6 p.m.), on the east side of Calle Las Damas, was the home of Rodrigo de Bastidas, mayor of Santo Domingo. It opened in late 1977 as a museum for treasures found on sunken ships. Note the trees that flourish in the courtyard you walk through to reach the small museum.

Farther along the Calle Las Damas, on the river side of the street, you will pass **Fortaleza Ozama,** restored as a park, and the **Torre del Homenaje,** dedicated to Queen Isabella in 1507 and home for Diego Colon while his palace was being built. Sir Francis Drake burned the tower when he pillaged the city in 1586. Modern day notoriety comes with the fact that the tower was the hovel where political prisoners were tossed during the reign (1930–1961) of Generalissimo Rafael Leonidas Trujillo. Turn right at the tower to stroll past the bishop's houses to the cathedral.

"**The Cathedral,** the most interesting building in Santo Domingo, is in its interior a grand old church, with pillars and arches and crypts and altars innumerable; and as we view its vast extent we can readily believe the accounts of the various historians, who give such glowing relations of its splendors in ancient days. Its exterior bears the marks of its great antiquity upon its form, not only in the weather stained walls, but in the quaint architecture," Samuel Hazard commented following his visit in the 1870s. The same is true today. Built in the style of a Roman church, between 1512 and 1540 from stone by workmen who left for richer Mexico and other Central American cities before they finished the job, the cathedral was embellished with gold and silver which has been snitched by subsequent city occupants, "principally . . . during the occupation of the French," Samuel Hazard claims.

As you enter through the side gates, you walk into a small chapel where Sir Francis Drake is said to have slung his hammock to sleep—waking long enough to rob, pillage, and threaten the Spaniards and to chop off both hands of the bishop's statue, which stands nearby. Drake called this room home for his tumultuous 24-day stay in 1586, when he tried to barter with Diego Colon for the safety of the town and ended up burning most of it down. A very nice "antikee," I was told by one guide, is the baroque Virgin, which dates from 1774. Look at the cherubs over one of the portals; their mouths form do, re, mi, fa, sol, la ti—and then you have to go back to "do." The choir used to stand above them. Below them, on the side of the arch, the three crosses mark the spot for political asylum. In the old days, if a prisoner could touch this spot, he would be given freedom and escorted out of the city.

The "bones of Columbus" used to be held here; they've now been removed to the new Columbus Lighthouse monument. When you step outside to look at the face of the cathedral, note the frescoes, which are said to date from 1586, and the statues that replace bronze ones Sir Francis Drake gets credit for taking. In 1512 the bell was put in the bell tower and the 5 bells there today still ring at regular daily intervals.

The plazas surrounding the cathedral have been fringed with some tourist shops and are the arena for the "hey, lady" sidewalk salesmen and the black-market money men. If you are on your own, sit for a few minutes in the park at the foot of the statue of Columbus (who is supposed to be pointing to the New World—north—but in fact is pointing right at the Hipotecaria Universal S.A. with the Bank of America on its right). A devoted Indian maiden languishes at the base, carefully putting the final touches to Columbus's name with a quill. This statue was erected in 1887, in lieu of a lighthouse, which had been suggested by historian Antonio del Monte y Tejada in 1852.

Casa del Cordon, so named because of the cord of the order of Saint Francis over its main door, is a bank, but it is a bank with a conscience. The building is faithfully restored as it might have looked when it was built in 1503 for Don Francisco de Garay. Diego Colon and his wife Maria lived here when the Torre del Homenaje was damaged and before the Alcazar was completed. Two of their seven children were born in this house. This is the house to which the ladies of Santo Domingo came to donate their jewels in hopes of staving off the rampage of Sir Francis Drake, who was then swaggering around town. The restored Casa del Cordon was reopened on March 16, 1974; trained guides can show you around the boardroom and the executive offices so that you can see how a 16th-century building has been adapted to 20th-century commerce.

The Columbus Lighthouse, on the sea side of Los Tres Ojos (see below), not far from the airport, is President Balaguer's dream and the realization of an idea that was first suggested in 1852. He intends for the lighthouse, which will be inaugurated in 1992 as part of the "Discovery of America" 500th anniversary celebrations, "to be to Santo Domingo what the pyramids are to Egypt." The elaborate plans, designed by English architect J. L. Gleave and implemented by Dominican architect Teofilo Carbonell, include six museums, a laser-beam lighthouse, and a chapel that holds "Columbus's bones." The fact is, no one knows for sure where the actual bones are located. Historian Samuel Hazard mentions in his book that, in 1783, Frenchman Moreau de Saint-Mery found a lead coffin that he claimed held Columbus's bones. He was probably right, but they could have been the bones of Bartolome (brother), Diego (son), or Christopher (the discoverer), since all were eventually buried together. For decades, Cuba claimed the bones (no longer accepted as fact), and you can visit an elaborate tomb holding "the bones" in Seville, Spain. One recent theory is that some of Christopher's bones are in Seville, and some in the Dominican Republic, the result of a hurried excavation of ruined tombs in Santo Domingo in 1795, when only part of the Columbus family dust was scooped up to be reburied in Cuba, whence it made its way eventually to Seville. (Thomas Dozier's article, "The Controversy on the Whereabouts of Columbus' Body," in an issue of the *Smithsonian* magazine, gives an interesting perspective on the saga.)

No matter where the bones actually are, once a year, Santo Domingo celebrates with a procession—and the 500th anniversary should be a big event.

Direccion Nacional de Parques maintains several open spaces in and around Santo Domingo. The **Parque Litoral del Sur** fringes the Malecon (Avenida George Washington) between the Hotel Santo Domingo and the center of the Colonial City, with a sidewalk promenade for most of that distance, but guests at the Dominicana will look over **Paseo de Los Indios** and the **Parque Mirador del Sur,** an ideal (and perfectly safe) jogging or bicycling area that stretches out in front of the hotel. You can take the train around the grounds for 20¢. The several restaurants and play areas scattered around the park are favorite gathering spots for Dominicans when they have some leisure time; the grounds are very well kept and benches are prevalent.

Parque Zoologico Nacional, at the northern rim of the city in an area overlooking the Rio Isabela, moved to its present site a couple of years ago. Universitaria Nacional Pedro Henriquez Urena administers the park, which has a lake for aquatic birds and an aviary for exotic and native birds as well as an African plain where the animals roam and a children's zoo. There's a train that tours the park (40¢ adults, 15¢ children). Especially for children, the **Parque de Atracciones Infantiles** is on the site of the former zoo and botanical garden, between Avenida Bolivar and Cesar Nicolas Penson in the center of the city. In addition to the animal exhibits, there are caves to prowl around and special rides including a ferris wheel and ponies.

Jardin Botanico Nacional Dr. Rafael M. Moscoso (Tues.–Sun. 9 a.m.–12 p.m., 2–5 p.m.; closed Mon.; 25¢ adults, 15¢ children; $1 boat; $5 carriage; 50¢ train, 25¢ children) is not too far from the zoo, in the Gala area of the city. You can tour the grounds by horse carriage, as well as by train and boat. There are more than 200 varieties of palm trees, in addition to a Japanese garden area and a research section that includes diagrams of the country, and special laboratories (speaking Spanish makes a difference, if you're serious about some research).

Parque Los Tres Ojos, off the Autopista de Las Americas on the way to Boca Chica and the airport, is on most tours, often included with the new Columbus monument. It is actually 4 "eyes," or caves, that were mentioned in early histories of the city. If you are interested in stalagmites and stalactites you might enjoy the "eyes." Follow the tours through and around the pools. There's a lot of climbing involved, so this is not an excursion for people with weak knees or weak hearts. Those people can content themselves with bargaining for some of the handmade items that will be offered the minute you step off your bus at the grounds. (If you want to glimpse Los Tres Ojos, allow an extra hour to do so on your trip to the airport.)

Plaza de la Cultura is an impressive combination of modern buildings on the outskirts of downtown Santo Domingo, in an area that once was property of Generalissimo Trujillo. There are 2½-hour tours of the area on Tuesdays and Saturdays at 2:30 p.m. Cost is RD$8.50, which includes museum entrance fees. **Museo del Hombre Dominicano** (check for opening hours, which change) should be on top of the list of out-of-the-sun diversions for anyone with an interest in Caribbean history. Dioramas, maps, and displays of artifacts found in excavations around the Dominican Republic and elsewhere in the Caribbean are attractively presented. Knowing Spanish helps if you want to know details; there are very few notices printed in English, and from my experience, even the guide's commentary is not complete. The **Teatro Nacional** is the hub of the symphony and opera life. Special performances by visiting artists are a highlight of the impressive season, which focuses mostly on Dominican artists. Check with the social director at your hotel or with the Dominican Information Center near the cathedral in the Colonial City for details about obtaining tickets. (If you really care about attending something, find out as soon as possible after you check into your hotel what performances are planned while you are in town.) In addition to the Museum of Dominican Man and the National Theater, the **Museum of Natural History,** the **Museum of Fine Arts,** and the **Public Library** are here—with the "Wind Rose Fountain" that looks like a dandelion gone to seed in the middle of the mall and mango trees around the grounds. (The U.S. Embassy is nestled nearby, in splendor among the Central Bank and government offices, including the Dominican IRS.)

Other "Places Worth Finding" include **Altos de Chavon** (see "La Romana" section), which can be visited in one long day from Santo Domingo (with a 2-hour drive each way), and those at the north coast, a 4-hour drive (or an hour's small-plane flight) north around Puerto Plata from Luperon, on the west to Cabarete on the east. (Allow at least 2 days.)

SPORTS IN SANTO DOMINGO include tennis, golf, and jogging at Paseo de los Indios. For sailing and scuba, you'll have to head for the beachfront areas such as La Romana, Puerto Plata, Punta Cana, and Samana.

Tennis courts can be found at the Jaragua, Dominican Concorde, Sheraton, Embajador, and Santo Domingo hotels, as well as at Gran Hotel Lina. Santo Domingo Country Club's 18-hole **golf** course is available for guests by special arrangement. Your hotel's activities desk can usually help with details. It's possible to drive (2 hours each way) to the excellent courses at Casa de Campo, but that makes a long day.

Scuba diving is possible, but the D.R. is not the best place to learn. Pool lessons are similar to those offered at other Caribbean resorts, but the offshore exploration is recommended only for experienced divers. La Caleta Reef and the reefs off Playa Palenque, where you can dive around ancient cannons, are two places that Scuba firms take their clients. (Check to see who is operating, and with what credentials, if you're interested in diving. *Buceo Dominicano* [T 809+521–2094] is one established firm.) If you are experienced and hire a guide, Cabo Frances Viego, Rio San Juan, and Playa Magante can be challenging and interesting. Check with your hotel activities desk for prices and details about scuba excursions, and resort or regular certification courses. At Playa Juan Dolio, the *Diver's Den,* on the inland side of the main road, has diving equipment and offers guides and instruction. For Puerto Plata, see p. 332.

Fishermen should zero in on Casa de Campo for access to the fleet of Bertram 35s or to Boca Chica, where *Andres Boca Chica Club* (T 809+685–4940) arranges boats and tackle. The *Club Nautico de Santo Domingo*'s Boca de Yuma Fishing International tournament out of the east end marina, usually takes place in May. Established more than 20 years ago, the tournament includes only white and blue marlins, sailfish, and tuna for points—and speaking Spanish is a definite plus if you want to have any fun with this one. (T 809+566–

1684.) Contact *Mundo Submarino* for specific facts about other fishing opportunities.

Horseback riding can be arranged through your hotel's activities desk. Paso Fino horses came to the Dominican Republic in 1493, when 25 of them limped off the ships of Columbus. From here, they went to Puerto Rico with Martin de Salazar in 1509, to Cuba with Diego de Velazquez in 1511, and to Mexico with Cortez in 1518. There are regional shows of Paso Finos around the country, with the *Feria Garadera* (National Cattle Fair) usually held in February on the Malecon at Ciudad Ganadera. Since this is where many of the Paso Finos are stabled, you can see the horses almost any afternoon between four and six when the owners and trainers ride them. In addition to the polo matches held at Casa de Campo resort on the southeast coast, there are matches at Sierra Prieta in the capital, on most weekends from January through April.

TREASURES AND TRIFLES: Treasures are emerging—and being designed—amid what had become a landslide of simple, sloppy, overpriced tourist items that included a lot of amber that wasn't. Among the true treasures you can find today are the items at **Planarte,** an arm of the Fundacion Dominicana de Desarrollo, Inc. (Dominican Development Foundation), which works with country folk in the development of crafts in leather and ceramics. In their shop near the center of the Old City you can find well-made sandals at about RD$20, picture frames in leather, handbags, and several small pottery items that are easy to pack for the folks back home.

El Mercado Modelo, with one entrance on Avenida Molla, is a marvelous melange of colors, sounds, smells, and samples of all kinds of Dominican workmanship, some of it quite good. The market covers a block, with entrances on 4 sides, and is a clutter of stalls where folks sell the expected amber, larimar (which is a light blue stone, polished and put into all kinds of settings), wood, straw and pottery, in all shapes and sizes. There are many tortoise-shell items (which U.S. customs will confiscate if they find them among your belongings) and some come from cow horn, which is OK to buy. One of my Dominican treasures is a pottery coffee set, with a neatly designed pot and sugar bowl and 6 small cups and saucers, with cups that seem more suitable for egg holders than for a healthy slug of coffee. Similar sets can be bought at the market. In addition to the intrigue involved in finding special items amid the clutter, there's added pleasure in mixing with the Dominican people. Even those who are persistent salesmen are pleasant. Be prepared to buy, but not until you've bargained—plenty. It's part of the game.

Plaza Criolla, on Avenida 27 de Febrero near Maximo Gomez, is a place to shop for quality crafts. There's a gathering of shops including two exceptional jewelry stores, offering good quality items, all of them handmade and many of them exceptional. Surroundings are pleasant, in recently built boutiques linked by pathways, not far from the Gran Hotel Lina. In addition to the pottery, jewelry, and other traditional items, there are some nicely made clothes—and a few comfortable cafes and restaurants (*La Fromagerie* is one).

There are interesting items, also, at **El Circulo de Colecionistas,** just off Calle de las Damas on Calle Mercedes (check to see if the courtyard bistro has reopened). Items available here include attractive coasters with historic maps and prints as design, some limited-edition maps and prints for wall hangings, plus other quality items. Other Dominican work to look for includes some tortoise-shell items (which, since the U.S. government lists tortoise as an endangered species, are illegal to bring back to the U.S.), some good quality handmade furniture, baskets and macrame work if you like it, and some of the sculptured stone birds and other items that children make. These last make up in effort what they may lack in art. Altos de Chavon, 2 hours' drive along the south coast from the city, is a 1980s creation of a 16th-century Spanish-Dominican village that is devoted to handcrafts and paintings. Although not as overwhelming (yet) as Haiti's street vendors, Santo Dominguenos who flock around you in the Colonial City and at any tourist attraction can be tiresome. If you stop to look, be prepared to have young, supersalesmen come from every corner.

The Bishop's Basket at Avenida Independencia and Danae has good quality handicrafts, sold in a shop that is sponsored by the Episcopal Church. There are many tourist shops around the cathedral area, and some of them have a few worthy items amid the clutter. The **Columbus Gift Shop** at the Alcazar is another such spot.

For furniture, ask to find **Manuel Caceres's** work. He took the cue from the furniture designs Oscar de la Renta innovated for the former Gulf + Western hotels, and uses Creole techniques when he works with pine, horn, conch, plantain fiber, agave, sisal, and palm tree thatch. Some of the chairs, stools and tables are small enough to bring home without too much trouble, but do not ship furniture if you aren't prepared for a lot of problems. The process takes forever, and you may never see your treasure.

If you are short on reading matter, and can't find anything interesting in the hotel shops, stop at **El Greco** on Avenida Tiradentes to look through their selection of English-language paperbacks. Track down a copy of *Santo Domingo Past & Present, with a Glance at Hayti,* written in 1873 by American Samuel Hazard, now sold in paperback, if you are interested in early Dominican history.

Amber is one of the Dominican Republic's natural resources. (There's an amber museum at Puerto Plata.) It appears in all manner of jewelry, as well as picture frames, boxes, and other trinkets. Amber is a lemon- to brown-colored petrified resin from a coniferous tree that has long since disappeared. It was burned as incense at the time of Moses; Greeks rubbed it with fur to make it magnetic; Phoenicians and Syrians prized it; Columbus noted in his diary on December 16, 1492, that he received some as a gift from the Quisqueya Indian chief; 17th-century German guilds count amber cutters in their numbers; and man has used it as an amulet for sore throats (and Moroccans are supposed to have worn it for safety). In China and Korea it means good luck—and in 1800 it was discovered in the Dominican Republic. In the past 35 years, the mines near the Cordillera Septentrional in the west, and in the north between Puerto Plata and Santiago de los Caballeros have yielded plenty of amber. So much that some people, notably Antonio Prats Ventos, a Dominican sculptor, are using huge pieces as the block from which artistic shapes are worked. The real McCoy is here. Be sure that's what you are buying, if that's what you are paying the high price for.

Two good jewelry shops are **Parentesis,** the studio of creative artist **Edison Antigua,** and **Maria Ambar** (Calle Duarte 9), a small place in a residential community where you can find high quality that is worth the high price. If you want to design your own jewelry, capable staff can give suggestions.

Duarte Street is one of the top shopping areas, if you like to bargain, and to rummage through a lot of not-so-good pieces to find a few treasures. Shopkeepers are Arabs, Chinese, Spanish—and sharp. If you want clothes made, bring a picture and allow a couple of days for fashions to be made and fitted. Check the social hostess at your hotel for the names of the people she knows, trusts, and can badger into finishing in a hurry if you are having troubles with your own authority.

El Conde Street, most of the length of it, is another major shopping avenue, but you have to know what you are buying. The street is a short walk from the cathedral plaza, in the Colonial City.

La Atarazana shops are strictly for tourists, but the merchandise has been culled from some of the commercial best available. Located in the attractive mall, built to look as though it might be an old shopping area, the shops across the road from the Alcazar are actually on the site of an arsenal, where the pillage from rich ports in the conquistadors' Caribbean was stored. Among the shops to look for are **Nader's Art Gallery** in what had been a convent (buy carefully; I thought there was a lot of high-priced junk here), open 9 a.m.– 12:30 p.m., 3–7 p.m. except Sun., **Artecentro** at #13, where crafts by the handicapped at the Centro de Rehabilitacion are sold (when you buy here, you're contributing to more than just your own supply of souvenirs), and the **Zodiac** at #17 and **Columbus Gift Shop** at #27, both with amber, black coral, and pink conch shell jewelry (some junk, I think, and a few good pieces) as well as other standard Dominican crafts. By decree 3050, duty-free status was granted to Atarazana shops, creating the fourth duty-free shopping area in Santo Domingo.

Other duty-free shops, most of them featuring liquor bargains, plus the usual perfume and Spanish Lladro figures, leather goods, cosmetics, cameras, and other items are at the **Embajador Hotel** (a small area), the **Centro de los Heroes,** which was the first duty-free shopping area and is a mass of overwhelming commerce where only U.S. dollars will do for transactions, and **Las Americas International Airport** at the departure lounge, which you reach after going through immigration. Deals offered at the special sales can be excellent. *However,* remember that you can only bring back a quota duty free, and duty and IRS tax on rum is high. Other airport offerings are silver and gold chains, watches, cameras, Sony radios, and Kodak equipment. Do your preparatory shopping in your hometown camera store to be sure that you are, in fact, getting the bargain you think you are. An interesting gift for a gourmet friend could be the oranges or figs bottled in Armagnac. As with all the free port areas, you can only purchase with U.S. dollars but the bargaining techniques effective elsewhere in the D.R. are useful here also.

ARRIVAL AT LA ROMANA can be either by car, along relatively good and usually straight roads, in just over an hour from the Santo Domingo international airport (2 hours from the city center); or by small plane, landing at the airstrip at Casa de Campo, amid the golf course. There is public bus service from the city for the 2-hour ride at a very modest cost. Day tours will sometimes take one way passengers on their buses.

HOTELS AT LA ROMANA are only 3, with Casa de Campo resort undoubtedly the best known.

★★★ **Casa de Campo** • *east of town* • has all the elements for the luxury life, but standards sometimes slip. Created under Gulf + Western's auspices, the property and its sister hotels (Hotel Santo Domingo and Hispaniola, both in the capital) are now part of the Florida-based Fajul family's venture. In addition to two 18-hole Pete Dye golf courses (one of which was built before the hotel accommodations), there are 13 tennis courts at a hillside area known as *La Terraza,* several swimming pools, with the main pool at the reception and restaurant hub, polo fields, horses for trailriding as well as polo, a fleet of boats for fishing and a yacht for day sailing, and evening activities on the grounds of the resort as well as at Altos de Chavon, about 20 minutes' drive from the hotel. There is no beach worth the name, although there is a span of sand called Las Minitas, about a 10-minute ride from the main cluster of rooms, and other beaches on offshore islands and elsewhere on the southeast coast. If there is a weak link with this resort, it has been the food, but the choices in restaurants both here and at nearby Altos allow for variety. *El Patio,* the informal restaurant near the reception area, is attractive with red and white checked tablecloths. Slow service is a fact of the country, so it doesn't bother me here and the scattered facilities aren't much of a problem if you slow down to Dominican pace (or rent a car so you can go when you want to instead of following the jittery schedule). Rooms vary, from "standard" hotel rooms near the main reception area to duplex and other apartments that are privately owned, but rented out in an owner's absence, to entire villas that are also rented on that basis. The resort covers some 7000 acres. Oscar de la Renta has a home here, near the 14th green; the Bludhorn family (he was president of Gulf + Western at the time of his death in late '82) have a home here, and several other notables nestle into elegant surroundings in season. The jet set Spanish/Latin atmosphere is at its peak in February and is available for everyone who can afford the high prices, or those smart enough to hone in on the special tennis, golf, and other ackage weeks and weekends that are being offered. Relax insofar as service expectations are concerned; it's not as good as it should be. *Resort.*

Club Dominicus • *on a lovely beach about 20 minutes' drive from La Romana* • has rooms in several stone cottages and other attractive buildings along one of the country's most gorgeous beaches. Little known to most Americans, the resort is popular with Canadian and European groups who enjoy the laidback lifestyle and the spectacular beach. The *Caribbean Newsletter* (page 9) will have further information when warranted. For this winter, count on a casual management style that allows for a great deal of freedom—and a beach-focused vacation, with watersports opportunities. The place is reached by following a dirt road for about 30 minutes from a turn off on the Casa de Campo road out of La Romana. *Resort.*

HOUSEKEEPING HOLIDAYS are possible at several of the luxurious villas at Casa de Campo. **Villas Lagos,** part of the 7000-acre Casa de Campo family, are several 2-, 3-, and 4-bedroom villas on the hillside, near the third golf course, which is still being constructed at press time. Attractively furnished and available with staff (cooks cost $50 per day), the villas are rented through Premier Resorts (T 305+856–5405 or 800+856–7083).

THE INN WAY: There's only one place that qualifies.

★★ **La Posada** • *at Altos de Chavon* • is a picture-perfect 10-room inn, in a 2-story building near the main plaza in the 16th-century-style village built a few years ago. Rooms are elegantly furnished, in a style that complements the 16th-century setting; some rooms are rented long term to artistic souls who enjoy the surroundings—and the quiet that settles over the village after the evening events are over and everyone else has gone "home." Lackadaisical staff requires that guests be self-sufficient but accommodations are attractive. *Inn.*

RESTAURANTS IN AND NEAR LA ROMANA   are many. Vacationers have a choice of the hotel restaurants at Casa de Campo (*Tropicana, El Lago Grill, El Patio Brasserie* at the main hotel area, plus snack places at *Las Minitas* beach and *La Terraza* tennis village), all of which serve average fare in sometimes impressive settings (depending on the restaurant). Far more interesting choices include:

Cafe del Sol • *beyond the church and up the wide staircase to the right, on the plaza at Altos* • is a favorite for snacks and drinks at any time of the day or night. Known for its pizza and sandwich plates, the cafe also serves crepes, ice cream concoctions, and a delicious fruit punch. A table on the patio, overlooking the plaza, is a prize spot on a pleasant evening (which is most Dominican evenings); there's limited space inside for those who want to be near the kitchen.

Casa del Rio • *at Altos* • in spectacular surroundings that are floodlit at night, is the fish restaurant, but it is much more. A table at window-side in the terrace dining room almost suspends you over the river, and the view by nightlight is awesome. Paella and fresh fish are specialties, and reservations are recommended in peak season. The walk here takes you past most of the sights of the village, but the reward for finding this place will be a memory that will last forever. Dominican earthenware is used for table service, and the tone is set by the stone walls and wood tables and chairs. Worth enjoying for atmosphere as much as for the food, which was excellent when I dined here, Casa del Rio is a must.

La Piazzetta • *just to the left of the Altos entrance walk and a few steps from Los Chinos* • is an Italian restaurant with an atmosphere that is elegant, in a building that incorporates touches from what one expects in an old Italian home: tiles, peasant cooking utensils and other touches affixed to the walls, and food service on attractive pottery with an interesting carafe for the house wine (and an expensive, and not too imaginative wine list). All right for show but not my first choice for good food, La Piazzetta is worth investigating prior to making your reservation. Count on about $20 minimum per person.

PLACES WORTH FINDING AT LA ROMANA include the sugar mill that gives the town its major industry, and Altos de Chavon, the 20th-century village created in the 16th-century-style.

The **sugar mill** can be visited by special appointment. If the idea appeals to you, check with the activities desk at Casa de Campo. If they aren't able to set things up, don't despair. Telephone the mill to ask for special permission, which is often granted if you can gather a small group of people who are genuinely interested.

Altos de Chavon is well worth a visit, even if you are based in Santo Domingo and have to devote the entire day to it. Guests at Casa de Campo can hop aboard the hotel's shuttle bus and be at the remarkable area in a carefree 15 minutes or so. Altos ("the heights") is a 1980s construction of a 16th-century Spanish-style village, built on the high banks of the Chavon River, just east of the town of La Romana. The awesome creation is a labor of love, partly initiated by the necessity for Gulf + Western to invest some of its profits from what has been called "the largest sugar mill-and-plantation in the world" in the country of origin and guided to its present development by the enthusiasm of the Bludhorn family. The first building to rise on the site of the new-old village was the small church, dedicated to the Polish patron saint, St. Stanislas. Cobbled courtyards were underway, and the church was almost finished when I first visited the project; now—only a few years after the concept was first discussed—there are interesting handicraft boutiques (with some items made by the artists who live in the village), art galleries with work by Dominican artists for sale, an Oscar de la Renta boutique, a huge 5000-seat amphitheater for special events, and a complete roster of cafes and restaurants. Don't miss the **Museum,** a regional museum of Taino Indian history and artifacts. Even if you have a natural aversion to museums, make time for this one. The displays are attractive, and the doses of history are punctuated with interesting artifacts and reprints of pictures supplemented with drawings and diagrams. Even my nephew, whose enthusiasm for museums does not rival his interest in golf and tennis, found the displays intriguing and palatably educational. Some of the displays are in an open-to-breezes foyer; the core is in an air-conditioned "deep freeze" and contains valuable finds including jewelry and cooking implements from the earliest Indian settlers. A schedule of special events (jazz and other musical performances, in addition to pageants, art shows, and opportunities for special dinners) is available through Casa de Campo resort. Even if there's nothing special planned, Altos de Chavon deserves your touring time.

SPORTS AT LA ROMANA center on golf and tennis, with access also to horseback riding, polo, and boats for fishing and sailing.

Golf came clearly into focus when Pete Dye's *Cajuiles I* opened at Casa de Campo on the southeast coast, with its 7 shoreside holes as part of the challenging 6774-yard course. Now there's a second 18 at *Cajuiles II,* inland and abutting the first course. Golf carts, pro, and clubhouse are all here, in full country club fashion. In season, there can be a wait for starting times. Costs are high, but quality's here. Greens fees are $47.50 for 18 holes, including a cart. Caddies are also available.

Tennis is possible at the 2 courts near the reception area or the cluster of top-grade courts up the hill at *La Terraza*, the tennis center for the resort. There are pros available for lessons, and ball boys to clean up your court while you're playing. A tennis shop has equipment for rent, but it's a good idea to bring tennis balls (which you can leave as a gift if you don't use them all). Check for details on special tennis holidays, but know in advance that there can be a problem with court time. You'll have to reserve well in advance for slots at 4 p.m. or later. At Casa de Campo the activities desk has details. (Catalina Island offshore has some good snorkeling rocks and reefs.)

Scuba diving is arranged through the activities desk, but don't count on facilities such as you may know them on some of the other Caribbean islands that specialize in the sport. Some knowledge of scuba diving is an asset here; you're diving in almost virgin territory, and wrecks of Spanish galleons have been located off some Dominican Republic shores.

Fishermen can head out on the Bertrams that are part of the fleet maintained for Casa de Campo guests and residents as well as for fisherfolk who may be working at the sugar mill.

Polo was the national passion during the Trujillo years, and there are still staunch supporters. Polo matches have been revived with all the elegant flourishes at the field at Casa de Campo. Here you can watch (or play) from September through May.

Horseback riding is well organized at *Cajuiles Dude Ranch* at La Romana (arrangements made through Casa de Campo activities desk, or if you want to make a day of it, through Hotel Santo Domingo, including a 2-hour ride each way from Santo Domingo to La Romana and back).

TREASURES AND TRIFLES at La Romana range from country craft items that are available market days at the square in town to top-quality ceramics, sculpture, weaving, paintings, and other crafts that are part of the lifestyle encouraged through Altos de Chavon. The Feria Artesanal that takes place in February is a worthwhile event. You will find some stores for resort clothes at Casa de Campo, with tennis and golfwear available at the respective sport clubhouses.

Altos de Chavon has several small shops with unusual stock that includes high-quality art. The village itself is a craft "museum," since everything has been built in the early '80s, although design is true to 16th-century style in many cases. Allow plenty of time to saunter around the patios and plazas.

See the section on "Santo Domingo" for additional shopping suggestions in the colonial city.

THE NORTH COAST

The north coast is where Christopher Columbus first touched the shores of the Dominican Republic, although his ill-fated settlement yielded to the more successful (and later) development at Santo Domingo on the south coast. Today, **PUERTO PLATA,** east of the original landing area, is the main port on the north coast, and a town that is an emerging resort area, following ambitious development plans of the national bank and the government. Samuel Hazard points out that "as far back as 1499 the town is spoken of as a flourishing place, and it is even said that Columbus, in one of his later voyages, himself traced the plan of the town, which was afterwards, in 1502, constructed by the orders of Ovando the Governor, who, in order to connect it with the interior, built a fine road. . . . In those days it was a lively place, being the port at which were embarked the products of the mines and the sugar from Santiago and La Vega—the Spanish merchantmen coming here in great numbers for cargoes. The port was originally discovered by Columbus in his first voyage and being overlooked by the high mountain . . . the top of which appeared at sea so white to the Spaniards, they thought it covered with snow, as it glistened like snow or silver. Being undeceived as to the snow, they called the port, from this circumstance, Silver Port (Puerto Plata)."

Hazard didn't think much of Puerto Plata when he visited in the early 1870s, but the town is the heart of a major tourism development program that is finally getting underway to be ready for vacationers in the early 1990's. By the mid-1500s, pirates had already ravaged the town and in 1606 the Spanish government destroyed it, to stop illegal trafficking with foreign powers. By the mid-1700s, the town gained some fame again when it became a free port, and by 1822, new homes began to appear on the grid streets as coffee plantations developed on the hillsides around the city. Most of the interesting wood buildings, with their overhanging second-story balconies, date from this time and all the traditional buildings are now under government decree for historic preservation. The boxy cement buildings that pass in this town as "modern" should have hit their limit. Puerto Plata is waking from years of sleep, with its prominence as a cruise port plus being the nearest town to the resort area of Playa Dorada, about 10 minutes' drive east, and the fact that more than 300 yachts anchor here during island cruising.

SOSUA, established by German Jews fleeing Nazi oppression during World War II, is now a flourishing community with a low-key style of living that appeals to many. When Trujillo issued the invitation to establish a community on the remote north coast of the Dominican Republic, few accepted his offer. Those who did have settled in, to produce the country's best cheese and sausages, and create a town. It's the curve of sand and the gradual development of the area that appeals to many who come here. Sosua has become a "packaged-comforts" holiday area that can be ideal for self-sufficient folk. The atmosphere is very casual, and popular with European and Canadian travelers as well as for residents of Santo Domingo. Many have vacation homes (and investments) here.

CABARETE, about 30 minutes' drive east of the airport, following the coast beyond Sosua, has also grown at a rapid rate in the past five years. The big attraction for Cabarete is windsurfing. The beach is littered with places to rent boards.

SAMANA PENINSULA, northeast of Sosua and Cabarete, is one of the several special areas in this intriguing country, but it's not for those who must have everything perfect, with pampering. The spine of land that stretches off the northeast coast of the country is rugged, sand-fringed, and ideal for anyone who likes rustic settings and virtually virgin countryside. Flatlands at the midsection of the Dominican Republic rise to mountains and a terrain that looks, from the small planes you can charter to fly here, like a lumpy, green quilt, patchworked with dirt roads. Coconut groves are appliqued along some sandy strands, many of which are accessible only by boat.

Samana, on the south coast of the peninsula, is a cruise port for a few ships. One of Balaguer's projects, many years ago, was to raze the former town and "build a new one." I, for one, long for the old small town where some of the wood houses could have been renovated to maintain a unique personality. What you see here today are boring stucco boxes, albeit 2-story buildings, with pockets for "freeport" shops stuffed with items for cruise passengers. (Don't count on a wide selection, but if you see what you want in the luxury-item roster, the price will be good.) Although the town's character is undefined, at the moment, the natural countryside is spectacular. There are specks of offshore islands, some of them used as beach havens for cruise passengers who don't care about shopping (picnics are planned), and other areas that can be seen if you hire an enterprising taxi driver and ask for a tour of the area. Don't expect a trumped-up tourist-type spot when you get out of town. It is rural.

AUTHOR'S OBSERVATION

The rapid and mind-boggling development along the north coast is suffering from the lack of any unified promotional program. In the absence of leadership from the government, insofar as a tourism plan is concerned, the individual owners are left to themselves. Since most have never been involved with tourism, and have no concept of "the big picture," the north coast seems cluttered and disorganized. Although the facilities can be fun for carefree experienced travelers, be sure to ask plenty of questions and be ready to improvise. Service is s-l-o-w almost everywhere in this country, but especially at places along the north coast. Be prepared to relax and enjoy the scenery; don't try to rush!

ARRIVAL IN THE PUERTO PLATA AREA will be at *La Union International Airport,* which has outgrown its once-huge size as tourism surges on the north coast. Expansion in mid-'87 was not enough, when it was completed, to ease the pressures of several flights arriving (or leaving) at the same time of day. Immigration formalities involve long lines and waiting. Taxis stand outside the entrance for the 10-minute drive to Sosua, or 25-minute drive to Cabarete, to the east (or the 30-minute drive to Playa Dorada resorts) and Puerto Plata to the west. There is a bank for exchanging money but don't count on its being open. If you are arriving on one of the group tours, buses will provide transportation. You will need your tourist card (for $10), which is issued through your arrival airline or at the airport.

CRUISE passengers will dock at the port in the town of Puerto Plata to be poured into minibuses for guided tours around the area. Frankly, there's not all that much to see. You can do about as well, better if you're an independent traveler and speak some Spanish, by walking as far as the market and taking a taxi if you want to go to the beach.

DEPARTURE is reasonably easy, from the modern terminal, but allow plenty of time and expect crowds of people. There are a few counters selling Dominican-made crafts and liquor after you have paid your departure tax of US$10 (Dominicans pay RD$15) and passed through immigration. The shops are not always open, however, so don't count on them as your only source.

HOTELS IN LAS TERRENAS, on the north coast of the Samana Peninsula, are best reached by private plane to the small airport. The ride by car is a long and bumpy one.

Portillo Beach • *on a lovely, long white sand beach* • opened a few years ago as the ultimate escape. Built by Maxine and Georges Taule, who were involved with the first steps at now-burgeoning Playa Dorada, the original buildings are cabins, designed for a beach-focused life. The recently built 2-story buildings hold standard hotel-style rooms. There's a disco for evening activity and watersports equipment plus bicycles for daytime use. The resort is off the beaten path; the beach and the rugged terrain provide most entertainment. Favored by adventuresome Europeans, this area is not well known to American travelers.
Atlantis, with 13 rooms, and **Chez Jeannot,** with 16 rooms, are two small spots with very reasonable rates.

HOTELS IN SAMANA are best reached by small plane from either Santo Domingo's Herrera Airport or, by previous arrangement, from Puerto Plata. Many residents from Santo Domingo drive out to this area for weekends.

Hotel Gran Bahia • *on Samana Bay* • is a very ambitious project, backed by Dominicans who are aiming high insofar as luxury is concerned. Given the track record for other ambitious projects in this country, I suspect it will be a while before this place opens. The tract of land is gorgeous, with plans to build an elegant central resort and sell off villa plots on the hillside. The *Caribbean Newsletter* (page 9) will have more details, closer to opening date.

HOTELS IN PUERTO PLATA area include an impressive group of resort properties as well as some small Dominican properties. Selected for development in the late 1970s, the Playa Dorada area, about 15 minutes' drive east of the town of Puerto Plata, and almost 30 minutes west of the airport, has over 4000 hotel rooms with more in the plans. Infratur, the resort development arm of the Dominican Central Bank, has been the conduit for World Bank and other development funds. Many millions have been invested in the area, with a lot more to come, following the seed money for resorts and infrastructure, including the airport and golf courses. What has been accomplished is amazing, with attractive resorts at Playa Dorada, and many privately owned restaurants and shops in Puerto Plata to provide diversions for the guests.

DOMINICAN REPUBLIC · · · 333

AUTHOR'S OBSERVATION

It's impossible at presstime to predict what's ahead for the winter '91–'92 insofar as status of hotels and restaurants. The lack of unified tourism promotion, and the severe drop in business last winter and in summer '91, means that many places closed, perhaps only temporarily. Many are having financial problems. The *Caribbean Newsletter* (page 9) will have ongoing comments about the Dominican Republic, but be sure to ask plenty of questions and double-check the answers to avoid getting duped this season.

For holiday spots in nearby Sosua and Cabarete see pages 339 and 341.

Bayside Hill • *at Costambar, on the west side of town* • gives each guest a sea view from the hillside. Planned for "adults only," many units have private Jacuzzis. Modern bedrooms with small balconies cluster around the pool and reception area. On-premise *Cafemba* (gourmet) and *El Casco* (grill room) offer mealtime options; the piano bar is lively when the guests are. *Resort.*

Discovery Bay • *at Punta Rusia, west of Puerto Plata* • is a relative newcomer, with attractive units that are intended for private ownership, to be rented in owners' absence. Best for independent travelers, who won't mind being a bit out of the mainstream. *Apts.*

★★ **Eurotel Playa Dorada** • *at the beach and near the golf course* • accepted guests in December 1985, but opened officially in April 1986. Its style reflects the typical architecture in Puerto Plata, making the hotel look more like a Victorian-style village than the standard resort. Taking cues (and curlicues) from Victoriana, the architects blended lacy wood fretwork and a palette of blues to greens to purples for the outside decor. Some rooms are very small, construction seems flimsy, and the place is showing signs of wear, but overall the place has a nice feeling. Upholstered furniture in the lobby area may have to yield to the weather (it must be moved when it rains), in favor of a more practical style. Shops, car rentals, and tour services are in and around the lobby; pathways lead to and around the several buildings of rooms, linking them to the central dining and entertainment areas near the pool. The beach is an easy walk from most rooms; although the golf course is a bit farther away, it's also within easy stroll. Several resorts—Villa Doradas, Dorado Naco, the Jack Tar Village, and the Playa Dorada Beach Resort among them—are near enough to walk to enjoy their restaurants and activities. There's a scuba source at the beach. *Hotel.*

Flamenco Beach Resort • *near the beach at Playa Dorada* • is planned to be a complete resort, when things get in full swing. Guests in the 310 rooms have expected modern comforts, including air-conditioning and color cable TV. All rooms have either terrace or balcony, and all guests have to walk to the beach. Pool is on-premises, as are several restaurants (*El Cortijo* has ambitious offerings; *La Giralda* is the main restaurant). *Hotel.*

Heavens • *at Playa Dorada, between Jack Tar and the Eurotel* • opened in early '88, as a 3-story property with suites-with-kitchenette as well as standard hotel rooms. Operating on an "inclusive" plan for meals, watersports, and daytime tennis (there's an extra charge for night tennis), the property has a pool. The beach is a short walk north; the golf course is across the road; and many other Playa Dorada hotels are within an easy walk. *Hotel.*

★★★ **Jack Tar Village & Casino** • *near the beach at Playa Dorada* • has its own tennis courts, pool, and action plan near the golf course. Following the popular all-inclusive week-long program, the Dallas- and Toronto-based Adventure Tours firm flies folks in for a good value holiday. With several white stucco, terra-cotta-roofed villas scattered around the grounds, separated from the beach with sea-grape trees and a wedge of the golf course, the resort has a residential feeling. The hotel hub is a huge thatched bohio and stucco-walled area where restaurants, pools, shops, nightclub, and all the action facilities are centralized. All are an easy walk from all the villas and from the 40 two-story units on the inland side of the pool. Package-plan, resort-pegged all-inclusive rates are charged. All rooms have Dominican art, created by people in Puerto Plata area who attended a special art school. Spend some time looking at all the furnishings and trim on the buildings; it's Dominican, made by hand, elegant, interesting, and worth purchasing if you can find a local source for some of the furnishings. *Resort.*

★★★ **Playa Dorada Hotel** • *on the beach* • offers beachfront and pool activities. Managed by Holiday Inn for part of its history, the property is now independent—with the Princess. Both have distinctly Dominican personalities. The lobby and courtyards are breeze-swept and attractive; pale pink paint and foliage-punctuation help create atmosphere. The 3-story buildings allow for sea view from most bedrooms, if you can see over the flourishing sea-grape trees that line the shore. Some rooms have balconies; others have a fencelike barricade across sliding doors that open to a foot-wide platform. The pool is popular, especially for children; informal cafe-style food is offered around the rim. Other dining areas have theme evenings. The golf course is a short walk from the entrance. Horse-drawn carriages are available for touring, as are taxis. *Hotel.*

Playa Dorada Princess • *a short walk from the Playa Dorada* • opened in December '87 as a Radisson hotel. Now offering all-inclusive and standard daily rates, the hotel is several 2-story buildings with bedrooms and suites as well as other buildings for restaurants (*El Pilon* coffee shop, *La Condesa* for more formal dining, and *La Raqueta Terrace* at the tennis courts). The pool has a swim-up bar; *La Tortuga Loca Beach Club,* linked by shuttle bus for those who prefer not to walk, provides snacks, changing rooms, and watersports. There's an additional charge for golf, which is within easy stroll of the complex. Count on the usual s-l-o-w service, and look into sports-focused and other package plans. *Hotel.*

Puerto Plata Beach Resort • *across the road from Long Beach, on the eastern fringe of Puerto Plata* • is one of the several north coast resorts built in Dominican-Victorian style, with buildings in several pastel shades and courtyards linking them. A pool is the heart of the hotel, in the center courtyard, for those who prefer that to the across-the-road beach. Although the restaurant is pleasant and worth noting, it's the lively disco that has been getting the most attention in recent seasons. (Check about current status.) The property is about 10 minutes' drive west of the Playa Dorada resort area (and golf course), but within easy walk of the in-town shops and restaurants. *Hotel.*

Victoria Resort • *near the 10th fairway of the golf course* • aims toward a plantation-house feeling, with its pillared entryway and elegantly furnished rooms. Tiled floors and louvered windows help the Caribbean-Dominican atmosphere, and private balconies are pleasant for sunning. The beach is a short walk from the hotel; restaurants and the tennis courts are on-premises. *Hotel.*

HOUSEKEEPING HOLIDAYS around Puerto Plata are varied. Life can be almost luxury, if you rent one of the new condominium units, or very casual in one of the shoreside bungalows that have been around for several seasons. Food will be fresh fish, which you can negotiate for with the local fishermen, or produce bought at the open-air market under a very modern shelter on a back street in Puerto Plata. Excellent kosher beef is cured and sold at Sosua, from stands you will see by the side of the road, in front of the substantial business ventures that supply meat products for the rest of the country.

Check for rental of villas at Playa Dorada and through the management of many of the hotels. Word of mouth can be the best way to find self-catering accommodations especially in Sosua where there are many. Plan for a couple of days in a hotel, with time to look at places on location, before booking.

Costambar • *west of the town at the foot of the station for the Isabel de Torres cable car* • is an assortment of buildings holding apartments available for sale as condominiums. Ask your travel agent about a multinight holiday package, with an apartment and other benefits at a good rate. Good for families, or other self-sufficient travelers, Costambar has a clubhouse and pool area that is popular with the many Dominicans who have bought units here. *Apts.*

★★ **Dorado Naco Aparta-Hotel** • *near the beach* • opened in the spring of '82. There are 62 1-bedroom units, 52 2-bedroom units, and 36 penthouses in this elaborate complex, with luxury the keynote and Mediterranean the style. Apartments are in 9 buildings, with a reception area that has a pool, shop, and other facilities. Located not far from the Jack Tar resort, and Dorado-Naco is worth investigating if you want an apartment on the north coast. *Apts.*

Playa Confresi • *near the beach, west of Puerto Plata* • is a collection of two dozen or so "summer" houses that are rented in owners' absence. Maid/housekeeper services are provided at modest cost. *Villas.*

Tropicana Caribe • *near the golf course at Playa Dorada* • links apartments with hotel management, for maximum conveniences. There's a Jacuzzi at the pool area, and a restaurant is convenient for those who don't want to use the kitchen facilities for home-cooked meals. The property was having start-up problems; the *Caribbean Newsletter* (page 9) will have news. *Apts.*

Villas Doradas • *near the golf course, at Playa Dorada* • rose amid the new developments a couple of seasons ago. The several housekeeping apartments put lodgers within easy walking distance of the other hotels. Modern kitchen areas make meal preparation easy enough, and balconies or patios turn into the living area when you tire of the nearby beach or the pool. *Apts.*

Villas Caraibe • *at Playa Dorada, near the golf course* • have been a couple of years in the building and opened last season. The 220 apartments are in several 2-story buildings clustered near the entrance to the Playa Dorado Beach Resort. *Apts.*

LOW-COST LODGING: Although overall rates in the Dominican Republic are lower than on other islands, especially when apartments are shared by several friends or a family, there are a few places that offer pleasant accommodations with very low rates.

Caracol • *on the seaside boulevard, near Long Beach* • has about 40 rooms in a comfortable hotel-style building on the inland side of the street. Rooms on the front of the hotel have sea view (and street noises). *Guesthouse.*

Hostal Jimesson • *on Calle Beller in Puerto Plata* • adapts one of the town's traditional Victorian houses at the reception area, with newly built rooms in a 3-story building in back. The 22 rooms have comfortable furnishings and private bath. Owned by Maria Jimenez Messon, who also owns the Plaza Meson restaurant and Cafemba Tours, this can be a nice nest in town, for those who want to settle into Puerto Plata as residents know it. *Guesthouse.*

Hotel Montemar • *a short walk inland from the shore* • has a new look, after Infratur funding lavished many pesos on what is the area's hotel training school. The lobby is attractive, with soft pastels of lavender and blue to accent the light wood and white walls. Recently added rooms doubled the size of the previous small hotel, and all facilities received a total new look at that time. Rooms are comfortably, if basically, furnished and have individual air-conditioning units. There's a lovely pool, a cafe dining area, and a more formal dining room where a piano player enhances some evenings. Service is slow (after all, these are students who are learning), but there is a wonderfully warm atmosphere among the enthusiastic students and I find this place comfortable and pleasant. *Small hotel.*

RESTAURANTS IN PUERTO PLATA are a varied lot, from the "safety" of the traditional hotel restaurants to the fun-and-casual bohio-style places that freckle the shore and street corners in and around Puerto Plata. Insofar as hotel food is concerned, all places have some coffee shop equivalant that serves grilled chicken, salad, and usually fried plantain (similar to a hard banana) chips.

Aqui Norma • *near town on the main road* • is a casual place for good Dominican food. Popular with residents, the place also welcomes vacationers.

De Armando • *on Separacion at A. Mota* • is the new name (and style) for what used to be La Carreta. Now enclosed, and air-conditioned, to make the most of the roadside view (and close out the gnatlike motor scooters' noise), the place has an elegant air, an extensive (and excellent) menu that features local seafood, and the same wonderful trio of Dominicans whose appearance is as entertaining as their music. Highly recommended!

Jimmy's • *on Calle Beller, in an attractive former home* • is the town's second elegant restaurant, where the extensive menu offers several interesting choices and the atmosphere makes it worth a reservation. Although some guests appear in casual clothes, this place warrants dressing up. It offers both good service and good food.

Jardin de Jade • *at Playa Dorada, near Villas Doradas* • is related to the very successful Chinese restaurant in Santo Domingo's Embajador hotel. Count on many choices, with traditional (very good) Chinese fare.

Portofino • *near Montemar Hotel* • has been a longtime favorite for Italian food, although on my last visit did not seem up to par. Okay for casual, pasta-style evening.

Valters • *on Hermanas Mirable, near Montemar Hotel, where Portofino once was located* • is another restaurant with pastas, some other Italian offerings, and steak as well as fish. More atmosphere than some of the restaurants, Valters is known as a fun spot spot when friends gather here.

Vivaldi • *on the main road into town* • is better known for its disco than for its food, although Chinese food is served at mealtimes.

PLACES WORTH FINDING in Puerto Plata are many, but there are a few spots you'll want to avoid. The **Fort of San Felipe** will be a stop on your minibus tour from the ship. Skip it, unless you're addicted to typical tours. Buttons, coins, and cannon balls are displayed in the few rooms inside, and you'll have to double in half to crawl through the low doors that separate the small rooms. Not for the claustrophobic, the fort can be interesting if you have nothing else to do that day, or if you wander around on your own. Cost for entry: a modest 25¢. There's a proliferation of sidewalk salesmen who will follow you up the hill and to the door of the fort (and will be there to greet you when you come out). Buy if you want, but there are no bargains. General Gregorio Luperon, who prances on horseback in the middle of the parking area, fought to overthrow the Spanish when they were in power from 1860 to 1865. He staggered from his deathbed at age 58, pulled himself upright saying, "I refuse to meet death lying down," and promptly dropped dead.

Isabel de Torres cable car runs on an independent schedule, which will probably include a cruise ship day, but don't count on it if you've headed north on your own. (And if you have flown into Puerto Plata, you've had your spectacular view from the plane window; that offered from the top of the tower is no better.) There's a fort built under the regime of Generalissimo Trujillo near the top of the tower.

SPORTS   around Puerto Plata include **golf** at the *Robert Trent Jones* course that is the focus for the Jack Tar, Dorado Naco, Playa Dorada Hotel and the area's other resorts, in addition to **tennis** which is available at most resort hotels including Jack Tar and the Playa Dorada Hotel. **Horseback riding** can be arranged through the resorts. **Scuba** is becoming popular, with hotels linked to dive operators. *Puerto Plata Diving Club* (T 212+982–8303) plans diving holidays. **Boardsailing** is best at Cabarete, about 50 minutes' drive east on the coast. The wind that comes in on this Atlantic coast makes watersports a challenge.

TREASURES AND TRIFLES   are appearing at a rapid rate, in response to the town's popularity as a cruise port and the developments at nearby Playa Dorada and other north coast spots. The top of the list, for quality and efforts, is the **Centro Artesanal,** in a building on John F. Kennedy. The place opened in September 1982, with help from the Banco Central and Infratur, and is a training area for quality craftsmanship. It is officially known as the **Fundacion Dominicana de Desarrollo,** and the specialties include ceramics, stone work, wood, and jewelry. Apprentices are trained by artists and, following their schooling here, are encouraged to set up shop, with funding from the organization, in other areas of the country. By all means, visit here to see the best that's offered.

Tourist Bazaar Boutique, on Calle Durate 61, not far from the central square, is in a marvelous, big Victorian former home. Each room on the first floor is filled with handmade items, with the ceramic figures some of the real treasures. Macrame, black coral, shell jewelry, amber, and larimar are all available, as are paintings and embroidered blouses—and the ubiquitous T-shirts. Upstairs is an Amber Museum, which should be a requirement for all visitors, preferably before purchase of the omnipresent "stone." Didi and Aldo Costa are the owners of this place, and one or the other is around most of the time. (They also have a shop at the Playa Dorada Hotel, but the selection here is far more extensive.)

Loa, in Victorian-style buildings about 5 minutes' drive along the road from the Playa Dorada hotels to the airport, has crafts (and cool drinks) in pleasant surroundings.

Other places worth finding for interesting purchases are **Paulette's** for baskets, **Macaluso's Gift Shop** for an assortment of items and several small shops that are around the Hotel Castilla on Avenida John F. Kennedy.

If you're looking for something unusual head for **La Fabrica,** where Bill Everett sells handwork from his house, and the studio of **Carlos Mena,** a commercial artist from New York who transplanted to Puerto Plata. **Mildred Casacate,** who studied art in Mexico, has been bringing local artists into her shop to work when cruise ships are in port, but ask around if you want to find her—and her workshop.

Casa Castilla, next to the Hotel Castille, not far from the town square, has imaginative hand-painted rocks for about $5. (A lot for a rock? You're right, but they're clever.) The shop also has paintings (framed), plus wrought-iron mirrors, some work done by local schoolchildren, and above average handwork. The **Amber House,** also on this street, has better than average workmanship for the inevitable amber jewelry.

HOTELS IN SOSUA are appearing at such a rapid rate that it's difficult to keep up with all the newcomers. Since many places offer apartments with kitchens in addition to rooms where guests rely on the on-premise restaurant, all types of lodgings are included in the list that follows. For rentals of housekeeping facilities, contact Gwen and Tom Urena at **North Shore Reality,** Sosua, Puerto Plata, DR, T 809+571-2292. In addition to considering places mentioned below, adventuresome travelers might want to arrive in town to book a room at some of the casual places or the sure-to-appear newcomers. The *Caribbean Newsletter* (see page 9) will have news about new hotels and other Sosua developments when pertinent.

★ **Alcazar** • *on one of the short side streets of the village* • offers a dozen simple rooms in a 3-story, recently built structure punctuated by a small pool. Worth considering if budget is a prime concern, the hotel is popular with young travelers. *Hotel.*

Los Almendros Beach Resort • *inland on the main road* • is built in enclave style, with its pool the social center. The nearest beach is a 10-minute walk from the hotel. Rooms are small, with closets in the bathroom. When there are 2 double beds, there's very little floor space. Planned by DeMarco Tours from Santo Domingo, the hotel hopes for tour groups. The pool makes the entry area attractive; it's an easy walk to the many restaurants, shops, and beach. *Hotel.*

★★ **El Mirador** • *in the hills overlooking town and beach* • gives a sense of privacy with the comforts of a resort. Your lodgings can be a regular room (shaved from one of the 2-bedroom units, a 1-bedroom apartment (without the second bedroom), or the entire unit. You'll want a car for mobility, although there's a restaurant, entertainment some evenings, a pool, and tennis courts on the premises. For the beach, you'll have to leave "home." *Hotel, apts.*

★★★ **Club Nautico** • *perched on the cliff at the western end of the long beach that is Playa Sosua* • is an enclave of apartments (air conditioned, with ceiling fans also) about a 5-minute walk from the beach. Built for private sale, the units are often for rent in owners' absence and are comfortably furnished for sun-and-sea living. Not all units offer sea view, since they've been built in two terra-cotta-roofed bands of white stucco units, one "behind" the other. The pool and main building are at the shoreline. *Apts.*

North Shore Hotel • *in town* • is a 3-story new building with a couple of dozen rooms. Linked with Tom and Gwen Urena's real estate firm, the hotel gives independent folk comfortable lodgings for a casual holiday. There's a small pool in the back of the property, with the building forming an L around it. Shops and many restaurants are outside the front door. *Hotel.*

Playa Chiquita • *a seaside inn* • is slightly removed from the hubbub of Sosua's center, but close enough to get into town for restaurants and shops. Much nearer is El Batey, a cluster of craft shacks that now caters to visitors. The daytime focus is on watersports and the small beach that fronts the property. Rooms are comfortable, with king-sized beds and TVs. A kitchenette makes snacking easy, but the social life centers on the open-air patio. *Apts.*

★★★ **Sand Castle Beach Resort** • *on the shore, with pool and beach* • was a newcomer in early '89, when the first part of the ambitious resort opened for guests. The main building perches near the beach, but gives guests a pool with patio. Rooms are on several levels, staggered back from the face of rocky cliff. Built for private ownership, the apartments are furnished for luxury living. Although there's a small dining table next to the kitchenette, most meals can be enjoyed on the terrace. Top-level rooms have the most privacy—and the longest walk, with the most steps, up and down to the beach. *Apts.*

★★ **Hotel Sosua** • *a short walk from Sosua's beach* • has proved to be an ideal hub for many. Most rooms in the original part of the 3-story hotel have an overhead fan as well as air conditioning and are attractively furnished. There's a small pool in the center area and a couple of cottages that are also part of the property. Breakfast is served, and special dinners are offered some evenings, but guests are encouraged to sample nearby restaurants. Owner Dolly Estrella is the source for *all* information; she's a member of one of Sosua's long-time families and a friendly host. *Hotel.*

Sosua Sol • *inland, not far from the beach* • is a collection of small bungalows and basic housekeeping facilities. Gathered into a sort of neighborhood, the place is popular with Canadians and others who want an informal place in the sun. Barbecues are popular entertainment at an area in the backyard; otherwise you're on your own to cook at home or sample restaurants within walking distance. *Bungalows.*

★★★ **Villas Los Coralillos** • *on the slope at one end of Sosua's beach* • give guests a good beach-and-sea view from most apartments. Villa #1 has the main living area on the walk-in level, with the bedrooms downstairs, and all with view. Other villas are similar, sharing the grounds with an attractive hill-capping restaurant and a small pool midway up the hillside. The main long beach of Sosua stretches out along the shore. *Villas.*

Yaroa Hotel • *in town, on a lane that ends at a rock-steep shore* • is modern and attractive. The hotel opened in 1986. The comfortable rooms give guests the option of swimming at the hotel's pool or walking a short distance to the beach. Attractively decorated with blond wood and white stucco, the place has a clean, neat appearance and a pleasant staff. *Hotel.*

Among the several very casual small spots are **Nino's Hotel Colonial,** across the road from Hotel Sosua in town, with 3 floors of basic rooms within easy walking distance of beach and bars; **Koch's Oceanfront Guest House,** down a dirt lane, near a huge breadfruit tree at the shore (but not the beach);

and **Pension Anneliese,** with 4 very clean rooms that are small, dark, and inexpensive.

HOTELS IN CABARETE are growing at a rapid rate. The *Caribbean Newsletter* (page 9) will have details when noteworthy places are open and running. *Punta Goleta,* this area's first hotel, has been joined by several small spots, all with a casual atmosphere. Action is directed toward the beach—and the fact that Cabarete aims to be the Caribbean's most famous and best equipped boardsailing area. (Several rental shops have sailboards along the beach and regattas are held when there are enough enthusiasts to participate.)

Cabarete Beach Hotel • *on the beach* • is a small and charming Canadian-funded guest house, with 8 rooms that have personal appeal. Most have sea view; all are ideal lodgings for folks interested in being shoreside, with the action. *Hotel.*

Residencia Goleta • *on the inland side of the road, closer to Sosua* • is a cluster of new apartments, with basic kitchen and small rooms. Built for private ownership, the units are for rent in owners' absence. *Apts.*

Punta Goleta • *at Cabarete, east of Sosua along the coast* • opened in December 1985. The once impressive property, with tennis courts, pool, restaurants, and beautifully furnished rooms needed attention, good management, and overall repair and housekeeping when I visited for this edition. The walk from your room, across the highway to the beach, is a reasonably long one, especially in the hot sun. Built by Dominican interests, the property will thrive with special interest groups or others who enjoy being in comfortable surroundings remote from man-made pressures and some distance from the nearest town. European and other international visitors join Dominicans here. *Hotel.*

RESTAURANTS IN SOSUA range from very casual cafes to places where you can get elegant fare at reasonable prices. Among those worth noting are:

★★★ **Cafe Sosua** • *on a side street, in an attractively decorated setting* • is probably the top restaurant in town. Serving dinner from 6 to 11 p.m., the chef features langouste in basil butter, fish "depending on whether Octavio wakes up or not," and pork entrees. Check the evening's offerings when you make your reservation.

Carlos Cafe • *on the main street* • serves from breakfast through dinner hours, with French toast and other offerings to start the day and seafood, steaks, and brochettes featured for more substantial meals. Under a thatched roof, some tables set you curbside. Cognac is served with your breakfast coffee; the bar is a focal point at other hours.

El Coral • *at Los Coraillos villas* • serves a well-rounded menu (seafood and steaks) in a very attractive setting. When the weather is pleasant, the terrace dining offers the best sea views.

Mora Mai • *at a crossroads shared with La Roca* • gives a Polynesian feeling with its decor. Red snapper is one popular entree. Fashion shows, music, and folkloric dancing are evening entertainments, with shows at 8:30, 9:30 and 10:30 in season and sometimes, also, in summer.

★ **Oasis** • *on a side street, in humble surroundings* • was closed for a while. If it is open when you visit, check to see if ownership still serves the seafood and Dominican specialties that made this casual spot a favorite.

La Roca • *at the village crossroads* • is the biggest eatery, and the focal point for the active social scene. The place has grown from a small (and slightly seedy) spot to be a beguiling clutter of wood, wrought iron, white paint, and copies of old prints of life in Puerto Plata. Open from 10 a.m. to 11 p.m., the place includes a snack bar and roadside bar as well as a regular restaurant.

Three cafe-style, open-air places in Cabarete are **El Jardin** • *in a flower-filled patio on the corner* • with a small, undercover area; **Mama Juana** • *near El Jardin* • featuring crab, chicken, ribs, and lobster, served at wood tables in a patio, curbside; and **Amigo's Bar and Restaurant,** also with sturdy wood chairs and tables and a snack-style menu.

NATURAL SURROUNDINGS and **SPORTS** along the north coast, east of Sosua, include several beaches, many of which have become focal points for resort and residential development. Although the caramel-colored sand on Sosua's beach has long been flecked with Dominicans selling barbecued chicken, sausage and other food, and the young boys who sell the fresh oysters (which they open and offer with a squeeze of lime), other beaches are white—and quieter. The beach at Cabarete is already recognized by boardsailors as being one of the best in the Caribbean. The steady breeze is usually on-shore and seas offer enough surf to be interesting for experienced board-sailors.

Sports on the Samana Peninsula include all the Hemingway-style offerings: **deep-sea fishing, diving, exploring,** and **sailing,** but don't count on the latest equipment. This area is for self-sufficient types looking for new frontiers. A sailing group hauls boats over from Santo Domingo for regular regattas off the beach at Cayacoa. Inquire from the Dominican Tourist Information Office about dates and contacts.

THE EAST COAST

For many years this coast has been remote, best known to Dominicans who save to buy passage on one of the boats that sets out from little-known coves to make the treacherous passage to the west coast of Puerto Rico, from which Dominican immigrants can travel easily into the United States. Insofar as tourism is concerned, Punta Cana came to the attention of New York labor leader

Theodore Kheel in the 1950s, when he opened a beachside hideaway to which his friends and a few knowledgeable (and acceptable) others could fly by private plane. These days, the coastline is marked for major development. It has the country's whitest and widest beaches, with one span (from Punta Cana to Macao) running for most of 25 miles. An offshore reef calms seas that are brushed to a frenzy by the prevailing tradewinds before they reach the sandy shore and the clarity of the waters defies description. Palms flourish where the sands break to green, and the area offers all the natural attributes of a prized sun-struck resort area.

ARRIVAL can be by car or by plane, depending on the day you travel and your timing. Here are some of the options: fly into Santo Domingo and drive, for four hours, east along the south coast passing La Romana and going through Higuey to the east end. With prior notice, hotels can arrange car meeting services. Otherwise take a taxi, for about US$40. Or fly into Santo Domingo and fly from there to Punta Cana on a smaller plane. Hotels can arrange for the hop from Santo Domingo's airport to the airport at Punta Cana. Or you can fly into Punta Cana's private-but-international airport from San Juan, Puerto Rico, which can be much pleasanter than passing through Santo Domingo. (American Airlines' Eagle service makes that link.) Or fly to La Romana from San Juan, Puerto Rico, and drive for over an hour east of there, through Higuey to Punta Cana. Or charter a plane from San Juan, Puerto Rico, to fly to Punta Cana. Or, if you're planning to stay at Club Med or can arrange for a seat on the plane, fly on their special American Airlines' flight direct from specific U.S. cities (New York is usually one). That flight does not operate daily, and has been operating only in winter. The *Caribbean Newsletter* (page 9) will have details on any other ways to reach this outpost.

HOTELS are self-contained resorts, each separate from the other, and there's little encouragement by "your" management to spend a day at one of the other places. For many years the Club Med was the only property; for this season its inclusive style is being mimicked by Bavaro Beach & Gardens and by the Punta Cana Yacht club. The *Caribbean Newsletter* (page 9) will have comments on new properties if and when they open.

AUTHOR'S OBSERVATION

Be prepared for windswept beaches. Although the breeze is not always strong, it can make the beach bustle in winter months.

Bavaro Beach & Bavaro Gardens Hotels • *fronting on their own beach* • comprise a resort city! The complex has more than 1000 bedrooms in dozens of buildings, many of which are five stories high. Some terraces face the sea, with a view over the beach-bordering trees; others overlook the gardens. The several restaurants serve Dominican produce adapted to Americanized-Dominican style—with sandwiches and a sort of hamburger joining heavily fried foods on the menus. There are pools around the premises and boats and boardsurfers at the shore. The gate-guarding services for this enclave are so austere that I was refused entry by a uniformed guard (with his feet on the table) for one of my survey visits. Registered guests have no trouble. *Resort.*

★★★ **Club Mediterranee** • *on the beach* • claims high marks for a full roster of fun in special surroundings at the eastern shore of the country, about 150 miles from Santo Domingo. The Club opened for the season of '81, pioneering this coast with gala festivities. You can count on plenty of action, akin to that offered by Club Meds on other islands (Guadeloupe, Martinique and Haiti, North Caicos, and New Providence). The prepaid week, with beads for on-the-spot cash, lures guests that fill the 600 beds in the cluster of 3-story buildings. This Club is a l-o-n-g way from anything else, but direct air service makes arrival relatively easy. Excursions offered for Club Med guests include a visit to Altos de Chavon, Higuey, and the capital (Santo Domingo). Inquire about the shoulder and other break-in-the-rate weeks when costs are less. *Resort.*

Punta Cana Beach Resort • *with 105 acres, including a band of beachfront* • has grown from its original few single-story houses to include dozens of private homes, which are rented in owners' absence, and a group of 2- to 3-story buildings with blocks of bedrooms. The lodging buildings cluster near the oversized thatched-roof social center, with its restaurants, cocktail area, and nearby pool, not far from the beach. The tennis courts are ready for play and the golf course is in the works (but will not be ready this season). Marketing to European tour operators should bring hordes of Spanish and other vacationers; U.S. visitors will find this to be a European-style beach resort, with most of the action gathered at one beach area, for this season at least. Watersports are offered, and can be fun when the wind lets up. *Resort.*

PLACES WORTH FINDING are many in this area, which has only recently known the heavy foot of mass tourism. The town of **Higuey** is still very much a Dominican market center, with a noteworthy cathedral that is a religious shrine and several casual restaurants (with more certain to open as soon as tourism warrants).

From the east end resorts, Santo Domingo is a long drive or a short flight. The resorts can help with finding drivers (or rental cars), but allow plenty of time—even a few days—for making arrangements.

GRENADA

Grenada Board of Tourism, Box 293, St. George's, Grenada, W.I., T 809+440–2001, fax 809+440–6637; #900, 820 Second Ave., New York, NY 10017, T 212+687–9554 or 800+927–9554, fax 212+573–9731; #820, 439 University Ave., Toronto, Ont., M5G 1Y8 Canada, T 416+595–1339, 1 Collingham Gardens, Earls Court, London SW5 England, 01+370–5164.

$ · · · US $1 = EC $2.65
Unless otherwise noted, $ refers to U.S. currency.

The weathered wood house stands, cared for amid the plants that bloom on its lawn, with a view to the sea over the north coast of the island. Its hilltop location allows for breezes to sweep through, too forcefully sometimes. Strong winds have blown the roof away—or sent the shingles flying—to be repaired and replaced at a later date.

Inside, the furnishings tell the family tales—of childhood picnics, birth, death, friendships, and marriages. Upholstery may show signs of age, but it's mellow with love and years of living. Antimacassers dress the arms of chairs; crocheted coasters await the sweat from a glass of rum punch. And the meal that Betty Mascoll arranges at Morne Fendue includes some of her longtime favorites, prepared by family recipes that are part of her kitchen's heritage.

Conversation, as well as the food, makes memories—of serving turkey to some Americans who were in Grenada over Thanksgiving, after the rescue mission of October '83, and of family outings to the beach and other island points in the days of childhood.

The past becomes the background, however, later in the day when you settle on a soft sandy south shore beach or enjoy a swim in the sea that laps the nearby shores. When the soft flesh of fresh papaya splits under your spoon, and you sample the sweet orange fruit, you'll enjoy another piece of the wealth of Grenada.

The real wealth of the country is the children. You'll see them walking to and from school, neat in their uniforms. Colorful ribbons often marshall the girls' hair into tidy bunches. And there are other children, like Peter, who stand around the waterfront in St. George's, selling spice baskets—leaving school for tourists' commerce.

Peter is a master negotiator; he's far more skilled than I. I did not want

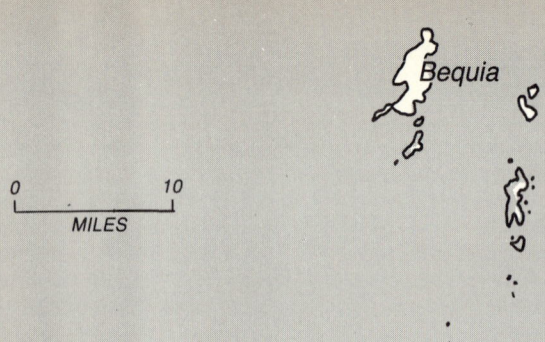
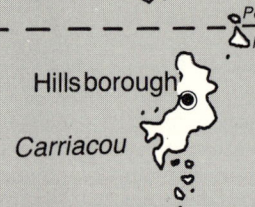
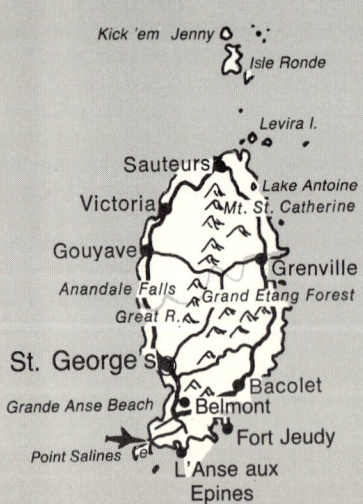

even one of the six small baskets, but I ended up with all of them. Why? We shared some conversation—about town, his life, and plans. And he has a wonderful smile.

He and others join the buxom ladies who sell spice baskets and other handmade items from the stands near the cruise ship landing. Tourism has brought them to town. Some of their counterparts, and their predecessors, work in spice plantations in the countryside.

Although some of the plantations have been modernized, it was not too long ago when the ladies would dance and shuffle around on the vats of cocoa beans, some of them humming softly but most just scuffing around, flicking the beans with their feet as they pranced on their lumpy boardwalk. Some estate managers used to hire a calypso band to play while the walkers worked. Walking the beans had been part of the cocoa process for decades—even centuries—since cocoa was sifted over Grenada, some say in the 1700s.

And nutmeg has been part of the spice of Grenada's life since the mid-1800s. Nutmeg was so important to the taste testing of the Englishmen that tales are told of 17th-century ladies carrying nutmeg in a filigreed silver case, and gentlemen quietly pulling their folding silver graters from their waistcoats to waft a few grains over a meal.

One local legend puts nutmeg into the hand of the Honorable Frank Gurney, who carried it from the Dutch East Indies to put it in Grenada's soil in 1843. Vats of nutmeg arils, carefully peeled (a whole skin gets a higher price), are sun-dried, before being shipped to countries where the husks will be processed as mace. The pulpy outside layer, just under the apricot colored skin, gets brewed with sugar for nutmeg jelly—tart and tasty—and sold by the ladies in St. George's market and elsewhere around the country.

Today's Grenada continues to be a study in contrasts, with rich traditions thriving amid the strident march to a modern future.

POLITICAL PICTURE: When the National Democratic Congress received the majority of votes in the elections of March 1990, Nicholas Brathwaite was chosen to lead the country. Prime Minister Brathwaite had served as head of state immediately following the trauma that ended Grenada's Marxist experiment in October '83. When the New National Party won 14 of the 15 seats in the Grenadian Parliament in the elections of December 1984, NNP leader Herbert A. Blaize became Prime Minister. He died in office in December '89. His successor, Prime Minister Ben Jones, called elections for March 13, 1990. Independent since February 1974, Grenada follows the British parliamentary system, wherein elections are called by the incumbent Prime Minister within a five-year period.

Following his election, Prime Minister Brathwaite moved swiftly to support tourism, with the appointment of both a Minister of Tourism and a Parliamentary Secretary for Tourism. Carefully planned development, with attention to the environment, is the basis for the country's tourism plan.

Prior to and immediately following independence, Sir Eric Gairy had been Grenada's political leader. His tirades about UFOs in the United Nations and elsewhere and his other personal crusades gained him notoriety, as did some of his business dealings at home. That did not stop him, however, from returning home to run for office in the elections held in December 1984 and again in 1990. (He was defeated.)

Grenada's flirtation with Marxism, including its bond with Cuba, the Soviet Union, and other countries in the Eastern block, proved to be an expensive experiment. A dispute over leadership within the leftist government led to a revolution in fall 1983 that resulted in the murder of former Prime Minister Maurice Bishop—and a request to the United States by the Eastern Caribbean countries and Jamaica for intervention, which took place on October 25, 1983. That vivid period of Grenadian history was relived through most of 1986 when those accused of Bishop's murder were put on trial (and key figures sentenced to death).

The late Maurice Bishop and his New Jewel Movement had taken over the government in a political coup on March 13, 1979, while Gairy was away from the island. The action was greeted with enthusiasm by most of the population who yearned for a dedicated government, honest in its pursuit of freedom and a better lifestyle.

The extent of the Marxist activities in this 133 square-mile, 3-island country took most of the world by surprise, and jolted the region—and those concerned with it—into acknowledging the economic problems and taking specific action to develop free-market economies and improving the standard of living for Caribbean nationals.

Grenada continues its development on a strong foundation of free enterprise and democratic principles, with a measure of technical and financial assistance from the United States, Canada, Britain, and other world powers.

ISLAND APPEARANCE: Grenada and its small partners in independence, Carriacou and Petit Martinique, are picture-perfect islands. While the central portions are mountainous or at least, in the case of the two small islands, hilly, white, powdery sand lines many coves. In Grenada's case, the best beaches are on the south coast, not far from the lovely West Indian capital of St. George's. Hillsborough, the main town on Carriacou, has a beach that runs parallel to its short main street. Palms join other tropical trees along the inland side of the beaches; they also grow in groves elsewhere on Grenada, where they are cultivated for their copra, coconuts, and other products. Bananas and other crops also flourish. Spices—nutmeg, cinnamon, cloves, bay leaves, and others—are one of Grenada's important exports; they give fragrance to the air in the parts of the country where they are being prepared for market. Although tourism has touched Grenada's southeastern shores, near the capital, it has not yet trampled with a heavy foot elsewhere on these islands, which are still true to their West Indian heritage. Grand Etang National Park is one of Grenada's greatest assets for those who enjoy nature.

Other areas of natural interest include the Levera National Park area, which benefits from reforestation and plans for hiking and walking trails as well as with other facilities for development of ecotourism, and Carib's Leap, a rocky promontory in the north where Caribs made their legendary jump into the sea rather than be taken by French invaders. The River Sallee Boiling Spring and the Mount Rich petroglyph are being made more accessible for visitors by improved trails, and Lake Antoine, another crater lake, flecks a dip in a mountain peak.

LIFESTYLE is Caribbean casual. The old-time British tradition of coat and tie (even in the hot tropics) is sometimes the fashion at formal functions, but conservative informality is the usual dress. The usual dress for social occasions is a mixture of men in open-neck shirts (no jacket) and ladies in cotton blouse and skirt or dresses. Grenadians enjoy a carefree and colorful social life that includes elegant parties at private homes and an interest in entertaining with style. If you are invited to a Grenadian party, chances are it will be a dress-up affair. At the hotels and around town summertime fashions are the usual dress, with bathing suits and beach wear limited to the shore or poolside. Grenadians dress up for going to town; in the countryside they live in simple surroundings. Tourists are obvious outsiders, whether they arrive on tour from a cruise ship or by rental cars.

AUTHOR'S OBSERVATION

This country is Grenada (Gre-*nay*-da); Granada (Gre-*nah*-da) is in Spain. The spelling is similar for good reason, but there is no reason for pronouncing it incorrectly once you know that, although Columbus passed by on August 15, 1492, and named the island Concepcion, the Spanish conquistadors called it Granada for the far-off port whose peaks they knew better. The French called the island they claimed from time to time Grenade, and the English, who ultimately took possession by the Treaty of Versailles in 1783, pronounced the French name of their new colony with its final "e" as an "a"—eventually spelling it that way. Grenada is Gre-*nay*-da.

MEDICAL FACILITIES The General Hospital is on a viewful hillside, near the churches and the St. James Hotel, in St. George's. Although much-needed new equipment and supplies were received after the tumultuous departure of the Bishop government, the hospital is too small for its needs. The Grenada University School of Medicine (T 809+444–4271), a U.S. school, stands on prime acreage on Grande Anse beach. (Some of the buildings are a former hotel.)

MONEY MATTERS: Eastern Caribbean currency is the local legal tender and you'll do best if you exchange at the bank where the official rate is about EC$2.65 to US$1, give or take a few cents for the current fluctuation. Brace yourself for long, slow-moving lines at St. George's Banks, however. Hotels happily accept payment in US$ but the exchange rate will not be in your favor, which may be of no concern on a small bill, but can tally up to significant proportions if the bill is substantial. Be sure you have checked the going taxi rate before you get in a car for a tour, and do some shopping around before you commit yourself on a rental car. Rates vary, and may be quoted in either US$ or EC$. Always ask "whose dollars."

COMMUNICATIONS are reasonably easy, with direct dial 809+44 for Grenada plus a 5-digit number. Although most hotels charge a premium for placing calls from your room (when there's a telephone there), it's easy to telephone from Grenada through the Cable & Wireless office in St. George's, or from telephones that accept the phonecard that you can buy from them in any of several denominations. Inserted in a slot when you place your call, the phonecard uses the amount required and is ejected when your call is finished. To use AT&T's USADirect service from Grenada, dial 872 to be connected to the AT&T operator through whom you may place a collect call to the USA or a call charged to your AT&T account. Many hotels and other businesses have facsimile machines. Mail service out of Grenada is slow, and you can count on 10 days or two weeks for mail from the U.S. Postage from the U.S. for airmail is 50¢ per half ounce.

ARRIVAL by air is to the international airport at Point Salines, not far from the capital of St. George's. This is the airport that had been started and almost brought to completion with Cuban assistance and Soviet support. If you have any lingering doubts about the intended purpose of that airport by the Marxist government of Maurice Bishop, take a good look at the length of the airstrip and the size of what is now in use as the passenger terminal. It would have been possible to keep (and maintain) an air force in the structure. Although the airport opened officially on October 25, 1984, the first anniversary of the U.S. rescue mission, it was several months later that regular big plane service was routine. *BWIA* and other carriers fly from New York and Miami. *American Airlines* has daily flights using its hub in Puerto Rico. *British Airways* started flying direct from London in April 1986. The small planes of *LIAT* link Barbados and other nearby islands. (The former Pearls Airport, in the northeastern quarter of the country, is no longer in use.)

Arrival formalities are akin to those on other islands: presentation of your proof of citizenship (passport is best), plus immigration card and return or onward ticket. Immigration officials continue to be businesslike and pleasant, as has been the case on all of my visits.

AUTHOR'S OBSERVATION

If you are overwhelmed by a clamor of taxi drivers when you arrive, as I have been on a couple of occasions, insist on being taken where you want to go by the driver of your choice. Always ask the fare *before* you leave the baggage claim area, so you know in advance both the amount and whose dollars (EC or US) are being quoted. If you have any problems, report the driver to your hotel manager and/or the Tourist Board office. Most Grenadians are very considerate of visitors' comfort.

CRUISE ships come into the pretty harbor of St. George's, the capital, in ever-increasing numbers. Some can tie up at the dock but most anchor offshore to bring passengers to the waterfront by lighter. Many of the ships based in San Juan stop in St. George's on their inter-island cruises. Your travel agent can advise on schedules. Natural scenery and a West Indian lifestyle are part of Grenada's appeal. The capital of St. George's is one of the Caribbean's most picturesque. (Be sure to be on deck with your camera for arrival.) Many 18th- and 19th-century buildings, in West Indian Georgian style, border the narrow streets; the marketplace is strictly local—and fascinating, for the produce as well as for the many people. Although the south coast beaches are the island's best, the spice plantations and verdant countryside are well worth touring. Grand Etang National Park will interest botanists and birders.

DEPARTURE from the modern and comfortable terminal at Point Salines involves return of the immigration card you filled out for entry, and being at the airport at least an hour prior to flight time. As the country warrants additional flights, the modern facilities will be expanded, but all the basics are here, in use and comfortable. The departure tax is EC$25.

TOURING TIPS: Grenada is a beautiful country, with verdant hills covered with bananas and other plantation crops. **Taxi** drivers can take you around; their knowledge can be helpful. Ask your hotel for suggestions for good drivers. Contact *Henry's Safari Tours* (T 809 + 444–5313, fax 809 + 444–4847), for a memorable day (or half-day) outing. Henry knows his country well, and happily shares his favorite hiking trails and little-known places in the hinterlands. Other contacts for tours include *Otway's Tours* (T 809 + 440–2558, fax 809 + 440–4179) and *Arnold's Tours* (T 809 + 444–1167, fax 809 + 444–4836). *M & C Travel Agency* (T 809 + 440–2371) can make arrangements for travel to nearby islands if you don't want to do it yourself.

Rental cars are readily available, at the airport or through your hotel. In addition to the *Avis* contact, *Spice Island Rentals* (T 809 + 440–3936), there are several local firms. Among them, *MCR Rental* (T 809 + 440–2832), *Hibiscus Car Rentals* (T 809 + 444–4233), and *David's Car Rentals* (T 809 + 444–4310) at the airport and at South Winds cottages are three to try.

Boat taxis are small, independently-operated motorboats that travel across the harbor at St. George's and from there to Grand Anse Bay. You can bargain your fare on the spot, or check first with the Tourist Board office about approximate charges. If you like small motorboats, and are reasonably adventuresome, returning from town to Grand Anse beach can be fun.

For traveling around the St. George's area, you may opt for riding the **public bus** that travels the island-rimming roads on the hotel-flecked south coast, but avoid the commuter hours, from 7:30 to 9:30 a.m. and from about 3:30 to 6:30 at night. It is possible to take the public bus (EC$1) from most of the south-coast hotels into St. George's, although taxis are ready and waiting—and are eager for your business. Most buses convene at the market in St. George's. Although the swarm of people and the unfamiliar (to visitors) signs may create confusion, it's easy to find someone who can help direct you to the correct bus for your route.

If you can find a couple of days for a visit to Carriacou, there's a choice of travel methods. One route is to the airport for the short **flight** (about 10 minutes) to Carriacou's airstrip. A more adventuresome route is on the **mailboat** that makes regular connections out of St. George's harbor to Hillsborough on Carriacou. The crossing can be rough, but certainly will be interesting if you enjoy island traveling. Check with the Grenada Tourist Board office in St.

George's for sailing times and costs. A third method can be a pleasant day sailing aboard a charter yacht.

LODGING can be in hotels, cottages, apartments, or yachts. There are no high-rise biggies, in the hustle-bustle sense; the country has, instead, a selection of some of the region's best small hotels, each with its own personality. Part of the 5-year development plan discussed by the Ministry of Tourism includes ecologically sound projects. At present, there are 1089 approved rooms; the plan is to have over 2000 by 1994. Among the major hotel projects being discussed, but not ready for this season, are *Liberty Club*, with a golf course, a 200-room British-financed project, *Riviera Resorts Ltd.*, on Grand Anse Beach, and a hotel and marina complex near the capital of St. George's. All are in the southern sector of the country. The *Caribbean Newsletter* (page 9) will have an update on these and other projects when they are close to opening. In the meantime, the only U.S. chain link is the Ramada on Grand Anse beach. Even this hotel, however, has a Grenadian style. Some of the guest houses offer very basic facilities, and might appeal to adventurous travelers.

Hotel bills carry an additional 10% to 15% for service and an 8% government tax.

―――――――― **AUTHOR'S AWARDS** ――――――――
Spice Island Inn has been a long-time favorite, for its pool suites, its beach, and its Grenadian hospitality; *Calabash* is another to note, with similar attributes but its own style; *Twelve Degrees North* can be ideal for independent folks who want access to a kitchen and a view from a private patio/terrace.

Information about places to stay is included under Hotels/Resorts, Housekeeping Holidays, The Inn Way, and Low-Cost Lodging. Stars are awarded within each category. (See page 11.)

HOTELS/RESORTS are small personality places, where self-sufficient travelers can have a pleasant holiday quietly mingling with the day-to-day routines known to Grenadians. Most places are on the beach, and all are within walking distance of the shore. This is no place for the sports enthusiast who must have a top-notch golf course. Grenadian hospitality is warm, genuine, and quietly administered.

★★★★ **Calabash Hotel** • *on the beach at L'Anse aux Epines* • has all the elements for an ideal Caribbean hideaway: rooms in several separate buildings scattered around the property, with the reception and social area wrapped in lush foliage and an elegantly Mediterranean-style pool area at the right side as you face the sea. Suites with private pool were added in 1990. The bedrooms are light and airy. Most rooms have twin beds, bath, sitting room with kitchenette, and porch. The beachside inn was created by an Englishman in 1964, when Grenada was an elitist hideaway. His plan—to have a maid serve breakfast in your cottage—is again in place, under the teamed ownership of Lynden

Ramdhammy and Leo Garbutt, with his wife, Lilian. The pleasant alfresco bar patio encourages lingering; the dining area is on a neighboring terrace. Among the daytime options, in addition to relaxing on the beach, are charter-yacht sailing, island tours, and trips into St. George's. Nightlife is island music some nights, and conversation with guests. *Hotel.*

★★ **Coyaba** • *on Grand Anse Beach* • provides comfortable rooms within a few steps of the lovely beach. Opened with 30 rooms in three 2-story buildings in 1988, Richard and Andre Cherman have created a uniquely Grenadian atmosphere in their pleasant hotel. Staff is well-trained and usually responsive. With the Ramada a short sand-scuff along the beach, the hotel is centrally located, but its pool and country-style dining area are the social centers for most guests who are content to stay on the premises or the beach. There's entertainment some evenings, especially in winter season. Local wood and products are used wherever possible, creating a nice atmosphere. Rooms have all modern comforts; many of the second floor units have a sea view. *Hotel.*

★★ **Horseshoe Beach Hotel** • *on a hillside, overlooking its sandy cove* • claims a picture-perfect setting. Approached through a foliage-trimmed entryway, the main house and dining room seem more like a private home than a hotel. Everything is done to enhance that image, including the decor and appointments in the rooms. Furnished with 4-poster beds and other West Indian–style furniture, rooms are to the right as you face the bay. The pool and beach are down the hillside. You'll want a car for mobility, although taxis can be called for specific journeys. *Hotel.*

★★★ **Ramada Renaissance Hotel** • *on the beach at Grand Anse* • is truly a renaissance—of the original Grenada Beach Hotel that was adapted (and rebuilt) into a Holiday Inn that fell on hard times during the Bishop years, to be hit by artillery during the October 1983 war and used as a barracks for U.S. and other troops thereafter! What you'll enjoy today is a beautiful resort, worthy of its place on one of Grenada's best beaches. The basic elements (pool, main building, and some rooms) have been totally refurbished—and rebuilt where necessary. A color scheme of soft pastels with beige complements the natural hues to create a comforting sense of hospitality. Although Grenadians add their own personality to the Ramada chain's training, the result is a pleasant mix of American efficiency softened (with that "no problem" philosophy) to West Indian tones. Expect rooms to have the U.S. style, although plumbing and power may operate with Caribbean glitches. The open-to-breezes dining terrace, within view of the beach, serves U.S. staples with many West Indian ingredients. If any place has evening action, this place will—especially in winter season and when there are groups in the house. *Hotel.*

★★★★ **Secret Harbour** • *on a hillside overlooking Mt. Hartman Bay* • was built by yachting interests in the early 1970s, and is once again in a yachting family. Purchased by the successful Moorings charter group, who got their start in the British Virgins and had already expanded to St. Lucia, Secret Harbour is better than ever with its lively marina and complete yacht chartering facilities. This place was built for luxurious living. The Mediterranean-style main house has a private-home feeling, with large patios and a breeze-swept dining room. The hillside bedrooms are suitelike, two to a building, with island-built four-poster beds, tiled floors, and an incomparable view from a private patio. There's a lovely pool just below the hill-capping main house; bedrooms make a band, just below on the hillside. Secret Harbor can be a perfect place for island life, for those who like to be with yachtsmen and can be satisfied with a small beach. Ask about time-ashore and time-afloat vacation combinations and learn-to-sail programs offered by the *Moorings* (see page 361). *Hotel.*

★★★★ **Spice Island Inn** • *on Grand Anse Beach* • personifies what Grenadian holidays are all about. This place is a perfect, romantic, beach-oriented hideaway. The reception/entrance area opens out to sand-and-sea, with the dining terrace to the left as you face the beach; the patio bar and the lounge are to the right. Expanding on the style that has made this place a popular hotel since it was created in the 1960s, owner Royston Hopkin has added more pool-studded suites to the original rooms in recent years. Not all rooms are right on the beach, but all are within a few steps. Private whirlpools are in most rooms, in addition—in some cases—to tiny, private patio pools. Spice has been my home for several visits and, although the staff training may need some attention, the facilities are what I dream about for the Caribbean. If there's a weak spot, it's with the food, but surroundings are pleasant even when the recipes and presentation could stand improvement. In June 1991, Royston Hopkin was elected Caribbean Hotelier of the Year by his colleagues, in recognition of his contributions to tourism and Grenada. *Hotel.*

HOUSEKEEPING HOLIDAYS have been a way of life for visitors to Grenada for several decades. The English started it, with the "cottages" they rented around the shores of Grand Anse Beach and other sandy coves, and wise Americans and Canadians followed the trend in the late '50s and through the '60s. Although the Cuban interlude slowed the U.S. rental enthusiasm, housekeeping holidays are, once again, a wonderful way to enjoy this special country.

As far as food shopping is concerned, you can find plenty of the locally grown fruits and vegetables at the market in St. George's. Some of the top stores to head for, when you're looking for produce are the *Food Fair* at the Grand Anse shopping center and markets in St. George's, but don't count on finding the shelves stacked with all the familiar names from home. All the staples will be there, plus many imports. Bring what you *must* have from home, and that includes steaks and beef from your hometown butcher (who can pack from his cold storage, wrapping the beef in newspaper to keep it cold for its journey to your refrigerator in Grenada).

★★★ **Blue Horizons** • *a short walk from Grand Anse Beach* • is a collection of nicely appointed apartments in several small buildings on a hillside and the newest block is in Mediterranean style. The reception and pool area, near the roadside, is the social center for British, European, American, Canadian, and West Indian guests who book most of the units. Ideal for families and others who want housekeeping quarters, Blue Horizons has a loyal group of repeaters. The homey atmosphere, with the attention offered by the Hopkins and their helpful staff, is part of what makes life at Blue Horizons so pleasant.

La Belle Creole, the hillside restaurant, is the viewful spot where most meals are served. Snacks are served at the lawn-surrounded pool and bar area. The beach is a few minutes' walk along the road to Spice Island. *Cottages, apts.*

★★ **Cinnamon Hill** • *at one end of Grand Anse Beach* • stretches up the hillside from a near-shore area. Each hillside unit has a spectacular view of the bay, and comfortable homelike accommodations. Completed a year or so before the Bishop government made "luxury" a bad word, the property languished during intervening years and is for sale at press time. The *Caribbean Newsletter* (page 9) will have details. *Apts.*

Flamboyant Hotel • *at the south end of Grand Anse Beach* • is a gathering of rooms, apartments, and cottages on the hillside, rising from one end of the spectacular beach. The 2-bedroom cottages are ideal for families or friends. Bedrooms are air conditioned; kitchens are well equipped. A pool near the hilltop can be a good dunking spot, if you choose not to make the hike down to (and up from) the beach. The beachside restaurant serves homecooked-style food. For independent travelers who want to be on the country's best beach, this place is it. *Cottages, apts.*

Hibiscus Inn • *within a few minutes' walk of Grand Anse, next to Blue Horizons* • is a cozy and comfortable cottage complex, ideal for vacationers who enjoy Grenadian hospitality. Janice Antoine helps with touring suggestions and offers tasty Grenadian recipes for mealtimes at her dining room. Each of the five cottages has two bedrooms; all are adequately, but not lavishly furnished. It's an easy walk to Grand Anse beach. *Cottages.*

Holiday Haven • *on the hillside above a quiet cove* • is an apartment cluster with a dozen rooms. Not far from Horseshoe beach, the property is owned by John Watts, a Grenadian who's been involved with the country's tourism since the 1960s. *Apts.*

La Sargesse Nature Centre • *on the south coast shore* • offers four very simple apartments for guests who enjoy hiking the nature trails and being surrounded by Grenada's flora and fauna. Nancy and Michael Meranski operate an on-premise restaurant that is a popular goal for lunch or dinner while touring. (You can swim at the quiet beach.) *Apts.*

Maffiken Apartments • *on a hillside near Grand Anse Beach* • are comfortably furnished for "at home" living. Units are slanted up the hillside; each has a private balcony (although top level can overlook the lower level neighbors). Units are air conditioned. It's a short (hot) walk to the beach. You'll want a rental car for touring. *Apts.*

Morne Rouge Aprtments • *on a hillside* • offer new units with housekeeping facilities for independent travelers as well as some cottages. Not open at press time, the *Caribbean Newsletter* (page 9) will have comments, when warranted.

No Problem Apartments • *on the road between the airport and Grand Anse Beach* • were built in the mid-1980s to offer modern, adequately furnished housekeeping apartments in 2-story buildings. Each of the motel-style units has a patio, but privacy depends on your location. There's a swimming pool on the premises, but you'll have to travel to get to the beach. A rental car will allow for complete mobility, although management was also offering free bicycles. (Check to be sure one's available, if biking appeals to you.) *Apts.*

True Blue Inn • *overlooking the sea, south of St. George's* • is a collection of one-bedroom apartments and a couple of cottages, all with pleasant island atmosphere. Opperating with an inn-like feeling, management helps with suggestions for settling into Grenadian life. Ideal for folks who want a relaxed, quiet place. *Cottages, apts.*

★★★ **Twelve Degrees North** • *on the hillside, overlooking beach and sea* • is tops for comfortable accommodations at a curve of sand, with pool-and-gathering area near the sea. All units slope down the hillside, giving you your own view out to sea. Joe Gaylord puts hospitality at the top of the list of priorities and there's plenty of it here. There are twin beds in bedrooms, modern bathroom equipment (that usually works), and a living room/terrace area that will quickly feel like home. Kitchen facilites are compact but more than adequate. There's no air-conditioning, but overhead fans and the trade winds more than take care of that problem. *Apts.*

THE INN WAY is Grenadian style. Several of the properties mentioned in the Hotel section qualify as inns insofar as atmosphere is concerned. Although they are not family managed, the imprint of the owners is ever present, and staffs know the value of genuine hospitality. Especially worth noting are *Calabash* and *Spice Island Inn*. *Twelve Degrees North* has an innlike feeling, in spite of the fact that it is housekeeping units. On the more informal roster, look at places such as the *St. James Hotel*, which remains true to a West Indian style that has been erased on too many islands in an avalanche of modern tourism.

LOW-COST LODGING: Grenada has several guest houses and small hotels that have been popular through the years with Europeans and others who like West Indian living. Although most of the modern hotels charge prices comparable to beach resorts on other islands, the small spots often charge West Indian prices. Some rooms will have a shared bathroom and many will not have a tub when they have a small stall shower. Mealtimes are often West Indian family style, where what's served is the cook's choice for that day. Among Grenada's small and relatively inexpensive hotels are:

Crescent Inn • *about a mile from St. George's and also from Grand Anse Beach* • has 14 rooms in a hillside building that is on the main route between town and beach (so that buses pass nearby). Rooms are various shapes and sizes, but they are clean and some are quite comfortable. *Guesthouse.*

Mamma's Lodge • *on the road between town and Grand Anse* • is owned by the family of Mamma of restaurant fame. The recently built stucco building has a handful of simply-furnished rooms. *Small hotel.*

St. Ann's Guest House • *near the yacht harbor and the Botanical Gardens* • is a homey inn with 15 rooms on the road between Grand Anse and town. The place is very simple, but pleasant. *Guesthouse.*

St. James Hotel • *near the fort in St. George's* • is a traditional Grenadian Hotel, with a lovely view over the rooftops of the capital to the harbor below. Rooms vary in size, shape, outlook, and appurtenances; 8 of the 16 rooms are doubles. This West Indian inn is neat, clean, and comfortable. *Hotel.*

RESTAURANTS are popular with Grenadians as well as with visitors, and although those of us from elsewhere may prefer the excellent island cooking, Grenadians go where the steak is good.

───────────── **AUTHOR'S AWARD** ─────────────
| Betty Mascoll's *Morne Fendue* is an island legend, and a vanishing style. You can dine informally on her recipes at her north coast plantation home.

★ **La Belle Creole** • *at Blue Horizons* • is the hillside restaurant where the Hopkin family recipes make maximum use of fresh local produce. Menu offerings are imaginative, intriguing, and usually delicious.

Bird's Nest • *in its own small building, near the Grand Anse Shopping Centre* • just outside the gates of the Ramada Renaissance and within walking distance of Spice Island Inn, specializes in Chinese food. Best when a group orders several different dishes (smoothed down with the local Carib beer), here are some specialties to try: lobster Cantonese (EC$15), curried lobster (EC$15), and any of several chicken dishes (all in the EC$5 range). A "Yin Wo" lunch combination, with fried rice, chicken, and chow mein, is about EC$6.50.

Coconuts • *in an old house on Grand Anse Beach* • has potential, but the "ghetto boys" lingering under the shade of the huge tree near the house make the atmosphere as you stroll up the beach less than welcoming. When I sampled offerings, pizza was a big seller. This place is worth investigating before settling in for a full meal.

Delicious Landing • *near the Post Office, on St. George's harbor* • is a casual, seaside place that was better for view and atmosphere than for its food when I visited. Bugs in a rum punch made that less than appealing, but bottled (and capped) Carib beer and some of the snacking food may seem palatable. Check to see if housekeeping has improved before settling in for mealtime. If you're looking for a comfortable cooling off place, with a good view of the harbor action, this might be a nice place to pause.

★★ **Mamma's** • *in her house in the Belmont hills of St. George's* • has been island famous for good (and spicy) West Indian food. Mamma passed away in June '90, but her daughters and other family members continue to run the place. Reservations are essential to assure a place in the small dining room.

Nutmeg • *upstairs, near the post office in St. George's* • is another island tradition that has modified its personality to fit the current trend. From yachting beginnings through revolutionary fervor to present-day Grenada, this place continues to be a very casual, in-town drinking, snacking, and meeting spot. It's windowside tables provide one of the town's best viewing perches, but don't count on much in the way of special "cuisine."

Morne Fendue, Betty Mascoll's home in the north, makes plantation dining possible, with advance reservations and a long drive. Inquire through your hotel about phoning ahead (440–9330) to make a reservation on a day you're touring. The experience—wonderful West Indian food served in a 70-plus-year-old plantation house—will be unforgettable.

Red Crab • *in the L'Anse aux Epines area, just outside the gates of Calabash Hotel* • is an island legend that has survived everything. Originally opened by a Brit and favored by yachtsmen and other visitors, the place has maintained its pub atmosphere through onslaughts of students (attending the Grenada Medical School) as well as Cubans, Soviets, and other sundry visitors prior to the arrival of the Americans and others in fall of '83. Loyal patrons—many of us— have enjoyed the Red Crab through all its personality changes. Fish and chips have been a staple, but a new chef has more pretentious offerings. Beer is chilled, and joins other beverages as favorites for those who settle at terrace tables—or in the pub-dark interior.

Rudolf's • *near the post office, in St. George's* • has had its ups and downs, and at times the food has been excellent, taking its cue from a European chef. Can't comment on current status, but the setting is nice and, when you're on the island, it's worth some on-the-spot inquiring.

Tropical • *on the road into town, near the harbor* • is a good place to sample Grenadian food, including spicy offerings and Chinese recipes at reasonable cost. Good for lunch or dinner, this place is popular with nationals.

Several small spots serve island food, which usually means very good island-grown ingredients with not-so-good presentation. Some places to try include a meal at **Roydon's Guest House,** the **Hibiscus Inn,** and the **St. James Hotel,** all of which warrant advance inquiry for reservations, and for *very* casual fare in town, look into **Ye Olde Farm House** on a side street near the market.

NATURAL SURROUNDINGS True to most people's image of what a tropical island should look like, Grenada's development is limited to the area around the capital of St. George's. Most of the rest of the country is still in its natural state, sliced by roads but otherwise undeveloped.

Botanical Gardens are a peculiarly English contribution to the former colonial outposts, and Grenada is no exception. The formal gardens near Government House, just off the road into St. George's from the south coast hotels, needed a lot of work when I last looked. Garden Club folk will be able to pick out areas of the original plan, but paths need tending and plants need care. Far more interesting is a private venture, **Bay Gardens,** on the outskirts of St. George's, in St. Paul. Owned by Keith St. Bernard, the gardens are filled with spice bushes and trees as well as flowering and other decorative plants. Tours are given, with guides who are knowledgeable about the flora. A walk through these gardens in the early days of your visit will heighten your interest in plants that grow *everywhere* in this country, usually with minimal attention.

Grand Etang, the crater lake that marks an island highpoint, is on the route that links the southwest coast's St. George's with the former Pearls Airport in the northeast sector. During the years of Grenada's close friendship with Cuba, the area around the lake was "off limits"; it was one area where Cubans were training Grenadians in guerilla and other warfare techniques. It's interesting to reflect on Grenada in those early '80s years, while walking along the bosky paths, some of which are well maintained and clearly marked. Not only is the lake beautiful, but the lush foliage of the surrounding area will be interesting for botanists, birders, and others who enjoy tropical life. The Visitors' Centre is a source for information about the area, as well as for an educational video describing the park. If you choose to follow the paths on your own, be sure to note Mt. Catherine and Mt. Sinai, two of the three highest peaks in Grenada.

Levera National Park includes an area of the shore in the northern part of the island. Its mangrove swamps are good birding areas; marked trails, which are supposed to be maintained, lead from the beach.

With assistance of the Caribbean Conservation Association and other organizations, Grenada has noted several areas for special attention as nature preserves. The *Caribbean Newsletter* (page 9) will have details on new places as they are readied for visitors.

Offshore areas of Grenada are virtually unexplored. Although some reefs surrounding the southernmost of St. Vincent's Grenadines (the Tobago Cays, for example), are frequented by yachtsmen, many of the reefs around Grenada, Carriacou, and Petit Martinique are almost virgin territory for scuba divers. A prime site is the *Bianca C*, a cruise ship that caught fire in 1961, and now lies in about 100 feet of water off the southwest coast. In the past couple of years, reliable firms have been established in St. George's and most hotels have some link with the area's certified diver-guides.

PLACES WORTH FINDING center on and around the coves of the capital.

ST. GEORGE'S, the capital, is in St. George Parish, in the southwesternmost of the country's six parishes. (The other parishes are St. Andrew, St. David, St. John, St. Mark, and St. Patrick.) The curve of the coast makes a huge bay, with an inner bay that is the harbor which some say is the bowl of a submerged volcano. In the harbor, the lagoon (home for charter yachts), and the Carenage (the waterfront village "square" where the boats were hauled in the old days), are prickled with yachts and service ships, carrying people and produce to and around the islands. The "newness" of town comes from rebuilding after Hurricane Janet, which swept through on a path that is far from the usual hurricane course, on September 22, 1955. The traditional look comes from the British, who took the city in 1763, the French, who took it back again, and the British who claimed it by treaty in 1784. Typical West Indian buildings, some of them tumbling against their neighbors, parade up and down the hills of towns, shoved apart from time to time to make a road now used by taxis, or more often by footfall. The waterfront where the interisland boats tie up, and the central market square, are focal points for daily life. **Bay Town,** connected to St. George's by the Sendall Tunnel, is where you will find the fish market on Melville Street.

Fort George, briefly called Fort Rupert in honor of the late Prime Minister Maurice Bishop's father during the Bishop years, will fascinate bulwark collectors. It was built by the French in the early 1700s, taken by the British, and is now the country's police headquarters, honeycombed with tunnels and complete with walls you used to be able to walk around.

For a drive-yourself excursion, dipping and weaving on Grenada's roads, with views and villages punctuating almost every curve, head up the west coast. You'll pass through a selection of fishing villages and small towns where both you and your car will be obvious outsiders, but don't let that deter you. **Mt. Moritz** (a white community on an island that is 98% black) is the first village north of the capital of St. George's, with Fontenoy just below. Beyond the old estate of Beausejour is **Halifax Harbour,** but it is **Gouyave** that is the goal for many visitors who want to visit the **nutmeg cooperative,** in a 3-story building at the edge of town. (Gouyave is the town's old French name, used today in spite of the fact that the British officially called this place Charlotte Town.) Beyond Gouyave, in the parish of St. John (which the French called by the name of the town), are acres of banana, cocoa, and nutmeg, and before you reach Gouyave, allow some time for a pause at spectacular **Black Bay** where volcanic sand makes a black line at the sea. The **Concord Waterfall,** high in the hills, tumbles down the Concord Valley as Black Bay River.

In the town of **Victoria,** there are some Indian rock carvings (just south, before you reach the town), and the country's highest mountain, **St. Catherine,** pierces the skyline in this parish of St. Mark (known to the French as Grand Pauvre). St. Patrick parish's town of **Sauteurs** is more noteworthy for history than for current sights. The scenery is spectacular, but it is the fact that this is where the Caribs leapt into the sea in 1652, rather than yield to the French, that is the story every Grenadian schoolchild knows. Beyond Sauteurs, known to the French as Bourg des Sauteurs or town of the leapers, there is **Levera Bay,** mentioned above, with its spectacular powdery beach, and the offshore small islands officially known as Green and Sandy.

Your choice now is to return back along the west coast, after your swim at Levera Bay, in time to see the sun set from some viewful terrace near St. George's. (A once-favorite view from the peninsula at Pointe Saline has lost some of its appeal since that site has become the location of the airport.) Continue around, through the Parish of St. Andrew (which the French knew as Grand Marquis). If you continue on around the east coast, you will follow the route from the old Pearls Airport through the **Grand Etang Forest Reserve** to the city, but detour for **Grenville,** where schooners set sail for Carriacou and other islands, and the nearby town of **Boulogne** with its cocoa experimental station and nursery for tropical plants. (Grenville is really worth an excursion of its own, if you don't want to pack all your touring into one exhausting day.)

Other places worth finding are the offshore islands on the south. Check at the Tourist Office to see about getting to the beaches of **Hog Island** or on **Calivigny.** Both small islands have been my goals on fishing boats, heading out from Woburn Village, in early Grenada visits. Although Cuban activity changed their holiday status, both offshore specks are once again restored to their natural state. **Glover Island,** off the True Blue Peninsula (the site of Expo '69, an expensive Gairy-administration exercise for Caribbean colleagues that helped put Grenada seriously in debt), is the third of the south-shore triumvirate, and its status, also, is worth inquiring about.

SPORTS have settled into a Grenadian pattern of watersports, soccer, cricket, and some tennis for local folk and tourists. Sailing put this place into print in yachting magazines a decade or more ago, and there's renewed enthusiasm for the sport now. The biggest of the charter firms—those with U.S. connections—are returning to sail north to St. Vincent, the northern mark on the course through the several Grenadine islands, and there are reputable firms from which to charter "your" yacht—as many European vacationers are realizing.

> **AUTHOR'S OBSERVATION**
> One of Grenada's most spectacular beaches, and the one most talked about, may seem to the novice to be three. The name is pronounced vaguely as "Lance-eh-peen," and will be spelled—in print—as Lance aux Epines, L'Ance aux Epines, and L'Anse aux Epines. All mean Cove of Pines, and I choose L'Anse aux Epines, the true French spelling, for this chapter.

Sailing is sensational between Grenada and the island chain of the Grenadines, which stretches northeast to St. Vincent. You'll have your nose into the prevailing wind for most of that route, but there are plenty of quiet coves on the lee side of the islands and the open-water areas make for lively sailing. This is a great arena for experienced yachtsmen, and others who would do well to consider chartering with skipper and crew. Among the most complete charter facilities are those offered by *The Moorings Grenada* (#402, 1305 U.S. 19 South, Clearwater, FL 34624, T 813+535-1446 or 800+535-7289), located at hillside Secret Harbour Hotel, with a marina below on Mt. Hartman Bay.

There are several yachts that charter on their own, out of these marinas as well as from the harbor at St. George's. Most of the hotels have lists of skippered yachts that are available for day or longer sailing.

Carriacou's Regatta, held on the first weekend in August (Britain's traditional August Bank Monday), is a sight to be seen if you can manage it. The island's hand-hewn work boats, with their hand-sewn sails, compete in a race series that also exemplify a seamanship unknown to Sunday sailors from most U.S. areas. The spirited races are separated by class, which usually means the size of the boat and the number of crew, but all are well worth watching.

Participation by outsiders is limited since crews are fiercely competitive, and usually comprised of close friends, but anyone is welcomed to the evening festivities held in the town of Hillsborough.

Snorkeling is spectacular off many beaches, but the flat, sandy shores of Grand Anse are not the best areas. Some of the rocky areas are more interesting, and your hotel and fellow guests can suggest the best of the nearby spots. As far as **scuba** is concerned, well-organized, professional resort facilities are available through *Dive Grenada* (T 809+444–4371) at the Ramada and *Grenada Aquatics Ltd.* (T 809+444–4219) at Coyaba. *Worldwide Watersports* (T 809+444–1339) offers a range of activities from its shop on Grand Anse beach.

Tennis courts can be found at the *Richmond Hill Tennis Club* and at the *Tanteen Tennis Club,* on the grounds of the special site cleared and built upon for Expo '69, a Caribbean Free Trade Association festival sponsored in Grenada. You can also use the courts at the Ramada Renaissance, Coyaba, Spice Island Inn, Twelve Degrees North, Calabash, and Secret Harbour, if you make arrangements ahead of time.

Golf can be played on the *Grenada Golf and Country Club* (T 809+444–4128) 9-hole course not far from the capital, but the condition of the course is not worth carrying clubs this far. Serious golfers should catch up on their reading, or go to another island where facilities are better.

TREASURES AND TRIFLES in Grenada are full of spice—literally. Known as the spice island, Grenada sells its fresh bay leaves, ginger root, ground coriander, pepper, cinnamon sticks, and other spices in neat baskets in local shops or in bulk at the market in St. George's. Considered treasures by any hometown culinary expert, fresh spices are plucked from the trees and bushes of this island. If you haven't latched onto any in the several markets and shops around the south, in and around St. George's, there are spices in baskets and glass jars for sale at the small shop at the airport. (If you're intending to buy spices, bring plastic bags with you. They are hard to find in Grenada.)

Spice ladies proliferate on the streets of St. George's, hovering around the exit to the cruise ship docks on days when a ship is in port. The going price for a couple of small spice baskets is $5, but be sure to bargain—and specify whether you're talking US or EC $.

For shopping on the streets of St. George's, **One Stop**, on Upper Grenville Street, sells good craftwork in wood, straw, tortoiseshell (which is illegal—as an endangered species—to bring into the U.S.), and other natural raw materials. Brooms, bowls, baskets, and beach dresses are also available.

Tikal, on Young Street, next to the Grenada Museum, carries imports from South American countries as well as some interesting paintings, Dominican Republic amber black coral batik items, the ubiquitous T-shirts (reasonably good quality), and "no shoes" feet decorations. The shop has good quality merchandise. Other places to prowl around before you make your final decisions on island straw work are **Pitts Handicraft** at the pier (where the torrents of tourists pour off the cruise ships) and the **Straw Market** at Granby Street, opposite the market square. **Sea Change Book and Gift Shop**, on street level at the waterfront, with **Nutmeg Cafe** over its head, is the best source for books and magazines.

Yellow Poui, an art gallery upstairs off Granby Street at Market Square, has expanded, with an interesting selection of local art.

Spice Island Perfumes, Ltd., on the Carenage (waterfront) in St. George's sells much more than just perfumes, although all of its product line smells good. Special herb teas, plus pomades, colognes, perfumes, soaps, etc., are attractively packaged and made from Grenadian-grown spices and herbs. Ideal gifts for the folks at home, the Spice Island products are easy to pack and very attractively packaged.

The usual store hours are 9 a.m.–12 p.m., and after lunch until closing time—worded that way because that is the way it is in Grenada. If it is important to you to get to a shop when it is open, research on location or phone the entrepreneur at home if necessary. Although you can usually count on places in downtown St. George's being open (and crowded) when a cruise ship is in port, shop hours are not dependable in spring, fall, and even summer, when the tourist season is slower. Shops frequented by Grenadians open, certainly for morning hours, and usually also in the afternoon—until about 4 p.m. or so. The island market, at Granby Street on Market Square, is at its liveliest on Saturday morning, but there is something sold there in the way of produce every day of the week.

CARRIACOU

Maxman leaned out the window of his car, his red cap accenting the ebony face. "Wanna ride?" I nodded, tossed my bag and myself into the back seat of his car, and slammed the door, all set to slumber. After all, it was about 6:30 a.m. and I had been traveling since a pitch-black 4 a.m. when I stumbled out of my hotel on the southwest shore of Grenada, near that island's capital of St. George's several years ago. The weaving and darting ride up and over the mountain route of Grenada to the old Pearls Airport was an hour-long endurance test, where only agile skirting of potholes by an experienced driver kept the car on some sort of path. There was a broken ribbon of traffic, mostly pedestrian, wandering along the way to . . . where? Maybe work? Maybe not.

The check-in at the Island Air counter at Pearls was casual at best, and capable of being overlooked at worst. Only a "You going to Carriacou?" to the man at my elbow yielded the essential information that "The plane's taking off." I scampered out to the runway, to gain permission to sit in the seat next to the pilot, the only seat left in the 7-passenger plane.

My arrival on Carriacou about 10 minutes after takeoff from Grenada was greeted with the sunrise. Spectacular! It seemed a shame that only a dozen or so of us were there to enjoy it, but others undoubtedly saw it from their vantage points. People get up early around these islands.

But not everyone. Two men were rocking on the terrace facing the sea when I finally figured out how to get behind the front gates and onto the patio of the Mermaid Inn. "Hi. Do you know where I can find somebody?" "No."

Continued gazes at the sea. Rock, rock, rock. Pause. "But someone will turn up around seven or so."

I pulled up my rocker next to theirs, and settled into what was obviously the local system. Slow rocking. I looked off to the wedge of green mountains that sat in the sea not far away, and watched a couple of sloops sail across the view. That was Union Island—where once there was a "rebellion" that made a 4-inch-long article in *The New York Times*. No one here even knew it was happening, and I suspect that the people on Union only knew it when they watched a small plane land at neighboring Palm, on a strip that had been closed for scheduled service because the clumps of grass on the strip had grown too high. (The plane carried the police from St. Vincent, several stepping-stone islands to the north and the seat of the government of which Union is a part.) The dissenters were arrested within hours.

So much for the effect of rebellion on daily life in the Caribbean. The main concern this morning was when I could get breakfast and get going—to explore Carriacou. Soon after Agnes arrived, she delivered my requested two eggs sunny-side-up with a selection of fresh-baked bread, still warm from Cecilia's stone ovens down the street. Conversation began, at the table I shared with the two previously unknown fellow travelers—and none of my pressures to do something seemed to be important anymore.

POLITICAL PICTURE: Carriacou is part of the country of Grenada, with the same central government. The island has its own administrator, and is earmarked for investment and attention as part of the country of Grenada.

MEDICAL FACILITIES: Carriacou's small hospital sits on a breeze-swept ridge in the Belair area, overlooking Hillsborough. Facilities are closer to clinic status. Serious problems that need a larger hospital's facilities are flown to Barbados aboard a charter plane.

MONEY MATTERS: U.S. dollars are in demand (as hard currency). Hotels, cab drivers, and others will be happy to have them. If you're staying for a while, you can change money into Eastern Caribbean dollars at the Barclay's Bank on the main road in town.

ARRIVAL on Carriacou can be aboard a small plane from Point Salines International Airport on Grenada or on the interisland flights from St. Vincent or from Barbados. The mailboat and other interisland craft make regular runs out of St. George's on the south coast of Grenada and south from St. Vincent, at the northern "end" of the string of Grenadine islands. Private, chartered yachts make Carriacou a port of call. If you are chartering through the Grenadines, you can count on your skipper to know the island.

HOTELS on Carriacou are certain to flourish, now that the government encourages investment in the tourism industry. The few small spots that will be open for this season only hint at what can come to this island. When there's news it will be reported in the *Caribbean Newsletter* (page 9). In the meantime here's the roster:

★★ **Caribbee Inn** • *at Prospect, northwest of Hillsborough* • can seem the perfect hideaway, if you're looking for a quiet place with good food, comfortable rooms, and amiable hosts. Wendy and Bob Cooper's 2-story inn has an island focus, with four-posters in the bedrooms, louvered windows that let tradewinds cool the air (with the help of overhead fans when needed), terrace dining that gives unobstructed views of the sunset beyond the sea, and friendly staff. Man Friday's bar and a lovely sandy beach are a short walk down the hill from the main building. Count on warm hospitality. *Inn.*

Cassada Bay • *on a slope on the south coast* • sits on a hillside, overlooking Manchineel and Great Breteche Bays. Used as a hideout for the last few Cubans, after the events of October '83, the former "Camp Carriacou" has been totally refurbished and spruced up as a back-to-basics, nature-oriented place, with a few cottages, a pleasant pool, and a main building where meals are served. Although it has the potential to replicate the successful operation at Maho Bay on St. John in the U.S.V.I., Cassada Bay is enjoyed only by intrepid travelers who search to find it and can be relatively self-sufficient when here. Although surroundings are ideal for birdwatchers and others who like prowling natural terrain, the best beaches are elsewhere. *Camplike.*

Mermaid Beach Hotel • *on the main street of Hillsborough, with a beach at the "back" door* • is legend-filled, and figures in many of my favorite island memories. It was, quite simply, an island home that became an inn, with basic comforts and a sea and yachting emphasis. During the difficult years, landholding owners left the island and the place has had an uneven record since that time. The *Caribbean Newsletter* (page 9) will have an update when warranted. The inn has always been a simple stucco structure, with a main house that has an appendage of a trio of rooms that reach toward the beach, and although changes are planned, this season should still find a small seaside inn.

Silver Beach • *on the shore, at one end of Hillsborough's main street* • added a second story to its shorefront building, with bedrooms that have a sea view and has refurbished for beach-focused vacationers. The original place was a few single-story stucco structures that offer very basic self-catering facilities. The basic-box building on the beach is a favorite hang out for local folk who enjoy the social life that gathers at the bar and restaurant, which is noted for its grilled fresh lobster. For casual housekeeping in natural Caribbean style, this place has a following. *Cottage apts.*

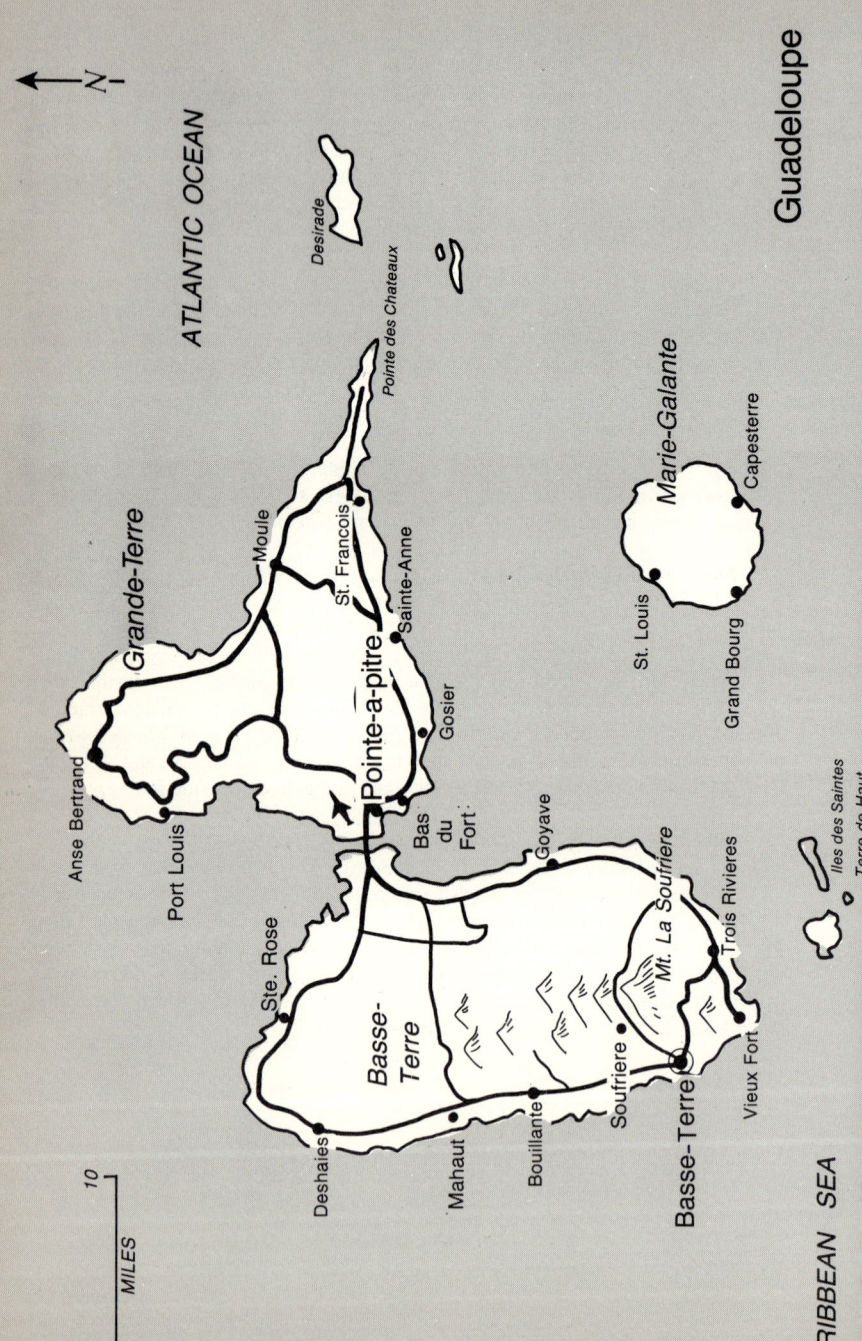

GUADELOUPE

Office Departemental du Tourisme de la Guadeloupe, 5 Square de la Banque, 97181, Pointe-a-Pitre, Guadeloupe, French West Indies, T 011+590+82.09.30; French West Indies Tourist Board, 610 Fifth Ave., New York, NY 10020, T 212+757–1125 or 900+990–0040, fax 212+247–6468. French Govt. Tourist Office, 9454 Wilshire Blvd., Beverly Hills, CA 90212, T 213+272–2661; #250, 1 Hallidie Plaza, San Francisco, CA 94102, T 415+986–4161; #630, 645 N. Michigan Ave., Chicago, IL 60611, T 312+337–6301; #205, 2305 Cedar Spring Rd., Dallas, TX 75201, T 214+720–4010; 1181 Ave., MacGill College, #490, Montreal, Quebec, Canada H3A 2W9, T 514+288–4264; #2405, 1 Dundas St., W, Toronto, Ontario, Canada NS 123, T 416+593–6427.

$ · · · US$1 = about 5.5 French francs (Confirm at travel time.)
Unless otherwise noted, U.S. equivalents are figured at the above rate.

It was years ago, at a mountainside inn above Basse-Terre, on the flanks of La Soufriere, that I first encountered French West Indian hot sauce, the pungent pepper potion that turns your mouth into a raging volcano and sends lava down your gullet.

I now suspect, considering the obeah known to the weed women of Guadeloupe (and most West Indian islands), that that established my addiction to the French West Indies—and, I might add, my respect for the perils of hot sauce and admiration of French Creole cuisine.

No waterfall in Guadeloupe's 74,100-acre National Park cascades more profusely than the tears did down my cheeks on that first encounter. I am older and wiser now. I slice the pepper paper-thin, pierce it with my fork, and waft it over some gourmet delight with the care many people reserve for vermouth when it comes near gin or vodka.

The French West Indies are like that. Their effects are felt immediately, and the impact carries extra voltage. The Antilles Francaises don't *intend* to be different; they just *are*. And most who head here on holiday from the English-speaking world are totally unprepared for a completely different culture, especially when some of the modern hotels are places that *look* just like home.

The French West Indies are tied to mainland France by the long tether of Air France and other airlines, with preferential rates for vacationing French people. Since the islands operate as *departements* of France, equal to the *departements* on mainland Europe, the French West Indies have the same social benefits: hospitals, modern low-income housing, vacation pay, tax benefits, educational opportunities, and a staggering government payroll.

"Bonjour" is the key to unlock the French West Indies. Without it, you'll survive, but you'll miss a lot of what's going on. With French in your kit-for-travel, you'll be a free agent, one able to negotiate with the market ladies, colorfully dressed in their madras layers, and sometimes offering herbs, spices, and piles of little black or white dolls on which to work your obeah.

―――――――――――――― AUTHOR'S OBSERVATION ――――――――――――――
For self-preservation, learn some French and use it. If you speak only English, it's important to know the systems and currency and to be travel-wise. Guadeloupeans seem to prefer to do business only in French, ignoring all other languages and the people who speak them. Systems may seem obscure, and confusion about fees is a natural result.

POLITICAL PICTURE comes into focus only when one looks carefully at mainland France, and then at Caribbean island politics in the past few years. The French islands receive the same benefits accorded to all French *departements,* but they are in the mainstream of Caribbean life, which means that they are affected by Cuba's brand of communism as well as by capitalism. The Communist Party has always been active in Guadeloupe, as it is in mainland France, and government policies are socialist, following the government of President Mitterrand. In addition to being a *departement,* the French West Indies are a region. Local elections are held for delegates to the Conseil Regional, the Conseil General, and for the Conseil Economique et Social. Two *senateurs,* four *deputes,* and two members of the Economic and Social Council represent this island group in the French parliament. Guadeloupe has an active independence movement that does not yet represent the majority. Although the dramatic activities in eastern Europe are far removed from the Caribbean, communication is such that disillusionment with the system has not gone unnoticed here. Party followers are seeking a revitalized platform. Vacationers will be unaware of local politics, except insofar as it affects the workings of the hotel and other services, which operate on strict hours with many holidays and long lunchtimes. Strikes are the means of registering protests to mainland France. The government is the island's major employer, but tourism is a significant source for jobs.

The French West Indies have a standard of living that equates with that of mainland France; the islands are the *departement* of Guadeloupe and its satellites of Marie Galante, Desirade, and the Iles des Saintes as well as the **Iles du Nord,** which are the French part of St. Martin and St. Barthelemy, 125 miles to the north. Martinique, to the south, is also part of the French West Indies. You'll see little of the poverty found on some of the other Caribbean islands. Medical services and education are patterned on the mainland's, with modern schools and equal opportunities for university in France. Unions and other groups on mainland France offer Guadeloupe and Martinique as places for the five weeks' paid holiday that all French salaried employees receive. The ties that bind to mainland France give these Caribbean *departements* a role to fill in Europe's Common Market, but no place in the Caribbean community in the middle of which the islands sit. It is easier for Guadeloupe to trade with Italy and Austria than with Trinidad and other countries a few miles north and south!

ISLAND APPEARANCE: First-timers will be surprised by the size of Guadeloupe, an "island" that is actually two big islands joined by the bridge that crosses Riviere Salee, and several small islets that fleck Grand Cul-de-Sac Marin and Petit Cul-de-Sac Marin, the bays that open up to the northwest and southeast of the bridge, respectively. Basse-Terre, the southwestern island, is mountainous and lush; its "low-land" name comes from its position, below the prevailing winds, not from its terrain. Grande-Terre, the easternmost island, seems flat by comparison; it was the site of most of the flourishing plantations in the 18th century—and is where the largest crop of hotels now grow. Although there are some nice beaches along the outer (western) coast of Basse-Terre, the best beaches are along the south coast of Grande-Terre, as far east as Pointe des Chateaux. Main roads are excellent; secondary roads are usually good. The main city, Pointe-a-Pitre, is busy (and often steamy); the capital of Basse-Terre, on the south coast of its like-named island, seems sleepy by comparison. Saint-Francois is becoming a tourism town; Sainte-Anne is smaller and more locally oriented. Other towns and villages are primarily local, and often dedicated to fishing.

AUTHOR'S OBSERVATION

Portions of Guadeloupe were pummeled by Hurricane Hugo in September 1989. Although most of the foliage has grown again, some of the big old trees were shattered by the winds. Many waterfront places in Ste.-Anne were badly damaged, and hotels in Gosier were also affected, but most soon rebuilt and reopened. People who knew the island before the hurricane may notice a few minor changes; newcomers will see no evidence of the bashing.

LIFESTYLE is French, and if you speak French you'll enjoy life in these islands more. Not only will you be able to understand what's going on (perhaps not in a conversation between Guadeloupeans because they will speak their patois, or dialect), but you will be able to read signs and menus.

This is creole country, and that means a lot of magic in the air—and in the recipes for living as well as for table. Obeah (witchcraft) is practiced by many in the countryside; weed women (who use herbs and other natural products for cures—and curses) are locally known as some of the most reliable medicine ladies; pageants and customs are colorful.

Clothes on the city streets are French. Midcalf sundresses, swirling skirts, or mini-skirts with T-shirts and sandals are the local fashion for ladies; European-cut trousers and loose-fitting shirts for men. And on the beaches: Nothing goes. Even visiting maidens from the country club cloistered set doff their bikini tops after a few days under the French West Indian sun. *Very* casual attire can be seen (if not admired) in hotel lobbies and around the cluster of vacation places at Gosier St. Francois and Bas du Fort. Wintertime travelers are usually a dressier group. Men seldom need jackets; open-necked shirts are acceptable everywhere. Some people choose to dress up for evening, and resort-wear pants, jumpsuits, and other usually fashionable outfits are often seen.

> **AUTHOR'S OBSERVATION**
> If you're unfamiliar with the ways of the French West Indies, write to the Tourist Board office for a copy (free) of *Helpful Hints for Visitors to Guadeloupe and Martinique*. The 28-page booklet is filled with tips to smooth the way for strangers.

MEDICAL FACILITIES: The large, multi-story hospital near Pointe-a-Pitre is fully equipped, following the procedures of mainland France. Medical services are comparable to those in all the *departements* of France. Specialists and surgeons make frequent visits to the French West Indies' hospitals, to diagnose and to perform the most intricate operations. There are clinics around the island and doctors are on call at all of the larger hotels. The smaller inns have their family doctors who are called in when guests need their services. Obviously, French is the language in the hospital, although many also speak English.

MONEY MATTERS: French francs are the currency of record, and travelers should use them (instead of dollars). The French franc to U.S. dollar ratio has fluctuated widely in the past couple of years. The ratio is about 5F to US$1 at press time, but be sure to check at the time you plan to travel.

Tipping is a troublesome matter here, as it is everywhere. Most restaurant bills include a 10% or 15% item for service. Ask when in doubt. *"Service compris?"* (Is service included?) will bring a *"oui"* (yes) or a *"non"* (no) from your waitress. If service is *not* included, an additional 10% to 15% is sufficient. You need add no more if the answer is *"oui."* In one or two restaurants, there is a notation on the menu that says *"Prix nets."* This means that each item carries its own service charge; you need not leave additional money when your bill is presented. For special service, from watersports personnel, for tennis, for some exceptional service at the hotel, or from a taxi driver a small additional sum may seem appropriate. In most instances, though, the fee you are being charged is more than enough.

For best use of your francs, do some research with your bank as to possible trends. It may be advantageous to buy your French francs or French franc travelers' cheques through your hometown bank, although you can also exchange dollars on arrival in Guadeloupe. The bank will give a better rate than hotels or restaurants, as is always the case, but there are so many holidays and unusual (to Americans) working hours that it may be difficult to get to the bank when it's open. Some tourist-oriented stores give a discount for purchases made with U.S. dollar traveler's checks and major U.S. credit cards; inquire before you purchase, and have some travelers' cheques in reserve if you're planning to buy a lot of perfume, etc. Be aware that places quoting prices in dollars may not have the most advantageous exchange rate, which is one advantage of transacting in francs.

COMMUNICATIONS by telephone are relatively easy from the U.S., by dialing 011 for overseas, plus 590 and the number. Obviously, speaking French eases the conversation. Be aware that surcharges on telephone calls made from your hotel are astronomical. If you *must* telephone from your hotel room, keep the message short and businesslike. It's far less expensive to purchase a *Telecarte* from *La Poste* (post office) in Pointe-a-Pitre, or other places where they are sold, to use in telephones designated for card use. About the size of a credit card, the Telecarte comes in several denominations. There are also facsimile machines, which the French know better as *telecopie,* telex, and other methods for business transactions. Radio programs are mostly in French, although it is possible to pick up programs from some of the nearby English-speaking islands.

ARRIVAL on Guadeloupe at Le Raizet Airport is usually easy and efficient. Immigration and customs formalities are standard: Stand in line to show your passport (the easiest and most effective proof of citizenship); your filled-in immigration form, which you probably will receive on the plane but may have handed to you on arrival; and perhaps your return ticket if you look like you might not have the wherewithal to support yourself while here. Porters are scarce, but you can find luggage carts (European airport–style) around the baggage claim area. *American Airlines* provides service through its San Juan hub, with an *American Eagle* link. Inquire at the French West Indies Tourist Office about charter services, often linked with Club Med vacations but also available only for air tickets.

Air Guadeloupe is available for charter flights to nearby islands as well as on scheduled service. *Air Caraibes* also flies to the satellite islands. *LIAT* includes Guadeloupe in its inter-island network. *Winair* and *Air St. Barths* also link smaller islands to Guadeloupe. The check-in area is at the left end of the terminal as you face the entrance. You can buy your ticket just before check-in, but allow at least 45 minutes before boarding time—and be prepared for the shock of reentry at the end of a day spent on one of the small spots. Guadeloupe's Raizet Airport takes on all the aspects of metropolitan France, with the unexpected hustle and bustle after a leisurely day on a remote speck.

CRUISE ships visit Pointe-a-Pitre, which has expanded port facilities to include a pedestrian mall, dockside shops and cafes, and other improvements. Pointe-a-Pitre is a busy place, and the seaside at Gosier and Bas du Fort or farther east on Grande-Terre's south coast may be more appealing. Although the coves on relatively flat Grande-Terre are great for sunbathing and swimming, Basse-Terre is far more intriguing for its Parc Naturel, dramatic shoreline, and walk-up volcano. Shopping is best along the sometimes confusing (and often hot) streets of Pointe-a-Pitre, but interesting and stylish resort fashions can sometimes be found amid the T-shirts and other trappings at the hotel boutiques.

> ### AUTHOR'S OBSERVATION
> When you arrive at the Office du Tourisme or at your hotel, ask for a copy of *Bonjour Guadeloupe,* in English. The fact-filled information booklet is published at regular intervals, and although it may not have all the latest hours and times, the basic information is sound. Armed with *Bonjour Guadeloupe,* supplemented by inquiries at the Office du Tourisme, your hotel's activities desk, and conversations with residents you may meet, you should be able to enjoy a holiday that is uniquely your own.

DEPARTURE from the modern airport involves check-in at least an hour in advance of flight time, and forfeiting the copy of your immigration form before you go through security and into the departure lounge. Guadeloupe has no departure tax. There are some shops, with French perfumes, scarfs, and other items, but don't count on the shops being open. Too often, in my experience, they have been boarded shut.

TOURING TIPS: *Be sure* to ask in advance at your hotel, the tourism desk at the airport, or at the taxi stand for the fare between where you are and where you want to go. Taxi drivers here, as almost everywhere, recognize a novice when they see one, and have sometimes charged what they think the traffic will bear. (For the ride from the airport to Gosier, expect to pay about 70F, to St. Francois 175F, and 40% more after 9 p.m.) Speaking French should save you anguish and money.

Rental cars are available through the activities desks at most of the big hotels. As everywhere, gas is expensive, but the investment is nothing by comparison to the going rates for hiring a car with driver, and having the driver wait while you swim, explore, or have a leisurely meal. If you want a car at height of winter, request it when you book your hotel. French is essential if you want to stray from the usual tourist routes (and even when traveling along some of them); your alternative is a lot of smiles, sign language, and silent prayers if you have a breakdown or otherwise need help.

> ### AUTHOR'S OBSERVATION
> Be sure to ask, and ask again, about add-on charges, which can almost double the first-quoted cost for your car rental. As is always the case, you'll get a better rate for a multi-day rental, but local taxes, mandatory insurance, and other extras can seem excessive. Shop around, if you care.

The main routes are well paved, but watch out for the Frenchmen who drive at breakneck speed down the middle—or squarely on your side of the road. Signposting is not always easy to understand. You may follow a well-paved road that dissolves into dirt. You won't be the first, and some of those dirt roads lead to the best places. Exploring types will love driving on Guadeloupe.

Another getting-around option includes the **public bus service,** which is relatively comfortable (buses are new, usually Mercedes vans). It's easy to travel from, for example, the Gosier hotels to Pointe-a-Pitre or, in the other direction, to Ste. Anne, or on to St. Francois. Routes are highlighted in writing on the side of the bus. All you need to know is the name of your town, and—with payment of a few francs—you're on your way.

For those who want commentary with their travel, **tour companies** that operate in Guadeloupe give efficient service, pick you up from your hotel, and deposit you back there after your carefully coddled day of exploring. All of the big hotels have tour company desks in the lobby area. If you're staying at a small spot, management usually helps with arrangements.

Neighboring islands are interesting excursions, even for a day. **Boat** services include regular ferries that depart from both the Quai de la Darse in Pointe-a-Pitre and from St. François, as well as from Trois Rivieres and Basse-Terre city, which are farther from most hotels and used mostly by residents. Day trips are possible to Terre de Haut (one of Les Saintes islands), Marie-Galante, and Desirade. The *Caribbean Express* ferry makes it possible to go to Dominica by boat, but it's not always possible to get there and back in a day. Check the schedule carefully; there are specials, but the regular schedule doesn't allow enough time on Dominica to see much.

Small planes are the fastest way to reach the neighbor islands. *Air Guadeloupe* makes the 15-minute flight to the satellite islands (Desirade, Les Saintes, and Marie-Galante), as well as longer flights to French St. Barths and St. Martin and to independent Dominica.

LODGING: Choices are endless, and similar in style to those of mainland France. Most of the resort hotels are on or near the beaches of Grande-Terre; a couple of places are in the mountains of Basse-Terre. Gosier was a small fishing village when its beaches caught the eye of hoteliers, several years ago. The "town" has now capitulated entirely to tourism, with guests staying at any of the several resorts along the beach or at some of the small guest houses in the town. Bas du Fort, between Gosier and Pointe-a-Pitre, is a newer resort area, with several hotels, apartments, and restaurants within walking distance of each other, and the marina the major focus. (The few beaches are not noteworthy, although Europeans seem to enjoy them.) The third big resort area is at Saint François, about 25 miles from Pointe-a-Pitre, where there's a golf course and marina; a fourth area is at and around Sainte-Anne, on the south coast of Grande-Terre, where Club Med is joined by a few hotels, some apartments, and many restaurants.

AUTHOR'S OBSERVATION

> Don't expect deluxe services, as you may know them at the best European hotels. White-glove service is not part of the Caribbean lifestyle, especially in the French islands where local politics make everyone equal. Most hotels are built in European style, which often means smaller bedrooms that Americans may find useful, a bidet in the bathroom, and lots of plastic and buffets in the dining rooms.

To avoid a shock when you check out, be sure to ask in advance about any surcharges on your bill. Local taxes and service charges are substantial; there's an 8F tourist tax levied per night.

AUTHOR'S AWARDS

On a hillside above the beachfront clutter, *Auberge de la Vieille Tour* is the "grande dame" of Guadeloupe's tourism, with more traditional style than most newcomers; *Residence Canella Beach* has pleasantly modern facilities and easy access to activity; and *Hamak*'s hideaway location is appealing when you have one of the sea view villas. For innlike surroundings that will appeal to francophiles, *Relais de la Grande Soufriere* is the best.

Information about places to stay is included under Hotels/Resorts, Housekeeping Holidays, The Inn Way, and Low-Cost Lodgings. Stars are awarded within each category. (See page 11.)

HOTELS/RESORTS have few special amenities, such as room service. Many meals at the bigger hotels are buffets. (You can count on a breakfast buffet.)

★★ **Arawak** • *on the Gosier shore, between Salako and Callinago* • opened in the early '70s and is a "skyscraper" on the shore, stretching to a 10th-floor crown of 6 suites that are *huge,* with terraces, and a choice of 3 sea-facing outlooks. Lobby facilities include a shop, a welcoming-bar area, and a terrace where a piano player entertains for evening relaxation. There's a pool near the 48-room annex (a boxy 3-story building with minimum-rate rooms) and the very active (very topless) beach. The 2 tennis courts get steady play, but those who want to head out to sea should check at the watersports pavilion on the plot of land near the Callinago side of the hotel. I don't think the regular rooms are anything spectacular, but if you get one facing the sea, the view makes up for the mundane furnishings. Top-floor suites are best. *Hotel.*

★★★ **Auberge de la Vieille Tour** • *on a hill at the Gosier end of a shoreside brace of hotels* • benefits from infusions of funds, and extensive renovation, under the French Pullman Company's banner. Always atmospheric, with the namesake mill marking its entrance, the reception area is welcoming, with the bar and restaurant area nearby; staff is well-trained. Most bedrooms are in units on the crown of the hill, with sea view, and a steep walk down to the shore and (often crowded) small beach. The few cottages, to the left as you face the sea, can be ideal for families and others who want a self-contained unit. The newer multi-story block of rooms is on the way down the hill, near the beach-view restaurant where buffet breakfast is offered. In addition to the sand patch, there's a pool, with a watersports concession nearby. Beach vendors sell assorted beachwear and other items. Tennis courts are in good condition. *Resort hotel.*

★★★★ **Club Mediterranee La Caravelle** • *at Ste. Anne, about 30 minutes from Pointe-a-Pitre* • was the innovator of all-inclusive style, which has been adapted throughout the region. Although the Club Med system allows for purchase of beads to exchange for drinks, rooms, meals (with mealtime wine), tips, taxes, and many activities are included in the prepaid fee. The activities plan is administered by GO's *(gentils organisateurs);* guests are GMs *(gentils membres);* and a membership fee is required for your first Club Med visit. Promoted throughout Europe, this club is very popular with French people and others who enjoy the action and lifestyle. Inquire about special air arrangements from the U.S. for an all-inclusive, multi-day stay. This property opened as a private hotel, built on a bluff overlooking the beach; it was adopted by Club Med in 1973 and has been repeatedly refurbished, and sometimes rebuilt and added onto, in intervening years. There's a pool just off the lobby; rooms are small and compact, with air-conditioners and small bathrooms. *Resort.*

★★★ **La Cocoteraie** • *on the shore at St. Francois* • aspires to be top-of-the-line, and the nicely furnished suites warrant accolades. Built for the 1990's traveler who knows (and wants) a luxury lifestyle, this place adds several nice touches—flower arrangements, noteworthy decor, pleasant furnishings—to a club-like setup not far from the golf course, and near the marina and other activities of resort-oriented St. Francois. Popular with Europeans, this place has yet to be discovered by many Americans. *Small resort.*

Callinago Beach and **Village** • *seaside, in Gosier* • opened for the '75 season, adding the village apartments soon after. The white stucco walls of the main part are softened by the planting in the center courtyard, where you'll find a couple of shops. The restaurant and bar, down the stairs from the lobby entrance and to the left, are sparse but adequate (I prefer the open-air drinking and dining nook that opens out to the pool and beach). The apartments are in several buildings around the patch of land. Be sure to ask for sea view, if you prefer that to the usual back of the neighboring building. Liveliest action here is when the folkloric group performs (otherwise you'll listen to the steel band). For scuba, check the concession at the beach. Other watersports available on the beach include waterskiing, windsurfing, pedal boats, and sailing. *Hotel, apts.*

La Creole Beach Hotel • *on the beach at Gosier* • is the name that came with a complete refurbishing of the former Holiday Inn. Its location, at one "end" of the string of hotels that includes the Arawak, Salako, the Callinago hotels, and Auberge de Vieille Tour, gives it a grainy sand patch as a beach. Rooms are in several bands to the right as you face the sea; all are large, with modern facilities—and often two double beds that were required of the Holiday Inn link. All rooms have narrow balcony or terrace, depending on your level, and require a good sense of direction to walk the long distances to find where your key fits. The tennis courts are in good shape, and night-lighted. The choice of restaurants, in addition to the beachside places, include a more formal (but not too) dining room that features island-style peppery cuisine as well as classic French. There are nightspots in and around Gosier and a casino nearby. *Hotel.*

Ecotel Guadeloupe • *inland near Gosier* • operates as a hotel school offering a unique holiday option. Everyone learns: The staff learns service; you learn French. Rooms at the Ecotel are modern, comfortable but not lavish, and many have views over pool or gardens. Although you're on the public bus route, you may feel more carefree with a rental car, especially if you want to escape to the beach. *Small hotel.*

★★★ **Hamak** • *on the shore at St. Francois, about 25 miles east of Point-a-Pitre* • is a cluster of single-story villas on or near the shore. The entrance has a clublike feeling, with a breezeway at the reception area; villas are to the right as you face the sea. Refurbished following Hugo's unwanted visit in '89, this place is in good shape. Near the Meridien hotel and convenient to the golf course, guests in the sea view villas have the prized rooms. (The others look at the plant-shrouded backs of the first row units.) All units have private patios, plus twin-bedded room and bath, with kitchenette. (Used for Presidential rendez-vous, this place is quietly discreet.) There are many restaurants in the area. *Small hotel.*

★★★ **Meridien** • *at St. Francois* • is one of the island's biggest hotels, and one of the few with full hotel services. Built for the American market, but used mostly by Europeans, the hotel opened in '74 and has been repeatedly refurbished since then. All bedrooms in the multi-story building have sea view (and tiny balconies). The large pool near the beach is the daytime social center. I've never had great food at the hotel's expensive restaurant, but there are several dining spots in the area. Breakfasts are buffet-style. The on-premise European-style casino opened in '77; there's other entertainment some evenings, usually in winter months. Watersports are offered, as are land tours. There are a few lobby shops. *Resort hotel.*

★ **Novotel Fleur d'Epee** • *at Bas du Fort* • is another of a French chain reaction for middle-income travelers. Nestling next to the PLM-Azur Marissol, the two properties are similar in tone: lively if the usually young crowd is, used by groups from Canada and Europe and *very* casual (bathing suits go almost everywhere, and tops go off when you're by the pool or at the beach). The 3-story Y-shaped building stretches along the coast on a manmade beach. The public areas are in the yawn of the Y, and filled (when the hotel is) with bathing-suited enthusiastic vacationers who wander in and out of the shops and other spots. Beach action includes volleyball and Ping-Pong, plus a selection of watersports and free use of pedal boats (which have been well used, from my glimpse), windsurfers, and Sunfish sailboats. The two tennis courts are free by day with charge for night-light. There are restaurants here and in the neighborhood. It will take you about 10 minutes by car to get into downtown Pointe-a-Pitre from here, and about the same time in the other direction to get to the Gosier hotels. *Resort hotel.*

★★ **Marissol PLM-Azur** • *shoreside at Bas du Fort* • is 15 minutes by car from Pointe-a-Pitre (Taxi 60F). The hotel opened as the Frantel Guadeloupe in December '75, on a manmade beach that is better than some of the God-given ones on this island. (Novotel is a neighbor.) There's a comfortable feeling, if you are happy in a place that supports the casual, carefree, sun-struck life, with tennis during daytime (charge at night), shuffleboard, volleyball, Sunfish sailboats, and pedal boats—plus the pool, beach, and Fitness Center. Since the area of Bas du Fort has many cafes, restaurants, and a few other hotels, this place can provide a convenient cost-conscious vacation home. *Resort hotel.*

★★★ **La Plantation Sainte Marthe** • *at Saint Francois* • is a multi-building newcomer with attractive furnishings and a pleasant airy, holiday feeling. Built for the French/European market, the property has an international feeling in its cafes, around its pool, and among the guests at the beach. Planned for vacationers who will enjoy the golf and other facilities nearby, the Plantation is a good choice for folks who enjoy big hotels amid an area that aspires to have country-club style. *Resort hotel.*

★★★ **Residence Canella Beach** • *at Gosier, near La Creole Beach* • opened for winter '91, with attractive buildings that have Victorian-style wood fretwork embellishing what would otherwise be standard stucco rectangles. Rooms have private patio/balcony areas. Bedrooms may seem smaller than the usual American size, but fabrics and accent colors are in soft Caribbean shades of turquoise, yellow, coral, and pink, and the feeling is a pleasant one. The pool, restaurants, and other public areas are airy and attractive. The "beach" is not one of the island's best, but you're at the hotel hub, with all the Gosier properties within walking distance and tennis courts on the premises. There's action nearby. *Resort hotel, apts.*

Salako • *at the shore at Gosier* • is wedged between Arawak and La Creole Beach. Named for the hat worn by the fishermen of Les Saintes, Salako opened in 1975. The public facilities range over a separate area, connected by walkways and including check-in and activities desk, shops, and several restaurants. Pool and 2 tennis courts supplement the beach for day activities. Tennis can also be your nighttime game (courts are lighted), but you may prefer the band that plays in the bar from 9:30 p.m.–12:30 a.m. (on Saturdays, it's a steel band). *Hotel.*

Touring Hotel Club de Fort Royal • *at Deshaies, at the northwest shore of Basse-Terre* • is far from everything except natural surroundings, on a site once occupied by another Club Med. The hotel could be ideal for folks who want days of hiking in the Parc National, and scuba diving or snorkeling in the pristine waters off the calm west coast, but inquire about status before booking. Planned for use by European groups, staying here will undoubtedly have aspects of a visit to a foreign country for most Americans. The *Caribbean Newsletter* (page 9) will have further comment, when warranted. *Resort hotel.*

HOUSEKEEPING HOLIDAYS on Guadeloupe allow for complete independence, with the freedom to sample the special cuisine at the many small creole and fish bistros, as well as at the haute cuisine French restaurants. **Agence Molinard,** with offices at Galeries Nozieres, B.P. 372, Pointe-a-Pitre, lists several seaside houses for long-term rental near the marina at Bas du Fort, as well as some houses elsewhere around Guadeloupe. There are individual homes, apartments, and villas available for week-long or longer rental through **Gites de**

France (contact the Office du Tourisme in Pointe-a-Pitre) and **M. R. Adolphe at Bungalows-Village,** Montaubon, Gosier, Guadeloupe, F.W.I., for places near the resort hotels of Gosier. Do *not* count on flourishes and fancy fixtures, or even, in some cases, hot water. Some places listed are second homes for Guadeloupeans who use their beach villas during very casual, carefree summer holidays but are happy to rent them to visitors during the winter months. Rentals will range from about F1500 for a small villa to about F2800 per week for a 4-bedroom villa.

Speaking French is essential, not only for negotiating the rental, but certainly for shopping for food and making arrangements with the maid and/or cook if you hire one with your island home.

Marina Baie de Boucanier • *at Saint Francois* • is a modern 3-story building with 42 apartments, each with balcony (or small patio if on the ground level). A pool is the daytime gathering place. *Apts.*

Residence Karukera • *on the road to Pointe des Chateaux near Saint Francois* • is a gathering of 44 bungalows, each with private porch and adequate housekeeping facilities. Best for independent Francophiles who choose to rent a car, the place can be comfortable for families and other groups who enjoy a back-to-basics life. *Bungalows.*

Sprim Hotel • *in Bas du Fort, 10 minutes' drive from Pointe-a-Pitre* • is a modest apartment cluster, with air-conditioned, comfortable units that put you within walking distance of tennis courts, watersports, a few boutiques, and several restaurants and cafes. A good choice for independent travelers who want a base with an option for light housekeeping. *Apts.*

★★ **Les Trois Mats** • *at St. Francois, an hour's drive east of Pointe-a-Pitre* • perks at the boardwalk of the marina and shares management with Hamak. All residents can cook at home, in one of the 36 studio or duplex units, or dine at one of the nearby restaurants. The 2-story buildings nestle up the shore (not beach). Each sets you up with an "outside" kitchenette, with cooking and sink facilities on the outside wall so that you cook and dine on your patio or porch. Ideal for self-sufficient types who like open-air living (bedrooms are enclosed, as are the living rooms of the duplex units) and the chance to walk to the Meridien, the casino, the golf course, and the beach (at Meridien). The restaurant serves snack fare, including breakfasts, if you prefer not to prepare your own. You may want to rent a car for a couple of days, but it's not essential for day-to-day living. There's a small commissary in the marina complex, but for stocking up you'll need to bring things from home or head to a market in St. Francois. *Apts.*

Village Soleil, or **Sun Village** • *in Bas du Fort* • rose from its hillock-top to open in December 1979. The several buildings that encircle the pool and gathering area hold 92 attractively furnished studios, suites, and a couple of duplex units that are suitable for 4 people. Village Soleil is comfortable for self-sufficient, nautical types who like being able to wander down the slope to the activity and restaurants at the Port de Plaisance, the Bas du Fort marina area.

Although the hotel is promoted in the U.S. as "Sun Village," signs on location and conversation about the hotel to residents (who speak French) refer to Village Soleil. On-the-spot dining is in *Le Boucanier,* a highly touted, open-to-breezes restaurant near the pool (a glass baffle protects from prevailing winds). *Apts.*

THE INN WAY: Francophiles will enjoy the very French West Indies' style of inns on Guadeloupe. Although the service may lack polish, some of the surroundings seem special. *Relais Creoles* is a local association of hotels with less than 50 rooms. Ask the Tourist Board office for one of the booklets describing these places. Although I don't feel that all the members qualify for my recipe for an inn (which includes hospitality and atmosphere as prized ingredients), there are a few worth special mention. Among my favorites are:

L'Auberge de la Distillerie • *on Basse-Terre, near Petit-Bourg* • is a special place that can appeal to folks familiar with inns around France. In the residential area, on Route de Versailles-Tabanon, the Auberge has a homey feeling, with wicker headboards on the cot-sized beds and over-stuffed furniture in the living room. The restaurant, *Le Bitaco,* has been popular with island cognescenti for its creole cooking, and the modest rates make this place popular with those who know and love their French West Indies. Speaking French is essential for comfortable communication. The pool is pleasant for on-premise cooling off; you'll want a car for exploring—and finding any beach. *Inn.*

Auberge du Grand Large • *at Ste. Anne* • is a French beachside place where life is casual and uncluttered. You can walk onto the Ste. Anne beach, a long stretch of sand that is shared with the village folk and the fishermen. This is a simple place, with the social area and restaurant decorated in creole style. The restaurant's colorful dining area tops placemats with madras-patterned napkin "hats," ready and waiting for your use at mealtimes. (Creole fare is featured at lunch and dinner.) Although rooms 2 through 6 are closest to the beach, they face the fence that discourages walk-in traffic. Rooms nearest the main building (where meals are served) are more protected from unwanted beach strollers. *Cottages.*

Relais de la Grande Soufriere • *above St. Claude, Basse-Terre* • has been one of my longtime favorites. Although it was closed for several years, its opening for the 1988 season was a boon for travelers. Built as a private home, the property is elegant and speaks of former prosperity. High ceilings, airy rooms, breeze-swept halls, and mansion surroundings are key assets. The grounds are filled with tropical flowers and well-tended plants; a pool marks the lawn. Nestling on a hillside just below the start of the walk up the flanks of the volcano and above the seaside capital of Basse-Terre, this charming inn will appeal to well-traveled folk who know and love France—and the Caribbean. *Inn.*

★★ **Relais du Moulin** • *at Chateaubrun, near Ste. Anne* • rests amid grazing grounds for cattle, and the horses that are available for riding. Marked by a sugar-mill tower that is the main reception office for the cluster of small buildings that hold the 40 rooms, the Relais provides a very special resting spot for those who want quiet, countryside surroundings. The small pool that punctuates the top of the rise on which the Relais perches can be lively with children or completely yours, depending on the house count. Rooms are neat, comfortable, and small—with a hammock strung on some of the porch areas. *Le Tap Tap* is the pleasant, poolside dining area. You'll want a rental car for mobility and plenty of books to read if you intend to stay "at home." *Cottage inn.*

LOW-COST LODGING: Variety is the keynote for Guadeloupe, where there is a local group of Gîtes de France, which are inexpensive lodgings. The tourist office has a list. Francophiles who like small spots will applaud (as I do) the establishment of Chaine des Relais de la Guadeloupe, now known as *Relais Creoles*. My favorites are mentioned above. Here are some lower-cost choices.

Auberge J. J. • *at Gosier* • is a 12-room inn where Jose and Josy Mormont are your hosts. The inn is clean, and the restaurant is more prominent than the lodgings when you glance up the entrance steps from the street. This inn is good for anyone who has traveled in France and would enjoy walking to activities in town.

Canibis • *in the countryside near Gosier* • can be comfortable for hikers and walkers and those who want to be near Grands Fonds. The 13 rooms in the recently built stucco building are simply furnished; most have small balconies.

★ **Cap sud Caraibes** • *not far from the beach at Petit-Havre* • is a small spot not far from Gosier. An on-premise pool is the cool-off place for guests in the dozen air-conditioned rooms.

Les Flamboyants • *in Gosier* • is a pleasant small spot that puts you near (but not in) all the hotel-resort action.

Grand Anse Hotel • *at Trois Rivieres* • is a gathering of small air-conditioned bungalows. A pool is the centerpiece; independent travelers who speak French may enjoy the outpost atmosphere. The ferry for the satellite islands (Terre de Haut and Desirade) leaves from the waterfront. *Bungalows.*

★★ **Le Rotabas** • *in Ste. Anne, on the south coast* • opened a few seasons ago with 20 comfortable bungalows, which were followed with another 24 around a central building that holds the restaurant and reception area. Francophiles familiar with the French-Mediterranean ambience will find reflections in this place pleasant. *Bungalows.*

★ **La Toubana** • *in Ste. Anne, about midway between Gosier and St. Francois* • makes the most of a viewful hillside location, punctuating it with an attractive pool surrounded by sturdy white painted woodslat furniture. The patio proves perfect for the bistro-style meals, and guests seem to enjoy the casual, countryside atmosphere when lodging in the bungalows. You'll want a car for island exploring, but if peace and quiet and book-filled hours sound appealing, this can be your place in the sun. *Bungalows.*

Les Marines de St. Francois • *at the shore in St. Francois* • is a community of 230 comfortable apartments, built to accommodate the growing group of French folk who come here for a month or more. The units are spacious and many have a lovely view; there's a pool on premises. *Apts.*

Relais Bleus du Madrepore • *at Bas du Fort* • gives you a comfortable apartment in a reasonable grouping of about 30 units, within easy distance of some of the country's best dining spots—and the action of the PLM-Azur Marissol and the Novotel Fleur d'Epee hotels. *Apts.*

RESTAURANTS on Guadeloupe range from exceptional to "tourist traps," and careful on-the-spot research pays off. There are places where French haute cuisine is served, but the spice of life, for my money, comes in the creole cooking that is the essence of the French West Indies. Time-honored French culinary methods have been adapted to Caribbean ingredients. Sauces are spicy, to cope with the tropical heat. Fish, beef, and chicken were curried and otherwise flavored to keep them edible in the days of no refrigeration, and the recipes have been refined to thrive today. Guadeloupe's *Fete des Cuisinieres*, held annually in mid-August, begins with the blessing of the platters of food prepared by the island's culinary experts and culminates in a bacchanal that follows the exuberant parade. Although the fete honors the island's best cooks, it is not the best day to sample the foods. Wait until the cook has returned to the kitchen to enjoy the best the Caribbean islands have to offer.

Special creole foods that appear on small bistro menus include *soupe du pecheur* (fisherman's soup), *blaff* (a French West Indian bouillabaise, *lambi* (conch, pounded tender and cooked), *ouassous* (local crayfish), *colombo* (curry, often des poissons, which means fish), *calalou* (a hearty soup, often flavored with garlic, that bears a resemblance to spinach soup), and langouste, the Caribbean lobster served in a variety of ways. *Accra*, a crispy, fried, spicy fritter, usually made with cod, is often served as an appetizer, as are other nibbles with names best known to the cook.

During peak winter season, reservations are advisable, especially for dinner. Summertime meals can usually be spur of the moment, especially if you're willing to wait a while if all tables are filled.

Chez Rosette • *in the village of Gosier, not far from most of the hotels* • has fallen into the doldrums, in my opinion. The place has expanded from a once-special tiny place run by Mme. Rosette Limol into a modern place that has capitulated to commercialism.

★ **Chez Violetta-La Creole** • *on the outskirts of Gosier, as you head down the hill toward Ste. Anne* • was a small and special spot until additions during summer of '80 nearly tripled the size of the place. Red-checked cloths cover tables, and various madras patterns parade around the room on waiters and waitresses. A meal might include, as one of my memorable ones did, a mouth-watering *poisson en papillotte* (fish cooked in a "paper bag" of aluminum foil), spicy *accras, colombo poulet* (chicken curry), and *soupe du pecheur* (a hearty soup with fish).

Also in Gosier, there are several small spots that warrant a visit if you enjoy experimenting and are enthusiastic about creole food and personality restaurants. Partly in response to the proliferation of hotels (and, therefore, guests) along the Gosier beach, several specialty places grow in the small houses of town and occasionally in newer buildings constructed as restaurants. Among those worth trying are **Le Baoule**, on the waterside of the road that goes through Gosier, and **La Mandarine**, a favorite for its Oriental tone. **Bach Lien** features Vietnamese food.

Among the favorites in the Saint-Francois area where there are more than 30 choices, are **Chez Honore**, a creole place with a pleasant atmosphere, and its relative, **La Langouste Chez Honore**, on the road to Pointe des Chateaux. (This place can seem perfect before, during, or after a day at the beautiful beach at its "doorstep.") Several shoreside spots have grown along the scenic road out to Pointe des Chateaux, the southeast finger of land that is a favorite for romantics. Among them are **Au Colombo**, a long-time favorite for its fish and lobster focus, as well as **La Mouette** and **Le Ranch Marty**.

On rugged, mountainous Basse-Terre, restaurants are sprinkled around the island, often in places where you least expect them. **La Mouina** is at La Retraite Baie-Mahault, to the north just after you cross over the Pointe-a-Pitre bridge to Basse-Terre, and the **Grand'Anse Hotel** at the beach at Trois-Rivieres. **Le Massoukou**, on rue Victor-Hugues in the town of Basse-Terre, and **Chez Ragouvin**, in the residential area known as Sainte-Claude above Basse-Terre, are two places worth trying for lunch during an island tour. **La Rocade, Chez Clara**, and **Le Relais** are informal bistros at the fishing village of Sainte-Rose, on the northeast shore of Basse-Terre after you've crossed from Grande-Terre, and **Aux Charmilles** and **Au Caraibe** are in the fishing village of Vieux Habitants on the southwest coast of Basse-Terre, before you reach the town of Basse-Terre but after you've driven through the scenic Col des deux Mamelles.

Returning to the island of Grande-Terre, where most of the hotels are located, the development of the marina and hotel community at Bas du Fort has birthed a series of good restaurants. **La Plantation** is a time-honored success story (see below), but others worth trying include **La Route du Rhum**, which takes its name from the yacht race that goes from mainland France to Guadeloupe and is located, not surprisingly, at the marina, and **Le Barbazar**, a casual and often fun place that is also at the marina.

★★★ **La Plantation** • *at the marina area at Port de Plaisance in Bas du Fort* • is where elegant surroundings help good food and service seem even better. Make your reservation early for a very special (and expensive) mealtime with pace-setting cuisine.

★★★★ **La Canne a Sucre** • *in downtown Pointe-a-Pitre at 17 rue Jean-Jaures* • was "discovered" by Craig Claiborne, former food editor of the *New York Times*, who heaped encomiums on the fish soup, the accra (fish fritters), and grilled lemon chicken, as well as on some of the desserts. If you are in town (or want to go there), check for a reservation. Entrees cost from 60F to about 85F, with wines running from 60F to 120F. Closed Sun. and Sat.

★★ **Auberge du Grand Large** • *on a side street off the beach at Ste. Anne* • is a bowered open-air spot for a good creole meal. You will have to have French firmly in command to know exactly what you are ordering (and to make your wants known), but a reservation here will put you in touch with creole atmosphere, near enough to the sea to have a swim for dessert.

★★ **Karacoli** • *north of Deshaies, on the "wing" of Basse-Terre* • is an informal, bathing-suit kind of place where you can leap into the sea while you wait for the next course to come—and the favorite food will probably be *poisson grillee* (grilled fish). Owner Lucienne Salcede speaks English, if you're timid about trespassing where you are not on firm footing with French, and the owner's recommendations will make a fine memory. (A good goal on your car rental day.)

NATURAL SURROUNDINGS include verdant countryside, beaches, and sprinkling of fishing villages around the shore, plus the satellite islands offering special sights of their own.

Basse-Terre, the westernmost wing of two-island Guadeloupe, is mountainous, verdant, and the site of the **Parc Naturel,** which is pinpointed by the 4813-foot peak of La Soufriere. There are more than 74,100 protected acres to the park, with the waterfalls at Carbet one of the hiking goals. If you're driving on your own, make your first stop the *Maison de la Foret* where you can get full details. You'll find the park headquarters by veering off at the sign on the main *traversee* which runs more than 10 miles through the park. For those who like to see their parklands in comfort, it's possible to drive along the well-paved roads, circle around to the town of Basse-Terre, and drive to the hillside suburb of St. Claude (note the affluent suburban homes, many of them well-kept models of turn-of-the-century French West Indian architecture). Your goal, before or after the drive up the mountain to the sulfur-seething vents in La Soufriere, might be Relais de la Grande Soufriere, which can be a special place for meals.

Any serious trek to and through the Parc Naturel should be preceded by a careful reading of the *Walks & Hikes* booklet (*Promenades & Randonnees*), with diagrams, description of sites, and suggested hikes with approximate times and a code for degree of difficulty. (Ask for the booklet at the Office du Tourisme.) Even those who don't hike will enjoy the 10-minute walk to the *Cascade aux Ecrevisses* (waterfalls) from the first parking pull-off after you head into the park from Pointe-a-Pitre, following the island-splitting, well-paved *traversee*. You can swim in the rock-lined pool at the base of the falls.

The **Parc Archeologique des Roches Gravees** (Engraved Rocks) is a wide spot off the road near the wharf at Trois Rivieres, which I find more interesting for the local boat service to Terre de Haut. (The rugged boat trip can be an exceptional travel experience if you like the sea and have an adventuresome spirit.) The rock carvings that "were more than likely carried out by the Arawaks" are more of a tourist lure than I care to spend time on. If you want to take a look, head to the wharf (*embarcadere*) where the boat departs for Les Saintes. (Trois Rivieres is about 30 miles from Pointe-a-Pitre.)

Heading east along the south coast of relatively flat Grande Terre there are fishing villages and, eventually, the easternmost point of two-island Guadeloupe, **Pointe des Chateaux**, where a majestic tumble of black rocks is etched on the horizon. The surf comes pounding in against the rocks, and after you have "oh-ed" and "ah-ed," there's not much more to do here—unless you want to slither off to the naturalists' beach or one of the several other soft-sand fringed coves that draw enthusiasts from the nearest hotels (Meridien, Hamak, etc.), about 20 minutes' drive away, or settle into one of the several small-but-expensive bistros and cafes that are scattered around the area.

PLACES WORTH FINDING: Pointe-a-Pitre is Peter's fishing village, taking its name from a 17th-century Dutchman who fled to these shores from Brazil, when the Portuguese laid claim to that colony. According to a local legend, when Peter came to Guadeloupe in 1654, landowner Houel du Petit Pre gave him a site on which to build his home and set up a fishing business. That site is the point of Peter, or Pointe-a-Pitre. During the Seven Years War, when British soldiers built a harbor at Pointe-a-Pitre, the town began to grow and, when the French reclaimed their land in 1763, the town continued to expand, following the original British design. Today, the city is the island's center of commerce.

An earthquake on February 3, 1843, destroyed most of the first city, but buildings soon reappeared according to the original plan, and the Basilique (church) that claims its place in the middle of the city, where rue Lamartine and rue d'Ennery would intersect (and do change names), dates from 1847. The structure, however, is more noteworthy for its presence than for its architecture, which was "improved" throughout the years to be basically boring today. Fires in 1899, 1906, and 1934 gobbled up many of the original wooden buildings, and a devastating hurricane on September 12, 1928, took care of most of what was left.

The city today is a steamy commercial center that I find overwhelming. It's best experienced around Place de la Victoire, where the waterfront activity is the vibrant heart of the matter. (The Office du Tourisme is located nearby.)

The marketplace, known as the **Marche**, is on rue Peynier, just south of Place de la Victoire. It's well worth a visit for anyone interested in leaping into the middle of this island's life. Fruits, vegetables, and other produce mingles with obeah dolls and other facts of local life, most of it displayed in the huge hand-made reed baskets that are a trademark for West Indian life. The market-women are even more colorful than their products, and most will respond kindly to a "Bonjour" and a smile.

AUTHOR'S OBSERVATION

If you want to take pictures in the marketplace, be sure to learn enough French to be able to ask if taking the picture is acceptable to your subject. Many Guadeloupeans believe in the occult and feel that taking a picture is taking the soul.

The **Musee Schoelcher**, also on rue Peynier, not far from the market, is an interesting building. The eclectic collection is being upgraded; it has been mostly artifacts and personal belongings from past times that can be interesting as a slice of life but are not much real value. Be prepared to find all the notices only in French.

Basse-Terre, the capital of this island, is a wonderful collection of 18th- and 19th-century buildings, some restored to previous elegance and others remodeled to be hybrids. There are several shops in Basse-Terre, but it is by no means as vibrant for visitors as downtown Pointe-a-Pitre.

As you travel around the island, **La Griveliere,** a coffee plantation that dates from 1726, is open to the public. Claiming an impressive portion of the mountainside, above Basse-Terre and near the Grand Riviere, the lush and well-tended plantation is a beautiful place for walks and a midday meal. (Phone 98.48.42 for reservations.)

Offshore islands are intriguing outposts that can be seen in a hurried day, flying over and back to Terre de Haut, Marie-Galante, or Desirade. (The flight to Terre de Haut takes about 15 minutes; Desirade and Marie-Galante are about 20 minutes.) A bag with your bathing suit and a towel, plus your tongue firmly wrapped around French is all that you need for an excursion to one of the small islands. (A group tour is *not* the ideal way to visit the small islands; *you* become the sight to see, and there is no way to mingle with the local life, which is about all there is to offer on these islands.)

Many of the tour desks at big hotels arrange excursions to neighboring Dominica and to St. Lucia for a day or two. Even if you are not staying at one of the biggies, it may pay to read their activities board. If there is space on one of the tours to get you to and from another island, the tour operator is usually very happy to have an extra fare. The alternative is to check with one of the travel agencies with offices in Pointe-a-Pitre.

Dominica is definitely worth finding, when you are as near as Guadeloupe, especially now that some small plane flights land at that country's Canefield Airport, only 5 minutes from the capital of Roseau. (Other flights swoop into Melville Hall Airport, for a 2-hour winding drive south to Roseau.)

SPORTS on Guadeloupe are resort-centered. If it's action you're after, the Club Mediterranee Caravelle is the place to make your reservation. It offers tennis, volleyball, sailing excursions, and all the usual watersports, and most are included in the all-inclusive price. Many of the larger hotels, especially those in the Gosier area, have added some, and sometimes all, watersports with their inclusive plans, but it's worthwhile checking to find out exactly what is included, if you want to scuba dive and boardsail. Guests at the hotels in Gosier and Bas du Fort have easy access to watersports concessions, which are at the shore in front of the properties.

Watersports take on a French panache on this French island. **Boardsailing** is *very* popular from many shores, and most of the larger hotels can arrange for rental. From the Gosier hotels, boards are rented from the shorefront concessionaires. Out of St. Francois, Meridien and other hotels have boards for rent, and concessionaires operate from the marina area.

Scuba assistance is available at most hotels. It's also noted as **plongee** (in French). The traditional favorite dive site is off Pigeon Island, an area made famous by Jacques Cousteau many years ago. Diving can be arranged from the beach at Malendure, on Basse-Terre, for Pigeon Island dives. Both *Chez Guy* and the *Nautilus Club* have facilities there. In addition, out of Gosier, the PLM Azur Calinago and La Creole Beach are two of several places with dive operators who offer resort and certification courses as well as independent dives with a guide. The Bas du Fort marina has a dive operator. One goal for divers is Les Saintes.

Golfers should reserve a room at the hotels in and on the fringes of the St. Francois course, which opened in early 1978. If you're staying at the Gosier hotels you will have almost an hour's drive before you can negotiate for your caddy and cart to play. Greens fees figure to about 200F per day, but ask specifically about charges if it matters to you. The 18-hole course was designed by Robert Trent Jones's group, and the pro is English-speaking (but all the caddies are not fluent in English).

Tennis enthusiasts will find courts at La Creole Beach, Arawak, Auberge de la Vieille Tour, and Salako at Gosier, and the PLM-Azur and Novotel in Bas du Fort. Meridien, Les Marines de St. Francois, and Hamak also have tennis courts, near St. Francois. Near Sainte Anne, Relais de Moulin and La Toubana have courts.

Yachting around Guadeloupe often involves heavy seas and stiff winds when you head out as far as Terre de Haut or some of the other satellite islands. Experienced charterers can take a good-sized skippered yacht for a few days or a week.

There are three main sources for charter yachts, namely Port de Plaisance at Bas du Fort near Pointe-a-Pitre, the Marina de Riviere Sens at Gourbeyre near the capital of Basse-Terre, and the Marina de St. Francois, on the southeastern shore. Sailing lessons are available through *Evasion Marine*, at the St. Francois marina. For charter yachts a few of the best contacts are *Vacances Yachting Antilles* and *Locaraibes* at Bas du Fort and *Emeraude Yachting* at Pointe-a-Pitre. Most of the larger hotels have suggestions for yachts that are available for day sailing. Port de Plaisance (Pleasure Port) was established in early '80 at the Pointe-a-Pitre side of the Bas du Fort nub of land. The private and charter yachts tied up at the marina make up an impressive fleet with many yachtsmen having sailed transatlantic to reach Caribbean ports. This area has taken over as the headquarters for yachtsmen (and yachting activity), leaving the Appontement du Carenage on the Gosier side of the capital mostly for boat work and local activity. Check the bulletin board at *Route du Rhum* cafe for notices about yachts looking for crew if you're an accomplished and/or adventuresome sailor looking for a bunk. The bulletin board is also a good place to find out about boats available for charter. Several of the skippers are happy to talk business, for a day sail or longer.

Guadeloupe came into sailing headlines as the western port for *La Route du Rhum*, a race from St. Malo on mainland France to Pointe-a-Pitre that has been held in fall, when yachts sailed transatlantic to arrive in early December. Check for information about future races if the adventure interests you.

TREASURES AND TRIFLES on Guadeloupe are best found in seething, steamy Pointe-a-Pitre, where most of the stores for residents are located, and along the street and lanes in Gosier, the former fishing village turned holiday hub. There are shops in the hotels for essentials, and many of those shops carry resort wear imported from France as well as a few local items. In the city, the fruits and vegetables, plus dolls on which to work your witchcraft with the "weeds" (herbs) the weed women use for theirs are sold at the local market, along with a selection of baskets that the local folk use for carrying their produce and brooms they use for their housekeeping.

Boutiques are gathered at several spots, but especially in a cluster known as **Galerie Nozieres** on rue de Nozieres. Schoelcher, Frebault, and Nozieres are the threads for most of the shops, but do not expect displays geared for visitor consumption. These shops feature household items and furniture as well as tropical clothes that visitors can buy (and use) for resort wear. Perfume is sold at **Phoenicia, Rosebleu, Coppelia, L'Artisan Parfumeur, Caribel,** and **Au Bonheur des Dames,** to name only a few stores. Most offer a 20% discount for U.S. currency traveler's checks and on some credit cards.

Jennifer, Raquel, Topkapi, Loft, and **Adonis** are fashion shops on rue de Nozieres; **Paul et Virginie** and **La Pagerie** are two of many on rue Schoelcher. **Au Caraibe** and **Champs-Elysees** carry an assortment of items, and fabric by the yard can be a good buy if you want to have something made up while you are here. (Ask at your hotel for the name of someone who sews; usually they will have some names and, failing that, check with the Tourist Office at Place de la Victoire.)

Across from the string of hotels that stretch out of the point from Gosier (nearest Callinago) is **La Galerie,** an attractive boutique, in its own small house, with an interesting selection of handmade dresses and other resortwear, plus some accessories and wall-hangings. The **Boutique des Arts Caraibes** is nearby, at the corner, with, as its name suggests, island-made items, many of them with a creole theme.

La Veranda, in Bas du Fort at Place Creole, has furniture as well as some unusual (and very attractive) small pieces, but the house in which the items are displayed is almost as intriguing as the merchandise. Anyone with fashion flair will enjoy time spent here.

The main feature with shops on Guadeloupe is *not* bargain prices, but fashion. The pret-a-porter (ready-to-wear) carries prices akin to those in Paris, and follows those fashion lines. Count on stores being closed from about noon until 2:30 p.m. or so, when they open until about 6 p.m. Most places are closed on Saturday afternoons.

LES SAINTES

When the first smudgy-faced child looks at you, silent with saucer eyes, and then looks down at his basket of warm tartes, called "tourments d'amour," it is difficult to resist pulling out a few francs to buy one. I've seldom hesitated, and sorrow some at the fact that commerce is now putting the tartes d'amour on the tables, sometimes just after you check into one of the small inns, and usually with a little thought to the several hands that have patted the pastry and put in the filling before cooking and handing it to me.

A tarte d'amour is a special pastry that, for me at least, is the symbol of a special island. **TERRE DE HAUT** is a few miles off the south shore of the western wing of Guadeloupe. The choppy ride across the channel to the cover that is the island's main town, known as Bourg, takes less than an hour. Departure ports can be either Pointe-a-Pitre or Trois Rivieres, which is more than an hour's drive from Pointe-a-Pitre, across the bridge over the Riviere Salee that divides Basse-Terre and Grande-Terre, heading southeast along the coast. An alternative route, followed by the day trippers who wash over the town in winter months, is to swoop onto the airstrip like a frigate bird dipping for food, after the 15-minute flight on *Air Guadeloupe* or *Air Caraibes* from the cosmopolitan (by comparison) Raizet Airport at Pointe-a-Pitre.

LODGING on Terre de Haut will be at a small spot, where speaking French will add a lot to your holiday. This is a low-key, hideaway island—the kind of place that now popular St. Barthelemy was before it was "discovered."

Among the hotels, housekeeping places, and inns are:

★ **Auberge des Anarcadiers** • *on the beach, near town* • is a cluster of less than a dozen pleasant rooms (with air conditioners). With watersports and a casual lifestyle the emphasis for most guests, the small hotel can be ideal for sun-seeking, self-sufficient folk. *Inn.*

★★ **Bois Joli** • *about 10 minutes' drive from the airport* • is away from the village, but a boat link with town makes the connection several times daily (and is far pleasanter than the short drive). The main house, with a few of the 21 rooms, is on the top of a hill, with viewful terrace and the main dining area. Down at the beach-lined shore, there are watersports facilities, and midway are a couple of cottages with a few rooms each. Surroundings are simple; the setting is superb. There's no "action," but there's plenty to do if you enjoy natural surroundings and like exploring, snorkeling, and swimming. *Inn.*

Jeanne d'Arc • *in the village* • is a boxy, cement-block building that provides 4-walls, bed, and few comforts for overnight guests. The terrace, at the "back" of the 10-room inn, is a lovely place to watch the fishermen work their nets and boats. For getting away—way away—from it all, this place has its assets.

Kanaoa • *at the northern "end" of the harbor cove, on the shore below the hill-capping Fort Napoleon* • is another of the informal lodging spots. Don't expect anything special. The dining terrace is at the seaside. Guests who linger around the premises can lounge on the "lawn." It's a longish walk around the cove to the village, but the view from a seaside room is spectacular. Most rooms have showers; only 3 have sea view.

La Saintoise • *at water's edge in the village, not far from where the boat from Trois Rivieres docks* • has 10 rooms, which have had a complete overhaul. This place can be ideal if you like casual surroundings and convenience to the village. (You are *in* it!)

UCPA • *from the seashore up the hillside toward Fort Napoleon* • is a covey of 2-room cottages with basic comforts that was, for a while, part of the PLM/Pullman group. As with other places on Terre de Haut, the sea—for fishing, windsurfing, swimming, snorkeling, and scuba diving—is the focus for most guests. Life at Los Santos is casual, French-Mediterranean, with the restaurant a gathering place after the day's activities are finished.

HOUSEKEEPING HOLIDAYS are possible on Terre de Haut, if you are lucky enough to get one of the apartments at **Village Creole,** next to Kanaoa on the harbor cove, where units are tidy and comfortable. There are 22 duplex units. If you rent one of these you can cook at home, after you've negotiated with the local baker and fishermen (in French), or you can go to one of the restaurants in Bourg, around the bay (and walk home).

For other homes to rent on Terre de Haut, contact the Office du Tourisme in Pointe-a-Pitre, Guadeloupe.

RESTAURANTS on Terre de Haut are small, and most specialize in seafood. As you stand at the main (small) square, where the boat from Trois Rivieres docks, there are several bistros and cafes to the left (with the sea at your back); Jeanne d'Arc and the airport are to your right. The midday dining time is right at noon; I found it difficult (impossible) to get much of substance after 2 p.m., until about 6 p.m., when places begin serving the evening meal.

NATURAL SURROUNDINGS: Since most of the island's dwellings cluster at the harbor of Bourg, as the village is known, the rest of the 3 mile by 2 mile island is left to nature—at least as of this writing. There's an interesting crop of cactus near Port Napoleon, as easy walk up a hillside just outside the town, and other flora of note around the island. The convoluted shoreline creates dozens of tiny coves, the best of them fringed with soft sand and many of them good for snorkeling and scuba driving. The island's high point, Le Chameau (at just over 1000 feet) can be hiked in a couple of hours, for a view over this island and its seven other Iles des Saintes, namely Le Pate, Ilet a Cabrit, Les Augustins, Grand Ilet, La Redonde, La Coche, and the only other inhabited isle, nearby Terre de Bas.

PLACES WORTH FINDING on Terre de Haut begin with the island itself. This is a gem for people who like their islands "pure." Bourg (town, in French) is the main metropolis—with its half-dozen short streets, its gray sand strand that separates sea from seawall and provides a platform for the fishing boats that get pulled up when the catch is completed, and the few small bistros that speckle storefronts. Chickens share the sandy streets with the dozen or so cars—and the day-trippers that come by small planeload from the Club Med and other Guadeloupean hotels.

Fort Napoleon (open 9 a.m. to noon daily; 30F entrance) was built in the 18th century, when British Admiral Rodney grappled with French Admiral de Grasse for supremacy of the seas. (Rodney sent de Grasse scuttling in the Battle of Les Saintes in 1782.) There's a small museum of island history and artifacts, but it is the fort walls and the buildings inside the walls that are worth the climb to get here. Club du Vieux Manoir, a French-based organization that moves into derelict forts and buildings and puts its members to work patching and pulling weeds from buildings and grounds, has a group that sets up camp here. For a small fee, campers/workers spend part of the day working on the restoration and the rest of the time enjoying their vacation on Terre de Haut.

HAITI

> Office National du Tourisme, Avenue Marie Jeanne, Port-au-Prince, Haiti, West Indies. Haiti Tourist Office's in the U.S. are closed at press time. The *Caribbean Newsletter* (page 9) will list contacts when known. Haitian Embassy, 2311 Massachusetts Ave. NW, Washington, DC 20008, T 202+332–4090. Caribbean Tourist Organization, 20 East 46th St., New York, NY 10017, T 212+682–0435; fax 212+697–4258.

$ · · · US$1 = 5 Haitian gourdes.
In the following text, $ refers to U.S. currency.

See pages noted for information on: Beach Hotels, p. 400; Cap Haitien, p. 411; Jacmel, p. 415; Port-au-Prince and Petionville, p. 404.

---- **AUTHOR'S NOTE** ----

> Haiti is dramatic—and different. Although adventuresome travelers will find Haitian art and history exciting, timid travelers will be more comfortable in calmer countries. It's no secret that Haiti is going through a difficult time, as the country grapples with democracy after 30 years of Duvalier dictatorship. Since early 1966, with the downfall of the government of the former President-for-Life, Jean Claude Duvalier, Haitian politics have been in turmoil. Prior to that time, the Duvalier family ruled, with its own "style" and ethics. At press time, it is impossible to predict the situation through the life of this edition. For that reason, coverage of Haiti is limited to basic facts, with a few tips on touchstones for your own research prior to travel. The expected personal comment will be forthcoming, in a special "Haitian Report" to be issued when the climate for tourism improves. The *Caribbean Newsletter* (page 9) will have details and updates when changes are evident.

The pyramid of purple eggplants and uniformly scarlet tomatoes rose from a woven basket in an arrangement suitable for the centerpiece of a gala dinner party. The Haitian woman carrying this burden on her head through the pulsing, dusty downtown of Port-au-Prince seemed impervious to the commercial chaos around her. So did the man who had linked eight chairs into a sort of hat, and his counterpart, whose headpiece was a load of intricately wrought iron. Haitian salesmen use their heads.

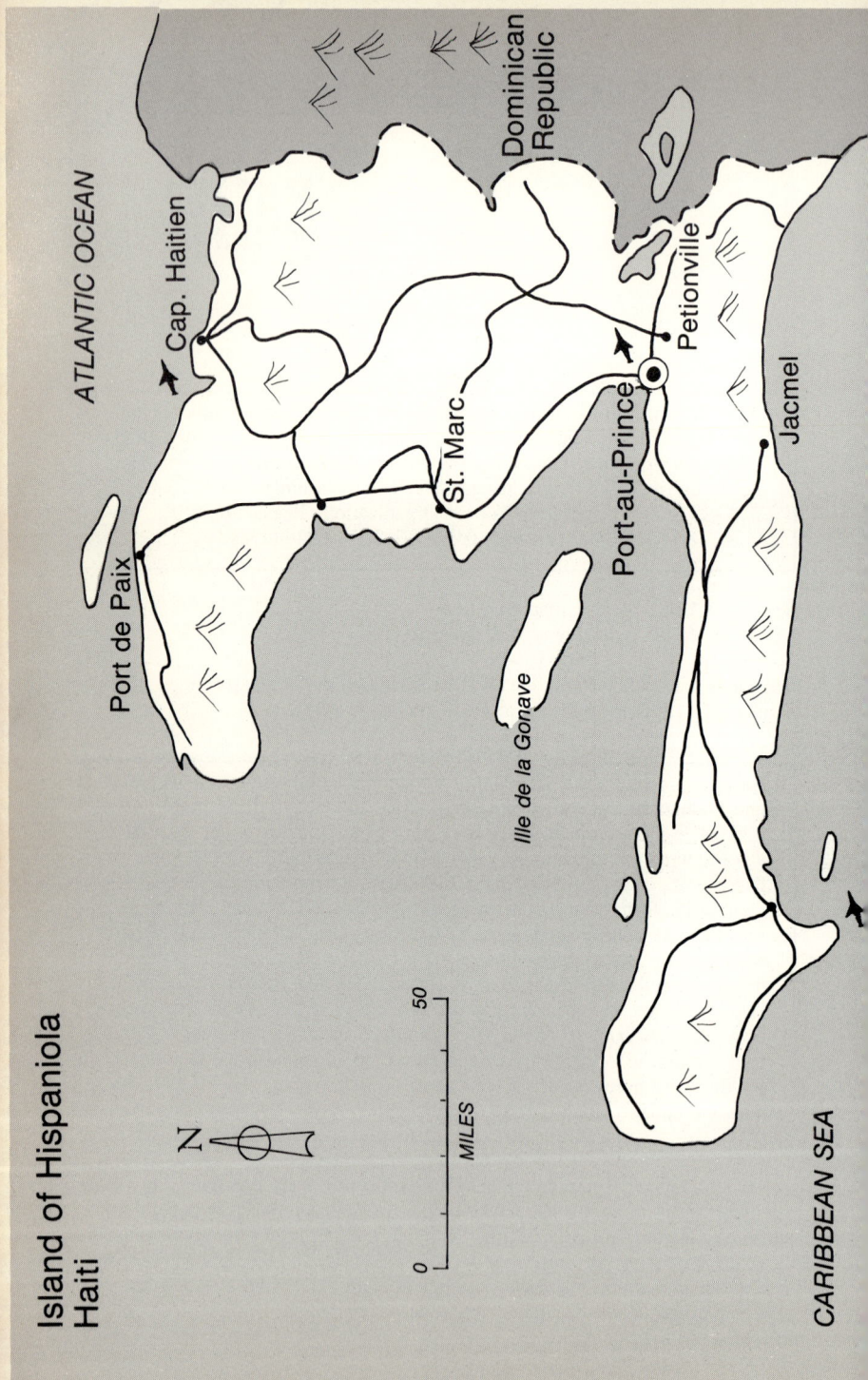

Sidewalk level gaps in the Victorian buildings that line the city's cross hatch of streets ooze with colorful fabric, plastic, spices, machinery parts, and almost everything else. Ready-made clothes dance in the breezes over doorways, in a city version of the kites that thread sky-high from small settlements around the countryside.

Outside of the city, the border of the paved road is embroidered with river-washed laundry draped over cactus hedges, and small adobe houses. Haitians "from the country" weave their lifestyle onto the asphalt road. Brilliant yellow-orange mangoes loll on wood slabs, waiting for sale. The juice runs down your arm when you bite into them, and the sea that laps the shores nearby is the best wash basin.

Haiti is a colorful country—sitting a few rungs up from the bottom of the list of most impoverished nations. It is full of people who use their wits (and perhaps witchcraft) to overcome substandard living conditions and whose priorities seem to be on something more immediate than material possessions. Having a big house is not a realistic goal for most Haitians, although it does seem to be top priority for some. Haiti's official tourism slogan has been "Vive la difference," and nowhere in the Caribbean is "la difference" woven more tightly into the web of life than it is in this country—the first Black Republic, declared independent by its free Negro King in 1804.

History in Haiti hangs over the foundations of a Republic built by four flamboyant Haitians and the abuses and conspicuous consumption of the Duvalier family. Toussaint L'Ouverture gained his nickname, some say, from the fact that he could make an opening (*ouverture*) in the lines of invading forces, which in the late 18th century were mostly French. He inspired Haitians to throw off the bonds of slavery. The rebellion began on August 14, 1791, with a holocaust that devoured plantations and destroyed the white privileged society, to end with the beginning of an independent Haiti. Toussaint was killed in France in 1802; Jean Jacques Dessalines declared Haiti independent in 1804—and himself Emperor Jacques I. Two years later, after he had been assassinated, Haiti would be divided, north and south. The northern section, with thriving Cap Francois, was claimed by Henri Christophe who took a crown for himself as King Henry I and set about building himself palaces and fortresses worthy of his kingdom. Alexandre Sabes Petion made his capital at the coffee port at the south. Simon Bolivar, who set out from the town of Jacmel to liberate South America, would promise Petion, in return for his protection, that he would free South America from slavery.

It is this dazzling legacy on which modern Haiti is built.

POLITICAL PICTURE: At elections of December 16, 1990, Jean-Bertrand Aristide, a popular Catholic priest known for his liberal theology, won an overwhelming victory. Before he could assume office, on February 7, 1991, there had already been a bloodless coup by a supporter of the former Duvalier regime, Roger Lafontant, who remained "in office" only a short time. President Aristide was installed in his office on the appointed day.

For almost 30 years, until early 1986, the Duvalier family had ruled this country with a system of their own definition, built on fear and favors. Francois Duvalier, known as "Papa Doc," controlled Haiti from 1957 until 1971, keeping his dictatorship in place by terrorism through his secret police force, known as the Tonton Macoutes. After his death, his 19-year-old son, Jean-Claude Duvalier, assumed the office of "President-for-Life" on April 22, 1971. Baby Doc's mother, wife of Francois Duvalier, was a strong force in the government until she was succeeded, in a much-rumored power play, by Michelle, wife of Jean-Claude. The Duvalier family left Haiti in the middle of the night in February 1986 for exile in France, where a now-divorced Jean-Claude lives in a villa on the French Riviera.

Graham Greene's novel, *The Comedians,* gives a good picture of Haiti under the Duvaliers, but the novel has yet to be written about Haiti's history since that time, as Haitians grapple with their newly imposed democracy, a system previously unknown to most of the population.

Following the Duvalier's departure, a National Governing Council assumed office, with Lt. General Henri Namphy as its spokesman and the military in control. The writing of a constitution occupied most of 1987. Successful national elections took place on January 17, 1988, after the widely publicized massacres that accompanied the aborted elections of November 1987. (This period is a blot on modern Haitian history; the army's prosperity resulting from their role with contraband, including cocaine, has been acknowledged as a plug in the funnel for United States aid.)

Leslie F. Manigat was inaugurated on February 2, 1988, following elections that everyone agrees had the tacit approval of the ruling junta. He was ousted soon thereafter, when Lt. General Prosper Avril assumed the presidency. After two coup attempts by Haitian army factions, Avril was finally overthrown in March 1990, to be followed by Mrs. Erpha Pascal Trouillot, a member of Haiti's Court of Justice. She left office just prior to the 1990 elections. The 7000-man army has traditionally been in control of the country, whether those orchestrating the scene were the henchmen of the Duvaliers or subsequent leaders. Time will tell whether or not this trend has changed.

Colorful and volatile politics are not new to Haitians. And, for the first time in almost 190 years, since Haiti became the world's first independent Black Republic in 1804, Haitians are struggling against awesome odds to build a free and democratic government

The country's needs are great. The right to organize free labor unions, in a country where $3 has been the average daily wage, is also linked to U.S. aid. Over 60% of the workforce is chronically unemployed, although Haitians prove to be good workers who learn fast.

Although the country has some of the Caribbean's most exceptional and charming hotels and the region's most interesting culture and art, tourism has suffered. Unfavorable publicity about Acquired Immune Deficiency Syndrome (AIDS), the continuing illegal immigration of Haitians into the U.S. prior to and following the Duvaliers' departure, and the inability of the government to make firm and fast decisions has not helped.

ISLAND APPEARANCE: Poverty will be the overwhelming first impression, not only from the hordes that wait at the airport but also from those you see in Port au Prince and around the countryside. This western one-third of the island of Hispaniola was once covered with the same fertile blanket of crops that still covers most of Haiti's neighbor, the Dominican Republic. However, indiscriminate harvesting and the raping of the hillsides for firewood, has meant that the once rich topsoil has disappeared. Low scrub-brush, accurately pictured in Haitian art, is all that survives on most mountainsides. The best beaches are along the north and south coasts, around Cap Haitien and Jacmel respectively, but many are not easy to reach. There are good beaches, also, along the northern lip of the lower "jaw" of Haiti and at the "back" of the mouth that is the Gulf of Gonave.

LIFESTYLE is a curious mixture of French and African customs. The recipe is distinctly Haitian, and that includes voodoo (spelled vaudou in French), which seems to pervade the air even though it has come in for its share of criticism following the Duvaliers' departure.

Clothes are casual, often with French flair, for the few affluent Haitians. Visitors will be comfortable in casual (not sloppy) tropical clothes, with sweaters or long-sleeved shirts for evening wear and mountain journeys. Bring jeans or some sturdy trousers if you plan to ride the nags to the top of Christophe's Citadelle at Cap Haitien, or horseback ride, or jungle-walk anywhere. Hiking shoes will be better than supportless sneakers if you plan to get into the hinterlands; crepe soles are better than leather for the streets in town and for any walking you will want to do around Haiti's rutted roads. Beach resorts are very casual. Some wrap over your bikini will take care of daylight hours—and at some spots will serve well into the evening. Keep luggage light; you should be able to buy some things if you find yourself short.

MEDICAL FACILITIES: Port-au-Prince has a choice of hospitals, but airlift to Miami is preferred by those who can afford it and have entry papers. The General Hospital is the biggest, but people with means usually go to Canape Vert Hospital. Hospitals receive donations of equipment and supplies from the U.S. and other countries, through government and private aid, but never enough. The Albert Schweizer hospital, in the countryside, is a continuing project of the Philadelphia-based Mellon family. Doctors come from U.S. training and hospitals to work in the country hospital. The project is a humanitarian effort that operates on private donations.

MONEY MATTERS: There are two ways to travel around Haiti. The first is paying in U.S. currency—which is what your hotel prices will show, and what art galleries and shops will want. U.S. dollars are also what the market ladies and the omnipresent street salesmen, young and old, will want. The Haitian gourde is worthless outside the country, although you may often receive gourdes as change. If you do exchange for small purchases on the road or in the markets, be sure to exchange only what you will use (or what you want as souvenirs). U.S. currency is in demand, and in a country where the annual average income is not much more than you pay a day for a hotel room, it's hard to bargain—even when you know that the local salesmen like it, think of it as a game, and price their merchandise accordingly.

COMMUNICATIONS are reasonably easy with direct dial on overseas lines to Haiti using 011 + the area code for Haiti, 509, and the city code, which is 1 for Port-au-Prince and Petionville, 2 for the Gonaive area, and 3 for Cap

Haitien, plus the specific number. From Haiti, AT&T's USADirect service is available by dialing 001 + 800 + 872-2881 to reach an AT&T operator to place a collect call, or charge the call to your AT&T account. Facsimile machines are used by many hotels and businesses. Phone calls within Haiti can be a challenge, since lines are often out of order and/or busy. Several newspapers bloomed with the new press freedom following the Duvaliers' departure.

ARRIVAL at the airport can be confusing. The most dependable air service is on *American Airlines* service, sometimes through San Juan with an *American Eagle* link. If you arrive as part of a special group, you'll be whisked through, oblivious of the ritual everyone else faces. If you come alone, speaking French (or Haitian creole) will help with some of the customs questions, if any are asked. Count on "people confusion" at the luggage pick-up and the departure areas. Customs will be cursory if you are an obvious tourist bent on having a good time and helping the local economy. Luggage will be lifted by handy porters, unless you get to it first. There's a tourist desk just beyond the immigration booths; helpful staff can answer questions, advise with hotel reservations if you've arrived without any (assuming the telephone is working), and head you in the right direction for rental car or a taxi to take you where you want to go. Ask what the fare should be, if you haven't noticed the posted sign listing all hotels and their official taxi rates from the airport.

CRUISE SHIPS come into Cap Haitien at regular intervals, depending on the local politics. The ground tour offerings are interesting—with a tour up to the Citadelle well worth the effort. **Royal Caribbean Cruise Line** links Miami to its resort area of Labadee, near Cap Haitien, using the *Song of Norway* and the line's other ships. There are also occasional stops at Port-au-Prince, where the town can seem overwhelming—and is certainly a juxtaposition of lifestyles from what you are enjoying on the ship!

DEPARTURE from either Port-au-Prince or Cap Haitien is reasonably easy, but the airport scramble described on arrival is also your final impression of this country. Be sure to unload any Haitian gourdes prior to arrival at the airport; no one will exchange them here. You'll be asked to return the copy of your immigration card just before you go through the security check into the departure area. There's a departure tax of $10. If you've succumbed to shopping, you may be burdened with plenty of packages, and you can count on most Haitians to be traveling with bundles.

Reconfirm your departure flight when you arrive and are still at the airport. Getting through by telephone may take the better part of your vacation, and if you do not reconfirm, your reservation may be canceled—especially at height-of-season winter. Be prepared to wait (bring a book, write your postcards) at all airports, not only for the intra-island services to Cap Haitien and elsewhere (when they operate), if you make those jaunts by plane, but also for your return trip away from Port-au-Prince. Haitians move at their own pace, which may not be the one you're used to.

TOURING TIPS: Taxis proliferate, but be sure before you get in one that you know what you will be paying. If you want to go touring, check with your hotel and/or the tourist office about a good guide unless you are more interested in experimenting than in having your facts straight. Taxi rates are set for regular tourist routes. If this is your first time in Haiti, and you consider yourself a timid tourist, sign on for a tour—which is usually you and your party in a car with driver/guide.

There are flights between the Port-au-Prince airport and Cap Haitien, as well as other Haitian towns, but do not expect the plane to be faster than driving. From my experience, by the time you get through waiting for the plane to depart, you could have driven.

There are **rental cars,** and experienced travelers may want to rent one. All the major firms (but by no means all the car rental firms in the capital) have a representative at the airport. Count on finding *Budget, National, Hertz,* and *Avis.* Be forewarned that many Haitians have gotten their cars in the past couple of years, and the paved roads are—for them—speedways, even when the roads curve continually. Driving is often in the middle of the road, and signposting is almost nonexistent. If you are staying at a beachside property and want a car for mobility, write in advance to the management to make arrangements for your car at the airport. It is possible to follow those routes with a minimum of inconvenience, and, unless you want to be confined to your beachfront accommodations, you'll need a car to get into Port-au-Prince or anywhere else.

Much is said about the **"tap-taps,"** the colorfully painted buses that the locals use. You certainly *can* use those buses yourself, but be prepared to be *very* conspicuous in this land where the average daily wage is about $2.50. You will probably represent more than the entire packed busload earns in a week! (For that reason, my recommendation is to take the taxis or even the autos that sell a seat-in-car for the regular runs between Petionville and Port-au-Prince, where the more affluent travelers are less obvious.)

LODGING in Haiti gives travelers a selection from places with more variety and personality than on any other island. Each place has its own personality. Most hotels are located in Port-au-Prince and its hillside (cooler) suburb of Petionville, where there are no beaches along the west coast, north of Port-au-Prince, and on the south coast (near Jacmel), as well as in the north at Cap Haitien.

In light of the many political problems, no hotels have high winter rates, in the accepted Caribbean terms. Most are reasonable; many of the small spots are inexpensive. All rooms carry a 10% government tax; most also add 10% gratuity.

AUTHOR'S AWARDS

Businessmen and reporters have outnumbered vacationers as guests at Port-au-Prince and Petionville hotels in recent years. My top choices of places to stay at this point in Haiti's history are *Villa Creole,* on a Petionville hillside and *Grand Hotel Oloffson,* a journalists' favorite in Port-au-Prince.

Information about places to stay is included under Hotels/Resorts, Housekeeping Holidays, The Inn Way, and Low-Cost Lodgings. Stars have not been awarded for Haitian hotels in this edition.

PORT-AU-PRINCE AND PETIONVILLE

No city in the Caribbean can be more confounding than Port-au-Prince, the capital of Haiti. The hillside "suburb" of Petionville, site for some of the hotels, has some breathing space and views, but it does not share the pulsating vigor of this country's seaside capital. Nestled among the many buildings and millions of people that flood the gridlike streets of the capital are several personality inns that offer warm hospitality, and a link with the very real life of this nation where every Haitian is a salesman of sorts and all are warm and friendly to obvious outsiders.

HOTELS/RESORTS   range in style from multi-storied to rambling homelike. Some have casinos, but don't count on the lively action seen at some other islands' casinos (Aruba and Sint Maarten, for example).

AUTHOR'S OBSERVATION
When the vacation climate improves, the *Caribbean Newsletter* (page 9) will have details on all lodgings and restaurants.

CastelHaiti Hotel • *on a hillside overlooking Port-au-Prince* • is Haiti's only "high rise." The Thebaud family built and own the property, with the hotel now in the hands of its second generation. The multi-leveled lobby, dining, and pool area leads down several steps to the small conference rooms. Most furnishings are Haitian made. Most rooms are up some stairs, and many have viewful balconies overlooking the sights of Port-au-Prince, which is only 5 minutes drive away. Located not far from the Grand Hotel Oloffson, CastelHaiti is in the heart of things—although its height and hillside put it slightly above the hubbub. Check the front desk about a minibus link to beach and town. Otherwise, take a taxi—and brace yourself for the short-but-steep road that curves up (or down) from this spot. *Hotel.*

El Rancho Hotel & Casino • *on the hillside in Petionville* • knew a brief reign as part of a Las Vegas gambling link. It's now owned by others with gaming interests. Opened in 1950, when it was little more than the Silvera home, the hotel now includes the original building (to the left, and suite-filled), plus bungalows bordering the pool area and an arm of lavishly appointed rooms in a 2-story wing to the right of the entrance. The hillside location allows for a lovely view over the plains, with Port-au-Prince below, and the 3 pools, plus tennis courts, casino, nightclub, dining facilities, and an entertainment program give this hotel resort potential. *Hotel.*

Grand Hotel Oloffson • *in downtown Port-au-Prince* • is assumed to be the friendliest spot in town. The white, 3-story Victorian building is rich with fretwork—and with legends, including those in Graham Greene's *The Comedians.* It was, a Frenchman, Roger Coster, who injected the first shot of modern individuality—discounting the entertaining tales about the 19th-century President S.D. Sam who built it as his palace and the fact that the hotel did hospital duty during an interlude from 1915 when U.S. Marines added the maternity wing. It was the late Al Seitz and his wife Suzanne, both Americans, who perpetuated the mystique for journalists and others in the arts and fast-lane professions. Now the inn is back in the Sam family, with Max Sam and Richard Morse responsible for the complete refurbishing and the new panache. Foliage-bordered steps lead up to the front porch, with the pool to the right as you climb. Bedrooms are in the main house and a few cheek-by-jowl cottages, some of which are air-conditioned. Each has its own personality, and some have other people's name—such as the Gielgud suite, and rooms named for Truman Capote, Anne Bancroft, Charles Addams, and a host of lesser lights who were guests at one time. The lobby bar is the place for gossip-swapping; atmosphere is casual—with cosmopolitan appeal. *Hotel.*

Le Plaza Holiday Inn • *on Rue Capois in Port-au-Prince* • braids Haitian traditions with the expected in-room comforts of the Holiday Inn chain. Furniture is Haitian woven reedwork and carved wood; food in the restaurant is Haitian-style, even when it reads to be as American as hamburger and club sandwich, and the pool is an oasis in the middle of a hot steamy, throbbing city. Favored by business folk and the reporters who flock to cover political turmoil, the hotel is masterminded by long-time friend and colleague Fred Pierre Louis whose Haitian heritage and business ability make him a good source for facts. Count on slow pace here, as everywhere in Haiti, and inquire about the Sunday night buffet, which has been a time to sample special Haitian-style offerings. A few shops in the lobby make it possible to buy necessities and some Haitian crafts, and all of town is an easy walk across the park. *Hotel.*

Prince Hotel • *in a residential area of Port-au-Prince* • preempted one of the city's marvelous mansions for some of the rooms, adding a newer building in 1980 for the rest. Designed and furnished in homelike Haitian style, the hotel maintains its family feeling. The paintings on the walls include many by the late Nanotte Chancy, the wife of the owner, Raymond. He and his daughter, Maryse, run this place, where guests can enjoy the pool, hotel-provided transportation to the beach, and the convenience of being within a few minutes of some of the city's best-known art galleries. The hotel's restaurant is popular for mealtimes. *Hotel.*

Royal Haitian Hotel & Casino • *at Martissant on the fringe of Port-au-Prince* • seems to have fallen on hard times, in my opinion. The big hotel with its adjoining casino building yearns for guests, but its location, out of the city amid a warren of shacks, causes a tweak in social conscience. The once-glamorous lifestyle seemed to have moved up the hill, when the legendary Mike McLaney took his casino operation to Chacounne in Petionville. *Hotel.*

Splendid • *in a residential area, about 7 minutes from the heart of downtown Port-au-Prince* • is a member of the prestigious French-based Relais et Chateaux group. Built at the turn of the century, the 52-room hotel was a Danish merchant's mansion before it became one of Haiti's first hostelries. *La Bougainvillee,* with its noteworthy tapestry and memorable food, is a restaurant worth finding! Although most of your meals will be served in the newer section of the main house (with view over pool and garden), there's an open-air dining area near the pool that is used for breakfast. The pool is pleasant for sunning and splashing. Twelve modern rooms were added in spring of '80. All the rooms have air conditioners, private bath, telephone, and radio, but the 7 rooms in the original old mansion have most personality. Wolfgang Wagner, the German-born hotelier who has called this home for more than 30 years, can head you in the right direction for island exploring. *Hotel.*

Villa Creole • *on the hillside in Petionville* • was opened almost 40 years ago by Dr. Reindall Assad, an accomplished medical doctor and head of the *Conseil National du Tourisme,* in the late 1950s when modern tourism got its start. The hotel is now owned and managed by Ariel and Roger Duval and Alicia Assad, a family team that is the hotel's second generation. Guests are "above" the bustle of seaside Port-au-Prince, although trips to town take only a few minutes by car. Bedrooms are air-conditioned; all have balconies or small porches. Most have a distinctively Haitian style. Some are bigger and better than others; I prefer those by the pool. Domestic marble is used in the deluxe bathrooms, and mahogany doors add a note of elegance. Breakfast is served on the pool terrace, near the almond tree; evening meals are in the restaurant. The tennis courts are in reasonable condition. Note the exceptional Haitian art, especially the intricate metal work behind the bar. This comfortable hotel seems to offer Haitian hospitality in a relaxed manner. El Rancho is a short walk away. *Hotel.*

HOTELS ON BEACHES along the coasts, north or west of Port-au-Prince, are a varied lot. Some Haitian beaches are pebbly, and some of the resorts bear a resemblance to places you would expect to find on the Mediterranean shores. Don't expect long stretches of Caribbean white sand.

Club Mediterranee Magic Isle • *north of Port-au-Prince at Montrouis* • was Le Club's 3rd Caribbean venture. (Other Club Med's are located in Martinique and Guadeloupe, the 4th Club Med is at Punta Cana in the Dominican Republic and the 5th is on St. Lucia.) The facilities include colorful, stucco units scattered at the beach, surrounding pools and public rooms, and 16 tennis courts. Inquire about the status of this Club, on a lovely beach, almost a 1½-hours' drive north along the shore from Port-au-Prince airport. The Club has been closed for long periods when business pulled back in response to political headlines. *Resort.*

Ibo Beach • *on Caique Island* • begged sand from nearby Gonave Island to make its beach, but its personality comes from its creator, the late Haitian architect Robert Baussan. On its own reef-rimmed island, the Ibo Beach is in 90 simple cottages with private bath (shower) plus sunning area. Getting here is a sort of safari—with a combination of car or jitney-bus, plus 20-minute boat ride with a liberal portion of waiting time, although Ibo Beach is half an hour from downtown Port-au-Prince. If scuba diving is crucial for a successful holiday, be sure to check about facilities prior to the time you travel. The real pros bring some of their own equipment, but there are masks, fins, snorkels, belts, regulators, etc., on location. There's a marina with sail and motorboats, plus equipment to service them. The triple-tiered swimming pool has a waterfall at one level, a kiddie-sized pool at another, and a third for those who really want to swim, about 15 minutes' walk from the dock. The three tennis courts are lighted for night play when you finish with dinner at the open-air casual, seafood-focused restaurant. Shuffle-board and minigolf round out the action options. Inquire about status; Swiss owners had grand plans. *Hotel.*

Jolly Beach • *on the sand, near Kaliko* • opened with about 20 rooms on the beach, adopting the name of a resort in Antigua where the Haitian owner, Raymond Polynice, had worked prior to coming home to open his own place. The formula is simple: beachside location, casual lifestyle, good food, and congenial atmosphere. The fact that you are about 45 minutes from Port-au-Prince makes town forays a day's excursion once you slow to island pace. *Hotel.*

Kaliko Beach Resort • *La Gonave Bay, about an hour's drive from Port-au-Prince* • is a group of multi-sided, comfortably furnished bungalows. All units are a short walk from a small beach, where watersports (especially scuba) are features. The place can be very quiet. Meals are served in the main pavilion, with tables on the narrow balcony as well as in the center of a room that does double duty as the entertainment center.

Kyona Beach • *about 45 minutes' drive from the airport and Port-au-Prince* • is near enough so some residents-in-the-know come here for alfresco dining. The thatch cover that keeps the occasional quick shower, and more often the steady sun, off your head while you dine is like a great big umbrella, with tables set beachside so you can watch the sea while you sup. Meals will be what manager and chef dream up. The 12 units are simple, so don't count on anything fancy for your beach break and be prepared for a quiet place. In addition to the beach, there's horseback riding (free), but don't count on tennis or organized sports. Scuba diving is possible, if you're sure of yourself and a good diver. A 50-foot sloop may be anchored offshore for day sails. *Cottages.*

The Bay Hotel • *also known as* **Ouanga Bay** *at Carries* • takes its second name from a Haitian vaudou word meaning "to touch with affection." On a Haitian beach more than an hour's drive southwest from Port-au-Prince, the Bay Hotel was "the first" place to open on the beach, in a sandy pocket not far from what had once been the holiday home of the former President-for-Life. The architectural style is hard to define. There are some buildings that are low single rooms and there are others that are balconied octagons, 2 stories with wood standing on a cement first floor. A thatched beach and watersports bar is pillar-supported, at the end of a boardwalk that leads out to sea. Inquire about the status of watersports. *Hotel.*

Taino • *at Grand Goave* • about 30 miles (an hour trip) from the airport, takes its name from one of the tribes of Arawaks, the first settlers on this and other Caribbean islands—before the Caribs ate them all—or drove them into the sea. The thatched-roof villas and wooded walkways give the place a rustic feeling. Built as big A-frames, units have either 3 or 5 rooms-with-bath, plus balcony or porch. There's a pool not far from the long stretch of sand bordered by trees and shared with the villagers, who sometimes set out for fishing excursions in their handmade canoes, carved from tree trunks. You can rent a pirogue to paddle your own canoe. Constantly casual (no dressing up necessary), Taino Beach Village has been popular with Europeans. *Cottages.*

Xaragua • *at Deluge not far from the Club Med* • looks like a piece of honeycomb and has had a history of being sometimes open and sometimes closed. Paul Latortue's hotel sits on a sandy shore almost 50 miles (and about 2 hours' drive) north of Port-au-Prince. Heralded by Haitians (and the few others that found this place, when it opened in '78) the Xaragua has h-u-g-e rooms with 2 queen-size beds, a balcony big enough for tables and chairs, and a spectacular sea view from all rooms. The 6 suites seem to be full-size apartments. Only 2 hours separate you from the north coast's attractions, Cap Haitian's Citadelle, and the ruins at Sans Souci. *Hotel.*

THE INN WAY is *the* way to stay in Haiti. Most of the best properties qualify as inns, with hospitality and atmosphere. Among the best, of course, is *Oloffson* (mentioned above), with its legendary history, but many others are also noteworthy. Here are two of my favorites:

Hotel Montana • *on the hillside route between Port-au-Prince and Petionville* • is a family-operated place with warm Haitian hospitalty. Surroundings are hotel style, with Creole atmosphere and plesant pool, dining room and facililties. Rooms are comfortable, with some offering a plesant view. Nadine Cardozza Riedel is on the spot to offer assistance. *Small hotel.*

Moulin sur Mer • *just north of Montrouis, on the shore near Club Med* • is on the grounds of an 18th-century sugar plantation. Opened first with the restaurant in the ruins of a sugar mill tower near the sea, the property now includes bedrooms in the *Moulin Club,* built in Haitian Victorian style with wood fretwork and comfortably elegant appointments. Each room has a private terrace or sundeck, and all allow for easy access to the sea. General Manager Dominique Carvonis is your capable and welcoming host. The hotel, about an hour's drive from Port-au-Prince and Petionville, helps with transportation—and Club Med is nearby for action, when it's open. *Hotel.*

LOW-COST LODGING: Since labor costs are very low and tourism has been in the doldrums while the country rebuilds its government, even the best Haitian hotels offer better value than many properties on islands where tourism flourishes. Most Haitian hotels are former residences. Many are wood-walled, and some are very simple. If you're looking for a *very* inexpensive place, inquire about current status at some of the following places.

Christopher • *on John Brown Road in Port-au-Prince* • has about 70 rooms with acceptable facilities. Gerard and Claude Desir manage this 7-story property, with swimming pool and hotel-style public rooms. *Hotel.*

Coconut Villa • *part way up the hill toward Petionville* • has about 50 rooms in 2-story buildings around the swimming pool. Some of the rooms have a lovely view over the town to the ocean. *Hotel.*

Doux Sejour • *on the hillside, between Port-au-Prince and Petionville* • has a few rooms with efficiency kitchens in addition to the standard hotel rooms. The central pool seldom has more than a few people around its patio. Robert Covington is your host. *Guesthouse.*

Marabou • *in Petionville* • is a 15-room inn just off the main square. It was opened several years ago by Mme Odette Weiner, a dedicated and extremely talented artist of dance who has sparked enthusiasm among Haitians and others, and who has created a dance company whose performances should be part of any Haitian visit. This place is very simple, with several rooms around the entry courtyard, and a small pool to one side. Best for those who know and love Haiti and are happy with island-style informality. *Guesthouse.*

RESTAURANTS are personality places in Port-au-Prince and Petionville, the seaside city and hillside suburb that are the heart of Haiti's tourist activity. Although (alas!) you can now find the standard fare of the Kentucky Colonel or Burger King variety, the specialties that make Haiti famous are spicy creole cooking, and some spectacular French service, sometimes with spectacular prices as well. Reservations are essential at all the small, special restaurants since personal service is part of what you are paying for and it's wise to be sure the place is open. Some of the meals at hotels are worth a reservation, especially the creole night and the lobster buffet at Villa Creole.

AUTHOR'S OBSERVATION

It is impossible, at press time, to comment on what's open or closed. Tourism is in the doldrums. Restaurants will be reviewed in the *Haitian Report*, mentioned in the *Caribbean Newsletter* (page 9).

La Belle Epoque • *on a side street in Petionville* • has been one of the capital's best restaurants, and reports are that it thrives in a new location on rue Borneo.

La Bougainville • *in the Hotel Splendid on rue N in downtown Port-au-Prince* • deserves special mention not only for the setting, but also for the food. Popular with businessmen who don't want to battle traffic to get out of town at noon, the poolside-but-covered dining room is at its best by night-light. Study the intriguing rope weaving that provides the focus for the "end" wall if you are interested in art forms. Call for reservations for dinner.

La Cascade • *on a side street in Petionville* • is the place to go if you're planning just one night out. The setting is lovely, with the gentle splashing of the courtyard's fountain accompanying the softly played symphonies as background music.

Le Chalet Restaurant • *12 Route de Laboule, on the Kenscoff Road, past the Petionville Police Station (follow rue Lamarre off rue Pan Americaine)* • occupies a homelike new building on the left-hand side of the road as you head toward Kenscoff. Stop by to look at the menu.

Chez Gerard • *off the square in Petionville* • settles its guests in an inside room, or on the alfresco porch where the trees dip into the dining area. Another home-turned-dining-spot, the atmosphere is that of a tropical hideaway.

NATURAL SURROUNDINGS in and around Petionville and Port au Prince involve getting into a car and driving—either north, out of the capital and up the coast, or inland and upland, through Petionville to Kenscoff and beyond. The density of population in and around Port au Prince, the seaside capital, can seem overwhelming, but when you head a few miles into the countryside you'll see a few people along the roadsides but not much in the way of real settlements. For horseback riding and hiking in the mountains, the best contacts are your Haitian hosts, who sometimes have country places where they welcome visitors. If you're on your own, stay to the reasonably well trafficked areas and inquire about places to go from Haitians whose opinions you respect. Many of the most natural areas are not in the orbit of the capital; they are most easily reached out of Cap Haitien, for places in the north, or Jacmel, for places along the south coast.

PLACES WORTH FINDING • *in Port-au-Prince and Petionville* • are a varied lot, with most of the cultural sights (art galleries and museums) near the sea in the capital. First-time visitors will want to take a tour (either taxi or group) because the logistics of getting from "here" to "there" can be confounding, and finding out when places are open is a full-time job best left to a professional. Day-long or longer excursions can take you from the capital to Jacmel, in the south, and even to Cap Haitien in the north, although two days is the minimum time, in my opinion, necessary to enjoy the special atmosphere and treasures in the north.

"*PORT-AU-PRINCE* has 30,000 to 35,000 inhabitants, and though it is the center of nearly all the foreign trade, it is a shabby, ill-kept, foul smelling, and most unwholesome place. It was shaken to pieces by an earthquake in 1842 and has been several times nearly burned up, but it retains its flimsy construction, speedily becomes dingy after being rebuilt, and reeks with filth at most times." The comments are those of Amos Fiske, in his *The West Indies*, published in 1899. While my own writing will not be as harsh, it is only an affection for the Haitian people that softens my sentiments. The city, in spite of an investment of millions of dollars for an exposition slated by President Dumais Estime and enthused over by Papa Doc for the 1950s, is a seething caldron of humanity that I usually find overwhelming. The brilliant white **Presidential Palace** is prominent, and best viewed across the huge park with its statue of the Maron, the Haitian slave blowing the conch shell heralding the uprising for independence which began in 1791, resulting in success in 1804. The vast and usually people-flecked park is known as **Parc des Heroes**; some claim that the Palace was designed by a Haitian architect to resemble the Petit Palais in Paris. The area has been the scene of protests and fighting during recent political battles. The main street of the city is Boulevard Jean Jacques Dessalines, named for the lieutenant of Toussaint L'Ouverture who has been called "the most powerful spirit" in Haitian history. Dessalines crowned himself Emperor in 1805, after he had proclaimed Haiti independent from France. In fact, it was Dessalines who named "Hayti," which had previously been known as Sainte Domingue. (Dessalines was a tyrant, who was murdered for his trouble on October 17, 1806, at Pont Rouge, the site of Bowen Field, which is the present military airport.)

Port-au-Prince is hot, dusty, and people-packed at midday. If you are interested in touring the town, head into the city streets at sunup and linger until midmorning before you head to beach or the hills—or your hotel pool, to emerge after the heat of the day.

AUTHOR'S OBSERVATION

The same laissez faire that makes this country appealing for a holiday can make an excursion to the museums an infuriating experience. Check, and double check, on hours that public buildings and stores are open (or not open) before you head for an entrance door to find it locked. A similar casual regard for hours makes meal service slow—and reservations (to be sure the place is open more than for a specific time) essential.

Cathedrale de la Sainte Trinite, rue Pavee at rue Jean Marie Guillox, is the country's best museum of Haitian art. The paintings that cover the walls are much more than decoration for the church; they represent the first real impetus for Haitian painting. The project was undertaken in 1951, and the painters took about a month to complete their works. Bishop Voegeli agreed to the decoration of his church, and the artists began their project while he was out of the country. When he returned, according to Rodman's commentary, he looked at the paintings with their religious themes and said, "Thank God they painted Haitians." The paintings were sponsored (at about $5000) by anonymous patrons. Wilson Bigaud's *Marriage of Cana* on the south transept wall covers almost 528 square feet, and incorporates two windows in the painting. (Bigaud, who was discovered at age 14 by Hector Hippolyte, started with a charcoal drawing and later covered the wall with paint.) The entire work was accomplished when he was 22, several months after the mural at the altar, which is one of the main murals in the cathedral. The 3 panels are painted with different approaches: Rigaud Benoit focused on detail in his painting of the Virgin and Child; Castera Bazile makes flat figures in his Ascent to Heaven, and Philome Obin, in the center panel of the Crucifixion, paints Christ without his beard. Overhead, tying the panels together, Gabriel Leveque sends his angels upside down, plunging between the windows with sprays of flowers. The *Last Supper*, logically, shows a white Judas betraying a black Christ, with his black Apostles. Obin painted this, and Bazile painted the *Baptism of Christ*. The intricate carvings of the choir screen were worked in 1954 by Jasmin Joseph as a memorial for Hector Hippolyte, one of the first Haitian painters to be recognized by the American artist DeWitt Peters, and a vaudou priest who painted black magic scenes. Philome Obin, born in Cap Haitien, was the other Haitian painter singled out by Peters.

When you are saturated with the paintings, and the people they represent, leave by the side door to walk across the street to the small shop that is operated by the Episcopal sisters. You can buy handicrafts made by parents of the children who attend the school as token payment for their tuition, but check for hours when the shop is open or knock at the door of the nearby residence to see if they can open up if you are serious about buying.

Le Centre d'Art, in an old house at 56 rue de 22 Septembre, (9 a.m.–5 p.m. Mon.–Fri.; 9 a.m.–1 p.m. Sat.), was the first organization to sell Haitian paintings, in the 1940s, when DeWitt Peters, who came to Haiti during the war to teach English, was director—Selden Rodman worked with him to encourage the popular arts. The Haitian elite was not enthusiastic about encouraging the development of the naive art we know today. Having been schooled on the French masters, they seemed to feel the style was too primitive. In spite of the lack of Haitian encouragement, William Calfee of the American University in Washington was invited to come to Haiti to instruct a group of local artists in the tempura technique. According to Selden Rodman's account, in his *Haiti: The Black Republic* published in 1954, five noted Haitian artists were set up in the upstairs rooms. Those who were painting primitives were given the stairwell, and Philome Obin was ensconced in the library. While the "professionals" fussed and dawdled, Benoit, Leveque, Bigaud, Bazile, and Obin excelled, using the clear, bright colors in fast succession to bring the unique world of Haiti alive on canvas with the touch of the brush.

The **Foyer des Artes Plastiques,** established in 1950, was a splinter group from the Centre d'Art, and today there are several schools—some of them as commercially oriented as the studios set up in the lower level of Issa Gallery.

Le Musee d'Art Haitien du College St. Pierre (check about hours, which change depending on interest and available funds) opened in May 1972. The Musee's main purpose is to house the works of art sponsored by Bishop C. Alfred Voegeli when he was at Sainte Trinite Episcopal Church and responsible for sanctioning the paintings on its walls, and encouraged by American artist DeWitt Peters, who is given the credit for focusing on the talents of Haitians and establishing the Centre d'Art in the 1940s. The modern boxy Musee seems almost too stark for the colorful paintings, but perhaps the blank walls (with their supply of fingerprints) are an acceptable foil for the work of the people. The museum opened with donations from private sponsors and Le Centre d'Art plus $10,000 from the discretionary fund of Knox when he was Ambassador from the United States, but its present status depends almost entirely on private donations. Although the Musee is owned by the Episcopal Church, the independent, self-perpetuating Conseil d'Administration is charged with funding and daily operation.

Musee Defly (open at midday, but check for specific times, which seem to be flexible), perches not far from the Champs de Mars and the Musee d'Art Haitien. Restored and refurnished, the gingerbread mansion gives us a chance to see surroundings suitable for turn-of-the-century life in downtown Port-au-Prince. Even if museums do not usually intrigue you, this is one to be sure to see if you're curious about the intricate artistry that is in the soul of Haitians. This is a place where the Haitian heritage could have been born.

Musee National (usually open Mon.–Fri. 8:30 a.m.–12 p.m.) holds its collection in what was once a Presidential mansion, but has been the home for the National Museum since its founding in 1944. The collection assembled in the several rooms has a naive quality that relates to the Haitian paintings. The eclectic displays cover centuries and events, in no particular order and with no apparent regard for prominence. The silver pistol with which Henri Christophe shot himself is one of the prize exhibits, as is one of the 7 anchors of Christopher Columbus's *Santa Maria,* which was wrecked on Christmas night 1492 off the shores of Cap Haitien. Henri Christophe's jawbone rests near his spurs, a few buttons, and some silverware from table service at Sans Souci, and then there are some personal effects of Toussaint L'Ouverture, the impressive fighter who drew the awe and eventual wrath of Napoleon, who ordered him to France for "special honors" which included his death. President Alexandre Petion's help to Simon Bolivar (who set off from Jacmel to liberate South America from Spanish oppression) is noted in another display with a sword given by Bolivar to Petion. A gold plate given by Lyndon Johnson to the late President Francois Duvalier is in another room, with a gold sword given to President Dumarsaid Estime (elected 1946) by Argentina's Juan Peron. Slave bells have been assembled in one of the hallways, where special prominence has been given to the bell used to herald Haiti's independence in 1804. There are a few artifacts from the country's earliest Indian settlers, as well as a room with dolls dressed in Haitian costumes of earlier times. You can count on finding a little bit of everything in this museum. While I am not a devotee of enclosed museums in tropical climates, this one has its charm.

Petitionville, up in the hills outside of shoreside Port-au-Prince, allows for interesting views, when you can glimpse them through the trees as the road climbs up through town and beyond. This residential area of private homes has a crop of hotels, most of them low-rise places that have grown with a residential feeling of their own.

Jane Barbancourt Castle, on the road leading to Kenscoff, is a commercial place. Taxis will take you here, tours will stop here, and your own curiosity will pull your self-drive into the parking area for a visit to what I can only call a tourist trap. The Barbancourt name came to Haiti with Louis in 1765, when he arrived in the then-French colony of Ste. Domingue from his home in Bordeaux, France. The sugar plantation he started near Arcahaie was where the family rum enterprise began, and it was Jane Barbancourt's grandfather who is credited with winning the international awards for L'Abbe Barbancourt. Rudolph Linge, with the Barbancourt connection, trained in a perfume factory at Grasse on the French Riveria for the liqueurs he blends! It's difficult to find pure rum here; the claim to commercial success is cordials—in a syrupy-sweet array of apricot, mango, coffee, and other flavors that I find best over ice cream (or in conversation). The huge rum casks, the castle walls, the chains and shackles are more like a Disneyland amusement than an authentic sight. For a hokey spot in the hillside, this place wins a prize.

Kenscoff is a different story, especially if you head here when the bus tours are not depositing their loads of cruise ship passengers. As you weave up the mountain road, the views at every curve can be spectacular. Friday is the big market day when the market ladies sell for the country folk as well as for the tourists. The array is slightly less overwhelming than the caldron at the iron market in Port-au-Prince, but the sales pitch is just as persistent.

The **Baptist Mission** near Kenscoff was started with the arrival of Eleanor and Wallace Turnbull in 1946. The projects, which now include some 60 churches and many small missions ministering to country people both spiritually and through the hospitals and schools, is supported by its headquarters in Grand Rapids, Michigan. Most visitors arrive in response to the wares sold at the handcrafts center, the outlet for work done at home by Haitians who live in the countryside. This is one of the better places to buy Haitian handcrafts, and well worth a visit. Talk with some of the staff who work here about the less obvious accomplishments of the Wallaces' mission. There's a cafe for cool drinks and simple fare.

SPORTS in Haiti are not highly specialized or finely tuned, especially with the downturn of tourism in the past few years. The same laissez faire that makes the country appealing, and puts its personality first, applies to the sports facilities. Don't count on the best court surface for your tennis, or immaculate ship-shape yachts for your sails—or even a meticulously manicured course for your golf. The best sports are those pursued by the rugged individualist who gets part of his kicks out of climbing the last mile or 2 to the Citadelle in the country's north, or bushwhacking along the south shore, in spots suggested by those who live in and around Jacmel.

There are interesting places to **hike,** and some of the hotel managers are your best sources of information about where they are. **Horseback riding** can be arranged from several spots, with one of the best places the stable the Baussan family maintain at their mountain retreat about 6000 feet high. The nags that meander up the route to the Citadelle are used only by the horse-hardy these days, now that the road weaves almost to the top of the peak. Check with Walter Bussenius at Mount Joli for information about horseback riding when you head to Cap Haitien.

Golf is available at the 9-hole Petionville Golf Club, where clubs can be rented along with your caddy. The course isn't worth hefting your clubs all the way to the country; if you're that much of a golfer, go elsewhere.

Snorkelers based in Petionville and Port-au-Prince set out for Sand Cay by boat from the dock near the International casino at the downtown waterfront. Check with the activities desk at your hotel about taxi and/or car arrangements to get to the boat in time for the usual 10 a.m. departure. Return is about 1 p.m., but if you want to head to the cay for a picnic lunch, you can make other arrangements for return (and bring a long-sleeved shirt and plenty of sun protection).

Scuba diving is not highly organized, but there are many sites of interest. Haiti has been popular with French groups and other Europeans. The several tiny Anacadian islands, in the gulf, have been designated as an underwater park area. They are reasonably accessible from most of the beachfront hotels, and detailed preservation rules are enforced. Haitian shores are almost virgin territory for divers. The north shore is intriguing as an area that was one of Columbus's landfalls, but winds and currents—and a lack of dive facilities—make diving out of that area a challenge.

Watersports are possible from the beach resorts southwest of Port-au-Prince (Taino Beach) and north of the city (Ibo Beach, Kaliko, Ouanga Bay, Xaragua, Moulin sur Mer, and Club Med) as well as on the north coast (Cormier Plage). You can snorkel from the sands, or go out with guide, by boat but inquire about facilities to avoid disappointment.

TREASURES AND TRIFLES are related to art, either painting or sewing, both done well in this country. However, for every treasure you find, you'll find yourself plowing through piles of trifles—and there comes a point when even they look good. Haitian art features bright, lively, clear colors in imaginative scenes, some so cleverly done that they look like the countryside you travel through when you head out of the city.

AUTHOR'S OBSERVATION

Individual entrepreneurs are what make Haitian shopping special. The artistic elements and love of color in every Haitian's soul come to full flower in the plying of a craft and in the selling. Sometimes (often) the actual purchase is only worth half the price you finally pay, but the ceremony of salesmanship is worth a good price of its own! Haitians are persistent salesmen, but they smile and bid you good day when they realize, finally, that you do not intend to buy. There's no grumpiness.

Prime products are crocheted skirts, blouses, blankets, shawls, almost anything, and the items for sale are strung from trees, walls, and arms. One of the best reasons I know for renting a car is so you can stop at will along rue Panamericaine which becomes Avenue John Brown as it slopes into Port-au-Prince from Petionville. Among the items for sale, in addition to the crochet work, are goatskin rugs, carved items of every sort, baskets, and other woven mats, hats, rugs, paintings (of course), and huge and heavy cement planters and urns. In all cases, bargaining is the only way to buy from the roadside merchants. Start at half the price and work up as they work down. The game takes time, and I, for one, have trouble bargaining when I think about the difference in the artists' and my own disposable income.

Art is half of the Haitian equation, whether it is the *naif* art seen in paintings, colorfully painted wood carvings, iron sculpture, or embroidery. It's also one of the country's most successful exports. You'll see Haitian art in galleries on most of the Caribbean islands where shopping is a major attraction. **Galerie Marassa, Inc.** has established a business for high-quality work.

In Port-au-Prince, two other names to know for Haitian paintings are **Issa** and **Nader**. Although both men know, collect, and sell the best painters, their shops and galleries are also full of large quantities of modest—but always colorful—work. Some of the artist names to note are Bottex, Obin, A. Bazile, and Dubic (there are several Dubics; Abner is one), but it's also worth knowing that artists often paint over the name of a well-known painter, even if it is not their own! A lot of the current painting is done to order, with painters knocking out several "in the style of" canvases and boards per day.

Le Centre d'Art at 56 rue de 22 Septembre (9 a.m.–5 p.m. Mon.–Fri.; Sat. 9 a.m.–1 p.m.), is worth an entire day (and is mentioned as one of the "Places Worth Finding" earlier). Not only is it a museum on the second floor (which has the Collector's Room), but the center is also a shop for better-than-average crafts. Search the lower level for works by budding artists. The main floor also has works for sale, with some of them unusual modern paintings.

Red Carpet has a store at the end of El Rancho's driveway near the town of Petionville.

There was a small shop just up the road in Petionville, where a woodcraftsman was carving furniture, spindles for chairs that would have cane seats and backs and the like. I neglected to get his name, but the shop is to the left as you face Red Carpet.

The **Iron Market** appalls me. In spite of the number of times I have girded up for this fray, I am still overwhelmed by it and am frank to admit that the entire caldron of humanity, most of it converging as I walk through the open arches, is too much. I am easily "intimidated" by young children, old women with no teeth, cripples of both sexes, and talkative salesmen, all urging me to buy. There is mahogany among the items to buy, but watch out for the bugs in some of the woodwork (which, if bought, should be stuffed into the nearest freezer for several days to de-bug). Be sure that you know what you are bargaining for—and in the Iron Market you *must* bargain (only fools and very rich people do not). As a swarm of life, the Iron Market is akin to the souks of the Middle East. You will find tap-taps, the colorful painted Haitian buses, parked outside a vast span that piles mangoes, pineapples, potatoes, and spices with sewing machines, shoes, plastic bags, and other items that appeal to the local folk. Tortoiseshell bracelets are a good buy, but you are not supposed to bring them back into the U.S. Customs may take them; tortoise is an endangered species.

Holy Trinity Gift Shop, at the Ecole de la Sainte Trinite (Holy Trinity School) near the Cathedrale, has an interesting collection of handmade items, many with detailed and sometimes colorful embroidery. Monies that come from goods sold at the shop go toward the scholarship fund for the school. Everything has been made by parents or students at the school, often as a partial contribution toward tuition expenses. You can have things made to order, but allow enough time. For information about items sold, with prices and—if the catalog is still available—some descriptions, write to Ecole de la Sainte Trinite, Box 857, Port-au-Prince. Although there's no charge, I'd suggest sending a contribution, at least to cover mailing costs. This entire venture is the province (as is the school) of members of St. Margaret's Convent in Boston, MA.

Ambiance, in a marvelous gingerbread house on property that runs between Avenue N and Avenue M in downtown Port-au-Prince, has an eclectic assortment of decorator items as well as some neatly tailored clothes. Haitian-made ceramic ashtrays and other pottery are especially interesting, as are the elegant beach and evening clothes. A high-quality shop, in interesting surroundings, Ambiance gets my vote for one-stop shopping—if you want something out of the ordinary. Be sure to ask to see the work of **Les Ateliers Taggart,** an enterprise of artistic and talented Daniel and Ginette Taggart. Their tapestries and the Haitian cotton items are original, impressive, and worth trying to find a way to carry home. (The firm also exports to U.S. stores.)

Mountain Maid Self Help Project has a link with the Baptist mission in Haiti. The shop and snack place is popular for cruise ship passengers, but is well worth a visit on the day you go up to Kenscoff. It's on the road up into the mountains, in Fermathe, and you'll find an impressive selection of quality wrought-iron work as well as hand-carved furniture that can be shipped (reliably) to arrive—eventually—on your doorstep. All the items for sale have been made by Haitians, usually at home. In addition to the usual mats and hats, inquire about the furniture that can sometimes be made to order. The Haitian chairs with woven seats are sturdy, useful reminders of your holiday here (and small ones can be shipped home with your luggage).

For last-minute shoppers: After you have come through Immigration at the airport, there are a few shops upstairs with good, representative merchandise (including full-sized chairs that can be packed for shipment on your plane). Macrame bags, a small supply of overpriced paintings if you "just have to have" one and don't much care what it looks like, and bottles of special Haitian rum—Barbancourt 3-star of course.

CAP HAITIEN

Called Cap Francois in the 18th century, Cap Haitien was a social and shipping center of wide repute, and was sometimes referred to as the "Paris of the Antilles." (The accolade was also given to Martinique's once-thriving town of Saint Pierre, before the volcanic eruption of 1902 destroyed that city.) At that time, the riches of Central America and Mexico lured adventurers farther to the west, and the thriving city of 25,000 people played host to visitors from Europe as well as to buccaneers and marauders. Burned to the ground in 1802, when Henri Christophe was waging the war of independence in the north, the town was to become his capital—and his monument (also the site of his grave)—in the first quarter of the 19th century. Even if you are making your main base elsewhere, this is the first-priority daytripper's goal.

After years of slumber, Cap Haitien awakened slowly in the late 1950s. The alarm was the jubilant celebrations of 150 years of Haitian independence, when costumed Haitians reenacted the battles and lifestyle of the celebrations of January 1, 1804, and Marian Anderson sang at Sans Souci. The Norwegian Caribbean Line, to be followed by other cruise lines, discovered the port in the early '60s. Cap Haitien proved to be not only a convenient halting spot when the fuel crisis hit, but also an interesting port for an ever-increasing cruise market. The Citadelle was the main attraction, and although not everyone made the then-rugged journey to the top, everyone did talk about it—and about Cap Haitien. In 1977, the new road from Port-au-Prince brought the journey from that city to a reasonable 4-hour drive, replacing a staggering and spine-snapping almost 12 hours.

HOTELS in Cap Haitien are few, and all are small, with the personality of the owner/management. The *Caribbean Newsletter* (page 9) will have facts and news about the following places when the tourism climate improves.

Brise de Mer • *at Carenage* • is an 18-room guesthouse by the sea. Roger and Maggy Pinkcombe are your hosts. Don't count on fabulous furnishings, or any lavish entertainment, but you can certainly count on getting your money's worth—and much more.

Cormier Plage • *at the beach* • is far removed from hectic day-to-day. Claiming a marvelous mile of white-sand beach, the thatched roof villas hold 32 elegantly furnished rooms. Wood slat roofs provide a cooling atmosphere; the tradewinds do the rest. Haitian woods, burnished to fine gleam, punctuate the white walls, and the suites are places you'll be pleased to settle. Jean-Claude and Kathy Diquemare are on the spot to help with suggestions for touring, and to set up any watersports activities. This hideaway hotel has been found by a few scuba aficionados; professional guide services (and teaching) are offered.

Hotel Beck • *in the hills, amid gardens* • offers the option for long walks around the grounds. There are 2 pools on premises, and beaches are about half an hour's drive or a boat ride along the coast. Kurt and Kuno Beck keep this place running with German-born efficiency, mingling enough of the natural Haitian nuances into the mood to create a special enclave out of the mainstream (which admittedly runs slowly) of the life of Cap Haitien. Guests who come here seeking solace and solitude may want to head for other hills on the days and evenings when cruise ships heave into view. Passengers are invited to this 12-room inn for a folklore and voodoo show!

Hostellerie du Roi Christophe • *at the edge of town* • was a home for Napoleon's sister, Pauline Bonaparte Leclerc, and her general-husband, whom Napoleon dispatched to Haiti to control the slave uprising, but it was also Henri Christophe's jail for insurgents who did not follow the rules of the new kingdom after war had been won and independence declared. The house was built in 1724, as home for French Governor de Chatenoy, and it still looks the part. The architecture is not the wood fretwork "gingerbread" style that you may have heard about (or seen) at Port-au-Prince. This is a sturdy stucco sanctuary that has been refurbished from time to time. The best rooms have a balcony (and air conditioners). Some of the moderate rooms face the generator, and the standard rooms with ceiling fans are the ones that are sometimes affectionately called the "dungeon" rooms.

Mont Joli • *on its own hill on the northern fringe of town* • is not far from the ruins of Pauline Bonaparte's palace (which shouldn't be confused with Habitation Leclerc, on the site of her estate at Port-au-Prince). The nearest beach is about 20 minutes drive. Most of the other escapades are longer excursions. The 45 twin-bedded rooms, many air-conditioned and all with private bath, are in several buildings around the hilltop, with villas, each with 3 bedrooms, kitchen, 2½ baths, and a dining area and porch-with-a-view. Meals are served near the pool, either on the terrace or in the restaurant.

Labadee Resort • *at Pointe Sainte Honore, near Cap Haitien on the northwest coast* • is the $5 million project of Royal Caribbean Lines. Planned as a beach-based "utopia" for cruise passengers, the resort was announced in late 1985 and partially opened for this season. Claiming a point where Christopher Columbus is said to have landed, the area has ruins of Fort Belli, 4 undeveloped beaches (3 of which will be used for snorkeling programs), dining facilities featuring thatched hut–casual atmosphere, and a stage for folkloric shows. In the plans are waterfalls, nature walks, and possibly a hotel. Beginning with the January 4th cruise, the beach area will be used for passengers who come ashore from the *Song of Norway*, the *Nordic Prince* and the *Song of America*.

NATURAL SURROUNDINGS: On the north coast can be of great interest to the truly adventuresome traveler, intent on seeing nature under rugged conditions. Even getting to the beaches means long, bumpy rides, usually down dirt and rutted roads, to shores where fishermen are your only neighbors (if you have neighbors at all). In light of the political and economic problems Haiti has faced in recent years, it's wise to check with hotels in Cap Haitien about the advisability of heading out on your own into the hinterland—or into the seas for snorkeling or scuba diving.

PLACES WORTH FINDING near Cap Haitien start with the famed Citadelle. **MILOT,** the town from which you get your start, is about 45 minutes' drive from your overnight base (Mont Joli recommended) at Cap Haitien. **Sans Souci Palace,** just outside Milot, stands in ruins, majestic even with its present coats of moss and mold. When Henri Christophe, king of the north (who was born on St. Kitts) ordered this place built in the early 1800s (completed 1813), he pictured himself regal in robes, surrounded by marble and mahogany, with chandeliers providing the physical light while he provided his country's emotional light. And that is the role he played. The closest anyone has come to re-creating that grandeur, according to some who tell about the ceremony, was when Marian Anderson stood on the remains of the grand staircase on January 1, 1954, to sing a celebration of Haiti's 150th anniversary. Sans Souci was Christophe's answer to the elegance (and excesses) of palace life in Europe. Versailles was one of his models, in lifestyle if not in design, and he picked up local clues from the palaces of Napoleon's sister, Pauline, married to General Leclerc and living a sybarite's life in Haiti. Although Christophe's dream may not have equaled the style of Europe's royalty as practiced on the Continent, it was far grander than anything the average Haitian had known. Selden Rodman noted that Sans Souci Palace "is built of brick overlayed with stucco four stories high and covers twenty acres of sloping ground from the sentry boxes flanking the regal steps to the royal stables which housed the King's £700 English carriage. . . . Completed in 1813, Sans Souci in Christophe's time had floors of marble and mosaic, walls of polished mahogany, and pictures, tapestries, and drapes imported from Europe. Under its floor, conduits carried a cold mountain stream—ancestor of air conditioning—to emerge below as a fountain. Installation of numerous bathrooms was a notable feature of the time." The ruins are impressive, but travelers with romance in their souls will want to make arrangements to get here at other than cruise-ship-visitor, top tourist time. A lot of the mystique is lost when guides and tourists vie for space on the moss-covered steps and around the grounds.

The **Citadelle,** hung on its clifftop like a monstrous freighter aground on a rock, overlooks the town, plains, and Caribbean Sea from its superior peak. Many of us who have made the four-hour muleback trek to some 3000 feet above sea level scoff at the fact that cars can now travel the rutted, bumpy road that winds through the hillsides and wraps around the ridges to a flat spot that leaves only a hefty half-hour ride on a pathetic nag to reach the haunting ruins. The fact that you still have to walk for about 20 minutes, and certainly have to walk all over the ruins, is small penance for what used to be a real pilgrimage of tourism. However, it is a *little* easier (although still an adventure) to see the Citadelle now that the road is at least cleared, and I am told (but have not yet seen) that "they are fixing up the ruins." I hope not too much, since the moss and weeds were part of what gave this place its personality, providing the punctuation marks for a period in Haitian history that saw a black man, born of free Negro parents on the island of St. Kitts, move from his job as a waiter in a small Capois hotel to become King Henry I, ruler of Haiti's north. It is claimed that he took the name Christophe from the formal name of his homeland (St. Christopher), the name Henry from his love of the English rule, and his portion of land from wars with Petion which left the latter with control of the south of Haiti. Christophe's ties with the fledgling United States included fighting in the Battle of Savannah during the American Revolution and hiring a Quaker lady as governess for his daughters, whom he called Princess Amethyst and Princess Athenaire. Devoted to creating a culture for his people in the early years of his rule, Christophe's Citadelle was the result of his eventual paranoia about invasions from the powers of Europe. The benevolent king turned tyrant to order, cajole, and whip hundreds of thousands of men into submission (and 20,000 to death) to build the Citadelle. The promontory is imposing, but it would have taken an incredible advancing force to come close enough to the monumental walls for any of the 365 cannons that were hauled to this place to have been useful. The walls are *thick.* Just how thick depends on whether you follow an official Haitian tourism office folder—"12-foot thick walls took ten years to build"—or Selden Rodman—"20-30 feet thick" and "tens of thousands toiled for sixteen years"—or the *National Geographic* article of January 1976, which states that "20,000 men died and hundreds of thousands of others suffered cruel hardships during some 15 years of pulling up stone, cannon, and supplies for the fortress" with "walls up to 20 feet thick. . . ."

Both the Citadelle and the ruins of Sans Souci have been designated as National Monuments, and the long-term restoration plan is in the capable hands of Albert Mangones, with assistance offered by the U.S. National Park Service.

AUTHOR'S OBSERVATION

Plan for your trek to the Citadelle in the early hours of the morning. As is the case with many Caribbean high points, the clouds settle (and the rains may come) on the peaks at midday and later. Although the ruins are impressive on their own, it's the backdrop of sea, mountains, and miles of space that makes the entire experience unforgettable.

JACMEL

Worthy goal for anyone who wants to see something of Haiti and the Haitian countryside, Jacmel is about 2 hours' drive from Port-au-Prince. (The southshore town used to be a tortuous excursion of 8 to 12 hours, depending on how many times your car broke down and how full the streams were that you and the car would have to ford.) Any Haitian taxi driver will take you, or you can drive yourself (if you know a lot about car maintenance and enjoy wiggling and weaving roads that oncoming Haitian drivers think they own and that cows, goats, and people don't realize are used by anything that moves faster than they do).

Selden Rodman, noted art critic credited with promotion of Haitian art, has a home in Jacmel. Rodman notes that "Albert Mangones, Haiti's leading contemporary architect, thinks that the country's Victorian Gothic, in its iron as well as wooden manifestations, owes more to New Orleans than to Paris. Much as I would prefer to see the credit go to America," he comments, "I am inclined to think the style came to Haiti from France—by way of Jacmel. The Renaissance II structure carries the date 1888. It was in that year that Alexandre Gustave Eiffel was completing the famous tower that bears his name; three years before, he had designed the skeletal structure of the Statue of Liberty. But this was engineering. The *art* of wrought iron, freed from its hitherto almost exclusive dependence on ivy and acanthus motifs, was being perfected in the workshops of such master craftsmen as the Moreau brothers, Emile Robert, and Edgar Brandt. Iron was 'in.' Art Nouveau was just around the corner. And Jacmel, perhaps without being conscious of it, became a repository for some of the fanciest experimentation in forged filigree and cast columns." Rodman points out that "Jacmel's glory is its dozen or so 'coffee places' built in the 1880s and 1890s out of cast iron columns, balconies and doors shipped from France and Germany as ballast for the incoming freighters," who would return to France with cargoes of coffee and other produce.

Note especially the Jacmel marketplace (which you can't miss—it's in the center of the town and all streets lead to it), and then saunter the zigzag road down to the sandy shore, past the shops that have a few good items for sale, and Selden Rodman's house, painted white, with the blue trim and a plaque that says "Renaissance II." The house has an art gallery on its first floor (9:30–11 a.m., 2–4 p.m. from Dec. 1 to Mar. 1) and is open for visitors on the second floor when he is not in residence (and sometimes, also, when he is). The beach at Jacmel is not much, by other Caribbean standards, in spite of the enthusiasm of local folk (Erick Danies among them) for building a "large hotel on the beach." Ask Erick Danies about the better beaches that are a drive along the coast. I have not seen them, but he says they are there—and spectacular.

HOTELS IN JACMEL are personality inns, and there are four I know at the moment that are worth writing about.

Cyvadier Plage Hotel • *about a mile from Jacmel* • is for folks who want to *really* get away. Located on the shore, with a pool, the hotel focuses on hiking, horseback riding, and special excursions arranged in response to the interests of the guests. Popular with French visitors, Cyvadier offers comfortable rooms with private bath in one of several single-story white stucco buildings. A thatched roof over the seaside bar makes it a pleasant lingering spot. Transportation for the drive from Port-au-Prince airport is included when you stay two weeks; otherwise count on at least $50 round trip, if you let the hotel know when you're arriving.

Hotel Craft • *in Jacmel* • carries its past as an important part of the present. Even when you sit on the small terrace, roadside, sipping a cool drink, the past pervades—and parades along in front of you with the people going to the market down the street. This is another world, one not yet stamped upon by the firm foot of tourism. The 12-room inn that Adeline Danies operates has simple wood walled rooms, not all with private bath, but #8 and #9 with balconies overlooking the street. The walk up to the rooms is on a wide mahogany staircase. Around the walls lining the staircase are family photographs, showing the grandfather, who had used what is now the attractive, airy dining room as his office, and the grandmother with some of her grandchildren.

★★ **Hotel La Jacmelienne** • *on the shore* • nestles into palm trees in an area punctuated with fishing boats and much better known to the Haitians who live in Jacmel than to the few tourists who find this enclave. Taking its cue from the former prominence of this now-sleepy town, La Jacmelienne attempts to recall an elegant era not known in Jacmel for many years. The pool has been pressed into cement casing at the edge of the gray-sand beach, with an attractive poolside dining and drinking area, and the arcades of the 2-story hotel as a background. On the inland side of the hotel, the small and simple homes of the Jacmeliennes who live in the area have been fenced off, but anyone living in a second-floor room can look into the "residential" area (where most of the living is done outside the small shacks) as you walk along the open-to-breezes hall. Rooms are designed to take advantage of trade winds, and to give every guest a very special sea view. Don't expect a lot of action, unless you head here with a cluster of friends. Jacmel is definitely not your "typical tourist town."

Manoir Alexandre • *36 rue d'Orleans* • is a decrepit mansion, peering over the far edge of the park, across the expanse from street-side Hotel Craft. The building is bigger than it looks from the park; it hangs down the hillside in a couple of balconied levels, the old wood frame held to the land with lush planting. This is the home of Mme. Alexandre Vital, and speaking French when you stay here will be helpful (essential, if you want anything special). The Vital name is one of Jacmel's most venerable. Grandfather Vital arrived from France in the 1870s, to set up a coffee business buying from the locals for less than 19¢ per pound and exporting his healthy portion of what's reported to have been 700,000 bags in 1900. The legends of Jacmel include many about the German owner of this house, who was asked to leave the country in 1910. The 5 rooms are simple, most have view but all do not have private bath. Ideal for adventuresome travelers who care more about people and a place with personality than about being pampered.

RESTAURANTS in Jacmel in addition to the dining rooms and terrace/porch areas of the small inns, include a few places in former private homes on the winding streets of town.

NATURAL SURROUNDINGS: This south-coast area is almost unknown to ousiders. Haitian friends advise that there are spectacular beaches along the south coast and some of them can be reached from Jacmel by Land Rover or horseback. When the climate for vacation travel is better, the *Caribbean Newsletter* (page 9) will have comments.

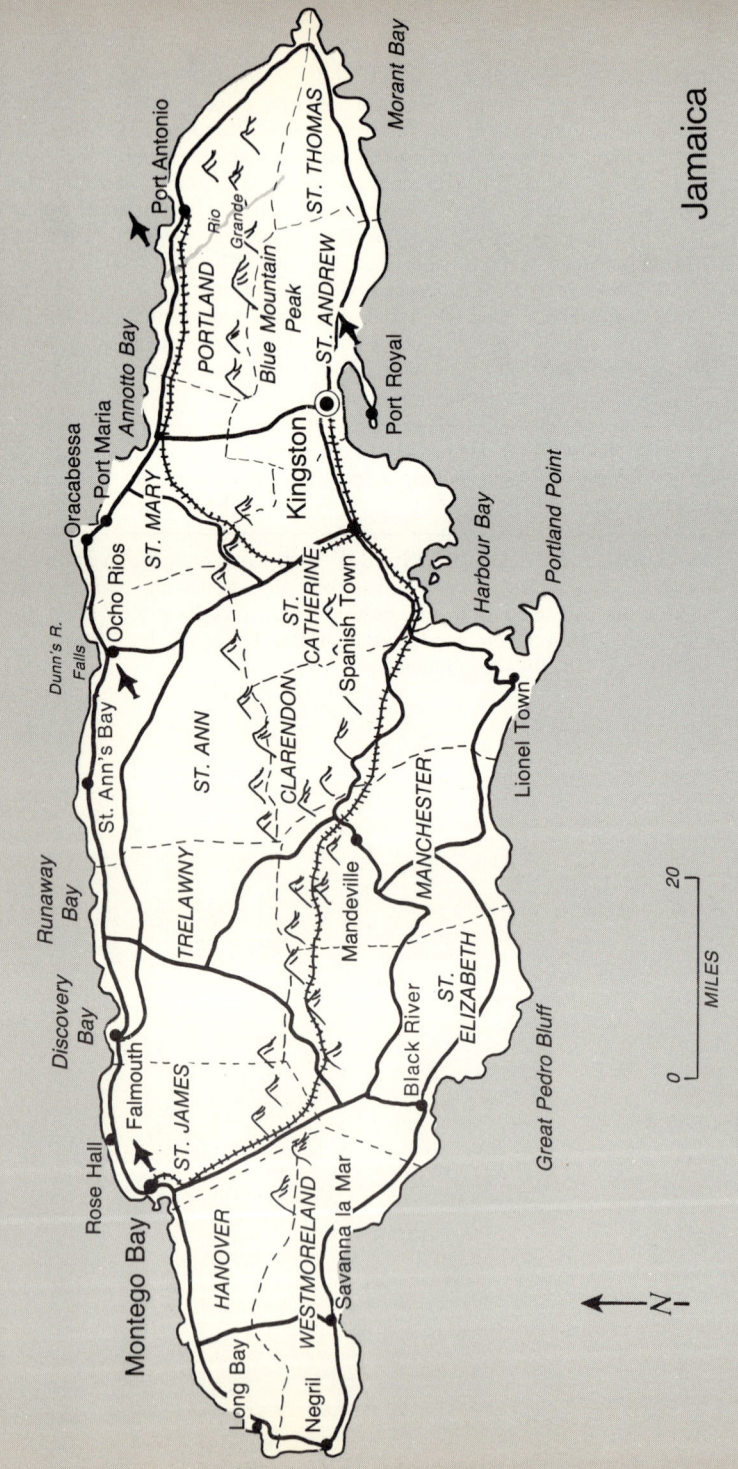

JAMAICA

Jamaica Tourist Board, Tourism Centre, 21 Dominica Drive, New Kingston 5, Jamaica, W.I., T 809+929–9200, fax 809+929–9375; #1207, 3440 Wilshire Blvd., Los Angeles, CA 90010, T 213+384–1123; 866 Second Ave., New York, NY 10017, T 212+688–7650 or 800+223–5225, fax 212+759–5012; 1320 S. Dixie Hwy., Coral Gables, FL 33146, T 305+665–0557; #1210, 36 S. Wabash Ave., Chicago, IL 60603, T 312+346–1546; 8411 Preston Rd., #605, LB31, Dallas, TX 75225, T 214+361–8778; Mezzanine, 1110 Sherbrooke St. W, Montreal, Quebec, Canada H3A 1G9, 514+849–6386; #616, 1 Eglinton Ave. E, Toronto, Ontario, Canada M4P 3A1, T 416+482–7850; Jamaica House, 63 St. James's St., London SW1A 1LY, England, T 01+493–3647.

$ · · · US $1 = about J$12. (See ''Money Matters'' below.)
Unless otherwise noted, $ refers to U.S. currency.

Along the north coast, Negril (p. 455) is about 2 hours' drive west of Montego Bay (p. 439). Lucea (p. 436), between Montego Bay and Negril, is about an hour's drive from each. Runaway Bay (p. 475) is about an hour's drive east of Montego Bay. Ocho Rios (p. 463) is another hour's drive east of Runaway Bay, making it about two hours east of Montego Bay. Port Antonio (p. 477), on the east coast, is about 2 hours' drive east of Ocho Rios. On the south coast, Kingston (p. 426) is about 2 hours' drive over the mountains from Ocho Rios. Mandeville (p. 437), in the mountains, is about 2 hours' drive from Kingston; about 2 hours, partially along the south coast, from Negril; and about 2 hours' drive into the mountains from Ocho Rios or Montego Bay. Trains run from Montego Bay to Kingston, stopping at Williamsfield, near Mandeville.

Suzette and Clareath were almost silent when they got into my car. They remained so while I did my best to engage them in conversation—about their neat school uniforms, about their names, about their journey to school (a 2-hour walk if no one picked them up), about *anything*. It was only when I asked them about their national anthem that we struck a mutual chord of sorts. Surely they knew it. Would they sing it for me? Giggles worked their way into very soft efforts, but only after I had made them laugh outright with my efforts to sing a ditty I knew. By the time we arrived at Rusea's campus, they were leading me into the second verse of their national anthem—enthusiastically offered to anyone who would listen.

Their schoolhouse sits amid historic buildings on the shore at Lucea. From a plaque near the welcoming stairs of the building that swallowed them, I learned that Martin Rusea was a French refugee who lived in Jamaica. In his will, dated July 23, 1764, he left his personal estate to the parish of Hanover. In 1777 this nondenominational school was established, to prepare students for the Cambridge (England) local exams. Today this historic section, near Fort Charlotte (built about the time of King George III's marriage to Queen Charlotte—in 1761), is the primary school with high-school age attending classes in a newer building out of town along the Negril road.

The hundreds of students in these schools—and the many others around the country—face an uncertain future. Although Clareath plans to be a nurse and Suzette wants to go into business, achieving those goals will take continued effort, determination, money, and a good measure of luck. Opportunities are not everywhere in this country.

Jamaica's 4411 square miles are home for 2,240,000 people who mix English, African, Chinese, East Indian, Lebanese, Welsh and Irish traditions and bloodstrains to present a culture and a citizenry that are uniquely Jamaican. Although independent from Britain only since August 6, 1962, the country has developed a distinctly Jamaican personality—with its ubiquitous reggae music, its innovative national dance troupe, its art and theater, its often exceptional use of the many Jamaican fruits and vegetables in what is now regarded as Jamaican cuisine, and its people.

For those who stray from the usual tourist paths, the country yields rich rewards.

POLITICAL PICTURE: Prime Minister Michael Manley's People's National Party won elections held February 9, 1989. Under the parliamentary system adopted from Britain, the next elections must be called before early 1994. Rumors at press time hint that, for personal reasons, the Prime Minister may call elections well before that date. Deputy Prime Minister P. J. Patterson seems to be the PNP's heir apparent. There is little in the PNP's present program that reflects the tumultuous years of their previous time in office, when friendship between the Manley government and Cuba's Fidel Castro made headlines.

For nine years prior to the '89 elections, the country had been run by the Jamaica Labour Party, with Edward Seaga as Prime Minister. These were years of dramatic changes in Caribbean politics, from a time when the region flirted with militant socialism/communism to a time when the capitalistic democracy known in the Western countries is accepted as the viable economic method for a better standard of living.

Jamaica's policies, no matter which party, seem to be firmly dedicated to the need to link public (government) and private sector investments to keep the economy moving, and to give full support to a dignified tourism as the best route to open employment opportunities and earn hard currency.

Jamaica became independent from Britain in 1962, and has grappled with the realities of building a viable economy since that time. The harsh measures required to build an economic base have not been popular, but are essential to gain approval for much-needed loans from the International Monetary Fund and other funding agencies. Although many middle-management Jamaicans left during the troubled years at the end of the 70s to settle in Miami and other U.S. cities, a new generation of Jamaican entrepreneurs is developing, largely in the tourism industry.

Drugs, including locally-grown marijuana (ganja) and imported cocaine and crack, provide quick fortunes for some Jamaicans, in spite of the government's efforts to curb that activity (with some U.S. assistance). The U.S.-initiated Caribbean Basin Initiative has been one route for business assistance, notably through funds available through Puerto Rico under U.S. Congress bill 936. Britain, Canada, and other countries also have sizeable aid programs in place for Jamaica. But the tourism industry is seen by most Jamaicans as their route to a better future.

ISLAND APPEARANCE: This is one of the most beautiful—if not *the* most beautiful—of the Caribbean islands. It has everything in the way of natural attributes. The Blue Mountain range rises from the seaside capital of Kingston, toward the east on the south coast; there are several small islets within easy boat trip from the capital. The longest span of beach is along the northwest coast, at Negril where the shore is ribboned with soft white sand. But there are also pleasant beaches, some of them small sand-fringed coves, along the north coast, from Negril to Port Antonio in the east and along portions of the south coast. The mountainous spine of Jamaica is remarkable, cloaked in verdant foliage, with centuries-old trees and many varieties of flowers, each blooming in its season. In the western interior, the karst country, with its pockets of limestone caves, seems stark by comparison. This area is locally known as the cockpit country. The most luxurious part of the country is its eastern sector, from Ocho Rios to Port Antonio, where tropical growth responds to the sometimes excessive rain. Rushing rivers cascade in remarkable waterfalls at Ocho Rios, near Port Antonio, and elsewhere in this part of the country. Small villages fleck mountainsides at many byway junctions. Most of the tourism facilities are along the north coast; the south coast is not well known to visitors although Jamaicans enjoy its beaches.

Jamaica received a severe pounding from Hurricane Gilbert in September 1988. Although the winds roared over the spine of the country, shaving the plantations, uprooting countless trees, and ripping the tin roofs off many Jamaican shacks when it did not grind them to pulp, the storm miraculously left the beaches intact and did relatively little damage to most of the seaside hotels. Because the full force of the wind traveled the length of the island, there were not the severe tides sometimes known in heavy storms. The warm climate and fertile soil responded to the return of the usual sunshine, however, and most foliage has grown again, masking the horror of the many huge trees that have gone. Visitors will see almost no evidence of Hurricane Gilbert.

> **AUTHOR'S OBSERVATION**
>
> The S.O.S. Children's Village Jamaica, founded in 1972 at Barrett Town in Little River on the north coast of Jamaica, and now with a second village in the Kingston area, is a community of children from 3 to 18 years old. All have been referred to the villages because living conditions in their homes were unsuitable. They live in one of the family houses, each with its own house mother. The S.O.S. kindergarten educates the small children; the older children go to school in the community, and all work on the farming project, where they raise goats, chickens, fruits, and vegetables for their own food and for income. The organization welcomes contributions, which are used to build additional houses and to maintain the community. If you're interested in the S.O.S. project, contact Ilse Kessler, Director of S.O.S. Children's Villages in Jamaica, Box 93, Stony Hill, Kingston 9, Jamaica, West Indies, or Heinz Simonitsch at Half Moon Resort, Montego Bay.

LIFESTYLE is uniquely Jamaican, with fashion and comfort equal priorities. The foundation for Jamaican customs is a British tradition that prevails in the courts of law, the parliamentary government—and in the love of cricket, polo, and afternoon tea. In the years since independence in 1962, Jamaicans have assumed the strong leadership of their country. The man on the street is an informed politician, and most people are willing to share some of their national traditions with visitors who seem interested. Insofar as clothes are concerned, the year-round warm climate dictates comfortable summer clothes, but that doesn't mean sloppy. Jamaicans know and enjoy style. The more affluent Jamaicans set a sophisticated pace. Most men wear neat, long-sleeved shirts, sometimes with jackets. Jacket and tie for men and dressy clothes for women are expected on some occasions, especially for dinner at the elegant places on the north coast and at some functions in the capital of Kingston. Jamaican women have always had a flair with clothes. Although long dresses are seldom seen, dressy clothes are popular for evenings around the pool. Be sure to cover up your beachwear when you go into town, even when weather is steamy.

Reggae is a fact of Jamaican life. The pulsating music got its start in this country, and it's played everywhere, in one version or another. Bob Marley, the talented musician generally credited with the creation of reggae, died from cancer a few years ago. He is regarded by many as a prophet and folk hero, and his music is still the favorite. The *Reggae Sunsplash,* held annually in late July in Montego Bay, has developed a strong following. If you like the music, inquire about the festival—and be sure to make reservations well in advance. Rita Marley, a talented singer in her own right, has continued the tradition of Bob Marley, as have his children. All are singing regularly, and Rita Marley has opened up the studio in Kingston for scheduled visits by outsiders.

"Meet the People" is a government-assisted program, with a special department in the Jamaica Tourist Board offices. The program includes over 600 volunteers and also has a special plan for young people to meet their counterparts. If you want to participate, contact the JTB office by telephone before you leave for the island or register with the tourist board office in the area you are visiting as soon as you arrive, so your interests can be matched with those of a Jamaican host. Talks with some of the "Meet the People" hosts revealed that some visitors who sign up don't show up, an imposition to hosts who often go to a lot of trouble for their guests.

MEDICAL FACILITIES: Kingston has the country's largest and most complete hospital, with operating rooms and other equipment. Most doctors have trained in Britain, Canada, or the U.S., although there are some trained in other countries. During the years with close Cuban friendships, medical assistance was offered by that country. The Kingston hospital is overcrowded, however, as are most of the country's clinics, which can be found in communities of any size. There is a private hospital in Montego Bay that had been noted by some for its innovative treatment for cancer. Since Jamaica is just over an hour's jetflight from Miami, some of the most serious cases are flown to hospitals in that city, when finances permit.

MONEY MATTERS revolve around the Jamaican dollar and the country's balance of payments problems. Check with the Jamaican Tourist Board prior to departure as to current value of the Jamaican dollar against the U.S. dollar, which has been about J$7 to US$1. Although you may have paid your hotel bill in U.S. dollars prior to your departure for Jamaica, you will be required to spend Jamaican dollars for additional charges and on-the-spot purchases *other* than your hotel bill. Money can be changed at banks or at your hotel. There are branch banks at the arrival areas at the airport, but there may be long lines if you arrive on one of the major airlines with a planeload of fellow passengers. When you travel away from the usual tourist routes, paying in Jamaican currency means that some prices, when equated with U.S. dollars, seem low. In the heavily touristed areas, however, items are priced for the visitors—and reflect not only the duties imposed on many items imported into the country but also the belief that visitors have money to spend.

COMMUNICATIONS links are reasonably easy from outside the country to Jamaica. A telephone call is as easy as dialing 809 + a 6-digit local number. Telephone calls within Jamaica are not always as easy to complete. The local system seems to have problems keeping up with the increased demand for phones and repairs. From Jamaica, to avoid sometimes excessive surcharges imposed at hotels, ask about AT&T's USADirect service, which is offered at some hotels and through dedicated telephones at the airports. To reach the AT&T operator from Jamaica, dial 0–800+872–2881. The operator can place your call collect, or charge it to your AT&T account. Facsimile machines are widely used. Many Jamaicans have satellite "dishes" for cable television; a few hotels have television sets in their rooms. Jamaica's newspapers are good and informative. Jamaica's *Gleaner* covers local and Caribbean news, with some international coverage also included. Newspapers arrive from London at regular intervals. U.S. newspapers can sometimes be found at the big hotels.

ARRIVAL can be to either one of two international airports (in Kingston or Montego Bay) on *Air Jamaica, American Airlines,* and other carriers. From there, you have a choice of flying on the small planes of *Trans Jamaica Airlines* to domestic airports at Negril, Boscobel for Ocho Rios, or Port Antonio, or of arriving at your hotel by car or jitney-bus from your arrival airport. Most of the resorts are best reached through the Montego Bay airport. Kingston is the most convenient arrival airport for the capital (obviously), and for the south coast hotels as well as for most travelers going directly to Port Antonio. (Some prefer to arrive in Montego Bay, and fly to Port Antonio.)

Kingston's Norman Manley International Airport (named for the father of PNP leader Michael Manley), has quite a different atmosphere from that of tourist-conscious Montego Bay. It is the country's business center, as well as being the preferred airport for most residents.

Montego Bay is the country's first-and-busiest vacation city. Donald Sangster International Airport can seem chaotic when several flights arrive at one time. For details about Montego Bay arrival, refer to page 440.

On the airplane, you'll be given a customs declaration for entry to Jamaica, with wording similar to the U.S. Customs forms used for reentry to the U.S., and an immigration card. At immigration, you'll be asked to present your proof of citizenship (passport is best), the filled-out immigration form, and your return or onward ticket. Customs officials are serious but polite and businesslike—and very hard on folks with items that are not for personal use. Gifts and items for Jamaican friends can be heavily taxed, so be sure to check with the Jamaica Tourist Board offices in the U.S. as to duties before you get taken by surprise.

CRUISE ships come into Montego Freeport, a landfill area near the center of Montego Bay, and into Ocho Rios, midway on the north coast, and occasionally to other ports in the country. Most of the "sights to see" are scattered around the country, inland from the coastal areas, so there are advantages to taking an organized tour or arranging for a knowledgeable taxi driver. Two of the many options, if you've done some advance planning and have enough time, are a ride up to Mandeville or a drive to Negril for a day at the beach. *Regency Cruises* has been using MoBay as homeport for some of its 7-day cruises for the past couple of years. Check for information about other lines that call at Jamaican ports.

The *real* Jamaica is some distance from the cruise ship piers, which are surrounded by expected shops and taxis wanting to take you touring. Montego Bay is a confusing, bustling city that's dedicated to tourism. Advance planning pays off. If you want to play golf, make arrangements from home, before you board ship, for a starting time and caddies to play at the Half Moon or Rose Hall courses. (Tryall's course has been private in winter months. Inquire about permission to play.)

DEPARTURE involves reconfirming your transportation route back to the airport. If you're staying in Ocho Rios or Port Antonio or elsewhere, the jitney-minibus is a popular method for getting to the airport. From Kingston hotels, taxis provide convenient service. If you've rented a car, be sure to ask if there are extra fees for airport drop-off.

Allow an hour-plus for check in. Lines are often long, and they move slowly. You'll be required to forfeit the copy of the immigration form you filled out on arrival and go through security check. If you have currency to exchange back to U.S. dollars, allow plenty of time to do so and be sure to have your receipt for the initial transaction to prove that you bought the currency you are exchanging. There is a J$80 departure tax.

TOURING TIPS: **Car rental** firms maintain booths at both airports, but you'll find the "service" a bit casual—and sometimes confusing, even when you're negotiating with the established international names like *Hertz, Avis, National,* and *Budget. Island Car Rentals* is Jamaica's biggest nationwide firm, but I've found the attitude of some staff to be imperious and annoying, and charges to be high. I've had very good luck, and good service, from Jean and Michael Casewell's *Econocar,* with the main office on 15 Arnold Road in Kingston and another office in Montego Bay.

AUTHOR'S OBSERVATION

Jamaica has the most expensive car rental rates in the Caribbean. Even with the high import duties on rental cars, the rates seem exorbitant—at about US$100 per day! Check your credit card's policy about insurance; some companies cover you when you charge with their card. That's one way to save a little. Otherwise, brace yourself for high costs.

Taxis are available at both Montego Bay and Kingston airports, and are on call through all hotels. Be sure to establish your touring rate *before* you get into the taxi. Don't be shy about bargaining on rates for touring. Although there are accepted rates for specific routes and for waiting time, it's often possible to work out some other arrangement.

Bus tours operate along the tourist-conscious north coast, using both huge buses and the minibus-jitneys. Some firms plan tours to the Maroon or Cockpit country (in the mountain highlands of the west) and to Kingston. Hotels can help with arrangements.

Flying *Trans Jamaica Airlines* between the country's domestic airports—Montego Bay and Kingston or elsewhere—gives a bird's eye view of this spectacular country.

LODGING choices range from very simple, small rooms in inexpensive guest houses to opulent luxury, with spectacular views, in some of the country's "Elegant Resorts," some independently owned hotels that have grouped for promotional purposes. There are attractive inns, comfortable small business-style hotels, and many types of resorts. In addition, there are dozens of lovely villas that can be rented in owners' absence, and an increasing number of apartments that have been offered as condominiums, to be rented for a week or two. And remember that Jamaica is the home of the Caribbean-style all-inclusive hotel, where one pre-paid fee covers "everything." There are nearly 20.

> **AUTHOR'S OBSERVATION**
>
> Do not be misled into believing that "all-inclusive" *always* means everything is included. Although the SuperClubs and the Sandals resorts do include drinks, entertainment, and everything except personal purchases, some of the other so-called all-inclusives have add-on charges for some things that you may feel are essential to your holiday pleasure. Always ask for complete details and about additional charges that will be added to your hotel bills. Government taxes and service and other charges are the usual add-ons.

Information about places to stay is included under Hotels/Resorts, Housekeeping Holidays, The Inn Way, and Low-Cost Lodging, for each area of the country, covered in alphabetical order. Stars are awarded within each category. (See page 11.)

KINGSTON

As the largest English-speaking community south of Miami, with about 700,000 people, Kingston fills a huge pocket on the south coast—at least a 2-hour drive from the north coast resorts and far removed in feeling. Contrary to the beach-oriented life of the north coast, Jamaica's south coast capital is culturally and commercially oriented. The seat of the government is here, as are the main offices for most of the national and international companies, the country's major freight port, and touchstones for the country's heritage.

Although its ghettos are the source for headlines when political activities heat up, the city deserves attention for far more important reasons. Its business, social, and cultural communities have developed a sophistication that earns Jamaica an important place in the Caribbean community. Kingston can be overwhelming to the uninitiated, but it warrants at least a few days' visit by those who have more than a sun-tanning interest in this country. Not only is this where reggae music was born, but the capital also claims an impressive National Art Gallery, Devon House (a restored 19th-century home-turned-museum), the Jamaica Folk Musical Pantomime, the National Dance Theatre Company, and regular performances at the Little Theatre, the Ward Theatre, the Creative Arts Centre at the University of the West Indies, and several other stages that make their headquarters here. In addition, historic Port Royal—an important 17th-century city across the bay—is being restored to the time of its pirate haven heyday when clever scoundrel Henry Morgan was its governor.

ARRIVAL AND DEPARTURE: The walk from your plane to the immigration desk is a long one. If you have carry-on luggage, bring wheels. The tourist board maintains a desk just beyond immigration with folders and other information that can provide useful facts for later on. At this point, there are porters to help with luggage. Taxis and shuttle buses for the long ride into Kingston wait outside the doors. Be sure to inquire as to costs before you are wedged into some vehicle. Vacationers with tour coupons from a travel agent will find life a bit (but not much) easier.

AUTHOR'S OBSERVATION

Jamaicans enjoy gathering around the doorway out of the airport. The sea of people can seem overwhelming for travelers not familiar with West Indian city airports.

When you leave from Kingston's airport, there are several small booths in the waiting area for last-minute purchases such as Jamaican rum, coffee, books, spices, toys, and other products. The restaurant is upstairs.

TOURING TIPS: From your Kingston hotel, you can negotiate with a taxi driver to tour around at your own speed, hitting highlights such as a drive up to Blue Mountain Inn (and maybe higher), as well as around town. A good driver can provide information that is more interesting than the "canned" patter offered on most of the sightseeing tour buses. Check with your hotel activities desk about boat trips to some of the nearby small islands for picnics, and plan to take the harbor ferry across to Port Royal if you're adventuresome. It's a fun journey for those of us who love Caribbean life.

Rental car firms maintain booths at the airport. You'll find representatives from the U.S. international firms in addition to some local firms. I've rented through *Econocar,* on Arnold Road in Kingston, and found Mrs. James and Jean and Michael Casewell to be helpful and pleasant. Driving British style (on the left) in downtown Kingston is not for everyone. It can be chaotic, and finding parking places is the real challenge if you don't pull into a designated parking lot. A car is ideal for touring the countryside, however, once you master the left-hand drive. Ocho Rios is about two hours' drive; around the coast to Port Antonio takes two hours or more.

Air service is on *Trans Jamaica Airways* between Kingston's local airport (not the International one) and Montego Bay, which takes almost four hours to drive, as well as to Port Antonio and the Boscobel airport east of Ocho Rios, but figure delays into the equation before you assume flying is fast.

HOTELS/RESORTS in Kingston range from high-rise hotels in the heart of the business areas to smaller spots that are popular with long-time Jamaican visitors.

★★★ **Jamaica Pegasus** • *on Knutsford Blvd., in the New Kingston area* • is a high-rise hotel that benefits from a British Forte Hotel connection. The lobby is studded with overstuffed furniture, upholstered in pastel tones that complement its sturdy structure. All is set off by the shiny marble floors. *Le Pavillion* is the lovely luncheon, high tea, and elegant dining area on the lobby level, while the *Surrey Tavern,* to the right of the entrance, continues to be popular for pub-style fare. The pool, on the lower level, gives a resort feeling to this city hotel, and the neighboring coffee shop serves good food with reasonably fast service. The top-floor restaurant has been closed for some time. The *Knutsford Club*, on the 14th, 15th, and 16th floors, offers lounge area and business services; the refurbished rooms on other floors can be pleasant, with views over Kingston to mountains or sea. A jogging track circles near the pool area; tennis courts are near the pool and at a neighboring club. Expect to enjoy a U.S.-style hotel, with Jamaican imprint. *Hotel.*

★★★ **Morgans Harbour** • *on the airport peninsula, across the harbor from Kingston* • appeals to yachtspeople and to those who want a convenient base for prowling around historic Port Royal. Lots of money has been spent on improvement for the marina facilities, especially the piers and restaurant. This is *the* spot for folks who want to get out to sea in Jamaica, whether for day sails to offshore islets or on multi-day sails. The newest (and attractive) viewful rooms are in buildings completed in 1990. Older rooms face onto the swimming area, a salt-water pool that has been enclosed and improved. The waterside bar-cafe-restaurant is a pleasant lingering area for all meals; evening entertainment includes barbecues, reggae evenings, and other events. Taxis take about 20 minutes to get to Kingston, on a U-shaped route past the airport and around the harbor. Ferry boats make the crossing in a matter of minutes, when your schedule fits with theirs. *Small hotel.*

★ **Oceana Kingston** • *near the shore in downtown Kingston* • is a high-rise hotel that opened under Inter-Continental Hotel management several years ago. Currently owned and operated by the Jamaican government, the hotel abuts the convention center and is a block from the National Gallery, the Institute of Jamaica and other downtown cultural arenas. The street-level restaurant is staffed with pleasant personnel and I found front desk staff helpful. The best of the standard hotel rooms are on upper floors, with a harbor view. Business offices occupy some floors. The New Kingston area, with Pegasus and Wyndham hotels, is about 10 minutes' drive, depending on traffic. This can be a good bet for business folk and those who come for conventions, but it may seem remote if you're expecting tourism style. *Hotel.*

Terra Nova • *on Waterloo Road* • in a residential area of Kingston, has long been popular for business luncheons and meetings. The pool that punctuates the front lawn seems seldom used, but the 32 rooms in the 2 wings and a 2-story back building are reasonably comfortable. You'll need a car or taxi for mobility. For comments on the *El Dorado* dining room, see "Restaurants" below. *Small hotel.*

★★ **Wyndham New Kingston** • *on Knutsford Blvd., near the Pegasus* • is a high-rise member of the Dallas-based Wyndham organization. The street-level lobby is airy, open, and tropical in feeling. The mezzanine lounge areas, with music playing sometimes for social hours, are conducive to leisurely lingering, especially at the bar. Planting by the pool and pool terrace adds a nice note, and the wicker furniture and plants make public areas pleasant. Rooms in the tower are preferable to the first-built (many years ago) rim of rooms around the pool. The presidential floors (15 and 16) provide a mini-version of the "executive floor" that's popular in some U.S.-based business hotels. The *Palm Court* serves pastas and other offerings; and the open-to-breezes *Macaw Terrace* is the place for breakfast and lunch as well as for simple suppers. Note that tennis is available at the courts near the pool and that phone and elevator service, when the hotel is full, has been wretched. *Hotel.*

THE INN WAY for Kingston is surprisingly pleasant, when you consider that this is the country's capital. There are a few small hotels that seem innlike in their appearance. The best have grown from a building that was once a private residence, to include some of the accepted assets of a pleasant inn. Regrettably, ownership/management in most cases seems more interested in the financial part of the business than in the joys of hospitality, but someone on the staff usually fills in with the friendly gestures. Here are my suggestions:

★★ **The Courtleigh** • *31 Trafalgar Rd.* • offers small-hotel hospitality within a short distance of the high-rise Wyndham and Pegasus. Most activity focuses on the restaurants and pool, with its nearby bar. Hanging baskets of greenery dress up the patio and alcoves of the white buildings. Bedrooms are in 1- and 2-story buildings; the best have a pool view (and all are sometimes within earshot of pulsating music from a nearby nightclub). In most rooms, the white-painted background is accented with bright colors. Popular with businessfolk, including wise Brits, Courtleigh can provide a nice nest amid city life. *Small hotel.*

★ **Four Seasons Hotel** • *on Ruthven Rd., near the New Kingston Shopping Center* • started as a lovely (and still recognizable) old mansion, with an impressive staircase that leads to the rooms. Rooms 11, 12, and 14 share a big, sunstruck, sparsely furnished terrace. Newer rooms are in a separate building. Breakfast, drinks, and snacks are served on the front and side porches; main meals are served in the air-conditioned dining room. *Small hotel.*

★★ **Ivor** • *at 2000 feet, on Jack's Hill, 20 minutes' drive from downtown* • is a very special spot. The Aitkens have opened their home, which dates from the 1870s, to welcome people who make reservations for lunch or dinner, and a handful of resident guests who are smart enough to reserve one of the few rooms. The view from the front porch is sensational—over the Liguinea plains to the sea. You can also look "behind" to the mountains. Ivor can be a comfortable home for birders and others who enjoy nature—naturally. As might be expected, you're treated like a house guest. The view is spectacular; the quiet palpable. *Inn.*

★ **Mayfair** • *in a residential area, on a cul de sac called West Kings House Close* • is a gathering of houses, with the reception area in the biggest (and original) house. The backyard pool is popular; there are lounge chairs on the lawn. Meals are served in the pub near the pool as well as in the main house dining room. Sybil Hughes and her staff help with tips about places to go and things to see. British and European guests are regulars; independent Americans who don't require high-rise hotel comforts are also finding this place. Rooms range from *very* basic to comfortable. Weekly buffets are popular with Kingstonians. A rental car will keep you mobile. *Small hotel.*

★ **Medallion Hall Hotel** • *53 Hope Rd., in a residential area* • is another former home turned inn. With the addition of a new dining room and an air-conditioned British-style bar, the small property has the potential to be a comfortable nest. I found the staff lackadaisical when I visited for this edition, but the rooms are attractive, the place convenient, and the rates reasonable. It's worth considering if you don't want the high-rise biggies. *Small hotel.*

LOW-COST LODGING: Except for Wyndham and Pegasus (whose international managers charge international city prices), all Kingston hotels charge very reasonable rates. In addition to Mayfair, Courtleigh, and Oceana, mentioned above, others to consider for *very* low-cost lodgings are:

Altamont Court Hotel • *on Altamont Crescent, behind the Wyndham and Pegasus* • has apartment-style rooms in a 2-story building. Furnishings are basic; some folks live here. *Apts.*

Indies House • *on Holborn Road in New Kingston* • is a former West Indian home modified to hold about a dozen bedrooms, each with private bathroom. It's possible to walk to Devon House and to shopping areas from the inn. *Guesthouse.*

★★ **Pine Grove Chalets** • *almost 45 minutes drive from Kingston, in the mountains* • has been rebuilt since its bashing by Hurricane Gilbert in September 1989. With comfortably simple bedrooms and a common area that can be used for small conferences, this place is sometimes used by Jamaican businesses and groups for special "think tank" sessions. Call from Kingston to find out about possibilities for lunch, and plan to hike in the area. If you want to stay for dinner, you'd better spend the night. The road is wiggly, scenic, and best driven in daylight. Great for folks enthusiastic about camping and being away from hustle and bustle. *Rustic Inn.*

Sunset Inn Apartment Hotel • *on Altamont Crescent, behind the Wyndham and Pegasus* • is a 2-story motel-style building. Units are simply furnished; some West Indian travelers use this as home for long-stay visits. *Apts.*

Tropical Inn • *on Clieveden Avenue, not far from the University of the West Indies* • has an assortment of rooms that includes some with kitchenette. All have TV and air conditioners, even when furnishings are not the most lavish. There's a restaurant on premises, as well as a small pool. *Guesthouse.*

RESTAURANTS in Kingston vary from local places best known to Kingstonians (and seldom visited by outsiders) to places that are popular with sophisticated business types who know (and expect) the best. Especially worth noting are restaurants at some of the small hotels, namely Courtleigh, and Terra Nova's *El Dorado*.

★★★ **Blue Mountain Inn** • *about 30 minutes' drive out Old Hope Rd. and into the mountains* • is romantic and elegant, both for the setting and for the food. The riverside inn is open only for dinner, and reservations are essential. Cocktails are usually served on the terrace, within sight of the river. (Bring bug repellent if you're bothered by mosquitoes.) The elaborate menu often rises to expectations; the setting always does.

Devon House • *near most hotels, on Hope Rd. at Waterloo, in the Kingston residential area* • is a special place for its restoration to 19th-century style. The dining areas are on the back porch or at *The Grog Shop* patio or air-conditioned Devonshire. Staff is dressed in 19th-century West Indian–style. Open for full meals, or a sandwich lunch, the place offers a perfect escape from 20th-century pressures. It's a good idea to make reservations for dinner. For lunch, when it's on the menu, the thin pancake-crepe called "roti" is a hearty meal, especially when filled with curried chicken!

★★ **El Dorado** • *at the Terra Nova Hotel on Waterloo Rd.* • is a pop-ular city place for business lunches or for expense account evenings. The dining room gives the appearance of an over-draperied elegant home, making the most of the decor of the rooms in which it is located. Food is served with some flourishes; this is one of the dressiest dining places in the city. The huge-sized menucard lists beef, chicken, veal, and fish, sometimes offered with imaginative sauces and always with Jamaican vegetables served in interesting ways. House guests enjoy breakfast on the porch.

Gordon's • *in the Petroleum Bldg., just off Trafalgar Rd.* • serves Korean food in very attractive air-conditioned light and airy rooms in the lobby of the building. Popular with Kingstonians, this place is good.

★★ **Heather's** • *on Haining Rd., near the Wyndham and Pegasus* • has grown beyond the former home it occupies, to fill the garden area with tables. The intriguing menu includes some Middle Eastern dishes with more standard fare. My sampling was excellent, finely spiced, and very filling.

Hot Pot Restaurant • *off Altamont Court, behind the Pegasus and Wyndham* • is known for good Jamaican food. The casual place is open for breakfast, lunch, and dinner. Traditional salt fish and ackee (salted cod and the Jamaican fruit that looks like, and is the texture of, scrambled eggs when cooked) is served, as well as other homestyle food.

Indies Pub & Grill • *on Holborn Rd., just off Trafalgar, in the New Kingston area* • is a popular local gathering place, for businessfolk and others. It's within walking distance of the Pegasus and Wyndham, so draws some visitors as well.

★★★ **Ivor's** • *on Jack's Hill, about 20 minutes' drive into the hills* • is a rare treat. Arrive before the sun sets, if you're going for dinner. The view is spectacular! Menu is family style, with one or two offerings each meal. Ask, when you make your reservation, about the selections. Food is prepared, and served, as it would be in a landed-gentry private home.

Jade Garden • *at Village Plaza, off Constant Spring Rd.* • is one of many good Chinese restaurants in Kingston. Some say it's the best, and my meal supports that claim. The atmosphere is pleasant, service good, and menu extensive, especially for the Szechuan (spicy hot) offerings, which are my favorites.

Kohinoor • *on Chelsea Pl., near the New Kingston Shopping Centre* • makes its name with Indian food, which Jamaicans enjoy with the full spice treatment. If you like Indian food, this is a place that cooks and serves it well.

MeeMee's • *off Old Hope Rd., in a shopping center* • is another Kingstonian favorite for Chinese food.

★★ **Norma's** • *in the patio behind a small building on Belmont Rd., near Pegasus and Wyndham hotels* • is a pleasant oasis. Not only is the food good, but the patio setting makes the most of decorating talents, with attractive flower arrangements, hanging baskets, and color-coordinated table linens. Corner tables are protected from the elements and strong sun with canvas tentlike shelters. The menu is elaborate, with local products prepared in interesting ways and delicious desserts. The place is popular with Kingston's "in" crowd so reservations are advised.

Rafaels • *on Hillcrest, in a residential area just off Hope Rd.* • serves Italian pastas and other offerings in the garden and in the house. Ice cream is a favorite, sold from a separate gazebo.

NATURAL SURROUNDINGS First-time visitors should rent a car or hire a taxi to drive up into the Blue Mountains, at least for a cool drink at *Ivors* or perhaps a stop at *Pine Grove,* for a meal and walking. The snakelike route offers spectacular views as you climb.

Check with the tourist office for reliable guides to take you hiking in the mountains. Jamaicans can add lore and expertise to routes that follow trails, which can link for a multi-night mountain expedition. It's also possible to raft and canoe along rivers, especially those on the south coast that are less publicized than the Rio Grande, near Port Antonio, and the Great River, near Montego Bay.

From Kingston, it's possible to go up to Mandeville for a day of hiking and birding or to Port Antonio, but both would be long days and both places benefit from a couple of days' stay. The south-coast beaches and the offshore islands (including Lime Cay) are daytime goals; scuba diving and snorkeling are good around the cays, but negotiating for a boat requires advance planning. Your hotel can help.

PLACES WORTH FINDING in Kingston are many, but they are scattered around the city and its environs, making a rental car (or a taxi driver/tour guide) essential.

Devon House is at 26 Hope Road not far from the New Kingston hotels and near Jamaica House, the prime minister's office. It's worth a couple of hours, not only for the historic house that has been restored to remarkable condition, but also for the display of crafts, paintings, and other Jamaican art and for the food possibilities, for ice cream, pastries, and other baked goods. The mansion, built in 1881, has been elegantly furnished with original period antiques (many of them from Barbados and some from Jamaica). Reopened, after total restoration, in time for the visit of Queen Elizabeth II and Prince Philip in January '83, the mansion and its surrounding buildings and grounds are reminiscent of Williamsburg, VA, and other historic U.S. restorations. Well worth a visit, even if you visit as an all-day excursion from Ocho Rios or another northshore spot, Devon House stands as a statement to the craftsmanship of Jamaicans. It was built entirely by Jamaicans, at the behest of George Stiebel, a man of modest birth who had traveled to Venezuela in search of work. He returned to his native Jamaica a rich man (some claim he had discovered gold), to incorporate into his new home all the best he had seen during his travels.

The National Gallery, downtown in the Roy West Building, is worth a couple of hours to anyone interested in Jamaica's cultural heritage. Opened on this site in November 1984, the art gallery holds impressive sculpture by the late Edna Manley, mother of Prime Minister Manley, as well as 65 pieces of the work of Kapo, a talented Jamaican who worked in Lignum Vitae, a rockhard wood known throughout the West Indies. (Leader of the opposition and former prime minister Edward Seaga recognized Kapo's talents early enough to own one of his first sculptures.) In a back room, Alvin Marriott's study for the Independence Monument is a fascinating work of people on people, rising to a pair on the top. I've particularly enjoyed Isaac Mendez Belisari's marvelous scenes of Jamaica in the mid-1800s and the pre-20th-century collection of portraits and scenes, especially one of "Merry-making Villagers" on St. Vincent in 1775 by Augustin Brunias.

Some other places that might be of interest, amid the commerce of downtown Kingston, are the **Institute of Jamaica** on East Street (the building also houses the National Library, which has an exceptional collection of West Indian books) and **Hope Gardens,** beyond the College of Arts, Science and Technology on Hope Road. The 200-acre park is not as well-kept as it once was, but the area allows for a nice change from the traffic and busy-ness of downtown Kingston. Best on Sundays, when Jamaican families spend the day, the gardens are laced with paths and dotted, in a back area, with a small amusement park that lures children. Given by the Hope family, soon after the abolition of slavery in the mid-1800s, the park once held an extensive orchid collection as well as a wide variety of tropical plants and trees. Only a few prized specimens remain.

Nature's Habitat, a privately financed recreation area at Hartlands, St. Catherine, is a fish farm that has been opened for the public. The acres of land are open for recreational fishing, as well as for bird watching and other nature pursuits. Picnicking is permitted, and is popular on weekends and holidays, for Jamaicans who have transportation.

The Bob Marley Museum, at 56 Hope Road, is the 19th-century home in which he lived with his family and friends. Pictures, furnishings, and tokens from his life are on display; the museum chronicles his life from the ghetto to his adult years as a Rastafarian and internationally known reggae musician. One feature on the grounds is a vegetable and herb garden with foods that were Marley favorites, and the juice bar that serves drinks enjoyed by the reggae artist (who was a vegetarian).

Port Royal, a thriving city in the 17th century when it was used by pirates and privateers, claims Henry Morgan as one of its lieutenant governors. He was knighted by King Charles II, who appointed him lieutenant governor in appreciation for seafaring exploits against the Spanish. Restoration has been underway for the past few years, as a project of the Friends of Port Royal and others. On one of my visits, Dawn strolled me around, explaining where the "widest and longest street in Port Royal" had been. It was called Lime Street, and plans are to excavate the street and pave it in brick and to line it with copies of buildings that might have been there when it was the busiest street of the West Indies. Although the realization of those plans (and others) is a long way off, rampant imaginations can call forth a lot of magic as you visit the small St. Peter's Church, built in 1754 on the site of an earlier church and housing four pieces of silver, more than 400 years old, that came with Morgan from Panama. It's well worth reading the tombstones, many dating from the 1825 yellow fever epidemic that decimated Port Royal. My favorite is at the church entrance, where a tablet notes the fascinating life story of Lewis Galdye Esq. "who departed this life at Port Royal the 22 Dec. 1739 aged 88. He was born at Montpelier in France, but left that country for his Religion and came to settle in this island where he was swallowed up in the Great Earthquake in the year 1692. By the providence of God he was by another shock thrown into the sea and miraculously saved by swimming until a boat took him up. He lived many years after in Great Reputation, Beloved by all that knew Him and much lamented at his death." At **Fort Charles,** there's a Maritime Museum with a few items documenting the area's early history, but the **Archaeological Museum** in the former Naval Hospital holds the most remarkable treasures, many of which have been culled from the sea floor in scuba expeditions over the portion of the city that washed into the sea in the earthquake of June 7, 1692. Also worth noting in this area is the artillery building known as Giddy House. Port Royal is out near Kingston's airport and, if you allow enough time when leaving the country, a couple of hours can be spent here. A ferry links Port Royal with downtown Kingston, from the pier near the Oceana Hotel.

Spanish Town, about half an hour's drive from Kingston, was called Villa de la Vega when Diego Columbus (Christopher's brother) presented the plan for the streets. Although most of the early Spanish buildings were shattered when the English took over the area in 1655, some of the names survive. Spanish Town is a residential area, and perceptive visitors will have to look around corners and through 20th-century life to see the treasures left (and there are many) from the early English years. Many of the buildings are marked for restoration and the place to start looking around is the center of the old town, Plaza Mayor. (Do not expect this place to be preened to perfection. Spanish

Town has had hard times in recent years, and although there are many buildings worth noting, there's a lot to be done before this town has reached its potential as a historic landmark.)

SPORTS for the Kingston area include **tennis** (at Wyndham, Pegasus, and the Liguinea Club, across the road from the hotels, in New Kingston), **squash** (your hotel can make arrangements for play on one of the 11 courts available), and **golf** (at 18-hole courses at the Caymanas Golf Club and the Constant Spring Golf Club). Although Kingston is a popular **yachting** center for Jamaicans, it's sometimes difficult for visitors to connect with resident sailors. The Royal Jamaica Yacht Club, near the airport and Morgans Harbour Hotel, has its regatta in August, but there's usually activity on weekends. Members of hometown yacht clubs can sometimes obtain reciprocal privileges. Lime Cay and other offshore islets are popular picnicking goals. Harbor cruises operate on request from Morgans Harbour Hotel, which is also the best source for day sailing and charters. There are some boats at the marina not far from Port Royal and near the airport, but most are privately owned. If you enjoy **polo,** matches are held regularly at the Kingston Polo Club at the Caymanas Estates, as well as at Chukka Cove and Drax Hall, both on the north coast.

TREASURES AND TRIFLES: Kingston is the "big city" for Jamaicans and, as such, the source for the country's most extensive selection of household furnishings and the items for daily life. For visitors, many of the shops hold welcome surprises in the way of handcrafts, fashions, and books about the Caribbean (with special focus on Jamaica, naturally). Although some of the shops in the heart of the old city, near the waterfront (and the Oceana Hotel, National Art Gallery, and the Institute of Jamaica) may be interesting, most shops of interest to visitors are in New Kingston, the area that has been built since the early 1960s, inland from the shore.

The **New Kingston Shopping Mall,** not far from Pegasus and Wyndham hotels and across the street (on Dominica Drive) from the Tourism Centre building, has several clothing and household shops with attractive items of interest to any shopper. Among the most interesting, when I looked for this edition, are a few places in a corner arcade on the second level. **Atash** was one spot with quality Jamaican-made items. On the street level, **Market to Market** is chock-full of food items, including spices, biscuits, baskets, coffee, candies—and an ice cream stand that I found irresistable. **Lee's New Kingston** is a large department store.

One of the many Jamaican designers worth looking for is the **Ital Craft Boutique,** at the Twin Gates Plaza on Constant Spring Road. Cindy Breakspeare and Donna Feltis Coore design accessories and clothes with style and imagination.

Around the New Kingston area, there are many clusters of shops in areas that Kingstonians refer to as "malls." Several stores gather around one parking area. The scene changes, but it's worth asking for tips about the best places for designers and handcrafts. The tourist office can give you suggestions about the latest list of Jamaican designers of summer fashions and accessories.

Lane's Shopping Mall is another one of several one-stop sources for daily items, including those carried in sundries shops and drugstores, where Jamaican-made skin creams include many with Caribbean aloe base. It's one of a half-dozen malls along Constant Spring Road.

The hotel gift shops and pharmacies at Wyndham and Pegasus have several books about Jamaica and the West Indies, as well as nicely packaged collections of spices, jams, jellies, and other Jamaican products. Artwork and ceramic pieces, especially the figurines of Jamaican women and men in typical market and lifestyle poses—are attractive and unusual.

Devon House's grounds hold several craft shops with high quality items, especially those of "Things Jamaican," a government-assisted craft association.

LUCEA

At a bend of the north-coast road, between Montego Bay and Negril (and about an hour's drive from each), lies the town of Lucea. Overlooked by most of today's visitors, the town has a rich history that led its Lucea Parish Church to celebrate its 260th anniversary in November 1985. Built on the site of an old Spanish church, its history closely follows that of Hanover Parish since the town was one of the most important in the early years of settlement.

Fort Charlotte, marking the entrance to Lucea Harbour, is down a nondescript road on the west side of town. Built in 1761, around the time of King George III's marriage to Queen Charlotte, the fort was transferred to Jamaica by the English War Office in 1862. The harbor, noted on a plaque as being "about three cables wide," was one of the most protected on the north coast.

Not far from Fort Charlotte, Rusea's Old High School (mentioned in this chapter's introduction) is still in use for classes. It was built in 1777 from funds given for education at the behest of Martin Rusea, a Frenchman who made his home in Jamaica.

Although tracking down the historical parts of Lucea may take a few minutes out of your drive between Montego Bay and Negril, time spent with Lucea's past will be well worth the effort.

West Palm Hotel • *as the road bends by Lucea Parish Church* • is on the Negril side of town, within walking distance of the fort. Built in 1983, Mr. Wilson's 2-story hotel offers tidy rooms, many with private bathroom, in a building that is known in its town for serving good Jamaican food. Rates are very reasonable, and are listed in Jamaican currency. *Small hotel.*

MANDEVILLE

Best known to Jamaicans, and to employees and business folk related to the bauxite companies, Mandeville is a surprise to visitors who think of Jamaica only as sandy beaches and resort activity. Both Alpart and Alcan, two multinational conglomerates that are involved with Jamaica's bauxite industry, have established communities here, and have punctuated this mountain town with country clubs, a golf course, and the other trappings of the good life. Cutbacks in the bauxite business have curtailed some of the social activities, but the mountain town has weathered (successfully) worse times than these in its history and the bauxite business is improving.

Mandeville's main attractions are not beaches (there are none, obviously, in the mountains), but its almost Alpine feeling. The air is clear and the mist that sometimes settles in the evenings is softened by the first rays of sunshine, giving the countryside a fairyland quality. The town seems to appeal most to European visitors and others who like hiking through the countryside, horseback riding, bird-watching, nature walks, and blissful peace and quiet with crisp air.

ARRIVAL AND DEPARTURE in Mandeville are best in a rental car, having first arrived at either the Montego Bay or Kingston airports. One route is to drive up from the south coast, which you can reach by driving from the Montego Bay airport to Negril and south around to Black River, where you turn north to drive into the mountains through "Bamboo Alley," a spectacular tunnel through stands of bamboo. Another route into the mountains, south from the north coast, takes you inland not far from Discovery Bay, to Browns Town and on through several villages to Mandeville. The drive up from Kingston is probably the fastest (but not the most interesting, in my opinion). Arriving here on your own is best. This is not a tourist town, but is a place with a strong sense of community.

HOTELS IN MANDEVILLE are small, with basic comforts but not much in the way of the expected Caribbean resort (beach and sea) facilities.

★ *Astra Hotel* • *on 62 Ward Ave., in a residential area* • has been a private home and now is one of Jamaica's special inns thanks to the hospitality of its owners. This place has been in the McIntyre family for several years, first with the senior members and now with Diana and Carey McIntyre-Pike (who live off-premises but maintain this inn in a homelike style). The staff is loyal and helpful; the surroundings are ideal for country walks, perhaps from Marshall's Pen (see below), horseback riding, tennis, and golf, thanks to assistance from the owners. Ask about the train ride to Montego Bay, the reverse of the excursion from that tourist town to mountaintop Mandeville. Count on substantial Jamaican food at mealtimes, and know that you are in a primarily residential (not tourist) area when you head for this spot. There's a pool on premises; the popular *Revival Bar* near the pool is a gathering spot for guests. *Hotel.*

Mandeville Hotel • *off the main town square, away from the bustle* • languished until it was taken over by the McIntyre family, mentioned above for their Astra. Gordon McIntyre is in charge here. Built as a commercial hotel, the 2-story stucco building (with wings of rooms) has a pool, television, and restaurant and bar for entertainment areas. Bedrooms can be linked as suites and/or apartments, a fact that appeals to long-stay visitors and to senior citizens, who find the Mandeville climate and lifestyle pleasant for winter holidays from Europe, Canada, or the U.S. The McIntyres' hospitality is the key to the charm of this hotel. *Hotel.*

★ **Marshall's Pen** • *in the countryside* • is a special spot. Check with Diana McIntyre-Pike at Astra for reservations. The 250-year-old house is set in 300 acres of countryside, surrounded by fields and wooded terrain favored by birdwatchers and others who like walking. Antiques fill the house, which is still very much home for Mr. Robert Sutton, who shows you the 1848 edition of the *London Illustrated* in which his great-grandfather's death is recorded. Some of the bedrooms have private bath; 5 are in two separate apartments. Meals are usually taken at Astra, and a car will make getting around possible. *Inn.*

HOTELS IN THE AREA   include a few on the south coast and a neighboring spa. All are easily reached out of Mandeville and, combined with the mountain town, present a Jamaica that is far removed from the tourism trappings of the popular north coast resorts.

Treasure Beach • *on the south coast* • has a dozen rooms on a beach best known to Jamaicans. The motel-style building offers basic service, with rooms that have private bathrooms and a building with a disco that is popular with Jamaicans, especially on holiday weekends. *Hotel.*

Villa Bella Hotel • *about 13 miles from Mandeville, in Christiana* • is a spa hotel of modest proportions. Best known locally for its curative springs, the hotel continues its tradition of afternoon tea, which is a good time for your first visit to look things over before booking a room. *Small hotel.*

Wilton House • *at Bluefields, Westmoreland* • is a lovely private home, punctuated with antiques and facing the sea from a rise on the shore. The peaceful, homelike surroundings are for those who crave a place removed from tourism's clutter. Owner Joyce McLeod Grulke is your hostess. The nearest beach is an easy walk down the shore-rimming road. *Inn.*

Natanias Guest House, between Bluefields and White House, on the south coast seaside, and **South Sea View Guest House** are two other places to stay along the little-known south coast.

NATURAL SURROUNDINGS   offer exceptional opportunities for visitors interested in birding or in walks and hikes and horseback riding. **Marshall's Pen**, mentioned above, is the first stop for an introduction to some of the offerings in this mountaintop area and then, with the help of Mandeville's residents, who know and love their special place, other expeditions can be arranged.

Two other places that can be enchanting for botanists and those who enjoy gardens are **Mrs. Stephenson's Garden,** a privately owned expanse of beautiful flowering plants, bushes, and trees; and the **Paul Cross Nursery,** not far away and also of interest. The **south coast beaches** are easily accessible from Mandeville and, since that area is one of the few where manatees can be found, at a point where the river meets the sea, snorkelers and scuba divers can also find a lot that's interesting.

South Coast Safaris operate wonderful excursions from their south coast starting point, up the Black River, through Salt Spring. The *Black River Boat Tours* take almost 2 hours, on a flat boat that brings you into the *real* country life of Jamaica. Another journey, to the dramatic, cascading **Y.S. Falls,** on a private estate, involves walking through the estate, for which South Coast Safaris has been granted permission. Make plans for a picnic lunch, and take your time enjoying the seven cascades that plunge into pools on each level. There are approved guides (paid by South Coast Safaris and tipped by you) at a kiosk at the starting point.

MONTEGO BAY

Jamaica's modern tourism got its start in Montego Bay, and for some the shoreline near the city is still the heart of a holiday. The resort area has grown from its roots in town to cling to the shores—both east and west on the north coast—and climb all over the reclaimed land of Montego Freeport that was intended to make this city one of the Caribbean's most alluring ports. Frankly, this town-turned-city of 30,000 is not one of my favorites because the bustle and tourist trappings make it difficult to know the Jamaica I love. The downtown area is a knot of commerce and, although bypass roads divert some of the traffic, it is confusing (and hot). There are some special small hotels amid the clutter, but most of the better resorts are east and west of the north-coast city. Check with the Jamaica Tourist Board at Cornwall Beach for their suggestions about what to do while you are in the area. In my opinion, after you've seen Sam Sharpe Square—which isn't a square at all, but is named for one of Jamaica's Emancipation patriots—then all that's left are the barnacles of buildings that house the heart of a tourism industry: shops, hotels, restaurants—some good, some excellent, some terrible.

The Cage, built on the northwest corner of Sam Sharpe Square in 1806, and the building used to imprison runaway slaves, is now a commercial building, but the structure is worth noting. Cast a glance at St. James Church, built in the late 1700s, at the Georgian house that stands at 16 Church Street, and at Burchell Memorial Baptist Church, while you leap around, sidestepping people and traffic.

ARRIVAL AND DEPARTURE: The Donald Sangster International airport has expanded to cope with increased traffic, but visitors walk "miles," including up and down stairs, a fact to remember if you have carry-on luggage. In recent seasons, a group of young Jamaican women, in colorful costumes, sing welcome songs—and rum is served while you wait in the immigration lines. There's a branch of the bank near the immigration desks and another downstairs near the luggage claim areas on the street level. Porters are usually available to help with luggage, but brace yourself for the fray that awaits outside the doors. If you are on a tour, with a travel voucher for another part of the country, go to the Jamaica Tourist Board desk where there is usually someone who can send you to the appropriate bus or jitney car. Expect to wait—and wait—and wait, until the transport is full. (There's no point in rushing through customs.) Several car rental desks are to your right, after you wade through the "Want a taxi?" folks (see "Touring Tips" below); taxis are waiting and buses and tour company desks are near the curb for seat-in-car travel to Negril, Ocho Rios, and Montego Bay.

Departure from Montego Bay may seem chaotic when many planes are leaving at about the same time (and most of them going on to Kingston before returning to U.S. cities). Once you have gone through immigration and security (where your hand luggage will be searched), there's an open area with plenty of seats, an active bar, and several attractive specialty shops. (See "Treasures and Trifles.")

TOURING TIPS: There's plenty to see and do, and plenty of tour companies, plus almost 50 **car rental** firms, to help you reach most of the sights. Plan ahead, with a bus company voucher from your travel agent, or be courageous. *Budget, Hertz, Avis, National,* and other name brands have their representatives stationed in the car rental area to the right of the exit from customs at the airport. There are also several independent car rental operators who don't have airport desks and must be reached by telephone. Their rates are sometimes lower for good, but not the newest, cars. *Econocar* is one I've used and found helpful. Figure on paying $100 and up for a day's rental; there are slightly better rates for a weekly rental. Be sure to ask how many miles are included in your daily charge. Cars vary insofar as upkeep, and all firms require an astoundingly high deposit or a signed, blank credit card slip against damages. Driving is relatively easy, on the left, British style; but drive defensively. Most Jamaicans drive fast, and apparently without much (or any) thought for others.

AUTHOR'S OBSERVATION

Being streetwise helps with negotiating for your car rental at the airport in MoBay. The several booths take on a bazaarlike status, and staff seem more anxious to talk with each other than to help customers. Be attentive, specific about your wishes, and patient. Don't count on speed, courtesy, or efficiency.

Touring companies run **shuttle bus** service to the north-coast hotels, from MoBay west to Negril and east to Ocho Rios and beyond. The charge has been about US$15 to Ocho Rios hotels (taxis charge over $60). Since devaluations can affect the price, inquire at the time of your travel, if price matters. Several companies (*Tropical Tours, JUTA, Greenlight,* and others) operate day-long and half-day tours that make it possible to see the major attractions with a group and driver. (See "Places Worth Finding" and know that anything in Ocho Rios or Negril is a relatively easy day trip by car or bus from Montego Bay.)

Taxis hover around the airport exit and most hotels, and anyone who asks if you need one will either be a driver or a friend of a driver. *Be sure* you have asked about the taxi fares—before you get duped. Taxis are supposed to accept Jamaican dollars, but most want U.S. currency and may give a better price if you pay in U.S. dollars. Fares are high but might make sense if several people share the cost.

Airplane service is available on *Trans Jamaican Airways* to Negril, Kingston's domestic (not the international) airport, Port Antonio, and elsewhere. Although the time in the air is much shorter, the ground delays can make the actual travel time about the same as driving. The view from the air, however, is a tour of its own, and well worth the experience.

HOTELS/RESORTS in the MoBay area (which stretches all the way from Round Hill to Falmouth) give you more choice for your money than any similar cheek-by-jowl lot of hostelries in the Caribbean. The only places with as many (perhaps more) rooms are the north coast of the Dominican Republic, east of Puerto Plata, and the San Juan strip of Puerto Rico, but the MoBay area hotels have more variety, and much better beaches than the Puerto Rican group. The all-inclusive resort with a special West Indian style was created in Jamaica, with the opening of Couples in the Ocho Rios area in 1978. Since that time, many other properties have adopted a single fee for a multinight stay, with room, board, sports equipment, entertainment, and almost everything else (sometimes even drinks) included. Most of the all-inclusives are in the MoBay area. Three of the "Elegant Resorts" are in the MoBay area, namely Round Hill, Tryall, and Half Moon.

AUTHOR'S AWARDS

Half Moon Resort is Jamaica's most compact, comprehensive beachside resort, with tennis, squash, golf, watersports, and a range of accommodations; *Sandals Montego Bay* is the liveliest and most airport-convenient of the inclusive resorts; *Tryall* is Jamaica's classiest "Elegant Resort," and small *Coral Cliff* continues to be a personal favorite for modest MoBay accommodations.

Doctor's Cave Beach Resort • *within walking distance of the beach* • was one of the first properties to settle near MoBay shores (although *not* on Doctor's Cave Beach). Now wedged between a cluster of shops, restaurants, tour offices, and neighboring hotels, this hotel is right in the middle of most MoBay resort activity. The basic structure (rooms in a few floors of assorted buildings within an easy stroll of the beach) is sound, and refurbishing gives a homey feeling to this 75-room hotel. The terrace restaurant in the back is pleasant, a pool is to the right of the entrance, and the atmosphere is usually comfortable. *Hotel.*

Fantasy Resort • *next door to Doctors Cave Beach Hotel* • had been Club Casa Montego until a total overhaul resulted in a grand (re)opening with the new name in May 1988. Now operating on a unique "modified inclusive" plan, the property is Jamaican style, with moderate charges that cover almost everything. The hotel's pool is pleasant for those who prefer an on-premise cooling-off place to walking across the road to the beach. The *Fantasy Disco* is popular for evening action; other activities are geared to meeting fellow guests. Lodgers in the 119-room hotel are convenient to the rest of the MoBay activity, which includes shops, watersports at Doctors Cave Beach, and nearby nightspots. *Inclusive hotel.*

The Gloucestershire • *on shore-rimming Gloucester Rd.* • occupies the site of the former Beach View, but is a high-density new complex where shops, bars, and restaurants add to the activity that centers around the pool. Famed (and busy) Doctor's Cave Beach is across the road. Good restaurants are within walking distance and on the premises. The best rooms in this 2- and 3-story complex are those with a sea view. Count on activity. *Hotel.*

★★★★★ **Half Moon Resort & Club** • *on the beach, about 10 minutes' drive east of the airport and town* • is a total resort, with all the atmosphere of a country club and lavish planting that gives the complex a Disney World feeling. The resort is really *three* resorts: the main beach area, with villas, the newest suites, and rooms; the former Colony Hotel now with duplex villas and pool, as well as a beach; and the Golf Club at the undulating course on the inland side of the road. Choices for lodgings include both wings of the main building, where most rooms have been redecorated using copies of Jamaican antiques, plus separate villas to the west and the east, which is the right as you face the sea. There's jitney service to take you to the villa complex, if you choose not to walk or drive your rental car. Tennis courts are midway between the main building (with restaurant, beach activities, and the social center) and the plantation-style pavilion-with-large-pool that is the hub for most of the property's villa rentals. Some of the apartments are duplex, furnished with copies of Jamaican antiques, and come with daily maid service. The resort has a long shoreline, with part of it a good beach, plus tennis courts, squash club, a golf course with club house, access to horseback riding for those who want it, and a full range of watersports (including scuba). Many of the several pools around the premises are for the private use of villa renters. The bigger pools—near the tennis courts and at the center of the villa complex—are for use by all the guests, but the expanse of the property means that pool areas are seldom crowded. Count on elaborate buffets (Sunday noontime is especially lavish), evening entertainment, and action if you want it. In response to the all-inclusive plans offered elsewhere, Half Moon and other "Elegant Resorts" offer a "Plantinum Plan," with all meals, drinks, sports, taxes, and service charges and the company of the other members for part of your stay. Ask for details if it sounds interesting. Austrian-born Heinz Simonitsch, managing director, has served as president of the Caribbean Hotel Association and was chosen as "1981 Caribbean Hotelier of the Year" by his colleagues. *Resort.*

Jack Tar Montego Beach Hotel • *5 minutes' drive west of the airport and 5 minutes' drive east of the center of MoBay* • is one of Jamaica's "club" hotels, where one fee pays for "everything" for the duration of your stay. The hotel is shoreside at the heart of MoBay's vacation action center. The multi-story former Montego Beach hotel incorporates the former Sunset Lodge hotel into its complex and gives guests all watersports, meals, and entertainment as part of the week-long holiday at good value rates. Most of the 127 rooms have sea view. A proliferation of shops and salespeople surround the roadside at the entrance of the hotel; the sand that makes the beach, when there is one, sometimes settles farther out to sea, but a sunning area is secured by a cement wall. If the price is right, this place may be okay if you prefer action to privacy. *Inclusive hotel.*

Reading Reef Club • *west of Montego Bay, east of Round Hill* • fills a pocket between sea and road with a couple of buildings that hold public areas and bedrooms. Sunbathers can enjoy a sea view from poolside; a small beach puts sand underfoot when you want to get into the Caribbean. Bedrooms are in a building to the right as you face the sea, either upstairs or ground level; most have water view. The Safari lounge is one pre-dinner gathering spot. The restaurant offers some diners a view of the sea. This is a pleasant spot, slightly removed from the heart of MoBay's action, but near enough to drive into town. Could be ideal for folks seeking a sunstruck hideaway. *Hotel.*

Rose Hall Holiday Inn • *on the MoBay side of Half Moon Club resort* • is a multi-building complex punctuated with bright orange splashes of color and plenty of activity, when enough package tour travelers have arrived to keep things lively. Shops fill the arcaded areas, the pool is on the beach side of the hotel, and guests here have access to evening entertainment, tour facilities, and other activities that appeal to those who like the Holiday Inn style with Jamaican flavor. Totally refurbished, and rebuilt where necessary, the hotel looks reasonably good. It's often used for bargain-priced air-and-hotel package plans. Buffets are a common mealtime pattern. *Resort hotel.*

★★★★★ **Round Hill** • *trimming a promontory, west of Montego Bay on the north shore road* • is, quite simply, gorgeous! Not only are most of the privately owned villas (for rent in owners' absence) tastefully decorated, but the bedrooms in the two-story wing off the seafront Great House are gems, furnished with copies of Georgian-Jamaican antiques. All rooms in the Great House have louvered sea-viewing windows, pretty fabrics, and dark wood furniture. The villas that rise up the plant-and-tree-covered hillside vary in size, furnishings, and maintenance. Some are extremely elegant; others need attention. The best of the lot, in my opinion, are pool-studded, with lush foliage to ensure privacy. Beachside barbecue evenings provide relief from more formal dining room, in a beachside pavilion. Food has been uneven, but may have improved for this season. Well-heeled families seem to enjoy this palace; small children are not always the favorite guests. Round Hill has been popular with CEOs and others who want to escape the pressure-filled business world; promotional-style write-ups in major travel magazines have had their effect on "mystique." *Classic hotel, villas.*

★★★★ **Sandals Montego Bay** • *on the beach not far from the end of the MoBay airport's runway* • is the pace-setter for fun-loving couples seeking a carefree, action-packed holiday at an all-inclusive price. This was the first of Butch Stewart's growing family of Sandals' resorts. (There are now two others in the Montego Bay area, two near Ocho Rios, and one in Negril.) The former Bay Roc hotel has been swallowed up in a rush of building and beach-fixing that has turned this property into one of Jamaica's most popular hotels. Packaged for multi-night stays "for mixed couples only," the property's management thinks of everything—from a boatload of fresh fruit and free drinks at the beach to elaborate buffets and special theme meals in the dining room, action in the disco until dawn, plus tennis courts, a squash court, health club, pool, beach, and Jacuzzis. Scuba lessons and other watersports are included in your price for 2, as are all meals. Awards are given for participation in the several contests and games, but it's your choice as to whether you compete. Rooms start with "superior," which is the least expensive, and include villas suites, some of which have a separate living room. Both 3-night and 7-night holidays are available. *Inclusive resort.*

Sandals Carlyle on the Bay • *at the shore, near the airport and sister resorts* • has been one of MoBay's established hotels since tourism came to this area in the 1950s. Taken into the Sandals family in early '87, the hotel is now all-inclusive, following the usual pattern where one fee pays for everything for a multi-night stay. It differs from the other Sandals resorts in that it is smaller, has no beach or watersports facilities on premises, and does not share exchange privileges with the other, more expensive Sandals. The several stories of rooms cup the pool; the sea is across the road. Shops freckle the street-level arcade; the balconied rooms facing the sea have the best view. Count on action options, including bus-shuttle into MoBay shops and excursions to Negril, Ocho Rios, etc. You're at the airport so no time is lost between arrival and getting on the beach, but be prepared for jet noises. *Inclusive hotel.*

★★★★ **Sandals Royal Caribbean** • *about 4 miles east of the heart of MoBay and not far from the airport* • was adopted into the Sandals family of Gordon "Butch" Stewart in early 1986. Built for elegance when it rose on these shores some 30 years ago, and totally rebuilt, with improvements, following Hurricane Gilbert's damage in fall '88, the 9-acre, beachside property is now flourishing for couples who choose a multinight holiday at a predetermined fee that includes all meals, drinks, sports, tips, and hotel taxes. The pool is the center of some of the daytime activity, but there's also a complete health club, tennis courts, shuffleboard, croquet, golf, and afternoon tea served on the lawn. The roar of airplanes from MoBay's airport is only a temporary intrusion, amusingly handled here and at neighboring Sandals Montego Bay by a hotel policy to wave to departing planes. (A side benefit is the convenience to your arrival and departure point, only 10 minutes' drive from here.) Open-to-breezes terrace dining is part of what this island is all about, and entertainment adds to the atmosphere. Rooms vary in size, shape, and location—with the sea view rooms my favorites. *Inclusive resort.*

SeaGarden Beach Resort • *next to Carlyle on the Bay, on the spur road that follows the shore, near the airport* • is the former Chatham hotel, which was briefly known as Club Paradise, with an all-inclusive plan. The plantation-style appearance of the main building is impressive; the one-fee-pays-all plan is in the middle range and applies for families. Grounds, on the inland side of the shore road, are well maintained, with a pool as the focus for the "backyard." It's easy to walk to nearby hotels, and to several shops and restaurants, but the spur road puts this place off the usual road-traffic pattern (although under the flight plan for the airplanes that land and take-off nearby). *Inclusive hotel.*

Seawind Towers & Beach Resort • *on the shore at Montego Freeport, west of the town* • includes colorful high-rise towers that have become a MoBay landmark as well as the 2-story buildings of the Beach Resort next door and the Seawinds Apartments across the road. Also in the neighborhood are Ocean Pines apartments, The Anchorage, and the new Bay Pointe apartments, as well as the MoBay Yacht Club and Marina. Standing on land dredged several years ago from the sea, the complex has grown into a resort town unto itself, with a yacht and beach focus. At the beachfront area in front of the towers, most of the action is watersports oriented, although dance lessons, volleyball, and other diversions are also offered when house-count warrants. Swimmers can choose between pools and the sea. Ask your travel agent about good-value vacations at this complex, where many of the 425 tower, bayfront, and garden rooms can be relatively inexpensive. General Manager Lucille Lue is president of the Jamaica Hotel Association. *Resort hotel, apts.*

★★ **Trelawny Beach Club** • *at Falmouth, almost half an hour from the Rose Hall and Half Moon area* • is another action-oriented resort, focusing on watersports (with use of equipment included in your rate), horseback riding, tennis (on 4 courts), craft classes, evening entertainment, special mealtimes, and other events. Jamaican wicker furniture, floral prints, and plenty of plants give a pleasant outdoor feeling to this place. Rooms are in the tower or four low-rise buildings that stretch to the sea. This can be a good value if the package price appeals. *Big hotel.*

★★★★★ **Tryall Golf & Beach Club** • *from shore to hillside, about 30 minutes' drive west of the MoBay airport* • may well be the Caribbean's most beautiful resort. Certainly it's one of the few that hints at the romantic side of 18th-century plantation life, set amid a challenging and beautiful golf course. With millions recently invested, following Hurricane Gilbert (which blew the roof off the Great House), the resort is rising to its true potential. The beach building holds a pleasant restaurant and is the source for watersports. A few of the privately owned villas, for rent in owners' absence, are on the shore; most are on the hillside, scattered on the fringes of the golf course that ranges over several acres. Villas range in size and style, according to the taste and needs of the owner. The golf course is open only for Tryall residents during winter season; tennis courts are in good shape, with a resident pro in winter season. The viewful hotel rooms are in a wing off the main Great House building, on the hillside, where there's a pool, small shop, and lovely restaurant. All reflect a Jamaican-Georgian style. *Classic resort, villas.*

★★★ **Wyndham Rose Hall Beach and Country Club** • *about 15 minutes' drive from downtown MoBay* • benefits from the infusion of funds from Trammell Crow's Dallas-based Wyndham hotel chain. Built several years ago, as a member of the Inter-Continental group, the physical plant has always been sound, with a golf course ranging inland, plus tennis courts near a lovely beach and pool. Bedrooms have been redecorated; phone service and room service continue to be amazingly slow. Buffets are popular for breakfast and other meals, at the beach-level dining room. Facilities make the hotel popular for conventions and groups. The golf clubhouse has a country-club atmosphere. Horseback riding is available near the hotel; a car or taxi will be essential for island touring. *Resort hotel.*

★ **Wexford Court** • *on the eastern fringe of the commercial heart of MoBay, west of the airport and best beaches* • has grown to become a multi-story lodging with kichenettes in some rooms and modern furnishings in all. Widely respected for its *Front Porch* restaurant, the hotel is popular with West Indian and other businesspeople. Owner Godfrey Dyer is actively involved with Jamaica's tourism programs. *Hotel.*

HOUSEKEEPING HOLIDAYS in the Montego Bay area range from small apartment clusters, often around a central pool, to some of the elegant villas that are privately owned and for rent in owner's absence. There are several sources for villa listings. Among the best, because they're specialists with many years of experience, are **Selective Vacation Services** (154 Main St., Ocho Rios, Jamaica, W.I., T 809+974-5187, fax 809+774-2359) and **Villas and Apartments Abroad** (420 Madison Ave., New York, NY 10017, T 212+759-1025 or 800+433-3020; fax 212+755-8316). Their Jamaican listings include a number of shoreside properties in Montego Bay, Ocho Rios, and other areas, as well as some of the elegant villas in the hillsides. Other firms with Jamaican listings include **JAVA** (Jamaica Association of Villas and Apartments, 370 Lexington Ave., New York, NY 10017, T 212+986-4317), and **LaCure Villas** (11661 San Vincente Blvd., Los Angeles, CA 90049, T 800+387-2726), which specializes in deluxe properties with staff. Although these firms do carry some of the same properties, each has its own listings and services.

When you set up housekeeping in Jamaica, even if you have a maid and cook, as is the case with all villas, try the local food. It's best at the villas, where your cook can use spices, vegetables, and fruits in the ways she knows best. If there are special foods you like (or must have), bring them from home. Although it is possible to buy chicken, fish, and lobster in Jamaica, beef at the supermarkets cannot compare with what you know at home, and canned ham, tuna fish, and other favorite items are worth bringing.

In addition to the apartments that are available at some of the hotels, and the elegance of the luxury villas at *Half Moon, Tryall,* and *Round Hill,* the following offer housekeeping facilities:

Bayshore Townhouse Apartments • *at the Ironshore property on the inland side of the shore-rimming road* • cluster around a pool. Some apartments are rented long-term, and children are welcomed. Units are basic, and although cooks are available, most people do their own cooking. There's a minimarket for basics, but you'll find more stock at nearby supermarkets. A car is recommended, although the public bus runs along the shore road. *Apts.*

Jamaica Vacation Villas • *west of Montego Bay* • are what some of the homes in the hills at Ironshore are called. There are about 150 villas scattered around the Ironshore development. About 35 of them are in the rental pool. Each is different, furnished to the owner's taste. Some seemed to me to reflect how much of the time the house is rented. There is great variety; be specific about your needs. All have private pool plus maid/cook and gardener. *Villas.*

Ocean Pines Villas • *on the sea at Montego Freeport within walking distance of Seawinds Hotel* • are 2-bedroom units with 2 baths and attractive furnishings. The units are privately owned, for rent in owner's absence. Maid service is provided, but if you want a cook, request one in advance. Children are welcomed. All the action of Seawinds is available for villa guests, and the shopping center and cruise ship pier are nearby for additional diversions. *Apts.*

Upper Deck • *a hill-covering of apartments overlooking MoBay* • offers air-conditioned housekeeping basics with kitchenette. Some units seemed a bit down-at-the-heels when I surveyed for this edition and many of the 100-plus apartments are rented on long term. You'll need a car, and an ability to drive serpentine roads, for mobility. *Apts.*

The Palms • *located shoreside, on a small span of private beach, across the road from the Rose Hall and Half Moon golf courses* • is a cluster of 1- and 2-bedroom apartments. Built by John Rollins, who spirited and financed the restoration at Rose Hall Great House, the units have small, efficiency kitchens. The living room sets the stage for relaxed beach and poolside life. A few of the units are privately owned and rented long-term, but several are available for rent. Convenient to both Wyndham Rose Hall Beach Resort and the Half Moon Club, The Palms can provide a peaceful place for relaxed living. *Apts.*

The Tallyman • *in Westgate Hills, overlooking MoBay* • offers 2-bedroom condominium units for rent in owners' absence. The apartments have all modern conveniences, including full kitchen. There's a pool at the center of the luxury units and management provides a shuttle bus for the 5-minute ride down to Montego Bay for shopping and activities. If you want real independence, you'll need a car. "Summer special" prices have been a very good value. The residential feeling can be ideal for those who know and love Jamaica and who want a place in the sun. *Apts.*

THE INN WAY in Montego Bay can be enjoyed at a couple of places, but you'll have to make some effort to bond with the staff to get the friendliest welcome. Making money seems to take precedence over hospitality for most of the area's hotel owners. Three worth noting are:

★ **Coral Cliff** • *at the western end of MoBay's resort-trimmed shore road* • continues to offer pleasant rooms in various shapes and sizes, an attractive breeze-swept dining veranda, and traditional Jamaican atmosphere. The dining area of the main house, with its fan-punctuated ceiling and sea-and-surroundings view, makes this place one of my MoBay touchstones. There's a small pool on the hillside; the beach is a short walk to the west, across the road. *Marguerites* restaurant is also across the road. Coral Cliff continues to offer good value to pleased patrons. *Inn.*

Richmond Hill • *perches on a hilltop* • with a magnificent view over all the hubbub and confusion of the city to the sea beyond. Surroundings are special, with an elegant former home atmosphere at the main house, where terrace dining wraps around two sides of the pool (opening to the view). Rooms are in several strands, with some down the hillside "under" the pool's platform; all are neatly furnished, with air-conditioning units if the breeze doesn't blow through the louvers enough to keep you cool. A rental car will give you maximum mobility, but you can easily take a taxi into the city that stretches out below, to the beaches, and to some of the other restaurants (there's good seafood served right here with romantic surroundings). *Small hotel.*

Toby Inn • *across the road from the Jack Tar Village and near Sandals Carlyle* • has rooms in several buildings surrounding a tree-punctuated lawn. Facilities include pool and restaurant, but all looked down-at-the-heels when I checked for this edition. The place has potential, but check on the current status before booking. *Small hotel.*

LOW-COST LODGING: Although some of the all-inclusive hotels can figure to good value, if you are a very active person and want to make full use of facilities (and food), some of the smaller and older properties have lower daily rates. For very inexpensive guest houses and rooms-for-rent, check with the MoBay Tourist Office at Doctor's Cave Beach on arrival. Here are a few suggestions for less expensive places in the MoBay area:

Belvedere • *near Walter Fletcher Beach* • has neatly attractive, simply furnished rooms in an L-shaped, 3-story modern building. There's a pool on premises, and a beach and tennis courts within easy walking distance.

Blue Harbour • *in the hills, above the shore activity* • offers simple surroundings, sometimes a clublike atmosphere (if the regulars are there when you are), and modest rates for 22 rooms.

Buccaneer Inn • *on the spur road shared with Sandal's Carlyle Beach and SeaGarden Beach Resort* • is a relatively new pool-punctuated, 48-room building. This is a laid-back place popular with travelers who like casual surroundings within easy footfall of the town's resort action.

Chalet Caribe Hotel • *about 10 minutes' drive west of Montego Bay city* • concentrates on scuba diving, and its location near one of Montego Bay's most spectacular reefs assures interesting underwater sights. With rooms that range from regular hotel style to studio and 1-bedroom apartments, the hotel gives its guests sea-oriented surroundings. There's entertainment some evenings when house count warrants, but the property can seem isolated if you don't have a car for mobility. Inquire about the special scuba program.

Ocean View Guest House • *on the Sunset Blvd., the upper road in MoBay* • has a dozen rooms, rented at modest prices. This is not your usual vacation retreat, but management does provide free transportation to the airport.

★ **Royal Court** • *on the hillside above the shore road* • is a pleasant small spot with a Jamaican home-style feeling. The white stucco building has grown around the pool, giving guests in the rooms, studio apartments, and suites a congenial atmosphere above the hubbub of MoBay's beachside. The floor to ceiling window wall that borders the dining room affords protection from breezes, but allows for a spectacular view while enjoying the Jamaican specialties served for guests. *The Grotto* is the on-premises evening spot, with music and entertainment some evenings.

Winged Victory • *on the hillside road in MoBay* • gives guests in some of its basic rooms a view over the rooftops of Montego Bay's hotel area and the sea beyond. Roma Chin Sue, the enthusiastic managing director, is not always on premises, and staff, when she's not, are willing to help when asked. The *Calabash* restaurant and a pool are on-premise; the beach is down the hill.

RESTAURANTS in the Montego Bay area are changing as the hospitality industry revives and more visitors are searching for good places to dine. Surveys for this edition proved that, when the food and atmosphere are worth noting (and that's not always the case), the restaurant is expensive. Jamaican wine, made from essence, is bottled under the brand name *Rosemont*. Although wine connoisseurs will scoff, it appears on most wine lists and is reasonably priced; the cost of imported wines is staggering (due to heavy duties). Only a few places have much of a wine list. Jamaican *Red Stripe* beer is one of the Caribbean's best; it's exported to other islands, but it's made here. Some, but by no means all, hotel dining rooms have good food.

AUTHOR'S AWARDS

My top choice for MoBay is the *Sugar Mill* at Half Moon's Golf Club for imaginative, attractive presentation of local produce. Coral Cliffs dining room offers the best value.

Calabash • *on Queen's Drive a few paces from the Diplomat restaurant* • specializes in seafood and Jamaican recipes, accompanied by background music on some evenings. A bright blue awning marks the entrance; about $25 per person will permit carefree dining.

The Diplomat • *in a mansion on Queen's Drive* • is hard to beat for all-time elegance insofar as surroundings are concerned. Ralph Chapman's home has been turned into a seafood and steak place, where surroundings were more elegant than the fare I sampled.

Front Porch • *at the Wexford Hotel on the city side of the hotel area of Montego Bay* • has spruced up and taken on glorified coffee shop overtones with hotel improvements and expansion. There's always some chicken dish, and usually the fish is excellent. Recommended for Jamaican food.

Gloucester House • *at the hotel complex amid the hubbub of MoBay's resort area* • creates a pub atmosphere in one air-conditioned area and a fancier style in the "Great House" and its terrace. Seafood is the specialty (along with satellite TV).

Gold Unicorn • *on Queen's Drive, MoBay's upper road* • is in a building intended to be a private residence. Although the limited menu offered slightly uneven selections (Hawaiian pork chops and U.S. grilled sirloin among them), the Jamaican Pepperpot (soup) and the conch fritters and the Gold Unicorn rum pudding were first rate. Better for view than for culinary expertise, this place is worth trying.

★★ **Marguerite's** • *across from Coral Cliff and within a stroll on any of the cluster of MoBay hotels* • is wedged onto a nub of shore. Some tables give diners a sea view. Food is sometimes more pretentious than tasty and the tab of about $40 per person may seem steep. The setting can be romantic (when company is).

★ **Pelican** • *on the shorefront drive* • is an air-conditioned restaurant that's not too far from Doctor's Cave Beach (but farther than you might want to walk at nighttime). Primarily of interest to residents, Pelican's offerings include sandwiches and snacks (including breakfast) as well as more elaborate offerings at evening hours. Check the menu before settling in to be sure it's your kind of place.

Round Hill • *east of Montego Bay's town* • has a beach cove dining room that is special. Be sure to telephone for a reservation if you hope to dine here. Spaces are usually reserved for resident guests, and there are times when outsiders are not welcomed. The surroundings have been better than the food when I've visited, but you may have better luck—and it's worth the experience.

Siam Restaurant and Jazz Club • *on the hillside, in a residential area above MoBay's shore* • has an exceptional menu, with well-prepared, attractively served Thai specialties. The flavorful light sauces and kabob presentation make the most of the basic chicken and fish offerings. Soups are also special.

Check for dates and times for the jazz performances, when this spot is at its best. Otherwise, evenings are quiet (and breeze-swept).

Tryall's Great House • *on the hillside overlooking the golf course, villas, and the distant shore* • has a picture-perfect setting, especially during lunchtime, when light meals are served near the pool and at the beach. (Because it's a distance from most hotels, dining here only makes sense if you're staying here or want an elegant place to stop for lunch when you have a rental car.)

★★★★ **Sugar Mill Restaurant** • *at the edge of Half Moon's golf course* • is for special occasions. The prize-winning recipes are justly praised. My ackee tart appetizer was memorable, and food presentation and setting add much to the meal, which features Jamaican produce in innovative recipes. Dinners are served by candlelight facsimile on the patio, under the trees. Note the waterwheel to the right as you enter. It's impressive, even when it is not turning.

Town House • *16 Church Street across from the Parish Church, in the heart of "old" Montego Bay* • was built in 1765, but the menu is strictly today. This place is attractive, with a nice patio for cocktail time and air-conditioned dining within the faux-Georgian interior. I've found the Jamaican (and very rich) lobster excellent, but there are steaks, spareribs, and other familiar U.S. fare offered as well as some local fish (usually fresh). Count on paying the equivalent of $40 per person for a feast; less for entree only.

On the days when you're touring toward Ocho Rios, plan for a luncheon or dinner stop at **Glistening Waters,** at Falmouth, if you like lobster and other fresh seafood in casual surroundings. West of Runaway Bay, **Aunt Mary's Blue Bird Restaurant** is a memorable roadside place by the sea that serves good lobster.

NATURAL SURROUNDINGS come in two versions in the busy MoBay area. The first is those places that are neatly packaged for tourism promotion, and most of those are mentioned below when we look at "Places Worth Finding." The real nature can be found by those willing to head into the hinterlands to walk and hike. A good guide is essential for an expedition into the karst country and other areas in MoBay's nearby mountains, not only because Jamaicans know the paths, lore, and local contacts better than outsiders, but also because these areas are prime *ganja* (marijuana) growing areas and many "farmers" aren't enthusiastic about outsiders' intrusions. Your best source for reliable and approved guides is the Jamaican Tourist Board and/or your hotel's manager. Birders should make arrangements to get to **Rockland Bird Sanctuary** (see below), where some of Jamaica's 250-plus species can be viewed at feeding time, from 3:30 to 5:30 p.m.

In addition to the landscape, offshore areas are being recognized by scuba divers. Some interesting reefs are near the north shore, both east and west of MoBay, but the best diving is in the caves and overhangs that are farther out. West of the city, Mariner's Reef is one favored area, and the Laughing Waters Lagoon is enjoyed by divers who head east.

PLACES WORTH FINDING around Montego Bay have been found by hundreds before you. Although the magic of "discovery" may have vanished with increasing tourism that has totally changed this once small resort on the north shore, there is comfort in knowing that many of the tourist attractions are regularly monitored by, and sometimes affiliated with, the Jamaica Tourist Board. The programmed pleasures you follow are part of the plan to show you Jamaica's "typical" experiences.

Appleton Express Train, following a route from Montego Bay almost 40 miles into the mountains, is a day's outing in comfortable train cars, with commentary and reggae lessons en route. Popular with groups, the journey is offered through the activities' desks at most hotels. Included is a tour of the Appleton rum factory, with a talk about how rum is made and a taste test.

Mountain Valley Rafting at Lethe, operated by *Great River Rafting and Plantation Tour Ltd.* (3 Strand St., Box 23, Montego Bay, T 809+952–0527) is a daytime excursion that includes an hour ashore for donkey rides and relaxation, while the **Evening on the Great River** is a gala party, available several nights a week in winter season (usually Tues.–Thurs.). Your price of about $30 includes transportation from your hotel to the river at shoreside, west of the town of MoBay. The ride includes paddling in a dugout canoe (worth a lot of laughs) upstream to the clearing where you walk through the "jungle" to reach your Jamaican feast with lively, colorful entertainment. As with the White River trip offered for guests in Ocho Rios, these trips are most fun if you've gathered a group at your home-base hotel, but if you're on your own go along anyway because you will be with sunburned vacationers from other hotels and introductions are easy when you're all at sea.

Cornwall Beach was created several years ago as a JTB project to accommodate the crowds that were smothering the nearby small patch of sand, Doctor's Cave Beach, which had given Montego Bay its fame as a beachside resort in the early 1950s. Cornwall is action-packed and lively, known as a place to meet-and-greet among the tourists who clog the streets of MoBay and the locals who want to be among them. It's not my favorite beach.

Maroon Country is for adventuresome, empathetic travelers. This mountain cockpit country is definitely off the beaten path made around the coastline by the usual tourist resorts. If you drive about 2 hours up into the hinterland you will reach a remote area where the first freed slaves, the Jamaican Maroons, created their own community and kept it secure with a guerilla war against the British in the 19th century. The area is unique, with its hilly terrain and many sinkholes and caves. The best way for first-time travelers to visit the Maroon country is to take an all-day bus tour. Contact 952–7780 for details.

Miss Lisa Salmon's **Rockland's Bird Sanctuary,** about 4 miles up the coast toward Anchovy, is a special pursuit for those who are intrigued by our feathered friends. Miss Salmon settled into her hillside retreat in 1952. Her original reason was to paint, but she found that the birds who were her tenants demanded more than full time. Her feeders drew grass quits, doves, and finches who told their friends about the new tourist resort for the birds. Visitors are invited to come, quietly, to observe and feed the birds—in the afternoon from 3:30 p.m. until just before sundown. If you want to make a special pilgrimage, call Miss Salmon to set a convenient time.

Great Houses in the MoBay orbit include Greenwood, Rose Hall, Good Hope, and Sign. These elegant former homes of plantation owners vary in style and furnishings, but all are fascinating for inveterate house tourers. **Sign Great House,** in the hills east of MoBay, is the simplest, with an overgrown cottage quality. It has been a hotel, but its status is uncertain at press time. **Greenwood,** about 15 miles east of MoBay and 7 miles west of Falmouth, was the private home of Richard Barrett between 1780 and 1800, and although much is made of the possibility that relatives of Elizabeth Barrett Browning may have visited here, this doesn't make any difference in your appreciation. The place is fascinating, with authentic furnishings, a collection of 18th-century musical instruments, and the island legends that surround the property. Inquire about visiting hours.

Good Hope Estate in the hills behind Falmouth, is closed to the public at press time, but ask when you're in the country. The house has spectacular lawns and gardens in their natural state. The estate was started by Thomas William, Jr., in 1755, and legends are rife (and carefully told by your guide). Among the buildings on the estate are the icehouse, the estate offices, the counting house, and the sugar works. Elegant Oriental rugs cover the wood floors, and mahogany furniture punctuates all rooms. The lower floor is said to have been a slaves' prison. The grounds are best seen on horseback, which can be arranged by appointment.

Rose Hall Great House, set inland from the resorts of Half Moon and Rose Hall Intercontinental, was restored to look better than it probably ever did. The fortunes and leisure time of a former lieutenant governor of Delaware, John W. Rollins, and his wife brought this place back to life—to the dismay of some Jamaican friends of mine who remember playing around the ruins, terrified by the legends of Annie Palmer's ghost. The legends are now politely recited by the well-trained guides who take you through the property, pointing out historic highlights and giving you prices for the restoration. (Read *The White Witch of Rose Hall* and *Morgan's Daughter,* both by Herbert deLisser, to set the tone for this sight, and try to ignore all the Hollywood theatrics that have been added in the name of restoration.) If this is the only Great House within your touring orbit, make a stop here—but if you can get to some of the others, they seem to me to have more life. In addition to the Great House's two floors to tour, there's a comfortable bar/lounge area where you can wait for your tour to start or linger when it is finished.

"Up, Up and Buffet" is what Norma Hilton Stanley has tagged her balloon ride at the end of a tether. The Hilton family plantation has been opened up to people who want to spend $45 for a day that includes pick-up at your Montego Bay Hotel, breakfast, a Jamaican-style lunch that should include roast suckling pig, rum punch—and the balloon ride, navigated by an official FAA pilot. The balloon ride gives a special view of one of Jamaica's verdant valleys and some nearby mountains. You're invited to walk around the plantation grounds and to tour the house. *Hilton High Day Tour,* Box 313, Montego Bay, is the contact.

SPORTS for Montego Bay area include golf, tennis, squash, watersports, horseback riding—and ballooning (see above). Insofar as specifics are concerned:

Deep-sea fishing can be arranged on boats out of Montego Bay. Your hotel is the best source for the boats available at the time you visit. See "Port Antonio" section of this chapter if you're serious about deep-sea fishing.

Golf is available at several courses around Montego Bay. Half Moon and Wyndham Rose Hall Beach Resort both have clubs that are hubs for their courses. There's a course at Ironshore, but inquire about condition. Tryall, west of Montego Bay, also maintains a challenging course that covers the sloping lawns from its hilltop Great House to the shore. Inquire about regulations and costs for play.

Horseback riding can be arranged through *Double A* and *White Witch* stables, both near the Holiday Inn, Half Moon, and Wyndham Rose Hall hotels, as well as through the other resorts. *The Rocky Point Riding Stables* are at the entrance to Half Moon. There are interesting plantation rides at Prospect and Brimmer Hall, if you want to make the drive to Ocho Rios, and *Chukka Cove,* near Sandals Dunns River resort, west of Ocho Rios, has polo ponies and regular horses for riding and lessons. (See "Ocho Rios" section.)

Sailing, once a popular sport off Jamaican shores, languished in the late '70s. The SORC (Southern Ocean Racing Circuit) Miami-Montego Bay race was reinstituted in March '83, however, and annual yachting events are now a regular feature. Inquire about day charters at your hotel's activities desk.

Scuba diving is the major focus of the Chalet Caribe Hotel (see "Hotels" above) where the *Poseidon Nemrod Divers* make their headquarters. In addition, Half Moon Club has a professional scuba-diving operation, with resort courses offered as well as dives for experienced divers. The Sandals all-inclusive resorts include scuba lessons free in the program, as do Trelawny and Seawinds hotels, and there may be more scuba activity by the time you visit. Be sure to ask when you book, if scuba is important to you. Divers are beginning to focus on this area.

Squash is offered at Half Moon Golf, Squash, and Racquet Club, where there are 4 international courts, and at Sandals.

Tennis is available at most resort hotels, with the courts at Half Moon among the best in the area. Tennis is included free at Sandals, and there are also courts at Rose Hall, Round Hill, Tryall, the Jack Tar Village, and many other hotels. Inquire about special tennis weeks, sometimes available in summer season. **Windsurfing** or **boardsailing** is popular from resort hotels in the area.

TREASURES AND TRIFLES include straw baskets, wood carvings, tie-dyed fabrics made into clothing and by the yard, plus T-shirts of all shapes, sizes, and slogans. In addition, there are some good-quality crafts, instigated by "Things Jamaican," a government-assisted design and production project. Stuffed dolls can be a joy for at-home children; pottery figures of Jamaican market ladies, field workers, and other local people and colorful ceramic fruits and vegetables are attractive reminders of time spent in the country; and an increasing amount of spices, jellies, coffee, and other local produce is finding its way into gift baskets and attractive packaging.

AUTHOR'S OBSERVATION

When you see something you like, buy it. Although the tourist shops tend to take on a sameness, they do not carry identical merchandise. Be firm with the street salespeople. When you see them coming your way, say "no, thank you" even before they start talking, if you're not interested in buying. Once you start looking, you're fair game for a tenacious sales pitch. *Always* bargain on prices with street salespeople; they expect it. Be sure about whose dollars are being quoted (Jamaican or U.S.).

There are some good values, but the onus is on you to do your research so that you know that you have found one. **Swiss Stores** punctuate tourist towns, specializing in Tissot, Patek Philippe, Piaget, Rolex, Omega, and other watches, as well as an eye-popping assortment of other jewelry and luxury items. Peter Bangerter, the man in charge of the several shops, has an eye for merchandise that could keep you in hock for decades. The selection is superior, and some of his specials are worthy of the claims made for them. This is a place to survey on the day you arrive and shop in just before you leave—when you have had time to think carefully about what you really want.

Caribatik, a batik studio started by Muriel Chandler from Chicago sells its fabric by the yard and made into clothes. There's a shop near Doctor's Cave Beach, and the studio is about an hour's drive east along the north shore, on the shore at Falmouth. You can't miss it when you follow the north coast road toward Ocho Rios.

At the **MoBay airport,** there's a bookstore-magazine shop just before you go through immigration. Other shops in the departure lounge include the *Coffee Mill* with high-quality food, coffee, and other items made in Jamaica, sold at standard prices (no bargaining); *Duty Free Shop,* with a selection of cameras and camera equipment, plus watches and the usual; a liquor shop where the selections of imported brands is better than that of the local Jamaican products; and a couple of places with a few Jamaican craft items. Insofar as local spirits are concerned, *Appleton Rum* is Jamaica's best; investigate *Rumona,* the very special Jamaican liqueur. *Tia Maria* is the popular coffee liquer. Cigar smokers should try *Royal Jamaican.* (See also "Treasures and Trifles" for Ocho Rios and Negril.)

NEGRIL

Long before the northwestern coast hit its stride with action-packed resorts, the once small village of Negril had been savored as a hideaway for peace-loving vacationers, including the hippies of the 70s who liked the grass that grows around here. For many years, the village of Negril was offbeat, barefoot, and natural—known to only a few travelers who wanted a no-frills holiday. In the late 1970s, Hedonism II opened at the eastern end of the long beach; it was followed by other properties, most of them small, sprinkled at intervals along the coast. Today there are hundreds of places to stay—including resorts, hotels, cottages, cabins, and thatched huts. Some places are condominiums, for rent in owner's absence; others are the last word in modern resort style; several operate on Jamaica's "all-inclusive" style. But be prepared for a thriving resort area; most vestiges of the former village are long gone.

As a very general guide, most of the familiar style hotels are east of the village; most of the funkier spots are along the narrow road that stretches west.

AUTHOR'S OBSERVATION

Although drugs are illegal in Jamaica, they are so omnipresent in Negril that it is almost impossible to stroll the beach without having several salesmen offer you the current assortment. Even when you express no interest, the sales pitch continues. Although the salesfolk are pleasant, and do leave eventually when you are firm with your "No, thank you," I found the attention as annoying as sandflies at sunset. Be prepared to be solicited, and be smilingly firm with your reply. The approach is not dangerous, it's simply an annoying fact of Negril life.

ARRIVAL AND DEPARTURE in Negril are usually by car or minibus, after the two-hour drive along the coast, west from Montego Bay's airport. If you haven't made arrangements ahead of time, check with the Jamaica Tourist Board booth at the airport, and do some comparison shopping on prices, for seat-in-car transport. If you are more than one, talk with the taxi drivers. Some will give a good price, if they want the business. *Trans Jamaican Airways* flies between MoBay and Negril, if small plane flying appeals to you. It's not necessarily faster, but the view is nice.

HOTELS/RESORTS IN NEGRIL grow faster than the marijuana in the hillsides. There's a new crop each season. Some are complete resorts, in the well-known island style; others are clusters of cottages; and some are very simple, rustic, laid-back places. The beach stretches east from the heart of town for several miles in an almost unbroken strand of white sand. Most of the higher-priced hotels and apartments are along that strand, forced to the beach by the shore-rimming road. West from the center of town, cottages and other small spots are cheek-by-jowl on the rocky shore and on the inland side of the narrow, twisting road.

As mentioned elsewhere, there's a bewildering list of extras tacked onto hotel bills, except at the all-inclusive places. Even there, you should ask in advance to find out exactly what is included. Many places add a "service charge"; something extra is warranted only when you have special attention. At *Grand Lido, Sandals, Swept Away,* and *Hedonism II,* you can count on a quality inclusive place; some of the others don't match the faclities at those places, although some come close to meeting the prices.

AUTHOR'S AWARDS

Grand Lido deserves mention for its unabashed pretense, with lavish decor in the central reception and restaurant area; *Sandals Negril* excels with its friendly, almost cozy, beachside atmosphere; and *Swept Away* has lovely sea-view bedrooms amid tennis and watersports facilities.

★★★★ **Grand Lido** • *the easternmost of Negril's hotels, on its own long beach* • has a pretentious pillared-and-marble lobby entrance that seems like a stage set. Officially opened in February 1990, the property is another in John Issa's SuperClub family. (He's the man who opened Jamaica's first all-inclusive hotel, *Couples,* east of Ocho Rios, in 1978, and brought big resorts to Negril, with *Hedonism II,* about that time.) No expense was spared on the main building and the grounds. The breeze-swept reception area is coated with Jamaican marble. The plan is to provide "power" people with ultimate luxury at an inclusive price. Most of the small but pleasant bedrooms are in 2-story buildings along Bloody Bay beach, between the main building and the tennis courts. Another group cup the small cove and pool that have been set aside for nudists. Three snack-drink-hot tub hubs are located on the grounds; all serve food and drink whenever you want it. A private yacht is available for guest use; classical music and other events are part of the activities program. Grand Lido aspires to become the replenishing place for the rich and powerful. *Inclusive resort.*

★ **Hedonism II** • *at the east end of the long beach* • was Negril's first inclusive hotel, appealing to the young, in spirit and in fact, with round-the-clock action. The mix includes drinking contests, toga parties, volleyball games, and constant daytime sports such as tennis, a fitness room, and watersports. Rooms in the several 2-story buildings are colorful, with basic furnishings, air-conditioning, private bath, and a roommate. (You can bring your own or be assigned one of the same sex.) The reception and activities area, including the exercise room and shops, is at the top of the slope, near the tennis courts and pool. The beach, an easy stroll down the hill, has an area for nude bathing and a small patch for bathing-suited folk. It was showing signs of overuse when I checked for this edition. Meals are often buffet and family-style. This Super-Club reminds me of a college fraternity party. (Other SuperClubs are *Grand Lido, Couples, Jamaica-Jamaica,* and *Boscobel Beach.*) *Inclusive resort.*

Negril Inn • *on the long white-sand beach* • operates on an all-inclusive plan, with daily rates that allow for transfers from MoBay's airport; a room with sea-viewing balcony or patio (depending on your level in the white stucco 2-story units); all meals, drinks, and cigarettes; watersports facilities, bicycles, and tennis and gym facilities. Multi-night packages are available; the plan is to give you carefree luxury at a prepaid cost. *Inclusive hotel.*

★ **Paradise View** • *on the long beach, next to Foote Prints* • is a pleasant 2-story cluster of small rooms with louvered windows and sliding glass doors.

The emphasis is on the beach and beach-style living. Watersports are a focus; the dining room is seaside. *Small hotel.*

★★★ **Poinciana Beach Hotel** • *on Negril's long beach* • offers both bedrooms and housekeeping units, most of them with sea views. The best rooms are in the newest buildings, officially opened in February 1990. Watersports are offered at the beach; the restaurant has made a name for itself by providing good Jamaican food. There's a pleasantly friendly atmosphere at this place, which both European and North American guests seem to enjoy. *Hotel.*

★★★★ **Sandals Negril at Coconut Cove** • *west of Hedonism II, on the long beach* • opened with fanfare in December '89. The inclusive resort incorporates two former hotels, the attractive Coconut Cove and neighboring Sundowner, with a chunk of new rooms built between them. The loft suites are split-level units, with sea view from the patio; deluxe beachfront rooms are in the 2-story block that had been Sundowner. The gourmet restaurant is on the Sundowner patio, incorporating part of its former lobby. Count on a comprehensive activities plan, and exchange privileges with Sandals' resorts in MoBay and Ocho Rios (you'll pay extra for transportation only). A "playmaker" is in charge of assuring that you have a carefree vacation. Jacuzzis, a sauna, racquetball court, tennis courts, pool, and a full range of watersports assure fun-filled days. The disco and evening entertainment keep things lively after nightfall. If a couples-only inclusive place is what you're looking for, this place provides that—on Jamaica's best beach. *Inclusive resort.*

★★★ **Swept Away** • *on the long beach of Negril* • is a welcome newcomer, planned for couples who want easy access to tennis, squash, and racquetball courts as well as health club facilities, a pool, and to watersports equipment such as windsurfers, small sail boats, and waterskiing boats. The attractive 2-story buildings that hold the 130 suites are angled to give many rooms a sea view. All rooms have either patio or porch, and all modern comforts. The beachside restaurant serves plenty of Jamaican fruits and vegetables, as well as other healthy food (and not-so-healthy pizzas). An alternative to action-packed places, this one of Jamaica's inclusive properties features sports and the good life. The beach is superb; the furnishings elegant. *Inclusive resort.*

Tree House • *on the beach, east of town* • is a combination of hotel rooms and self-catering units, most in rondavels, with the huge tree-house-style reception, dining, and drinking building the focal point for action and entertainment. Some of the cottages have a very rustic feeling, with basics but not many flourishes. The rooms are also basic, with private (but small) bathroom. A good location for watersports, beach strolls, and neighboring lodgings for dining options. *Hotel, apts.*

★★ **T-Water Beach Hotel** • *on the east side of the town, at the beach* • is a large complex with a split personality, having grown from a few casual cottages to a full-fledged hotel devoted to sea-and-beach living. Facilities include a pool, an attractive dining room, and a room for games and slot machines.

Traditional Jamaican recipes are featured in the restaurant. Scuba and other watersports are offered nearby along with boardsailing and waterskiing. *Hotels.*

HOUSEKEEPING HOLIDAYS IN NEGRIL range from very simple, camplike facilities to comfortable apartments and cottages. Be sure to make specific inquiries, depending on your own vacation preferences, or—better yet—make a reservation at a hotel for a night or two, to look around and see for yourself. Some places are popular with folks who enjoy ganja; others are more conservative. There are no elegant villas similar to those you can find in the Montego Bay environs and in Ocho Rios, but many choices. **Villas and Apartments Abroad** (420 Madison Ave., New York, NY 10022, T 212+759−1025) has Negril listings.

In addition to a well-stocked Jamaican supermarket, fresh fruits, vegetables, and fish are sold at the open-air market and at stalls and shops around town.

Banana Shout Cottages • *on the rocks, west of town* • are a half-dozen single-story units, the best three of which are perched where rocks shear to the sea. Cement steps make it possible to walk down the rockface into the sea. Rooms have ceiling fans and a cozy, camplike atmosphere.

Country Cottages • *on the long beach* • are simple lodgings with basic comforts, offered at a reasonable price. Good for very casual seaside living. The beach restaurant serves Jamaican food, including jerk pork and chicken.

Crystal Waters • *a Country Cottage neighbor, on the beach* • has few self-catering units, with basics but not many flourishes. The price is modest, management is helpful, and the place appeals to young travelers—and the young at heart. *Cottages.*

Drumville Cove • *near the west point's lighthouse* • is a collection of personalized cottages, with a variety of offerings, ranging from basic to well-furnished homes. There's a fresh-water pool. *Cottages.*

Native Son Villa • *on the beach, near Foote Prints Hotel* • is a group of buildings planned by Jamaican Wesley Burton and his wife, Sarah. The first villa has 3 bedrooms, each with air-conditioning and ceiling fans. A housekeeper is included with the rental, for one week or longer. *Apts.*

Negril Beach Condos • *just east of the village, at the western end of the long beach* • began as Negril Beach Club, but adapted to condos as a cash-flow measure a few years ago. Most units are Jamaican-owned; many are for rent by owners. The 2- and 3-story basic buildings have standard air-conditioned rooms with overhead fan, modern bathroom, and sliding glass doors to the patio. There are some standard hotel rooms, but studios and the 1- and 2-bedroom apartments have full kitchen facilities. There's a pool next to the beach; a restaurant and bar that's lively when the house guests are; and tennis courts on the premises. Topless sunbathing is part of the property's style. *Apts.*

Summerset Village • *on the rocks west of the town* • is an assortment of tree houses, thatch cottages, and basic bungalows with a relaxed vacation atmosphere. There's a freshwater pool for on-the-spot dunking, and easy access to the sea. The beach requires more of a journey. All rooms have kitchenette and are cooled by ceiling fans. *Bungalows.*

Villas Negril • *on a hillside above the supermarket shopping complex* • have a Mediterranean appearance, with tile roofs and white stucco walls. The many 2-story buildings are cheek-by-jowl on the hillside; maintenance has slipped some in recent years—and the villas showed signs of wear when I checked for this edition. The on-premise pool and tennis courts are social hubs. The restaurant and bar area are also popular for renters. Okay if you want a basic housekeeping apartment slightly removed from the shoreline activity. *Apts.*

Others worth investigating are **Negril Sands, SunQuest Cottages** and **Firefly,** on the town side of Crystal Waters, not far from Charela hotel; and **Caribella Cottages,** near Firefly. On the inland side of the shore-rimming road, three neighbors with comfortable cottages are **Moonrise Villas, White Sands Villas** (with studios and some cottages on the beach in addition to the newer units on the inland side), and **Villa Mora Cottages.**

THE INN WAY in Negril includes both small hotels and some places that provide rooms with kitchenettes. Here are a few places where management seems to care about providing Jamaican hospitality.

★★ **Charela Inn** • *beachside, about 30 minutes' stroll or 5 minutes' drive along the beach east of town* • opened as a Spanish-style home turned inn, with some rooms upstairs, over a dining area, and others on the ground floor, stretching back from the beach. Expansion planted 2-story room-filled units near the parking area in 1989. All rooms are within a few steps of the beach. All have private bath; some rooms are large; most are air-conditioned. The restaurant is popular for its alfresco setting and Jamaican additions to what seemed to be a mostly vegetarian menu when I sampled. Beachside lunches are popular. *Hotel.*

★ **Foote Prints** • *on the beach* • is a family venture that started with one building, and now has three with several rooms in each. Bedrooms have standard furnishings, with ceiling fans and/or air conditioning. Second floor rooms have the best view; some have sea view. The beachside restaurant serves basics. Comfortably convenient, midway on the strand, a room here puts most activities within an easy beach stroll. *Small hotel.*

LOW-COST LODGING: There are many *very* inexpensive, slightly seedy rooms-for-rent. My suggestion for choosing one is to book a hotel room for a night or two, and look around to pick out something suitable for yourself. Many of the places listed under "Housekeeping Holidays" figure to low cost when the apartment charge is shared with several others. Some places with attractive surroundings and modest cost are listed below.

Mahogany Inn • *not far from Negril, along the long beach* • is a small spot, with motel-style rooms, staggered back from the beach so that most have easy sand-and-sea access. Bedrooms have ceiling fans—and carpeting (which is difficult to keep tidy). The dining room, on the second story of the reception area, has a nice sea view.

Negril Cabins • *near Bloody Bay, on the inland side of the road* • are rustic, with an atmosphere expected in a woodsy camp. Louvered shutters allow for maximum breeze; furnishings are wood, simple, and nice. Jamaican food is the restaurant's specialty.

Negril Gardens • *along the beach, east of the village* • is a cluster of attractive rooms, with a pool near the beach and lovely planting around the grounds. Bedrooms are comfortable, air-conditioned, and neatly furnished, with scatter rugs on the floor. There's good restaurant, and a schedule of activities such as volleyball and watersports when guests show an interest.

Ocean Edge Resort Hotel • *on the cliffs, west of the village* • has less than 20 rooms and cottages, each within sea sounds and with a spectacular sea view. Seafood is the restaurant's specialty. There's a sundeck near the Jacuzzi for sun-and-pool; watersports are offered nearby.

Rock Cliff Hotel • *on the rocks, west of the village* • has comfortable, carpeted rooms and a lovely kidney-shaped pool. Most bedrooms are in 2-story blocks around the pool, with a view from the patio. A conical roof caps the breeze-swept dining area, where seafood is a specialty. The *Cliff Bar* perches seaside, for spectacular sunset viewing.

Hotel Samsara • *on the rocks on the west end* • puts the bedrooms in individual cottages that are reminiscent of tree houses; they're upstairs. There's a swimming pool in the rocks, with ladder steps down to the sea. Satellite TV is a touted feature of the *Jah Beer Garden;* atmosphere is casual and *very* laid back.

RESTAURANTS IN NEGRIL: There are dozens of places to eat. Hotel dining rooms—most of them open to the breezes—are the dressiest of the lot, but even at the hotels men seldom wear jacket (never tie), and women wear what they please. Most places are very casual, offering a range from jerk pork and chicken (which is barbecued Jamaican style) to full-course meals.

Negril nests to try for meals are **PeeWee's,** a small spot (a couple of tables under a shed) on the inland side south of the town; the **Banana Spout** (also casual); and certainly **Rick's,** which draws all the visitors and some long-time residents in Negril at sunset time. Perched on an enviable west-facing promontory, splashed with the sea, very casual Rick's is open for lunch and dinner, at least at high winter season. Food is far from gourmet-style. It's snacks, sandwiches, and fried. Others worth checking are **Cafe au Lait, Erica's, The Yacht Club,** and **Chicken Lavish,** but don't count on finding much gourmet cooking.

NATURAL SURROUNDINGS, in addition to those in the sea, are highlighted at the **Great Morass,** a swampy area that is a nature preserve. It's reasonably good for birding, but most people heading to Negril are interested in more active pursuits, so it may be difficult to find someone knowledgeable about the flora and fauna. Check with the tourist board.

Insofar as underwater sights are concerned, the rocky west end of town has many good snorkeling areas, especially since the water is usually calm, and therefore very clear. Sponges and sea fans can be spectacular at many of the overhangs, and the caves and ledges are popular with divers. Whaler's Reef and Mariner's Reef are two of several noted dive sites. Qualified dive masters have scuba centers.

PLACES WORTH FINDING are in the town of *Savannah-la-Mar,* heading west and south, and the sights mentioned for Montego Bay, a couple of hours' drive east along the north coast. There are few organized "tourist attractions" in the Negril area, where most of the activity is sea-and-sun oriented. Savannah-La-Mar is relatively untouched by tourists, and the countryside you'll pass through is some of Jamaica's most beautiful. This is an area little known to most, but overlaid with fields of cane and other crops.

SPORTS in Negril are mostly sea-centered. *Grand Lido, Hedonism II,* and *Sandals* offer everything, including *Nautilus* equipment for exercising. *Swept Away* has the area's most comprehensive sports focus. In addition to the expected **yacht sailing, boardsailing, scuba diving** (with lessons, if you want them), and other **watersports,** there's **horseback riding** and **tennis** at the resorts. (Only golf is lacking at this end of the island.)

The *Negril Scuba Centre* has its headquarters at the Negril Beach Condos. *Neptune Water Sports* operates from Negril Gardens. *Blue Whale Divers* is next to Charela and *Rays Water Sports* is at Poinciana. Most beach hotels and apartments have access to the full range of watersports, including scuba lessons and diving excursions for proficient divers. Along the beach that usually lines the coast from *Hedonism II* past *Sandals* to town (except when sea-action has temporarily taken it away), there are individual entrepreneurs who offer sailing and other watersports. Bargain, and enjoy—but don't expect equipment to be in top-notch shape.

TREASURES AND TRIFLES in Negril are legion. Selection varies between well-made clever items and outright junk. You can buy both from the salespeople who set up their stalls near the beaches and in the village of Negril. You'll find a surfeit of carved wood heads, bowls, plates, and platters, plus plenty of woven baskets—with and without the name of the village woven in colored raffia. Flour-sack shirts and skirts have been "the rage" of recent seasons, with rapidly rising prices—and local grass (*ganja*) is surreptitiously sold along the beach, in town, and almost everywhere else. You don't even have to look eager to be approached. Buying is illegal here; but a proposal a few years ago to make 2 ounces of ganja legal drew laughs from those in the know. (I suspect that ganja is the most lucrative local product offered for sale in Negril.)

Hedonism II shops have reggae records, better quality (and higher priced) woodwork and baskets, plus some resort wear made in Jamaica, and stacks and stacks of T-shirts, with the marijuana leaf "Weed of Wisdom" or "Ganja University" being top sellers.

The local supermarket is the place to buy Jamaica's *Pick-a-Peppa* sauce (which is such a popular export that it's often scarce "at home"), local jams and jellies (good gifts for the homefolks), Jamaican coloring books (for young children), and *Appleton* or another Jamaican rum, which will cost much less than the per drink price at any of the hotel bars.

OCHO RIOS

This thriving community is many things to many people. Vacationers know it best for the hotels, each with its own personality, and the restaurants, shops, and other entertainment options. Residents, those who live in the elegant homes in the hills, live a life apart from the visitors, even though their community is supported by funds left by vacationers.

AUTHOR'S OBSERVATION

It's with great regret that I admit that I think Ocho Rios looks trashy and cluttered. Unbridled building in the past couple of years has turned the main road through town into a gnarled mess of traffic, both pedestrian and car-bus-truck. I'm reluctant to think about possible pollution to the seashore, now that "every" inch has been covered with some kind of a resort. There are few traditions left; this place has capitulated to tourism.

Ocho Rios was not named, as many commonly suppose, for eight rivers. There are many rivers flowing to the shore in the area of the town but not eight. *Las Chorreras,* Spanish for the waterfalls, is the earliest town, the one that Don Ysassi, the last Spanish governor, made his headquarters, just before he and his men fled from the shores at Runaway Bay (named for their hasty departure) for more secure settlements at Cuba. The town was spelled Chereiras by the English in records of 1744, and Cherreras by 1800 when a fort was built for protection from invasions on the north shore. By 1841, the almanac lists the town as Ocho Rios and comments that "It is an old harbour sheltered to windward and affords anchorage to vessels of thy burthen."

By 1886 "The people here complained of want of employment. Some go sixteen miles to get work on sugar estates at St. Mary's. A few years ago it would have been described as the most advanced in the intelligence and prosperity of its population. But it has suffered perhaps more than any other from the drought and also from the diminished value of its staple pimento." Today the town has stretched from its once small hub to be a vacation town of note, and a cruise ship port.

ARRIVAL AND DEPARTURE IN OCHO RIOS are by **car** or **minibus**, usually from Montego Bay airport, but give some thought to a Kingston departure (about a two-hour drive through the mid-island mountains), allowing a few hours for Devon House, the National Gallery, Port Royal, and lunch at Morgans Harbour before an afternoon flight. You'll have to make special arrangements with a taxi driver unless you've taken a rental car, and plan to return it at the Kingston airport. The almost two-hour ride along the north coast from Montego Bay can be pretty, if you're not overwhelmed by the heat from being packed into a small jitney bus. If you have a voucher from your travel agent for transportation, be prepared to wait—interminably—at the airport for your bus driver to decide to leave for the ride east. Cost for a seat in a car is about U.S.$20. Taxis are available, and charge J$392 or more for the journey.

Air arrival is possible at the small airstrip at Boscobel, which is served by *Trans Jamaican Airways,* but Boscobel is on the eastern side of Ocho Rios, and flying will probably take longer, with ground waiting time and taxi to your hotel, even though the flight is short (and interesting).

TOURING TIPS for the Ocho Rios area include shopping around for rental cars, if price matters. There are almost a dozen **car rental** agencies and most hotels have some link with one or more of them. *Sunshine* (T 974–2980) is in town with an office, also, in Montego Bay (T 952–4218). *Martins Jamaica* (T 974–2594) is the local representative for the *Dollar Rent a Car* system, and *Caribbean Car Rental* and several other firms also rent cars. *Watson's* shuttle bus links most of the Ocho Rios hotels with town on a schedule that is convenient for shoppers, and there are taxis at all hotels. *Tropical Tours* is one of the companies offering bus tours to places of interest around Ocho Rios and even to Montego Bay for the Governor's Coach and other sights in that area. All the big hotels have tour desks; you can sign on through those desks even when you are staying elsewhere.

HOTELS/RESORTS in Ocho Rios can be exceptional. Some offer visitors the Caribbean's most beautiful surroundings and the best service. Others give only the basics. Two lovely hotels—Plantation Inn and Jamaica—Inn are tucked into the trees along the shore, and there are places up in the hills or at the beach where you can enjoy a "home" of your own. Several all-inclusive resorts, where one fee covers "everything," follow the lead of Couples, Jamaica's first (and pacesetting) all-inclusive hotel.

The sheer volume of hotel rooms in the Ocho Rios area makes it difficult to distinguish one property from the other, not in looks (which are quite different) but in style, which depends on management, staff, and hospitality. The many new-and-big resorts operating on the inclusive plan make price a deciding factor in some cases, since each tries to outdo the other insofar as what they offer. A lot depends on who else is vacationing at the place when you're there.

AUTHOR'S AWARDS

Sandals Dunn's River is a top choice, because it is compact, with a friendly staff, on a lovely beach with a spectacular pool and plenty of action; *Couples* deserves special marks because it was the first of Jamaica's all-inclusives and keeps in shape; and *Jamaica Inn* is a favorite for its classic '50s style of Caribbean hotel. For small spots, I'll choose *Hibiscus Lodge*, for good value and pleasant surroundings "the inn way."

★★★ **Boscobel Beach Resort** • *on the shore, near the Boscobel airport, about a 10-minute drive east of Couples* • is one of John Issa's SuperClubs (which include *Couples, Jamaica-Jamaica, Grand Lido,* and *Hedonism II* in this country, and *Couples II* on St. Lucia). Using the core of the former Playboy Club, Boscobel Beach gutted the interior, added entertainment areas, rooms, and other facilities, and emerged for the winter of 1986–87 as an all-inclusive family resort. There are separate, but related, areas for small children, for teenagers, and for adults. While the whole family can play together, they need not stay together. Facilities are comprehensive but compact. Sports, craft classes, entertainment, and meals are offered at various places on the grounds. Ideal for families since each member can pursue his/her own activities, to convene at mealtimes. Convenient to the airport used by *Trans Jamaican Airways,* the hotel is linked by air and car (2½-hour drive) to Montego Bay. Check for package plans, some of which include Air Jamaica flights. *Inclusive resort.*

★★★★ **Couples** • *on its own beach, about a 15-minute drive east of the town of Ocho Rios* • was the trendsetter for Jamaica's all-inclusive hotels. Since January 20, 1978, when the former Tower Isle hotel emerged as the Couples resort, this place has led the pack of copy-cats that numbers over a dozen all-inclusive places, in this country alone. John Issa and his team created and perfected a popular pattern for Jamaican vacations. The resort strives to stay ahead of the rest—and to appeal to couples of all ages (not only honeymooners). Included in your multinight fee are rooms, all meals, drinks, entertainment, watersports including scuba, tennis, volleyball, and a fun-packed daily schedule that leads to a floor show each evening. Mealtimes are buffet except for dinner; food is plentiful, good, and Jamaican-grown whenever possible. Although it's easy to meet other guests, it's also possible to have some privacy. An offshore island is favored by sunbathers; the beach and pool are popular for bathing-suited folk. Some exercise equipment stands near the Jacuzzi. Trips to town are arranged by the hotel; taxis are available for other touring. Rooms are well maintained; they are regularly refurbished and in good condition. *Inclusive resort.*

★★★ **Enchanted Gardens** • *at Carinosa Gardens, in the hills above Ocho Rios* • is a cluster of elegantly furnished apartments, opened mid-'91 as an inclusive resort. Near Shaw Park Gardens, the grounds were opened as a nature reserve prior to building the villa-apartments, which are offered for private sale to be rented in owners' absence. Managed by Frank Rance, who left SuperClubs to open his own FDR resort at Runaway Bay and now has a management company, the property aims for upscale vacationers who want a one-price-pays-all place with deluxe aspects and who don't care about being away from the beach. (There's a pool.) The *Caribbean Newsletter* (page 9) will have further news, when warranted. Inquire about exact elements of the plan. *Inclusive resort.*

★★★★ **Jamaica Inn** • *at the western fringe of town* • is a traditional Jamaican-elegant hotel, with a strong band of regular visitors, thanks to the loyal staff who are the heart of this place. The steadying influence of the ownership team (the Morrows) keeps the inn on an even keel. The first 35 of the 50 rooms opened on this beach in the season of '51, but constant painting and polishing keeps them at top quality. The 2-story wings of rooms that stretch from the main reception area face onto the lawn and beach. Rooms are comfortable, colorful, neat, and pleasant with a balcony or terrace for reading, snoozing, sipping, or entertaining some of your fellow guests. The lounge area, to the left as you walk in, passing the check-in desk, has the cozy feeling of a country home, with comfortable couches, puzzles for playing, and backgammon board. There are facilities for tennis, Sunfish and snorkel gear at the beach, and entertainment most evenings in winter (when guests put on their best finery). Dinner by candlelight on the terrace, and a rum punch, brought to you at your bidding as you bask in the sun at the beach before you order your lunch, set the special tone that makes this place worth the investment. *Classic hotel.*

★★★★ **Plantation Inn** • *east of the main part of town* • trims a portion of the shore with an elegant hotel, with 65 special rooms and 14 suites, some with 2 bedrooms. The surroundings, from the entrance through the lobby and out to the sea-view patio with pool nearby, are picture-perfect, but noise from neighbor Sandals' motorboats sometimes shatters the seaside calm. Opened in 1955 and maintained for many years with a Bermuda link, the hotel is now owned by the Watson family from Kingston. Afternoon tea has been one time-honored tradition; music some evenings near the pool is a newer one. To reach the sandy cove of beach, you have to climb down a winding and flower-festooned series of steps; after your swim, it's an uphill climb to tea on the terrace. Tennis courts are located on the lawn near the entrance; a few shops (including a hair salon) are to the left as you drive through the gates. Planned for luxury living, Plantation Inn is one of Jamaica's "Elegant Resorts." *Classic hotel.*

★★★ **Radisson Cibonney** • *in the hills, with entrance across the road from Sandals Ocho Rios* • seems more like a residential community with private club status than like a resort. The core is the oversized main house, with villas scattered around the hillsides like chicks around their mother hen. The pool-punctuated main building, in Great-House style, holds the reception area, restaurants, entertainment centers, shops, and some of the guest rooms. Most rooms are a jitney ride (or long hot walk) from the main house, in 3-bedroom villas, each with its own pool. (The property claims 33 pools.) Guests sharing a villa should be (or will soon be) close friends; the small pool is for use by all villa residents. A rental car will allow for instant access to the beach, which is down the hill and across the road, as well as for getting around the grounds and for exploring elsewhere. Check for special package rates, which Radisson has in hopes of luring guests to this lovely hillside perch. *Resort.*

Ramada Ocho Rios Resort & Beach Club • *on the shore at Ocho Rios* • is the result of merging the former Mallards Beach Hotel and the Divi Resort into one 750 room resort planned for conventions and other groups. The two high-rise hotels joined under the Ramada umbrella in spring 1991, to enjoy a rainfall of several million dollars for extensive rennovations, with plans for re-opening by late 1991. Every aspect of the resort came under careful review, with new and better restaurants and shops as well as a much-needed clean-up of beach and pool areas. The resort claims a wedge of land on the west side of town which features: a pleasant beach, a long shoreline, and easy access to dozens of shops, restaurants, and nightspots (all within an easy stroll through the busy part of vacation-focused Ocho Rios and not far from the cruise ship pier). The *Caribbean Newsletter* (page 9) will have post-opening comments, after the resort is in full swing in early 1992. Expect to find all modern comforts in the bedrooms and a full range of activities for public areas. Top floor rooms gave the best view. Check for status if you plan a late 1991 vacation. *Big hotel.*

★★★★★ **Sandals Dunns River** • *on the shore, west of Ocho Rios* • is the reincarnation of a prized piece of shorefront property, slightly removed from the clutter of town. Although some of the stately palms along the entrance drive went with Hurricane Gilbert's visit in September '88, prior to becoming part of the Sandals family, the grounds are vast, the beachfront good, and the setting gorgeous. Gordon "Butch" Stewart has gone all out at this spot. The pool is vast, the decor spectacular, and the range of activities has been planned for sports-minded couples, and all others, with the last word in equipment and programs. The core of the hotel was the Arawak hotel in '58, and then the Jamaica Hilton for almost 25 years. It became an Americana property in 1985, and part of the Savoy group after that. Ocho Rios is a 5-minute drive east, but there's little reason to go there. On-premise are several excellent tennis courts, a lovely long beach, big pool, complete watersports, and a full activities schedule. The entrance building is the core, with bedrooms in this and other buildings. The highest floors have a sea view. *Inclusive resort.*

★★★★ **Sandals Ocho Rios** • *amid foliage at the shore, east of the town center* • is another member of Gordon "Butch" Stewart's successful all-inclusive resorts. Following its sister resort in Negril with its formal opening (in early 1990) the property incorporates all the flourishes gradually added to the other Sandals resorts, with a "partymaker" in charge of the entertainment and a full range of daytime and evening activities. Bedrooms are in several 2- and 3-story buildings; most face the sea. In addition to your room, all meals, activities, watersports, drinks, tips, and taxes are included in the one price, whether it is for the week-long or the shorter holidays. *Inclusive resort.*

★★★ **Sans Souci Club** • *on and above a sand-bordered cove, about 2 miles east of the Ocho Rios shopping hubs* • entered a new phase in 1990, with new Jamaican owners who have expansion plans and cost-cutting management concerns. The *Caribbean Newsletter* (page 9) will have an update when procedures are in place. The setting is one of the Caribbean's most beautiful, with the original multi-faceted buildings angled on the hillside so that each room has its own special view, of either lush tropical planting or the sea—often of both.

Built as a club, with each suite privately owned, the hotel has a spa program and talks of adding new units by the beach, which is a band of hard-packed sand that slopes so gradually into the sea that you walk a long way to reach knee-high. There are two pools, one at the thermal springs near the sea-level spa and another just below the top-of-the-hill reception area, in the lobby of the main building, which is in plantation Great-House style. Tennis courts are near the beach pavilion at the shore, near the watersports area. Entertainment is offered most evenings in winter; check if it matters for summer months. Touring assistance is available at a lobby desk. Count on climbing plenty of steps, through gardens and around the grounds, and check for status of the expansion plans to assure that you're not vacationing on a construction site. *Resort.*

★★★ **Shaw Park Beach Hotel** • *on a pleasant beach at the east end of town* • takes its name from a legendary hotel that used to stand inland, on the hillside in the middle of what are still Shaw Park Gardens. The beach hotel rose on this spot of shoreline in the season of '59, with a string of 2-story units with modern furnishings and an action plan focused on the beach and sea. Fame rested for several seasons on the fact that scenes for the movie made from Ian Fleming's *Dr. No* were shot at a creek down the sand, but life now percolates to a lively mix of British and European visitors (Germans and others), and other international guests. Dining is alfresco on the seaside terrace near the beach. Sailing can be arranged through the watersports concession; windsurfers scoot along the sea surface from here; and there are tours to the White River for the boat trip and island buffet. Bus tours take guests along the road (15 min.) to Ocho Rios for shopping, but otherwise daytime visitors stretch out to enjoy the sand and sea. The hotel has a lively, action-packed plan during winter months when things often operate with a full house. *Resort hotel.*

HOUSEKEEPING HOLIDAYS in Ocho Rios are easy and elegant. There are more villas in the Ocho Rios area than in any other part of the country, and supermarkets are well stocked. Especially popular are the villas at Mammee Bay, near the Eden II (within walking distance, if you like strolling the beach), but there are houses in the hills as well as heading east along the coast. Sources for villa rentals include **Villa and Apartments Abroad** (420 Madison Ave., New York, NY 10022, T 212+759–1025 or T 800+433–3020, fax 212+755–8316); **Selective Vacation Services** (Box 335, 154 Main St., Ocho Rios, Jamaica, T 809+974–5187, fax 809+774–2359); **Jamaica Villa Vacations** (8101 Milwaukee Ave., Niles, IL 60648, T 312+965–2100); and **La Cure Villas** (11661 San Vincente Blvd., Los Angeles, CA 90049, T 800+387–2726). In addition to the many villas that are listed with these firms, there are apartments.

Fisherman's Point • *next to Turtle Beach, at the shore near Ocean Village* • is a group of condominium units in buildings, in a village style that has Victorian overtones. Although there are no phones in rooms (and walls are thin so sounds travel), furnishings are comfortable and the location is good for families with young folk who want to be near the action. Apartments come in several sizes, sometimes changing by locking a connecting door. Kitchen equipment is adequate, with cutlery and dishes. *Apts.*

Sandcastles • *in the heart of things at Ocho Rios* • is a complex of 3-story buildings, each built in a square with an atrium core from which stairways lead to the upper floors. The studios, suites, and 1-bedroom apartments are modern, comfortably furnished, and ideal for vacation living. A large pool near the reception area is the social center, for those who want a gathering place, but it's easy to walk "everywhere," especially to the beach. Although reception staff seemed diffident when I visited, maids were pleasant and the set-up makes it possible to be independent. Worth considering for comfort and convenience, if you want a place of your own in Ocho Rios. *Apts.*

Turtle Beach Towers • *at the shore at Ocean Village, west of the center of Ocho Rios* • stand at the end of the sandy strollable strand that passes Inn on the Beach and stops at Club Americana and Mallards. The high-rise towers are air-conditioned, and look like modern apartment buildings in Miami or a lot of other cities. They are filled with studio, 1-, and 2-bedroom apartments all furnished with the basics. Ocean Village Shopping Center is at your feet; you can do all your shopping at the supermarket. *Apts.*

THE INN WAY is possible in Ocho Rios. There are a few places that offer the hospitality and congenial surroundings usually associated with good innkeeping. Here are four to consider:

Arawak Inn • *on the inland side of the road, across from the entrance to Sandals Dunns River* • has bedrooms in a 3-story building, with a pool at its feet. Meals are served at the *Garden* restaurant; the neighboring disco draws the late-night crowd from around Ocho Rios. *Small hotel.*

★ **Hibiscus Lodge** • *on the shore* • is in the heart of busy Ocho Rios. The original house, wood-walled West Indian, is a charmer. Most bedrooms have balconies and stretch along the cliff side, so they have sea views. Best known for its *Almond Tree* restaurant, the inn is convenient to most in-town activities. Porch sitting, sea-viewing, and reading are naturals here, although all the touring options are available. Favored by wise Europeans who like the small spots, Hibiscus Lodge is one of the area's best bets. *Inn.*

★★ **High Hope Estate** • *at St. Ann's Bay* • is one of those special places that most people learn about by word of mouth. Set on 51 acres, in the hills above Ocho Rios area, the estate is elegant, with pool, well-manicured lawns, and black wrought iron accenting the white walls. The view through the arches is spectacular and the setting is reminiscent of the 15th-century "Venetian Villa" the place claims as its model. The entire villa can be rented including staff plus 3 meals and tea daily, or you may have just a room or two. It's a 10-minute drive to the beach. *Inn.*

LOW-COST LODGING: Many of the apartments, such as those at Turtle Beach and Fisherman's Point, allow for inexpensive holidays for families and others who share a unit. In addition, the tourist board sometimes has listings of apartments and rooms-for-rent in other places around Ocho Rios.

For standard hotel services, here are a few small spots with pleasant personalities—and reasonable rates:

Inn on the Beach • *at Ocean Village* • is mentioned because it settles into the hub of activity, within a short walk of Club Americana, Mallard's Beach, and the Turtle Beach Towers, all linked by beach and road. Location on the beach puts it in the traffic pattern for beach vendors. Rooms are motel style.

The Little Pub • *near the clock tower in the heart of Ocho Rios hubbub* • is a complex best known for the restaurant and for the dinner theater. In addition, there are less than two dozen rooms, upstairs at the heart of the action. Furnishings are basic, rooms are on the small side, and air-conditioning is essential, both to block out town noises and for cooling. Good for folks who want to be within a few steps of evening entertainment and patio breakfasts, lunches, and dinners; you'll have to walk to the nearest beach (past the Ocean Village shopping area).

Pineapple Penthouse Hotel • *on the hillside near town* • has a pool for cooling off, and about two dozen rooms for guests who want a small hotel at reasonable rates. There's an on-premise restaurant, but most action is elsewhere.

RESTAURANTS in Ocho Rios are interesting and varied. Service is dependably s-l-o-w, but the atmosphere is usually exceptional enough to make the evening special. In winter months, reservations are essential and should be made a day in advance for the most popular places (which includes most of those mentioned below). At the chain hotels, hamburgers, etc., are popular, but be sure to try Jamaican "jerk pork" or "jerk chicken," both spicy barbecues that are pungent and good. Many hotels—notably Plantation Inn, Sans Souci, and Jamaica Inn—have candlelit "formal" dinner service, with Jamaican produce as well as imports. Reservations are essential for dinners at any of these three.

Almond Tree • *at the Hibiscus Hotel near the Catholic church on Ocho Rios* • is one of the most popular dining depots. The atmosphere on the terrace is pleasant in evenings, even when you have to wait at one of the swinging chairs by the bar. Food is best at dinner; I found lunchtime offerings fairly mundane—although the view and surroundings are special.

Evita's • *on the hillside, above the pier* • moved from the MoBay area, to serve pasta and other Italian-style specialties from this perch. Casual and fun, when your fellow travelers are.

Little Pub • *at the main road shopping area* • has a nice atmosphere, with chairs on the terrace and music playing most evenings, but the service can be lax. Menu varies and is sometimes too ambitious, but the fish feature was good when I last sampled.

Piccolo Mundo • *almost 10 miles east of downtown Ocho Rios* • was known as Moxon's in its previous life. Now Italian fare (of uneven quality, when I sampled) is offered. Dining is in a private home and terrace setting.

Parkway • *near the town market* • is known for its Jamaican food. Popular with locals who stop here on their way to or from the produce market across the road, the place has the appearance of a diner, and offerings that are typically country Jamaican.

The Ruins • *in Ocho Rios, amid gardens that are worthwhile just for viewing* • is a popular spot. Although the place seats close to 100, the tiered arrangement makes for a cozy atmosphere. Music is a part of most evenings; luncheons are nice when the weather is; and food takes its cue from the Oriental heritage of the owners, with many good Chinese entrees on the menu. Reservations are essential in season. Highly recommended, especially if you're planning only one night out.

Tradewinds • *amid the clutter of Ocho Rios, near the market* • serves delicious curried lobster and other local fare. Open for breakfast, lunch, and dinner, the back courtyard is casual.

NATURAL SURROUNDINGS have been carefully packaged for vacation and other visitors, thanks to the Jamaican government's recognition of the importance of tourism to the economy. **Dunn's River Falls,** west of the town of Ocho Rios, have cascaded over their rocks and rills for centuries and, although the foliage received a severe pruning thanks to Hurricane Gilbert in September '88, they're still spectacular. If the thought of wallowing around in fresh-water pools formed by the falls as they tumble down a 600-foot drop appeals at all, head for the area with a handful of friends and start climbing from the roadside ticket window at beach level. (Guides are available, if you want an experienced person to show you each footfall.) Your human chain snakes up the rocks, slipping and sliding all the way. Bathing suits are proper attire, although the folk who live in the village at the top of the falls make this wet climb as their daily commute—in their regular clothes. Anyone who jogs and is staying within a reasonable distance could consider heading here for variety. One climb up and your legs will get their wanted workout. The beach on the other side of the road is a reasonable swimming spot, but the falls are better. Booths for crafts sales are near the parking area.

Fern Gully, a few miles inland on the winding road to Kingston from Ocho Rios, also received a bashing from the hurricane but is fully recovered, once again with lush foliage. The area has only a hint of its former appeal, however, because exhaust from automobiles and trucks is taking its toll.

Shaw Park Botanical Gardens, up in the hills west of the town, are on what used to be a famous plantation. The well-tended gardens appeal to botanists and others who like tropical flora, but their appeal has been somewhat curbed by the opening of nearby Carinosa Gardens. Shaw Park has 34 acres, with views, streams, ponds, and plenty of plantings. (The hotel that once stood on these grounds gave way to the new, and not nearly as enchanting, Shaw Park at the beach.)

The best way to see the natural Jamaica is to rent a car or hire a driver to head for Mandeville for the day, or to go up into the hills to some other place. Although the coastline is dedicated, in many areas, to tourism, even a few miles into the back-country reveals an entirely different Jamaica. Insofar as walking and hiking in this area, check with the tourist office and/or your hotel for recommendations about routes and guides. The interesting, gnarled back-country is also the area where the *ganja* (marijuana) farmers proliferate, and they are not usually enthusiastic about outside, unknown visitors.

Insofar as offshore sites are concerned, there are several popular scuba-diving places off the north coast, both east and west of Ocho Rios, since the area is at the east end of the deep trench between the Cayman Islands and Jamaica. For experienced divers, The Mountain rises almost 60 feet from the edge of the Cayman Trench, and for snorkelers and novice divers, the sea-life at Laughing Waters Lagoon is varied and colorful. Reefs, caves, overhangs, and walls are well known to dive masters, who can take you to prime sites when seas are clear and currents propitious.

PLACES WORTH FINDING around Ocho Rios have been found by the tour operators. All are well marked, well promoted, and well peopled at the tour times. Even if you are a loner, some places are still worth seeing—but on your own terms and time.

Firefly, on the coast at Port Maria, just east of Oracabessa where banana boats used to load, and about 35 minutes' drive east of Ocho Rios, is Noel Coward's home-turned-museum. Donated to the Jamaican government on his death on March 23, 1973, the home holds memorabilia of the famous playwright, actor, director, painter. The 4½ acres include his tomb—and a lot of memories of the life of the man who wrote *High Spirits* (a musical version of his play, *Blithe Spirit*), *Quadrille,* and other plays here. Sir Noel lived in Jamaica for the last 25 years of his life.

"Jamaica Night on the White River" is a special, and truly "tourist" evening, where you step into a longboat to putt-putt up the river for drinks and dinner in a side-of-the-river setting that takes on a whole new personality, helped along by those of you who come in the boats and the sound of the steel band that greets you. You can buy a ticket for this evening (usually Sundays, but check) at your hotel activities desk if it has not been included in your package tour. You will be picked up at and returned to your hotel and—even if you can't go with a group of friends from your own lodging—the evening can be a fun one if you're in the mood for it. (Slather yourself with your favorite mosquito deterrent if those pesky intruders bother you.)

Spice plantation tours should be on the activities program for any first-time Caribbean visitor. **Prospect Plantation** offers a complete and enthusiastic tour, with talks about all the produce and a horticulture lesson that will not be too pedantic but will let you know something about all the trees and bushes you will look at during the rest of your stay. The usual conveyance is a truck-turned-bus-called-jitney where you bounce around in the back, sometimes sipping a rum punch (which you can certainly get at the "filling station" that is the last stop). You will see a local boy climb a coconut tree (fascinating, for the first time), and then will taste fresh-cut sugarcane in season, a favorite for all the schoolchildren you will see munching it as they walk along the roadside. Count on spending about $20 for the tour. Inquire about the possibility of pickup at your hotel, but the usual route is to take a taxi to either plantation, with arrangements for the cab to pick you up when you're finished. If you like horseback riding, that can be the ideal way to tour the plantation.

SPORTS in Ocho Rios include all the offerings. There is **golf** available at the Upton Golf course, which makes up in viewful golfing what it may lack in challenges (the courses at Half Moon, Rose Hall, and Tryall are reportedly better).

Horseback riding amid the plantations is available at Prospect, just east of the town, but do not expect to ride the finest horses. The mounts are easy and relatively comfortable; even a novice can enjoy the experience. Riding is also available at *Upton Country Club. Chukka Cove,* just west of Eden II, is a full-fledged stable with rings and rides. Although the specialty is polo, with lessons and chances to play, Danny Melville and Yvonne Whittingham also teach show jumping and basic riding. The stable can arrange guided trail rides and treks for those who want them and, with about 40 well-cared-for horses, this place is a truly professional operation.

Sailing is possible from the beach at the Americana and Mallard's Beach hotels. **Boardsailing** is available from many of the hotels, including Sans Souci, Shaw Park Beach, the Sandals and SuperClub resorts, and others.

Scuba diving is offered through most hotels and by concessionaires at the beach near the Ramada. Courses start in the pool and with table talk, and then head out to sea when beginners are trained and begin to be comfortable with the equipment. All equipment is available for rental, but the pros bring some of their own.

Tennis is available at most resort hotels, the *Sandals Dunns River, Sandals Ocho Rios, Plantation Inn, Sans Souci, Shaw Park, Cibonney, Ramada,* and others among them. Nightlights make it possible to play late in the day. Bring tennis balls from home to leave behind; they're expensive when they are available, in Jamaica.

TREASURES AND TRIFLES in Ocho Rios are part of the planned tourist scene, as is the case in Montego Bay. Most of the real bargains have long since gone, but the game of bargaining can still be played at the straw market stalls and with the beachside vendors, with a modicum of fun (and profit) for all. The **Ocean Village** market is a warren of stalls with strawwork, sun smocks, shorts, shirts, wood carvings, jewelry, and other handmade items for sale. If you pay attention, you can avoid being taken completely. Although the shops that honeycomb **Pineapple Place,** on the shoreside of the main road, and **Coconut Grove** on the inland side and a short walk east of Pineapple Place, have some luxury goods (crystal, china, Wedgwood, perfumes, etc.), the best buys these days are some of the Jamaican-made goods. For those who want T-shirts, Jamaica has them all—including a large selection in colors and size for ''Weed of Wisdom'' and ''Ganja University'' as well as several other slogans. The T-shirts of Jamaica are well made and do not shrink too much when washed (because they are cotton, count on *some* shrinkage). Going price is $3.50 for small and $5 for adult size. Buy when you see what you want. Although the shirts are "everywhere," the stock and slogans vary.

Harmony Hall, a 19th-century Victorian-style Great House that has been painstakingly re-created, serves as a center for the best crafts of Jamaica. Opened in late '81, the house is worth visiting just to look at the restoration, but the real focus is the shop and art gallery, with changing shows of Jamaican artists and craftsmen as well as several unusual items that make perfect gifts for the folks at home. Responding to the inspiration and enthusiasm of a team that includes Annabella and Peter Proudlock, Harmony Hall continues to thrive as a pocket of culture on the north coast. This is a good source for books about Jamaica, as well as for Jamaican art and for cards with drawings of Jamaican scenes. The house is on the main road, east of Ocho Rios and very near Couples Resort.

When you buy liquor by the bottle, you will be paying the standard rate paid by all who live here *unless* you buy "in bond," which means you make up your mind a couple of days (at least) before you plan to leave. Place your order and pay for it, receiving a slip of sale in return. Your package of liquor purchased will be available for pickup *at the airport* or the place your ship docks. (I have found that the peace of mind that comes with having whatever I thought I needed securely packed with my luggage was worth more than the $1 I might have saved.)

Straw baskets, mats, hats, etc., are sold by the ladies who make them, at the **straw market** near the Ocean Village Shopping Center, not far from the Family Food supermarket. You'll find all kinds of straw work; several varieties of flour-sack shirts, skirts, hats, etc., carvings that have been toned with shoe polish, and black coral that is rubbed with Noxon. Bargain for everything: the rapid increase in prices has put some of the poorer-quality merchandise into the "rip-off" category.

AUTHOR'S OBSERVATION

A warning about the street and beach vendors: put your sales resistance into your pocket with your wallet when you go shopping, and use them at the same time. Some of the sales folk will slide up to you as you saunter, offering you a gleaming selection of trinkets, etc., that are surreptitiously slipped from their pocket, or a covering/polishing cloth. During a flurry of whispered conversation that could not have taken more than 10 minutes, I negotiated for a selection of 6 etched "gold" bracelets. Both the salesman and I knew they were not the gold he said they were; only he knew where they came from, and only I knew how much I wanted them. The same sales process is in effect for *ganja,* Jamaica's marijuana, which is illegal but freely offered—even when you show no interest. If you consider shopping a sport, as I sometimes do, then the streets and shores of Ocho Rios have a lot to offer. If you're looking for real bargains, you'll be disappointed.

The expected resort clothes and island trinkets are sold in the air-conditioned, commercial shops at Ocean Village, near the *Turtle Beach, Fisherman's*

Point, and *Ramada* hotels on the west side of town, and at big hotel boutiques. At the Ocean Village center, there's a branch of the **Ruth Clarage** shop, plus **The Craft Cottage** (with some high-quality handicrafts), **Jamotique** selling spices, coffee, rum, and other Jamaican-made items, and **Ting 'n Ting** has lightweight summer clothes. Special Jamaican items that are sold (and priced) for local consumption are Pick-a-Peppa spice, sauce found in the best grocery stores at Ocean Village, and the firm and well-made market baskets and reed brooms used by Jamaicans for their own housekeeping. You can buy those on the street. The Jamaican reggae records include some labels not easily found at home. Costs are about J$30 for LP records and J$6 for 45s. Tapes are also sold.

RUNAWAY BAY AND DISCOVERY BAY

Nestling on the north coast within a few minutes by bus or car from the shopping centers and attractions of Ocho Rios, and about an hour's drive east of Montego Bay airport, the cluster of hotels at the area known as Runaway Bay offer comfortable accommodations and all the vacation options—including golf. For "Housekeeping Holidays" and other information, see listings under Ocho Rios, and know that all the action of MoBay is also within reasonable drive.

HOTELS/RESORTS:

Ambiance • *nestled on the shore* • is an eclectic mixture of Jamaican life-style with a restaurant that aspires to French standards. Most bedrooms are in 2- and 3-story buildings; the best have sea-view balconies. There's a pool on the premises, and a golf course not far down the road. Popular with Canadians and Europeans, this place is not well known to most U.S. visitors.

Caribbean Isle • *next to Ambiance, on the coast* • is well known to Canadian groups who come here on low-cost air-and-hotel packages. Bedrooms are in 3-story buildings; the best have sea views. There's a pool, as well as swimming from the shore. (The beach washes out at this spot, so there's not much sand.)

Club Caribbean • *on the shore* • reopened after almost complete rebuilding, and new ownership, following Hurricane Gilbert's devastating "visit" in September '88. Now looking better than ever, with several rooms near the pool and others a few steps away, the hotel is Swiss-owned and often enjoys European guests. *Resort hotel.*

Eaton Hall Resort • *on the north shore, about an hour's drive east of downtown MoBay and west of Ocho Rios* • has had several personalities. Some rooms rent on an inclusive plan, with all meals, drinks, and sports equipment figured into one sum, but you can also have a room with breakfast only. In addition to the hotel rooms, many of which have sea view from their balconies, there are villas around the grounds. *Hotel.*

★★★ **Jamaica, Jamaica** • *on the north shore at Runaway Bay* • danced into the season of '85 with a thoroughly Jamaican focus. The action-packed resort occupies the former Runaway Bay Hotel and Golf Club, but those who knew it then will barely recognize it now. A waterfall, Jacuzzi pool plus a place for swimming short laps, exercise room, and other activities have been built into the lobby, where you'll also find a bar, shops, and activities desks. Rooms span two low wings toward the sea, but many bathrooms have been outfitted with gigantic bathing tubs. The beach has soft sand; a golf course is nearby and a "Golf Academy" vacation is offered. Tennis courts are here—and the shoreside beach bar is one of several favorite gathering areas. The Jamaican theme is carried out with all food, entertainment, and a special arrival packet of Jamaican-made shorts, shirt, and a few gifts. Built for fun, this place has action!

HOUSEKEEPING HOLIDAYS are possible at many villas and a few apartment and villa clusters.

Caribbean Village • *at the shore* • is a community of octagonal bungalows with peak roofs. All are adequately furnished for beachside living. *Bungalows.*

★★ **Franklyn D. Resort** • *west of Jamaica-Jamaica and east of Eaton Hall* • was a newcomer for the 1990 season. A cluster of 2- and 3-story buildings hold studio, plus 2- and 3-bedroom apartments, all with full kitchens. There is a restaurant, near the bar area at the pool, but couples who stay here are encouraged to use their own kitchen facilities. Owned by Frank Rance, one of the original team for the SuperClub resorts, this place adopts the all-inclusive formula for family vcations, with extensive facilities and activities. Rooms have small balconies; those with the prettiest pool-and-sea view are also exposed to the evening entertainment noise. Some units are duplex; all are attractively furnished. *Apts.*

★★★ **Portside Villas** • *at Discovery Bay, west of Runaway Bay, along the coast* • cling to the shoreline, pinned there by the coast-rimming road. Studios and larger apartments are available, with the newest units rising up the hillside on the inland side of the road. My favorites (9 D and E among them) are some of the older units on the seaside, not far from the pool and restaurant. Surroundings are pleasant at this oasis. *Apts.*

★ **Sunflower Villas** • *on the shore, not far from the Runaway Bay Golf Course* • are a collection of 1- to 5-bedroom villas, some of which have a small but private pool. Airport transfers are included in the rental cost. Maids and cooks are available, for carefree housekeeping holidays. *Cottages.*

THE INN WAY: is possible at one pleasant spot that is uniquely Jamaican.

★★ **HEART Academy** • *near the shore at Runaway Bay* • is a special project with a remarkable flair. The small hotel and restaurant is operated as a hotel training school by HEART, which stands for Human Employment and Resort Training. Guests should be prepared for slow-but-willing service, while the students learn their new field. Since the kitchen help is also students, you'll sample some new recipes with the experience. Bedrooms are pleasantly furnished and very comfortable. The pool is a great asset; Cardiff Hall Beach is down the road. (The hotel offers car service.) Well worth a visit, reservations for meals and the few rooms are essential. *Inn.*

NATURAL SURROUNDINGS include the places mentioned for both Montego Bay and Ocho Rios, since they are within day-touring distance of Runaway Bay and Discovery Bay, and the several snorkeling areas and scuba sites, made exceptional by such things as a huge anchor from a Spanish ship, which sits in about 50 feet of water, and a sunken boat that went down about 40 years ago and is now home for assorted sealife.

PORT ANTONIO

The easternmost town of Jamaica has been the secret salvation for shattered souls and those in search of a quiet place with a special ambience, for centuries. Known as a thriving banana shipping port at the turn of the century, and as a cavorting hideaway for Erroll Flynn and others in the 1950s, Port Antonio is, once again, coming to the attention of the exceptional few who want a place in the sun with its own personality. The town sleeps, with its beautiful surroundings secure—even after the onslaught of Hurricane Gilbert in September 1988.

Why go? Because the area is beautiful and unspoiled, with comfortable resorts, and out of the mainstream of resort and commercial life. Jamaican and off-island guests share all the facilities, some of which are exceptional, all of which are clean, neat, and near some interesting natural sights. Among the most fascinating are Blue Lagoon, which is deep, deep blue, even after Hurricane Gilbert's visit; Nonsuch Caves; and the Gardens of Athenry; and the Rio Grande with its river rafting.

ARRIVAL AND DEPARTURE in Port Antonio takes time. Your choices are either to drive around from the airport at Kingston, approximately 3 to 4 hours driving, or to come from Montego Bay, along the coast road in almost 4 hours, or to fly from either city's airport to Ken Jones Airfield, just west of the town of Port Antonio. From there you'll need a taxi to get to your hotel unless your hotel has arranged ground transportation for your arrival.

HOTELS in Port Antonio are a half-dozen personality places that aspire to luxury living and a couple of small spots mentioned below under "Low-Cost Lodging." The taxes and service charges in effect here are similar to those throughout the country.

AUTHOR'S AWARD

Trident Villas, a lovely, uniquely Jamaican hotel is a gem.

Admiralty Club & Marina • *on Navy Island, in the harbor of Port Antonio* • has a legendary history as the private retreat of Errol Flynn during his swashbuckling days in Jamaica. He bought the long-term lease on the island from the British Navy. The several seaside villas on the 64-acre island have modern comforts, overhead fans, and sunning patios. There's an island restaurant and bar, but the food was not gourmet when I tried it. A small boat links the island with Port Antonio on 24-hour service, but you may have to wait around a while until the boatman is ready to carry you across. Best for back-to-nature types who enjoy the carefree lifestyle, the place has been operating on an all-inclusive plan. *Resort.*

Jamaica Palace Hotel • *on a nub of land near the town* • aspires to the grand life. The 2-story main buildings have a surfeit of arches and pillars, in a style that reflects the imposing plantation Great Houses of yesteryear. The huge pool has an outline vaguely reminiscent of the country's; suites have patios or porches, and color TV that sometimes works. Grounds assets include tennis courts, a lively disco, and a restaurant noted for top-notch cuisine. *Hotel.*

★★★★ **Trident Villas** • *on the shore, 10 minutes' drive from town* • with 28 rooms plus 2 suites and 7 rooms in a Castle, is one of the Caribbean's most beautiful resorts, Earl Levy has created a gem, with Jamaican-made copies of the antiques, polished silver punctuating important points in the enclosed dining room, choice chintz and other fabrics for drapes and appointments in the public rooms and bedrooms, and a smiling, attentive, and helpful staff. White stucco walls are counterpointed with brown umbrellas and chairs on the dining terrace—and around the pool. Peacocks parade on the grounds. There's a small beach at a cove reached by strolling across the lawns. Rooms are elegant; each one is different. F, G, and H are on the second floor; the Tower building has 4 rooms, one of which is a gorgeous suite with oriental rugs scattered around. Although the setting is spectacular, you may feel lonely if you need more than your traveling companion or a good book for company. House count is often low. *Villa hotel.*

HOUSEKEEPING HOLIDAYS in the Port Antonio area are very popular, with several privately owned homes for rent in owners' absence, and villas and apartments also available. The Port Antonio branch of the Jamaica Tourist Board can help with referrals. Houses bordering and near Blue Lagoon are the most popular.

Dragon Bay • *east of the town, near the shore* • is a collection of villas, each with 2 bedrooms and a suite. The property has been a Spanish-affiliated Marbella Club at a time in its recent history, but it's now operating with individual villas. Best for self-sufficient small groups of family and/or friends, the place can seem isolated if you want lots of action. There are tennis courts and a beach-lined cove for swimming, in addition to the pool on the lower lawn. The *Caribbean Newsletter* (page 9) will have further details when management firms up. *Villa hotel.*

★★★ **Fern Hill Club** • *on the hillside, east of town* • is a collection of very comfortable villas and suites, each with a private whirlpool, satellite T.V., and plenty of privacy. Operated by Canadian Airtrain International, the property is upscale all-inclusive, with flight from Montego Bay to Port Antonio and return included in your 7-night fee. Activities arranged for guests include trips to Reich Falls and other area sights, and visits to a private Jamaican club with a casino (dice and cards) in Port Antonio. This place is a true hideaway, beloved by those who've found it. *Small resort.*

Frenchman's Cove • *east of town* • is a large tract of lovely, verdant land, with villas and cottages scattered near the shore, perching on rocks and overlooking the sea. Opened in the '60s with an offer that "two people can spend $2000 for two weeks" for ultimate luxury in the first real all-inclusive plan, the property had fallen on hard times in recent years. Once elegant homes were shorn of their classy furnishings and many villas fell into disrepair. Rumors of new owners at press time bring hope for the future; the *Caribbean Newsletter* (page 9) will have news when it's a fact. *Villas.*

Goblin Hill Villas at San San • *on the hillside, southeast of town* • are attractive 1- and 2-bedroom units, each with kitchen, in white stucco buildings that gather near the pool, amid lovely lawns and tropical planting. There's a main house with restaurant area and check-in reception. Each apartment has maid and cook service. The beaches (and Blue Lagoon) are down the hill at the shore, a short drive away. New management provides a clever package, with car-and-driver to meet guests at the Kingston airport for the drive to the villas. The car is then yours for your stay, to return to the airport on your own or with a driver, as you choose. These villas are comfortable for get-away lodgings, with all the conveniences of a big estate. *Apts.*

THE INN WAY: is possible, in traditional island style as Jamaicans know and like it.

Bonnie View • *on a hilltop reached by a steep and wiggly road* • claims a viewful spot and caps it with a building that holds the dining room-with-terrace and the check-in area, stringing most simple rooms off an L-stem at the back. The pool is on the back lawn. Bedrooms are basic; few have views, but all are near the pool.

LOW-COST LODGING: For very inexpensive lodgings, check with the tourist office when you arrive in town to see what they have for listings of rooms-for-rent.

DeMontevin Lodge • *on a hillside in a residential part of town* • is a classic Victorian building with a definite personality, which is that of the host. The several bedrooms (on the second floor) vary in size, outlook, and furnishings, but all position guests in family-style surroundings for meals in the main dining room, where Jamaican food is the specialty of the house. Most bedrooms have private bath, and some are quite spacious. This inn offers house-like surroundings, with little formality. *Guesthouse.*

NATURAL SURROUNDINGS at the east end got a thorough bashing with Hurricane Gilbert's visit in September 1988, but a lot of the new growth makes an interesting study of how quickly foliage grows in Jamaica's climate. Because the east end has fewer tourists, the landscape has not yet been as trampled as other areas along the north coast. This is a good area for birdwatching, hiking, and the like. The nearby Rio Grande is where the rafting got its start (adapted from the strictly business procedures of floating bananas and other crops down the river from their inland plantations). Although Blue Hole, a spectacular deep lagoon, was damaged by the hurricane, the rocky area is still impressive, especially if you have not known it prior to the wind and water damage. There are also the Nonsuch caves to explore and two remarkable waterfalls, Reich (pronounced "reach") Falls, on Driver's River, and Somerset Falls. Both are inland river attractions with natural pools for cooling off after, or during, the climb.

PLACES WORTH FINDING include boat-linked Navy Island, site of the Admiralty Club, just offshore, with a nice sunning and swimming beach. The town of Port Antonio has several wonderfully Victorian buildings, some of them recently restored. Most are shops; one (DeMontevin Lodge) is a simple hotel. The drive around the east coast south to Kingston is little known to most tourists, although the road is reasonably good and the coastal scenery is pretty. One spot that is popular with Jamaicans is Boston Beach, where jerk pork—Jamaica's uniquely barbecued pork—was first acclaimed. (It's now been joined by jerk chicken and fish, but the pork was what started the local equivalent to "Kentucky Fried Chicken.") Reich Falls, inland following a dirt and rutted road, is worth an hour's diversion.

SPORTS in Port Antonio are in the hands of your hotel, and there's not a lot that is highly organized here. The Deep-Sea Fishing tournaments are annual spring and fall events, drawing boats from Miami, the Bahamas, the Cayman Islands, and Caribbean countries. The Jamaica Tourist Board will have details.

MARTINIQUE

> Office Departemental du Tourisme de la Martinique, B.P. 520, Fort-de-France, Martinique, F.W.I., T 011+596–63.79.60.; French West Indies Tourist Board, 610 Fifth Ave., New York, NY 10020, T 212+757–1125 or 900+990–0040, fax 212+247–6468. French Govt. Tourist Office, 9454 Wilshire Blvd., Beverly Hills, CA 90212, T 213+272–2661; #250, 1 Hallidie Plaza, San Francisco, CA 94102, T 415+986–4161; #630, 645 N. Michigan Ave., Chicago, IL 60611, T 312+337–6301; #205, 2305 Cedar Spring Rd., Dallas, TX 75201, T 214+720–4010; #490, 1181 Ave., McGill College, Montreal, Quebec, Canada H3A 2W9, T 514+288–4264; 1 Dundas St., W., Suite 2405, Toronto, Ontario, Canada M5G 1Z3, T 416+593–4717.

$ · · · US$1 = about 5.5 French francs (Confirm at travel time.)
Unless otherwise noted, U.S. equivalents are figured at the above rate.

It was just after dawn when I stood on the pier at Fort-de-France, waiting for the ferry to leave for Anse Mitan. Two schoolboys, neat in their uniforms, pranced along the waterfront, pausing at the pier long enough to dangle a hair-like string to tempt the fish. The croissants that were offered by a lady from her booth were snapped up by many; I waited until mine could be joined by the strong black coffee I knew was waiting at one of the shelters along the beach, after the boat ride across the harbor.

The sun is warm, even at 8 a.m., and the air is clear. The hulking ferry, the "tourist boat," lumbered across the harbor from its dock at Pointe du Bout, a few paces from the entrance of the Meridien hotel and at the doorstep of the marina where boats from the world unite. It first appears as a speck near the land across the sea. With each minute it looms larger, carving the sea as it speeds toward Fort-de-France.

"My" boat, on the other hand, is small and wooden, with flecked paint and sea-worn sides. The seating is haphazard; no one seemed to mind that I stayed on the hatchcover for the crossing. I liked it there. The sea spray hit my face but not the folded newspaper I held for the ticket taker. I sheltered the paper, and glanced at it, a reminder that I was in France, only when I knew it was safe from the sea. This island is as French as the rest of the nation on the mainland of Europe; and travels here are best when they're in the lap of the locals.

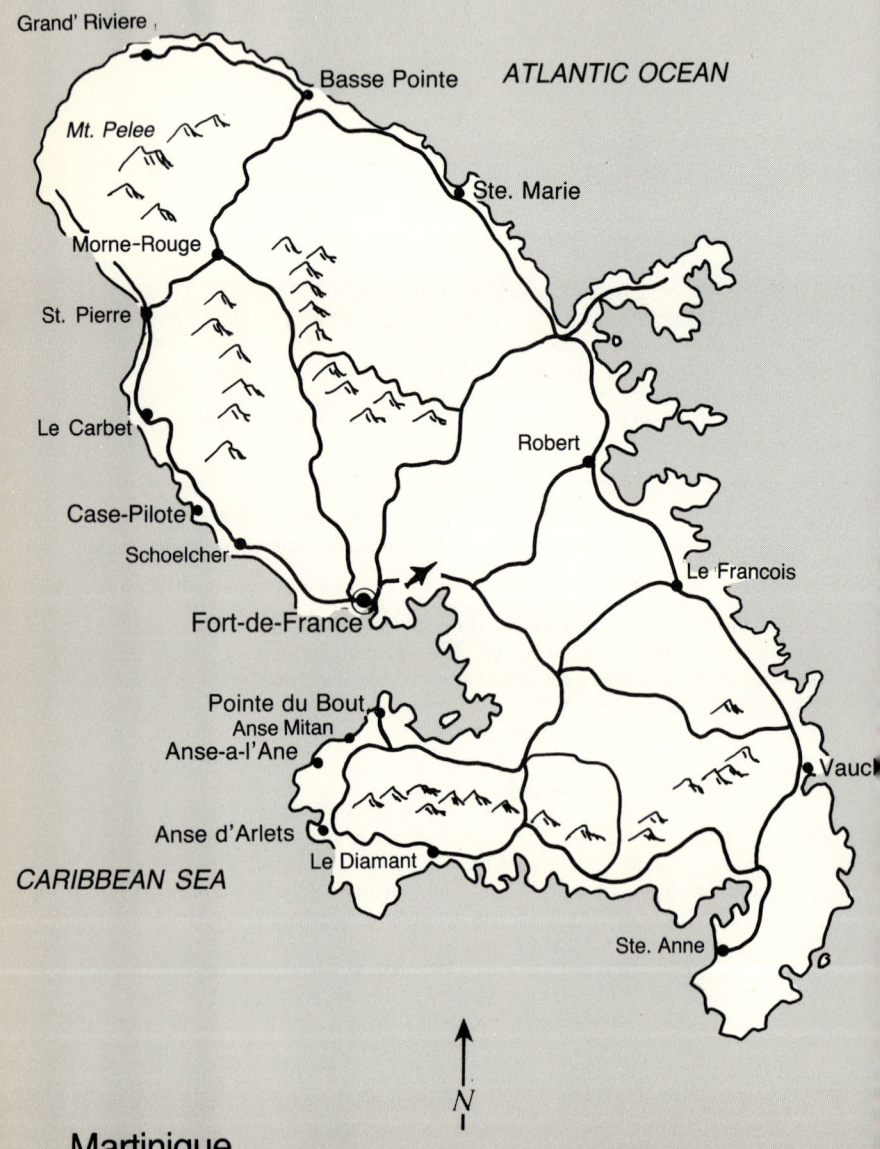

Martinique

Martinique has always been a community of the sea, but these days outsiders outnumber the fishermen on the sand of many shores. You have to head out—away from Pointe du Bout and the other tourist nests, to the far south, to Tartane on the east coast, and even to the north to Le Precheur or Grand' Riviere to find the "real" Martinique, and the soul of this special place.

> **AUTHOR'S OBSERVATION**
>
> *Helpful Hints for Visitors to Guadeloupe and Martinique,* a 28-page booklet packed full of good information, is available through the French West Indies Tourist Board at 610 Fifth Ave., New York, NY 10020. Write for your copy so you can have it in-hand when you arrive.

POLITICAL PICTURE: The economics of mainland France have their effect on the French West Indies and the elections of May 1988 were reflected in Martinique. President Mitterrand's policies are implemented in these islands, where the local Communist party has long played a part in the government. Since government is the major employer, prosperity continues as long as the money holds out. Tourism from mainland France has always been strong because French business policy includes long, paid vacations and the islands are favorites for Frenchmen who can have sun and sea with familiar language, currency, and customs. Visitors help the local economy by creating a need for new facilities, which provide jobs in the burgeoning tourism industry. Talk of independence is being nurtured by the very active left. A smoke screen of Castro-from-Cuba involvement in the already firmly entrenched Communist Party is a fact of local life, but enthusiasm for the system wanes, as a reflection of the new European order. Many of Martinique's communist party members live with most of the so-called capitalist trappings. Socialism is, and has long been, the system for schools, housing, medical care, and other governmental functions, as is the case in France.

ISLAND APPEARANCE: Although some shores are palm-studded and many in the south and east are beach-fringed, this island has more variety than many vacationers expect. Mt. Pelee rises from the northwestern shore and, from the several seaside hotels south of Fort-de-France on the southwest coast, it is an imposing sight, especially on the few days when its peak is not shrouded in clouds. The northern sector of the island is the most verdant, with the rain forest and the Parc Naturel, ranging over the several volcanic remnants that are led by Mt. Pelee to the lower foothills and eventually to the flatter lands in the south. Rocher du Diamant (Diamond Rock) juts from the sea off the south coast, and the tail of salamander-shaped Martinique curls off the south from the east coast toward the west. The deep and protected harbor punctuated with the island's capital of Fort-de-France is traversed several times daily by ferry boats taking passengers to the neighboring tourist centers at Pointe du Bout, Anse Mitan and Anse a l'Ane. Although once acceptable beaches are often washed out by sea surges near the major hotel areas around Pointe du Bout, long soft-sand strands still line shores in the south and some coves on the east coast. As with sister-island Guadeloupe, main roads are well paved and sign posted; secondary roads are also usually good.

LIFESTYLE is uniquely Martiniquais, taking the cue from mainland France but adding elements from a Creole Caribbean history. French is the language of the island, and speaking some is essential for transactions outside the well-traveled tourist routes. Although there will be some staff who speak English at the hotels, it is seldom the primary language. Knowledge of French is valuable for understanding directions, reading menus, or carrying on a complicated conversation. Familiarity with the style of life on mainland France will add to holiday pleasures here, not only because many fellow vacationers will be from Europe but also because many customs are patterned on those of the mother country.

"Service" (the tip) is often included on bills presented for meals. Sometimes the sum is added as a final item, at a standard 10% or 15%; sometimes prices include the service. There is usually some notation on the menu, but do not be shy about asking "Service compris?" (Is service included?). If the answer is "Oui," you need not leave more. If it is "Non," then consider adding 10% to 15% to your bill. That's plenty for the service tip, especially when some staff members are not above saying "Non" just to get more money. Finding your answer printed on the menu is most reliable.

Clothes are chic and casual on the best-dressed folk. There are several small boutiques (some of them in the larger hotels) where women can buy suitable French-style sun dresses and cotton evening wear, but there's not much in the way of men's fashions. Jackets for men seem to be a thing of the past, except for the most formal occasions. Even the best restaurants do not require coat and tie. Open-neck shirts go everywhere (and T-shirts are also in many dining rooms these days). On the beach, anything—or nothing—goes. Although there are no official naturalist beaches in Martinique (where nude bathing is acceptable), most Americans will be wide-eyed over the topless bathing on some beaches and at all of the major tourist hotels. European women—and now, also, a lot of Americans—think nothing of doffing bikini tops along with their sandals when they sit on the beach.

MEDICAL FACILITIES: As with its sister island, Guadeloupe, medical facilities around Martinique are among the best in the Caribbean. The status as a *departement* of mainland France makes the island appealing for professionals trained in the best medical schools and hospitals of France and elsewhere. There are exchange programs with the mainland, whereby professionals come to the island on regular visits. Le Meynard, near Fort-de-France, is regarded as Martinique's top hospital, although there are clinics and other hospitals around the island. Obviously French is the first language, but most doctors and many other hospital staff are fluent in English as well. The larger hotels have a doctor on call; owners and managers of the smaller properties have close contact with their own physicians. *Medecin* and *Pharmacie* are two words worth knowing.

MONEY MATTERS involve the French franc. Check with your local bank about trends and equivalents for the time you intend to travel. At press time, the franc is about 5 to US$1. Convert to French francs at the bank for the best local rate, unless you've bought French franc traveler's cheques prior to departure from home. (Doing so can take the exchange rate-checking pressures off your holiday plans.) Some stores give discounts if you pay in U.S. dollar traveler's cheques, so having *some* traveler's cheques, or using your credit card (which is usually converted at a favorable rate), can pay off if you're planning a lot of purchases.

COMMUNICATIONS are reasonably easy, by direct dial, overseas telephone. From the U.S., dial 011 + 596 (the area code for Martinique), and the local telephone number. Within Martinique, telephone service is usually good, although not all the small places have telephones.

For overseas phone calls from Martinique, inquire about *Telecarte,* a plastic card (like a credit card) to be used in the special "telecom" phone, which you'll see noted in and around Fort-de-France. The card is sold at **La Poste** (the Post Office) and other designated places in 40-unit and 120-unit amounts for 30.8F and 92.4F, respectively. A U.S. call costs about 11.5F per minute.

Newspapers from France arrive daily on the transatlantic flights. Radio programs will be in French, unless you tune into one of the English-speaking programs beamed from nearby islands or the British Broadcasting Company (BBC) or Radio Interference Confidentielle, which began broadcasting some programs in English in January 1985. There is local television. Some hotels provide T.V.

ARRIVAL on Martinique puts you into expanding Lamentin Airport, about five miles from downtown Fort-de-France. When things are working as they should, you'll find phones that usually work, cafes that are open, shops that have a few things (mostly liquor and perfume) worth looking at (and even buying), and a busy place where French-speaking visitors will be most comfortable, but those speaking only English can survive.

The Immigration procedures are fairly standard: show your identification (passport is best), your return ticket, and your arrival card, which states where you will be staying. After immigration, proceed to the customs area to claim your luggage for inspection. Customs formalities may seem tedious, especially when officials go through everything.

CRUISE passengers may disembark at the pier at the fringe of the capital at the new cruise ship area (for a taxi ride into Fort-de-France) or aboard the ship's shuttle boat if the vessel has anchored offshore. In either case, Fort-de-France, the capital, is the main shoppers' goal, but the ferries that leave from the waterfront for either Pointe du Bout or Anse Mitan will take you (in about 20 minutes) to the resort and marina area.

DEPARTURE from Lamentin Airport involves arriving more than an hour before flight time, for the inevitable waiting in line for check-in. The terminal is usually bustling. Immigration will take the carbon copy of the form you filled in for arrival, and there will be a security check before you are inside the departure area—within reach of several duty-free shops with a limited selection of liquor, watches, perfume, and the like. There's a restaurant upstairs (not the cafe near the check-in counters), *before* you go through immigration formalities.

TOURING TIPS: Martinique is an ideal island for **self-drive cars.** Roads are well paved and signposted. Gas is always an extra charge, and it's very expensive. Unlimited-mileage rentals are advisable if you want to do a lot of touring. It's easy to put 200 kilometers on your car in a day.

Most **rental cars** are in top condition. You'll find the expected international names—*Budget* (T 596+63.69.00), *Avis* (T 596+51.26.86), *Hertz* (T 596+51.28.22)—as well as several local firms. In addition to booths at the airport, there are places to rent cars at Pointe du Bout and through most hotels.

AUTHOR'S OBSERVATION

Be aware of a possible bait-and-switch scheme. My *Budget* car rental was quickly and efficiently arranged at the airport (I was on the road, driving away within 20 minutes), at an agreed upon rate. When I returned the car, just before boarding my plane to leave Martinique, I was told that the person who gave me the car had misquoted the rate. My charge was considerably more and, because I was heading for a plane, I did not have time to "fight it out."

Taxis are ready and waiting at the airport when you arrive. Many taxi drivers speak some English, but ask in advance about the appropriate fare for your ride, to avoid being overcharged.

Taxi drivers in Martinique can be like taxi drivers anywhere; if they know you are a novice, they also know you are "fair game." When you know the approximate fare, you can just present it as though of course both you and he know what it is. (Be sure you have French francs—which you should be able to get at the exchange booth at the airport when you arrive if you haven't gotten some at your hometown bank before you leave.)

If you are cost-conscious, and traveling light (and you should do the latter, even if you don't have to worry about the first), there are several reasonable ways to reach a Pointe du Bout hotel from the airport. Taking a taxi direct is fastest, and most expensive at about 142F (because the taxis have to drive all around the huge bay of Fort-de-France). Alternatives are taking a taxi into Fort-de-France (figure 56F), or better yet, if you're very adventuresome (or poor) the **bus** that makes the run from town to the airport at regular intervals for a few francs. At the pier at La Savane (the park) wait for the **boat** across to Pointe du Bout, or Anse Mitan (the neighboring beach), and walk from the dock to your hotel. None of the Pointe du Bout hotels are far from that boat dock; if you disembark at Anse Mitan, you'll be at the beach and can stroll along it to your hotel.

Between the cluster of Pointe du Bout hotels and the city of Fort-de-France, there is frequent boat service. The charge is 18F round trip (11F one way) to Pointe du Bout and Anse Mitan. The journey is far preferable to the around-the-bay road that takes about half an hour by car.

The major hotels have an activities board that shows day-touring options. Although many of the excursions (to neighboring island Dominica, for example) are set up for groups that book package tours, individual travelers can often get space if they inquire a day or two in advance. The small bus tours that thread sites of Martinique are interesting, and often give commentary in English as well as French so that you can learn some of the historic background.

Public bus service, often aboard small Mercedes buses, is good, inexpensive, and can be an interesting way to travel if you are not pressed for time and speak good French. Villages on the routes are written on the side of the bus. The main depot is in Fort-de-France at the waterfront not far from the Office du Tourisme.

AUTHOR'S OBSERVATION

Ask at your hotel for a copy of the monthly *Bienvenue en Martinique,* published by the tourist office. The fact-filled newspaper in French *and* English for visitors is valuable for finding out what's where and when.

LODGING on Martinique ranges from very simple homes turned inn, some of them historic, to big and brassy modern hotels that look as if they should have finger-snapping service but don't. Fellow guests are more apt to be vacationing working-class French and other Europeans or French-speaking Canadians than Americans. Although the surroundings may seen familiar, you are in France, and French ways prevail. Socialism also prevails. No hotel offers the level of luxury that can be found at some of the exclusive resorts on more capitalistic islands, which is far below the level of luxury known at the best European or American hotels. Many of the hotels that claim to have the best "service" also offer most meals—and certainly breakfast—buffet style.

If you want to avoid the franc-to-dollar gamble, inquire about buying an air-and-hotel-room package from your hometown travel agent. *Fete Francaise* holidays, assembled with a nudge from the French West Indies Tourist Office and the cooperation of some local hotels, can offer good value, but read the small print carefully to be sure what you are getting for your investment.

The greatest concentration of hotels and restaurants is in one of three areas. The best known, and busiest, is the Pointe du Bout and Anse Mitan area, with beach and marina across the harbor from Fort-de-France. There is also a community of properties near Sainte Anne, on the west side of the southern hook of the island. The third area, now developing with many new hotels and apartments, is Le Diamant, a bulge in the southern part of the west coast, where there are many small restaurants and a few big resort clusters. In addition to these three areas, there are also a few places scattered around Tartane/Trinite and north of Fort-de-France.

For those who want to be where the action is, the several hotels in Pointe du Bout and the Club Mediterranee in the south at Ste. Anne are the busiest places. For those who seek peace and quiet in traditional surroundings, there's an inn in the north and a few in the south that offer another, quieter, less cluttered world. And for those who prefer housekeeping, there are several options—including campers that you can rent to drive around the island and stop where and when you feel like it.

In addition to the posted room rate, count on a hefty room tax, plus a per night tourist tax and a service charge (even though you get very little "service").

AUTHOR'S AWARDS

Bakoua gets my top vote, for offering highest quality with local flavor; *Le Fregate Blue* is a perfect hideaway for independent travelers wishing to stay in a private home setting; *Anchorage* is ideal for settling into a French-style seaside vacation. Fanciful *St. Aubin,* near Trinite, deserves mention for offering a quiet retreat.

Information about places to stay is included under Hotels/Housekeeping Holidays, The Inn Way, and Low-Cost Lodging. Stars are awarded within each category. (See page 11.)

HOTELS/RESORTS are very apt to have European-style small rooms and narrow beds. Room service rarely exists; meals are often buffets.

★★★ **Anchorage Hotel** • *within walking distance of the beach, near Ste. Anne* • is actually five small hotel buildings, each with about 40 rooms. Several pools punctuate the complex, which was built in 1989. A group of shops and a restaurant *(Le Grill de Belfard)* are at the crossroads in this residential area. Rooms are duplex suites and/or standard hotel rooms. All are air-conditioned, have kitchen facilities, and are attractively decorated. This place gets high marks for attractive rooms in a vacation setting. *Resort hotel.*

★★★★ **Bakoua Beach Hotel** • *on a hillside rising from the shore at Pointe du Bout* • earns top accolades, once again, for offering a true island experience with concern for creature comforts. Totally renovated in summer '90 by new owners (the French Accor company), the public areas are tastefully furnished in a pleasant plantation Great-House style, with wood furniture, madras and other fabrics discretely used, and tile floors in the lobby area. Bedrooms came in for their share of sprucing up as well; even the oldest are in good shape. The beach seems small when guests fill the patch. There's a nice holiday atmosphere around the property, which was one of the first when Guy de la Houssaye opened it in 1965 with 27 rooms, 30 employees, and a distinctly Martiniquaise personality. Subsequent additions changed it from a cozy hotel to a busy resort, with a full range of watersports, evening action, pool, beach, tennis, and restaurants. Capping the hilltop, the reception area is near the bar and a dining terrace; a pool is nearby. Many of the rooms are in a wing off the main building; others are down the hillside, nearer the beach. A wing of rooms stretches at right angle to the first-built block so that guests share views of each others balconies (and each other). Breakfasts are buffets, as are some other meals. Food is reasonably good. Tennis courts are on the marina side of the hotel. Pointe du Bout and the ferries to Fort-de-France are a short walk from the rooms. *Resort hotel.*

★ **La Bateliere Hotel** • *on the shore at Schoelcher, north of Fort-de-France* • owned by French banks, is high-rise and handsome. Opened in the late 1960s as a Hilton, the multi-story hotel sits on a rocky shore about 10 minutes' drive from downtown Fort-de-France. All bedrooms are air-conditioned; most overlook the activities of the entrance to the bay. The lobby has bars, shops, and entertainment; a freshwater pool supplements a man-made beach for swimmers. Tennis courts are lit for night play; boats depart from the hotel's pier for fishing, sailing, and motorboat excursions. Car rentals and tours can be arranged through the activities' desk. The casino was the island's first; there's also a disco. *Hotel.*

★★ **Carayou PLM Azur** • *at Pointe du Bout* • wraps the French chain around the east side of the marina. The uninteresting strips of buildings, with brown doors and railings, have settled into flourishing planting over the years. Rooms are cozy (small), but modern. (One problem is that when you close your louvered windows, you've cut out all the natural light.) Action options include tennis, a very small beach (often windy), active watersports with scuba facilities, and opportunities for strolling around at the marina, trying restaurants and shops, and talking to boat people. The *Cafe Creole,* near the pool, is a pleasant resting spot, with swinging wicker chairs and big overstuffed furnishings under the dunce cap roof at the upstairs bar. *Le Boucaut* is the restaurant (where you should get a table with a view of Fort-de-France). *Le Vesou* disco has caves, caverns, and a peek-through hole to the sea. All of Pointe du Bout is a short stroll from your room; golf is a short ride to the course at Trois Ilets. Made for the middle-income market, groups get good rates. *Hotel.*

★★★ **Club Mediterranee Les Boucaniers/Buccaneer's Creek** • *at Point Marin near Sainte Anne* • is a long and winding route south, about an hour from the airport. Planned for sun seekers, the enclave is so self-contained that some boosters make the dubiously complimentary but accurate claim that you can spend a week here without even knowing you are on Martinique. In addition to the familiar Club Med formula of GOs (staff, called *gentils organisateurs*) and GMs (guests, known as *gentils membres*), with a *Chef de Village* in charge of the recipe and a long list of activities often announced on loudspeakers, there's a beach for sunbathing au naturel and the option to make a long and hot walk into Ste.-Anne, a small fishing village now turned to tourism. The disco, at a thatch-and-terrace open-air spot, serves creole food until 12 p.m. when the pulsating ear-pounding rhythms start. There are snacking and sitting places around the grounds, in addition to the patio restaurant. Waterskiing, volleyball, tennis, yoga, calisthenics, and other team sports can keep you moving from dawn to dusk, with a few spare minutes for the shops where you can buy the *pareo* (the piece of cloth that you will learn to wrap over suit and/or self as your all-purpose garb), suntan lotion, magazines, and a selection of other tourist-tested items. There's a library for quiet times, but most vacationers head to the sun, for socializing. In addition to the island tours (half-day into Fort-de-France, full-day touring sights), there are visits to neighboring islands: Dominica by plane and the Grenadines by boat, one of several that leave from the dock to cruise through the Caribbean's most spectacular sailing area. Your home for the week, which you buy at all-inclusive rates, will be in a 2-bed, air-conditioned, simply furnished, often small room. *Inclusive resort.*

★★ **Diamant-Novotel** • *on the south of the west coast bulge of Diamant* • benefits from the French Novotel chain connection, with groups from France and other places keeping things active at the hotel. A trio of 2-story rectangular buildings hold the modern bedrooms, which have TV, direct-dial phones, and thin walls (so you can hear your neighbors). Try to avoid the rooms in building 3 that overlook the garbage pick-up area. A large free-form pool is the daytime social center; beaches here are not the best. There are tennis courts, but they reportedly need resurfacing. Breakfast and a few of the evening meals are buffets. There's a small shop in the lobby area and many seafront and other restaurants in nearby Diamant, a short ride west. *Resort hotel.*

★ **Ecole Hoteliere de la Martinique** • *at Anse-Gouraud near Schoelcher* • can be a comfortable place both for those who are learning the hotel business (and share their enthusiasm with you by giving wide smiles) and for guests who want to learn French (which you can do while the staff practices their English). The white stucco building is surrounded by lush, tropical planting, and the lobby has been decorated with bamboo-style furniture made in Martinique, and there are attractive bar and dining areas where the students practice their skills. The pleasant pool in the garden to the right as you enter is an ideal cool-off spot, but you'll need a car for mobility or island touring. The 14 bedrooms are modern, comfortable, and well maintained, and you won't find a better buy than this spot on this or many other islands. The hotel school closes for a few weeks in summer. (Most of the staff will speak some English; it's part of their hotel training.) *Hotel.*

★★ **L'Imperatrice Village** • *at the southern end of Anse Mitan* • is a community of rooms and apartments, built as cottages in pseudo-Victorian style. Pastel paint livens the village; porches are a favorite living area for the small, cozy-looking units. Not far from the activity of Anse Mitan, and slightly farther from Pointe du Bout, it seems like a long hot walk to either. (You may wish for a rental car.) An ownership link to the L'Imperatrice in town, this property is a favorite for French who enjoy a casual, carefree holiday with reasonable (not lavish) comforts. *Bungalow hotel.*

★★★ **Meridien Trois Ilets** • *at Pointe du Bout* • mesmerizes with an action plan that gives vacationers free watersports equipment (including windsurfers), several dining depots, and casino-plus-disco for after-dark dalliance. Meridien management regularly pulls the sand back onto the small stretch of beach, and tries to keep it there with a cement and stone groin that some use for sunning. The pool is ringed with umbrellas that help keep the sun off. Dining facilities range from the French idea of a coffee shop (which looks like home, but doesn't act like it) to *La Case Creole,* overlooking the sea, and *La Capitane,* the terrace restaurant, where the menu is huge, the prices are high, and the quality ranged from average to fair. Surroundings in the restaurant are certainly not tropical; it has the aura of a New York spot. Rooms all have small balcony and sea- or marina-view; there are several tennis courts and the whole range of activity around the marina to enjoy. The boat to Fort-de-France makes the 20-minute run several times daily. *Resort hotel.*

HOUSEKEEPING HOLIDAYS on Martinique range from apartments at places like PLM Azur La Pagerie (see below), to the several homes, most of them second homes for Martiniquais families, rented through the **Villa Rental Service** of the Martinique Office du Tourisme (B.P. 520, Fort-de-France, Martinique, F.W.I.). Other sources for self-catering places are **Logis Vacances Antilles** (T 011+596+63.12.91), which lists free-standing homes as well as studio and larger apartments, and **Gites de France** (T 011+596+73.67.92), operating with a system similar to that in mainland France, with listings around the island. Do not expect furnishings and facilities exactly like what you have at home. Most of the homes for rent on Martinique have been built on or near the sea, many of them in the hills overlooking the sea. Beaches on Martinique are not the Caribbean's best—at least those that are near Fort-de-France or any other hub of action are not. A home of your own in Martinique is ideal if you speak French (or want to struggle along with it to learn how to speak French), like to read, and do not insist on a beach at your doorstep. Most of the homes have tepid water (sun-warmed, not heated) and adequate but not lavish furnishings, and you will need a rental car for mobility.

For stocking up, you will find good French bread, and should be able to track down a fisherman who will keep you supplied with fish and langouste (as the local lobster is called). There are few supermarkets as you know them at home, but there are good stores for provisioning.

★★ **Alamanda** • *on Anse Mitan* • offers two dozen attractive studios, conveniently located on a beach enjoyed by residents. Several casual bistros and cafes join a few other small lodgings in this low-key area that has become popular for boardsailing and other beachside activities. *Apts.*

★ **Bambou** • *on Anse Mitan* • is dozens of tiny bungalows planted in the grassy area behind the open-air beach pavilion where the cafe allows for *soupe de poisson* (fish soup) or other local fare and a glass of wine—in your bathing suit. There's also a small pool for hotel guests. This very casual spot has basic accommodations at reasonable costs for folks who want to spend a vacation unfettered by dressing up and social events. Speaking fluent, colloquial French will add to your sense of belonging. Several shoreside bistros join this one at Anse Mitan, and the casino, marina, and action of the Pointe du Bout hotels is a short walk away. *Bungalows.*

★ **La Pagerie PLM Azur** • *at the Pointe du Bout marina* • has refined its mix from the 200-plus apartments to a management arrangement for only a portion of the units that make a beehive out of a piece of land not far from the Bakoua and Meridien hotels, at the marina near the boating activity. Walls are thin in the several 3-story buildings in which the apartments are located, and the facilities may seem spartan to Americans who expect lots of space. These units can be ideal for casual folk who aren't fussy about snappy service and who enjoy a bathing suit lifestyle. *Apts.*

Le Panoramic • *above Anse a l'Ane, across the harbor from Fort de France* • is a band of 2-story buildings, with simply furnished apartments, each with a porch and all with basic kitchen equipment. Planned for independent folks, the apartments are up a serpentine road above the beach (where small ferries leave on schedule for Fort-de-France). There's a pool near the rooms. You'll want a car for touring—and food purchases; there are several restaurants nearby. *Apts.*

Residence Grand Large • *on the south shore at Sainte Luce* • offers 18 comfortable, modestly furnished, studios that can be ideal for Francophiles who enjoy being some distance from most of the tourism developments. (The area is half way between Diamant, to the west, and Sainte Anne, to the east, but you'll need to look carefully to avoid missing the highway turn-off.) A car is essential for mobility, although the public bus does pass nearby on its intermittent service. *Apts.*

★ **Rivage Hotel** • *at Anse Mitan* • has rooms with kitchenettes, amid the bistros, near the beach. Compact and basic, these units are well located. *Apts.*

Village Club Anse Caritan • *on Anse Caritan, near Ste. Anne* • was built in the early 1980s with French travelers in mind. The several buildings that hold the rooms are above a lovely beach, near a once sleepy village that has developed restuarants and boutiques in response to resort development initiated by Club Med. The air-conditioned modern rooms are small, by U.S. standards, and show signs of age. They are well known to French families who enjoy the beachside living, with small kitchens and narrow beds. Activities for children are planned, as are some buffets and other adult events. *Apts.*

THE INN WAY can be wonderful, especially in historic surroundings or in some of the personality places that are members of the *Relais Creoles,* an island association of hotels with 50 rooms or less. A booklet giving brief descriptions of the members is available from the French West Indies Tourist Office. Interior decorating has not been a primary concern, although some places are beginning to make some efforts.

Here are some places I think are Martinique's best inns.

★★ **Diamant les Bains** • *on the south coast near the village of Diamant* • is perched at a bend in the shore-rimming southwest coastal road, with a nice view of Diamond Rock. Atmosphere has been added to a boxy white stucco building with wood fretwork in Victorian style. Guests at the back of the house (not the street side) have a lovely sea view. Rooms are neat and furnished simply. The restaurant serves both creole food and seafood. A car is essential for exploring, but you can walk into town from here. *Small hotel.*

★★★ **Le Fregate Bleu** • *a short distance off the main road, north of Le Francois on the east coast* • can be an ideal hideaway for well-heeled travelers who want a quiet place. Owned by Charles and Yveline de Luxy de Fossarieu, who masterminded Leyritz Plantation for many years, the inn has a pleasant pool, a lovely view of three offshore islets from each room's private balcony, and a mixture of antiques and functional furniture. You'll want a car for mobility. *Inn.*

★★ **Leyritz Plantation** • *in the north, at Basse-Pointe* • captures a historic setting to offer vacationers an extraordinary experience. The place is popular for lunch on day excursions, which may detract if you've sought out this lofty plantation perch for its spectacular isolation, but the grounds are spacious so there's room to get away. It takes a couple of hours to wind the 40 miles north from the airport or Fort-de-France, at a substantial taxi fare, but the journey can be a pleasant and interesting drive in a rental car. Lawns slide from the main-house doors into lush tropical foliage that would completely take over if things were not carefully tended. Most guests are content to sit by the pool, participate in the spa program, wander around the gardens, read, or go off to a beach with a picnic lunch and a will for leisure time. There's a tennis court, but arrangements have to be made elsewhere for waterskiing, snorkeling, scuba, and sailing equipment. The bedrooms are in the former slave quarters, which have been turned into 15 small cottages, and in newer buildings that have been added in the old style. *Inn.*

Le Madras • *at the fishing village of Tartane, on the east coast peninsula* • has grown from being a seaside bistro to a full-fledged restaurant, with several rooms upstairs and in a stucco block next door. You're at a pleasant beach, far away from most of tourism's clutter (except when tour buses drive past to one of the cafes down the road). *Inn.*

★ **Manoir de Beauregard** • *Chemin des Salines, near Ste.-Anne* • maintains a private home atmosphere, with comfortably modern rooms. Although the place often looks neglected it does have charm. There's no action here, but some available nearby if you want to go to the shops and bistros of Ste.-Anne. If the other guests are total strangers when you arrive, chances are they will be so when you leave, unless you are fluent in French and exceptionally outgoing—and they want to be, too. The core of the inn, and what has made it special, is the 18th-century main house. A speck of a pool is a cool-off spot; French and creole food are served alfresco at the back of the house, but reports continue to call it "average." All rooms have antique furnishings (or copies), most have 2 double four-poster beds and, for those who stay in the newer wing, a small terrace. Taxi fare from the airport (30 miles north) is pricey, but once here, you can walk to Ste.-Anne. The nearest beach is Plage des Salines, about 3 miles south. *Inn.*

★ **St. Aubin Hotel** • *at Petite Riviere Salee* • is an unusual gem, sitting on a hillside overlooking the seaside village of Trinite. You'll need a car for mobility; the public bus that passes along this road continues, eventually, from Trinite to Fort-de-France, but the ride involves a day's excursion. Otherwise, settle into this former private home on the hillside to swim in the pool, or walk around the grounds (a clearing among plantation fields) to look carefully at the fanciful gingerbread fretwork that trims the eaves of this marvelous pink-beige house. The veranda is perfect for rocking in the soothing tradewinds, and you can count on special island recipes in the dining room. All rooms have private bath, but each room has its own personality, depending on the view and the furnishings. (You'll probably take most of your dinners here unless you like driving wiggly island roads in the dark.) *Inn.*

LOW-COST LODGING   There are many small spots, not only in Fort-de-France (the capital), with ferry boat links to the beaches at Anse Mitan, but also in the area around Pointe du Bout's marina and in the foliage that lines Anse Mitan. Places with a few rooms can also be found around the island, often at fishing villages and on breeze-swept hillsides. Adventuresome travelers can have a wonderful time with a rental car and no planned itinerary, stopping for meals and overnight when a place seems suitable.

Insofar as inexpensive places are concerned, in addition to the housekeeping set-ups mentioned above, here are a few of the many:

Auberge de L'Anse Mitan • *at Anse Mitan on Trois Ilets* • is an old-timer, at the end of the popular Martiniquais beach of Anse Mitan across the bay from Fort-de-France. Ferries make scheduled trips. The inn has 20 air-conditioned rooms with bath/shower in its 3-story beachside stucco main house, where the open-to-breezes dining patio is at beach level, and 2 one-bedroom cottages along the beach (often taken on long-term rental). This is a very casual inn where you should ask (and pay extra) for a room with a sea view.

Le Balisier • *on Victor Hugo street in Fort-de-France, amid boutiques and restaurants* • shares walls with neighboring buildings. Lodgings are in small and simply furnished rooms with narrow beds and showers in bathrooms. Rooms on the front have city street view (and noise). The 19 rooms are okay for budget watchers who don't need to be on a beach.

Calalou • *on Anse-a-Ane, just west of Anse Mitan* • focuses on the beach and sea life, offering comfortable small nests that include some recently built additions and the core of a long popular place.

Caraibe Auberge • *on the shore at Anse Mitan* • is a small spot with rooms in a 2-story building. Second-floor rooms on the beach-facing side of the building have a view of the sea; others look inland. There's a pool at the inland edge of the beach.

Dunette • *on the shore at Ste.-Anne* • is a modern stucco building with simple rooms, the best of which face the sea. There's a dining patio at the shore, within sound of sea, and the place is better with offering simple comforts than with atmosphere and hospitality. Independent travelers might enjoy it.

Imperatrice • *facing the park in Fort-de-France, near Lafayette* • is a traditional downtown French West Indies hotel, spruced up in recent years but still with some atmosphere from the past. The rooms facing the Savane give guests a good view of the park activities, but you'll pay a price with street noises.

Lafayette • *facing the park, a few doors from Imperatrice* • has shops on its street level. Rooms range from small singles to doubles that are especially nice if you have a view overlooking the park. You're a short walk from the ferry boat dock, plus most of the boutiques and stores. The on-premise restaurant is worth booking.

La Malmaison • *neighbor to Lafayette, facing the Savane* • provides small rooms of varying shapes and furnishings. Rooms overlooking the Savane are viewful, but can be noisy.

Victoria • *in Didier, a residential area of Fort-de-France* • has reasonably comfortable rooms, but some can seem stuffy when the breeze drops. A road cuts off part of what used to be a beautiful view from this hillside, where lodgings might appeal to businessfolks who need to be in town for meetings. There's a pool and a restaurant that I've heard is good. (I haven't tried it.)

RESTAURANTS on Martinique share the unique French West Indian offerings known on Guadeloupe. Here, as on Guadeloupe, the informal bistros offer some of the best eating experiences for my vacation dollar. The cluster of restaurants at the marina of Pointe du Bout have capitulated to commerce, in some cases, although the small spots near Anse Mitan can seem fun. The simpler, older surroundings at some of the country villages and those places slightly off the beaten path are often excellent.

AUTHOR'S OBSERVATION

Food seems expensive, since all prices are in francs and the dollar exchange is low at press time. Count on more than 80F for luncheon, and at least 160F and probably more for a complete dinner.

If you want to follow the "when in Rome" principle, you enjoy soft drinks or wine, rum (usually as "poonch" or a "planteur"), and *biere*.

The accepted accompaniment for main meals is wine, which you can order by the carafe in the casual places and will be expected to order by the bottle, from the wine list, in the best French tradition at the more formal restaurants. For a bistro lunch, you may get by with French beer (*Kronenbourg* from the Alsace is sold here and *Lorraine* is locally brewed), and bottled water appears on most mealtime tables, but you will have to order it (for about 4F). The French West Indies *ti-punch* is the classic drink. Pronounced "poonch," the drink is a potent potion that is served with the ceremony of English tea in the traditional places: On the table will be set a tray with a small bucket of ice, a small carafe of what will prove to be sugar syrup, a plate with limes, and a bottle of powerful rum. Your host—or you—can mix the ingredients in the small shot-sized glass provided for the purpose. Water is not usually part of the recipe, but a generous squeeze of lime with your rum and sugar syrup on the rocks is. A *planteur*, also popular, is rum and fruit juice.

496 · · · MARTINIQUE

AUTHOR'S AWARDS

For dining on Martinique go to *Le Matador* for the spicy creole cooking; to *L'Ami Fritz* for its seafood presentation, atmosphere, and setting; to *Le Mouina* for its special surroundings and superb filet de sarde and other offerings.

L'Ami Fritz • *at Brin d'Amour, Trinite* • is worth the drive. Daniel Rebert made a name for himself (and his cooking) at two other locations—Anse d'Arlets and Anse Mabouyand—before moving here to adapt the charming home to his special restaurant. French imports are features, as well as local seafood, in a menu that takes cues from Alsace. Call for reservations.

L'Amphore • *along the narrow road from the end of Anse Mitan toward Bakoua Hotel* • is better known to residents than to tourists. Its locale seems out of the mainstream. My meal was exceptional, with the usual *poisson grille* (grilled fish), bread, salad, and wine. Owner Guy Dawson also claims Villa Creole.

Aux Fines Gourmandises • *marked by a Patisserie sign, on rue Victor Severe* • is the place to find if you're in Fort-de-France and want to have your midday meal as the locals do. You can dine well, automat style, pushing your tray and choosing your meal (so you don't need fluent French to sit at one of the nearby tables). Entrees were about 30F when I looked. Another place for good food, snack style, is across the street, marked by the awning that says *"plats emporter"* (plates-to-go).

La Belle Epoque • *in a residential area of Fort-de-France, on the Didier Rd.* • is also known as **Le Restaurant Rosso**, taking the name of its owner. Local *langouste* (lobster) and *ecrevisses* (crayfish) are specialties, but other typically French fare is also offered. The restored 19th-century house makes the surroundings special.

★★ **La Biguine** • *on Route de la Folie, just off Blvd. General de Gaulle, in Fort-de-France* • opened in 1984 and has received accolades from many. Gerard Padra, who had worked at Bakoua Hotel, features creole dishes (try the chicken fricassee for a modestly priced entree) and more elaborate fare. White walls are set off with brown accents, for a slightly sterile but refreshingly simple decor. Although the place can be pricey, it's possible to dine on his daily special for about 60F.

★ **La Bonne Auberge Chez Andre** • *near the beach at Anse Mitan* • is between 2 small houses on a side street not far from the Pointe du Bout marina. Your fish will be grilled, and whatever you order will be simple and good. Although the menu is written in English and French, the waitress or waiter will respond best to French or slow and precise English. Count on about 80F for a full lunch (in bathing suit with cover-up if you want) and 150F for dinner.

La Caprese • *in Fort-de-France, at rues Gallieni and Perrinon* • serves a simple lunch, with salads and other light fare, and becomes a cafe with piano bar at twilight and into the evening. Full dinners are served. The place is popular with residents, as well as with guests in the rooms upstairs. The restored Palais Creole is owned by Mounia, who made her name as a model for Yves St. Laurent.

Le Cantonnais • *set back from the boardwalk at Pointe du Bout's marina* • is an air-conditioned Chinese restaurant favored by residents. The menu is extensive, the food good, and if you want a break from creole cooking, this may be worth a try.

La Cave Roi • *at 4 rue Garnier* • is a wine bar, serving special cheeses as well as foie gras and other delicacies with your choice of wine. Inquire about entertainment on weekends. Plans were to have a piano bar for Friday and Saturday nights.

Davidiana • *on the boardwalk at the Pointe du Bout Marina* • is the new name for a space long occupied by Mme. Sidonie. M. and Mme. Choukroune continue the bistro style, now popular for informal meals in an alfresco setting, in sight of the many yachts and marina activity. In addition to salads, French-style sandwiches, and pizza, full meals feature seafood, chicken, and meats with tasty sauces—and fresh French bread. Location makes this place special.

★★★ **D'Esnambuc** • *in Fort-de-France* • is up the stairs near the building on the corner to your left as you get off the ferry from Pointe du Bout. It is on venerable ground. For several years, the location was that of Le Foyal (now closed), the most famous haute cuisine restaurant in the city. D'Esnambuc has good food, but the surroundings are crowded, especially at lunchtime, and closed in so that you could be anywhere. There's a view of the harbor if you capture a window table, and a lot of noise if the place is full. Look it over before you make your reservation here, but count on above average French cooking and good seafood—with wine—for your meal.

★★ **Le Foulard** • *at Schoelcher, northwest along the coast from Fort-de-France* • is named for Victor Schoelcher, a leader in the 1848 abolition of slavery in the French West Indies. The taxi fare can be high from a Pointe du Bout base (but not from Fort-de-France), and you'll have to make arrangements for the taxi to return for pick-up. If you drive yourself, be sure to get specific directions. The restaurant is unpretentious, and therefore not easy to find. Call for a reservation and inquire about the evening's special, which should be preceded (if you are hungry) by the soupe de poisson. Pastries and bread can become an addiction.

La Grand' Voile • *near the Yacht Club, on the waterfront in Fort-de-France* • has new owners and a new menu, but the location—upstairs, where the best tables are by the windows with a good view of the harbor—remains unique. The *Caribbean Newsletter* (page 9) will have an update on style and offerings. Count on high prices for gala dinners and good wines.

Lafayette • *in the hotel of that name facing the Savanne in Fort-de-France* • is attractive—and very expensive. Tableware is elegant and decor suggests fine European restaurants. Located one floor up from street level, the restaurant's elaborate menu includes main courses bathed in delicate sauces, some with fresh herbs, and fine wines. At a tally close to 2000F, this place set four of us back about $400 at the rate of exchange when we dined. Brace yourself.

La Mouina • *on route de Redoute, just outside Fort-de-France* • opened to rave reviews in early '88. Magdelaine and Guy Karchesz make this place special, not only with the decor they've chosen for the one-time house, but also for the al fresco patio dining. Creole and traditional French specialties are attractively served, with fish a menu staple and domestic produce used in interesting ways. My bonito *en Papillote* was excellent.

★★★ **La Matadore** • *at Anse Mitan, the turn-off from the Pointe du Bout road* • is across the road from its birthplace not far from the beach. Francois (the former chef at Bakoua) and Raymonde Crico serve lively creole specialties as well as local langouste (lobster). Count on good, fresh fish, and the chef's special (whatever it may be) to be excellent—and the atmosphere to be favored by residents who know good food.

Plantation de Leyritz • *in the northern quarter of Martinique* • is an 18th-century estate that has developed its dining for groups and tourists. Food is served in a building near the pool, and reports were good when I stopped by for this edition. Satisfied diners liked their meal; I was too late for mine. I suspect the place is better for dinner (if you are staying here), then it is when it is full of day-trippers who arrive for lunch and fill the place with lively conversation.

★★★ **Le Tiffany** • *outside Fort-de-France* • is a gem, with prices in keeping with the excellence. Surroundings are almost reason enough to make a reservation for dinner here, but food preparation and service are also superb. A traditional French West Indian house has been preened to perfection (and painted pink and white). Plan ahead for a dinner reservation and hope that the place is open (and your wallet can cope with prices) if you are on Martinique at other than peak-season winter.

Other places to head for when you're touring the island are **Mme. Edjam's** in Basse-Pointe (almost at the northern tip of the island, at the village near the turn off for Leyritz) and Mme. Palladino's **Le Colibri,** in Morne des Esses, a worthy goal for Creole cooking in typical homelike surroundings on the day you tour the north. The place has had a shower of publicity in U.S. newspapers and magazines, so calling for a reservation is essential to assure a seat. **Poi et Virginie,** a casual thatch-roofed seaside spot at Ste.-Anne, a short walk from Dunette Hotel and at a corner of the town's main square, is related to **Filets Bleus,** both good spots for a memorable meal if you're staying in or driving around the south.

NATURAL SURROUNDINGS There's a lot on this island to interest the naturalist. Not only is the area around **Montagne Pelee** fascinating for the flora and fauna on the flanks of the volcano, but adventuresome travelers can follow the road from Morne Rouge up about 2500 feet, to start hiking for almost six hours to reach the top. Check with the Office du Tourisme to get a reliable guide, since the path is often overgrown and can be treacherous for the uninitiated. Speaking French helps, since your guide will probably be most comfortable conversing in that language.

Parc Naturel Regional de la Martinique is the designation given to the verdant area around Mt. Pelee, in the northern section of the island (in the vicinity of Leyritz Plantation). Check with the Office du Tourisme for information about hikes and walks and other activities that are planned from time to time. Anyone interested in island flora and fauna should at least make the drive north, coming down the windward side of the island from Leyritz. Cecile Graffin, tireless French West Indies touter in the New York City tourist office, tells of a six-hour hike along the shoreline trails in the vicinity of Grand' Riviere and Le Precheur on the northwestern tip of the island. It took her half an hour to return to the starting point by boat!

In addition to the northern area, including the peaks and flanks of Mt. Pelee, the Parc Naturel includes **Presqu'ile de la Caravelle,** a peninsula jutting into the sea on the east coast and an area now undergoing development for recreational facilities for the Martiniquais. Plans include a marina in addition to full watersports facilities for scuba and waterskiing as well as tennis and other facilities, but at this writing you will find only beautiful scenery, the small fishing village of Tartane, and some dirt roads leading to remote coves and the ruins of the 18th-century Chateau Dubuc.

Jardin de Balata is a remarkable botanical garden that covers several acres with gorgeous anthurium lillies, hibiscus, heliconia, orchids, and other tropical blooms, each in its season, as well as with huge ferns, palms, and other trees. Well worth a visit, the gardens will appeal to nature-lovers and birders who should schedule plenty of time to wander the grounds. Named for a hardwood tree that is a sapodilla relative, the gardens have been created since the 1960s and are owned by Jean-Philippe and Marie-Claude Thoze, who have also restored the typical Creole house on the premises. Balata Gardens are reached by following route 3 north out of Fort de France, past the prominent hillside cathedral of Sacre Coeur. Check with your hotel for times when the property is open to the public.

At the south coast hook of land that curls east to west, there are some lovely beaches at **Les Salines.** Most of them are "empty" during the week, although the ones reached by paved road are enjoyed by Martiniquais and others on weekends. (Those reached by dirt road are almost always reasonably underpopulated.)

The drive along the south coast, heading around the west coast past Anses d'Arlet to work back east toward Trois Ilets and Pointe du Bout, is a lovely one with many nice views and plenty of places to pause for a picnic or photographs. One unique natural sight is Rocher du Diamant (Diamond Rock). The Rock, according to my mentor Sydney Clark, is "a historic oddity offshore . . . rising 600 feet sheer from the sea. Here, in the year 1804, Captain (later Admiral)

Samuel Hood, in command of a British fleet, landed a garrison of 120 men, together with cannons and ammunition—a most hazardous undertaking for those days—bidding them hold the rock against the French. They held it for almost a year and a half with such unfaltering heroism that Hood commissioned it as the sloop-of-war HMS *Diamond Rock!"*

Insofar as **underwater sights** are concerned, the French West Indies have been favorites for the Cousteau followers since Jacques Cousteau first dived in these waters a couple of decades ago. Diving, which is *plongee* in French, is very popular. The area off the west coast below Mt. Pelee is noteworthy. When the volcanic eruption of 1902 covered the town with ash, it also threatened many ships anchored in the harbor. Dozens went to the deep, some too deep but others at sites where they can be searched today.

In the south, the area around Rocher du Diamant is noteworthy, as is the area off the southwest coast fishing village of Anse d'Arlets. Reputable divemasters can suggest other noteworthy sites.

PLACES WORTH FINDING on Martinique are a marvelous mixture of small fishing villages, legitimate and interesting historic sites, and plenty of verdant tropical countryside—occasionally shored with beaches. The big tourist hotels have activities desks where you can sign on for a group tour, with daily options that vary according to the prevailing plan, but there's a lot to be said for striking out on your own—in a rental car—especially if your French is fluent. Martinique is a very special island, where the French flair is so ingrained in the lives and looks of the people that even the smallest villages have an ambience all their own, more reminiscent of places on the French Riviera than of other Caribbean islands you may know.

Musee de la Pagerie (daily except Mon., 9 a.m.–5:30 p.m.; 8F) at Trois Ilets is on the site of the house where Napoleon's Josephine was born, but don't be misled into thinking that the present museum was her birthplace. It was the former kitchen for a plantation on the site, built after the 1860 hurricane blew the former plantation to bits. The gigantic African tulip tree may have stood on the property when she played here, but the museum and most of its collection are the result of a local doctor's interest in the famed Martiniquaise. In addition to costumed dolls in cases, and letters written by Napoleon to his wife (whom *he* called Josephine; her birth name was Marie Josephe Rose), there are mementos and portraits of Beauharnais (Josephine's first husband), comments about Josephine's two children (one of whom married Napoleon's brother to become Queen of Holland and mother of Napoleon III), and her divorce from Napoleon in 1809.

The small museum is a short drive from the hotels at Pointe du Bout and Anse Mitan, on the road to the airport. You can allow an extra hour or more for a visit and to pause for a stroll around the gardens with pond that you pass on the way to get to the museum. Known as the Parc Botanique, the compact garden nestles near the golf course, and is worth a look if you are interested in tropical flowers (and the gates are open). The road off the main road at Trois Ilets is well marked. A guide is usually available—and even in French, with a few words in English, can help with highlights.

Mont Pelee is the peak that put the island into the headlines in 1902 when the volcano erupted. The northeast-coast site is about an hour's drive up the coast from Fort-de-France. For most, the **Musee Volcanologique** (daily 9 a.m.–noon, 3–5 p.m.; 5F) tells the story in vivid enough displays. There are twisted and tortured clocks that stopped at the hour the volcano erupted (8 a.m.), as well as before and after photographs that are hard to believe when you look at the sleepy village that has taken the place of once-thriving Saint-Pierre. The pictures and remnants give another dimension to the most monumental event in Martinique's history, and you can stroll through the couple of rooms in a quick 20 minutes.

Saint-Pierre is described as "the quaintest, queerest, and prettiest withal, among West Indian cities," by Lafcadio Hearn. He comments about the town being "all stone-built and stone-flagged, with very narrow streets, wooden or zinc awnings, and peaked roofs of red tile, pierced by gabled dormers. Most of the buildings are painted in a clear yellow tone, which contrasts delightfully with the burning blue ribbon of tropical sky above; and no street is absolutely level; nearly all of them climb the hills, descend into hollows, curve, twist, describe sudden angles. There is everywhere a loud murmur of running water, pouring through the deep gutters contrived between the paved thoroughfare and the absurd little sidewalks, varying in width from one to three feet. The architecture is quite old; it is 17th century probably and it reminds one of a great deal of that characterizing the antiquated French quarter of New Orleans. All the tints, the forms, the vistas, would seem to have been especially selected or designed for aquarelle studies, just to please the whim of some extravagant artist. The windows are frameless openings without glass; some have iron bars; all have heavy wooden shutters with movable slats, through which light and air can enter as through Venetian blinds. These are usually painted green or bright bluish-gray." Lafcadio Hearn's description of the town in the 1880s continues; the town does not. When Mont Pelee erupted on May 8, 1902, the entire thriving metropolis of Saint-Pierre, known at that time as the "Paris of the West Indies," was extinguished by clouds of poisonous gas, horrendous heat, and a blanket of hot ash. Today Saint-Pierre is a small village, with a big history—and its interesting small museum.

In *FORT-DE-FRANCE,* **La Savane** is the town's central park. Tourism has touched the shoreside section, across the road from the place the ferries dock from Anse Mitan and Pointe du Bout. That end is cluttered with shoppers' stalls stuffed with Haitian carvings and other tourist trinkets. At the other side of the park, not far from the imposing **Schoelcher Library** with its intricate facade, leisure time is enjoyed by the islanders who linger on the benches that have been sifted around the sometimes well-trimmed gardens.

Musee Departemental de la Martinique (Mon.–Fri. 8 a.m.–noon, 3–6 p.m., Sat. 8 a.m.–12 p.m.; 5F) will fascinate anyone interested in island archeaology. Relics retrieved from the early Arawak and Carib civilizations have been organized in display cases, with some explanation (usually in French, but simple enough for anyone with rudimentary knowledge of the language to decipher). Documentary films and slide talks are sometimes sponsored by the musee; check with the tourist office, which is along the waterfront in a special building you can easily find, if you walk along rue de Liberte to the shore. **Musee Gauguin** (daily 10 a.m.–5:30 p.m.; 5F) is off the shore-rimming-road south of St. Pierre and is near the place where Gauguin lived and painted for four months in 1887. A nice interlude after a day of natural sights, the small museum holds the expected memorabilia—letters and small items relating to his life on the island—as well as some copies of his painting while here.

Fishing villages are liveliest in the morning, when the fleet has returned with the catch and the stalls are set up at the shore. At their best when you go on your own, so that you can mingle with the local folk (who will look you over because you will look different), the villages are perfect places to settle into one of the small cafes that set up seaside to serve the fresh grilled fish—sometimes served with lime and usually best with a fiery shot of rum. Places like **Marin** not far from Ste.-Anne in the south, and **Vauclin** or **Le Francois** on the west coast are special spots to sample the Antilles Francaises. Both are about as different from the tourist tempo at Pointe du Bout as you would wish to get (and a detour for a broiled langouste at Les Brisants near Le Francois can put the final touch on a perfect island day).

SPORTS on Martinique stretch from north to the south, and from the calm western coast of the *departement* to the rugged east. While most of the sports that need special equipment (scuba diving, which is known as *plongee,* boardsailing, and yacht sailing) are centered on the resorts, the individual sports (horseback riding and hiking) can be found in the country, in places seldom seen by most tourists but well known to the Martiniquais. Action centers are the areas of Pointe du Bout and Anse Mitan, both a 20-minute ferryboat ride from the waterfront of Fort-de-France, and the Club Med in the south.

Sailing centers on the Pointe du Bout marina, where yachts can be chartered at *Soleil et Voile* (T 596+66.09.14), operating from their own boat moored at the Pointe du Bout marina. Other firms chartering out of this marina include *Karacoulis* (T 596+66.03.85), *Tropic Yachting* (T 596+66.01.72), and *Star Voyages Antilles* (T 596+66.00.72). Crewed boat charters are priced to include fuel and water, and have high quality radio and other equipment on board. When you charter, be sure to ask for a copy of the French guide to cruising the Antilles; if your language is not French, there is an English guide by Wilensky that is an essential companion. Yachtsmen can track down charters simply by walking along the piers. *West Indies Bird,* a 39-foot sloop, has been available for charter through *Caribtours,* from their office near the entrance to the Hotel PLM Azur La Pagerie, and the watersports desks at PLM Azur Carayou, Bakoua. Meridien can also arrange for day and longer sailing on bigger boats.

Although the deep bay marked by Fort-de-France is a yachtsman's favorite, the favored cruising area in this part of the Caribbean is the several specks of the Grenadine islands. Some firms include flights to St. Vincent in your charter fee so that you can board at the best sailing area, and not have to pound your way across the often rugged seas from Martinique, southeast to St. Lucia and on to the north of St. Vincent, where you sail down the coast to reach the string of Grenadines that stretch out from the south. For true yachtsmen with club credentials from home, the *Club de la Voile de Fort-de-France* is at Pointe Simon, and the *Yacht Club de la Martinique* is on blvd. Chevalier Ste. Marthe. Ste.-Anne is a burgeoning yachtsmen's goal.

Scuba has surged to the forefront of water activities in the French West Indies, as you might expect from an area that can benefit from knowledge of Frenchman Jacques Cousteau who developed the underwater lung. The French instructors are licensed in international scuba organizations such as the World

Underwater Federation and the French Federation of Underwater Sports. Spirotechnique and scubapro regulators are used, and although the bilingual instruction is excellent, the teaching procedure varies slightly from what you may be used to in your hometown pool. Boats often go to Anses d'Arlets and the Ramier inlet where there is a wreck as well as plenty of coral. At Carbet, just south of St. Pierre, there are scuba facilities at Club Marouba and near the Christophe Colombe hotel. French instructors take experienced divers to spots off the coast at St. Pierre (to shipwrecks like that of the *Roraima*) and farther north at Le Precheur. Club Med, on the south coast, includes basic scuba lessons in its week-long all-inclusive holiday (no extra charge), but complete novices may find that the group technique does not give the very special personal touch that some beginners may need.

Snorkeling is good off many shores, but especially off the beaches at the south near Ste.-Anne, and at some of the small coves that cut into the west coast around the point below Anse Mitan at les Anses d'Arlets.

Glass-bottom boat excursions are offered from Meridien and La Bateliere hotels, with morning, afternoon, and sunset two-hour journeys.

Deep-sea fishing has not been organized for tourists as it has been in some places. The Pointe du Bout area hotels have access to fishing boats, so check through your hotel when you arrive on Martinique, and ask around at the marina to see if there's some news on this subject. For adventuresome tourists who speak French, it may be possible to go out with one of the local fisherman when he goes to collect his nets, but this is *hard* work (as you can see when you stand on shore and watch them return) and not a sightseeing expedition. Your space and your brawn are important.

Golfers should book at Pointe du Bout hotels if being near the 18-hole Robert Trent Jones course is important. The course opened for the season of '77–'78. *The Empress Josephine Golf Course* (T 596+76.32.81) undulates over several acres (6640 yards) near the village of Trois-Ilets. Greens fees for 18 holes are 180F per day, with a weekly rate of 910F. Facilities include club house, with lockers, pro shop, and a new restaurant/bar. Electric carts can be rented; tennis courts are floodlit for night play. The Club Med may negotiate some special rate, but if you go on your own from that southern spot, you will have almost a 300F taxi fare to get to and from the course; playing golf on the day you rent a car turns out to be the most economical way to play from the south coast.

Hiking is popular with the Martiniquais, and guided walks are arranged through the Parc Regional. Check at the Office du Tourisme on the waterfront in Fort-de-France for details about possible hikes, dates, and times. The day will be a lot pleasanter if you speak some French, but it is possible to survive without it. One of the popular hiking areas, with some occasionally marked trails is Presqu'ile de la Caravelle Nature Preserve, on the east coast. Hikes are also planned around and up the flanks of Mont Pelee in the north.

Horseback riding is "outlawed" on beaches in France—and that applies to the French West Indies, but there are plenty of interesting trails inland. If you ride at *Ranch Jack Galochat,* near Anses d'Arlets, which is less than half an hour's drive from the Pointe du Bout hotels, you can canter around on small and nimble creole horses. Do not count on English Riding School technique. The Antilles Francaises consider horses a means of transportation and the method of riding is not showmanship as much as survival. *Black Horse* (at La Pagerie) is another stable near most hotels and *La Cavale* has horses near the Diamant-Novotel in the south.

Tennis is very popular and most big hotels have courts. La Bateliere has six courts and the hotel's location just north of the city of Fort-de-France and across the harbor from most of the tourist activity has led to a focus on tennis. Diamant-Novotel also has courts. Other courts are available at Bakoua, Meridien, and PLM Azur Carayou in the Pointe du Bout area. There are courts at the Golf Club, and Leyritz has one court at its mountainside inn. The Club Med has 6, with 4 of them floodlit.

Boardsailing, the surfboard-and-sail sport that got its start in California in the late 1960s, has put a fringe of colorful sails at all the major tourist beaches. The sport is so popular, in fact, that the International Windsurfing Championships were first held in Martinique in 1978, and there are special events at regular intervals. There are several small booths (or tables) for rental and instruction on Anse Mitan and Meridien, PLM Azur Carayou and La Bateliere have windsurfers, as does the Club Med.

Pilots who would like to take a Cessna or Cherokee from the *Aero Clubs de Martinique* or *les Ailes de la Martinique* will have to have a French license, which you can get on the spot from the local civil aeronautics board (but allow at least a day to track down the person and price).

TREASURES AND TRIFLES on Martinique are clustered along the side streets of Fort-de-France, running parallel to the sea from rue de la Liberte, bordering La Savane, especially along rue Victor Hugo, rue Blenac, and rue Antoine Siger.

La Savane, the park that's the heart of Fort-de-France (across the road from the ferry pier), is a lively market bazaar most days. Individual entrepreneurs sell madras clothes, jewelry, and a wide variety of colorful, often good quality, crafts. Bargain on most prices; it's part of the ritual.

Roger Albert, at 7 rue Victor Hugo, is one source for perfume, china, Lalique, Lladro, Limoges, other crystal, household items and top-quality imports from France and other points. The store has been offering duty-free merchandise to visitors for almost 40 years, enlarging at regular intervals to make shopping easier for the hordes of cruise passengers who flock here when their ship's in port. The list of imports can seem overwhelming, with most luxury items represented, but not always in all styles, sizes, and/or patterns. If you are searching for a special item, contact the store in advance to find out if it's in stock—and the price. (Be sure to check your hometown store's price also.) The store gives a 20% discount on the French franc price when you buy with U.S.-dollar traveler's checks or credit card.

Cadet Daniel, at 72 rue Antoine Siger, also carries Limoges china and Lalique crystal in addition to Baccarat, and gold and silver jewelry plus some less expensive (but imaginative) creole jewels. And Cadet Daniel also advertises a "20% discount for payment in traveler's checks and credit cards."

Merlande, a department store near the Cathedral, is air-conditioned and well stocked. Although planned for residents, visitors can find a good selection of perfumes and other French products.

Au Printemps, with no direct link to the name you may know from mainland France, is at 12 rue Schoelcher, by the cathedral. It is one of the few department stores in the Caribbean that I think is worth my shopping time. I have found some excellent values (often at sales) and some interesting, and reasonable, French fashions and imports from elsewhere, sold at prices that big chain reactions can afford. **K-dis** on a main route parallel to the waterfront is a discount department store, which can be interesting if you like knowing what residents buy.

The **Caribbean Art Center,** also called Centre des Metiers d'Art, is in its own building opposite the Tourist Office on Boulevard Alfassa, which is the main waterfront road. The selection sold here is all handmade, and although there's been a change in quality (some of the naivete has gone with the standardization of designs) as the place has gotten more commercial, there are interesting colorful wall hangings as well as a number of paintings, wood bowls, carvings, and other items that have been made on the island. For one-stop shopping for island-made items, this is the place to find.

Most shops close at about noon, to open again at 2:30 p.m. or so, except on Sat. when the morning hours are all the time you'll have for shopping.

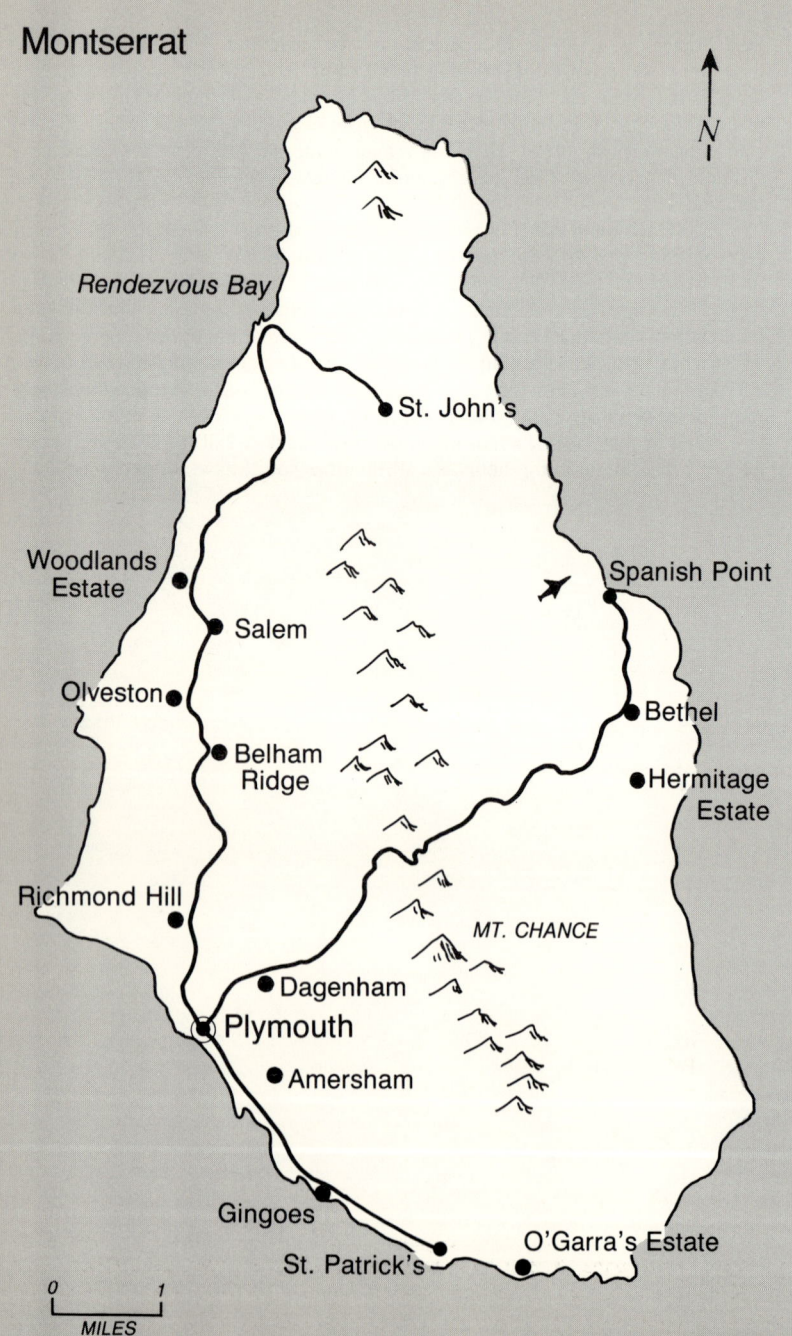

MONTSERRAT

> Montserrat Tourist Board, Box 7, Plymouth, Montserrat, W.I., T 809+491–2230, fax 809+491–2337; Box 666, Station A, Toronto, Ont., Canada M5W 1E4, T 416+868–1852; Caribbean Tourism Organization, 20 East 46th St., New York, NY 10017, T 212+682–0435, fax 212+697–4258; High Commission for Eastern Caribbean States, 10 Kensington Court, London W85DL, England, T 01+937–9522.

$ · · · US$1 = EC$2.65
Unless otherwise noted, all prices are in U.S. dollars.

Lights were ablaze at the hotel when I arrived after nightfall on November 4, 1989. The hearty Saturday night barbecue (with a choice of chicken, steak, or fish) was served for guests who included 50-plus men from the Yorkshire (England) Electrical Company who, with U.S. teams, helped string new power lines around this 11-by-7-mile British Territory. The former lines were yanked from their posts and draped over the landscape; posts joined uprooted trees that lay in the fields like spent matchsticks.

    It's accurate to say that Hurricane Hugo trashed this island. Although Montserratians were awestruck for months by its impact, and many will feel its affects for years to come, a spirit of sharing and replenishing flourished. Everyone helped. "My house was okay, but I'm helping the rest of my family rebuild," John-Five, a taxi driver, told me. Everyone was touched. Miraculously, there were only 10 deaths out of a population of 12,000, and each of those can be attributed to extenuating circumstances (either old age or, in one case, youth flirting with disaster by attempting to ride a log along a raging river).

    "My children were under the bed, after our roof blew off," LIAT employee Peter Galloway told me. "These days, when there's a strong wind, they are afraid." A fellow passenger on the 10-minute flight from Antigua to Montserrat told how she began putting things in plastic bags when her roof started to leak, but soon the wind tore the galvanized metal roof from the walls. She was soaked for several hours—from about 2 or 3 a.m. until almost midday—while the storm pummeled Montserrat. "Everything was ruined, but we are alive," she noted with a gentle smile.

    The taxi-van that provides livelihood for Adolphus Moreson escaped serious damage. Dents were pounded out and, after repainting, the van looks like new. "When the road was cleared, about four days after the storm, I drove from my home [near the airport] to Plymouth," he told me as we drove along the now cleared roads. "I couldn't stand it. When I got there I turned around and came home again. Everything was smashed. The hillsides were brown."

By early November breadfruit trees sprouted the first of their post-Hugo huge waxy leaves; denuded stately palms were sending out tender green shoots as the first new fronds; and broad-leaved bright-green vines were wrapping rubble that included slabs of tin roofs, scattered over the countryside by winds that some put at 200 miles per hour.

St. Anthony's Anglican Church was packed for the 8:15 a.m. service on "Harvest Thanksgiving" Sunday, November 5. Although the minister noted the lack of harvest in Montserrat this year, he assured his congregation that "God's harvest didn't fail. There's been a little hiccup in this part of the world, but 'Harvest Thanksgiving' is more than gifts from the field. It's a chance to share—and this year Montserrat shares the harvest from elsewhere in the world."

Although it dwindled as time passed, initial aid was swift. British ships arrived with supplies, anchoring offshore to lighter goods to the island. The town pier was destroyed and the chief minister began negotiating for funds to build a much larger port, suitable for cruise ship visits. Canadians brought materials to assist with rebuilding the airport terminal, a new roof for the hospital, and repairs for schools. U.S. aid helped with clearing the roads, and with rebuilding. A hospital ship stood offshore, providing medical assitance.

Montserrat has been called the "Emerald Isle," not only because of its heritage (settled by indentured Irish fleeing Cromwellian persecution) but also because of the lush robe of crops and foliage on its once verdant mountainsides. After Hugo's shearing, the island began putting on a new cloak of green foliage. Today it is difficult for newcomers to notice Hugo's effect. Life is back to normal.

POLITICAL PICTURE is put in focus by Chief Minister John Osborne, whose People's Liberation Movement controls the majority in the government, which follows the British system. The opposition party is the Progressive Democratic Party. Montserratians living in Canada, England, and the United States also play a role in local politics. The chief minister has spoken in favor of independence for his island, which now holds the status of British Crown Colony, also referred to as a British Dependent Territory, but the majority of island residents seem to prefer the links with Britain. The communist line promulgated on many Caribbean islands appears here through George Irish, whose affection for Cuba is widely acknowledged. Although there are periodic "differences of opinion" among local politicians, Montserrat has quietly and steadily improved the standard of living for its citizens, and appears to be one of the more stable island communities in the region. The island has a resident governor, the queen's representative, but its daily affairs are in the hands of its chief minister and other locally elected officials.

ISLAND APPEARANCE: Montserrat is, once again (now that new growth has replenished areas shorn clean by Hurricane Hugo, on September 17, 1989), an "Emerald Isle" of green mountains sitting in the sea. Crops and foliage flourish on its volcanic peaks, which are only occasionally trimmed with a road. Never known for white sand beaches, since there are none that are accessible, shores plunge steeply to the sea or are fringed with brown-to-gray volcanic sand when the waterline slopes. Although soft underfoot, the dark sand can seem startling to white-footed travelers. Plymouth, the seaside capital of this British territory, is the only settlement of note, and there are only a few hotels.

AUTHOR'S OBSERVATION

Icterus oberi, the Montserrat Oriole, has been the pivot point for a domestic conservation program, sponsored and supervised by RARE Center for Tropical Bird Conservation, working through the Montserrat National Trust. Put in place soon after the devastating visit of Hurricane Hugo on September 17, 1989, the program that was administered by Montserratian Rose Willock succeeded in creating national awareness of the oriole and its habitat. Check with the Montserrat National Trust in Plymouth, Montserrat, for assistance with hiking to areas known to be oriole habitats. For information about the program, contact RARE Center (1529 Walnut St., Philadelphia, PA 19102; T 215+275-8087).

LIFESTYLE is uniquely West Indian. The population of 12,000 moves along at its own pace, gradually improving the quality of life for all. Although things may have progressed beyond the days when a Montserratian told me there could be no thievery because if someone appeared with something new, everyone would know where it came from, life is mutually supportive and peaceful. The island is mercifully untouched by the heavy foot of tourism. Life has proceeded naturally to full integration, with a pattern of daily life reminiscent of rural life in the USA and Canada.

MEDICAL FACILITIES: The small hospital in Plymouth is reasonably well equipped and staffed by doctors who have had training in Britain, Canada, and the U.S. Although serious medical emergencies warrant chartering a plane to go to Puerto Rico or Miami, minor problems can be handled on Montserrat. There is a family feeling on this island that gives a sense of well-being.

MONEY MATTERS focus on the EC$. Change your greenbacks at the bank and spend local. This is not a tourist island (although visitors are welcome). One of the several small courtesies to your hosts is to follow their system instead of imposing yours. Exchange is fixed at about EC$2.65 to US$1, but you will find some shops giving only EC$2.50. Taxi fares have climbed, as they have on all islands due to increased costs (figure about EC$20 to Plymouth; EC$35 to Vue Pointe, and about EC$100 for an island tour).

COMMUNICATIONS are far more sophisticated than the size of the island might suggest. Direct-dial telephone service to Montserrat uses the 809 code + 491 for Montserrat, followed by the local 4-digit number. From Montserrat, in addition to placing calls from your hotel (with a surcharge), you can purchase a phonecard from Cable & Wireless in Plymouth, to place calls yourself, on the telephones designated for card use. AT&T's USADirect system works from Montserrat to the U.S. by dialing 1+800+872–2881 to reach an AT&T operator who will place your call either collect or charged to your AT&T account. Facsimile machines are used by many businesses. Telex and cable are also handled through the island-based Britain-affiliated Cable and Wireless Ltd.

ARRIVAL at Blackburne Airport is unfettered by the presumptuous routines of busier resort areas. The 15-minute flight from Antigua sweeps in with a breathtaking pass at the north-coast mountains before gliding onto the tarmac strip. Antigua-based Caribbean carrier *LIAT* (Leeward Islands Air Transport) makes the flight five or more times daily, sometimes leaving ahead of schedule, so be at Antigua's airport when they tell you to be there! (LIAT also sometimes leaves late, so come prepared for lingering.) Round-trip Antigua-Montserrat is about EC$150, but fitted into your U.S.-purchased fare, the difference between fare to Antigua and to Montserrat can be only a few dollars.

Blackburne Airport is at the northeast coast, near the site of one of the early Arawak settlements (as shards found on the site have proved). The tidy terminal is sufficient for service these days; immigration is quick and easy (your U.S. passport gets a shamrock stamp), customs perfunctory—even when you are bringing in food for meals at the house you've rented.

CRUISE ships are not a common sight in Montserrat's Plymouth harbor. Only a few small ships (usually those that are island-based) stop here, and they anchor offshore, bringing passengers ashore in small boats.

DEPARTURE involves flight check-in, forfeit of Immigration slip, payment of a $5 departure tax, and a wait in the breeze-swept lounge. Don't count on shops. The few items for sale include Antiguan rum and Montserrat condiments.

TOURING TIPS: First-timers should take a taxi, not only to get where you're going, southwest across the island, but also for the lore and the option to have a lot of questions answered. If you advise your hotel about your time of arrival (and manage to arrive, with the erratic plane connections, pretty close to that time), chances are they will have someone there to meet you. If not, negotiate yourself, but be sure the fare is understood (and know whether the dollars are EC or US) before you start riding. Years ago, when he was one of a few drivers, Adolphus Moreson shared stories about his childhood on Montserrat and I often ask for his help these days. Ask for him—or for Peter Galloway, who works at the airport. Once settled at your hotel, you can rent a car for maximum flexibility (and should have arranged for one in advance if you have rented a home to set up housekeeping). In height of winter season, write in advance for your car reservation as well as for hotel/home overnights.

Rental cars are available through villa-renting firms as well as through the hotels. Three local firms with rentals are *Ethelyne's* (T 809+491–2855), *Jefferson's* (T 809+491–2126), and *Pauline's* (T 809+491–2345).

LODGING: Your choice is one of two resort-style hotels, one commercial hotel, and a few guest houses—or rental of a villa or apartment-condominium, often with access to a pool.

A 10% service charge and a 7% government tax will be added to the room rate.

AUTHOR'S AWARD
Vue Pointe continues to be my favorite place in Montserrat, not only because the rooms are comfortable, but also because the Osbornes are very involved with their hotel, and hospitality is assured.

Information about places to stay is included under Hotels/Resorts, Housekeeping Holidays, the Inn Way, and Low-Cost Lodgings. Stars are awarded within Montserrat as the properties relate to their counterparts on other islands.

HOTELS: There are only three full-service hotels in Montserrat.

Flora Fountain • *on Lower Dagenham Rd. in Plymouth* • sits on a corner with its entrance up the side street. The 2-story stucco building has a center court (where the fountain sometimes operates). The bar is popular with some local folk; the dining room is an area of tables in the patio and under cover, near the bar. Bedrooms are upstairs, with basics but not much style. Air-conditioners can be essential when there's no breeze and to keep street noises out. Used mostly by businessfolks, this place offers in-town rooms, within a few steps from a bank. *Small hotel.*

★★ **Montserrat Springs** • *on the hillside, overlooking Plymouth* • began life as the Emerald Isle hotel and went through a phase as a health clinic. The hotel provides comfortable and attractive lodgings, in standard hotel rooms and housekeeping villas, with a pool as the focal point for those who want to linger on the premises, and a weekly all-you-can-eat barbecue evening as part of the entertainment. Rebuilding after Hugo resulted in many improvements, including new furnishings. *Hotel, Apts.*

★★★ **Vue Pointe Hotel** • *on a hillside, about 10 minutes' drive north of Plymouth* • has been the island's number one hotel for two generations. The place continues to be a hospitable, family-run inn where guests have been returning to their favorite winter retreat for long enough to create a house party feeling. The Osborne family (Cedric, Carol, and their children) continue to provide their friendly style of Montserratian hospitality. A complete overhaul of the dining area makes that open-to-breezes area comfortable, with good food attractively served. Bedrooms are in an assortment of octagonal cottages or in a trio of stucco blocks, each with 4 rooms. Cottages A, B, C, and D are on the lowest level, with view and an easy walk to *The Nest,* as the shoreside bar area is known. The tennis courts and gray-black sand beach are nearby. Scuba diving is an offering in recent seasons, and evening entertainment includes a weekly (in winter) cocktail party at the Osbornes' nearby home as well as a lavish buffet evening and island-style entertainment on several evenings. There's a pool at the hilltop main building, where the restaurant and shop are also located. Tradition continues to be the hallmark here, where a relaxed, low-key tone prevails. *Hotel.*

HOUSEKEEPING HOLIDAYS in Montserrat keep several real estate firms in business. A rash of apartment and condominium units have been built in recent years, sparked by the fact that Canadians and people from the United States have built second homes here. The house-rental-in-owners'-absence business thrives. There are all kinds of houses for rent, most of them with small private pool. Some of the firms with listings of villas and apartments for rent are Jacqui **Ryan** (Box 425, Plymouth, Montserrat, W.I., T 809+491–2055), Neville **Bradshaw** (Box 270, Plymouth, Montserrat, W.I., T 809+491–5270), and D.R.V. **Edwards** (Box 58, Plymouth, Montserrat, W.I., T 809+491–2431), who lists several villas as Montserrat Estates. In the U.S., contact **Villas and Apartments Abroad** (420 Madison Ave., New York, N.Y. 10017, T 212+759–1025 or T 800+433–3020; fax 212+755–8316).

When you're investigating houses, know that the less expensive places are priced that way for a reason—and it's often that the location is inconvenient, that the rooms are small, that the view is nonexistent, or that you'll be without some of the qualities you've come to the Caribbean to find. ("When it's in the low price, it's not much of a much," according to Jacqui Ryan when she was showing me around.) Most houses are *not* air-conditioned because people on this island have been smart enough to continue the tradition of building to take advantage of tradewinds. Most bedrooms have double (sometimes triple) exposure so that cross-ventilation is a fact. Kitchens are modern (some places have freezers), appointments are adequate-to-luxury, and a rental car is essential if you want to get around. Count on spending from US$40 to US$60 per day for your car, depending on size and shift, with no charge for mileage and a hefty wallop for gas.

Many of the houses are in the area around Vue Pointe Hotel in the hills north of Plymouth. If you rent one of those places, you can shop in the "supermarkets" of Plymouth, or at the local market where fresh produce and fish are offered by market ladies, or at the small shop in Salem. If you can't survive without your U.S. steaks and beef, bring them from home, packed by your favorite butcher from his cold storage and plunked into your own refrigerator when you arrive. The same goes for other special foods you can't do without, but you should be prepared to pay some duty, which will be levied by an understanding customs officer on arrival in Montserrat. Most customs officials are aware of the housekeeping needs, and are not too harsh on vacationers who are obviously bringing food for their own use.

Alliougana • *on a hillside across the road from the golf course* • is an ambitious luxury development, planned for 74 private villas. Mentioned here because you'll hear about it when you arrive, the development didn't look like it would be open for this edition. The *Caribbean Newsletter* (page 9) will have information when there's some progress on the site. *Villas.*

★ **Belham Valley Hotel** • *across the road from the golf course, just north of Plymouth* • has been better known for its restaurant than for its apartments, in several cottages gathered near the main-house dining areas. *Jasmine* and *Frangipani* are two small studios; *Mignonette* and *Hibiscus* each have 2 bedrooms and a small sitting room. All have recently been spruced up, with the arrival of new owners with New England (U.S.) links. *Cottages.*

★ **Lime Court Apartments** • *in the center of Plymouth* • is across the road from the Legislative Building and a few doors down from the Tourist Board offices. Units include one with 2 bedrooms, private baths, kitchen with electric oven, washing machine, large living room, and a plant-filled veranda. You won't need a car unless you head for the hills (and even then a taxi can take you). Other apartments are wedged into whatever space could be made available to provide 1- and 2-bedroom units in a small plot in Plymouth. Some units are rented long-term, but the convenient location warrants inquiries. *Apts.*

★★★ **Montserrat Villas** • *north of Plymouth* • are several attractive, freestanding villas, for rent in owners' absence. Each is tastefully furnished, with most of the comforts of home. Villas vary in size, but none is more than 2 bedrooms. A rental car puts you in touch with town and touring. *Villas.*

★ **Shamrock Villas** • *on a hillside overlooking Plymouth* • are condominiums with view. Plans for a pool and tennis courts at the base of the hill-clinging development are slow to be realized, but the white cement units, furnished in the taste of the owners, are ready and waiting: 1- and 2-bedroom units, plus 2-story townhouses with bedroom and balcony on the second floor. You'll need a car for mobility (you have a shelter to park it under). Maid service is not included, but maids are available at about EC$25 per "day," which is about 9 a.m. to 2 p.m. *Apts.*

★ **Woodsville Apartments** • *north of Plymouth* • claim a sheer hillside, giving renters a nice view over Montserrat's green landscape. The lower road is the main route between town and the golf course. Although traffic noises float up to your apartment, there aren't too many vehicles at this stage in Montserrat's development. Most units are privately owned, for rent in owners' absence, and all are comfortably furnished with basics. There's a pool at the top of the hill; you'll want a rental car for mobility (and marketing). *Apts.*

THE INN WAY is the way in Montserrat. Vue Pointe has all the best assets of an inn, although it's a full-service hotel.

LOW-COST LODGING got badly battered by Hurricane Hugo. Although **Coconut Hill** has plans to reopen for this season, there's nothing completed at press time. The *Caribbean Newsletter* (page 9) will note places suggested for rooms at modest cost when I've seen some to recommend.

Oriole Plaza Hotel • *in Plymouth* • was built on the site of the former Wade Inn, with a small area of shops and the hotel intertwined. Stuccoed cement block is the sturdy construction; rooms are functional, with private bath and basic furnishings. A restaurant and bar are on the street level. Named to honor Montserrat's endemic oriole, the hotel is a nice addition for businessfolks and others who want to be in town and don't care about a lot of atmosphere.

RESTAURANTS are limited, with one of the best being **Belham Valley Restaurant,** on the road that borders the golf course. Located in a former home, the atmosphere is pleasant and the food, on the evening I dined there, was exceptionally good. Offerings are imaginative and an evening here can be a special one. Be prepared for leisurely service, and a friendly atmosphere.

Vue Pointe Hotel's Wednesday night buffet is popular with outsiders, as well as with the hotel's guests.

Emerald Cafe, over the bridge on Parliament Street, occupies the street level of a building and fills its back courtyard with tables. I enjoyed a hearty meal of mountain chicken (domestic frogs' legs), cooked in a spicy West Indian sauce. The best offerings are the traditional Montserratian recipes, but there are also sandwiches and salads. It's worth stopping in while you're in town to check on the menu for dinner—and to make a reservation. There's nothing fancy about this place, but it does what it does well—in the style of the island.

NATURAL SURROUNDINGS: This island offers much to people who like to prowl around verdant countryside. Although local guides can be helpful with reaching specific points, there's no reason why visitors couldn't wander around many of the places independently. Only when you get into the hinterlands and out-of-the-way places will you find that your road dissolves; local folks know the best routes for these jaunts.

Two goals for those in search of natural sights are the Galway Soufriere, as one of the volcanic peaks is known, plus Galways Plantation, the Great Alps Waterfalls, and the beaches at Carr's Bay and Rendezvous Bay.

As for the **Great Alps Waterfalls,** the challenge is getting there, in spite of what the folders say about excellent walking paths and modern roads. Although the route is easier than it used to be, it's still a hike to be enjoyed at leisure, with time to relax and drink in the tropical surroundings. The start is near Shooter's Hill Village, where guides are usually available. (Check with the tourist office to make specific arrangements.) This jaunt is a good picnic expedition and, if you plan to climb, sturdy walking shoes will ease the path.

Galway Soufriere, a phenomenon of interest to those intrigued by sulfur vents, perks not far from the village of Upper Galway in the middle of the southern half of the island. The road to reach this spot can be slippery, but is navigable, although not enthusiastically by timid drivers. The rugged volcanic rock is a sharp contrast to the small village cupped in verdant hills, and your reward at the end of the 20-minute walk to the crack in the rocks is bubbling vents, very strong hot water, strong-smelling sulfur fumes, and a roaring and rumbling guaranteed to send you back to more peaceful surroundings. This is another excursion that should be considered for enjoyment of nature-en-route for those who are comparing Caribbean volcanoes.

Galways Plantation, a privately owned estate on the flanks of the Soufriere, is well worth visiting. Tireless efforts in recent years by Dr. Lydia Pulsipher from the University of Tennessee and others are bearing fruit. A glimpse of the mid-17th-century life known by the Irish settlers in Montserrat is emerging, thanks to excavations, research, and coordinated studies. The sugar plantation was founded by David Galway with Irish indentured servants as the first land workers, and stone ruins are yielding the form of the community. The plantation, which claims to be "the only Irish plantation in the new world," was thriving in the 18th century when Irish settlers worked with Africans in the fields to raise the crops. The ruins of the sugar boiling house, Great House, a windmill, and other buildings as well as two graveyards have been uncovered. Speculation on the "houseyard" system of cooperative communities has proved interesting as a social system known around the island until very recent times. Ask at the tourist office and at the National Trust office about the summer field school and other participatory projects.

Foxes Bay Bird Sanctuary, established as part of the Montserrat National Trust in 1979, lies north of Plymouth at Richmond Estate. The sanctuary includes 15 acres of mangrove swamp. Egrets, herons, cuckoos, and kingfishers are among the birds sighted, but cows have encroached on the area and pleasant birding is inhibited by the need to look down more often than up.

PLACES WORTH FINDING will be those that your hosts and Montserratian friends tell you about. Plans should start with rental car, easily arranged and easy to negotiate around the usually well-paved and adequately marked roads.

Plymouth is worth some wandering time, especially on Saturdays when the market is in full swing. The clock tower and other restored buildings along the waterfront in the area of the town's original core are effective reminders of the 18th-century lifestyle.

Montserrat Museum (Wed. and Sun. p.m.; T 809+491–5334 for other times), in a sugar mill on Richmond Hill, is the place to start any touring. The museum was created with the obvious devotion (and talent) of the late Walter Connell, a "new" Montserratian whose interest in island history brought together a fascinating, well-displayed collection of artifacts. The first exhibit inside the mill is a map showing the location of Montserrat, and your location on the island. From that point, you whirl around cases with shards and relics unearthed on island prowls, with pictures of Montserratian life in the 1900s and some copies of advertisements of Montserrat Lime Juice from 1885 (about the time when island production was tallied at an astounding 180,000 gallons exported to Crosse and Blackwell in England). Although limes have been the biggest business for Montserrat, the island's era as a sugar producer is recorded not only with pictures and commentary, but also with the 150-year-old donkey saddle with its rack for sugarcane, traded with an elderly Montserratian for the new saddle he wished for. Maps and comments on the migration and culture of the island's first settlers (the Arawaks) help put the move from South America through the Caribbean islands from about 500 to 1500 A.D. into perspective. The diagrams are interspersed with exhibits showing witchcraft ceremonies and items actually found at the Arawak settlement unearthed near the island's airport. This is also the place to note some relics and newspaper comment about the Pan Am jet that crashed into Chance Peak on a swoop into Guadeloupe in September 1965, and a photo of the black Lady of Montserrat at St. Patrick's Catholic Church.

> **AUTHOR'S OBSERVATION**
>
> It's almost impossible to set foot on this island and not want to share in its past, present and future. Here's one way: contact the Montserrat National Trust, Plymouth, Montserrat. You can reach the museum curator by writing Box 120 in Plymouth. The National Trust has about 150 members, most of them local. The annual membership fee is EC$5. Interest and membership are welcomed from visitors.

The small museum is easily reached in about five minutes from downtown Plymouth. Manned entirely by volunteers and supported by private donations, the museum was started in October 1975. It opened in the restored mill, with special display cases designed by and built under the watchful eye of Walter Connell, an American whose enthusiasm sparked the museum project, and has educated thousands of visitors since opening day. Among the most interested viewers are the troops of schoolchildren who come through to learn about their heritage and to note the original artwork from their local stamps. (The Montserrat National Trust has tracked down an almost complete collection of stamps, many of which are kept in the bank vault when not on display.) For intrepid historians who make it up the two short flights of very narrow wood steps, the top-floor research library's wall displays (to pad the echo) were drawn by island schoolchildren on bags supplied by the late Walter Connell. If the recounting of exhibits makes it sound like a lot, know that the total collection is housed in a typical small mill, and that you can almost touch wall to wall in the mill with arms outstretched.

SPORTS in Montserrat are usually the do-it-yourself variety, unless you get involved in some of the local tennis matches and can find space on the two courts at Vue Pointe Hotel or the two at Montserrat Springs. Hiking and climbing are natural pursuits on an island that has verdant hinterland, several dormant volcanoes (the best known is Galway Soufriere), and the Great Alps Waterfalls (which have become relatively touristy with walks and markers).

Golf is played on the new 9 and the old 9 (which total to 11, played in 2 versions). The Montserrat Golf Club course stretches out at the foot of the Vue Pointe Hotel's hill and ranges over a respectable length. The clubhouse is in an old cotton gin. (Note the hand slots for pulling the machinery in the clubroom near the downstairs locker rooms.) There's a small "19th hole" bar area, and a pricing system that lets you play for EC$30 greens fee, EC$3.50 for club rental. Caddies with blue caps (the best) command EC$5. Sat. is caddies' day. Otherwise, the course is used mostly by retirees who live nearby and by visitors.

Sailing, scuba, and the expected **watersports** are not highly organized as on other Caribbean islands, but scuba has become a new activity at Vue Pointe. Charter yachts occasionally cruise over from Antigua and elsewhere, and there are Sunfish sail races on Sundays from the Yacht Club. (Don't expect formality at this Yacht Club.)

TREASURES AND TRIFLES are a fascinating assortment of items, on this island where handcrafts have become a way of life for many. Downtown Plymouth is flecked with small shops that nestle amid traditional West Indian architecture to offer good quality items. Sea Island cotton, which has been part of the island's history, is now part of its present with an attractive shop called **Montserrat Sea Island Cotton Co. Ltd.** on the main square of town. Amid the displays, you can find placemats, tablecloths, napery, hand towels, blouses, and assorted other items made from the sturdy woven cotton.

Montserrat Tapestries, upstairs in one of the Plymouth buildings, is a hardwork venture by a U.S. couple where colorful yarns are pulled into designs on tote bags, wall hangings, rugs, and other items. Items can be made to order. Be sure to bring room measurements and color swatches if you want something made to order.

Sugar Mill, upstairs in a breeze-cooled Plymouth loft, has a collection of interesting island-made items, many of them from Haiti and others from batik and silk-screen studios on other islands. The shop also has some U.S. imports for local home furnishings, plus postcards and easy-to-pack gifts.

Fine Furniture can make household furniture to order, but allow enough time and have definite ideas of what you want, be it bed or table.

Leather items, including very attractive (really!) leather flower pins and earrings, are a popular craft item. The workshops at **Cultural Frontier** or **Productions Tannery** give you an opportunity to watch the craftsmen at work. (These places may have been joined by, or superseded by, others. If you're interested in the leather work, inquire when you arrive in Montserrat.)

Outside town, **Sunny Ltd.** specializes in embroidered items, with their firm at Fort Barrington. They produce shields, emblems, and other items for export, as well as special machine-embroidered items following a design you may supply.

If island history with a local outlook interests you, search for *History of Alliougana—A Short History of Montserrat* by Howard Fergus, the first Speaker of the Legislature under a government expansion in 1974. Another book edited by Fergus is *Dreams of Alliougagana,* an anthology of prose and poetry. His newest title, *Montserrat—Emerald Isle of the Caribbean,* is available in places where books are sold, for EC$24.

Carol's Corner at Vue Pointe Hotel also specializes in finding good quality work by island craftsmen. The shop carries the leather jewelry and some Sea Island cotton items, in addition to sundries that can save the guests from trekking to town for essentials.

Cockleshell Bay
0
2
MILES
Newcastle
Beachlands
Cotton Ground
Brick Kiln Village
Fountain's
Village
Nevis Peak
Coconut Wa
Gingerland
Charleston Jetty
Charlestown
Fig Tree Village
Indian Castle
N
Nevis

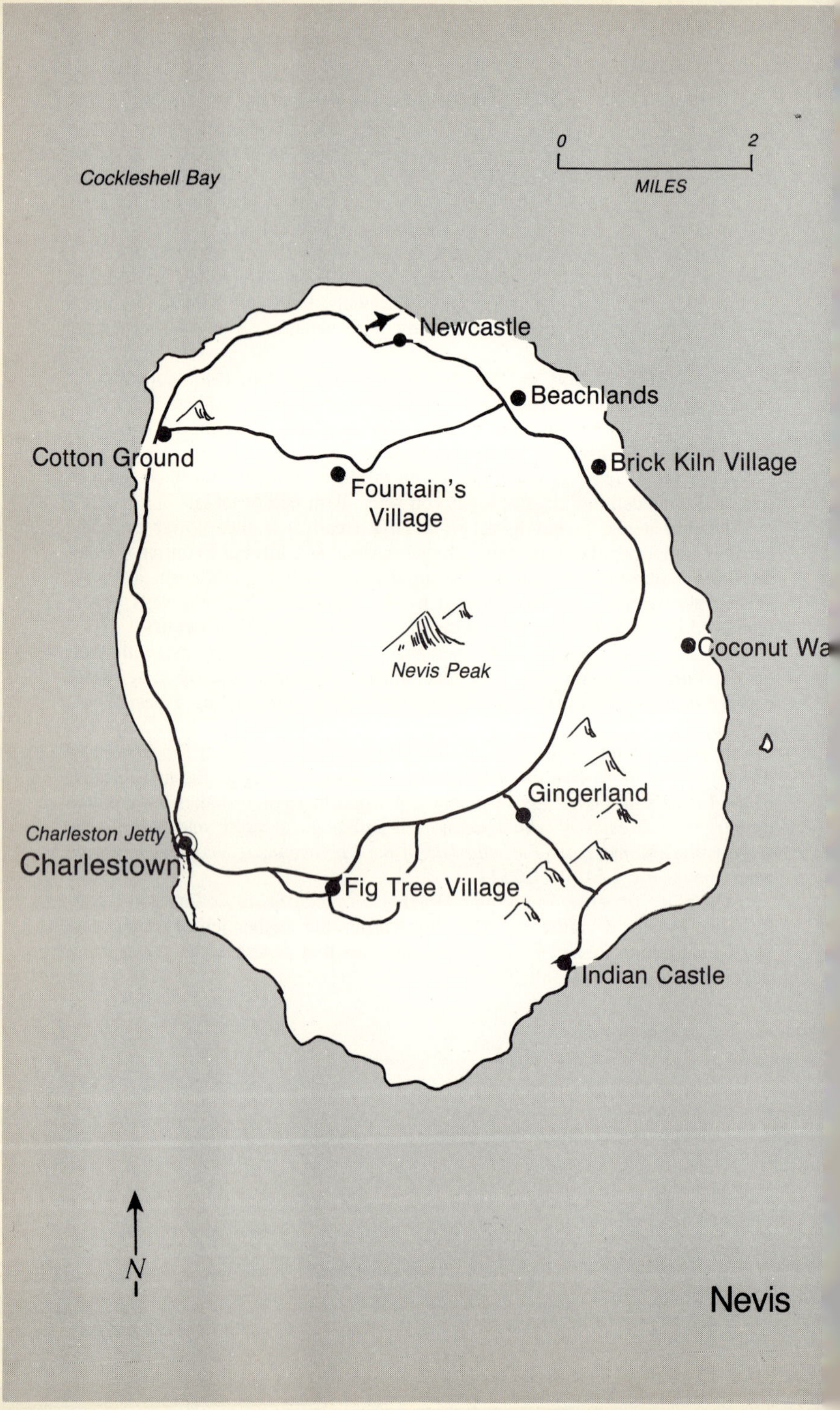

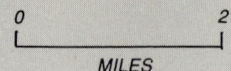

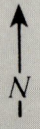

NEVIS

St. Kitts-Nevis Tourist Board, Charlestown, Nevis, W.I., T 809+465-5494, fax 809+465-8794; 414 East 75th St., New York, NY 10021, T 212+535-1234; High Commission for Eastern Caribbean States, 10 Kensington Court, London, England, W85DL, T 01+937-9522; #508, 11 Yorkville Ave., Toronto, Ontario, Canada, T 416+921-7717.

$ · · · US$1 = EC$2.65
Unless otherwise noted, $ refers to U.S. currency.

Nevis has its head in the clouds, and that's what gave the island its name. Although the earliest map—the Mapus Mundi—splotches "Nieves" as a name across an area that could refer to Saba and other islands in the neighboring seas, it's Nevis that has claimed the name as its own. During his second voyage to the New World, Columbus hung the tag on the cloud-covered peak, here or elsewhere, that reminded him of the snow (nieves) of the Sierra Nevada of Spain. The first settlement—Jamestown—was swept into the sea by a 1680 tidal wave, according to island records, and although it may be interesting for scuba divers, there's nothing on land to note from that time. Charlestown's 17th-century prosperity was as the depot for flourishing slave trade in the British Leeward Islands. Records in the late 1600s count as many as 8000 slaves prepared and sold on the market at the west-coast town, and notes made about life in the early 1600s show that slaves were being used in those years on British plantations here and on other islands.

But it's Alexander Hamilton that forges the American link to Nevis. He was born here and spent his early childhood on Nevis before heading off to St. Croix to work in a relative's hardware store. Much is made of Admiral Nelson wooing and winning Fanny Nisbet, daughter of a prominent merchant, but the present church at Fig Tree Hill probably wasn't standing here in 1787 when they were married across the road at Montpelier Estate.

The historical facts are only of passing interest to most visitors who search out Nevis for peace, quiet, and a go-slow pace that is contagious. Although the 20-mile "rim" road that circles the island and goes inland for a portion of its route can be driven in less than two hours, there are some people who never make it. Not because they can't, but because there are too many spots to linger—and the only people who speed around the rim in the 10-mile-per-hour race are those that are heading to the airport—where they will probably wait for a while.

POLITICAL PICTURE is a stable one. Elections called for February 1989 supported the policies of the incumbent government; under the British parliamentary system, adopted by independent St. Kitts-Nevis, elections do not need to be called until early 1994. The Peoples' Action Movement of Prime Minister Kennedy Simmonds continues in office, with Nevisian Simeon Daniel, head of the Nevis Reformation Party, known as premier of Nevis. The St. Kitts-Nevis coalition holds 10 seats in the government, with the opposition claiming 2. It was the government of Prime Minister Simmonds that led St. Kitts-Nevis into independence on September 19, 1983, as an independent country within the British Commonwealth. (Although part of the original three-island Associated State set up by Britain in 1967, Anguilla split from St. Kitts and Nevis, to officially obtain separate status as a dependent territory in January 1981.) The two-island nation claims approximately 50,000 people and 104 square miles on its islands. Nevis is only 36 square miles.

ISLAND APPEARANCE: Whether you arrive at the small airport at the shore in the northeast or by ferry at the pier in Charlestown, you'll feel as though you have stepped back in time. This is still a quiet, rural island, even with the big leap into tourism by the new *Four Seasons Hotel*. Charlestown, the only town of any size, shutters up about 4:30 p.m. and is slow paced even before that hour. A magnificent grove of palms will be splintered by the plan for the island's first large hotel, but the volcanic Nevis Peak, almost in the center of the island, should remain untrammeled for years to come. Count on pleasant beaches on a few coves and hotels with a plantation appearance and a house-party atmosphere.

LIFESTYLE is relaxed, with cues from a British history. Tourism has not stepped on Nevis with a heavy foot although the new Canadian project seems to be one firm footprint. Charlestown, the main town, is the commercial center, but the commerce is mostly West Indian; visitors are in the minority. The pace of life is s-l-o-w whether you live here or visit. "Good Morning," or another appropriate greeting, should start any transaction, and is also part of the ritual of passing someone in the street. Be prepared for candlelight dinners even if a place *usually* has electricity. (Power outages are a fact of life, as is the case on many islands.) The island water supply can be sporadic, but all hotels have mastered that situation. You will always have plenty of water to drink, but what comes out of the faucet may be a trickle, or only a drop or two at times when there are power problems that inhibit pumping. What you wear at your resort is a matter between you and the management, but for exploring the island—or even a quick trip to a nearby beach—covering up the bathing suit indicates your awareness of the local sensibilities. Nevis is home for about 10,000 people, most of whose families have lived here for generations. Many island families are very religious and not ready for (or happy about accepting) the freewheeling, carefree, unfettered life that can be the routine on some other islands.

AUTHOR'S OBSERVATION

Be prepared for dinners to be social occasions. Since most hotels are small, a house-party atmosphere prevails. Some places have family-style meals, where guests sit at suggested tables with other guests. In all cases, the cocktail hour and after-dinner coffee are times when guests meet and talk with one another.

MEDICAL FACILITIES are limited to the small Alexander Hamilton Hospital in Charlestown, which benefits from links with hospitals in the U.S., Canada, and Britain insofar as donations of supplies and funds are concerned. Doctors' offices in Charlestown serve as clinics for minor problems. Nevisians usually go to St. Kitts for operations and for more complicated medical problems; visitors often charter a small plane to fly to Puerto Rico or Miami.

MONEY MATTERS will be conducted in Eastern Caribbean currency at local spots, but your hotel expenses will be billed in U.S. dollars, as will purchases in shops that usually deal with visitors. Ferry boat fares and local purchases should be transacted in Eastern Caribbean currency, which you can get from the bank in Charlestown at a slightly better rate than that offered by your hotel.

COMMUNICATION via telephone involves dialing the 809 area code + 465 and the 4-digit number for Nevis. Phones on the island or between St. Kitts and Nevis are another story. SKANTEL, a joint system between the local government and British-based Cable and Wireless, Ltd., maintains the phone, telex and telegraph systems. Overseas calls can be made from their offices. The Cable & Wireless phonecards can be purchased from their office in Nevis, for use in the telephones designated for card use. The phone will "use up" the amount required, and return the card for additional calls, if there's a balance left. AT&T's USADirect system can be accessed by dialing 1–800+872–1881 to reach the AT&T operator who can place your call, either collect or charged to your AT&T account. Not all places have telephones, and many that do also have them "out of order" often. Most hotels now have facsimile machines. Radio stations are in English, but you can also pick up nearby French and Spanish stations. There is local television, produced at a studio on St. Kitts, as well as cable T.V. facilities.

ARRIVAL can be by air or sea, depending on whether your jump-off point is Antigua, where you'll fly over, or St. Kitts, where you have the choice of the ferry that links the capital of Basseterre with Nevis's Charlestown or the small planes that link the airports. The ferry makes the crossing in about 45 minutes. It is reasonably comfortable, inexpensive, and operates on a dependable schedule. Newcastle Airport on Nevis is little more than a small wood building and an airstrip on the northeast rim of the island, just across the channel from the south coast of St. Kitts. A subsidiary of Antigua-based *LIAT* (Leeward Islands Air Transport), *4-Islands Air* links Antigua's airport to Nevis on a loosely followed (and frequently changing) schedule. *Carib Aviation* (Box 318, St. John's,

Antigua, West Indies, T 809+942–3147) provides charters from Antigua. *Winair* flies from Sint Maarten several times weekly, and to St. Kitts daily, in about 30 minutes, and *Air BVI* links Tortola and Nevis. Flights link the big airport on St. Kitts with San Juan, Miami, New York, and other cities.

CRUISE ships anchor offshore, bringing passengers to Nevis in small boats. Only the smaller cruise ships—and some of the windjammers—make Nevis a regular port of call.

DEPARTURES are relaxed. You either go to the small airport an hour or so before flight time, or walk down to the pier for the scheduled ferry for Basseterre, St. Kitts. It's a good idea to make a few inquiries prior to your planned departure to be sure that the schedule is as you expect it to be. There are often changes. There's a departure tax of $5 when you leave St. Kitts-Nevis. If you are going to the sister island, there's no tax to pay.

TOURING TIPS: There's only one main road on Nevis. It makes a ring around the island, near the coast for most of its route. Spurs stretch off to reach hotels and a few sights in the hinterlands, but don't count on much in the way of paving on some of the spur roads. **Rental cars** can be arranged through your hotel, but request your car when you make your reservation if you are vacationing at peak season. I've had very good luck with *TDC Car Rentals*. Their Nevis office is to the left as you leave the boat dock and, though their main office is in Basseterre, St. Kitts, you can use a car for the day on the "other" island with one rental agreement. Cars can be scarce. Driving is on the left and the cost for your local license is EC$30.

Taxis take you anywhere you want to go and will wait (or come back to get you) if you're planning to stay for a while. Most Nevisian inns have links with "their own" drivers. Rates are set by distance; drivers, from my experience, usually stick to the rules. On recent travels, Curtley Maynard (T 809+469-5343) provided prompt and pleasant service.

Horses can be rented for rides along the shores and into the verdant midsection of Nevis. True island aficionados make the run between St. Kitts and Nevis on the local **ferry** that makes daily crossings between Charlestown, on Nevis, and Basseterre, St. Kitts. The alternative is the small-plane service between the two islands' airports, but the schedule often makes it difficult to do that trip in one day from either starting point.

Flights to nearby islands (which are many) can be arranged by charter through *Carib Aviation* (T 800+469-9295).

LODGING in Nevis is unique for the Caribbean area. With the arrival of the Four Seasons resort, Nevis has its first resort-style hotel. All other properties have the best qualities of inns, with management (usually the owners) taking a keen interest in the guests. Most of the hotels are in the hills, as was the case when plantation houses were built in the 18th and 19th centuries, to take advantage of the breezes. No one thought, in those years, of being near a beach (which was usually buggy). Each spot has its own personality, and most have Nevisian history intertwined, either with the buildings or the owner and sometimes both. There's nothing on the island for those who need manufactured entertainment; everyone turns in by dark—unless there's some house-party-type entertainment at your chosen inn, or a big do that sounds interesting in Charlestown or one of the local places. An islander's island, Nevis welcomes anyone who wants to fit into the accepted pace—which is slow, relaxed, and tropical.

Most hotels include a 10% service charge, and the 7% government room tax, but something extra for special service by some member of the staff is always appreciated.

───────── **AUTHOR'S AWARDS** ─────────

Montpelier gets my vote for picture-perfect surroundings in the hills, with traditional plantation lifestyle; *Nisbet Plantation* is better than ever, with the addition of new and attractive units nearer the beach; small *Hermitage* is a nice hideaway, with pleasant pool and quiet surroundings; and the Victorian-style bungalows at *Oualie Beach* are back-to-basics comfortable, at the shore.

HOTELS/RESORTS on Nevis include a half dozen of the best inns in the Caribbean, plus one new resort.

★★ **Golden Rock Hotel** • *at Gingerland* • is a way of life, not only for Pam Barry but also for those who find this place. The estate has an intriguing history, helped along by Pam's great-great grandfather, Edward Huggins, who built the main house in 1815. Your choice of rooms can include one of the 10 in the 5 cottages nestled into the flourishing gardens near the pool, or one of the 2 rooms in the stone-walled sugar mill, where the focal point of the top floor is the "oldest mahogany 4-poster bed in Nevis." The lawn-level mill room has 2 mahogany 4-posters. These beds have canopies, and all rooms have modern plumbing and other comforts. Nevisian craftsmen have furnished the other rooms with 4-poster beds fashioned from bamboo, sisal rugs on the floors, and adaptations of island products for other furniture and decoration. The social center is the Golden Rock Courtyard and the Estate Long House, where most meals are served family style. *Cottage inn.*

★★★★ **Montpelier Plantation Inn** • *in St. John's Parish* • about 15 minutes' drive from Charlestown, claims fame as being near Fig Tree Church where Admiral Nelson married local belle Fanny Nisbet, on March 11, 1787. According to local lore, an estate flourished on this property at that time; a plaque noting "Montpelier House" and its history stands near the spot. James and Celia Milnes Gaskell appreciate the good life and do their best to share it with you. A huge swimming pool punctuates the top of the estate at about 650 feet and carefully tended landscape is punctuated with colorful tropical blooms. The main house is open to steady and pleasant breezes, with mill nearby and moss-marked stone walls that exude history. The main room encourages lingering, as do the chairs on the breeze-swept porch. The 19 bedrooms are in several small buildings. Although furnishings are basic and decor may seem spartan, folks familiar with the real Caribbean will find this place comfortable. Some rooms have sea view (if the foliage is pruned). Overhead fans can be supplemented with air conditioners. Showers are small in some rooms, and privacy may require keeping your curtains closed since some rooms are along the path to others. *Cottage inn.*

★★★★ **Nevis Four Seasons Resort** • *along Pinney's Beach and inland, north of Charlestown* • has gained a following in its opening season ('91). It's the island's first full-fledged resort, with a golf course ranging over acres on the inland side of the road, and the 2-story bands of rooms along the beach, amid a grove of stately palms. The taxi-and-boat lift from the St. Kitts airport to the dock at Basseterre for the ferry to the dock in Nevis seems to work to the satisfaction of most guests. (It's also possible to fly directly to the small airstrip on Nevis from Antigua, St. Kitts, or St. Croix, or to take the regular ferry that runs daily between St. Kitts and Nevis.) The Toronto-based company has lived up to its quality reputation with attractive landscaping, plus pool, tennis courts, and full resort facilities on this once-quiet site. Ask your travel agent about special package plans that may bring the high rates to more reasonable levels. *Resort.*

★★★ **Nisbet Plantation** • *at Newcastle, on the northeast side of the island* • shares the attentions of owner David Dodwell, with his successful Reefs in Bermuda. Famed as a place where, in the mid-1700s, Fanny Nisbet used to come to play (her uncle owned a house on this site), Nisbet is now a hideaway haven. The beach that rims the shore, marking one boundary on the 30-acre plantation, proves perfect for shell-strolling, morning jogging, setting off for swimming, or enjoying a lobster, conch chowder, or a rum punch at the beachside restaurant. It's the site for the Sunday barbecue, with steel band in season, and a good place for lunch most days. The main house's terrace gives guests a lovely view across the lawn and gardens, through the avenue of palms, to the shore. The original 20 cottages, most of which are octagonal buildings with 2 rooms per cottage, have been joined by newer units and a pool. The main house has a cozy comfort, with a book-lined reading room, a dining room furnished in 18th-century antiques, and a congenial bar that often operates on the honor system. Management sets the tone for this place. You're only 5 minutes from the airport. A plantation atmosphere prevails; guests spend their days horseback riding, exploring, swimming, hiking, fishing, sailing, or swinging in a hammock. The tennis courts get frequent use, often early in the morning when the "pong" of tennis may be your wake-up call if your cottage is within hearing distance. *Cottage inn, apts.*

★★ **Old Manor Estate** • *at Gingerlands* • formerly known by an earlier resident's name of "Croney," was extensively renovated and rebuilt by Texas funds and ingenuity before its sale to Vicki Knorr, who is the current owner and on-the-spot manager. Innkeeping is casual, and wear and tear on some of the once magnificent refurbishing has taken its toll, but the small pool is pleasant, and the surroundings can be impressive if you're prepared to overlook maintenance and landscaping. Bedrooms are in assorted buildings and vary according to the size and shape of the original part of the plantation. A few are upstairs; some are furnished with big 4-poster beds; others combine for suites or apartments; all have private bathroom. The original Great House, built in 1832 when the property was a thriving plantation, yields its patio for alfresco dining. You'll need a car or access to taxis for mobility; otherwise, the quiet atmosphere is ideal for reading or ruminating.

HOUSEKEEPING HOLIDAYS in Nevis are possible not only in individual homes, for rent in owners' absence, but also at resort-style places. There's plenty available in the way of fresh fish, lobster, conch, and locally grown vegetables and fruits; these basics, wooed to perfection by a Nevisian cook, will make canned items you might have brought from home superfluous. One contact for rentals is Sylvia Doore at the **Nevisian Agency,** Charlestown, Nevis, West Indies, T 809+465-4423. Another source for self-catering units, both bungalows and more lavish villas, is **Bentley Associates** (4 Cayon St., Box 384, Basseterre, St. Kitts, West Indies, T 809+465-4100).

Here are a few of the villa and/or apartment clusters:

★★ **Hermitage** • *in the Fig Tree area* • has been the homestead of the Lupinacci family, one-time managers of Zetland. Several rooms are in the main house and some in separate West-Indian Victorian style buildings with lacey wood fretwork near the pool. The main house, in eclectic style that shows influences from several carpenters, has separate stone stairways from several rooms, and a personality of its own. According to some island tales, this is the oldest house on Nevis; ask the Lupinaccis for details. *Apts.*

★ **Hurricane Cove Bungalows** • *rising up the hillside, near Oualie Beach* • are comfortable units that appeal to a back-to-basics lifestyle. Kitchens are modern and complete; the units are built of wood, in chalet style. Since they are staggered up the hillside, each of the 1- and 2-bedroom units has a view. A 3-bedroom villa, with private pool, should be ready for this season, and other villas will be built as interest warrants. Owned by Bob and Althea Turner, the units are capably managed by on-the-spot Nevisians. *Bungalows.*

Mt. Nevis Hotel Condominiums • *at Newcastle* • opened with several studio apartments and deluxe bedrooms in units intended for private ownership. There's a beach and marina facilities, plus restaurant, at Newcastle Bay, and a pool and pleasant restaurant on the premises. More typical of today's building style than some of the more traditional places, the 2-story blocks at Mt. Nevis offer expected modern comforts in standard hotel-style rooms. *Apts.*

★★ **Oualie Beach Club** • *on the beach, with a view toward St. Kitts* • is the beach house, with bar, restaurant, and nearby shop, plus a collection of homey West Indian–style cottages. Each has a living area plus bedroom and private bath—and a deck that's ideal for leisure times. You're at the beach for easy swims. The place has charm. *Cottages.*

Rest Haven Inn • *near Charlestown* • has 12 efficiency apartments with kitchen units, but check to be sure all's in order before you plan to cook "at home." The hotel operates a dining room, and all drinks and meals are available there. (See "Low-Cost Lodging" for the hotel-style rooms.)

Zetland Plantation • *at Gingerland just south of the "middle" of the island* • gives you the freedom to live as you choose, preparing a few meals in your apartment or dining at the Manor House. The property has new owners who have great plans for this place. The *Caribbean Newsletter* (page 9) will have news when factual. The 15 plantation suites, with rooms that can link or lock, offer adequate accommodations for family vacations. There's a pool within a few steps of the Manor House and your room, as well as a mood-setting sugar mill with rooms. A courtesy bus makes the link between hilltop and the beach and/or Charlestown, and touring can be easily arranged by taxi, or horseback, or a car. *Cottages.*

THE INN WAY is the only way for most places on Nevis. Although mentioned under "Hotels," most places are inns. Certainly *Montpelier, Golden Rock,* and, perhaps, still, *Nisbet* (although the addition of its newest rooms near the beach may change some of the atmosphere) excel at traditional innkeeping. In addition, *Hermitage* has all the assets of an inn, with on-location owner-managers and sincere hospitality that is based on something more than just the money you'll spend. *Oualie Beach,* also, has an innlike atmosphere, when the owners are in residence and attentive.

LOW-COST LODGING: Places that are really "low-cost" are also very spartan on this fashionable island. The Tourist Office has a list of some of the Nevisian guest houses, but I'd suggest looking before booking. Winter prices are geared for U.S., Canadian, and European visitors who are wealthy enough to pay for peace and quiet. A couple of shoreside places do charge reasonable rates for island motel-style accommodations:

Pinney's Beach Hotel • *at one end of a gray sand beach that sometimes washes out with strong sea surges* • is a series of bungalows and rooms that needed a lot of work when I checked for this edition. An air-conditioner is essential for cooling in some rooms, which are angled in such a way as to cut out any breeze. The restaurant and evening action are popular with local folk, so rooms nearest the social areas can be noisy in evenings.

Rest Haven Inn • *on the shore at the outskirts of Charlestown* • has expanded from a simple hotel to include a string of comfortable motelstyle units. The pool is a focal point for those who don't want to head to the beach; the restaurant and terrace dining area are known for good Nevisian cooking.

RESTAURANTS on Nevis are at the hotels, especially *Hermitage, Nisbet, Montpelier,* and *Oualie Beach,* where advance reservations are required, or at a couple of simple spots in Charlestown. **Caribbean Confections** is an in-town meeting and greeting place, noted for home baked breads and ice cream. **Octagon Restaurant and Bar,** on the bayfront in Charlestown, serves good local food. It's a popular lunch place. Another pausing place is **Unella's,** a casual spot upstairs, overlooking the waterfront, but I'm not impressed by other eateries I tried. There's no island I know of where all hotels make better use of island produce and offshore fish and lobster. Each inn offers its own variations; you're encouraged to wander.

NATURAL SURROUNDINGS: Most of Nevis is in its natural state. Only the shoreline around Charlestown has met the intrusion of modern development, not only with the expansion of the town but also with the recent plans for the Four Seasons hotel to the north on the west coast. The hinterlands, however, are still pretty much virgin territory. The tourist office in Charlestown can give you details about walking and hiking on the flanks of Nevis Peak, but be prepared for heat and take along some sun protection and a hat to ward off relentless rays. Those who enjoy horseback riding find that a pleasant way to explore the countryside. Although most of the property is privately owned, permission is often granted for crossing private estates. Ask your hotel owner for specific suggestions about walks—and for names of people who can accompany you if you want to climb the peak.

PLACES WORTH FINDING on Nevis include the other hotels, most of which represent interesting modern adaptations of once impressive plantation estates such as Old Manor, Montpelier, Golden Rock, and Nisbet; the town of Charlestown, sleepy today and hardly hinting at its 17th-century prosperity; perhaps the Morningstar Nelson Museum and the Fig Tree Church, but more probably the verdant hills and wild growth on mountainsides with an occasional spectacular view over the Caribbean sea.

CHARLESTOWN is a grid of short streets fringed with West Indian wood buildings, most of them small and filled with the commerce of a West Indian town. The place comes alive when the ferry from Basseterre, St. Kitts, chugs into port (at the end of a 45-minute ride that costs about EC$10). The ferry is the local service, used by Kittitians and Nevisians to get back and forth to market and home, since most jobs are on St. Kitts—and some of the fun is on Nevis. (Market collectors will want at least a whisk through the Charlestown market, to the right as you walk off the pier. The prime market day is Saturday, but Tuesdays and Thursdays are also active.) When Queen Elizabeth visited Nevis, on February 22, 1966, and more recently on October 23, 1985, the entire town dressed for the occasion—and the October visit has been its biggest recent event. Although the action at Pier 2 is the town's liveliest, walk over to **Memorial Square** and the **Court House,** with the library on its second floor. There's a plaque on a wall that mentions a visit by the Jamestown (Virginia) settlers, who spent almost a week here before they continued on to settle in Virginia.

Alexander Hamilton Museum, at the shore in Charlestown, is fascinating, not only for the collection of Hamilton memorabilia and other glimpses of Nevisian life of the past, but also because the building has been painstakingly restored and is worth seeing. The top floor is used for meetings of the local government officials; the museum—with its diagrams, pictures of 18th- and 19th-century life on Nevis, and touchstones from the life of the island's most famous native son—has attractive displays that can be interesting for all ages.

Fort Charles is for ruin collectors, since you have to walk through an overgrown field (passing garbage and goats, when I walked through) to find the ruins—and nothing has been done to restore the little that is left (a cannon, a few walls, some stones, and the site). The **Bath Hotel,** built in 1778 and the place in the West Indies to recoup and regroup in the 18th century, is open most days. The Tourist Office can advise on status. In the 18th century all the top people came to the spa at Nevis, where commerce was contracted and gossip shared. The major building you look at these days was restored/rebuilt in the 19th century and the fledgling museum inside is worth a glance. The springs are still gurgling, the basic structure is still sound, and you can have a sulfur bath for EC$5, but no one has yet turned this potentially elegant hotel into the top resort it could be. (Someone tried around the 1900s, but the place didn't stay open for long.)

Fig Tree Church is actually St. John's Church at Fig Tree Hill. The faded register has a couple of documents—namely one dated 1787 that supposedly tells that Horatio Nelson, Esq., was married to Frances Herbert Nisbet, widow, but speculation continues about the document, since the original register is so blurred and illegible that the present "statement" is mostly supposition.

The **Morningstar Nelson Museum,** in a room of the private home of a Philadelphia lawyer, Robert Abraham, contains an eclectic collection of Nelson memorabilia. Included among the pictures, tokens, and Nevisian artifacts, is an invitation to Nelson's funeral. (There's no charge for the museum, if it's open when you're in the area, but donations are gratefully accepted.) It's worth venturing up the road just to look—from the outside—at the attractive home that has been molded around the turret of an old stone mill.

SPORTS on Nevis are what you dream up yourself, although the marina in the plans (and underway) at the Fort Charles area bodes well for sailors and watersports. Check with your hotel management about other possibilities for boating. The hoteliers have their contacts for whatever access to sea sports are available at the time you visit. **Snorkeling, boardsailing,** and **scuba** are popular off the beaches, and around the shores if you are experienced and have brought your own equipment. *Scuba Safaris* (809+469-9518) offers a full line of dive options, plus **glass-bottom boat** trips, from Oualie Beach Club.

The **golf** course may be ready in early 1991, but be sure to check if playing is crucial to your holiday happiness. There are **tennis** courts at Four Seasons, Montpelier (check to see if the court has been fixed), Nisbet, and Golden Rock. **Horseback riding** can be arranged through Garner's Estate or at Cane Garden, for trail rides around mountains and plantations.

TREASURES AND TRIFLES on Nevis center on Charlestown.

The Sand Box Tree, on Chapel Street, may well be your one-stop source for island treasures. Not only are the warm-weather dresses, wraps, and shirts attractive and colorful, but the assortment of other items that includes a few "antiques" as well as handmade items changes constantly and offers some variety. This is Kitty Burke's venture, and it's attractive and worth a visit.

The **Nevis Crafts Studio,** in a yellow house on the inland side of the road through Charlestown, has an intriguing selection of island-made items. In conversation with Michael Brooks (who carves calabash shells) and Ashley Liburd (whose bamboo wind-chimes fill the air with "music"), I learned that the eight craftsmen who started the cooperative in November 1978 have been joined by others for a total of about 25 members. Aided by an Inter American Foundation grant and other donations, plus the profits from their sales, the group is working with other Nevisians, especially young people, to encourage high-quality handcrafts and individual entrepreneurs. Any profits from purchases made here go for a good cause, and items for sale are interesting and well made. Expect to find pottery, baskets, bamboo items, shellcraft, macrame, and other items—all of which can be brought into the U.S. duty free under the customs allotment.

Caribbee Clothes is a Nevisian enterprise that claims to be the island's major employer (35 people). Started over a decade ago by Betty Robey, the shop and workrooms have been owned by Tip Todd, who moved south from a high-pressure job in New York to oversee (and labor at) the enterprise. A search for "new identity," responding to fashion changes, leaves this place with what I felt was mediocre merchandise. It's worth a look, however.

Caribbean Confections supplies food, jam, chutney, jelly, and other island-made edibles.

The Arcade, in Charlestown near Memorial Square, carries the colorful Caribelle, Batik fabric and fashions made on St. Kitts. The **Nevis Handicraft Cooperative,** next to the Tourist Office on the main square, is one source for Nevisian pottery and other handwork. The **Workshop for the Blind** is a hard place to leave without having bought something. Head here only if you are prepared to buy; the crafts are the only livelihood for the elderly and infirm who weave local grasses into mats, hats, etc.

Nevisian pottery, sun-baked-clay bird ashtrays and other small items, make ideal gifts for the folks at home. You'll find it in the handcraft shops and can go to the source if you ask directions. Mrs. Elena Jones, now in her 70s, was the originator of the Nevis pottery. Her disciples include her niece, Almena, and others who now make most of the items for sale.

Nevis Philatelic Bureau, in a modern air-conditioned building near the pier in Charlestown has collections of Nevisian stamps that will appeal not only to stamp collectors but to anyone intrigued by this island. Artists' renderings of island scenes—including the hotels, local boats, birds, and other uniquely Nevisian subjects—appear on colorful stamps, sometimes affixed to postcards with the same picture. Inquire about special issues; many are worth framing.

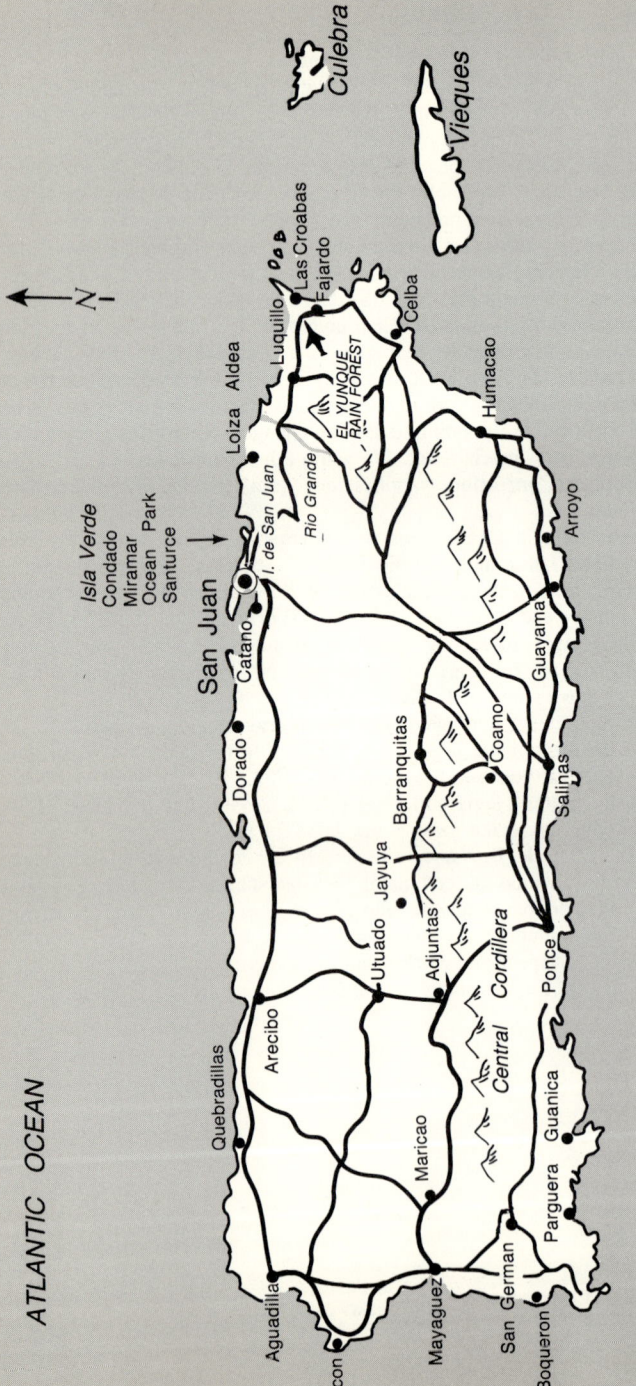

PUERTO RICO

Puerto Rico Tourism Company, Paseo la Princesa, Old San Juan, Puerto Rico 00902, T 809+721–2400, fax 809+725–4417; 575 Fifth Ave., New York, NY 10017, T 212+599–6262 or 800+223–6530, fax 212+818–1866; 200 S.E. First St., Miami, FL 33131, T 305+381–8915; #2204, 233 N. Michigan Ave., Chicago, IL 60601, T 312+861–0049; #560, 3575 W. Cahuenga Blvd., Los Angeles, CA 90068, T 213+874–5991; 11 Yorkville Ave., Toronto, Ontario M5C 1C3, Canada, T 416+969–9025.

$ · · · U.S. currency is used.

See pages noted for information on: Condado and San Juan, p. 538; Culebra, p. 568; Dorado, p. 556; Humacao (Palmas del Mar), p. 560; Mayaguez, p. 564; Ponce, p. 562; Vieques, p. 569.

Daniel Rodriguez lives near El Yunque, the mountain that is better known as the site of the rain forest. His small home in Rio Grande is Puerto Rico in microcosm because of the "little people" he creates. He is a skilled artist who molds pieces of wood into re-creations of country people he has known—vendors, women with several children, men participating in a cock fight, a woman drying the family's clothes on the ground in the sun. Each piece that comes from his *Artesania Otoniel* is signed "Daniel" if he has played a role in its creation. His earlier work is the best. When he started his craft, he gently coaxed his knife and other tools to bring out the personality of the people. He still enjoys that work the best, and new members of the traditional Puerto Rican country life sometimes join the earlier pieces that he has kept (most have been sold), when he has time to caress the character out of the wood he works. These days, in answer to modern commerce (and the need to make a living), he has established a sort of assembly line. Arms, legs, torsos, babies, food carts, horses for the three kings, and even the parts of the three kings themselves are carved by Rodriguez; his apprentices put the pieces together, in a sort of jigsaw puzzle of people, to make "men," "women," and "children" who will immigrate to the U.S. mainland as souvenirs in our suitcases.

A kneeling lady whips her washing on a rock. I catch a glimpse of her and of a pregnant mother with babe in arms and another tugging at her skirt, as I pass the bookcase where she sits in my house. Daniel Rodriguez's people are a constant reminder of the "other" Puerto Rico, the Puerto Rico of the country, the Puerto Rico that seems remote from the cluttered commerce, but which is, in fact, tethered to the resort areas for the livelihood tourism provides.

POLITICAL PICTURE: Elections will be held in November 1992. Governor Rafael Hernandez Colon won the election in November 1988, for his second consecutive term. (The governor had also been in office 1972–76.) His Popular Democratic Party (PDP) supports the Commonwealth status of Puerto Rico, while the party of former governor Carlos Romero Barcelo, the New Progressive Party (NPP), is pro-statehood. Puerto Rico's Independence Party has support in some quarters, although the actual vote in recent elections has been small; it is acknowledged to have the support of Cuba and other socialist/communist interests. Puerto Ricans will have the opportunity to vote on the island's status some time in the near future, but the date is uncertain at press time. Governor Colon has been strong in his support of tourism, giving a virtually free hand to the very effective Puerto Rico Tourism Company, a quasigovernment body that runs Puerto Rico's tourism like a business. Since tourism is labor-intensive, and unemployment has been a major challenge in Puerto Rico, the vacation business offers the best hope for an improvement in the economy.

Puerto Rico is unique. Links with the U.S. are more economic than emotional, but they appear to have dominated the past three decades. The ground swell of "national" (meaning Puerto Rican) feeling has little clear definition—except to keep Spanish as the island's first language, which was assured by legislative act in spring '91, and to try to maintain traditional customs. Known as the "poorhouse of the Caribbean" in the 1940s and early '50s, Puerto Rico responded to the herculean efforts of its workers and U.S. industry subsidiaries under "Operation Bootstrap," a program that created a Puerto Rican middle class by building an island economy to raise the standard of living and by offering education and skills-training. Many Puerto Ricans now hold executive positions in their own or major multinational companies. Puerto Rico has interacted in a very positive way with Jamaica and other Caribbean countries, taking a cue from the Caribbean Basin Initiative, by coordinated manufacturing with piecework done in those islands, where wages are lower, and final assembly accomplished in Puerto Rico, where labor has achieved a high degree of skill in recent years. Latin links to the Dominican Republic, Cuba, and places in Central America go back for centuries, long before Puerto Rico "became American" after the Spanish American War in 1898. With its U.S. and Puerto Rican allegiances, this 3500-square-mile-island, with its 3.2 million residents, seems almost schizophrenic.

ISLAND APPEARANCE: If you can squint to block out the clutter that surrounds the burgeoning city of San Juan, with its traffic jams and uncontrolled building, this island is one of the Caribbean's most beautiful—once you head for the hills and other coastlines. Puerto Rico is a lot more than San Juan, which is a speck at a midpoint on the long north coast. Dramatic mountains rise in the middle of the island, with portions of El Yunque peak affiliated with the U.S. National Park system. Although a domestic "keep our island clean" program would be of great benefit, the rural countryside—when you head into the spine of mountains that stretches the length of the Commonwealth—is lush and fascinating for those who enjoy islands with a unique personality. The Spanish affiliation is still strong away from the areas that have developed for tourism. The road system benefits from the U.S. connection, with a good network and wide and well-paved main roads and highways. Signposting is excellent, but travelers must know some Spanish since most directions appear in Puerto Rico's language. Most *paradores* (government-assisted system of country inns) are worthwhile goals for meals or overnight accommodations away from the knots of tourism. Puerto Rico's offshore islands of Culebra and Vieques present yet another face of this complex Commonwealth. These two satellites are rustic and popular for a back-to-basics island life.

LIFESTYLE in Puerto Rico has a Spanish flair, especially when you go to the countryside, away from the Condado/San Juan tourism veneer. Not only is Puerto Rican–style Spanish the language of the country, but there are also local village festivals that take their cue from Saint's Days, and where the evening paseo is still part of village life. Even such developed towns as the northwest coast's Quebradillas and the south coast's San German, to mention only two, center the social life for the community on the central plaza or park. Until recently, the young people would come to the park in evenings, if not to stroll—girls in one direction, boys in the other—as was the custom of their parents, then at least to look at—and perhaps to meet—their counterparts.

To understand the customs that are still part of Puerto Rico, visit the small museums and homes in Old San Juan, where some of the traditions are explained, and then take a car to drive into the country, away from the usual tourist routes. Even the country's most sophisticated citizens continue the tradition of their childhood (and long before) of the celebration of San Juan Bautista Day, the day of the patron saint of Puerto Rico. Families and friends gather for festivities, fun—and the midnight swim, walking into the water backward to keep evil away for the year.

Roadside stands sell traditional Puerto Rican foods on the busy route from the airport to the commercial caverns along the north coast, and in the mountains and fishing villages. Artisans are encouraged to practice, and perhaps learn again, the handicrafts of their fathers. Puerto Rican culture continues—with encouragement from the island's dynamic Instituto de Cultura Puertorriquena, with its head office at the convent on San Jose Plaza in Old San Juan.

Many of the houses in small villages in the mountains are painted the pastel colors that were popular around the turn of the century. Although municipal governments have focused in recent years on a cleanup and improvement campaign that benefits visitors as well as residents, you will find small-town life still carries many of the customs of many years ago. Children are sheltered by their parents and nightlife as it is known in the sophisticated centers is nil.

Clothes are casual, colorful, and comfortable. Blue jeans and shorts are worn, in all shapes and sizes, on Ashford Avenue, that commercial thread through Condado's hotel area. Anything that is comfortable in warm weather appears on the streets of Old San Juan. Puerto Ricans will not wear sundresses and other half-dress in their cities; often tourists do. In churches and cathedrals covering the arms and back is the custom, as in any Catholic country. Beachwear is best only at the beach or pool. When you're touring in the country, you will find that people dress conservatively. Evenings at the better resorts are dress-up affairs, although there are plenty of places in Old San Juan and the Condado-Isla Verde areas where you can go for dinner in casual clothes (*Kentucky Fried Chicken, Burger King,* hotel coffee shops, and the assortment of snack places that rim the roads around the cluster of hotels). Jacket and tie are not required at many places, although most men do slide into something respectable when they go to one of the top spots, or to a concert, play, or another social event where residents and visitors mix. Dress for women in the evenings is usually a skirt or pants-with-style. Long dresses are usually seen only at some special hotel function, one of the gala evenings of "your" convention, or a social event. At beach and poolside, anything goes—even hair curlers (in too many places).

MEDICAL FACILITIES The Commonwealth has excellent health care facilities, comparable to those available in many metropolitan cities of the U.S. mainland. The greatest concentration of (and best equipped) hospitals are around San Juan, but there are also hospitals in Mayaguez, Ponce, and other areas. In the San Juan area, both the Presbyterian Hospital on Ashford Avenue, near most of the hotels, and Pavia Hospital on 21st Street, in the commercial area, are fully equipped for heart problems and have intensive care units. The Municipal Hospital and Veterans' Hospital are neighbors in the Hato Rey area of the capital. Your doctor can advise you about colleagues who may be practicing in Puerto Rico, if you want a name contact for your travels. All of the hotels have a doctor on call.

MONEY MATTERS If you travel with a lot of cash (U.S. dollars are the island's currency), keep it in the hotel's safe deposit boxes, or in travelers' cheques. Credit cards are widely accepted, especially in the San Juan area hotels, restaurants, and shops, but do not count on using personal checks. Make arrangements with a local bank if you will need a lot of cash.

COMMUNICATIONS are akin to those on the U.S. mainland. Phone service to Puerto Rico is via the 809 area code + the 7-digit Puerto Rico number. Facsimile machines are everywhere. New York and Miami newspapers are available through major hotel newsstands (often at high prices), and the *San Juan Star* is a good newspaper, with international as well as local news. Television is available in many hotel rooms, with Spanish-speaking San Juan stations as well as U.S. programs. Radio is in Spanish and English. Puerto Rico's telecommunications network has Telex, cable, and computer facilities.

ARRIVAL in San Juan is on big planes that come into the modern terminal from all parts of the world. The "new" terminal opened officially on January 17, 1983, with two levels, and an arrival ramp to alleviate some of the car and bus congestion. Ongoing modernization has made most of the airport look like a U.S. small-city terminal, especially since the commitment of *American Air-*

lines to the region. Since *American* uses Puerto Rico as a hub for Caribbean island links, and *Delta, US Air,* and others also have frequent flights, it is easy to reach San Juan from most major U.S. cities and to travel throughout the Caribbean from here.

American Airlines concentrates its check-in and gates in its expanded and efficient terminal, making it easy to make connections for onward flights. In addition to convenient, and relatively quick, connections, the American complex has its own baggage claim area and a convenient pickup station with options for ground transportation, plus the convenience of the Admirals Club (for members only) and access to the *American Eagle* commuter airline check-in area, if you are flying within Puerto Rico or to other islands on the small-plane services.

Having friends and relatives come to the airport for an arrival or departure is very much a Puerto Rico custom, and gathering at the gates makes arrival or departure for the rest of us something of a slalom course. The walk is long, and if you have carry-on luggage that gets heavy, bring luggage wheels—or your own porter.

In the terminal, the Puerto Rico Tourism Company has an information office, where you can get the current copy of *Que Pasa* (a fact-filled book that will become your thumb-worn bible), and if the bar is open for service, a free Puerto Rican rum potion. Thus armed, head for the fray—the luggage tug that finds you either stamping on your best friend (or some stranger) or standing back to be the last to claim your suitcase.

When you and your luggage are reunited, walk past the sometimes-checking-checks clerk at the gate, and locate transportation to your hotel. Minivans, offering seat-in-car services, go to hotels in the San Juan area. Hyatt's Dorado hotels and Palmas del Mar also have their vans. If you take a taxi, ask the fare for your destination before you get into the cab. And ask to have the meter running, if it is not. San Juan cab drivers can be a challenge.

AUTHOR'S OBSERVATION

In addition to shops, a wide range of airline ticket counters, and a selection of places to drink and dine (on average food), San Juan's airport has the *International Hotel,* a hermetically sealed honeycomb of rooms that can provide overnighting if you have a very early flight, or arrive on a late, late flight and are heading on the next morning.

CRUISE passengers are right in the heart of historic San Juan when the ship docks here. Facilities are among the Caribbean's best, with shops, phones, restaurants, etc., an easy walk from the shipside. Beaches require a taxi ride. This island offers far more than most people expect. Highlights, in addition to walking around Old San Juan, include San German (for the *Porto Coeli* church and museum), the agricultural station at Mayaguez on the west coast (for tropical flora), the art gallery in Ponce on the south coast, and the mountainous middle part of the island, with a visit to one or more of the *paradores* (government-assisted inns) and, perhaps, to El Yunque National Park, the Camuey caves, and/or the Taino Indian sites. At the east end, El Faro lighthouse and Las Cuevas natural park are worthy goals.

Most of the major cruise lines, and many of the smaller ships, sail from San Juan to other islands. Most cruises are 7 days; a few are longer.

DEPARTURE from San Juan is a routine U.S. airport procedure, but count on long (and slow) lines if you are checking in on one of the major airline flights for the mainland or Europe. Luis Munoz Marin International Airport is comparable to U.S. mainland airports, except that its bustle is created mostly by Puerto Ricans attending traveling friends and relatives and vacationers heading between U.S. mainland cities and island destinations (this one and others). Although *American Airlines'* check-in area is reasonably efficient, several of the island-based carriers are not as businesslike with their procedures. You'll have to assume some initiative to get what you want, if it's anything extraordinary (like finding out what time the flight is *really* going to leave).

In spite of the fact that Puerto Rico is an island (and a receptacle for illegal immigrants from Dominican Republic and other non-U.S. neighbors), the U.S. immigration officials on duty in the area you pass through to board your flight seem to me to spend more time chatting with their buddies or reading their newspapers than in checking passengers. There are no formalities for leaving Puerto Rico for the U.S. mainland.

Don't count on more than snack food at the airport. I find the eating areas to be tacky and unappealing. The few shops have mostly T-shirts and other typical tourist items.

TOURING TIPS: The situation for transportation from the airport is much improved, although it can lapse into the long familiar chaos on occasion.

AUTHOR'S OBSERVATION

In spite of continuing efforts by the Tourism Company and other interested community leaders, taxi drivers continue to do what they please in Puerto Rico. You are within your rights to insist on a metered rate, although many drivers at the airport tell you there's a flat rate to nearby hotels. As of this writing, there is no flat rate—and the metered rate is usually less than they quote on their flat rate. Don't be hoodwinked into overpaying! Write down the driver's name and number, plus date and time of ride, and contact the Puerto Rico Tourism Company.

Choices for transportation from the airport are three: a rental car; a taxi, ready and waiting although the gathering spot is not always easy to find; or the minibus/van. The fare for the bus/limousine service is about $5 for a trip to San Juan, but it is not always easy to find the minibus; a taxi costs about $10. If you are heading to Dorado, Palmas, or one of the outlying areas, reasonable transportation choices for first-timers are two: by bus/limousine (there is usually one waiting if you are expected on the flight), or by small plane. Advance arrangements (through your travel agent, or by writing the hotel) are advisable, but not foolproof, so be patient. You should know—before you assume that flying is faster—that although your time in the air is about 15 minutes, the waiting time to connect with the pilot, to board, and to take off puts the total travel time about the same—between one and two hours, depending on traffic and takeoff time. Those who know the routes to Palmas and to Dorado can pick up their rental car and arrive at either place within the hour.

American Eagle and *Sunaire* fly between San Juan and Ponce or Mayaguez. Those two airlines, plus *LIAT* and others, fly to most islands east and south.

Rental cars are available through a variety of sources. The names you know (Hertz, Avis, Budget, National, etc.) are easy to find. You can telephone as follows: *Hertz* (T 791–0840), *Avis* (T 721–4499), *National* (T 791–1805), *Discount,* (T 726–1460), *Budget* (T 791–3685). From my experience, their rates are highest, and good values are available from some of the smaller operations with only a dozen or so cars. Two firms worth noting are *Thrifty* (T 791–4241) and *Target* (T 783–6592). I have had good luck with *Charlie* (T 728–2418), *L&M* (T 725–8307), and some of the other local rental offices in the busy Condado and Isla Verde areas, although their cars are not always the latest models.

Investigate the several **small-plane air services** to neighboring islands. There have been some good-value (and fun) day shopping excursions to both St. Thomas and St. Croix, to take advantage of the U.S. Virgin Islands' special duty allotments. Check through your hotel, or at San Juan's International Airport by going from desk to desk, about the best excursion fares to islands including the British Virgins, the U.S. Virgins, St. Maarten, St. Kitts, and several other places, as well as to Vieques and Culebra from the Isla Verde airport, a few miles closer to San Juan city center.

To reach Vieques and Culebra, Puerto Rico's offshore islands, small domestic airlines fly from Isla Grande airport (near the bridge between the Caribe Hilton and the Condado Plaza in San Juan) on schedules or by charter. There is also ferry service from Fajardo, a town on the east end of Puerto Rico, for a ride that takes about an hour and costs less than $3.

AUTHOR'S OBSERVATION

If you are driving, or taking a taxi, to the airport on weekdays, between 4 and 6:30 p.m., allow plenty of time. Automobile traffic in and around the airport, and especially on the gnarled routes from Old San Juan to Isla Verde, can be overwhelming; cars crawl, tempers rise and the cacaphony of horns can bring city realities all too clearly into focus even though this is a lovely tropical island.

Roads around the countryside are good and usually well posted; rental cars give you a chance to be independent. There are some tours into the interior (check with your hotel activities desk), if you prefer to head inland with a guide. The most popular areas are the El Yunque area for the rain forest and, for those with an interest in the island's history, to the mountain village in the midwestern part of the island, near the Taino Indian ballpark.

In addition to the **taxis** that wait outside the doors of most of the big hotels, there is frequent **bus service** from well-posted stops, marked with the colorful *LeLoLai* tourism symbol, running between most of the Condado and Isla Verde hotels and downtown Old San Juan. The cost for the tourist bus is 50¢.

LODGING in Puerto Rico gives you more choice for your money than almost any place in the Caribbean. You can choose between action-packed, 24-hour casino cavorting high-rise hotels or small spots within a few steps of discos and the beach. You can head for the hills, to some of the government-encouraged *paradores*, small country inns that are typical of their region, or you can tap top elegance (for this Commonwealth) at the north coast or the southeast. You can book into a tennis clinic, or concentrate on golf, or you can see the new Puerto Rico, that is old to traditionalists, but little known to the hordes of tourists that sweep through the San Juan strip. There's no island that has more variety with accommodations than Puerto Rico, and few that have as much.

When it comes time to pay your bill, almost all Puerto Rican hotels accept credit cards. If payment by card is crucial, ask in advance. There's a 6% room tax, but what you give for service is at your discretion. It's reasonable to leave about $1 per day for the maid who cleans your room.

AUTHOR'S AWARDS

Puerto Rico has a greater range of good places than any other Caribbean island. In the San Juan area, my votes go to the *Condado Plaza Hotel & Casino* for glitz and glitter in the Las Vegas style, and to the *Excelsior* for good value with an excellent restaurant. *Gallery Inn* deserves special mention as a very unique inn in Old San Juan. Around the island, I'll choose *Hyatt Dorado Beach* for its classic Caribbean beach-and-palm style with high quality, and to *Horned Dorset Primavera*, a pace-setting inn on the west coast that has the feeling of an elegant private home.

Information about places to stay is included under Hotels/Resorts, Housekeeping Holidays, the Inn Way, and Low-Cost Lodging in specific areas around the island. Stars are awarded within each category. (See page 11.)

SAN JUAN AND CONDADO AREA

The name San Juan is used for everything between the airport and the old city. In fact, there are several small districts, plus the big zone called Santurce, that cover that area. The addresses in the hotel comments include the districts, namely Condado, rimming the Atlantic, with Ocean Park to its east at the shore and Miramar to its southwest, on the inland side of the lagoon. All are east of the bridge (Punta dos Hermanos) that separates San Juan Antiguo (old San Juan) and modern San Juan from the Condado and Miramar sections. The area nearest the airport, east of San Juan/Santurce, is known as Isla Verde and is in the Municipality of Carolina. (All the others mentioned are in the Municipality of San Juan.) You can drive from the airport to the tip of Old San Juan in about 20 minutes, traffic willing (but the ride can take an hour or more).

The Condado area has gone through a nu[mber of phases], from elegant resort to seedy and back to a thriv[ing area with] overtones. The severe drop in business in the e[arly 1980s] caused local folks to concentrate on reassessmen[t that is] still underway. The Condado aspires to be a livel[y area] along the lines of Miami Beach, Atlantic City, a[nd other] centered resorts. There's a special atmosphere to Sa[n Juan, with its] Caribbean sea and beaches along the shoreline.

The next few years promise more improvements [and the Carib-]bean Newsletter (page 9) will have an update on devel[opments].

★★★ **Ambassador Plaza Hotel & Casino** • *in the Condado area* • swallowed up the former Howard Johnson Hotel, leaving only the ice cream link and a HoJo restaurant as tokens from the past, to become a deluxe hotel with a pleasant, marble-tiled lobby and rooms in the tower capped by the swimming pool. Several dining choices open out to street level: *Giuseppe*'s features northern Italian, with plenty of pastas; *Jade Beach* is the Chinese offering; and the 24-hour American-style Howard Johnson restaurant serves American snacks, sandwiches, and full meals. Air-conditioned bedrooms have TV and all modern features. The new look is a good one; this place is worth a try, for value, comforts—and ice cream. *Big hotel.*

★★★★ **Caribe Hilton** • *not far from Old San Juan, on the grounds of Fort Geronimo* • has been the headlight for tourism development in the San Juan area since it was built in 1948. Extensive building and refurbishing in '91 resulted in a huge, glitzy casino, new dining rooms, and expanded lobby cafe. The three high-rise blocks of 707 rooms cup the swimming pool, beach, tennis courts, health club, shops, restaurants, convention halls, and casino. Business people appreciate the Vista executive floors, with deluxe suites as well as comfortable standard rooms, a hostess/manager assigned to the floor, plus valet and other special services. The summer *Youth Camp* for 9- to 13-year-olds (mid-June to mid-August) is free for guests, and other children's activities plans are offered during school vacations throughout the year. Guests enjoy assorted games (volleyball, etc.), lessons that include dance, palm frond weaving, rum drink mixing, and tours of the hotel's facilities. Most rooms are in top shape with beige tones, plants, and air conditioning as well as services of a "bellman," the order-when-you-want drink dispensers that computer-tally your takes on your bill when you turn the key. This hotel opened in December '48, added rooms in '63, and the 18-floor tower rooms in '72. If there *are* problems, they will probably be tedious lines at check-in and check-out if you hit either counter at busy times, an occasional "brisk" staff member, and clutter that is sometimes left around the pool and beach area long after the loungers have gone. Check for special programs during summer months, and inquire about multi-night packages that may apply for your visit. *Big hotel.*

Carib Inn • *near the airport, in the Isla Verde area* • is a multi-story hotel, within walking distance of the beach. Rooms are the expected hotel style, with furnishings that show signs of wear. There's a pool on the premises, plus

...nese restaurant, a coffee shop poolside, a health club, and several ...rts that are in good shape. *Hotel.*

★★ **Clarion Hotel & Casino** • *in the Miramar area* • inland from the shore, is a full-service multi-story hotel (the tallest in San Juan), with a grand view from its *Windows of the Caribbean* top-floor restaurant. Popular with business travelers, the hotel provides office services and a large pool, plus a health club facility. Bedrooms on the upper floors are the most viewful. *Hotel.*

La Concha • *on Ashford Ave., in the Condado area* • and its neighbor, *Condado Beach,* benefit from extensive building and renovation in recent years, but there's still work to be done on staff attitude, in my opinion. The lobby area seems to collect assorted "hangers on," which detracts from a resort atmosphere. The hotel has 224 U.S. hotel–style, air-conditioned rooms in a tower where top-floor rooms have a nice beach-and-sea view. Third-floor rooms have easy access to tennis courts and large pool. A neighboring shopping arcade holds *Budget* car rental and a branch post office as well as shops. (The underground parking area for the convention center is a convenient "hotel" for your rental car.) *Big hotel.*

★★ **Condado Beach Hotel** • *on Ashford Ave. next to the convention center* • has a venerable history and, with new owners and investment, has a chance to return to a prominent place on Puerto Rico's tourism roster. In 1919 the Hotel Vanderbilt was built on this site, and although most of the surroundings have changed beyond recognition, photographs available at the hotel show life and festivities of that time. By the early '50s, when the tourism tide was beginning to rise, entrepreneurs saw the potential for Condado. The hotel was tied to the newer La Concha by the convention center, and a wing of new rooms was appended to the left as you look at the historic facade (with your back to the bustle of Ashford Ave.). Sea-view rooms with balcony are the best. The lagoon rooms have a "view" of modern commerce. There's a pool, plus the beach, which is thin at this part of the coast. All the action of the Condado area and the convention center are within an easy walk. *Hotel.*

★★★★ **Condado Plaza Hotel & Casino** • *on Ashford Ave., within easy walk of the convention center, shops, and restaurants* • has a mystique akin to that of Disney World, with adult action that includes restaurants, casino, nightclubs, floorshows, slot machines, and the world. A glass people-tube stretches between the shoreside hotel and its inland Siamese sister-building of bedrooms. The *Lotus Flower* Chinese restaurant has been consistently good. Try for a table with a lagoon view. Other restaurants are *Capriccio's* for Italian food, *Tony Roma's* for barbecued ribs and chicken (across the road from the casino), *Sweeny & Son* for seafood (with an oyster bar), *Las Palmas* for pizza, and *La Posada,* which doubles as a steak place at night and a coffee shop by day. The nightclub has classy Vegas-style floorshows; there's a disco, *Isadora,* a San Juan favorite. Count on action—even outside the casinos—and know that your one of the 558 rooms will be U.S. style, with air-conditioning, lagoon or sea view (I prefer the lagoon view here because of the activity), and all modern conveniences. Two tennis courts are on the lagoon side. *Resort hotel.*

Condado San Juan • *between shore and Ashford Ave., near the Condado Plaza* • needed a lot of work when I checked. Carpets are tattered, cement and tile chipped, and staff attitude seemed lax. The former Ramada link has been broken. Check before booking. *Hotel.*

★ **Dutch Inn Hotel & Casino** • *just off Ashford Ave.* • offers housekeeping apartments as well as regular hotel rooms in two tall, skinny towers. If your room is on one of the upper floors, you may have a view of the sea; otherwise you're within walking distance of the beach, shops, and action in the Condado area, and at a hub where you'll find the *Greenhouse* restaurant, open for all meals, which are served amid hanging plants and other greenery. Expect the usual amenities, with an instant coffee- or tea-maker in your room if you don't have the complete kitchenette. *Hotel, apts.*

El Convento • *across from the Cathedral in Old San Juan* • could be charming, but it wasn't on my recent survey. Modified from a 17th-century convent, the site is convenient for stepping into history, and for shops, galleries, and cafes. Used as base for some cruise lines' passengers, before or after sailing, there's a "transit" feeling here. A tacky-looking plastic roof covers the once-airy (always hot) courtyard, which has a small pool. Food served in this area is only average. Air-conditioned rooms can be pleasant, when you have one with a good view. With firm, capable management and investments in decor, this place could be a gem. The *Caribbean Newsletter* (page 9) will have comment, when changes are made. Ramada's management agreement was terminated at the end of '90; at press time, there are rumors of a sale. *Historic hotel.*

★★★★ **El San Juan Hotel & Casino** • *on the shore at Isla Verde, near the airport* • brings glitzy luxury trappings to the San Juan area. The Palm Court lobby offers a wine bar—and piano music for those who want to linger. It's the hub for the lively casino, *La Galeria* shopping arcade, *Le Pavillion* gourmet restaurant (with aspirations toward elegant service), and other services. The reception area is to the left of the entrance. The large pool, and Condado's beach, are also in that direction, as are other restaurants (*Dar Tiffany* steak and seafood restaurant, *Back Street Hong Kong* for Oriental food, and *La Veranda* near the beach among them). Bedrooms are large and comfortable. Some spacious suites have whirlpools; others have a private garden area. Ocean and pool lanais, on the ground level nearest the beach, have a private terrace—and a villa style. The "new" El San Juan is about a 5-minute drive from the airport. Tennis courts, watersports, beach, and big pool are focal points for daytime diversions; restaurants, nightclubs, cocktail areas, casino, and floor shows occupy evening hours. *Resort hotel.*

Excelsior • *across the lagoon, in Miramar* • is popular with businesspeople who know and appreciate good value and pleasant surroundings. Air-conditioned bedrooms in the 10-story hotel have TV, telephone, kitchenettes, and modern comforts; all are tastefully decorated. Breakfast is served around *El Gazebo* in the pool area. *Augusto's* (see "Restaurants") is one of Puerto Rico's best dining choices. *Apt. hotel.*

Olympia Court • *in Miramar, about 5 minutes' ride from the Condado hotels* • is a multistory tower with under 100 rooms, some of them with self-catering facilities. Businesspeople and others who want the option of cooking "at home" nest here, as do price-conscious travelers from the West Indies and elsewhere. *Hotel, apts.*

★ **El Portal** • *in the Condado area, within a short walk of the beach* • is a small, multi-story hotel with modest rates, modern and clean air-conditioned rooms, and reasonably comfortable surroundings. There's a sunning area on the roof, with umbrellas—and a barman, when business warrants. A privately owned coffee shop next door is used for the complimentary continental breakfast and, while it's not elegant, it is genuinely Puerto Rican and pleasant. Rooms have TV and are modern. *Hotel.*

Hotel Pierre Best Western • *on a side street in the Condado area* • has a devoted following of businessfolk who know this hotel to be efficient, convenient, and good at taking messages, with a secretarial service. There's a pool. Some rooms have kitchenettes; all have T.V. The *Montenegro* restaurant is next door; the Best Western link makes reservations easy. *Hotel.*

★★ **Radisson Normandie Hotel** • *next to the Caribe Hilton, on the outskirts of Old San Juan* • assumed a meaningful role as the place for San Juaneros to hold important social events soon after it opened in 1988. The heart of the new hotel is the former Normandie Hotel, built by its owner as a tribute to his wife and, in its day, a magic, romantic spot. Efforts have been made to reestablish the art deco era, with a top-quality restaurant with European chefs and a center-area coffee shop that is appealing. Bedrooms have sitting areas, minibars, T.V., and comfortable furnishings in tones of mauve, beige, and gray-green. There's a pool at the back of the building, and a small patch of sand for swimming in the sea next door to the Hilton. *Hotel.*

The Regency • *next to the Condado Plaza, on the beach in the Condado area* • has suite-style rooms. The ones with sea view are my preference. Front desk prides itself on message-taking ability, a service that is much appreciated by visitors with appointments. The hotel is within easy walking distance of the convention center and all the Condado action, there's a restaurant called *Royal Palm* on the premises. Surrounded by shops, and the Condado Plaza's casino and restaurants, a room in the Regency offers convenience within slightly more subdued surroundings. *Hotel.*

★★★★ **The Sands Resort & Casino** • *on the beach at Isla Verde* • is big, brassy, beautiful, and active. Opened in the '60s as the high-rise Americana Hotel, the property has been linked with several chain reactions. The newest adoption included a complete overhaul, with white marble on the floor (and white walls and halls) for the reception area. The pool and several restaurants are on the beach (lower) level. The casino and nightclub provide expected glitz. Being near the airport makes this a convenient spot for a last-minute swim before departure, and the action of its neighbor, the El San Juan, gives guests some choices. Tennis courts and beach activities are on-premises; fishing boats, sailing, and scuba diving can be arranged. Bedrooms have either beach-and-sea or mountain-and-inland view; if you have a preference, state it. *Resort hotel.*

Travel Lodge • *in Isla Verde, across the road from the beach* • offers reasonably priced accommodations with the expected U.S. chain conveniences of restaurant, a room with big beds and modern bathroom, and some hints of Puerto Rico in the shops and other trappings. This 91-room 8-story spot has a pool not far from El San Juan Hotel. Several fast food restaurants are nearby. *Hotel.*

HOUSEKEEPING HOLIDAYS may be in individual homes, as is the case on the north coast, west of the capital, near the Dorado Hyatt property, where homeowners occasionally rent their villas. More often, self-catering facilities are in high-rise condominiums or in some of the hotels, where a few rooms have kitchenettes. Since branches of well-known U.S. supermarket chains are in Puerto Rico, and daily patterns are akin to those known in Miami and other cities of the south; lifestyle is American—with Spanish-language overtones.

Among the hotels with apartments are the *Dutch Towers,* the *Regency,* the *Excelsior,* and the *ESJ Towers,* west of the El San Juan hotel. One source for apartment/condominium rentals in the Isla Verde area is Mrs. Francis Gilroy (3405 East Dr., Douglas Manor, NY 11363), who also has a small shop in the area where most of her rentals are located.

For places with kitchenettes in small hotels, see the individual mentions under "Low-Cost Lodging."

THE INN WAY: *Paradores Puertorriquenos* (T 809+721–2400 or 800+443–0266) are unique in the Caribbean. The government-assisted inns are scattered around the countryside, at coffee plantations in the mountains, at the seaside near one-time fishing villages, and in historic towns. Although these small properties do not yet, in my opinion, have the high standards warranted by such a program, paradores are wonderful places for a day trip or overnight, when you want to see the real Puerto Rico. For comments on the paradores, see pages 557 and 564.

Although there are no paradores in the San Juan-Condado area, inquire about **Gelabert's Bed & Breakfast,** which is planned to be in their house, where 15 rooms will be available for guests. Located in Old San Juan, on Caleta de las Monjas (Street of the Nuns), the place should be open for this winter.

★★ **El Canario** • *on Ashford Ave., near the high-rise hotels* • sits amid the the hustle and bustle of the Condado area, offering its guests simply furnished rooms at modest rates on a bed-and-breakfast plan. A few rooms have been added to the original main house; the hotel looked run-down when I checked for this edition. There's a small courtyard for sunbathing, and all the action of the area casinos, shops, restaurants, snack places, etc., on and along the street, and beach nearby.

★ **El Canario by the Lagoon** • *on a side street in the Condado area* • is a small, 5-story building in a residential part of this hotel-studded area. You can walk to all the big places, plus restaurants and shops. Although small, rooms are pleasantly decorated; TV and telephone, private bathroom, and continental breakfast are included in your rate. *Small hotel.*

★ **El Canario by the Sea** • *at 4 Condado Avenue, almost on the beach* • is a 4-story block of small-but-pleasant rooms that provide reasonable comforts; most have air-conditioners. Complimentary continental breakfast sometimes includes homebaked breads, but always allows for tea or coffee. Most rooms have TV and, although compact, all have basic facilities and a pleasantly informal, guesthouse atmosphere. Part of a trio of like-run inns, this place is independently managed, within walking distance of the rest of its relatives but closest to the beach. Good value for cost conscious travelers. Plenty of fast food places and classier restaurants are within walking distance. *Small hotel.*

Casa de Playa • *on the beach in Isla Verde, not far from the airport* • is a newly fitted 2-story building, in Spanish style. Suites have kitchenettes; air conditioned rooms have private bath, TV, and reasonable comforts. Within easy stroll of several restaurants, plus lively casinos and nightlife, this place offers good value. *Small hotel.*

★★ **The Gallery Inn** • *on Blvd. del Valle in Old San Juan* • was once known as *La Cueva del Indio,* and it's unique. Not only is it the gallery of talented artist Jan D'Esopo, but the colonial building has been painstakingly restored and is full of antiques—and the owner's paintings and sulpture. Each of the 6 rooms has its own personality (3 are suites) upstairs in the historic house. Within an easy stroll of all the old city's sights, this place is very special—and meals prepared by Jan D'Esopo are a memorable occasion (possible by reservation only). *Inn.*

LOW-COST LODGING: Puerto Rico has more hotel rooms in all shapes and sizes than most other Caribbean islands and, although most are priced for U.S. mainland consumption (which means top dollar in winter), many of the smaller hotels have rates that seem reasonable when compared with the big-and-famous places. There are a few big hotels that have reasonable rates (when they are compared with high-rise neighbors); and several small guest houses and inns in the San Juan-Condado area are reasonable.

The San Juan-Condado area guest houses have a very local personality. Many are favorites for homosexuals; others are best known to people from nearby islands who have been coming to their Puerto Rico "home" for years. In all cases, rooms may be viewless, which makes an air conditioner essential. If you haven't been in this area before, I'd suggest booking at one of the small hotels mentioned above, and looking for yourself to see whether the laid-back style appeals to you.

Arcade Inn • *on Taft St., in the Condado area* • is a former private home with stucco structure and several air-conditioned rooms, plus a couple units with kitchenette. You can walk to the beach. *Guesthouse.*

Arcos Blancos • *in a couple of former homes on a side street in the Condado area* • has 19 attractive rooms, some of them small, and a pool. It's a short walk to the beach at the end of the road, and you're not far from some excellent restaurants. Favored by a homosexual clientele, the inn has enthusiastic repeat visitors. *Guesthouse.*

Atlantic Beach Hotel • *on Vendig St. in the Condado area* • is a reasonably priced block of rooms within a few steps of the busy beach. The view from the seaside restaurant was more interesting than the food when I tried it, but this place offers basic hotel rooms at modest rates within a short walk of all the casino and nightclub action. *Small hotel.*

Casa Blanca • *on the inland side of the shoreside Condado hotel area* • is an 8-room guest house, near the Condado action—and shorefront. The rooms vary, as you would expect in a home-style place. Good for folks who'd rather spend disposable cash on casinos, discos, gala dining, and shops than on bed and board. *Guesthouse.*

Green Isle • *on Villamar St., in the Isla Verde area* • offers a handful of simply furnished air-conditioned rooms, some with kitchenettes. There's a pool, but you can walk across the highway to the beach shared by the Sands hotel and several high-rise condominium complexes. *Guesthouse.*

International Airport Hotel • *at the airport* • gives you a reasonably quiet, adequately furnished room on the 3rd floor of the terminal building. Although it can be welcomed lodging for in-transit travelers, there's nothing about this 57-room hotel that makes it ideal for vacationing, except its convenience. (Isla Verde resorts are only 5 minutes from the airport.) *Small hotel.*

Numero Uno • *on Santa Ana St., in Ocean Park* • is within easy walk on the beach. Ken and Liz Austin are hosts at this small spot where repeat guests feel very much at home. Rooms are comfortable, even when small. *Guesthouse.*

El Prado Inn • *on Calle Luchetti in the Condado area* • is a combination of standard bedrooms and units with kitchenette, within walking distance of the hotel-hub action. All rooms benefitted from a total refurbishing in fall 1988. There's a pool on premises; continental breakfast. *Guesthouse.*

El Prado by the Beach • *on Yardley Pl. in the Ocean Park area* • is another home-turned-inn. The several rooms are in a Spanish-style main house, with comforts even when the rooms are small. Continental breakfast is included in the modest overnight rate. You can walk to the beach. *Small hotel.*

RESTAURANTS in the San Juan-Condado area include all kinds, some serving very good international food, as well as French, Spanish, Chinese, and other regional cuisines. Each of the big hotels has several restaurants including one that features elegant dining at high prices and at least one coffee shop. The profusion of fast-food places equals that of any city in the U.S. You'll be able to find all the familiar names: *Kentucky Fried, Burger-King, Arby's, Ponderossa, Baskin-Robbins,* and others.

Count on metropolitan city prices for the better San Juan restaurants. Some restaurants, especially those in Old San Juan, offer exceptional atmosphere. Many are enclosed, air-conditioned, dark—and expensive. The only dining bargains come from the roadside stands that sell empanadas and pastillitos or fresh pineapples, oranges, and other fruits.

Mesones Gastronómicos are government-acknowledged typical restaurants, usually in the countryside and marked by a sign showing a knife, fork, and spoon with the words "Meson Gastronomico." Ask at the Tourist Office for a list. They're fun; food's good.

AUTHOR'S AWARDS

Among the many places for meals, two noteworthy restaurants in San Juan are *Augusto's,* an independent restaurant in the Excelsior Hotel, and *Il Perugino,* a small cafe off a patio on Cristo Street in Old San Juan. Both serve good food with style.

There are well over 100 restaurants in the busy San Juan-Condado area. Each season brings more, and many of the new places are exceptionally good. In addition to the suggestions offered by the concierge in the bigger hotels, consult the listing in the monthly *Que Pasa* magazine, distributed through the tourist office.

If you want some special meals in San Juan, here's what I'd suggest:

Ajili-Mojili • *at the corner of Joffe St., in the Condado area* • specializes in good, nicely served Puerto Rican cooking. Very popular with residents at lunchtime, the place is also open for dinner. Call ahead for reservations.

Al Dente • *on Racinto Sur, in Old San Juan* • is one of a cluster of atmospheric restaurants in restored old buildings near the cruise ship piers. Italian food is the specialty here.

Amanda's Cafe • *in Old San Juan, on Calle Norzagaray* • provides good meals, snacks, and sipping potions near Fort San Cristobal. Unusual entrees include adaptations of Puerto Rican country food and Mexican-style offerings.

Ambrosia • *at 250 Cristo St. in Old San Juan* • is a comfortable cafe with pleasant atmosphere, and reasonably good food. Although pasta and other Italian staples are on the menu at all times, fresh fish and other offerings are also interesting.

Amadeus's • *106 Plaza san Jose, near the Dominican Convent, at the top of Cristo St.* • is as popular as a gathering spot as it is for food. Puerto Rican specialities are served with talent. I've enjoyed making a meal of delicious and different appetizers, using local produce.

★★★ **Augusto's** • *at the Excelsior Hotel, on Avenida Ponce de Leon* • gives its patrons pleasant, uncluttered surroundings and neat table settings as a complement to the innovative food offerings. Appetizers and entrees blend nouvelle cuisine with Puerto Rican favorites. Desserts are special. (Augusto was chef at the Caribe Hilton's best restaurant prior to opening this place.)

★ **La Casona** • *609 San Jorge Street, in Santurce, not far from Condado's Ashford Ave. hotels* • serves important fare in homelike surroundings. The inside rooms are air-conditioned; the garden area is not, but it's pleasant. Count on an international, with emphasis on Spanish style.

Chart House • *across Ashford Ave. from the Palms Hotel* • serves slabs of roast beef, as well as steak, lobster tails, fish, and other offerings in huge portions. Salad, baked potato, and the "usuals" are available to tag onto the entree. Owners restored/rebuilt an imposing private home to create atmosphere on the several floors and balconies, but until the former Dupont Plaza reopens (across the street), it's difficult to predict how busy this place will be.

La Chaumiere • *on Tetuan, in Old San Juan* • serves French-style specialties in an elegant setting near the Tapia Theater. *La Creperie,* upstairs, is popular for light dining at theater (and other) times.

★★ **Los Faisanes** • *1108 Magdalena, on a spur road off Ashford Ave.* • specializes in pheasant, but the menu has many other offerings, which are attractively presented. Dark and air-conditioned, the dining room is more formal than the service, which fluctuates between pretentious and lackadaisical. Food has been good (and pricey) when I've been here.

★★★ **The Gallery Inn** (also called La Cueva del Indio) • *on Blvd. del Valle in Old San Juan* • is a unique and special place where advance reservations are mandatory. Jan D'Esopo's home can be yours for a special dinner—if you are part of a group of as many as 60 and have planned ahead. Primarily an art gallery, the inn is just off the upper road leading past the forts in Old San Juan. Although its ground-level rooms are filled with the work of local artists, the upper floors are the D'Esopos' home. Meals are usually prepared at the discretion of Jan D'Esopo, although special favorites can sometimes be selected when you make arrangements in advance. Not open to the public for walk-in traffic, the inn can be an unforgettable experience. Phone 809+722–1808 or 809+725–3829 for further details.

★ **La Mallorquina** • *207 Calle San Justo, in Old San Juan* • has been on the restaurant roster longer than any other place (more than 140 years); it still has a cozy atmosphere and reasonably good food. The oft-touted speciality, the soupy, spicy rice dish known as *Asopao,* is still tops on the menu, although it's been better on some of my tries than on others. The menu features Puerto Rican favorites, which means a lot of heavily fried and high calorie offerings.

★★ **Montenegro** • *on De Diego, next to the Pierre Hotel* • fills a building formerly occupied by the legendary Swiss Chalet, with a menu that includes interesting (and tasty) preparation of local fish and poultry. The air-conditioned dining area is attractive, with white stucco walls accented with dark beams (from the former Swiss life). Desserts take their cue from the Puerto Rican's affection for a very sweet mealtime finale. Convenient to all Condado hotels.

El Patio de Sam • *at 102 San Sebastian, near the Dominican Convent at the top of Cristo St.* • is a San Juan legend. Now spruced up, with air-conditioning and other comforts, the casual restaurant is noted for its hamburgers and other snack plates. This is a favorite late-night spot, as well as a place that's popular for lunch and dinner.

Picayo • *in old San Juan* • is a local "hot spot" enjoyed for its New Orleans' style Cajun recipes.

★★★ **Il Perugino** • *at 202 Cristo St., off a shop-surrounded alcove* • is a cafe-style restaurant that's small, and can be noisy. The several tables are clustered in one small room, with the bar along part of one wall. Popular with classy San Juaneros, the Italian restaurant brings a measure of style and sophistication to Old San Juan, with its European feeling. Reservations are recommended, especially for dinner.

★★★ **Ramiros** • *1106 Magdalena, just off Ashford Ave.* • makes a name for himself not only on his restaurant but also with his special preparations, done to specific request when you stop by ahead of time to give suggestions. Otherwise, content yourself with the chef's choices, which include intricate preparations attractively presented, with emphasis on flavor as well as eye-appeal. Count on the basics—beef, fish, chicken—prepared in nouvelle ways. A good choice.

Yukiyu • *at 311 Racinto Sur* • serves Japanese sushi and sashimi as well as other Japanese-style offerings. The decor recalls an upscale Japanese restaurant. This is a first for Old San Juan; my sampling was tasty and attractively served.

La Zaragozana • *San Francisco 356* • not far from the cathedral in Old San Juan, can seat as many as 100 people on the dark wood chairs that pull up to red-cloth-covered tables, nested in the darkened rooms of this air-conditioned special spot. The bar, where you will wait if you arrive for dinner on a busy evening, is on the left, curving to the back dining area. Food is flambe and with flourishes, taking its cue from the elegant restaurant that used to occupy a private home setting in pre-Castro Havana. When the tide turned, the brothers took their bourgeois habits and classic recipes to a side street in Old San Juan, where the violin trio still plays as you linger over a late-night dinner. The red snapper flambeed with sherry and a soupcon of lemon was ideal on a recent visit, and you must have the Cuban-style flan (which colleague Carlos Diago claims gets its special flavor from creole eggs and the Cuban touch). The high prices you pay seem to me to be for one of Old San Juan's best values, considering setting, service, and food.

El Zipperle • *at 352 Roosevelt Ave., in the Hato Rey area* • is best known to residents and others with cars. Combining both Spanish and German styles on the menu, this place ends up being distinctly its own. Paella (seafood and rice) is a favorite for many, but expect to find sauerbraten and other European offerings as well. Check the wine list, which is reportedly excellent. Figure the cost of your taxi into the cost for dinner, unless you have a rental car.

NATURAL SURROUNDINGS: The congested San Juan area is not the first place (or the best place) for visitors to find "nature," but the **Botanical Garden** has well over 200 plant species, including those in the orchid garden. It's located in Rio Piedras, a once independent community that became part of San Juan in 1951. Be sure to reconfirm the opening hours for the garden, before you attempt the traffic-clogged roads to the Agricultural Experimental Station where it is located. Easy day trips from a San Juan hotel are by car to **El Yunque,** the mountain whose flanks are blanketed with the Caribbean National Forest, and to the **Pinones Forest Reserve,** east of San Juan and west of the Loiza River, that is noteworthy for its acres of mangroves. Farther east, privately-owned **Las Cabezas Nature Reserve** is well-organized for visitors, with a reception building in the style of the U.S. National Park facilities. A bus-train takes groups through the area, explaining the various plants, shrubs, and landscapes, and stops for a visit at scenic El Faro, a lighthouse perched on a promontory with a good view of the isles to the east and of the surrounding land. It's possible to get from the San Juan area to Ponce and other places along the south coast for a day's visit, either by driving (with an early start and late return) or by flying to Ponce and renting a car from there. If you head as far west as Mayaguez or want to go to San German and the southwest, plan to stay overnight so you'll have time to do more than pass by the sights. If you fly to Mayaguez, it's possible—but not advised—to see something in a very long day of touring.

PLACES WORTH FINDING in the San Juan/Condado area begin with Old San Juan, which has undergone extensive restoration and refurbishing in preparation for the Columbus year. The restored 16th- and 17th-century buildings represent the most authentic picture we have of the community known to the Caribbean's early Spanish settlers. Even the old city of Santo Domingo, in the Dominican Republic, settled before San Juan, does not represent a truer picture of an early Caribbean community. Most of Santo Domingo's buildings were rebuilt, albeit according to old plans and lines, because the original city had been almost completely destroyed. In Old San Juan, the original buildings that were tumbling together until the 1950s had survived that long not because of a manmade plan but because the original forts—El Morro and San Cristobal—perched on clifftops. Their walls plunged to the shore or the sea, the town's early buildings were not destroyed, and no suburban sprawl from any century could be built on at least three sides of this peninsula. (When you see what has oozed out of the fourth side of the city, the commercial knot you twist through to get in and out, you can appreciate the wisdom of the Spanish settlement on the promontory.)

In addition to the many 16th- and 17th-century homes now restored and filled with boutiques, restaurants, and—in a few cases—apartments, there is Casa Blanca, on a site of the house built for Ponce de Leon, the newly restored **Ballaja** building, near the Dominican Convent, and the **Beneficienca,** which is the new home for the Instituto de Cultura Puertorriquena. The Dominican Convent dates from 1523, and San Juan Cathedral, although mostly 19th century, is on the site of the first wood church (1520). Tapia Theater, built in 1832, has been restored to its 19th-century appearance and is used for 20th-century performances, and La Fortaleza, where Puerto Rico's governor lives, has been home for the chief ruler of Puerto Rico since the first community was established here. The first tower was ordered built by Spain's Carlos I in 1540.

AUTHOR'S OBSERVATION

Old San Juan's narrow streets are sometimes clogged with traffic. But portions of the seven-square blocks of Old San Juan are turned into pedestrian areas for several hours each day. Jitney buses follow regular routes along the main streets; you can get off and on at will.

The **Dominican Convent,** from the 16th century, is a convenient start for any walking tour through the history of Old San Juan. Art exhibits are often shown under the arcades around the edge of the center courtyard. The small museum (ancient sheet music, convent study room, altarpiece) to the right as you enter is reminiscent of old Spain, and the walk is all downhill from Plaza San Jose, where the convent is located.

Museo Pablo Casals (101 San Sebastian; Mon.–Sat. 9 a.m.–12 p.m.; Sun. 1–5 p.m.; free) on Plaza de San Jose opened in early 1978 as a memorial to the beloved cellist who spent the last 20 years of his life in his adopted country, Puerto Rico, and created the Casals Festival, held in June and highlight of the Commonwealth cultural season. Pablo Casals left his native Spain in protest over the policies of dictator Generalissimo Francisco Franco, to settle in his mother's home island in 1956, and was not to return until a couple of years before his death. In addition to photographs, musical scores, and memorabilia, the small 16th-century house has a special library of tapes from the Festival Casals. Highlight for those devoted to the famed cellist's work will be his cello, which is upstairs in a glass-enclosed display. (The case is propped up in a ground-floor corner.)

Casa Blanca, perched on a bluff overlooking San Juan harbor, claims to be the oldest continuously inhabited residence in the western hemisphere, but that seems to me to be a loose claim since the place is a museum now, and was closed for a lot of its recent history while undergoing complete refurbishing and repair. Be sure to see this house if you have any interest in early history. Although Ponce de Leon never lived here, the house that stands on the site of a simple 24-square-foot wood and thatched structure was supposed to have been built for him. When the thatched building burned, in 1521, stone was used for the new building, started in 1523. The fortress was added later, with the prestige of being called a fort. The approach to the house, through the gardens (and past the building where concerts are sometimes held), is a world apart from commercial San Juan. The views out the windows and from the balconies of the house lure students and others to the parapets to talk and read. Inside, the furnishings are typical of what might have been in the house, but none of them are original.

La Rogativa, the statue at the end of Caleta Las Monjas, a right turn as you head from the Plaza San Jose, commemorates the saving of Puerto Rico when it was surrounded by the Dutch. The women lined up with candles to march behind the bishop, giving the impression that there were a lot of soldiers at the top of the fortress when, in fact, there were none.

After you've looked at the statue (and the view over the wall), wander down Calle Recinto Oeste (past the old San Juan gate, the oldest gate in the original walls), which is sometimes open for cars (which then drive around the outside of the walls at sea level).

La Fortaleza, the governor's residence and office, at the walls at the end of Calle Fortaleza, is open for guided visits at specified hours. The main halls are shown, but not the private residence of the governor, which is upstairs.

Casa del Libro (255 Calle Cristo; 11 a.m.–5 p.m. Mon.–Fri., 2–5 p.m. Sat. and Sun.) is almost as interesting for its 16th-century setting as for the collection of books and prints that fill the first-floor cases. Primarily of interest to bibliophiles, this special spot rates near the Casals Museum in perfect presentation of dedication to a single subject. One item of interest is the decree relating to Columbus's second voyage, signed by King Ferdinand and Queen Isabella, but there are also pages from a Gutenberg Bible and an impressive collection of 15th-century Spanish books in special rooms upstairs.

La Casa de los Dos Zaguanes (House of Two Entrances) at the corner of Luna and San Jose (Tues., Thurs., Fri., Sat., Sun., 9 a.m.–12 p.m., 1 p.m.–4:30 p.m.) opened in August '78 as the first part of a planned museum of Puerto Rican heritage. The three floors will eventually house folk art, early Indian artifacts (some on loan from a Taino Indian collection that had been held at the Smithsonian), and perhaps a traveling collection from the Ponce Museum. On opening day, most of the Taino artifacts from the collection of George Latimer, U.S. Consul in Puerto Rico in 1836, held at the Smithsonian, were in place in the museum, as well as a *duho* (Taino ceremonial stool), which was repurchased from a collector in the Dominican Republic, and a grinding stone found by Ricardo Alegria, first director of the Instituto, during digs at Cueva Maria de la Cruz in Loiza. Be sure to look at the 18th-century buildings that house the collection; they're prize examples of life in this residential area in the 18th century. (A $25,000 Citibank donation helped bring the museum to birth.)

AUTHOR'S OBSERVATION

If seeing a particular museum is important, be sure to check opening hours in advance. In spite of the times and days listed in *Que Pasa*, and with information given to me by the very efficient staff of the Puerto Rico Tourist Offices, I have come to places to find them closed. You can count on all museums closing *exactly* at closing hour, so don't plan to make a last-minute sprint through some hallowed premises.

For "Places Worth Finding" around the island, consult the regions as they are mentioned below.

SPORTS around this big island have the variety you'd expect in a place that is home for 3.2 million people and is prepared to welcome more than 2 million tourists a season. For the planned seaside sports, the best spots are at the resort hotels, either those of the Condado area, where facilities are offered at a couple of easily accessible hubs (you can count on El Centro, the convention center, to be one), and at the Dorado hotels—Hyatt's Dorado Beach and Cerromar—as well as at Mayaguez for the west-coast area, La Parguera for the southwest coast, Palmas del Mar at the southeast, the town of Fajardo at the east, and Rio Mar on the northeast coast.

There are a dozen **public beaches** with lockers, showers, and facilities for your use as well as, of course, for the people who live here. Facilities at the public beaches are closed Mon. (or Tues., if Mon. is a holiday), but are open 9 a.m.–5 p.m. in winter and 9 a.m.–6 p.m. in summer. Isla Verde and Luquillo beaches are easily accessible from San Juan; Isla Verde is a taxi ride from Condado hotels, and Luquillo can be a goal on the day you rent a car. Humacao Beach, not far from the Palmas area on the southeast, and Punta Guilarte Beach on the south coast near Arroyo have fewer facilities than the north coast beaches, but if you're touring out this way, they are good cooling-off spots. El Tuque Beach, about four miles west of Ponce is talked about, but frankly, when I looked at it, it was an uninviting stretch of pebbly shore. Cana Gorda, near Guanica, was more interesting although not quite as easy to find. Boqueron Beach on the west coast at Boqueron Bay is not too far from Punta Higuero, between Aguadilla and Rincon, and one of the few good surfing beaches in Puerto Rico. Cerro Gordon Beach, west of the Dorado-Cerromar hotels, is a popular spot for vacationing Puerto Ricans; most visitors who book into either Dorado Beach or Cerromar will find those strands satisfactory, even though they are small. Sardinera Beach, on Route 698, is also near Dorado, and Punta Salinas is the beach that stretches between the Dorado area and Catano, on the coast. (If you drive out here, you'll see a sprinkling of the trucks that sell *chicharrones* and other Puerto Rican favorites for snacks at the beach.) The best white sand beaches by far are those on Vieques, Culebra, Icacos, and the other islands off the east coast of Puerto Rico. The first two are small-plane trips, if you want to make a day trip of it, and Icacos is a nice day sail/picnic lunch spot from Fajardo.

For **snorkeling** and **scuba,** the most central spot for San Juan visitors is the *Caribbean School of Aquatics* at La Concha, with its headquarters on the promenade just past the coffee shop and pool as you walk through the lobby and out the "back" door. These people have been operating scuba courses for almost 20 years and have a basic course that any average swimmer can easily conquer. Advanced courses are offered, and there is also the option for non-scuba folk to go along on the dive boat if there's space. Snorkel equipment can be rented, if you haven't packed your own; a complete set figures at about $25 per day. For those who want a day at sea that is relaxing, there's an "All Day Snorkel and Scuba Safari" that departs from La Concha at 8:30 a.m., driving for more than an hour east to Innovation's marina at Fajardo. Lunch, guides, boat ride, transportation to and from are all included for the $35, and you're back by 5 p.m. or so.

The San Juan Bay Marina near the Radisson and Caribe Hilton is home for the *Caribe Aquatic Adventure*, (T 809+724–1882) with scuba and snorkel guides and instruction. Most of the scuba is at the reefs off the shore near the hotel, with beginners starting their session with pool time and lectures. From the Mayaguez Hilton, on the west coast, there are scuba tours to nearby sites, and some training in the pool when there's a group that warrants it. Scuba here will be more interesting for experts, and is best when the sea is not rough. Operating out of ESJ Towers, at Isla Verde, near San Juan, *Castillo Watersports* (T 809+791–6195) plans excursions to waters off east end's Fajardo. Others offering scuba courses are *Carlos Flores* at the Puerto Chico Marina on the east coast at Fajardo and *Coral Head Divers,* out of the Marina de Palmas, at Palmas del Mar on the southeast coast. (Frankly, all the building and bodies on the north coast near San Juan fuzz up this water; the other areas are less peopled, and therefore clearer for good scuba.)

For **sailing,** check at the *Villa Marina Yacht Harbor* at Fajardo. The classiest sailing is offered at *Palmas del Mar,* where some of the boats that come into the new marina will take day charters, and there is a small fleet of "sail-yourself" boats for use (rental) by experienced sailors. The scene changes, but the excellent facilities are ready and waiting. Some big yachts call this place home this season.

La Parguera on the south coast talks about its "U-Drive-It-Boats," but don't count on all the equipment to be in next-to-new shape. While they're a lot of fun, the 16-foot aluminum boats with their 6 hp outboards have had hard use. From La Parguera there are boats to charter, with captain, to head out of the lagoon to open sea.

For **deep-sea fishing,** Fajardo and the Palmas marina are the places to start. Captain Mike Benitez (T 809+724–6265), Puerto Rico's best-known deep-sea captain, operates out of the Club Nautico de San Juan. At the San Juan Marina Fishing Center, next to the Club Nautico, by the traffic circle at the west end of the Condado area, facilities have been spruced up. There are several boats listed for deep-sea fishing charters for about $300 for 6 for a day, with captain, mate, rods, bait, and ice. (You bring lunch and drinks.) Stop by the day before to finalize the arrangements. *Maragata Yacht Charter* (T 809+850–7548) and *Karolette Deep Sea Fishing* (T 809+850–7442) head out from the marina at Palmas del Mar, on the southeast coast.

Golf courses are plastered over rolling terrain at the east and west. The four Dorado courses are the biggest cluster—and all can be played on golfing holidays at either Cerromar or Dorado Beach Hotels. The pro shops at both resorts have full facilities—and a list for sign-up times, which are essential in winter months and when golfing specials fill the house at package rates from April 16 through December 15. At the far west, the former U.S. military course, on what was Ramey Air Force base and is now Punta Borinquen resort, is available for all. The pro shop is at the crest of the hill, with restaurant and facilities. Club Rio Mar's course is along the shore on the northeast coast, about 45 minutes' drive from San Juan, but the most peaceful place of all of them, in my opinion, is the 18-hole course at Palmas del Mar, spread out between the beach units and the golf and tennis units that make up part of that resort. The expanded pro shop has a snack area as well as the expected rental equipment, lockers, caddies, and shop. Check on the status of the 18-hole course that wraps around three sides of the former El Conquistador Hotel near Fajardo on the east end. (At the 11th hole, golfers can stare El Yunque in the eye and blink at the Caribbean to the left.) The other courses pale by comparison to this group, but if you are going to be at Mayaguez, you can plan on the 9-hole country club course, and there's a 9-hole course at Caguas.

Tennis players who want the best facilities should check arrangements for the courts (and tennis packages) at the Hyatt's Dorado Beach and Cerromar and at Palmas del Mar. In the San Juan-Condado-Isla Verde area, there are courts at several hotels including the Carib-Inn near the airport in the Isla Verde area and the Caribe Hilton, which has its tennis club, with local members (and a high cost on court use). There are courts atop the roof at La Concha, as well as at The Sands, Condado Plaza, El San Juan, and elsewhere. If having easy access to a tennis court is at the top of your list of activities for a happy holiday, be sure to find out if there is a court—and how many of them are available *on the premises*. There are high costs for all, and the fee is sometimes more reasonable if you are overnighting at the court site.

For **horseback riding,** the *Palmas del Mar Equestrian Center* has over 40 horses. You can ride you along the shore and into the country on good trails; the paradores in the mountains have access to horses (which will be enjoyed if you have ridden before, but may not be well-trained enough if you are a timid rider), and riding is possible from Mayaguez. *Rancho Borinquen* at Carolina will pick you up in San Juan for the hour long ride west to their stables.

At Guayama, on the south coast, the *Paso Fino Horse Show* takes place in late February—early March. Those interested in watching (and riding) the remarkable smooth-gaited horses should plan a visit to Guayama. The Puerto Rico tourism office can provide names of stables.

If your interest is **horse racing** instead of horse riding, head for El Comandante at Canovanas, about 45 minutes' ride east of San Juan, for races on Wed., Fri., Sun., and holidays. (Clubhouse admission $3; grandstand $1.)

TREASURES AND TRIFLES are hidden in the cobbled streets of San Juan and at surprising places in the countryside, as well as at some of the hotel boutiques and the artisan markets. Although there's nothing duty-free in the Commonwealth of Puerto Rico, shops, markets, and special fairs yield some interesting handcrafts and a selection of worthy prints and paintings by Puerto Rican artists. Be sure to get a copy of the artists'-workshop map, available free from the tourism offices. Clearly marked are the studios (around the island) of artists who welcome visits.

If you find the offerings overwhelming, as I sometimes do, head for La Forteleza, in Old San Juan and stroll along Calle Fortaleza and Calle Cristo to name only two of many streets. You'll find some attractive small shops (and some junky ones, unfortunately). At **Jose Alegria's Studio** (#152), you can find high-quality sculpture, a few antiques (and some copies), as well as paintings. The Alegria brothers were prime movers in the restoration of Old San Juan; their enthusiasm and campaigns to rebuild date back some 30 years.

Glance right when you reach Calle Fortaleza, to note the few boutiques that border the road that leads to the governor's home (open for public visits at specified hours; see "Places Worth Seeing"). The majority of the stores can be found when you turn left.

Along Calle Fortaleza, look especially for **La Casita,** with what has become a Caribbean staple of embroidered clothing, batiks, and other colorful island-style clothes; **Casa Joscar,** where careful looking may yield some "treasures" among the supply of ceramics, Puerto Rican santos (carved saints), and other souvenir items; **Ultra** for the couturier names (Cardin, Givinchy, and others); **Chantilli,** with some good-looking jewelry amid some average, apparently popular styles; and **Puerto Rico Arts & Crafts,** where your own taste will dictate whether or not you find a treasure. One place worth perusing, if you have any interest in handmade lace, is **Aguadilla en San Juan** (#352 Calle San Francisco).

On Calle Cristo, the outlet stores for Ralph Lauren, Hathaway, and London Fog sometimes have good merchandise at less-than-U.S. prices, but items are often surplus stock and less popular lines.

One of the real browsing pleasures in Old San Juan is art gallery and small museum hopping. The area is literally packed with them, but many of the best are folded into restored buildings with little or no signposting. Ask at your hotel's activities desk. Check the *San Juan Star* (newspaper) for details about current shows.

AUTHOR'S OBSERVATION

Getting a taxi in Old San Juan can be a problem if you wait to find one cruising. The in-town taxi stand is at Plaza de Colon, where you can usually find one or more waiting.

La Plazoleta, Puerto Rican Craft Center, at Pier 3, at the Customs House in Old San Juan, is a hive of handcrafts. A lot of the work is high-quality, and the area is certainly worth browsing around. Inquire about the shops and galleries forecast for **La Princesa,** where the Tourism Company is located.

Shops in the Condado area are overwhelming. The mixture of outright junk and *very* high-quality merchandise can be confusing, especially when some stores carry both. For handcrafts, the **Artisans Fair,** established in late 1977 at the patio on El Centro, the Condado Convention Center, takes place some weekends, from about noon–5 p.m. Work varies, depending on which artisans have set up shop the week you are there, and if you see something on Saturday, don't wait until Sunday to buy it. There's a chance that both artisan and item may not be there. Some of the papier-mache tropical fruits, birds, etc., affixed to a piece of old wood to hang on a wall were colorful and worth looking at on a recent stroll, but there may be other things that will appeal more to you.

With the artisans' map in hand, you can drive around the countryside visiting more than 100 craftsmen at their workshops. Some studios are devoted to wood carving (be sure to find Elipidio Collazo, in Jayuya, for a look at the carved birds), others to ceramic, santos, jewelry, furniture, and hammocks (which are made in Yabucoa and San Sebastian).

THE NORTH COAST

DORADO, on the north coast, west of San Juan, and far removed from the hustle and bustle of the city (although only half an hour's drive when traffic is willing), is a small town that hasn't changed much since the advent of the *Dorado Beach* and *Cerromar Hotels*. Although there are a couple of restaurants, bars, and shops that might interest adventuresome travelers, most visitors will only drive through on their way to the elegant resorts.

ARRIVAL at Dorado and Cerromar hotels can be either by car or the resort's limousine, about 45 minutes' drive from San Juan's International Airport, or by small plane to the airstrip within minutes of the hotels. The flight is interesting for sightseeing, but don't count on it to be much faster. By the time you check in, find the pilot, board the plane, and take off, you could have driven to Dorado.

HOTELS at Dorado are two, both started under Rockefeller impetus and now important Hyatt links. Dorado Beach was the first built, with an elegance that is being restored under Hyatt's watchful eye. It had yielded to the convention fervor at the time sister Cerromar was built.

★★★★ **Hyatt Dorado Beach** • *on the shore* • opened almost 30 years ago when Laurance Rockefeller spotted this plot, then known as Finca La Sardiniera, the grapefruit plantation of Dr. Alfred Livingston. Rockefeller was encouraged to lend his class and cash to Puerto Rico's tourism plans by building a luxury resort in an "unknown," depressed area, with tax assistance and a $1.3 million loan from the Industrial Development group. Rockresorts set the pace and kept the stride for several years, before selling to Eastern Airlines who sold to Regent International, experts in doing things with class, who then sold to Hyatt, who brought this place back to top-of-the-line. *Su Casa,* a restaurant that was the former home of Clara Livingston, whose family built the place in 1928, now features Puerto Rican specialties prepared with care well-known in French cuisine. Sunday's champagne brunch on the poolside terrace is lavish. Lunchers can settle at the golf shop's snack area, or the *Terrace* at Dorado, near its beach, with a rattan and airy look. Food has been attractive, well served, and offered at prices you'll soon get used to. Two 18-hole golf courses, tennis courts, and opportunities for dining at a choice of restaurants are on these premises, and you have all of Cerromar's action (golf, tennis, casino, supper club, disco) a shuttle-bus ride away. You don't need a rental car, but may want to take one for a day of touring. Shuttle buses roam the property. Ask about the vacation plans offered from April through mid-December. *Resort.*

★★★★ **Hyatt Regency Cerromar Beach** • *on the shore, about a 10-minute ride from Dorado Beach* • claims the "longest freshwater swimming pool in the world." The 1776-foot-long pool, which opened officially September 9, 1986, includes 14 waterfalls, plus 4 waterslides, a swim-up bar, and assorted other entertainments. In 1972, when this 8-story, 506-room hotel opened, it was planned for conventions. Its size and scope dwarfed its discrete and elegant sister resort, Dorado Beach, as it brought a new focus to the north coast area. With the investment of many millions in this and the sister resort, Hyatt keeps these properties in good shape. The two 18-hole golf courses join the two 18-hole courses at Dorado Beach (for a total of 4), and 14 tennis courts here are supplemented by 7 more at Dorado, linked by shuttle bus. The fitness center has a full range of equipment and there are bicycles for riding around the grounds. An open-air bar and cocktail lounge overlooks swans and flamingos in a manmade lake and the *Orchid Pavilion* is joined by the 3-tiered *Garden Terrace* for restaurant choices. *Costa de Oro,* the supper club, has nightly entertainment and *Club Coqui* is the on-premises disco that thrives when the place is full. Inquire about sport vacations, especially the packages offered from April through mid-December. Insofar as bedrooms are concerned, rooms at the ends of the Y-shaped arms are a long walk from the center hub, but every room has a seaview balcony. Complete redecorating resulted in the addition of radios as well as other conveniences. It's safe to say that this place is better under Hyatt's leadership than it was when it opened! For an action-packed resort that can rival U.S. theme parks, this resort claims a place of its own at the top of the list for making the most of the Caribbean's—and Puerto Rico's—natural assets. *Resort hotel.*

LOW-COST LODGING: Although there are several small spots that are popular with Puerto Ricans, who come to the north coast sea and mountain resorts for their own family outings from San Juan, most of the places are not ideal for North American families unfamiliar with the Puerto Rican lifestyle.

THE INN WAY: Although the government-assisted paradores should (and could) be top-quality inns, all could benefit from staff training and culinary classes, in my opinion. The area's Paradores Puertorriquenos are mostly in the mountains, easily reached from the main north-coast roads. Here are several that can be pleasant luncheon or overnight goals (others are mentioned on page 565–7):

Parador Banos de Coamo • *in the mountains at Coamo* • was built on the site of hot springs enjoyed by President Franklin Roosevelt and others. The historic buildings were incorporated into newer ones a few years ago. Lush planting tends to make the rooms dark. There's an air-conditioned restaurant in addition to the pool patio snacking and sipping place. Electronic games by the check-in area appeal to children (but not to me). This place needed attention when I checked for this edition. *Inn.*

Parador Casa Grande • *in Utuado, near the ancient Taino Indian ballpark* • opened in late '87 with comfortable rooms in a rural mountain setting. There's a pool and plenty of area for walks and hikes. *Cottage inn.*

Parador La Familia • *at the east end, at bend of the road on the way to Las Croabas* • is a homelike building that is as popular for its restaurant as for its tidy rooms. The 2-story building sits at the edge of the road, across from a gas station, in an area not far from Las Cabezas Nature Preserve. Ideal when you are roaming with a rental car, this spot will be difficult to reach by public transport. *Inn.*

Parador Guajataca • *at the shore, near Quebredillas* • expanded from a once small family home where the traditional cooking and the family's hospitality made the place popular with nearby residents. Bedrooms are in a motel-style wing, with windows that cloud with sea spray. The pool is popular with Puerto Rican families, who enjoy vacations here. *Small hotel.*

Parador Hacienda Gripinas • *on a former coffee plantation, in the mountains* • has a few small rooms with basic comforts and a lush location where the ubiquitous tree frog, the coqui, adds its voice to the symphony of natural sounds. Popular as a lunchtime goal, this place offers peace and quiet most evenings. *Inn.*

Parador Matorell • *near the beach at Luquillo, east of San Juan on the north coast* • is a 2-story house with bedrooms of varying shapes. All are small and, since the building is new, the atmosphere comes from the hospitality—and easy access to the beach. *Guesthouse.*

Parador Vistamar • *on a hillside, near the coast and Parador Guajataca* • has expanded in recent years to include modern rooms in 2- and 3-story blocks in addition to some rooms in villas. The viewful restaurant is on the top floor of the highest building; the menu offers Puerto Rican specialties. There's a big pool and a view of the sea from many rooms. *Small hotel.*

RESTAURANTS in the Dorado area include a few typically Puerto Rican places near the beach known as Playa Cerro Gordo.

La Familia • *on route 690, en route to Playa Cerro Gordo* • is a small white building on the left side of the road as you head toward the beach. Known for its seafood and steaks, the restaurant is a favorite with Puerto Rican families for the midafternoon Sunday meal.

Los Naborias • *on route 690, a little closer to the beach than La Familia, but on the same side of the road* • offers a feast of Puerto Rican specialties. The elaborate menu lists offerings in Spanish with English translation. Expect plentiful portions for your entree, which will run from $12 to $18 or more. The plantain and breadfruit tostadas are excellent, as are other typically Puerto Rican snacks.

La Terraza • *on Marginal St., parallel to route 693, not far from the beach* • is open to breezes, and serves seafood as the specialty. The grilled fish with spicy sauce was excellent on one visit.

NATURAL SURROUNDINGS are fascinating, when you get away from the built-up area around the busy city of San Juan. Although route 2, heading west from the city, is bordered by shops and other commercial ventures for much of its length between San Juan and Aguadilla, at the west, the spur roads leading into the mountains offer a glimpse of a world where lush tropical growth borders the road.

PLACES WORTH FINDING from a Dorado base include all the sights of Old San Juan (see page 549), about 45 minutes' drive to the west, plus noteworthy places in the neighboring mountains and the observatory at **Arecibo**, which can be visited by appointment or on tour, at 2 p.m. Tues.–Fri. or Sun. 1–4:30 p.m. It's farther west, heading first along the coast and then inland. (The hotel activities desk can provide information and arrange for your visit.)

Parque de las Cavernas del Rio Camuy will be of great interest to spelunkers and nature-lovers. A 268-acre area in the northwestern limestone hills has been designated a Commonwealth Park by the Land Administration. Its most famous attraction is an area where the Camuy River carved huge caves, some of which can be visited, with a guide to lead and point out the most remarkable stalagmites and stalactites. Although comfortable walking shoes are essential, there are not a lot of steps inside the cave and touring is reasonably easy.

EAST AND SOUTHEAST COAST

The drive from north coast San Juan, east on route 3, follows the coast for part of its route. It can be an interesting ride through the "real" Puerto Rico. It takes almost an hour to get away from the suburban sprawl that has cluttered the sides of the road along the north coast with modern commerce and clogged it with traffic, which can be thick and slow on weekends, but life in the east is slower paced and can be pleasant. In addition to Luquillo Beach, and El Yunque (the mountains), allow some time to visit Las Cabezas Nature Reserve, which deserves at least an hour. The highway south makes it possible to speed to Humacao (for Palmas) or Ponce in about an hour's drive from the San Juan area, but you'll miss the glimpse of the real Puerto Rico that the coastal drive offers.

ARRIVAL at the eastern part of the island is best by **car**. **Taxis** make the trip, and the resorts usually have a limousine that can hold several passengers and carries them at reasonable cost. The **ferry boat** that links the islands of Vieques and Culebra out of Fajardo can be an interesting excursion for adventuresome travelers who have a few days to wander, and there's a small airport at Palmas.

HOTELS in the southeastern part of the country include some of the government-assisted paradores, each of which takes its special personality from its location and management, and one complete resort, Palmas del Mar, at Humacao on the southeast coast, plus the big plans for the El Conquistador development near Fajardo. There are a few business-style hotels at Ponce.

★★ **Candelero** • *near the beach at Palmas* • aims to be a country-club style hotel. The lobby is lovely, opening onto a golf green and offering comfortable chairs to sit in to enjoy the breeze. During winter season, Candelero shares in activities planned for the Palmas complex, including performances by dance groups and poolside cookouts. Although it's a short walk to the beach, many rooms have sea view. Guests have the use of the golf, tennis, and other facilities, including the several restaurants, of the Palmas resort. Popular with small groups for meetings and conventions since it opened in '81, the hotel is also a goal for many Puerto Rican families on weekends. Both the coffee shop/restaurant and the bar area are by the pool. Candelero offers lodging for vacationers in search of golf, tennis, horseback riding, and rest, without the social scene that thrives at the northwest coast Dorado. *Hotel.*

El Conquistador Resort and Country Club • *on and over a clifftop at Las Croabas* • expects to open, with fanfare, on October 12, 1992, as a 950-room resort with a "south of Spain" appearance, in five different styles. The basic core for the 500-acre resort has been in place for a couple of decades; it knew a former life as a big resort linked to the El San Juan, in *its* former life. What will open on the 500th anniversary of Columbus's landing in the New World will be a totally new resort, patterned on the resort-city concept made popular in Hawaii. The *Caribbean Newsletter* (page 9) will have an update, closer to the planned opening.

Puerto del Rey Marina and Beach Resort • *near Fajardo, on the east coast at Demajugua Bay* • will be a new town when it's finished. The multimillion dollar project, partially financed by Germany's Bayerishe Vereinsbank and Britain's Trafalgar House, includes a huge, fully equipped marina with 700 slips, plus restaurants, shops, condominium units, and a 325-room hotel. Only the marina will be operating for this season; it's one source for charter yachts and setting out for Vieques, Culebra, or the U.S. Virgins St. Thomas and St. John, all within easy sailing distance. The *Caribbean Newsletter* (page 9) will have news as plans develop.

★ **Villas at Palmas** • *in clusters around the grounds* • are available with a tennis, golf, beach, or marina/sailing focus. Part of the original concept when Sea Pines developer Charles Fraser started this place (he later pulled out), many condominium units are for rent in owners' absence. All are tastefully furnished. Since units are cheek-by-jowl, depending on the sports focus, you may find that noises tend to intrude on an otherwise peaceful holiday. Your neighbor's choice of music may not be yours. There are commissaries on premises for basic stocks, but you'll find that nearby supermarkets (for which you'll need a rental car) have everything. The several restaurants provide plenty of dining choices when you no longer want to cook at home. Villa vacation plans give good value for 1-, 2-, or 3-bedroom villas. Best rates are offered at other than February–March months. Among the contacts for villa rentals are Palmas' office at 600 Third Ave., New York, NY 10016, 800+221-4874 or 212+983-0393.

THE INN WAY: Palmas Inn • *on the hilltop* • has the potential to be a charming inn, with its small pool, restaurants, and the reception area. Junior suites have a sun terrace, regular rooms have a lovely view. The design is impressive; the housekeeping is improving. The 23 rooms overlook one of the several activities areas of the Palmas resort (with another pool plus restaurants, the casino, and nearby beach); there's a small, almost-private pool at the hilltop, near *Azzuro,* an Italian luxury-style restaurant. The golf courses, marina, tennis courts, and all facilities are on the grounds, but a healthy hike from here.

RESTAURANTS at Palmas are varied, and include the Golf Clubhouse and the Beach Bohio for hot days, hamburgers, and sandwich or snack fare.

Avo's Piano Bar • *at the hilltop restaurant* • is a lingering spot that is at its best when Avo Uvezian is playing. The restaurant and bar received a social jolt with the opening of the casino and the disco. Both are active when the guests are.

Azzuro • *near the main reception area, on the top of the hill* • aspires to be the best restaurant in the Palmas complex. It is the priciest; some of the Italian-style specialties are quite good.

Le Bistroquet • *near the tennis courts* • occupies a wedge of one apartment building and fills it with French atmosphere. Owner Robert Gaffori (who opened the marina's cafe) features adaptations of nouvelle cuisine.

Cafe de la Plaza • *just over the crest of the hill from the Palmas Inn* • amid a cluster of villas (near one of the commissaries), serves Puerto Rican specialties.

Daniel's at the Marina • *at the Palmas Yacht Club* • is a particular favorite, not only because the setting at the marina with tables on the terrace is pleasant, but because the food is excellent if you follow the expertise of the chef. Hamburgers and more mundane offerings are available if your palate can't handle the delicate tastes of French cuisine, but the poisson a l'estragon (fish with tarragon) and the soupe de poisson (fish soup) made me recall some of my most-treasured-memory meals from the French West Indies. Daniel's small cafe is a worthy goal on a day of touring from San Juan.

Le Grill • *at the marina* • serves barbecue and other basic fare.

Las Garzas • *at Candelero Hotel's poolside* • serves expected coffee shop/hotel restaurant offerings often at low coast.

NATURAL SURROUNDINGS can be glimpsed from the highway that links the busy Munoz Marin International Airport to the southeast-coast resorts, but the landscape includes at least one area that should be on the program for anyone interested in Puerto Rico's flora. The Luquillo Mountain range is better known to most visitors by the name of one of its peaks, **El Yunque.** Although the honors for highest peak in this area go to **El Toro** (at least 2532 feet), the trails on the flanks of El Yunque, and its tourism facilities, make it more popular. The Caribbean National Forest includes El Yunque, El Toro, and several other peaks in its 28,000-acre tract. Portions of the park make it the only tropical rain forest within the U.S. Forestry system. It is laced with trails, some of which require binoculars, patience, and plenty of time to spot, the trees and vines flourishing in the forest are studded with orchids and dozens of other flowers. The area is popular with Puerto Ricans on weekends and holidays, but is otherwise quiet and reasonably untrammeled. The place to start touring is the Sierra Palm Visitor Center, clearly posted off the main mountain-climbing road.

Also worth visiting from the Palmas area is Las Cabezas Nature Reserve, an easy drive north up the west coast, for a look at the several ecological systems that thrive in the 316-acre park. Tours operate several times daily; allow 3 hours.

SPORTS in the Palmas area are partially covered when we looked at sports in a general way for all of Puerto Rico, but you should know when you head here that the 6660-yard, 18-hole **golf** course is good, the **tennis courts** superb, and the marina is filled with yachts that are often available for charter. The bulletin board at the Yacht Club posts names of boats available for **fishing** and **charter sailing.** *Coral Head Divers,* at the Palmas' marina, takes care of **scuba** excursions. The *Equestrian Center* has horses for **riding.** Although full resort courses are offered, the facilities are best for folks who already know something about the sport.

THE SOUTH COAST

Easily reached by high-speed road in little more than an hour, or by plane service from San Juan's International Airport, the south coast claims the island's second city, ***PONCE.*** The small plaza that once marked the center of the now-sprawling city had been fringed with some attractive noteworthy buildings, but many buildings around the town have now been modernized so that their most interesting architectural features have been destroyed. Over the past few years, a vital interest in historic preservation and the potential for tourism have given this city a welcome face lift. More than $450 million has been invested in *Ponce en Marcha,* not only to restore historic buildings but also to install an infrastructure that can accommodate the future growth. The plans have focused on the beach area, the historic center of the city, and the Vigia area, where the view is the attraction. Several new hotels have been rumored; a few are under way, to open late this year.

Caja de Muerto Island, popular for its beach, now has dozens of shacks where food and drinks are sold, as well as a boardwalk to link the ferry landing to the shore. Hiking trails are planned on the island, as are facilities for scuba diving in an area planned to be an underwater park.

On the third Sunday of each month, a street festival is held on Ponce's Calle Isabel, where many of the original buildings have been restored.

Castello Serralles is one sight of visitor interest, but there are many others in the area.

ARRIVAL for most visitors is by car, either after an hour-long journey on the highway that links San Juan to Ponce, or on the more leisurely route around the coast, taking a full day or longer, with plenty of pausing en route. By air, planes land at Mercedita Airport, not far from town.

HOTELS IN PONCE are limited to one in the center of town and two on the outskirts, although other properties are projected to be open during the life of this edition. There are plans for a long-dormant Intercontinental hotel to come to life again, with a new access road and a new name. Hilton's plans are mentioned below. Already in operation are:

★ **Days Inn Hotel** • *near the shore, just outside town* • has been built on the popular U.S. mainland formula, for a moderately priced hotel. Air-conditioned bedrooms are modern, with basic comforts expected by the businessfolks and others who use this property. Not much on atmosphere, this place offers a dependable nest. *Hotel.*

Melia • *in Ponce on Ave. Cristina* • just off the old city square with its much-photographed, freshly painted red-and-black-striped firehouse and the city's cathedral. The Old-World commercial hotel rises from a street-level band of shops and has an interior courtyard. Balconies overlooking the street have flower boxes, and noisy traffic. Air conditioning is essential, and if you're driving, this is no place to consider unless your car will fit in another room. There's NO place for it on the street.

Hilton International • *at the La Guancha area of the shore* • expects to open for fall 1992, with 256 rooms. Plans include a golf course, and full resort facilities. The *Caribbean Newsletter* (page 9) will have an update, closer to opening date.

Holiday Inn • *on Highway 2 in Ponce* • is the businessman's base. It is a "just-like-home" Holiday Inn: pool, plastic-packaged glasses and jellies, soap wrappers, air-conditioned boxy rooms, and all. Nowhere near the center city (where the Ponce Museum and interesting square are), but there's a parking area. You'll be on a hill, overlooking El Tuque "beach," which focuses on its public pool because the shoreline is mostly rocks.

THE INN WAY: In the mountains north of Ponce, **Gripinas** (page 558) could be a lunchtime goal. Other paradores within reasonable driving distance are **Parador Villa Parguera** and **Parador Posada Porlamar** (see page 566) both on the southwest shore.

NATURAL SURROUNDINGS are best enjoyed during the 165-mile drive along the **Cordillera Central,** an east-west route that links several roads into a scenic journey through rural landscape. Highlights are the mountain views and a few of the towns that are not on the usual tourist route. Covering the entire route makes a long day, however, and there are not a lot of areas that are clearly marked for walking paths (although local folk can share their knowledge of the area, if you speak Spanish). Consider linking segments of this journey with one or more of the paradores, for lunch if not for overnight. Near Salinas, on the southeast coast, the **Aquirre Forest** might be of interest for birding at the neighboring **Jobos Bay Sanctuary,** but the most rewarding birding area in the island is west of Ponce, at the **Guanica Forest and International Biosphere Reserve.** Several endangered species of birds are reportedly seen here.

(Places mentioned on page 562 and page 566 are easy to reach from lodgings on the southeast coast.)

PLACES WORTH FINDING in the Ponce area include the two paradores that offer good places for lunch or dinner during a drive in the mountains, and, in the city, the very impressive **Ponce Museum** in a building designed by Edward Durrell Stone. The central patio and curved stairway are particularly impressive, as is the collection. Included in the collection are many Puerto Rican works of art as well as noteworthy works by the impressionists and other widely recognized international artists.

THE WEST COAST

The west coast city of *MAYAGUEZ* will be a surprise to first-timers traveling around the countryside. Best known to businesspeople who head here for appointments, Mayaguez intrigues many visitors with its spectacular gardens at the agricultural station, the small villages along the coast, and the opportunity to sample some good Puerto Rican food. This area is well worth a visit if you are an adventuresome traveler not hooked on casinos and gala nightlife (which can only be found in surfeit in San Juan).

Tours to nearby areas can easily be arranged, but your best bet here is to rent a car and take off on your own. Routes into the mountains are easy and interesting to follow, even when wiggly and not well marked. The Spanish road signs can be mastered by nonlinguists who like word puzzles and have some confidence. The nearest beach is a 20-minute drive, and golf at Aguadilla is closer to 45 minutes, with the 9-hole course at Cabo Rojo only half an hour.

ARRIVAL   can be by small plane or by a long day's drive along the north coast to curve south for Mayaguez. There are rental cars available at the airport in Mayaguez (as well as in San Juan or Ponce).

HOTELS/RESORTS   in Mayaguez are limited to several small spots, one chain name, and a gem of an inn.

★★★ **Horned Dorset Primavera** • *on the west coast, about 20 minutes' drive north of the Mayaguez airport* • is a pace-setter as an elegant inn in Puerto Rico. Making the most of the Spanish Colonial architecture, owners Kingsley Wratten and Harold Davies have created a hacienda atmosphere. Well-tended gardens are punctuated with the pool; the veranda on the seaside (over the small beach) is peaceful for apertifs—and watching the sunset. The name is adapted from the owners' northern New York state hotel. The breeze-swept main house has a welcoming staircase leading to the second-floor dining room, which is used for gala evening dinners. Breakfast and lunch are served on the ground floor, often accompanied by soft classical music. Bedrooms are in several nearby buildings; the best have seaview. All are tastefully furnished.

★ **Mayaguez Hilton** • *on a hillside, a short drive inland* • makes a very different impression from the standard high-rise, action-packed places in the San Juan area. As you curve up the hill of route 104, turning inland off Route 2, the main road from the Mayaguez airport (10-minute drive), you approach what looks like a quality country club. Opened on June 14, 1964, and completely refurbished in 1988, the hotel has a huge swimming pool, 2 tennis courts (night-lighted), a casino, and comfortable air-conditioned rooms that give you a view from one end of the modern double-bedded box. Request one of the pool-view rooms with balcony for the favored outlook; lanais are convenient to the gardens but in a hot pocket. At the modern 5-story hotel, the *Rotisserie* serves island food and the expected grilled beef and lobster, but the special treat has been the Chef's Table arranged by advance reservation. *Hotel.*

THE INN WAY   can be found at the paradores, although management involvement is not as warmly hospitable as it could be, in my opinion. Noted for typical Puerto Rican country atmosphere, the paradores are assisted, through a special department within the Tourism Company with training to offer reliable standards of service and accommodations. Some of the paradores noted in "The North Coast" (page 557) section can be reached easily on a pleasant coastal drive. Choose a time when commuter traffic will not clog the road; mid-morning weekdays are much better than weekends.

Hacienda Juanita • *in the mountains at Maricao* • is about an hour's scenic drive up and out from Mayaguez. The parador has 21 rooms in wood-frame buildings in a U-shape around a courtyard. The main house holds the dining area, plus a porch where hands of bananas sometimes hang from the beams, to be picked for snacks when ripe. The pool, and the fact that there are riding horses nearby, makes this place a favorite for some Puerto Rican families. *Inn.*

Parador Oasis • *in San German* • is about an hour's drive from Mayaguez (or from Ponce). Modern "improvements" almost mask a 200-year-old one time family home. Latticework and arcades are features of the dining area, along with startling primary colors at and around the pool. Bedrooms vary; some are quite tacky. *Small hotel.*

Parador Perichi • *in Joyuda, between Cabo Rojo and Mayaguez* • is a relative newcomer to the list of paradores. The inn is known locally for the Puerto Rican specialties in its restaurant, and is a favorite place for residents who enjoy watching the west coast sunsets from here. *Small hotel.*

Parador Boquemar • *at Boqueron, near Cabo Rojo south on the west coast* • is well located both for excursions to the coast and to the historic town of San German. The 2-story stucco building is helped along with awning and balconies. On-premise daytime entertainment focuses on the swimming pool, with a special area for children. *Small hotel.*

Parador Villa Antonio • *at Rincon, a popular surfing area* • has both studio apartments and regular rooms at what has become a popular seaside resort for retired folk and Puerto Rican families. Although the inn is not right on the shore, it provides a rural setting within easy sea access. *Small hotel.*

Parador Villa Parguera • *at La Parguera, near Lajas* • has attractive rooms in a loft style, plus garden rooms in an older building. The lawn is punctuated with a pool. There's a play area for children. The oft-touted Phosphorescent Bay is a short boat ride from the dock. *Small hotel.*

Parador Posada Porlamar • *next to La Parguera* • is simple, with friendly owners. Most rooms are in a refurbished (rebuilt) building as the shell for the 19 rooms and interior public area. The restaurant features Puerto Rican recipes, with variety. *Small hotel.*

Parador El Sol • *in Mayaguez* • is a small building on a busy street near the city square. The small pool is near the reception desk. Bedrooms are basic, with private bathroom. The in-city location makes the dining room popular with business folk. *Small hotel.*

NATURAL SURROUNDINGS in the west are some of the island's most fascinating. Top of the list, and not often accessible for visitors, is **Mona Island,** a nature preserve that is almost 50 miles offshore. Prized inhabitants are sea birds, and several endangered species including a large iguana no longer seen elsewhere in Puerto Rico. Check with the tourist office about permission to visit Mona; it is usually granted only to scholars and others with serious interest in the flora and fauna.

There are walking and hiking trails in the **El Bosque Guajataca,** northeast of Mayaguez, and there are dirt roads that some people enjoy following in the **El Bosque Cambalache,** farther east, beyond Arecibo (making this place as accessible from the north coast and the San Juan area as from here). Heading into the mountains from Mayaguez, the road is held to the slopes with hairpin turns. Although **El Bosque Maricao** is not as lush as some of the other forested areas, it is home for dozens of birds and is, therefore, popular with those who want to add to their list.

PLACES WORTH FINDING in Mayaguez are midway on the west coast, in Puerto Rico's third city (after San Juan and Ponce). As the port for an agricultural region, the city has become industrial. Its traditional Spanish-style square, Plaza Colon, hides in a baffling maze of one-way streets and horn-honking traffic, but is worth finding if you have the stamina. The 16 bronze statues, including Greek maidens with hand held high, supporting a now-electrified street lamp, were cast in Barcelona, Spain, to stand tall here in the 1890s. Columbus (Colon) stands in the middle of the square and the whole sight is best to see—if you can plan it—in May or June when the jacaranda trees, known to Puerto Ricans as la reina de las flores (queen of the flowers), are in bloom.

A Taino Indian town stood at this shore (and one information source claims that the town takes its name from a Taino cacique, or chieftain, Mayagoex), but was conquered by the Spaniards, who claimed the port area as their own. At one end of the square is the refurbished city hall, at the other, the **Cathedral of la Virgen de la Candelairia.**

Halting spots from Mayaguez, south on the west coast, curving east on the south coast, include those villages and beaches along the shore road, which is not well marked but is sometimes marvelously scenic and always interesting. The alternative is Route 2, which is straight, fast, and boring.

SAN GERMAN, in Puerto Rico's southwest quarter, is about three hours' drive from San Juan, via Ponce, and an easy hour southeast from Mayaguez (perhaps a midmorning halt on the way to lunch in the mountains at *Hacienda Juanita*). The town was settled on orders of King Ferdinand, and named (some claim) for his second wife, a French woman named Germaine de Foix, whom he married in 1505 after the death of Isabella. The first San German was settled on shore, but the town moved inland in 1570 to safer surroundings after ravages by French privateers and attacks by the resident Indians. The ancient **Porta Coeli church** claims to be the second oldest church in the New World (Santo Domingo's cathedral in the Dominican Republic is the first). Today San German is blissfully removed from the commerce of the cities. The Inter-American University is the main focus of modern activity, but this is a town about which Evalyn Marvel could write, in her 1960 *Guide to Puerto Rico and the Virgin Islands,* "along the tree-lined esplanade of the central plaza of San German, especially on a Sunday evening, the young people gather to promenade—the girls, arm-in-arm, circling clockwise and the boys counterclockwise, primly flirting as they pass. On the stone benches sit the chaperones, watching with vigilant but tolerant eyes—for it was the same when they were young, and their mothers and grandmothers before them." The Sunday paseo is still a ritual although not in a formal way. Small-town life exists, and many are eager to preserve it.

Museo de Arte Religioso, in the old Porta Coeli church (Tues.–Sun. 9 a.m.–noon, 2–4 p.m.; free) is well worth the wander up the two dozen old brick steps at the end of the esplanade. Built as an all-inclusive fortress, church, and monastery, following the 16th-century custom, the building was restored through the efforts of the Instituto de Cultura Puertorriquena. Little is left of the monastery, built in 1609, to the left of the church, but you can see the arched wall and the gate. The ancient church, which some date to 1583, has been plucked and painted so that it is almost too perfect, but the restoration has been authentic, under the watchful eye of the Institute. The altar is particularly worth noting, and the collection of ancient *santos,* the carved saints and holy figures that decorated the churches (and homes) in the old times, is one of Puerto Rico's most extensive. There's an exhibit area showing paintings and prints of churches from the 16th through 19th centuries.

PUERTO RICO'S ISLANDS

CULEBRA, a 7- by 4-mile cove-crimped island off Puerto Rico's east end, was settled in 1880. The first governor, appointed from Vieques, was killed in 1887, and from that point on the independent Culebrans appointed their own top official. In 1903, when the U.S. Navy came in, Culebrans were moved to new settlements, one at the east end and another in the midsection on the south coast. This second was known as Dewey, locally called Puebla and originally a swamp. Although there are 900 residents on the island, there are more Culebrans living on St. Croix, one of the United States Virgin Islands about 70 miles southeast, than on home territory. Dewey (Puebla) is not much to look at: a few small stores, a couple of boxy buildings, and a couple of casual places to stay. When you swoop through the pass in the twin hilltops to land at the small airstrip, you won't notice the town anyway. If you focus on anything except the peril of landing, you will notice the spectacular strand of Flamingo Bay and the protected hurricane harbor that is a pocket of sea, poked into the south shore at Ensenada Honda ("deep bay").

ARRIVAL ON CULEBRA is fastest by **small plane,** usually from Isla Grande airport (which is *not* the International Airport) aboard *Flamenco Airways* or another local airline. It is also possible to take a **ferry boat** out of Fajardo, a town on the east end, for an inexpensive hour-long ride. If you decide to take the ferry, the bigger problem is negotiating with a taxi driver to drive you from your San Juan arrival point to Fajardo at a fare that is less than the national debt.

ISLAND APPEARANCE: Culebra is one of several small islands that fleck the seas between the east end of Puerto Rico and the western tip of St. Thomas, in the neighboring United States Virgin Islands. It's a lumpy island, where scrub growth makes hillsides green when the relentless sun and lack of rain have not conspired to turn the landscape brown. Several deep coves are bordered with wide bands of soft, white-powder sand and other areas are peppered with tiny islets that are best known to scuba divers and lobster fishermen. This remains an islanders' island, with little in the way of spruced-up development.

HOTELS are very basic—and usually inexpensive.

Posada La Hamaca • *on the waterway that joins Sardinas Bay and Ensenada Handa Bay* • has a few bedrooms and some rooms with kitchenettes. You'll have to cook for yourself or snack in your room. There's no restaurant. *Small hotel.*

HOUSEKEEPING HOLIDAYS   are possible at some rental homes, but there's only one development organized for visitors.

Culebra Island Resort • *near the water, on a hillside* • is a grove of Douglas fir houses that grew from the shoreside hill at Ensenada Honda in fall of '73. Best way to get to what used to be called Punta Aloe is by boat, from the small airstrip near Dewey (if they know you're coming, they'll send the *Boston Whaler* over the lagoon). Each house has angles, plenty of trade winds blowing through, plus adequate furnishings, beds for 6 people, a couple of hammocks, and a full-fledged kitchen for cooking up the lobsters you progged that morning. A small commissary fills basic needs, but bring the meat you want from home. Planned by a coterie of academics from midland U.S.A., this is a perfect place for self-sufficient types who want a quiet spot with tropical breeze, good view, and plenty of time for resting and reading.

Tamarindo Estates • *on the beach* • is a collection of air-conditioned cottages, with lovely views and a quiet, relaxed style. Weekly rates are reasonable.

LOW-COST LODGING   borders on being shabby.

Coral Island Guest House • *near the ferry terminal* • gives you a balconied room with a view overlooking the action of town, such as it is. The place is made up of two 4-bedroom apartments where scuba types and other low-key folk enjoy informal surroundings with a sea focus.

Two other small spots with very simple quarters are **Villa Fullazoza** (Box 162, Culebra, PR 00645) and the **Red Roof Guest House** (Box 248, Culebra, PR 00645).

PLACES WORTH FINDING   on Culebra are related to the sea. They include **Punta Molines** at the northwest and **Punta del Soldado** at the south in the middle. Both are exceptional for snorkeling, but bring your own equipment. The small offshore cay called Culebrita, reached by fishing boat or a motorboat that your hotel may have at the ready for excursions, is good for lobster progging.

The biggest news on Culebra has involved no longer getting bombed, which the island was regularly—until U.S. Navy exercises were stopped by Presidential order in response to irate Culebrans in 1975. You can count on peace and quiet, and no planned activities, when you holiday here.

• • •

VIEQUES is about 20 miles long and 1 to 4 miles wide, depending on where you measure. The beach-trimmed island sits almost 7 miles off the east end of Puerto Rico. In its earliest history, Vieques was a home for Arawak tribes, and relics from the early settlements are discovered from time to time. The island has always been independent, and has often had a flourishing economy. In the 17th century, the protected coves made Vieques a favorite haven for pirates, who set up a signal system, with eye-sighting possible over the seas and islands as far as St. Croix. During much of its history, Vieques has been self-sustaining. Five sugar mills employed most of the local population, and a cosmopolitan community included Europeans from England, Germany, France, and other countries. The island continues to have an agricultural economy, with tomatoes and other produce easy to grow. When its economy was flourishing, Vieques had as many as 25,000 people. Today the count is closer to 7500, with "about 40% unemployed." Since all residents have some land, anyone can grow enough food—and meat is readily available from the 15,000 head of cattle that range on the island and fish are plentiful off-shore. Although water is now piped in from San Juan, Vieques has wells and three small reservoirs. The few visitors who find this place come in search of peace and quiet, a lifestyle that exists even though the island occasionally makes Puerto Rican newspaper headlines (when its spirited and vocal residents disagree with government policies).

The U.S. Navy has a Vieques base that has become a cause celebre for the independence movement and for people who want Vieques to move into the mainstream of development. Some want the island to become a free-port shopping area for Puerto Rico, others are looking to small industries, a few of which have already established here. Visitors will be blissfully unaware of most of the local causes, however, and will have the island beaches almost to themselves. The main town is Isabel Segunda, named for Isabella II, who was Queen of Spain from 1833 to 1868. It's a slow moving collection of shops and stores that comes alive when the ferry boat lands or departs. Otherwise, the island's main attraction is its beaches. The small town of Esperanza, on the south coast, is the area most popular with visitors. It's basically a fishing village, where fishermen can sometimes be talked into taking passengers for scuba or snorkeling excursions. The few cafe-style restaurants and shops make this the shoreside center for guests at the few inns in the area.

POLITICAL PICTURE deserves special comment because, although the Viequenos are Puerto Ricans and vote in the island elections, they have very strong politics of their own which cross the main island's party lines. The hottest issue on Vieques is the U.S. Navy and its presence on the island. There are some that like it; others do not. Those who are pro-Navy seem to side with the Independistas and the anti-Navy folks appear to be pro-Statehood. During the "poorhouse" years, referred to in the "Political Picture" comment earlier in this chapter, many industrious Viequenos left their island. The fishermen and farmers who stayed have built their island in its present style, and have given it its personality.

LIFESTYLE is very casual and friendly. Residents are helpful and cordial, as long as you do things their way. Speaking Spanish helps—a lot.

ARRIVAL AND DEPARTURE is on a small plane usually linking with San Juan area's Isla Grande Airport, which is very near the Caribe Hilton Hotel, just outside the Old City. There is talk about service, also, from Isla Verde International Airport, where international flights arrive. The *Caribbean Newsletter* (page 9) will have further information, when it materializes. There is also ferry boat service linking the islands and Fajardo, at the east end of Puerto Rico, for an almost 2-hour ride. The boat is the most popular way for residents and their friends to travel.

TOURING TIPS: *Publicos* are a combination bus and taxi, where you can hitch a ride in a car with other folks going your direction. Costs are modest. There are also private **taxis** available, and **rental cars** are available through *Budget* and *Thrifty* (about $45 per day). Check at *Nelson's T-Shirt* shop for Suzuki jeeps.

HOTELS are limited to a handful of places, including some very modest spots.

★★ **La Casa del Frances** • *on a knoll not far from Esperanza* • was built in the late 1800s by a plantation owner from the French West Indies. It became the home and sometime inn called Sportsman's House, with Mr. Wemyss as host, in the 1950s. In September 1976, Irving Greenblatt of Boston became part owner, a position he has now secured with complete ownership. He is on premises some of the time. (A manager has the full-time responsibility.) When you pull up to the front door of the Victorian house, with its courtyard and flourishing planting, it's like arriving as a house guest for a country weekend. Rooms on the main and first floors have high ceilings and overhead fans. Furnishings are simple, but adequate, and the pool at the back of the house vies with the rockers on the porches for your time. Horseback riding can be arranged as can scuba. Good swimming is only as far away as the nearest beach. Meals are served as house count warrants (and wishes). *Inn.*

Villa Esperanza Beach Resort • *at the shore, on the site of a sugar mill* • is in a state of flux at press time. The *Caribbean Newsletter* (page 9) will have an update. The main building, with the reception area, was part of the sugar mill operation when that was an island source of revenue. Sailing, scuba lessons, windsurfing, and other watersports, are available at the beach. What had been a pineapple factory, and was used by the *Lord of the Flies* movie company for one of the sets, will be covered tennis courts. There are about 50 villa apartments, most of which share a common wall with the neighboring unit, giving enough privacy to exude an independent feeling, but not enough distance to do away with your neighbor's noise. Bedrooms are arranged so that units can be rented as one 2-bedroom villa or two 1-bedroom units, on a ground floor, first-floor basis. This place is at the beach, and a short stroll from the cafes and shops of Esperanza.

HOUSEKEEPING HOLIDAYS: Both the **Sea Gate** (741–4661) and **La Lanchita** (741–8449) offer housekeeping accommodations. Other places can be found, but it's best to see them before booking.

LOW-COST LODGING:

The Trade Winds • *on the beach at Esperanza* • is a pleasant guest house with casual atmosphere.

Ocean View • *in Isabel Segunda, near the ferry dock* • is popular with business folk who like the air-conditioned simple hotel-style rooms, and the convenience of being in town. Perched on the shore, most rooms have a sea view. There are informal restaurants nearby to supplement the dreary on-premise dining facilities. *Small hotel.*

Sea Gate • *with sea view* • is a 2-story block of basic apartments, which can make a comfortable home for a back-to-basics holiday. *Guesthouse.*

RESTAURANTS include those at the hotel and a few, very informal places that specialize in Puerto Rican food, including fresh fish and lobster in many guises. Among the places to find at Esperanza are **La Central**, a very casual cafe on one corner, **El Quenepo, Bananas** (which also has a few rooms for rent), and the **Trade Winds**. In Isabella Segunda, **Cayo Blanco** is a bar/restaurant, with plastic cloths on the table and Arroz con Jueyes (which is land crab) for $3.50. **El Yate** is another informal place, near the ferry dock, and **Lydia** reportedly bakes "the best" bread. In Puerto Real, **Cerromar** is a barnlike restaurant favored by residents who enjoy typical Puerto Rican cooking, with lobster, fried plantain, and other specialties.

NATURAL SURROUNDINGS: The island has three protected coves, known as hurricane holes to yachtsmen, and many interesting areas for scuba diving. Phosphorescent Bay is "about 50 times better" than the like-named place on the south coast of Puerto Rico, and there are other places that Vieqenos know best.

PLACES WORTH FINDING include the beaches, especially **Sun Bay** where there's a campsite, plus pavilions for changing clothes and other facilities. Garbage and vandalism had changed the once pristine atmosphere, when I visited for this edition. **El Fortin,** the partially restored fort on a high spot in the town of Isabella Segunda, could be charming, if the work is ever completed and the fort has a purpose (such as a cafe/restaurant). At presstime, it's interesting to walk around, and as a photographic sight. Otherwise it won't require much time.

SPORTS include horseback riding and watersports, with most of the diving in the hands of *Vieques Divers* at Esperanza. Costs for a resort course are about $60, with an open water course at $200 and a basic certification course at $175. Night dives cost up to $40 per person, for experienced divers, and nighttime boating excursions, such as to Phosphorescent Bay, are $10 per person. Windsurfers rent for $15.

SABA

Saba Tourist Office, Windwardside, Saba, N.A., T 011+599+4-2231; Saba Tourist Information, % Medhurst, 271 Main St., Northport, NY 11768, T 516+261-7474 or 800+344-4606.

$ · · · US$1 = NAf1.77
Unless otherwise noted, all prices are in U.S. dollars

When the *Blue Peter* made its official, but sporadic, stop at Saba more than 30 years ago, you hung over the side to lunge into a rocking small boat for the plunge to the shore, such as it was. About the only thing you could be sure of was that the Saban seamen were competent—and that you would get wet. These days, when a handful of people wedge into a Winair plane to swirl to the airstrip on the finger of sea-rimmed Saban rock, there's the same "moment of truth." I noticed the stolid face of the Saban octogenarian who sat next to me on a recent flight. The typical Saban straw hat with its stovepipe shape couldn't hide the permanent crinkles in his suntanned face, and his blue eyes darted around the brim in a look that could only be classified as controlled panic. This was his first flight. When he had left Saba a few months earlier, for a bout in the hospital at Philipsburg on Sint Maarten, he had gone by boat. No such luck for him coming home, but at least he was coming home. The final swoop—after the wide spiral down to take stock of the strip—is awesome. But so is this island. It's the top of a volcano and like nowhere else.

POLITICAL PICTURE is pegged to that of Sint Maarten, where most of the commercial ventures are located. As noted under Statia and Sint Maarten, Saba has one delegate, the island's senator, to the Netherlands Antilles Staten that meets in Curacao. Saba's share of the coffers is small—but then so is its population, recently numbered at 1097. The island does have its own Island Council in charge of local problems and development and a new interest in tourism, which must be limited to day visitors for volume since overnight accommodations are limited.

ISLAND APPEARANCE: Only Nevis shares a similar circular shape, with the island rising to a volcanic peak at tis center. Unlike Nevis, however, Saba has no beaches. Its mountainsides sheer into the sea and continue sharply downward. Secondary peaks rise, only to fall into valleys where the few towns nes-

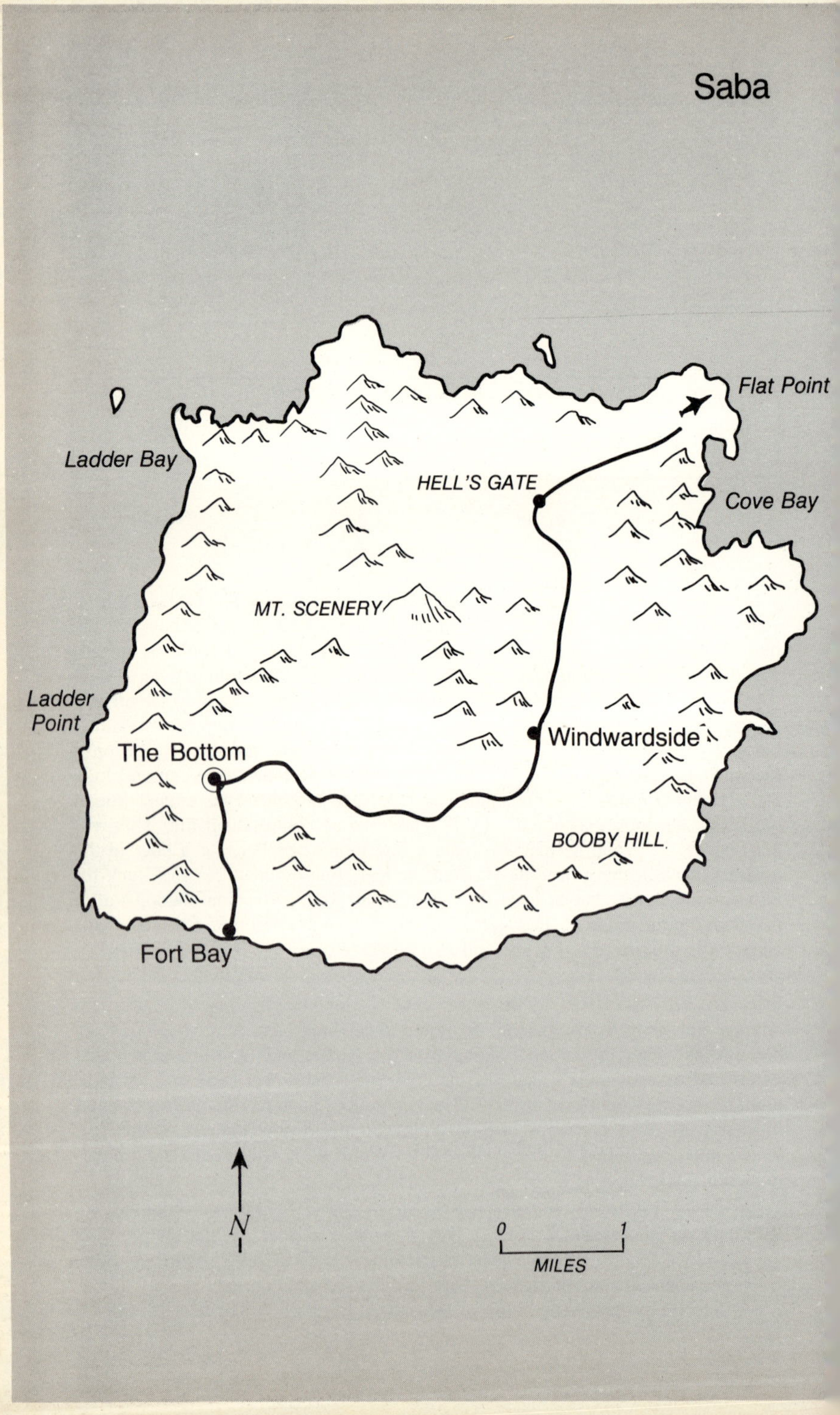
Saba
Flat Point
Ladder Bay
HELL'S GATE
Cove Bay
MT. SCENERY
Ladder Point
Windwardside
The Bottom
BOOBY HILL
Fort Bay
N
0
1
MILES

tle. Since the style of architecture is Victorian, and most houses are small, white boxes, there's a make-believe quality about this island. The flanks of the mountains are draped with an occasional walking/hiking path and the cross-island road wiggles up, around, and over like a string of cranberries on a Christmas tree.

LIFESTYLE is conservative, with outsiders seeing little of what goes on behind the shuttered windows of the small houses that speckle the communities. The older Sabans are a very special people who keep pretty much to themselves. The most adventuresome souls headed out, from the island's earliest history, to become some of the world's most remarkable seamen, and to send money back home so that the family homestead could be built and maintained. Take time to talk with your taxi driver, and anyone you meet, and you will be richly rewarded—especially if you have been wise enough to blend in here for a couple of days so that you are not "one of the day trippers."

MEDICAL FACILITIES: Sabans go to Sint Maarten for most serious medical problems. The cliniclike hospital at The Bottom has limited facilities, although the facility is neat, as you would expect from the Dutch. The nearest extensive facilities are in Puerto Rico, which requires a charter plane for the hour-plus flight. There is a decompression chamber on Saba.

MONEY MATTERS are conducted mostly in U.S. currency, with a sprinkling of Netherlands Antilles guilders or florins. (The words are used interchangeably and noted as NAf or Afl.)

COMMUNICATIONS by telephone are much more dependable than mail. Dial overseas 011 + 599 area code plus 4, and a 4-digit Saban number. The Netherlands-efficient *Landsradio* makes phoning overseas from Saba relatively easy. Calls can be placed, and paid for, at their office. Don't count on international news, or much in the way of TV.

ARRIVAL on Saba is one of the few adventures left in the civilized Caribbean. The small strip, hacked from the only "flat" land on the island, is plastered like a Band-Aid on a knuckle of land that protrudes into the sea. The name of the airport—Juancho Yrausquin Airport—is almost longer than the strip, which is served several times daily by the gnat-sized planes of *Windward Island Air Service,* locally known as Winair. The STOL (Short Take-Off and Landing) flights dip in and out with tourists and a handful of residents at regular intervals, but make your reservations in advance at the ticket counter in Sint Maarten if you have not booked through your travel agent. The time you wait after check-in and before the plane takes off is longer than the 15-minute flight, but be there when they tell you to or you may find that "your" seat has been sold to someone else. There are days when the flights are very full—and on those days, if you're flying one of the bigger Winair flights (about 19 passengers), the flight stops first at Statia, since the Saba airstrip does not encourage full-plane landings. If all this makes you think you'd rather go by boat, you should know that there's boat service from Sint Maarten aboard *Style,* a 50-passenger speedboat popular with daytrippers who pay $45 for a round trip. The seas are often rough across the 25-mile span that separates this place from Philipsburg, Sint Maarten, the nearest port. The crossing to Saba's Fort Bay is not in any way reminiscent of a trip on the old *Queen Mary*. Sailboats and cruising yachts cross from the area around Bobby's Marina, at the western curve of Philipsburg, on day trips that depart from Sint Maarten about 9 a.m. and return about 5 p.m. Your hotel and/or the Tourist Office (near the Post Office and pier in Philipsburg) can give on-the-spot details.

AUTHOR'S OBSERVATION

If you depart for Saba through Sint Maarten's airport, do not pay the $5 departure tax, which Sint Maarten's unscrupulous "toll takers" may request. There is no departure tax (because Saba is a related Dutch territory), but those who staff the "departure tax" booth happily extract one from any travelers not savvy enough to resist. Simply tell them you are going to Saba and they will wave you on to the immigration desk where your boarding pass confirms that you are Saba bound.

DEPARTURE is casual, from the airstrip to busy Sint Maarten. There's a departure tax of $1 when you're returning to Sint Maarten, or $4 for non-Dutch destinations.

TOURING TIPS: Take a **taxi,** not only because the serpentine roads bend and weave with perilous regularity, but also because the local lore you can pick up from a good driver is one of the best reasons for coming to Saba. If you prefer a car (rather than a van), as I do, telephone ahead or ask on arrival for Joyce Gomez (T 599+4–3209), a Saban brought up in Curacao. Her well-kept Toyota has been my chariot for Saba visits. Although a tour costs about $25, a trip from the airport to Fort Bay, which carries you the 5-mile length of the island's only road, costs $10.

It's possible to **rent a car** from *Emile's* at The Bottom, but only long-stay visitors with a particular mission will see the need for a rental car. Most folks slow down to a pace that allows for taxis, walking, or riding with whoever may be heading your intended direction.

THE INN WAY is all there is on Saba. Each has its own small and special personality, and all are ideal for a real getaway vacation, if you do not insist on beaches. (This island has none.) There's a 5% government tax and often a 10% to 15% service charge.

Stars are awarded according to facilities for Saba, as they compare to other islands.

AUTHOR'S AWARD

Captain's Quarters is a charming inn with a Saban soul.

★★★ **Captain's Quarters** • *at Windwardside* • claims a notch on the hillside at the lower edge of town, about 1000 feet above sea level, which is high enough to be caught in the clouds that sometimes get hooked on the peak. The atmosphere is Caribbean inn at its best, with one of Saba's traditional wood homes, built in the early 1900s, as the core. Tied together by blooming bougainvillea and other tropical plants, and a management style that allows friendly independence, the 10-room inn includes two newer buildings across the narrow road, plus a pool near the popular bar-and-gathering area. Most meals are served on the patio appended to the original house, under a sun- and rain-sheltering roof that is masked by flourishing plants and trees. Mealtime can be an occasion. Caribbean lobster appears as salad as well as in the shell, and soups are special. The comfortable common rooms in the main house are furnished in the style of a sea captain's home, with cozy corners ideal for reading. The two newer buildings allow for more conventional rooms, with small terraces that offer views from the mountainside to surrounding seas below. Popular for scuba divers, nature lovers and others who want a quiet island retreat, Captain's Quarters remains true to its Saban personality—with the help of a loyal team. *Inn.*

Cranston's Antique Inn • *at The Bottom* • is an imposing Saban home with a half dozen rooms, each furnished with 4-poster bedsteads and other trappings of an earlier age. Built in a style well known to New England (in the U.S.), the inn has a long tradition of local management. There are overhead fans to swirl breezes, and an informal, inn-like atmosphere that appeals to self-sufficient travelers who like island life. Not quite as polished for the "Saban tourist" as Captain's Quarters, Cranston's also has more modest rates. Good for vacationers who enjoy a guesthouse style. *Inn.*

★ **Scout's Place** • *at Windwardside* • takes its name from Scout Thirkield, one of the first of the "new wave" to discover Saba, many years ago when he came here from Sint Maarten which he thought had gotten too crowded (even then!). Scout spirited Captain's Quarters to fame, and then left to open up this spot. He's now turned things over to Saban Dianna Meadero, and the casual atmosphere continues. The terrace is popular with day-visitors who know and love Saba, especially those who come over on business. A band of new rooms, built in spring of '87, allows for balconies (and private bathroom with hot water). Expect very simple surroundings, with an "old attic" feeling. Hot water has not been one of the luxuries, although it is planned for the new rooms. *Inn.*

HOUSEKEEPING HOLIDAYS offer a special experience. Several of the perfectly proportioned, small wooden Saban cottages are available for rent. Many are in Windwardside. Check with the tourist office for their listings of "Houses and Apartments" for rent and ask about SabaVillas and the new Queen's Garden Villas on Troy Hill. (Telephone numbers below require a 011+599+code before the number.) Here are some of my favorites:

Benny's Hideaway • *in Windwardside* • has two bedrooms and a lovely front porch that encourages mind meanderings. Weekly rental through David Johnson at Hell's Gate (T 4–2254) is $300.

Carpenter's Cottage • *in Windwardside* • is another typical small cottage, with one bedroom and a back porch that has a sea view. Weekly rental through Mrs. Angela Johnson (T 4-2229) is $200.

English Quarter • *on the fringe of Windwardside* • has 3 bedrooms and ocean view as well as a view over the town of Windwardside. Rental from Carl Anslijn (T 4-2206) is about $150 per week.

Juliana's Apartments • *next to Captain's Quarters in Windwardside* • are modern, with private bathroom. For details, contact Juliana Johnson at T 4-2269.

Rainbow Cottage • *in Windwardside* • with one bedroom, hot and cold water, a fully equipped kitchen and a viewful back porch. The weekly rental through Mrs. Angela Johnson (T 4-2229) has been $200.

LOW-COST LODGING is available with the cottages mentioned above, while rooms at rock-bottom cost can best be found on the spot (by talking with local folk) or by inquiring at the tourist office.

NATURAL SURROUNDINGS on Saba start with the island itself. Any time spent here will be special—and you'll be one of less than 10,000 who find this peak this year. **Mount Scenery** is the highest point, at 3000 feet, and one serpentine road connects the pier, the airport, and the four villages. Those who enjoy walking and hiking will want to climb the 1064 steps-and-slant up and out of Windwardside to Mount Scenery. The up-and-down climb takes about 2 hours. Another angular exercise is the climb down from The Bottom to Ladder Bay, the original landing point for boats in the old days (before the Fort Bay facilities), with steps down most of the way to the water's edge and a heart-pumping climb back up.

The Saban landscape allows for experiences with many types of vegetation, from the secondary rain forest with its many bromeliads to a treefern brake and on through the palm brake to the elfin woodland or cloud forest. Birders can spot some 60 species, with the Garnet-throated hummingbird and the Trembler native to the top of the mountain.

AUTHOR'S OBSERVATION

The *Saba Conservation Foundation* has taken the lead with preserving and managing the island's natural resources, including the vegetation on Mt. Scenery and the Saba Marine Park, established in June 1987. Membership is US$10; sponsorship is US$100; life members pay US$1000. For further information, contact the Tourist Office in Winwardside on Saba or the Marine Park Office at Fort Bay, Saba.

PLACES WORTH FINDING: The **Saba Museum,** in a sea captain's house a short walk up from Captain's Quarters in The Bottom, is charming and well worth a visit. Rooms are furnished in traditional manner, reminiscent of America's northeastern sea towns, with everything scaled to Saba's small size. Opened in early 1978, the museum's collection is small but fascinating.

Visitors intrigued by Saba flora, fauna, and history should visit the **Queen Wilhelmina Library,** either in Windwardside (near the school and the old people's home) or not far from the tourist office in The Bottom. Both libraries have a special section for West Indian history and science.

SPORTS on Saba in the conventional sense have been nonexistent until recently. Although there are always hills to hike and paths to wander, scuba enthusiasts can sign on with *Saba Deep* (011+599+4–3347) which maintains its dive shop at Fort Bay, or with Joan and Louis Bourgue who operate *Sea Saba* (011+599+4–2246) with a dive shop at Windwardside. They take divers out in their 24-foot dive boat. A single tank dive costs about $40; 2-tank dives are $70. Lessons are given, but it's a good idea to contact one of the dive shops in advance to set up your time. Special scuba holidays are offered for groups, using the Captain's Quarters inn as base.

TREASURES AND TRIFLES on Saba are limited. There are a few shops in Windwardside, most notably **The Upper Room, Around the Bend,** and the **Island Craft Shop,** all of which carry some of the Saban "lace," a handcraft that is actually drawn work where threads are pulled to create the open spaces. Once a traditional pastime of Saban women, drawn work is now offered on handkerchiefs, table linen, aprons, and bread basket liners. There are a few women who sell on the street and from their homes, in addition to the work that is offered in some of the shops.

Saba Artisans seem to have capitulated to the ubiquitous T-shirts, but their talents have been put to better use with fabric by the yard, designs for shirts, beachwraps, and other items of higher quality. Their studio is near Cranston's Inn at The Bottom.

Mrs. Freda Johnson (Box 517, Windward Side, Sába) does exceptional drawn work, in Saba's traditional manner. She will do items to order, and is very reliable.

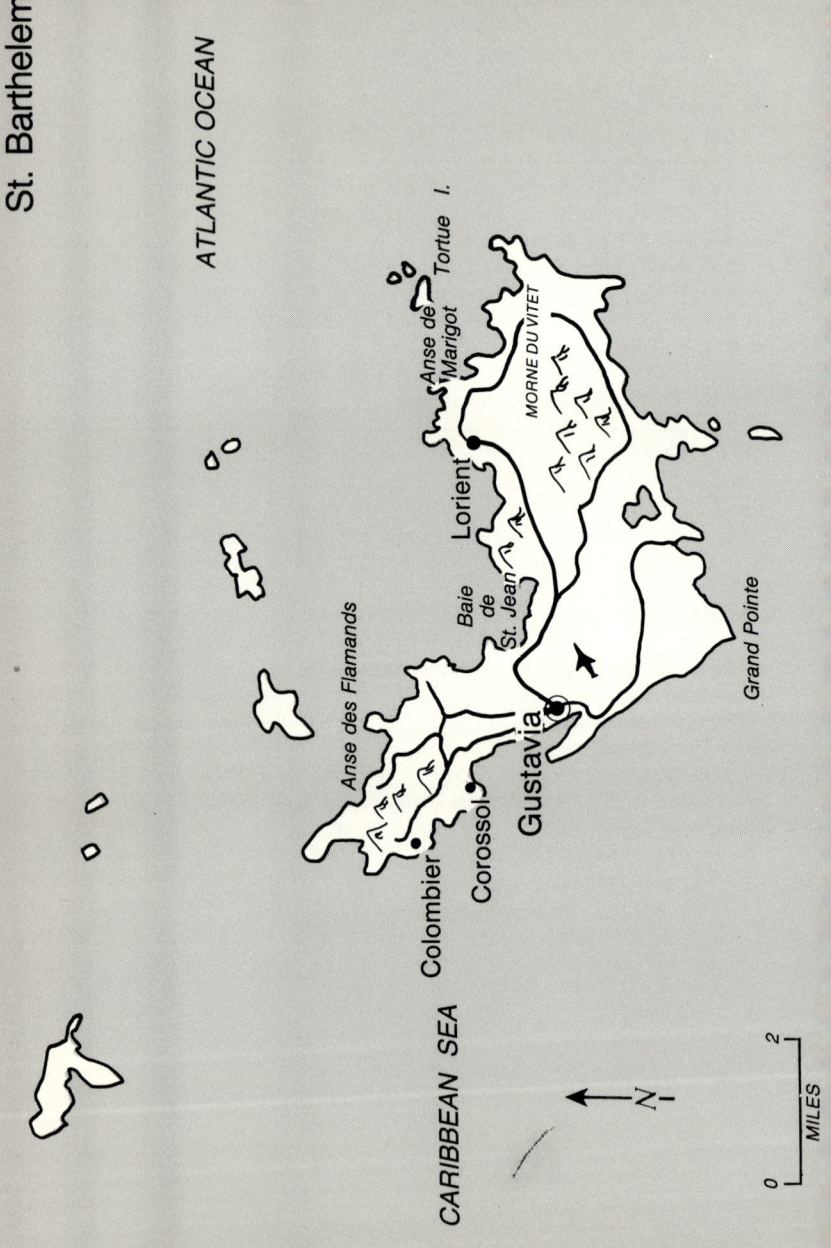

ST. BARTHELEMY

L'Office Municipal du Tourisme, rue August Nyman, Gustavia, 97133 St. Barthelemy, French West Indies, T 011+590–27.60.08; French West Indies Tourist Board, 610 Fifth Ave., New York, NY 10020, T 212+757–1125; French Govt. Tourist Office, #303, 9454 Wilshire Blvd., Beverly Hills, CA 90212, T 213+271–6665; #630, 645 N. Michigan Ave., Chicago, IL 60611, T 312+337–6301; #205, 2305 Cedar Spring Rd., Dallas, TX 75201, T 214+720–4010; 1981 Ave. McGill College, #480, Montreal, Quebec, Canada H3A 2W9, T 514+931–3855; #2405, 1 Dundas St. W. Suite 2405, Toronto, Ontario, Canada M5G 1Z3, T 416+593–4717.

$ · · · US$1 = about 5.5 French francs. (Confirm at travel time.)
Unless otherwise noted, U.S. equivalents are figured at the above rate.

"The little inhabitants find many sweet things in these islands. The air is wonderfully good there, serious diseases are unknown. They live a long life in good health. They derive their own food from their cattle and fowl, they plant and grow all kinds of things, and no crop ever fails. Several of them were producing indigo which sold quite well before the war. Most families have several children, which means that when the islands are well enough inhabited, we will be able to obtain from them quite a lot of cattle, fowl, and staples." So said Francois Roger Robert, administrator of the Isles d'Amerique, as the small French-claimed islands were known in the 1700s. The quotation comes from *Histoire de St. Barthelemy* by Georges Bourdin, published by Porter Henry. The glimpse into the island's early history can be verified today, even though many of the facts have changed. Tourists are today's crop.

A few years ago the man who grew lettuce with a sun-blocking palm frond roof over his several flats of crisp green leaves had a crop that was cultivated according to the weather. When the occasional evening shower fell, he had a crop; when it didn't, he didn't. Most of the lettuce and other fresh vegetables and fruits are imported now and the *AMC*, or *Sodexa*, or *Le Mono Shop*, or *Le Gourmet*, as the *Libre Service*, (or "free service") supermarkets are called, carry an imposing selection of produce and special items (notably cheese) from France, as do markets elsewhere on the island.

The lady on the Lorient road has a following that makes an almost daily pilgrimage to the corrugated tin house set back from the road. Once inside, the "perfume" in the air is overwhelming. The fresh-baked bread may just be emerging from her ovens, which she tends in her cotton frock reminiscent of those known in her ancestral home of Brittany. A wide-brimmed straw hat, the mark of the older women of St. Barths, serves as her baker's cloche. The modern kneading and baking equipment is her only nod to the 20th century; her bread and her bearing are traditional.

The Gustavia bakery near the Post Office is bigger, but there are other bakeries, now, in town and at communities around the island where the recipes and customs of France are adapted to the Caribbean climate. The language and currency remain distinctly French. No matter how you negotiate, the purchase is what is important—and the special sweet breads, perhaps warm and crispy palmiers, are the prize.

Although small hotels and cottage communities that used to drape the laundry over nearby bushes or on lines strung between the palms are now tossing the clothes in the dryer and although the bistrolike restaurants buy much of their produce from U.S. and other wholesalers, the atmosphere in St. Barthelemy is still in shades of the past. Time has not stood still, but it has certainly slowed to a reasonable pace.

AUTHOR'S OBSERVATION

The discrepancy between the spelling of the nickname of St. Barthelemy—St. Barths or St. Barts—puzzles travel professionals as well as firsttime travelers. Since French is the language of this island, and in French pronunciation the "th" has the sound of a single "t" in the word St. Barthelemy, I have used the French nickname—St. Barths, pronounced with a hard "t" sound.

POLITICAL PICTURE: Although the island is officially linked with the French *departement* of Guadeloupe, St. Barths seems to go its own way, with elections for mayor and other officials responding to the will of registered residents. Elise Magras is the efficient and helpful *directrice* of *L'Office Municipal du Tourisme*. Municipal revenues come from a 4% wharf fee on imports, in addition to the funds that come from the central government in France through Guadeloupe. Local needs revolve around roads, hospitals, schools, and the like, and seem to be satisfied with a minimum of publicity. Most visitors will be unaware of local politics.

ISLAND APPEARANCE: St. Barthelemy has a little bit of a lot of things, but not a lot of anything—except French chic. You'll get the best overview of the island from the right side of the small plane as it swoops through the mountain cleavage to land on the short airstrip. Gustavia is a horseshoe-shaped harbor, now fringed with boutiques and bistros and flecked with yachts. Although the island is hilly, and roads are draped at perilous angles on the several slopes, there's no real mountain worth the name. Many of the deep coves are sand-fringed; most of the beaches are less than a mile long, but several are perfect places for peace and quiet. Only a few—Baie de St. Jean, for one—have seaside bistros and watersports activity. The beaches have more sea-grape trees than palms, and the midsection is usually green, sun-burning to brown only when the tropical rains bypass the island.

LIFESTYLE on St. Barths includes some homage, still, to a past that weaves a few traditions of Sweden and French Normandy and Brittany, but those vestiges are fast disappearing—except insofar as holidays are concerned. You will see an occasional older woman dressed in the traditional white bonnet (a *caleche*) and black dress if you go to Corossol and may notice the platter-flat straw hats, with small crown and black band, being worn by a few women in town. It's difficult not to notice the lean (almost gaunt), weather-worn faces of the venerable past that mingled the earliest French (from Normandy and Brittany) with the Swedes who settled here. The recent wave of tourism, building up to cresting point in the past five years, finds many ex-Palm Beach and other elegant resort-area types from the U.S. in addition to wise and wealthy French and other Europeans and others who do *not* want a high-pressure, action-packed place. St. Barths is still special, but total concentration on tourism has made changes.

Unlike most Caribbean islands, the population of St. Barths is mostly white (as you'd suspect with settlers from Brittany, Normandy, and Sweden). The native families stay pretty much to themselves, linking to the tourism community through their stores, car rental firms, hotels, restaurants, and cottages or apartments for rent.

Reservations are essential for the dinner hour, which is late (9 p.m. or so) for residents, but can begin as early as 6:30 p.m. for American visitors. During height of season (February, March), you'll need a reservation at the best places; at other times check to be sure that the place is open.

MEDICAL FACILITIES: The small hospital is on a hillside in Gustavia. Most doctors are from France, and equipment is better than that in hospitals of similar size on other islands. Speaking French helps if you are fluent in the language, but most of the staff also speak English. Since the nearest big island (Sint Maarten) does not have extensive facilities, a charter plane to Puerto Rico is suggested for serious problems when time and money permit the flight.

MONEY MATTERS revolve around the French franc. Be sure to check with your local bank for the exchange rate at the time you plan to travel. It's a good idea to purchase French franc traveler's cheques (which your hometown bank can obtain for you with a little advance notice), and pay your on-location costs in the local currency, especially if you want freedom from the "what's the franc worth today" conversation. Hotels do figure their rates in U.S. dollars for the U.S. market (and travel agents). Restaurants and shops will accept dollars in payment for bills, but their exchange rate may not be as favorable as that of the bank. Bring your pocket calculator if you care.

584 · · · ST. BARTHELEMY

AUTHOR'S OBSERVATION

Daily living is expensive, not only when the franc to dollar exchange favors the franc, but because island enterpreneurs jack up their dollar prices annually—as high as the traffic will bear. As long as St. Barths continues to be the classy "in" place, you can count on restaurant and rental prices to be top of the Caribbean's line. For this season, at least, the island is still French-chic and special!

COMMUNICATIONS are best accomplished in French, although many people do, also, speak English. St. Barths is reached by direct dial 011 + 590 + the 6-digit local telephone number. Facsimile machines are used by many hotels and other businesses. You can find some French newspapers and magazines, but count on paying a high premium for any U.S. city papers, if and when you can find one. Radio stations are in French, but your own portable can pick up St. Maarten and the U.S.V.I.'s.

ARRIVAL by plane will be to the small and slanting airstrip that has a hillside at one end and the sea at the other. If you are in transit through Sint Maarten, *you do not have to pay their departure tax.* But, if you overnight on that Dutch/French island, you will have to pay $5 to get on your St. Barths' flight unless you fly from the French side's small airstrip at Esperance near Grand Case. The present air terminal on St. Barths opened in late '84. Although small by comparison to the hubbub of nearby Sint Maarten, it is tidy, efficient, and easy to negotiate. It's close enough to the Baie de St. Jean to allow for walking access from the beach. Small planes are the only planes that swoop into the airstrip at St. Barths. *Winair* and *Air St. Barthelemy* fly to and from Sint Maarten several times daily; *Air Guadeloupe* comes up from its namesake island, which is a much longer distance than that from Dutch Sint Maarten or from Esperance Airport, a small strip on the French side of St. Martin that is occasionally used by charters or other small planes. There are flights, also, from St. Croix and St. Thomas, the neighboring U.S. Virgins, and air links with Anguilla.

CRUISE ships visit Gustavia harbor, sending passengers ashore in launches, and there is boat service to Gustavia from Philipsburg, Sint Maarten, as well as from Marigot, on the French side (which is a slightly longer trip since Marigot is on St. Martin's north coast and St. Barths lies to the south).

DEPARTURE by air involves check in about an hour before flight time (which you should reconfirm to be sure there have been no changes in the schedule), with time for socializing, with coffee or something stronger, at Joe Felix's airport cafe. During busy times, there is almost shuttle service, so if you arrive early you may get on the "first section" of one of the several-times-daily flights. Departure by boat is from the pier at Gustavia. There is a departure tax of 10F, but if you are *in transit through Dutch Sint Maarten, you do not have to pay the Dutch side's US$5 departure tax.*

TOURING TIPS: **Renting a car** is the best way to be mobile and there are almost a dozen individual entrepreneurs, some representing the well-known international firms, operating from tiny booths at the airport. **Taxis** are readily available, but there's a lot to be said for being able to travel at whim. Cars are often minimokes or other small vehicles that rent for $35 to $45 per day with reductions for weekly rental. Although rental car operators seem to prefer being paid in dollars (and will be if you use a charge card), you can sometimes figure a better rate if you pay in francs. Among the rental firms are *Henri Greaux* (T 27.60.21), the local Hertz representative, *Maurice Questel* (T 27.64.05), *Soleil Caraibe* (T 27.65.06), *St. Barth Location de Voitures* (Car rental) (T 27.71.43) and *Carlos Car Rental,* the firm of Charles Robert Greaux (T 27.61.90). Avis and Budget have their links also.

――――――― **AUTHOR'S OBSERVATION** ―――――――
Tropical St. Barth, an annual magazine, available through L'Office du Tourisme and elsewhere, is a fact-filled, dual-language magazine that is as useful for its information as it is for its French lesson.

LODGING on St. Barths is in personality places with style. Imaginative, attractive architecture adds to the atmosphere at most places. Independence is the strongest accent—for guests as well as managers. Although many properties have been built in recent years, there are no high-rise hotels and, unless politicians are able to break the rigid building regulations, there will be none here. Victorian-style wood fretwork enhances even the boxiest building; favorite paint colors are white or pale pastels. Style follows that of traditional West Indian buildings; many rooms have overhead fans and louvered windows instead of air conditioners.

There's no government tax at press time. Most hotels add 10% to 15% service charge.

――――――― **AUTHOR'S AWARDS** ―――――――
Guanahani, festooned from hillside to shore, is a full-fledged resort with style; small, elitist *Castelets* is unique, with hilltop surroundings and elegant atmosphere; and *Emeraude Plage* is a personal favorite because owners remain true to their original purpose of providing natural hospitality where guests can be totally—and easily—"at home."

Information about places to stay is included under Hotels, Housekeeping Holidays, the Inn Way, and Low-Cost Lodgings. Stars are awarded according to facilities. (See page 11.)

HOTELS usually blend in with their surroundings. There are a couple of 2-story rectangular boxes that perch on the edge of a beach, and a couple of places with several small buildings, nestled amid foliage. For smaller hotels, refer to "The Inn Way" below.

★★ **Hotel Baie des Flamands** • *at Anse des Flamands* • rests at the end of a snakelike road that weaves down from the hilltop near the airstrip and about

3 miles up and down from Gustavia. Wind sweeps across the beach so that the louvers are often closed for the spray-clouded windows in the upstairs dining area. Pool sitters bask in the sun, protected on the inland side of the 2-story building. The modern French architecture is uninspiring, as were the silk bougainvillea flowers on the dining room tables, but the promotion of the place by a U.S. firm assures that you will be grouped with fellow Americans—if that's what you want on this delightfully French island. Families are encouraged with special rates for children. *Hotel.*

★★ **Grand Cul de Sac Beach Hotel** • *on the beach at Grand Cul de Sac* • is more typical of a "hotel" image than the other personality inns on this island. Modern facilities assure the basic creature comforts (twin-bedded rooms, tiled baths, etc.), but I find more atmosphere at some of the other spots. Inquire about special summer programs that include extras with a basic room-and-breakfast rate for multi-night stays. All rooms have kitchenettes, but meals are included for some daily rates. St. Barths Beach is a neighbor. *Hotel.*

★★★★ **Guanahani** • *rising from the shores of Anse de Grand Cul de Sac* • is a community of villas, angled for maximum view. In some cases, that has made air conditioning essential since the building faces away from prevailing breezes. The pool and neighboring restaurant are near the shore, which is often wind-swept and sometimes short on sand (when wave action takes the beach away). Be aware that rooms 62 through 74 are convenient to the pool and have a lovely view, but others may not be as viewful. A hotel shuttle can carry you from hilltop check-in to your room, but count on hillside walking if you haven't rented a car. Some units are ideal for total privacy; others that have a "private" pool also have easy access to neighboring units. Planned for luxury living, the place appeals to those who follow names. *Cottage hotel.*

Jean Bart Hotel • *on the hillside above Baie de St. Jean* • is a collection of foliage-surrounded buildings on the hillside, above a cluster of boutiques and shops and across the road from the beach. Built in '78, when there was not much building along the slope, the bedrooms are in units near the hillside pool. Tropical growth hides the buildings, but you are a short walk downhill to the beach. One of the biggest properties on the island, this place participates in package air-and-hotel holidays. *Hotel.*

★★★ **Manapany** • *rising from Anse des Cayes, on the north coast* • is a community of villas with 2 bedrooms and 2 bathrooms, plus an open-to-breezes living area and a small kitchen. Your viewful porch has deck chairs for sunning; some also face a private pool. Narrow doorways follow French building customs, but may seem claustrophobic for space-loving Americans. Beautiful landscaping punctuates the public buildings with colorful planting, giving the feeling of a modern West Indian village. It can be a hefty hike up from the beach, depending on where your cottage is located. The pool, tennis court and main social hubs are near the beach, where one of the restaurants is located; another is mid-way on the hillside. Brace yourself for a wind-swept shoreline; this end of the bay faces into prevailing winds. You'll need a car for touring. *Cottage hotel.*

St. Barths Beach Hotel and Tennis Club • *at Grand Cul de Sac* • is big for St. Barths, and stretches like 2 shoe boxes at beach edge, a good drive from anyplace else. Owned by Guy Turbe, St. Barths Beach has become its own action center, with windsurfers enjoying the steady breezes, snorkelers and scuba enthusiasts starting out from beachside, and tennis enthusiasts leaping around on the hot asphalt court. Built in a more standard U.S. hotel format than many places on this island, the hotel appeals to the action-oriented. The 36 rooms offer private bath and balcony with the usual spartan-modern French design. You're about 4 wiggly, shore-rimming miles from Gustavia and a little less from the airport. *Hotel.*

HOUSEKEEPING HOLIDAYS on St. Barths are the experts' way to vacation. The specialty of this island is the fact that most visitors "fit in." **Sibarth** (Box 55, Gustavia, 97133 St. Barthelemy, F.W.I., T 011+590+27.62.38) specializes in rentals. **WIMCO** (Box 1461, Newport, RI 02840, T 401+849–8012), is a U.S. firm with an extensive list of villa and apartment rentals on this and other islands. Among the 150 or more properties listed are a U-shaped villa with two air-conditioned bedrooms with private bath in one wing, a master air-conditioned bedroom with bath in another, and a connecting elegant living/dining room that looks out through sliding glass doors (always opened) to the sea. When you contemplate rental, be sure to spell out your interests, be specific about your requirements, and contact a reliable, knowledgeable rental source far in advance of your vacation time. Demand is great. Booking a year in advance for February and March is not too early.

A group of houses owned by Mr. Joseph Ledee (who lives in the house behind the picket fence at the edge of the airport) and his sister, Mme. Linders-Ledee, are available for rent. Each of the houses owned by Mme. Linders-Ledee has two bedrooms, and rentals can be arranged by contacting her *Boutique sur le quai* in Gustavia. There are several houses for rent through Joseph Ledee; he can be reached through Box 158 Vitet, St. Barthelemy, T 011+590+27.74.29. Operating as *Villas St. Barth,* Mr. Ledee's listings are around the island, and include Colibri, at Pointe Milou, with 2 bedrooms and a Jacuzzi, plus Cactus, at Colombier, with 3 bedrooms, and many others. In addition, many self-catering units are sprouting on the beaches at Baie de St. Jean and Lorient.

One of the joys of housekeeping on St. Barths is that the fresh French bread is only as far as Gustavia or the village of Lorient, both with bakeries that bake daily. Good produce can be bought from names you will quickly learn and from the Thursday and Friday open market at the waterfront.

AUTHOR'S OBSERVATION

> Excellent prepared meals, as only the French can do them, are offered not only at the delicatessen counters in the supermarkets, but also through *La Rotisserie,* convenient at the St. Jean boutique cluster as well as in Gustavia, and through *Gout Illimite* (Taste Unlimited) in Gustavia. In both cases, stop by in the morning to order and pick up your dinner after you leave the beach at 4 p.m. or later.

Auberge de la Petite Anse • *on Flamands beach* • is not too far from Gustavia, on an up-and-over-the-hill route ending at the road to Flamands. The project perked with the first 4 villas in spring of '79, and others followed along as time and money permitted for a present total of 8. Decor is reminiscent of J. C. Penney, with gold rayon curtains and dark furniture. Porches on second-floor units are perfect for twilight sea-watching. You can stock up with staples at a nearby *epicerie* which is a long-but-possible walk from home base. Florville Greaux, owner also of Presqu'ile in Gustavia, is the one to find for further facts. A car is recommended for mobility. *Cottages.*

★★★ **Emeraude Plage** • *at Baie de St. Jean* • is one of my longtime favorites. From the time when it was only one small cottage shared by Genevieve Nouy's family when they vacationed here from their home in Guadeloupe, this place has continued to offer happy homelike surroundings. It was my parents' winter salvation for more than a dozen years, while the place grew from 7 buildings, each with 2 efficiency units, to the present 24 units, 3 of which have 2 bedrooms each. One beachside villa has a couple of rooms, making it ideal for families; others have comfortable bedroom with modern bathroom, plus living patio with a kitchen unit enclosed by shutters when not in use. Perfect for pursuing a Robinson Crusoe dream with modern comforts, and favored by people who are comfortable with themselves, Emeraude Plage has a loyal list of repeat guests who make finding a winter room a challenge. Well maintained, and hidden from the strollers on St. Jean beach by a flourishing grove of sea-grape trees, the units are ably managed by Genevieve Nouy, Christian Greaux and a supportive team who seem to enjoy providing warm (and welcoming) hospitality. When a frenzied life makes me dream of getting away, this is one place that comes quickly to mind. *Cottages.*

Les Islets Fleuris • *in the hills, above Lorient* • is a cluster of view-full studio apartments, gathered around the swimming pool. You'll want a car to get to the beach or elsewhere. Rooms are comfortable and breeze-swept; your sundeck is good sized. Although most units are studios, there's one "sea view suite" with a separate living room. *Apts.*

Jardins de St. Jean • *near the Baie de St. Jean* • are a cluster of studios and 1- and 2-bedroom villas with kitchens and terrace living, plus a spectacular view of the sea. It's a downhill walk to the beach (and an uphill walk afterward), but the breeze-swept hillside makes the location superb. Shoreside bistros offer dining options for those who won't want to cook at home. Open for the '85–'86 season, the community started with 10 villas, and rapidly grew to 20, to hold at that number for a while. *Villas.*

Hotel Karl Gustav • *in Gustavia, on the hillside near the clock tower* • was a season's newcomer for '90–'91, with a dozen very comfortable suites. Intended for guests who know, understand, and will pay for classy elegance, this small spot is within walking distance of the port action and the many restaurants around Gustavia. Shell Beach is nearby. *Apts.*

Kerjan Cottages • *on Baie de St. Jean* • are tucked into a wedge of beach-fronted shoreline, next to Tom Beach and a short walk from Emeraude Plage and Filao Beach. The 5 cottages offer bedroom with modern bathroom, patio living area with basic kitchen facilities. Located at the part of the bay where taxi drivers drop their cruise ship passengers, the neighboring cafe and water-sports equipment lure those in search of action. *Cottages.*

Marigot Sea and **Marigot Bay** • *below Pointe Milou, overlooking the shore* • are two collections of cottages, with the name relating to the location. Since all are recently built, the units are comfortable, with private bathroom and breeze-swept sundeck. *Cottages.*

Terrasses de St. Barth • *in the St. Jean area that is becoming the island's prime beach-and-cottage* • are several studios and 1-bedroom units for self-catering folk. As with others in this area, the proliferation of cafes, bistros, and places to shop make the location convenient, but peacefully yours if you don't feel sociable. *Apts.*

Tom Beach Hotel • *on Baie de St. Jean* • was a newcomer with the 1983–1984 season, but its owners—the Magras family—are one of the island's original families. The shingle roofs and walls wrap around a dozen small units, each with kitchenette and easy access to the beach. Good for cozy twosomes, but not so great if you want space around you. *Cottages.*

Villas Creole • *on the beach at St. Jean* • is an ambitious multi-villa project planned by the Tom Beach owners. Most pool-flecked villas are planned for the hillside, above the beach and behind the central buildings that will be the social and reception center. Mentioned here when it was first under way, a few villas are available this season. *Villas.*

Villas Moreno • *on Pointe Milou, a point that pokes into the sea* • are built within sea sounds, but you'll have to walk around the road to the beach. Clinging to the hillside, the wooden decks are lovely places for relaxing. Units are comfortably fitted with all the basics. *Cottages.*

★★★ **Village St. Jean** • *overlooking Baie de St. Jean* • clusters on the hillside, up a short but steep cement drive from the road, on the other side of which is the Baie and its long white sandy strand. Opened with a few units in the 1970s, the Village is now several separate redwood units, some *(Terrasse* or *Jardin)* with kitchen, air-conditioned double bedroom, and breeze-swept deck; others (hotel rooms) with twin beds, air-conditioned room, and refrigerator, with balcony, and the best of the group with its own Jacuzzi-pool. Furnishings are outdoor-comfortable, with a casual tone. There's a commissary on the hilltop, and *Le Patio* restaurant for terrace (and indoor) dining near "home." Entertainment focuses on congenial guests. Car is essential for mobility; otherwise stay at home or walk down to (and very slowly up from) the beach. Planting puts you in seemingly very private quarters; views are magnificent. *Apts.*

White Sands Beach Cottages • *on Anse des Flamands* • are a few cottages within walking distance of the activity of Baie des Flamands hotel. The area has long been popular with residents, who frequent the small food store, enjoy cookouts at the beach, and windsurf offshore. The place is pleasantly informal. *Cottages.*

THE INN WAY is the "in" way for St. Barths. Repeat visitors enjoy coming "home," with a familiar staff to welcome them. Since only a few of the places to stay have 50 rooms or more, most places qualify as inns. Each of those mentioned below has its own personality, which usually takes its cue from that of the owner/manager.

Hotel Baie des Anges • *on Baie des Flamands* • is a small spot (9 rooms) on a beautiful, often wind-swept, beach. A few of the rooms have kitchenettes; others are simple bedrooms that leave you free to sample the nearby bistros and other restaurants around the island. *Guesthouse, Apts.*

★★★ **Castelets** • *on Morne Lurin* • stands on a hilltop, above the town of Gustavia. A "straight up" road makes the arrival somewhat harrowing, but the view is spectacular. Castelets is a gem for people with money, ably managed by Mme. Genevieve Jouany, who leaves you pretty much to yourself, unless you need some help. This can be the sybarite's dream, if the sybarite does not need a beach and the sea at his doorstep to enjoy the Caribbean (and I do). There's a small pool. The evening meals (reservation only) are elegant, gourmet affairs by candlelight and after 9 p.m. (Price should be no concern, but figure on at least 300F for dinner.) Luncheon is served, in style, for about 250F. Most units have kitchens; some are 2-bedroom duplex units with living room, balcony, and private (elegant) bath; others are one air-conditioned bedroom with kitchenette and living room with terrace, and then there are 2 small rooms in the main building. Each room has a tape deck. A car's essential if you want to leave this aerie. *Inn.*

Club Hotel La Banane • *just off the shore road, near Autour de Rocher* • uses its pool as the focal point for a cluster of charming West Indian-style buildings. The main building is used for reception area and dining place, with wood tables set with colorful creole-style napery. Tropical foliage surrounding the buildings gives the feeling of being far removed from the action centers, but they are only a few minutes away. You're near, but not on, a beach. *Inn.*

Eden Rock • *on Baie de St. Jean* • is an island tradition with an "unusual" personality. It sits on the rocks in the middle of the shoreline at Baie de St. Jean. The house is historic as the home of Remy de Haenen, an island legend himself. His inn was the island's first, and in the early days he would meet you in Sint Maarten to fly you over in his own plane. Island antiques fill the main house, and less valuable, more functional four-posters and other furnishings make the several small rooms livable. One of the separate bungalows, just below the main house on the rocks as they slant to the sea, is an ideal hideaway, if you don't demand ultramodern plumbing and fancy furnishings. *Inn.*

★★★ **Filao Beach Hotel** • *on Baie de St. Jean* • sifted onto the shore between Emeraude Plage's cottages and Eden Rock hotel for the '81–'82 season. Owned by a group including the former Mayor and managed by veteran hotelier Pierre Verdier, the Filao has a pool at its heart. Your patio puts you in public view with most lodgings. The single-story half-circle of rooms cups the pool, with the shore and sea beyond. Breakfast and lunch are served there. Location on the eastern end of Baie de St. Jean has meant that seas swirl the sand from the shore, leaving this place "beachless" when surges take out the sand. The hotel is a member of the highly esteemed *Relais & Chateaux.* Small hotel.

★★★ **Francois Plantation** • *in Colombier, near the shore* • opened in the season of '88 with a dozen attractive rooms, not far from the workshop of artist Jean-Yves Froment. The on-premise restaurant is elegant, expensive, and staffed by proven experts. Long-time residents Francois and Francoise Beret have added a top-notch address to this island's lodgings. *Inn.*

★★★ **L'Hibiscus** • *in Gustavia* • grew at the corner of rue Thiers and rue Courbet, a block inland from Gustavia's port, for the season of '80–'81. It's the punctuation mark at the foot of the town's historic Swedish clock tower. Quickly claiming a devoted following among those who want to be within a walk of all the Gustavia options, the inn offers its guests a spectacular harbor view from the balcony of the second-floor rooms. Modern architecture blends with Gustavia's traditions. The air-conditioned rooms offer the choice of fan-swirled balmy breezes and are punctuated with patterns designed by island-famous silk-screen artist Jean-Yves Froment. Count on classy ambience, cultivated French atmosphere capably administered by Muriel Labastire, and the convenience of kitchen equipment in your room if you prefer cooking at home to dining at the inn's noteworthy *Restaurant du Vieux Clocher* or another one of the many interesting dining depots. *Inn.*

Hostellerie des Trois Forces • *at Vitet, out of the mainstream* • has a dozen 1-bedroom cottages, named for the signs of the zodiac, and a menu in the dining room that is primarily vegetarian. Ceiling fans cool the cottages; furnishings are rustic and comfortable. This palce has a relaxing, restful atmosphere—and a pool. *Cottages.*

Sea Horse Hotel • *near Marigot beach* • is cozy comfortable, and pool-studded. With the appearance of a private home, this place is peaceful and pleasant. *Inn.*

★★★ **El Sereno Beach** • *at Grand Cul de Sac* • saturated its small space on the shoreline with a cluster of neat-and-new units. It opened in summer of '80 and now has owners from Lyon, France. Guests have a choice of two-stroke pool or a sliver of a beach. Not designed in traditional style, the pool has an island in the middle and skull-cracking depth. Rooms gather around a small court, punctuated with pool, dining depots, and a beach-oriented bar. Elegance with European style has been the keynote here. Hotel guests are joined by outsiders during daytime hours when windsurfing provides a colorful (and active) panorama. (Club Lafayette, a source for windsurfers, is next door.) *Small hotel.*

★★★ **Taiwana** • *at Anse de Flamands* • has captured elegance and made it available for guests. With 9 attractively furnished rooms, a few of which face the beach (all are adjacent to the pool), the hotel offers almost idyllic surroundings and a special, sun-struck seaside bistro. Price keeps the riff-raff out. If you search for class and are willing to compensate well (with cash) for privacy, consider this. *Inn.*

★★ **Tropical Hotel** • *overlooking Baie de St. Jean* • nests in the lush foliage on the first rise of the hill road that leads up to a cluster of units that is Village St. Jean. A newcomer to the '81 roster, Tropical folds its guests into small but adequate rooms and offers full American breakfast. Beaded curtains make the break for your closet; there's not enough room for a door, but most vacationers will probably head downhill to the Baie de St. Jean where there's plenty of beachside activity including some good restaurants. There's a small pool (dunking size), and a center court that offers a verdant heart for the hotel. Catherine Cevaer is the inn-keeper, and she's cultivated a French Riviera atmosphere along with the tropics. *Small hotel.*

LOW-COST LODGING: "Low cost" becomes a relative term when it's used with reference to St. Barths! There's not much that's truly inexpensive, although some of the cottages allow for multi-person occupancy that can bring costs down. In addition to some of the places mentioned under "Housekeeping Holidays," here are others to consider:

Les Mouettes • *at Lorient* • offers apartments on the shore, but you'll have to walk to find the good beach. Named for a kind of bird, the units are comfortably furnished and offer lovely sunset views from "your" balcony.

Hotel La Normandie • *at Lorient* • is an 8-room French inn, within a short walk of a lovely beach. Not for fussy travelers, this place is comfortably casual and has done some wing-sprouting in recent seasons with music in late afternoon and evenings. There's a small pool, and a large portion of island hospitality for anyone who puts good value ahead of well-known name. Meals are available, and the house offering is usually reasonable.

Hotel Le P'tit Morne • *in the hills above Colombier* • is for self-sufficient folk who can settle in easily to island life, French West Indies' style. Owner Joe Felix, for those who like to tie island legends together, came from his native St. Barths to work at St. Thomas's Mountain Top in the 1950s when it was a small hotel; he wisely returned home well over a decade ago, to operate the cafe at the airport, this small inn, and Chez Joe in town. This aerie may seem like a long way from anywhere, but the view is spectacular, the hospitality is genuine, the rooms are comfortable, and there's a pool for days when you prefer not to drive the wiggly road to town or an island beach.

Presqu'ile • *in Gustavia* • parks at the waterfront, on the far side of the harbor as you head down the hill. It's a navy type place that has led a seaman's life. More than a casual barefoot and boating spot, the small hotel which starts on the second floor (climb the narrow stairway at the left of the building) reminds me of the waterfront at Marseilles—with a West Indian personality. Bargain rates (by comparison to others on this island) make it interesting for French-speaking casual, sea-oriented folk. The rooms are basic: walls, floor, window, narrow bed, and sometimes private bathroom-with-shower.

Sunset • *on the waterfront at Gustavia* • is a lovely 8-room inn, with comfortable furnishings in today's island fashion. Tastefully decorated to maximize space (and the window's view, when available), bedrooms vary in size and shape. Some have air conditioners; others have overhead fans. On the second floor of a refurbished traditional West Indian wood building, Sunset can prove ideal for those who prefer in-town access to beach location if the place hasn't been taken over by long-term rentals, as sometimes happens.

RESTAURANTS on St. Barths are small, and very special, with high prices and quality. Good food and elegant ambience reign supreme at some places; good food and bistro surroundings in others. As the trickle of tourists threatened to swell into a flood, it was "dammed," at least temporarily, by high prices.

AUTHOR'S OBSERVATION

Check for new names when you arrive on the island. Each season brings a few special spots. Reservations are recommended at all times for dinners on St. Barths. During peak season winter, places may be "full" and at other times an advance reservation assures that there will be food and the place will be open. Many places accept cash only (no credit cards).

L'Ananas • *in Gustavia, on rue Thiers* • is a longtime favorite. Small (a dozen tables) and very special, chef Luc Blanchard prepares culinary delights with full flourishes.

★★★★ **Castelets** captures top spot for location and looks. Food service at Castelets is elegant (and you'll be more comfortable if you are too). The once perilous drive to this perch has been repatterned to weave back and forth in a series of switchbacks up a precipitous slant that in previous seasons made some taxi drivers turn down a trip up. This dress-up spot at the top of the world has a perfect view, pristine table settings, and priceless food.

Au Port • *upstairs on rue du Centenaire* • near the corner of the base of the U-shaped harbor. Both filet mignon and veal have been excellent on recent visits and this place continues to have a devoted following.

Aux Trois Gourmands • *on the far side of the harbor, near the ruins of a fort* • is an elegant caterie where Christophe Gasnier, a protege of Paul Bocuse, holds forth. Larger than many in-town spots, this place benefits from pink-and-white decor, crystal on the table, and a fine waterside view.

Au Bon Coin • *overlooking the beach at Lorient* • warrants an advance search by daylight to find the place so you know where it is when you come back after dark. The location is lovely; the food samplings worth the drive.

Le Bistro • *near Eden Rock on Baie de St. Jean* • and wedged on the roadside, has its following for good food in very casual surroundings.

Bar de l'Oubli • *across from Loulou's Marine and diagonally across from Le Select* • is a cafe in the best French tradition. Coffee, pastries, and light foods are served from morning well into the night, with a dinner priced at a modest, for St. Barths, 70F.

Capitaine Monbars • *on rue de Roi Oscar II, in Gustavia* • is the successful (and expensive) enterprise of the owner of the catering service Gout Illimite. Putting already proven culinary expertise to work in the restaurant guaranteed a popular place, since Hillary's catering is well known and highly respected among dedicated St. Barths' visitors.

La Cremaillere • *near Gustavia's harbor on rue General de Gaulle* • is the place to settle in for the local lobster bisque, frogs' legs, and for other, more elaborate fare, if you've made a reservation.

L'Escale • *next door to La Marine, in the Yacht Club* • serves pleasant meals at a refreshingly moderate price. The harborside location allows for plenty of boating activity as your mealtime entertainment.

Francois Plantation • *at Colombier* • makes the most of its hillside location with nicely presented offerings served by a well-trained staff. Although the tally may seem high, the surroundings are classy and the investment should create happy memories.

★★★ **La Langouste** • *above street level on Quai de la Republique in Gustavia* • is a special spot serving good langouste (local lobster) and poisson grille (grilled fish). Annie Turbe is part of the family that owns St. Barth Beach and other island businesses.

Le Patio • *at Village St. Jean* • is primarily for the convenience of guests at the village. If you're looking for a new place to try, stop by and see what they're offering (and if they're open). This place seems to be an on-again off-again operation.

Restaurant du Vieux Clocher • *at L'Hibiscus hotel* • under the Swedish clock tower that is a famous Gustavia landmark, has a set menu at *prix fixe* *avec vin* for about 120F. Menu offerings warrant high praise among those who prefer steak, lobster, veal and chicken without a lot of fancy sauces.

★★ **Le Pelican Gourmand** • *beachside at Baie de St. Jean* • is owned by the Mayor and frequented by island residents. It's a favorite for many who enjoy good food in a Breton-style setting. Reservations are required. Figure 150F or more per person. A cafe-style Pelican, next door, serves on a covered deck at sea's edge, with informal atmosphere and salads (and hamburgers) as specialties.

Le Sapotillier • *on rue du Centenaire in Gustavia* • is a long-time favorite, taking its name from the tree that shelters those who dine in the patio. Mousses are special here, whether fish (as an appetizer) or white chocolate (for dessert), and this is one of a few places where quality continues to be tops.

Taiwana • *on the beach at Baie des Flamands* • is an open-air bistro that puts you near a pool, amid flourishing plants. Poisson grille (grilled fish) is a favorite and the place is a club-of-sorts for locals-in-the-know. A luncheon or beverage will be your only way to enjoy these splendid surroundings, unless you're lucky enough to stay here. Prices are lofty and staff attitude borders on haughty. Reservations are essential.

Tamarin • *on the road to Salines* • is a good lunch stop, if you find yourself out this way without a picnic. It's not open for dinner at press time. The *Caribbean Newsletter* will have news.

Topolino • *on the inland side of the road along Baie de St. Jean* • serves pizza, barbecues, and creole dishes on a pleasant, open-air, cafe-style patio, sheltered from sun by a West Indian-style roof. Pleasant, for casual fare.

In Gustavia, **Chez Joe** and **Eddy Snack** are worthy casual snack spots that will give you good salads and other simple fare.

Chez Francine • *on Baie de St. Jean* • has become a haven for tour bus lunches on days when tour groups come off cruise ships. It's a better bet as a beachside bistro when the buses are elsewhere.

Santa Fe • *in the hills* • with a viewful perch that is almost as perfect as Castelets, serves mouth-watering hamburgers and other snack-style food. It's a popular place with repeat visitors.

La Toque Lyonnaise • *at El Sereno Beach* • is *very* pricey, but highly praised for exceptional cuisine in the style of French masters. A dining experience, at the pool-and-beach setting, tallies to 200F per person.

Alsace • in the St. Jean area, serves good food at reasonable prices. For creole cooking (spicy, with sauces), two favorites for those who live here are **Chez Tatie** and **Jacki**, with a slight edge in some people's minds for Jacki's.

AUTHOR'S OBSERVATION

Things slow down (and sometimes stop completely) on St. Barths in the fall. Several of the inns are closed and restaurants open when they feel like it and/or when business warrants. In spite of the "silence," the fall has been my favorite time for St. Barths.

NATURAL SURROUNDINGS: Except for the enthusiasm for tourism that has embroidered the harbor at Gustavia and the roadsides at St. Jean with lodgings, bistros, and boutiques, large portions of the island are in a natural state. Since most land is privately owned, it's important to check with the tourism office about suggested walks and hikes, and to gain permission to cross private property. Footpaths are part of a master plan for activities, with trails that branch out from La Petite Anse. It's wise to ask about the degree of difficulty for the walk/hike. Some of the planned trails cover rugged terrain.

Insofar as offshore sites for snorkeling and scuba diving are concerned, St. Barths is surrounded by reefs that are popular feeding grounds for several kinds of fish, most of them colorfully garbed. **Pain de Sucre** is one of the best dive sites, partly because of the sheer drop-off, the cave, and the proliferation of corals and sponges. **Les Petits Saints,** several small islets off the western thumb of Gustavia harbor, are home for turtles and several fish. Among the many other sites are an area off Colombia, with walls and caves where the Atlantic and Caribbean meet, and the wall off Gros Ilet.

PLACES WORTH FINDING on St. Barths are mostly the ones you discover yourself, as you prowl around the island. There are small villages (Corossol, where the ladies who weave the baskets and mats swarm around your car) and special beach-lined coves, but the enchantment of St. Barths is that it is a solitary place to share with someone special. This is no place for tour groups and hordes of tourists.

St. Barths Museum, at Gustavia Point, is charming, with costumes, household items, and furniture from days past.

SPORTS on St. Barths succumb to the sea, either in it, on it or under it. **Boardsailing** has taken over here, as on many Caribbean islands. Flocks of sails fleck the sea at Baie de St. Jean, at the *St. Barth's Wind School* on the beach at Tom Beach Hotel, and others head to *Wind Wave Power,* at St. Barth's Beach Hotel. Boardsailors have been known to try their boards and sails at almost any shore. **Scuba diving,** known as "plongee" on the French-speaking islands, is offered through *La Marine Service* (T 27.70.34) in Gustavia and *La Maison de la Mer* (T 27.81.00) as well as at the beach at Baie de St. Jean. *The Reefer Surf Club* (T 27.77.25) is headquarters for the *St. Barths Sport Agency,* which offers help with tennis, surfing, diving, hiking, and other activities.

Yachting is very popular in seas around St. Barths. Not only is the protected harbor ideal, with Gustavia as a horseshoe, but there are several coves to welcome sailors from Sint Maarten, Antigua, and elsewhere. *Saint-Barth Association du Plaisance,* a yachting group, was formed in 1988 to continue to build the Route du Rose, an annual November trans-Atlantic regatta of tall ships out of St. Tropez, on the Mediterranean coast of France, as well as to focus on other yachting events and on maintenance of the port and facilities. Both *La Marine Service* (T 27.70.34) and *La Caleche Yacht Charter Agency* (T 27.62.38) are sources for charters of a day or longer, as well as for **deep sea fishing.** Day charters usually run about 700F per person with a minimum of four people. Motorboat rentals can also be arranged through La Marine Service.

Tennis is available at St. Barth's Beach Hotel, Club Taiwana, and Manapany, Guanahani and Le Flamboyant Tennis Club.

Golfers should ask about the driving range and putting green above Gouverneur. Equipment can be rented. The island's too dry and hilly to have much of a course.

TREASURES AND TRIFLES on St. Barths are tucked into several small shops of Gustavia, and sold from even smaller places in some of the villages around the island. In Gustavia, check to see what's being sold at **la Caleche,** where Brook and Roger Lacour have their home and apartment rental office. The usual selection includes clothing as well as some specialty items and island designed fabrics worked into summer fashions from St. Kitts and Nevis. Merchandise is top-quality in the now expanded quarters.

Two books, as welcomed for gifts as they are for personal possessions, are the very impressive *Fils de Vikings a St. Barth* by Jeanne Audy-Rowland, published in 1985 by Paris-based Dargaud Editeur, and *Histoire de St. Barth,* with French and English text, by Stanislas Defize as one of Les Editions du Latanier. Both books are available in stores in Gustavia and in the shopping centers at St. Jean and across the road from the airport.

Among the luxury French items available in Gustavia are Hermes scarfs, beach towels, change purses, ties, etc., at **La Fonda** (phone 27.66.15) and the Souleiado provincial designs, along with some Dior items and Sevres crystal at **Vestibule** on Rue de la Republique (phone 27.67.45). **Le Poinsettia** at St. Jean has clothes and other resort items, and the **Smoke & Booze** is known locally for supplies of tobacco and liqueur.

Allow some time to visit **St. Barth's Pottery** in Gustavia, and try to time your visit when they are working in the studio. The items are for sale, and special items can be made to order if you allow enough time.

ALMA Optiques, near the waterfront, takes care of the "usual" perfume, camera (including Kodak), watches, and crystal routines. If you're in the market for any of those luxury items, visit the shop to check the prices (which are usually a shade or two below the better-known shopping havens in the U.S. Virgins and Curacao). St. Barths' reputation as a smugglers' port since the time of the buccaneers is worth remembering when you shop for imported items.

Stop at the studio of **Jean-Yves Froment,** in Colombier, for handblocked island prints, painted and printed T-shirts, and other island-made designs. The fabric can be purchased by the yard, or made up in shirts, skirts, and other clothes.

The delicately woven reed work is unique to St. Barths. Although a lot of the work is whipped together by sewing machine these days, it is still possible to find some of the handsewn items that I find far preferable. Hats, mats, baskets are the usual items for sale, and bargaining when you buy from the women at Corossol is part of the process for purchase.

La Cave de Saint Barthelemy is a find for anyone who wants to buy good wine. In an enormous cement-block building that looks more like an airport hangar than a wine cellar, you can find some of France's best vintages, at very reasonable prices. Worth toting home to the States (considering the relatively low tally that customs adds to wines), the vintages are certainly ideal for "at home" consumption while you are in residence here. Located between Lorient and Grand Cul de Sac, La Cave is worth a visit if you are serious about wine.

Postcards made from the painting/collages of **Margot Ferra Doniger** are worth buying, if you can't track down (or afford) one of the exceptional works of art in the original. Available in most shops where postcards are sold, the special scenes of St. Barths help recall this island's unique quality long after you've left its shores.

ST. CROIX

> Division of Tourism, Christiansted, St. Croix, USVI 00820, T 809+773-0495, fax 809+778-9259; Frederiksted, Customs House Bldg., Strand St., St. Croix, USVI 00840, T 809+772-0357; 3460 Wilshire Blvd., Los Angeles, CA 90010, T 213+739-0138; #500, 900 17th St., N.W., Washington, DC 20006, T 202+293-3707; Virgin Islands Government Tourist Office, 235 Peachtree Center, #1420; #907, 2655 Le Jeune Rd., Coral Gables, FL 33134, T 305+442-7200; Gaslight Tower; Atlanta, GA 30303, T 404+688-0906; #1270, 122 S. Michigan Ave., Chicago, IL 60603, T 312+461-0180; 1270 Avenue of Americas, New York, NY 10020, T 212+582-4520, fax 212+581-3405; 2 Cinnamon Row, Plantation Wharf, York Pl., London SW11 3TW England, T 01+978-5262.

$ · · · U.S. currency is used.

The sun scattered diamonds of light on the sea. At the horizon end of that glittering path, a parade of yachts—all shapes and sizes—moved across my view. It is a Sunday in September, and I am almost sleeping—supported by the salty sea, glimpsing the sailboats over my toes as I float. From this vantage point, it's hard to comprehend the devastation that followed Hurricane Hugo's visit in September 1989.

It is early, and most people are either sleeping, in bed or on the deck of one of those yachts, or floating in the sea as I am. Those people who are bent are probably curling around a cup of coffee, perhaps at one of the Christiansted hotels, where your juice, eggs, and bacon may come with yachting conversations shared with strangers who turn into friends after a few converging breakfasts.

St. Croix can be a somnolent spot. Not far from where I float, the sea laps at the shores of Christiansted, the town that was planned by the Danes, in an area known before that as Ay Ay by the Indians who were here and then by a handful of settlers—French who gave it its name, and English in 1645.

Even after the Danish claim, English, Scottish, and Irish outnumbered the Danes about five to one. English has been the language of the street.

The best-looking buildings in town are forced to stay that way. They're part of a National Historic Site, overseen by the U.S. National Park Service. The Danes made the plan, adapting the buildings they knew at home to the Caribbean breezes and sun—and to the ballast brick that became the building material. The arcades are from the 18th century; the people who walk under them are definitely 20th century.

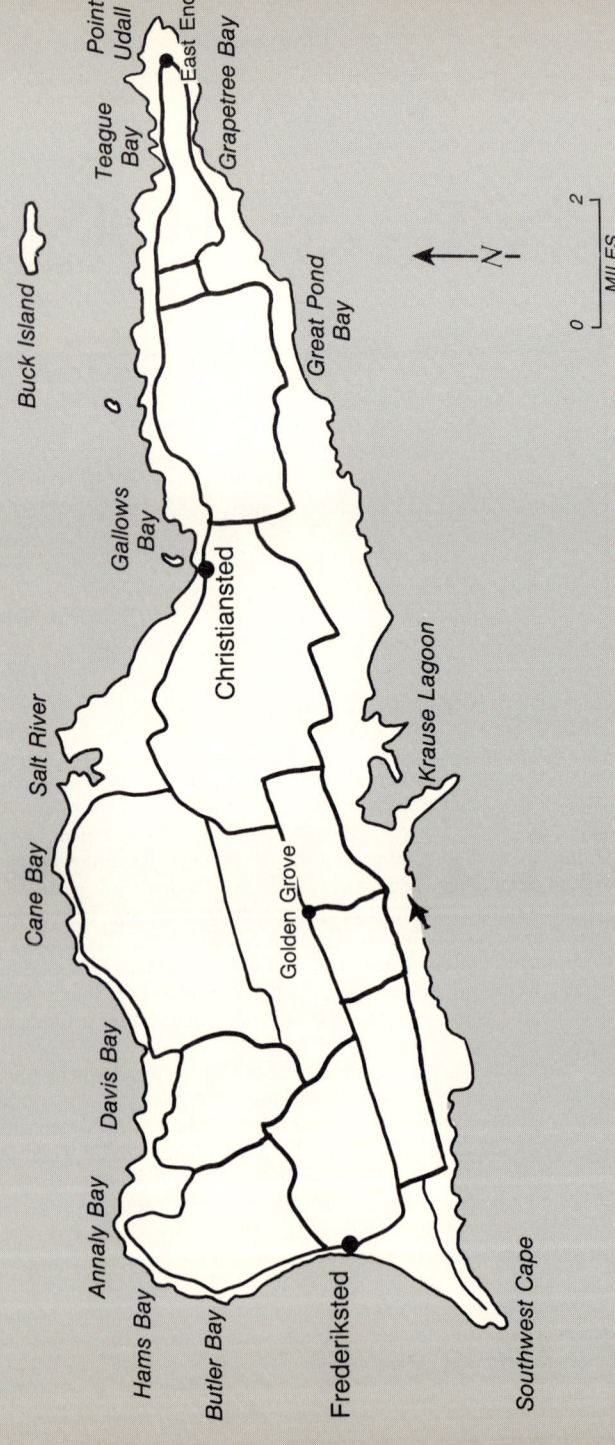

POLITICAL PICTURE: Citizens in the U.S. Virgin Islands (St. Croix, St. John, and St. Thomas) hold elections every four years. Incumbent Governor Alexander Farrelly was returned to office in elections held November 1990.

Purchased from Denmark in March 1917 for $25 million, the U.S. Virgin Islands are an unincorporated territory of the United States. Although elected representatives handle the day-to-day operations, the islands fall under the jurisdiction of the U. S. Department of Interior. Key areas of concern, as in many U.S. cities, are education, public works, drugs, and crime. The U.S. two-party system, with Democrats and Republicans, is the accepted one here, but there is sometimes an Independent party candidate and often, also, candidates from splinter groups responding to special interests.

Tourism is the major source for funds and employment, especially since the Harvey Alumina and Hess industrial complexes on St. Croix have curtailed operations, but the territorial government is still the largest employer. A U.S. Government matching funds policy for rum sales, another plum for Virgin Islands coffers, has been effected by the opening of rum markets to other Caribbean islands, but protectionist measures assured the privileged position for Puerto Rico and the U.S. Virgins. There are tax incentives for investment by U.S. firms and individuals within the U.S. Virgin Islands, and plans are under way for industrial parks on St. Croix.

ISLAND APPEARANCE: Within the 21-mile length of the island, there's history punctuated with two 17th-century forts, one plantation Great House museum restored to its 18th-century ambience, a Botanic Garden and a natural rain forest, two small towns, each with its own personality, and miles of shore often rimmed with soft-sand beaches. There's also an overlay of modern development, with resorts, condominiums, shopping centers, and branches of chain stores well known to many U.S. mainland communities. The surge of building gives this island an "American suburbs" aspect, although West Indian stone sugar mill towers have been restored as homes, restaurants, and punctuation marks for hotels. Surrounding seas have become an area of study as well as pleasure, with research facilities on the island. Offshore Buck Island is designated as a national monument; an underwater trail is clearly marked for snorkelers and scuba divers. Christiansted, the island's main town and the seat of the local government, devotes several blocks to history, with 18th-century Danish buildings preserved as a U.S. National Historic Site, although those buildings not devoted to government or museums are shops, restaurants, and small hotels. Sleepy Frederiksted, a smaller town with many Victorian-style buildings, is the island's major cruise port; it's about 30 minutes' drive from Christiansted.

LIFESTYLE is American island-casual, after years of U.S. affiliation (since the pre-1917 Danish days). Although residents applaud the convenience of *Grand Union, Woolworth, Kentucky Fried,* and the rest of the chain reactions known to every town in the U.S.A., the Americanization of these islands has wiped out all of the foreign flavor and has contributed to a sophisticated lifestyle with problems familiar to many U.S. cities. Attempts were made to revive interest in things Danish a few years ago, but the prevailing atmosphere is distinctly American tourist, especially in Christiansted. There are a couple of Danish restaurants, some street names, and—of course—the names of Charlotte Amalie (the capital, on St. Thomas) and the towns of Christiansted and Frederiksted.

Clothes are casual, with the ultra-elegant resort wear of *Vogue* (and yesteryear) seen on occasion (usually at private parties). Downtown, small-restaurant attire is neatly informal. Most men disdain the coat and tie, favoring an open-necked shirt; and some women dress up, with casual skirt-and-blouse or T-shirt and skirt combinations. Blue jeans and shorts are popular for boats and beach. As with all island areas, it's pleasanter for everyone if bare chests and bare feet are limited to pool or beach (and the bare chests are usually on men only, except at a beach or pool of your own, in the U.S. Virgin Islands). The U.S. affiliation means U.S.-style summer resort clothes are the style here also.

MEDICAL FACILITIES: The St. Croix hospital at Sunny Isles, about 20 minutes' drive from downtown Christiansted, was built in the early 1980s, and has been rebuilt following extensive hurricane damage (in September 1989). It replaced the former Charles Harwood Hospital, which is used mostly for management and psychiatric patients. Although the hospital is relatively new, staffing and equipment leave much to be desired. Islanders often go to the hospital on St. Thomas for more serious matters. Visitors would probably prefer the hospitals in Puerto Rico or Miami, when time and budget permit. Medical charters can be arranged out of St. Croix. Many doctors have offices in and near Christiansted; hotels usually refer medical problems to doctors known to management.

MONEY MATTERS: The dollars that disappear are U.S. variety, and everyone is overly eager to have them. Some places take credit cards, but don't count on their acceptance everywhere. Many small spots are accepting only cold, hard cash. Traveler's checks are a convenient (safe) way to carry "cash."

COMMUNICATIONS are easy, with direct dial from overseas to St. Croix using 809 + 77 + 5 digits for the local number. Facsimile machines are business essentials. Local television comes out of studios on St. Thomas and the U.S. mainland. New York and Miami newspapers are available, but they are double or more the cost of hometown purchase.

ARRIVAL on St. Croix is by air, for most, landing at Alexander Hamilton Airport, midway between Christiansted and Frederiksted, in the southern part of the island.

AUTHOR'S OBSERVATION

The seaplane service that used to scoot out of Christiansted harbor, linking Charlotte Amalie (St. Thomas), Cruz Bay (St. John), and San Juan (Puerto Rico) on several times' daily flights, has been revitalized with owners from Puerto Rico, but service has not been completely restored. The *Caribbean Newsletter* (page 9) will have details when warranted.

Mid-island's Hamilton Airport is open to tropical breezes, except for the air-conditioned enclosed upstairs restaurant. The luggage pick-up area seems fairly primitive for such a busy airport. You'll be responsible for plucking your luggage from the conveyor belt and taking it to one of the waiting taxis.

In addition to the major carriers—*American, Continental, Delta,* and others—there are several feeder airlines that make easy links between St. Croix and other islands. Among those flying between San Juan, Puerto Rico, and St. Croix are *American Eagle, LIAT,* and *Sunaire.*

At Alexander Hamilton Airport, there are car rental desks for easy car pick-up, but the rates tend to be scalper-high in winter ($65 per day on a recent winter visit). The information desk at the airport has folders, and sometimes a person, to help with on-the-spot directions and news.

AUTHOR'S OBSERVATION

> Taxi fares are printed on the wall near the luggage pick-up. The charge is for a seat in a car, and you'll sit there until the car is full before takeoff for town or your hotel. The alternative is to "buy" the car yourself, at top dollar. Ask, before you get in the cab, about current fares; charges can change from the posted rate. Christiansted is about 20 minutes' drive east; Frederiksted is about 15 minutes' drive west.

CRUISE ship arrival is usually at the pier in Frederiksted, the smaller of the island's two towns, which has been rebuilt after Hugo's visit. Smaller ships had been using Christiansted's Gallows Bay pier, but the storm ended that. At press time, no lines had announced plans to return. The two towns are about half an hour's drive from each other. There is public bus service that takes almost an hour, allowing for stops. In Frederiksted, where all the larger cruise ships dock, you can walk along the cement pier (in the hot sun) to the shops along the waterfront and back street of town; there's a beach beyond the historic fort at the fringe of town. Better beaches require a car or other transport. Christiansted's grid of streets are appliqued with shops, cafes, and inns. In addition to golf at Carambola, a visit to Whim Greathouse, and perhaps the Botanic Garden, St. Croix's greatest attraction is Buck Island Underwater Park.

DEPARTURE by air is usually from Alexander Hamilton Airport, where there is a (cafeteria style) restaurant, upstairs before you go through security formalities. There are also a few shops, including one where you can buy liquor.

If you're on a direct flight to the U.S. mainland, you will go through U.S. customs in St. Croix. If your flight stops in Puerto Rico, you'll go through U.S. customs there. Because the U.S. Virgin Islands are exempt from customs duties as they are applied on items coming into the mainland (thanks to terms continued since the islands' Danish rule and maintained through heavy lobbying in Washington), it's necessary to go through customs *even though you are within U.S. territory.* The customs formalities are reasonably routine; the waiting area after you have passed through customs at Hamilton airport is drab. Do any wandering, eating, or last minute shopping before customs. The customs allotment is $1200 in duty-free goods, per person, plus five liters of liquor.

TOURING TIPS: Unless you're a downright novice, avoid the island tour. You can drive around on your own with a rental car for a day, heading to the opposite end of the island for midday (to Frederiksted if you're in the Christiansted orbit, and to Christiansted if you are staying in the peaceful, less-touristed Frederiksted area) and see all there is to see. Two tour companies offering round-the-island excursions are the *St. Croix Safari Tour* (T 773–5922), leaving daily at 9:30, across from Government House in Christiansted and *Travellers' Tours* (T 773–3986). Most of the touring options have to do with the sea, with trips to Buck Island, a day sail, scuba and snorkel excursions, and perhaps a day trip to St. Thomas, soaring out of the Christiansted harbor in the belly of the sea plane.

Taxis have regulated rates, but ask before you get in as to what they are. **Rental cars** can be a good bet. During all but the busiest season (Christmas and February), shopping around can yield varying prices and conditions for car rentals. I've had good luck with *Budget Car Rentals* and *Olympic Car Rental*, at the Caravelle Hotel. The names you know *(Hertz, Avis, National,* and *Budget)* have booths at the airport as well as offices in Christiansted. Their rates are usually the highest, especially at their airport desks at peak season (winter) but they have specials. Inquire about discounts, available—sometimes—for airline employees, some businesses, and, it sometimes seems to me, for the color of your eyes! Many small hotels have their own routes for car rental, and if you're booking there, let them make arrangements. Your U.S. driving license is sufficient documentation for V.I. car rental.

Driving is on the *left,* a surprise in a U.S. area, but a relic from the early days when, presumably, carts and cattle followed the European system.

LODGING on St. Croix can be in the heart of Christiansted, surrounded by historic 18th-century Danish buildings, or along the coast, where most places focus on the shore. Christiansted lodgings are beachless, except for Hotel on the Cay, which has a tiny patch of sand. The boating center is at Christiansted, as are most of the restaurants. Frederiksted, at the southwestern "corner," is quiet, in spite of the fact that the rebuilt cruise ship pier is located at the town. Some properties scattered at the shoreline have beaches; most have seaviews, and a short walk to the nearest beach. The unwelcome visit of Hurricane Hugo, in September 1989, was followed by extensive rebuilding and redecorating, which means that most places are in good shape.

There's a 7.5% government tax on all rooms. Some hotels add a "fuel surcharge," which seems to me to be a way to extricate a little more money (since any well-run property should be able to figure the cost of fuel into the room charge). Tips for service are at your discretion at most places.

AUTHOR'S AWARDS

Buccaneer continues as my top choice for this island, because it's true to its traditions and respected history; and in Christiansted, my choice is *King Christian,* which bears the indomitable imprint of the enthusiastic Sperber clan.

ST. CROIX · · · 605

Information about places to stay is included under Hotels/Resorts, Housekeeping Holidays, The Inn Way, and Low-Cost Lodging. Stars are awarded within each category. (See page 11.)

HOTELS/RESORTS on St. Croix are personality places, built to take advantage of the landscape—and the beach areas. Although some hotels are clustered around a swimming pool and/or social center, none of the properties is high-rise, U. S. city style. Here are the properties with standard hotel services:

★★★★ **Buccaneer Hotel and Beach Club** • *on the shore, near Christiansted* • is one of very few Caribbean properties that continues to be nurtured by one family's ownership, as has been the case since the hotel opened in 1948. Miraculously open throughout the storm and in its aftermath, the property has been an estate since 1653 when Charles Martel, a Knight of Malta, built a hospice here. After years as a French Great House, the property became a sugar factory when the Danes took over; in 1733, Governor von Prock added the mill that stands on the hilltop today. According to family records, Shoy bought the property from von Prock as a cotton plantation. It later became a cattle ranch, which has been owned by the Armstrong family since 1922. In 1948, they opened the first 11 rooms for guests. The present owners, the Robert Armstrong family, are the 8th and 9th generations to live here.

Buildings have been added, in styles that maintain the plantation feeling and positioned to take advantage of the lawns sloping from the hilltop Great House to the shores' two beaches. A golf course now blankets portions of the grounds and there are watersports facilities at one of the beaches. Tennis courts are near the beach, and scuba lessons that start in the hilltop pool quickly move to the offshore reefs and Buck Island areas. Spa facilities and shops are near the hilltop pool; there's a boutique near *The Mermaid*, the patio American-fare restaurant at the watersports' beach. Hamburgers, hot dogs, and snacks are offered at the *Grotto* on neighboring Beauregard beach. The "best" restaurant is the air-conditioned *Brass Parrott*, which I find dreary. (I prefer the open-air terrace area.) Rooms range from those on the hilltop, in the main house, and in a band of linking units, to other buildings on the slope and a border of beachside units (my favorites) perched at the sea. If a country club setting is what you're after, this place offers it. Inquire about special sports, honeymoon, and other package plans, especially during summer months. *Resort hotel.*

Carambola Beach Resort • *on the north coast's Davis Bay* • was closed at press time, and up for sale. *The Caribbean Newsletter* (page 9) will have details. Opened in late 1987, Carambola rises at a favorite north coast, sea-smashed beach, on a portion of a 28-acre tract. The first view of the hotel, as you curve down the hill to the sea, is of a "pile" of red roofs, capping the several small buildings that make up the resort: the main building, with shops, restaurants, social areas, and pool, and several satellite buildings that hold the rooms.

★★★ **Cormorant Beach Club** • *on the beach, about 3 miles northwest of Christiansted* • puts you in beautiful surroundings, by the sea. The beachside location appeals to swimmers, who also have a choice of the pool. The alfresco dining and drinking area offers options for leisure time. Tastefully furnished bedrooms, with fluffy robes and other amenities, are a short walk from the reception building. Second floor's my preference; beach-level rooms require night-bolting, which means the air conditioner hums for cooling. The nearby neighborhood's not much, but the sea view and hotel surroundings are lovely. *Resort hotel.*

Divi St. Croix Beach Hotel and neighbor **Grapetree Bay Hotel** • *on the south shore near the east end* • have been closed since Hugo hit. The *Caribbean Newsletter* (page 9) will have further news, when warranted.

★ **Hotel on the Cay** • *on its own tiny island, in Christiansted harbor* • is a self-contained complex, with a wonderful view of Christiansted harbor. There's a small beach (for those who like to swim in the harbor), with colorful sailfish and a beachside restaurant. Tennis courts are to the left as you step off the hotel's small ferry boat (to the right as you come from your room). Overhead (literally) is the pool. The main dining room and bar are up the hill, on the site of the historic inn that Paul and Nora Gilles operated from the 1940s through the 1960s. Bedrooms are modern and airy, with good views from most, but the hotel is not for anyone who must count steps or who wants to hoot and holler after 1 a.m., when the last boat returns from town. (The first boat leaves for town about 6 a.m.) Check for package tours and other valueful offerings. *Hotel.*

St. Croix by the Sea Hotel • *on the shore, north of Christiansted* • has a venerable history, as one of the first hotels of the island's modern tourism. It opened in the early 1950s. After 40 years of ups and downs, including recent time as an all-inclusive property and the severe beating by Hugo, the hotel has reopened with new management. Seaview rooms have been refurbished and rebuilt where necessary, with ceiling fans and cable TV. The bar and cafe near the seaside pool is a popular gathering area. Although the "beach" still suffers from Hugo's visit, surroundings are sea-oriented and comfortable. The *Caribbean Newsletter* (page 9) will have comments, when the season's in full swing. *Hotel.*

HOUSEKEEPING HOLIDAYS on St. Croix are easy to arrange, with a cottage, house, or apartment base. Many homes are offered complete with maid and gardener. The condominium units come with maid service, groundskeepers, and on-the-spot managers in most cases. A few apartments are family-owned and operated, with fewer than a dozen units. The result, for those who want to cook their own meals, is a long list of possibilities.

Among the rental firms worth contacting are **Island Villas** (Caravelle Arcade, Christiansted, T 809+773-8821 or 800+658-7313, fax 809+773-8823) and **Pivar Real Estate,** 1112 King St. Christiansted, T 809+773-9617 or 800+537-6242, fax 809+778-8066.

Housekeeping in the U.S. Virgin Islands has the advantage of excellent supermarkets for shopping in a system similar to home. You may pay more for what you buy, but at least you can find plenty of food. It is not as easy, however, to find good local produce. The Cruzan market ladies still set up their stalls at the rebuilt marketplace off Company Street in Christiansted, where you can buy spices and homegrown fruits and vegetables. Otherwise, word of mouth will lead you to local sources for special items; the staples you can buy in the supermarkets at several modern shopping centers around the island.

You'll want to rent a car for mobility at most places.

Arawak Cottages • *north of Frederiksted* • are modest cottage-style places next to the great old house that is Sprat Hall. Guests here have the option of making a dinner reservation at the big house enjoyed by Sprat Hall guests. *Cottages.*

Carambola Villas • *on the vast grounds of the planned development* • are elegant, free-standing villas, built for private ownership but for rent in owners' absence (or to prospective owners). Check with Carambola Rentals (T 809+773–6887 or 800+323–7241) for details as to size, location, status, and charges.

★★ **Chenay Bay** • *east of Christiansted, on the north coast* • has a new look, with ownership by Richard and Vicki Locke. Several gray-washed cozy cottages are set up the hillside, rising from the shore-and-pool level, where there's also a social bar and snack-style restaurant. Tennis courts are nearby. Each cottage has basic furnishings, with bedroom/living area, private bathroom, and a small porch. Ideal when you're yearning for the simple, uncluttered life, this spot is peaceful, pleasant, and convenient to town and action—when you rent a car. Good for families—and for back-to-nature holidays, scuba, snorkeling, and boardsailing are popular. There is a small beach, but you have to walk out "miles" in knee-high seas to find water deep enough to really swim. *Cottages.*

★★★ **Club St. Croix** • *on the beach north of Christiansted* • is attractive, with condominiums for rent in owners' absence (or in hopes that you'll buy). Choices include 2-bedroom, 1-bedroom, and studio, all with modern kitchen facilities and most with a sea view. What's open for this season is the first part of an ambitious project that will eventually top 300 condos with restaurants, tennis courts, swimming pools, etc. *Apts.*

★★ **Gentle Winds** • *about a 15-minute drive northwest of Christiansted* • is a community of several apartment-filled buildings, shoreside on the north coast near Salt River where Columbus landed. Although Hugo made his mark, some units are back to normal. The units are a safe and convenient distance from any noises from the beachside pool, snack shack, and open-air dining pavilion near the reception area and small shop. Units come in 2- and 3-bedroom versions that divide into separate rooms, each with its own door to the outside and plenty of privacy. Tennis courts are a good distance from the shoreside buildings, near the entrance gates. *Apts.*

King Frederik • *in Frederiksted* • sits on the shore, off the east end of Frederiksted's waterfront drive (turn left at the big tree if you are coming into town from the airport or from Christiansted). Since the road is the only one you can take, the house-scattered area is the only confusing part. Guests can saunter into town in an easy (and hot) 10 minutes. The cluster of 16 efficiencies and 1-bedroom apartments stands in a couple of buildings, arranged so that every balcony has some privacy and most have sea view (if not soundproofing). The hotel is popular with a homosexual clientele. Your welcome gift (rum and fresh flowers) is geared to getting you started with "at home" living; the rest of the stocking-up is up to you. There's a long stretch of sand that can wash out with the sea, but it comes back at regular intervals. *Apts.*

Granada Del Mar • *near Christiansted* • is within a few miles of downtown Christiansted. A family of 4 can slide comfortably into one of the 10 2- and 3-bedroom units with kitchen. Check with Betty and Jack Green about latest news of places to eat when you're tired of cooking at home. (You'll want a car for mobility; pool and tennis court can provide daytime activity.) *Apts.*

Mill Harbour • *at Estate Golden Rock near Christiansted* • is a complex of condominiums for rent in owners' absence. Check for status.

Schooner Bay • *on a hillside at the fringe of Christiansted* • has many units on long-term rentals. The cheek-by-jowl arrangement of 2- and 3-bedroom apartments has a pool and Jacuzzi as focal points. Built with vacation living in mind, the units have full kitchen. The Gallows Bay shopping area, with restaurants, is at the foot of the hill. *Apts.*

Sugar Beach Club • *near Christiansted* • sits on the shore next to Mill Harbour (with which it shares a high wire fence and proximity to the play yard of the nearby housing development). About 10 minutes' drive from downtown Christiansted, the resort's 25 units include 2-bedroom, 2-bathroom units with complete housekeeping facilities (dishwasher, washer, and dryer with kitchen). Shaped like a question mark, with the pool at the scoop, the units have balconies with sea view and—although basic construction is typical Cruzan '70s—the elements are here for good value, self-sufficient holidays. The neighborhood (residential, with moderate income multi-story buildings) leaves a little to be desired.

★★ **The Waves** • *on the north coast* • shares a shoreline with Cane Bay Reef and puts guests in rooms that seem to hang over the sea. The 10 housekeeping units, in two 2-story blocks, are home for scuba divers and others. Bigger units have full kitchens; others have kitchenettes. New owners have put a lot of energy (and money) into this congenial small spot.

★★★★ **Villa Madeleine** • *at Teague Bay* • is a new (1990) group of beautiful villas around an attractive appointed main house that serves as reception area, restaurant, and lounge. Villas are elegant pool-studded and very comfortable. On a saddle of land, the complex allows for hilltop view of both north and south coasts. *Villas.*

THE INN WAY is Christiansted's style, with several personality places within walking distance of each other on the main and side streets of the Danish-Colonial area. There are also a few inns worth noting on the fringes of the island, away from town.

Anchor Inn • *in a cul de sac off King St., nudging Christiansted's waterfront* • is a tight cluster of rooms that puts guests in the heart of the town's activities. Opened in 1968 as the Old Quarter Hotel, the place became the Anchor Inn in 1974. The 30 bedrooms vary in shape and size, as they are angled to fit into a small patch of real estate. Air-conditioners are essential, especially for those rooms with "view" blocked by neighboring buildings. An on-premise restaurant, operated by a separate owner, is one of the town's most popular, especially if you can get a table on the sea view porch. *Small hotel.*

★ **Cane Bay Reef** • *on the shore, near the beach* • is modern apartments that are comfortable, light, and airy. Each has kitchen facilities. There's a small pool on premises; the beach is a reasonable stroll along the road. The building is a 2-story block at sea's edge. *Apts.*

★ **Caravelle** • *on the Christiansted waterfront* • is ideally located for in-town activity. Bedrooms are modern, viewful, and convenient. Top floor rooms have a vaulted ceiling that allows for overhead fans and additional light, making these rooms very pleasant, in my opinion. Within easy stroll of shops, the historical buildings, and the many in-town restaurants, the hotel's own *Banana Bay* is a cheery and pleasant place to dine. It's at the waterfront, which gives daytime diners plenty of yachts and watersports to watch.

★ **Club Comanche** • *in the heart of Christiansted* • has weathered many storms since its core was built in the mid-1700s and, after recent renovations, has a courtyard entrance, and several cozy rooms. Purported to have been a doctor's house in the 1700s, the inn was opened with 7 rooms in 1948 by Ted Dale and Guy Reynolds, two modern-Cruzan pioneers. Now owned by Dick Boehm, who piloted the Comanche restaurant to popularity, the rooms are an eclectic lot. *Inn.*

Holger Danske • *on Christiansted's King Cross St.* • is closed at press time. The *Caribbean Newsletter* (page 9) will have further information when warranted.

★★ **King Christian Hotel** • *on Christiansted's waterfront* • looks better than ever with the post-Hugo rebuilding. Friendship with the Sperbers, and now with others on the staff, is one reason I return, but this is a place where all guests are important. The original building dates to the Danish era although renovations prior to and since the Sperbers' arrival permanently altered all but the street-level arches. The 3-story building gives top-floor guests an ever-changing panorama of Christiansted harbor and Hotel on the Cay. The comfortable rooms have telephone and TV; new decor included white walls accented with fresh pastel fabrics and window shades. A small pool fills most of the back courtyard. The hotel has no restaurant but breakfast catering is done by the neighboring *Taste Place,* a popular island snack spot, and *Chart House* is next door for meals. Many restaurants are an easy stroll from here. Watersports are arranged through *Mile Mark Charters,* the thriving business of Miles and Mark, sons of Betty and Irwin Sperber. *Small hotel.*

★★ **Pink Fancy** • *on Christiansted's Prince St.* • survived Hugo with minimal damage. The original Pink Fancy was a favorite in the 1950s; Nan and Wendell Snider continue in that spirit, with friendly and helpful attention. A small pool is the gathering spot; the bar/reception desk is at one end. All rooms have kitchen facilities; each has its own personality. The 18th-century exteriors are intact (or rebuilt in that style) and painted white, with pink shutters and roofs; the interiors are modern and cozy. This pleasant inn is within easy walk of everything in Christiansted, but the neighborhood's not the greatest. *Inn.*

★ **Sprat Hall** • *north of Frederiksted* • is a special kind of place, as the Merwin family's homestead, turned inn, now operated by Judith and her husband. Bedrooms are furnished in home like fashion. Room #5 is huge, airy, typically West Indian, with a huge four-poster bed and minimal furnishings. Main rooms at Sprat Hall are furnished with mahogany tables and chairs in the dining room and other liveable furnishings. *Arawak Cottages* (see above) are on the grounds. *Inn.*

LOW-COST LODGING is a relative term for St. Croix, as it is for the others of the U.S. Virgin Islands. Since pricing is done on U.S. standards, you may not get as much for your money as you do on some of the other islands where Canadian, British, and West Indian travelers have encouraged a spate of very simple, reasonably priced places. Although places such as Anchor Inn, Club Comanche, Kings Alley, Sprat Hall, and Arawak Cottages, all mentioned above under ''Hotels'' or ''Housekeeping Holidays,'' would fall into the low-cost category on some islands insofar as their services, rooms, and facilities are concerned, on St. Croix they are not inexpensive. Here are a few places that are (or should be) low-cost lodgings:

Danish Manor • *on Christiansted's Company St.* • is favored by value-seeking vacationers who like a guest-house atmosphere. Rooms are small and tucked into spaces around a speck-sized courtyard. Fellow guests are often young, friendly, and sports oriented, giving this place a congenial atmosphere. Most rooms have TV; all the restaurants and action centers of Christiansted are within a few steps of the gate.*Three Dolphins* restaurant faces the street.

Frederiksted Hotel • *on 20 Strand St. in Frederiksted* • is at the east end of Frederiksted's waterfront. Although the best of the modern, motel-style rooms in this 3-story building has a sea view, the nearest beach is a hot walk to the other end of town. Rooms are air-conditioned, with 2 double beds and a kitchen area that has refrigerator and sink but no cooking unit. On-premises facilities include a speck of a pool, a cement slab for sunning on comfortable lounge chairs, and a poolside bar where breakfast is sometimes served, depending on house count.

The Moonraker Hotel • *on Queen's Cross Street in Christiansted* • has a convenient location, and simple rooms with no view. Air conditioning is essential. All rooms open onto a balcony-walkway overlooking a courtyard that could be very attractive (but isn't as of this writing). Several casual restaurants and lingering places are within a short walk. *Moonrakers* streetside restaurant is a popular gathering spot. Good for self-sufficient types who want a place in town.

Villa Morales • *just off the main road between Frederiksted and Christiansted, near the airport* • is a once-private single-story home with several simply furnished rooms. The Morales are known for their West Indian cooking. The bus runs along Centerline road, not far from the front door, if your budget doesn't include renting a car to get to beaches and anywhere else of note.

RESTAURANTS dot Christiansted and are scattered elsewhere on the island, with a few in Frederiksted. The list varies with each season. Ask on arrival for new nooks, but count on the following (and on parting with between $25 and $40 for a full meal at one of the better spots).

AUTHOR'S AWARD

Christiansted is a veritable market basket of dining depots. My favorite in recent samplings is *Kendricks*, where I found service, food, and presentation to be very special. Figure $40 per person for all the flourishes, although you can eat well for less.

A word to the wise before pulling up a chair to table: look and learn before you leap through the door. Ask to see the menu and look at what others are eating to see if the offering is what you want for *your* dinner. Reservations are essential if you want to eat at one of the top spots at 8 p.m. or later on Saturday nights, and at the other hours if there is a special place where you *know* you want to eat. Without reservations, you will find a table at one of the eateries at some time during the evening, but it may be very early or very late.

★ **Banana Bay** • *on the waterfront, at Caravelle Hotel* • has true island atmosphere with its menu of shrimp, swordfish, and assorted steaks. Breakfast is a special time to watch the harbor activity.

★★ **Chart House** • *at the harbor in Christiansted* • is a popular seaside dining spot that nests near King Christian's hotel. The best seats are along the waterfront with a captain's view of the charter-boat fleet that moors offshore, but all are in an enclosed area that has sea-breeze air-cooling (through windows). Food ranges from steak to lobster and around in that orbit, with a hearty salad bar.

★★★ **Comanche Restaurant** • *upstairs across the Strand from Club Comanche hotel* • is an island staple, with consistently good U.S. style fare. (Steak, veal, chicken, fish, best with special sauces.) The atmosphere benefits from a few wicker peacock chairs to supplement banquettes and straight-backed wooden ones. Overhead fans help the tradewinds around the open-but-covered deck. There's a bar to ring around while you wait for your table. Count on being cozy with your neighbor; tables are tightly knit with weaving waiters. Reservations are essential in winter season. Plan on parting with $40 per person, at least.

Dino's • *in an old house near the fort* • serves Italian offerings with casual style. A good place to go with friends—or to be among them.

★★★ **Kendrick's** • *on Queen's Cross, between King St. and the Strand* • specializes in island foods, attractively served in a pleasant setting. Ballast brick steps lead upstairs next to Cavanaghs' shops to a plant-filled area and a few small rooms where your meal is served. The setting is cozy and comfortable, and my sampling of the food was worth another visit. I like this place.

Tivoli • *upstairs at the Pan Am Pavilion* • has ferns and other foliage growing where patrons, tables and chairs are not. Plan in advance for the essential reservation for delicious dinners which can include scampi, lobster, and—strange though it seems—Hungarian goulash. Count on from $20 or more for the lobster; all main courses hover in that range.

★★ **Top Hat** • *Company St., near the Christiansted market* • is only open for winter months. The owners travel at other times. In 1966 Bent Rasmussen was one of 2 Danish chefs to participate in a cultural exchange with the once-Danish island of St. Croix. He stayed, and eventually opened Top Hat on the second floor of a traditional Cruzan house (stairs up the left side of the building). The place was expanded to include several rooms, with Bent *still* working over the hot stove and wife Hanne elegant as the overseer of the dining room. Ask her for the suggestion for the evening—it will be superb; and order wine to accompany whatever you've chosen. Figure on $45 per person, and relax secure in the knowledge that you're in the best restaurant on the island.

Sprat Hall's Beach Club • *on the west coast, north of Frederiksted* • offers the chance for a swim, a good beach, and filling but certainly not gourmet food at lunchtime. Specialties were grilled fish (a hearty hunk of some big catch), salads, and a lobster, or chowders. Bathing suit cover-up is acceptable lunchtime dress.

NATURAL SURROUNDINGS: Hurricane Hugo devastated St. Croix when it roared through in mid-September 1989. A tornado, spawned from the hurricane twisted homes and landscape across the mid-section of the island. But, as happens in this part of the world, nature heals all wounds. Although some of the big trees were reduced to rubble by Hugo's wrath, foliage once again flourishes. Flowers are blooming and smaller shrubs mask some of the damage. As far as natural surroundings are concerned, the rain forest in the northwest sector is worth visiting, but walking alone is not recommended. The best way to visit, other than driving along the paved (but pock-marked) road, is on horseback.

The eastern sector of St. Croix has very different flora from the rain forest in the west; it is almost desertlike, with cactus and other growth that thrives in dry climate. Although the south coast does not have many hotels, there are a few places where views are magnificent (most notably heading east, soon after passing the Divi hotel), but the shore has been ruined by the industry planted here in the 1960s. An area well known for bone-fishing was destroyed by the Hess and Harvey developments. The area's best site is Buck Island (see Places Worth Finding below), which *is* a natural site, although it is carefully controlled by the U.S. National Park Service—and often cluttered with sail and other tourist boats that reach it on daily excursions. If you're seeking nature at its pristine best, look to the non-American islands.

PLACES WORTH FINDING: If you have an interest in the Danish history of the Virgin Islands, track down a copy of *Three Towns,* subtitled *Conservation and Renewal of Charlotte Amalie, Christiansted, and Frederiksted of the U.S. Virgin Islands* at the Christiansted library. During the early 1960s a team from the Royal Danish Academy of Fine Arts in Copenhagen came to the Virgin Islands, following a visit by two of its members, to document the early history and town plans in hopes that present development would be carried out with some thought and concern for the original intentions of the Danish architects. The Rockefeller Foundation made a sizable contribution to the study, as did a number of Danish and other American interests. The National Park Service has copies of the study on file if you are unable to find one to purchase. Most of the research was conducted by a team of 25 teachers and promising young Danish architects who spent two months in the islands, beginning in May 1961. Subsequent shorter visits completed the survey, published in 1964.

 CHRISTIANSTED was established "on November 16, 1733 [when] the Directors of the Danish West India and Guinea Company sent instructions for the colonization of the newly purchased island of St. Croix [from the French] to Frederick Moth, who was to be the island's first governor. Moth was ordered to choose a suitable location for a fort and a town, which was to be called Christiansted [in honor of King Christian VI]. The town site was to be subdivided into regular building lots and the lots were to be sold with the stipulation that buyers were to build on their lots within five years from the date of purchase.

 "Moth explored the island between June 20–24, 1734, and chose the site of a former French village on the north-central shore of St. Croix as the site for Christiansted. Moth described the area as large enough to contain a town the size of Copenhagen and promised that Christiansted would be well laid out with streets as straight as those in Christiania, now Oslo, Norway. He also proposed that the best buildings should be built in the immediate vicinity of the fort, while the poorer class of buildings was to be located on the outskirts of town." It's easy to see that plan today, as you wander from the fort area, west on King Street to St. John's Episcopal Church. The report goes on to comment that the town had only 20 residents by 1742, probably "due to the fact that prices for building lots in town were considered relatively high in comparison with prices for plantations." By 1800 the town had 5284 inhabitants, which was close to its high point of 5806 in 1835, after which time the population declined, to rise again to the 5000 figure in the resurgence of the 1960s. Today there must be close to 6000 people packed into Christiansted, and many more when the tourism tide is running full. Spared the 19th-century fires that leveled Charlotte Amalie on St. Thomas, and Frederiksted on the northwest shore of St. Croix, Christiansted stands today almost as it looked in the late 1700s. The core of buildings around the fort are part of a National Park Service tract.

On the waterfront in Christiansted, at the **Scalehouse,** is the local office for the Virgin Islands Department of Tourism.

AUTHOR'S OBSERVATION

The Tourist Office staff ranges from helpful to lounging while they talk with friends, but even if no one says a word, there's a lot of printed information to pick up. If you persevere, the staff on duty can usually provide details. When in doubt, ask for "Walking Tour Guide," a blue and white folder that tells you most of what you need to know; *This Week in St. Croix,* the pink sheet which is nowhere near as fact-filled (or topical and accurate) as the St. Thomas yellow sheet, but is better than nothing (and free). You can find most of the worthwhile sights in Christiansted on your own.

The Scalehouse was the Customs House. The present building was constructed between 1855 and 1856 on the site of a former wooden house. It was completely restored (on the outside) and refurbished (on the inside) in early 1978. The scales on which imports were weighed for taxes stand in the entryway.

Fort Christiansvaern (National Park Service headquarters, Mon.–Sat. 8 a.m.–4 p.m.; guided tours start here at regular intervals), big, ochre-colored, and basking in the Caribbean sun, is impossible to miss. It was built of ballast bricks in the 18th century, with some additions (and the first of its countless coats of paint) in the 19th. There's not much inside in the way of furnishings, but there are tales to be told about the battles waged from its parapets, where you can now stand to look out over the Hotel on the Cay and the boats as they set sail for Buck Island or return at sunset.

The Danish Customs House, the most elegant Danish building on the waterfront, was the public library until books, use, and U.S. government funds made the new Florence Williams Public Library on King Street possible. Part of the first floor dates from 1751, but the rest of the building dates from the early 19th-century prosperity. Photographic displays join art for decor in upstairs rooms; the Park Service doles out information at the street-level entrance.

The Steeple building (museum open Mon.–Fri. 9 a.m.–4 p.m., Sat. 9 a.m.–noon; free) got a complete going-over in the mid-1960s and again after Hugo. It stands as tall now as it did when it was erected as the first Lutheran Church in 1753—well, not quite as tall. The steeple that gives it its present name was added, for the first time, in 1794. The building began falling into disrepair when the town's (and island's) financial base dissolved with the liberation of the slaves—and the problem with working the sugar plantations—in the 1840s. After years as a bakery, a storage area, and a building to be used for whatever need was next, the former church was a shambles. Providing the launching pad for your historical appreciation of St. Croix and the U.S. Virgin Islands became its purpose after complete renovation in 1964 (Fred Gjessing, architect; Herbert Olsen, historian). You can breeze through three centuries in less than 20 minutes, so simplistic are the billboards on which the National Park Service chooses to tell the tales. Pictures, costumed mannequins, and wall cabinets with a few relics make up the entire exhibition. Note the polished ballast brick underfoot—and if you come in after a rain, walk *carefully;* the footing can be perilous. Among the exhibits: Indians of St. Croix 1000 years ago; the King's Life Guard, testimony to 184 years of rule by Denmark, which you can see on the map, is 3500 miles away. The Danish West India and Guinea Company was granted the Royal Charter in 1671, at the time when there was a united Denmark and Norway. In one cabinet, I noted that "an 1853 customs record at Elsinore Castle shows that there was trade with the West Indies." Elsewhere you can note that "about 100 people from Denmark and Norway went to St. Thomas in 1672." In 1733, the Danes purchased St. Croix from France and the first colonists arrived on September 1, 1734. The Danish West Indies government divided St. Croix into 150-acre plantations and sold them, mostly to English settlers who came here from nearby islands. A map of 1754 shows the island with what looks like a piece of graph paper superimposed; that's how straight the early boundaries were between plantations that still carry names like Anna's Hope, Hannah's Rest, Wheel of Fortune, Two Williams, Judith's Fancy, Betsey's Jewel.

Government House (government offices; reception hall) is two private homes joined together sometime in the early 1830s. The most impressive part of the present Government House, the building facing King Street, is also the oldest. John William Schopen's home, built in 1747, was purchased by the Danish government in 1771 as a suitable Governor's residence. By the end of that century, the island's prosperity and the demands of the government required more space. Planter-merchant Adam Sobotker's dwelling at the corner of King Street and Queen's Cross Street was acquired in 1828 by Governor-General Peter von Scholten, the man who freed the slaves. The connecting link was built a few years later, as is obvious when you stand in the ill-kept garden area in the center of the U-shape of the present Government House complex. The most interesting (and most photographed) part of Government House is the welcoming staircase that leads up to the reception hall after you walk through the iron gates at King Street. The hall is used regularly for government functions, but visitors are allowed in at other times to look at the mirrors and chandeliers given in 1966 by the Danish government to replace the originals—which were returned to Denmark at the time of the transfer (1917). Although the jigs and quadrilles popular in the Danish days no longer provide the focus for a gala evening, there's plenty to recommend peeking in the windows if you are not invited to some government function. This room is spectacular when the lights are lit and reflected in the mirrors, with the festive folk attending.

AUTHOR'S OBSERVATION

Alexander Hamilton, who clerked in a Christiansted hardware store when he came up from his birthplace, Nevis, is claimed as a local boy made good. The fact is that Hamilton's hardware store is only a name and a plot of ground. The new and commercial building that stands on the site was rebuilt after a fire in the early 1960s and bears no resemblance to the store that Hamilton knew. Noting his presence here in boyhood years is about as much as any local historian can claim.

Florence Williams Library is big, boxy, modern, air-conditioned, and to my eye, very out of place in Colonial Christiansted. References made to the "Old Danish School" refer to a building that had stood since the 1800s, the home of a merchant who fell on hard times. The house was sold at auction on July 3, 1846, to the Royal Danish Treasury for Funds and Education. Modern "progress" tore the old and interesting building down in 1972 so the bigger-and-better library could be built. I mention today's building only for the historic volumes it holds (many of which were destroyed, along with other books, by Hurricane Hugo), and certainly not for the way it looks. The only old part of this building is the ballast bricks from the former structure.

Buck Island Reef is a National Monument, administered by the National Park Service, U.S. Department of the Interior, and a spectacular day excursion. A fleet of boats sets out from Christiansted daily for Buck Island.

The day is fun, both for neophytes and for underwater experts. Your personal prowess will make the decision about whether you tag along on a guided tour, flipper-to-flipper throughout the marked trail, or whether you and a pal head to the deep areas away from the commercial, relatively shallow marked trail. In all cases, strict National Park Service preservation rules apply: no plucking, picking, or pinching of fish, coral, or anything else you find.

AUTHOR'S OBSERVATION

The St. Croix Landmarks Society has open membership (single $20, family $30, sponsor $50, and on up). For details, contact the Society by mail (Box 242; Christiansted, St. Croix, VI 00820). St. George's Village Botanical Garden memberships for individuals are $10, associate $25, junior—under 18—$2.

Whim Greathouse (on Centerline Road, 2 miles E of Frederiksted; winter daily 10 a.m.–5 p.m.; summer Tues.–Sun. 10 a.m.–5 p.m., Sun. 2–5 p.m.; $3 adult, children $1, under 12 free; small shop on premises). A marvel, if you know what this place looked like when a group of concerned citizens took an interest in it in the early 1960s. Under the aegis of Walter and Florence Lewisohn, part-time Cruzan residents with a full-time interest in preservation of the island's history, the St. Croix Landmarks Society got more than itself off the ground. Whim Greathouse restoration was the prime focus for the first years of the society, and all fund-raising, including that from sale of Florence Lewisohn's books and booklets (*The Romantic History of St. Croix* is one) and from the annual House Tours, was dedicated to furnishing the Greathouse and reviving the plantation buildings. You step into another century when you step out of your car for a tour of the house, small museum, working sugar mill, and grounds. The sketchy history of the man named Christopher MacEvoy gets embellished with each recounting. The presumed facts are these: MacEvoy built the house about 1794; the man was wealthy enough to move to England in 1811, to buy a refinery and castle in Denmark, and to return occasionally to St. Croix where legends about him and his assumed bachelorhood are prevalent. The 18th-century house is furnished with antiques from the period, many of them from Cruzan homes—some made on the island, copied from popular European styles of the era, and others imported to St. Croix from European centers. The building, with its three-foot-thick walls, might have been intended as the core of a bigger estate house, but the fact is that MacEvoy lived in what we can see—complete with a moat around its perimeter. Delores was my guide for one tour of the property. She is a Cruzan teenager, one of three daughters of a family who lives on the estate. Although she goes to school in Frederiksted she was my teacher for some of the lore: about the Exportware that fills cabinets in the first room (it came on the trading ships), about the 1830s sugarcane prints (they are from Antigua, where the process was different from that of St. Croix, but are interesting nevertheless), about the table setting in the dining room (Bing & Grondahl from Denmark), the rum in St. Croix today (molasses comes from Puerto Rico because cane is no longer cultivated on St. Croix), about the bedroom, with its mirrors, mahogany bed, wood floors, and open windows (the bed was Mrs. Limpricht's and she was the wife of a Danish Governor; the planter's chair is a modern reproduction; and the room reminded me of Room 5 at Sprat Hall up the coast past Frederiksted), and about the items in one of the corner cabinets—especially the Queen Margarethe cup. Margarethe (1347–1412) was Queen of the united Norway, Sweden, and Denmark. The cup has eight sides, one for each of the Queen's ladies and one for herself. There's a print of Danish Prince Valdemar's arrival on St. Croix in the late 1800s, and a print of Bernstorf, an estate in Denmark that looks like Whim. The museum's few open and airy rooms are filled with treasures and with memories of plantation life now gone.

Because there was no working mill in the U.S. islands, Walter Lewisohn and others involved in the Landmarks Society at the time trekked through the Caribbean in search of a representative one. A mill with sails was found in Nevis, transported block by numbered block to Whim Estate, and reconstructed on the grounds to show what the 115-plus mills that were on St. Croix in the sugar king days looked like.

The plantation museum shows the step-by-step process for sugar cane to rum, with appropriate caldrons, wheels, and a pot-still punctuating the illustrations that make the whole process very clear.

AUTHOR'S OBSERVATION

For an interesting island entertainment, check to see when art shows, concerts, and receptions will be held here. All are welcome to attend. Open House Tours are held in February and March, providing an opportunity to see several exceptional island homes, some restored mills and plantation houses, others new and built to make the most of spectacular views and plantings.

St. George Village Botanical Garden (Box 338, Frederiksted; on St. George Estate; open 7:30–3:30, free admission; inquire about the date for the monthly visitor luncheon and tour for $6). On the day when you rent a car, head for these gardens. The minute you turn right off Centerline Road, about 11 miles from Christiansted (or left about 4 miles from Frederiksted) and head through the stone gates, into the area defined for the gardens, you have a glimpse of just how rich the flora of this island can be. The surroundings are the perfect setting for occasional Sunday concerts (inquire about dates when you arrive on the island, or write ahead if it makes that much difference to you). Given to the Botanical Garden, Inc., in 1972, the estate is complete with meandering stream, great-house ruins, and a historic garden that includes cassava, corn, and sweet potatoes known to the earliest Arawak settlers as well as representative contributions made by later English, Dutch, French, Spanish, and Danish settlers. Bicentennial Memorial Trees are some of the newest plantings, but there's always room for more on this estate, tended mostly by volunteers. I guarantee that a few hours here will give you an entirely different impression of this rural island where approach to the town of Christiansted was through an avenue of stately royal palms as recently as 15 years ago. (In 1977 a furor was created when road-widening activities mowed down too many of the few remaining royal palms. Some survived, but today's emphasis seems to be more on speed than on saving.)

FREDERIKSTED, according to the Danish survey *Three Towns,* follows a plan submitted by Surveyor Jens M. Beck, who had also been involved in the Christiansted plans. His plans for this west-end town, which the Danish West India and Guinea Company ordered established on October 19, 1751, to be named in honor of Danish King Frederik V, had "two symmetrical parts separated by a lagoon and a proposed fort." Although customs duties were remitted to builders who established in Frederiksted, and work was started on the fort and warehouse that were supposed to make the location more appealing, there were only two houses in Frederiksted by 1755. Many of the buildings that had been built by the 1860s (when the population numbered about 3000) were washed away in the tidal wave of 1867 or wiped out by flames on October 1 and 2, 1878, when labor riots resulted in conflagrations that completely consumed many of the wood buildings. Frederiksted has never been the thriving commercial center that its sister-town to the northeast has been, although this town holds the favored harbor. Even today, when the deepwater pier juts into the sea off Frederiksted's waterfront, most of the cruise passengers that do land here head to Christiansted, in buses supplied by the local tour companies. Hurricane Hugo's damage to buildings and trees is still visible, although the worst ravages have been cleared away.

Victorian Frederiksted was built after the labor riots, and unless someone gets some local zoning into firm effect fast, many of the enchanting wood-fretwork buildings will be demolished or "refurbished" beyond recognition by an unimaginative Public Works department. That government department has already done its architectural damage to the fort area, where a prominent, modern, and—to my eye—ugly resting pavilion has been erected. Presumably, it is for cruise ship passengers, who have plodded along a hot cement pier to reach the town park. The only redeeming factor is that when you sit at this "pavilion," you can't see it.

Fort Frederik is to look at from the outside. Construction was started in 1752, but enthusiastic if unskilled restorations have all but covered the original attributes—except for the shape. The most recent sprucing up was bicentennial inspired, in 1976. Because this port was Danish in 1776, claims are made (but not supported as strongly as those of Sint Eustatius) that the first foreign salute to a fledgling U.S. flag was made here on St. Croix. The story is that an American brigantine was in this port for supplies at the time independence was declared. A hastily hand-sewn flag was hoisted when the British flag was hauled down, and the local population responded with cheers. This fort claims to be the location at which Governor-General Peter von Scholten read his "freedom for the slaves" proclamation on July 3, 1848.

Victoria House is far more interesting to look at than the fort. It is on Strand Street between Market and King streets, is privately owned and in very bad repair, but it is a remarkable example of just how elaborate Victorian fretwork could become. Some of the original house dates from 1803, but most was burned in the riots of 1878, and some fretwork and structural elements were damaged by Hugo.

Walking the streets of Frederiksted is the best way to see the town, pausing to note some of the remarkable wood buildings and blinking to overlook too many modern, commercial boxes that threaten to destroy the one thing this town has going for it. One of the worst examples of modern trends, in my opinion, is the Kentucky Fried depot that has painted an old arcaded walkway with the ubiquitous red and white stripes. Fortunately, it is on King Street, so it's not the first sight you see.

SPORTS on St. Croix: The surrounding seas provide the playground for most of the Cruzan sports. A stroll along the boardwalk of Christiansted yields a dozen or more alternatives for heading out, on, and under the Caribbean. **Sailing** is usually by the day, with Buck Island the goal. Boats are skippered and varied; whatever sails into port usually goes out on charter. *Annapolis Sailing School* (Box 3334, Anapolis, MD 21403; T 800+638-9192) operates in Christiansted, with headquarters at its own building at 31E Kings Cross Street. The firm specializes in lessons, with beginners learning on 24' Rainbows and other lessons on O'Day 37s and the Gulf Star 50, which is used for 5-, 7-, and 9-day cruises. Beginners stay at a Christiansted hotel for a land-based portion before heading out to sea for more practical lessons.

Mile Mark Watersports, the business of Miles and Mark Sperber, enterprising sons of indefatigeable Betty Sperber (owner of King Christian Hotel and spark behind most of the positive promotion for St. Croix), provides services to Buck Island and all watersports. What they don't have on their own businesslike roster, they will put together for interested guests, if it's humanly—and safely—possible.

Boardsailing (alias windsurfing) is popular at most beaches. *Tradewindsurfing Inc.* has its headquarters at Hotel on the Cay, in Christiansted harbor. The firm offers lessons, rental, package plans, and many other watersports features. *Mistral* has a fleet at Chenay Bay.

Sport fishing ($350 full and $225 half) is a feature of *Caribbean Sea Adventures,* now owned by Mile-Mark, but also look into the sport fishing offered through boats that moor at the waterfront.

AUTHOR'S OBSERVATION

Names and numbers change. Allow a day for researching to find the deal that's best for you. Wander along the wharf and talk to the boating people. There's a great variety in boats and skippers; prices are controlled by the National Park Service so should be standard.

Scuba around St. Croix has its devoted followers. *Skindiver* magazine, one of the divers' Bibles, detailed nine prime sites in one feature by Jim and Cathy Church. "The diving ranges from colorful, shallow reefs to plunging walls," they noted, before singling out King's Reef, on the western coast, with "a 45 degree drop-off where you can dive from about 40 to more than 100 feet. The slope is rich with corals, seafans and gorgonians. The marine life includes large French angels, eels, lobster and turtles."

Several hotels have special scuba package holidays, usually in summer. Among those to investigate are the Waves, Buccaneer Hotel, Hotel on the Cay, King Christian, Anchor Inn, and Sprat Hall.

Golf gets gold stars on St. Croix, where the golf facilities now called *Carambola* (formerly Fountain Valley; Box 337, Frederiksted, St. Croix, USVI 00840, T 809+778–0747) offers one of the best facilities in the Caribbean. The course was laid out by Robert Trent Jones over 10 years ago, to be part of Rockefeller plans. Greens fees grow from $50 for 18 holes, $30 for 9, plus carts and club rental. Inquire about 3- and 5-day packages that include cart, greens fees, club storage and cleaning, golf clinic, a cocktail and a cap! The course is in good shape. Pro and pro shop are on-premises, with golf carts and full equipment for rent (expensive). *Buccaneer Hotel's* 18-hole course is enjoyed by hotel guests and by others by reservation. Check at the pro shop for club rental, lessons, etc. Cost for non-guests is $25, plus $14 cart rental. *The Reef* has a 9-hole course and charges $12 for 9, $20 for 18.

Tennis is popular. Every patch that's big enough for a court or two is being plastered with one. The best bases for tennis enthusiasts (and places worth inquiring about special tennis weeks, especially in spring, summer, and fall) are the *Buccaneer Beach Hotel,* where courts are lighted for night play, *Gentle Winds, Chenay Bay,* and *Hotel on the Cay,* which has the courts nearest to Christiansted. Guests in downtown hotels can take the 5-minute boat ride for $1 round trip and pay extra for court time.

Horseback riding happens to be the love (and living) of Jill Hurd, who grew up at Frederiksted in the homestead (Sprat Hall) near the corral. She knows her trails and her horses well. An afternoon riding from *Jill's Equestrian Stable* (T 809+772-2880), on the grounds of the Merwin family estate and in the neighboring countryside will be time well spent. A punch ride goes through the rain forest and around old sugar mill ruins; Mt. Victory is a little longer when you include Rose Hill, but you can go only as far as Mt. Victory and back. Beginners should check on the lessons before heading out on the trails; jumpers can also take lessons.

TREASURES AND TRIFLES fill boutiques and stores in Christiansted, Frederiksted, and at U.S.–style shopping centers mid-island. Offerings are original and handcrafted in some cases.

AUTHOR'S OBSERVATION
Remember in the United States Virgin Islands you can purchase up to $1200 duty free, including five liters of liquor per person plus one liter of Virgin Islands spirits. Items made in the Virgin Islands can be brought back to the states in any amount; they are not dutiable. Check with U.S. customs for further details.

When you walk along Christiansted's King Street, the main (and one-way) road through town, be sure to look in every open doorway; some of them lead into alleys-turned-shopping arcade where you'll find several boutiques, each with its own specialty.

The **Gallows Bay** area, east of Christiansted, has a few attractive shops, including clothes and gifts. **Whim Greathouse Gift Shop** (at the Estate off Centerline Rd. near Frederiksted) has note cards, tote bags, door knockers, bags of raw sugar (locally known as Muscouada), pineapple-patterned porcelain, steel band records, and a fascinating collection of books and pamphlets about St. Croix and other islands. Ideal for one-stop quality shopping for a cause.

The **St. Croix Botanical Garden** also has a shop. Frederiksted shops are scattered around several alleys. It's best to call ahead to be sure when places are open if you are going to make the 16-mile, half-hour drive from Christiansted for something special.

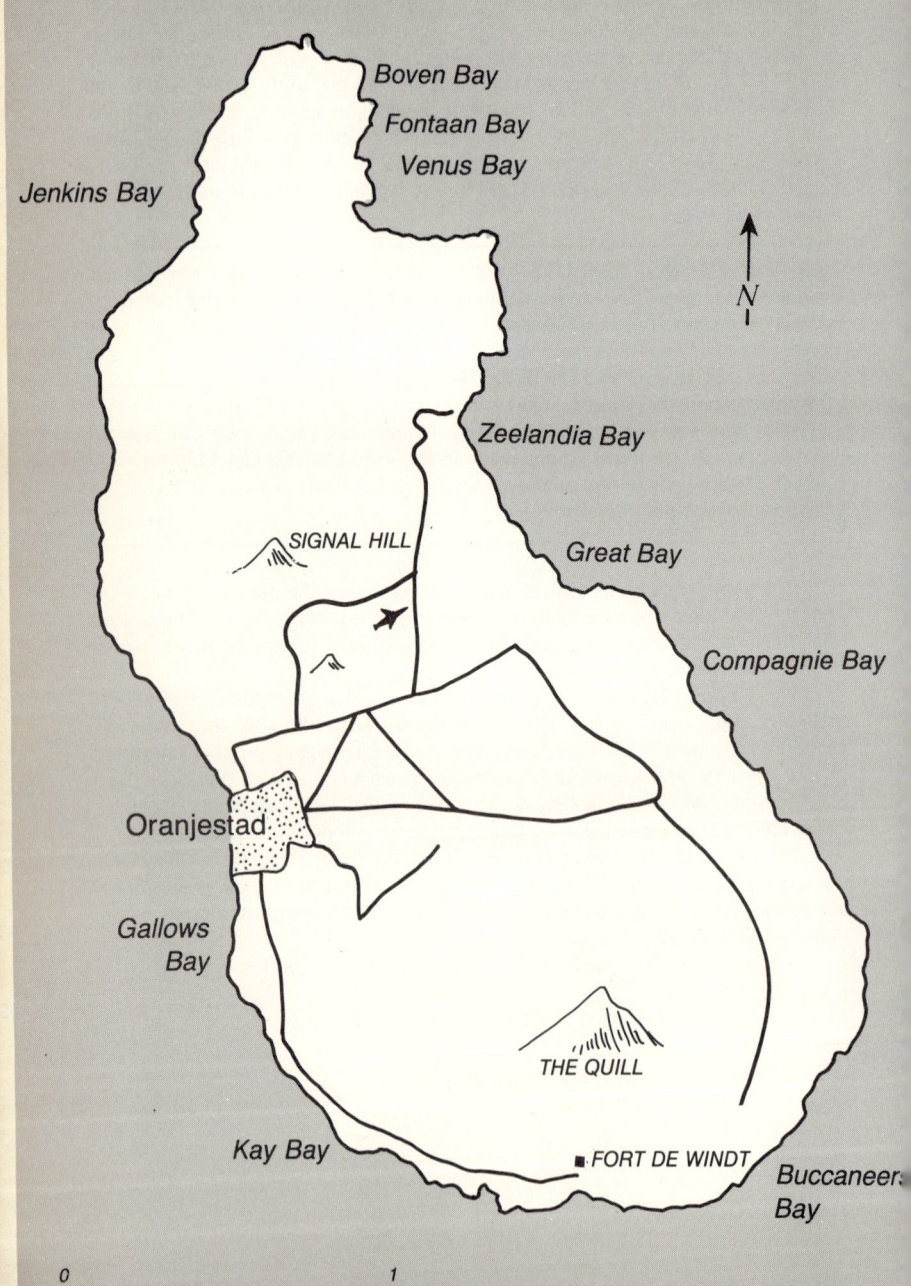

SINT EUSTATIUS

> Sint Eustatius Tourist Office, Fort Oranjestad 3, Sint Eustatius, N.A., T 011+599+38.24.33, fax 011+599+38.23.24; % Medhurst Assoc., 271 Main St., Northport, NY 11768, T 516+261-9600 or 800+344-4606; 243 Ellerslie Ave., Willowdale, Toronto, Ont., Canada M2N 1Y5, T 416+223-3501.

$ · · · US$1 = NAf1.77
Unless otherwise noted, all prices are in U.S. dollars.

When Christopher Glover perches on one of the 18th-century cannons at the ruins of Fort de Windt, he does it with a jaunty turn that hints of an adventuresome island past. Glover drives a taxi on Statia, as he has since 1971, more by happenstance than choice. In the 1920s, when he dreamed of leaving Antigua for a future in the United States, he hopped a boat to St. Kitts for Statia, where ships bound for U.S. ports stopped with greater frequency than at other islands. Love for a woman and opportunity for work conspired to keep him here, although most of his 11 children now live in the U.S., Canada, the Netherlands, and elsewhere in the world.

Glover's tales of Statia are sprinkled with 18th-century facts that tie this island to St. Kitts, a few miles off its southern shore, and with other nearby islands where British, French, and Dutch battled for holdings—and history.

On Statia in the 18th century, the Dutch had built a dike, behind which the good life thrived. In the years following Statia's official recognition of an American Brig-of-war, on November 16, 1776, Admiral Rodney punched a hole in it, and after he plundered what he could, the French followed, intermittently with the Spanish, the Dutch, the English—and so on for 22 changes in rule, which returned eventually to the Dutch.

Although there was some rebuilding after the Rodney episode, commerce and its contributors moved elsewhere. From the 1830s on, when freedom of slaves made plantation life impractical and the importance as a transshipment port for a rebel nation had passed, so also passed Statia's golden era. The once bustling Oranjestad harbor at water's edge began its final decline. Even in the 1900s, the pillaging continued. Stones from former mansions were sold to neighboring Saba in the 1940s, when that island began building its miraculous serpentine roads. Further sales of whatever had a market elsewhere helped the continued destruction of the Lower Town.

Pride in Statia is part of the island's spirit these days, even though the island seems the last on the list for economic favors doled out by the central government of the Netherlands Antilles based in Curacao. About two-thirds of the 1480 Statians now living on the island are without regular employment and most of those who work are employees of the government. Cash is in short supply, but friendly West Indian hospitality is not.

POLITICAL PICTURE changed slightly with elections held in April 1991, but visitors will notice little difference. In November 1985 Statia won the right to send its own elected Senator to the Staten that meets in Curacao for the government of the Netherlands Antilles. Special pleas have made some impression in recent years, but you'll still find the roads, electricity, and other infrastructure a little more rustic than on other islands—and a lot different from what you'll find on Sint Maarten.

ISLAND APPEARANCE: Still true to itself, Statia's 8 square miles seem virtually untouched after the cluttered commerce of Sint Maarten. Gray-to-butterscotch sand borders segments of the east-coast shore, with one running north from the Old Gin House hotel; yellower, coarse sand rims a section of the wind-battered western shore below Maison sur la Plage. The island's trademark is "The Quill," the volcanic cone that rises in the southern sector; the north landscape is harsh, with few to no roads and little of interest. Restorations of the 17th-century fort and some 18th-century buildings in the small cluster that is bluff-capping Oranjestad make the sleepy town interesting.

LIFESTYLE in Statia is uncluttered, simple, and relaxed. The handful of visitors who come here hasn't made a big dent in the lifestyle, although on the days when cruise ships stop by or when the windjammer anchors in the bay the town has added action. Those are days to go climb The Quill, in my opinion.

MEDICAL FACILITIES: Don't count on much on Statia. There is a small hospital on the outskirts of Oranjestad, but residents with serious problems are usually referred to Sint Maarten. Visitors may want to charter to fly to Puerto Rico or Sint Maarten (a 15-minute flight) to pick up a major airline for Miami.

MONEY MATTERS used to be conducted in blue beads in the earliest history. Now U.S. currency is the key, although the official currency is the Netherlands Antilles guilder or florin, noted as NAf or Afl, at 1.77 to US$1.

COMMUNICATIONS are reasonably easy, if the people you want to reach have access to a phone. From overseas, direct dial is with the 011 overseas code + 599 + 3 and a 4-digit number. Facsimile machines are used by businesses. On the island, it's almost easier to walk or ride to find the person than to try to phone other places on Statia. Overseas calls are easily accomplished through the helpful staff at *Landsradio,* the Dutch-motivated communications center, with offices in Oranjestad.

ARRIVAL at Sint Eustatius's airport usually involves a *Windward Islands Airways* or *LIAT* flight from Sint Maarten, unless you fly over in a charter plane. This airstrip, unlike some of the neighboring ones, is on flat land. The airport terminal is a small, breeze-swept building. Perfunctory immigration (since you are presumably coming from Sint Maarten where you've gone through the official clearance) includes a request to know when you are planning to leave. That's not an inhospitable gesture; often it's so that officials are sure there's a plane to carry you out.

AUTHOR'S OBSERVATION

The contrast between Sint Maarten's airport and tiny Statia might seem overwhelming for first-timers. *There is no departure tax* for visitors going from Sint Maarten to Statia, although the "departure tax" collectors will often request the $5 fee. Be sure to tell them you are going to Statia (which is also Dutch and part of the same territory); for immigration, you only need to show your boarding pass.

CRUISE ships occasionally anchor off the shore below hilltop Oranjestad, bringing passengers to shore in lighters. Four-masted schooners and small ships make this a port-of-call. Check with your travel agent for specific itineraries. Once ashore, climbing The Quill is the island's greatest challenge. Otherwise, a drive around might be interesting before a swim and a stroll through town.

DEPARTURE: Check-in for your return flight is informal. It's wise to look at the sky around plane arrival time. Sometimes flights arrive—and leave—early; you can still make the flight if you are in the town as long as you start for the airport when you spot your plane in the sky. There's a departure tax of $5, payable when you leave Sint Maarten for the U.S. or elsewhere.

TOURING TIPS: The 10-minute **taxi** ride into town will deposit you at Oranjestad, the heart of the matter, if you want to wander around on a day trip (or even if you're staying overnight). The new crop of taxi drivers, many of whom hover at the airport, are not above overcharging, so be sure you know the going rate for the ride you want. Figure $25 for a good tour of the island. When you leave for the airport on return, allow an hour or so for a grand circle tour, and you'll have seen the highlights. **By foot** is the best way to get around, not only from Oranjestad down to shoreside (for Old Gin House, its restaurant, and Golden Era), but also to climb "The Quill." Be sure to buy the *St. Eustatius Guide* for its "Nature Treks" and information.

LODGING on Statia is limited to a trio of inns, each with its own personality, and a ragtag lot of apartments and rooms for rent. Although some of the apartments have been built in recent years, few show much imagination as far as style and decorating are concerned. You can count on basic comforts. There is no big hotel on Statia.

Information about places to stay is included under the Inn Way, Housekeeping Holidays, and Low-Cost Lodging.

AUTHOR'S AWARD

The Old Gin House has atmosphere and charm, making it my favorite for this island.

THE INN WAY is the only way on Statia.

★ **Golden Era** • *on the shore at Lower Town, next to the Old Gin House* • is 2-story pinky-beige stucco building, with 20 rooms angled for sea views from the small balconies. Air-conditioners are often essential, since rooms have no cross ventilation. Boxy rooms have expected comforts (private bath; twin-beds). The seafront dining room specializes in West Indian cooking, although sandwiches and other American-style standards are also offered. Popular with scuba divers and others for whom costs count, this small hotel has the basics. *Small hotel.*

★ **Maison sur la Plage** • *at Zeelandia, on an east-coast hillside* • has a French personality, as its name suggests. Owner Michelle Grecca sets the tone, with the help of chef Pierre Arragon who sets (and prepares) the menu. Considered a lunchtime favorite for daytrippers drawn by easy airport access (in about 5 minutes' drive), the restaurant warrants dinner reservations if you've planned a longer island stay. Rooms in several single-story buildings in a band near the pool are furnished with the basics. The windswept (Atlantic) beach is long and often surf-bashed; competent boardsailors may be drawn to these seas, but a stroll along the beach is far more appealing to most. The social area around the pool is dotted with tropical plants, and homey touches soften the atmosphere of the main building where meals are served on the porch and in the dining room. This can be an o.k. nest for self-sufficient folks who prefer a sea and surf to the convenience of walking in town. *Small hotel.*

★★★ **The Old Gin House** • *on the shore, down the hill from Oranjestad* • set the style for Statia's tourism, with decor and dining intertwined with the personalities of owner John May and his partner, the late Martin Scofield. The few seaside rooms in the original Old Gin House, which takes its name from a cotton gin on the property, are my favorites, with overhead fans, small balconies, and tasteful decor. Other rooms are in the newer 2-story building on the inland side of the narrow shore-rimming road, with the pool and Mooshay Bay evening dining room. Resurrected from and created amid the ruins of an old cotton gin in 1976, the dining room is punctuated with Dutch pewter, antiques, a few of Martin's paintings, and other touches that hark back to the 18th century when Statia was in its heyday. Candlelight and murmurs from the fountain in the nearby pool add elegant touches to the evening meal. Breakfasts and mid-day meals are served at the original seaside bar and restaurant. Daytime activities focus on walks, hikes, scuba diving—or reading and relaxing; nightlife is as lively as the other guests. Guests can enjoy jogging or strolling along the gray sand beach that stretches off on one side of the property and is bordered by sea-battered ruins of an 18th-century prosperity. It's an easy climb up the old road to Upper Town (the commercial hub, such as it is, of Oranjestad). *Inn.*

HOUSEKEEPING HOLIDAYS are possible in houses built for that purpose as well as in a few traditional homes for rent in owner's absence. The Tourist Office is one source for individual home rentals.

Alvin Courtar Apartments • *near the airport* • are upstairs, in a cement-block building. The sparsely furnished units might appeal to cost-conscious scuba divers, who will need transportation to get to the beach, about 10 minutes by car from here.

Cherry Tree Villa • *in Oranjestad* • is a 2-bedroom villa with modern comforts that include an open-to-breezes hot tub. Used in conjunction with scuba-diving holidays, the villa is available for individual rental as well.

Lens Apartment • *in the Cherry Tree area* • is a reasonably modern, modestly furnished apartment operated by Mrs. Hilda Lens.

Sugar Hill Apartments • *inland, on the hillside* • are efficiency units owned by Rita Williams. Located in a residential area, a rental car is essential for any mobility.

Henriquez Apartments include a group near the airport, about 5 minutes' ride from town and shore, with a recently built block of nine 1-bedroom units and four 2-bedroom units and another cluster of two 3-bedroom units and two 2-bedroom units, with modern basic kitchen equipment. Rates are very reasonable on daily or longer basis.

LOW-COST LODGING: Low-cost lodgings include the apartments mentioned above as well as a few guesthouses around Oranjestad. It's best to find rooms when you arrive, so that you can look at accommodations yourself. Although most taxi drivers will know of places with rooms for rent, the tourist office can also help if you stop by the Oranjestad office or find anyone manning the airport booth. Two places to look at are **Daniel's Guest House**, with 2 bedrooms near town, and **Richardson's Guesthouse**, about 2 miles from the airport and a distance from town.

RESTAURANTS: Don't count on a lot of gourmet choices on Statia. Reservations are not required at most places, but are suggested for the hotels (so they have a head count). Don't expect to use your credit card; be prepared with cash. The best meals are dinner at the **Old Gin House** and lunch, so you can enjoy the view, at **Maison sur la Plage.** The small places in town serve mostly Americanized home recipes. Ice cream and homebaked bread are two big sellers. Kim Cheng's **Chinese Restaurant** on Prinses Weg is popular, as is the **Stone Oven,** a bar and a restaurant with West Indian–style food. **Talk of the**

Town has a coffee-shop style, and **L'Etoile** and **Statia Bar** serve whatever the cook feels like brewing.

NATURAL SURROUNDINGS: "The Quill" can be a challenging climb for reasonably fit vacationers interested in flora and fauna. Although an occasional iguana can be spotted, it's birds that are most interesting on the verdant flanks of the volcanic cone, which reaches to about 2000 feet, and elsewhere on the otherwise quite flat island. Some of the best places for birding are along the south coast (where there's a spectacular view toward St. Kitts, even when few birds can be spotted). Insofar as surrounding seas are concerned, the few divers that have found this island seem intrigued by the sharp drop-off, to almost 1000 feet, offshore below The Quill on the south coast. The White Wall is another sharp drop-off that has lured divers. There are several shipwrecks, only seven of which can be reasonably charted, off the shore below the present town of Oranjestad, not far from the Old Gin House. The greatest concentration of wreckage is known as *The Supermarket*. (The town, as noted elsewhere in the chapter, is where Admiral Rodney ordered the plunder and sacking of ships in the harbor as well as the entire once thriving community, in the late 1700s.)

PLACES WORTH FINDING on Statia: "The town consists of one street, a mile long, but very narrow and disagreeable, as everyone smokes tobacco and the whiffs are constantly blown in your face.

"But never did I meet with such variety; here was a merchant vending his goods in Dutch, another in French, a third in Spanish, etc., etc. They all wear the habit of their country and the diversity is really amusing . . . From one end of the town to the other is a continuous mart, where goods of the most different uses and qualities are displayed before the shop doors.

"Here hang rich embroideries, painted silks, flowered muslins, with all the manufacturers of the Indies. Next stall contains the most exquisite silver plate, the most beautiful indeed I ever saw. . . . ."

Statia's Oranjestad? Yes. Today? Definitely not! The notes are those of an English lady of the 1700s, from her *Journal of a Lady of Quality*. You can find copies of the pertinent section of the journal in the new and well-stocked library in Oranjestad's Upper Town.

Today, the fort, churches, and a few shops are in Upper Town (also known as Oranjestad), some 300 feet (90 meters) up a sheer bluff-face from the sea, safely over the hill from boat-based marauders. Even with the utmost effort, your sightseeing will be limited to a saunter around Fort Oranje—now the seat of the local government and the heart of town gossip at mail time, which is midmorning at the Post Office, and a visit to the recently restored (and rebuilt) **Doncker-De Graff House,** home for a collection of artifacts and memorabilia from Statia's past assembled and maintained by the Sint Eustatius Historical Foundation. Opened officially in early September 1985, the house has been restored to recall the 1700s, when Oranjestad was a bustling city. Simon Doncker was a wealthy local merchant whose impressive home stood as testimony to the affluence of the era and the elegance of the island's life. Johannes de Graff, commander of Sint Eustatius, acquired the property in April 1776. De Graff is best known these days as the commander who responded, that following November, to the arrival and 13-gun salute of the American brigantine *Andrew Doria*. Links between Statia and the United States during the fight for independence were strong, and were rewarded by the wrath, blockades, and pillaging of British Admiral George Bridges Rodney. That series of acts would reduce prosperous Statia to ruins from which she would never return. At the house the high ceilings, louvered shutters, and yellow ballast-brick walls have all been restored or reconstructed. The parlor and bedroom are furnished as they might have been in that era, and an 18th-century as well as a West Indian garden mark the grounds around the house. The house is reason enough to come to Statia for at least a day. Contributions for the maintenance of the house and its museum collections are gratefully received and can be given or sent to the **Sint Eustatius Historical Foundation** (Box 171, Sint Eustatius, Netherlands Antilles).

If you are interested in archaeology and early Caribbean history there are special exhibits devoted to those subjects. Check with the local Tourist Office or with the Historical Foundation near the pier in Lower Town about any interesting digs that may be under way during the time of your visit. Some relics dated to I,-HA.d.H,-I 300 have been unearthed in the midsection of the island, and, although too much material was tragically bulldozed into the sea to make way for the pier, there are probably many more early items to be unearthed. The rich history of this island, where society thrived in the 18th century, lies under its surface. Among the most interesting 18th-century ruins are those of the synagogue built in 1738 and recently excavated.

SPORTS on Statia are limited, but **scuba diving** is offered by *Dive Statia*, on the bay, next to the Old Gin House. Mike and Judy Brown operate dive plans with most of the guesthouses and apartments. Mazinga's shop also has some equipment for rent, but experienced divers will want to bring their own.

You can **snorkel** among the ruins of the Lower Town; the parts that have slid into the sea can be clearly noted from the fort ramparts on a day when the sea is calm. Then there's the experience of **climbing** Mount Mazinga and of going down into "The Quill," which is the core of the dormant volcano. This is the high point of the island, rich with verdant growth and an impressive herd of land crabs that are hunted at night by flashlight and end up on table, in stews and other local dishes.

Beaches can give you Atlantic surf, or Caribbean calm—and plenty of silver-gray, "black" sand where yours will be the only footprints. You'll share the roads with Statians and a few donkeys, which had been the local transportation for most people.

Don't count on golf or tennis.

TREASURES AND TRIFLES on Statia are limited. The blue beads discovered a few years ago are hard to find today, but if you take the time to find some of the local folk interested in historic digs, you may share with them the glee of finding *real* treasure. The rubble of the town blasted into the sea has still not been sifted as it should be, and someone on the spot might be able to send you to some areas where other settlements are known to have existed.

There's not much in the way of interesting shopping for offshore residents' tastes, but the March '87 opening of **Hole In The Wall,** near the Roman Catholic church in Oranjestad, holds some promise. Its selection includes island-designed fabrics by the yard, as well as island-fashioned resortwear, and other attractive handwork. Another shop worth a visit is **Surfside,** next to the Old Gin House at the shore, where a few books and postcards join resortwear, straw hats, and other items for sale. The **Handcraft Shop,** at the hilltop's edge with a lovely view out to sea, also has a few interesting items, mostly of wood or straw, and **Mazinga's,** which was the only store for many years, includes a "drugstore"-style assortment of goods presumably of interest to residents as well as, perhaps, to some visitors.

ST. JOHN

> St. John Visitor's Bureau Information Center, Box 200, Cruz Bay, St. John, VI 00830, T 809+776–6450, fax St. Thomas 809+774–4390; Virgin Islands Government Tourist Office, 3460 Wilshire Blvd., Los Angeles, CA 90010, T 213+739–0138; #500, 900 17 St., NW, Washington, DC 20006, T 202+293–3707; #907, 2655 Le Jeune Rd., Coral Gables, FL 33134, T 305+442–7200; #1420, 235 Peachtree Center, Gaslight Tower, Atlanta, GA 30303, T 404+688–0906; #1270, 122 S. Michigan Ave., Chicago, IL 60603, T 312+461–0180; 1270 Avenue of the Americas, New York, NY 10020, T 212+582–4520, fax 212+581–3405; 2 Cinnamon Row, Plantation Wharf, York Pl., London SW11 3TW, England, T 01+978–5262.

$ · · · U.S. currency is used.

The ferry waits, straining at its lines secured to the Red Hook pier. Those who board carry the trappings for their day: bathing suits stuffed into easy-to-carry bags for the day-trippers; suitcases filled for the resort life; shopping bags from a St. Thomian supermarket for the residents; and hotel plans, tightly rolled to be unfurled on the beach where building is under way.

Within moments, the ferry pulls from the pier—leaving the bustle of St. Thomas for the smaller and quieter island of St. John. The ride takes only 20 minutes, but the sea separates lifestyles.

The panorama is ever changing, as sun and clouds cast shadows over the boat-flecked ocean. Seas known to Columbus, Sir Francis Drake, and others are now the yachtsman's playground as charter yachts carve their way from cove to cove around the several British and American Virgin Islands.

At Cruz Bay, the main town on St. John, friends and taxi drivers are waiting, clogging the exit from the pier. Ferry boat arrivals are the big event of the day, rivaling the mail delivery at the post office. The first hints of a tourism invasion are having an effect on this once remote island, but to those who see it for the first time, it still seems quiet and natural.

St. John had about 400 residents in the early 1950s when the island caught the eye (plus heart and wallet) of Laurance Rockefeller. Caneel Bay had a fishing camp, enjoyed by a handful of St. Thomians and some off-islanders who sold their property—held as the Rhode Island Charity Preserve—to Rockefeller

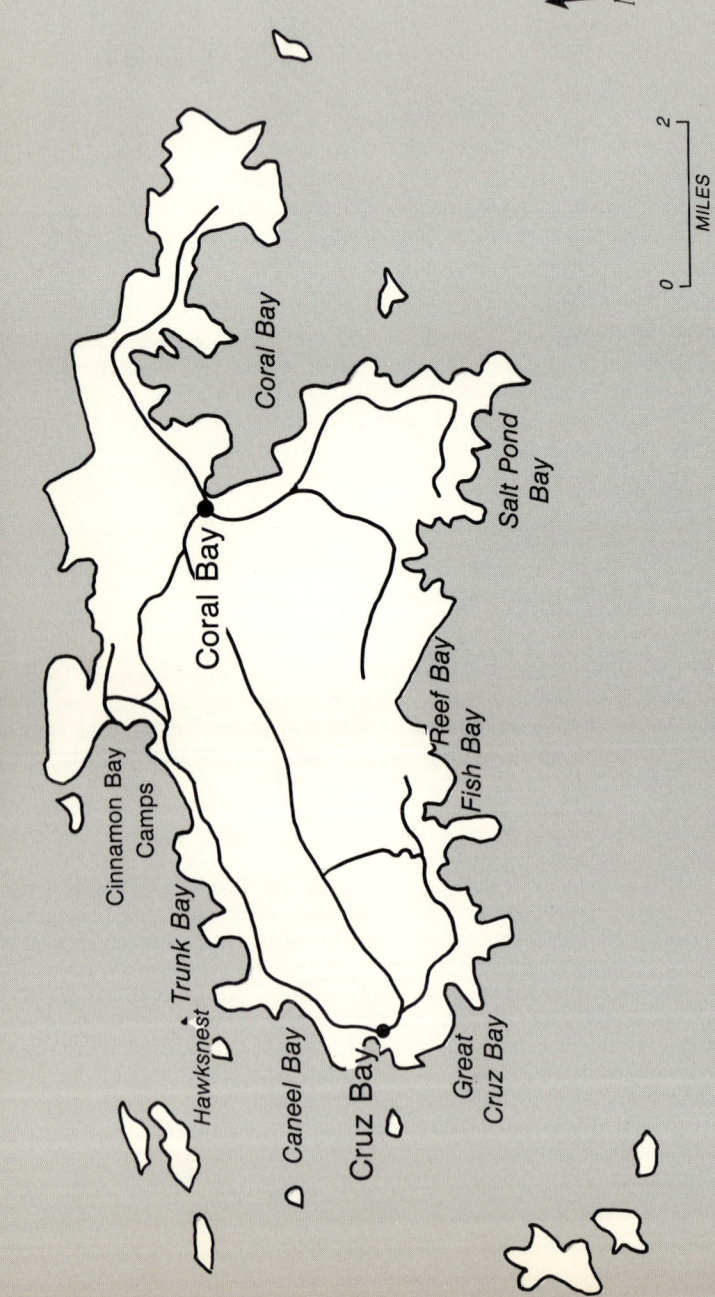

in 1952. The late George Simmons, Administrator of St. John for the better part of 20 years, told about an excursion of his boy days from St. Thomas to St. John. It took 24 hours and depended on the winds. Most people never made the trip. If you were born here, you stayed here. The island had no electricity until Rockefeller guaranteed that Caneel would use enough to make an underwater cable worth the investment. And even then, in the early days, lights only went on for a few hours at night.

The 20th century has come to St. John, in a flurry of small shops, cafes, and inns. Island businesses allow for expected 1990s comforts but this island is still out of the mainstream, preferring to leave the clutter of commerce to St. Thomas, its sister across the channel. Even with its new developments, St. John is an ideal place to step off the treadmill of "civilized" life.

POLITICAL PICTURE: The governor (see "Political Picture" for St. Thomas) appoints an administrator who lives at Cruz Bay, and oversees improvements for roads, water supply, electricity, schools, and hospitals. Although it is part of the United States Virgin Islands, governed through the capital at Charlotte Amalie on neighboring St. Thomas, until recent years St. John has quietly slept in the sun. Not so now! With the opening of the island's first new-and-big hotel a couple of years ago, tourism surged, clogging the main streets of small Cruz Bay most days, and especially when cruise ships are in port. As of this year, resorts and the few hotels "gather in their wagons" come nightfall.

ISLAND APPEARANCE: St. John is a picture-perfect island, with palm-flecked beach-rimmed shores where the sand is often the texture and color of talcum powder and verdant mountains wear colorful flowers and exotic greenery. It is also, since 1956, the site of the 29th National Park in the United States' system. Although larger than many expect (at 20 square miles, it is smaller than St. Thomas), St. John has only a few areas that are developed for tourism. Since almost two-thirds of the land is in the National Park, the only settlement of note is at Cruz Bay, which, even with the increased construction of the past few years, is still a small town.

LIFESTYLE has become more sophisticated in recent years, although it is still casual and calm when compared with St. Thomas. Now that Caneel Bay has been joined by the Hyatt, Cruz Bay shops and restaurants cater to upscale visitors as well as residents. The National Park and the campgrounds lend a note of natural simplicity while the remoteness of the south shore and places scattered around the island support the natural independence of most residents (and many visitors). Things are changing, but the island has not yet lost its "away-from-it-all" feeling. While dress code at the luxury resorts will be country club style, informality is the keynote for most of the island.

MEDICAL FACILITIES: There's only a small clinic at Cruz Bay. Medical problems require either on-the-spot treatment by a local doctor or a boat and taxi/ambulance ride to the hospital of St. Thomas. The only air service out of St. John (where there is no airport) has been by seaplane, which may not be expedient for emergencies (and is not operating at press time).

MONEY MATTERS are conducted in U.S. currency.

COMMUNICATION is easy by phone, if the people you want to reach have access to one. Direct dial to reach St. John is 809 + 776 + 4 digits. Facsimile machines are standard for businesses. Radio and TV are available.

ARRIVAL AND DEPARTURE are by boat, usually from and to Red Hook landing, St. Thomas, but also by ferry from the waterfront at Charlotte Amalie. The crossing from the east end of St. Thomas (Red Hook) operates hourly, and takes about 20 minutes (at $2 each way). The first trip leaves from Red Hook at about 6:30 a.m. weekdays (slightly later on weekends) and from Cruz Bay (to get to St. Thomas) at about 7 a.m. The last crossing from St. John is at 10 p.m. The 45-minute ferry ride from the waterfront at Charlotte Amalie to Cruz Bay costs $5. The public ferries go to the village of Cruz Bay, the island's main town. The Caneel Bay ferry goes, obviously, to Caneel Bay and is more luxurious (and more expensive at about $10 each way). Hyatt also operates its own ferry between the hotel and St. Thomas. If you're a nautical type, the best way to arrive at this island is under sail, easily arranged on a day excursion out of St. Thomas (several charter firms have day sails, with lunch provided at about $30 per person).

CRUISE ships stop off St. John's shores, but most service is on the small ships with an island home port. The main attractions are beaches and the National Park walks.

TOURING TIPS for St. John involve taxi or rental car, and you should be prepared for the fact that both survive on the day visitors and other tourists. **Taxi** drivers lounge around the park, just left as you leave the ferry, and may move when you approach. Be sure to ask the rate before you get into a car, and expect the rate to be higher than what you've been quoted for similar distances on St. Thomas. Be ready to negotiate, after you have been told the fare. You *may* be able to get a better price.

Best values usually come with a seat-in-car arrangement with one of the jitneys that operate on day tours. Those drivers are also near the park, if they are not hustling as you arrive in Cruz Bay.

The National Park Service, about 5 minutes' walk to the left after you get off the ferry at Cruz Bay, is your source for lectures, guided walks, and suggested hiking routes. There are booklets as well as helpful staff to answer questions. One 5-hour hike offered three times weekly starts at Centerline Road and leads past an old sugar mill to Reef Bay, with a boat return to Cruz Bay. There are also snorkel trips and historic tours as well as posted trails you can follow on your own.

Car rentals are available through almost every entrepreneur in Cruz Bay! *Hill's Rental and Taxi* (T 776–7947), *Varlack's Car Rental* (T 776–6695), *Spencer's Jeep Rental* (T 776–6628), and *Roosevelt Jeep* (T 775–3708) are some of the several places. (The last two share a small shack-office near the post office.) There are also scooters and Hondas for rent. *Cruz Bay Scooter* is one firm with motor bikes from $5 to $10 per hour or $22 to $36 per day.

AUTHOR'S OBSERVATION

Car rental firms were charging more than those on St. Thomas when I visited. The going rate was about $45 per day, but that fee is negotiable, if you have enough time to bargain.

LODGING choices range from the established Caribbean-style luxury of Caneel Bay and the recently built Hyatt operation to an assortment of small spots that charge more than warranted because the demand for rooms is great. Both of the camping facilities—Cinnamon Bay and Maho Bay—offer well-maintained natural surroundings, and several of the recently built apartment-condominiums have all the comforts of home. Most of the places to stay are in and around Cruz Bay; only a few are scattered elsewhere.

All hotel bills carry a 7% government tax; most leave the amount of tip to your discretion.

AUTHOR'S AWARDS

Caneel Bay is the best there is, for style, landscaping, and the several beaches; *Maho Bay Camps* makes the most of natural surroundings, with basic comforts assured; *Gallows Point* is my favorite for the independence of viewful housekeeping within an easy stroll of town.

Information about places to stay is included under Hotels/Resorts, Housekeeping Holidays, The Inn Way, and Low-Cost Lodgings. Stars are awarded within each category. (See page 11.)

HOTELS/RESORTS are two, one recently gathered into the Hyatt family and the other maintaining a style set when Laurence Rockefeller first opened it, almost forty years ago.

★★★★★ **Caneel Bay** • *claiming a beach-embroidered peninsula surrounded by the National Park* • is a beautiful, 170-acre estate. Coral stone buildings are tucked unobtrusively into the natural surroundings with a sense of calm over all. Although the main reception and dining area is not far from the dock, most bedrooms are in other buildings scattered around the grounds within easy stroll, and sometimes right on, one of the several white-sand beaches. There are 7 tennis courts (as well as hammocks) on the grounds; golfers can enjoy a "Golf Day" by taking the ferry across to St. Thomas to play the course at Mahogany Run. Watersports are easily arranged at the beach near the main house; fishing, sailing, and boardsailing are all available. Evening entertainment ranges from island music for dancing to special buffets, but all is finished by 10 p.m. or so; quiet conversations are the only social activity around the midnight hours.

Caneel Bay Plantation opened in December 1956 on a beach-lined cove that had been a small and private fishing camp. It was the creation of Laurance Rockefeller and the management company was Rockefeller's Rockresorts. (The name is now owned by others, with a more commercial goal.) The first rooms were the beachside accommodations, still standing and several times refurbished, nearest the reception and dining pavilion. Rockefeller interests' gradually purchased almost 5000 acres, eventually presenting most of that acreage to the U.S. government to be the 29th National Park. The resort has expanded and remodeled through the years to include the once-private Turtle Bay Estate House (formerly owned by the Oppenheimers), plus rooms on Scotts Beach, Hawksnest Beach, and other areas, discretely hidden around the grounds. The emphasis on privacy (and luxury) appeals to the world's famous, who filter in here during the height of winter season. For low-key luxury on a tropical island paradise, this place has few rivals. Inquire about package rates that include a vacation split between Caneel and its British Virgin sister, Little Dix, as well as about combination yacht and land vacations. *Classic resort.*

★★★★ **Hyatt Virgin Grand Beach Hotel** • *at Great Cruz Bay* • opened for winter '87, exactly 30 years after luxury leader Caneel Bay; it burst into full bloom for 1988 and was adopted into the Hyatt family in early 1990. I knew this cove when it was a quiet sailboat anchorage and was stunned by the first development. Hyatt's management can provide funds and expertise to make this property into a classy, active resort, with tennis, pool, beach, and a full roster of watersports. Planned by the architects responsible for Stouffer's Grand Beach Hotel on St. Thomas, the resort has clusters of room-filled units around the bay, with some also up the hillsides. Most of the rooms have been built to take advantage of the grounds-and-sea view. Brick paths link buildings; gardens and lawns need constant tending. The formal dining room is in the main reception area—in a building that looks like a Hollywoood stage set. Those closest to the beach are in the 1510–27 and 1610–27 blocks. The sand-lined cove is good for swimming and sunning; private patios or terraces provide a bedroom-connected sitting area. This place needs group and convention business to survive. Everyone must arrive via St. Thomas, which requires a relaxed mind-set. Great Cruz Bay, incidentally, is neighbor to, but not part of, Cruz Bay, where the island's main town is located. *Big resort.*

HOUSEKEEPING HOLIDAYS range from very simple studio apartments to lavish homes for rent in owners' absence. There are camping facilities at Cinnamon Bay in the National Park and at Maho Bay Camps on Maho Bay. You'll find local grocery stores with familiar items, but count on high prices as a result of the procedures involved with getting items here. The St. Thomas supermarkets have all the basics at slightly better prices, if you want to take the ferry over for a shopping spree.

Several firms on St. John handle rentals. Among those listing several homes are **Holiday Homes**, Box 40, St. John USVI 00830, T 809+776–6776, **Caribbean Villas & Resorts,** Box 458, St. John, USVI 00830, T 809+776–6152 or 338–0987.

Conrad and Gladys Sutton (T 809+776–6479) have a hillside house for rent.

Check for specifics about exactly what is included with your rental. Maid service is usually part of the deal, and beach gear is sometimes included, as is a rental car.

Battery Hill • *on a hillside overlooking Cruz Bay* • provides eight 2-bedroom apartments in a cluster completed by CDC in early 1987. Offering viewful, comfortable apartments, these units can be an ideal base for independent housekeeping. *Apts.*

Bethany Condominiums • *in the hills, about a 5-minute drive from Cruz Bay* • are 9 efficiency apartments with a beautiful view, a steady breeze, and the comfort of knowing that the on-premises *Upper Deck* restaurant serves meals some evenings. *Apts.*

Carla's Cottages • *at Estate Bethany* • capture a viewful spot on the hill overlooking Cruz Bay. Comfortable enough to be called "home" for as many as 6 compatible people, the cottages gather around a Jacuzzi pool and become a "club" when regular renters return in winter months. *Cottages.*

Cruz Views • *just off Centerline Road, within walking distance downhill to Cruz Bay* • gathers ten units—both 1-bedroom and 1-bedroom-plus-loft—beside a common swimming pool. Offering most of the comforts for Caribbean living within easy walk of town and beach, the units are managed by CDC. *Apts.*

★★★ **Gallows Point** • *on the southern arm of Cruz Bay* • is a collection of attractively furnished villas, each privately owned but for rent in owners' absence. All units have a sea view, with the best looking toward St. Thomas. (Those facing the Cruz Bay harbor have the clamor of the first morning ferry as well as the town's evening activities wafting in on the sea breeze.) Apartments have modern kitchens, comfortable bedrooms, and a spacious living area, which includes a porch or terrace, depending on the level. The C and D units have a loft bedroom; A and B, on the lower level, are smaller and less expensive. There's a small pool on premises and, although there's no beach here, you can walk down steps into the sea for snorkeling and swimming. You're within walking distance of town and viewing distance of sailboats coming and going in the boat-flecked harbor. Guests in units 4, 5, and 6 are nearest the noise of the on-premise restaurant. Called *Ellington's,* it's named for mystery-writer Duke Ellington and his wife, Kay, who ran a legendary inn on this spot from 1948 to 1978. Under its present management, the place draws folks from St. Thomas for dinner, after which they catch the last ferry home. *Villa apts.*

Gifft Hill • *with a hillside view, about 5 minutes' walk from Cruz Bay* • punctuates each villa with a private pool, and allows for island-flecked views through arched openings. Planned and managed by CDC, the villas are for rent in owners' absence. Tiled floors are ideal for easy housekeeping, bathrooms have garden showers and ceiling fans supplement air conditioning units in the bedrooms. These homes allow for luxury living on your own.

★★ **Lavender Hill Estates** • *on a hillside overlooking Cruz Bay* • is a cluster of a 1-bedroom suites, built as condominiums and available for rent in owners' absence. On 4 levels, slanting up the hillside, the units are in two banks, with a small pool in the middle. Craig and Laurie Crandall are on the spot to assist with hospitality. It's an easy stroll down the hill and along the beach-fringed shoreline, to Cruz Bay. (You can also follow along the road, if you'd rather.) *Apts.*

★★ **Maho Bay Camp** • *on the hillside rising from Maho Bay* • is a gathering of rustic cottages, with fabric walls on a wood frame and basic furnishings that appeal to nature-loving folk. Every effort has been made by owner/originator Stanley Selengut and his team to keep the ecological balance secure. Boardwalks link the community, with water pipes and other essentials attached to the underside to avoid trench digging. Cottages are casually comfortable, with basics plus cooking arrangements. Toilets and showers claim their own building. There's a folksy atmosphere, respected by outdoor types and helped along by the on-the-spot managers and by fellow guests. All unite in appreciation of nature—and of spectacular surroundings of sea, beach, and carefully protected tropical growth. A series of special events—weeks that focus on folk music and tales, astronomy, ecology, chamber music—have filled recent summer seasons, with special prices for grandparents with children and others. Space is at a premium in winter months—and will soon be, also, in summer. Book early if this sounds like your Robinson Crusoe place. *Cottages.*

The Nut Tree • *near Frank Bay Beach* • has a few apartments, each with space for 4 people. There's a swimming pool on the premises and you're only a short walk from Cruz Bay town. For casual lodgings at a reasonable cost, this place can be comfortable. *Apts.*

Selene's • *up the hillside, overlooking Cruz Bay* • offers a half-dozen small apartments, built for tropical living. Each room is cooled by a ceiling fan, which pulls the breeze through louvered windows. The apartments are simply furnished, with double bed, living area with a couch that converts to another bed, a kitchen, and a bathroom. Four units have balconies. *Apts.*

Serendip Apartments • *on the hillside* • are away from the Cruz Bay action. They're comfortably (not lavishly) furnished. Rent a jeep for bouncing and weaving around island roads. (It may take you a couple of days to recover.) *Apts.*

Villa Bougainvillea • *overlooking Cruz Bay* • is a 2-story building with 2-bedroom apartments on the first and second floors. Air cooling is by ceiling fan, which copes well except on the hottest days. The second-floor apartment has the best view, which is a spectacular span of yacht-flecked sea and offshore islands. *Apts.*

THE INN WAY is possible on St. John at two small spots where wintertime prices are defined more by demand than by decorating. Several of the housekeeping places also have the warm hospitality usually associated with inns. Consider *Maho Bay, Gallows Paint,* and *Selene's,* to name three.

The Inn at Tamarind Court • *on the inland side of Cruz Bay village* • offers both bedrooms with shared bathroom and slightly spiffier lodgings where you have private bathroom and larger rooms, sometimes with cooking facilities. Complimentary breakfast is served in the entry courtyard. Be forwarned that, unless they've changed since I checked in (and immediately out again), the single rooms without private bathroom are cell-like, hot, and not worth the approximately $50 winter charge—even when breakfast is included. The atmosphere is friendly; the place is simple. *Inn.*

★ **Raintree Inn** • *in Cruz Bay, by the Catholic Church* • is a combination of efficiency apartments (3) and simple bedrooms, each with private bath. Convenience to all the restaurants, shops, and small-town life of Cruz Bay can be an added attraction, although the place is not as quiet as some of those out in the hills. Fun for the young-in-heart or in fact, rates are modest and the inn is convenient for anything in town. *Inn, apts.*

LOW-COST LODGING can be found at the National Park campgrounds as well as in simple inns and several of the places mentioned above for their housekeeping apartments. It's often possible to find a room when you arrive on St. John, by checking with the tourist office which is near the post office, around to the left from the ferry dock. **Virgin Island Bed & Breakfast** (T 809+779–4094) specializes in homestay holidays. **Bamboo Inn** is a Cruz Bay guest house better known for its food than for its rooms.

Cinnamon Bay Campgrounds • *on and near the beach* • was opened officially in 1964. Currently operated as a concession by Rockresorts (the company that operates Caneel Bay Plantation), the National Park campgrounds include forty 10′ x 14′ tents with camp cots, linens, ice chest, grill, picnic table, propane gas stove, and basic utensils, plus forty 15′ x 15′ cottages, with screen and cement block "walls," four narrow twin beds, and a housekeeping package that is similar to that provided for the tent sites. There are also some bare sites, for those who choose to travel with camping equipment. Reservations should be made well in advance, but they are accepted last minute by phone at (T 809+776–6330) when there are sites available. A deposit is required for tents and cottages. The commissary at the campgrounds stocks basic foodstuffs. It's near the cafeteria, information center, showers, and watersports center, where you can rent sailboards, Sunfish, snorkel and scuba gear. Park rangers lead guided walks around the island, discussing flora, fauna, and history. Beaches are, in a word, spectacular.

Cruz Inn • *within walking distance of the Cruz Bay dock* • is one of a few small spots that offer simple accommodations at a reasonable cost (for St. John). There are guest rooms as well as efficiency and 1- and 2-bedroom apartments in this cluster. Complimentary breakfast is included in your rate; the Bamboo Bar is the guests' gathering spot.

Sea Breeze Villas • *perched on a hillside* • with a wonderful view, give you independent housekeeping and free transportation to the beach. Although they are not lavish, the units are new and comfortable.

RESTAURANTS on St. John range from the special dining at some hotels to several small spots in and around Cruz Bay. Catering services and specialty restaurants thrive during the peak season winter months; since summer season is apt to be slower, some places close. For hotel dining, **Caneel Bay** serves buffets in addition to the a la carte meals at its restaurants, and the **Hyatt Virgin Grand** has an elegant dining room as well as poolside dining on special evenings and other events. Other places to consider are:

Cafe Roma • *in Cruz Bay* • has pizza and pastas, including lasagne and spaghetti with special sauces. Veal, chicken, fish, and shrimp are also offered.

Ellington's • *at Gallows Point* • a short walk out of Cruz Bay past the cemetery, serves seafood and other specialties in an attractive room overlooking the sea. Although the place is open for lunch, dinners are more interesting and the activity can be fun.

The Farm House • *in Cruz Bay* • occupies space formerly claimed by Franks. It's at Joe's Discount Liquor store. Offerings are not too exciting.

The Lime Inn • *at Cruz Bay's Lemon Tree shopping area* • allows for patio dining, with salads, soups, sandwiches, and quiche favorites for lunch and slightly more elaborate offerings at dinner hour. Wednesday night is usually "Shrimp Night." There's a band most Saturdays. A gathering spot and a cool-off place while waiting for friends, this place has a cafe atmosphere.

Mongoose Restaurant • *at Mongoose Junction shopping area, just beyond the National Park headquarters* • serves fish and local lobster on a wood deck at the back of the shops. Since the place is open for breakfast, lunch, and dinner, as well as for snacks at other times, the menu runs the gamut of expected American-style offerings, sometimes with European-style sauces and presentation.

Paradiso • *upstairs at Mongoose Junction* • is a relative newcomer with an atmosphere akin to sun-spots in the U.S. Count on steak, chicken, and pastas.

Pussers • *at Wharfside Village* • follows the publike pattern known to sailors and others who stop at Road Town or West End on Tortola, in the nearby British Virgins.

Redbeard's Saloon • *on the waterfront at Coral Bay* • has been a comfortably casual place where darts or pool help create a social center for town.

Sugar Mill • *on the grounds of Caneel Bay* • is more exotic for its setting than for its menu, which is American-style with hamburgers, etc.

The Upper Deck • *at Bethany Condominiums* • is open some evenings for dinner by candlelight on the deck. The place is up the hill in Cruz Bay, so the view at sunset can be spectacular.

NATURAL SURROUNDINGS: St. John is truly an American paradise for travelers who like the security of the U.S. National Park Service precincts, with well-tended walking and hiking paths and plenty of places to roam. The trails are well marked, and all represent reasonably easy hikes. As you might suspect, the areas nearest Cruz Bay, and heading north along that west coast, are the best marked and most traveled. Hurricane Hole, on the south coast of a finger of land that points west, is a favorite charterboat anchorage and Coral Harbour, the island's second village, is just now starting to expand, as people flee the increasing commerce of Cruz Bay. Although the hinterlands have been explored, they still seem almost virgin territory in some areas. Before you set out on any prowls, ask at the Virgin Islands' Government Tourism Office near the post office at Cruz Bay for the map folder about St. John. (Try writing to one of the U.S. offices if you want the map in advance.)

The National Park Service Visitors' Bureau, to the left as you get off the boat at Cruz Bay, sets the stage for what you can see. In typical "basic information" displays, the history of St. John stretches around an airy room, with special exhibits on flora and fauna. Ask about the guided tours, operated by park rangers when there is enough interest. (Check also at the Cinnamon Bay Campgrounds, if you are staying there.)

Coral Bay was the site of the original settlement, some say by the Arawaks in A.D. 200. This was the main town for the European settlers who had their plantations on St. John, under grant from the Danish government. You'll need a four-wheel-drive jeep to find Coral Bay Overlook, and the rest of the sights worth seeing—including Reef Bay Estate, a hiking goal, where the remains of one of the island's steam-operated sugar mills is almost buried in tropical growth. The Estate House, built around the 1830s, is closed, but the grounds are open for visitors who want to poke through an unattended area.

The most spectacular sights for St. John are underwater, for those who want to don snorkel gear to follow the underwater tags that mark the trail.

PLACES WORTH FINDING are mostly natural ones. There were never impressive buildings in the small towns of Cruz Bay and Coral Bay, but there are some interesting ruins scattered around the island. They include sugar mill towers, the ruins at **Fort Berg,** jutting into the harbor at Coral Bay, and other ruins at **Estate Catherineberg.** Probably the most impressive, and certainly the most accessible and best restored is **Estate Annaberg,** within the confines of the National Park. There are records of ownership that date to 1786, when Benjamin Lind, who spent most of his time at his estate on St. Thomas, was owner. Guides are sometimes available to take you around the grounds, pointing out the slave quarters, the site of the village, the windmill and a horsemill, as well as cisterns, an oven, and other remnants. Your imagination will be helped along by pictures showing the estate as it might have been in the 18th century. (Check with the National Park Service if you want to be sure to find a guide on the premises. Otherwise use the printed folder as your guide.)

Also worth noting is the **Moravian Church at Emmaus,** not far from Coral Bay. Built in the late 1700s, the chapel is one of the Caribbean's oldest in constant use. The Moravians were one of the Protestant sects that came into the West Indies, many in the late 18th century, to educate and care for the slaves. (The established colonists brought their church affiliations—mostly Catholic or Church of England—with them, but slaves were not usually permitted to participate in those services.)

SPORTS are mostly sea-centered on St. John. A prime seaside action hub is at the National Park service campsite, a favorite for boardsailing and snorkeling.

Scuba diving can be arranged through a quartet of firms, one at Caneel Bay, one at Coral Bay, and two in Cruz Bay. *Jim Travers Caneel Bay Diving* (Box 550, St. John 00830, T 809+776-6111) has two dive boats at Caneel, as well as some rental equipment. At Coral Bay, Estate Zootenval plans dive packages with David Bruer's *Coral Bay Watersports* (Box 569, St. John 00830, T 809+776-6857). The Cruz Bay firms are in town (*Cruz Bay Watersports,* Box 252, St. John 00830, T 809+776-6234) and at the Cinnamon Bay campgrounds (*St. John Watersports,* Box 70, Cruz Bay, St. John 00830, T 809+776-6256), and both have dive boats that take divers out to the offshore sites. Prime attractions include Carvel Rock, 2 miles north of Cruz Bay, and a drop off Congo Cay that sinks about 85 feet. Eagle Shoal is a good place off the south shore of St. John and Fishbowl Reef and Stevens Cay are other favorites. The wreck of the *Rhone,* a British steamer that went down off Salt Cay in the British Virgins in 1867, is a big attraction, not only for divers heading out from the British Virgin dive shops but also from St. John.

Sailing is part of the plan for Caneel Bay with special "Best of Both Worlds" vacations that allow for either 3 or 7 nights aboard a 40′ or 50′ Hinckley yacht. *St. John Watersports* in Cruz Bay is the source for this and other plans. Even if you aren't staying at Caneel Bay, aspiring sailors would be wise to check there to find out what yachts they have listed. Chances are that at all but peak times yachts available for charter will be glad to have "outsiders" aboard. If you can't find the yacht you want at a base at St. John, it may make sense to take an early-morning ferry to Red Hook to pick up a day sail out of that (St. Thomas) marina. See the "sailing" section for St. Thomas.

Deep-sea fishing can also be arranged through Caneel Bay. Check with their activities desk soon after arrival, even if you made your wants known when you booked at the hotel.

TREASURES AND TRIFLES on St. John run the gamut between elegant resort clothes and exceptional hand-crafted items to the ubiquitous T-shirt and shell jewelry. It's all here, sometimes in the same shop.

As a result of special customs regulations for U.S. possessions, visitors to the U.S. Virgin Islands can bring back up to $1200 worth of dutiable goods. Items made in the U.S. Virgin Islands are not dutiable, so most of what you buy from craftsmen on St. John can be brought back to the United States mainland in any amount. A flat 5% duty is charged on the first $1000 over your duty-free exemption. Check your home state for its restrictions on liquor import. The federal government allocation from U.S. possessions is five liters of liquor, which is considerably more than the general allowance of one liter.

Wharfside Village, to the right as you enter the harbor, is the newest shopping center. It has a couple of eating places, in addition to several shops and some offices.

Two other shopping hubs amid the potpourri of commerce in Cruz Bay are the crossroads in the center of town, near the Lutheran church, and Mongoose Junction, a couple of jogs to the left and about a 10-minute walk from the Cruz Bay dock.

Mongoose Junction is a cluster of small shops with a few exceptional artisans making and selling wares. The cluster has been popular enough to warrant a recent doubling in size. It's past the National Park Service station. Be sure to search out **Rudy and Irene Patton.** They design and work silver and gold jewelry; expensive but worth it. **Donald Schnell** ceramic studio usually has someone making pottery while you watch, and the craftsperson will make a special bowl or planter if you state your interests and give enough time. **The Canvas Factory** has all sorts of canvas totes for sailing, tennis, or other activities. This place is also a source for watersports activities. **Fabric Mill** makes wall hangings and other items from unusual (and attractive) fabrics and **The Clothing Studio** has filmy cotton clothes, many with hand-painted motifs by Linda Smith and others. *Mongoose Junction* restaurant has been mentioned under "Restaurants" above, but **Marcellino's Bakery,** at the entrance to the restaurant, is also a favorite snacking source—with ice cream, hot dogs, cookies, and other edibles.

In the center of town, across from the social welfare building, **Batik Caribe** sells fabric designs from the studio in St. Vincent. Yards of colorful fabric sometimes join smocks and shirts as a greeting by the doorway. **Stitches** is the place for T-shirts, Indian cotton dresses, and an assortment of shorts and shirts. It's wedged between the social welfare building and *The Back Door* snack spot.

The Lemon Tree, to your right (with the sea at your back), is a collection of a few shops, with *The Lime Inn* the area's main attraction. **Pink Papaya** has a delightful colleciton of Haitian and other colorful painted tinware, place mats, paintings, and assorted handicrafts.

Out on the island, **Caneel Bay Gift Shop** has chic clothes, mostly imports from the States, Mexico, and elsewhere in the Caribbean. Elegant resortwear is here in limited but colorful quantity at prices fitting for the island's most luxurious resort.

Two exceptional books about St. John are *St. John Backtime* ($14.95), compiled by Ruth Hull and Rafael Valls, with legends from the island's history, and *Impressions of a Happy Island* (about $40), written by West German industrialist Peter Ernst under his pseudonym Peter Buruba (using the name of his estate). The photographs are spectacular.

ST. KITTS

St. Kitts-Nevis Tourist Board, Box 132, Basseterre, St. Kitts, W.I., T 809+465−2620; 414 E. 75th St., New York, NY 10021, T 212+535−1234; 3166 S. River Rd., Des Plaines, IL 60018, T 708+699−7580 or 800+582−6208; #508, 11 Yorkville Ave., Toronto, Ontario, Canada M4W 1L3, T 416+921−7717; High Commission for Eastern Caribbean States, 10 Kensington Court, London W85SL England, T 01+937−9522

$ · · · US$1 = about EC$2.65.
Unless otherwise noted, $ refers to U.S. currency.

The silence that wrapped around us was broken only by bird calls and an occasional snap of bamboo. Shifting winds had added pressure from another side, and some of the older stands of bamboo were responding to the force. Overall, although winds rustled the tops of the trees that surrounded us, it was quiet at the floor of the tropical forest through which we walked.

The narrow path threaded up from where we left our jeep, along a vine-tethered valley to the waterfall. Long before turning the last link, sounds from the waterfall were clear. They added another tone to the rain forest symphony, while the sight of tall trees, lush vines, occasional orchids, and fans of ferns, added another sensation.

It takes 45 minutes to an hour to climb to the waterfall, and an equal amount of time to return part way and walk out another valley where stands of bamboo make a lacy archway. The hike up the volcano, which comes in view as you look toward northern peaks through parting trees, takes about 9 hours, with a picnic lunch on the crater's lip—at 2800 feet.

The history and the hinterlands of St. Kitts are far more impressive than its better known shores and beaches.

In 1623, Sir Thomas Warner stepped ashore with a small group of British settlers, which included his wife and a son who would later go to a new settlement in Antigua. They established Old Road, where a marker can sometimes be seen amid a tangle of brush and where the sea pounds against what's left of an old fort's walls. The island had been known to Spaniards, and then to the French, British, and Dutch, but no one had settled until the Warner group arrived. Not long afterward, when Sieur d'Esnambuc brought his crippled ships ashore to careen and repair, the Frenchman and his sailors stayed, and others from nearby French settlements followed. The split personality still known on

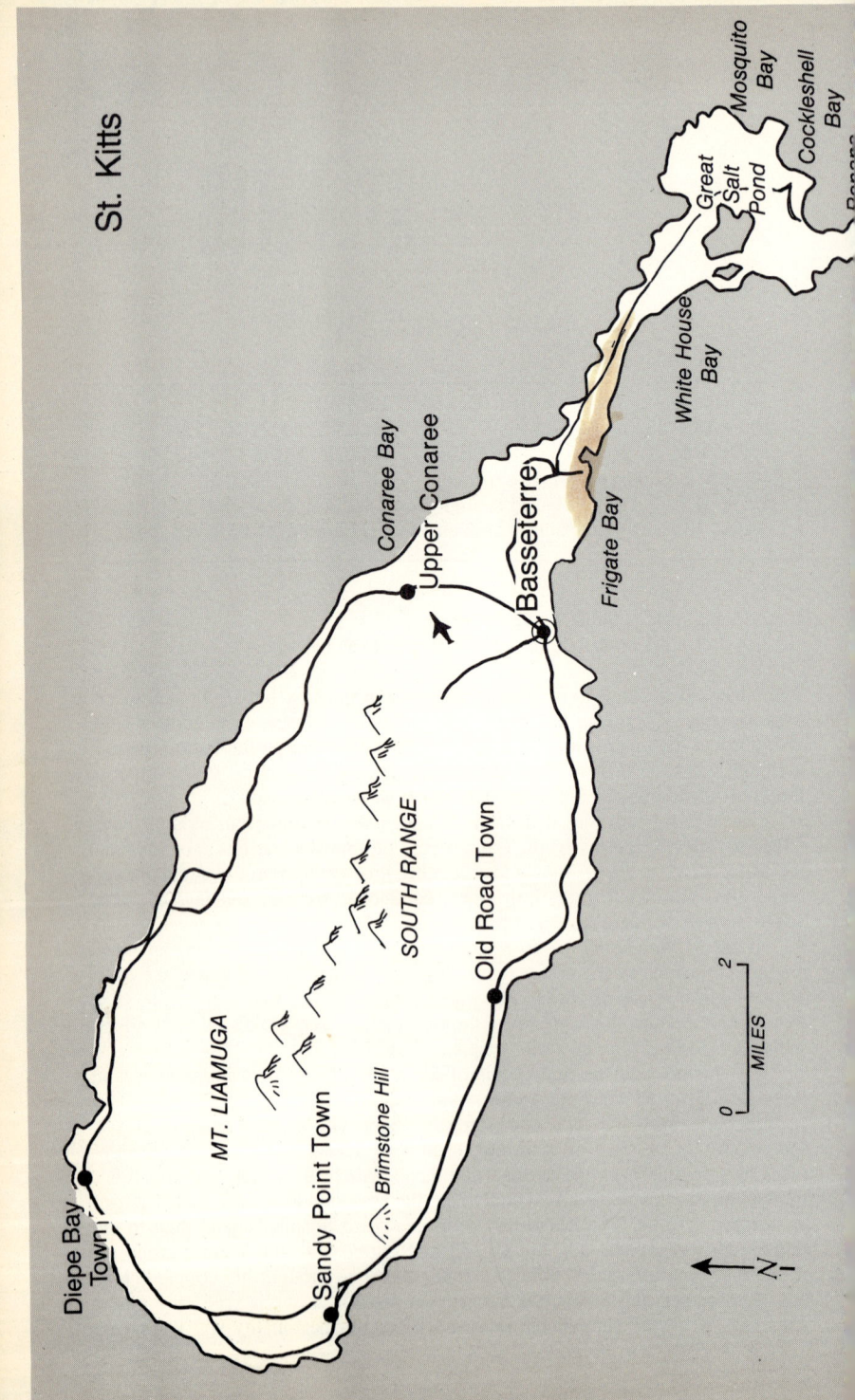

Sint Maarten/St. Martin to the north was known also on St. Kitts. The British held the middle; the French claimed both ends—and named Basseterre (the low land).

Even today, this West Indian island turns to its own tune; there's little that's touristy about it. Since Basseterre became the British capital in 1727, the town has known the floods and fires familiar to many 18th- and 19th-century West Indian towns. A few buildings—and the street plan—date to the rebuilding after the fire of 1867, and some of the newer changes at the shore came after the earthquake and floods of 1974. Renovations in recent years help restore the 18th-century ambience, and craft and other shops, plus attractive restaurants, put 20th-century life in town.

Developments on Frigate Bay, at the wrist of its paddle shape, attest to the country's tap dance with tourism—and although sugar and peanuts have replaced the first crops of logwood and salt, it seems safe to say that it will be a while before tourism overwhelms this primarily agricultural island.

POLITICAL PICTURE: The People's Action Movement won the elections of February 1989, giving PAM solid national support for three terms. St. Kitts-Nevis patterns its government on the British system, where terms are for five years unless a vote of confidence is required by the opposition before that time is up. Prime Minister Kennedy Simmonds is head of the two islands' government, with a coalition that includes leaders from the Nevis Reformation Party, namely Simeon Daniel as Minister of Natural Resources. St. Kitts-Nevis became an independent country on September 19, 1983, led by Prime Minister Simmonds who had served for the previous three years as Premier of the two-island nation when it was an Associated State of Britain. Under the People's Action Movement, St. Kitts-Nevis has known steady and stable development, with an increase in tourism facilities (and revenues) as well as tax incentives for investment in small-but-labor-intensive industries including agricultural ventures and joint ventures with Kittitians and Nevisians. The two-nation country stands to benefit from the Caribbean Basin Initiative. The active Chamber of Commerce and other business groups have played an important role in sponsoring regional business conferences.

ISLAND APPEARANCE: The volcanic mountains of the north slope to plains at the midsection of the island, only to rise again—although not quite as high—in the southern hills. Although there's junglelike growth on the flanks of the volcanoes of the north, the plains are blanketed with crops (traditionally sugar) and the southern hills are often parched by the strong sun. Shaped like a cricket bat, the island's tourism development has centered on an area known as Frigate Bay, a few miles south of the west-coast capital of Basseterre, where the face of the cricket bat yields to the grip. A beautiful new road has been carved and paved, with U.S. government financial and technical assistance, from Frigate Bay to the south coast. Views from the road are sensational, rivaling the California views from San Francisco to Monterey. Most of the rest of St. Kitts is still in its traditional state, with small villages along the coastal roads and the markets of Basseterre a focal point for many Kittitians. Although the best beaches are along the south coast, facing sister-island Nevis, across the 5-mile channel, there's soft sand lining other coves in the southern sector, granular golden sand at the beaches at Frigate Bay, on both the windy east and calmer west coasts, and gray sand on the beaches in the far north. This is an island that continues to be true to itself, still untrammeled by tourism.

LIFESTYLE has some remnants of what was basically British, although there is a Kittitian modus operandi that comes with the confidence of knowing that this island was the first English settlement in the islands—Sir Thomas Warner established his small community in 1623. In the 1950s and 1960s, when the late Premier Robert Bradshaw became the spokesman for the workers on the sugar plantations and set up new systems in the country, St. Kitts established a "new" lifestyle. More obvious on St. Kitts than on rural Nevis, the customs that will appear for the sensitive traveler include the familiar greeting, either a "good morning" or a "good afternoon," to anyone you pass, and certainly before starting any business transaction in a hotel, restaurant or shop.

There is tremendous (and justified) pride among Kittitians and Nevisians about accomplishments over the recent past with an orderly political development and a firm tourism infrastructure. The market day ritual that you can note in downtown Basseterre is just as much a fact of life for island residents as the golf course and tennis courts at the Frigate Bay area are for vacationers.

Tourists are still in the minority on both St. Kitts and Nevis. Emphasis seems to be more on fitting into the system that is working here than on parading through town, either Basseterre or the Nevisian town of Charlestown, in peacock finery or beach clothes.

Clothes are comfortably casual tropical wear. Coat and tie may be worn by some for business meetings, and at formal evening occasions, but the more common attire is a neatly comfortable open-neck shirt for men and skirts or dresses for social events for women. Touring togs are, of course, whatever is comfortable—with resort finery appearing for an occasional dinner at the Golden Lemon or a special elegant evening at Rawlins or Ottley's Plantation.

MEDICAL FACILITIES: The John Franks Hospital, on the northwest side of Basseterre, is adequate for most needs of the local population, but visitors with serious medical problems may want to charter a flight to hospitals in Puerto Rico or Miami. There are no decompression facilities for scuba divers.

MONEY MATTERS revolve around Eastern Caribbean currency. Although there may be slight variations, due to the nibble for exchange services at the hotels, stores, and banks, the rate is "pegged" to the US$ and therefore fairly steady. Many places accept credit cards although it is always wise to inquire before assuming that cards can replace cash, and if you want to cash a personal check, be sure to ask the hotel's owner/manager in advance. When you are dealing with taxi drivers, always ask *in advance* to be sure whose dollars you both are talking about. There is a departure tax of EC$13.50 or US$5.

COMMUNICATION by telephone from overseas to St. Kitts uses 809 area code +465 and a 4-digit local number. The telephone system is operated and maintained by SKANTEL, a joint venture between Britain's Cable and Wireless and the St. Kitts-Nevis government. Overseas phone calls can be made from SKANTEL's office in Basseterre or by purchasing a phonecard from that office to use in phones equipped for that service. To use AT&T's USADirect Service from St. Kitts, dial 1–800+872–2881 or use the designated phone at the airport. Facsimile machines are used by most hotels and many businesses. There is local television as well as cable TV; satellite links bring some U.S. programs to the island. Radio stations are in English, with Spanish (from Cuba and Puerto Rico) also heard. Telex sytems are effective. News magazines and newspapers are available at *Wall's* bookstore in Basseterre and at the shop at the *Jack Tar resort.*

ARRIVAL on St. Kitts is relatively easy. The 8500-foot airstrip was completed in 1976 and is adequate for big jets. When you get off your plane, you will be directed to immigration (a slow process, especially if you arrive on one of the small *Winair* or *LIAT* planes with the relatives and friends of the immigration officials), and then to the ramps for customs clearance.

AUTHOR'S OBSERVATION

There is a tourism desk near the immigration officials' area. It is usually staffed at the time of plane arrivals. Answers are forthcoming if you are pleasantly persistent; the free printed information is helpful.

Although you can make arrangements for rental cars through the tourism desk, no firms operate at the airport. You must take a taxi into town to pick up your car. (See "Touring Tips" below for facts about taxi fares.) Any one of the taxi drivers usually waiting just outside the customs clearance area will be willing to take you where you want to go—at a price. Ask about the fare in advance if you haven't been advised by your hotel when you made your reservations, and always inquire whether the price you are being quoted is in EC$ or US$. Most price quotations—except at strictly tourist traps—are in EC dollars because this is still an islander's island

CRUISE ships arrive at the Deep Water harbor, not too far from the shops in the capital of Basseterre. Taxis line up for island touring and for the day at Frigate Bay with beaches, tennis, golf, and a casino. Plan ahead to include a mountain hike, for something special on St. Kitts.

DEPARTURE from the international airport involves the usual: Check-in at least an hour ahead of scheduled departure, even for regional small plane flights, and then payment of your EC$13.50 or US$5 departure tax (unless you are going to sister island Nevis), and forfeiting the copy of your immigration card. The departure lounge has a few shops and a snack bar but they are not always open for small plane departures.

If you are going to Nevis, the ferry that operates between Basseterre and Charlestown (on Nevis) takes about 45 minutes. The service is popular with residents, and costs about EC$10 each way.

TOURING TIPS: First-timers will undoubtedly want to hire a taxi driver for an island tour, not because there's any difficulty following the ring road that wraps around the bulk of the island but because the lore from taxi drivers is worth the price of the ride. Tipping is not necessary unless some special service is involved. Kittitian drivers own their cars, and except for what they pay for purchase, maintenance, license, running costs, and union dues, the fare is theirs.

AUTHOR'S OBSERVATION

Be savy with taxi negotiations. Immediately clarify whose dollars (US or EC) are being quoted, and check with more than one driver to find a rate. If you are taking a taxi into Basseterre to get a driver's license before picking up your rental car, be aware that there's a relatively high charge for more than one stop.

Since most car rental firms are a short walk from the police station, where you get your license, have the taxi leave you (and your luggage) there. After you get your license and pick up your car, you can return to get your luggage. Your local driver's license costs US$12 or EC$30, after you fill out a form and present your valid hometown license. (When the airport car rental booth is staffed, as it never has been for my arrivals, you may be able to purchase your driver's license there.) The license is valid for one year.

There are several **car rental** firms. I've had courteous and efficient service from *TDC Car Rentals* (T 809+465–2511), where Shirley Romney has helped me with rentals on several occasions. TDC has a unique service that allows you to use one of their cars on Nevis for a day and have it in exchange for your multi-day Kittian rental of one of their small cars. Other local firms include *Caines Garage* (T 809+465–2366), *Island Moped & Auto Enterprises* (T 809+465–2405) and *Sunshine Car Rental* (T 809+465–2193). There are also links with the well-known U.S. firms such as *Hertz*, *Avis*, and *Budget*, but the "big name" association also often means higher rates.

Local bus services will not appeal to most tourists, especially those pressed for time. Waits are long and rides are stop-and-start affairs. Hitchhiking is prevalent.

Mopeds are popular; helmets are not, but should be. Roads are potholed and moped riders looked hot (and scorched) when I saw them. Your hotel can make arrangements for a moped rental; *Jack Tar's Royal St. Kitts* hotel has a fleet and *Island Moped* (see above) rents from offices on Sprott Street.

For **inter-island transportation** between St. Kitts and Nevis, pros travel on the official ferry service for 45 minutes between Basseterre and Charlestown; others take the small planes of *LIAT*, *Winair*, or one of the charter firms. The flight is only 10 minutes. LIAT's links with the rest of its route make excursions to other islands such as Antigua, Sint Maarten, and St. Thomas easy.

LODGING on St. Kitts offers the extremes—from one lively all-inclusive resort to a few quiet, elegant plantation houses, with options, also, for housekeeping in an apartment of your own. Most of the new resort development is centered in the Frigate Bay area, at the neck of the cricket-bat shape of the island. With the opening of the spectacular new road that has been paved to the south coast, resorts will develop in that area, but there's no big news for this season. The *Caribbean Newsletter* (page 9) will have details when any plans are definite and under way. Most of the plantation-style inns are set in the hills of the midlands and north, with gorgeous views and nature's sounds.

There's a 7% room tax on hotel rooms; some places also add a 10% to 15% service charge. Always ask whether the service/tip is included.

AUTHOR'S AWARDS

Ottley's Plantation Inn is a glorious newcomer, in the hills facing east, on the east coast; *Rawlin's Plantation,* in the north, facing northwest, continues to be peaceful and pleasant; *Frigate Bay Beach* would be my choice for lodgings near the resort activity of Frigate Bay.

Information about places to stay is included under Hotels/Resorts, Housekeeping Holidays, the Inn Way, and Low-Cost Lodgings. Stars are awarded within each category. (See page 11.)

HOTELS/RESORTS have an individual style. Some have grown from one-time small spots; others have been built since 1980, with resort patterns in mind. Two hotels are near Basseterre; most are at Frigate Bay, southeast of the capital, near the golf, tennis, beaches, watersports—and casino. The southern peninsula is targeted for development, but most places won't open for this season.

Casablanca • *on the south coast* • is planned as a big resort with full flourishes. The *Caribbean Newsletter* (page 9) will have details as things progress.

Bird Rock Beach Resort • *perched on the shore, below a residential area off the road toward Frigate Bay* • is a newcomer, with balconied buildings growing on a hillside. Some rooms have kitchenettes, but the restaurant serves all meals. The beach is tiny and private; there's also a pool. You'll want a car for mobility. *Apt. Hotel.*

★ **Fort Thomas Hotel** • *on the hillside site of a one-time fort, on the northern side of Basseterre* • was opened in the late 1960s, to be the island's premier hotel. Although it was briefly managed by Holiday Inn, the government-owned hotel is now locally managed. Used as a center for meetings and small conventions for West Indian and other groups, and by tour operators for package vacations, the hotel is showing some signs of wear. The pool is large, and active—with guests (including families) and loudspeaker music. Bedrooms with sea-facing balconies have a nice view over the pool; *Ocean Terrace Inn* is across the road. *Hotel.*

★★ **Frigate Bay Beach** • *on the hillside, a short walk from the east coast beach* • opened, with a few rooms, in early '83, and is now a gathering of several 2-story white stucco buildings. The best rooms overlook the pool and/ or the sea down the hill and beyond; a few face the parking area. Rooms 104 and 105 are nearest to the pool and the open-to-breezes dining pavilion. Although not on a beach (as the name suggests), all units put guests within easy walk downhill to the beach and not too far from the golf links and tennis facilities around and near the Jack Tar Royal St. Kitts Resort. *Hotel.*

★★★ **Jack Tar Village** • *at Frigate Bay, south of Basseterre* • is the island's only total resort, with a casino—plus tennis courts, pool, surrounding golf course, and nearby beaches (on both the east and west coasts of the narrow neck of land). The resort offers a round-the-clock activities plan for its guests who book for the all-inclusive week-or-longer vacations. Modern U.S.-hotel style rooms are in several buildings that cluster around the main recreation and dining center, where shops, taxis, rental cars and mopeds can also be found. Horseback riding is included with other offerings for daily sport, and evening activities revolve around the casino and planned island-focused events. The artificial ponds were murky and unappealing when I checked for this edition. Be prepared to trek to the beach or to wait for the hotel's intermittent jitney service, if you haven't rented a car or moped. The nearest beach is windy with Atlantic sea swells when the tradewinds follow their traditional pattern. The hotel is about 20 minutes' drive from Basseterre and the airport. *Resort hotel.*

★ **Ocean Terrace Inn** • *on the northern hillside, overlooking Basseterre* • has grown from the original small house to become a multi-room hotel, with bedrooms in houses on the inland side of the road as well as appended to the original house and in a separate block on the hillside. (In addition, Fisherman's Wharf on the waterfront below OTI, is part of this family's ventures). The Pereira family are involved in the hotel, and they are what gives it personality. The sloping lawns, waterfalls, Jacuzzi and a large pool, flower-filled gardens, outdoor patio bars, and upper terrace (near the original house) are what creates the atmosphere. Inquire about the status of the menu choices. This place was a favorite for island food, prepared in family style. At *Fisherman's Wharf* you'll stand in line, in casual surroundings, to have grilled chicken, steak, or fish and your choice from vats of vegetables. Always popular with businessmen, the hotel is convenient to town. *Hotel.*

Sandals St. Kitts • *on the south shore* • is being built, following the purchase in early 1989 of the former Banana Bay Beach property from OTI's Colin Pereira and others. Jamaican Gordon "Butch" Stewart will plant a version of his popular inclusive-plan hotel on the two bays that were an admired hideaway until the road broke through the southeast peninsula. The *Caribbean Newsletter* (page 9) will have an update when warranted.

★★ **Timothy Beach Resort** • *at one end of Frigate Bay's west coast beach* • is a cluster of buildings, with suites, studios, and regular rooms. There's an open-to-breezes restaurant, with entertainment some evenings. The tiny air-conditioned check-in area is a welcome relief after a hot drive to this seaside place, where watersports are available on the beach. Near *Jack Tar Village* and the golf course, the units are comfortably (not lavishly) furnished. *Hotel.*

ST. KITTS · · · 653

HOUSEKEEPING HOLIDAYS have always been popular on St. Kitts, but until recent seasons, most facilities have been reminiscent of a summer shore beach place. There are several small cottages along the east shore's Conaree Beach, which was littered with trash when I checked for this edition, and a few apartments elsewhere, but most of the modern places with housekeeping facilities are in the Frigate Bay area. Although there are commissaries linked with many of the apartment rental places, it's a good idea to bring some meat, solidly frozen and packed with the help of your local butcher, and a few other basics if you are addicted to some favorites.

★ **Fisherman's Wharf** • *below Ocean Terrace Inn, on the shore at Basseterre* • are privately owned units for rent in owners' absence at the seaside *Fisherman's Wharf Restaurant,* with its shop and watersports facility. Built of wood in modern style, the apartments and the public areas have the feeling of an old West Indian wharf. The 1-bedroom apartments have sea views from the kitchen and balcony, plus easy access to the restaurant, at the right as you face the sea from the units, and to OTI, up the hill. *Apts.*

Gateway Inn • *on the road approaching Frigate Bay* • is a motel-like band of housekeeping units with TV and well-equipped in an area that looked hot to me. A fitness center is across the road. *Apts.*

★★★ **Golden Lemon Villas** • *at Dieppe Bay in the north* • are elegantly furnished, as you can expect from any project undertaken by Arthur Leaman. The first-built units stand to the left, as you drive down the short road through Dieppe Bay to the shore. The newer units are to the right, with the Golden Lemon Inn to your back. All are sensational, but my personal preference is for the newer units, where lofty ceilings, white walls, and spacious, breeze-swept rooms help create an ideal vacation home. Highly recommended, for decor and for proximity to one of the island's most charming inns. *Villa apts.*

★ **Island Paradise Beach Village** • *on the east coast shore at Frigate Bay* • is a collection of 1- and 2-bedroom apartments, each with its own patio or balcony, depending on level, and modern kitchen. There's a pool near the beach, which can be blustery when prevailing tradewinds are strong. Buildings 1 and 2 as well as 17 and 18 are closest to the beach, with 11 at the back of the U-shape, nearest the road, where a mini-market and a few casual restaurants can be found at the small shopping center. The Pizza Bar & Restaurant is at the complex; the *Jack Tar resort* and golf course are nearby. *Apts.*

★ **Leeward Cove Condominiums** • *on the east coast at Frigate Bay* • is a cluster of 2-story white stucco buildings that show more imagination (with architecture) than some of the new buildings in this area. The 1- and 2-bedroom apartments are near the beach, golf, tennis, and activity centers of the resort area of St. Kitts, with Ram's mini-market as a source for food supplies. The palm-studded grounds are an asset; you'll want a car for mobility. *Apts.*

Palm Bay Condos • *at the south end of the Jack Tar Village, in the Frigate Bay area* • are a fortress of units at the edge of the golf course. Built in early 1990, the project is a long-term one, with units for sale, to be rented in owners' absence. *Apts.*

★ **Sea Lofts** • *on the beach* • overhang their beach-level base, like birds standing on one leg. The unusual architecture allows for a fresh approach. Interiors have attractive "summer house" fabrics and rattan furniture. Built for sale, to be rented in owners' absence, the complex will have tennis courts and a pool. Check for status. *Cottages.*

★★ **St. Christopher Beach Hotel** • *on the east coast beach at Frigate Bay, near the roundabout for the south peninsula road* • is a 3-story cluster of units, with a pleasant and classy appearance. The units are commonly furnished, with 1 or 2 bedrooms, which can be adapted as owners' wish. You're within walking distance of both the *Jack Tar Village* and, in the other direction, the "other" beach (west coast), and across the road from the golf course. *Apts.*

★ **Sun 'n Sand Beach** • *on the east coast at Frigate Bay* • is a community of small white stucco cottages, with an informal restaurant at the beach and *The Dog House* at the roadside collection of shops. As neighbor to Leeward Cove and Island Paradise, Sun 'n Sand also is in the orbit of the Jack Tar resort. Individual units are privately owned, for rent in owners' absence. Due to placement and design of the cottages, air conditioning is essential, so units hum. *Apts.*

THE INN WAY is popular for St. Kitts (as it is for sister island, Nevis), where many historic buildings that were in reasonable shape have been restored and refitted for guests. The Great House, as the main plantation house was known, is usually the social center, with a living-room style reception area and the main dining room. The out-buildings have been restored, or built in old style in some cases, to hold bedrooms, in addition to those in the Great House. These inns are some of the Caribbean's most charming.

★★★ **Fairview Inn** • *mid-island, on the west coast north of Basseterre* • was the first real inn, when Fred and Betty Lam opened a family house for guests. The Lams continue to offer Kittitian cuisine and hospitality, in a place that has been my "home" on several visits through the years. As the place grew from the homelike traditional Kittitian wood Great House, with open balconies and breeze-swept rooms, to include several motel-style cottages around the grounds, it has held on to its personality. The large pool near the main house is the focal point for evening entertainment. A few slot machines have been tucked inconspicuously in a lower, one-time cellar, where a dart board is another diversion. Renting a car allows for easy island touring to reach Basseterre and the best beaches. Popular with repeat vacationers, Fairview is about 10 minutes from Basseterre. *Cottage inn.*

★★★ **Golden Lemon** • *on the north coast, at Dieppe Bay* • is a decorator's dream—really. Painstakingly rebuilt and maintained by New York interior designer Arthur Leaman, the inn is special not only for its antiques and its daily flower arrangements, but also for the "way away" feeling that's maintained as soon as you pass through the gates of the property. The original 17th-century building is the core of this special inn. Exceptional meals are served in the dining room and on the terrace. There's a small pool in the back courtyard (where breakfast can be enjoyed), and a gray sand beach on the point at Dieppe Bay, a Kittitian fishing village named by French settlers for their better-known bay across the Atlantic. Each room, whether it's in the main building or in one of the recently built satellites, has its own personality, plus patio or gallery, modern bath, and overhead fan to keep the tradewinds whisking through the open windows. The Lemon Court apartments are on the right and left as you look seaward from the main house. The Lemon cluster is in a simple village, about 15 miles north of the airport and about 45 minutes' drive north of Basseterre. (Young children are not invited.) *Inn.*

★★★ **Ottley's Plantation Inn** • *on a hillside facing the east coast* • can be enjoyed as soon as you turn onto the road leading up to the grounds. It nests on the hillside, and comes into view from turns on the narrow road that leads up, through the cane fields of the plantation. The recently restored house holds most of the guest rooms on the second floor. The first floor and its verandas are used for living rooms, meals, and tea. Other bedrooms are in the separate small buildings scattered on the grounds, not far from the beautiful pool. Although you're a long ride from the beach, this place can be a perfect (and romantic) hideaway haven. *Inn.*

★★★ **Rawlins Plantation** • *in the north, facing west on a slope of an estate* • has been restored and maintained with its plantation architecture intact. Having been in the Walwyn family for "300 years or more," the property is now owned by Paul and Claire Rawson, who continue a rich tradition. A neighboring homestead was incorporated into Rawlins a few years ago, keeping its name (Mount Pleasant) and joining Cotton House, the Mill, and other buildings in providing the rooms for guests. The cozy Great House has been tastefully expanded to add more dining space; memorable meals are served there and on the bordering porch, overlooking the spring-fed pool and wide expanse of lawns and fields. (The grass tennis court is nearby.) Not for those who need action, or who expect pretentious surroundings, this place is perfect for any who know and love the traditional West Indies. Country walks and reading are the main on-premise activities. Plan ahead for mid-winter weeks; they're often booked by savvy repeat visitors. *Inn.*

The White House • *north of Basseterre, in the hills* • is a newcomer, although the Great House has been standing for over 250 years. Attractively restored, with 4-poster beds in some rooms and antique-style furniture in all, the wood buildings have been painted the traditional white. English-style fabrics are used for accents. There's a pool amid the manicured lawns, and a grass court for tennis. Less than a dozen guests give this place a homelike feeling; it can seem like your own vacation home. Management arranges transportation to nearby beaches for those who choose not to stay home to read. *Inn.*

LOW-COST LODGING is available in a couple of simple hotels and in some cottages and apartments around the island. Since St. Kitts is still an islander's island, it might be a good idea to survey the scene yourself, from a base at one of the better-known hotels, before making a reservation.

Canne-A-Sucre • *in Basseterre* • has 10 simple rooms and a convenient location. This place is popular with West Indian businessfolk and others who come through from other islands.

Conaree Cottages • *on the Atlantic Coast at Conaree Beach* • are geared to shoreside, casually comfortable living. Some cottages have regular American and British visitors who have been coming to these out-of-the-way lodgings for years. You'll want a car for mobility, but won't need anything more than a taxi if you're content seaside. There's a real outpost feeling here.

On the Square • *on Independence Square* • is a narrow building of rooms in the heart of town. Not for everyone, this place might appeal to budget-minded adventurers.

Tradewinds • *at the Atlantic coast's Conaree Beach* • are open-to-breezes cottages that are adequately furnished for shoreside living. There's nothing fancy about this place, but the units appeal to a handful of German and other European visitors as well as to self-sufficient Americans and Canadians who like natural surroundings.

Guest houses in Basseterre that warrant further checking before booking are **Ilan Pine's Guest House,** the **Part View Guest House,** and the **Windsor Guest House.** All are small, very simple places with rooms for rent.

RESTAURANTS on St. Kitts range from hotel-style standard to atmospheric excellence to restored historic buildings where owners serve local food. You can count on some truly special food at a handful of places, but reservations in advance are essential at peak season in winter (and advisable at other times since some of the smallest places don't serve every night).

Among the hotel dining rooms where reservations are worth the effort are **Rawlins Plantation, Ottley's Plantation, Fairview,** and the **Golden Lemon,** all atmospheric inns in the northern sector where a rental car is essential unless you negotiate with a taxi driver to take you there and pick you up at an appointed time.

Anchorage • *on the west beach at Frigate Bay* • is very casual, with local lobster at a beachside setting that allows for a dip in the sea to wash up after grappling with the spiny specialty. When I last sampled, the cost was EC$28, for a whole broiled lobster, with coleslaw and french fries. A favorite spot for a local-fish lunch, Anchorage also serves sandwiches and a regular snack-bar menu. Count on very simple, open-air surroundings.

Ballahoo • *upstairs, over Caribelle Batik's Bay Road shop in Basseterre* • offers luncheon specials at about EC$10, and dinners from EC$20. Seafood and West Indian food are specialties but my creole fish on a recent sampling was only mediocre. The roti (a filled crepe) looked better. The balcony is the best place to dine.

Fishermen's Wharf • *at OTI, on the seaside at Basseterre* • is patterned after successful wharf-side restaurants on U.S. shores. Offering local fish prepared in several styles, as well as imported seafood and some other items, the place is built at water's edge. Wooden picnic tables and benches are placed on a deck and booths are at another nearby area. This can be a fun spot, and is popular with those who know the island well.

Georgian House • *on Independence Sq.* • is a gem worth inquiring about when you visit. Its future is uncertain, following the death of its talented and indefatigable creator, Georgie Bowers, who painstakingly restored the house to its elegant 18th-century style. At its prime, Georgian House served memorable meals in the back courtyard, and in the attractively appointed main-floor rooms, which were furnished with copies of Georgian antiques. The *Caribbean Newsletter* (page 9) will have further comment when there's news about the restaurant.

★★ **The Patio** • *on a residential road at Frigate Bay* • is a home turned restaurant, with creative Helen Malliahau in charge. Meals are served in the back patio room. Be sure to arrive before dark to appreciate the garden. Prices for the main courses range between $23 and $30, which included duckling and lamb en croute when I visited. Most appetizers are under $10; each course is an extra charge. This is a wonderful (and pricey) place for a special occasion; reservations are required, sometimes a day or more in advance.

The Palms Patisserie • *just off the Circus (as Berkeley Square is called) in Basseterre* • is a delightful snacking area, with pastries and other light offerings sold from display cases where you can see the specialties.

There are a few simple spots at the east coast, south of Basseterre, in the Frigate Bay area near the apartment and cottage places.

NATURAL SURROUNDINGS are noteworthy on St. Kitts. At least two firms (*Kriss Tours* T 809+465–4042 and *Gregory Pereira* T 809+465–2754) provide tours with guides, to get into the rain forest and on the flanks of the volcano in the north. Hurry to the south, before the new roads have their full effect—of increased homesite building, more hotels, and the inevitable scattering of the birds and other wildlife that have had this place pretty much to themselves. As of this writing, the south peninsula road is spectacular. It makes for easier access to good birding areas.

Mount Liamuiga, in the northwest, peaks at 3792 feet. It can be climbed from either Harris Estate or Belmont Estate, in the northeast, but it's wise to have a guide for the trek through thick, orchid-flecked forest to the lip of the neighboring volcanic peak, at about 2000 feet. The guide helps with exploring inside the crater, where portions of the "path" are navigated by hanging on to vines and trees. There are wild monkeys, in addition to some birds, although the birds are not as plentiful as you might expect. Monkeys, mongooses, and other wildlife enjoy the eggs.

Another verdant area that is a good walkers'/hikers' goal is Dos d'Anse Pond at Verchilds Mountain. It can be reached from Molineaux, Lambert, or Wingfield estates, in the midsection of the island.

Ruins of the one-time home of Chevalier de Poincy do more than many rebuilt sites to move the imagination. Lost amid a tumble of overgrowth and, each in its season, brilliant tropical blooms, the area is near Basseterre. Carved stone steps, now moss-gilded and time-worn, once led up to the gardens of the 17th-century French governor who lends his name to the Poinciana, a tree also known as the Flamboyant. The tourist office can give directions and local contacts for visits to the site.

The southeastern peninsula has been the best area for nature walks. Although some portions are used as grazing land for cattle (which are a shock when encountered at remote locations), this area is a playground for Kittitian green monkeys and deer. The monkeys dart and play along the dirt roads and in the hinterlands, especially around the salt ponds where birding is also interesting.

Insofar as offshore sites for divers are concerned, this is almost virgin territory. Since fishermen use nets and lines, plenty of colorful fish escape the trawlers and heavier equipment used commercially in some other areas. For fascinating coral, the grid iron is an 11-mile stretch along the often rough Atlantic side, off Conaree shore. Monkey's Shoal, a spectacular circular reef, lies in the channel between Nevis and the south shore of St. Kitts. Several shipwrecks are noted on a map available through Ocean Terrace Inn.

PLACES WORTH FINDING on St. Kitts are going to be those you find for yourself or those you visit with an island guide, perhaps walking or hiking in the mountains. Among the places to head for are the fishing village at Dieppe Bay in the north, plus some of the small towns you pass through as you drive around the rim road from Basseterre north on the west coast and south on the rugged and windy east coast, and coves and beaches you can reach only by boat at the midsouth section and along the south shore, facing Nevis, which lies across the two-mile channel. Many of the villages were the original settlements of this island that proudly calls itself the Mother of the Caribbean (because many early settlers on other islands came from the original Sir Thomas Warner 1623 settlement on St. Kitts). Today the villages are quiet settlements. The inland villages, encouraged to move to the rim road for better transportation to school and commerce, are again surviving; many of the people who moved obediently to the shore at the strong urging of the Bradshaw government returned to their more familiar, if less modern, communities in the hillsides, near the heart of the old plantation where they recognized their favorite trees, streams, and way of life.

BASSETERRE, the capital of St. Kitts-Nevis, was in the French portion of the island when the north and south sections were held by that country and the midsection was English. Extensive restoration has brought to life some of the most interesting buildings, especially those around **Independence Square,** formerly known as Pall Mall Square, where the lines of sectioning in the park still follow the 18th-century tradition of special areas for slaves and freemen. Some of the renovations in the unique houses that rim the square (notably Georgian House) have made the space available for artists and small shops, as well as for private homes and a couple of restaurants. The archives room in the Government Headquarters is the place to find if you are interested in documents relating to the island's early history. (Call for an appointment to be sure the archives are open and there's someone on duty.)

St. George's Anglican Church, on Cayon Street, which runs parallel to the waterfront, reached easily by walking up Church Street, was built as it now stands in 1867, on the site of a church which was first built in 1670. When you wander around the grounds and look at the old wood pews and decoration, modern commerce seems to be in another world. Note the gravestones in the unkempt cemetery—with Woodley (1795), Cunningham (1847), Pilington (1748), and others reminiscent of the previous planter-dominated world of St. Kitts-Nevis.

For ruins around the island, check for permission to prowl around **Fort Smith** on the St. Kitts Sugar Factory grounds. There used to be rusted cannons here, as well as some old stairs and walls, with some bits that might be from some 18th-century pottery, but it was a couple of years ago that I climbed around this site, so things may have changed. Check at the Tourist Board office, or ask at your hotel, if poking around old sugar mill ruins seems like an intriguing pastime for your holiday.

AUTHOR'S OBSERVATION

If you want to prowl around the ruins and restoration, wear rubber-soled shoes (something firmer than sneakers) for the cobbled walkways, and bring some mosquito repellent if you plan to explore after a rain or on a humid day.

Brimstone Hill, a fortress built on the top of a cliff on the western coast of St. Kitts, continues to claim its spectacular outlook with imposing silence. It was the site of special celebrations in 1983, in honor of its 200th anniversary of a French defeat and was officially dedicated as a National Park during Queen Elizabeth's visit on October 25, 1985. Walking around the fortification, the parts that have been restored and the parts still left in weeds and disrepair, recalls the past when English and French jockeyed for control of this fort. The English built the first battery on the hill starting in 1689, after they'd tossed the French out of this part of the island. By 1736 there were 49 cannons on the hill and, during the French seige of the fort in 1782, some 600 troops of the Royal Scots and the East Yorkshire brigades plus 350 militia lived in and fought from here. Even with all that might the English surrendered—with dignity, however. In keeping with war maneuvers of the time, the French reportedly stood by while the English forces—all of them—marched valiantly out of their fort and down the hill, a ceremony that was to be repeated in 1783, when the French were defeated by the British and *they* marched safely to French enclaves elsewhere on the island. The fort was damaged by the hurricane of 1834 and abandoned in 1852, to come back into Kittitian and Caribbean prominence when the Island Resources Foundation, based in St. Thomas, focused on the prominence of the remains and helped raise funds for a partial restoration of the Prince of Wales Bastion in the early 1970s.

Romney Manor, along the west coast about 20 minutes' north of Basseterre, is a sight worth seeing even if you do not go inside the batik workshop (but you should if you haven't on a previous visit). Grounds and building are classic and well maintained, making both a special experience. The turn-off (to the right coming from Basseterre) from the shore-rimming road is marked.

SPORTS are mostly watersports, with hiking, tennis, golf, and horseback riding your land-based options. Frigate Bay, the ambitious project for developing a resort hotel/private home community at the handle of the cricket-bat shape of St. Kitts, is the hub for planned action, but there are places around the island as well

Golf is the prime possibility, with an 18-hole Trent Jones designed course, the clubhouse at the Jack Tar Village plus caddies. Don't count on all the accoutrements you find at your local country club, or perfectly manicured course or greens, but count on being one of the few on what has the potential to be an exceptional course.

Tennis courts have been added, and the existing ones resurfaced, at the Jack Tar Village, and there are also courts at the Olympic Club and the St. Kitts Lawn Tennis Club. Rawlins Plantation and White House have grass courts.

Scuba courses are offered through OTI from *Fisherman's Wharf.* Facilities include a few boats, as well as equipment for rent. Experienced divers may want to bring their own equipment. *Caribbean Watersports* at the Jack Tar Royal St. Kitts Hotel can help with all watersports, from boardsailing and snorkeling to scuba diving, sailing, and deep-sea fishing.

Sailing and **boating** are possible, on picnic cruises as well as for a day sail to Nevis. David Stanger's *Canona,* a 40-foot catamaran, is also available for picnic cruising and for a beach barbecue on nearby Nevis. He can be reached through the *St. Kitts Boat Building Company* on the Bay Road. Most of the boat outings are aboard motorcraft that are available through Fisherman's Wharf.

Boardsailing is the specialty of Paul Webster at *Caribbean Island Windsurfing,* based at the Fort Thomas Hotel.

Horseback riding is offered through *The Stable* at Palmetto Point (T 809+465–3226) and Vandell Berry at *Kriss Tours* on New Street in Basseterre (T 809+465–4042). Your hotel can put you in touch with someone if you are interested in riding, but don't count on facilities for lessons.

For **hiking** and **walking,** contact Kriss Tours (T 809 465–4042) or Gregory Pereira at Ocean Terrace Inn, but avoid the days when cruise ships are in port and bunches of people make a trek.

TREASURES AND TRIFLES on St. Kitts range from the exceptional wall hangings and printed fabric for clothes and other uses designed at **Caribelle**

Batik, with studios at 17th-century Romney Manor and a shop near the clock in town, to the simple handcrafts that make up in earnest attempt what they may lack in finesse. Caribelle's studio at Romney Manor is worth an excursion, with a stop at the Carib petroglyphs carved on the stones, up the road to your right as you pass through Old Road Town heading northwest on the west coast. The batik and tie-dying (wax painting on fabric which is then dipped in color vats) is fascinating to watch, and the designs are worked on West Indian Sea island cotton which used to be made in the islands—and is now made elsewhere occasionally from cotton grown here. Prices for T-shirts hover around $10; sundresses can be $35 or more; wall hangings range from $15 to $30 and up. The shop in Basseterre is near the Circus.

Rose Cameron Smith's Gallery, next to Georgian House on Independence Square, sells Rosie's clown prints and drawings of Kittian scenes as well as a good selection of work by other local artists. Rose Cameron Smith came from England to settle in St. Kitts, at least for part of the year, a couple of seasons ago. With a flair for capturing the special character of West Indian scenes, buildings, and people, Rose parlays her expertise with watercolors into a commercial venture that gives vacationers something of quality to buy.

A Slice of Lemon on Fort Street, at the Circus, is a very special shop which will be no surprise to any readers who already know just how unique the Golden Lemon Inn at Dieppe Bay has become. Martin Kreiner's considerable talent sets the tone. Elegant jewelry with interesting design is a specialty.

Palmcrafts, at "the Circus" in downtown Basseterre, has enough interesting items to offer one-stop shopping for purchases for all your friends at home. Culling the best from this and other islands' handcrafts, the small store is packed with "the best" available from Haiti, St. Vincent, and other spots. Although prices reach the highest ranges, there are shell bracelets and other items at reasonable cost. One specialty at the shop is products of the Kittian Kitchen, a local venture packaging jams, jellies, and spices.

T.D.C. Duty Free Shop, on Bank Street, has cameras, binoculars, china, crystal, and other imports displayed in a rather prosaic setting. Before buying be sure you know your hometown discount store's "best price." **Ram's** also has a duty-free shop near the Tourist Board office—for the winning gamblers to spend their money on crystal, perfume, china, and other luxury items that have not been readily available heretofore, and **Kassabs** also has a wide selection of imports for Kittian homes—and visitors.

Wall's Bookstore, with an around-the-corner entrance marked as Deluxe Records, is a Kittitian tradition, and your source for reading matter including an interesting selection of paperbacks. This is one reliable source for books about the area. Of special interest for island recipes are the *St. Kitts International Women's Association Cook Book* and the *St. Kitts & Nevis Independence Cookbook.* Locally printed *Discover St. Kitts—Christopher Columbus' Favourite Island* is available at Wall's as well as elsewhere. Its price is about EC$21. Investigate the records by West Indian artists and ask to see Betty Lam (who with husband Freddy is responsible for Fairview Inn). This is her family store.

David Coury & Company, on College Street, has the British-made cotton, small-flowered print Liberty fabric by the yard, and **The Sport Shop** at West Street Square has a selection of sports equipment for sale.

Among the shops selling crafts, I found some better-than-average offerings at **The Unique Boutique** on the Frigate Bay Road, and at the **Craft House Emporium,** the display and sales area for the handicraft industry of St. Kitts-Nevis.

Two local items that are of interest to many visitors are the islands colorful stamps, available through the St. Kitts Philatelic Bureau in Basseterre, and Rothchilds' "Spirit of St. Christopher," which made its debut in early 1988, in a classy looking bottle. The cane spirit, distilled at its "home" near the sugar factory not far from the airport, is offered at all the island's inns. Enjoyed both as an apertif and as an after-dinner drink, it's worth considering as a gift—something more exotic than the usual rum—for the folks at home.

ST. LUCIA

> St. Lucia Tourist Board, Box 221, Castries, St. Lucia, W.I., T 809+452–9568; 9th floor, 820 Second Ave., New York, NY 10017, T 212+867–2950 or 800+456–3984; #425, 151 Bloor Street, W, Toronto, Ontario M5S 1S4, Canada, T 416+961–5606; c/o High Commission for Eastern Caribbean States, 10 Kensington Court, London W85DL England, T 01+937–1969.

$ · · · US$1 = about EC$2.60
Unless otherwise noted, $ refers to U.S. currency.

The west-coast road has not been known for its smooth paving. In fact, its reputation for potholes, washouts, and hairpin turns had sent me along the main north–south road on most visits, even though that meant hooking back up the coast when I reached the south-coast town of Vieux Fort.

The day was glistening, the hour was early, and I had done a survey of sorts—questioning a series of friends, taxi drivers, and a cluster of total strangers gathered at a gas station—before I left the commerce that is Castries.

Adopting a role as the morning shuttle bus, I picked up my first neatly dressed pair of schoolgirls as they stood by the road not far from my hotel. Iluma was in form one and Bertha in form three, I learned, before they proudly told me that their tidy white blouses and red skirts were in honor of the Canadians who provided funds for their school.

It was not long after I left them at their school, to be sent on my way with waves and smiles, that I picked up Jane and Letitia. Both had their hair neatly plaited in several braids, gathered with colorful beads as is the fashion among their friends. We were soon joined by as many of their friends as could fit into the car, as we plucked them from the children who ribboned the road. The car was full by the time we drove up the hill to their school, south of Castries.

It was here that I was joined by Valerie Leon, a teacher with 44 children, ages 9 to 13, in one class. She teaches them six subjects, for eight hours a day, five days a week. "I like my weekends," she added with a smile.

"I don't know what the government can do with all these children," she noted as we drove past several clusters in the khaki and black uniforms that designated their school. They almost filled the narrow road through the cane fields, and did fill the front yard of the Roseau Combined School where Valerie Leon teaches.

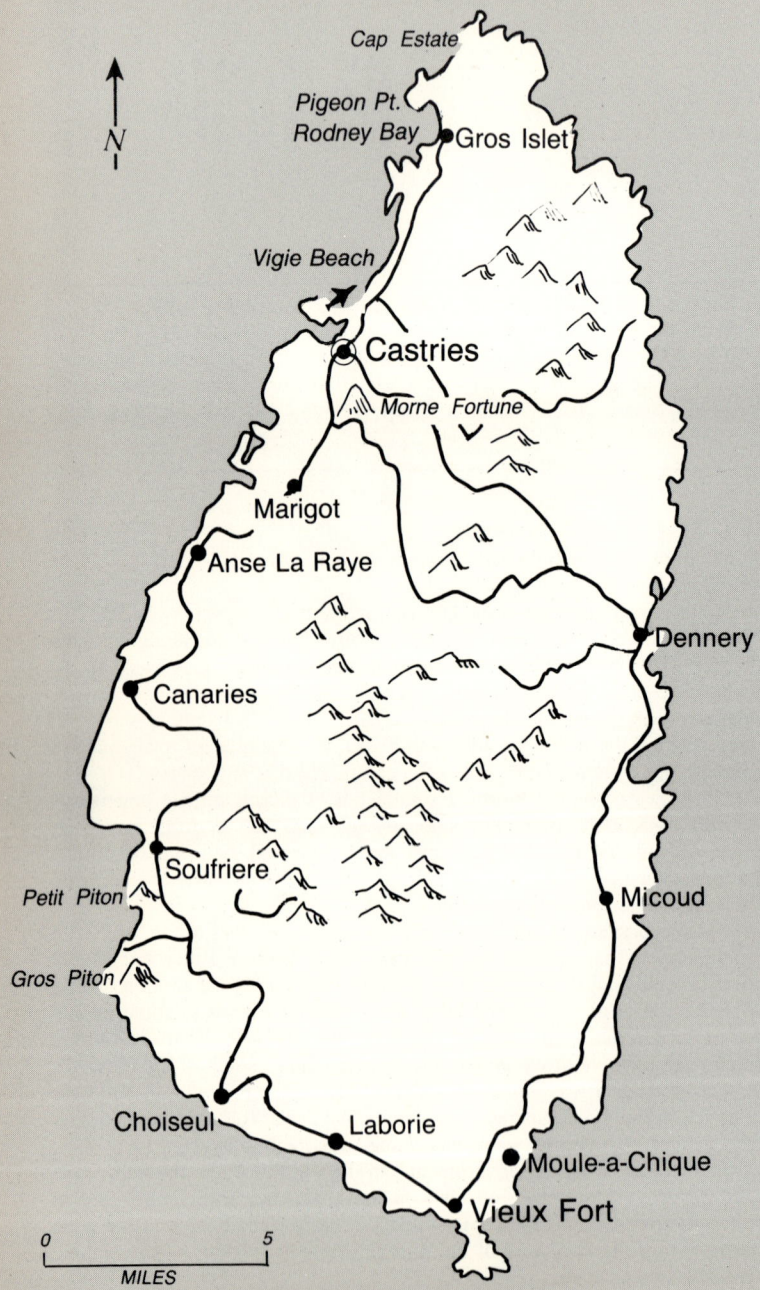

It was miles later that I encountered Leo, George, Danny, and Hendrison. I had driven through spectacular scenery, weaving around the coastline road, up and down, around the curves, often with the sea in view and always joyful at the next beautiful view. The rutted road made driving slow but possible—until I hit a spell of washboard that was broken by the four boys frantically waving me to stop.

"You have a flat tire," they said, turning my anguish to joy when they claimed they could fix it. And fix it they did, with smiles, chatter, and speed. My tip, which included my gratitude as well as their skill, was far too much, of course. But the conversation and the entertainment were worth it.

It's not only the children that mark the shores and hillsides of this island. On the Cas-en-Bas estate, near Lavoutte Bay at Gros Islet, there's an intriguing three-level sugar mill. They say that animals turned the mill by walking around the top level (most St. Lucian mills weren't powered by wind). The middle level held the hearth, the boilers and the rest of the heavy equipment and the lower level is lined with vats and canals—for the molasses that was crushed and boiled, leaving the bagasse that was rich in nutrients and used for fodder. Today the place is in ruins, and few know it is here. Sugar was finally abandoned as a St. Lucian crop in 1960, almost 200 years after it was first planted.

It's banana plantations and plantations prickling with the coconut trees that provide the source for the copra that make the quilt in shades of green that lies over St. Lucia. Those have been the crops for the past few years, but the newest crop is tourists, well fried in coconut oil, which is sold with lessons about the application by wily young St. Lucian salesmen who saunter along the beaches.

POLITICAL PICTURE: In early April 1987, Prime Minister John Compton's United Workers Party won reelection by one seat. Elections must be called by spring 1992, but have not been announced at press time. The *Caribbean Newsletter* (page 9) will have an update. The UWP holds nine elected seats in the present government, with eight held by the main opposition party, the St. Lucia Labour Party. The Progressive Labour Party, led by charismatic, Marxist-leaning one-time deputy prime minister George Odlum, lost the one seat they had previously held. Although the prime minister did not receive the overwhelming mandate he had hoped for, he continued with plans, with leaders of the other Eastern Caribbean States, to forge a political unity within the OECS, in order to ensure the economic viability of the smaller independent, formerly British Caribbean countries. St. Lucia is headquarters island for this alliance.

St. Lucia shares economic problems faced by most Third World countries, with a need for hard currency (primarily U.S. dollars) to buy in the world market. Tourism is regarded both as a valuable source for employment, in what has been primarily an agricultural economy, and for dollars.

Since independence from Britain in 1979, St. Lucia has operated with a bi-cameral system, with 17 elected members in the House of Assembly and 10 appointed members in the Senate. The Attorney General, also known as the Minister for Legal Affairs, is elected; the Prime Minister is chosen by his party.

ST. LUCIA

AUTHOR'S OBSERVATION

The question of whether or not to have gambling casinos keeps coming up for heated debate. It seems to me that some government folks want it, for reasons I suspect I understand. However, my conversations with people around the country indicate that those who are aware of the effects of casinos are not in favor of building one in St. Lucia. Certainly the Catholic church is opposed (and 98% of the people are Catholic). Many people are aware that gambling appeals to a different group from those who now make up St. Lucia's visitors. When there is definitive news on this issue, the *Caribbean Newsletter* (page 9) will mention it.

ISLAND APPEARANCE: St. Lucia is one of the Caribbean's most beautiful islands; it is lush and tropical, with stately palms at many shores and around the countryside. Tourism clusters at only a few areas of the 238 square miles of this oval-shaped country, specifically the west coast, where the shores are washed by calmer seas (since the prevailing winds blow against the east coast). Other areas of development, in addition to those around the capital of Castries, are in the north—at coves from Cap Estate to Pigeon Point to Vigie Beach—and south of the capital, around Marigot Bay and Soufriere, as well as on the southeast coast, just north of Vieux Fort. Small villages cluster at protected coves along both the east and west coasts. Although some of their residents may work at the hotels, many people earn their livelihood from the sea and from field work. Vast tracts make a patchwork of the mountainous midlands, covering fertile valleys and small plains with agriculture. Sugar plantations are important, as are copra plantations (coconuts, which are used for their husks more than for their meat); the island can grow most of its own produce. Although the main roads are reasonably good and well paved, they may dissolve into potholes (or dirt) when you drive away from the most settled areas.

LIFESTYLE in St. Lucia is a mixture of French Creole customs, a token from the days of French rule and the present proximity to French neighbor Martinique, and English tradition. Over the basic French and English, there is a liberal layer of modern independence. Government efforts for domestic education about the benefits (and liabilities) of tourism have been on-going. When you head into the hinterlands, however, you will be an obvious outsider—welcomed, but looked at askance. Only Castries caters to commerce, but it does so with its own West Indian character.

Clothes are comfortably casual. Business dress in downtown Castries is more casual than it used to be, but you will still find men in business suits and women in "proper" dresses. St. Lucians put on their best for the excursion to town—especially if it is market day. Colorful resort wear and shorts are conspicuous, marking you immediately as an outsider. At the luxury hotels (*La Toc, Le Sport, Windjammer*, and others), most of your fellow vacationers will be North Americans and Europeans who dress up for the tropics. Evenings can be dressy, especially if you are with a group who likes to be more formal in the evenings. Jacket and tie are seldom required. Men often wear a short-sleeved shirt, often in conservative style.

AUTHOR'S OBSERVATION

St. Lucians speak English, but you may not be able to understand it. The dialect is their own, as is the case for each island of the English-speaking Caribbean, but the colloquialisms link French and African words and sayings with perhaps-familiar English words. When you're trying to make your wants known to staff at your hotel, and to people you may talk with elsewhere, speaking slowly—and without too many Americanisms—will be the easiest route for clear communication.

MEDICAL FACILITIES: There are several hospitals and clinics around the country, with the two largest being in Castries—Victoria Hospital on the road up the Morne, in La Toc area—and in Vieux Fort, where St. Jude's Hospital is located in the Augie (pronounced "Oh joy") area. Hospitals are patterned on the British system, and most doctors have trained in Commonwealth counties or other places with British ties. At a research hospital on the top of the Morne, the hill that rises from Castries, extensive research has been done in times past on schistosomiasis, a disease known in tropical countries that comes from a small worm that lives in streams and burrows into the skin. The larger hotels have links with local doctors. Visitors with serious medical problems sometimes fly to Barbados, Puerto Rico, or Miami.

MONEY MATTERS: Since most of the stores, restaurants, and other services are for residents first—and tourists also—$ and ¢ refers to EC currency. Some places (notably Bagshaw's shop) will also print U.S. prices, but most leave you to figure equivalents for yourself. Although you can pay your hotel and services in U.S. dollars at the end of your stay, it's wise to change some money at the bank or through your hotel cashier to have the currency of the country for purchases when you are touring. Banks give the best exchange rate, but often charge a small fee for their service.

COMMUNICATIONS are reasonably easy between St. Lucia and overseas, with international contact via telephone. From the U.S. there is direct-dial with the 809 code plus 45 and a 5-digit local number. Cable & Wireless Company issues plastic credit-card sized phone cards, for use in designated coinless phones. The cards can be purchased in several amounts, to be used for as many calls as can be covered by the card you buy. Facsimile machines are in common use by hotels and other businesses. Telex and telegraph are handled, also, by British-based Cable & Wireless Ltd. in league with the St. Lucian government. Overseas telephone calls can be made easily from their offices in Castries and at Pointe Seraphine, the cruise ship dock, where AT&T has USADirect telephones and there are other public telephones as well. Mail can take a week or longer from the U.S., and requires 50 cents for a normal airmail letter. Radios pick up not only English-language stations but also French (from neighboring Martinique) and Spanish programs. Satellite dishes bring in television, and VCRs are popular. Don't count on much in the way of international newspapers. What's available at the more luxurious hotels will be priced at a premium.

ARRIVAL at St. Lucia's airports offers you options, depending on your starting point. For most hotels, the small Vigie airstrip at Castries, about 5 minutes' drive from downtown and no more than 20 minutes from most hotels, is by far the most convenient. It is used by smaller planes, including those of *LIAT, American Eagle,* and other inter-Caribbean island carriers. The big jets from major international destinations do not land here, however. *American, British Airways, BWIA,* and other major carriers fly into Hewanorra (Hugh-an-*no*ra) Airport at the south, which was a U.S. military base, Beane Field. My St. Lucian friends say the drive between Hewanorra and Castries (where most hotels are located) takes 45 minutes, but I find it difficult to cover that distance—when I don't know what's around the next curve—in less than an hour and a half. Although it is possible to charter a small plane for a scenic length-of-the-island flight, by the time you load, fly, land, and unload, the time for travel is about the same as driving.

CRUISE ships come to St. Lucia in ever increasing numbers, encouraged by the extensive facilities at the Pointe Seraphine Tourism Complex, on the northern fringe of the capital of Castries, where there are shops, telecommunications facilities (telephones, telex, etc.), as well as taxis and a London double-decker bus that links the port with town.

From a Castries hub, it is easy to go north, to spend the day at the beaches, as many passengers do (using the *St. Lucian* hotel near Rodney Bay and other properties). Unique to St. Lucia, however, is a journey south, to the area inland from the southwest coastal town of Soufriere for a ride to the sulphur baths and the volcano, or a boat trip out of Castries along the coast to Soufriere. Refer to "Places Worth Finding" and "Natural Surroundings" for other suggestions for day touring in St. Lucia. There's far more to enjoy on this island than the beach.

AUTHOR'S OBSERVATION

In this country, "dollars" are not U.S. dollars. The "dollar" reference is usually to Eastern Caribbean dollars, valued at about EC$2.60 to US$1.

DEPARTURE by plane can be from either Vigie Airport, near Castries, for other Caribbean islands, or Hewanorra International Airport, at the southern part of the island for flights to North America and Europe. You'll need to allow at least 3 hours from your Castries area hotel to Hewanorra to abide by the advance check-in requirements *and* the drive south. You will be asked to forfeit the copy of your immigration card and pay a $5 departure tax. There are a few shops at Hewanorra (including Mrs. Joseph's cafe, which serves the best fried egg sandwich I've eaten, and hearty roti), but you'll have better luck with purchases made when you see items you like in your travels.

TOURING TIPS: As on other islands, your options for getting around include taxi or rental car (and you'll drive on the left). Main roads are good, and taxi fares between the southern airport, where most of the big planes land (at Hewanorra), and Castries are about EC$90 per car (for 1 to 4 people).

Rental cars can be arranged at either Hewanorra or Vigie airports, where you can buy a local driver's license from immigration on presentation of your valid hometown license and a payment of EC$30 or US$12. Plan to buy your license before going through immigration, to save some time. Although the big-name car-rental firms *(Avis, Hertz, Budget, National)* do have representatives, it's sometimes possible to negotiate better rates from local entrepreneurs. *Sly's Car Rental* (T 809+457–5057), with rates posted at US$29 per day, plus *Royal Rent-a-Car* and *Island Car Rentals,* are some I've noticed on recent visits. I've had helpful service from John Elliot's *National Car Rental* offices, where I picked up my car on arrival at Hewanorra and left it, when I departed, at Vigie airport and from *Budget* at Hewanorra.

Roads are not well signposted, but the main road that is the backbone of the island is easy enough to follow (just stay on the paved part); the side roads often dissolve into rutted routes of dry and dusty dirt, but the rewards at the end may be a remote fishing village or a sandy cove. (Avoid swimming on the surf-pounded east coast, unless you're with an island resident who knows the area. The surf may be tempting, but the undertow can be treacherous.)

For quick trips between airports, inquire about chartering a **small plane.** Local air taxi services make a "bridge" with small plane service between the airports as well as to neighboring islands.

The **taxis** available for several versions of "round-the-island" tours are a wise investment for first-timers since learning something about what's where, and the island's fascinating history, is well worth the fee, which you should negotiate before getting into the cab. Drivers are willing to wait while you prowl at some spot that interests you. Often their conversation adds a lot to the experience. For those who like the water and want a quick glimpse of the highlights, I suggest the trip from Castries on one of the sightseeing **boats.** (The boat trip, plus a taxi drive overlooking the east coast from Hewanorra Airport to a northwest coast hotel, will give you an idea of the island, but there's nothing to compare with prowling around on your own.)

LODGING choices range from small and simple, but new and often pleasant, guest houses to resorts that aspire to luxury, with a few attractive inns, a couple of price-inclusive hotels, and several housekeeping places in the mix. Most of the action is around the capital of Castries, on the west coast, in the northern half of the island. The biggest of St. Lucia's airports is, as mentioned above, on the southern tip of the island. Long anticipated development of that area has yet to be realized, although the Club Med is being joined by at least one other multi-room project now underway.

It's possible to be in the middle of plenty of tourist-oriented activities—or to be away by yourself, in truly tropical surroundings. This island offers many good choices.

There's an 8% tax on your room rate; many hotels also add a service charge of 10% or 12%. If you've had very special service, it's appropriate to leave something more.

AUTHOR'S AWARDS

Windjammer Landing is my top choice for luxury living, not only for its appearance but also for its staff and atmosphere; in the south, *The Hummingbird* is an inn at the shore of Soufriere, with comfortable rooms; and I still enjoy the informal, West Indian *Islander,* which I think is one of St. Lucia's best values.

Information about places to stay is included under Hotels/Resorts, Housekeeping Holidays, the Inn Way, and Low-Cost Lodgings. Stars are awarded within each category. (See page 11.)

HOTELS/RESORTS include one dazzling newcomer, a couple that have resort facilities (golf, tennis, watersports) and three that operate on a price-inclusive plan, where one multi-day fee covers room, meals, and most other costs. Most hotels are on good swimming beaches.

★★★ **Club Med St. Lucia** • *on a southeast beach, near Vieux Fort* • appeals to the young at heart or in fact, with an action plan that focuses on windsurfing, in addition to all other watersports, plus tennis, archery, games, and plenty of daytime and night-time activity. Filling a hotel that was originally built in the 1960s, Club Med opened in 1986 with completely refurbished facilities. Foliage now wraps around the multi-story buildings that rise, beachside, giving guests sea-view rooms. Ground-floor rooms open onto the beach. The strand of wind-swept sand stretches for "miles" to the right and left; calmer facilities on the west coast are used for most boating activities. This place operates on the "beads for purchases" principal that the French-inspired Club Mediterranee made famous, but be aware that you'll be asked for the equivalent of $5 for some drinks! All-inclusive at Club Med includes room, meals, and activities. Mixed drinks are extra. Vieux Fort is a few minutes away; Hewanorra airport is almost next door. *Inclusive resort.*

★★★ **Club St. Lucia** • *on a west coast cove at Cap Estate* • has grown into a full-fledged classy resort, with a new reception area, a top-notch sports complex with tennis courts (to which St. Lucians can belong, as a club), and rooms with modern comforts in several single-story bands of buildings around the grounds. There's a pleasant beach, with pool nearby, and an area that has shops and an activities center. The restaurant is planned for buffets, with several serving centers and attractive tiling, with overhead fans to cool. Some of the acreage has been planned as a nature preserve, with a small pond and no buildings. Popular with British and European travelers, this place is good for families and others who want everything within easy distance. Most of the complex opened in early '91, although some of the older villas that are on the hillside are popular with repeat visitors who have known them to be cozy quarters. *Inclusive resort.*

★★ **Couples II** • *on the shore at Vigie Beach* • clipped a page from the successful formula at Jamaica's north-coast resort, and turned the former Malabar Beach Hotel into a clublike all-inclusive multi-day holiday-for-two resort. Craig Barnard, son of the owner of the property when it was one of St. Lucia's first (and most popular) small hotels, joined with Jamaican John Issa and his team to keep the tempo moving and the resort in first-class shape. Included in your prepaid holiday is room for 2, all drinks, cigarettes, food, and fun. There are watersports facilities, tennis courts, and a program of evening entertainment that includes disco and other dancing as well as floorshows, buffets, and pool-time pleasures. Rooms are in several units, some of them 2-story motel-style, but all with basic comforts. *Couples II* is a good value for those who want to be where there's action. The resort is a short distance from the capital of Castries and small Vigie airport (used by LIAT and other local airlines); the big airport with links to the U.S. and other major destinations is about an hour's drive to the south. *Inclusive resort.*

★★★ **Cunard's Hotel La Toc & La Toc Suites** • *on the west coast, south of Castries* • falls short of being St. Lucia's leading property because of service and maintenance, in my opinion. All the physical attributes are here: golf course, tennis courts, watersports, choices for restaurants, and some attractive rooms. The beach area is tricky for swimmers when surges bring surf and undertow. Opened as a beachside hotel of several 3-story blocks in the 1970s, the property has expanded to include apartment suites in several buildings on levels up the hillside. Most rooms have a sea view; the best suites have a plunge-pool. Castries is about 10 minutes drive away. Taxis are on-premises for island tours; there's also a rental car desk near the lobby-area shops. *Bagshaws* silk screen studio is up the rocks at the north end of the beach. Used by convention groups and tour programs, the hotel also offers enough entertainment for families with teenage children. *Big resort.*

★★ **Halcyon Beach Club** • *on the shore, just north of Castries* • best known to British and European groups, has all the elements for a pleasant beach-and-sun holiday in expected doses. The planting that thrives around the entrance lends a pleasant Caribbean tone, and the activities desk and lobby shops provide entertainment. There are choices for dining, with sea view places the best. Rooms are in cottagelike buildings as well as in standard hotel style in low-rise finger buildings. Those nearest the beach are best for my money, but all are within easy walk from the sea. A popular home for travelers on package tours from Britain, Europe, Canada, and the U.S., the hotel seems to have its guests' happiness in focus. Count on a good vacation here. *Resort hotel.*

Jalousie Hotel • *between the Pitons, near Soufriere* • may be open for this year, but it is still being built at press time. The luxury villas are on the hillside, overlooking a lovely beach. Controversial since ground was cleared for the first buildings, the planned resort sits between the trademark mountains that rise from St. Lucia's southwest shore. Environmentalists are horrified and the Organization of American States and other groups recommended *against* any development in this area, but the infinite wisdom of St. Lucia's politicians prevailed. The villas are being built. The *Caribbean Newsletter* (page 9) will have an update.

★★ **Pullman Morgan Bay** • *on the west coast at Choc Bay, a few miles north of Castries* • effectively walls out the rest of St. Lucia with its sea-facing blocks of rooms. On a lovely beach, looking toward Pigeon Island-Point, the new resort includes air-conditioned rooms with TV, direct-dial phones, and small balconies. Swimming pools are near the beach, with a couple of restaurants, and the sports center. Plans are to have squash courts, tennis courts, a gym and dance studio, croquet field, bocce court, and places for archery and for basketball, plus all watersports, but all were not in operation at press time. The *Caribbean Newsletter* (page 9) will have details, when the place has been open for a while. Pullman, a French-based chain with resorts on neighboring Martinique, as well as on the other French West Indies, will market the property in Europe as well as in the U.S. *Resort hotel.*

★★★ **Royal St. Lucian** • *on Reduit Bay, north of the St. Lucian hotel* • has polished marble floors in its breeze-swept lobby, and pastel decor throughout the public rooms and bedrooms. Planned in a U-shape, with a large pool in the center, the rooms are in 3-story buildings, with the best—elegant suites—at the tip of the southern arm, closest to the sea. One suite has a private pool; others have balconies and great sea views. The dining room is elegant, with a decorative element of sails. Planned as a deluxe property, facilities and staff seemed willing. Facilities of sister hotel, *St. Lucian,* are next door and, although entirely separate, can be enjoyed by Royal guests. *Resort hotel.*

★★ **Le Sport** • *on a cove on the northwest coast at Cap Estate* • focuses on exercise, spa treatments, and general attention to health and fitness, but that shouldn't intimidate anyone. The surroundings needed attention when I checked for this edition. Hopefully, stained carpeting, chipped tiles, cracking cement, and other problems will have been repaired (or replaced) by the time you visit. A circular driveway leads to the entrance and the airy lobby and reception area; dining areas and the beach are downstairs. Exercise classes and the juice bar are in a separate building along the beach. Originally built as a classy hotel with international style, the former Cariblue was taken over by Craig Barnard (owner of *Couples II*) to be refitted for its new role. Most rooms are positioned above a nice curve of sand to give guests a lovely sunset view south and west over the sea. There are plenty of steps to climb between beach and room and/or tennis courts; the Cap Estate golf course is nearby. This self-contained resort has its European following. *Inclusive resort.*

★★★ **St. Lucian Hotel** • *at Reduit beach, the island's best* • is an action-oriented hotel with several small restaurants, a yacht marina, and a gathering of smaller hotels nearby. Combining what had been two low-rise beach hotels (a former Holiday Inn and the St. Lucian) and linking them with a new bank of rooms, the property is self-contained, with restaurants, tennis courts, shops, and watersports all on premises. You are within walking distance of the Rodney Bay marina with all its activity. Groups book here summer and winter, which means any lone ranger can find other people here—even during the slowest travel times. (Cruise ship passengers also use this beach when they are in port.) Count on a friendly, informal atmosphere. The disco offers top decibel gaiety when outside enthusiasm warrants. You will be about 7 miles north of Castries, so town is a taxi ride or shuttle-bus trip away. (Cap Estate's 9-hole golf course is about 5 miles north.) *Resort hotel.*

Vigie Beach Hotel • *at the south end of Vigie Beach* • also calls itself the *New* Vigie Beach as a tip of the hat to extensive refurbishing. It's a lower cost Halcyon relative. Always nicely located, at one end of a curve of beach shared with *Couples II* (and all of St. Lucia on weekends and holidays), the place has been spruced up with paint and necessary maintenance. When staff attitude is good, this place can be a comfortable, reasonably priced nest. Guests lodge in two flanks of rooms, most with a pleasant beach and sea view. You're across the road from the Vigie airport. *Hotel.*

★ **Villa Apartments** • *in Castries* • perches on a patch on the flanks of the Morne, and gives you mountain breezes and a spectacular view of town and the Caribbean, up and over the heat of downtown Castries. The apartments, usually on long-term rental, are casual, comfortable, and very West Indian. Tucked into a 2-story building that stretches out in back, the apartments are air cooled. **Villa Beach Cottages,** north up (and on) the west coast, about 15 minutes' drive from town, offer beachside lodging. A rental car is recommended if you want to be mobile, but there's plenty of traffic that passes by the driveway, so you can probably hitch a ride to town if you want to. *Apts.*

★★★★ **Windjammer Landing** • *on the shore, north of Castries* • is gorgeous, classy, and a welcome addition to the Caribbean lodgings list. The public/reception area, overlooking the beach, is reminiscent of a multi-room Mediterranean mansion, with white stucco walls, terracotta tiles on the floors, attractively recessed footlights at the steps and in some alcoves, and many designer touches. The dining area is within sight and sound of the sea; a free-form pool looks pretty, by sunlight or nightlight. Living units are scattered around and up the hillside, and therein lies the only problem: transportation between the main house and your house. The walk is hot (but possible); the steep driveways can be intimidating to novice island drivers; the hotel's jitney requires waiting until it's ready. But that's a small inconvenience for a place that seems pretty close to perfect otherwise; after all, you're supposed to be relaxing. This place is beautiful—and pricey. *Classic resort.*

HOUSEKEEPING HOLIDAYS can be ideal on an island with plenty of fruits, vegetables and rural markets. Life is easy and pleasant, and there are adequate to luxury places to rent. For stocking up, the markets in town have fresh vegetables, there is a good bakery near the Vigie airport for marvelous crusty St. Lucian bread (which shows its French influence), and fish and chicken are relatively easy to come by.

Houses for rent range from luxury accommodations (some of them condominiums rented in owners' absence at Cunard's *La Toc,* mentioned above) to villas at Marigot Bay Resort to the simple small apartments and cottages away from the tourist hubs, in villages such as Soufriere and Gros Islets. Rental firms with many listings include **Tropical Villas,** Box 189, Castries, St. Lucia, W.I.; T 809+452–8240; **Eastone Overseas Rentals,** 274 Madison Ave., New York,

NY 10016, T 212+683–9150; and **La Cure Villas,** #1010, 11661 San Vicente cBlvd., Los Angeles, CA 90049, T 800+387–2726. Although some of the apartments are new, many have been built for European guests and may seem small for U.S. visitors. Villas also vary.

Bois d'Orange Holiday Villas • *inland, perched on a hill* • are often booked for long-term rental. They're up a hill, between the main road and the shore (where *Windjammer Landing* claims its place). There's a pool on premises. Surroundings are simple. You'll find the basics in a 1- or 2-bedroom villa, but the restaurant (a separate concession) has been charming. *Apts.*

Caribbees Apartment Hotel • *on the hillside at La Pansee, above Castries* • offers 10 studio apartments in a band of buildings that cups the pool and a gardened area. Rooms are supplied with the basics, with a small kitchenette for home cooking. There's a minimarket on premises. You'll need a car if you want flexibility, but the hotel provides transportation to the beach if all you want is beach-and-back. (Management can handle the car rental, as well as boat trips and other activities.) This can be a comfortably casual home base. *Apts.*

Dasheene • *near Soufriere* • is in a state of flux at presstime. The *Caribbean Newsletter* (page 9) will have further comment when warranted. The villas that are Dasheene are privately owned, furnished according to the tastes of the individual owners, with maximum use of the breathtaking view of the Pitons and the mountain air that wafts around. You'll have to drive to the beach. *Apts.*

Harmony Apartel • *at Rodney Bay, north of Castries* • claims a wedge of land on the harbor, across from the marina, within walking distance of (but not on) the beach shared by the *St. Lucian* hotel. The compact apartment community gives you either a 2-bedroom or 1-bedroom unit, with ground level offering convenience of easy walk-out-the-door-to-the-pool at the expense of privacy. For that reason, I prefer one flight up. Opened in '80, Harmony encourages (and appeals) to families whose small children cavort around the grounds. A small snack place is on-premises, and good restaurants are nearby if you're tired of cooking. *Apts.*

Morne Fortune Apartments • *also known as Top O' The Morne, where they are located* • occupy one of the hilltop's historic buildings. The exterior was restored, and the interior gutted to be filled with comfortable living quarters, about 5 minutes drive up from Castries to a viewful perch. The 1- and 2-bedroom apartments offer full kitchen facilities, in addition to a glorious view from the balcony. The "Fortune Package Plan" includes a rental car. You're not too far from the Green Parrot and other Castries restaurants. There's a small pool. *Apts.*

Tarpion Reef • *on a hillside, on the southern fringe of Castries* • is a block of self-catering apartments with air conditioning in the bedrooms. Living areas are open to breezes. There's a small swimming pool, and reportedly good snorkeling near the offshore reef. The on-premise restaurant serves local-style offerings, if you choose not to do your own cooking. A courtesy bus links this place to Castries. *Apts.*

THE INN WAY is changing. There are a few properties with less than 50 rooms that provide the traditional hospitality that makes inns special. And there are some other properties that have the appearance of a charming small hotel, but diffident management and a paycheck-oriented staff. I've sampled both. Here are "inns" to consider.

★★★ **Anse Chastenet** • *rising from a small west coast cove, north of Soufriere* • was a very special place when I first found (and wrote about) it, in the early 1970s. Thankfully, it still has an outpost, Robinson Crusoe quality, in spite of some additions, occasional refurbishing, and management quirks. It also, now, has a scuba focus, with divers departing by boat from its curve of sea-washed gray sand. Rooms are in a trio of beachside buildings (#9, #10, and #11, with 9C closest to the beach), as well as in several airy hillside cottages, separated from the beach by 100-plus steps as are the beautiful new wood units, with attractive furnishings. From the south coast's Hewanorra Airport, the bend-and-weave, often pot-holed road takes about an hour to drive. "Our guests love it," I was told; I don't. If you can arrange it, the pleasantest arrival route is by boat from Castries, but getting luggage ashore is a minor challenge best solved by not bringing much. The beachside alfresco dining area is attractive, with Madras napery, but flies were pesky when I dined. There are a couple of shops at the beach pavilion; tennis courts and the professional dive shop are nearby. The traditional dining deck is up the hillside in the original hotel building, where wood-and-reed chairs, wooden tables, and Madras-covered cushions set a Creole tone. The reception area is also here, as is a tree house–style, open-to-breezes library and activities' board. For divers and those in search of an away-from-it-all vacation, this is a place to try. *Inn-hotel.*

East Winds • *on the shore, north of Castries* • has had its ups and downs. The several rondavels at the beach have the basics, with kitchenettes, in various stages of repair. The beach is lovely, but sandflies can be annoying. A garden area at the entrance is a pleasant introduction to pool and beach. *Cottage inn.*

Green Parrot Inn • *in the hills above Castries* • made its name as a restaurant and still serves good food when the owner/chef cooks. The motel-style rooms were an afterthought; they offer expected basics for businessmen and others to whom price and food are important. There's a pool, but you'll want a car for mobility (and beaches). *Small hotel.*

★ **Hummingbird Beach Resort** • *on the northern fringe of Soufriere* • grew from its popular restaurant to include a couple of simple rooms plus a few cottages with bedrooms. Room #4, with mosquito netting over the bed and a soft coral-and-beige color scheme, was my home on one visit. Sea sounds can be heard in the rooms; a private deck-porch is pleasant for relaxing times. There's a small pool, a good restaurant, plus public beach and sea, which are separated from the grounds by a "keep out" wire fence and a guard. *Cottage inn.*

★★ **Islander Apartment Resort** • *north of Castries, near Reduit beach* • can be a comfortable home for folks who want basic surroundings and a pleasantly informal atmosphere. Some of the rooms have kitchenettes on the patio, with the bedroom and bath behind the screen doors. A pool, amid gardens, bordered by some of the single-story units, is the social center, with the restaurant and terrace bar on one side. Popular with West Indian and other travelers who know and enjoy good value, this place can be a pleasant vacation home within walking distance of the beach, several restaurants, and all the action of the *St. Lucian* hotel. I've stayed here, and enjoyed the dependable St. Lucian hospitality. *Hotel, apts.*

★★★ **Marigot Bay Resort** • *at Marigot Bay, south of Castries* • has long been one of my favorite places for a casual, nautical hideaway. *The Moorings* charter yachts line up at piers and anchor in the bay, along with other yachts that enjoy the protected harbor. With a shoreline that is studded with palms, plus many other trees and tropical plants, the several small buildings that hold the bedrooms are almost hidden from view. The resort includes what had been a couple of independent sailing-oriented properties whose single-story buildings had a home-style feeling. The approach road leads down a steep hill into what had been Hurricane Hole, a self-contained 12-room resort of several small buildings and a central reception area. It's a short walk to the pier to pick up the row-boat sized shuttle (with an outboard motor) that takes you across the harbor, to the charter boat office and the "other" small hotel. Lodgings on the Moorings' side of the cove are in a recently built shoreside building that serves as the charter boat office or in separate and special villas that rise from the shore, where a maid keeps house in your private surroundings. *Dolittles,* the cove-side restaurant, is the place for any evening action. *Club Mariner* also has its restaurant, and a place for entertainment. Because I enjoy the casual comfort of this place, Marigot Bay resort gets top marks from me. *Cottage resort.*

LOW-COST LODGING: On this island, many of the places mentioned under "Housekeeping Holidays," above, allow for reasonably priced vacations, when the apartment or villa is shared by a family or several friendly folk. In addition, the St. Lucia Tourist Board has listings of many of the small spots, but vacationers not familiar with West Indian small hotels should look first before booking for an extended stay.

★ **E's Serenity Lodge** • *on the hillside not far from the coast road, north of Castries* • is a special place with comfortable rooms with fans. Elsie Vitalis is a good hostess; she welcomes her guests like family. *Guesthouse.*

RESTAURANTS in and around Castries are personality places that count as much on their atmosphere as on their food. In recent years St. Lucia has nurtured a crop of bistrolike dining depots that cluster at several locations, namely north of Castries between Reduit Bay and Rodney Bay, where you'll find several choices; and on the southeast coast at the village of Soufriere where you'll find many personality places. The area around Rodney Bay has a dozen or more restaurants, with several a short walk from Reduit Beach (*St. Lucian Hotel,*

Islander, Harmony, etc.) and others on the far side of the marina, between the marina and the main north coast road.

The real phenomena in St. Lucia, however, is **Gros Islet,** a fishing village that has opened many of its houses and rum shops as *very* casual restaurants. Friday night is the "Jump Up" for the village; restaurants are open (and packed), there's music in the streets, and the local folks encourage visitors to share in the fun. Gros Islet's "Jump Up" is the only opportunity, in today's Caribbean, for vistors to enjoy natural West Indian enthusiasm and hospitality on a regular basis. Although I'm wary of the sale of marijuana and other drugs at the fringes of this fete, it's still—as of this writing—a wonderfully spontaneous evening, a chance to enjoy the *real* Caribbean in a style that is *not* antisceptically packaged for tourism.

―――――――――― AUTHOR'S AWARDS ――――――――――
San Antoine, on a hillside above Castries, is a viewful spot with offerings that rise to the occasion; *The Hummingbird* offers good food in a pleasant seaside setting at Soufriere.

A-Frame • *at the marina, on the road north of Castries* • is breeze-swept and yachtsmen-filled. The "picnic table" style on the deck draws many of the boat people, and others of their ilk. Count on casual atmosphere, reasonable prices (for St. Lucia's tourist area), and varied menu with snacks as well as full meals.

A Pub • *near the Islander and other hotels* • is a gathering spot for boat people and visitors who enjoy a Caribbean-style pub, serving fish and chips and other fare in casual surroundings that are pleasant.

Afterdeck Bar & Grill • *at the marina, on the road north of Castries* • has several shops and snack places as neighbors in a recently built cluster to cater to yachting folk. With an ownership link to *San Antoines,* you can count on good food here. Grilled meals are served on a wood slab. Open-to-breezes tables are near the yachting activity.

Anse Jambette • *on the beach, near Canaries village* • is worth asking about. If it's open (which isn't always), link it with a day of swimming at the beach. West Indian–style fish and vegetables are offered by reservation. For a delightfully informal island experience, try this.

Capones • *between Reduit Beach and Rodney Bay* • opened with flourishes in March '85, with a glitzy setting conceived by the successful formula used at Rain. The speakeasy atmosphere is helped along by serving staff costumed in 1920s attire, and the menu is decidedly Italian—with pasta emphasis and high prices. A nearby ice cream parlor, with traditional trimmings, serves pizza by the slice, with tables on the "lawn" at the entrance to both places.

Charthouse • *at Rodney Bay's marina* • offers grilled steak, chicken, ribs, or fish, with baked potato, salad, and dessert. The place is popular with those who enjoy U.S.–style staples. (Prime tables, in my opinion, are those nearest the marina.)

Eagle's Inn • *at the "end" of the Reduit Beach Rd., at the Rodney Bay channel* • is a small spot that specializes in St. Lucian–style recipes served on the patio, within view of the channel. There's music and entertainment some evenings.

Ginger Lilly • *near the beachside hotels, north of Castries* • is a Chinese place enjoyed by many. The menu is extensive; the food standard fare.

Green Parrot Restaurant • *up the winding road to the Morne, about 15 minutes' drive out of and above Castries* • is in an unusual setting next to the St. Lucia perfume factory. The restaurant, to the left as you walk up the steps after you've parked your car, is set up for elegant service but didn't rise to expectations when I sampled it for this edition. Food focuses on local specialties. Ask for the chef's special. Prices run about $25 for an entree, but with full meals will be much higher (and are quoted in E.C. currency).

★★ **Humingbird** • *at Soufriere, on the road out to Anse Chastenet* • has a tropical, West Indian atmosphere, with a sea-and-yacht view from most dining tables. There's a small pool, where guests can play (if you've planned ahead with a bathing suit), and menu items that range from interesting hors d'oeuvres served antipasto style to a multi-course meal with St. Lucia's pumpkin soup (which is squash to most North Americans) or some other homemade offering. The birds chirp, the sea laps at the shore, and the thatched roof lends a pleasantly rustic atmosphere.

Jimmie's • *at the Castries marina* • is breeze-swept and pleasant, for lobster or local food served on wood tables on the patio or inside. The bar lures yachting folk and their ilk.

Key Largo • *at the Rodney Bay marina* • serves pizza and other Italian-style fare in plesant surroundings, on a small patio with a pizza oven as focal point and yachts for a background.

Marina Steak House • *neighbor to the A-frame* • is in a former private home, built in A-frame style. Well-cooked steaks share the menu with barbecued items, fish, and Teriyaki chicken.

★ **Rain** • *on the square near the Catholic church inland at downtown Castries* • is a St. Lucian institution. Planted in a special small, wood frame white-painted building more than a decade ago, the restaurant is casual, with a very special Somerset Maugham slightly decadent atmosphere. The 2nd-floor balcony is the prize spot—not only to read from the blackboard to learn the day's offerings, but also to watch the view over town. Count on everything from hamburgers to a multi-course "Champagne Banquet" with several wines.

Depending on your dining hour and personal tastes, you can have breakfast, lunch, or dinner here—and can sample ice cream, delicious desserts, and a panoply of rum and other concoctions. White walls, wicker, and pinpoints of color, plus interesting pictures, posters, and notices make this place a "must" stop on any St. Lucian visit. Fortunately, Rain is open from about 10 a.m. until late evening, when the atmosphere changes with the light.

Plantation House • *in the main house, near the pool, at Bois d'Orange, off the road north of Castries* • is tidy, airy, and creole in feeling, with white walls, orange and madras fabric accents, and good local food.

★★ **San Antoine** • *in the hills, overlooking Castries* • stands on the site of mid-1800s Great House, incorporating the stone walls that remained after a 1970s fire into the sensational surroundings. This is a place for a lingering lunch (if you want to enjoy the view) or a leisurely romantic dinner. The route up to, or down from, this spot is along winding roads above Castries. Breezes sweep the terrace area, while inside tables are set with napery and tableware intended to recall the 1800s. My meals have been very special, with imaginative preparation and presentation of fresh ingredients. Lasagne and fettucine join various more standard offerings on the food list, and desserts are hard to refuse. (They're presented in style aboard a covered cart.)

The Still • *on a side street in Soufriere* • is a long way to go from Castries for dinner, especially to a place that is best when you're part of a large, fun-filled group, but it gives you the opportunity to dine in refurbished ruins of a plantation house. For most visitors, this is a luncheon stop on a day of touring. Guests can arrange for special dinners here, where the verdant growth disguises the remains of the 1900s' rum distillery.

NATURAL SURROUNDINGS: Except for the beach-fringed coves north and south of Castries, on the calmer west coast, most of St. Lucia remains in its natural state. First-time visitors can sample verdant tropical growth by following the marked paths that lead from San Antoine, a hillside restaurant above Castries, but that's a pretty tame walk. The Pitons, two often photographed peaks rising dramatically from the southwest coast, can be climbed. The tourist office can help with finding a reliable guide, often available through the Forestry service. (Plan a few days in advance to assure yourself of a guided hike.)

Although some of the northern cap of the island has been divided for homesites, there are many areas that are untrammeled. The 40-acre Pigeon Island has become Pigeon Point, with landfull making a causeway between the former island and the west coast at Gros Ilet, but the area continues to be a bird sanctuary; many of this area's rock formations are dramatic.

The most impressive terrain is in the south, at the rain forest at Mahaut and in the volcanic areas around Soufriere. Mt. Gimie is St. Lucia's highest peak, but Piton Canaries and Piton Tromasse are the most dramatic. They are joined by Mt. Houlom as part of the preserve that make up the rain forest—and provide a home for the endangered, colorful St. Lucian parrot *(Amazona Ver-*

sicolor) and other birds. The area is also rich with orchids and various kinds of tropical flora.

The Sulphur Springs are a popular tourist site, especially for those who have never seen a volcanic sulfur vent. Tours drive into the 7-acre crater to see several pools, with the hot springs a much-touted focus. Diamond Falls and Diamond Baths, waterfalls and a natural pool that are a result of the volcano's past eruptions, are walking goals, along paths that have been trod by most who leave the beaches to explore St. Lucia. Sea birds nest at Moule a Chique, a dramatic cliff-bordered peninsula at the southern hook of the island.

The St. Lucia National Trust maintains the Maria Islands Nature Reserve, on the Atlantic side of the south-coast town of Vieux-Fort. Included in the area are about 25 acres of Maria Major and 4 acres of Maria Minor, home for a native lizard and a non-poisonous snake, among other fauna. Frigate birds, terns, doves, and other bird species thrive in the Reserve. Your hotel can make contact with the Interpretive Centre for visits, which are permitted except at nesting time.

Plantations are still a mainstay of St. Lucia's economy; crops flourish in the rich soil of the valleys. Not far from Castries, in the north, the Marquis Plantation offers guided tours, with commentary about the crops and the historic plantation lifestyle.

Insofar as nature offshore is concerned, dive masters take their clans to sites off Soufriere including the shelf that drops off the beach at Anse Chastenet hotel, as well as to shipwrecks, Piton Wall, the Keyhole Pinnacles, and elsewhere. Strong currents make the diving suitable only for experts and at other times only because these seas remain relatively unexplored.

PLACES WORTH FINDING: The best view over Castries is from the top of the Morne Fortune (the mountain that rises behind the town), but the Morne itself is not much to look at, having been subdivided into building lots in the last half of the '60s. There's part of Fort Charlotte, started in 1794 and named for the mother (Queen Charlotte) of Edward, Duke of Kent, that is worth a wander, but otherwise watch a cricket match or a football/soccer game played by some of the young people who attend the school and university in some of the refurbished buildings, note the hospital (which has been used for a St. Lucian government-Rockefeller Foundation study of schistosomiasis) and head for a beach. The hospital is in what was a barracks building; the Batmen's Quarters, shown on a map of 1846, are the museum for the **St. Lucia Archaeological and Historical Society;** the Canteen (on maps of 1846) is a lecture hall for the university, and the Combermere Barracks is a technical school. Although most of the authentic historical feeling has been lost with the new building uses, the site *is* worth visiting, mainly for the views on the way up and from the top. (Typical of new uses for old buildings, the Top of the Morne apartments are in what was the headquarters building, erected in 1891 but unrecognizable for its venerable past now.)

CASTRIES has been burned and rebuilt so many times in its history that there's not much of historic interest, as far as buildings are concerned. The town thrives as a West Indian port, with the fishing boats lining up in the morning on the north side of the harbor (easily seen as you drive out of town to the hotels on the northwest shore). Find the town square, a couple of streets back from the waterfront, for the most interesting buildings. One is **Cathedral of the Immaculate Conception,** built in 1894 on the site of previous churches and completed in 1897. The wood inside is worth noting, if you like imposing buildings. Otherwise, look from the outside (you can't miss it) and head for the upper porch at Rain restaurant to watch the meandering activity around the square. The **Market,** at the north end of town, is the only other sight of note. The market building was formally dedicated in 1894 by Sir Charles Bruce, but it will be difficult to imagine an imposing proper Englishman in the middle of the fray you'll witness on market day. Take time, when you wander around here, and be sure to look at the buses as they get stuffed to the splitting point before they head out of town back to the villages.

AUTHOR'S OBSERVATION

Invest $3 in *St. Lucia Historic Sites* (1975) by Robert Devaux, published on behalf of the Saint Lucia National Trust. The ponderous book lists sites, monuments, buildings in a strictly functional fashion, but the background information will be interesting if you want to explore on your own. Inquire at the Tourist Board if you have trouble tracking down a copy.

Moule-a-Chique, the southernmost point, near Vieux Fort, is an interesting ride for the view, but the lighthouse perched at the point, and the stone buildings you can note around it, were built in 1911, so there's no point in heading here for history. The view, along the shores where Halcyon Days reigns supreme, and out to sea is spectacular.

For a more interesting route, in my opinion, drive through **Vieux Fort,** a village with small buildings, cluttered with people, chickens and sometimes pigs on dirt roads; with shops tucked into the wood West Indian buildings (Agatha's Art & Boutique; Kitch Tailoring Boutique, Charles Supermarket, all small and surviving on local business). **Laborie,** another village, about 25 minutes' drive west, has an imposing Catholic church at the turn in the road as you snake around the coast. Follow the road up, down and around the shore toward **Choiseul,** a town which rumor claims is destined for a big hotel. The waterfront street in Choiseul spills into the sea, there's a handcraft center on the hill as you head into town, and then you'll wind past the graveyard, the Catholic Church, and the fishing boats, nets and traps at the shore. (About 1½ hours along this route, you'll come to the turnoff for Dasheene apartments—see "Housekeeping Holidays.") **Soufriere,** half-burned in the 1900s, is a clutter of pastel houses set on the shore. The town was the earliest French community, and is a goal these days for the sulphur vents at the volcano in the hills where your guide will either talk about—or actually perform—cooking an egg in the steam. At **Diamond Estate** (a banana plantation) there are mineral baths that periodically come into conversations as "about to be developed." At the moment, you can wallow if you want, but there's nothing fancy or even very organized about the facilities. (The claim is that Louis XVI used the baths during a French reign over St. Lucia, in the years of English-French squabbling over possession of the island.)

SPORTS simmer down to a complete list, with a little of everything, and among the Caribbean's best for some. **Sailing** facilities are centered around *Sunsail, Tradewinds,* (T 809+452–8424), *Austro Yachting,* and *Via Carib* at Rodney Bay and Marigot, where *The Moorings Yacht Charters* nests their yachts at an historic harbor with some of the Caribbean's most picturesque surroundings. The planned programs include crewed yachts with 7-night itineraries, combination crewed yacht and hotel (at Marigot Bay Resort) accommodations for multinight vacations, as well as bareboat (a yacht you sail yourself) and flotilla programs where several yachts cruise Morgan 46s with the lead boat a Morgan 60. For full details on The Moorings programs, contact their U.S. office (1305 U.S. 19 South, #402, Clearwater, FL 33546, T 813+536–1187 or 800+535–7289).

Several independent yachts offer themselves for day charters, with skipper, crew—and lunch. One source for finding out which yachts are around when you are is *St. Lucia Yacht Services* at the Vigie Marina (452–5057). Another is *Tradewinds Charters,* mentioned above.

Other **boat trips,** fun for nonsailors as well as those who love the sea in social settings, include the 140-foot, square-rigger *Unicorn,* which sets out from Castries to cruise south down the west coast to Marigot Bay and Soufriere (the character ship offers an open bar and a lot of fun for its lively day; a good investment of about $50), and *Vigie* a motor yacht, makes pretty much the same run. The price is the same, and although the character of the craft isn't as impressive, the day can be a good one if you've gathered with friends.

Boardsailing is popular off many of the west coast beaches. Contact the St. Lucian Hotel for information. They have equipment and offer lessons. There's good windsurfing from the Club Med, at the southern tip of St. Lucia. Proficient boardsailors enjoy the challenges of both Caribbean and Atlantic sea and winds.

Golfers have a choice, of the well-maintained nine holes at Cunard's La Toc, just south of Castries, or the often-parched nine holes at Cap Estate on the island's northern tip near Le Sport Hotel. Greens fees at Cap Estate depend on whether you come from an obviously American hotel or whether you live locally. Going rates have been the E.C. equivalent of the $12 per person per day, with a reasonable weekly charge. Both courses have clubhouses, the Cap Estate arrangement being more independent of the hotels than the setup at La Toc, which is obviously part of one.

Horseback riding can be arranged at *Trim's Riding Stables* (Cas-en-Bas and at Cap Estate, 452–8273). Rene Trim leads trail rides and a weekly picnic trip on the Atlantic (east) coast plus other planned rides and lessons.

Tennis courts are at Le Sport, Cunard's La Toc, Halycon Beach, Vigie. Lucian, the St. Lucian, and Couples II in the Castries area, and at the Club Med on the south coast, near Vieux Fort and Anse Chastanet, on the southwest coast, at Soufriere.

Scuba diving is organized through your hotel, probably with *Scuba St. Lucia* (at Anse Chastanet, 454–7354) *The Moorings Scuba Centre* (at Marigot Bay, 453–4357) or *Buddies* (at the Vigie Marina, 452–5288). If you want details in advance, phone them. The resort course (to give beginners confidence to make at least one dive) is about $50, with dive tours on the west coast figuring about $50 with the price variation depending on the location and your expertise. Dive packages of about six dives cost about $150, but check for details when you arrive and phone in advance to be sure of equipment availablility. Anse Chastanet Hotel has special scuba week-long, dives included, holidays and a film processing lab for underwater photographers. Instruction, gear rental, and boat rentals are part of the watersports operation.

TREASURES AND TRIFLES were centered only in Castries until a few years ago, when hotels added boutiques and craft shops on their premises and **Pointe Seraphine,** the cruise ship area, became the best place to shop. It has a duty-free complex where your can find luxury imports from around the world as well as island-made items. There are 20-odd shops clustered around the courtyards that makes for easy strolling from one place to the next. Among the crafts are clothing made by island steamstresses, silk-screened and batiked fabrics, woodcarving (some of it Haitian), straw work, and other items of varying quality. One Pointe Seraphine boutique is the **Island Connection Boutique,** with a shop also on Monigraud Street in Castries. Included in the wares are coasters, wall-hangings, and other items with island scenes drawn by Barbados resident Jill Walker and the NafNaf comfortably casual resortwear, which is also available at chic shops in Mt. Martin/Sint Maarten and elsewhere. Although it can be lively when a cruise ship's in port, the complex is "dead" at other times. Downtown Csatries is a mixture of shops for residents and shops where tourists may find something to buy, but commerce is mostly geared for residents. **Noah's Arkade** on Jeremie Street has some interesting West Indian books (and a complete Penguin paperback collection), plus flour-sack shirts, plenty of carved wood figures, St. Lucian pottery of good quality, and an unusual selection of bowls, mats, and hats.

The Bagshaws silk-screen designs first made news over 20 years ago, when the Bagshaws retired to St. Lucia from U.S. pressures. They put their considerable talents to work incorporating island themes into colorful designs, screening the patterns on plain fabric, and selling placemats, wall hangings, and eventually shirts, skirts, and yard goods. Today the shop and studio that sit on the shore on a hill outside Castries (you can walk along the beach from La Toc if you plan ahead and bring your money and a cover-up for shopping) burst at the seams with tourists when the cruise ships are in port. At other times, you can wander around on your own to pick through the piles of merchandise, priced in US$. There's a room to the right as you enter the shop that has had some sale items worth looking at; otherwise, I've found the consistently good and interesting designs to be the birds and flowers that were some of the Bagshaws' first. If you're a nonshopper, you can swing in the wicker chairs on the porch or peek at the studio operation if it's open and running when you're here.

Ruth Clarage, at La Toc, carries the well-made, colorful Caribbean fashions well-known to those who knew Jamaica in the old days. Clothes include men's jackets, children's clothes and fashions for the ladies. Other places to find attractive, comfortable, warm-weather clothes are **Windjammer Clothing** and **Top Banana,** both in hotels.

The **Castries Market** is well worth a wander, but not slung with cameras and in your colorful tourist togs. You'll look different enough as it is, even if you are dressed conservatively and try to look inconspicuous as you poke around the piles of fruits, vegetables, fish, and handwork, made by people who trek weekly to Castries in hopes of selling and/or bartering for their weekly needs. On one visit through the market, I found some sturdy wood and reed chairs which, although bulky to bring home, have withstood the ravages of time. They are handmade and solid.

The **West Indian Sea Island Cotton Shop,** on Bridge Street, has a good selection of silk-screened and other fabrics, some of which can be made to order to the pattern of your choice (often by copying a dress you brought with you) while you're here.

Caribelle Batik, and its **Koconuts,** has its workshop and sales shop for the island-designed fabric at Howelton House out Old Victoria Road, and another shop at the *St. Lucian Hotel.*

Y. De Lima, on William Peter Blvd., the block-long esplanade in the center of town off Bridge Street, has the expected crystal, china, watches, etc. for tourist purchase. Check on prices, and don't count on a complete selection of all patterns. If you want a specific pattern or item write to the store in advance of arrival to find out it it's in their stock. Cox and Company is a department store to prowl if you are interested in household sundries.

The **government handicraft center for strawwork**—including woven grass rugs rolled up to carry out—is a marvelous place to poke around, for baskets and other items, at prices you can bargain about. The small shop is at the waterfront, toward the main Castries market.

The **Arts & Crafts Development Centre,** near Choiseul on the southwest coast, deserves special mention. Talented St. Lucians are encouraged to create their specialties, be it wood carvings, tapestries, baskets, dishes, or something else. With the help of the U.S. Peace Corps, and teaching of basketweaving and other crafts by Taiwanese, the center was thriving when I stopped by. There are items for sale; visitors are also encouraged to go into the workshops to watch works-in-progress.

SINT MAARTEN/ ST. MARTIN

> Sint Maarten De Ruyterplein, Philipsburg, Sint Maarten, N.A., T 011+599+552-2337, fax 011+599 52-4884; Sint Maarten Tourism Representative, 275 7th Ave., New York, NY 10001, T 212+989-0000, fax 212+627-1152; 243 Ellerslie Ave., Willowdale, Toronto, Ontario, Canada, T 416+223-3501.
>
> St. Martin Tourist Information Bureau, Waterfront, Marigot, F.W.I., T 011+590-87.53.26; St. Martin, French West Indies Tourist Board, 610 Fifth Ave., New York, NY 10020, T 212+757-1125. (Refer to Guadeloupe chapter for F.W.I. offices elsewhere.)

$ · · · US$1 = NAf1.77 or about 5.5 French francs
(Confirm at travel time.)
Unless otherwise noted, all references are to U.S. dollars.

The view from the second-floor balcony would make a marvelous painting. Luxury sailboats bob at anchor, with hand-built island freight boats as a counterpoint. Baskets of vegetables are piling up at the waterfront, with the help of an assortment of men and boys who lift the cargo when conversation permits.

The scene played out almost at our feet, but the view toward the calm and quiet of neighbor island Anguilla permitted a sense of peace. We could savor crisp salad and grilled fish, served with island limes, and sip wine while we watched the activity below. The price for the meal seemed obscene, but it did include the waterfront entertainment. Somehow the total, although higher than it might have been, was acceptable.

This island is like that. There are moments that are priceless—and usually there's no charge for them. Other encounters, often involving taxis, restaurants, and hotel rooms, come at high cost, but there are ways to skirt those costs if your pocketbook can't stand it.

Sint Maarten/St. Martin seems like a massive construction site, so fast has building on this island moved. The island continues to (over) build with awesome statistics and development. French and Dutch cultures are sometimes braided in amusing ways (and other times stand impressively separate, even when shar-

ing nearby plots of land), but the 37-square-mile island has an overwash of American commerce that threatens to overwhelm the best of the two countries' traditions.

In the 17th century, after the Dutch had laid claim to the south part and French from settlements in Guadeloupe claimed the north, people used to walk back and forth between French Marigot and Dutch Philipsburg. Probably not every day, but often enough to bring news—and to make it.

Scottish John Philips, for whom Philipsburg is named, always claimed that the island should be under one flag, but the 1648 division treaty held—at least for most of the island's history. When Salomon Gibbes, a Swede, was commander of the colony at Sint Maarten he saw to it that Barthelemy Curet, a Frenchman with debts on the Dutch side, was locked in the Philipsburg jail. A covey of Curet's cronies marched from Marigot to plead his case, and while the council debated, they strolled past the jail and stole the jubilant sinner, parading him and another prisoner on a flag-waving march back to Marigot.

Not long after 1793, after the Dutch had secured their possession from the Spanish but were still squabbling with the English, Commander Rink ordered a march on Marigot by his Orange Company guard. His purpose was to protect the entire island from English invasion (and his Dutch colony from problems with the French), but his immediate project was to march with his men, dragging a cannon to French Fort Louis, which the Dutch would name Fort Willem Frederik. For a few years, St. Martin was governed by the Dutch, with an administrative council of Frenchmen who reported to the Philipsburg-based island council.

The roles reversed with the political waves of Europe. When the power of France welled over the Netherlands at the end of the 18th century, Guadeloupe ordered the Dutch to give up their claim to French St. Martin and to become the occupied part themselves. A garrison of Frenchmen lived in Sint Maarten and built themselves a fort. That period lasted until 1801, when the English invaded—to clear the air during their occupation of less than a year.

By 1802, sides would be separated again, according to the treaty of 1648. The Frenchmen of St. Martin would continue with their own language, coins, and customs; the Dutchmen on Sint Maarten would do the same with theirs, and the trade, then transports, then tourists would continue to cross borders without noticing more than the view.

AUTHOR'S OBSERVATION

Comment about the spelling of Sint Maarten (Dutch) and St. Martin (French) is constant and confusing. In this chapter, when a place is on the Dutch side, the island will be referred to as Sint Maarten; when it is on the French side, St. Martin will be the spelling, but you can drive from Marigot, St. Martin, to Philipsburg, Sint Maarten, in about half an hour on weaving roads and barely know when you've crossed the border, which is noted only with "welcome" signs. Whichever spelling is used, the other "country" is a stone's throw away, perhaps not politically, but practically.

POLITICAL PICTURE: Politics plays an important role in Sint Maarten today. At least one local politician (Claude Wathey) had a firm hold on the tourism strategy for the Dutch part of the island for many years but he was voted out, and is now a vocal opposition member. His Democratic Party was defeated in elections held April 12, 1991. The Dutch side is now governed by a coalition of the St. Maarten Patriotic Alliance and the Progressive Democratic Party.

The French side is governed by a *sous-prefet* who eventually reports to Guadeloupe, seat of the government of one French *departement*. Substantial changes, some of them improvements, in the past few years have brought an interesting tourism to St. Martin, with bistros, small hotels, huge resorts, and a casual, seaside focus akin to that of the French Riviera. Although the French side has been a Caribbean area with a very special French flavor, building in the past few years has yanked it into the forefront of modern Caribbean tourism. Sint Maarten is the largest and most developed of the northern triumvirate of the Netherlands Antilles. The three "S islands" (Sint Maarten, Saba, and Statia) are grouped as the Dutch Windward Islands. (They, in fact, mingle in the Caribbean Sea with what the British refer to as the Leewards.) The three islands send senators to the Staten that convenes in Curacao (Sint Maarten has 3 senators; Saba and Statia each have one). Sint Maarten's allegiance to North American commerce is strong, with firm links forged with U.S. entrepreneurs, through the big hotels and certainly with the casinos. Commercial interests with other parts of the world include a longtime liaison with a Japanese group for a fishing operation based near Philipsburg, and ventures with European, Arab, and other countries.

The Dutch claimed Sint Maarten in 1631, and used it as a way station between their community of New Holland in Brazil and New Netherlands (New York) on the east coast of North America. Dutchmen came over from their colony at Christiansted, St. Croix to settle Sint Eustatius in the late 1630s, and they claimed Statia in 1640. Sint Maarten (Dutch) continues to yield to Americanisms which include Kentucky Fried, Burger King, Pizza Hut, and a tempo that keeps time with U.S.–style, warm-weather condominium life. The casinos on the Dutch side can be fun although some are becoming as frenetic as Las Vegas or Atlantic City.

ISLAND APPEARANCE is best when you look offshore, or out the airplane's window. There are some spectacular views of Saba, Statia, St. Barths, Anguilla, and some of the smaller islets when you drive around the island. From the road that climbs up from the airport area heading toward Philipsburg, you can see the offshore islands of Saba and Statia as well as get a good view over Simpson Bay Lagoon toward Marigot; from the eastern road out of Philipsburg, weaving out to Oyster Pond, there are spectacular views toward French St. Barthelemy; and from Grand Case and Marigot, the view toward Anguilla is lovely. Beautiful white, soft-sand beaches rim most coves, but they've been bordered on their inland side by hotels and/or condominiums in recent years. Boutiques, restaurants, cafes, hotels, and clutter gather like barnacles along the narrow roads in the towns of Philipsburg, Marigot, and Grand Case. Building scars are now destroying the once pristine, although often sun-parched, hillsides of the northeastern quadrant, which is French. The entire 37-square-mile island seems to me to look more like a construction site than like a Caribbean paradise. Sint Maarten/St. Marten is fast losing, or has already lost, most of what it once had in the way of natural beauty.

LIFESTYLE is Americanized on the Dutch side of Sint Maarten, and French on the French side. Speaking French can be fun (but is not essential) on the French side of the island. Speaking English is common practice on the Dutch side, where you will only hear an occasional word of Dutch.

Ties with Holland are most obvious with place names (Juliana Airport, for example), food, and holidays. Most of the Netherlands' official holidays are celebrated in Sint Maarten (but not necessarily on the French side of the island). The French holidays are celebrated on the French side where a French atmosphere prevails. An impressive list of strictly local holidays, some geared to political rallies and other occasions, also appear on the calendar. The Dutch side's stores will carry extravagant displays of Dutch cheeses (check the supermarkets), Bols gin, and Heineken and Amstel beer. Dutch devotion to the dollar or guilder, or whatever the going currency happens to be, is typical of the homeland and reflects its commercial history. On the French side, supermarkets and many shops are true to French style, imports, and currency (the French franc). Sint Maarten is small in size but big in impact in the vacation world.

AUTHOR'S OBSERVATION

The coalition government voted into office in April 1991 promised a war against crime and the problem is being addressed. It has not, however, been solved. Crime, rudeness, and high prices continue to make me wonder if this island has exchanged sincere smiles for dedicated dollar signs.

Clothes for Sint Maarten/St. Martin are Caribbean casual, and sometimes elegant. Jackets are seldom seen these days, especially during summer season, but some men wear them for some of the official government functions, or special resort evenings during the winter season. Men seldom wear ties. Women can enjoy dressing up in resort clothes in the evenings. Fashionable resortwear, with European panache, is worn some places, usually for parties at a private home. Mini-skirts, dressy pants, and calf-length summer dresses are common sights. Daytime wear is comfortably casual, but please—for the sake of residents if not for other tourists—no bathing suits in shopping centers or on the streets of town or bare chests in dining areas. Keep the bare-look for the beach and cover up when you go to town or island touring.

MEDICAL FACILITIES vary depending on which side of the island you are on. The French side's hospital near Marigot is related to services on Guadeloupe, with the most extensive facilities on Guadeloupe. This hospital is regarded as an adjunct of the Guadeloupe hospital, where specialists come from mainland France at regular intervals and most doctors have trained at hospitals in Europe. On the Dutch side the small hospital on the main street in Philipsburg, on the waterfront, has been replaced by a modern hospital built near the

Belair Hotel, on the outskirts of Philipsburg, to the west. It has excellent facilities. North American visitors with serious problems often fly to hospitals in Miami, Puerto Rico, or other U.S. cities.

MONEY MATTERS: Although the Netherlands Antilles guilder or florin, noted as NAf or Afl on price tags for merchandise (and in the supermarkets), is the official unit of currency for the Dutch side, and the French franc is the official currency for the French side, the U.S. dollar bridges the gap and is accepted everywhere. You may get change in the local currency (especially on the French side), but you can use dollars to pay bills. When you pay with dollars on the French side, the exchange rate is not often in your favor. Credit cards and travelers' checks are accepted most places.

AUTHOR'S OBSERVATION

Be attentive when you pay bills. On one gas transaction, the attendant accepted U.S. dollars for a cost that was on the meter in guilders. Only when he was specifically asked did he admit that we had overpaid. And in restaurants, when you use a credit card, the "service charge" that is on your bill for 12% or 15% is lumped with the cost of the meal; the "service/tips" space is blank. If, in accepted U.S. style, you add 15% service, you will have paid either 27% or 30%! Even when I've asked, some waiters have said that service is *not* included. They're wrong; it usually is! Be aware of scams—in this very tourist-oriented island.

COMMUNICATIONS include links between Dutch and French systems making intra-island phoning tedious. Direct dial from overseas to the French side involves the 011 overseas code + 590 + the 6-digit number; for places on the Dutch side, the routing is 011 + 599 + 5 and the 5-digit number. Getting in your car and driving to the place you're trying to call is sometimes more reliable than the local phone system. Facsimile machines are widely used, but count on mailed letters to take 10 days or more. Air mail from the U.S. is 50¢ for the first half ounce.

ARRIVAL at Princess Juliana International Airport, on the Dutch side, will bring you into an area where appendages have been added to the original terminal to make the big "new terminal."

Immigration officials are stone-faced, strictly-business, often rude types who look at you—and the Immigration card you have filled out on the plane (keep the copy for departure), your proof of citizenship (passport is best; voter's registration or a notarized copy of your birth certificate will do; driver's license is *not* sufficient since it does not prove citizenship)—and then take up the next in line. Luggage claim takes a while since the carts to get the luggage from the plane are not sufficient to bring a fully loaded cargo to the terminal with anything resembling speed and this island's tourism has outpaced its people's ability to cope. The Sint Maarten Tourist Bureau information booth, usually (but not always) open from 7:30 a.m.–9 p.m., has leaflets and staff to answer questions about hotels, rates, and facilities. Check there or with one of the tourism aides about cab fares before you get in a car.

AUTHOR'S OBSERVATION

If you are going to British affiliated Anguilla or French St. Barths, or "out of the country" for the day, you will have to pay the $5 departure tax, fill out all forms, and go through Immigration *again* when you reenter Sint Maarten that evening. Since Saba and Statia are both Dutch, there is no $5 to pay for those day excursions. If you leave to come home the following day (or whenever you leave), you will be hit with *another* $5 departure tax. (You do not have to pay the $5 if you are "in transit.") I find that system annoying, although I'll grant that it is good for Sint Maarten's coffers.

CRUISE ships usually anchor offshore and bring passengers into the main street of Philipsburg by small boat. One result of this procedure is that, on some cruise itineraries when the sea is rough, the port may be skipped in favor of smoother seas (or better docking facilities) elsewhere. Some ships, if they are small enough, can dock at the pier at the left arm of Philipsburg Bay, as you face the sea from shore. Passengers on those ships are closest to Philipsburg for shopping and restaurants. Beginning with winter 1987–88, an occasional small cruise ship began to come to Marigot, a fact that is certain to destroy the final remnants of a sleepy town if or when the calls increase.

DEPARTURE, even for a day trip to another island, involves check-in at least 45 minutes before flight time, passing the immigration folks (which you must do even for Saba and Statia which are still Netherlands Antilles territory) to pay your $5 departure tax even for day excursions to non-Dutch islands, and waiting for planes that are often delayed. Be sure to listen for your flight, and make inquiries if you're uncertain. The small plane operation is reasonably casual, and announcements are not always clear.

For international flights, it's wise to check in at least an hour in advance since lines are often long, and the process for check-in can be a slow one. There are restaurant and shopping facilities *before* you go through immigration, and pay your departure tax, as well as after.

There are several shops (liquor, watches, jewelry, and Dutch cheese) at the airport, as well as a good restaurant, *Cafe Juliana* (upstairs), but all must be visited *before* you go through immigration and security check. Once inside that area, you are *not* allowed out.

TOURING TIPS: Plan to rent a car if you want mobility. **Taxis** are expensive and in my opinion seem to be a "law unto themselves." If you are going to one of the hotels near the airport, you may have some trouble finding a driver willing to take you from the airport.

If you are planning to tour by taxi or to go to one of the several good restaurants around the island for dinner, negotiate the fare in advance, and ask if the driver will come back for you at a specified time. It's difficult and time-consuming to wait for a cab on call.

As far as **rental cars** are concerned, many firms have booths at the airport as well as offices downtown and contact desks at major hotels, but, since the taxi union has a stranglehold on the airport, no rental firm can provide a car there. You'll have to take a taxi to the rental firm's office or wait for a car to be delivered to your hotel after you've checked in.

AUTHOR'S OBSERVATION

It's worth shopping for the best price at other than peak season. During peak winter months (February and March), when cars are at a premium, you may find your car "gone" even though you have reserved in advance. In my experience, if you wave your coupon and insist, a car will be produced—probably one for someone arriving on the next flight.

In addition to local car rental companies with *Hertz, Avis, Budget,* and *National* affiliation, there are independent companies. On more than one recent visit, I've rented from *Opel Car Rental* (T 011+599-54-2644), with offices near the end of the runway (but too far to walk there from the airport). Ask for Rolando, and be sure to discuss the best rate. Time spent chatting about types of cars, length of rental, and the weather can sometimes help with your rental rate. I've also used *Risdon* (T 011+599+52-3578) on several occasions, but have found their rates to be among the most expensive. Most firms have new cars, well maintained and usually delivered clean and in good condition.

AUTHOR'S OBSERVATION

Thievery has reached such proportions on this island that many cars have broken locks; some rental firms will warn you about parking in certain places. I'd suggest leaving nothing of value in your car at any time. Some rental firms demand a deposit for gas. You'll save money if you fill the tank before returning your rental, but be forewarned that some gas stations will happily accept U.S. dollars in the amount that their tanks show in florins—thereby multiplying your cost by 1.7! Be wise and be wary.

It's possible to walk from the airport to both *Budget* and *Speedy Car Rentals* car pick-up areas, if you turn right and walk along the road when you come out from the luggage claim area.

Mopeds can be rented, by day or week, through *Moped Cruising N.V.* (T 011+599+52-2330). Be forewarned that although main roads around the island are in good condition, the backcountry or remote beach roads on both sides are often little more than dirt lanes with perilous potholes. Signposting is not ideal, but it's hard to get too lost on an island this size.

LODGING choices include "everything," from posh, elegant 5-star places to cozy guest houses on the shore and around the island. Included also are an increasing number of self-catering places, partially because there's a shortage of hotel workers and also because there's less payroll for owners. Many apartment clusters have resort facilities: tennis courts, pools, watersports, restaurants, and shops.

In general, the atmosphere on the French side, near and in Marigot and Grand Case, is more European/French than the Americanized Dutch-side hotels. French investors (and hoteliers) practice the procedures well known in mainland France, and their clientele is often European.

For the best values, inquire about package plans, no matter which hotel you choose. Most properties have some plan where "extras" are included for those who ask about them and where rates are favorable for multi-night stays.

Tourism facilities have been a fact of life for Dutch Sint Maarten since the late 1950s, although the rampant, apparently uncontrolled, building since the early 1980s makes those early hotels seem old-fashioned. The French side's interest in tourism has shifted into high gear only since 1986, with formation of its own hotel association, separate and distinct from the hotel association of the Dutch side. Expect to find construction "everywhere." The *Caribbean Newsletter* (page 9) will have updates when new places open.

AUTHOR'S OBSERVATION

Monies that are being invested in Sint Maarten/St. Martin have obviously not come only from "successful tourism." It's worth giving some thought to possible sources. Some of the hundreds of rooms now available will probably be offered in multi-night packages at bargain rates. Ask your travel agent about good deals that may be offered at the "last minute."

Some of the smaller properties do not accept credit cards for payment. Be sure to inquire in advance, especially if you are staying at housekeeping clusters, where you must pay your bill with travelers' checks, cash, or personal check.

There's a 5% tax on your room rate; many hotels also add a service charge, which ranges from 10% to 15%. Ask if your maid and others who've been helpful get that sum.

AUTHOR'S AWARDS

For location and potential, *La Samanna* is back on my list, for its promise to offer ultimate luxury; the small *Horny Toad* is a personal favorite, because its owners know what hospitality and friendly atmosphere are all about; I like *Oyster Pond* because it has exceptional food and is away from most of the clutter.

Information about places to stay is included under Hotels/Resorts, Housekeeping Holidays, the Inn Way, and Low-Cost Lodgings. Stars are awarded within each catgegory (See page 11).

HOTELS/RESORTS on Sint Maarten/St. Martin include once small places that have added appendages to become big hotels, places that were built to be big resort hotels with casinos, places that are intended for time share, and compact hotels with style. There are a couple of price-inclusive hotels, but *be sure you know exactly what is included*. It may not be "everything," as is the case at the best inclusives.

★★ **La Belle Creole** • *on a point of the French side, near Marigot* • opened in March 1988, after many false starts. More than 30 years ago, this "Mediterranean village" was started, under the auspices of Claude Phillipe, well known maitre d'hotel in the '50s at New York's Waldorf Astoria. As his fortunes fell, so did the plans for this place—and it stood, a shell subject to the vagaries of weather and trespassers, until U.S. domestic Hilton Hotel Corp. took it over as the first in its chain of Conrad International hotels. (The name "Hilton" for overseas properties is owned by another company.) Although glamorous and dramatic when it was first planned, the property is trapped by the fact that newer and more impressive places have been built in intervening years. I feel this place falls short of its mark, with pretentious surroundings, anticipated service unrealized by too many on the staff, a mediocre beach, and rooms scattered around the grounds linked by stone walkways that make walking in heels treacherous. *Resort hotel.*

★★★ **Caravanserai** • *near the airport, with a small beach* • perches at the end of the runway, within earshot of the many roaring planes. The hotel has two pools near the shore and attractive public and dining areas. With a cosmetic investment of $2.4 million, the property benefits from much needed attention. Rooms are attractively furnished, with my preference being those that have a view out to sea. (Some look into public areas and lack any privacy. A few have kitchens.) Originally opened for the season of 1965, when the island's tourism was in its infancy, the once small inn has grown with the times, to flourish with trappings demanded by luxury-loving guests. You're near Mullet Bay for golf and tennis. *Hotel.*

Club Orient • *near Le Galion* • offers beach-in-the-buff. The chalet-style cottages provide simple shelter for those who want a nudist holiday. The beach is open for others who want "naturalist" surroundings; you won't need much (anything) in the way of clothes. Bring plenty of sunblock. *Cottages.*

Club Le Grand Beach Resort • *on the shore east of Marigot* • was the Grand St. Martin hotel until it adopted the inclusive plan, to offer guests a multinight holiday at one fixed price for lodging, food, drinks, watersports, etc. Ask specifically what is included if this type of holiday sounds interesting. You're within walking distance of Marigot, at a beach-lined curve of shoreline that is punctuated with several two-story buildings that hold the bedrooms and apartments. There's a pleasant pool, plus on-premise restaurants seaside. *Hotel.*

Coralita Beach • *at Baie Lucas on the French side* • is closer to Philipsburg (about 5 miles) and Juliana Airport than it is to Marigot (almost 10 miles). The 40 rooms are big, modern, and air-conditioned; whether on first or second floor, all have sea view and either small balcony or small patio—and big sea breeze. Facing the prevailing winds, the rooms are slightly protected by having the pool area and the slope of sand in front of them, but count on plenty of breezes. There's one tennis court; buffets and barbecues with music some evenings; and gathering areas that are seldom peopled (from my experience) but comfortably furnished. Check on status; the property needed care. *Hotel.*

★★★ **Divi Little Bay Beach** • *on the beach, about 5 minutes from Philipsburg* • was one of Sint Maarten's first island hotels when it opened in '55, but with its adoption into the Divi family (with hotels in Aruba, Barbados, Bonaire, Cayman Brac, and other islands) developments shifted into high gear and newly built rooms and time-share units cover most of the land. Major investments soon after the adoption resulted in welcomed cosmetic improvements; I'm not so sure about the expansion planned for the fort area where timeshare units blanket the hill. The location—on a beach within easy distance (even a long walk) from Philipsburg—is an asset for those who want to be near town. Rooms in several buildings around the grounds vary in view, size, and location. My favorites continue to be the ones to the left as you face the beach. Other rooms are in 2-story units to the right, facing the beach and in cottages and other buildings up the slope rising from the shore. The property has tennis courts, pools, shops, and a refurbished casino. Morning joggers can lope along the beach shared with neighbor-resort Belair. Count on watersports and other activities and on beachchairs being at a premium during height of winter season when the span of sand gets crowded. *Resort.*

★★ **Flamboyant Bounty I** • *at Baie Nettle* • occupies property that began under the Radisson banner. Operating as an all-inclusive hotel, the property houses its guests in modern rooms, in pseudo-Victorian style-buildings. There's a pool on the premises; the beach is a short walk away. Restaurants serve standard fare, often buffet style. Be sure to ask exactly what's included, which should be drinks, all activities including watersports, plus room, meals, tips, and taxes. Transportation between airport and your hotel is included in the prepaid fee. *Inclusive resort.*

★★ **Flamboyant Bounty II** • *at Cul de Sac, on the way to Meridien L'Habitation* • opened as the Belvedere hotel, in an out-of-the-way location at the eastern shore. Operating on the all-inclusive plan, the property provides modern room, meals, drinks, watersports, activities, plus tips, taxes, and transfers between airport and hotel, which is at least a 35 minute ride. This property is slightly less expensive than *Bounty* I above, probably due to its location, which is pleasant but not in the thick of things. A trip to tiny Ilet Pinel, an offshore isle, is an extra charge, but can be arranged through local boatmen. *Inclusive resort.*

Galion Beach • *at Baie de l'Embouchure* • supplies *huge* rooms around a central area that houses the restaurant, terrace for sunning while dining, the water sports center plus one tennis court and several l-o-n-g strands of sand (Club Orient's beach, nearby, is for naturalists). The hotel is on a cove, about 10 miles from the airport and about 7 weaving miles from both Philipsburg and Marigot. The nationality—and local language—is French, although a sprinkling of North Americans have been known to nest here. The beaches are spectacular, the hotel's own atmosphere quiet, and too spread out to be cozy. *Hotel.*

★★ **Great Bay Beach Resort** • *at the western end of Philipsburg Bay* • has an uncertain future at presstime. Check before booking. There's a casino plus occasional evening entertainment, pool and beach, and shops on the lower level, below the reception desk at the entrance. Rooms vary, from those in the multilevel building to the left of the entrance, where some rooms overlook the parking lot and others look to the sea, and rambling off to the right, where my room had a sea view (and a sewage-type smell some evenings). The walk to town is as easy as strolling along the beach, with a choice of cafes and restaurants to use as pausing places. Although on-premises dining depots include a coffee shop and an air-conditioned "formal" dining area, I say "skip them" and head to others in nearby Philipsburg.

★★ **Maho Beach Resort and Casino** • *near the airport, at the shore* • has received infusions of funds and a new look with renovation. The action-oriented resort hotel stands at one end of the airport runway, which implies planes swooping in and out nearby. New rooms built at the beach (the Islander timeshare set-up) supplement those near the tennis courts and in the main building, where most rooms have sea view. The huge new Las Vegas–style casino across the road is one source for evening activity; restaurants and the events programs are others. There are shops on premises, and recent construction has almost covered this area with buildings. Popular for package tours, groups, and conventions, this place can be lively when there are lots of guests around. The casino and timeshare sales create an overwhelming atmosphere of bustle. Count on U.S.-style offerings in the restaurants and Baskin-Robbins ice cream and many other snack choices at the shopping area. *Big hotel.*

Marine Hotel Simson Bay • *on the lagoon side of Baie Nettle* • is a newcomer for this season, with almost 200 studio and duplex apartments and full hotel services. The 2-story buildings are not on a beach, but there's a pool. *Apts.*

★★★★ **Meridien L'Habitation** • *on l'Anse Marcel, a French side cove* • was adapted by the French chain in early '91. Almost the size of a small town, this place is used by groups and for meetings (including one by Presidents Bush and Mitterrand). Reached by driving an up, over, and around route to a northeast coast cove, the resort includes several attractive buildings full of studios, apartments, standard hotel rooms, public areas with cafes and restaurants, a marina, watersports area, pools, a good beach, and "everything." A French insurance company is the money behind the project, and most rooms, built in international style with Victorian-style lattice-work on the buildings, are attractively furnished. Most are quite large; many have small kitchenettes. Action, with French flair and atmosphere, is part of the plan with the lovely long beach and the pool area two daytime focal points. The hillside pavilion is the site of spa and health club, with pool, exercise equipment, and staff. The disco and one of many restaurants are also at the hillside center. *Big resort.*

Mont Vernon Hotel • *at Orient Bay, on the northwest shore* • is several bands of 3-story buildings that give most rooms a sea view (and the sometimes stern sea breezes that sweep in on this shore). Opened in early 1990, the hotel's 227 suites are attractively furnished with shades of Caribbean sea and flower hues. Beach-level rooms have easy access to the shore, where sea-covered coral can be rough underfoot; upper-level rooms have sea-view balconies. A beach pavilion is the daytime action hub, with windsurfers and other watersports equipment for rent. The on-premises dining room provides most of the evening action for those who prefer not to drive the long and wiggly route to Philipsburg or to Grand Case (which is nearer) in the dark. *Hotel.*

★★★ **Mullet Bay Resort and Casino** • *on 170 acres near the airport* • is a vast resort with the island's only golf course, tennis courts in good condition, a beach with watersports, a swimming pool, several clusters of shops, many restaurants, and rooms in a couple of dozen blocks scattered around the grounds. You'll want a car, unless you enjoy waiting for the shuttle bus—or long walks (in the hot sun, by day). Originally planned as an exclusive winter playground for the Ford family and their friends, this place has grown way beyond its first phase, through a period as part of the Sheraton chain, to a present situation that involves Arab ownership and a new high-rise tower of rooms at the lagoon. Used by convention groups who can be patient with the fragmented layout, this place can be good for families who rent one of the housekeeping elements or with people on a package plan. In winter months, the white sand beach can be people-flecked (and crowded) when the house count is high; surf often swallows huge chunks of sand, returning it days later. There are several well-kept tennis courts. The golf course is only for use by registered guests, residents with membership, and cruise passengers who buy time for a round. *Big resort.*

PLM-Azur St. Tropez • *near Marigot, on the French side* • is closed at press time. The *Caribbean Newsletter* (page 9) will have any news. The property is a big one.

Le Privilege • *on Anse Marcel, near the Meridien* • is a tony newcomer with comfortably furnished rooms and good service. *Small hotel.*

Hotel Royal Beach • *at Baie Nettle, west of Marigot* • is a relative newcomer, with air-conditioned, ocean-facing rooms. *Le Cayali* restaurant has potential; *Le Titiri* is the cozy bar.

★★★★ **La Samanna** • *overlooking Baie Longe, northwest of Mullet Bay* • was the pace-setter for Caribbean luxury when it was built in the mid-1970s, and it reigned supreme for several years. It is still elegant. Tropical foliage surrounds the main check-in area, in a white stucco, Mediterranean-, almost Greek-, style building on the highest hill. The building is sectioned off with a sea-viewing dining terrace, attractively furnished with wood-and-rush chairs and sea-blue cloths on tables. Color accents take their cue from the brilliant bougainvillea blossoms that cascade nearby. The lounge/bar area overlooks the tiled pool; you can linger near the bar or on the poolside terrace. The talcum-powder-white sand of Baie Longe stretches for what seems like miles. Some of the bedrooms needed attention when I last looked, but most have white walls with colored accents; many have a private sunning terrace. The late Jim Frankel was the talented creator of this place, which set the pace for Anguilla's Malliouhana and Cap Juluca. *Classic resort.*

★ **Sint Maarten Beach Club Hotel & Casino** • *in Philipsburg* • is wedged next to the Holland House and the casino, amid shops and restaurants. The beachview rooms that give this place the "beach" in its name are above the casino, at the seaside. There's also a pool, open-air bar area, and dining depot here, but the other 1-bedroom units are across the road, above the elegant shops that line the entryway and around popular *Fandango* restaurant. The 2-bedroom oceanview suites are "the best" and go for top rate. *Hotel.*

★★ **Summit Hotel** • *facing on Simson Bay Lagoon, not far from Mullet Bay* • is several 2-story buildings surrounded with lush tropical growth. Although the hotel is not on a beach, guests can ride on the hotel's jitney service or walk along the dirt road to a nearby one. There's a pool on premises for cooling off; tennis courts are in good condition. The buzz from jet skiers frollicking on the lagoon is an unfortunate addition of recent seasons, marring the atmosphere of the poolside bar and restaurant. Theme nights include music for dancing; buffets are popular, especially for barbecue night. A rental car puts all places within easy distance. Often included in advertised package plans, this hotel offers a hospitable nest near the action at reasonable cost. Bedrooms are modern, air-conditioned, and comfortable. Sliding glass doors that are the entrance for some mean that curtains must be pulled for privacy.

Treasure Island Hotel & Casino at Cupecoy • *on the inland side of the road, northwest neighbor of Mullet Bay* • is in bankruptcy proceedings at press time. The *Caribbean Nesletter* (page 9) will have an update when warranted. It is a community of rooms and apartments, with shops, restaurants, and the casino on the inland side of the road. *Resort.*

HOUSEKEEPING HOLIDAYS on Sint Maarten/St. Martin offer the only way I know of to keep costs under control. In addition to many very lavish houses, there are hundreds of apartments and cottages for rent. Before signing up, be sure to get an island map and find the exact location of the property you're considering. Some locations are better than others, and shorefront is preferred for my vacation dollars.

Several stores, both small and large, cater to the home market, but count on high prices for everything. *Food Centre,* near Philipsburg, is huge and fully stocked, especially with Dutch cheeses, meats, and other items, while *K-dis* on rue de la Republique in the French side's Marigot focuses on French imports (and seemed less expensive when I scouted prices). In addition to these two supermarkets, there are many small spots with specialties. Freshly baked bread, both U.S. style and French, is best when bought daily.

The best source for island villa, cottage and apartment rentals, with very reliable comments and care, is Judith Shepherd's *St. Martin Rentals* (Pelican

House, Beacon Hill at Burgeaux Bay, Sint Maarten; T 011+599+55-4330; fax 011+599+55-5443). Be as specific as possible about price, needs, and location preferences to get her best advice.

Almond Grove • *in the hills, above the east shore of Simpson Bay Lagoon* • may be your ideal haven, if you're not one of those folks who demands sand outside your door. Each house has a full kitchen (with washing machine nearby), and living area that includes either 1, 2, 3, or 4 bedrooms. Located midisland, about 3 miles from the airport and less than that from the French side's capital of Marigot, Almond Grove guests will need a car. There's a pool on premises and *Spartaco* restaurant for dinners. *Villas.*

★ **L'Anse Marigot** • *at Baie Nettle, west of Marigot* • is a cluster of new apartments with kitchenettes. Units include both studios and 1-bedroom suites, upstairs over a bank of shops and cafes. *Apts.*

★ **Beachside Villas** • *on Simpson Bay* • offer clustered apartments, with courtyard, 2-bedrooms, full kitchen, and a laundry room—all on a nice beach. A good spot for families or a comfortable home for a foursome. *Apts.*

Belair Beach Hotel • *at Little Bay Beach* • was built in the season of '81, with deluxe suites that have 2 bedrooms and TV. With 18 suites per floor, the 4-story building has a castlelike appearance, with crenellated roofline. The management plan allows you to rent one of the Belair condominiums when the owners are elsewhere and take your meals at home or at the *Sugar Bird* restaurant at the beach, which is friendly, reasonable, and pleasant for some meals. Count on a beach and sea views. The upper floors have more privacy; ground level gives you the convenience of walking out to the beach, but all passers-by can look in if your drapes aren't drawn. In addition to the restaurant, next-door neighbor Divi Little Bay Beach Hotel has a casino, tennis courts, and beach activity that includes all watersports. *Apt. hotel.*

Captain Oliver's • *overlooking the cove of Oyster Pond* • is another of the French-inspired newcomers, with a flock of cottage units that opened for business in late 1988. Built near a popular open-to-breezes restaurant at a marina, the units are most comfortable for yachting types and others who do not need to be on a beach. (You'll want a rental car to reach one—and every place else, except for the yachts.) Units are attractive, with kitchenettes, narrow twin beds, and modern European-style bathrooms. *Apts.*

★★ **Cupecoy Apartments** • *wedged between the sea/rocks and the road, near Mullet Bay* • is a border of privately owned units, some of which are for rent in owners' absence. Formerly affiliated with the ill-fated Treasure Island Casino complex, these owners split away prior to the bankruptcy proceedings. These apartments were built on the shore in the early 1980s, but the beach they claim is a "sometime" matter, depending on the sea surges and how much sand has been swept away. The top-rate sea view rooms are the best, for my vacation dollar, but other accommodations are modern, spacious, and furnished for easy resort living. The place can be good for families who want a place in the sun. There's a pool on premises. *Apts.*

★★★ **Dawn Beach Hotel** • *at the beach, on the east coast* • is several single-story dwellings scattered near the shore and hotel's hub, and apartments in other buildings on the hillside. Each unit has its own table and chairs that share the small patio with the grill, for outdoor cooking. Units nearest the beach are preferable, in my opinion, since they allow for easy access to a wonderful powdery shoreline. The main social hub, with pool, puts you on a second level for mealtime offerings. For independent housekeeping (with a rental car essential), this place could be pleasant, especially if you don't mind sharing close quarters with your neighbors. Many privately owned villas and condominiums are included in the rental pool. *Cottages.*

Esmeralda Resort • *on Orient Bay* • is a collection of villas amid a few private homes. The pool and other common buildings, with shops and restaurants, lend a country club atmosphere. *Villa resort.*

Gardens at Nettle Bay • *on the shore, just west of Marigot* • is one of several new spots that opened in late 1988. Built on shorefront acreage that was cleared of mangroves and other brush and planted with condominiums, apartments, shops, and hotel rooms, the units are part of a new French-built community. The *Caribbean Newsletter* (page 9) will have comments when developments in this Nettle Bay area take on a life of their own, other than that of a building site. *Apts.*

★★★ **Grand Case Beach Club** • *on the shore at the northeast edge of the village* • is a group of 3-story beachside buildings, with rooms and apartments of varying sizes. *Le Panoramique* dining pavilion perches on the prominent point. Open on all sides, the pavilion can be a pleasant place to look out to sea—and over most of the blocks of rooms and the shoreside of Grand Case village. Units are attractively furnished, with modern comforts, reasonable space, and, for most rooms, a balcony or terrace view of the sea. On the spot managers, Michael and Sheila Acciani, guide an ambitious project; this place is no longer the cozy outpost that lured the first season's guests, but that success led to this. *Apt. hotel.*

Holland House • *on Great Bay Harbor at Philipsburg* • fills a sliver of beachfront, amid the shops and restaurants of the Dutch town with stacks of hotel rooms and apartments. Top floor rooms with sea view share a wood deck, which can be pleasant if your neighbors are. When you open your sliding glass doors, your room becomes "common property." Efficiency kitchens are tucked into one niche of the room; beds are narrow (Dutch-style) and rooms facing the street can be noisy—and obviously viewless. Lobby staff is casual, in a style common on Sint Maarten, the bar at the shore edge, near the small pool, seems to be a "local hangout," with assorted types draped around the bar and a few flip comments from the bartenders didn't do much for the atmosphere. The *Tulip Restaurant* overlooks the bay. (Sint Maarten Beach Club's *Peacock Casino* is next door, amid shops and cafes.) *Apts.*

★ **Laguna Beach Hotel** • *at Baie Nettle, west of Marigot* • is one of several new places built in pseudo-Victorian style near the shore. Basic kitchenettes placed, in French style, on the small patio, are part of all units; there are a few bistros and some shops in the complex. The marina is a reasonable walk from here. *Apts.*

Marina Royale • *at the marina in Marigot* • has apartments that are often rented for longer term. Small, European-style rooms are upstairs over marina-bordering shops and cafes, with a view of yachts and other action. This place looked slightly seedy when I inspected for this edition. (The nearest beach is a 10-minute walk west out of town or across the sea on its neighbor island of Anguilla.) *Apts.*

Parapel • *near Marigot* • is a small spot where each air-conditioned unit has TV and a kitchenette. Pink-and-white is the color scheme for these units, which were opened in early '89. *Apts.*

Pelican Resort and Beach Club • *covering most of 13 acres, shoreside at Simson Bay* • has plastered a once beautiful hillside with multi-story buildings reminiscent of big cities in the U.S. The emphasis seems to be more on making money for the developers than on preserving any semblance of natural surroundings; timeshare units blanket the hill. From its start, with one building in December '81, the project now includes hundreds of units with pools, shops, marina, tennis courts, watersports, restaurants, and a mind-boggling hive of activity. Accommodations vary, from shore-rimming, seaview units including apartments and villas, to others that are on the hillside, some with sea view and others overlooking neighbors. The entry gates suggest an exclusive resort, but the place takes on tenement overtones. If you like high-density condominium communities, this place may be for you. *Huge apt. hotel.*

Petite Plage • *along the shore at Grand Case* • shares a cove with expansive Grand Case Beach Club. The 18 apartments are adequately furnished; emphasis is more on hospitality than on show. Some of the units are occupied on year-round rentals, and shorter-term guests are encouraged to feel "at home." Many do, year after year. Planting surrounds the 2-story buildings; most units have sea view. *Apts.*

The Point on Burgeaux Bay • *on an arm of land between airport landing strip and beach* • has penthouse, 1- and 2-bedroom suites, with a shared pool. Perched on the rocks at the southeastern end of a curve of beach, the seaview from The Point includes Caravanserai Hotel at the far end of Burgeaux Bay. It's a short walk to the beach, which is not the island's best. Good for self-sufficient types who like convenience with a far-away feeling. *Apts.*

Pointe Pirouette Villa Hotels • *on Simson Bay Lagoon, near Mullet Bay and the Summit Hotel* • are five villa clusters that appear to be one community. Although each cluster has its own personality—some have private piers into the lagoon—each is a cluster of elegantly furnished apartments, built in tasteful Mediterranean style. Once you're in residence, it's possible to forget that the units cling to a wedge of land backed by the busy resort life at Mullet and nearby places. Semi-private and, in some cases, totally private pools allow for exclusive living; a car is essential for mobility. *Villas.*

Royal Islander Club • *at Maho Reef Hotel beside the airport runway* • is a complex of timeshare apartments. La Plage was the first of several buildings; the "club" and the expansion of Maho Reef with its huge casino threaten to plaster any available land with buildings in an area that has festered with development. Apartments are for rent in owners' absence, and pressure to purchase seems relentless. *Apts.*

Royale Louisiana • *on Marigot's rue de la Republicque, near the marina complex* • rises above the many shops. The reception area is a booth at street level; bedrooms are one or two flights up. Streetfront rooms have small balconies (and street noises), as is the case with neighboring La Residence. Although there's some beach nearby (west along Marigot's waterfront) the best beaches are a long walk or short ride away—or on Anguilla, easily reached by shuttle-boat from the harbor. *Apts.*

Town House Apartments • *at one end of Great Bay in Philipsburg* • cluster as the curve of sand stretches toward Great Bay Hotel. Shingle roofs, lush courtyard planting, and clever unit arrangement provide homey privacy although the several units occupy a relatively small space. The 2-bedroom, single-story lodgings are condominiums for rent in owners' absence; all are comfortable and adequately furnished. A mix of owners and renters allows for congenial atmosphere, with the convenience of being able to walk along road or beach to Philipsburg's restaurants and shops. *Apts.*

The Village at Oyster Pond • *on the road that ends at Oyster Pond Hotel* • is a cluster of 3-story wood-and-fretwork buildings planned as condominiums by a building company known as Laissez Faire NV. Potential investors should be sure to look at construction, which will seem okay for vacationers in these first few seasons. A car is essential; the road to reach these lodgings is wiggly, pot-holed, and very hilly once you turn off the main east side road between the Dutch and French sides. *Apts.*

THE INN WAY is multi-faceted on this two-nation island. Inn-keeping at places with fewer than 50 rooms depends more on hospitality by the management/owners than on the structure. Although there are a couple of traditional inns, most of the properties are not architectural beauties. Some places have kitchenettes; others offer the meal services that many vacationers want—and expect. Several properties—all small, but some with apartments and others with only bedrooms—have joined, for promotional purposes, as the *Inns of Sint Maarten/St. Martin.* Among the group at press time are *Beachside Villas, Great Bay Marina, Horny Toad, The Jetty, LaVista, Marty's Boon, Oyster Pond, Passanggrahan,* and several others. Check with the tourist office for a current roster; the *Caribbean Newsletter* (page 9) will feature my new discoveries. In the meantime, here are some suggestions.

★ **La Belle Grand Case Hotel** • *between road and sea at Grand Case* • is a small gem with viewful, attractively furnished rooms that have bedroom and large sitting room or area. Rooms 7, 8, and 9, on the top floor, are my favorites. With a car for mobility and the beach as your lawn, this place can be a comfortable home. *Small hotel.*

Beach House • *on Front St. in Philipsburg* • has a few small apartments in a wedge between the road and the town's bordering beach. Although the harbor is nice to look at, the sea serves several purposes. *Apts.*

★★★ **Horny Toad** • *on Simpson Bay beach, next to the airstrip* • is a special spot, thanks to the hospitality offered by Betty and Earl Vaughan. Guests in the 8 apartments, each with its own personality, are often repeaters who have found their island "home." Daytime activities can be as peaceful as reading a book in the shade of a palm tree or trips to neighboring islands (or around this one). The long and lovely beach is the focus for most, for early morning swims and for late afternoon socializing, when that appeals. The two-story building that holds most rooms is painted white, with blue trim and glass louvered windows. Second-floor seaview rooms are my favorites. A couple of cottages next door are also managed through the Vaughans. Count on friendly atmosphere and low-key living. A couple of food shops, several fast food places, restaurants, and *Opel Car Rental* are within walking distance of the property. *Apts.*

★ **Hotel Hevea** • *near Chez Martine in Grand Case, on the French side* • is a small inn with attractively appointed rooms and a comfortable guesthouse feeling. Within easy stroll of several restaurants and on the premises of one, the inn is ideal for self-sufficient art-appreciating types. *Guesthouse.*

The Jetty • *on the east end of Philipsburg* • stands near the marina in a 4-story white block that hardly hints at the comfortable rooms within. Best from the inside, the units give renters a balcony with harbor view and a kitchen for homecooking. There are plenty of restaurants, in addition to provisioning places, within easy walk, so a car's not essential except to get to the beach. *Apts.*

★ **Mary's Boon** • *on a strip of beach-lined land that backs up to the airport runway* • appeals to folks who want a breezy room by the sea, with an atmosphere reminiscent of New York's Fire Island. Manager Rush Little runs an informal inn for independent types who may (or may not) want to gather at the shoreside honor-system bar for conversation around the mealtime. The alfresco patio/porch is the place where meals are served, and there's a low-key, private-home feeling about this place. Rooms are opened to breezes, which is wonderful when not punctuated with the airplane engine roar. The long beach is superb, when seas haven't taken it out. *Rooms, Apts.*

★★★★ **Oyster Pond** • *overlooking the sea, near Dawn Beach* • is an inn, with a coterie of nicely furnished rooms and a pleasant courtyard that doubles as a breakfast and sipping spot and a new wing of 20 attractively appointed rooms. The main house bedrooms are off the center court or up the stairs around its rim, with several offering gorgeous views toward St. Barths. There are a couple of duplex rooms, with special decor. The dining room, under shelter off the courtyard, is elegant by candlelight, and service can be special (offerings usually are). Chef Paul Souchette was honored as chef of the year by the Caribbean Hotel Association in 1990. A sand-filled patch is the nearest sunning spot; a pool is on a lip of land. Dawn Beach is nearby. An oasis on an island that has capitulated to tourism, you'll want a car, unless you prefer isolation, and should count on a hilly drive from this elegant perch to anywhere else. (You're almost equidistant from Philipsburg and Marigot when you're here.) *Inn.*

★ **Pasanggrahan** • *on Great Bay in Philipsburg* • is a legend to longtime visitors. Now pinched between new buildings and the sand-fringed sea, the place clings to some of its earlier charm. Most of the 21 rooms are in a 2-story band to the right as you face the sea; others are in a nearby building. Lingering and dining on the patio is pleasant, and the location is amid many restaurants and shops. With the increase in tourism, the public beach along Philipsburg's waterfront is sometimes crowded, especially on cruise ship days and at height of winter season. The sea is studded with charter yachts; I question its "purity" for swimming since it receives spill-off from town and boats. *Guesthouse.*

Residence • *near the marina in Marigot* • gathers a handful of small rooms around the restaurant in the second-floor courtyard of a building on one of Marigot's best shopping streets. The feeling is definitely French. *Inn.*

LOW-COST LODGING: The best bet for cost-conscious travelers is to rent an apartment, controlling food costs by dining at home. Most inexpensive rooms are spartan. Street noise is a problem for small spots in Philipsburg, Marigot, and along the main street in Grand Case, where local folks may hassle visitors. A few small hotels are less expensive than some of the biggies, but prices are not necessarily cheap. Here are some to investigate further:

Les Alizes Guest House • *on the beach at Grand Case* • is a small stucco building, with sliding doors. The 7 air-conditioned rooms are adequate for those intending to spend days on the beach. A color TV in the tiny lobby is the main entertainment. There are many good restaurants within easy stroll; car rental can be arranged on premises.

Beausejour • *at Marigot's waterfront, near the market* • is one of the few oldtimers that has not modernized or expanded beyond recognition—at least as of this writing. The 10 very simple rooms are worth considering if you know West Indian islands and can cope with the French-style informality. Rooms are on the second floor, next to the restaurant that offers home-style food.

Bico Guest House • *near the Pondside Elementary School in Philipsburg* • is on a dirt side street in the heart of town, not far from George's Guest House, mentioned below. Only worth considering if price is a critical consideration and hotel/resort services are not.

Caribbean Hotel • *on Philipsburg's main artery* • is above shops on a traffic-clogged street. The on-premises *A-1 Grill* occupies a portion of the balconied second story. Boxy, basic rooms are also on this level. Timid travelers should inspect on site before booking.

Hotel L'Ermitage • *down a sea-ending alley in Marigot* • has very simple rooms at prices advantageously negotiated on the site. The check-in area is at Lakes' Store where rue de l'Anguille links with rue de la Liberte. Air conditioning is essential in the small rooms which, when the door is closed, have no air circulation. The alley is shared by pricey, pleasant, seaside *Poisson d'Or* restaurant.

George's Guest House • *across from Pondside Elementary School on a back street in Philipsburg* • is in the heart of downtown, if that's what you want. Most small rooms have air conditioners, which are essential for comfort. This place has simply spartan surroundings.

Palm Plaza Hotel • *on a main street in Marigot* • looked rundown when I checked for this edition. The *Caribbean Newsletter* (page 9) will have an update when warranted. The 3-story building holds about two dozen air-conditioned rooms, some with kitchenettes and some facing the street (and noises). A center courtyard cups a low-key cafe. On a main road ending at the waterfront, the hotel is near shops, restaurants, and the shuttle-boat to Anguilla. The nearest beach (with watersports) is a walk through town, heading west.

RESTAURANTS on Sint Maarten/St. Martin are beyond count, with over 100 dining options. Many menus show French flair (especially, but not exclusively, on the French side), but you can also find Chinese, Italian, recognizable American hamburgers and hot dogs, as well as Kentucky Fried Chicken. Count on spending substantial sums, however, even for simple fare. Restaurants price as though they had to make whatever profit they can in the three-month height of season (Jan., Feb., Mar.), even though they have good summer business too. If you figure $40 per person as an average, you will occasionally be able to eat for less, and will often pay more for dinners. You can taxi to Philipsburg, to wander to one of several restaurants, or to Marigot or Grand Case to do the same, but for all other dining depots, a rental car or taxi is essential.

AUTHOR'S OBSERVATION

I believe that most restaurant prices on this island are out of bounds. On top of that outrage, always ask whether or not service is included in the bill that's presented to you for meals. The often-awesome meal prices are made even more unpalatable by a tendency to add a service charge into the food amount written on your charge-card slip, leaving the service section blank in hopes that you will add *another* 15%. Be aware—before you overpay.

AUTHOR'S AWARDS

Le Perroquet, on the airport road, is a favorite for food and service. I have dined happily and comfortably here on more than one occasion. *La Rhumerie* has also proved to be consistently pleasant.

Les Alizes • *in Marigot* • features Vietnamese food in pleasant surroundings. Prices are high and offerings were not spectacular on my visit.

Antoine • *next to the pier in Philipsburg* • facing on Front Street and housed in one of the old wood West Indian buildings, makes up in location what it may lack in gourmet cuisine. The menu reads well, but the actual presentation wasn't up to my expectations. The lunch with salads and sandwiches is a safe bet.

Auberge Gourmande • *on the French side at Grand Case* • is one of many dining choices in this small village on the shore. Among the offerings are the hearty soups and the main entrees that are special that day, with the typical poisson grille always good (it's grilled fresh fish).

★★ **Le Bec Fin** • *upstairs on Frontstreet, with a sea view* • has a French menu (on the Dutch side), with rack of lamb and duck to delightful entrees. Fish soup is a pleasant starter, and lobster is always offered. This place has a link to Marigot's La Calanque.

Baie d'Along • *on the sea, just west of Marigot* • serves Thai food in a simple stucco-boxy home.

Bertine's • *in the hills near Grand Case* • is a small and special spot that is making a name for itself for hospitality (it has a few rooms), as well as for its sunset view and creative menu. Offerings make good use of any fresh produce available. Christine and Bernard Poticha (from Chicago) are your hosts.

★★★ **La Calanque** • *on the shore road at Marigot* • a few doors away from La Vie en Rose, was the first to offer outstanding food in special surroundings. The service can be slow, but the food lived up to expectations when I dined here. If you're planning for dinner, stop by early to make your reservation; height-of-season space is scarce. (And plan on parting with the equivalent of 120F per person for a memorable meal.)

Captain Olivers • *on the lagoon at Oyster Pond* • is a shoreside place at a burgeoning marina. Once "alone" on this shore, the place is being surrounded by apartments, cottages and condominiums. Seafood, salads, and steak are joined by French specialties on the international menu.

Chesterfield's • *on the road to Pointe Blanche* • near the marina on the east curve of Great Bay, serves down-to-earth seafood and sandwiches from 11 a.m. until well after midnight and more ambitious specialties such as duckling, steak, and seafood, at normal dining hours. Popular when it was the "new place in town"; check here for publike activity.

L'Escargot • *on the inland side of the west end of Front Street, Philipsburg* • is in a wooden West Indian building wrapped with a band of red, white, and blue for the tricolor and/or the Dutch flag. The wall coverings around and over the bar where you will wait for the table you reserved (or linger after your meal) are worth noting. Count on spending $40 per person for dinner, and if you get out with less, consider yourself lucky. You're expected to order wine, but a carafe of the house potion will keep the waiter happy if it pleases you.

Hevea • *on the inland side, at the western end of Grand Case* • serves special meals to a few lucky patrons. Surroundings are attractive and the menu interesting. Prices are high.

Key Largo • *between road and sea, at the western side of Grand Case* • has a beautiful setting and an annoyingly diffident attitude on the part of management. High prices and mediocre offerings were off-putting on a recent visit. This place had been the Ritz Cafe.

La Maison sur le Port • *at Marigot* • provided pleasant dining for a luncheon with friends on a recent visit. My broiled lobster was $17.50 for about 5 mouthfuls of lobster meat; lobster salads also had only a couple of bites-worth but the price was more reasonable. Prime lure for this place is its portside location in Marigot, and alfresco dining in pleasant surroundings.

Messalina • *on the Marigot waterfront* • focuses on pretentious Italian style, with tableware and setting as memorable as the food. As with neighboring Vie en Rose, prices are sky-high.

Mini Club • *in palm fronds, seaside, at Marigot* • is an island original, known to me since an early visit to St. Martin more than 20 years ago, but suffering from too much fame and building on my most recent visit. Entrees include the inevitable grilled fish or lobster, and include more ambitious undertakings with veal, beef, lamb, and chicken. French cheeses are a nice way to drift from dinner. The Wednesday and Saturday buffets, served from 7:30 p.m., are feasts for those who reserve in advance.

★★★ **La Nacelle** • *nestled on the island side of the road from the sea at Grand Case* • marries exceptional surroundings (now that they have been restored) with some of the island's best cuisine. A meal here will be memorable.

La Nadaillac • *at waterside in Marigot, in the Galerie Pergourdine* • is a pleasant French bistro, with tables on the terrace and Chef Malard, who brings his native Perigord cuisine to Caribbean island surroundings. Not open for luncheon, La Nadaillac makes a ceremony of dinner and is open until the latest hours.

★★★★ **Le Perroquet** • *on Simson Bay Lagoon near the airport* • starts your meal with a complimentary flute of champagne. Menu offerings are interesting, and my selection (of ostrich) was superb. Standards are high; fish, veal, beef and chicken appear in special sauces. Worth the investment.

★ **Il Pescatore** • *on the shore at the west end of Philipsburg* • serves delicious homemade pasta, and flavorful entrees on an open-to-breezes deck at the beach. My salmon in mustard sauce was delicious, and linguini in clam sauce comes highly recommended. Appointments are attractive, with pottery fish plates as the table setting, and the meals have been excellent on evenings I've enjoyed. Owned by Massimo Vezzosi, this atmospheric spot has links to elegant shops in town.

★★★ **Poisson d'Or** • *at seaside in Marigot* • can be an ideal setting for an elegant evening, with cuisine (and prices) to match. Meals are served on the veranda, as well as in the main room, and the impressive wine list makes a selection seem mandatory. *Ris de veau* proved delicious, as did the mushroom souffle, and lobster medallions with basil are memorable. Symphonies playing softly as background music helped set a scene that is accented by local art hanging on the walls of the main room. Reached by an inauspicious alley off the main road, Poisson d'Or is worth finding.

La Residence • *on rue de la Republique in Marigot* • serves in a lovely patio setting. Fish soup is standard. Lobster and other offerings are popular entrees.

★★★ **La Rhumerie** • *at Colombier, on a spur off the main road between Marigot and Grand Case* • is settled in the countryside. The creole setting suggests some of the specialties of the chef, such as *accras* (spicy conch fritters), *crabes farcis* (stuffed crabs), and other items familiar to French West Indian cuisine. You'll need a car to reach this spot, but it's well worth any effort. The homelike setting is lovely; the food delicious; the evening mealtimes special. Call ahead for reservations in season, and be sure the place is open at other times.

Thai Garden • *between Marigot and La Belle Creole* • looks like a Thai temple. Its menu features, obviously, recipes from the homeland.

La Vie en Rose • *on a corner at Marigot, near the openair market and Vendome shop* • offers pleasant surroundings and special meals, featuring the fish that is this island's main offering. Be sure to dine upstairs; the street level seems like a tacky American coffee shop. Reservations are essential if getting a table on the balcony is important (and even with a reservation, on a winter evening you'll have to wait, from my experience). Count on $50 for 2, if you want to dine well. Careful control over entrees can bring a check for less.

★★★ **The Wajang Doll** • *in a small house at the west end of Philipsburg* • serves Indonesian specialties and more traditional food in a pleasant shoreside setting. The tone is set by the memorabilia collected in Indonesia by the owner, and the rijsttafel offered is a representative sampling of the bigger spreads served elsewhere. Well worth a visit, the Wajang Doll offers a break from the more familiar French or American cuisine.

The restaurant list is legion, and the best spots on this island are going to be the ones you find yourself. The above list includes some—but by no means all—of the places worth trying. For casual, comfortable yachting informality (and seafood) check the **Seafood Galley** on the beach, east of Pasanggrahan and just west of Bobby's yacht marina at Philipsburg; **Sam's Place** on the shoreside of Front Street, has new owners but you'll still find hamburgers, etc. in very informal surroundings; and the **West Indian Tavern,** across Front Street, serving onion soup and lobster salad, etc. in a congenial publike setting in a balcony, house, and garden (backgammon and darts for entertainment). For Chinese food in Philipsburg, try Steven Suen's **The Majesty,** in air-conditioned, boxy surroundings at the west end of Front Street, where the menu includes some Javanese and Spanish specialties mixed in with the expected Chinese. In Philipsburg, there are several small hamburger and snack places seaside, tucked into halls and houses. On the French side, both at hotels and at the small bistros, the French food is supreme.

NATURAL SURROUNDINGS: Hurry, before the entire island is covered with cement, to find the few remaining natural places, most of which are on the French side of the island. Thanks to some conscientious efforts by an association of interested citizens, a foundation has been formed to preserve the few remaining traditional buildings—and some of the landscape. If you're interested in learning about the activities, contact Mrs. Sheila Acciani at Grand Case Beach Club, Grand Case, St. Martin (T 011+590+87.51.87). Among the few areas still in a natural state are Ilet Pinel, reached by small boat from French Cul de Sac, and a few of the other offshore islets where birds nest.

AUTHOR'S OBSERVATION

Due to safety problems in recent years, I don't encourage exploring or relaxing on the most remote beaches—unless you've discussed it with island residents and they've been enthusiastic about the adventure.

Insofar as hiking and walking on St. Martin are concerned, the partially restored ruins of the hill-capping fort above Marigot are a worthy goal, but the fort at Philipsburg has been blanketed at its base by condominium/timeshare apartments! The parched hillsides rising from Anse Marcel (Habitation Hotel) have been suggested as hiking areas, but I'm more enthusiastic about flying from this island to Saba, Statia, St. Barthelemy, or Anguilla to find your "natural surroundings."

Divers also head out from these shores to sites best reached by boat. Local dive-masters are experienced at finding many of the unmarked sites, most of which are shipwrecks (especially the British frigate *Proselyte*), caves, fascinating reefs, and ravines. Other shipwrecks are recent, having been sent to the deep to become coral-encrusted fish condominiums to lure divers. There's no dramatic wall-diving around St. Martin/Sint Maarten.

PLACES WORTH FINDING on Sint Maarten/St. Martin are the beaches, for my vacation dollar, and they are powder ribbons at the shore end of dirt roads and overgrown paths on both the Dutch and French sides of the island.

Except for minimal ruins of a couple of forts, there's not much in the way of buildings to prowl around.

The Courthouse/Post Office in Philipsburg marks where Sint Maarten's first courthouse was built in 1793. As Commander William Hendrick Rink wrote when he requested funds from the government of the Republic of the United Netherlands, it was unseemly for the Island Council to continue to meet in the home of its commander, especially since *his* home, near the present inn at Mary's Fancy, was too far from town to expect the council members to walk. Rink countered the Netherlands' chastisement that the colony was lax with its taxes with the fact that, since the weights and scales had no housing, the salt air and strong sun had ruined them. People had taken to weighing and doing business in their homes, and it was obviously impossible for the weighmaster to chase all over town to be present at the weighing. The new courthouse Rink requested could hold the weights and scales and keep taxation under control. The third reason Rink gave for his need for a courthouse was that the garrison was too small to guard the jails in Philipsburg *and* at Fort Amsterdam, and prisoners were escaping. The jail could also be in the new courthouse. Rink won his case—and the money to build the courthouse—by 1793. A hurricane lifted the lid in 1819 and funding in those less prosperous years took until 1826, when restoration was supervised by Samuel Fahlberg, well known to islanders from this area as a cartographer, artist, civil engineer, and physicist. The Fahlberg restoration tore down the former (and partially ruined) second story and built a wood-beam version with a small balcony in front and the bell tower which Dr. Jan Hartog points out, in his *The Courthouse of St. Maarten,* was requested by the Council who wanted to follow the "modern" fashion in the 19th century—by making their announcements after a peal of bells instead of a roll of drums. Changes for 130 years were relatively minor, but the restoration in 1969 changed the lines of the building. Workmen got carried away with piling cement block on top of cement block and added 3 extra layers to the wood-flashed core they were recreating on the second floor. The building you look at from De Ruyter Square has an "imposing" second story that is the result of misreading the plans. The air conditioning is obviously new, but the stamp windows are where the weighing room used to be and packages fill the area where the jail cells used to be.

Other islands are the best places worth finding if you have time and inclination for an excursion from your Sint Maarten/St. Martin base. A day trip to Saba or Statia is as easy as booking a morning-over and afternoon-return flight, making arrangements with a local taxi for touring when you arrive. Flights in all cases are well under 20 minutes, as is the case also with French St. Barths and with St. Kitts, half of the two-island country of St. Kitts-Nevis. Anguilla can easily be reached by plane flying north in about 7 minutes or by boat, in about 20 minutes, from Marigot. (All the other islands are south and a little east.)

Count on the boat schedules to be *very* flexible in all but peak season winter months; if you want to go to one of the six islands by boat, your best bet is to check the day you arrive to see what day the boat goes to your chosen island and plan the rest of your excursions around that. Writing ahead is no assurance; plans change at the last minute. Airfare figures to about $35 round trip for the farthest distance—Nevis; all others are less with Saba and Statia at $30.

SPORTS on Sint Maarten/St. Martin set off from one of the Caribbean's best collection of beaches. Although there's no strand that stretches as far as the Caymans' Seven Mile Beach, there are not many coves on Sint Maarten/St. Martin that don't have at least a small patch of talcum sand, and all are open to everyone, no matter whose property you walk through to get there. Pack a picnic for some of the beach days; unless you've beached by a hotel, there are no food concessions and bringing something from home port makes the day trip possible.

Scuba and **snorkeling** thread out from water sports concessions at the hotels. *Patrick's Watersports* at Le Galion Beach Hotel has boardsailing, yacht sailing, waterskiing, and "the only nude snorkel trips in the Caribbean." *Ocean Explorers* (T 011+599+54-5252) arranges snorkeling and diving trips out of Simson Bay, not far from the airport, and *Watersports Unlimited N.V.* (T 011+599+52-3434) is a full service diving and sports operation based at Sint Maarten Beach Club in Philipsburg (and an easy walk from Holland House, Pasangrahan and other Philipsburg hotels). Scuba trips and boat rentals are specialties. Belair Hotel, on Little Bay, also has full watersports facilities. Mullet Bay's beach concession *Maho Watersports* (T 011+599+54-4280) offers on-the-spot options for guests. Novices can sign on for the three-hour Resort Course, given in Mullet Bay when the sea is calm, or at the pool otherwise. Your offshore dive is a second part of the experience, arranged the next day with one of the instructors. Divers depart from the Mullet marina by boat for dive sites offshore. Among the special spots for experienced divers are the wreck of HMS *Proselyte,* which sank in the early 1800s and has coral-encrusted cannons and anchors that are favorite havens for colorful fish. The Alleys, underwater cliffs, and ledges are another spot, and Hens and Chickens, on the windward side, are surrounded with elkhorn coral.

If you are interested in going farther afield, it is possible to make arrangements to go to St. Barths, Anguilla, and Flat Island, in addition to the areas around Dog Island, Prickly Pear, Scrub, Sandy Island, Five Island, Barrel-Beef, and others.

Snorkeling is best at the coral reefs, but is not its most spectacular off the resorts where the powdery sand slopes into the sea and the waves often churn the waters. There are regular snorkel trips arranged by both firms mentioned above, or you can head out on your own from some of the uncluttered coves you find yourself.

Glass-bottom boat rides are offered on lagoon and sea. Departure port is the Mullet Bay marina, behind building 66. The watersports facility at Mullet Bay has the most complete facilities, with waterskiing, jet skiing, sunset sailing, scuba, and snorkeling easily arranged. Only a rolling surf curbs the man-made activity at Mullet's beach.

Sailing: For latest information on the sailing fleet that sets sail or heads out under power from Sint Maarten/St. Martin shores, check first at the Sint Maarten Tourist Bureau on the waterfront, not far from the Courthouse/Post Office in the middle of Philipsburg's Front Street, and then, if you want to make a thorough survey, head over to the French side to check with the hotels near Marigot for information on yachts setting sail from this north side, usually to Anguilla. A worthwhile investment for serious sailors is the *St. Maarten Area Cruising Guide,* available for $10 from Virgin Islands Plus Charters, 239 Delancy St., Philadelphia, PA 19106. *Wathey Travel Service,* on the square near the Tourist Office in Philipsburg, arranges boat trips, and most hotels can help with information. Among the yachts available for day sailing are *Gabrielle* out of Great Bay Marina, on $55 day cruises; *Quicksilver,* a 61-foot catamaran that sails to St. Barths for $45; the *White Octopus,* a 75-foot motor boat; and *Barco Manana,* a 46-foot Trimaran that sails to Anguilla for a barbecue on the beach (and charges $45 for adults; $20 for children under 12 years). The Anguilla departure is from Marigot. Many boats pick up at the Town Pier and sometimes from the hotels if there is a big enough group to make a special boarding stop worthwhile. The Tourist Board can give you on the spot details

Watersports Unlimited, based at the St. Maarten Beach Club, has boats for sailing as well as boardsailing and dive equipment. *Dynasty* charters operate from Port la Royale Marina in Marigot.

The Moorings, with marinas on St. Lucia, Tortola, and Grenada, has a well-run charter operation at Captain Oliver's on Oyster Pond. For details, contact their U.S. office (1305 U.S. 19 South, #402, Clearwater, FL 33546 T 813+536–1187 or 800+535–7289).

Bahamas Yachting Services operates from a base next to Bobby's Marina in Philipsburg. The fleet of CSY 44s (cutters) and Morgan 46s (ketches) can take six easily, and are available either bareboat or with skipper. *Stevens Yachts* has a marina for their well-known Caribbean charters (skippered, with crew, or with the opportunity to sail yourself). *Lagoon Cruises and Watersports* offers "Sail in St. Maarten" specials, with boat rental and a sailing school operating on the lagoon. Contact the Sailing Master at Mullet Bay or ask at your hotel's activities desk. The usual complement of Sunfish and other small sailboats are available at Mullet Bay, Sint Maarten Beach Hotel, and Little Bay Beach on the Dutch side; and at Le Galion on the French side.

St. Maarten Watersports and Waterski Club offers parasailing (where you are towed aloft with the help of a parachute and a long line attached to a speeding motor boat) on Simpson Bay Lagoon in addition to waterskiing. The firm also gives scuba lessons and guided dives to several offshore sites.

Deep sea fishing can be arranged through Bobby's Marina, at the east end of Philipsburg.

Golfers must stay at Mullet Bay. Guests at other hotels are not allowed on the course, unless invited by an MB registered guest or resident member. The course undulates at the heart of the vast Mullet Bay complex, and is said by some to be the heart of the resort. Count on costs to be high.

Tennis courts speckle many of the resorts. Mullet Bay has a group of courts and tennis shop. Other hotels with courts are Divi Little Bay, La Samanna, Great Bay, Caravanserai, Oyster Pond, Dawn Beach, Maho Beach.

TREASURES AND TRIFLES on Sint Maarten/St. Martin on the Dutch side are neatly organized, and although the lark of discovering something "no one" else has found may no longer be the prime pursuit on the streets of Philipsburg, shops offer some of the Caribbean's most unusual good-quality items, especially jewelry (if you know your gold). The island has, in its French- and Dutch-based shops, more top quality fashions and furnishings than any other Caribbean destination. The several shops are within a short walk of each other: most are air-conditioned and—if you avoid the days when the cruise ships are in port—there is plenty of space to wander.

AUTHOR'S OBSERVATION

To make your shopping time count, spend some time perusing the green *St. Maarten This Month,* published regularly, available free, and full of suggestions for shops and restaurants.

Shopping on the French side is very different from the calculated commerce of the Dutch. First, although the most tourist-oriented stores will welcome U.S. dollars, credit cards, and traveler's checks, the common currency is the French franc. Shops sprawl around Marigot; those that cater to residents are mixed with the ones that focus on visitor interest. Count on hours to be flexible on the French side. From my experience, places seldom open at 8 a.m. as posted, and often shutter completely for lingering lunch between noon and 2 p.m. (unless a cruise ship has docked in Philipsburg).

PHILIPSBURG shops can seem to be an overwhelming clutter, on first glance(s). If you're serious about shopping, take some time to look carefully. There *is* a lot of "trash and trinkets," which may be what you're looking for, but there are also several shops that sell luxury items at prices way below the usual mainland U.S. cost. Among the places to look for the best there is, head straight for **Maurella Senesi,** at Royal Palm Plaza on the western end of town and at Cupecoy and Mullet Bay. The Italian-designed jewelry is exceptional, and attractively displayed. **Domina,** next to Holland House and Great St. Maarten beach, has leathergoods, including handbags, suitcases, leather calendars, belts, shoes, wallets, and so forth. **Maximo-Florence** has two shops, one on Front Street and another in the Promenade Arcade. Both carry leather goods, especially shoes. Local folks, and wise visitors, get pick-up bargains at the June special on shoes and other merchandise brought in especially for local consumption at *very* low prices (which is not the case with the usual merchandise). **Oro de Sol,** a favorite among those who known and like elegant design and perfect workmanship, features Ebel Swiss watches, as well as Villeroy & Boch porcelain and top quality linens and other housewares. The shop in Marigot is much bigger than the boutiques in some of the hotels.

There *are* a few bargains to be found, but here—as everywhere—wise shoppers should do research at home, with their local discount store, to be sure that the price they are paying in Philipsburg *is,* in fact, lower than that offered at home (where repairs, if needed, will certainly be easier to negotiate).

Shops on the Dutch side are open 8 a.m.–noon. daily except Sun. and Sat. when many shops close at noon. Shops at the hotels are sometimes open evenings, so check if it is important. Do not count on the airport shops to be open when you depart. Although most are open when there's airport activity, all have small staff and when they are sick (or late) the store's not open. When a cruise ship is in port, most tourist shops are open, even on Sundays, on the Dutch side—and sometimes (not always) on the French.

GRAND CASE has one narrow main street, a link in the main road around the rim of the island. Although quaint wood cottages in typical West Indian style are embroidered on both sides of the road, most of them are filled with restaurants and a few small inns.

MARIGOT is a maze of shops. The historic part of town had a street plan that was like two ladders lying side by side, with a long strut against the sea. Although each rung, as well as the lengths, are trimmed with several shops and restaurants, most of the chic French shops for avant garde fashions are at the *Marina Royale,* an area at the western end of town that has been created in the past couple of years. Although boats are tied up at the finger piers, and cafes line the harbor's edge, a maze of small shops fills the street level of all of the 2- or 3-story buildings that surround the marina. European imports, and mostly those from France, are the main lure for shoppers. Haitian paintings are also popular. Resort clothes, with trend toward fashions known at St. Tropez and elsewhere on the Mediterranean's riviera, are everywhere, as is sensational underwear.

Rue de la Republique, one street inland from the main sea rimming one and "ending" at the marina, is the primary shopping street, with small boutiques that specialize in art and artifacts, clothes, leather goods, fashion's names, and imported food delicacies. Trendy resortwear including hand-painted smocks top the list of clothes, but there are also trinkets, as well as elegant (and very expensive) jewelry, the best watches, sandals, beachwear, perfumes, and the best of Europe's housewares.

ST. THOMAS

Division of Tourism, Box 6400, Charlotte Amalie, St. Thomas, VI 00801, T 809+774–8784, fax 809+774–4390; #412, 3460 Wilshire Blvd., Los Angeles, CA 90010, T 213+739–0138; #500, 900 17th St. NW, Washington, DC 20006, T 202+293–3707; #907, 2655 Le Jeune Rd., Coral Gables, FL 33134, T 305+442–7200; #1420, 235 Peachtree Center, Atlanta, GA 30303, T 404+688–0906; #1270, 122 S. Michigan Ave., Chicago, IL 60603, T 312+461–0180; Virgin Islands Government Tourist Office, 1270 Avenue of the Americas, New York, NY 10020, T 212+582–4520, fax 212+581–3405; 2 Cinnamon Row, Plantation Wharf, York Pl., London SW11 3TW England, T 01+978–5262.

$ · · · U.S. currency is used.

Main, Mizzen, and Fore was the way sailors used to refer to the three hills in the harbor of St. Thomas, referring to their placement on the waterfront by terms best known to nautical folk. In 1672, when the town was founded, it was called Tappus by the Danes—for the "Tap Houses" that endeared the community to pirates and others who sought solace (and refuge) here. Only later was it renamed for their Queen, Charlotte Amalia.

These days, although the hillsides have been frosted with ever increasing layers of buildings, those three hills are still obvious to any of the thousands of cruise ship passengers who stand on the deck as their floating hotel hoves into port—as hundreds do each year.

Touchstones from the past give St. Thomas its firm foundation. The trademark stone tower surrounded by a hotel on Smith's Hill was built by Eric Smidt in 1666 and Fort Christian, the rust-red citadell standing at the shorefront, has 1671 over its arched doorway at the clock tower.

Far better known as a trading port than as a plantation island during those 17th-century years, St. Thomas returns to its past history for its present appeal. Shops fill the stone warehouses that stretch from the waterfront boulevard to the main street, and narrow alleyways are flecked with cafes or festooned with merchandise for sale.

Today this island's pleasures have adjusted to the stateside tempo. The roads to most beaches are paved. And there are hotels, plus condominiums around the shores almost everywhere on this island. Even the shores have changed;

the sand drifts out at regular intervals, as if recoiling from the surge of people. Hamburgers, hot dogs, and Kentucky Fried Chicken have taken over from the onetime specials of souse, calaloo and fungi. And the day of the "do-it-yourself" beach picnic has almost gone. There are places to buy your food on most beaches these days, and most people do that.

The simple life of the past has vanished from the U.S. Virgins—and so has most of the extreme poverty of those days. Natural pleasures have been packaged for sale. Tourism may have crowded some beaches, but it has also created jobs.

You have to head out of town—way out—to find the leisurely life that Caribbean converts come south to find. And you'll find comfortable, small hotels on most of those sandy strips these days.

POLITICAL PICTURE: Democratic Governor Alexander Farrelly was re-elected to his office in November 1990. Born on St. Croix, Governor Farrelly has been a practicing attorney on St. Thomas. His lieutenant governor, Derek Hodge, had been an active senator in the Virgin Islands legislature. Eric Dawson was appointed as Commissioner of Commerce, the department responsible for tourism, which is the territory's most important industry. As a result of active lobbying and historic legislation, exports of Virgin Islands rum are the measure for substantial funds for the operating budget of the Virgin Islands government, in spite of the fact that sugar cane is no longer cultivated in these islands. The government is the major employer.

Although Virgin Islanders do not have a vote in U.S. national elections they vote for their governor, lieutenant governor, and the members of the legislature. They also elect their representative in Washington, who lobbies for Virgin Islands' interests. Purchased from Denmark in March 1917 for $25 million, the U.S. Virgin Islands are an unincorporated territory of the United States. Elected representatives handle the day-to-day operations, but the area is under the jurisdiction of the Washington-based Department of Interior. Tax incentives for businesses assembling part of the product in the U.S. Virgin Islands have led to a spate of small industries.

ISLAND APPEARANCE Mountainous St. Thomas, once covered with tropical growth, is now threaded with roads and bandaged with condominiums, hotels, shopping centers, and homesites. Only the western end remains reasonably rural, but even there paved roads reach many once isolated coves. The eastern end of the island is fringed with hundreds of yachts, most of them for charter. Although many of the best beaches, along the cove-bitten south and east coasts, are bordered by hotels or condominium communities, the horseshoe-shape of Magens Bay, on the north coast, remains in natural state. A hub of commerce since the 17th century, the capital of Charlotte Amalie blisters with boutiques, cafes, and liquor stores, housed in buildings once used to store pirate treasure. Roads make hairpin turns as they drape over the mountainsides, affording spectacular sea-and-neighboring-island views to passengers in the hundreds of cars that often clog the streets of and around the town. Today, St. Thomas appears to be a sunny island suburb of its caretaker, the U.S.

LIFESTYLE is American suburban. St. Thomas is like any small town in sunny climates, U.S.A., except that the population is about 85% black. You will find most of the fast-food chains, with the usual hot dogs and hamburgers. Supermarkets akin to those you know at home can be found on the outskirts on Charlotte Amalie, as well as "in the country" at Estate Tutu and in other areas around the island.

The warm and sunny weather means that casual clothes are the daily uniform, with bathing suits best on beaches (*not* in town). Although dinner hours in the best dining rooms at the big hotels (Bluebeard's, Stouffer's Grand Beach, Frenchman's Reef) occasionally call for dressing up, dress code is casual at most places. Events at private homes are occasionally elegant, dress-up affairs. "Fashion" elsewhere is in the eye of the beholder.

The main word of advice is to travel light. Leave all the gaudy jewelry, etc. at home, and bring as little as possible in the way of baggage on your island vacation here, as at most places in the Caribbean.

AUTHOR'S OBSERVATION

St. Thomas is once again a commercial depot as it was in early Danish days, and as such has become a haven for seedy types. I do not recommend wandering around alone, on foot, along the waterfront outside of the well-traveled routes, especially at less busy hours. The same petty crimes that plague cities in the States are prevalent in these islands. There have been instances of robbery and worse crimes along the waterfront between town and the St. Thomas marina, especially in the area around the low-cost housing development. If you're timid about heading for the hills, to some of the island's top restaurants in your rental car, after dark, hire a cab and ask him to return for pickup at an appointed time.

There is no gambling in the U.S. Virgin Islands. Nightlife is informal/spontaneous. You'll seldom find big-time nightclub entertainment; if you find it at all, it will be at Frenchman's Reef, Stouffer's Grand Beach Hotel, or perhaps at Bluebeard's Castle. Otherwise, hotel entertainment—when there is any—is a steel band or some other local music for dancing a couple of evenings, and maybe a limbo or two.

MEDICAL FACILITIES: The hospital in St. Thomas is reasonably well equipped, but often overcrowded and understaffed. Most doctors practicing in St. Thomas have been trained at U.S. medical schools; many have offices in Charlotte Amalie. St. Thomas is about half an hour's flight from Puerto Rico and just over two hours' flight from Miami.

MONEY MATTERS a lot, and you will need plenty if you want to be carefree about dining out and renting cars, sailboats, snorkel gear, etc. Credit cards are accepted at many (but not all) restaurants and at the better stores, but cash is the essential commodity. If you have a lot of cash, keep it under cover, and consider leaving some at the front desk of your hotel. Traveler's checks are advisable since they're only negotiable with your signature.

COMMUNICATIONS are as easy as direct dialing 809, with the 77 code for the USVI plus a 5-digit number. Facsimile machines are commonly used. The *Virgin Islands Daily News* has local news, as well as major wire service international news. New York and Miami newspapers are available at some hotels and at newsstands, but expect to pay triple the cover cost or more. There are television production stations on St. Thomas, and many U.S. mainland network programs appear on St. Thomian TV channels. Cable TV is also available. VCRs and satellite pick up are common to homeowners, and in some hotel activities' rooms. There are several good Virgin Islands radio stations; you can also pick up the Spanish-speaking stations from Puerto Rico.

ARRIVAL is into a new terminal, with modern facilities. It's been over 10 years in the work stage, and more than 20 in talk. Extended runways and blasting "mountains" make it safe, which some said it was not prior to the building of a 76-acre bulkhead into the sea and the carving of the mountain that was at the other end of the runway. *American, Pan Am, Continental,* and Chicago-based *Midway* are among the major carriers; Puerto Rico's flocks of small-plane commuter airlines fly 30 or more flights per day into St. Thomas. *Sunaire, Express, American Eagle,* and other regional carriers dart in and out on a regular basis. There are small planes available for charter. Arrival "formalities" for U.S. citizens are nonexistent. This is a U.S. area and you need no identification.

CRUISE ships can dock at either of two piers, to the right or the left of the center of town as you come into port. If your ship comes in on a day when there are several others in port, you may be anchored outside the harbor, with service by lighter (small boat) into the Charlotte Amalie waterfront. For passengers coming into the West India dock, the walk into town is along the waterfront, past one of the low-cost housing developments where there has been some trouble in the past with muggings and the like. Take the taxi shuttle into town for shopping. For those who arrive at the Crown Bay pier, a taxi to town is advisable since the walk is along the main road, which is hot and noisy.

Clipper Cruise Line is one of several of companies sending smaller cruise ships out of St. Thomas. For information on the weekly cruises, with Sunday departures, visiting British and American Virgin Islands, contact Clipper Cruise Line, 7711 Bonhonne Ave., St. Louis, MO 63105, T 800+325–0010.

DEPARTURES by plane involve, first, double-checking to be sure your flight is departing on schedule, especially if you are flying aboard one of the inter-island airlines. Plan to be at the airport an hour or more ahead of schedule, in anticipation of slow-moving lines at ticket counters. There are no immigration formalities (this is a U.S. territory), but there will be a security check, especially for some of the major airlines. If you are returning non-stop to the U.S. mainland, you will clear customs in St. Thomas. (Customs procedures are required since the USVI status as a duty-free port makes it possible for goods to be sold without U.S. duty imposed. See shopping comment for details on the special customs allotment from the USVIs.) If your flight goes through Puerto Rico, you will go through customs there.

TOURING TIPS: First-timers would be wise to sign on for a half-day tour to get their bearings and find out what's where. From that point on, if you want to be mobile, consider **car rental.** All the big names have representatives at the airport *(Hertz, National, Avis, Budget),* and I have found staff to be helpful and prices, even at peak of winter season acceptable. For friendly and capable St. Thomian service, I've returned several times to *Sea Breeze* car rentals. Their office is in a trailer parked near their rental cars, by the Super Foods store on the Crown Bay side of town. If you telephone them (T 774–7200), George or Karen Dennis will arrange to pick you up at the airport or cruise dock to come to their office for your rental car. Others to consider are *Sun Island Rentals, Dotson Car Rental, Atlantic Car Rental,* or *All Island Rent-A-Car.* Some hotels have special arrangements for rental cars for their guests.

Mopeds can be rented for about $20 per day through *General Moped* (Box 7970, St. Thomas, USVI 00801, T 809+774–6990).

Taxi fares are posted at the airport. If you can't find the sheet, be sure to ask the dispatcher. Years of being in the tourism business seems to have resulted in "fair practices" by St. Thomian taxi drivers, at least from my experience. You'll seldom find a driver willing to share the local lore as is the case on less touristed islands, but you'll also be charged standard rates, unless you ask for special tours or other services. If you want a driver for half a day or for an island tour, be sure to negotiate the fee in advance. There is a set fee for so many hours, but if you and your driver get along, there's sometimes room for special treatment (with an expected special reward for the driver).

Know in advance that the mountains that give St. Thomas its spectacular vistas—the views *are* awesome, even to those of us who have been coming here for a couple of decades or more—make driving a "Grand Prix" event. Roads are winding, can be "straight" up and down, are usually potholed, and seldom properly banked. In addition, island drivers are apt to stop dead in the middle of the road to chat with a friend or drive on your side of the narrow route. Driving is on the left; your hometown license is valid for legal driving here.

AUTHOR'S OBSERVATION

Careful reading of the yellow sheet *St. Thomas This Week* should be your first priority on arrival. Available free through your hotel, and usually at the airport, the fact-filled weekly guide has all the necessary tidbits about restaurants, activities, and shops. For copies by mail, send $2 to Box 1627, St. Thomas, VI 00804.

LODGING on St. Thomas can be in historic buildings, modern hotels, friendly inns, and all shapes, sizes, and styles of apartments. Since the island has provided shelter for visitors since its heyday as a pirate haven, in the 16th and 17th centuries, you can expect an assortment of places to stay. In some cases, older hotels need sprucing up; in others, a swipe by Hurricane Hugo (in September '89) forced extensive rebuilding and redecorating. The greatest concentration of inns and hotels is in a south coast harbor, at Charlotte Amalie, the capital, but there are also many places to stay east on that coast, all the way to Red Hook and the easternmost point, where new buildings are cheek-by-jowl. There are a few places west of town, at the beach near the airport and on a nub of land that juts toward Water Isle.

Ask your travel agent and the Virgin Islands Tourist Information offices about multi-night packages, some of which include airfare in the price of a value-full holiday. Many hotels have 800 toll-free telephone numbers for easy reservations.

In addition to your room rate, expect to find a 7.5% government tax on your bill. A few hotels add a service charge, but always ask what it covers. If one of your maids or another person has given special service, an extra tip is appropriate.

AUTHOR'S AWARDS

Bolongo Bay Resorts is a Caribbean success story. It's a well-run family-operated trio of properties that includes the original beachside Bolongo Bay, plus apartments at one end of the bay, and Limetree, which operates as this island's only price-inclusive property. *Island Beachcomber* is my choice for a traditional small Caribbean hotel, and the comfortable and attractive *Sapphire Beach Resort & Marina* has both a sensational view (toward St. John) and a lovely soft-sand beach.

Information about places to stay is included under Hotels/Resorts, Housekeeping Holidays, the Inn Way, and Low-Cost Lodgings. Stars are awarded within each category. (See page 11.)

HOTELS/RESORTS are a varied lot, with two very big hotels *(Frenchman's Reef* and *Stouffer's Grand Beach)* and a handful of 100-plus-room properties that offer U.S.-style rooms at a complex that usually has a pool, several restaurants, and evening entertainment, and sometimes also is on a beach, with tennis courts. The island's only golf course is at Mahogany Run, on the north side.

★★ **Bluebeard's Castle** • *on a hill in the capital, with a view over Charlotte Amalie* • is a cluster of several buildings, some new and timeshare set-up, around the original mill tower. Although the view from the dining terrace still recalls the hotel's early (and simpler) years, the capitulation to time-share, office space, meeting rooms, and shops has cluttered the hilltop. The location, within minutes of downtown (shops, dining depots, boats to St. John and the British Virgins) is convenient; the tennis courts are in good shape; the rebuilt pool-with-Jacuzzi can be a pleasant place to cool off after a day of touring; and views from the balcony or patio of an air-conditioned room (especially those of the newest building, closest to town) help create a comfortable vacation home. Tropical foliage adds a soothing touch, as does the sugar mill tower. Staff I encountered seemed to be simply doing their job; the hotel's friendly personality apparently hasn't survived the recent changes. *Hotel.*

★★★ **Bolongo Bay Beach Club** • *on a south shore beach* • has expanded from an original formula that included housekeeping rooms (now refurbished and joined by a 3-story wing) but has maintained the original "small hotel" feeling. In addition to watersports, with scuba lessons, a yacht moored at the beach, and a live-aboard dive boat at the pier, there are tennis courts. The small pool at the beach is below the alfresco restaurant; beachside barbecues are dining choices for guests who choose to stay "at home." A rental car will make day touring easier. This place has a very special atmosphere, thanks to careful attention and concern for their guests (and staff) by Joyce and Dick Doumeng, chosen as "Caribbean Hoteliers of the Year" by their colleagues in 1988. Inquire about the "club" plan, plus scuba, honeymoon, adventure, and other package plans. *Small resort.*

★ **Elysian** • *on the south coast's Cowpet Bay, toward the east end* • aspires to elegance, and could reach it, once construction is completed. (Be sure to ask about status when you call for reservations.) Planted near the beach at the heart of a collection of dozens of condominiums that blanket the hillside like an amphitheater, the hotel is 2- and 3-story buildings gathered around a central pool and noteworthy, appealing restaurant. The attractively furnished sea view units have large and modern bathrooms, comfortable bedrooms (some with Murphy beds that pull from the wall), a living area, and viewful verandas that make the top-floor rooms the best, in my opinion. Some rooms have kitchenette, and all require a climb up or down from and to the beach-pool-restaurant area. When the condominiums are full in mid-winter, you'll have to be out early to claim your space of beach; at other times, there should be room enough. Watersports are offered beachside. *Resort.*

Emerald Beach • *on Lindbergh Bay Beach, near the airport* • has been abuilding for a couple of years. It stands next door to long-time favorite Island Beachcomber, and intends to open for this season (although it's not open at press time). The 3-story buildings are filled with rooms, in the standard stacked-shoebox fashion. Although decorating can make them special, it's the sea view from the upper floors that is worth claiming. You'll hear airplanes, but you're on the beach. The *Caribbean Newsletter* (page 9) will have an update after the expected opening.

★★★ **Frenchman's Reef Beach Resort** • *on the southeastern point of Charlotte Amalie harbor* • was the island's first conventional hotel when it came into the Holiday Inn franchise, but it now operates on its own and is good at what it does. Built according to U.S. big hotel standards, the massive property sits like a stationary cruise ship at the entrance to Charlotte Amalie harbor. The deluxe *Windows on the Harbor* restaurant has a lovely view—and memorable offerings. Everything is here, including conference rooms, shops, pool, beach, a center for around-the-island activities, restaurants, nightclub, boats for excursions, and a helipad for helicopter touring. Everything, that is, except gambling, which this place looks as though it should have. The big rooms (air-conditioned, carpeted, big beds, modern bathroom) have a view either of the harbor or the open Caribbean Sea. All facilities at this big place are geared to groups—and to those who want the expected U.S. modern hotel-style services. Included in multinight package holidays, Frenchman's Reef is a city unto itself, with an elevator ride down the hill to its beach and tennis courts. (For information about sister *Morningstar Resort,* at the beach, see below.) *Resort hotel.*

★★★ **Limetree** • *on the south shore* • is one of the Bolongo Bay Resorts, with Richard Doumeng in charge. The first hotel to offer inclusive pricing in St. Thomas, Limetree allows for multi-night stays, with room, meals, drinks, watersports, tennis, and entertainment included in one established price. There are no extras, except what you buy in the shops and a car rental or special tour, if you want one. Rooms are in seven 3-story buildings, separated from the beach by the pool and a shop-punctuated social area. The sea-view, hill-capping reception and restaurant building, once a private home, has an elegant atmosphere in evening hours. *Inclusive hotel.*

Mahogany Run • *on the north side of St. Thomas* • has had its ups and downs, not only on its golf course. From the moment the golf course was ready, people planned vacations at this resort—and that was long before most of the other facilities were finished. The *Caribbean Newsletter* (page 9) will have news, when warranted. The resort has tennis courts, golf, and some activities for condominium guests (whether they are owners or renters-in-owners'-absence). A rental car is essential for spontaneous mobility. Don't count on a lot of group activities (unless you arrive as part of a group). Nearby hotels—The Inn at Mandahl and Magens Point—offer additional dining diversions, and Magens Bay beach is a reasonable distance downhill, with the hotel's shuttle bus making a regular connection. You're in the hills when you are here, with spectacular views—but no beach within easy footfall. It takes about 15 minutes to cross the spine of this mountainous island to reach Charlotte Amalie. *Apt. resort.*

★★ **Morning Star Beach Resort** • *on the beach, below Frenchman's Reef Hotel* • is a close relative of the big hotel on the hill. The beach is the one used by Frenchmen's guests, and bill signing can be done between properties. The rooms are beautiful (and expensive). On the site of a legendary St. Thomian hotel, this entirely new complex still has an independent hotel feeling, with its own reception desk at the beach for those staying in one of the several clusters of modern rooms. The dining terrace, on the second floor of the main beachside building, offers a beautiful setting and a menu that includes blackened redfish with other offerings. Watersports, tennis, and other beachside activities take place here, whether you are staying up on the hilltop at Frenchman's Reef or here. *Resort.*

★★ **Point Pleasant** • *overlooking Smith Bay at the east end* • has expanded from modest beginnings in February '74 to be a community of apartments-for-rent-in-owners'-absence. These 15 acres of property are now building-studded. From the hillside perches, you have the prize island view with nearby pool (one of 3 on the premises) and a huff-and-puff walk up from the beach to your room. It's pretty going down past the pool, along the path that has been tended to make it a botanical walk. The sloping hills stretch to include Water Bay's shore from Sugar Beach to Pineapple Beach with all its action (including that of the Stouffer's Grand Beach Hotel). The main building (which isn't where the reception desk is located) holds 12 1-bedroom, 1-living room, 2-bath villas and 6 studios; all have complete kitchens. Newer units, in small groups sifted around the grounds, are similar; all are privately owned. Guests can sign up for the complimentary cars, and for snorkel and sailing equipment that is paid for with your rate. The *Agave* restaurant has a panel of rock garden and, on the other "wall," a dramatic view over bay and islands; it has become one of the favorite St. Thomian rendezvous for those in the know. A tennis court is at the start of the Point Pleasant drive when you turn off the main east end road; you'll need a ride (ask the bellman) or a lot of stamina to get to the courts with energy enough to play. *Apt. hotel.*

★★ **Ramada Yacht Haven** • *on the waterfront, near downtown Charlotte Amalie* • benefits from a $2 million investment, with new bathrooms for all rooms and extensive decorating. Its bubblegum pink paint job is hard to miss; hopefully strong sun will soothe the original harsh color. Restaurants that had been concessions have been gathered into the Ramada management contract, which bodes well for much-needed improvements. The waterside *Pastels* restaurant gives a swan's-eye view of yachts in the harbor. It's too early to comment on food. There's a pool in the "center" of the biggest batch of rooms; other rooms give a view of the yacht-packed marina and all the activity of the harbor of Charlotte Amalie. Swimming in the harbor is not recommended; you'll need a car to get to nearby beaches. The public bus passes by the entrance of the hotel for rides into town or out to east end beaches and other marinas. *Hotel.*

★★★★ **Stouffer's Grand Beach Hotel** • *on a Pineapple Beach curve, at the east end* • opened with a Wyndham management that gave way to the Stouffer chain in late '86. As the island's only true resort hotel for conventions and other groups, the property sprawls along the beach, back from the sand to pool-studded areas, and up the hillside for rooms with sea-and-offshore-island view. On the site of the former Pineapple Beach Resort, the new property overwhelms anything left from that former life, with its several 2-story units decorated in putty and rust tones and a focus on beach, sun, watersports, and tennis. There are plenty of "road maps" to help you find your way as you walk around the expanding grounds. Some privately owned housekeeping units are gathered into the complex, to be rented in owner's absence. Avis has a base here, for your rental car. The *Pavillion Restaurant* features expected American fare; *Baywinds* and *Smuggler's Grill* are in the condominium area; and a *Beach Boutique* is one source for sign up for watersports and fishing trips. This place has packaged the best of the Caribbean in a U.S. style that many find comfortable. Inquire about multinight package plans, especially during summer months. *Resort hotel.*

Virgin Isle Hotel • *on a hillside "above" the airport* • was walloped hard by Hugo, and has not reopened at presstime. Rumors are rampant, but when any news is firm the *Caribbean Newslletter* (page 9) will note it.

Windward Passage • *at the waterfront in Charlotte Amalie* • spruced up and rebuilt, where necessary, after Hugo blew past in fall '89. The rectangular building rims a cafe-dotted courtyard, where street-level arcades lead to shops and offices. Ask for one of the rooms that has been recently redone, preferably one on the harborside, where the view is fascinating (but brace yourself for traffic noises). The motel-style bedrooms are air-conditioned, with phones, TV, and other trappings that appeal to businessfolk. A rooftop pool provides an oasis; beaches are a drive from here. *Hotel.*

HOUSEKEEPING HOLIDAYS make a lot of sense in St. Thomas where food is easy to find (even when it is expensive) at local supermarkets with the name you may know from home—Grand Union, for one—and a large selection of familiar name brands. It's no surprise that the fodder-filled shelves go hand in hand with a long list of comfortable comdominium units that can be yours for a week or two (or longer, permanently, if you want to buy). A rental car is advisable for mobility, but it is not essential at most places.

Some housekeeping places have been included under the hotel coverage, when management and additional facilities give you leadership at the resort. Investigate Bolongo Bay, Mahogany Run, Point Pleasant, Pavilions and Pools, and Pineapple Beach.

Among the firms listing places for housekeeping on St. Thomas are **Moran Villa Rentals,** Box 936, St. Thomas, USVI 00801, T 809+774–0933 and **Van Dyck Vacation Villas,** Box 1073, St. Thomas, USVI 00801, T 809+775–5440.

★★ **Anchorage Beach Villas** • *built on the shore near the St. Thomas Yacht Club* • offer one of the best bets if you want a "home" of your own. Most units are owned as condominiums, with some for rent in owners' absence. All are tastefully furnished, and the 2-bedroom units with a spiral of stairs leading to the upper level can be fun (if you're agile). The 4-story units are in several banks with the pool as a focal point and soft sand beach. *Sib's* by the sea serves barbecues, steaks, and seafood. There are tennis courts nearby; you'll need a car for mobility. *Apts.*

Cabrita Point • *on an east-coast cove* • is part of the new rash of shore-side condominium units. Located not far from Red Hook and all the yachting activity, the 2-story units are painted white and use planting to maximum advantage. Opened in March '88, the units grow near the central building that serves as reception area and gathering spot. *Apts.*

★★ **Cowpet Bay** • *at the east end* • captured an entire cove when it was built a few years ago. The 1-, 2-, and 3-bedroom villas are privately owned, and most of them are occupied (or rented directly) by the owners. However, if you want to be part of a self-sufficient residential community at the east end of St. Thomas about 25 minutes' drive from downtown Charlotte Amalie, near the *Elysian* hotel, investigate this place. All apartments have views, terraces, and very attractive homelike furnishings. In addition, you have the use of the tennis courts, beach, restaurants, and shops on the premises. Good for families because there is something for everyone to do. *Apt. resort.*

Crystal Cove • *at the east end, near Sapphire Beach* • is a complex of studios, 1- and 2-bedroom apartments, each one air-conditioned, and all privately owned for rent in owner's absence. The four 2-story buildings are at the lagoon, within easy stroll of the beach. There's a pool as well as tennis courts on the premises. A good spot for families with teenagers and for couples, this place requires a car for any mobility (although the public bus does make its rounds along the main road up the hillside). *Apts.*

★ **Magens Point Hotel** • *Magens Bay Road* • hangs over the far side of the mountain, with a view of the British Virgins and, if you could see through the trees, over that ribbon of white sand that is Magens Bay Beach, a possible (but hot) walk down the hill. The island-famous poolside *Green Parrot Restaurant* continues to lure patrons from over the hill. Your room will be someone's condominium or time-share unit, in one of a few blocks, with a balcony so you can look at the spectacular view. Appointments are colorful; beds are 2 huge doubles; bathrooms modern. The tennis courts and a pool are near your room. Hotel provides transportation to Charlotte Amalie for shopping and to Magens for sun by the sea and has an enviable location not far from the golf course at Mahogany Run. *Apts.*

★★ **Sapphire Beach Resort & Marina** • *on a beautiful beach, with a view toward St. John* • opened with fanfare in March '88, with the first of five beachfront buildings of what has grown to be over 200 for condominium sale. Just to the right of the registration desk, restaurant, shops, and a watersports facility, as you face the beach and sea, the units have their living area facing the beach with bedrooms at the back. Duplex units claim the second and third floors. Planned for luxury living, these units are attractive, with both beach and marina for activities. *Villa apts.*

★★ **Secret Harbour** • *not far from Red Hook on the south coast near the east end* • is about a 20 minute drive from the capital. The restaurant has a superb setting on an elevated stone terrace beachside. Most rental units are in the third part of an elaborate condominium development and are owned on either a club plan, where owners have a certain number of days at a low daily fee (and the unit is in the "hotel" group for the rest of the time) or on a maintenance plan where you pay extra for use of the tennis courts. This is a good spot for housekeeping if you have a car. *Apts.*

Watergate Villas • *on the south coast* • share the shore with Bolongo Bay. They are about 15 minutes' drive along the winding road east of Charlotte Amalie and, although some were decapitated by Hugo, things are normal now. These clifftop villas were started before the name became so infamous. Sam Schattner, owner of the Watergate Restaurant in D.C., is the man behind this project. John Randal McDonald, architect for Christiansted's Hotel on the Cay and many homes on St. Croix, designed the complex of several 2- and 3-story clusters to weave over and around what nature put here. The view south is spectacular. The decor of each apartment is the owner's choice, so where you stay will be distinctly your "own." Rental costs vary according to size, shape, and length of stay. All renters have the use of the tennis courts and freshwater pool. Luxury on the rocks. *Apts.*

THE INN WAY takes on special meaning for St. Thomas, where modern Caribbean inn-keeping was a fine art in the 1950s and 1960s. There are a few places from those days that still excel at the art. And, within the past couple of years, several other small spots have taken advantage of some of the historic houses, using them as homes for attractive restaurants while adding a few bedrooms for folks who want comfortably casual surroundings. Most of the best inns are in Charlotte Amalie, which makes transportation to a beach necessary for those who choose not to spend their days by the speck-sized pools that punctuate most inns.

Here are several places worth considering;

★ **Blackbeard's Castle** • *on a hilltop in Charlotte Amalie* • stands on historic ground, with its trademark mill tower. The dozen rooms surround the swimming pool and cafe-style restaurant. Popular for lunch-with-a-view, the inn provides transportation from between Emancipation Park and its hilltop during mealtimes. The piano bar is pleasant. *Inn.*

Danish Chalet • *on a hillside in Charlotte Amalie* • has a homelike atmosphere, with Frank and Mary Davis welcoming nautical types and others in search of friendly surroundings. Count on comfortable rooms with all the basics, and helpful suggestions for tours and shopping. Rooms vary in size, shape, and outlook. *Guesthouse.*

★ **Galleon House** • *on Government Hill, in Charlotte Amalie* • is a small spot with a guest house feeling. Some rooms are in the original main house, a short walk along an up-and-down path from the hill-wrapping road. (Enter at the entrance for *Fiddle Leaf* restaurant.) Other rooms are in new units built above the main house on the hill. Good for independent folks who like homey surroundings, this place provides comfortable lodgings at a reasonable price. The public bus runs from town past the beaches for those who choose not to have a car. *Inn.*

★ **Harbor View** • *in the hills of Charlotte Amalie* • was a private home of the A. H. Lockhart family before it became an inn in the late 1930s. J. Antonio Jarvis, in his 1949 book, described Frenchman's Hill as a "residential district of fine stone houses and splendid views," and goes on to point out that "several streets of stairs as well as regular roads serve this section of the city." The "splendid views" are still here, once you are inside the "famous old mansion first built by the Huguenots," but the streets of stairs—now paved and about one car wide—are sided by dozens of people in dozens of humble homes. A taxi or rental car can take you up to Harbor View from the downtown marketplace in about 5 minutes, but it's no place to walk. Mealtime, especially dinner, can be special, with food served on fine china, and the wine you are expected to order served in elegant goblets. Lounges on the terrace make waiting for dinner pleasant and are comfortable for after-dinner coffee. Bedrooms vary in size; some of the air conditioners (essential because of the pocket-size rooms, some with no view) can be noisy, but the ambience makes it possible to overlook a lot if you like to travel "the inn way." Furnishings are mostly wicker, with colorful fabrics. *Inn.*

★★ **Hotel 1829** • *on Government Hill in Charlotte Amalie* • continues an island tradition, in some of this island's most traditional surroundings: old stone steps, front porch, ballast-brick walls in the bar and other main-floor rooms. The bowered courtyard is worth looking at when you climb up the front steps, and you can take a quick pace or 2 to the left or right to sit on the porch or in the inside dining room, or at the backgammon boards or the bar. Bedrooms are a varied lot, all carved a little smaller with the addition of private bath and all spruced up with a recent overhaul. Air conditioners hum to keep it cool in some of the tiniest boxes; 2 rooms overhang the entry steps and make up in view what they lack in quiet. Baron Vernon Ball, a world champion at backgammon, owns this place. A small pool cools houseguests between trips by car to nearby beaches. You can walk down Government Hill to town. *Inn.*

★★★ **Island Beachcomber** • *on Lindbergh Bay beach, near the airport* • was virtually flattened by a tornado spawned by Hurricane Hugo in September '89. When lesser folks would have given up, Michael and Lorette Resch revived the enthusiasm and spirit for hard work that caused them to start building this place in 1957, and rebuilt the small hotel better than ever. The planting, which received a "severe pruning" by Hugo, is flourishing in the center courtyard; the always popular beachside bar is again a congenial gathering place; all the bedrooms in the 2-story, L-shaped building are completely new. The restaurant continues in its separate beachside building. The warm hospitality engendered by the Resches makes this small spot very special. It's a favorite place for a long list of devoted repeat guests—and for me. The beach, replenished since Hugo, is glorious for early morning and all-through-the-day swimming. Thatched bohios replace the line of sea-grape trees that Hugo yanked away. For her excellence at inn-keeping and her commitment to the community, Lorette Resch was chosen "Hotelier of the Year" by her colleagues in the Caribbean Hotel Association in 1984. *Small hotel.*

Mafolie • *on the hillside above Charlotte Amalie* • makes the most of a mountainside location, with one of the most popular St. Thomian eateries (*The Frigate*) as part of a small inn, with pool. The walk down to town is possible, and some have walked up the winding, narrow road, but most vacationers rent a car for a couple of days if they've chosen to call this home. The several rooms come in all shapes and sizes, wedged into any spare inch of overhang. Air conditioning is essential for most of the pockets, a very few of which have any decent view. For a viewful hillside hotel, the rooms at Mafolie might fill the bill. *Inn.*

★ **The Mark St. Thomas** • *on a Charlotte Amalie hillside, next to Blackbeard's* • is a historic house turned inn. The main floor's dining room has proved popular for light dining, in the Spanish "tapas" style, as well as for the expanded and imaginative menu for gala meals; the few rooms are attractively furnished to make the most of the view over rooftops toward the harbor. This pleasant place would appeal to those who know and like small inns. *Inn.*

★★★ **Pavilions and Pools** • *at the east end* • turns a dark and vine-covered wall to the road but hides an oasis within. Not only is the place sufficiently removed from the island's crass commercialism, but once you pass through the archway that leads to the check-in desk and get to the waterfalls and the first of several pools, you are in a romantic world. Each room with its private small pool is planted and screened so that you can be completely unaware of anyone else except for an occasional noise or two. There are 2 floor plans: Type A with 1200 square feet, and a $16' \times 18'$ pool of your own; or Type B, known as the International Pavilion, with 1400 square feet of space, with a $20' \times 14'$ pool. Special winter package rates give you a bottle of liquor if you stay 3 nights, and a gallon if you linger for 7. The pavilion part of your pavilion-and-pool has an airy living-dining room, a kitchen with good equipment, and bedroom, with both bath and dressing room. All units have one glass wall that looks out on your patio and pool. *Villa hotel.*

LOW-COST LODGING in St. Thomas ranges from *very* simple surroundings that border on camping-out to comfortable small hotels where owners make an effort to keep costs moderate for small bedrooms in friendly surroundings. Moderate for St. Thomas figures to about $50 for 2 in winter months, with some better bargains from April 16 to December 15. The places mentioned below are some of my favorites, but they represent only a few of several small spots. The hotel and guest house list available through the tourist office in spring and fall has further facts and phone numbers; issues of the Virgin Islands *Daily News* can be a source for details on places with inexpensive rooms for rent.

Beverly Hill • *on the grounds at Contant, up in the hills overlooking the airport and sea* • has 12 rooms, 5 of which have air conditioners (which you may not need in the breeze-swept hills). You'll want a car for mobility, but this place could be nice for independent folk who want a homelike atmosphere.

Bunker's Hill View • *on a hillside in Charlotte Amalie, an easy walk from main street* • clings to the slope below Galleon House. Guests in the front-of-the-house rooms have a view overlooking the rooftops of town. Air conditioners in the 18 modest but comfortably furnished rooms help to overcome street noises. Good value and convenience for self-sufficient folk.

Heritage Manor • *in Charlotte Amalie* • is another small spot with a devoted following. The place has been repainted and spruced up to provide comfortable bedrooms and a viewful setting.

Island View • *with a bird's-eye view from a mountainside* • is a special small spot with a pool and warm hospitality. Rooms are cozy and comfortable.

Miller Manor • *hanging on a viewful hillside* • is another in-town hotel with decades of hospitality. Rooms are a varied lot; repeat guests have their favorites. Surroundings are basic, furnishings simple.

Villa Blanca • *high in the hills, overlooking Charlotte Amalie* • was once a private home, and still has that feeling. In spite of the height, you're only 5 minutes by car from downtown. Pleasant and homey, this small spot can seem very comfortable. *Guesthouse.*

Villa Fairview • *on a hillside in Charlotte Amalie* • is an oldtimer that continues to offer pleasant, small rooms in a traditional St. Thomian setting. Informal living is part of the pleasure of this place. Rooms vary in size and shape, but all have the basics and are popular with singles and the young in heart or in fact.

West Indies Inn • *in Frenchtown, on the western side of town* • open as Villa Olga, with a scuba focus. The name's changed, but the focus hasn't. The 2-story block of air-conditioned rooms on the hillside is punctuated with a small pool, behind the sea-level West Indian house that holds the check-in area and the casual gathering bar and snacking spot. Better meals are served at the *Chart House,* a short walk down the road.

RESTAURANTS on St. Thomas are some of the most atmospheric restaurants in the Caribbean, and while I prefer alfresco to being buttoned into an air-conditioned room, island residents like (and support) those small dark spots. There's a place for both, but my preference goes to terrace and open-air dining, where you may sacrifice something in gourmet food, but you gain a lot in total ambiance.

You need a car to get to many restaurants around the island, but there are several good places within easy walk of each other in the capital of Charlotte Amalie.

Among the many pubs and other places worth sliding into for a cool drink, a snack, or a full-fledged meal in casually comfortable surroundings are **Sparky's Waterfront Saloon, Harbourfront,** and the **Greenhouse,** all on the waterfront, or several spots on Back Street, otherwise known as Vimmelskaft Gade.

The **Virgin Isle** and **Frenchman's Reef** offer what's known on this island as a West Indian buffet on Friday night; **Limetree** does a similar show on Saturdays; **Stouffer's Grand Beach** serves its West Indian buffet on Wednesday and has other eventful evenings.

The collection of places at Compass Point, out toward the east end on the south coast, is worth noting. The hutlike, Robinson Crusoe atmosphere of the places, most of them appearing to have been built from trees and palm fronds, sets the easy tone. The most successful way to make a selection is to wander (by car) out to the area to menu-read before settling down at any table. Among those worth noting are **For the Birds, Raffles** (rebuilt following an April '86 fire), **Windjammer** (with a German chef), and the casual **Dockside Inn.** For traditional local food, stop at **Eunice's,** now in much larger, newer quarters than her original roadside stand, on the East End road near Sapphire with another restaurant near Crown Point, in town.

Agave Terrace • *at Point Pleasant, on the east end* • is a delight for dinner (arrive before dark, so you can find it—and see the view) and for Sunday brunch with jazz. Seafood is a specialty at this hidden spot.

Cafe Normandie • *in Frenchtown* • is in the settlement named for the community of farmers from St. Barths who lived here years ago. The air-conditioned dinner restaurant and the streetside **Le Bistro** cafe are on the site of what had been a sailor's drinking bar in the early days of St. Thomian tourist fame (in the 1950s). Expect to find good food, high prices, and cozy atmosphere at the Normandie and hamburgers at Le Bistro.

Chart House • *on the point, through Frenchtown* • opened in '81, in a building constructed on the ruins of the original Villa Olga, in the late 1970s. The menu features steaks, lobster tails (not local), shrimp, roast beef, with salad, baked potato, and monstrous portions of everything. A good place if you're hungry for "good old American food," and want plenty of it.

Fiddle Leaf • *on Government Hill, just up from the main shopping streets* • occupies a foliage-sheltered nest that has held good restaurants for several decades—from the time the original Galleon House opened here in the 1950s. Good wines and sometimes pretentious service give flair to mealtimes. Offerings show imagination, with unusual pairings of flavors. Basics are tastefully dressed fish, chicken, and meats. Nice surroundings; expect high prices.

The Frigate • *at east end, across from the entrance to the St. John ferry dock at Red Hook* • features steaks (some say the best on the island), fish plus lobster tail, teriyaki chicken, salad bar, and a baked potato. Count on a cost ranging from just over $10 for the chicken to close to $20 for the best steak.

Harbor View • *up a wiggly, narrow road weaving from the marketplace* • is a longtime favorite. For one thing, I like the view—especially at cocktail time, when you can lounge on one of the settees and watch the lights go on downtown. Continental is featured, and the goblets, tableware, and china will be enough to inspire raptures—if you are affected by that kind of thing. It's only fitting to order wine—and to make a reservation to be sure you'll get a table at one of the 2 sittings. This is #1; expense be hanged (closed Tues.).

Hotel 1829 • *on Government Hill in town* • has been here since before 1829. The terrace tables are surrounded by the first to arrive for dinner; if you want one, arrive early for your reservation (and ask for a terrace table when you call); the inside room, with its stone walls and overhead fans, has atmosphere, but it can be hot if the breeze isn't steady. Atmosphere is enough reason to walk up the steps from Emancipation Park, or wind up the road toward Government House. (Don't plan to park in front; space is limited.) Food ranges from roast beef to chef's specials (closed Sun.).

L'Escargot • *hanging over the sea near what's locally known as the sub base west of Charlotte Amalie* • has its following, and the view on the harbor and the souffles may warrant it. Try lunch, but look out for long lines even with reservations at dinner.

The Mark • *up Blackbeard's Hill* • serves memorable meals in attractive surroundings. Reservations are essential for mid-winter. Count on an impressive menu and appealing presentation.

Piccola Marina Cafe • *at Red Hook's ferry dock* • is a fun spot, as much for the atmosphere in the area as for the variety of food that Pat La Corte presents to her visitors. Pasta is popular, with several sauces, and breakfast is a great time to settle into local life (service starts soon after 7 a.m.). Sunday brunch is the only meal served, but it's on from 10 a.m. to 3 p.m.

Hook, Line & Sinker • *at Frenchtown's waterfront* • is another seaside place with casual cooking. The feature here is chili, along with hamburgers, salads, and other expected snacking fare. The fun is the nautical atmosphere that comes from charter yachts and their followers.

Raffles • *at Compass Point* • makes the most of ceiling fans, huge-backed peacock chairs, and other wicker-and-greenery decor to set off the food that includes salads and seafood as well as some exotic-sounding sauces on the standard chicken, beef, and veal. Piano playing adds the tone for most evenings.

NATURAL SURROUNDINGS: Although views are spectacular, from the climbing mountain roads, there's not much here to intrigue those in search of nature in its purest state. St. Thomas has developed for modern commerce and 20th-century living. There are natural areas on the north coast, especially heading west, but travelers who take the ferry over to St. John will be more richly rewarded.

St. Thomas is where Caribbean scuba diving got its start. During the 1940s, the island was a base for the U.S. Navy's Underwater Demolition Teams. They learned and practiced their trade in the clear surrounding seas. At least one of them (Joe Vogel) stayed on, to set up the first dive operation on St. Thomas in the 1950s. Clear seas, with visibility from 60 to 120 feet and some 60 noted (and popular) dive sites, lure thousands of vacationers into these waters. Although some sites can be visited from shore, many of the most dramatic are the reefs and ledges around neighboring islets such as little St. James, Packet Rock, Saba Island (not to be confused with the Dutch island of Saba), Buck Island (not the bigger and better-known island of the same name, some 40 miles south off St. Croix), Sail Rock, Thatch Cay, St. John, and several of the British Virgin Islands.

PLACES WORTH FINDING on St. Thomas: The handful of historic sites are huddled in downtown Charlotte Amalie, and can be checked off in a couple of hours. The rest of the sights are of the "oh" and "ah" version: mostly scenic and Gray Line is one of several sources for tours. Before you head out for your sightseeing, stop at the Hospitality Lounge, facing Emancipation Park (where von Scholten's proclamation of July 3, 1848, was read) in what is still called the Grand Hotel building (although the street level is now occupied by Irmela's Jewel Studio). Invest in *St. Thomas on Foot and by Car*, by Randall

Koladis, if you can find a copy. The compact, attractive book is not only fact-filled, but it is small enough to be a reasonable traveling companion.

Government House (open daily during working hours) is more impressive from the outside, where you can clearly note the intricate wrought-iron railings that border the balconies. The best place to stand to look is the small park across the road. The street on which Government House faces is narrow from the old days, and constantly clogged with the governor's car (when he's at Government House) and the cars of those who hover around him. Built in 1867, the 3-story house is impressive when viewed from Bluebeard's Castle (where you can pick it out from the others by its red roof, and U.S. and Virgin Islands flags flying). In the main foyer, when you climb the entrance stairs, are several panels of local woods, listing the Danish governors since 1672 on one panel, with a gap for 1807 to 1815 when the British ruled these islands. On another, from April 9, 1917, the United States chain of command is listed. On October 7, 1955, Republican John David Merwin, born on St. Croix, was the first native-born governor appointed to the Virgin Islands.

A glimpse at all the above will take you about five minutes. Then walk up the stairs at the back of the foyer, to the reception room (Mon.–Fri. 8 a.m.–noon, 1–5 p.m.) on the first floor. In frames around the wall of the lovely hall you can note signatures of Danish governors from 1733. (During one of my visits, a 20th-century Dane was checking out the signature of one of his ancestors who had been governor of the then-Danish West Indies in the early 1900s.) J. Antonio Jarvis's paintings of the Virgin Islands, plus paintings by island residents Ira Smith, Donaldson, and Camille Pissarro are on the walls, but the best picture is the harbor, seen through the open windows. The reception room was redecorated in 1969, when chandeliers were electrified and the walls were painted mustard color (woodwork is white). The chandeliers were last cleaned for the visit of the Queen of Denmark. The new frames around the pictures are the result, I was told by one custodian, of the fact that the old frames "were held together by termites holding hands." Flowers, gleaming silver, and other homey touches make the halls seem less awesome than they otherwise might.

As you leave, sign the register—along with others who have said "Beautiful Spot. I love it"; "After a ten-year absence, it is good to come back to V.I."; "Gorgeous"; "Happy to be here"; and—as noted by Mr. Honnig from Copenhagen—"Most interesting and beautiful."

Virgin Islands Museum (Mon.–Fri. 9 a.m.–noon, 1–5 p.m., free) is worth seeing more for the historic fort it sits in than for the artifacts it displays. There's no priceless collection of pirate treasure, but there are a few prints, bits and pieces of Indian and Danish eras, and a display that explains the history of the islands. The entire museum fits in a couple of small cells. Fort Christian itself stands sentinel at the waterfront, near the firehouse and just below Government House on its hill. The fort was completed by the Danes in 1672 (they had started construction in 1666), but the fort you see is the result of a scrub-and-polish routine in 1874 that dismantled a tower and reconstructed the ground plan to include several courtyards. From the 1670s, the fort was the hub of life in Charlotte Amalie. Anyone who *was* anyone was here: the governor and his fellow rulers, the blacksmith, other craftsmen, and most of the town's wealthy. The entire population gathered inside the 22-to-33-inch-thick walls when there were hurricanes, fires, pirates roaring through town, or some other holocaust that threatened peaceful days. Governors lived here; prisoners were jailed here. (The governor now lives in Government House.) A spin through the fort won't take more than an hour.

Coral World (daily 9 a.m.–5 p.m., Tue., Fri., Sat. 9 p.m.–midnight; $8 adults, $6 children); is a manmade marvel well worth paying the high fee to see, especially if you're not one of those who will don snorkel mask or scuba tank to go underwater to see freely. The cement and glass tube that was poured into the reefs just off Coki Point was a blasphemy to many of us who had headed out to this once remote east end spot for an idyllic snorkel-for-two. However, credit has to go to the builders, who splashed a minimum of reef-wrecking cement on the natural habitat of the fish this commercial venture was created to exploit. These days, as you wind your way down the staircase to the sea floor, the view out the windows is an absolute marvel. You are *inside* an aquarium—and the only place like this one is the owners' similar structure in Israel's Bay of Eilat. As you walk out to the dome, you have a spectacular view of St. John and the neighboring British Virgin Islands, and before you get to either of these places (since I have dealt with the best part first), there are the 21 aquariums in the Marine Garden area, all filled with corals, sponges, sea urchins, and fish plucked from the sea to survive here where they can be seen without scuba apparatus. The expected commercial ventures (shops and restaurants) flourish on your extra cash. The entire excursion can be a very expensive one if you've paid the full fee at the gate. Ask at your hotel, and check package tours including other things you might want to do to get a better rate.

Special considerations around and away from the island of St. Thomas include a day in Old San Juan, Puerto Rico, which is offered on tours conveniently arranged through the local travel agents. If you are a do-it-yourselfer, you can buy a round-trip air ticket, and arrive at the San Juan airport to taxi to town on your own.

Other open-air excursions to places worth finding are by boat, to St. John for the day or to the British Virgin Islands: Jost Van Dyke (on Mon. and Sat.), Tortola (daily), or Virgin Gorda (Wed. and Sat.). For U.S. St. John, choices range from an organized tour (purchased with the assistance of your hotel, or directly from one of the downtown travel agents) with pickup at and delivery to your hotel; to a day sail you put together with some friends; to a ferry ride from east end's Red Hook (either the boat to Cruz Bay, or to Caneel Bay for the buffet)—and walk, taxi, or rental jeep ride around St. John. You'll need the wheels for longer excursions, but be sure to allow an hour or two for a leisurely stroll around the streets of Cruz Bay. The town still represents an islander's island village. A day on Tortola can be via boat aboard the *Bomba Charger* or *Native Son,* with taxi for touring; and then there's seaplane service to Tortola, St. John, or St. Croix's Christiansted and taxi or rental car to tour that 21-mile-long island; plus an endless list of other options that you can dream up as you sit on the beach.

SPORTS on St. Thomas started to get organized about the same time the first record blue marlin was hauled in, in the early '60s. Today the island's south and east end coves are home port for yachts and source for charter boats for fishing as well as watersports concessionaires.

Sailing spokes out from the expensive slips at the St. Thomas Marina near Ramada's Yacht Haven Hotel, the casual moorings at the Avery Boat Yard across the harbor of Charlotte Amalie on the fringe of Frenchtown, and out at the East End, where only Sir Francis Drake Channel separates you from St. John, and trade winds send you tacking to reach some of the British Virgins. Among those who carry listings of charter boats are the Virgin Islands Water Safaris, which claims to be the Virgin Islands' largest list (with 600 bare boats and 200 crewed boats). Charlie and Marty Peet can be reached in St. Thomas by dialing 800+524-7676. Other reliable sources for yachts are Jim and Mary Kellogg whose *Easy Adventures* operate out of Anchorage at Cowpet Bay (Estate Nazareth, Route 6, St. Thomas, USVI 00802; T 809+775-7870) and Joan Woodson, operator of Virgin Island Water Tours, whose *Fairwind Charters* (T 800+524-2028) lists about 200 power and sailing yachts that are, or can be, in Virgin Islands waters. Her contact is Box 7332, St. Thomas, USVI 00801; T 809+776-3650.

The *Virgin Islands Charter Yacht League* (T 809-774-3944) has a membership of about 200 craft, ranging in size from 40 to 100 feet, and most of them dock regularly in St. Thomas. This is said to be the largest crewed-yacht charter fleet in the world. If you're roaming around the island in November, it's worthwhile checking for dates of the Annual Charterboat Show, at the St. Thomas marina.

For day sailing, *True Love* is one of the old stand-bys, as is Jane and Steve Marsh's *Nightwind*, a yawl that is moored at the St. John ferry dock at Red Hook. *My Way, Rose,* and *Typhoon III* are sloops to look for; *Billy Bones* is one choice, if you want to sail on a schooner. *Tropic Tours,* with offices at hotels and in town, is a good one-stop source for day sail information.

Boardsailing has burgeoned here as elsewhere on Caribbean shores. *Cowpet Bay's Beach Hut* is one source for lessons-and-rental, but *Aqua Action* (at Secret Harbour) can also arrange for boards. Magen's Bay is the north coast source.

Fishing is easy to arrange through your hotel or directly at the east-end marinas. August is the month for the USVI Blue Marlin Tournament, an annual international event since the early 1970s. Know before you go that a 1282-pound Atlantic blue marlin was taken 20 miles off St. Thomas in the Puerto Rico channel by Larry Martin of Pompano Beach, Florida, on August 6, 1977. The catch was the ninth world record blue marlin to be caught off St. Thomas since John Battles took his 814 pound fish in the early '60s. The *Fish Hawk,* captained by Al Petrosky, is island known and *Boobie Hatch, The Rogue,* and *Caribbean Soul* are others to ask about.

Scuba got its start in St. Thomas, when the Navy's Underwater Demolition Teams trained in the clear seas offshore. That was years ago, but many of those who trained stayed, and some of them took the first of the leisure scuba groups out to explore not only reefs but wrecks. Bolongo Bay holds scuba weeks, using the 68-foot *Mohawk II* as home for a few days and the hotel for the rest of the week, with instruction and good facilities. Other spots in and around town to sign on for special scuba sessions are at *Joe Vogel's* shop (Box 7322, St. Thomas; T 809+775-7610) at the West Indies Guest House, *Watersports Centers* at Frenchman's Reef and out at Sapphire Bay (Box 8088, St. Thomas; T 809+775-0755) and the *Virgin Islands Diving Schools* (Box 9707, St. Thomas; T 809+774-

8687 or T 809+774–7368) operation across the road from the St. Thomas hotel; *Caribbean Divers* (Red Hook, St. Thomas; T 809+775–6384), *Aqua Action* (Box 12138, St. Thomas; T 809+775–6285), and *Chris Sawyer Diving Centre* (Estate Frydenhof, St. Thomas; T 809+775–7320). Contact by mail or phone with any of the firms can set you up for lessons, or a diving pal for any special outings during your vacation.

The diving ranges from the shore dives possible off the east end's Coki Point, where the reef starts about 100 feet offshore to Sail Rock, a little over 3 miles off the west end of the island, where the "rock" sinks some 90 feet underwater. Spratt Point off the southern side of Water Isle is a place to find lobsters at night as well as plenty of colorful fish during daylight hours, and the Little St. James Ledges offers sights to see from 10 to 40 feet below the surface. Among the wrecks that have become coral-encrusted and fish-filled are the R.M.S. *Warrick,* a packet ship that wrecked on what is known as Packet Rock in 1816, and the wreck of a plane in 1981 that now lies in the sea off Fortuna Beach, west of the airport. All of the dive sites in the waters around the British Virgins and St. John are possible day excursions from St. Thomas as well.

Tennis has taken over. Almost every place that has a patch has a court, but you can count on good courts at *Bluebeard's Castle, Stouffer's Grand Beach, Bolongo Bay, the Cowpet Bay Tennis Club, Frenchman's Reef, Lime Tree, Sapphire, Secret Harbour,* and at the *Yacht Club* at the East End. The public courts on the shore between the St. Thomas marina and town are available for play. Check for special tennis weeks at the hotels with courts; most of them have good values—with some instruction and other bonuses.

For **golf** Mahogany Run on the north shore abutting Magen's Point Hotel is the island's course. The first 9 holes were "ready" in mid-80, with the back 9 ready in early '81.

TREASURES AND TRIFLES: "Know Before You Go" is the title of a U.S. Customs Service pamphlet giving facts and typical duties for bringing items purchased overseas back into the United States. Although they are part of the United States, the U.S. Virgin Islands have a special customs regulation that is a remnant from the agreement of transfer from the Danes in 1917. The "free port" status was to continue. That means that goods come into Virgin Islands ports at very low or no duty. When the goods are sold in shops, theoretically they come to you without extra charges, but the profit added by Virgin Islands' shopkeepers in recent years has gradually edged the price up so that some of those "bargains" are not. Know your hometown "best price" for a camera, watch, or whatever before you make your island purchase; you may find the cost about the same as your local discount house. On the other hand, the selection of items for sale in the former pirate warehouses of Charlotte Amalie (and even at Christiansted and Frederiksted on St. Croix) is astounding! The crowd of shops downtown is exceeded only by the crowd of shoppers on cruise ship days, all of them carrying the bulging shopping bags like so many children after a successful Halloween "trick or treat." When you have been in the U.S. Virgin Islands, you may bring home duty free $1200 worth of merchandise including five liters of liquor and an extra liter of Virgin Islands spirits. There is a flat 5% duty charged on anything over your exemption. In addition, items made in the U.S. Virgin Islands can be brought back in any amount.

They are not subject to duty and you can mail, each day if you wish, gifts valued at not more than $100 to friends.

I confess to being overwhelmed by the surfeit of shops in Charlotte Amalie. During several separate forays for this edition, I succeeded only in being completely confused. Many of the small shops open and close or leapfrog from one location to another. Good craftsmen work here for a while, and then seem to wander on. And, sad to say, there is an increasing amount of what I have to call junk, which succeeds only, in my opinion, in camouflaging the good items, making them harder to ferret out. Think of this place as a Middle East souk, and you'll be braced for what is here.

AUTHOR'S OBSERVATION

Two indispensable aids for St. Thomas shopping are a copy of *St. Thomas This Week*, the fact-packed yellow guide published by Margot Bachman and tirelessly researched by her team. Copies are sometimes available from the Virgin Island Tourist Offices in the U.S., or by writing to St. Thomas This Week, Box 1627, St. Thomas, VI 00801. (Enclose $2 to cover air-mail postage.) Another valuable contact, if you have a specific purchase in mind, is the Retailers' Association, Box 1287, St. Thomas, VI 00801 whose motto is "shop with confidence." Member stores are the highest caliber, and all have exemplary ethics.

First, let's look at the lay of the land: Think of the Charlotte Amalie waterfront as a comb, with the back of the comb as Main Street, or Dronningen's Gade as it was known to the Danes. The "teeth" of the comb are the old warehouse buildings that stretch from Main Street to the waterfront, with alleys with "pretty" names flecked with boutiques and shops. Now flip the comb over, with Main Street still Main Street, and head back into the hills, for another set of "teeth" that are the buildings that line the roads heading away from the water. *All* those narrow streets are fringed with shops, food places, an occasional small hotel—and commerce.

That's the general layout for town. There are also shopping centers around the island, notably at **Estate Tutu** where a craft center that started around **Jim Tillett's** silk screened fabric studio has burgeoned into a nice cluster of shops, and at **Compass Point,** a cove with a nautical flavor along the south coast, east of town. And then there are the shops that cluster near the cruise ship dock, across the road at the base of the hill, as well as at the **Havensight Mall** where many of the Main Street shops have branches and the several buildings hold hundreds of air-conditioned shops.

If you're looking for fashion and designer names, be prepared to sift through (and wander past) a lot of lesser lights.

Insofar as jewelry is concerned, be sure you know your gold and precious stones before you settle for some that are not. A personal favorite source for jewelry of exceptional quality and design is **Irmela's Jewel Studio,** near Emancipation Park, in what is known as the Grand Hotel (because it *used* to be a hotel, years ago). Irmela Neumann, who started the first small shop in the early 1960s, now has several designers working with her, and their original settings for special stones are memorable. Allow some time, if you want a special piece made for you.

If you're overwhelmed by the thought of conquering all that commerce, my suggestion is to head straight for the **A. H. Riise Gift Shops** and stores and get your bearings. That name stands for tradition in St. Thomas, and the family-owned real estate has expanded to include the buildings that house most of the better shops right in the heart of town.

Insofar as handcrafts and art are concerned, check for dates of the **Arts Alive Festival,** held in fall and at other times at Tillett Gardens, east of town.

It's worthwhile remembering that items made in the Virgin Islands—and that includes Irmela's island-made jewelry, Zoro's sandals, Jim Tillett's silk screen fabric, and a host of other items—are duty free. You may bring those items home in any amounts you can afford.

Final note: Two of the traditional "best buys" for the U.S. Virgin Islands, and especially St. Thomas, are liquor and perfume. A word of warning, however: Be sure you know your hometown prices for perfumes, and whether you want pure scent or cologne, for example. It's easy to become confused and to loose your "scents." Insofar as liquor is concerned, check your hometown laws on taxes that might be imposed when you bring your bottles back into your state. There's no problem bringing back, duty free, your five liters plus one liter of spirits made in the Virgin Islands, or even with paying duty on what you buy over that, but some states have the right to confiscate the liquor.

ST. VINCENT AND ITS GRENADINES

St. Vincent Department of Tourism, Box 834, Kingstown, St. Vincent, W.I., T 809+457–1502, fax 809+457–2880; 801 Second Ave., New York, NY 10017, T 212+687–4981 or 800+729–1726, fax 212+949–5946. 14347 Hay Meadow Circle, Dallas, TX 75240, T 214+239–6451; #504, 100 University Ave, Toronto, Ont., Canada M5J 1V6, T 416+971–9666; 1 Collingham Gardens, London SW5 OHW, T 01+370–0925.

$ · · · US$1 = about EC$2.60
Unless otherwise noted, $ refers to U.S. currency.

See pages noted for information on: Bequia, p. 756; Canouan, p. 758; Mayreau, p. 759; Mustique, p. 759; Palm Island, p. 760; Petit St. Vincent, p. 761; Union Island, p. 762.

"Pssst, lady. Want a head of lettuce? Tomatoes? Nice ripe mango?" Once you've established that you are a looker, not a buyer, the market ladies at the far end of Kingstown's main street take pleasure in showing you what's what.

The heaps of fruits, vegetables, and spices, clustered by kind, have probably grown in the fertile Mesopotamia Valley that is the backdrop for this West Indian town. And the women have carried them to market, walking or riding the wood-slatted bus, gaily painted, perhaps with "Patience and God" on its forehead, and certainly open to the trade winds—and to all passersby.

The pros will tell you that Saturday is the only day to go to market in Kingstown, St. Vincent's south-coast capital. But for most of us, any day will do. In fact, the piles of ruby-red tomatoes and coral carrots, and the bubbles of cabbage that nestle against dasheen, breadfruit, mangoes, and papaya are almost overwhelming when the Saturday crowd comes in to buy. It's much more fun on other days, when the market women have time to talk, which they will do, easily and animatedly, even when they know you are not going to buy.

And outside, close to the wharf, there's the fish market—and there used to

St. Vincent and its Grenadines
Baleine Falls
La Soufriere
Georgetown
Chateaubelair
Troumaca
Barrouallie
Penniston
Layou
Ft. Charlotte
Kingston
Sans Souci
Biabou
Mesopotamia
Ratho Mill
Calliaqua
Indian Bay
Young Island
Bequia
Mustique
CARIBBEAN SEA
Canouan
ATLANTIC OCEAN
Palm Island
Petit St. Vincent
Petit Martinique
Hillsborough
Carriacou
Conference I.
Grenada's Grenadines
0
10
MILES
Kick 'em Jenny
Isle Ronde
N

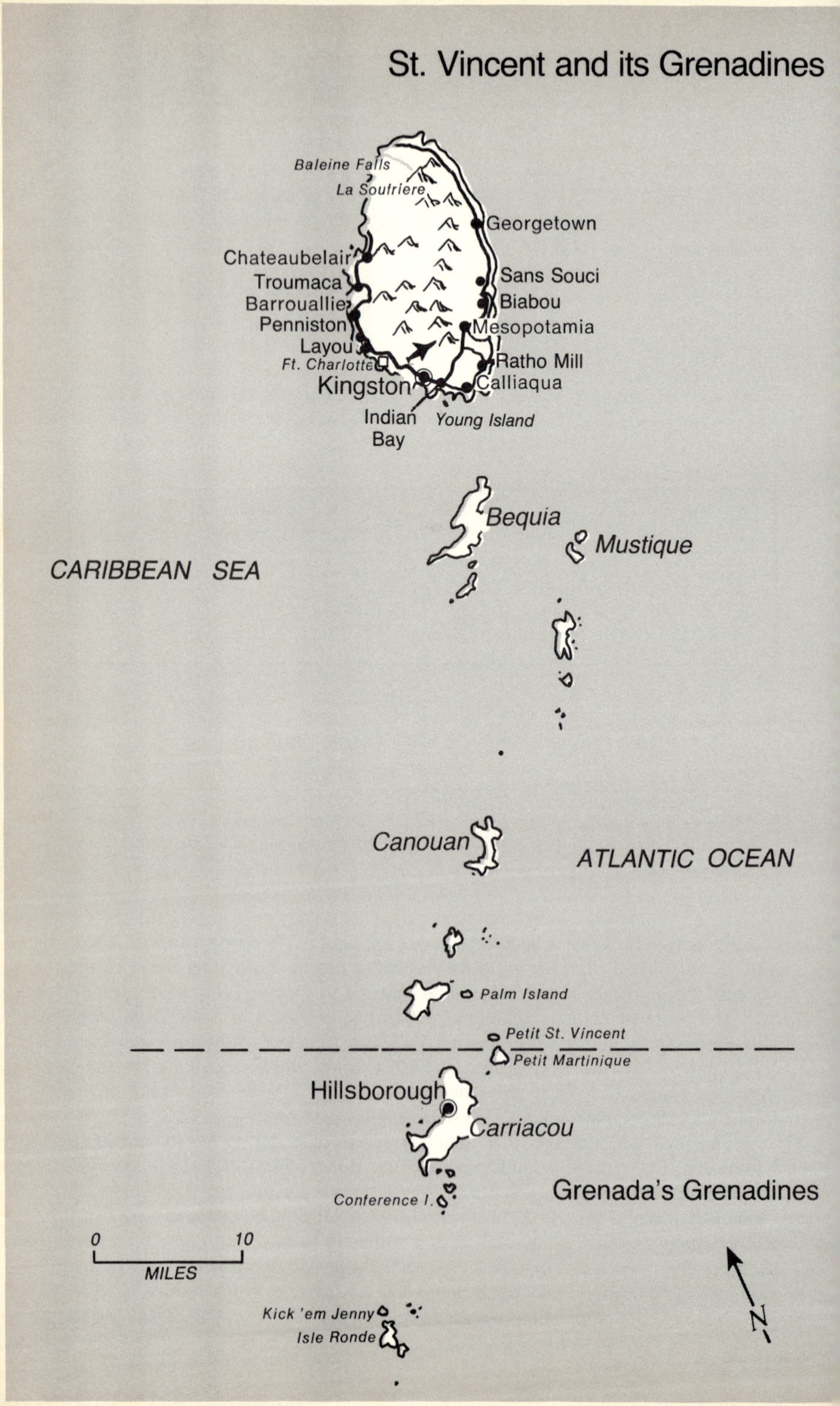

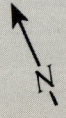

be many charcoal ladies, hands, face, and clothes blackened with their product, which was sold for cooking fuel for braziers used in most Vincentian homes.

At the other end of Kingstown, the first part of town you pass when you drive in from most of the small hotels, there are the boat docks. Once touched only by island schooners, the islands are now linked by motorized craft that travel on schedules. Some of the local boats still fit you in between cases of Heineken beer, sacks of potatoes, and tanks of bottled gas—all destined for the satellite islands, the chain of the Grenadines.

Boat schedules used to be "trade secrets" but there are now regular departures. The fare to Bequia is EC$5 one way on weekdays and EC$10 Sundays.

POLITICAL PICTURE: This multi-island grouping became the independent country of St. Vincent and the Grenadines on October 27, 1979, after having been an Associated State of Britain since 1967 when the group was granted that status along with most of the other formerly British West Indian islands. Following the British system of five-year terms, with elections called in response to the confidence of the people. Prime Minister James Mitchell will continue for his second five-year term following elections in May 1989, when his New Democrats Party won all of the 13 seats. He had served as prime minister for a term starting in July 1984 and, prior to that, for a term that began in 1972, interrupting the long tenure of former Prime Minister Milton Cato. This multi-island country has stayed out of the mainstream of Caribbean politics and development, although its location—at the northern end of a string of islands that "ends" at Grenada, with its satellite islands of Carriacou and Petit Martinique—has meant that its citizens have paid close attention to developments elsewhere. St. Vincent's Grenadine islands stretch south like the tail of the kite, making them appealing as a sailors' landfall and for those who like to explore reasonably remote islands.

ISLAND APPEARANCE: The main island—St. Vincent—is one of the Caribbean's most beautiful. It has all the attributes of Jamaica, in smaller portions. The mountains rise to the volcano in the north; their flanks are blanketed with plantation crops that flourish in soil made even more fertile by fairly recent volcanic eruptions. Bananas, copra, limes, and cotton are among the export crops for St. Vincent. Agriculture continues to be an important industry; tourism is limited to a few small hotels and outpost-island resorts, most of which are reached by boat. The country claims one of the Eastern Caribbean's four endangered parrots, now the focus of an island-wide conservation campaign. The southcoast capital of Kingstown is the only large town, although there are fishing villages along the reasonably protected west coast. The east coast is battered by the relentless Atlantic seas; the coastline sheers to the sea as dark volcanic rock in many places. St. Vincent has mostly dark to black volcanic sand beaches, except for a few coves on the south coast.

The several sister islands offer the contrast—of flatter terrain and miles of beautiful white soft-sand beaches. These islands are natural places for tourism development, although access is sometimes a multi-stop air or sea expedition.

LIFESTYLE on St. Vincent has been modified from the centuries of British heritage by the trends of newly independent Caribbean countries. Vincentians, and the sprinkling of people on the several Grenadines that are governed from St. Vincent's Kingstown, have a lifestyle that is uniquely Vincentian. You can count on cricket and football/soccer to be popular local sports, but you can also walk down to the far end of Kingstown, the opposite end of town from the banana-loading docks, and perhaps hear the young children practicing hymns at one of the trio of churches (Methodist, Anglican, and Catholic). Schoolchildren are uniformed, neat, and smiling, although curious about those of us who wander in their midst—intruders from another country.

This is a verdant island where almost anything grows. When you drive into the country, you will see lush plantations and a simple lifestyle that finds Vincentians living off the land they till.

For those interested in the island's history and past traditions, St. Vincent and Bequia have two of the few remaining Caribbean communities where men go out after whales, bringing them back to shore as the Portuguese fishermen did in the old days out of New Bedford, MA, and their own Azores in the Atlantic. When a whale is sighted, life among the old generation reaches a feverish pitch—with capture and cutting part of a time-honored ritual where danger mixes with daily activity.

The Carib community that has lived for generations on the slopes of St. Vincent's volcano in the north of the island was moved south in April 1979 when ominous rumbles resulted in a gigantic plume of ash in the air. Some of the younger Caribs did not return; the older generation who live on the flanks of the volcano have been integrated into modern Vincentian life as have the Caribs on the reservation in northeastern Dominica.

Clothes are casual. St. Vincent is not an island for peacock finery. Most of the small hotels and resorts are sea oriented (often sailing, certainly swimming), and only Young Island, for Vincentian hotels, aspires to be a resort-style property. What you dress up in there for dinner is up to you, but the rule used to be—and still is for some—that barefoot elegance sets the pace. Some of the Grenadine resorts (notably Cotton House on Mustique and Petit St. Vincent on its island of the same name) have been enclaves of the good life and still are, although they've slipped some in my opinion, in the past couple of years. When you venture into Kingstown, or any of the small villages around the country, conservative daytime wear is most appropriate. Vincentians are kind and welcoming people, many of whom have an annual income that may be less than the total value of the clothes in your suitcase.

MEDICAL FACILITIES: The General Hospital, at the west end of Kingstown, is the government hospital. There's a private hospital near the Botanical Gardens, in Kingstown, and a hospital run by the nuns in George Town. All the hospitals were built during the time when the country was a British colony. They are overcrowded and understaffed, as is the case with many of the facilities on the smaller islands. Barbados, almost 45 minutes' flight on a small plane, has the nearest big hospital. From Barbados, patients who can afford it fly to Miami or to London, depending on their loyalties—and tolerance for the flight. There are clinics on some of the Grenadine islands, but they may have only a nurse in charge.

MONEY MATTERS: When you are staying at Young Island, Petit St. Vincent, and other resorts, you can use your familiar greenbacks, but if you venture out of those compounds, you will find that Eastern Caribbean currency is legal tender—in the market, shops, restaurants, and anywhere in the country.

AUTHOR'S OBSERVATION

Using the local currency is regarded as a common courtesy by the people of recently independent countries. Flashing U.S. dollars around represents a lifestyle some West Indians resent, although you will find no resentment to you as an individual.

COMMUNICATION by telephone from overseas is direct dial 809 area code + 45 for St. Vincent and a 5-digit local number. It is reasonably easy to make contact with those who have phones on St. Vincent and some of the Grenadines. Cable & Wireless sells a plastic phone card, for use in phones that do not accept coins. The cards can be purchased in several amounts and are useful until your calls have totaled that amount. AT&T's USADirect can be accessed from designated phones at the airport and elsewhere. Many businesses have facsimile machines. Mail service is slow (and costs 50 cents Air Mail for ½ ounce from the U.S.). Telex can be effective. International newspapers are hard to find on St. Vincent, and almost impossible to find in the Grenadines. International newsmagazines are available in bookstores on St. Vincent, but the most extensive supply can be found in neighboring Barbados.

ARRIVAL on St. Vincent is usually via Barbados for visitors who come from the U.S., Britain, and Europe. At the Barbados airport, there is a courtesy desk in the immigration area for visitors continuing on to St. Vincent. It's advisable to check baggage only to Barbados, to claim it yourself before delivering it to the airline or charter flight for St. Vincent (which can be done at the St. Vincent information desk near the baggage claim area). Be prepared to "take charge" of your own transit from Barbados arrival to departure for St. Vincent, with luggage check and confirmation of flight time two important rituals. If your connecting flight is delayed, rest assured that there is a comfortable restaurant at the Barbados airport, in addition to shops and snackbar. The major carrier between Barbados and St. Vincent is *LIAT*, Leeward Islands Air Transport, the Antigua-based airline that comes in for more than its share of raps. It has become "fashionable" to share jokes about LIAT, and while I have had my problems with delayed flights, indifferent staff, and the whole list of complaints, I find LIAT flights part of what the Caribbean is all about today. Most people are *trying* but in many instances, no one really knows what to do next, so *you* must have your own action plan. *St. Vincent Air Services,* also known as Mustique Airways and Air Martinique, offers seat-in-plane service on their small planes. Arrangements can be made through hotels and at the St. Vincent airport. *Air Martinique* flies from Martinique to Union Island for boat links to PSV and

Palm resorts. There are other small charter airlines that are available, but you will pay a premium, usually, for your personal flight. One reasonably dependable, regular service for the Grenadine island destinations is *Inter-Island Air Service* (IAS, and a LIAT subsidiary). It operates an island-hopping flight between St. Vincent and Grenada.

St. Vincent's E. T. Joshua Airport arrivals building was expanded to open, officially, on Independence Day, October 27, 1979, but it is still small by comparison to, for example, the major international airport in Barbados. Customs inspectors take their work seriously—even when there are only a handful of you to clear. The system is methodical. On a couple of occasions, the inspector would not look at the first piece of luggage until everything from the plane had been put at the luggage claim area and taken to his counter. This may have changed, but if not—relax. You'll get where you're going sometime.

The St. Vincent Tourist Board information desk is usually manned for flight arrivals (but not always if you have chartered a plane). Leaflets and information are available; ask about taxi fares. The departure lounge is comfortable, with bar, post office, and a branch of St. Vincent Craftsmen's shop (which is not always staffed).

CRUISE ships occasionally come into St. Vincent, and the boat service from the Kingstown docks down the Grenadine islands as far as Grenada is an exceptional experience, enjoyed by many of us who like our islands "natural." Regular Grenadine "ferry" services include the *Admiral,* and the *Friendship Rose,* to one or more islands, in addition to charter yachts. Don't count on any luxuries for the motor service, and sailors know what to expect from yachting through the islands. (See "Touring Tips" below.)

DEPARTURE involves LIAT (Leeward Islands Air Transport) and that can mean delays, and changing schedules. Be sure to double check the flight you *think* you are on, if you are making connections for onward flights from Barbados. If you have a close connection, consider chartering. Your hotel can help with arrangements. There's a departure tax of EC$15, to be paid when you check in for your return flight. Immigration officials will take the copy of the card you filled in when you arrived. Security systems are fairly casual for these small plane flights.

When you arrive in Barbados, there are snackbar-style restaurant facilities in the transit lounge. The good restaurant is outside the customs area, but worth the effort if you have a long wait between planes. The nearest hotels to the airport in Barbados are Crane Beach, Ginger Bay, or, slightly farther, Marriott's Sam Lord's Resort.

TOURING TIPS: When you step outside the airport door, taxis will be waiting. If your hotel expects you on a certain flight, they may have made arrangements for a driver to ask for you. Check with the Tourist Board desk before you wade into the sea of drivers outside. Cab fares to all hotels are reasonable; there's no place that's more than about 15 minutes' drive from the door.

Bequia and the offshore Grenadine Islands are another excursion. If you're headed there, be sure to travel light, unless you *like* to lug suitcases, crates, etc. through the several stages involved in getting from Barbados to St. Vincent airport to the docks for the boat service to some of the islands with no airfields. Boats at the Kingstown dock include the mailboat that makes the run to Bequia, Canouan, Mayreau, and Union, to return to St. Vincent two times weekly in each direction, in addition to the Friendship Rose Edwina, Admiral, and island-built schooners that will take you to Bequia along with the freight. None of the escapades are geared for resort wear; dress for rugged travel in warm countries (jeans, shirt, and not much luggage).

For touring around the "big" island of St. Vincent, take a taxi if you are a first-timer, and check with your hotel to find the name of a tried and true driver whose lore will add to your experience. Once you know the roads (signposting is limited or nonexistent), you can **rent a car,** but be prepared for roads that weave and are potholed and expensive gas (with small cars you won't use much). The Vincentian **minibus** service runs along the road past the driveway for most hotels (Young Island's dock included), and you can pay about EC$1 for the 20-minute ride into Kingstown.

On Bequia, taxis will take you touring, and you can walk (or hitchhike—cars are limited) around near Admiralty Bay.

LODGING on St. Vincent and its Grenadine Islands is in places with personality. There are no big and boxy hotels. The choices make up an astounding collection of Caribbean luxury—the kind that makes you marvel at how anyone *dared* to attempt to bring freezers, fresh running water, and electricity to island outposts—and small and simple surroundings, suited to the inevitable power failures, sudden tropical downpours, and dearth of fresh water that are facts of life in island communities where modernization comes at a high price—emotionally as well as financially. For years, I have fled to hideaways on St. Vincent and its islands—to luxuriate in the sure knowledge that nothing elsewhere would be/could be important enough for anyone to succeed in finding me. You will find hospitality the highlight in these islands.

Most of St. Vincent's hotels, cottages, and inns are on the south coast, within a few minutes' ride from downtown Kingstown if they are not actually in the town. There are a couple of places outside the town—one on the golf course (which has had an open-and-shut history that warrants a check on current status before you carry your clubs south for play), and another on a black-sand windward cove. Most vacationers will find themselves in the cluster of small places that look toward the Grenadines.

On the Grenadine islands, there are a few places to stay—some simple and some simply perfect luxury.

―――――――――――― **AUTHOR'S AWARDS** ――――――――――――
Petit St. Vincent provides an elegant escape; *Young Island* is everything a small island resort should be; and *Grand View* is a uniquely Vincentian inn with special island food.

There's a 5% government tax on all room rates; many hotels also add a service charge, which is usually 10%. If you have special service, a bit more is appreciated, but hand it to those deserving folks, so you know they receive it.

Information about places to stay is included under Hotels/Resorts, Housekeeping Holidays, the Inn Way, and Low-Cost Lodgings. Stars are awarded within each category. (See page 11.)

HOTELS/RESORTS on St. Vincent are few; most places qualify for what I've called the "Inn Way." There are no modern, high-rise hotels here, but you'll find plenty of hospitality.

★★ **Sunset Shores** • *on the shore* • with a view of Young Island, sat firmly on a yellow sand beach on St. Vincent's southern shore in the season of '73. This property is family-managed as well as family-owned. You'll be staying in one of the garden-level rooms that U-shape around the pool. Accommodations are motel style, air-conditioned, and comfortable but not luxurious. There will probably be entertainment some evenings, especially in winter, but most of the activity here—as at other hotels—is what you stir up yourself. Kingstown is about a 10 minute ride, either by taxi, rental car, or the bus that runs on its own schedule past the end of the drive. *Small hotel.*

★★★★ **Young Island** • *about 200 yards off the south shore of St. Vincent* • is one of the Caribbean's first "whole island" resorts. This islet is a small spot on which the first of about two dozen cottages were built in the early 1960s. The wood-frame villas have louvered windows through which the tradewinds blow, and when they slow an overhead fan takes over. Most showers are bamboo enclosed, but open to the sky; newer rooms have regular showers. Colorful fabrics counterpoint the wood walls, and punctuate beachside areas. It's the beach, the breezes, and the relaxing atmosphere that make this place special. Some of the loyal staff have been here since the place first opened, and that includes the Vincentian-born general manager and part owner Vidal Brown, who began work here as a boy when the place was built. (His partner is Vincentian surgeon Fred Ballantyne.) While a few of the cottages curl around the shoreline, others are set back from the foliage-fringed pool, rising up the hillside from the shore so that each has its own spectacular view of the south coast of St. Vincent, that island's most settled area, as well as a private sunning terrace. An *African Queen*-style ferry makes the 5-minute link several times daily, with a schedule that's decided by when you (or the hotel's staff) want to get to the other side. The atmosphere in the dining areas, both the sunstruck tables nestled among the foliage at the edge of the beach and the other tables in the dining room behind the beachside bar, is informal: "No tie, no shoes" for guests, and usually, also, for owner Vidal Browne, his family, and staff. A few small bistro-cafes on the St. Vincent shore provide diversions for the dining hours, just a shuttle-boat ride from your room. Some watersports are available at the beach (boardsailing and snorkeling especially), yachts for charter rest at anchor in the channel, and there's a tennis court over the brow of the hill. More for well-heeled boating and barefoot types than for the pampered and perfect set, this place is an islanders' island, a pricey Robinson Crusoe place. Inquire about the special multinight package plans, with many extras for honeymooners, and at some seasons. *Classic resort.*

HOUSEKEEPING HOLIDAYS have been popular ever since there has been tourism to St. Vincent. Surroundings are usually simple and sea-oriented, even when the beaches are just a patch of sand. You'll buy food at the Kingstown market, from a fisherman you meet and from people suggested to you by the manager of the place you rent. If you have favorite foods you cannot live without, bring them with you—but know that you can get a good supply of island vegetables and spices at the market, depending on the season.

Emerald Valley Resort & Casino • *in the country, in the Penniston Valley* • is a dozen cabins and a casino that is sometimes popular with West Indians and a few tourists (and is sometimes closed). Check for status.

Indian Bay Beach Hotel • *at the shore of Indian Bay* • has 1- and 2-bedroom units, not far from Yvonette Apartments. There's nothing fancy about the surroundings, down a road that slopes to the sea, off the main route between airport and town, in sleeping surroundings that allow vacationers to relax as the Vincentians do. Don't expect a U.S. modern apartment. *Apts.*

Tropic Breeze Hotel • *on a hillside, about 10 minutes from town* • overlooks the Grenadines to the south, and puts you in your own apartment with kitchenette, with the option to eat all your meals at the hotel's restaurant. Insofar as physical details are concerned, rooms are in 1-bedroom apartments and a unit that makes up for 3 bedrooms to take care of 3 couples or a family who want to be in an apartment-style complex. You'll need a car if you want to be mobile. Kingstown is about 15 minutes' drive down the hill, curling around the airport to town. *Apts.*

Yvonette Apartments • *at Indian Bay* • clutch a piece of shoreline. The units are a cheek-by-jowl group that climb over a small slope, offering the option for 1, 2, or 3 bedrooms. All apartments have balconies, a kitchen with adequate equipment (and a propane stove), and enough furniture to give you a comfortable, casual place to enjoy but not worry about. You'll need a car or access to a taxi, to get into Kingstown and around the island. The road that leads to the shore and Yvonette is a winding route from the main road between airport and town. *Apts.*

THE INN WAY is Vincentian style. Both hotels have "inn" overtones. What follows are small places with homelike atmosphere.

CSY Marina • *at Blue Lagoon* • is the home port for Caribbean Sailing Yachts, the operation that is headquartered in the United States. The overnight facilities were built with yachtsmen in mind, for providing a place to overnight before you head to sea (or when you return from your sailing). The 19 rooms were built in the late 70s and a scrub-up in one of the billets is welcomed after a week or two of sailing. Rooms are upstairs, over the yacht service area, not far from the convening area where sailors swap sea stories. They're basic, with no real holiday spirit. *Small hotel.*

Cobblestone Inn • *in Kingstown* • has had its ups and downs since it was sandblasted back to the pirate-era ballast-brick walls. *Basil's Bar* on the main waterfront street is a gathering place for local folk; bedrooms are up the courtyard stairs on the second level. They vary in size and shape. All *must* have air conditioning for any air circulation. Room #3 (twin-bedded, on the front of the building with street noises and waterfront view) and #4 (on the back with less noise and no view), are the best of the lot. The coralstone walls in many rooms add a nice touch, but a "down at the heels" tone was noticeable on my recent visit. The place is popular with Vincentian businessfolk and with barefoot and boating types who take off for sea from the waterfront piers. *Small hotel.*

★★ **Grand View** • *on a hilltop, with a view south to sea* • is within easy distance of Kingstown, although far removed from the town's bustle. The house was part of an estate, and was once used for drying cotton. Today, the comfortable West Indian style rooms are breeze-swept and viewful, with new rooms added for this season. There's a small but pleasant pool in the "backyard," with clusters of chairs gathered for sitting areas and a shelter that provides a perfect perch for watching visiting yachts—and sunsets. The small bar near the reception area at the front of the house has its following among the businessfolk who find this a favorite island lodging. There's a rim of sand at the shore below this hilltop perch that's an easy walk, down or up the hill. Island recipes are featured in the dining room, where service is traditional West Indian family-style, with vegetables from a serving dish and a standard evening offering served to all. (My dinner of pumpkin soup, cornish hen with fixings, carrots with curry, and bread pudding for dessert makes one more happy Vincentian memory.) Located on the main south coast road, about 10 minutes from the airport and slightly longer from town, Grand View can be ideal for anyone seeking good value in comfortable, hospitable West Indian surroundings. (This continues to be one of my favorite traditional West Indian-style havens.) *Inn.*

The Last Resort • *on a sandy shore not far from Kingstown or the airstrip* • overlooks yachts anchored in the protected passage that separates this shore from Young Island. Formerly known as Coconut Beach, this casual spot has had a much-needed spruce-up. Turn off the main road at the sign and weave down for about 3 minutes toward the shore to find the place. Ask for one of the 10 rooms that are closest to the sea. Tucked under and around palm trees and other tropical planting at the shore, the others can seem boxy if you get one in the back, but bright colors liven up the inside, and chances are you'll spend most of your time on the seaside deck or the sands. *Small hotel.*

Mariner's Inn • *at shoreside, near the Young Island dock* • has a main building that is informal and salty, as it has been since it opened several years ago and a block of newer, self-catering rooms in a boxy, stucco building at the roadside entrance. The bar atmosphere can be *very* island casual depending on who is "hanging around," and that's been medical students who lived in some of the rooms in recent seasons. The inn offers sea-oriented surroundings that have bordered on "scruffy," plus dancing, music, and perhaps a shoreside barbecue some evenings. The indoor dining area is open to the breezes and features island food. There's a small patch of sand where you can slide into the sea, but don't count on a long stretch of powder here. You'll have to go to the Grenadines to find that, but you are within a 15-minute drive of Kingstown and can take the public bus that passes along the main road outside the entrance if you don't want to rent a car or taxi. *Small hotel.*

★ **Umbrella Beach Hotel** • *on the south shore, near the Young Island dock* • makes the most of a charming, simple West Indian house and some new additions. The handful of rooms are furnished with basics, tidy with paint, and good for self-sufficient folk who enjoy small hotels. Rooms 1, 2, and 3 are on the inland side; #8 faces the sea. Most meals are offered next door at *The French Restaurant,* breakfast is served in your room or on the sea-rimming patio. *Guesthouse.*

★ **Villa Lodge** • *on a hilltop near Kingstown (and Grand View)* • is a home-turned-inn, with rooms in various shapes and sizes, all neat, and some with a view of the water. (Number 7 has a lovely view of Fort Duvernette, the rock hump near Young Island.) The 3 rooms off one side of the original house have doors leading out to the pool path; #1 is a big double room that can easily take 3 people. Count on sincere West Indian hospitality from the Brisbane's inn, and you can walk down the hill to the shore for swimming if you prefer that to the pool. The bus into Kingstown runs past the end of the driveway. Surroundings right here are conducive to quiet evenings "at home," either joining the other guests (and the Vincentians) who settle around the bar, or enjoying your own company after a good West Indian meal. *Inn.*

LOW-COST LODGING: There are a few small hotels in Kingstown that have very reasonable rates for simply furnished, traditionally West Indian accommodations. In addition, some of the places mentioned above, under "Housekeeping Holidays," have very reasonable rates, especially for longer stays.

Haddon Hotel • *on a hillside overlooking the main road into Kingstown* • has 17 rooms, some of them singles and all furnished with basics only. You can walk along the road to town, but will need the local bus or a taxi to get to the beach. *Guesthouse.*

★ **Heron Hotel** • *across from the banana-loading docks in Kingstown* • has been a longtime favorite of mine. It hasn't changed much in all the years I've known it, except to carve a piece out of several rooms to allow for a private bathroom. Reached through a narrow archway off the main waterfront street, the hotel is upstairs to your left. The breeze sweeps through opened louvered windows into the sitting room (with TV), and most bedrooms are off the hall that rims a center court (which could be attractive, but isn't). This typically West Indian hotel has its own inimitable style. *Guesthouse.*

Kingstown Park Guest House • *in the hills of Kingstown* • is a private home with 20 rooms for rent. Some are in the main house; others are in neighboring buildings. Although the old wood house shows signs of wear, it has a style all its own that appeals to folks who want to step back in time to the traditional West Indies. Owner Mrs. Nesta Paynter is a Vincentian who can share tales of the past. *Guesthouse.*

RaWaCou • *rising from a gray sand beach on the windswept Atlantic coast* • has 10 cottages that might be enjoyed by folks with pioneering (and nature-loving) instincts. Reached by a steep road, this place is only recommended for independent (and self-sufficient) travelers who enjoy out-of-the-way places. A thatched-roof restaurant at the main building is the social center, and new owners promise improvements. Horseback riding. *Bungalows.*

RESTAURANTS on St. Vincent feature West Indian food sometimes dressed in Italian or French flourishes. Some of the most comfortable places for outsiders are the hotel dining rooms. If you are unfamiliar with the ways of West Indian islands, you'll find the dining room at Young Island the most typical of what you expect of Caribbean resorts. However, the food will be better—if you want to sample local recipes—at places such as **Grand View** and **Villa Lodge.** Stop by a day before, or certainly in the morning, to see if you can have a West Indian meal that night.

The French Restaurant is this island's best place for dinner, in my opinion. Located at the south shore, near the Young Island dock, the West Indian house has several tables on its porch. When I sampled on a recent visit, entrees included fish with dill (EC$40), local lobster (EC$50–70, depending on size), crab farci (stuffed crab for EC$22), and other well-prepared offerings. Vegetables include plantain (a member of the banana family) au gratin and pureed sweet potato, both of which were tasty. The wine list is extensive.

Stilly's Aquatic Club, also near the Young Island dock, is an easy place to have a snack or more in shoreside surroundings. It breaks loose as a bar and sometime disco at night.

In Kingstown, **Cobblestone** serves meals and its Basil's Bar has a following. Check with Doreen McKenzie at the **Heron** about the possibility of a simple, family-style meal with her overnight guests if you have not booked here. She may be able to take an extra reservation. The sandwich-and-soup lunches are a noontime favorite for many who find themselves in Kingstown then, but don't count on any food service between 2 and 6 in the afternoon.

NATURAL SURROUNDINGS: Most of St. Vincent is still in a natural state; tourism has not stepped on this island with a heavy foot—yet. For a glimpse of what can be found in its natural habitat around the country, visit the **Botanic Garden,** founded in 1765 in the foothills of the mountains that rise behind Kingstown. Legend claims that the huge breadfruit tree is an offspring of one brought, with several other plant species, by Captain Bligh (of *Mutiny on the Bounty* fame) when he came to the West Indies in 1793, after infamous travels in Tahiti. The garden covers almost 20 acres and is a propagation center for ornamental plants and trees as well as fruit-bearing, food-bearing species.

In recent years, the tourism department has worked with interested citizens and other government departments to define and maintain walking and hiking trails and to provide guides. Although the system has not worked perfectly, the interest is in place, and checking with the tourism officials in Kingstown should yield more specific information about trails and the status of facilities, not only on St. Vincent, but also in the Grenadine islands. The colorful St. Vincent parrot, Amazona Guildingii, can be spotted in some of its natural habitats, but it is only one of the many birds that lure nature-lovers into the remote parts of the country. The Whistling Warbler can also be seen.

There are trails in the **Buccament Valley** that start near the top of the valley to thread through the rain forest, while rivers and streams in the **Mesopotamia Valley** hold their own fascination. Although the standard taxi tours drive through the valley, it's much more rewarding to walk and hike away from the road and settlements. **Grand Bonhomme** is the highest mountain; the **Yambou Gorge** is popular for picnics; and views to the sea are spectacular.

Falls of Baleine are well worth the day's outing. Inquire about making the excursion by boat as soon as you arrive on St. Vincent. (It may take a couple of days to get things organized). The boat trip from Kingstown area along the west coast is almost enough reason to make the journey. Views are spectacular. But the falls are a bit of magic. This can be a bathing suit-and-sneakers excursion where diving into the sea swells that make a landing a challenge are part of your experience. The *MV Admiral* usually comes into the shore. Following the riverbed to the base of the falls is a short (ten-minute) rewarding walk, with an opportunity to wallow in the pools at the base of the falls when you reach the "end." This is a special experience, well worth whatever the going rate happens to be.

The **volcano** in the north (see "Sports") is a real excursion and not a place for passive sightseeing. The area was restricted, except for rescue missions and volcanologists during the April '79 activity, but things are now back to normal. Hire a small plane at the airport and fly over the area; driving up and back is a back-breaking ride, not worth the excursion unless you are intrepid.

Insofar as scuba and snorkeling are concerned, the Grenadine islands offer far better sites than the island of St. Vincent, where seas off the windward (east) coast can be treacherous, with strong undertow and often strenuous surf. Indian Bay, off the south coast of St. Vincent and just north of Young Island, is one of several areas where multicolored fish hold their daily "carnival," sashaying around the rocks and reefs, but far more dramatic coves can be found in the Tobago Cays, in the southern Grenadines, where the cornstarch-white sand provides a perfect foil, and reefs are popular feeding grounds. Coves off Bequia are also popular, as are the reefs, walls, shipwrecks, and caves known to divers who live in the Grenadines.

PLACES WORTH FINDING are concentrated in and around the capital of Kingstown. Although you can wander around Kingstown happily on your own, looking and lingering at whim, for your first foray into the countryside stop at the Tourist Board and ask them to suggest a driver if you have not already made arrangements through your hotel. Having a Vincentian take you around, to give some local commentary, will make all the difference in the first run. From that time on, you can rent a car and get around easily on your own.

ST. VINCENT

> **AUTHOR'S OBSERVATION**
> Do not take just any taxi driver; some are better versed in island lore than others, and it is worthwhile, if you are taking time from your vacation to ride around in a car, to make inquiries in advance and ask around to be sure you find a driver you like.

KINGSTOWN is several villages, at least as I see it. First is the port area, around and down the road from the banana boat loading docks. The most fascinating part is the schooner dock, where you should be at 8 a.m. or earlier—whether you want to sign on to go down island, or just look around. Everything gets loaded—early; and you can sign on on the spur of the moment if you like spontaneous travel.

    The St. Vincent Library, in a building where trade winds blow through the second floor while you check up on West Indian history or other subjects, is one of several Carnegie libraries dotted around the formerly British West Indies as part of a behest from the Andrew Carnegie fortune.

    The cluster of churches at the west end of town, the "other" end from the docks, set an entirely different tone. Most of the churches also have schools (you will see neatly uniformed children in play yards and around the area on weekdays, morning, noon, and mid-afternoon). **St. George's Cathedral,** the Anglican church, has interesting plaques on its walls and stones in its graveyard of English/Scottish days. The view from the graveyard of **St. Mary's Roman Catholic Church,** built in an intriguing combination of several styles, is interesting. The Catholic church was the dream of Belgian monk, Dom Carlos Verbeke, who obviously carried with him European visions of the house of God. The **Methodist Church,** on the third "side" of this area, is simple, with its louvered windows usually open to the breezes.

    Fort Charlotte, up and out from Kingstown, is the standard tourist stop for anyone who takes a cab (or a cruise ship tour). It's the view that is awe-inspiring. A small collection of artifacts and documents has been assembled as a museum in the former dungeon. Part of the fort is used as a jail. The drive to get here is matched (or exceeded) by the curling route you will follow around what's known as Mesopotamia Valley, a lush plant-filled "bowl" where Vincentians farm on the slant and reap some of the healthy crops you can witness at the local market.

    St. Vincent Museum, planted in an interesting West Indian house in the middle of the Botanical Gardens where the Caribbean's first breadfruit tree grows (the nut was left by Captain Bligh, legend claims), is worth a visit. The Botanical Gardens claim to be the oldest in the western hemisphere, having been founded in 1765 with a link to Britain's famed Botanical Gardens at Kew, outside London. Be sure to make an appointment to meet the museum's enthusiastic director, Earle Kirby, if you want more legends and lore than appear on the meager identification tags on displays in the simple museum. Among the treasures in the small museum are early Arawak Indian artifacts, and items from the culture of some of the tribes (Tainos and Ciboneys). All items have been unearthed around St. Vincent and its Grenadines, and the $1 donation seems too small a price to pay for this opportunity. Allow some time to saunter around the Botanic Garden, well worth a walk in their own right.

Whaling villages on the leeward (west) side of the island are not the typical tourist traps. If you head here, take humility with you. Not many outsiders come to these villages, and you will be obvious whether you mean to be or not.

Liberty Lodge is not your typical sightseeing goal, but it is definitely a place worth finding, or at least finding out about. Located in the hills behind Kingstown, the Lodge is a self-help project for Vincentian adolescents who had been spending their childhood getting into trouble around the docks. Sparked by the enthusiasm of some local citizens and a few interested island visitors, Liberty Lodge became a residence for delinquents, who learned animal husbandry, agriculture, and carpentry, plus other useful crafts at their own community in the hills. To quote from the mimeographed folder given to me by Colonel Anderson, retired chief of the Vincentian police and a prime mover in the project, "In November 1969, a group of ten juveniles ranging from 10–16 years, who had all been known to the police, were called together to discuss their participation in a scheme which was to provide training for them in a different environment." The environment was the Lago Heights Police Post, no longer used for training officers and available as a mountainside residence for the boys. The youths have worked toward building their community and raise food for sale to hotels and stores in Kingstown so that the project is partially self-supporting. If you have the opportunity and the interest, inquire about the Liberty Lodge project, either through your hotel manager or directly from Andy Anderson, if you can find him while you're on the island. (Check at the offices of Argyle Associates on James Street, or write to Box 530, St. Vincent, W.I.)

SPORTS are sea-oriented. They focus on sailing—not only out of St. Vincent, but certainly around the Grenadines. Bequia is a favorite anchorage for many yachts, in spite of the feeling on the part of a few captains I have talked with that the reception among yachtsmen is not as warm as it used to be. (There seems to be competition among anchoring yachtsmen for the charter business.)

Sailing is very popular (and professional) in these island-flecked seas. Among the multi-yacht charter firms are *Bimini Yacht Charters, Dolphin Yacht Charers,* and, out of Bequia, *Frangipani Yacht Services. Caribbean Sailing Yachts* is one source for professional advice and well-kept yachts. CSY sends you out with capable skipper in one of the 35 special CSY 44s, designed for these waters with information supplied by CSY owner Van Ost and his crew. The firm got its start in a dentist's office in Tenafly, NJ, and CSY tried the idea of full-service chartering in Essex, CT, in 1967. From there, the senior Van Ost went to St. Thomas, pulling up anchor from there to head to Road Town, Tortola, in the British Virgins, in 1969. At that time, services stretched south to the port at St. Vincent and the fleet was expanded to include the Carib 41s that the firm had pioneered in the island cruising-for-comfort market. Full details on the varieties of sailing programs, including bare boat, boat with skipper and sail-and-learn programs can be obtained from the CSY mail drop at Box 491, Tenafly, NJ 07670, or at Blue Lagoon, St. Vincent, W.I.

Pleasure cruising is sometimes available on motor boats to go up the coast or to the Grenadine islands. Tobago Cays, cruising to the Falls of Baleine, Mustique, deep-sea fishing, and Bequia are usually offered at fees that range from about $35 per person up to $60 (for the longer excursions to, for example, the Tobago Cays). Inquire at the tourist office or your hotel on arrival.

Scuba diving facilities are no match for those on Bonaire, the Caymans, and St. Thomas, although the waters in the Grenadines and even off the coasts of St. Vincent offer spectacular sites. In the past couple of years, some pros have settled here and the start for what can become a flourishing scuba center is solid. Contact *Mariner's Aquatic Sports* near the Young Island dock at Villa, or *Dive St. Vincent* with an office at CSY's marina.

Golf is not a prime sport at this time since the course at Aquaduct, about 45 minutes' drive from Kingstown and most of the hotels has been allowed to dissolve into bad condition. The location is gorgeous, in the valley surrounded by mountains, but be sure to check on the status of the course before you lug clubs this far. Financing has plagued this operation from its start and condition of the course reflects the problem. If you are a golfer, a trip here to rent some clubs and play a few rounds can make a pleasant day *if* the course is in condition for play.

The **tennis** court over the hill on Young Island is used by YI hotel guests even when its surface is "variable," but otherwise it bakes in the sun. There are public courts (asphalt) on the way into Kingstown, and there are courts at the Aqueduct area, but St. Vincent is not a tennis island—yet. Grand View Hotel's addition of tennis (and squash) facilities reflects a new interest.

Hiking on this island yields special rewards for anyone who has arrived armed with long pants, long-sleeved shirt, sturdy climbing shoes—and bug spray or repellent of some kind. The slopes of the north coast's volcano have become a sort of pilgrimage goal; only those who have conquered the paths and seen the lake at the top can really claim to have seen St. Vincent.

TREASURES AND TRIFLES: **St. Vincent Craftsmen,** a handcraft cooperative, inspires some of the best-quality handcrafts in the Caribbean. When the St. Vincent government focused on local handcrafts in the late 60s, they recognized the need for retraining in some of the skills that had been part of the earliest traditions of the people of these islands. Responding to cooperation from the United Nations agency charged with teaching skills and defining products, St. Vincent's craftsmen relearned some of the earliest skills. Mr. Malcolm Benjamin, from the U.S., was the first director of the Vincentian operation, and with the assistance of Lennox "Scully" Hunte and two Peace Corps workers, the fledgling industry was born. Handmade items of highest quality are sold from the shop on the grounds of the Old Cotton Ginnery, inland along the road leading from the banana-boat docks in Kingstown, and from the second shop at the airport. It is possible to head out into the country to visit some of the home industries, and that can be the most rewarding way to visit the "real" St. Vincent.

Batik Caribe is a shop on the main street of town that sells batik designs on fabric. You can buy clothes ready-made or fabric by the yard.

Noah's Arkade, next door to Batik Caribe, has high quality handicrafts from St. Vincent and other Caribbean countries, as well as an interesting selection of books about the country and the West Indies and some resortwear by St. Vincent "Casuals" and others. This can be your one-stop place for shopping. Variety in price and consistency for quality are hallmarks of this shop.

In the Cobblestone courtyard, there's a **Stecher's** store (you'll find them on St. Lucia, Trinidad, and other Eastern Caribbean isles as well). That's your best source, in my opinion, for the traditional luxury items: crystal, china, etc. You'll find Spode, Finnish Ittala, and other known names in limited selection. Prices are fair, and probably less than you'll pay at your hometown store, but the real reason for looking here is that the selection is interesting, and *that* you probably won't find in your hometown village.

Two sources for interesting, typically Vincentian gifts are the **local markets,** where you buy domestic peanuts, sun-dried and bottled, as well as West Indian hot sauce. Ask about other local products bottled or canned for easy carrying home. The second source is the **Post Office,** where Vincentian stamps showing local scenes are interesting, pretty, and easy to carry home.

THE GRENADINES

The several islands rising from the seas between the south coast of St. Vincent and the northern shore of Grenada are some of the prettiest in the Caribbean. Although most of the Grenadine islands are tied politically to St. Vincent, like the tail of a kite, a few—namely Carriacou and Petit Martinique—are satellites of Grenada. Most are fringed with protected coves, dusted by sand that is as white as talcum powder and about the same consistency. Because the seas are diamond-clear, offshore reefs are favorite places for snorkelers and scuba divers. Known for many years to only a few yachtsmen, these islands are now favorite areas for people sailing out of Martinique and other islands. Unfortunately, trash and other remnants of tourism are the result.

Insofar as coverage of these islands is concerned, I have chosen to talk about Bequia as an island, with its inns and places of interest, and then "go" to Canouan and the other islands alphabetically. Cotton House, a small inn, is mentioned in the coverage of its island of Mustique, which is followed in turn by Palm Island (resort on an island that is officially Prune) and Petit St. Vincent (resort and island). Union Island follows, with its few small places, but look also at the chapter on Grenada if you want to know about places on *its* Grenadine islands of Carriacou and Petit Martinique, within sight and easy boat ride from Union.

Having said that, you should know what every Vincentian schoolchild knows: the order of the islands that string south, as you can see them or sail them from St. Vincent, are Bequia, Petit Nevis, Quatre Island, Battowia, Baliceau, Savan, Petit Canouan, Canouan, the Tobago Cays and Sail Rock, Mayreau, Union Island, with Palm Island and Petit St. Vincent nearby. (South of PSV is Petit Martinique, the "first" of Grenada's Grenadines as you head south, soon to be followed by Carriacou, Saline, Frigate, Large, Diamond, Ronde, Caille, and Les Tantes, before you hit the southern "mark," Grenada.) Only a handful of these islands have housing of any kind for visitors, but most have spectacular powdery sand beaches, most of them unpeopled most of the time. Snorkeling and scuba are almost as exceptional as the sailing around here.

BEQUIA

Old-timers know that you have to jump into the water quickly to bind the mouth of the whale to keep it from sinking and to make it easier to tow. And they know that once the whale is beached on Petit Nevis, carving quickly is crucial. A clutch of sharks can devour at least half of a beached whale in one Caribbean evening. That may not matter in your daily life, but it does in the life of the Bequia whalers. This is an island of the sea. Tradition puts the folk into boats at an early age to pluck up lobsters, fish, and even whales that head south on their annual migrations. Your landing at Port Elizabeth after the crossing from Kingstown on St. Vincent will be casual. You may find one of the 30-plus taxis that formed into an association a few years ago—or you may not. It really doesn't matter because you can take off your shoes and walk in the water to the nearest small inns and you shouldn't have brought much in the way of luggage anyway.

There's a tourism booth near the shore and a few shops in the village that is Port Elizabeth, but mostly this town is a quiet, casual place, lingered over by yachtsmen who make this their first landfall after a trans-Atlantic crossing, and by some who call this harbor home port for chartering around the Grenadines.

The best of Bequia is lolling in the sun, watching, listening and learning how it's done. If you care, you can learn how to cook breadfruit or how to catch a local lobster; you can listen to whaling tales and you can learn how to build a boat—from trees cut to planking size and framed up on the beach. If you're lucky, you may even be around for a boat christening, when all the neighborhood comes to the shore to break down the scaffolding to drag the boat to the sea and to celebrate with more revelry and joy than most people show for a child.

ARRIVAL on Bequia is by boat, either on one of the motor launches that brings you, freight, and the mail across the Bequia Channel from Kingstown, St. Vincent, or on an island schooner. Some boats are sturdy, hand-hewn versions perhaps with a tree-trunk mast, and others are sleek, modern fiberglass yachts for charter. Construction of a much heralded airport is under way. The *Caribbean Newsletter* (page 9) will have further facts when available.

LODGING on Bequia is in a special group of personality places. There's amazing luxury at a couple of cottage/house "resorts" and simple, comfortable shoreside lodgings at a trio of inns. You can count on reasonable rates, casual life, and plenty of time to relax with no pressure to do anything.

AUTHOR'S AWARDS

Frangipani, is a favorite for yachtsmen—and for me. I like the casual, island-style brand of hospitality. If you demand picture-perfect surroundings and don't care about being at Bequia's heart, consider *Spring Estates*.

Bequia Beach Club • *at Friendship Bay* • is a small spot with a sea focus. Opened a couple of years ago on a beach formerly known only by Friendship Bay Hotel, this place can be a comfortable nest for outdoor types. *Small hotel.*

★ **Frangipani** • *at Port Elizabeth* • is one of my favorite inns because it has the courage to be exactly what it is and doesn't fuss a lot to become something others may think it should be. What it is is the childhood home of Prime Minister James "Son" Mitchell, and what it can be is your vacation home. Marie Kingston is the owner/manager. The rooms in the main shoreside building are simple, with bath down the hall from the 6 rooms in the main house. Behind the open-to-breezes gathering spot there are a couple of cement-block cottages with rooms-with-bath and modern conveniences for fussier travelers who want more privacy than a room in the house affords. When you sit by the sea, sipping a cool rum punch dusted with fresh grated nutmeg and waiting for your lobster salad, all will seem right with the world. Frangipani has been a yachtsmen's haven for a decade or more, a place for barefoot and boating types that has become one of the world's few constants. *Inn.*

★ **Friendship Bay** • *on a cove it calls its own* • has new owners, but the same sea-oriented, relaxed atmosphere. The place has been purchased by Eduardo and Joanne Guadagnino, who have Canadian connections. There is a tennis court, and there are prime snorkel and scuba areas not far offshore, but the beach—and the books you bring with you—will be the main daily diversions. Count on varied cuisine, with a focus on fish and local vegetables. Rooms are furnished simply, and most have a sea view. *Hotel.*

★ **Plantation House** • *on the shore at Port Elizabeth* • has new owners, but the location of the former Sunny Caribbee remains the same. The small enclave stretches along the shore at Port Elizabeth not far from the main dock. Ideal as a casual, comfortable place for sea-oriented folk who want to spend their time stretched out at the shore, this is a place where guests spend time perched on stools at the seaside pavilion, or snorkeling and sailing somewhere else. The cottages that parallel the shore are simply furnished, with sea-breeze cooling and private bath. Some entertainment is planned for a few evenings at height of winter season, but don't expect a lot of action. *Cottage hotel.*

★ **Spring on Bequia** • *amid a plantation setting* • is a gathering of stone buildings, with Great House the main building—and the setting for the restaurant and bar area, as well as four of the 10 rooms. Other rooms are in Fort and Gull buildings, and each room has private bath as well as a sunning terrace. The tennis court and pool are near Great House; the beach is a stroll away, at Spring Bay. Owned by Dick and Nina Rudolf, Minneapolis residents, the property is operated from November through June by Candy and Rosie Leslie, their daughter and son-in-law. If you're looking for a quiet place to rest and revive, this may fill the bill. Surroundings are plantation lush, with foliage and flowers around the buildings and plenty of space for walks and relaxing. *Villas.*

HOUSEKEEPING HOLIDAYS on Bequia can (and do) involve house-owning for a handful of people who have found this island and love it. There are several small places to rent; some should be surveyed when you spend your first vacation on Bequia from a base at one of the hotels. For those who know and like island life, where entertainment options are natural, private homes are available for rent in owners' absence. **Villas & Apartments Abroad** (420 Madison Ave., New York, NY 10017; T 212+759-1025 or 800+433-3020, fax 212+755-8316) lists a couple of properties near Friendship Bay in their roster of homes for rent.

SPORTS on Bequia will be sea-centered. There may be professional scuba firms by the time you arrive, but if it's crucial to your holiday fun, be sure to contact the hotel of your choice with specific questions about exactly what facilities are available, certification of the instructors, and quality of equipment. **Snorkeling** is spectacular off almost every cove. There are several places best reached by boat, and anyone at Frangipani or the other hotels can put you aboard something to get around to the best reefs.

Yachts bob at anchor in the harbor. Although the fleet changes, you can assume there will be something in port, and that arrangements can be made for at least a day sail, if not for longer. If you want to be sure of a charter, contact the CSY marina at St. Vincent to have a specific contract for your time.

Do not count on golf, tennis (although there is one court at Friendship Bay), or organized sports. This is not an "organized" island—and there are those of us who love it because of that fact.

TREASURES AND TRIFLES on Bequia are led by **Crab Hole**, started by Linda Lewis and purchased in late '79 by Carolyn and George Porter, who have hired Barbara Station as manager. The shop continues to produce, with the help of the Bequians, marvelous, colorful applique designs as well as silk-screen work and other high-quality crafts, and the expanded selection makes a visit even more interesting than before. There isn't anything in this small seaside shop (which you can reach by walking to the shore between Caribbee and Frangipani) that I wouldn't like to own—and it is worth dropping anchor in port just to see what is for sale.

CANOUAN

Arrival on Canouan is best by boat. That route gives you plenty of time to slow down so that you can move at the local pace. The mail boat chugs through the Grenadines with freight and passengers twice weekly. Arrival is scheduled (as I write, but that may change) for Monday and Thursday in Canouan, with departures north for St. Vincent on Tuesdays and Fridays. Alternative route is to fly to Barbados, to charter to fly to the airstrip on Canouan, via one of the ports of entry in St. Vincent, Mustique, or Union Island, or to fly to St. Vincent from Barbados and then arrange for a small plane flight.

Canouan Beach Hotel • *on a beautiful white sand beach* • was a newcomer in the season of '84, when its first few villas opened for guests. With the addition of new units, the hotel is ready to offer informal hospitality to those who seek a quiet island, before it breaks into the big time resort arena. For this season, this spot is a pleasant get-away place, on an island that's big enough to allow for exploring, birding, and plenty of swimming, snorkeling, and some fishing. *Cottages.*

Crystal Sands Beach Hotel opened in December 1977 as the first place with overnight accommodations for visitors. The main building has the small reception room and the place for whatever the evening entertainment happens to be (often it's just the other guests). Daytime entertainment focuses on swimming, sailing, snorkeling, and scuba if you've brought your own equipment and are proficient (no facilities/teaching for beginners). There are 10 rooms in 5 villas; each room mirrors the next, with twin beds, private entrance, private bath and comfortable—not lavish—beach-oriented surroundings. *Small hotel.*

MAYREAU

Truly a Robinson Crusoe island, with little but spectacular beaches, diamond-clear seas, and sunshine made bearable by ever-constant tradewinds, Mayreau has one of the Caribbean's most glorious escapes.

Saltwhistle Beach Resort • *bordering a white sand beach* • is for the world's weary, providing the budget can stand it. Perked to perfection on this shore by an enterprising group of Canadians, the resort focuses on fishing, sailing, windsurfing, and other watersports. Rooms are in several villas and one main building, all low-rise and low-key, with good meals served at appropriate hours and congenial company for those who want it. This is a perfect escape. You'll need suntan lotion, sunglasses, and a sense of peace. *Small resort.*

MUSTIQUE

Arrival on Mustique is accomplished in a small plane or a seaworthy boat. People are flown in direct from Martinique or via St. Vincent and/or Barbados, depending on what's convenient for you and the size of your group. A roundtrip Air Martinique flight from that French West Indian isle has been about 500 French francs.

★ **Cotton House** • *on a hilltop* • captures the prize spot on the 3-by-1½-mile island it occupies, but good management was lacking when I visited. The island was originally pushed to prestigious planes by Hon. Colin Tennant, who opened the main house as a private club in 1968. He held the helm through the early days of development, when the late Oliver Messel's considerable decorating talents were lavished on the verandas and public rooms of the 18th-century farm buildings he transformed. The public was invited to stay here beginning in 1972, in one of the several 18th-century houses or new ones built to look like them around the main building. They hold most of the twin-bedded, air-conditioned guest rooms. (You won't need the air conditioning; the overhead fans are enough.) About ¼ mile from the main house, at Ansecoy Bay, there's a beach cottage nestled in the palms—and it is its own resort, for rent with a maid and an assurance of privacy. The swimming pool supplements the sandy coves, and the atmosphere here now has a layer of French, gleaned from Guy de la Houssaye, part-owner of Martinique's Bakoua Hotel and, since 1977, the lessee of this island resort. You can count on a quiet, away-from-it-all, island atmosphere on this island and the same kind of carefree holiday that has lured Princess Margaret, Prince Andrew, and others here. *Inn.*

HOUSEKEEPING HOLIDAYS on Mustique are a special brand. If you want to live in the style of royalty, rent Princess Margaret's house, Les Jolies Eaux, between Geliceaux beach and Deep Bay; it has 3 large bedrooms, plus one smaller one, all opening out onto the center courtyard, which leads to a terrace. The living room, at the "back" of the terrace, has a dining terrace of its own (with table that can seat 12) as well as sundeck and balcony surrounding the room for maximum sightseeing. The view is spectacular, and the beach that stretches out at your feet is "the island's best beach" according to some. You can walk to any one of a selection of sandy coves, or use the car that comes with your week's renting. Cost for height of season is about $2000, with staff; after April 15, rates drop to $1500, which isn't a lot when you consider that you can live like a princess. **Villas and Apartments Abroad** (420 Madison Ave., New York, NY 10017, T 212+759–1025 or 800+433–3020, fax 212+755–8316.)

PALM ISLAND

Arrival on Palm Island is best by sailboat, but if you're heading here from home, you'll probably travel the full-day route via Barbados with a flight charter on Tropicair Service (arranged by the hotel if they know when you are coming) to fly to Union Island, where you cross the one-mile span of sea in about five minutes by motorboat. The cost for the Tropicair flight on a "share charter" basis is about $90 per person each way.

★★ **Palm Island Beach Club** • *at the shore* • is testimony to the dream—and hard work—of John and Mary Caldwell. (Try to track down a copy of

Desperate Voyage, John Caldwell's book about sailing for 106 days over 8500 miles in a small boat with two kittens for company, from Panama to Australia to pick up Mary as his wife.) This 110-acre island was known (and still is known on many charts) as Prune Island, but its rebirth as Palm Island Resort was in 1968 when the first rooms were built and the small inn began accepting overnighters who came ashore from yachts. An airstrip, no longer used, was built in the early stages, and the tennis court plus the provisioning shop if you want to cook at home in one of the separate villas were added as time permitted. What's here now is a place that has a wonderful Robinson Crusoe atmosphere. (Be prepared for sandflies and other pesky bugs at the beach especially at twilight after a rain.) While Palm Island may lack some of the luxury of nearby Petit St. Vincent, the casual Caldwell atmosphere offers its own special brand of hospitality. Bring some books, your snorkel mask and fins (if your own are your favorites), and languish seaside for a relaxing vacation. The evening entertainment is as lively as the guests, and there's an occasional barbecue, perhaps with a band if one happens to sail by. A special sailing package holiday gives you a beach villa and a sailboat to sail on your own or with a crew (your pleasure). Your choices for lodging are the Beach Club building that runs like a beachside hotel or one of the several housekeeping villas. Among the villas for rent are Rum Corner or Tropical Villa (2 bedrooms near the beach), Palm Villa or Sea Villa (2 bedrooms on the beach), and Sun Villa (4 bedrooms on the beach). *Resort.*

PETIT ST. VINCENT

Arrival on Petit St. Vincent is the end of an excursion. By the time you settle into your cottage, you will have packed and parted from your hometown, flown to Barbados to connect, hopefully expediently, with a charter or multihop scheduled service for the 45-minute flight to Union Island where the PSV boat meets you for the 20-minute ride (included in your tariff) to the shore where you can climb (or ride the jeep) to your cottage. And after that, you deserve to be pampered.

★★★★ **Petit St. Vincent Resort** • *on its own island, near Union Island* • has been a special spot since it accepted its first guests a couple of decades ago. Hazen Richardson is your host on this 113-acre island, and he and the long-time staff are running a complex they've been operating for several years. Each stone cottage has been designed for comfort and eye appeal. The blue-bitch stone used for the building-plus-patio follows a design by Swede Arne Hasselquist. The main building on the hillside is the social center, with the restaurant and other areas. There are no phones to bother you. A flag system is used for communication between your cottage and the main house, with a red flag assuring privacy and the yellow pennant, raised when you put your written order in your mailbox, assures that you won't be bothered until your order is ready. Tennis, badminton, snorkeling, sailing, windsurfing, Ping-Pong, horseshoes, darts, volleyball, and a choice of several more remote islands to sail to and explore are part of your holiday package here. This is a picture-perfect island "country club" where the world's weary wealthy can come to relax and retread. Problems with staff attitude seem to be a thing of the past. *Classic resort.*

UNION ISLAND

Arrival on Union island can be by plane, yacht, or by the interisland mail boat that starts (or ends) it run at St. Vincent. Clifton Harbour is the island's main town, but it's a speck by comparison to other places you've seen in these islands. The only other "village" of note is Ashton, on the south shore, but it's the beaches (and the airstrip) that draw some folk here. In addition to being the jumping-off point for vacationers heading to Petit St. Vincent and Palm Island, Union has a couple of overnighting spots of its own.

This small island's claim to fame is its December '79 "rebellion," which I "witnessed" from nearby Carriacou. I sat on the terrace at Mermaid Inn, enchanted by the sight of Union, peaceful and majestic, set in the Caribbean sea an easy sailing distance away. Two days later, when I returned to Grenada, the pilot of my plane told of his flight into the grass strip on Palm Island, usually "off limits" for planes since the surface is not well kept. He had followed a Tropicair pilot onto the "strip," and his passenger list included police from St. Vincent, who had to cross to Union to quell the "rebellion" of a handful of renegades. Jokes on Carriacou about the "marijuana marines" brought laughter to all who know the islands well, and no one locally seemed to waste much time worrying about a serious "revolution." Prime Minister Milton Cato declared a "state of emergency" for St. Vincent and its Grenadines, as much to curb any over-enthusiastic malcontents (displeased with the elections that returned Cato to office with a landslide vote) as for any other reason.

HOTELS on Union Island are an informal lot. Only one is a "real" hotel; the others are simple spots mentioned in Low-Cost Lodging.

Anchorage • *on the shore at the "other" side of the airstrip from the shedlike terminal* • is a French-style place, favored by yachtsmen from Guadeloupe and Martinique. The 10-room, multibuilding inn has a marina, where sailors tie up for a meal at Anchorage, plus refueling and supplies. Sharks glide with turtles in a special pool at the shore, providing a diversion of sorts for those who take the time to look. Not for fussy travelers, this place may appeal to folks in search of an island outpost. *Small hotel.*

LOW-COST LODGING on Union Island can be in a room-for-rent at one of the small guest houses or at a couple of small, shoreside hotels.

Clifton Beach • *on the shore at the settlement of the same name* • is a string of motel-style buildings, with simply furnished rooms and a restaurant that features local lobster and fresh-caught fish.

Sunny Grenadines • *at Clifton Beach settlement* • claims a 2-story building with a few rooms, and other units nearer the shore. The "beach" is not the greatest, but convenience to town puts all nearby islands within easy reach by local boat, at rates and routes you can negotiate on the dock.

Trinidad
Tobago
CARIBBEAN SEA
Las Cuevas Bay
Maracas Bay
Blanchisseuse
San Souci
Toco
Galera
Maraval
Tunapuna
Arima
Port-of-Spain
Sangre Grande
Caroni R.
Trinidad
Piarco Plain
Manzanilla Point
Gulf of Paria
Calxton Bay
Pointe-a-Pierre
San Fernando
Pitch Lake
Point Fortin
Rio Claro
Princess Town
Mayaro Bay
Siparia
Basse Terre
N
0
10
MILES

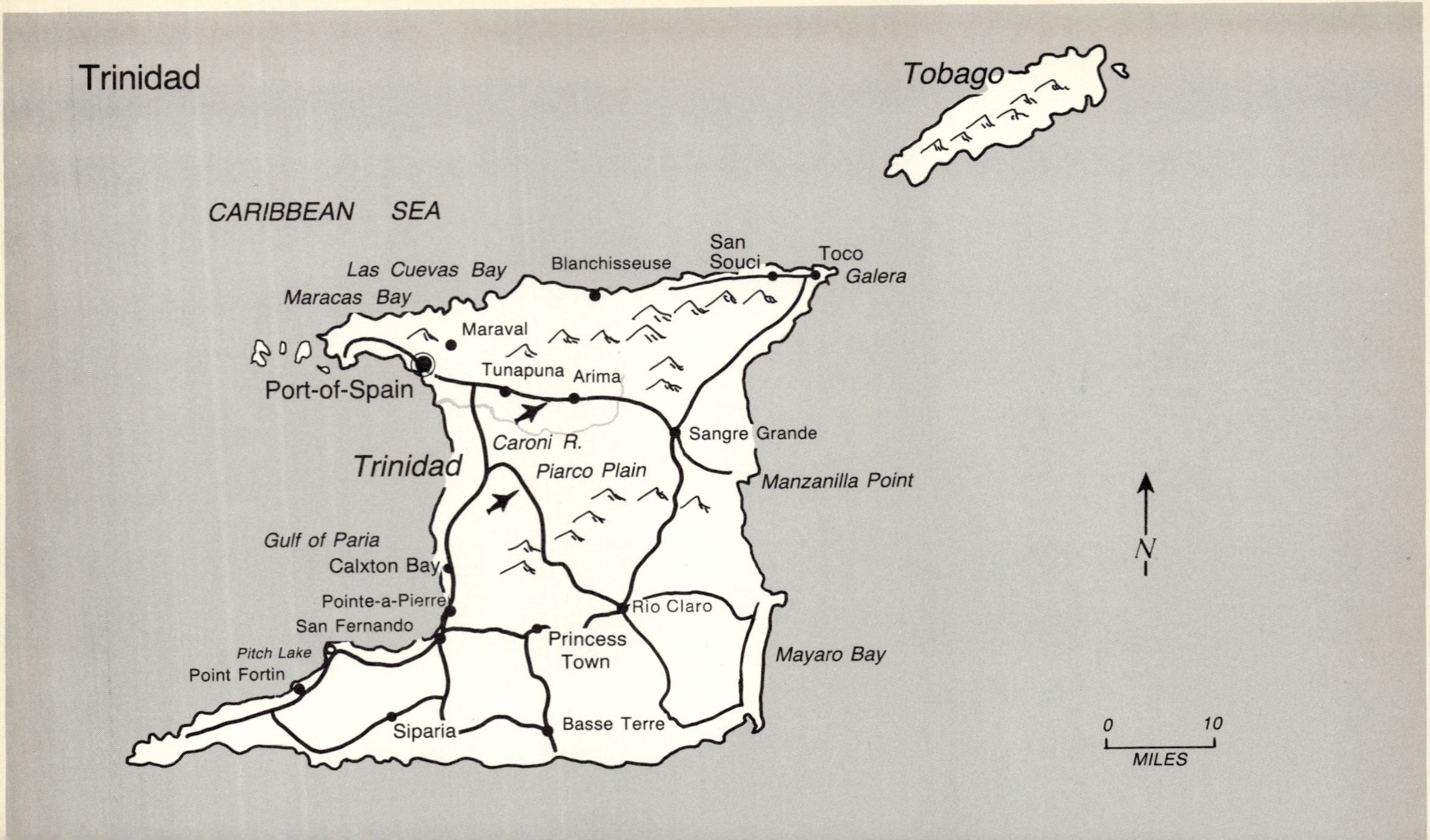

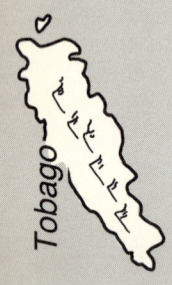

TRINIDAD

Trinidad & Tobago Tourism Development Authority, Cruise Complex, Box 222, 1D Wrightson Rd., Port of Spain, Trinidad, W.I., T 809+623–1932, fax 809+623–3848; #310, 330 Biscayne Blvd., Miami, FL 33132, T 305+374–2056; #1508, 25 W. 43rd St., New York 10036, T 212+719–0540 or 800+232–0082, fax 212+719–0988; #102, 40 Holly St., Toronto, Ontario M4S 3C3, Canada, T 416+486–4470 or 800+268–8986, fax 416+440–1899; 20 Lower Regent St., London SW1Y 4PH, T 01+839–7155.

$ · · · US$1 = TT$4.20
Unless otherwise noted, $ refers to U.S. currency.

Humphrey Bogart could have sauntered with confidence down Frederick Street to Independence Square in Port of Spain, brushing shoulders with East Indians, West Indians, Chinese, Africans, South Americans, French, British, Portuguese, Lebanese, Syrians, and a handful of mid-Europeans, the melange that makes this city so special. He could have dallied, as we all do, at some downtown roti stand, where one "chef," sometimes serving through a chicken-wire "screen," hands you the crepe-thin pancake that is folded around spicy, curried shrimp, chicken, beef, or some other stuffing. Some of the roti stands are small buses or trucks that have been turned into possibly mobile snack stops, that don't seem to move from their place at Independence Square.

Roti stands nest amid department stores, yard goods outlets, and luxury shops that sell crystal, china, and other European imports along with gold that is fashioned into jewelry in the workshops upstairs. And the roti stands are sometimes patched on the side of well-known restaurants, where the take-out counter caters to those who want just snack food; they are never far from even the most luxurious Port of Spain restaurants, those places that are in trimmed up traditional houses, where hanging plants, historic pictures, and an elegant aura vie with the cuisine for your attention. (And where the cost for a dinner is almost 200 times the cost of a roti which can make a reasonable supper.)

The best way to respond to Trinidad's special tempo, which can be overwhelming to the uninitiated, is slowly. A first look is best from afar: from the hillside Hilton's terrace or the top of the downtown Holiday Inn, overlooking Queen's Park Savannah and the seething city with huge ships at anchor in its port. This is a country of contrasts. Rugged, jutting mountains plunge to the seaside. There's the Asa Wright Nature Center (walks, talks, and simple accommodations), the Caroni Swamp Bird Sanctuary (boats coast through to spot the scarlet ibis), and one of the West Indies' most cosmopolitan capitals at bubbling Port of Spain.

POLITICAL PICTURE: When the National Alliance for Reconstruction was voted into office by an overwhelming majority, Prime Minister A. N. R. Robinson, born in Tobago, became leader of the country. Monumental economic problems and fractionalized government, which tries to be all things to all people, has led to discontentment. The kidnapping of government ministers by a small faction of Muslim malcontents in July 1990 shocked the local folk and the world community, in spite of the fact that all were released and the perpetrators jailed.

For many years, Trinidad & Tobago enjoyed unprecedented prosperity among Caribbean nations, based on its oil revenues. The economy of the republic hit some rough bumps, however, when oil's boom years dried up at about the same time that Trinidad's reserves were almost depleted. In 1983, Trinidad's oil revenues dropped over 26%, to about $2.4 billion, and unemployment rose to more than 11%. Former Prime Minister George Chambers was elected to his office in fall of '81, after a term as an appointed prime minister following the death of the country's longtime, legendary leader, Dr. Eric Eustice I. Williams. During his terms, the once strong People's National Party lost much of its following and the splintering of parties that began in his terms has not yet been repaired.

Trinidad & Tobago, led into independence by Dr. Williams (on August 31, 1962) soon after he pulled his area out of the fledgling West Indies Federation in the late '50s (as did Jamaica), has always been a maverick nation. At some point, however, the new government must acknowledge the need to address the country's serious economic challenges, working with the European Economic Community and other world bodies to move ahead.

Throughout recent years, Trinidad & Tobago has shown little interest in tourism, which has become a source for employment and hard currency for all the other Caribbean islands, but the new government indicates that policies will change. Private business continues to be the goal for many Trinidadians, who acknowledge that the country needs to become more efficient. The nation's 1.2 million people are an interracial community that is about 45% black, 40% East Indian and 15% "all other," which includes whites, Chinese, Syrians and others.

AUTHOR'S OBSERVATION
Trinidad & Tobago has several newspapers, if you want to be informed about local and Caribbean news. The *Trinidad Guardian* follows a conservative pattern, and the *Express* has a more sensational style. A daily purchase of either (or both) and some of the spicier papers will supply facts for putting this country (and its neighbors) in perspective.

ISLAND APPEARANCE: Far more fascinating and much larger than most people imagine, Trinidad offers an amazing variety of landscape. The mountain range that ripples along the north of the country, and stretches out onto the northwestern peninsula, is traversed by roads that make it reasonably easy to reach the north-coast beaches from the capital. The northern islands, a series of dots that once made a land-bridge to the coast of Venezuela, have caves, beaches, and terrain of interest to birders, while the midsection of the island, on its west coast, has long been known and respected for its Pitch Lake. The packed sand that rims the east coast stretches almost to the south, into areas little known to most visitors. Clearly defined nature centers—at Caroni Swamp and in the mountains near Arima—have facilities to make bird-watching and traveling through the areas possible. Although beaches are better on the sister island of Tobago, Trinidad's dramatic variety makes it worth some attention.

LIFESTYLE in Trinidad includes both the sophistication of the well-to-do in Port of Spain and the oil towns and the country culture of farmers and fieldworkers. Cosmopolitan Port of Spain, the capital, is the most fascinating city in the Caribbean. It is a port city, with the large strands of commerce woven into the tapestry of customs that keeps Indians, Asians, Africans, Europeans, North Americans, and others mixing and mingling on the streets and in shops and restaurants. Many cultures follow the traditions of their homelands, sometimes adapting Oriental fishing festivals, for example, to the Trinidadian countryside, or the Hindu marriage rites to the dirt roads of small villages. Port of Spain is a "formal" city, not necessarily in the coat-and-tie sense (although that, too, was the case until the ubiquitous shirt-jac became the style a few years ago), but certainly in the sense of formal business procedures. It is customary to make appointments, even though they often run on Caribbean time—late.

Trinidad is not the typical tourist island. Trinidadians have known prosperity from oil, natural gas, a steel plant, many small businesses, and big plans for petrochemical industries. And yet, public services (transportation, telephone, water, electricity) are in such disarray as to be archaic at best and amazingly inefficient at worst. Too much has come too fast. The nation takes itself seriously in many ways, although few Trinidadians appear to value "a hard day's work." There is, however, a sense of humor that is uniquely Trinidadian. No one knows how to have a good time better than West Indians, and the pre-Lenten carnival in Trinidad sets a pace unmatched in the Caribbean. Some say that the exuberance of Trinidad's Carnival is close to that of Rio, with equally elaborate costumes and lively street marches.

AUTHOR'S OBSERVATION

If you want to know about Trinidad's Carnival before you attend one, be sure to track down a copy of Erroll Hill's excellent and informative *Trinidad Carnival: A Mandate for National Theatre,* published by the University of Texas Press, Austin, Texas. Also interesting is the annual Carnival guide. Copies of the previous year's guide are sometimes available through the Tourist Board offices.

Clothes are warm-weather conservative, with "proper" attire on the streets of Port of Spain and around the countryside. This is not a city for shorts and resort wear; it is a place where suits, shirt-jacs, and sometimes short-sleeved shirts are the businessman's "uniform," and skirts and blouses, or conservative dresses are the daily wear for women. For evenings at most restaurants in Port of Spain, clothes are dark colors, but not formal. Although evening pants appear at some after-dark affairs, they are usually partially covered with elegant, fashionable tops. Long skirts are still worn at some places (and certainly at formal business or government receptions). As a general rule, conservative can't go wrong.

MEDICAL FACILITIES: The Port-of-Spain General Hospital, on Charlotte St., is the major government hospital for Trinidad and Tobago. And there's a newer Eric Williams Medical Complex at Mt. Hope. There are district hospitals around the country in places such as Arima, Couva, Mayaro, and elsewhere. Although many doctors were trained in Britain and Commonwealth countries, some were trained in other European and South American countries. The hospitals are often crowded and understaffed. For serious medical problems, those who can afford it fly to Miami.

MONEY MATTERS: After arrival at the airport make your first stop the National Commercial Bank, conveniently located just after you pass through customs. (There's a charge levied for exchanging US dollars for TT dollars at the bank.) Traveler's checks get a slightly higher rate than bills. You can change money at the hotel, at banks, or, when you are in Port of Spain, at the bank near the Tourist Board offices, on Frederick Street. Do not expect Trinidadians to transact business in U.S. currency. For an occasional purchase, U.S. dollars will be accepted, but in the shops in this country, $ and ¢ refers to TT.

On hotel and restaurant bills, 10% is usually added for service, although the section for "service charge" is deceivingly blank. Ask, if you're unsure about whether or not service had been included in the total, or risk overtipping by more than twice the expected / accepted amount.

COMMUNICATIONS by telephone from overseas are often easier than domestic telephone service. From overseas, dial 809 + 62 and a 5-digit Trinidad number. Facsimile machines are popular; Telex is also used. Television is international by satellite. Problems with the domestic telephone service, which has been slow to respond to the rapid growth of the country, can make setting up appointments difficult. It may be easier to get in the car, if you're up to facing the traffic problems. There is local television, and some hotels arrange for sets in your room.

ARRIVAL at Trinidad's Piarco International Airport is orderly, and more efficient than it once was. Although Piarco has been cloned to double its former size, it is still inadequate for such a complex country. There are slow lines for immigration formalities here, as there are at most Caribbean and U.S. airports.

Immigration officials are businesslike when you hand them your immigration card with your proof of citizenship and passport. You will be asked to show your return ticket (to prove you will not be a drain on the economy), and to advise your local address. When you've claimed your luggage, make a quick stop at the Trinidad & Tobago Tourist Board airport office for a map, a discussion of taxi fares and bus routes, and some advice about anything special that is taking place while you will be in the country. You have a choice of shuttle bus, for TT$17, or taxi for TT$40 or more. If you decide on a taxi, head for the taxi dispatcher, and ask the fare for reaching your destination. (The taxi drivers that sidle up to you offering their services are not above overcharging outrageously.)

Count on traffic jams during your 45-minute ride to town. The road between the airport and downtown is a knotted route that has been a driving hazard for 20-plus years that I have known it, and there's no improvement in sight except that buses have priority for a special route. The eventual solution will be a six-lane road that can take the considerable industrial traffic (big trucks) plus the people trying to go home or get to work—and *that* "dance" takes place twice daily.

CRUISE: Port-of-Spain has a new cruise port facility with modern docks, and a shopping complex, on Wrightson Road, not far from the Holiday Inn. Few cruise ships make this country a port of call, however.

DEPARTURE from Piarco takes stamina. Count on traffic if you have to catch a plane in early morning, midday, or after 4:30 p.m., even with the completion of the four-lane highway. Allow plenty of time—at least an hour from downtown. A bus shuttle leaves Port of Spain for the airport to link with major flights. Cost is TT$17. Reconfirm your flight when you *arrive* in Port of Spain, and again by telephone (if you can get through) or at the downtown or hotel ticket office, and be sure to check in early. Planes from Port of Spain are often crowded, especially at peak travel times, and the cluster that convenes around the ticket counters can include a lot of people who have been waiting "for days" as well as you with your valid ticket. The departure tax is TT$50.

In addition to the expected liquor and perfume shops, just before you have cleared immigration, there are flowers for sale (packaged to comply with U.S. Dept. of Agriculture restrictions) and a place where you can get a haircut or shampoo and set if you've allowed enough time—or your plane is late. But be forewarned: you will have to carry your hand luggage plus purchases up three banks of narrow stairs to the vast room that serves as departure lounge—and then down another stairway to ground level, before climbing up again to board your plane!

TOURING TIPS: Trinidad is "huge" and varied. First-time travelers will do best to link up with a good taxi driver, to learn lore as well as sightseeing lanes. It's difficult for the novice to find what's where, and you may be so independent that you miss all the highlights. Parking in downtown Port of Spain is "impossible." Even walking has its hazards, with all the building and bustle that goes on in this fascinating city. There is a hefty fine for parking illegally in Port of Spain, so try for a space in one of the parking garages.

If you've signed on for one of the special promotion packages, chances are at least a half-day of touring is included. Take it. In this two-island country, there *are* many sights to see, and to learn about. Cars are a fact of life in Trinidad, where many people are making good money—and although gas prices have tripled from a joke-low charge when Trinidad felt flush with its oil reserves, people still drive everywhere.

Car rentals are available through several reliable companies. You'll pay about TT$170 per day, plus TT$50 for a minimum two-day insurance coverage, plus your gas costs. In addition, you'll be expected to post a deposit against any car damage.

LODGING in this country could be a lot more interesting than it is. Port of Spain, the capital, is the site for most hotels, which have been built to accommodate business people—and such visitors who care to come. But all the elements are here for an exceptional hospitality industry. Unusual buildings in the city, and around the countryside, are part of Trinidad's intricate and varied culture; they could become attractive inns. At the moment, however, there are a couple of major hotels in Port of Spain, both members of U.S. chains, plus some small hotels and one or two inns, with more potential than they realize. Out in the countryside, there is one exceptional nature center, with the possibility for others in other areas. This fascinating country is different in many ways; the lodging industry is one of them.

The government tax on hotel rooms is a modest 3%. In addition, many hotels add a service charge. Ask in advance, to be sure that those who are most helpful are being acknowledged.

AUTHOR'S AWARDS

> *The Trinidad Hilton* is the country's top hotel; it's where the action is.
> The *Normandie* is noted as a small hotel, with good restaurant and shops.
> *Mount St. Benedict* is an unusual spot for those in search of nature and peace.

Information about places to stay in included under Hotels/Resorts, Housekeeping Holidays, the Inn Way, and Low-Cost Lodgings. Stars are awarded within each category. (See page 11.)

HOTELS/RESORTS are mostly in Port of Spain; there are a few places to stay near the beaches and at business locations around the country.

★ **Chaconia Inn** • *at 106 Saddle Road-Maraval* • backs up to the mountains, on a valley road in a residential area. The complex of stucco buildings is partially hidden behind the front entrance wall with Chaconia Inn "written" in the special logo of the hotel. When you've parked your car (or the taxi driver has parked his), you'll walk past the reception desk into the pool area, an oasis at heat-of-the-day in suburban Port of Spain. Furnishings are modern, with TV available for most rooms, and kitchenettes in 16. All rooms are air-conditioned, some have better views (over the pool with a peek at the mountains) than others, and there are 10 2-bedroom suites if you're a family of 4 or more. A ribbon of rooms rims the road on the opposite side from the main complex. The restaurant serves Trinidadian and international (steaks, chicken) food. *The Baron* pub is dark, and a drawing card for Trinidadians who know and like this spot; the roof patio is used for special barbecues and open-air dining at modern plastic tables with gently curving chairs—perched like chessmen on a black and white checkerboard floor. *Hotel.*

Farrell House • *on the outskirts of San Fernando* • was opened by the government in '83, to accommodate businessmen who come out to this part of the country. The 57-room hotel has 40 boxy, motel-style rooms, plus 11 suites and 6 cabanas near the pool. Part of a development plan for the nearby Point Lisas area, the hotel has "always" been a haven for oil men and others who make the hour-from-the-airport drive to San Fernando. It used to be a small outpost hotel. Not your "typical tourist" place, Farrell House can give you a glimpse of the "real" Trinidad when you tour the country. *Hotel.*

Holiday Inn • *on Wrightson Rd., in Port of Spain* • punctuates a part of portside Port of Spain, near the cruise ship complex. Modern, with its 14th-floor *La Ronde* restaurant sometimes revolving as it was built to do, the top floors permit an overview of the port activity—and the bonus of a view of the Venezuelan coast on clear days. The *Calypso Lounge* on the 12th floor, is air conditioned, and by night, with the city lights, there's more atmosphere than at lunchtime. The lobby restaurant serves a good local-recipes businessfolks' lunch. The rooms follow a standard format, for size and facilities (including TV) with the 9 suites the most luxurious air-conditioned units. Fully booked at carnival times, when "mas" bands parade past the lobby doors and the parking lot is sometimes turned into a party scene. The hotel seems to cater mostly to businessfolks. The pool provides the cooling-off place, popular at lunchtime for people who have to be in town. Other action options are limited to shuffleboard and dancing evenings when the band plays in the nightclub on the top floor. *Hotel.*

★★★ **Hilton International Trinidad** • *in Port of Spain* • captured the top of a hill and slants its rooms down the flank (although the floor numbers go up), making the hotel unique. The "upside down" Hilton, where you go *down* to the 10th floor, and *up* from there to the first, was built in 1961, to open at the time of the country's independence. From the opening of the first cluster of rooms the Hilton has had its following. Most of affluent Trinidad comes to the Hilton, if not to drink, dine, and dance, then to do business with some of the salesmen and others who stay here. Although you'll find full resort facilities (tennis courts, pool, tour desk, shops, disco for dancing, coffee shop, potentially elegant *La Boucan* dining room where food and service vary from acceptable to mediocre, and a full complement of air-conditioned rooms with view), the atmosphere is far more substantial than the frivolous just-for-fun veneer at most Caribbean hotels. There's no beach (Maracas is a good picnic lunch excursion over the northern mountain range), but you are overlooking the Queen's Park Savannah where, with binoculars, you could follow the cricket matches and the horse races. Most of the rooms are twin-bedded, but there are singles, studios, and double-bedded rooms if you request them, plus a 4-bedroom combination and some 1-bedroom and 2-bedroom suites that give you a dining room. Most rooms have self-service bar/refrigerator, and TV is available at an extra charge. The drive from the airport *should* take under 45 minutes. *Hotel.*

★★ **Kapok Hotel** • *6–18 Cotton Hill, St. Clair, Port of Spain* • stands about 8 stories tall on a side street just off Queen's Park Savannah, and a short walk from the zoo and the Botanic Gardens. The arcade of shops and *Cafe Savane* on the street level almost hide the lobby entrance, but the restaurant on the 8th floor makes it worthwhile going through the small lobby and up in the elevator even if you are not overnighting here. For those who check in, there's a small pool fringed with a cement sunning area at the back of the house, and 6 suites among the air-conditioned rooms that open off the carpeted halls. This is not a typical tourist hotel, nor is it a fancy spot, but the surroundings are suitable for businesspeople and others who want the experience of Trinidad and easy access to downtown Port of Spain, plus good food. *Hotel.*

★★ **Normandie Hotel** • *on the outskirts of Port of Spain* • is a legendary hotel, with a venerable history, but what you see today is a totally revamped and refurbished hotel on the original site. The pool that punctuates the inner core of the property is the focal point for some guests; businesspeople and long-term visitors have found this to be a comfortable Trinidadian home. Bedrooms vary from viewless to loft-style to standard hotel with basic furnishings, private bath, and a view over the pool. A bank of shops adds activity to the inner lobby. The air-conditioned dining room serves well-prepared Trinidadian specialties and international fare. *Hotel.*

Queen's Park Hotel • *on Queen's Park Savannah, Port of Spain* • has come to the attention of Veronique and Joseph Fernandes, part of the owning family, and innovative and welcome plans are being discussed. This place *could* be a gem. At presstime it's an old-fashioned West Indian hotel. The *Caribbean Newsletter* (page 9) will have any news.

THE INN WAY in Trinidad is unique. There are a couple of places that qualify as inns, in my opinion, for their hospitality, and a few others because they look the part, although management stays in the background. Here are a few Trinidad inns worth noting:

Monique's Guest House • *next to Chaconia, on Saddle Rd. in residential Maraval* • began as a private home, with the Charbonnes' hospitality offered in genuine Trinidadian measure. They are willing to do all possible to help you enjoy (and understand) their country, as they know it. The house has white stucco walls and a terra-cotta tile roof, which gives it a Mediterranean feeling. The bedrooms vary in size and shape, but all have homey comforts. A car service passes nearby for rides into Port of Spain, if you don't want a taxi. There's a pleasant pool on premises. *Guesthouse.*

Mount St. Benedict Guest House • *in the mountains above Tunapuna* • never fails to enchant me, partly because it seems so calm at its lofty perch with the monastery nearby. The inn, known as the PAX Guest House, is not so heavy on religious overtones that it need turn away the profligates. Some of the dozen rooms have sinks in the room and a shared bath; others have private bath. Decor is basic; meals are served family style from whatever was bought in town that day or plucked from the hillside gardens. Best rooms for the view are #1 and #7, looking out on the valley and hills. A veranda runs along the front of the house, and on the second floor where the bedrooms are located. The first hut built on this hillside perch, way above the hubbub of Port of Spain or even Tunapuna, was a 15-by-9-foot thatched-roof structure built by monks who had fled the oppression in Brazil in the early 1900s. The Abbey of Mount St. Benedict celebrated its Diamond Jubilee in 1972. Anyone with a little time at Piarco Airport can get up to this spot in about 45 minutes, for lunch between planes or for an overnight. The church, monastery, and school are a short walk up from the guesthouse, which is mentioned here because it is used as a home base for bird-watching tours. Details are available from Wonderbird Tours (T 212+727–0780) in New York City. *Guesthouse.*

LOW-COST LODGING: Since Trinidad is only beginning to focus on North American tourists (and the U.S. dollar), most hotels have reasonable rates. Those that have traditionally had a West Indian clientele have rates that are priced for that market, but visitors used to hotels and motels around the U.S. should look first before booking some of the smaller properties. There's a recently formed association of **Bed & Breakfast** places. For facts, phone 809+637–9329 (Grace), or 809+628–3731 (Gottfried), or 809+633–5256 (Victor). Trinidad has exceptional nature areas, and the Asa Wright Nature Centre's lodgings are unique in the Caribbean.

Asa Wright Nature Centre • *at Spring Hill Estate in Arima* • is a special preserve, 1200 feet up in Trinidad's mountains, 7 miles north of Arima and about 40 minutes' drive from Piarco airport, but about 2 hours from Port of Spain. The property was part of a private plantation purchased from Mrs. Wright to become a nature preserve for birding and flora. Administered by the Royal Bank Trust Company as a recreation and study area, the Nature Centre is a unique Caribbean spot. Accommodations are simple, dress is informal, as you'd expect at a place that concentrates on the woods and virgin terrain that covers the slopes of this mountain area. In addition to nature lovers who find this place on their own. *Wonderbird Tours* (200 Fifth Ave., New York, NY 10036, T 212+727–0780) and *Caligo Ventures* (387 Main St., Box 21, Armonk, NY 10501–0021, T 800+426–7781 or 914+273–6333) operate nature tours spending a few nights at the center before continuing to Tobago. Overnight accommodations at the center on your own are very reasonable, priced for Trinidadians and others who come here in study groups. *Camp.*

Bel Air International • *at Piarco Airport* • is a "catch-all" hotel into which I have fallen on a couple of occasions when I have been stranded at the Port of Spain airport and was unwilling to battle the traffic to head back to the capital. The hotel has a popular restaurant, a basic pool, and very informal rooms, some of which are better than others. Don't count on much in the way of vacation amenities or "decor," but there will be bed, chair, and private bathroom at a reasonable rate. This is not a vacation hotel, but could be o.k. for business or in-transit travelers. *Guest house.*

Errol J. Lau Hotel • *on Edward Street in Port of Spain* • is a downtown, multi-level hotel that has basic rooms in a boxy building. Check further before booking one of the 18 rooms. *Small hotel.*

Timberline Cabins • *on the road near Maracas Bay* • are popular with nature lovers who enjoy walks in the wilderness and camplike facilities. Ask the Tourist Development Authority for further details. *Cabins.*

RESTAURANTS on Trinidad range from some special spots to La Boucan at the Hilton, and the revolving restaurant (that sometimes doesn't) at the top of the Holiday Inn (both of which sound like they should be more elegant than they are, in my opinion) and can include the roti stands that proliferate along the streets of Port of Spain, and the ears of cooked corn sold from carts at the edges of Queen's Park. (You can recognize the corn carts by the strings of children lined up to buy their favorite after-school treat.) Any country that mingles West Indian, East Indian, Chinese, African, European, Syrian, Venezuelan, and an assortment of other nationalities is bound to have a varied food menu also—and Trinidad does.

AUTHOR'S OBSERVATION
Although there are some restaurants that are popular for businesspeople at lunchtime, there are only a few places suggested for dinner. The depressed economy and security problems have affected Trinidadians' desire to dine out.

A visit to the local markets—the Indian market on Saturdays at Chaguanas, the Beetham Highway market at the fringe of the commerce of Port of Spain, and an assortment of other markets—gives you the best preparation for what may appear on your table. If you are adventuresome, and interested, take some time to travel around to see the raw materials before you make your dining choices—and be prepared to find lavish use of mangoes (julie mangoes are special in Trinidad), coconuts, avocados, plaintains, fig bananas, and all the fresh fruits and vegetables that grow in the Trinidad countryside and on Tobago. Roti is a crepelike "pancake" filled with chicken (with bones), goat, shrimp, beef, chickpeas, liver, potato, and an assortment of other mixtures, usually heavy with curry. The filled roti is folded, so that nothing oozes out the sides until your first bite, which, if you're trained, is an inhaling nibble.

Cafe Savane • *claiming the quarters previously occupied by the street-level restaurant at the Kapok Hotel* • doesn't have much in the way of a view, but is good for mealtime.

Chaconia Inn • *106 Saddle Rd.* • has special Trinidadian menus, but call in advance to be sure that what's on when you plan to be there is something you want to try.

Mangal's • *at 13 Queen's Park East* • makes an impression even before you know it's a restaurant. The imposing Victorian mansion is almost interesting enough to warrant a visit, no matter *what* the restaurant serves. But if you like spicy, hot Indian food, this is the place to dine. The Indian food comes with a Trinidadian accent. Count on a lot of curry, ginger, and hot sauce, all favorites for local palates and tasty, although explosive when unexpected. Dining at Mangal's is best if you've done some homework on Trinidadian food, and that is as easy as talking with some of the residents. Count on roti, which will be served with more flourishes (but not as much local flavor) in this white-tableclothed restaurant.

Rafters • *claiming the corner of Woodford St.* • which had been occupied by Renaldo's Bistro and Alfies, serves continental food, and is one of the few noteworthy restaurants in Port of Spain.

Shay Shay Tien • *at 81 Cipriani Blvd.* • has a good Chinese menu, with Trinidadian soul (and spices). Some discussion at noon, when you plan to dine at night, can result in a bonus menu; count on simple surroundings and a check that multiplies as you order a taste of this and a taste of that, which is the only way to dine. (If you are on your own, have an aperitif and look at what others order before either pointing or asking about something you see that looks good.)

Tiki Village • *on the 8th floor of the Kapok Hotel, not far from Queen's Park Savannah* • serves Polynesian-style food. It's the atmosphere here that is as interesting as the food. The place is dim, by night light, which helps to add to the romance/intrigue and view out the 8th-floor windows. The menu varies to include a selection that is grilled on your own flaming brazier set at the center of your table. Tiki Village attire is casual, comfortable but not dressy. Count on paying about TT$35 or more per person, for as much food as you can eat, with a Trinidadian beer or two.

The flock of fried-chicken stands expands with every season. Not only can you find **Kentucky Fried** and **Chicken Unlimited** in downtown Port of Spain, but on the major country roads (and at any cluster that calls itself a village) you'll find others. As one of my Trinidadian informers observed, "all the different chickens taste the same" except for Kentucky Fried.

For Trinidadian creole cooking in very casual surroundings (no place for camera and colorful tourist trappings), search out the **St. Clair Snackette,** on the corner of Marli and Picton Streets, where "we serve beef, chicken, shrimps, liver, potatoe roti" is painted on the streetside wall. Samuel Daniel led me here the first time, and I've come back for more, and not been disappointed yet. Also in downtown Port of Spain is **Cuisine Creole** in a "sealed" air-conditioned room at 31 Abercromby Street. This is a lunchtime spot with buffets of local food including callaloo (the West Indian spinach-style soup that varies from island to island), and mauby and sea-moss beverages. Surroundings at any of the strictly local spots are downtown West Indian style, with emphasis more on good local cooking than on interior decoration.

Long Circular Mall (yes, that's what it's called), near the United States Ambassador's residence on the fringe of Port of Spain, is an air-conditioned shopping center that is peppered with interesting, and relatively inexpensive, dining and drinking spots. A fringe of snack stands—**Bubblicious** (ice cream),

Chinatown Express, Chicken Unlimited, Take Five, and **Mario's Pizza**—surrounds a "sea" of orange plastic tables and chairs on the lower level "Food Fair" area; **Ships Tavern** is publike and pleasant, and the **Swiss Chalet,** on level 3, is open from 10 a.m. to midnight, serving on red checked tablecloths with an atmosphere true to its name.

NATURAL SURROUNDINGS: Touring the four corners of Trinidad can be one of the Caribbean's most fascinating excursions—if you're an exploring type who's good on car maintenance and very self-sufficient. Arm yourself with a good road map and a sense of direction (even a compass, if you have one). This is a huge country to explore. Its natural surroundings are unique, with hints of mainland South America (to which Trinidad was once joined) as well as the island ecology that has developed through more recent centuries.

> **AUTHOR'S OBSERVATION**
>
> Directions you will get from local folk may be as detailed as turning "at the third row of palms" or "the second bay" or "when you pass Burney's Parlour" or another verbal help-along—and these directions are given, assuming you understand the local dialect of Trinidadian English.

Among the sights you can expect to find are rugged surf pounding hard-sand shores that sometimes become the road you drive along as well as bird sanctuaries, caves, verdant mountainsides with thick forests, plummeting waterfalls, and the unique pitch lake.

Right in the capital of Port of Spain, **Royal Botanical Gardens,** across the north road around Queen's Park Savannah, stand on what was Paradise Estate. The government purchased the land in 1816 and, when Sir Ralph Woodford (for whom Woodford Square is named) was governor, he established the 70-acre garden. A few of the original buildings remain, refurbished and put to new uses, but in the early 1800s, when the governors lived in the estate house, the garden surrounded their domain. The propagating and experimental stations have been moved to the University of the West Indies at St. Augustine, not far from Tunapuna in the direction of the airport, so what stands here is an extensive selection of trees, plants, and shrubs. (Charles Kingsley, who spent time in Trinidad in 1869–70 while he was working on his novel *At Last,* makes reference to the Botanic Gardens.) There are guides to take you around, and their services are essential if you want to learn about the plants, even though the patter may get tiresome toward the end of the grand tour. Note especially the flower beds around the bandstand (and check to see if there is any event at the bandstand while you are in Trinidad). All the park gardens could have used a good plucking and pruning when I looked, but they are in far better shape than their counterparts in, for example, Kingston, Jamaica.

Emperor Valley Zoo occupies a small section of the gardens, near the west entrance, at the opposite "end" of the south rim of the park from the Governor General's House. Its claim to fame is the collection of indigenous animals, which is more interesting than could have been assembled on many islands because it is commonly accepted that Trinidad was once part of South

America. The reptile collection gets a lot of attention, but I am not an enthusiast of caged animals and have not spent much time here.

AUTHOR'S OBSERVATION

Binoculars and insect repellent are two invaluable items for travel in Trinidad & Tobago. No slur intended on hotel housekeeping; the reference to both is for those who want to head into the hinterlands, to the Asa Wright Sanctuary in the mountains, to the Caroni Bird Sanctuary, or on birding walks, perhaps along the old road between Hillsboro Dam and Castara on Tobago. You'll want long trousers, sturdy shoes, and a long-sleeved shirt (plus rain gear for Asa Wright) if you give any thought to reasonable comfort.

Asa Wright Nature Centre, at Spring Hill Estate, seven miles north of Arima and a good hour's drive from Port of Spain, in the northern range of Trinidad mountains, has marked mountain walks and guides to take you on special excursions. Telephone ahead of time if you are planning to go on your own or with your own small group to be sure that there's someone available when you want to visit. The "dry" season, when flowers are at their best and weather is more dependable, is from January until May, and perhaps in mid-fall (Oct.–Nov.), but be sure to have lightweight rain gear, long trousers, long-sleeved shirts, and sturdy shoes for your mountain hiking. There is a supply of plastic raincoats at the Centre for those who forget to bring their own, but if you are serious about birding and the flora, come prepared. Count on humidity—lots of it—and very simple man-made surroundings amid spectacular natural ones. Some Audubon and other groups make arrangements for time here, but anyone is welcome to come up to wander—and many Trinidadians do. You can sit on the veranda and notice squirrel cuckoos, toucans, and other birds, but you will have to wander around with your binoculars and patience to find some other kinds.

Caroni Bird Sanctuary, where you can see the scarlet ibis, the heronries of the white and blue heron, as well as streaked herons and hundreds of other birds who live in this 437 acre swampland, is less than 10 miles south of Port of Spain. I made my first trip here in one of the small boats of David Ramsahai & Sons, moved to wake up in time for the 4:30 a.m. departure party by the Ramsahai folder which said "You are planning a vacation away from the maddening crowds. Come visit with us; enjoy the cultures of the world in a nutshell Trinidad. . . . First stop on this spectacular journey is at the feeding grounds, a stretch of shallow water in which small fish, crabs and shrimps abound: hundreds of Ibis pecking at their unsuspecting prey, is a sight to behold. Southwards, flying in unionism [sic] against the blue skies, the Scarlet Ibis appear on the horizon. The Ibis at home. The sun sets. Enveloping us in a beautiful cloak of peace. Other species of birds are Egrets, Herons, Spoonbills, Jacamas, Kingfishes and more and more in the deeper waters of the river; Tarpon, Salmon, Mollet, Snookers and others make good fishing. Our boats depart 4:30 a.m. and 4 p.m. each day of the year. Come, be our guest, we are anxious to share our good fortune with you." The only problem with all of this is that the David Ramsahai heartfelt enthusiasm is hard to come by these days. Tours to the

Caroni Swamp by Hub have turned into routine affairs—a job for the driver/guide and sometimes a bore for you. If you are lucky enough to get a good guide, know your birds, or can go with someone who does, the experience can be fascinating. Tours operate on regular "schedules" and you'll have to plan in advance.

> **AUTHOR'S OBSERVATION**
>
> There are several companies that have tours: 4 hours departing at 3 p.m. daily for the Caroni Swamp, 4 hours for the "Down the Islands" boat cruise, a golfer's package, a day on Tobago, etc. Richard Charleau's Pan Kaiso Maki Service (7 Almond Dr., Morvant; T 809+624–3825) is personable and helpful.

Blue Basin, about 45 minutes' drive into the Diego Martin Valley, is a freshwater pool reached by a half-mile hike from the parking area. The road through the estate that leads to the parking area for the hike is bordered by hibiscus hedges, and the entire excursion (which can take about three hours) will provide a glimpse of "another" Trinidad. Take the Western Main Road through Four Roads and get directions from there, if you haven't mapped out your route with the experts beforehand.

Lopinot (pronounced lo-PEEN-oh) offers a special glimpse of life in Trinidad. The area, made up of villages of Siree, La Pastora, and Lupinot, is about 16 kilometers from Port of Spain and about eight miles from Piarco Airport. It offers a *Brigadoon* setting in a valley in the mountains of the Northern Range. Many of the less-than-1000 people who live here are descendants of the slaves brought into this valley by a French settler in the 1800s. The Compte de Lopinot Charles Joseph took his band of slaves along a river path, into lush country where he started his plantation. Today the area is a natural botanic garden, with brilliant *immortelle* vivid in March and April, and coffee, cocoa, cashews, and other crops growing most of the year. Birds, butterflies, and other fauna live in their natural state, untroubled by modern commerce. The church originally stood on another site, in another mountain village. In 1948, when government plans for a dam threatened to blow up the church, the local priest put a curse on the project—and the village people moved themselves and their church to Lopinot. (The dam, incidentally, was never finished.) The caves here are a special site, toured by donning helmets with miners-light (and wearing sturdy shoes) to follow your guide through the dark halls. Because it is not too far from the airport, Lopinot is a reasonable goal if you find yourself at Piarco with a long wait between planes (perhaps from Tobago to elsewhere).

Caura Valley and the North Coast Road are two other driving routes to follow for a look at rural Trinidad. Both trips can be made in a morning or an afternoon (allow about three hours for each).

Pitch Lake is downright ugly. Unless you're heading out this direction (in the southwest, at the north shore of the southern peninsula) for another reason, there's no need to come here to see this. It is interesting (to me) to note that the pitch from the lake used to be carved out in huge hunks (sometimes 6 feet by 6 feet), put into mining cars that ran on tracks across the "lake," and then put on trucks to be taken to ships at Port of Spain. Water fills in the gaping holes, and eventually the pitch seeps back up, displacing the water and making it impossible to tell just where the cut was made. Intriguing? Maybe, but nothing to spend your vacation time looking at. (The Pitch Lake was known in Sir Walter Raleigh's time, and used to caulk his ships and those of others, as well as for paving streets of many cities in the U.S. in more recent history.)

PLACES WORTH FINDING on Trinidad are an endless list, shortened only by your own enthusiasm for things like Victorian buildings and bustling ports or outpost villages in back country where signposting and conversation are limited. Most visitors miss the most interesting sights, not only because they are not packaged in Hub and other travel service tours, but also because it takes time to relax into the hinterlands of this big and complex country.

PORT OF SPAIN is the starting point for most visitors. To understand some of the country, it is necessary, I suppose, to put your hand to its heart—even though it is overwhelming. **Beetham Highway Central Market,** at the south end of the city, was moved to its present quarters a few years ago, and although it is a short ride from where you are apt to be, the market still seethes when there are products for sale (and that is almost every morning). You can view piles of spices, fruits, and—when the season is right—sorrel that a local housewife will be able to tell you how to make into the popular West Indian party drink.

A trio of squares (some of which aren't squares at all) are focal points for downtown Port of Spain, but were also the sites for most of the July '90 "aberration": **Woodford Square,** bordered on one side by a part of Frederick Street (near the Tourist Board office), and the Houses of Parliament, plus Holy Trinity Cathedral (Anglican) and Red House, prominent, impressive, and the seat of the government. The building dates from 1906. The other two squares are **Independence Square,** which is mostly a parking lot and stall market (with food—including roti—for sale), and **Columbus Square,** behind the Catholic cathedral (started in 1832), with its expected statue of Columbus, the island's discoverer in 1493.

National Museum & Art Gallery, on Frederick Street between Gordon and Keate Streets, in what used to be known as the Royal Victoria Institute, is worth a visit to look at the carnival costumes if you aren't around to see the real things prancing and dancing through the streets at the pre-Lenten festivities. Carnival is the soul of Trinidad; the more you understand about it, the closer you are getting to finding the key to Trinidadian outlook on life. Since part of the costume is the action of the wearer, these exhibits are sterile by comparison to the real thing, but better than nothing. The rest of the displays (some ancient relics from early settlers, maps of the area at the time of discovery, and painting and sculpture by modern local artists) are also worth seeing.

The assortment of **Victorian houses** that have been stitched around the edges of Queen's Park have suffered from modernization and from government plans that, in a burst of activity at the time of independence, tore down venerable buildings in the mistaken notion that new would be better. In my opinion it is not: the new buildings are boring, cement boxes. The Victorian mansions left standing, and now adapted to new causes (museums, restaurants, etc.), are fascinating to view from the outside even when you cannot enter. (But you can enter the National Museum in the Royal Victoria Institute and Mangal's restaurant, both in Victorian mansions at the park's edge.) You'll have to be content to look from the outside (unless you can get special permission to enter) at Roodal Residence, a gingerbread-fretwork house, and some of the other mansions.

SPORTS on Trinidad are limited to land sports, unless you sign on for the motorboat ride (check at the Tourist Board) to the islands that string out toward Venezuela from the northwest peninsula. There are some boats (and huge ships) at the marina and boatyards in Chaguaramus former U.S. Naval base turned recreation and shipbuilding area for Port of Spain. It is not easy, however, for you, the average tourist, to get a line on a boat for charter, unless you find something offered at your hotel's activities desk.

Cricket is played (fanatically) at the Oval Cricket Ground on St. Clair Avenue, and elsewhere around the island in more casual surroundings. If you want to watch a match (or part of one) ask at the Tourist Board for dates, places, and times.

Golf is played at the Moka course, about 10 minutes' drive from the Trinidad Hilton, and even less from the Maraval hotels, since the golf course is in that suburb. Popular with Trinidadians, the course is in demand on weekends, when starting times can be a problem. Play here is a good way to meet some residents, especially if you're in Trinidad on business and have a local contact who can set up the game. Otherwise, you'll find the course good, but the others around the club slightly standoffish, especially if you arrive with your own foursome and seem to be having your own fun.

Horseracing takes place regularly on the Race Course in Queen's Park Savannah and elsewhere around the country. You can view the Queen's Park events with binoculars from your room at the Hilton, but half the fun of the Trinidadian experience is lining up at the gate as almost everyone else in town does.

Tennis is available at the Hilton's courts (nightlighted and in almost constant play), as well as at some of the private clubs (on invitation only). Check for special tennis holidays at the Hilton if you play a lot and are interested in a break on rates for a combined Trinidad & Tobago holiday.

Swimming at beaches in Trinidad is an excursion, no matter where you're staying. There's a long stretch of sand at Maracas Bay (where there is also talk of a hotel that has yet to rise on these shores), but you will have the place pretty much to yourself, except on summer weekends when it's popular with Trinidadians. Bring a picnic from your hotel, and hire a taxi to take you over the northern mountains, on the wiggly route to the north-shore sands. There are other beaches along the leeward coast, along the peninsula that starts with Chaguaramas, and at the small islands at the northwest tip, but the sand is not the powder-smooth strip that you find on Tobago. (Even Trinidadians head to Tobago for weekends.) Along the northeast shore, there are unpeopled beaches around Balandra and Toco, and at the coast around Manzanilla and Mayaro, but swimming is suggested only for strong swimmers and competent self-sufficient sportsmen who like challenges. There's nothing set up for tourists, even in the way of food and facilities, and certainly no "lifeguards."

Scuba enthusiasts should check with the Tourist Office about sites, guides, and equipment. As interest in the sport develops, facilities are improving.

TREASURES AND TRIFLES are most easily found in gift shops at the hotels. Shopping here is not the usual trick-or-treat game played on many of the islands known as "freeport" or "duty-free" shopping centers. Most of the central portion of the city, especially around Independence Square and Frederick Street, was ransacked and burned during the July 1990 hostage-taking and riots.

Shopping malls have the largest selection of merchandise, both clothing and crafts. Long Circular Mall, near the American Embassy on the fringe of Port of Spain, is a comfortable place for one-stop shopping in air-conditioned comfort. Before you gasp at the idea of a "hometown-style shopping mall" for exotic Trinidad shopping, let me assure you that the best shops (**Stecher's** and others) have branches here, that the several restaurants make pleasant halting spots, that there's a lot to be said for air-conditioning after a few minutes in the downtown heat, and that the **Tru Valu Supermarket** that is an appendage on one side has some of Trinidad's most interesting "take home" items: Angostura bitters, local hot sauce (which is fiery hot), Old Oak rum plus Carypton (a liqueur made from oranges), bottled rum punch and Trinidad-made wines, some special canned vegetables not known to your local market, spices, and other domestic items.

The imagination and ingenuity that is channeled into the elaborate carnival costumes every year contribute to some of the Caribbean's most interesting fashions. If you have the time and inclination, it is possible to talk with some of those who work on carnival costumes about some interesting patio wear that will certainly *not* be just like what you see in your hometown. You can have clothes tailored in several shops. Ask at your hotel for recommendations.

For the traditional luxury "duty-free" items, check at **de Lima** shops and at **Stecher's,** now stretching through the Eastern Caribbean with samples of the wares that sell at Frederick Street locations as well as at the Hilton and other places. You can count on a good selection of watches, jewelry, crystal, china, and all the elegant trappings of the luxury life. As for the prices, be sure you know what comparable merchandise would cost at home. The prices will be better here—but just how much depends on your best deal in your hometown.

Expect the shops in Port of Spain to be open Mon.–Fri., 8 a.m.–4 p.m. Some are open until 5. Do not plan to buy liquor or food on Thursday afternoon (those stores close at noon), but you can buy liquor and food Saturday afternoon, when all the other stores close (at noon). Check if you're searching for some special item, and you can count on the shops in the Hilton arcade to be open at hours that appeal to the hotel guests; there's some variety, but inquire in advance if you're counting on a last-minute purchase on, for example, a Sunday.

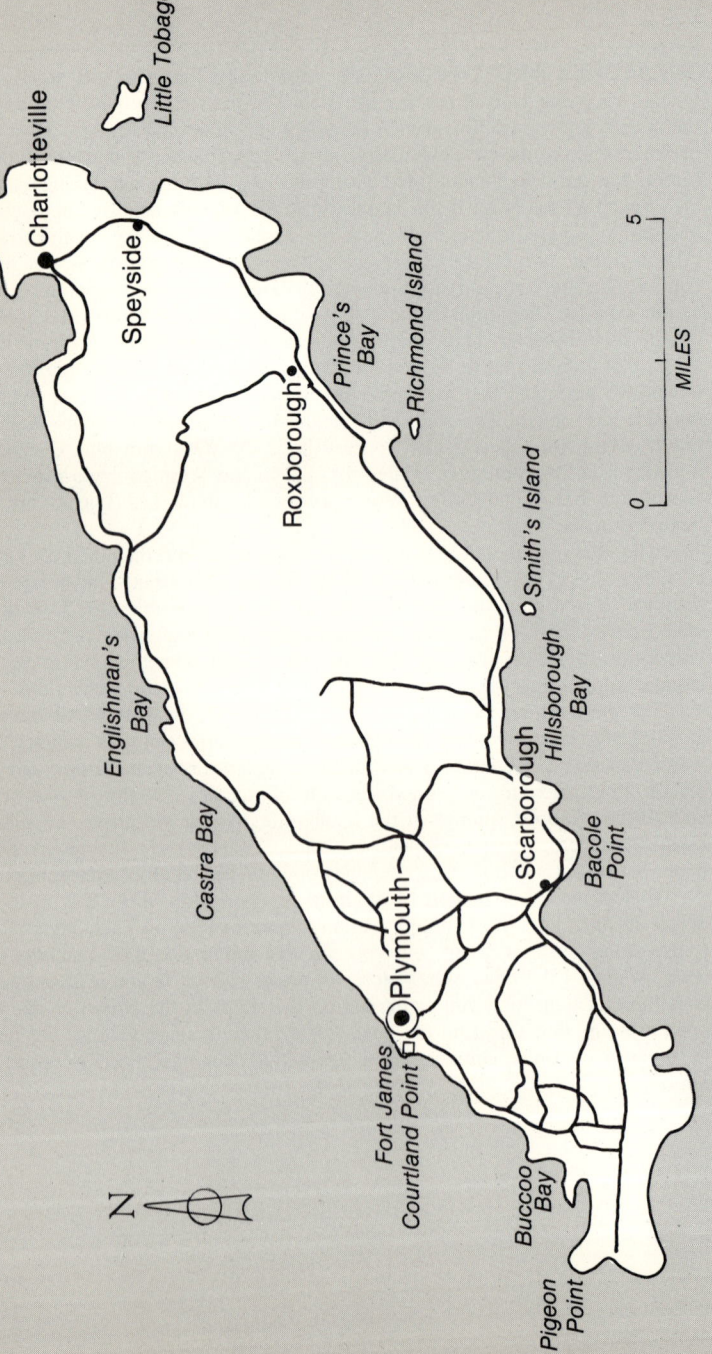

TOBAGO

Trinidad & Tobago Tourism Development Authority, Cruise Ship Complex, Box 222, 1D Wrightson Rd., Port of Spain, Trinidad, W.I., T 809+623-1932 or T 800+537-3505; Tobago Tourism Information, Scarborough, Tobago, W.I., T 809+639-2125; #310, 330 Biscayne Blvd., Miami, FL 33132, T 305+374-2056; #1508, 25 W 43rd St., New York, NY 10036, T 212+719-0540 or 800+232-0082, fax 212+719-0988, 40 Holly St., Toronto, Ontario M4S 3C3 Canada, T 416+486-4470 or 800+268-8986, fax 416+440-1899; 20 Lower Regent St., London SW1Y 4PH, T 01+839-7155.

$ · · · US$1 = TT$4.25
Unless otherwise noted, $ refers to U.S. currency.

Emil Robinson eased his truck from Trinidad's St. Vincent Street pier onto the ferry boat. It was dark, and his day in Port of Spain had been spent driving from place to place. The gasoline was relatively inexpensive, but the cost of the cement, lumber, pipes, and other elements for his house cost a lot. Traffic clogged most roads, so wedging into a confined space on the Tobago ferry was a welcomed relief. The ferry would leave about midnight, and six hours later, just after dawn, he could drive to his homesite and unload the pieces for his new house.

"Driving" from Tobago to Trinidad to pick up building materials and other items has proved to be the fastest way to get them. Shipping between the two islands that make up the one nation of Trinidad & Tobago has always been slow, and now that demand for consumer goods is high in both places, unless you "go fetch" yourself, you can wait weeks for delivery.

Although joined to Trinidad by constitution, Tobago has a personality distinctly its own. Popular as a weekend retreat for cosmopolitan Trinidadians, it wasn't until sugar crop failures at the end of the 19th century that Tobago chose annexation to Trinidad over its own independence. When David Codrington revs up the "twin" engines (an Evinrude 25 and a Yamaha) on his Tobago-built glass-bottom boat, his "Johnson's Sea Tours" long-sleeved T-shirt flutters in the breeze. His wide smile and flashing dark eyes are shaded with a plastic leopard cap, but there's nothing else fake about this 2½-hour trip to the coral gardens of Buccoo Reef. The boat leaves Buccoo Village with an assortment of visitors from the nearby hotels and the trip is one of the few planned activities for visitors on Tobago. This is a place where you can do as you please.

Perching over Scarborough, at the end of a road that curls up and around, is Fort George, built by the British and imposing even in ruins. Children festooned the branches of the flamboyant tree that stood by the parking area, and their saucer eyes hovered over huge smiles as we said "good morning" and wandered on our way. Their laughter, oblivious of our pursuit, provided the melody for the constant rustle of the palm fronds in the trade winds. And, later in the day, as the sun started to go down, we watched the fishing fleet return at Turtle Beach. We sipped a potent rum punch, with a sprinkling of island-fresh grated nutmeg, while we watched the fishermen hauling in their catch. We lingered until dark, staying as long as Redman Deman did. He was sewing the fishing nets after the catch was in, as he had been doing "plenty years," and certainly long before the hotel was built on this shore.

POLITICAL PICTURE: Trinidad & Tobago became one independent country in August 1962. Separated by several miles of sea and linked politically only since 1803, the island of Tobago has an independent streak. From time to time, in recent years, there have been rumbles about "going it alone," forming a unit separate from Trinidad, Tobago's sometimes overwhelming sister island. When former Prime Minister George Chambers assumed office, upon the death of former Prime Minister, Sir Eric Williams in March 1981, he noted in his acceptance speech that "with regard to Tobago, while we adhere unswervingly to the concept of a unitary state. . . . we shall seek in a spirit of equality to overcome the apparent obstacles to improvement of the administration and development of the sister isle. To this end, steps will be taken to initiate appropriate dialogue." That dialogue was loud and clear, with the elections of December 1986 when the National Alliance of Reconstruction party was elected to office and Prime Minister A. N. R. Robinson, a Tobagonian, became the head of government. Unlike Trinidad, where an impressive percentage of the population is of East Indian descent, most of Tobago's populace is of African descent, a fact that will be obvious to even the most cursory visitor. Tobago was not damaged by the political "games" in Trinidad in July 1990, except by cancelled bookings at hotels.

ISLAND APPEARANCE: Tobago is more like the "typical" Caribbean island than like its cosmopolitan sister, Trinidad. Although the midsection is hilly—almost mountainous—and only discards its green cloak when steady sunshine has turned its planting brown, there are butterscotch-colored beaches along many of the north-coast shores. There are also a few beaches on the south coast, but they are apt to be coral fringed and no good for swimming. At only 116 square miles, the island is much smaller than Trinidad. Tobago's population is primarily of African descent, without the vast array of cultures that make the fabric of Trinidad so dramatic.

LIFESTYLE on Tobago is more casual, less cosmopolitan, than that of Trinidad. Customs reflect the African heritage of most of the people. Tourism is the island's major industry, albeit tourism from nearby Trinidad. Hotel facilities look like those found on other Caribbean islands, and the beaches, tennis, golf, and scuba are the main interests for most vacationers. The pace of life on Tobago is distinctly island-Caribbean: slow.

Here, as on other Caribbean resort islands, beachwear should be confined to the beach, with "proper dress" for island touring and in-town visits.

MEDICAL FACILITIES The hospital near Scarborough is a district hospital, much like the ones in outlying areas of Trinidad. It has enough to handle with the population on Tobago, many of whom fly to Trinidad for more serious medical problems. Most of the doctors have been trained in South America and Europe, as well as in Britain and Commonwealth countries. There are no decompression facilities for scuba divers.

MONEY MATTERS: Trinidad & Tobago dollars are common currency here, although most hotels will take payment (at least at the front desk) in U.S. dollars. It's best, for local courtesy as much as for cash-on-hand, to change to TT dollars, however, and that can easily be accomplished at the airport, before you fly to Tobago, or in Port of Spain if you are adventuresome enough to take the six-hour ferry ride. (The airport bank is next to the Tourist Office, in the main building, which is a short walk from the Tobago departure/arrival rooms.)

COMMUNICATIONS: Tobago's problems parallel those of Trinidad (see page 722). It is reasonably easy to call Tobago from overseas, using the 809 area code + 63 and a 5-digit domestic number. Telex is also effective. Insofar as mail is concerned, allow ten days or longer, and replies can take "forever." It is not always easy to find the Trinidad newspapers on Tobago. If you want them, your hotel may be able to help.

ARRIVAL on Tobago from Trinidad can be by boat, on the ferry that departs from the St. Vincent Street pier in Port of Spain and makes the crossing to Tobago's Scarborough in about five hours, or by plane from Trinidad's Piarco International Airport to the recently lengthened runway. Arrival at Tobago's Crown Point airport is easy, with the aura of the holiday place this island has come to be—for Trinidadians as well as for us from the outside. The airport benefits from an expansion program that makes it easy to negotiate; your luggage will appear in the air terminal soon after you do. Make arrangements in advance for a rental car for pickup at the airport if you want instant mobility; otherwise—and especially on your first visit—be sure to check to see if your hotel has pick-up service before you take a taxi. You won't have any trouble finding a taxi; drivers will all but tug on your arm when you walk from the luggage area.

AUTHOR'S OBSERVATION

When you are traveling to Tobago, if you do not fly direct on a charter or one of the nonstop services, check in early for the flight, which will take half an hour or less, depending on the size and speed of the airplane. If you make your reservation *in your hometown* to include the trip to Tobago, on your Trinidad ticket, you will not have to pay extra. Otherwise, your round trip Trinidad to Tobago return will cost about TT$75.

With one of the reorganizations of BWIA, the former Trinidad & Tobago Air Services was merged into Trinidad & Tobago Airways Corporation, which operates as an arm of BWIA. Nealco, a small local carrier, also flies regularly. A result has been improved Trinidad-Tobago air service, with several-times-daily shuttle service referred to as "Air-bridge" service, leaving at least every hour (and at peak times more often). Advance reservations are not essential (although they are advisable if you are unfamiliar with island airlines); you can go to the airport and go "on the next flight."

Cruise ships will be able to stop in the recently dredged Deep Water Harbour at Scarborough. The *Panorama* ferry makes the crossing between Port of Spain, Trinidad, and Tobago in 4½ hours.

DEPARTURE is reasonably easy, since most hotels are not too far from the airport. Be sure to reconfirm your flight, as much to be sure that the schedule is as you think it is as to be sure you're listed on the flight. Count on tedious check-in if you are traveling on weekends, when Trinidadians like to come to Tobago, or at height of winter on a big plane. There is a TT$50 departure tax.

TOURING TIPS: Tobago is a beach and sand island, but prime sites on this islanders' island include Scarborough and Charlottesville, which is at the east end of the island. **Taxis** are happy to take you wherever you want to go. Calvin Anthony, at Grafton Beach, has been a careful and pleasant driver for me on a couple of occasions.

AUTHOR'S OBSERVATION

It pays to do your homework on taxi fares. Ask at the Tourist Office desk and a couple of other places before you get into "your" taxicab.

Rental cars are available, at about TT$170 per day, plus TT$50 for a minimum two-day insurance, plus your gas. *Rodriguez Rentals,* at Turtle Beach hotel and elsewhere (T 809+639–8507), has 4-wheel drive and normal cars, at about US $38 per day. *Singh's* has the car rental concession at Grafton Beach hotel.

Otherwise, you'll tour by boat. Out of Pigeon Point, there are several boats that make the run to Buccoo Village for the trip. Going rate is TT$75.

LODGING on Tobago offers variety, from the looks of luxury to small, casual Tobagonian style, with a cosmopolitan climate created by an influx of vacationers from Europe who head here on charters and special tours. You'll find the expected resort facilities, including a beach, tennis, and golf at Mt. Irvine, but better beaches are at Grafton Beach and Turtle Beach.

As is the case with hotels on Trinidad, all bills are subject to a 3% government room tax, and most charge 10% or 15% service as well. Inquire when you check in to avoid a surprise when you check out.

AUTHOR'S AWARDS

Turtle Beach is the only full hotel right on a long beach. *Grafton Beach* makes exceptional use of domestic teak and location, and *Blue Waters Inn* is the best choice for serious scuba divers.

HOTELS/RESORTS are comfortable, with facilities in good condition (or new).

★★ **Arnos Vale** • *rising up the hillside, on a northwest cove* • has all the elements for an idyllic resort but the place is currently on lease to an Italian tour company. The *Caribbean Newsletter* (page 9) will have news, when there's a change. The comfortable, casual, island inn ranges from hilltop to beach, with a knee-bending walk or a short, hotel-supplied ride between the two.

Crown Point Hotel • *at Store Bay, near the airport* • has been refurbished and offers full guest facilities, with a pool, the beach, restaurants, and a water-sports program.

★★★ **Grafton Beach Resort** • *on a northwest coast bay, from beach to hillside* • was a newcomer for late '89. All the comfortable rooms, in 1-, 2-, and 3-story buildings are air-conditioned, with balcony, overhead fans, and TV. Trinidad teak has been used throughout, for a design that incorporates a tropical lifestyle and modern comforts. Pool is appealing; taffy-colored beach is a walk from all rooms. *Resort hotel.*

★★★ **Mount Irvine Bay Hotel** • *on a north shore bay* • has most of the elements to be a top-flight resort, and has been extensively refurbished for this season. The resort meanders over a prize piece of property, about a 15 minute taxi ride from the Crown Point Airport, and abutting the Tobago Golf Course, commonly referred to as Mount Irvine Golf Course. This resort puts you near the shore (you can walk to the beach), amid a cosmopolitan atmosphere helped along by the fact that many of your fellow guests, especially in winter months, will be Europeans. Rooms are in any of several units scattered around the grounds. Most have new fabrics and decor. There are houses for rent in the hills (see "Housekeeping Holidays") that give you access to the hotel facilities. The terrace around the mill-with-roof is your dining area, with changes in personality between dawn (breakfast) and dusk (dinner). The pool nearby is the setting for some of the evening entertainment, all of it local, natural, and informal. A couple of shops in the lobby and a bar to the left of the reception desk are the activity in the main building (except for the addition of a tour desk). The *Shamrock and Palm* down one of the lanes, toward the rooms and the "back" of the house, comes alive as a disco some evenings, when house count warrants. There's a lot of walking involved to get from here to there, and especially to the beaches, with the best—a long quiet strand you can have to yourself—a stroll down the road, cutting to the shore to go over the hill at the public beach area. Bring your dress-up clothes if you like the resort life. This is one place where winter season vacationers wear them. *Resort.*

★★ **Sandy Point Beach Club** • *at Crown Point* • perches at the end of the Crown Point airport runway. As long as the flights are limited to daylight hours, the noise is not deafening—but beware when traffic warrants more flights and bigger planes. From the outside, the complex (built in season of '78) looks like a cloister; white walls, tiny odd-shaped windows, and red tile roofs. Units are stacked and nestled against each other to take up minimum ground area for maximum housing density. The 20 suites give duplex living, with the bedroom up a narrow staircase. The 22 studio apartments are attractively, if simply, furnished in Scandinavian-modern style. All rooms are air-conditioned (a necessity since the angles shut out a lot of the breeze) and the bigger units have television. Modern kitchen equipment makes housekeeping relatively simple (but getting foodstuffs involves an excursion). The open-air, terrace dining at the shoreside is pleasant on warm evenings—and at lunchtime. The pool's nearby, and a small beach settles below the pool (unless waves have temporarily washed it out). Maxitaxi runs regularly to Scarborough, at rates that are less than taxi fares. *Hotel.*

Tobago Premier Resort • *on the northwest coast* • is planned, but not started at press time. The *Caribbean Newsletter* (page 9) will have news when warranted.

Tropikist • *at Crown Point* • touches the shore (but not a good beach) at the side of the Crown Point airport runway. Motel-modern-style rooms are in 2-story blocks, with sea views. Popular with Trinidadian families and with value-conscious travelers, the hotel is geared for casual travelers who do not demand luxury. You *can* walk to the airport, and to Crown Point hotel. *Hotel.*

★★ **Turtle Beach** • *at one end of a long stretch of sand at Courland Bay* • has a pleasant, relaxed Caribbean atmosphere, at a beach used by leatherback turtles for egg-laying, usually in April and May. The butterscotch-brown beach is also used by fishermen in early morning hours, and by sunbathers as the day wears on. Comfortable air-conditioned rooms are in 2- and 3-story buildings with either a balconied or terraced unit, modern furnishings, and sea view. Public rooms are furnished for beachside living. There's a pool, in addition to the beach, for swimmers. The hotel has been popular with Europeans, Canadians, and other folk who have found this spot either through a charter or their own informed travel agent. It's a pleasant place, with a very friendly, helpful staff. *Hotel.*

HOUSEKEEPING HOLIDAYS on Tobago can be in a luxury home, where someone else is on tap to help with the daily routine, or in an apartment, where you cook your meals yourself. There are some spectacular homes built as part of the development of Mount Irvine that provide sweeping views of Caribbean seas and sunsets as well as the option to head to the main hotel for meals if you tire of what your maid/cook fixes. And there are homes on isolated coves, away from any connection with community activities, where you can have a housekeeper and someone to tend the grounds or do what's necessary yourself. Other options include efficiency apartments, part of the development at Crown Point.

There's no supermarket in the U.S. sense of the word, but the Friday market in Scarborough proffers more than enough for adventuresome chefs. Your fresh produce may come from someone you meet in a nearby village or the market lady you find serves you best at Scarborough. Strange though it seems, you may have difficulty tracking down a good source for fresh fish. The best beef may be what you bring from your butcher at home, and a canned ham and any other special foods you think you can't live without can come in with your luggage.

Tobago Estates Agency Ltd. (Box 160, Scarborough, Tobago, W.I.; cable TEAL, Tobago, W.I.) has an extensive listing of houses and apartments available for rent near the Mt. Irvine Hotel. Several of the properties are fully furnished (and staffed) within a stroll from the golf course and the resort facilities.

Horizons • is one of the houses for rent at Mt. Irvine. The 3 air-conditioned bedrooms are perfect for 2 couples or a large family, and the modern kitchen has a bar area opening to the living/dining room and view. The maid comes in for breakfast and stays through lunch, but she can help with fixing the dinner you serve yourselves (unless you go to the hotel or another spot to dine). Figure about $130 per night Dec. 16–Apr. 15; $100 at other times. **Sunset Lodge** is another Mount Irvine house (3 bedrooms—2 share a bath and the bedrooms have air conditioners). Costs for this one are $100 winter, $70 summer. Both Horizons and Sunset are listed with Mrs. Martin, Box 160, Scarborough, Tobago, W.I.

Man-O-War Bay Cottages • *Charlottesville, Tobago; T 809+639–4327* • are among the listings of homes for rent. The 3 2-bedroom cottages and one 4-bedroom cottage are near a good beach, not far from the village of Charlotteville about 1½ hours' banding, weaving, and often bumpy—but scenic—drive from the airport. You'll want a car if you care about mobility, but if you want the real island life, take a taxi (about TT $30) and concentrate on your beach and the people of Charlotteville. *Cottages.*

Carefree Cottage • *at Speyside across the road from the beach* • is a simple, adequately furnished 2-bedroom cottage with maid service available. Write to Captain and Mrs. James Davies, Speyside, Tobago, for details about this cottage about ½ mile from town. *Cottage.*

Arcadia • *on Orange Hill Road in Scarborough* • Tobago's main town, has a swimming pool and 5 double bedrooms with 4 full baths. Ten people can settle in comfortably, to be assisted with the housekeeping by a maid who knows where to buy what in town. Information about the estate (including the gatekeeper's cottage) is available through Mrs. Eamon O'Connor, Northside and Valder Hall Roads, Scarborough, Tobago, W.I.

Samaan and Flamboyant Cottages • *on a coconut estate called Prospect* • is about 8 miles from the airport and a little more than 3 from Scarborough. Each cottage has 2 double air-conditioned bedrooms and 2 baths, but you'll need a rental car for transportation to the beach and to Mount Irvine (even though the golf course is next door. Contact Otto Weeks, Box 219, Scarborough, Tobago, W.I.

Tree Tops • *on the shore, near Scarborough* • is a group of wood cottages near the shore, with restaurant and some central facilities. Good for independent folk; you'll want a car for mobility. *Cottages.*

Crown Point Condominiums claim the spot of a former small hotel, near the end of the runway and right on the beach. Completely revamped a few years ago, the housekeeping units are simple but adequate, in a variety of shapes and sizes. You'll either cook for yourself, wander down the beach to Crown Reef to dine at the hotel, or get in a car you've rented to go to one of the other hotels. The Trinidadian-owned complex sold many units to local people who use this setup as a weekend retreat, renting it out to off-islanders at some times during the year. A good bet if you want apartment-style surroundings on the shore. *Apts.*

THE INN WAY on Tobago is not as good as it could or should be, given the scenery, the possibilities for attractive inns, and the need for pleasant small places for visitors who want to share Tobagonian hospitality. Here are a few places I think qualify as "inns," certainly by their number of rooms—which is well under 50 in each case.

★ **Blue Waters Inn** • *at Batteaux Bay, near Speyside* • is truly a tropical retreat. With less than a dozen rooms in 5 cabins, plus 4 small cottages and 18 double rooms, guests get to know each other easily. There's a restaurant, where meals are served family-style, and an emphasis on nature, the beach, scuba diving, and peace. This place is an hour's serpentine drive east of Scarborough and the airport. *Small hotel.*

★ **Kariwak Village** • *near Store Bay* • is a clever concept, with 18 bedrooms in 9 octagonal buildings arranged like cupcakes on a piece of Store Bay. The social center for guests in the cottages is an attractive main building with restaurant and bar, plus facilities for entertainment when it's scheduled (and that will be when house count warrants). Count on this to be a favorite for Trinidadians who weekend here, and ask manager Allan Clovis about the vacation village. He designed it. *Small hotel.*

Richmond Guest House • *inland, on a hilltop of the north coast* • is one of Tobago's traditional houses, with rooms for rent and typical hospitality. You'll need a taxi or rental car for beaches or other sites. There's a pool. Rooms 2 and 3 have the best view.

LOW-COST LODGING: Because tourism has not yet stepped with a heavy foot on Tobago, there are many very rustic places to stay quite inexpensively. The best way to find the most reasonably priced places is to head down to negotiate on your own, or to book a room for a few nights at one of the known places and look around for something more suitable for a long stay.

Here are a few of the small spots:

Cocorico Inn Guest House • *on a side street in Plymouth* • is a reasonably new stucco building, with a restaurant at the street level (front) of the building, and rooms upstairs and around the pool at the back. It's a short distance from the beach. The owner has a couple of cottages for rent for longer stays.

Coral Reef Guest House • *on Milford Road* • has focused on scuba divers, offering inexpensive rooms for folks who spend most of their daylight hours "at sea." The 14 rooms are pleasantly furnished, and helpful information is offered by your hosts.

Della Mira Guest House • *on the hillside near Scarborough* • is a collection of stucco buildings with hotel-style rooms at reasonable cost. The place is also known for its nearby *La Tropicale* nightclub and the hairdressing salon that is part of the family enterprises.

RESTAURANTS on Tobago are going to be hotel dining rooms for most vacationers, especially if you have your room on the MAP, which gives you breakfasts and dinners daily.

At **Buccoo Village,** there's a snack shop that used to post a sign that said, "People are people and should be treated like people 'cause we all are the same people, as I was saying . . ." The place is **Hendricks**, the roti and bakes (crusty pastries with filling) are usually good, and management gives no credit—everyone pays cash. If you don't like *very* informal island surroundings, forget about this place.

Arnos Vale is one special setting for dinner, but ask, while you're on the island, if they're accepting reservations for their delicious Italian fare. They sometimes limit to house guests.

For dining in local Tobagonian cottages, visit **Blue Crab,** in Scarborough, up on the hill heading out of town toward the hospital.

Two other noteworthy places are **Papillon,** on the northwest connector road, near Mt. Irvine, and the **Old Donkey Cart** on Bacolet Street in Scarborough, noted for its wines and good local food. You can get a good sandwich at the **Tobago Golf Club,** at the entrance to the Mt. Irvine Hotel drive, at about half the price (and twice the service) of those served at Mt. Irvine. **John Grant's** place, across the road from the Crown Reef Hotel, had a patio full of diners when I looked in and their food looked good.

NATURAL SURROUNDINGS: Natural Tobago is still intact, although some sites are threatened by the plans for tourism expansion. Exploring this island, to get your bearings and to decide on places for additional visits, is best by car, whether you drive yourself or hire a taxi. Places I've enjoyed include **Rocky Point, Bacolet,** with its beach, and **Englishmen's Bay,** a small beach on the north side with large rocks and deep white sand. All these sites are within 10 miles of Mt. Irvine hotel. There are at least three waterfalls—Argyle, King's Bay, and Rainbow—that have become hiking/walking goals.

Insofar as other walks and hikes are concerned, nothing much is well organized at presstime, although the Field Naturalist Club of Trinidad & Tobago has worked with the Forestry Division to plan specific treks, sometimes including expedition to two offshore specks, St. Giles island and Little Tobago island. Check with the tourist board and with your hotel for specific details. The *Caribbean Newsletter* (page 9) will have information about treks when their dates are announced in advance. Insofar as nature tours organized for Tobago are concerned, contact *Caligo Ventures* (387 Main St., Box 21, Armonk, NY 10501; T 914+273–6333) and *Wonder Bird Tours* (200 Fifth Ave., New York, NY 10010; T 212+727–0780). **Buccoo Reef** "ain't what it used to be," but if you are not a reef expert, it can be fascinating. Although conservation "laws" have now been instituted, they came too late for parts of this reef, and some of the interesting coral had already been plucked to be taken home, or at least to shore, for sale. Some of the fish, too familiar with bigger fish in funny-looking snorkel masks, have fled. If you have never glimpsed the underwater world, the shallow reefs at Buccoo are interesting; if you've been diving elsewhere, you'll find this pretty tame by comparison. A number of local entrepreneurs make the trip at low tide on boats out of Buccoo Village—including the Johnson brothers, who are brothers in spirit if not in fact. You can drive to the village or take a taxi from your hotel to pick up one of the boats. No matter who your skipper and mate are, the craft will probably be locally built, with a hefty engine (and a hotshot driver). Snorkelers tumble over the side into waist-high water armed with a pair of tattered sneakers so that they don't step on spiky sea urchins, and fins and mask that have been shared with countless others. Some folks choose to bring their own equipment. The tour almost always includes a stop on the return at Nylon Pool, so called because its water is clear—a fact which I've never understood being touted here since the water is superb at most places along this leeward shore.

PLACES WORTH FINDING: There's not much that has been "packaged" for tourism, insofar as museums and the like are concerned, but there are 18th-century ruins of a couple of forts, and some villages that are worth exploring, for those who are interested in Caribbean history and life.

Fort James, perched on a point at Plymouth, on the northwest coast, is mostly ruins, but the view from here is interesting. The original fort was built by the British in 1768, occupied by the French, and is well signposted by the Trinidad and Tobago Tourist Board. The visit will take about 10 minutes, tops, but is worth a stop for the view across the bay toward Turtle Beach.

Fort King George, built by the British in 1777 above the town of Scarborough, is far more interesting, although also in ruins. Follow the winding road up past the hospital and on up to the top of the hill, where the parking area is clearly marked. The fort was captured by the French, who occupied it from 1781 until 1793, and called it Fort Castries. The British recaptured it in 1793, the French in 1802–3, the British again controlled it from 1803 to 1854—and so goes the history of Tobago. Buildings and ruins have markers so you know when you are looking at the Officer's Mess, the Lighthouse, the Bell Tower. The gardens, the chirping of birds, the giggles of children who live at this hilltop, and the spectacular views along the shore and out to the Atlantic need no signposts.

When you head up to Arnos Vale, don't turn at the entrance, but head on another mile or so following a narrow track over a stone bridge for about fifteen yards to the **old sugar mill ruins,** where you can note a plate that claims that the equipment was made in Glasgow in 1851. The boiler had a canopy over it, supported by 6 metal Doric columns.

At **Grafton,** up a very rough track, the late Mrs. Alefounder, an intrepid Englishwoman, used to welcome visitors at bird feeding time. The estate continues to be open, following her death. Check through your hotel if you are interested in making a visit, and be prepared to step into another world. Up-ended rum bottles are strung to tree limbs and other props for suitable water bottles, and birds swoop through and around the open kitchen walls and through the house. There's a huge tree in the front (near where you'll park) that is a bird "hotel," with several varieties pecking and nesting among the foliage, sharing space with iguanas and other Caribbean animals. An experience not to be missed, if you have any interest in Caribbean birds.

SPEYSIDE, on the northeast coast, is about an hour's drive east of Scarborough, the departure point for the boats to **Bird of Paradise Island.** Do not head here expecting to see the rare bird of paradise; although the place was stocked several years ago, sighting the birds today is rare. The island seems to have to its own lure for people who like tromping around remote laces.

At *CHARLOTTEVILLE,* about 2 hours from most of the hotels, along a hardtop road on the southeast coast, there's the **Government Rest House,** very clean and right at the beach, for snacking and drinking. If you can raise the boatman and have enough time, ask him to take you around to **Lovers Beach,** which you can only reach by boat (but be sure to make arrangements for him to come back to get you!).

SPORTS on Tobago range from very professional golf at the Mount Irvine course, to tennis (also at that hotel) and some scuba facilities, but there's not much in the way of organized sailing. Check with the Johnson brothers at Buccoo Village about going out in a boat; they can make arrangements if anyone can.

Golf at Mount Irvine was pushed into prominence by television, with part of a tournament filmed on *Wide World of Sports.* A few people are still talking about it as a claim to fame, but most visitors are content to register at the nicely appointed clubhouse to set out on the 18-hole, 6,780-yard, par 72 course. (The Bermuda grass on the greens was "imported from Georgia" and takes constant attention in the Caribbean sun.) Winter months, when the homeowners around Mount Irvine Estates are in residence and the hotel is full, sometimes require sign-up times, but most days you can have the place pretty much to yourself—paying a premium if you are a guest at other than Mount Irvine (about $15 greens fees).

Tennis is available. There's a court at Mount Irvine, and at Turtle Beach, Grafton Beach, Arnos Vale and Crown Point, but don't count on lots of action, and bring tennis balls.

Scuba is centered at Sandy Point Beach Club, Crown Reef, Turtle Beach, and Mt. Irvine, where arrangements can be made, and at *Blue Waters Inn* (for serious divers), near the island's most spectacular reefs. *Tobago Dive Experi-*

ence and *Paradise Sea Sports* are two dive sources. Experienced divers who bring their own equipment can find challenging sites, but don't count on the last word in high-powered organization.

TREASURES AND TRIFLES   on Tobago are limited to what's available at the market and a few small shops in Scarborough plus whatever items have been brought in for tourists to the shops at Mount Irvine and Crown Point area hotels. Check the stock at the small shop at Buccoo Village where the person I talked with said she could sew up dresses and other clothes for anyone who bought fabric, knew what they wanted, and had the time (and inclination) to wait for the work to be done. Shopping is not a main attraction for Tobago.

Cotton House, on the Bacolet Road, east of Scarborough, has colorful batiks in island styles, and good jams and other condiments are sold in many shops.

TURKS AND CAICOS ISLANDS

> Turks & Caicos Tourist Board, % Ministry of Tourism & Development, Front St., Grand Turk, Turks & Caicos Islands, West Indies, T 809+946–2321, c/o The Keating Group, 14th floor, 425 Madison Ave., New York, NY 10017, T 212+888–4110 or 800+441–4419; 48 Albemarle St., London, England W1X 4AR, T 01+629–6355.

$ · · · U.S. Currency is used.

It was in the late 17th century that Bermudians began to farm the salt from these islands. They divided their tracts with ballast bricks and let the combination of strong sun and soft, dry breezes conduct the evaporation process. As recently as the late 1960s, salt rakers were working the flats—to harvest the crop that was an important source of income. At the time of the American Revolution, Turks Island salt was a valued commodity for Bermudian commerce with the North American colonies. It was used for curing (and preserving) beef and fish.

These days the flow of trade has reversed—and salt is no longer the crop. It's suntans and scuba diving that lure vacationers south to rapidly expanding tourism facilities on these flat, sun-parched islands. Surrounding reefs are acclaimed as almost-virgin diving territory and sea sponges, coral heads, and a carnival of colorful fish constantly entertain.

POLITICAL PICTURE: The Turks and Caicos islands make up one British Crown Colony with a self-governing status similar to that of the Cayman Islands, Anguilla, Bermuda, and Montserrat. Approximately 8000 people vote in the Turks and Caicos islands. Elections held in February 1991 resulted in a change of government. The Progressive National Party won the majority of votes, putting Chief Minister Charles Washington Misick in charge of the government. His quick appointment of a tourist board and a director bodes well for vacationers.

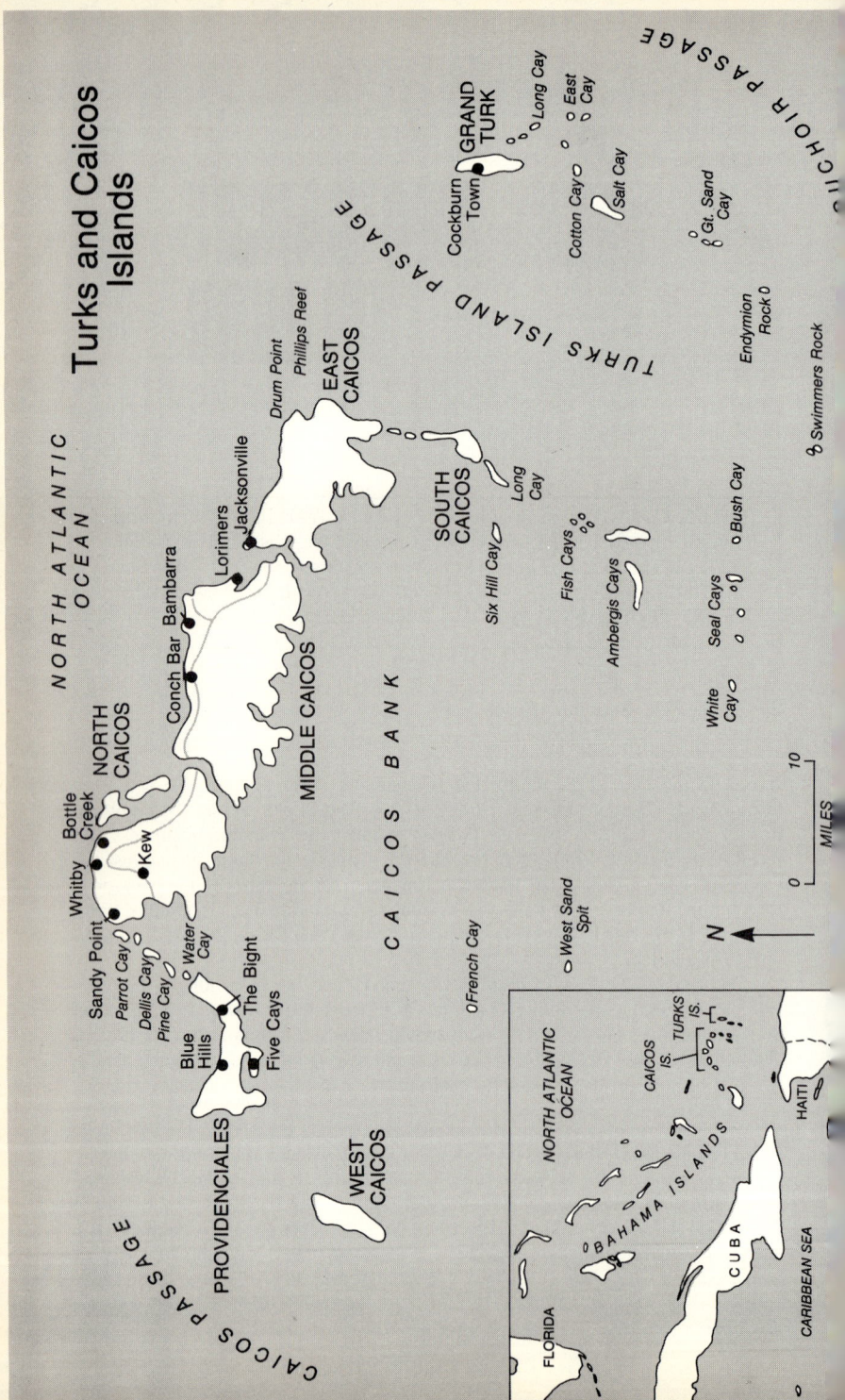

ISLAND APPEARANCE: The 30 Turks and Caicos islands, islets, and cays claim about 166 square miles of land and about 5000 square miles of ocean. The islands lie less than 30 miles southeast of the Bahamas, mingling with them in the northern part of the territory, and about 130 miles north of the coast of Hispaniola, the island shared by Haiti and the Dominican Republic. Most of these islands are flat and sand-fringed, with a desertlike climate, terrain, and scrub growth. There are salt ponds on some islands and limestone cliffs on others. The nine major islands are in two clusters: Grand Turk and Salt Cay in one; Pine Cay, Providenciales, and South, East, West, North, and Middle Caicos in the other. A 22-mile-wide channel separates the two. Grand Turk is the seat of government and Provo is the most developed in terms of tourism. Middle Caicos has limestone cliffs and caves that were known to the Lucayan Indians. Pine Cay, about a mile wide and two miles long, lies approximately 10 miles from Provo. It's privately owned and one of the smallest populated islands.

LIFESTYLE: Proximity to Florida and the Bahamas has yanked these islands into a world-wise, Americanized lifestyle. The focus for most entrepreneurs is the sea, traditionally for fishing and now, for some, smuggling and drug-running. For visitors, the sea is the main focus; life is casual, with resortwear de rigeur at the classiest resorts and very casual warm-weather clothes popular elsewhere. Lifestyle is informal, with few pretenses.

MEDICAL FACILITIES: There's a hospital on Grand Turk and facilities at the U.S. base, but most vacationers with serious health problems will probably prefer hospitals in nearby Florida. Hyperbarics Medical International has set up a multi-lock decompression chamber on Provo.

MONEY MATTERS: U.S. dollars are legal tender. Check with your hotel about the use of credit cards; not all places accept them. Hotels have a 7% government tax and many add 10% for service.

COMMUNICATIONS: From the main islands—South Caicos, Grand Turk, and Provo—there's direct-dial telephone and facsimile service to the U.S. and elsewhere. Direct-dial from the U.S. is T 809 + 946 + a 4-digit number. Many of the smallest islands do not have direct-dial phone service, although all are linked by radio phones. From Turks and Caicos telephones, it's possible to use AT&T's USADirect service from some hotels, and designated phones at marinas and the Provo airport. Postage from the U.S. is overseas airmail rate of 50 cents for the first half-ounce.

ARRIVAL: Getting here is *not* half the fun. Careful planning and a relaxed mind-set are essential for reaching these islands. Florida is the easiest jump-off point. *Pan American* flies from Miami, several times weekly, to Providenciales (known as Provo) and Grand Turk. From Provo, small charter planes stretch to basic strips on other islands such as Pine Cay. *Cayman Airways* flies out of Miami and Grand Cayman. *Bahamasair* flies between Nassau and South Caicos.

You'll need some proof of citizenship (passport is best) and a return ticket to show on arrival.

CRUISE: None of the major cruise lines stop here at presstime, but there are dive boats that set out from Grand Turk and Provo, stretching to the best dive sites, off the shores of the other islands.

DEPARTURE: Reconfirm your flight to be sure that the schedule has not changed and/or that your charter pilot remembers his committment. There's a departure tax of US$10.

TOURING TIPS: The first challenge is traveling interisland, which is fastest by plane but more dependable by boat. The airstrips on the inhabited islands are known to pilots out of Florida and the Bahamas, and charter services operate from Grand Turk and Provo for day trips to other islands. Insofar as attractions are concerned, the **Caicos Conch Farm,** where Queen Conches are cultivated in underwater pastures, was started on Provo in 1984; its visitor center was opened by H.R.H. Princess Alexandra during her visit in November 1988. Iguana Island is a favorite boating excursion out of Provo; Fort George Cay and Little Water Cay, both noted for their resident iguanas, are easily reached from Pine Cay.

There are **rental cars** on Provo through *Pride Rent-A-Car* (T 809+946–4214) and *Provo Rent-A-Car* (T 809+946–4404). Grand Turk also has rental cars. Driving is on the left. Taxis are plentiful.

LODGING in the Turks and Caicos is usually in a small spot, and always in a place with its own personality. The only biggies—and they *are* big—are the *Club Med* and the *Ramada Hotel,* both on Provo.

There's a 7% government tax on hotel rooms; some hotels add a service charge, but some do not. Always ask and, if someone has given you special service, a token of your appreciation is usually happily received.

Information about places to stay is included for each island, with categories as they apply. Stars are awarded in relationship to similar properties on other islands. (See page 11.)

GRAND TURK

The easternmost of the major islands, Grand Turk is also the seat of the government. Cockburn Town, the capital, is a sleepy, sun-baked village with some stucco block buildings and a few buildings in the traditional West Indian wood-with-shutters style.

HOTELS/RESORTS: Many of the lodgings on Grand Turk are small and basic, taking their personality from the owner/manager.

Columbus House • *on Pond St. in Cockburn Town* • is a small spot with a clientele of devoted divers who enjoy being next to a dive shop and the beach. Basic rooms have overhead fans for cooling. The restaurant/bar area is a local gathering spot; this place is very casual. *Small Hotel.*

Kittina Hotel • *on Duke St. in Cockburn Town* • has a couple of large suites, but most of the rooms are motel-style, in a recently built 2-story strip. About 20 have kitchen facilities; some are air conditioned; all have overhead fans. The pool supplements the beach for swimmers. Bicycles and scooters can be rented on premises. This place is popular with businessfolk and visiting dignitaries. (Its name comes from owners Kit and Tina Fenimore.) *Small Hotel.*

Pillary Beach Hotel • *on a lovely beach* • has modern and comfortable rooms for rent. Facilities are quite simple, but the rate is more reasonable than many places. *Guesthouse.*

Salt Raker Inn • *on the beach* • fills a 150-year-old beach cottage with comfortable, casual rooms that have overhead fans, air conditioners, and a small refrigerator. One of the original T & C inns, this place has a devoted following of island aficionados. *Small hotel.*

HOUSEKEEPING HOLIDAYS: If you have favorite foods, bring them from home. Although it's usually possible to link up with a source for fresh fish and lobster, most of the staples are stocked from Florida suppliers at premium prices. One local real estate firm with listings is *Prestigious Properties Ltd.* (T 809 + 946–2463).

Island Reef Resort & Tennis Club • *on the windward side, about 10 minutes from Cockburn Town* • is a shorefront cluster of modern, air-conditioned studio apartments and 1- or 2-bedroom villas. The clubhouse is the core, with restaurant, pool, and tennis court. The acreage includes "an 8-mile beach," but it's apt to be windy. Rates include continental breakfast, although units have cooking facilities. Some also have TV. *Apt. hotel.*

LOW-COST LODGING can be found at a couple of small spots.

Guinep Tree Lodge • *on the shore* • takes its name from the tree that stands at its gates. The West Indian wood home, with peaked tin roof, second-level balcony, and louvered doors and windows is a traditional island guest house. *Guesthouse.*

Turks Head Inn • *on the main beach-street of Cockburn Town* • has a dozen rooms with overhead fans and private bathrooms. Popular with back-to-basics folks, Turks Head is island-casual. *Small hotel.*

NORTH CAICOS

HOTELS/RESORTS   are small spots. Only one aspires to greatness.

   Ocean Beach Club • *at Whitby* • is an apartment hotel, with condominium units rented in owners' absence. All units are furnished for independent living, with sliding glass doors (and screens) for sea views. There's a pool at the main house and tennis, watersports, and fishing available. The outside walls of the 2-story units are a combination of stone and shake shingle. *Apts.*

   Pelican Beach Hotel • *on the beach* • has a half-dozen units for independent housekeeping. Rooms are modern and boxy but adequate. There's a restaurant on the premises. *Apts.*

   ★★★ **Prospect of Whitby** • *on North Beach* • takes its name from a British pub in London. Opened in the late 1970s, the hotel proved to be an ambitious project for an outpost island; it wore out the funds and enthusiasm of a series of owners/investors and now is owned by a group that reopened the place in early '89, after a complete overhaul. The restaurant is best in winter, when the chef caters to the affluent guests. Each of the attractively furnished bedrooms has two double beds. The freshwater swimming pool is one gathering place; there's also a long beach. Tennis courts are near the main building; a full range of watersports is available. *Small resort.*

PROVIDENCIALES

HOTELS/RESORTS   Until the opening of Club Med, the island had only a few guest houses. Now Provo is marked for big plans by some of the name chains.

   ★★★★ **Club Mediterranee Turkoise** • *on a beautiful beach* • brought the island into holiday headlines when it opeend in the mid-1980s. Adapting the all-inclusive, action-filled formula to a once isolated island, this Club Med excels with special vacation plans for scuba divers and watersport enthusiasts. Popular with a young clientele (in fact or at heart), this Club Med has a devoted following. Built on a village principle, with the restaurant, pool, shops, and activities centers in the core buildings, the Club lodges its divers in the units along the beach, near the dive shop. *Resort.*

   ★★★ **Le Deck Beach Club** • *on Grace Bay* • has grown from a popular French-style restaurant to include attractively furnished rooms for vacationers in search of innlike surroundings. The pool is a popular gathering spot. Air-conditioned rooms have cable TV. *Small hotel.*

★★ **Erebus Inn** • *overlooking Turtle Cove, on the Provo hills* • was one of the original small spots. The newest of its three dozen motel-style rooms are air-conditioned; all have overhead fans. The sunstruck tennis courts are lighted for night play. The pool is a welcome cooling-off place. *Small hotel.*

★★ **The Mariner Hotel** • *on the south side of the island, overlooking Sapodilla Bay* • benefits from careful planting that lends cooling shades of green to the sun-washed landscape. The wood-and-stucco buildings hold two dozen comfortable modern rooms, cooled by overhead fans. There's a small pool set into a wooden deck, with umbrella tables nearby. The enclosed restaurant features homebaked breads. *Small hotel.*

Parrot Cay • *on its own 1200-acre isle* • is a 20-minute boat ride from Provo. Building at presstime, the resort expects to open 50 luxurious rooms in fall '92. The *Caribbean Newsletter* (page 9) will have details as things progress.

★★ **Ramada Turquoise Reef Resort & Casino** • *on Grace Bay* • opens for this winter season, with 228 rooms. The resort-style lobby and the casino set a new style for Provo, where life has been casual and sea-centered. The casino will be the first for these islands when it finally opens. The *Caribbean Newsletter* (page 9) will have details as the ambitious plans progress. For now count on restaurants, pool, modern and comfortable rooms—and the beach.

★ **Third Turtle Inn** • *on the shore* • has a venerable history as a dive resort and is making headlines following purchase by the royal family of Oman. Plans to expand by more than 150 rooms have been put on hold for now. The *Caribbean Newsletter* (page 9) will have details when plans are firm.

Turtle Cove Yacht & Tennis Resort • *on Sellar's Pond at Turtle Cove* • is for yachting types and travelers who enjoy watersports. The marina is the action hub, with sail, motor, and dive boats setting out from the finger piers. Air-conditioned rooms have a garden view. There's a freshwater pool; the clay tennis courts are nightlighted. *Alfred's Place* is the bar/restaurant. Plans have been approved for 100-plus new units across the road, up on the cliffside, but nothing's underway at presstime. *Small hotel.*

HOUSEKEEPING HOLIDAYS: *Island Pride Supermarket* is one source for staples, but bring your favorites from home if you care about costs. *Prestigious Properties Ltd.* (T 809 + 946–4379) has listings of cottages and villas for rent.

★★★ **Admiral's Club** • *at Turtle Cove* • is on the shoreline rocks, although the start of "27 miles" of soft-sand beaches are within a few minutes' walk from the hotel. Built as condominium units for rent in owners' absence, the 1- and 2-bedroom apartments are in 2-story motel-style buildings, made reasonably attractive with wood fretwork. All units have screened patio or balcony, depending on the level. Air conditioners and/or overhead fans help keep things cool. Units are simply furnished with rattan furniture; all have kitchen facilities. Management rents color TVs. *Apt. resort.*

Treasure Beach Villas • *on almost 9 miles of beach, east of Turtle Cove* • are 1- and 2-bedroom villas scattered along the shoreline. Each is fully equipped, with comforts of home. Thatched *bohios* provide some shelter from the relentless sun on the beach. Both tennis courts and swimming pool are on the premises. *Villas.*

Other clusters with villa rentals are **Chalk Sound Villas, Nautilus Villas,** and **Provo Villas,** all with links to dive operators and other watersports.

LOW-COST LODGING:

Island Princess Hotel • *on Grace Bay* • has almost 100 motel-style rooms, for those who like a casual atmosphere. *Hotel.*

PINE CAY

HOTELS are limited to one of the region's best hideaways, which has no phones or radios. The island has no cars.

★★★★ **Meridian Club** • *on 2 miles of white sand beach* • is a sensational spot, for those in search of quiet in a classy setting. The property began to make headlines as early as 1968, when the original developer, Irish-born Liam Maguire, cleared the land for a pace-setting resort that was to focus on bone-fishing, deep-sea fishing, and flying. More than 150 homesites were part of his posh plan, which proved too ambitious for available funds. The Meridian Club evolved, through subsequent owners, to its present 23 private homes and 15 hotel guestrooms (13 beach-front suites and two ocean-view units), with a dock, dive shop, air strip, and hotel services. Thatched bohios provide shade near the freshwater pool at the 2-story clubhouse, where dinner is served; coffee and drinks are usually served on the upstairs porch. Rattan furniture and Indonesian-style pastel fabrics enhance the public and hotel guest rooms. Bicycles and electric golf carts are available for exploring; sailboards and small sailboats are at the beach. There are tennis courts. Don't count on your luggage arriving when you do; bring bathing suit and other essentials with your carry-on belongings. *Small resort.*

LOW-COST LODGING can be found at **Smith's Cottage,** which has a half-dozen units.

THE OTHER ISLANDS

On **MIDDLE CAICOS**, low-cost lodging can be found in one of the 4 rooms at Taylor's Guest House.

On **SALT CAY**, the village of Balfour Town has sun-bleached stucco-and-wood buildings.

Windmills Plantation, on a gorgeous beach, has less than a dozen beautiful rooms, with a pool and a luxurious style. Isolated on this off-beat spot, guests should be self-sufficient. From Grand Turk, the 9-mile flight to Salt Cay takes 5 minutes. For low-cost lodging, investigate the few rooms at *American House*. In addition, some residents operate informal bed-and-breakfast places. The Tourist Office can supply names and phone contacts.

On **SOUTH CAICOS**, inquire about the *Admirals Arms Hotel* and *Harbor View Hotel*.

NATURAL SURROUNDINGS Most of the Turks and Caicos islands are better known for their long soft-sand beaches and spectacular offshore reefs and caves than for the landscape. Provo, less than 600 miles southeast of Miami, has rolling hills that rise from the shoreline—and a ten-mile barrier reef. There's an impressive cave to explore on Middle Caicos.

Near Pine Cay, remnants of an 18th-century British fort create a popular snorkeling and scuba-diving site. Shelling is good on many of the remote beaches, and the salt ponds may seem fascinating to those unfamiliar with the flat "pans" where water evaporates from the salt crop as it is baked in the sun. There are 33 areas that have been designated as sanctuaries and national parks. One of the largest areas is Princess Alexandra National Park, formerly known as Leeward National Park, which includes Mangrove, Donna, and Little Water cays.

PLACES WORTH FINDING: Archaeologists enjoy prowling around the Arawak Indian settlement on Pine Cay. On Provo, Cheshire Hall is noteworthy as the ruin of a late 18th-century plantation great house. Otherwise, the small towns of Cockburn, Balfour, and perhaps the newer Turtle Cove may seem noteworthy to some island vacationers.

SPORTS: **Scuba diving** is the number-one sport around these islands. On Provo check with *Provo Aquatic Centre* (T 809+946–4455), *Provo Turtle Divers* (T 809+946–4232), and/or *Third Turtle Divers* (T 809+946–4230). On Grand Turk the leaders are *Blue Water Divers* (T 809+946–2432) and *Omega Diving* (T 809+946–2232). *Neal Watson's Undersea Adventures* (Box 21766, Ft. Lauderdale, FL 33335–1766, T 305+763–2188 or 800+327–8150) is one of several dive operators that put together vacations on Provo. *ITR Dive Desk* (4 Park Ave., New York, NY 10016, T 212+545–8437 or 800+223–9815) sells dive packages for the hotels the firm represents.

Sailing enthusiasts should note the late-May South Caicos regatta. **Deep-sea fishing** is challenging.

TREASURES AND TRIFLES: Shopping is not a primary reason for coming to these islands.

DIRECTORY OF HOTEL REPRESENTATIVES

Many hotels have toll-free numbers (800 numbers), which you can learn by dialing 800+555-1212 to ask for the hotel by name. Although every effort has been made to have the hotel directory accurate, a number of factors contribute to make the task difficult. In all cases, be sure to check details with the hotels involved. *Only they can provide* the correct last-minute facts.

AC—Accor International
2 Overhill Rd.
Scarsdale, NY 10583
914+472-0370
800+221-4542

A/WI—American/Wolfe International
1890 Palmer Ave.
Larchmont, NY 10538
914+833-3303
800+223-5695

BR—Bounty Resorts
47 Sherman Hill Road
Woodbury, CT 06798
203+266-0100
800+462-6868

BT—Barcelo Tour and Hotels
150 SE Second Ave., #806
Miami, FL 33131
305+374-0045
800+336-6612

BW—Best Western
Box 10203
Phoenix AZ 85064
800+334-7234

CA—Caribbean Inns
Box 7411
Hilton Head, SC 29938
803+785-7411
800+633-7411

CI—Caribbean Information Office
3166 S. River Rd.
Des Plaines, IL 60018
708+699-7570
800+621-1270

CH—Conrad International
1851, 301 Park Ave.
New York, NY 10022
212+980-6680
800+445-8667

CM—Club Mediterranee
Box 4460
Scottsdale, AZ 85261
800+528-3100

CO—Concorde Hotels
Suite 2530
551 Fifth Ave.
New York, NY 10017
212+697-7405
800+228-9290

CU—Cunard Sales
555 Fifth Ave.
New York, NY 10017
212+880-7500

DM—David Mitchell & Co.
200 Madison Ave.
New York, NY 10016
212+696-1323
800+372-1323

DIRECTORY OF HOTEL REPRESENTATIVES

DD—Divi Hotels
54 Gunderman Rd.
Ithaca, NY 14850
607 + 277–3484;
800 + 367–3484

DR—Dominican Republic Hotel Representatives
7204 N.W. 79th Ter.
Miami, FL 33136
305 + 887–7999;
800 + 327–9826

EM—E & M Associates
211 East 43rd St.
New York, NY 10017
212 + 599–8280
800 + 223–9832

ER—Elegant Resorts of Jamaica
1320 S. Dixie Hgwy. #1100
Coral Gables, FL 33146
800 + 237–3237
305 + 666–0447

FH—Forte Hotels
5700 Broadmore
Shawnee Mission, KS 66202
913 + 831–3535
800 + 225–5843

FR—Flagship Resorts
43 Kensico Dr.
Mt. Kisco, NY 10549
914 + 241–8771;
800 + 729–3524

FDR—F.D.R. Holidays, Ltd.
147 Merrick Rd.
Freeport, NY 11520
516 + 223–1786
800 + 654–1337

GT—Golden Tulip
140 East 63rd St.
New York, NY 10021
800 + 344–1212
212 + 715–6900

HRS—Hilton Reservations System
Waldorf Astoria Hotel
New York, NY 10022
800 + 445–8667
212 + 594–4500

HI—Holiday Inn Reservations
757 Lexington Ave.
New York, NY 10022
800 + 238–8000
800 + 223–9815
212 + 840–6048

HY—Hyatt Resorts Caribbean
341 Madison Ave.
New York, NY 10017
212 + 972–7000
800 + 233–1234

IL—International Lifestyle
Box 534
Freeport, NY 11520
800 + 858–8009;
516 + 868–6924

ITR—International Travel & Resorts
4 Park Ave.
New York, NY 10016
212 + 545–8469
800 + 223–9815

JdL—Jacques de Larsay, Inc.
622 Broadway
New York, NY 10012
212 + 477–1600;
800 + 223–1510

JT—Jack Tar Resorts
1314 Wood St.
Dallas, TX 75202
214 + 670–9888
800 + 527–9299

LH—Leading Hotels
747 Third Ave.
New York, NY 10017
212 + 838–3110
800 + 223–6800

LRI—Loews Reservation Int'l
One Park Ave.
New York, NY 10016
212 + 545–2222
800 + 223–0888

M—Meridien Reservations
4201 Cambridge St.
Fort Worth, TX 76155
817 + 355–8300
800 + 543–4300

MD—Mondotels Inc.
1500 Broadway
New York, NY 10036
212 + 719–5750
800 + 847–4249

DIRECTORY OF HOTEL REPRESENTATIVES · · · 807

MH—Marriott Hotel
420 Lexington Ave.
New York, NY 10170
212+490-3350;
800+847-4249

MO—The Moorings
1305 US19 South
Clearwater, FL 33546
813+530-5651 or
800+535-7289

O—Omni Supernational
Box 7862
Omaha, NE 68114
800+628-2216

PLM—Pullman International
1500 Broadway
New York, NY 10036
800+223-9862
212+575-2228

PR—Premier Hotel Service
2600 SW Third Ave.
Miami, FL 33129
800+773-6437;
305+856-5405

RA—Ramada Inns
2655 Le Jeune Rd.
Coral Gables, FL 33134
800+272-6232

RH—Radisson Hotels
2223 North 91 Plaza
Omaha, NE 68134
402+393-8700
800+333-3333

RL—Ralph Locke
Box 800
Waccabuc, NY 10597
914+763-5526
800+223-1108

RM—Ray Morrow
360 Main St.
Ridgefield, CT 06877
203+438-3793;
800+243-9420

RMI—Resorts Mgt. Inc.
201½ East 29th St.
New York, NY 10016
212+696-4566
800+225-4255

RR—Robert Reid
10606 Burt Cir.
Omaha, NE 68114
402+498-4300;
800+223-6510

RS—Reservations Systems Inc.
6 East 46th St.
New York, NY 10017
212+661-4540;
800+223-1588

RSC—Resort Sales Council
141½ Main St.
Norwalk, CT 06851
203+847-9445
800+622-7836

RRS—Resort Representation Services
2100 North East 28th Ave.
Miami, FL 33180
800+327-5746

RI—Rockresorts, Inc.
501 E. Camino Real
Boca Raton, FL 33432
305+395-3000
800+223-7637

RVI—Resort Villas International
30 Spring St.
Stamford, CT 06901
203+965-0260

SA—Sandals Resorts
7610 SW 61st Ave.
Miami, FL 33143
305+284-1300
800+726-3257

SHR—Selective Hotel Reservations
302 East 48th St.
New York, NY 10021
212+758-4375

SH—Sheraton Hotels
1700 Broadway
New York, NY
800+334-8484

SMR—Sint Maarten Beach
Box 1087, 149 Oak Dr.
Bowling Brook, IL 60439
312+759-7300
800+222-9902

DIRECTORY OF HOTEL REPRESENTATIVES

SR—Sands Resorts
551 Fifth Ave.
New York, NY 10176
212+986–8822
800+443–2009

SS—Sea & Sun Resorts, Ltd.
Box 30609
Jamaica, NY 11430
718+917–8222
800+223–0757

ST—Stouffer Hotels Reservations
29800 Bainbridge Rd.
Solon, OH 44139
216+248–3600
800+468–3571

TL—Travel Lodge
5700 Broadmore
Shawnee Mission, KS 66202
913+831–3535
800+225–3050

VN—Vacation Network
1501 West Fullerton
Chicago, IL 60616
312+883–4095;
800+423–4095

WH—Wyndham Hotels
5775 NW 11th St.
Miami, FL 33126
305+262–1397;
800+822–4200

HOTEL QUICK-REFERENCE CHARTS

Details below are for guidance only and are subject to confirmation by each property. Although every effort has been made to have information as accurate as possible, rates should be reconfirmed prior to making reservations. Lodging rates are lower during summer season, from mid-April, through mid-December.

KEY

The following codes are used throughout the directory:

EP = no meals
CP = breakfast only; sometimes the "continental breakfast" of bread or rolls, butter, jam, coffee or tea; inquire about full American breakfast
FP = full American breakfast only
MAP = breakfasts and dinners daily included in the rate
AP = all meals each day
AP+ = all meals plus drinks, watersports, activities, etc.

all-incl = all inclusive rate, usually for several days, with room, all meals, entertainment, and sports included in one price
apts = apartments, usually with living room plus 1 or 2 bedrooms
brm = bedroom
cot = cottages, meaning free-standing units
st = studio units with kitchenette
units = the living/sleeping areas
villa = a free-standing unit, often luxurious
wk = weekly

ANGUILLA, BRITISH WEST INDIES

	phone 809+	rooms	winter rate for 2	rep	page
Anguilla Great House *Cove Bay* Anguilla, B.W.I.	497–6061	25	$200–230 EP	CI	63
Cap Juluca *Box 240, Maunday's Bay* Anguilla, B.W.I.	497–6666	90	$390–1500 CP	FR	63
Carimar Beach Club *Box 327, Mead's Bay* Anguilla, B.W.I.	497–2881	23 apts	1-brm $285 EP	EM	65
Casa Nadine *The Valley* Anguilla, B.W.I.	497–2358	11	$25–30 EP		68
Cinnamon Reef *Box 141, Little Harbour* Anguilla, B.W.I.	497–2850	22	$225–300 EP	RL	64

809

HOTEL QUICK-REFERENCE CHARTS

	phone 809+	rooms	winter rate for 2	rep	page
Coccoloba Plantation *Box 332, Barnes Bay* *Anguilla, B.W.I.*	497–6871	51	$360–760 CP	ITR	64
Cove Castles *Shoal Bay* *Anguilla, B.W.I.*	497–6801	12 villas	$490–690 EP		66
Cul de Sac *Box 173, Blowing Point* *Anguilla, B.W.I.*	497–6461	6	$250 EP		66
Dolphins *Box 105, Sandy Hill* *Anguilla, B.W.I.*		villa			66
Easy Corner Villas *Box 65, South Hill* *Anguilla, B.W.I.*	497–6433	20 apts 1–3 brm	110–160 EP apts	ITR	66
Ferry Boat Inn & Apts *Blowing Point* *Anguilla, B.W.I.*					
Fountain Beach *Shoal Bay* *Anguilla, B.W.I.*	497–3491	10 apts	$210–320 EP	ITR, CA	66
Harbour Lights *Island Harbour* *Anguilla, B.W.I.*	497–4433	3 apts	1-brm $125 EP		
Inter-Island Hotel *South Hill* *Anguilla, B.W.I.*	497–2259	12	$50–60 EP	ITR	68
Lloyd's *The Valley* *Anguilla, B.W.I.*	497–2351	14	$70 EP		68
Loblolly *Box 81, Sandy Hill* *Anguilla, B.W.I.*	497–4250	2 apts	$450 wk		66
Malliouhana Beach Hotel *Box 173, Mead's Bay* *Anguilla, B.W.I.*	497–6111	51+ villas & suites	$480–720 EP suites	DM	64
The Mariners *Box 139 Sandy Ground* *Anguilla, B.W.I.*	497–2671	50	$420–630 EP Apt	ITR, CI	64
Masara Resort *Kartouche Bay* *Anguilla, B.W.I.*	497–3200	11	$175 EP 1 brm	ITR	67
Maybern *South Hill* *Anguilla, B.W.I.*	497–2350	9	$36 EP	CI, ITR	68

HOTEL QUICK-REFERENCE CHARTS · · · 811

	phone 809+	rooms	winter rate for 2	rep	page
Palm Grove Apartments *Sea Feathers Bay* *Anguilla, B.W.I.*	497–4100	22 apts	$100 EP	VV	67
Rendezvous Bay Hotel *Box 31, Rendezvous Bay* *Anguilla, B.W.I.*	497–2549	20 + villas	$100–175 EP	ITR	65
Rainbow Reef Villas *South coast* *Anguilla, B.W.I.*	497–2817	4 2-brm villas	$950 wk EP 155 EP	ITR	67
Rose's Place *Island Harbour* *Anguilla, B.W.I.*					67
Sea Feathers *Sandy Hill* *Anguilla, B.W.I.*	497–4400	villas	$145–190 EP		67
Sea Grape Villas *Box 65, Mead's Bay* *Anguilla, B.W.I.*	497–6433	10 apts	$575 EP	ITR	67
Shoal Bay Resort *Shoal Bay* *Anguilla, B.W.I.*	497–2011	15 apts	$195 EP	ITR	67
Shoal Bay Villas *Shoal Bay* *Anguilla, B.W.I.*	497–4250	9 villas	$230–270 EP		67
La Sirena *Box 200, Mead's Bay* *Anguilla, B.W.I.*	497–6827	27 villas	$180–215 EP	ITR	68
Skiffles *Lower South Hill* *Anguilla, B.W.I.*	497–6110	5 apts	$150 EP	219+ 642-4855	68
Yellow Banana *Box 63, Stoney Ground* *Anguilla, B.W.I.*	497–2626	12	$30–40 EP		68

ANTIGUA, WEST INDIES

	phone 809+	rooms	winter rate for 2	rep	page
Admiral's Inn *Box 713, English Harbour* *St. John's, Antigua, W.I.*	463–1027	14	$96–180 EP	ITR	88
Antigua Mill Inn *Box 319* *St. John's, Antigua, W.I.*	462–3044	33	$90–100 EP	RR	88

HOTEL QUICK-REFERENCE CHARTS

	phone 809+	rooms	winter rate for 2	rep	page
Antigua Village *Box 649, Dickenson Bay* *Antigua, W.I.*	462–2930	64 apts	$170–255 for 1-brm	RR, CI	85
Barrymore Hotel *Box 244, Fort Road,* *St. John's, Antigua, W.I.*	462–4062	36	$78–84 EP	ITR	89
Barrymore Beach Apts. *Runaway Beach* *Antigua, W.I.*	462–4101	20	$135–285 EP, 1 brm	ITR	85
Beachcomber *Box 10, Coolidge* *St. John's, Antigua, W.I.*	463–0100	24	$60 EP		89
Blue Acres *Hodges Bay* *Antigua, W.I.*					85
Blue Heron Beach Hotel *Box 185, Johnson's Point* *Antigua, W.I.*	462–8564	40	$205–235		79
Blue Waters Beach *Box 256, Soldier Bay* *Antigua, W.I.*	462–0290	48 + villas	$295–335 MAP+ villas	CI	80
Boon's Point *Soldiers Bay* *Antigua, W.I.*					85
Bougainvillae *All Saint's Road* *St. John's, Antigua, W.I.*					
Carlisle Bay Villas *Carlisle Bay* *St. John's, Antigua, W.I.*					85
Catamaran Hotel *Box 985, Falmouth* *Antigua, W.I.*	463–1036	13	$60 EP		89
Copper & Lumber Store *Box 184, English Harbour* *Antigua, W.I.*	463–1058	14 apts	$160–280 EP	ITR, CA	85
Curtain Bluff Hotel *Box 288, Old Road* *Antigua, W.I.*	462–8400	60	$495–560 AP+	212+ 289–8888	80
Dian Bay Apartments *Box 231, St. John's* *Antigua, W.I.*	463–2003	22 1 & 2 brm apts	$118–130 EP	ITR	86
Emerald Cove *Nonsuch Bay* *St. John's, Antigua, W.I.*					86

HOTEL QUICK-REFERENCE CHARTS

	phone 809+	rooms	winter rate for 2	rep	page
Falmouth Harbour Beach Apts *Box 713, St. John's* *Antigua, W.I.*	463–1027	25 apts	$110–120 EP	ITR, CI	86
Galley Bay *Box 305, St. John's* *Antigua, W.I.*	462–0302	30 incl villas	$298–388 AP+	RR	80
Galleon Beach *Box 1003, Freeman's Bay* *Antigua, W.I.*	463–1450	32 2-brm cots	$160–210 EP	ITR, CI	86
Halcyon Cove Beach & Casino *Box 251, Dickenson Bay* *Antigua, W.I.*	462–0256	153	$195–250 EP	RS	81
Halcyon Heights Apartments *Box 1345* *Antigua, W.I.*	462–0250	24 apts	$150 EP		87
Half Moon Bay *Box 144, Half Moon Bay* *Antigua, W.I.*	463–2101	100	$295–595 MAP	RR	81
Hawksbill Beach Hotel *Box 108, St. John's* *Antigua, W.I.*	462–1515	75	$280–365 CP	ITR	81
Heritage Hotel *Heritage Quay* *St. John's, Antigua, W.I.*					87
Hodges Bay Club *Box 1237, St. John's* *Antigua, W.I.*	462–2300	26	1-brm $200 2-brm $250–300		87
Inn at English Harbour *Box 187, English Harbour* *Antigua, W.I.*	463–1014	28	$245–300 EP	RR	89
Joe Mikes *Nevis St., St. John's* *Antigua, W.I.*	462–1142	12	$39 EP		90
Jolly Beach *Box 744, St. John's* *Antigua, W.I.*	462–0061	475			81
Jumby Bay Resort *Box 243, Long Island* *Antigua, W.I.*	462–6000	38	$600 AP+	516+ 626-9200	82
Long Bay Hotel *Box 442, Long Bay Beach* *Antigua, W.I.*	463–2005	20+ 5 cots	$290–330 MAP	RL	82
Lord Nelson Inn *Box 155, Coolidge Airport* *Antigua, W.I.*	462–3094	16	$80 EP		89

HOTEL QUICK-REFERENCE CHARTS

	phone 809+	rooms	winter rate for 2	rep	page
Marina Bay *Runaway Bay* *Antigua, W.I.*					87
Mill Reef Club *St. John's* *Antigua, W.I.*	463–2081	on request			82
Piggotsville Guest House *Clare Hall, St. John's* *Antigua, W.I.*					90
Pillar Rock *Deep Bay* *St. John's* *Antigua, W.I.*	462–2326	60	$130–250 EP	ITR	87
Pineapple Beach *Box 54, Long Bay* *Antigua, W.I.*	463–2006	36	$330–420 AP+	ITR	83
Ramada Royal Antiguan *Deep Bay* *Antigua, W.I.*	462–3733	285	$200–350 EP + sts, villas	RA	83
Runaway Beach Hotel *Box 874, St. John's* *Antigua, W.I.*	462–1318	50+ cots	$75–190 EP	RB	83
Sandals Antigua *Dickenson Bay* *Antigua, W.I.*	462–0267	149	$2995–3995 wk all-incl	SA	83
Sand Haven *Runaway Bay* *Antigua, W.I.*					87
Sandpiper *Crosbies Estate* *St. John's* *Antigua, W.I.*	462–0939	24	$240–280 MAP		84
St. James's Club *Box 63, Marmora Bay* *Antigua, W.I.*	463–1430	105	$385–425 MAP		84
St. John's Court *Old Fort Rd., St. John's* *Antigua, W.I.*					90
St. Mary's Guest House *St. Mary's St., St. John's* *Antigua, W.I.*					90
Siboney Beach Club *Box 222, St. John's* *Antigua, W.I.*	462–3356	12 apts	$140–220 EP	AWI	87

HOTEL QUICK-REFERENCE CHARTS · · · 815

	phone 809+	rooms	winter rate for 2	rep	page
Spanish Main *Independence Ave.* *St. John's, Antigua, W.I.*					90
Time Away Apts. *Runaway Bay* *Antigua, W.I.*					88
Trade Winds Hotel & Apts *Box 1390, St. John's* *Antigua, W.I.*	462–1223	21 apts	$150–300 EP		88
Trafalgar Beach Villas *Box 1585* *St. John's, Antigua, W.I.*	462–2531	56	$110–250 EP	ITR	
Yepton Beach *Box 1427, St. John's* *Antigua, W.I.*	462–0037	38 incl apts	$120–155 EP	RR	88

ARUBA, NETHERLANDS ANTILLES

	phone 011+297+	rooms	winter rate for 2	rep	page
Americana Aruba Hotel & Casino *Palm Beach* *Aruba, N.A.*	82–4500	206	$140–200 EP	AM	105
Amsterdam Manor *Palm Beach* *Aruba, N.A.*					105
Aruba Beach Club *Druif (Eagle) Beach* *Aruba, N.A.*	82–3000	133	$130–180 EP		105
Aruba Concorde Hotel & Casino *Palm Beach* *Aruba, N.A.*	82–4466	490	$165–175 EP	CH	105
Aruba Holiday Inn & Casino *Palm Beach* *Aruba, N.A.*	82–3600	390	$145–195 EP	HI	106
Aruba Palm Beach *Palm Beach* *Aruba, N.A.*	82–3900	202	$150–250 EP	RS	106
Best Western Talk of the Town *Oranjestad* *Aruba, N.A.*	82–3380	62	$120 EP	RL	109
Bucuti Beach *Manchebo Beach* *Aruba, N.A.*	82–3444	60	$170–220 EP	RL	106

HOTEL QUICK-REFERENCE CHARTS

	phone 011+297+	rooms	winter rate for 2	rep	page
Bushiri Bounty Hotel *Oranjestad* Aruba, N.A.	82–5216	154	$155 all-incl	BR	106
La Cabana Beach & Racquet Club *L.G. Smith Blvd. 250* Aruba, N.A.	83–9000	440		ITR	106
Carnicon Hotel *Palm Beach* Aruba, N.A.		460	not open at presstime		107
Casa del Mar *Druif (Eagle) Beach* Aruba, N.A.	82–7000	32		LE	107
Caribbean Palm Village *Noord area* Aruba, N.A.	83–2700	170	$70–110 EP	ITR	110
Divi Divi Beach Hotel *Druif (Eagle) Beach* Aruba, N.A.	82–3300	204	$200–280 EP	DD	107
Divi Tamarijn Beach Hotel *Druif Beach* Aruba, N.A.	82–4150	204	$200 EP	DD	107
Divi Dutch Village *Druif (Eagle) Beach area* Aruba, N.A.	83–2300	70 apts	$200st+ $300 2 brm	DD	110
Edward's Seaview Apartments *Malmok* Aruba, N.A.					111
Golden Tulip Aruba Caribbean *Palm Beach* Aruba, N.A.	82–2250	406	$175–600 EP	RR	108
Harbortown Resort & Casino *Oranjestad* Aruba, N.A.		246	$220 EP up	ITR	110
Hyatt Regency *Palm Beach* Aruba, N.A.					108
Manchebo Beach Hotel *Mancheloo Beach* Aruba, N.A.	82–3444	72	$150 EP	RL	108
Mill Resort *Box 1012* Aruba, N.A.	83–5033	99		800+ 447-3234	110
Paradise Beach Village *Manchebo area* Aruba, N.A.					109

HOTEL QUICK-REFERENCE CHARTS · · · 817

	phone 011 + 297 +	rooms	winter rate for 2	rep	page
Plantation Bay Beach Resort & Casino *Palm Beach* *Aruba, N.A.*	83–6528	420		PR	109
Playa Linda *Palm Beach* *Aruba, N.A.*	83–1060	194 apts	$160 EP for 4		110
La Quinta *Manchebo area* *Aruba, N.A.*	83–5010	235	$240–375 EP 2 brm	ITR	111
Ramada Renaissance Hotel *Palm Beach* *Aruba, N.A.*				RA	109
Sailboard Vacations *Malmok* *Aruba, N.A.*					111
Sonesta Hotel, Beach Club & Casino *L.G. Smith Blvd. 82* *Oranjestad, Aruba, N.A.*	83-6000	302		LRI	109
Sunset Village *Oranjestad* *Aruba, N.A.*					111
Vistalmar *28 Bucutiweg* *Aruba, N.A.*	82–8579	8 apts	$60		111

BARBADOS, WEST INDIES: Barbados Hotel Association Reservation Service takes bookings for its members through 800 + 462–2526.

	phone 809 +	rooms	winter rate for 2	rep	page
Abbeville Hotel *Hastings, Christ Church* *Barbados, W.I.*					140
Angler Apts *Derricks* *Barbados, W.I.*	432–0817		$75–80 EP		136
Asta Apartments *Hastings, Christ Church* *Barbados, W.I.*	427–2541	60 apts	$110 EP	AWI	136
Atlantis *East Coast* *Barbados, W.I.*	433–9445	16	$50–60 AP		138

HOTEL QUICK-REFERENCE CHARTS

	phone 809+	rooms	winter rate for 2	rep	page
Bagshot House *St. Lawrence Coast, Christ Church* *Barbados, W.I.*	435–6956	16	$90–160 EP		139
Barbados Beach Village *Fitts Village, St. James* *Barbados, W.I.*	425–1440	88	$155–235 EP	ITR	129
Beachcomber Apartments *West coast, near Holetown* *Barbados, W.I.*	423–0489	9 apts	$150 1 brm EP; $250 2 brm EP	RR	136
Berwyn Guest House *Rockley area; Christ Church* *Barbados, W.I.*					140
Best Western Sandy Beach Apts. *Worthing, Christ Church* *Barbados, W.I.*	428–9033	89 apts	$175–270 EP	BW	137
Buccaneer Bay *St. James Beach* *Barbados, W.I.*	432–7981	29 apts	$225–325 EP 1-brm apts	ITR	129
Caribbee Beach Hotel *Hastings, Christ Church* *Barbados, W.I.*	436–6232	28 + 20 apts	$85–100 EP	RR	140
Casuarina Beach Hotel *St. Lawrence Gap, Christ Church* *Barbados, W.I.*	428–3600	82	$130–160 EP	ITR	137
Cobbler's Cove Hotel *St. Peter* *Barbados, W.I.*	422–2291	38 sts	$450–1100 MAP	RR	129
Coconut Creek Hotel *Box 429, Derricks, St. James* *Barbados, W.I.*	432–0804	45 + 4 apts	$260–310 MAP	DM	129
Colony Club *Box 429, Porters, St. James* *Barbados, W.I.*	422–2335	76	$290–425 MAP	DM	130
Coral Reef *St. James* *Barbados, W.I.*	422–2372	75	$310–480 MAP	RL	130
Crane Beach Hotel *Crane, St. Philip* *Barbados, W.I.*	423–6220	25	$190–360 CP	RR	139
Cunard Paradise Beach Hotel *Black Rock, St. Michael* *Barbados, W.I.*	429–7151	172	$145–200 EP	LRI	130
Discovery Bay *Holetown, St. James* *Barbados, W.I.*	432–1301	84	$310–415 EP	ITR	131

HOTEL QUICK-REFERENCE CHARTS · · · 819

	phone 809+	rooms	winter rate for 2	rep	page
Divi South Winds Beach Hotel *St. Lawrence, Christ Church* *Barbados, W.I.*	428–7181	166	$225–290 EP	DD	131
Eastry House *St. Peter* *Barbados, W.I.*	422–2201	34 + 9 apts.	on request	A/WI	131
Fairholme Apartments *Maxwell, Christ Church* *Barbados, W.I.*	428–9425	11 + 20 apts	$40–70 EP		141
Flamboyant *Garrison, near Bridgetown* *Barbados, W.I.*	427–5588	8 + 5 apts	$25–50		141
Ginger Bay Beach Club *Crane area, St. Philip* *Barbados, W.I.*	423–5810	30	$200 EP	ITR	132
Glitter Bay Resort *Porters, St. James* *Barbados, W.I.*	422–4111	99	$345–475 EP	ITR	137
Grand Barbados Beach Resort *Box 639, Bridgetown* *Barbados, W.I.*	426–0890	138	$140–600 EP	ITR	131
Half Moon Beach Hotel *Dover Beach, Christ Church* *Barbados, W.I.*	428–7131	36	$115–145 EP & apt	AWI	132
Heywoods Resort *St. Peter Parish* *Barbados, W.I.*	422–4900	306	$190–225 EP	ITR	132
Hilton International Barbados *Needhams Point, St. Michael* *Barbados, W.I.*	426–0200	185	$170–350 EP	HRS	132
Inn on the Beach *Holetown, St. James* *Barbados, W.I.*	432–0385	21	$140–220 EP	ITR	
Island Inn *Aquatic Gap, near Bridgetown* *Barbados, W.I.*	436–6393	25	$160–180 EP	RR	139
Kings Beach Hotel *Mullins Bay, St. Peter* *Barbados, W.I.*	422–1690	59	$235–255 EP	ITR	133
Kingsley Club *Cattlewash* *Barbados, W.I.*		7			139
Mackston Apartments *Hastings, Christ Church* *Barbados, W.I.*		6 apts			141

HOTEL QUICK-REFERENCE CHARTS

	phone 809+	rooms	winter rate for 2	rep	page
Maresol Beach Apartments *St. Lawrence Gap, Christ Church* *Barbados, W.I.*	428–9300	12 apts	$400–800 wk		141
Margate Garden Apartments *Hastings, south coast* *Barbados, W.I.*	429–2758	25 apts	on request		141
Marriott's Sam Lord's Castle *St. Philip* *Barbados, W.I.*	423–7350	259	$190–220 EP	MH	133
Nautilus Beach Apartments *Bridgetown* *Barbados, W.I.*	426–3541	14 apts	$60–75 EP		141
Ocean View Hotel *Hastings, Christ Church* *Barbados, W.I.*	427–7821	40	$60–95 EP		139
Pineapple St. James *Vauxhall, St. James* *Barbados, W.I.*	432–7948	130		ITR	131
Rockley Resort & Beach Club *Golf Club Road, Worthing* *Barbados, W.I.*	435–7880	288 apts	$170–210 EP	ITR	137
Royal Pavilion Hotel *St. James* *Barbados, W.I.*	422–5555	75	$445–930 EP	ITR	133
Sand Acres Beach Club *Maxwell Coast Rd.,* *Barbados, W.I.*	428–7141	20 apts	$110–150 EP	RS	137
Sandhurst Apartments *St. Lawrence Gap* *Barbados, W.I.*	428–8246	21	$700–805 wk	SHR	138
Sandpiper Inn *St. James* *Barbados, W.I.*	422–2251	46 inc. apts	$340–545 MAP	RL	134
Sandridge Apartments *Road View, St. Peter* *Barbados, W.I.*	422–2361	50 incl apts	$75 rm EP $120–160 apt EP	RR	138
Sandy Lane Hotel *St. James* *Barbados, W.I.*	432–1311	110	$600–750 MAP	TF	134
Sea Breeze *Maxwell Coast Road* *Barbados, W.I.*	428–2825		$70–120		141
Sea Foam Haciendas *Worthing, Christ Church* *Barbados, W.I.*	428–5362	12 2 brm apts	$90–120 EP		138

HOTEL QUICK-REFERENCE CHARTS · · · 821

	phone 809+	rooms	winter rate for 2	rep	page
Seaview Hotel *Hastings, near Bridgetown* *Barbados, W.I.*	426–1450	19	$75 EP		140
Settlers Beach *St. James* *Barbados, W.I.*	422–3052	22	$400 EP	RL	138
Southern Palms *St. Lawrence, Christ Church* *Barbados, W.I.*	428–7171	95	$195–310 EP + 2-brm	RR	134
Sunset Crest Resort *St. James Coast* *Barbados, W.I.*	427–4710	288 apts	1-brm 65–70 + more	AWI	142
Tamarind Cove *Box 429, Paynes Bay, St. James* *Barbados, W.I.*	432–1332	55	$280–495 MAP	DM	135
Treasure Beach Hotel *Paynes Bay, St. James* *Barbados, W.I.*	422–1346	27 apts	$255–375 CP	RR	135
Windsurfing Resort *Oistins, on the south coast* *Barbados, W.I.*	428–7277	15	$80–140 EP		142
Yellow Bird Apts *St. Lawrence Gap* *Barbados, W.I.*	435–8444		$60–90 EP		138

BARBUDA, WEST INDIES

	phone 809+	rooms	winter rate for 2	rep	page
Coco Point Lodge *Barbuda Island* *Antigua-Barbuda, W.I.*	462–3816	32	$400–600 AP+	212+ 696–4750	157
The Earls *Codrington, Barbuda Island* *Antigua-Barbuda, W.I.*	461–1115 461–1144		$130 EP $890 wk		159
The K Club *Barbuda Island* *Antigua-Barbuda, W.I.*	460–0300	12 villas	$100–1500 apt daily	212+ 752–3525	158
Sunset View Resort *Codrington, Barbuda Island* *Antigua-Barbuda, W.I.*			$75 EP		159

BONAIRE, NETHERLANDS ANTILLES

	phone 011+599+	rooms	winter rate for 2	rep	page
Bachelor's Beach Apartments *Belnem* *Bonaire, N.A.*	Wash, DC 202+ 244-5046	4	$600 1 brm $750 2 brm weekly	202+ 338-0690	167
Black Durgeon *Kralendijk* *Bonaire, N.A.*					168
Bonaire Beach Bungalows *Belnem* *Bonaire, N.A.*	7-8585	4	$122-133 2 br	717+ 586-9230	167
Buddy's Dive Resort *Box 231, marina area* *Bonaire, N.A.*	7-8647	10 apts	$75 EP	ITR	168
Captain Don's Habitat *Box 88, Kralendijk* *Bonaire, N.A.*	7-8290 or 802+ 496-5067	70	$100-175 cot $50 bunk EP	800+ 327-6709	165
Carib Inn *Box 68, J.A. Abraham Blvd., Kralendijk* *Bonaire, N.A.*	7-8819	9	$59-89 EP suite $89-115	ITR	
Coral Regency Resort *Kaya Gobernador 90, Box 380* *Bonaire, N.A.*			$190 EP 1 brm	RR	
Divi Flamingo Beach Hotel & Casino *Kralendijk* *Bonaire, N.A.*	7-8285	150 incl apts	$105-180 EP	DD	166
Harbour Village Beach Hotel *Kralendijk* *Bonaire, N.A.*					166
The Point *Airport Road* *Bonaire, N.A.*		174	$300 EP	RSC	166
Hotel Rochaline *Box 27, Kralendijk* *Bonaire, N.A.*	7-8286	20	$50 EP		
Sand Dollar Condotel & Beach Club *Box 175, Kralendijk* *Bonaire, N.A.*		38	$125 up		167
Sorobon Beach Resort *Box 14, southeast coast* *Bonaire, N.A.*	7-8080	23 apts + studios	$120-150 EP		166
Sunset Inn *Box 115* *Bonaire, N.A.*	7-8291	17	$80-120 EP	ITR	

HOTEL QUICK-REFERENCE CHARTS · · · 823

	phone 011+599+	rooms	winter rate for 2	rep	page
Sunset Beach Resort *Kralendijk* *Bonaire, N.A.*	7–5300	88	$100–160 EP	ITR	167
Sunset Ocean Front Apts. *Kralendijk, Box 333* *Bonaire, N.A.*	7–8291	12 apts	$130 1 brm $175 2 brm	ITR	167

BRITISH VIRGIN ISLANDS, BRITISH WEST INDIES

	phone 809+	rooms	winter rate for 2	rep	page
Admiralty Estate *Box 158, Road Town* *Tortola, B.W.I.*	494–0014	30 apts.	$150–175 EP	ITR	183
Biras Creek *Box 54, Virgin Gorda Island* *British Virgin Islands, B.W.I.*	495–3555	32	$395–595 AP	RL	198
Bitter End Yacht Club *Box 46, North Sound, Virgin Gorda* *British Virgin Islands, B.W.I.*	494–2746	32	$280–360 AP	BE	198
Brandywine *Box 151, Road Town* *Tortola, British Virgins, B.W.I.*	495–2301	8	on request		183
Cane Garden Beach Hotel *Cane Garden Bay, Box 570* *Tortola, British Virgin Islands, B.W.I.*	495–4639	30	$50 EP		184
Castle Maria *Road Town* *Tortola, British Virgins, B.W.I.*	494–2553	30 incl apts	$65–70 EP		185
CSY Yacht Club *Box 157, Road Town* *Tortola, British Virgins, B.W.I.*	494–2741	8	$70 EP	201+ 568–0390	184
Diamond Beach *North Shore* *Virgin Gorda, B.W.I.*					184
Drake's Anchorage (Box 2510) *Mosquito Island, off Virgin Gorda* *British Virgin Islands, B.W.I.*	494–2254	10	$220 AP	617+ 661–4745	195
Fischer's Cove Beach *Box 60, The Valley, Virgin Gorda* *British Virgin Islands, B.W.I.*	495–5252	8	$185 MAP + cottages $150 up	312+ 296–2271	198
Fort Burt *Box 187, Road Town* *Tortola, British Virgins, B.W.I.*	494–2587	7	$50–70 EP	ITR	184

HOTEL QUICK-REFERENCE CHARTS

	phone 809+	rooms	winter rate for 2	rep	page
Fort Recovery Estates Box 239, Road Town Tortola, British Virgins, B.W.I.	495–4354	12 villas	$130 EP 1 brm	ITR	183
Frenchman's Cay Resort Road Town Tortola, British Virgins, B.W.I.	495–4844	1–4 brm villas		EM	183
Guana Island Club Box 32, Guana Island Tortola, British Virgins, B.W.I.	494–2354	15	$385 AP	914+ 967–6050	186
Guavaberry-Spring Bay Homes Box 20, Virgin Gorda British Virgin Islands, B.W.I.	495–5227	14	$100–150 EP + weekly rate		199
Harbor Vieco Tortola British Virgin Islands, B.W.I.					185
Jolly Roger Inn West End, Tortola British Virgin Islands, B.W.I.					185
North Sound Resort Box 1077, North Sound, Virgin Gorda British Virgin Islands, B.W.I.	495–7421	villas	$700 wk; $2500 mo	416+ 673–5400	
Little Dix Bay Box 70, Virgin Gorda British Virgin Islands, B.W.I.	495–5555	84	$615 AP	RI	198
Long Bay Box 433, Long Bay Tortola, British Virgins, B.W.I.	495–4252	44	$210–305 MAP	800+ 786–4753	181
Mango Bay Resort Box 1062, Drake's Channel, Virgin Gorda British Virgin Islands, B.W.I.	495–5672	8 villas	studio $110 1 brm $315	RR	200
Maria's By The Sea Wickham's Cay, Road Town Tortola, British Virgins, B.W.I.	494–2595	10	$80 EP		185
Marina Cay Box 76, Marina Cay Tortola, British Virgins, B.W.I.	494–2174	16	$235–335 MAP	FR	186
Mariner Inn Box 139, Road Town Tortola, British Virgins, B.W.I.	494–2331	40	$110–140 EP	MO	181
Maya Cove Apartments Box 399, Maya Cove Tortola, British Virgins, B.W.I.	495–2518	15	$30 EP		183
Necker Island Box 1091, Virgin Gorda British Virgin Islands, B.W.I.	494–4492		for 110 $7000 apt	RMI	196

HOTEL QUICK-REFERENCE CHARTS · · · 825

	phone 809+	rooms	winter rate for 2	rep	page
Nanny Cay Resort & Marina *Tortola* *British Virgins, B.W.I.*	494–2512	41 apts	$150–170 EP	800+ 786–4753	183
Olde Yard Inn *Box 26, Virgin Gorda* *British Virgin Islands, B.W.I.*	495–5544	12	$160–200 MAP	CA	200
Peter Island Resort & Yacht Harbour *Box 211, Peter Island* *Tortola, British Virgins, B.W.I.*	494–2561	52+ villa	$425–525 AP	800+ 346–4451	186
Prospect Reef *Box 104, Road Town* *Tortola, British Virgins, B.W.I.*	494–3311	131	$110–170 EP	LRI	182
The Reefs *Anegada Island* *Tortola, British Virgins, B.W.I.*	none	12	$120 AP		194
Rockview Holiday Homes *West End* *Tortola, British Virgins, B.W.I.*	495–4220	22	$910 wk and up		183
Rudy's Mariner Inn *Great Harbour, Jost Van Dyke* *British Virgin Islands, B.W.I.*					194
Sandcastle at White Bay *Jost Van Dyke* *British Virgin Islands, B.W.I.*			$150 AP		194
Sandy Ground *Jost Van Dyke Island* *Tortola, British Virgins, B.W.I.*	494–3391	8 houses	$900 wk		195
Sea View Guest House *Box 59, Road Town* *Tortola, British Virgins, B.W.I.*	494–2483	20 incl. apts	$33–45		185
Sebastians on the Beach *Box 441, Apple Bay* *Tortola, British Virgins, B.W.I.*	495–4212	26	$100–170 EP	908+ 462–2000	184
The Sugar Mill *Box 425, Apple Bay* *Tortola, British Virgins, B.W.I.*	495–4355	21	$130–190 EP	ITR, CA	184
Treasure Isle Hotel *Box 68, Road Town* *Tortola, British Virgins, B.W.I.*	494–2501	40	$105 EP	HTR	182
Village Cay Resort *Box 145, Road Town* *Tortola, British Virgins, B.W.I.*	494–2771	13	$80 EP		182
Way Side Guest House *Road Town, Tortola* *British Virgin Islands, B.W.I.*	494–2875	20	$20 EP		185

CAYMAN ISLANDS, BRITISH WEST INDIES

	phone 809+	rooms	winter rate for 2	rep	page
Ambassadors Inn *Box 1789, George Town* *Grand Cayman, B.W.I.*	949–7577	15	$75 EP		218
Beach Club Colony *Box 903, West Bay Beach* *Grand Cayman, B.W.I.*	949–8100	41	$158–268 EP	RR	211
Beachcomber Apartments *Box 1799, West Bay Beach* *Grand Cayman, B.W.I.*	947–4470	23 apts	$265–375	ITR	213
Brac Reef Beach Resort *Box 235, Cayman Brac island* *Cayman Islands, B.W.I.*	948–7323	40	$99 EP	800+ 327–3835	227
Britannia Golf Villas *Box 1698; at Hyatt Resort* *Grand Cayman, B.W.I.*	949–7440	25 apts	$315 1 brm $475 up 2 brm	HY	213
Buccaneer's Inn *Box 68, Cayman Brac island* *Cayman Islands, B.W.I.*	948–7257	36	$90 EP	CRS	227
Caribbean Club *Box 504, West Bay Beach* *Grand Cayman, B.W.I.*	947–4009	18 villas	$235–300 EP	CRS	213
Cayman Kai Resort *Box 1112, North Side* *Grand Cayman, B.W.I.*	947–9556	42 apts	$120 1 brm $200 2 brm		213
Christopher Columbus Apartments *Box 1091, West Bay Beach* *Grand Cayman, B.W.I.*	947–4394	27 apts	$225–350 EP	ITR	214
Colonial Club *West Bay Beach* *Grand Cayman, Cayman Islands,* *B.W.I.*	947–4660	24 apts	$300–340 EP		214
Coral Caymanian Apartments *Box 1093, West Bay Beach* *Grand Cayman, B.W.I.*	949–4054	11 apts	$110–175 EP 1 brm	RR	214
Dillon Cottages *Little Cayman Island* *Cayman Islands, B.W.I.*		2	$300 wk	CRV	229
Discovery Point Club *Box 439, West Bay Beach* *Grand Cayman, B.W.I.*	947–4724	45 apts	$125–225 EP	ITR	214
Divi Tiara Beach *Cayman Brac Island* *Cayman Islands, B.W.I.*	948–7553	33	$180–190 EP + Dive	DD	228

HOTEL QUICK-REFERENCE CHARTS

	phone 809+	rooms	winter rate for 2	rep	page
Eldemire's Guest House Box 428, George Town Grand Cayman, B.W.I.	949–5387	7	$55 EP		218
George Town Villas Box 1169, George Town Grand Cayman, B.W.I.	949–5172	54 apts 2 brm	$310 EP for 4	ITR	214
Grapetree/Cocoplum Apartments Box 1802, George Town Grand Cayman, B.W.I.	949–5640	51 apts	$175 EP 1 brm + others	ITR	214
Grama's B+B George Town Grand Cayman, B.W.I.					218
Grand Pavilion Hotel & Beach Club Box 69, West Bay Road Grand Cayman, B.W.I.	947–4666	56	$160–200 EP	RSI	211
The Great House West Bay Beach Grand Cayman, B.W.I.					214
Harbour Heights Box 688, West Bay Beach Grand Cayman, B.W.I.	947–4295	46 apt 2 brm	$175 for 4	CRS	215
Holiday Inn Grand Cayman Box 904, West Bay Beach Grand Cayman, B.W.I.	947–4444	215	$198–238 EP	HI	211
Hyatt Regency Grand Cayman West Bay Road Grand Cayman, B.W.I.	949–1234	240	$225–385 EP	HY	212
Indies Suites Box 2070, Georgetown Grand Cayman, B.W.I.	947–5025	40	$190 1 brm $210 2 brm CP	ITR	215
Island House Resort Box 194, West Bay area Grand Cayman, B.W.I.	949–3017	11	$70		218
Island Pine Villas West Bay area Grand Cayman, B.W.I.					215
Lacovia Condominiums West Bay Beach Grand Cayman, B.W.I.	949–7599	55 apt	$235–325 EP	ITR	215
Lime Tree Bay Box 1557, West Bay Rd. Grand Cayman, B.W.I.	947–4045	65 apt	$185 up	RR	215
London House Box 1356, West Bay Beach Grand Cayman, B.W.I.	947–4060	20 apt	$200 up	CRS	215

HOTEL QUICK-REFERENCE CHARTS

	phone 809+	rooms	winter rate for 2	rep	page
Morritts Tortuga Club *East End* *Grand Cayman, B.W.I.*					216
Pan-Cayman House *Box 440, West Bay Beach* *Grand Cayman, B.W.I.*	947–4002	10	$180 up	CRV	216
Pirate's Point *Box 1375, Little Cayman Island* *Cayman Islands, B.W.I.*	948–4210	8	$320 AP	CRS	229
Plantana *Box 1793, West Bay Beach* *Grand Cayman, B.W.I.*	947–4430	49	$170 up	ITR	216
Radisson Resort *Box 709* *Grand Cayman, B.W.I.*	949–0088	315	$220–300 EP	RH	212
Ramada Treasure Island Resort *Box 1817, George Town* *Grand Cayman, B.W.I.*	949–7955	290 incl apts	$140–380 EP	RA	212
The Retreat at Rum Point *Box 46, North Side* *Grand Cayman, B.W.I.*	947–9135	23 apts	$185 EP		216
Sam McCoy's Diving & Fishing Lodge *Little Cayman island* *% Grand Cayman, B.W.I.*	948–3251	7	$100–180 AP	412+ 834–4064	230
Seascape *West Bay Beach* *Grand Cayman, B.W.I.*					216
Seaview *Georgtown* *Grand Cayman, B.W.I.*					219
Silver Sands Beach Apts. *Box 205, West Bay Beach* *Grand Cayman, B.W.I.*	949–3343	42 apt	$280 2 brm	ITR	216
Southern Cross Club *Little Cayman Island* *Cayman Islands, B.W.I.*	948–3255	10	$250 AP	317+ 636–9501	230
Spanish Bay Villas *North West Point, Box 952* *Grand Cayman, B.W.I.*	949–3272		$160–195	HW	216
Spanish Cove Resort *Box 1014, North West Point* *Grand Cayman, B.W.I.*	949–3765	46+ 12 apts	$195 up EP	HW	212
Sundowner Apts		13 apts		RR	

HOTEL QUICK-REFERENCE CHARTS · · · 829

	phone 809+	rooms	winter rate for 2	rep	page
Sunset House Box 479, George Town Grand Cayman, B.W.I.	949–7111	43	$90–130 EP		218
Tamarind Bay West Bay Grand Cayman, B.W.I.	949–4593	28 apts			
Treasure Island Condos West Bay Grand Cayman, B.W.I.	949–8316		140–225 2 brm	ITR	
Tarquyn Manor Condominiums Box 1362, West Bay Beach Grand Cayman, B.W.I.	947–4038	20 apt	$205–290 EP 2 brm	ITR	217
Turtle Beach West Bay Grand Cayman, B.W.I.	949–8098	25 apts		RR	
Victoria House Box 636, West Bay Beach Grand Cayman, B.W.I.	947–4233	23 apts	$155–192 EP 1 brm	ITR	217
Villas of The Galleon Box 71, West Bay Beach Grand Cayman, B.W.I.	947–5185	75 apts	$225 up	RR	217
Villas Papagallo Box 952, North West Point Grand Cayman, B.W.I.	949–8098	44 apts	$205 up	RR	217
West Indian Club Box 703, West Bay Beach Grand Cayman, B.W.I.	949–2494	9 apts	$230 up	CRS	217
Windjammer George Town Grand Cayman, B.W.I.					219
Windsor House Apartments George Town Grand Cayman, B.W.I.					218

CURACAO, NETHERLANDS ANTILLES

	phone 011+599+	rooms	winter rate for 2	rep	page
Avila Beach Hotel Box 791, Willemstad Curacao, N.A.	961–4377	45	$90–135 EP	U	271
Coral Cliff Boca Santa Marta Curacao, N.A.	964–1610	35	$75 CP	ITR	271

	phone 011+599+	rooms	winter rate for 2	rep	page
Curacao Caribbean Hotel & Casino *Box 2133, Willemstad* *Curacao, N.A.*	962–5000	200	$160–300 EP	ITR	272
Holiday Beach Hotel & Casino *Box 2178, Willemstad* *Curacao, N.A.*	962–5400	200	$145–155 EP	ITR	272
Hotel Holland *F. D. Rooseveltweg 524* *Curacao, N.A.*	98–8044	40	$50–65		272
Landhuis Daniel *Willemstad* *Curacao, N.A.*					273
Otrabanda *Willemstad* *Curacao, N.A.*			$75 EP		
Las Palmas Vacation Village *Box 2179, Willemstad area* *Curacao, N.A.*	962–5200	98	$105–135 EP; villas $165–175 for villas	LRI	272
Lions Dive Hotel & Marina *De Ruyterkade 53* *Curacao, N.A.*	961–1644	72	$110 EP	ITR	273
Park Hotel *Frederikstraat 84, Willemstad* *Curacao, N.A.*	962–3112	86	$30 EP		274
Princess Beach Hotel *near Willemstad* *Curacao, N.A.*	961–4944	202	$140–225 EP	ITR	273
Sonesta Beach Resort *Willemstad* *Curacao, N.A.*			check on status		273
Trupial Inn *Groot Davelaarweg, Willemstad* *Curacao, N.A.*	967–8200	74	$44 EP; apts $55		273
Van der Valk Plaza *Box 229, Willemstad* *Curacao, N.A.*			$100–120 EP		273

DOMINICA, WEST INDIES

	phone 809+	rooms	winter rate for 2	rep	page
Anchorage Hotel *Castle Comfort, in Roseau* *Dominica, W.I.*	448–2638	36	$50–60 EP	RR	288

	phone 809+	rooms	winter rate for 2	rep	page
Castaways Hotel *Box 5, Roseau* *Dominica, W.I.*	449–6244	29	$100 EP	ITR	288
Castle Comfort *Box 63, Roseau* *Dominica, W.I.*	448–2188	10	$70 MAP		292
Coconut Beach *Portsmouth, Box 37* *Dominica, W.I.*	445–5393	15 apts	$65 EP		289
Continental Inn *37 Queen Mary St., Roseau* *Dominica, W.I.*	448–2215	10	$30–40 EP		
Emerald Pool Hotel *Box 20, Roseau* *Dominica, W.I.*	448–4943	10	$25–65 EP		290
EverGreen *Roseau, Box 309* *Dominica, W.I.*	448–3288	10	$70 MAP		290
Fort Young Hotel *Roscay* *Dominica, W.I.*	445–6244	33	$80–110 EP		288
Hamstead Country House *North coast* *Dominica, W.T.*					292
Layou Valley Inn *Box 196, Roseau* *Dominica, W.I.*	449–6203	6	$70 CP $95 MAP	ITR	290
Papillotte Wilderness Retreat *Box 67, Roseau* *Dominica, W.I.*	448–2287	6	$50–60 EP		291
Picard Beach Cottages *Portsmouth* *Dominica, W.I.*	445–5142	18 cots	$100–150 EP 1–4 people	RR	289
Portsmouth Beach Hotel *Box 34, Portsmouth* *Dominica, W.I.*	445–5142	76	$60 EP	RR	289
Reigate Hall Hotel *Box 200, Roseau* *Dominica, W.I.*	448–4031	16	$70–140	ITR	289
Riviere La Croix Estate Hotel *Box 100, Roseau* *Dominica, W.I.*			closed at present time		291
Sans Souci Apartments *L'Aromant* *Dominica, W.I.*		6 apts			290

HOTEL QUICK-REFERENCE CHARTS

	phone 809+	rooms	winter rate for 2	rep	page
Sisserou Hotel *Box 134, Castle Comfort* *Dominica, W.I.*	448–3111	20	$70 CP		289
Springfield Plantation Inn *Imperial Road, in the mountains* *Dominica, W.I.*	449–1401	13	$95 MAP + apts		291
Sunshine Village *Portsmouth* *Dominica, W.I.*					290
Vena's Hotel *48 Cork Street, Roseau* *Dominica, W.I.*	448–3286	14	$15–20 EP		292

DOMINICAN REPUBLIC (REPUBLICA DOMINICA)

	phone 809+	rooms	winter rate for 2	rep	page
Alcazar *Sosua* *Dominican Republic*					339
Los Almendros Beach *Sosua* *Dominican Republic*					339
Bayside Hill *Puerto Plata* *Dominican Republic*					333
Bavaro Beach Resort *Higuey, Punta Cana* *Dominican Republic*	682–2162	600	all incl	BT	344
Bavaro Gardens *Higuey, Punta Cana* *Dominican Republic*	682–2162	401	all-incl	BT	344
Boca Chica Resort *Boca Chica Beach* *Santo Domingo, D.R.*	523–4522	135	$200–220 EP	ITR	311
Bolivar *Av. Bolivar 62* *Santo Domingo, D.R.*					310
Cabanas Playa Cofresi *Santiago Highway* *Puerto Plata, D.R.*	586–2898	60	$60 up		336
Cabarete Beach Hotel *Cabarete (north coast)* *Dominican Republic*		8			341

	phone 809+	rooms	winter rate for 2	rep	page
Caracol *Puerto Plata* *Dominican Republic*					336
Casa de Campo *Aptdo. Postal 140, La Romana* *Dominican Republic*	682–9656	128 + apts + villas	$195–395 EP	PR	326
Hotel Cervantes *Calle Cervantes 202* *Santo Domingo, D.R.*	668–2261	171	$90 EP		310
Club Dominicas *La Romana* *Dominican Republic*					326
Club Nautico *Sosua* *Dominican Republic*					339
Club Mediterranee *Punta Cana (east end)* *Dominican Republic*	687–2767	300	$2300 wk all incl. AP+	CM	344
Continental *Maximo Gomes 16* *Santo Domingo, D.R.*	689–1151	100	$62–105 EP	RR	311
Costambar *Puerto Plata* *Dominican Republic*	586–2911	107	all incl		335
Decameron *Playa Juan Dolio* *Dominican Republic*	529–8531	280	$190–210 AP+	ITR	312
Discovery Bay *Punta Rucia, D.R.*		24	$260 EP	ITR	333
Dominican Concorde *Avenida Anacaona* *Santo Domingo, D.R.*	532–2331	316	$90–185		307
Don Juan Beach Resort *Playa Juan Dolio* *Dominican Republic*	686–6191				312
Dorado Naco Aparta-Hotel *Playa Dorada* *Puerto Plata, D.R.*	586–2019	202	$90–120 1 brm $130–160 2 brm	800+ 322–2388	335
El Embajador *Avenida Sarasota 65* *Santo Domingo, D.R.*	533-2131	309	$80 EP	O	307
Eurotel Playa Dorada *Playa Dorada, North coast* *Puerto Plata, D.R.*	586–3663	402		305+ 591–1954	333

HOTEL QUICK-REFERENCE CHARTS

	phone 809+	rooms	winter rate for 2	rep	page
Flamenco Beach *Playa Dorada* *Puerto Plata, D.R.*	586–6319	310		O	334
Gran Bahia *Samana* *Dominican Republic*				DM	332
Gran Hotel Lina & Casino *Maximo Gomez at 27 Febrero* *Santo Domingo, D.R.*	689–5185	220	$105–200 EP	LRI	308
Heavens *Playa Dorada* *Puerto Plata, D.R.*	586–5250	150	$240–290 AP+	ITR	334
Hotel Hispaniola *Box 1493, Av. G. Washington* *Santo Domingo, D.R.*	533–7111	165	$86–96 EP	PR	308
Jack Tar Village *Playa Dorada* *Puerto Plata, D.R.*	586–3800	197		JT	334
Hotel Jimmeson *Calle Beller* *Puerto Plato, D.R.*					
Metro Hotel and Marina *Playa Juan Dolio* *Dominican Republic*	809+p	180	$80 EP	O	312
Hotel Montemar *Avenida Hnas. Mirabal* *Puerto Plata, D.R.*	586–2800	60	$75	0	336
Hotel Naco & Casino *Av. Tiradentes* *Santo Domingo, D.R.*	562–3100	108			308
Napolitano *Av. G. Washington* *Santo Domingo, D.R.*	687–1131	72			311
Hostal Nicolas de Ovando *Calle Las Damas* *Santo Domingo, D.R.*	687–7181		$50 EP		308
North Shore Hotel *Sosua* *Dominican Republic*					340
Palmas del Mar *Playa Juan Dolio* *Dominican Republic*	689–0055	26	$60–100 EP		312
Playa Canes *Playa Juan Dolio* *Dominican Republic*					

HOTEL QUICK-REFERENCE CHARTS

	phone 809+	rooms	winter rate for 2	rep	page
Playa Confresi *Puerto Plata* *Dominican Republic*					336
Playa Chiquita *Sosua* *Dominican Republic*	689–6191				340
Playa Dorada Beach Resort *Playa Dorada* *Puerto Plata, D.R.*	586–3988				
El Portillo *Playa Las Terrenas* *Samana Peninsula, D.R.*	688–5715	26 cot			332
La Posada *Altos de Chavon, La Romana area* *Dominican Republic*	682–9656	10	$90–130 EP	P	327
Puerto Plata Beach Resort *Box 600, Puerto Plata* *Dominican Republic*	586–4243	216	$60–100 EP	ITR	335
Punta Cana Beach Resort *Punta Cana Beach (east end)* *Dominican Republic*	686–0084	350 + 50 villas	$180–230 MAP	ITR	344
Punta Garza Beach Club *Playa Juan Dolio, Postal 1340* *Dominican Republic*	533–2131	46	$50–75 EP		313
Punta Goleta *Cabarete (north coast)* *Dominican Republic*	531–3036	128 + 3-brm villas	$125 EP	800 + 874–4637	341
Playa Dorada Hotel & Casino *Playa Dorada* *Puerto Plata, D.R.*	586–3988	225	$120 EP	800 + 628–2216	334
Playa Dorada Princess *Playa Dorada* *Puerto Plata, D.R.*	586–5350	336	$120 EP	800 + 628–2216	324
Ramada Jaragua Resort, Casino & Spa *Avenida G. Washington* *Santo Domingo, D.R.*	686–2222	355	$170–210 EP	RA	
Sand Castle Beach Resort *Puerto Chiquito, Sosua* *Dominican Republic*	571–2549				340
San Geranimo *Box 15, Av. Independencia* *Santo Domingo, D.R.*	533–8181	72			311
Hotel Santo Domingo *Box 2212, Av. A. Lincoln* *Santo Domingo, D.R.*	532–0511		$125–150 EP	PR	309

HOTEL QUICK-REFERENCE CHARTS

	phone 809+	rooms	winter rate for 2	rep	page
Sea Shells *Playa Juan Dolio Dominican Republic*	529–8851	71	$100 AP	ITR	313
Sheraton Santo Domingo *Box 1493, Av. G. Washington Santo Domingo, D.R.*	685–5151	260	$90–300 EP	S	309
Hotel Sosua *Sosua Dominican Republic*					340
Sosua Sol *Sosua Dominican Republic*					340
Sosua Palm Village *Sosua, D.R.*		224		LRI	
Talanquera *Playa Juan Dolio Dominican Republic*					
Tropicana Caribe *Playa Dorada Dominican Republic*					336
Victoria Resort *Box 22 Puerto Plata, D.R.*	586–5145	120	$135–345 CP	RR	335
Villas Caribe *Box 589, Playa Dorada Puerto Plata, D.R.*	586–4811	130	$85–110 EP		336
Villas Doradas *Box 1370, Playa Dorada Puerto Plata, D.R.*	586–3000	207	$90–120 EP	O	336
Villa Los Coralillos *Sosua Dominican Republic*					340
Villas del Mar *Playa Juan Dolio Dominican Republic*	529–3735	52	$50 EP		313
Yaroa *Sosua Dominican Republic*					341

GRENADA, WEST INDIES (Grenada Hotel Association; 800+322–1753)

	phone 809+	rooms	winter rate for 2	rep	page
Balisier *Richmond Hill, St. George's Grenada, W.I.*	440–2346	15	$70–95 EP	ITR	

HOTEL QUICK-REFERENCE CHARTS

	phone 809+	rooms	winter rate for 2	rep	page
Blue Horizons *Box 41, Grand Anse* *St. George's, Grenada, W.I.*	444–4316	32	$120–145 EP	ITR	354
Calabash Hotel *Box 382, Anse aux Epines* *St. George's, Grenada, W.I.*	444–4334	34	$250–430 MAP	RL, ITR	352
Cinnamon Hill *Box 292* *St. George's, Grenada, W.I.*	444–4301	20 apts	$121 1 brm EP	ITR	355
Coyaba *Box 336* *St. George's, Grenada, W.I.*	444–4129	40	$150 EP	ITR	353
Crescent Inn *Box 336, Belmont* *St. George's, Grenada, W.I.*	444–3089	12	$60 EP	ITR	356
Flamboyant Hotel *Box 214* *St. George's, Grenada, W.I.*	444–4247	46	$85–105 EP + apts	ITR	355
Gem Holiday Beach *c/o BBC & GEM; Mourne Rouge* *St.George's, Grenada, W.I.*	444–4224	20	$50–70 EP + apts	ITR	
Hibiscus Inn *Box 279, Morne Rouge* *St. George's, Grenada, W.I.*	444–4233	10	$80–90 EP	ITR	355
Holiday Haven *St. George's, Grenada, W.I.*	444–4325	12	$400 EP wk		355
Horseshoe Beach Hotel *Box 174, L'Anse aux Epines* *St. George's, Grenada, W.I.*	444–4244	18	$110–125 EP	ITR	354
Maffiken Apts *St George's* *Grenada, W.I.*					355
Mamma's Lodge *St. George's* *Granada, W.I.*					356
Morne Rouge *St. George's* *Granada, W.I.*					355
No Problem Apartments *Box 280* *St. George's, Grenada, W.I.*	444–4634	20 apts	$85 EP	ITR	356
Ramada Renaissance Beach Resort *Box 441, Grand Anse Beach* *St. George's, Grenada, W.I.*	444–4371	186	$150 EP	RA	354
La Sargasse Nature Centre *St. George's, Grenada, W.I.*	444–6458	4 apts	$50 EP		355

	phone 809+	rooms	winter rate for 2	rep	page
St. Ann's Guest House *Paddock* *St. George's, Grenada, W.I.*	444–2717	15	$35 CP		357
Siesta Holiday Apts *Box 27* *St. George's, Grenada, W.I.*	444–4646	25	$70–95 EP	ITR	
St. James Hotel *Grand Etang Road* *St. George's, Grenada, W.I.*	444–2041	14	$46 EP		357
Secret Harbour *Box 11, L'Anse aux Epines* *St. George's, Grenada, W.I.*	444–4439	20	$1075 wk Apt	ITR	354
Spice Island Inn *Box 6, Grand Anse Beach* *St. George's, Grenada, W.I.*	444–4423	56	$320–450 MAP	ITR	354
Southwinds Apts. *St. George's* *Ganada, W.I.*	444–4310			ITR	
True Blue Inn *True Blue* *St. George's, Grenada, W.I.*					356
Twelve Degrees North *Box 241* *St. George's, Grenada, W.I.*	444–4580	8 apts	$130 EP 1 brm	ITR	356
Wave Crest *St. George's* *Grenada, W.I.*	444–4116	apts	$55–85 EP	ITR	
Carriacou Island Caribbean Inn *Prospect, Carriacou Island* *% Grenada, W.I.*					364
Cassada Bay *Hillsborough, Carriacou Island* *% Box 279, Grenada, W.I.*	443–4433	18 units	$85 MAP		365
Mermaid Beach Hotel *Hillsborough, Carriacou Island* *% Grenada, W.I.*	443–7484	12	$65 MAP	ITR	
Silver Beach *Hillsborough, Carriacou Island* *% Grenada, W.I.*	443–7337	18 incl. apts	$90–105 EP	ITR	

GUADELOUPE, FRENCH WEST INDIES (ANTILLES FRANCAISES)

	phone 011+590+	rooms	winter rate for 2 $ or F	rep	page
Arawak *Gosier* *97190 Guadeloupe, F.W.I.*	84.24.24	160	$145–180 CP		374
Auberge du Grand Large *Route de la Plage, Ste. Anne* *97180 Guadeloupe, F.W.I.*	88.20.06	10	$100 CP	ITR	379
Auberge J.J. *Gosier* *97190 Guadeloupe, F.W.I.*	84.14.85	12			380
Auberge de la Vieille Tour *Gosier* *97190 Guadeloupe, F.W.I.*	84.23.23	80	$150–200 CP	PLM	374
L'Auberge de la Distillerie *Petit Bourg, Basse-Terre* *97170 Guadeloupe, F.W.I.*	94.25.91	15	$100–120 EP		379
Callinago Beach PLM-Azur *Gosier* *Guadeloupe, F.W.I.*	84.25.25	40	$88–102 EP	PLM	
Callinago Village PLM-Azur *Gosier* *97190 Guadeloupe, F.W.I.*	84.25.25	93 st 22 duplex	$102–118 EP	PLM	
Canabis *Gosier* *97190 Guadeloupe, F.W.I.*	84.11.83	13			380
Cap sud Caraibes *Petit Havre* *97180 Guadeloupe, F.W.I.*	88.96.02	12	$130 CP		380
Club Mediterranee La Caravelle *Ste. Anne* *97180 Guadeloupe, F.W.I.*	84.21.00	300	$2640 wk all incl AP+	CM	374
La Cocoteraie *Ste. Anne* *97180 Guadeloupe, F.W.I.*					375
La Creole Beach Hotel *Box 19, Gosier* *97190 Guadeloupe, F.W.I.*	011 +590+ 84.26.26	156	$186–246 CP	JdeL	375
Ecotel Guadelôupe *Gosier* *97190 Guadeloupe, F.W.I.*	84.21.21	44	748 CP	BW	375
Les Flamboyants *Gosier* *97190 Guadeloupe, F.W.I.*					380

HOTEL QUICK-REFERENCE CHARTS

	phone 011+590+	rooms	winter rate for 2 $ or F	rep	page
Grand Anse Hotel *Trois Rivieres* *97114 Guadeloupe, F.W.I.*	92.92.21	16			380
Hamak Beach Hotel *Saint Francois* *97118 Guadeloupe, F.W.I.*	88.59.99	56	$300–350 EP	JdeL, CA	376
Marina Baie de Boucanier *Saint Francois* *Guadeloupe, F.W.I.*		42 apts			378
Les Marines de St. Francois *St. Francois* *97118 Guadeloupe, F.W.I.*	88.59.55	230 apts	F2867 wk	RR	381
Marissol PLM-Azur *Bas du Fort* *97190 Guadeloupe, F.W.I.*	90.84.44	200	$104–148 EP	PLM	376
Meridien St. Francois *Saint Francois* *97118 Guadeloupe, F.W.I.*	88.51.00	272	$160–230 EP	M	376
Novotel Fleur d'Epee *Bas du Fort* *97190 Guadeloupe, F.W.I.*	90.81.49	180	$158 EP	AC	376
PLM-Azur Village Soleil (Sun Village) *Bas du Fort* *97190 Guadeloupe, F.W.I.*	90.85.76	100 apts	$70–85 EP	PH	378
Plantation Ste. Marthe *Ste. Anne* *97180 Guadeloupe, F.W.I*					377
Relais du Moulin *Chateaubrun, near Ste. Anne* *97180 Guadeloupe, F.W.I.*	88.23.96	40	$125 CP	JdeL, ITR	379
Relais Bleus de la Grand Soufriere *Saint Claude, above Basse Terre* *Guadeloupe, F.W.I.*	80.01.27	22	F 400–500 EP		379
Relais Bleus du Madrepore *Bas du Fort* *Guadeloupe, F.W.I.*	90.81.46	30 apts	F580–680		381
Residence Canella Beach *SNC LaVerdure, BP 73B* *Gosier, Guadeloupe, F.W.I.*	83.48.40	150 units	$130 up	ITR	377
Residence Karukera *Pointe des Chateaux* *97118 Guadeloupe, F.W.I.*	88.44.03	30 apts	$154–180		378

HOTEL QUICK-REFERENCE CHARTS

	phone 011 + 590 +	rooms	winter rate for 2 $ or F	rep	page
Residences du Lagon *Saint Francois* *Guadeloupe, F.W.I.*		20 villas			
La Rotabas *Box 30, Ste. Anne* *97180 Guadeloupe, F.W.I.*	8.25.60	44	$150 EP	ITR	380
Salako *Gosier* *97190 Guadeloupe, F.W.I.*	84.22.22	120	$185 CP	JdeL	377
Sprim Hotel *Bas du Fort* *97190 Guadeloupe, F.W.I.*	90.82.90	25 apts	$99–123 CP	ITR	378
La Toubana *Ste. Anne* *97180 Guadeloupe, F.W.I.*	88.25.78	32 units	$207–245 CP	ITR	380
Touring Hotel *Fort Royale* *97190 Guadeloupe, F.W.I*					377
Les Trois Mats *Saint Francois* *97118 Guadeloupe, F.W.I.*	88.59.99	36 apts	$150 EP	JdL	378
Village Soleil *Bas du Fort* *97190 Guadeloupe, F.W.I.*					378
Terre de Haute, Les Saintes islands Guadeloupe					
Les Anacardiers *Terre de Haut, Les Saintes Islands* *% 97137 Guadeloupe, F.W.I.*		10	F550–750		388
Bois Joli *Terre de Haut, Les Saintes Islands* *% 97137 Guadeloupe, F.W.I.*	99.50.38	21	$108–120 CP	ITR	388
Jeanne d'Arc *Terre de Haut, Les Saintes Islands* *% 97137 Guadeloupe, F.W.I.*	99.50.41	10	F320 CP		388
Kanaoa *Terre de Haut, Les Saintes Islands* *% 97137 Guadeloupe, F.W.I.*	99.51.36	14	F250 CP		388
PLM-Azur Los Santos *Terre de Haut, Les Saintes Islands* *% 97137 Guadeloupe, F.W.I.*	99.50.40	54	$120 EP	PLM	389
Le Saintoise *Terre de Haut, Les Saintes Islands* *% 97137 Guadeloupe, F.W.I.*	99.52.50	10			388

HOTEL QUICK-REFERENCE CHARTS

HAITI, WEST INDIES

	phone 011 + 509 +	rooms	winter rate for 2	rep	page
Bay Hotel/Ouanga Bay *Box 1605, Carries* *Haiti, West Indies*	12–5774	40	on request		401
Hotel Beck *Box 48, Cap Haitien* *Haiti, West Indies*	32–0001	23	$65 MAP		412
Brise de Mer (Pension) *Carenage #24, Cap Haitien* *Haiti, West Indies*	32–0821	16	$34 MAP		412
Castel Haiti *Box 446, Port-au-Prince* *Haiti, West Indies*	12–0393	90	$49–75 EP	ITR	398
Club Mediterranee Magic Isle *Box 1575, Montrouis* *Haiti, West Indies*	12–4400	350	$1600 wk AP + all incl	CM	399
Christopher *Box 962, Port-au-Prince* *Haiti, West Indies*	12–1452	83	$50–60 EP		403
Coconut Villa *Delmas 19, Port-au-Prince* *Haiti, West Indies*	16–1691	50	$42–46 FB	ITR	403
Cormier Plage *Box 70, Cap Haitien* *Haiti, West Indies*	32–1000	32	$80–90 MAP	ITR	412
Hotel Craft *Place de l'Eglise, Jacmel* *Haiti, West Indies*	18–2641	12	$40 MAP		416
Cyvadier Place Hotel *near Jacmel* *Haiti, West Indies*			on request		416
Doux Sejour *Box 601, Petionville* *Haiti, West Indies*	17–1560	30	$36 EP	AA	403
El Rancho *Box 71, Petionville* *Haiti, West Indies*	17–2080	105	$75–175 EP	ITR	398
Grand Hotel Oloffson *Box 1720, Port-au-Prince* *Haiti, West Indies*	13–4000	22	$50–100 CP	ITR	399
Hostellerie du Roi Christophe *Box 34, Cap Haitien* *Haiti, West Indies*	32–0414	18	$58–75 MAP	ITR	412

HOTEL QUICK-REFERENCE CHARTS · · · 843

	phone 011 + 509 +	rooms	winter rate for 2	rep	page
Ibo Beach *Box 1237, Caique Island* *Haiti, West Indies*	17–1200	60	$75 CP	ITR	401
Hotel La Jacmelienne *Rue Ste Anne, Jacmel* *Haiti, West Indies*	12–4899	30	$98 MAP		416
Jolly Beach *Box 15418, Petionville* *Haiti, West Indies*	12–9653	20	$88 MAP	HTR	401
Kaliko Beach Resort *Box 338, La Gonave Bay* *Haiti, West Indies*	12–5773	40	$94–75 MAP	ITR	401
Kyona Beach *Box 1647, Nationale #1* *Haiti, West Indies*	12–6788	20	$65 CP	ITR	401
Manoir Alexandre *36 rue d'Orleans, Jacmel* *Haiti, W.I.*	18–2711	6	$50 MAP		416
Marabou *Petionville* *Haiti, West Indies*			on request		403
Mont Joli *Box 12, Cap Haitien* *Haiti, West Indies*	32–0300	45	$80 EP	ITR	412
Hotel Montana *Box 523, Petionville* *Haiti, West Indies*	17–1920	70	$70–85 EP	ITR	402
Moulin Sur Mer *Route Nationale, Montrouis* *Haiti, West Indies*	12–1918	28	$60–90 EP	ITR	402
Le Plaza Holiday Inn *Box 338, Rue Capois, Port-au-Prince* *Haiti, West Indies*	12–4606	80	$65–90 EP	HI	399
Prince Hotel *Port au Prince* *Haiti, West Indies*					399
Royal Haitian & Casino *Box 2075, Martissant, Port-au-Prince* *Haiti, West Indies*	14–0258	75	$90 CP		399
Splendid *Box 1214, Avenue N, Port au Prince* *Haiti, West Indies*	15–0116	40	$85–100 EP	RS	400
Taino Beach Hotel *Box 1253, Grand Goave* *Haiti, West Indies*	12–7009	59	$80 MAP		402

HOTEL QUICK-REFERENCE CHARTS

	phone 011 + 509 +	rooms	winter rate for 2	rep	page
Villa Creole *Box 126, Petionville* *Haiti, West Indies*	17–1570	70	$70–100 EP	ITR	400
Le Xaragua *Box 1734, Deluge* *Haiti, West Indies*	12–5000	48	$90 MAP		402

JAMAICA, WEST INDIES: Reservations can be made at many Jamaican hotels through the Jamaica Reservation Service, 800 + 526–2422

	phone 809 +	rooms	winter rate for 2	rep	page
Admiralty Club and Marina *Box 188* *Port Antonio, Jamaica, W.I.*	993–2667	25	$85–140 EP		478
Altamont Court Hotel *Altamont Crescent* *Kingston, Jamaica, W.I.*					430
Ambiance *Box 20, Runaway Bay* *Jamaica, W.I.*	973–2066	80			475
Arawak Inn *Mammee Bay* *Ocho Rios, Jamaica, W.I.*	972–2318	20	$50–80 EP		469
Astra Hotel *Box 60, 62 Ward Av.* *Mandeville, Jamaica, W.I.*	962–3265	22	$50–90 EP	JRS	437
Banana Shout *Negril* *Jamaica, W.I.*					459
Bayshore Townhouse Apartments *Ironshore* *Montego Bay, Jamaica, W.I.*					447
Belvedere *33 Gloucester Av.* *Montego Bay, Jamaica, W.I.*	952–0593	27	$60–70 EP	RR	448
Blue Harbour *Box 212* *Montego Bay, Jamaica, W.I.*	952–5445	22	$46–55 EP		448
Bonnie View *Box 82* *Port Antonio, Jamaica, W.I.*	993–2752	26	$50 EP		479
Boscobel Beach Resort *Box 63* *Ocho Rios, Jamaica, W.I.*	974–3291	120	all incl	EX	465

HOTEL QUICK-REFERENCE CHARTS · · · 845

	phone 809+	rooms	winter rate for 2	rep	page
Buccaneer Inn *Montego Bay* *Jamaica, W.I.*		48			448
Caribbean Isle *Runaway Bay* *Jamaica, W.I.*	973–2364	23			475
Caribbean Village *Runaway Bay* *Jamaica, W.I.*					476
Chalet Caribe Hotel *Box 365, Reading* *Montego Bay, Jamaica, W.I.*	952–1365	30	$40–60 EP	HTR	449
Charela Inn *Box 33* *Negril, Jamaica, W.I.*	957–4277	26	$110–140 EP	RR	460
Chukka Cove Villas *Box 160* *Ocho Rios, Jamaica, W.I.*	974–2593				
Club Caribbean *Runaway Bay* *Jamaica, W.I.*	973–3507	116	$196–214 MAP	ITR	475
Coral Cliff *Box 253* *Montego Bay, Jamaica, W.I.*	952–4130	32		HTR	448
Couples *Tower Isle, St. Mary* *Ocho Rios, Jamaica, W.I.*	974–4271	139	$1990–2240 per wk AP-plus	EX	465
Country Cottages *Negril* *Jamaica, W.I.*					459
Courtleigh *31 Trafalgar Rd., Kingston 10* *Jamaica, W.I.*	926–8174	39	$55 EP	JRS	429
Crystal Waters *Negril* *Jamaica, W.I.*					459
DeMontevin Lodge *21 Fort George St.* *Port Antonio, Jamaica, W.I.*	993–2604	13	$25 EP	JRS	480
Doctor's Cave Beach *Box 94* *Montego Bay, Jamaica, W.I.*	952–4355	75	$90–110 EP	RR	441
Dragon Bay *Port Antonio, Jamaica, W.I.*					479

HOTEL QUICK-REFERENCE CHARTS

	phone 809+	rooms	winter rate for 2	rep	page
Drumville Cove *Negril* *Jamaica, W.I.*					459
Eaton Hall Beach Hotel *Box 112* *Runaway Bay, Jamaica, W.I.*	973–3404	36+ 16 villas	$195 MAP		475
Enchanted Garden *Carinosa Gardens* *Ocho Rios, Jamaica, W.I.*				FDR	465
Fantasy Resort *2 Kent Ave., Box 61* *Montego Bay, Jamaica, W.I.*	952–4150	119	$115 EP	ITR	442
Fern Hill Club *Port Antonio, Jamaica, W.I.*	993–3243	18	$700–800		479
Fisherman's Point *Ocean Village area* *Ocho Rios, Jamaica, W.I.*		apts			468
Foote Prints in The Sand *Negril, Jamaica, W.I.*	957–4300	apts		JRS	460
Four Seasons Hotel *Box 190, 18 Ruthven Rd.* *Kingston 10, Jamaica, W.I.*	926–8805	35	$40 EP		429
Franklyn D. Resort *Runaway Bay, Jamaica, W.I.*	973–3067	110		FDR	476
Frenchman's Cove *Box 101* *Port Antonio, Jamaica, W.I.*	993–3224	30+ villas		JRS	479
Goblin Hill Villas *Box 26* *Port Antonio, Jamaica, W.I.*	993–3286	44			479
Gloucestershire House *Gloucester Rd.* *Montego Bay, Jamaica, W.I.*	952–4422		$95–115 EP	ITR	442
Grand Lido *Box 88* *Negril, Jamaica, W.I.*	957–4317		$500–550 AP+; $3360–3760 wk; all incl	EX	457
Half Moon Resort *Box 80, Rose Hall area* *Montego Bay, Jamaica, W.I.*	953–2211	197	$250–380 EP	ER, RR	442
Heart Academy *Runaway Bay* *Jamaica, W.I.*	973–2671	20			477

HOTEL QUICK-REFERENCE CHARTS · · · 847

	phone 809+	rooms	winter rate for 2	rep	page
Hibiscus Lodge *Box 52* *Ocho Rios, Jamaica, W.I.*	974–2269	20	$55 EP		469
High Hope Estate *Box 11, St. Ann's Bay* *Jamaica, W.I.*	927–2277	7	$	818+ 888–3762	469
Hedonism II *Box 25* *Negril, Jamaica, W.I.*	957–4200	280	all incl	EX	457
Indies House *5 Holborn Road* *New Kingston, Jamaica, W.I.*	926–2952	14	$35–45 EP		430
Inn on the Beach *Box 342, Turtle Beach* *Ocho Rios, Jamaica, W.I.*	974–2782	46	$66 EP	JRS	470
Ironshore Resort Villas *Box 108* *Montego Bay, Jamaica, W.I.*	952–2854	13	$220–243 EP; 2 brm	ITR	
Ivor Jack's Hill *Kingston, Jamaica, W.I.*					429
Jack Tar Montego Beach Hotel *Box 144* *Montego Bay, Jamaica, W.I.*	952–4340	127	$125 all incl	JT	443
Jamaica Inn *Box 1* *Ocho Rios, Jamaica, W.I.*	974–2514	45	$350–400 AP	RM	466
Jamaica-Jamaica *Box 58* *Runaway Bay, Jamaica, W.I.*	973–2436	152	all incl	EX	476
Jamaica Vacation Villas *Ironshore* *Montego Bay, Jamaica, W.I.*	952–2500	many villas	on request	HTR	477
Jamaica Palace Hotel *Box 277* *Port Antonio, Jamaica, W.I.*	993–2020	80			478
Little Pub *Box 256* *Ocho Rios, Jamaica, W.I.*	974–5826	25			470
Mahogany Inn *Negril, Jamaica, W.I.*					461
Mandeville Hotel *Box 78* *Mandeville, Jamaica, W.I.*	962–2460	60	$40–90 EP	JRS	438
Marshall's Pen *Mandeville, Jamaica, W.I.*					438

HOTEL QUICK-REFERENCE CHARTS

	phone 809+	rooms	winter rate for 2	rep	page
Mayfair Hotel *Box 163, Kingston 10* *Jamaica, W.I.*	926–1610	30	$40–50 EP	JRS	429
Medallion Hall Hotel *53 Hope Rd.* *Kingston 6, Jamaica, W.I.*	927–5721		J415.65– 552.60		430
Montego Bay Club *White Sands Beach P.O.* *Montego Bay, Jamaica, W.I.*	952–4310	60	$95–125 EP	ITR	
Morgans Harbour *Port Royal* *Kingston 1, Jamaica, W.I.*	924–8464	20		JRS	428
Native Son Villas *Negril* *Jamaica, W.I.*					459
Negril Beach Club *Box 7* *Negril, Jamaica, W.I.*	957–4220	80	$80–130 EP	AWI	459
Negril Cabins *Negril, Jamaica, W.I.*	957–4350	10 apts	$55	VN	461
Negril Gardens *Negril, Jamaica, W.I.*	957–4408	54	$125–135 EP		460
Negril Inn *Negril, Jamaica, W.I.*	957–4209	46	$140 AP		457
Ocean Edge Resort *Negril-west* *Jamaica, W.I.*					461
Oceana Kingston *Box 986, 2 Kings St.* *Kingston, Jamaica, W.I.*	922–0920	250	$80 EP	HTR	428
Ocean View Guest House *Box 210, Sunset Ave.* *Montego Bay, Jamaica, W.I.*	952–2662	12	$28–30 EP		449
Ocean Pines *Montego Freeport* *Jamaica, W.I.*					447
The Palms *Box 186, Rose Hall* *Montego Bay, Jamaica, W.I.*	953–2160	24 apts	$125–320	ITR	447
Paradise View *Negril, Jamaica, W.I.*					457
Pegasus Forte *Box 333, 81 Knutsford Av.* *Kingston 10, Jamaica, W.I.*	809+ 926–3690	350	$140–155 EP	FH	427

HOTEL QUICK-REFERENCE CHARTS · · · 849

	phone 809+	rooms	winter rate for 2	rep	page
Pineapple Penthouse Hotel *Box 263* *Ocho Rios, Jamaica, W.I.*	974–2727	24	on request		470
Pine Grove Chalets *Blue Mountains* *Kingston, Jamaica, W.I.*	922–8705				430
Plantation Inn *Box 2* *Ocho Rios, Jamaica, W.I.*	974–2501	79	$195–240 MAP	ER	466
Poinciana Beach Villas *Negril, Jamaica, W.I.*	957–4256	villas	$85–230		458
Portside Villas *Discovery Bay, Jamaica, W.I.*	973–2007	316 apts, villas	$92 st. 103 1 brm	ITR	476
Radisson Cibonney *Ocho Rios, Jamaica, W.I.*		286	$550–700 AP+	RH	466
Ramada Resort & Beach Club *Ocho Rios* *Jamaica, W.I.*				RA	467
Reading Reef *Montego Bay* *Jamaica, W.I.*					443
Richmond Hill *Box 362* *Montego Bay, Jamaica, W.I.*	952–3859	23	$75–85 EP	WI	448
Rose Hall Holiday Inn *Box 480, Rose Hall* *Montego Bay, Jamaica, W.I.*	953–2485	516	$85–115 EP	HI	443
Rock Cliff Hotel *Negril-west* *Jamaica, W.I.*					461
Round Hill Resort *Box 64* *Montego Bay, Jamaica, W.I.*	952–5150	101	$260–435 CP	ER	443
Royal Court *Box 195* *Montego Bay, Jamaica, W.I.*	952–4531	25	$60–85 EP	ITR	449
Samsara *Negril-west* *Jamaica, W.I.*					461
Sandals Dunn River *Box 51* *Ocho Rios, Jamaica, W.I.*		256	$2150–2840 wk, all incl.	SA	465
Sandals Montego Bay *Box 100, Kent Av.* *Montego Bay, Jamaica, W.I.*	952–5510	243	$2015–2480 wk, all incl	SA	444

	phone 809+	rooms	winter rate for 2	rep	page
Sandals Carlyle Beach Hotel *Box 412* *Montego Bay, Jamaica, W.I.*	952–4140	52	all incl	SA	444
Sandals Negril *Negril, Jamaica, W.I.*	957–4338	199	$2150–2840 wk, all-incl	SA	458
Sandals Ocho Rios *Box 771, Main St.* *Ocho Rios, Jamaica, W.I.*	974–5691	238	$2015–2280 wk, all-incl	SA	467
Sandals Royal Caribbean *Box 167* *Montego Bay, Jamaica, W.I.*	953–2231	190	$2015–2280 wk, all incl	SA	444
Sandcastles *Ocho Rios* *Jamaica, W.I.*					469
Sans Souci Hotel, Club, Spa *Box 103* *Ocho Rios, Jamaica, W.I.*	974–2353	67	$240–450 EP	FDR	467
Sea Garden Beach Resort *Box 300, Kent Avenue* *Montego Bay, Jamaica, W.I.*	952–4780	100	all incl.	800+ 433–4643	445
Sea Grape Villas *Tower Isle* *Ocho Rios, Jamaica, W.I.*		4 villas	$150 EP $2200 wk.	800+ 637–3608	
Seawind Beach Resort *Box 1168, Montego Freeport* *Montego Bay, Jamaica, W.I.*	952–4070	430 incl. apts	$95–155 EP	RR	445
Shaw Park Beach Hotel *Box 17, Cutlass Bay* *Ocho Rios, Jamaica, W.I.*	974–2552	118	$150–238 EP	RM	468
Singles *Negril* *Jamaica, W.I.*				FDR	
Summerset Village *Box 4* *Negril, Jamaica, W.I.*	957–4409	35	$40–175 EP		460
Sunflower Beach Resort *Box 150* *Runaway Bay, Jamaica, W.I.*	973–2171	80	$100 EP	ITR	476
Sunset Inn Apartments *Altamont Crescent* *Kingston, Jamaica, W.I.*					430
Swept Away *Long Bay* *Negril, Jamaica, W.I.*	957–4061	125	$2350–2550 wk AP+	800+ 526–2422	458

HOTEL QUICK-REFERENCE CHARTS

	phone 809+	rooms	winter rate for 2	rep	page
The Tallyman *Box 880, Westgate Hills* *Montego Bay, Jamaica, W.I.*	952–0722	18 apts	$140 EP 2-brm	212+ 832–2277	447
Terra Nova *17 Waterloo Rd.* *Kingston 10, Jamaica, W.I.*	926–2211	35	$70–150 EP	ITR	428
Tree House Club & Cottages *Box 29* *Negril, Jamaica, W.I.*	957–4287	cots	$95–250 EP	RR	458
Toby Inn *Box 467* *Montego Bay, Jamaica, W.I.*	952–4370	28	$50–55 EP	JRS	448
Treasure Beach *South coast* *Jamaica, W.I.*					438
Trelawny Beach Club *Box 54* *Falmouth, Jamaica, W.I.*	954–2450	350	$220–240 MAP	LRI	445
Trident Villas *Box 119* *Port Antonio, Jamaica, W.I.*	993–2602	28 villas + suites	$250–500 MAP	FR	478
Tropical Inn *19 Cliveden Ave.* *Kingston 6, Jamaica, W.I.*	927–9931	24	$55 EP		430
Tryall Golf & Beach Club *Sandy Bay Post Office* *Hanover, Jamaica, W.I.*	952–5110	50 rms + villas	$280–360 MAP	ER	445
Turtle Beach Towers *Box 73* *Ocho Rios, Jamaica, W.I.*	974–2801	120 apts	$121–132 EP apts	ITR	469
T-Water Cottages *Box 11* *Negril, Jamaica, W.I.*	957–4270	69 incl st	$85–105 EP		458
Upper Deck *Montego Bay, Jamaica, W.I.*		106 apts	$75 EP studio	RR	447
Villas Negril *Box 35, Negril Square* *Negril, Jamaica, W.I.*	957–4250	60 apts	$60–85 EP	RM	460
Villa Bella Hotel *Christiana* *Jamaica, W.I.*					438
West Palm Hotel *Box 107, Fort Charlotte Rd.* *Lucea, Jamaica, W.I.*	956–2321	15			436

HOTEL QUICK-REFERENCE CHARTS

	phone 809+	rooms	winter rate for 2	rep	page
Wexford Court *Box 108, Gloucester Ave.* *Montego Bay, Jamaica, W.I.*	952–2854	38	$100–110 EP	ITR	446
Wilton House *Box 20, Bluefields* *Westmoreland, Jamaica, W.I.*	955–2852	4	$80 MAP		438
Winged Victory *Box 333, 5 Queen Dr.* *Montego Bay, Jamaica, W.I.*	952–3891	27	$90–225 EP	ITR	449
Wyndham New Kingston *Box 112, Knutsford Blvd.* *Kingston 10, Jamaica, W.I.*	926–5430	400	$95–200 EP	WH	428
Wyndham Rose Hall *Box 999, Rose Hall* *Montego Bay, Jamaica, W.I.*	953–2650	500	$100–120 EP	WH	446

MARTINIQUE, FRENCH WEST INDIES (ANTILLES FRANCAISE)

	phone 011+596+	rooms	winter rate for 2 $ or F	rep	page
Alamada *Anse Mitan* *97229 Martinique, F.W.I.*	66.03.19	24	F490 EP		491
Anchorage Hotel *Ste-Anne* *Martinique, F.W.I.*	76.73.74	200			488
Auberge de L'Anse Mitan *Anse Mitan, Trois Ilets* *97229 Martinique, F.W.I.*	66.03.19	20	F300 CP		494
Bakoua Beach *Pointe du Bout* *97229 Martinique, F.W.I.*	66.02.02	100	$220–250 CP	AC	488
Baliser *Fort-de-France* *97200 Martinique, F.W.I.*	71.46.54	23	F274 EP		494
La Bateliere *Schoelcher* *97233 Martinique, F.W.I.*	71.90.41	215	$110–200 CP	RR	488
Bambou *Anse Mitan* *97229 Martinique, F.W.I.*	66.01.39	118	F400 CP		491
Calalou Hotel *Anse a l'Ane, Trois Ilet* *97229 Martinique, F.W.I.*	76.31.67	36	F860–930 MAP	ITR	494

	phone 011 + 596 +	rooms	winter rate for 2 $ or F	rep	page
Carayou PLM-Azur *Pointe du Bout* *97229 Martinique, F.W.I.*	66.04.04	200	$100–125 EP	PLM	489
Cariabe Auberge *Trois Ilets* *97229 Martinique, F.W.I.*	76.03.19	19	F290–430 CP	ITR	494
Club Mediterranee Les Boucaniers *Point Marin* *97180 Martinique, F.W.I.*	76.72.72	300	$2300 wk AP + all incl	CM	489
Diamant Marine Hotel *Diamant* *Martinique, F.W.I.*				AC	
Diamant Novotel *Pointe de la Chery, Diamant* *97223 Martinique, F.W.I.*	76.42.42	174	$162 EP	AC	490
Diamant Les Bains *Diamant* *97223 Martinique, F.W.I.*	76.40.14	24	F350–450 CP		492
Dunette Hotel *Ste. Anne* *97227 Martinique, F.W.I.*	76.73.90	18	F430–480 CP		494
Ecole Hoteliere *Fort de France* *97200 Martinique, F.W.I.*					490
Le Fregate Bleu *near Trinite* *Martinique, F.W.I.*			$200–225 EP		492
Imperatrice *Place de la Savane, Ft. de France* *97200 Martinique, F.W.I.*	63.06.82	24	F350 CP	ITR	494
Imperatrice Village *Anse Mitan* *97229 Martinique, F.W.I.*					490
Lafayette *5 rue de la Liberte, Ft. de France* *97200 Martinique, F.W.I.*	73.80.50	24	F345 CP	ITR	495
Leyritz Plantation *Basse-Pointe* *97218 Martinique, F.W.I.*	75.53.92	25	$112–168 CP	JdeL	493
Le Madras *Tartane* *Martinique, F.W.I.*					493
La Malmaison *rue de la Liberte* *97200 Martinique, F.W.I.*					495

HOTEL QUICK-REFERENCE CHARTS

	phone 011+596+	rooms	winter rate for 2 $ or F	rep	page
Manoir de Beauregard *Chemin des Salines* *97227 Martinique, F.W.I.*	76.73.40	32	$126 CP	RR	493
Meridien Trois Ilets *Pointe du Bout* *97229 Martinique, F.W.I.*	66.00.00	303	$130–150 EP	M	490
Le Panoramic *Anse a l'Ane* *Martinique, F.W.I.*					491
La Pagerie *Pointe du Bout* *97229 Martinique, F.W.I.*	66.05.30	98	$70–80 EP	PH	491
Residence Grand Large *St. Luce* *Martinique, F.W.I.*	62.54.42	18	F285 EP		492
Rivage Hotel *Anse Mitan* *97229 Martinique, F.W.I.*					
St. Aubin Hotel *Box 52, Petite Riviere Salee* *97220 Martinique, F.W.I.*	69.34.77	15	$150 CP	ITR	493
Victoria Hotel *Rond Point, Ft. de France* *9112678 Martinique, F.W.I.*	60.56.78	27	F300 EP	ITR	495
Village Club *Anse Caritan* *97227 Martinique, F.W.I.*	76.74.12	94 apts		ITR	492

MONTSERRAT, BRITISH WEST INDIES

	phone 809+	rooms	winter rate for 2	rep	page
Alliouqana *Plymouth* *Montserrat, B.W.I.*		not open at press time			505
Belham Valley *Plymouth* *Montserrat, B.W.I.*					
Coconut Hill Hotel *Box 337, Plymouth* *Montserrat, B.W.I.*	491–2144	9	on request		506
Flora Fountain Hotel *Box 373, Church Street* *Plymouth, Montserrat, B.W.I.*	491–3444	18	$90 EP		511

HOTEL QUICK-REFERENCE CHARTS · · · 855

	phone 809+	rooms	winter rate for 2	rep	page
Lime Court Apartments *Box 250, Parliament Street* *Plymouth, Montserrat, B.W.I.*	491–3656	8 apts	on request		513
Montserrat Springs Hotel & Villas *Box 259, Plymouth* *Montserrat, B.W.I.*	491–2481	29 + villas	$140–210 EP + apts	ITR	511
Montserrat Villas *Box 58* *Plymouth, Montserrat, B.W.I.*	491–2431	45 villas	2 brm $725 wk		513
Oriole Plaza Hotel *Plymouth* *Montserrat, B.W.I.*					
Shamrock Villas *Box 180, Plymouth* *Montserrat, B.W.I.*	491–2434	50 apts	$550–800 wk		513
Vue Pointe Hotel *Box 65, Plymouth* *Montserrat, B.W.I.*	491–5210	12 + 28 cot	$196–236 EP	RR	511
Woodsville Apts *Plymouth* *Montserrat, B.W.I.*					513

NEVIS, WEST INDIES

	phone 809+	rooms	winter rate for 2	rep	page
Cliff Dwellers *Tamarind Bay* *Nevis, W.I.*	469–5262		closed at press time	617 + 262–3654	516
Croney's Old Manor Estate *Box 70, Gingerland* *Nevis, W.I.*	469–5445	14	$175 EP, $210 MAP	ITR	524
Four Seasons Resort *Pinney's Beach* *Nevis, W.I.*	469–1111	196	$330–385 EP	800 + 332–3442	524
Golden Rock Estate *Gingerland* *Nevis, W.I.*	469–5346	16	$175–200 EP	ITR	523
Hermitage *Figtree Parish* *Nevis, W.I.*	469–3477	11 incl apts	$335–745 MAP	RR, ITR	525
Hurricane Cove Bungalows *hillside* *Nevis, W.I.*	469–9462	6 apts	$115–350 EP	ITR	525

HOTEL QUICK-REFERENCE CHARTS

	phone 809+	rooms	winter rate for 2	rep	page
Montpelier Estates *Box 474, St. John's Parish* *Nevis, W.I.*	469–5462	16	$350 MAP	203+ 438–3793	523
Mt. Nevis Hotel *Box 491, Newcastle* *Nevis, W.I.*	469–9373				525
Nisbet Plantation *Newcastle* *Nevis, W.I.*	469–5325	30	$298–398 MAP	AWI	524
Oualie Beach Club *Oualie Beach* *Nevis, W.I.*	469–9735	15 cots	$115 EP	ITR	525
Pinney's Beach Hotel *Charlestown* *Nevis, W.I.*	469–5207	48+ 7 cot.	$135 MAP		526
Rest Haven Inn *Box 209, Charlestown* *Nevis, W.I.*	469–5208	43+ 7 cot.	$60–100 EP		525
Zetland Plantation *Gingerland* *Nevis, W.I.*	469–5454	26	$225–310 MAP		525

PUERTO RICO

	phone 809+	rooms	winter rate for 2	rep	page
Ambassador Plaza *1369 Ashford Av.* *Puerto Rico 00907*	721–7300	150			539
Arcade Inn *8 Taft Street* *Santurce, Puerto Rico 00914*	725–0668	19			544
Arcos Blancos *Condado* *Puerto Rico 00902*					
Atlantic Beach Hotel *Vendig St., Condado* *Puerto Rico, 00907*	721–6900				545
Candelero Hotel *Box 2020* *Humacao, Puerto Rico 00661*	852–6000	102	$240 EP	212+ 983–0393	560
Caribe Hilton International *Box 1872* *San Juan, Puerto Rico 00903*	725–0303	707	$120 EP & up	HRS	539

HOTEL QUICK-REFERENCE CHARTS

	phone 809+	rooms	winter rate for 2	rep	page
Carib Inn *Box 12112, Loiza St. Station* *Santurce, Puerto Rico 00914*	791–3535	225	$80–100 EP	ML	539
Casa Blanca *57 Caribe* *Condado, San Juan, PR 00902*	722–7139	7	$55 EP		545
Casa de Playa *Isla Verde* *Puerto Rico*					
La Casa del Frances *Box 458, Barrio Esperanza* *Vieques, Puerto Rico 00765*	741–3751	19	$45–60 CP		571
El Canario Inn *1317 Ashford Av.* *Condado, San Juan, PR 00902*	722–3861	25	$80 CP		543
El Canario by the Lagoon *4 Calle Clemenceau* *Condado, San Juan, PR 00907*	722–5058	40	$85 CP		543
El Canario by the Sea *4 Condado* *Condado, San Juan, PR 00902*	722–8640	25	$80–95 CP		544
Clarion Hotel and Casino *Box 3368* *San Juan, Puerto Rico 00904*	721–4100	155	$90–265 EP		540
Condado Beach Hotel *Ashford Av.* *Condado, Puerto Rico 00907*	721–6090	248	$183–208 EP	O	540
Condado San Juan *1045 Ashford Av.* *Condado, Puerto Rico 00907*	723–9020	96			541
Condado Plaza Hotel *999 Ashford Av.* *Condado, Puerto Rico 00907*	721–1000	560	$185–220	800+ 468–8588	540
La Concha *Box 4195, Ashford Av.* *Condado, Puerto Rico 00907*	723–6090	224	check for status		540
El Conquistador *Las Croabas* *Puerto Rico*		950			560
El Convento *100 Cristo St.* *Old San Juan, Puerto Rico 00902*	723–9020	100	$90–130 EP		541
Coral Island Guest House *Box 396 Ferry Terminal* *Culebra Island, PR 00775*	743–3176	5	$45 EP	617+ 773–0565	569

HOTEL QUICK-REFERENCE CHARTS

	phone 809+	rooms	winter rate for 2	rep	page
Culebra Island Villas *Box 207; (Punta Aloe)* *Culebra Island, Puerto Rico 00775*	742–3112	10 units	$495–795 wk	908+ 458–5591	569
Days Inn *Ponce* *Puerto Rico*					563
Dutch Inn *55 Condado Av.* *Condado, Puerto Rico 00907*	721–0810	102+ 44 apts	$110–145 EP	LRI	541
Excelsior Hotel *801 Ponce de Leon Av.* *San Juan, Puerto Rico 00907*	721–7400	140 incl apts	$122–148 EP	ITR	541
Gallery Inn *Blvd. del Valle* *Old San Juan, Puerto Rico*	722–1808	6	$80–125 EP		544
Green Isle Guest House *36 Calle Uno* *Isla Verde, Puerto Rico 00913*	726–4330	17	$50–80		545
Hyatt Dorado Beach *Dorado, Puerto Rico 00646*	796–1600	300	$300–450 MAP	HY	556
Hyatt Regency Cerromar Beach *Dorado, Puerto Rico 00646*	796–1010	504	$200–400 EP	HY	556
Holiday Inn *Km 255.2, Highway 2* *Ponce, Puerto Rico 00731*	844–1200	120	$100–130 EP	HI	563
Horned Dorset Primavera *Rincon* *Puerto Rico 00743*	823–4030	22	$230–270 EP	CA	565
International Airport Hotel *Munoz Marin Airport* *Isla Verde, Puerto Rico 00913*	791–1700	57	$60 EP		545
Mayaguez Hilton *Route 2, Km 152.5, Box 3629* *Mayaguez, Puerto Rico 00709*	832–7575	145	$140–170 EP	HRS	565
Melia Hotel *Box 1431, 2 Christina St.* *Ponce, Puerto Rico 00731*	842–0260	77	$60–70 EP	AH	563
Numero Uno *Santa Ana Street* *Ocean Park, Puerto Rico 00911*	727–9667				545
Ocean View *Isabel Segunda* *Vieques Island, Puerto Rico*	741–3696	32	$40 EP		571

HOTEL QUICK-REFERENCE CHARTS · · · 859

	phone 809+	rooms	winter rate for 2	rep	page
Olympia Court *603 Miramar* *Santurce, Puerto Rico 00907*	724–0600	86	$50–60 EP	AH	542
Palmas Inn *Box 2020* *Humacao, Puerto Rico 00661*	852–6000	23 suites	$290 CP	212+ 983–0393	561
Palmas del Mar Villas *Box 2020* *Humacao, Puerto Rico 00661*	852–6000	103 apts	1-brm $295 wk $1365	212+ 983–0393	560
Paradores: see end of Puerto Rico lodging listing					
Pierre Hotel *Condado* *Puerto Rico 00907*	721–1200	184	$110–125 CP	BW	542
El Portal *Condado area* *Puerto Rico 00907*					542
El Prado Inn *Calle Luchetti* *Condado, Puerto Rico 00907*	721–9010	22			545
El Prado Beach *Yardley Pl.* *Ocean Park, Puerto Rico 00907*					545
Radisson Normandie Hotel *Box 50059* *San Juan, Puerto Rico 00902*	729–2929	182	$155–230 EP	RH	542
The Regency *1005 Ashford Av.* *Santurce, Puerto Rico 00907*	721–0505	129	$95–130 EP		542
Sands Hotel & Casino *Isla Verde Rd. 187, Isla Verde* *Santurce, Puerto Rico 00914*	791–6100	429	$390–435 AP+	ITR	542
El San Juan Hotel *Box 2872, Isla Verde* *San Juan, Puerto Rico 00913*	791–1000	392	$200–280 EP details		541
Travel Lodge *Box 6007, Loiza St. Station* *Santurce, Puerto Rico 00913*	728–1300	91	$100–150 EP	TL	543
Villa Esperanza Beach Resort *Box 1569* *Vieques Islands, Puerto Rico 00765*	754–9810	50	$76–96 EP	ITR	571
Paradores: (for reservations at all paradores, dial 800+443–0266 or 809+721–2884)					
Parador Boquemar *Route 307* *Boqueron, PR 00622*	851–2158	41	$45 EP		566

HOTEL QUICK-REFERENCE CHARTS

	phone 809+	rooms	winter rate for 2	rep	page
Banos de Coamo *Rte. 546; km 1* *Coamo, PR 00640*	825–2186	46	$55 EP		557
Casa Grande *Utuado, PR 00761*	894–3939	19	$45 EP		557
Parador El Sol *9 East Mariano Riera* *Mayaguez, PR 00708*	834–0303	40	$45 EP		566
Parador La Familia *Las Croabas* *Puerto Rico*					
Hacienda Gripinas *Route 527; km 2.5* *Jayuya, PR 00664*	721–2884	19	$40 EP		558
Parador Guajataca *Route 2; km 103.8* *Quebradillas, PR 00742*	895–3070	38	$55–65 EP		558
Hacienda Juanita *Route 105; km 23.5* *Maricao, PR 00706*	838–2550	21	$40 EP		565
Parador Matorell *6A Ocean Drive* *Luquillo, PR 00673*	889–2710	7	$45–56 EP		558
Parador Oasis *Calle Luna* *San German, PR 00753*	892–1175	52	$58–66 EP	ITR	566
Posada Porlamar *Carr. 304* *Lajas, PR 00667*	899–4015	18	$45		566
Parador Perichi *Route 102; km 14.2* *Cabo Rojo, PR 00708*	851–3131	15	$40 EP		566
Parador Villa Antonio *Rincon, Puerto Rico*					566
Villa Parguera *Route 304* *La Parquera, PR 00667*	899–3975	50	$60 EP		566
Parador Vistalmar *Route 113; Km 7.9* *Quebradillas, PR 00742*	895–2065	56	$55–118 EP	ITR	558

HOTEL QUICK-REFERENCE CHARTS

SABA, NETHERLANDS ANTILLES

	phone 011 + 599 +	rooms	winter rate for 2	rep	page
Benny's Hideaway *Windwardside* *Saba, Netherlands Antilles*		2 brm cot			577
Carpenter's Cottage *Windwardside* *Saba, Netherlands Antilles*	46–2229	1 cot.			578
Captain's Quarters *Windwardside* *Saba, Netherlands Antilles*	46–2201	10	$125 CP	ITR	577
Cranston's Antique Inn *The Bottom* *Saba, Netherlands Antilles*	46–3218	6	$55 CP	ITR	577
English Quarter *Windwardside* *Saba, Netherlands Antilles*	46–2206	3 brm cot			578
Juliana's Apartments *Windwardside* *Saba, Netherlands Antilles*	46–2269	10 apts	$75–95 EP	ITR	578
Queen's Gardens *Troy Hill* *Saba, Netherlands Antilles*	46–2236	10 units			
Rainbow Cottage *Windwardside* *Saba, Netherlands Antilles*	46–2269	1 brm cot	$45 EP $250 wk		578
Saba Villas *Troy Hill* *Saba, Netherlands Antilles*		50 villas			
Scout's Place *Windwardside* *Saba, Netherlands Antilles*	46–2205	15	$55–85 CP	ITR	577
Sharon's Ocean View *Hell's Gate* *Saba, Netherlands Antilles*	46–2238	4	$70 CP	ITR	

ST. BARTHELEMY, FRENCH WEST INDIES

	phone 011 + 590 +	rooms	winter rate for 2, $ or F	rep	page
Auberge de la Petite Anse *B.P. 117, Anse des Flamands* *97133 St. Barthelemy, FWI*	27.64.60	16 apts	F300 EP		588

HOTEL QUICK-REFERENCE CHARTS

	phone 011+590+	rooms	winter rate for 2, $ or F	rep	page
L'Auberge Normandie *Lorient* 97133 St. Barthelemy, FWI	27.61.66	8	F375–475 EP		592
Hotel Baie des Anges *Baie des Flamands* 97133 St. Barthelemy, FWI	27.63.61	9	$150–180 EP	RR	590
Hotel Baie des Flamands *Anse des Flamands* 97133 St. Barthelemy, FWI	27.64.76	24	$95 EP	RR	585
Castelets *Mont Lurin* 97133 St. Barthelemy, FWI	27.61.73	10+ villas	$100–240 CP	212+ 571-0336	590
Club Hotel La Banane *Lorient* 97133 St. Barthelemy, FWI	27.68.25	4 cots	$286–357 AP	RR	590
Eden Rock *Baie de St. Jean* 97133 St. Barthelemy, FWI	27.60.01	6	F250 EP		590
Emeraude Plage *Baie de St. Jean* 97133 St. Barthelemy, FWI	27.64.78	30 cots	$90–115 EP	WI	588
Filao Beach Hotel *Baie de St. Jean* 97133 St. Barthelemy, FWI	27.64.84	30	F2100–2900 EP	DM	591
François Plantation *Colombier* 97133 St. Barthelemy, F.W.I.					591
Grand Cul de Sac Beach Hotel *Box 81, Grand Cul de Sac* 97133 St. Barthelemy, FWI	27.60.70	16	$158–254 EP	ITR	586
Guanahani *Box 81, Grand Cul de Sac* 97133 St. Barthelemy, FWI	27.66.60	80	$380–430 CP	LH	586
L'Hibiscus *Rue Thiers; B.P. 86, Gustavia* 97133 St. Barthelemy, FWI	27.64.82	11	F800 CP		591
Hostellerie Trois Forces *Vitet* 97133 St. Barthelemy, FWI	27.61.25	12 cots	$140		591
Les Islets Fleuris *Hauts de Lorient* 97133 St. Barthelemy, FWI	27.64.22	7	$95–250	ITR	588
Jardins de St. Jean *St. Jean* 97133 St. Barthelemy, FWI	27.70.19	22	$140–225 EP	ITR	588

HOTEL QUICK-REFERENCE CHARTS · · · 863

	phone 011+590+	rooms	winter rate for 2, $ or F	rep	page
Jean Bart Hotel *Baie de St. Jean* *97133 St. Barthelemy, FWI*	27.63.37	50	$195–216 EP	ITR	586
Karl Gustav Hotel *Gustavia* *97133 St. Barthelemy, F.W.I.*					
Kerjan *Baie de St. Jean* *97133 St. Barthelemy, FWI*	27.62.38	5 apts	on request	WI	589
Manapany Cottages *Anse des Cayes* *97133 St. Barthelemy, FWI*	27.66.55	24 cots	$160–260 EP		586
Marigot Bay/Marigot Sea *Point Milou* *97133 St. Barthelemy, F.W.I.*					
Les Mouettes *Lorient* *97133 St. Barthelemy, FWI*					592
Le P'tit Morne *Colombier* *St. Barthelemy, FWI*	27.62.64	12 apts	F900 wk		592
Presqu'ile *Place de la Parade, Gustavia* *St. Barthelemy, FWI*	27.64.60	14	F300 CP		593
La Residence *Petit Cul de Sac, Box 81* *97133 St. Barthelemy, FWI*		20 apts	$225 EP 1 brm	ITR	
St. Barths Beach & Tennis Hotel *Box 81, Grand Cul de Sac* *97133 St. Barthelemy, FWI*	27.60.70	36	$254 CP	ITR	587
Sea Horse Hotel *Marigot Beach* *97133 St. Barthelemy, F.W.I.*					
El Sereno Beach *B.P. 19, Grand Cul de Sac* *97133 St. Barthelemy, FWI*	27.64.80	20	$225–285 EP	ITR	591
Sunset *Gustavia* *97133 St. Barthelemy, FWI*	27.60.18	8	F525–630 CP	JdeL	593
Taiwana *Anse des Flamands* *97133 St. Barthelemy, FWI*	27.65.01	9	on request		592
Terrasses de St. Barth *St. Jean* *97133 St. Barthelemy, FWI*					589

HOTEL QUICK-REFERENCE CHARTS

	phone 011+590+	rooms	winter rate for 2, $ or F	rep	page
Tom Beach *Box 94, Baie de St. Jean 97133 St. Barthelemy, FWI*	27.70.96	12	F600–800		589
Tropical Hotel *Baie de St. Jean 97133 St. Barthelemy, FWI*	27.64.87	20	$170–195 EP	ITR	592
Villas Creole *Baie de St. Jean 97133 St. Barthelemy, FWI*					589
Village St. Jean *Baie de St. Jean 97133 St. Barthelemy, FWI*	27.61.29	25 villas	$100–300 EP	CA	589

ST. CROIX, UNITED STATES VIRGIN ISLANDS: (For 800 toll-free numbers, dial 800+555-1212)

	phone 809+	rooms	winter rate for 2	rep	page
Anchor Inn *58 King St., Christiansted St. Croix, USVI 00820*	773–4000	30	$141–156 EP	ITR	609
Arawak Cottages *Box 695, Frederiksted St. Croix, USVI 00840*	772–0305	8 cots	$120		607
Buccaneer Hotel & Beach Club *Box 218, Christiansted St. Croix, USVI 00820*	773–2100	156	$175–310 EP	RL	605
Cane Bay Reef Club *Box 1407, Kings Hill St. Croix, USVI 00850*	778–2966	9	$75 EP $450 wk		609
Carambola Beach & Golf Resort *Box 3031, Davis Bay, Kingshill St. Croix, USVI 00850*	778–3800	150	$402–505 EP	800+ 447–9503	605
Caravelle Hotel *Queen Cross Street, Christiansted St. Croix, USVI 00820*	773–0687	44	$79–105 EP	RR	609
Chenay Bay Beach Resort *Box T, Christiansted St. Croix, USVI 00820*	773–2918	20 cots	$98–105 EP	800	607
Club Comanche *1 Strand St., Christiansted St. Croix, USVI 00820*	773–0210	42	$65–145 EP	AWI	609
Club St. Croix *Estate Golden Rock, Christiansted St. Croix, USVI 00820*	773–0333	54+	$189–289 EP	ITR	607

HOTEL QUICK-REFERENCE CHARTS · · · 865

	phone 809+	rooms	winter rate for 2	rep	page
Cormorant Beach Club *108 La Grande Princess, Christiansted* *St. Croix, USVI 00820*	778–8920	38	$350–500 MAP	DM	605
Danish Manor *2 Company St., Christiansted* *St. Croix, USVI 00820*	773–1377	37	$59–135 CP	ITR	610
Frederiksted Hotel *20 Strand Street, Frederiksted* *St. Croix, USVI 00840*	772–0500	40	$82–90 EP	800	610
Gentle Winds *Christiansted* *St. Croix, USVI 00820*	773–4102	25 apts	$245 EP up	800	607
Granada Del Mar *La Grande Princesse, Christiansted* *St. Croix, USVI 00820*	773–7472	36 apts	$160 2 brm		608
Holger Danske *1 King Cross St., Christiansted* *St. Croix, USVI 00820*	773–3600	44	$95–135 EP	BW	609
Hotel on the Cay *Box 4020, Christiansted* *St. Croix, USVI 00820*	773–2035	55	$163 EP	800	606
King Christian Hotel *Box 3619, Christiansted* *St. Croix, USVI 00820*	773–2285	38	$75–105 EP	800	609
King Frederik Beach Hotel *Box 1908, Frederiksted* *St. Croix, USVI 00840*	772–1205	22	$65–115 EP	800	608
Mill Harbour *Estate Golden Rock, Christiansted* *St. Croix, USVI 00820*	773–3800	86	$180–220 EP	RR	608
Moonraker Hotel *Queens Cross Street, Christiansted* *St. Croix, USVI 00820*	773–1535	16	$45 CP		611
Pink Fancy *27 Prince St., Christiansted* *St. Croix, USVI 00820*	773–8460	13	$120–150 CP	800	610
Queste Verde—see Estate Queste Verde					
St. Croix-by-the-Sea *Box 248, Christiansted* *St. Croix, USVI 00820*	778–8600	65	$138–158 EP	AWI	606
Schooner Bay *Gallows Bay, Christiansted* *St. Croix, USVI 00820*	778–7670	44 apts	$190 EP	800	608

HOTEL QUICK-REFERENCE CHARTS

	phone 809+	rooms	winter rate for 2	rep	page
Sprat Hall *Box 695, Frederiksted* *St. Croix, USVI 00840*	772–0305	9	$110–140 EP	AWI	610
Sugar Beach *Estate Golden Rock, Christiansted* *St. Croix, USVI 00820*	773–5345	45 apts	$120 st $160 1brm	800	608
Waves at Cane Bay *Box 1749, Kings Hill* *St. Croix, USVI 00850*	778–1805	10	$85–95 EP		608
Villa Madeleine *Box 3109, Christiansted* *St. Croix, USVI 00822*	773–8141	41 apts			608
Villa Morales *82 Estate Whim, Frederiksted* *St. Croix, USVI 00820*	772–0556	8	$30 EP		611

SINT EUSTATIUS, NETHERLANDS ANTILLES

	phone 011+599+	rooms	winter rate for 2	rep	page
Alvin Coutar Apts. *Oranjestad* *Sint Eustatius, N.A.*					627
Cherry Tree Villa *Oranjestad* *Sint Eustatius, N.A.*					627
Golden Era *Box 109, Lower Town, Oranjestad* *Sint Eustatius, N.A.*	38–2345	20	$88 EP	ITR	626
Maison Sur la Plage *Box 157, Zeelandia* *Sint Eustatius, N.A.*	38–2256	10	$80 EP		626
The Old Gin House *Box 172, Lower Town* *Sint Eustatius, N.A.*	38–2319	20	$150 EP	EM	626

ST. JOHN, UNITED STATES VIRGIN ISLANDS

	phone 809+	rooms	winter rate for 2	rep	page
Battery Hill *3 Ad–1, Box 458, Cruz Bay* *St. John, USVI 00830*	776–6152	8 apts	$195 EP	800	637
Bethany Condominiums *Box 254, Cruz Bay* *St. John, USVI 00830*	776–6318	6	$50 EP		637

HOTEL QUICK-REFERENCE CHARTS

	phone 809+	rooms	winter rate for 2	rep	page
Caneel Bay Plantation *Box 120* *St. John, USVI 00830*	776–6111	171	$310–510 EP	RI	635
Carla's Cottages *Estate Bethany* *St. John, USVI 00830*					637
Cinnamon Bay Campgrounds *Box 720, Cruz Bay* *St. John, USVI 00830*	776–6330	111	$59 cot $49 tent $10 site	RR	639
Cruz Inn *Box 566, Cruz Bay* *St. John, USVI 00830*	776–7688	14	$40–75 EP		640
Cruz Views *15A Estate Enighed, Cruz Bay* *St. John, USVI 00830*	776–6152	10 apts	$125 EP	800	637
Gallows Point *Box 58, Cruz Bay* *St. John, USVI 00830*	776–6434	60 apts	$225–300 EP	ITR	637
Gifft Hill *Estate Blucksburg, Cruz Bay* *St. John, USVI 00830*	776–6152	5 cots	$2100 wk for 6	800	637
Hyatt Virgin Grand Hotel *Great Cruz Bay* *St. John, USVI 00830*	776–7171	264	$450–500 AP+	HY	636
Inn at Tamarind Court *Cruz Bay* *St. John, USVI 00830*					639
Lavender Hill *Box 320, Cruz Bay* *St. John, USVI 00830*	776–6969	10 apts	$180–225 EP		638
Maho Bay Camp *Maho Bay* *St. John, USVI 00830*	776–6240	99 apts	$65 EP	800	638
The Nut Tree *Cruz Bay* *St. John, USVI 00830*		apts			638
Raintree Inn *5A Cruz Bay, Box 566* *St. John, USVI 00830*	776–7449	11	$50–75 EP		639
Sea Breeze Villas *Cruz Bay* *St. John, USVI 00830*					640
Selene's *Box 30, Cruz Bay* *St. John, USVI 00830*		apts			638

	phone 809+	rooms	winter rate for 2	rep	page
Serendip *Box 273, Cruz Bay* *St. John, USVI 00830*	776–6646	10 apts	$75–105 EP $490–693 wk		638
Villa Bougainvillea *Cruz Bay* *St. John, USVI 00830*					638

ST. KITTS

	phone 809+	rooms	winter rate for 2	rep	page
Bird Rock Beach Hotel *Box 227, Basseterre* *St. Kitts, West Indies*	465–8914	24	$95–175 EP	ITR	651
Blakeney Hotel *Box 281, Basseterre* *St. Kitts, West Indies*	465–2222	11	$25–30 EP		
Canne a Sucre *Basseterre* *St. Kitts, West Indies*		10			656
Casablanca *South coast* *St. Kitts, West Indies*					651
Conaree Cottages *Conaree Beach* *St. Kitts, West Indies*		cots			656
Fairview Inn *Box 212, Basseterre* *St. Kitts, West Indies*	465–2472	30	$100–120 EP	ITR	654
Fisherman's Wharf *Basseterre* *St. Kitts, West Indies*					653
Fort Thomas Hotel *Box 407, Basseterre* *St. Kitts, West Indies*	465–2695	64	$90–100 EP	ML	651
Frigate Bay Beach *Box 137, Frigate Bay* *St. Kitts, West Indies*	465–8935	64 incl apts	$95–190 EP	ITR	651
Gateway Inn *Frigate Bay* *St. Kitts, West Indies*					653
Golden Lemon *Dieppe Bay* *St. Kitts, West Indies*	465–7260	16	$275–280 MAP	800	653

	phone 809+	rooms	winter rate for 2	rep	page
Island Paradise Beach Village *Box 139, Frigate Bay* *St. Kitts, West Indies*	465–8004	36	$600–750 wk		653
Jack Tar Royal St. Kitts Resort *Frigate Bay* *St. Kitts, West Indies*	465–2651	100+	$250 AP+	JT	652
Leeward Cove Condominiums *Box 123, Frigate Bay* *St. Kitts, West Indies*	465–2654	12 apts	$100–140 EP	AWI	653
Lemon Court *Dieppe Bay* *St. Kitts, West Indies*	465–7260	apts			
Ocean Terrace Inn *Box 65, Basseterre* *St. Kitts, West Indies*	465–2754	52	$135–200 EP	AWI	652
Ottley's Plantation *Box 345* *St. Kitts, West Indies*	465–7234	15			
Rawlins Plantation *Box 340, Mount Pleasant* *St. Kitts, West Indies*	465–6221	8	$375 MAP	AWI	655
Sandals St. Kitts *Cockleshell Bay* *St. Kitts, West Indies*			check for status		652
Sea Lofts *Frigate Bay* *St. Kitts, West Indies*					654
St. Christopher Beach *Frigate Bay* *St. Kitts, West Indies*					658
Sun 'n Sand Beach Village *Box 341, Frigate Bay* *St. Kitts, West Indies*	465–8037	34 apts	$140 EP or $900 wk for 4	RR	654
Timothy Beach *Frigate Bay* *St. Kitts, West Indies*					652
Tradewinds Cottages *Box 208, Conaree Beach* *St. Kitts, West Indies*	465–2681	5 cots	$300 wk		656
White House *Basseterre* *St. Kitts, West Indies*					655

ST. LUCIA

	phone 809+	rooms	winter rate for 2	rep	page
Anse Chastenet *Box 216, Soufriere* *St. Lucia, West Indies*	454–7355	37	$270–300 MAP	RL	675
Bois d'Orange Holiday Villas *Box 98, Castries* *St. Lucia, West Indies*	452–8213	11 apts	on request		674
Caribees Apartment Hotel *Box 547, Castries* *St. Lucia, West Indies*	452–4767	10	$60 EP		674
Club Mediterranee St. Lucia *Vieux Fort* *St. Lucia, West Indies*	455–6001	256	$1900 wk AP+ all incl	CM	670
Club St. Lucia *Box 915, Anse Becune* *St. Lucia, West Indies*	452–0551	156	$260–330 AP+	ITR	670
Couples II *Box 190, Malabar Beach* *St. Lucia, West Indies*	452–4211	86	all incl	ML	670
Cunard La Toc Hotel & Suites *Box 399, Castries* *St. Lucia, West Indies*	452–3081	200+ 56 apts	$150 up EP	LRI	671
Dasheene *Box 225, Soufriere* *St. Lucia, West Indies*	454–7444	villas			674
East Winds *La Brelotte Bay* *St. Lucia, West Indies*	452–8212	10	$390 AP+	ITR	675
Green Parrot Inn *Box 648, Castries* *St. Lucia, West Indies*	452–3399	30	$90 EP		675
Halcyon Beach Club *Box 388, Choc Bay* *St. Lucia, West Indies*	452–5331	180	$140–165 EP	ITR	671
Harmony Apartel *Box 155, Rodney Bay* *St. Lucia, West Indies*	452–8756	9 st + 12 apts	$85–132 EP	RR	674
Hummingbird Beach *Soufriere* *St. Lucia, West Indies*					675
Islander Apartment Resort *Box 907, Reduit Bay* *St. Lucia, West Indies*	452–0255	60 incl apts	$110–120 EP	ITR	676

	phone 809+	rooms	winter rate for 2	rep	page
Jalousie Resort *Soufriere* *St. Lucia, West Indies*					671
Marigot Bay Resort *Box 101, Marigot Bay* *St. Lucia, West Indies*	453–4357	47 cots + apts	$125–140 EP	RR	676
Morne Fortune Apartments *Box 376, Castries* *St. Lucia, West Indies*	452–3603	12 apts	$70–80 EP		674
Pullman Morgan Bay *Choc Bay* *St. Lucia, West Indies*		240		PLM	672
Royal St. Lucian *Reduit Bay* *St. Lucia, West Indies*					672
Le Sport *Box 437, Cap Estate* *St. Lucia, West Indies*	452–8551	102	all-incl.	800+ 544–2883	672
St. Lucian Hotel *Box 512, Reduit Beach* *St. Lucia, West Indies*	452–8351	192	$150 EP		672
Tarpion Reef *Castries* *St. Lucia, West Indies*					674
Vigie Beach Hotel *Box 395, Vigie Beach* *St. Lucia, West Indies*	452–5211	57	$60–100 EP	ITR	673
Villa Hotel *Box 129, Castries* *St. Lucia, West Indies*	452–2691	10			673
Windjammer Landing *Castries* *St. Lucia, West Indies*			$260 EP 1 brm $350 EP 2 brm	EM	673

SINT MAARTEN, NETHERLANDS ANTILLES and ST. MARTIN, FRENCH WEST INDIES

	phone For N.A.: 011+599+ For F.W.I.: 011+590+	rooms	winter rate for 2	rep	page
Les Alizes *Grand Case* *97150 St. Martin, F.W.I.*					704

HOTEL QUICK-REFERENCE CHARTS

	phone For N.A.: 011+599+ For F.W.I.: 011+590+	rooms	winter rate for 2	rep	page
Almond Grove *Box 427, Cole Bay* *Sint Maarten, N.A.*	53-3517	16 homes	$150 EP and up	RW	699
Anse Marigot Hotel *Baie Nettle* *St. Martin, F.W.I.*	87.92.01	96	$175-275 EP	ITR	699
Beausejour *Box 67, Marigot* *97150 St. Martin, F.W.I.*	87.52.18	10	$35 EP		704
The Beach House *Front St., Philipsburg* *Sint Maarten, N.A.*	52-2456	8	$85-95 EP	ITR	703
Beachside Villas *Simpson Bay, near airport* *Sint Maarten, N.A.*	54-4294	14 apts	$380 EP	ITR	699
Belair Beach Hotel *Box 140, Philipsburg* *Sint Maarten, N.A.*	52-3362	72 apts	$245-350 EP	IH	699
La Belle Creole *Pointe des Pierres, Marigot* *97150 St. Martin, F.W.I.*	87.58.66	156	$265-580 CP	CH	694
La Belle Grand Case *Grand Case* *97150 St. Martin, F.W.I.*		apts			703
Captain Oliver *Oyster Pond* *97150 St. Martin*	87.40.26	30 apts		ITR	699
Caravanserai *Box 113, Philipsburg* *Sint Maarten, N.A.*	54-2501	85	$165-215 EP	RR, ITR	694
Caribbean Hotel *Philipsburg, Box 236* *Sint Maarten, N.A.*	52-2028	35	$40-45 EP		705
Club Orient *Baie de L'Embouchure* *97150 St. Martin, F.W.I.*	87.33.85	61 cot & st	$120-325 EP		694
Coralita Beach *Box 32, Baie Lucas* *97150 St. Martin, F.W.I.*	87.31.81	24	$125 EP	ITR	694
Cupecoy *West Bay* *Sint Maarten, N.A.*					699
Dawn Beach *Box 389, Philipsburg* *Sint Maarten, N.A.*	52-2929	155 apts	$200-290 EP	ITR	700

HOTEL QUICK-REFERENCE CHARTS · · · 873

	phone For N.A.: 011+599+ For F.W.I.: 011+590+	rooms	winter rate for 2	rep	page
Divi Little Bay Beach Hotel *Box 61, Philipsburg* *Sint Maarten, N.A.*	52–2333	120	$195–225 EP	D	695
Esmeralda Resort *Orient Bay* *St. Martin, F.W.I.*		64 suites		203+ 847-9445	700
L'Ermitage *Rue de la Liberte, Marigot* *97150 St. Martin, F.W.I.*	87.57.58	10	$50–60 EP		703
Flamboyant Bounty I *Baic Nettle, Marigot* *St. Martin, F.W.I.*			$370 all-incl.	BR	695
Flamboyant Bounty II *Cul de Sac* *St. Martin, F.W.I.*			$310 all-incl.	BR	695
Galion Beach *Baie de L'Embouchure* *97150 St. Martin, F.W.I.*	87.31.77	54	$130–230 EP	RR	695
Gardens at Nettle Bay *Baie Nettle, Marigot* *97150 St. Martin, F.W.I.*					699
George's Guest House *4 Union Road, Philipsburg* *Sint Maarten, N.A.*	54–5363	9	$353 EP		705
Grand Case Beach Club *Grand Case* *97150 St. Martin, F.W.I.*	87.51.87	76 apts	$180–285 EP		699
Grand Case Beach Motel *Grand Case* *97150 St. Martin, F.W.I.*	87.53.54	6			703
Le Grand St. Martin *Marigot* *97150 St. Martin, F.W.I.*	87.57.91		all-incl.	RS	705
Great Bay Beach Resort & Casino *Box 310, Philipsburg* *Sint Maarten, N.A.*	52–2446	225	$180–290 EP	ITR	696
Great Bay Marina *Box 277, Philipsburg* *Sint Maarten, N.A.*	52–2167	7	$70 EP	ITR	
Hotel Hevea *Grand Case* *97150 St. Martin, F.W.I.*	87.56.85	8			703
Holland House *Box 393, Philipsburg* *Sint Maarten, N.A.*	52–2572	55	$153–235 EP	ITR	700

	phone For N.A.: 011+599+ For F.W.I.: 011+590+	rooms	winter rate for 2	rep	page
Horny Toad Guest House *Box 397, Simson Bay* *Philipsburg, Sint Maarten, N.A.*	54–4323	8 apts	$180 EP	ITR	703
The Jetty *Philipsburg* *Sint Maarten, N.A.*	52–2922	15 apts	$180 up	ITR	703
Laguna Beach Hotel *Baie Nettle, Marigot* *97150 St. Martin, F.W.I.*	87.91.75	62 apts	$134–209 CP	ITR	701
Maho Beach Hotel & Casino *Box 306, Philipsburg* *Sint Maarten, N.A.*	54–2115	247 incl apts	$195–395 EP	SS	696
Marine Hotel Simson Bay *Baie Nettle, Marigot* *97150 St. Martin, F.W.I.*					696
Mary's Boon *Box 278, Philipsburg* *Sint Maarten, N.A.*	55–4235	12	$150 EP	ITR	703
Mary's Fancy *Box 420, Cul de Sac, Philipsburg* *Sint Maarten, N.A.*	52–2665	10	$110–220 EP		
Meridien L'Habitation de Lonvilliers *Box 230, Anse Marcel* *97150 St. Martin, F.W.I.*	87.78.00	253	$300–395 CP	M	696
Mont Vernon *Chevrise Baie Orientale* *St. Martin, F.W.I.*	87.42.22	227	$235–320 CP	212+ 840–0281	697
Mullet Bay Golf, Beach & Casino *Box 309, Philipsburg* *Sint Maarten, N.A.*	54–2801	622	$210–300 EP	GE	697
Nettle Bay Beach Club *Box 474, Marigot* *St. Martin, F.W.I.*	87.94.04	192 apts	$125–225	ITR	
Ocean Club *Cupecoy Bay* *Sint. Maarten, N.A.*		20 villas		203+ 227–7017	
Oyster Pond Yacht Club *Box 239, Philipsburg* *Sint Maarten, N.A.*	52–3206	20	$170–310 CP	DM	703
Oyster Bay Hotel *Oyster Pond* *97150 St. Martin, F.W.I.*	87.54.72	150 cots			
Palm Plaza *Marigot* *97150 St. Martin, F.W.I.*	87.51.96	21	$80 EP		705

HOTEL QUICK-REFERENCE CHARTS

	phone For N.A.: 011+599+ For F.W.I.: 011+590+	rooms	winter rate for 2	rep	page
Pasanggrahan *Box 151, Philipsburg* *Sint Maarten, N.A.*	52–3588	26+ 4 apts	$114–148 EP	ITR	704
Pavilion Beach *Grand Case* *St. Martin, F.W.I.*		16 suites	$150–225 EP	ITR	
Pelican Resort & Casino *Box 431, Philipsburg* *Sint Maarten, N.A.*	54–4309	514	$190–320 EP	ITR	701
Petit Plage *Grand Case* *97150 St. Martin, F.W.I.*	87.50.65	18 apts		PH	701
PLM-Azur St. Tropez *B.P. 50, Marigot* *97150 St. Martin, F.W.I.*	87.54.72	118	check on status		697
Point on Burgeaux Bay *Burgeaux Bay, near airport* *Sint Maarten, N.A.*	54–4335	apts	$150–290 EP	RR	701
Pointe Pirouette *Simson Bay Lagoon* *Sint Maarten, N.A.*	54–4207	villas	$150–455 EP	RR	701
La Residence *Marigot* *97150 St. Martin, F.W.I.*	87.70.37	20	$112–134 CP	ITR	704
Royal Beach *Baie Nettle* *97150 St. Martin, F.W.I.*	87.89.89	80		PLM	697
Royal Islander *Box 2000, Philipsburg* *Sint. Maarten, N.A.*	55–2318		$250–360 EP	ITR	702
Royale La Louisianne *Marigot* *97150 St. Martin, F.W.I.*	87.86.51	68		AC	702
La Samanna *Baie Longue* *97150 St. Martin, F.W.I.*	87.51.22	11 rooms 40 apts + 6 villas	$480–720 EP	DM	697
Seaview Hotel *Box 65, Philipsburg* *Sint Maarten, N.A.*	52–2323	45	$95–120 EP	ITR	
Simson Beach Marine Hotel *Simson Bay* *Sint Maarten, N.A.*				AC	
Sint Maarten Beach Club & Casino *Box 465, Philipsburg* *Sint Maarten, N.A.*	52–3434	78 apts	$190–230 EP	SMR	698

HOTEL QUICK-REFERENCE CHARTS

	phone For N.A.: 011+599+ For F.W.I.: 011+590+	rooms	winter rate for 2	rep	page
Summit Hotel *Simson Bay Lagoon, Philipsburg* *Sint Maarten, N.A.*	54–2150	60	$75–90 EP	ITR	698
Town House Apartments *Box 347, Philipsburg* *Sint Maarten, N.A.*	52–2898	12 apts	$175–250 EP	ITR	
Treasure Island Hotel *Cupecoy, Box 14* *Philipsburg, Sint Maarten, N.A.*	54–3219	256 incl. apts			698
Village at Oyster Pond *Oyster Pond* *Sint Maarten, N.A.*		check for status			702
La Vista *Pelican Key Estate* *Sint Maarten, N.A.*	54–3005	24	$180–290 EP	ITR	

ST. THOMAS, UNITED STATES VIRGIN ISLANDS:
For 800 toll-free numbers, dial 800+555–1212.

	phone 809+	rooms	winter rate for 2	rep	page
Anchorage Beach Villas *Route 6* *St. Thomas, USVI 00801*	775–3300	28 apts	$225–315 EP	800	725
Beverly Hill Guest House *Contant 105* *St. Thomas, USVI 00801*	774–2693	12	$45		729
Blackbeard's Castle *Box 6041; Blackbeard's Hill* *St. Thomas, USVI 00801*	776–1234	15	$110–195 CP		727
Bluebeard's Castle *Box 7480, Charlotte Amalie* *St. Thomas, USVI 00801*	774–1600	130	$185–220 EP	LI	721
Bolongo Bay Beach Club *Box 7337, Bolongo Bay* *St. Thomas, USVI 00801*	775–1800	77 + apts	$200–260 CP	ITR	722
Bunker Hill View Inn *9 Commandant Gade* *St. Thomas, USVI 00801*	774–8056	18	$47–65 CP		729
Cabrita Point *East end* *St. Thomas, USVI 00801*					725
Carib Beach Hotel *Lindbergh Bay* *St. Thomas, USVI 00801*	774–2525		$125–175	RR	

HOTEL QUICK-REFERENCE CHARTS · · · 877

	phone 809+	rooms	winter rate for 2	rep	page
Cowpet Bay *Box 7699, East End* *St. Thomas, USVI 00801*	775–6220	21 apts	$250–345 EP 2brm	800	725
Crystal Cove *Sapphire Bay* *St. Thomas, USVI 00802*					725
Danish Chalet Inn *Box 4319* *St. Thomas, USVI 00801*	774–5764	13	$50–75 CP		727
Domini Hus Guest House *4 Domini Gade* *St. Thomas, USVI 00801*	774–2661	7	$35 CP		729
Elysian Cowpet Bay *Box 51, Red Hook* *St. Thomas, USVI 00802*	775–1800	60 apts	$275–550 EP	ITR	722
Emerald Beach *Lindbergh Bay* *St. Thomas, USVI 00801*					
Frenchman's Reef Beach Resort *Box 7100, Charlotte Amalie* *St. Thomas, USVI 00801*	776–8500	512	$220–280 EP	800+ 524–2000	722
Galleon House *31 Kongens Gade; Box 6577* *St. Thomas, USVI 00801*	774–6952	9	$50–95 CP	800	727
Harbor View *Box 1975, Charlotte Amalie* *St. Thomas, USVI 00801*	774–2651	8	$100 EP	WI	727
Heritage Manor *Charlotte Amalie, Box 90* *St. Thomas, USVI 00801*	774–3003	4	$60 EP		729
Hotel 1829 *Box 1567, Charlotte Amalie* *St. Thomas, USVI 00801*	774–1829	12	$70–180 EP		728
Island Beachcomber *Box 1618, Charlotte Amalie* *St. Thomas, USVI 00801*	774–5250	50	$110 EP		728
Island View Guest House *11 Contant; Box 1903* *St. Thomas, USVI 00801*	774–4270	15	$50–60 CP	800	729
Limetree Beach Hotel *Box 7307, Frenchman's Bay* *St. Thomas, USVI 00801*	776–4770	84	$370–390 AP+	ITR	723
Mafolie *Box 1506, Charlotte Amalie* *St. Thomas, USVI 00801*	774–2790	20	$60–70 EP		728

HOTEL QUICK REFERENCE CHARTS

	phone 809+	rooms	winter rate for 2	rep	page
Magens Point Hotel *Magens Bay Road* *St. Thomas, USVI 00801*	775–5500	54	$160–300 EP	ITR	726
Mahogany Run—Fairway Village *Box 7517, North Coast* *St. Thomas, USVI 00801*	775–1200	25 apts	$140–160 EP	800	723
Mahogany Run—general villas *Box 7517, North Coast* *St. Thomas, USVI 00801*	775–1200	50 apts	$202–228 for 1brm	800	723
The Mark of St. Thomas *Charlotte Amalie* *St. Thomas, USVI 00801*	774–5511		$150–225 CP	800 + 343–4085	728
Miller Manor Guest House *27 Princess Gade* *St. Thomas, USVI 00801*	774–1535	22	$42–45 CP		729
Morning Star Beach Club *Morning Star Beach* *St. Thomas, USVI 00801*		96		212 + 986–7676	723
Pavilions and Pools *Star Route, East End* *St. Thomas, USVI 00801*	775–6110	25	$230–255 CP	RR	729
Point Pleasant Resort *Smith Bay, East End* *St. Thomas, USVI 00801*	775–7200	150	$215–315 EP	RR	723
Ramada Yacht Haven Hotel *Box 7970, Charlotte Amalie* *St. Thomas, USVI 00801*	774–9700	150	$125–160 EP	RA	724
Sapphire Beach Resort *Box 8088, Route 6, East End* *St. Thomas, USVI 00801*	775–6100	81 apts	$250–320 EP for st + villa	800	726
Sea Cliff Beach Resort *Box 2325, Water Isle* *St. Thomas, USVI 00801*	774–1207	95	$225 up	IH	
Secret Harbour Beach Hotel *Nazareth Bay Estate, Box 7576* *St. Thomas, USVI 00801*	775–6550	50 apts	$135–265	EM	726
Stouffer Grand Beach Resort *Box 8267, East End* *St. Thomas, USVI 00801*	775–1510 •	297 incl apts	$295–875 EP	S	724
Villa Blanca *Charlotte Amalie* *St. Thomas, USVI 00801*					730
Villa Fairview *Charlotte Amalie* *St. Thomas, USVI 00801*					730

HOTEL QUICK REFERENCE CHARTS · · · 879

	phone 809+	rooms	winter rate for 2	rep	page
Watergate Villas *Bolongo Bay, South Coast* *St. Thomas, USVI 00801*	775–2270	120 apts	$100–375 EP	800	726
West Indies Inn *Box 4976, Charlotte Amalie* *St. Thomas, USVI 00801*	774–1376	14	$90–145 EP	AWI	730
Windward Passage Hotel *Box 640, Charlotte Amalie* *St. Thomas, USVI 00801*	774–5200	150	$135–230 CP	800	724

ST. VINCENT AND ITS GRENADINES, WEST INDIES

	phone 809+	rooms	winter rate for 2	rep	page
CSY Marina *Blue Lagoon* *St. Vincent, W.I.*	458–4031	20	$70 EP	201+ 568–0390	747
Cobblestone Inn *Box 867, Kingstown* *St. Vincent, W.I.*	456–1937	20	$60 CP		748
Emerald Valley Resort *Penniston Valley, Box 1081* *St. Vincent, W.I.*	458–7421	12	$180 EP		747
Grand View Beach Hotel *Box 173, Kingstown* *St. Vincent, W.I.*	458–4811	12	$210 CP	RR, CA	748
Haddon Hall *Box 144, Kingstown* *St. Vincent, W.I.*	456–1897	18	$70–90 EP		748
Heron Hotel *Bay Street, Kingstown* *St. Vincent, W.I.*	457–1631	15	$55–65 MAP		749
Indian Bay Beach Apartments *Box 538, Indian Bay Beach* *St. Vincent, W.I.*	458–4001	8 apts	$50–75 EP $300–500 wk		747
Kingstown Park Guest House *Kingstown* *St. Vincent, W.I.*	456–1532	20	$40–70 EP		750
The Last Resort *Box 355, Kingstown* *St. Vincent, W.I.*	458–4231	11	$60 EP		748
Mariner's Inn *Box 868, Villa Beach* *St. Vincent, W.I.*	458–4287	17	$50–60 EP		748

	phone 809+	rooms	winter rate for 2	rep	page
RaWaCou *Stubbs, Atlantic Coast* *St. Vincent, W.I.*	458–4459	10	$75–95 EP		750
Sunset Shores *Box 849, Villa Beach* *St. Vincent, W.I.*	458–4411	19	$165–180 MAP	RR	746
Tropic Breeze Apartments *Box 761, Queens Drive* *St. Vincent, W.I.*	458–4631	12 apts	$40 EP	RR	747
Umbrella Beach Hotel *south shore* *St. Vincent, W.I.*		10			748
Villa Lodge *Box 222, Kingstown* *St. Vincent, W.I.*	458–4641	10	$75 EP	RR	748
Young Island *Box 211, Young Island* *St. Vincent, W.I.*	458–4826	29	$300–485 MAP	RL	746
Yvonette Apartments *Box 71, Indian Bay Beach* *St. Vincent, W.I.*	458–4021	7 apts	$40 EP 1 brm		747

BEQUIA

	phone 809+	rooms	winter rate for 2	rep	page
Bequia Beach Club *Friendship Bay, Bequia* *St. Vincent Grenadines, W.I.*					757
Frangipani *Port Elizabeth, Bequia* *St. Vincent Grenadines, W.I.*	458–3255	11	$35–65 EP		757
Friendship Bay *Bequia* *St. Vincent Grenadines, W.I.*	458–3222	27	$175–225 MAP	RL	757
Plantation House (Sunny Caribbee) *Port Elizabeth, Bequia* *St. Vincent Grenadines, W.I.*	458–3425	25	$60 EP	EM	757
Spring Estates *Bequia* *St. Vincent Grenadines, W.I.*	458–3414	12 apts	on request MAP		757

CANOUAN

	phone 809+	rooms	winter rate for 2	rep	page
Canouan Beach Hotel *Canouan, Box 530* *St. Vincent Grenadines, W.I.*	458–8888	43	$428 AP+	ITR	759
Crystal Sands *Canouan* *St. Vincent Grenadines, W.I.*	457–9240	10 apts	$60–90 EP		759

HOTEL QUICK REFERENCE CHARTS · · · 881

	phone 809+	rooms	winter rate for 2	rep	page
MAYREAU					
Salt Whistle Bay *Mayreau* *St. Vincent Grenadines, W.I.*		26		800+ 387–1752	759
MUSTIQUE					
Cotton House *Box 349, Mustique* *St. Vincent Grenadines, W.I.*	458–4621	19	$475–550 AP+	RL	760
PALM ISLAND					
Palm Island Beach Club *Prune Island* *St. Vincent Grenadines, W.I.*	458–4804	24 & villas	$250 AP+		760
PETIT ST. VINCENT					
Petit St. Vincent Resort *Petit St. Vincent* *St. Vincent Grenadines, W.I.*	458–4801	22 cot	$630 AP+	513+ 242–1333	761
UNION ISLAND					
Anchorage Yacht Club *Clifton, Union Island* *St. Vincent Grenadines, W.I.*	458–8244	10	$150 MAP		762
Clifton Beach *Clifton, Union Island* *St. Vincent Grenadines, W.I.*	458–8235	12			763
Sunny Grenadines *Clifton, Union Island* *St. Vincent, Grenadines, W.I.*	458–8327	10+ apts	$40 EP		763

TRINIDAD, WEST INDIES

	phone 809+	rooms	winter rate for 2	rep	page
Asa Wright Nature Centre *GPO Bag 10, Port of Spain* *Trinidad, W.I.*	212+ 840–5961	18			773
Bel Air International Hotel *Piarco Airport* *Trinidad, W.I.*	644–4771	58	$60–90 EP		773
Chaconia Inn *106 Saddle Road, Maraval* *Port of Spain, Trinidad, W.I.*	622–5474	48	$75–110 EP	RR	770

	phone 809+	rooms	winter rate for 2	rep	page
Errol J. Lau Hotel *Edward Street, Port of Spain* *Trinidad, W.I.*	625–4381	18	$35 EP		774
Farrell House *San Fernando, Point Lisas* *Trinidad, W.I.*	659–2271	51	$50 EP		771
Hilton International Trinidad *Box 442, Port of Spain* *Trinidad, W.I.*	624–3211	431	$130–180 EP	Hil	771
Holiday Inn *Box 1017, Wrightson Road* *Port of Spain, Trinidad, W.I.*	625–3361	253	$95–105 EP	HI	771
Kapok Hotel *6–18 Cotton Hill, St. Clair* *Port of Spain, Trinidad, W.I.*	622–6441	65+ suites	$70 EP		772
Monique's Guest House *114 Saddle Road, Maraval* *Port of Spain, Trinidad, W.I.*	629–2233	8	$30 EP		772
Mount St. Benedict Guest House *Tunapuna* *Trinidad, W.I.*	(212)–840–5961	15	$45 AP		772
Normandie Hotel *10 Nook Ave.,* *Port of Spain, Trinidad, W.I.*	624–1181	54	$70–90 EP	ITR	772
Queen's Park Hotel *Queen's Park Savannah* *Port of Spain, Trinidad, W.I.*	630–8583	35			772
Timberline Cabins *Maracas Bay* *Trinidad, W.I.*					774

TOBAGO, WEST INDIES

	phone 809+	rooms	winter rate for 2	rep	page
Arnos Vale *Box 208, Scarborough* *Tobago, W.I.*	639–2881	25 + 3 suites			787
Blue Waters Inn *Batteaux Bay* *Tobago, W.I.*					790
Cocorico Guest House *Box 287, Plymouth* *Tobago, W.I.*	639–2961	16	$55–95 EP	ITR	791

HOTEL QUICK REFERENCE CHARTS · · · 883

	phone 809+	rooms	winter rate for 2	rep	page
Coral Reef Guest House *Milford Road, Scarborough* *Tobago, W.I.*	639–2536	14+ 8 apts	$70 MAP		791
Crown Point Condominiums *Box 223, Crown Point* *Tobago, W.I.*	639–8781	109 apts	$130–150 EP	ITR	787
Crown Reef Hotel *Store Bay* *Tobago, W.I.*	639–8571	114	$130–220 EP	RR	
Della Mira Guest House *Box 203 Scarborough* *Tobago, W.I.*	639–2531	14	$30–35 EP		791
Grafton Beach *Grafton* *Tobago, W.I.*					787
Kariwak Village *Box 27, Scarborough* *Tobago, W.I.*	639–8545	20	$45 EP		790
Mount Irvine Bay Resort *Box 222, Scarborough* *Tobago, W.I.*	639–8871	110	$174–534 EP	RR	787
Sandy Point Beach Club *Box 223, Crown Point* *Tobago, W.I.*	639–8533	42	$60–70 EP	RR	787
Tropikist Beach Hotel *Crown Point* *Tobago, W.I.*	639–8512	33	TT$100 EP		788
Turtle Beach *Box 20, Scarborough* *Tobago, W.I.*	639–2851	125	$130 EP	RR	788

TURKS AND CAICOS ISLANDS: For information, dial 800+441–4419

	phone 809+	rooms	winter rate for 2	rep	page
Admiral's Club *Turtle Cove, Providenciales* *Turks and Caicos, B.W.I.*	946–4375	9	$100 up		801
Club Mediterranee Turkoise *Providenciales* *Turks and Caicos, B.W.I.*	946–4491	298	$2900 wk all incl AP+	CM	800
Columbus House *Pond Street, Cockburn Town* *Grand Turk, Turks and Caicos,* *B.W.I.*	946–2789	10	$55 EP		799

HOTEL QUICK REFERENCE CHARTS

	phone 809+	rooms	winter rate for 2	rep	page
Le Deck Beach Club *Grace Bay, Providenciales* *Turks and Caicos, B.W.I.*	946–4629	26	$155–280 FP	ITR	800
Erebus Inn *Turtle Cove, Providenciales* *Turks and Caicos, B.W.I.*	946–4240	36	$80 EP + villas		801
Guinep Tree Lodge *Cockburn Town, Grand Turk* *Turks and Caicos, B.W.I.*	946–2977	6			799
Island Princess Hotel *Grace Bay, Providenciales* *Turks and Caicos, B.W.I.*	946–4260	80	$80–150 EP		799
Island Reef Resort *Cockburn Town* *Grand Turk, Turks and Caicos,* *B.W.I.*	946–2055	21 apts.	$85–105 EP	RR	799
Kittina, Box 42 *Duke Street, Cockburn Town* *Grand Turk, Turks and Caicos,* *B.W.I.*	946–2232	45	$85–140 EP	ITR	799
The Mariner Hotel *Sapodilla Point, Providenciales* *Turks and Caicos, B.W.I.*	946–4488	25	$110 EP	ITR	801
Meridian Club *Pine Cay* *Turks and Caicos, B.W.I.*	946–4128	12	$275–350 MAP		802
Ocean Beach *Whitby, North Caicos* *Turks and Caicos, B.W.I.*	946–4880	5	$100–150 EP	RR	800
Ocean Club Condos *Box 240, Providenciales* *Turks and Caicos, B.W.I.*	946–5880	apts	$135–240 EP	RR	
Parrot Cay Resort *Parrot Cay, Provo* *Turks and Caicos, B.W.I.*				FR	801
Pelican Beach Hotel *North Caicos* *Turks and Caicos, B.W.I.*	946–4692	6	$160 EP		800
Pillary Beach Hotel *Cockburn Town, Grand Turk* *Turks and Caicos, B.W.I.*	946–2629	16			799
Prospect of Whitby, Box 21 *North Beach, North Caicos* *Turks and Caicos, B.W.I.*	946–4250	28			800

HOTEL QUICK REFERENCE CHARTS

	phone 809+	rooms	winter rate for 2	rep	page
Ramada Turkoise Reef Resort *Grace Bay, Providenciales* *Turks and Caicos, B.W.I.*	946–5555	230		RA	801
Salt Raker Inn *Cockburn Town, Grand Turk* *Turks and Caicos, B.W.I.*	946–2260	10	$60–95 EP		799
Third Turtle Inn *Providenciales* *Turks and Caicos, B.W.I.*	946–4230	13	$125 AP		801
Treasure Beach Villas *Providenciales* *Turks and Caicos, B.W.I.*	946–4325	18			802
Turks Head Inn *Cockburn Town, Grand Turk* *Turks and Caicos, B.W.I.*	946–2466	7	$55 EP		799
Turtle Cove Yacht & Tennis Resort *Sellar's Pond, Providenciales* *Turks and Caicos, B.W.I.*	946–4203	24	$95–175 EP		801
Windmills Plantation *Salt Cay* *Turks and Caicos, B.W.I.*					803

NOTES

NOTES

NOTES

NOTES

NOTES

NOTES

NOTES

NOTES

NOTES